California Prehistory

California Prehistory

Colonization, Culture, and Complexity

Edited by

Terry L. Jones and Kathryn A. Klar

Published in Cooperation with the Society for California Archaeology

AltaMira Press

A Division of

ROWMAN & LITTLEFIELD PUBLISHERS, INC.

Lanh

th, UK

AltaMira Press
A division of Rowman & Littlefield Publishers, Inc.
A wholly owned subsidiary of The Rowman & Littlefield Publishing Group, Inc.
4501 Forbes Boulevard, Suite 200, Lanham, MD 20706
www.altamirapress.com

Estover Road, Plymouth PL6 7PY, United Kingdom

British Library Cataloguing in Publication Information Available

Library of Congress Cataloging-in-Publication Data

California prehistory : colonization, culture, and complexity / edited by Terry L. Jones and Kathryn A. Klar.
p. cm.
Includes bibliographical references and index.
ISBN-13: 978-0-7591-0872-1 (cloth : alk. paper)
ISBN-10: 0-7591-0872-2 (cloth : alk. paper)
1. Paleo-Indians—California. 2. California—Antiquities. I. Jones, Terry L. II. Klar, Kathryn.
E78.C15C297 2007
979.4'01—dc22
2006034418

∞™ The paper used in this publication meets the minimum requirements of American National Standard for Information Sciences—Permanence of Paper for Printed Library Materials, ANSI/NISO Z39.48-1992.

Contents

Illustrations

FIGURES

TABLES

Preface

THIS VOLUME IS THE RESULT OF A FOUR-YEAR ODYSSEY that began at a meeting of the board of the Society for California Archaeology (SCA) in the spring of 2003. As board members were shaking off the effects of a very successful annual get-together, they began planning for the following year's meeting. As it happened, the year 2004 would mark the 20-year anniversary of the publication of the two most important scholarly landmarks in the study of California prehistory: *California Archaeology* by Michael J. Moratto (with contributions by David A. Fredrickson, Christopher Raven, and Claude Warren) and *The Archaeology of California* by Joseph L. and Kerry Kona Chartkoff. At its 2004 meeting the society would recognize those authors' contributions as well as review progress made in the field of California archaeology in the decades following publication of the 1984 volumes. Indeed, so much had been accomplished that the time seemed right for a major reevaluation of California prehistory. As a step in that direction, the 2004 annual meeting would feature an all-day symposium devoted to a 20-year update on California archaeology.

In 1984 both Michael Moratto and the Chartkoffs found that summarizing California archaeology was a daunting undertaking. In 2003, with 20 years of additional research from a large, diverse archaeological community, such a summary seemed even more overwhelming, and the SCA board appointed a committee to define the topics to be addressed in the session and to develop a list of individuals with the appropriate background to cover them. Ultimately 43 scholars agreed to participate in the symposium. As they prepared for the session, many participants were concerned about the monumental effort required to shape their regional and topical syntheses into a tangible written product. Those involved in early symposium planning thought that an Internet site might provide a useful outlet for disseminating the symposium's contributions. Although they appreciated the value of technology and recognized the growing importance of web-based scholarship, most of the symposium participants felt that a traditional book would be the most appropriate venue for such an important update. The SCA board agreed, and the planners moved forward with the idea that the symposium would culminate in a book. The session was held on Saturday, March 20, at the Riverside Convention Center. Following introductory comments, 14 papers were delivered on 10 regional and four specialized topics (paleoenvironment, linguistics, trade, and rock art). During the symposium, David A. Fredrickson presented the Martin A. Baumhoff Special Achievement Award to Michael J. Moratto and Joseph Chartkoff for their 1984 publications and subsequent contributions. Chartkoff and Moratto also provided commentary on the day's proceedings.

The presentations at that symposium became the chapters that constitute this book. Since certain topics were not adequately addressed by the papers, additions were made to the volume including treatments of coastal paleoenvironment (Chapter 3), Paleo-Indian technologies (Chapter 5), and DNA (Chapter 19). The 20 chapters in this book cover 10 geographic regions (Northwest, San Francisco Bay Area, Central Coast, Central Valley, Northeast, Sierra Nevada, Northern Bight, Southern Bight, Mojave Desert, and Colorado Desert) and eight specialized topics (terrestrial and marine paleoenvironments, Paleo-Indian settlement and technologies, linguistic prehistory, trade, rock art, and DNA). These chapters represent the labor of 53 contributors, accomplishing what six were able to do in 1984. We have attempted to build a comprehensive volume that incorporates a wide range of views and builds on, but does not replace, the 1984 books. We hope that archaeologists and interested nonprofessionals in and outside of California will find this new book useful. If it becomes half as important as the 1984 texts or remains viable for half as long, we will have accomplished our goal of bringing the study of California's remarkable prehistory up to date.

Acknowledgments

A VOLUME OF THIS SIZE AND SCOPE REQUIRED THE efforts of a large, diverse group of people. First and foremost we thank Michael J. Moratto and Joseph and Kerry Chartkoff, not only for their efforts in developing the first synthetic treatments of California archaeology in 1984, but also for their contributions to the current effort, which include the very thoughtful introduction in Chapter 1. Moratto and Joseph Chartkoff also provided constructive comments on many of the early drafts of other chapters. Also critical to the overall success of the project were members of the board of the Society for California Archaeology: Karin Anderson, Richard Fitzgerald, Shelly Davis-King, Amy Gilreath, Janine Lloyd, Dana McGowan, Elena Nilsson, Vicki Beard, and Stacy Schneyder. The board helped formulate the project's original vision and facilitated its completion. Mike Lerch, the program chair for the 2004 meeting, was instrumental in this regard as well. Crucial to the early planning of the SCA session at Riverside were three members of the symposium selection committee: Richard Fitzgerald, William Hildebrandt, and Lynn Gamble.

A small army of California archaeologists and other specialists provided technical assistance for the volume. For their efforts in this area, the editors and contributors would like to thank Richard Ambro, Jeanne Arnold, Leo Barker, Stan Berryman, Ethan Bertrando, Gary Breschini, William Bright, Colin Busby, Catherine Callaghan, James Cleland, Marie Cottrell, Owen Davis, Michael Delacorte, Jelmer Eerkens, Sally Evans, Kathy Flynn, Donna Garaventa, Alan Garfinkel, Jerry Gates, Mark Giambastiani, Roberta Greenwood, M. C. Hall, Trudy Haversat, John Hildebrand, Bill Howard, Bill Hyder, Jerry Johnson, Terry Joslin, Russ Kaldenberg, Doug Kennett, Chester King, Georgia Lee, Michael K. Lerch, Janine Lloyd, Kent Lightfoot, Susan Lindström, Meg McDonald, Connie Millar, Rick Norwood, Allen Pastron, Aimee Potter, Heather Price, Seetha Reddy, David Rhode, Eric Ritter, Bill Roop, Rich San Felipo, Joan S. Schneider, Adella B. Schroth, William Shipley, Jay von Werlhof, Claude Warren, Larry Weigel, Kenneth W. Whistler, David Whitley, Eric Wohlgemuth, Andy Yatsko, Robert M. Yohe II, Andrew York, and David Zeanah.

An equally large number of technical illustrators contributed to the volume; we are particularly thankful to Tammara Norton and Rusty Van Rossman, Jack Meyer, and Nelson Thompson for special assistance. We are also deeply indebted to Brian F. Codding for his fine cartographic work. Copyright permissions were obtained from:

- Bancroft Library, University of California Berkeley (Figures 8.2, 10.3, 14.2)
- Center for Archaeological Research at Davis (Figure 18.2a)
- Houghton Mifflin Company (Figure 1.1)
- J. Paul Getty Museum, Los Angeles (Figure 12.3)
- Malki Press (Figure 18.3a)
- Modoc County Historical Society (Figure 11.3)
- National Anthropological Archives, Smithsonian Institution (Figures 9.3, 16.3)
- Phoebe Apperson Hearst Museum of Anthropology and the Regents of the University of California (Figure 7.2)
- San Luis Obispo County Archaeological Society (Figure 18.2b)
- Santa Barbara Museum of Natural History (Figure 13.1)

We also want to thank the four senior scholars who provided thoughtful, constructive comments on the concluding chapter: David A. Fredrickson, Victor Golla, Michael J. Moratto, and Joseph L. Chartkoff. Any mistakes in interpreting their suggestions are strictly our own. During the two decades between the current and past syntheses, California anthropology lost a number of influential scholars, including James A. Bennyhoff, William Bright, Franklin Fenenga, Bert Gerow, Mary Haas, Clement Meighan, Fritz Riddell, Delbert True, and William J. Wallace. We feel their loss.

We are indebted to the editors and other personnel at AltaMira Press, particularly former editors Mitch Allen and Rosalie Robertson, and current editor Jack

Meinhardt, Sarah Walker, and Jehanne Schweitzer for their considerable efforts in bringing the volume to fruition. Finally we would like to thank the 53 contributing authors for their remarkable efforts in synthesizing the prehistory of a large, complicated place. Thank-you to all!

CHAPTER 1

Archaeological Progress since 1984

Michael J. Moratto and Joseph L. Chartkoff

Perhaps best known as the title of George Orwell's apocalyptic novel, 1984 is memorable for other reasons as well. In that year Ronald Reagan was reelected president of the United States, the Bell Telephone Company was broken up, and the Olympic Games were held in Los Angeles. The year 1984 also heralded the first two books offering a comprehensive survey of California's archaeological record: *California Archaeology* by Michael J. Moratto and *The Archaeology of California* by Joseph and Kerry Chartkoff.

Two decades later, the Society for California Archaeology (SCA) recognized the importance of these books by hosting a special symposium at its annual meeting, held at Riverside's venerable Mission Inn. That session included 14 papers written by more than 40 prominent scholars. While the papers were given to commemorate the twentieth anniversary of the books' publication, their topics emphasized what had been learned since 1984. The SCA symposium thus reflected two decades of progress by California's increasingly vibrant archaeological community.

California archaeology has grown phenomenally; indeed, "so much has been done and learned since 1984 that even a concise summary of major accomplishments would run to hundreds of pages" (Moratto 2004:xliii). Moreover, as Arnold et al. (2004:1) have observed, "This rich output of published work, virtually all of it about hunter-gatherer groups, may be the world's largest body of archaeological research on one region's hunter-gatherers."

The chapters in the present volume summarize many areas of active research and the new information gained. They highlight the challenges facing scholars who try to keep abreast of the rapid advances. Although up-to-date overviews of California prehistory are now more difficult to achieve than they were in 1984, they are also more needed.

Another book on the subject is Brian Fagan's *Before California* (2003). Although less comprehensive in scope than the 1984 books, it is more current and is written in an accessible style for a broad audience. Still, the field would benefit greatly from newer summaries and syntheses. The present volume is, we believe, a contribution of exceptional value in this regard.

SOURCES OF CHANGE

Whereas subsequent chapters in this volume detail perspectives and knowledge gained since 1984, this introduction offers a general overview. Much recent progress has emanated from the sheer volume of archaeological work done in California since the mid-1980s. Two factors contributing to this development are California's dramatic economic growth and federal and state environmental laws requiring consideration of archaeological and other cultural resources. Consequently the database has grown exponentially for all time periods and all regions of the state. Applying new theoretical approaches, methods, and techniques has resulted in the elaboration and refinement of testable models that help us understand human adaptations. The nature, timing, and causes of culture change have turned out to be more complex than previously thought, and our views of archaeological patterns have changed as new data have been gathered and processed.

Applying innovative technologies to the discovery and analysis of archaeological remains has also helped transform our perception of California's past. Methods already in use have been enhanced to yield data with greater precision and accuracy (e.g., the refinement of radiocarbon [^{14}C] dating, protein residue analysis, artifact replication and functional studies, and the geologic sourcing of obsidian through trace element analysis). New technologies and methods have also provided kinds of data not previously available (e.g., the analysis of mitochondrial DNA to characterize human populations and determine their biologic affinities, accelerator mass spectrometry ^{14}C dating of small organic samples, and studies of radiolaria and other microorganisms to build sea-surface paleotemperature chronologies and thus infer past distribution of marine fishes and mammals). New kinds of data have led to progress that goes beyond the quantitative increase of traditional categories of information. For example, refined dating methods have led to accurate correlations of human responses to environmental change in various parts of the state.

The intellectual ferment in California since 1984 has stimulated the ongoing evolution of theoretical perspectives on the development of prehistoric cultures. Many California scholars have actively contributed to the growth of archaeological theory, and their findings regarding hunter-gatherer dynamics have gained worldwide influence (Arnold et al. 2004; Chartkoff 1992). Concepts such as evolutionary ecology, optimal foraging theory, resource intensification, gender differentiation in prehistoric economic systems, and causal factors in the rise of hunter-gatherer social complexity have been systematically explored and applied to California's archaeological record (Arnold 1992a; Basgall 1987; Hildebrandt and McGuire 2002; Raab and Jones 2004; Waechter 2005; Wohlgemuth 2005).

THE PRESENT VOLUME

Many scholars have joined in this effort to present current views of California prehistory based on research progress since 1984. Two chapters examine past environments as they relate to cultural ecology; six chapters variously cover the initial settlement of California, early lithic technologies, linguistic prehistory, trade and exchange systems, rock art, and DNA studies; and 10 chapters explicate cultural developments in particular geographic regions. Here we touch briefly on key findings reported by the contributors as a way to highlight in statewide perspective some of the recent archaeological advances. Our comments follow the order of chapter presentation.

Past Environments

Probably no aspect of California archaeology has progressed as far during the past few decades as our understanding of prehistoric environments and their effects on human activities. Prior to 1980, the majority view was that only a few long-term, large-scale (panregional) environmental changes occurred in the Far West during the time of human occupation: (1) the Terminal Pleistocene shift from glacial to postglacial conditions, (2) an Early Holocene Anathermal Period of warming temperatures, (3) a Middle Holocene Altithermal marked by elevated temperatures and xericity, and (4) a Late Holocene Medithermal interval typified by relatively moderate climates, like those of today (Antevs 1953, 1955). Anthropologists tended to view California as a set of rather stable landscapes on which culture change over time reflected such factors as immigration, the expansion or contraction of ethnic territories, and regional economic specialization. Thus a widely held assumption just a few decades ago was that "after 2000 B.C. there were no large-scale climatic disruptions and that the chief reasons for cultural variance in the several regions, besides 'normal' change through time, were based upon the necessarily differing cultural adaptations to the regional environments" (Elsasser 1978:57). In that context it is not surprising that many scholars resisted Moratto, King, and Woolfenden's (1978) assertion that cultural changes inferred archaeologically may be correlated with paleoenvironmental shifts in California, and that at least some of the former may have been adaptations to the latter.

We have come a long way since then. As a result of countless studies in many disciplines, it is now well established that precipitation and temperature regimes, quantities of surface water, vegetation series, and faunas in all parts of California have been dynamic and have fluctuated significantly, with episodes of dramatic, often rapid change, during the past 15,000 years. Those seeking to understand human prehistory in California, therefore, must not only ascertain and precisely date the social and economic patterns evinced by the archaeological record, but also examine such patterns with reference to contemporary local environments and their possible influence on cultural behavior. A particularly apt example of this approach is the study of ecologic relationships between human demographic crises and the Medieval Climatic Anomaly marked by severe droughts (ca. A.D. 892–1112 and 1209–1350) in the southern Far West (Jones et al. 2004).

In Chapter 2, authors G. James West, Wallace Woolfenden, James Wanket, and Scott Anderson consider Late Pleistocene and Holocene environments. They remind us that hunter-gatherers depend entirely on nature for water, food, and other necessities, and then show that the occurrence, location, and abundance of plant and animal taxa and other essential resources "have been re-sorted dramatically since the last glacial maximum (LGM), [and] are therefore of critical importance to understanding the behavior of California's prehistoric cultures." West et al. discuss how past climatic shifts have affected the resources needed for human survival and provide region-by-region summaries of environmental change over time. Chapter 2 is the most comprehensive statewide overview ever compiled of environmental dynamics and their relationships to cultural adaptations in prehistoric California.

Chapter 3 is organized in two parts. First, Patricia Masters examines the tectonic, climatic, and marine forces that shaped California's coast south of Morro Bay during the millennia since the LGM. In the second part, Ivano Aiello offers a comparable paleogeographic survey of the central coast from Point Sur northward to Bodega Bay. The authors of this chapter adduce and synthesize a great deal of new information derived from recent studies of coastal geomorphology, Holocene climates, postglacial sea levels, shoreline movement, marine currents and paleotemperatures, the formation of coastal habitats, and the ever-changing biodiversity and abundance of species in various settings. This effort shows how local manifestations of coastal evolution could have influenced human carrying capacity, economic practices, and settlement patterns over time. It also portends an exciting future for coastal archaeology not only by framing a dynamic context for new interpretations of prehistory but also by opening new avenues for studies of cultural ecology, settlement, subsistence, Pleistocene land use, and myriad other research domains. This chapter, which could not have been written 20 years ago, is a foundation on which future archaeological work along the coast must rest.

Ancient Cultures

Our knowledge of the initial human settlement of California (i.e., how and when this part of the Pacific Rim was first colonized) also has increased greatly since 1984. In fact, most of the older received wisdom about the origins, antiquity, routes and modes of travel, and cultures of the earliest Americans has been thoroughly revised or supplanted entirely by newer concepts. This paradigm shift is taken up in Chapter 4 by Jon Erlandson, Torben Rick, Terry Jones, and Judith Porcasi. A generation ago the archaeological consensus was that toward the end of the last Ice Age, small groups of people from northeastern Asia had trekked across Beringia (the Bering "land bridge" that connected Siberia and Alaska at times of low sea levels) and then, around 12,000 to 11,500 years ago, drifted southward through an ice-free corridor paralleling the Canadian Rockies. From there, populations fanned out across the Great Plains and beyond. As their numbers increased, these intrepid bands radiated outward to the coasts and to more southerly latitudes. In accordance with this model, the first Californians were perceived as big-game hunters from the interior who entered the state from the north and east approximately 11,000 years ago.

The model presented by Erlandson et al. is quite different, reflecting current knowledge. Scholars now aver that ethnically diverse peoples from eastern and northern Asia migrated to the New World not only by crossing Beringia on foot but also by traveling offshore along the coast in seaworthy boats. Moreover, in light of data now available from sites in North and South America, occupation of the coast almost certainly preceded the opening of the ice-free corridor by at least 2,000 to 3,000 years. California thus would have been directly on the route taken by America's first colonists. In this regard, Erlandson et al. cite archaeological evidence of people living on the Northern Channel Islands some 12,000 to 13,000 years ago. This confirms the use of boats for sea travel in the California Bight at least 120 centuries ago. Such findings, as well as other discoveries of ancient cultural remains on the mainland coast, permit archaeologists working in California to enhance our knowledge about the earliest peopling of the Americas.

So what have we learned about California's most ancient cultures? Many archaeologists concerned with this question during the early 1980s thought that the state's earliest inhabitants were probably derived from big-game hunters farther east, and that their lithic technology—distinguished by large, lanceolate ("Clovis-like") fluted points—denoted a widespread culture that gave rise to more diverse adaptations. To be sure, in the mid- to late twentieth century some ministers of archaeology were preaching that California was first settled 40,000 to 200,000 years ago, but the march of science in recent years has laid waste to such notions. However, science has also been harsh on the "Clovis-first" dogma and its corollary that fluted points identify a continent-wide mother culture.

Chapter 5 provides a refreshing summary of current thinking about this perennial issue. In part 1, Michael Rondeau critically reviews what is currently known (and what has, perhaps without sufficient basis, been assumed) about the several hundred fluted points found in diverse settings throughout the state. In part 2, Jim Cassidy describes a fascinating microblade complex from Early Holocene archaeological deposits on San Clemente Island. Cassidy opines that "this tool kit is fully consistent with the Paleo-Arctic Tradition and contains all of the technological elements required for watercraft construction and maintenance." One of the remarkable things about this complex is that microblades are anything but typical of California; they are patently exotic.

> The technique of manufacturing a series of thin, parallel-sided microblades from a single piece of

stone is an efficient way to produce high-quality cutting edges. . . . [By using approximately] one pound of rock to produce microblades, as much as 1,300 centimeters of cutting edge can be produced (Hester and Grady 1982:169). In the arctic it is virtually impossible to obtain new sources of stone for about eight months of the year because the land is frozen and blanketed with snow during the winter months. By using the stone to produce microblades, these early arctic people were able to carry a small and comparatively lightweight supply of microblade cores with them and be assured that new hunting weapons could be manufactured and old weapons repaired through the long and difficult winter [Dixon 1993:60].

By contrast, California has numerous sources of abundant, high-quality toolstone available year-round. The microblade complex on Santa Catalina Island thus indicates the arrival of people who probably came from a very different climatic regime, most likely far to the north.

Based on their respective studies, Rondeau and Cassidy conclude that two separate lithic technologies (and by inference two distinct economic strategies) "can be linked with the earliest human occupation of California: fluted points from the interior and the coast (but not the islands) and a microblade complex currently identified only on San Clemente Island." These findings are not surprising in light of the remarkable cultural diversity evinced by Late Pleistocene and Early Holocene archaeological remains discovered recently in varied geographic settings throughout North and South America (Bonnichsen et al. 2005; Dillehay 1989, 1997; Dixon 1999; *Current Research in the Pleistocene* and *Mammoth Trumpet,* various issues). When California is viewed in the larger context of American archaeology, we would expect future investigations to reveal evidence of pronounced cultural diversity before 10,000 years ago.

Languages in California's Past

Anthropologists have long recognized that archaeology plays an important role in elucidating linguistic prehistory and, conversely, that the methods and results of historical linguistics may enhance archaeological reconstructions of the past. California is perhaps the best laboratory on earth for investigating relationships among past societies, their languages, and other aspects of culture. Interest in this research domain began during the late nineteenth century and was pursued intensively during the twentieth. General syntheses include those of Dixon and Kroeber (1919) and Moratto (1984:529–574). (See also Foster 1996; Shipley 1978.) In Chapter 6 of the present volume, Victor Golla (1) provides a state-of-the-art review of California's linguistic prehistory, focusing on six "primary language-family relationships represented in aboriginal California," and (2) proposes "a reconstruction of prehistoric events and developments that would account for the observed linguistic situation."

Golla notes that "while the calibration of linguistic dates with archaeological dates is fraught with difficulties, some correlations are clearly more probable than others, and where there is a congruence of linguistic and archaeological dates the correlation may be considered firm." He then moves on, first, to discuss native California languages and their relationships and, second, to build on and update previous models of the population movements, linguistic borrowing, and internal diversification that resulted in the historically observed geolinguistic mosaic of California. Readers will find that Golla's synthesis diverges in some important respects from earlier ones, a result of knowledge gained from more recent linguistic studies.

One such point of divergence is that linguists now deem the Chumashan family to be an isolate rather than a part of the Hokan stock, and not demonstrably related to any other language. Yukian in the North Coast Ranges was so identified long ago, but the isolated status of Chumashan is a more recent determination (Campbell 1997). Both of these linguistic groups seem to have deep roots in California's past, and either or both may be the ultimate products of languages spoken by some of California's earliest inhabitants. This and many other aspects of Golla's reconstruction offer a rich lode of data and hypotheses that could, and we think should, inform and guide archaeological research in California for many years to come.

Regional Prehistories

Each of the next 10 chapters presents an overview of a particular region (Figure 1.1), emphasizing the directions and results of archaeological work since 1984. More than just adding new archaeological data, however, Chapters 7 to 16 also employ current theoretical approaches, methods, and techniques. Consequently the overview authors are able to define cultural manifestations, pose and answer research questions, and provide explanations that were unattainable 20 years ago.

Advancing knowledge, however, also generates difficulties. For one thing, the more we learn, the more we have to face the complexity of the archaeological data. As we are now aware, there is no single cultural

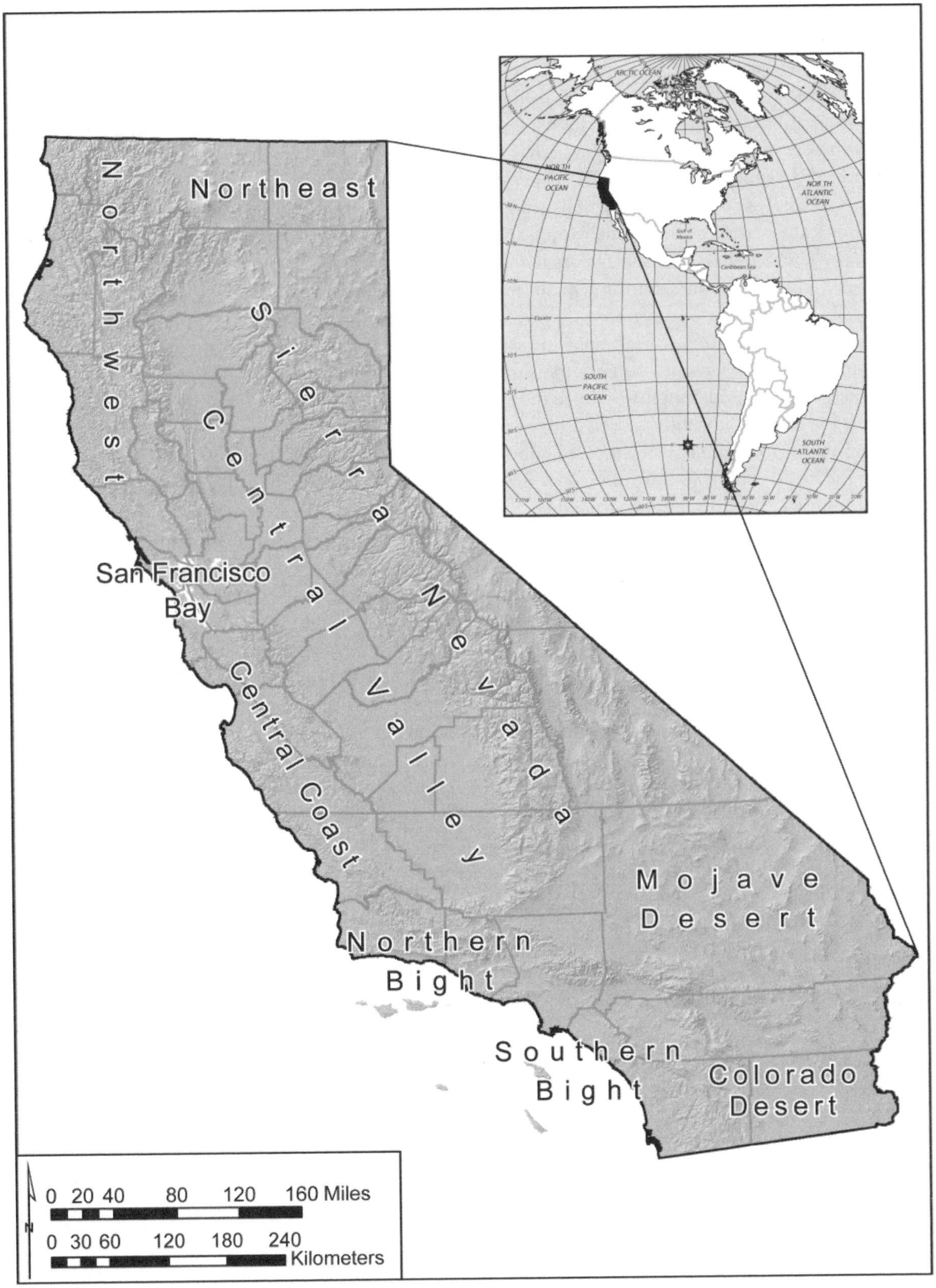

Figure 1.1. California's Place in the Americas, modified from the HOUGHTON MIFFLIN EDUCATION PLACE® website (www.eduplace.com/ss/maps/pdf/americas.pdf). Copyright © Houghton Mifflin Company. Reprinted by permission of Houghton Mifflin Company. All rights reserved. The map may be printed and copied for classroom use. Any other use of the material is strictly prohibited unless written permission is obtained from Houghton Mifflin Company.

sequence (i.e., chronology) for any region of California, and most regions encompass many localities and sequences. Moreover, each region has its own peculiar history and traditions of archaeological work so that theoretical orientations, research foci, methods, and taxonomic schemes vary enormously. The archaeological record itself (which reflects cultural behavior, diverse environmental conditions, and the vicissitudes of preservation) also varies greatly both within and among regions. The net effect of these factors is that there are many Californias, both environmentally and archaeologically. Thus, while the regional overviews in this volume convey a sense of the attested cultural variability, the same overviews advise us to be wary of broad generalizations and simplistic explanations. Complexity is the essence of California prehistory.

Any attempt by us to summarize the major findings presented in the regional overviews would risk stealing the authors' thunder (not to mention expanding the introduction into a book of its own), and so we will only highlight a few aspects of each chapter.

Chapter 7 by William Hildebrandt examines six major cultural patterns and their space/time distributions in northwestern California. Although more is known about some localities than others, Hildebrandt describes the patterns with admirable clarity and relates them to environmental changes, economic shifts, and population movements. Given the large number of native languages spoken in northwestern California, it is not surprising that much of the archaeological record seems to indicate the arrival and spread of certain societies (e.g., Pomo and Athabascan groups) at the expense of others (most notably the Yuki). Having synthesized regional prehistory, Hildebrandt proceeds to discuss important themes or objectives for future research. He thus provides a concise yet substantial update of Fredrickson's (1984) classic overview of the north coastal region.

Few if any parts of the state have witnessed culture histories as complicated as those of the San Francisco Bay region, and perhaps no other area of equal size in California has been studied as intensively by archaeologists during the past 20 years. To synthesize the major results of these studies, Randall Milliken and 13 coauthors have prepared Chapter 8. The new dating scheme, fresh interpretations of the social context of shell mounds, and other innovations arrayed in Chapter 8 extensively revise our understanding of Bay Area prehistory.

Of California's many regions, the Central Coast was one of the least known archaeologically in 1984, and neither of our books said much about it. But during the past score of years numerous studies have yielded a great deal of information about diachronic changes in settlement patterns, subsistence, trade, and relationships between human land uses and evolving coastal environments. The corpus of new data is synthesized in Chapter 9 by Terry Jones, Nathan Stevens, Deborah Jones, Richard Fitzgerald, and Mark Hylkema. Of particular interest in this chapter are the recent insights into Early Holocene adaptations, evidence for prehistoric population movements in the region, impacts of human predation on target species, and the emergence of complex socioeconomic patterns in late prehistoric times.

The Central Valley is the subject of Chapter 10 by Jeffrey Rosenthal, Gregory White, and Mark Sutton. This is a large, naturally diverse province in which cultural sequences have been defined for only some localities (e.g., the Sacramento–San Joaquin Delta and western Merced County) while others remain poorly known. Rosenthal et al. fit archaeological components and phases into five "periods" (actually stages with ascribed time limits): Paleo-Indian; Lower, Middle, and Upper Archaic; and Emergent. They then discuss a series of themes, mostly related to subsistence and demography, that have been the focus of recent investigations. Chapter 10 summarizes a wide range of data, but it does not cohere very well as a synthesis. This is not to fault the contributors, but rather to say that the Central Valley is too large and archaeologically varied to be treated as a single region. Although we too accepted the valley as a cultural region in our 1984 books, Chapter 10 provides enough new data to suggest that separate Sacramento Valley, Delta (or, perhaps, Bay/Delta), and San Joaquin Valley regions might better accommodate future syntheses.

Chapter 11 by Kelly McGuire surveys northeastern California prehistory. This corner of the state was probed sporadically beginning in the 1940s, but archaeological research has been intensive and sustained only since the 1970s. Thus, as in other regions, much of the synthesis is based on data acquired recently. McGuire places diverse local chronologies in a framework of six periods: Early Holocene; Post-Mazama; Early, Middle, and Late Archaic; and Terminal Prehistoric. Chapter 11 provides a lucid assessment of recent archaeological findings in northeastern California, thus building on and updating Raven's (1984) synthesis. Comparing the two works shows that during the past 20 years scholars have pursued innovative research, especially as related to obsidian analysis, while continuing to study long-established topics such as prehistoric boundary maintenance (at the juncture of the Great Basin, California, and Plateau culture areas) and population movements.

The Sierra Nevada provides another example of the extent to which our command of regional prehistory has been transformed since 1984. In Chapter 12, Kathleen Hull portrays the Sierra as a cultural province linked closely to both the Central Valley and the Great Basin. Hull's summary of archaeological advances since 1980 showcases our improved knowledge of local cultural sequences (beginning in the Early Holocene), more precise correlations of natural and cultural changes over time, and refinements in obsidian studies used to date archaeological assemblages and elucidate prehistoric trade. The author also discusses lithic technology, bedrock mortars (and inferred acorn use), social organization, and demography. Although organic remains are rare at high elevations in this region, the abundance of habitation sites, milling features, and obsidian artifacts make the Sierra Nevada particularly well suited for studies of changes in settlement systems, population levels, and environmental conditions over time. Since the Sierra Nevada covers such a vast area and encompasses so much cultural variation perhaps it, like the great Central Valley, should be subdivided into two or more archaeological regions when the next synthesis is contemplated.

Coastal southern California is the subject of two chapters. The Northern Bight and adjacent portions of the Transverse Ranges are covered in Chapter 13 by Michael Glassow, Lynn Gamble, Jennifer Perry, and Glenn Russell, while the Southern Bight is considered in Chapter 14 by Brian Byrd and L. Mark Raab. In both regions, a great deal of archaeological work, mostly in the context of cultural resource management (CRM) projects, has been done over the past 20 years. The research often has been guided by new theoretical perspectives related to social evolution or cultural ecology. As Glassow et al. observe, the investigations have "resulted in substantially more knowledge about the prehistory of the Northern Bight than was the case 20 years ago. Indeed, articles in prominent journals and books published by well-known presses have brought national and international visibility to the region." The same may be said of recent archaeological progress along the Southern Bight. In both areas the past two decades have witnessed phenomenal advances in environmental reconstruction (see also Chapters 2 and 3) as well as in our understanding of Late Pleistocene and Early Holocene occupation of the coast, human adaptation to natural changes over time, the development of maritime cultures, intra- and interregional exchange systems, craft specialization, and the emergence of remarkable social complexity. In sum, Chapters 13 and14 not only provide exceptional regional syntheses but also reveal how much has been learned since 1984 and why archaeological research in California has now assumed such a prominent role globally in the advancement of knowledge about prehistoric hunter-gatherers.

The desert regions of California are also the subjects of two contributions. Chapter 15 by Mark Sutton, Mark Basgall, Jill Gardner, and Mark Allen deals with aspects of Mojave Desert prehistory, while Jerry Schaefer and Don Laylander devote Chapter 16 to recent archaeological advances in the Colorado Desert. As in other regions of the state, an enormous amount of archaeological work has been undertaken in the deserts since 1984. For example, Sutton et al. point out that large-scale surveys and excavations at Fort Irwin in the central Mojave Desert "have made it the most thoroughly investigated . . . [area] of comparable size in western North America."

Two decades ago, Warren's (1984) chapter in Moratto's book provided an archaeological synthesis of the entire desert (i.e., virtually all of arid southeastern California). So much new information has come to light during the intervening years, however, that a comprehensive, chapter-length synopsis is no longer feasible. For this reason, Sutton et al. do not attempt a systematic update of Mojave Desert prehistory, but instead discuss just a few of the topics that have been studied intensively in recent years: paleoenvironment, chronology, linguistic prehistory, and the evolution of cultural systems. Archaeological findings relevant to these topics are temporally ordered and discussed with reference to eight periods, ranging from Pleistocene to Late Prehistoric. For the Colorado Desert, Schaefer and Laylander face a slightly less formidable literature and endeavor to synthesize the major findings since 1984. They discuss such research issues as the prehistory of Lake Cahuilla, toolstone procurement at Obsidian Butte and other sources, trade and travel, ceramics, and cultural relationships with neighboring regions.

Trade and Exchange Systems

Returning to a statewide perspective, Chapter 17 by Richard Hughes and Randall Milliken examines prehistoric trade and exchange, or "prehistoric material conveyance." The authors do not attempt a comprehensive synthesis of the data related to their subject, "which has increased by orders of magnitude" since 1984, but instead highlight dating and methodological issues. Accordingly, Chapter 17 captures what has been learned about the chronology, dynamics, and social context of material procurement and conveyance in prehistoric California. Hughes and Milliken show how studies of the voluminous data on obsidian and shell beads, when combined with state-of-the-art analytic methods and revised correlations with newly refined cultural sequences in various parts of the state, have enhanced our understanding of prehistoric cultural evolution in California. Twenty years ago a simple progression from small populations to ever-larger ones, with increasingly complex sociopolitical and economic systems over time, was generally assumed. Now we can see that the course of prehistory witnessed many fluctuations as population levels rose and fell, political systems and economies waxed and waned, and regional interaction networks emerged and declined. Within these dynamic contexts, material conveyance also was influenced by a host of local factors. Invigorated by all that has been learned since 1984, we stand on the threshold of learning even more about the economic systems of ancient California.

Rock Art

Prehistoric rock art is found throughout California, although the types and styles, quantities, and settings are highly variable among and within regions. Studies of rock art can yield insights into aspects of culture seldom accessible to archaeologists: cosmology, religion, shamanism, ritual, and aesthetic expression, to name a few. Rock art motifs may also portray clothing (including ceremonial regalia), tool use, events, activities (e.g., mountain sheep hunting), and astronomical observations. Not surprisingly, rock art in the American West has attracted scholarly interest for well over a century. While several important overviews were published before the 1980s (e.g., Grant 1965; Heizer and Baumhoff 1962; Heizer and Clewlow 1973; Steward 1929), the majority of rock art research in California has been done during the past quarter century.

Our 1984 books repeatedly mention rock art and comment on its inferred functions and cultural contexts, but the scope of our work precluded topical overviews of the subject such as the one that Clewlow (1978) wrote for the *California* volume of the *Handbook of North American Indians* (Heizer, ed. 1978) or Fagan's cleverly titled chapter "Art on the Rocks" in *Before California* (Fagan 2003). In Chapter 18, Amy Gilreath presents an up-to-date synopsis of California rock art and its significance. This treatment is organized according to rock art categories, with discussions of small decorated rocks (incised slates and painted pebbles), pictographs, cupules, petroglyphs, and earthen art (stone alignments and geoglyphs). The author considers the geographic distribution and, as data permit, the age, cultural tradition, style, social context, and function of various rock art forms. Above all, Gilreath reminds us of the people who left behind this evocative and durable record of their humanity and views of the cosmos. We anticipate that future rock art studies will yield even more fascinating insights.

The Promise of DNA Analysis

In 1984 few if any Californianists were using DNA data in archaeology. Now, some two decades later, mitochondrial DNA (mtDNA) analysis plays a major role in interdisciplinary research designed to elucidate prehistory. For a sterling example of the explosive growth since 1984 of new methods and knowledge related to California's human past, we need look no further than molecular anthropology, particularly as it relates to mtDNA.

During the twentieth century anthropological research in California focused on relationships among race, language, and culture, as well as their distribution in time and space. A central concern was with phylogeny—reconstructing the family tree of societies and cultures. Archaeology played a key role in this research, as did historical linguistics, but there were many obstacles to progress. Not the least of these was the assumption that "race" (actually, human populations), language, and culture covaried, and that from the identification of any one (e.g., a distinctive archaeological assemblage) the presence of the others (i.e., the corresponding ancient language and population) could be inferred. Over the years, critics rightly admonished that California ethnography is replete with cases where "race," language, and culture are *not* coincident. A classic example comes from northwestern California, where remarkably similar ways of life are shared by the linguistically and biologically distinct Yurok (speakers of an Algic language), Hupa (who speak an Athabascan tongue), and Karuk (belonging to the Hokan linguistic stock). Another case in point involves the spread of the Wailaki group of Athabascan languages southward into lands long occupied by Yukian people who seem to have lost their own ancestral language(s) in the process.

Historical linguistics and archaeology are powerful, especially when they join forces. However, the former is limited in what it can reveal about the prehistoric distributions of culture and populations, just as the latter is mute with respect to the idioms of the subject peoples. Archaeology has made human remains available for study, but analyses of these remains by traditional methods (e.g., comparative osteometry and odontometry, statistical analysis of nonmetric skeletal traits, etc.) has not always proven satisfactory. Even when samples of human remains from a skeletal population were sufficiently large for statistical purposes, there was the vexatious problem of determining the extent to which the observed measures and indexes actually reflected genetic penetrance (i.e., inheritance). The objective has long been to compare the remains of individuals representing defined populations as a means to characterize the genotype (e.g., Brace et al. 2004), but osteological data are at best a proxy record of population genetics. In brief, phenotypes are not simply genotypes cast in bone. The analysis of mtDNA largely avoids the proxy issue by identifying and comparing genetic material directly. This does not mean that we should discard the osteological data acquired so meticulously over the years. It does mean, however, that we have a new, very promising method at our disposal for the study of human population distributions and movements in prehistory.

This exciting development is the subject of Chapter 19 by Jason Eshleman and David Glenn Smith, which considers mtDNA from living Native Californians and its implications for prehistoric population movements. Eshleman and Smith provide an especially lucid discussion of mtDNA and pertinent analytical procedures, and then apply their mtDNA data to test models of prehistoric population movements derived from both linguistic and archaeological sources. We found it fascinating to compare the models of prehistory based on mtDNA with Golla's presentation of linguistically based models in Chapter 6. Prehistorians will find much of value in a comparative appraisal of these two chapters and their respective interpretations of the data.

SOME FINAL THOUGHTS

The chapters in this volume review changes in our understanding of specialized fields such as rock art and linguistic prehistory as well as cultural developments in particular regions. Not every topic or corner of the state is included, but the collective updating at this level cannot be found anywhere else. The new findings replace simple models with more sophisticated ones and give rise to many important questions about what caused the various patterns, processes, and fluctuations evident in the archaeological record. Pursuit of these questions is fostering an increasingly dynamic intellectual environment in California archaeology. It is helping make California archaeology a world-class influence on archaeological thought, particularly as regards hunter-gatherer studies.

The accelerating pace of research, along with the fact that so much has been learned during the brief interval since 1984, suggests that even more will be discovered in the next 20 years. Who could have imagined in that Orwellian year that archaeologists would soon discover cultural deposits 120 centuries old on San Miguel Island, or assemblages like those of the Paleo-Arctic tradition on San Clemente Island, or widespread evidence of demographic stress linked to Medieval-era droughts, or indications of Polynesian seafarers visiting the California coast a thousand years before the Spanish "discovered" this fabled land? And who can imagine what still awaits our spades and trowels? In Chapter 15, Sutton et al. raise the possibility of pre-Clovis occupation(s) in southeastern California. Perhaps future discoveries will confirm the presence of humans in California 15,000 or even 20,000 years ago, and perhaps not. But if this does happen, the paradigm shift will send us back to the intellectual drawing board. If we keep an open mind while adhering to and refining our scientific methods, the future could prove very exciting.

As time passes and we continue to expand the horizons of California archaeology, we should pause now and then to reflect gratefully on the vision and editorial labors of Terry Jones and Kathryn Klar as well as the efforts of the contributors who prepared the following chapters. Theirs is an immensely significant contribution to our field, for they have not only synthesized a great deal of information but also have charted numerous directions for future research. This volume will surely serve for years to come as the definitive reference work on California prehistory.

CHAPTER 2

Late Pleistocene and Holocene Environments

G. James West, Wallace Woolfenden,
James A. Wanket, and R. Scott Anderson

An understanding of the environments in which past societies interacted is crucial to a full comprehension of prehistory. While all parts of the environment are interrelated to a greater or lesser extent, those that provide subsistence and material resources for survival form the critical articulations to human societies. The manner in which human groups choose to interact varies widely even within the same environment. In prehistoric California aboriginal populations apparently made choices that were closely tied to the abundance of and production from native taxa. The occurrence, location, and abundance of these native taxa, which have been resorted dramatically since the last glacial maximum (LGM), are therefore critically important to understanding the behavior of California's prehistoric cultures. Our goal in this chapter is to provide a broad outline of terrestrial environmental change, focusing primarily on vegetation history, at varying degrees of resolution for the known prehistoric period.

California is the most topographically, climatically, and ecologically heterogeneous state in the country. It has many regional climates (Mitchell 1976), ranging from those associated with the temperate rain forests of the northwest coast to high glaciated peaks to the low hot arid deserts of the southeast portion of the state (Figure 2.1). These climatic-biotic conditions are multifactorial, but are primarily the result of latitude, topography (including elevation and exposure), substrate, organisms (plants and animals including humans), and distance from the ocean. Regional climates are influenced by both large-scale and regional-scale climatic processes, and their response to global-scale forcing is likely controlled by the response of both large- and regional-scale processes (Diffenbaugh and Sloan 2004). Latitudinal constraints are partly mollified by elevation allowing for a greater range of many plants while the effects of the ocean greatly dampen diurnal and seasonal variation. Substrate affects the distribution of many plant species and gives rise to disjunct populations of related taxa. Organisms also have had a role in California's diverse vegetation by transporting seeds, spreading diseases, pollinating plants, altering soil structure and composition, and through inadvertent and purposeful burning. In fact many California plant taxa depend on fire for successful reproduction.

California's precipitation, with minor exceptions, comes from Pacific cyclonic storms that begin in late fall and end by late spring, and is out of phase with much of the growing season for most domesticated plants. A series of mountain ranges—Coast, Transverse, Peninsular, Cascade, and the Sierra Nevada—parallel the Pacific coast and trap moisture from Pacific storms. This creates a rain shadow in the Great Valley and especially across the deserts to the east. The result is a humid to arid gradient from coast to desert and from lower to higher mountain elevations. There is also a latitudinal precipitation gradient from north to south (Kahrl 1979; Koltermann and Gorelick 1992) as the number of frontal storms increases northward (Houghton 1969). At the annual to decadal scale there is considerable variation in this pattern; when events such as El Niño occur, warmer sea surface temperatures are accompanied by high precipitation in southern California and drought in the Pacific Northwest. The general California pattern of wet winters and dry summers has led to unique vegetation types that contain plants that have evolved to cope with severe summer drought, when virtually no precipitation occurs. While parts of California, primarily the Sierra Nevada and portions of the state that overlap into the Great Basin and southern deserts, receive some summer monsoonal moisture, the amount is small, highly variable from year to year, and most often localized. Presently in the southeastern deserts about a quarter of the annual precipitation is received from, or is associated with, tropical storms from the south, which usually occur in late summer but may appear as late as October (Court 1974). Along the coast fog drip may help some taxa survive the summer drought, but the area affected by this phenomenon is very restricted. The California unimodal precipitation pattern appears to have occurred throughout the Pleistocene

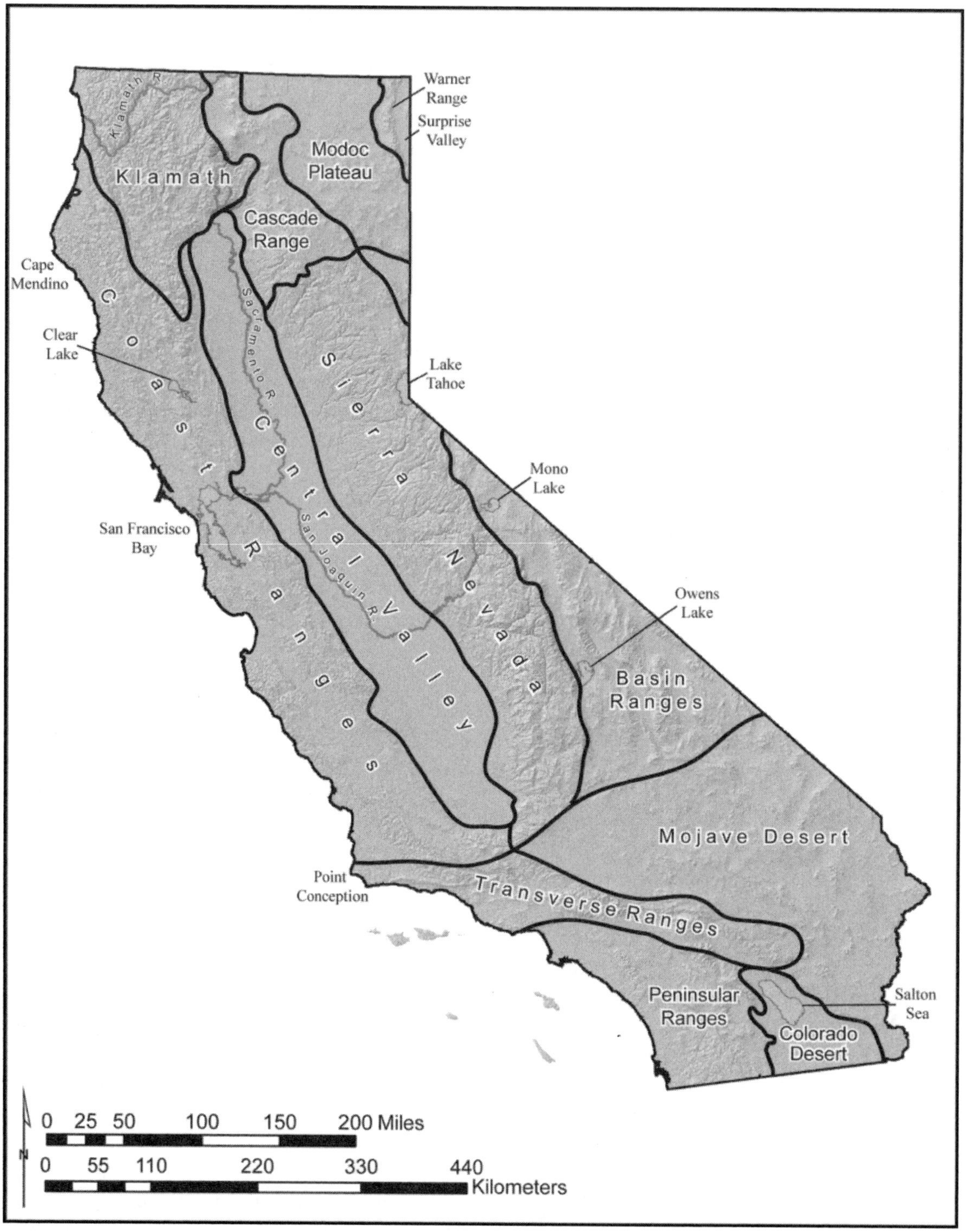

Figure 2.1. Topographic/geomorphic regions of California.

and Holocene epochs (Quaternary Period), although the length of the wet season has undoubtedly varied, as has the frequency of convectional storms in the interior and southern deserts. The other major climatic variable, temperature, while not totally independent, has also varied through time and season. Additional variables affecting California's climate and vegetation are solar insolation, atmospheric gas composition, and particulate matter such as volcanic aerosols, all of which have changed since the LGM.

However, it was not climate that prehistoric populations were interacting with per se, but the effects of climate on the biophysical environment. For aboriginal California, Baumhoff (1978), who examined the state by environment and culture area, pointed out that the critical element is vegetation since it forms the basis of the cultural ecosystem. We will take a similar perspective in this chapter and will focus heavily on vegetation in our examination of selected records of environmental change since the LGM. We plan to examine the dynamic nature of environments at the landscape scale in which prehistoric populations interacted since late Pleistocene times by adding a temporal perspective to Baumhoff's 1978 analysis.

ENVIRONMENT, CLIMATE, AND HUMAN BEHAVIOR

There are few simple unilinear relationships between environment and human behavior, nor is there a simple one-to-one relationship between climate and vegetation. Instead, the relationships in most instances are gradational and vary at differing temporal and spatial scales. Climate systems vary spatially from local to global, and vegetation responds by varying from the functioning of a single plant to global biomes. Seasonal to millennial oscillations of climate affect vegetation, although vegetation has its own internal oscillations such as succession. This multidimensional relationship is most often nonlinear and indirect where the mean state may change as external forcing factors (e.g., solar radiation, volcanic aerosols, or orbital variation) change (National Research Council 1999). Because of this, changes can cascade through ecosystems resulting in greater variability and instability affecting other parts or subsystems in both positive and negative ways, but the outcome is not always predictable. For example, the physical changes associated with El Niño years can have significant effects with considerable spatial variation on marine and terrestrial productivity, benefiting some taxa while devastating others.

Plants respond to climatic change through migration (latitude, longitude, and elevation shifts), adaptation through natural selection, extinction, extirpation, and changes in density. Their association with other plants has been dynamic, and the composition (presence and density of species) of vegetation types has varied temporally. There is conflicting evidence that plants making up vegetation types are restricted assemblages of species that coexist at equilibrium and undergo change by abrupt shifts from one apparently stable state to another or that vegetation types are open, continuously changing, nonequilibrium assemblages of species whose presence, absence, and relative abundance are governed by individualistic species response. For the timescale we are concerned with here, climatic forcing can be seen as the primary cause of such changes. Regardless of the ultimate cause and mode of change, evidence strongly suggests that vegetation types undergo profound composition changes, sometimes gradual, sometimes abrupt, on timescales of decades, centuries, millennia, and longer (Hubbell 2001).

California proxy vegetation records such as pollen and macrofossils in lake, marsh, and meadow sediments and pack rat middens, and tree ring series are a story of shifting species compositions, distributions, densities, and relative abundance. These proxy records suggest that the diversity of plant species over the past 20,000 years appears to have been about the same, but their assemblages changed because the plant associations disassembled and reassembled with varying dominance patterns and composition in response to climate variation. Most species responded individualistically at their own rate, some lagging behind others, and never quite in equilibrium. Because of this individualism and the previous occurrence of anomalous climatic parameters not historically observed, especially during the last glacial period, many former plant associations have no modern analogs.

As California's climate changed, plants responded according to their adaptive tolerance by remaining in place, changing their density, shifting their local ranges, migrating longer distances, or being extirpated. Migration was often rapid, as high as an estimated 400 meters per year, which is more than expected from present observations and seed dispersal characteristics. Therefore the range limits of many species responded rapidly to climate change. This rate is partly determined by the life histories of species. In general, trees live longer than shrubs, which in turn live longer than perennials and annuals. Most trees, therefore, have tended to persist against climate change longer than other plant life forms, leading to a more protracted alteration of tree species composition in forests.

Topography often influenced the type of response. In the mountains, the predominant vegetation response was contraction and expansion of populations along elevational gradients, whereas in the lowlands and desert basins, response was primarily latitudinal migration. Also regional climate in the mountains has been modulated according to topographical complexity, resulting in a mosaic of vegetation types. This heterogeneity can buffer the effects of climate change on vegetation.

The interactive relationship of human populations with plants has been dynamic and intimate, and may have affected vegetation composition and density, primarily through burning. Aboriginal populations may have altered the structure, density, and composition of some vegetation types. However, purposeful burning beyond natural fire frequencies is difficult to tease out of the known paleofire records, and its attribution to humans is mostly circumstantial. While the ethnographic record has been relied on for examining the anthropogenic effects on vegetation, its time depth and the scale of effects remain unclear.

CHRONOLOGICAL CONSIDERATIONS

A number of bio/geochronologic schemes, mostly based on global or hemispheric scales, have been put forth to temporally constrain and characterize the climate-vegetation-landscape changes that have taken place during the Quaternary. While all of the schemes have value and contribute to an understanding of the changes over time, most of them have been developed elsewhere and have been applied by some to California with little recognition of the variation that occurs at global, regional, or landscape scales.

Ice Sheet Chronology

Climate records of cores taken from Antarctic and Greenland ice caps have provided high-resolution information on temperature, precipitation, atmospheric composition, dust, and moisture levels for over 250,000 years. Chronological control for these cores is based on counts of the annual layers of ice, correlation with tephra from dated volcanic eruptions, and isotopic data. The core findings have been used to derive hemispheric-scale temperature, precipitation, dust, and atmospheric composition records of millennial to decadal resolution. The isotopic record of ice cores has demonstrated that climatic conditions of large magnitudes can change rapidly in timeframes of less than a human life span (Alley et al. 1993, 2003).

Marine Oxygen Isotopic Stages

Chemical and microfossil analysis of marine sediments from deep ocean basins and plains have provided continuous, high-resolution records of glacial-interglacial cycles through the entire Quaternary (Imbrie et al. 1992). Variations in the temporal distributions of microfossils, primarily foraminifera and radiolarians, reflect past temperatures, salinities, and productivity of the oceans. Oxygen-isotope ratios ($\delta^{18}O$) extracted from the carbonate tests of foraminifera provide estimates of continental ice volume and, through the use of a transfer function, temperature. Based on these observed shifts, a series of temporal and qualitative stages has been developed with correlations to orbital variations. These stages seem to reflect global or hemispheric climatic shifts, but more regional-scale isotopic records have been developed from mussel shell recovered from archaeological contexts (Jones and Kennett 1999).

Blytt-Sernander Late Glacial and Holocene Chronology

The original, well-developed, and widely used postglacial sequence was put forth by Blytt in 1876 and Sernander in 1910 based on the stratigraphic superposition of plant remains and oxidized layers found in Scandinavian bogs (Faegri et al. 1989). In 1916 L. Von Post, the "father of palynology," elaborated on the initial work and used pollen grains as well as plant macrofossils to refine the sequence. Von Post (Faegri et al. 1989) showed that samples from different deposits variously characterize vegetation; some contain regional pollen grains of the dominant trees, others local pollen and spores of marsh and aquatic vegetation. He focused on the regional pollen spectra because they better reflect changes in climate. Today, as the result of numerous studied sections, the Blytt-Sernander chronology has become more refined and is better understood in terms of ecological processes of plant succession in response to climate and other factors. It has served as the standard for northwestern Europe and has been applied to other areas, including California.

Antevs's Geologic-Climatic Dating

Antevs's (1955) late and postglacial scheme (Anathermal, Altithermal, Medithermal) is based on geomorphic studies in the southwest and intermountain basins of the West and has been widely used by archaeologists. Most of the original scheme is based on correlated data without absolute independent dates since his work was done prior to and into the early period of radiocarbon age determinations. As a result, some of Antevs's interpretations of chronology and climate have been challenged and refined based on new approaches and higher-resolution analysis. Nonetheless, his basic scheme has stood the test of time at least as a relative sequence, if not an absolute one. Antevs's ages and regional climatic interpretations have survived at a general level for large-scale comparative purposes.

Climatic Models

Climatic modelers have long attempted to explain Quaternary climate change as a result of variations in the earth's orbit (Berger et al. 1984; Imbrie and Imbrie 1980). Such changes are sufficient to force shifts in climate at the global scale. The pattern of glacial oscillations is widely assumed to be driven by the seasonal and latitudinal distribution of incident solar radiation according to periodic variations in the earth-sun geometry. In general, global ice volume grows with low summer insolation and high winter insolation and vice versa, giving rise to glacial and interglacial periods. The present Holocene climate phase, which began approximately 10,000 years ago, is the latest interglacial.

During the last deglaciation, summer solar radiation increased and winter solar radiation decreased from near present levels 18,000 years ago to a summer maximum and winter minimum 9,000 years ago. According to digital atmospheric general circulation models (GCMs) (COHMAP Members 1988; Kutzbach and Guetter 1986), maximum summer insolation 9,000 years ago caused above-average warmth. From their GCM, a rise in global temperature affects atmospheric circulation and consequently the position, orientation, and steepness of temperature gradients and precipitation patterns on a regional scale. While the northwestern United States became dry, the monsoons expanded and delivered increased summer rainfall to the Southwest, with resulting changes in vegetation.

THE FOSSIL PROXY RECORD

Since the instrumental climate record for California extends back less than 150 years, proxy records must be used to reconstruct climate prior to that time. The unknowns and uncertainties involved with proxy data, particularly when comparing records from different types of proxies (multiproxies) or from different regions, must be considered. This is especially significant when the resolution of data is low and uncertainty of interpretation is high.

Because of the long memory of some components of the climate system—heat capacity of the oceans, atmospheric gases and dust, ice sheets and the biosphere—conditions may persist for decades, centuries, or millennia, long after an externally forced climate shift has occurred. While there is evidence that climate may change abruptly within a decade, parts of the system have considerable inertia and reflect little response. Plants appear to respond at their own threshold; some species may show little or no change while others may respond more immediately to climate shifts from external forcing, such as solar variation or changes in the earth's orbit. If the climatic shift is too abrupt and there are no internal or external mechanisms for coping with rapid change, extinction or extirpation of a species may occur. Internal forcing, such as mutualism or other factors, may further constrain range shifts or other responses (such as an increase or decrease in density) of some taxa to climate change.

Interpretation is based on the geological concept of uniformitarianism, which states that the present is the key to the past. For the time frame addressed here, there do not appear to be significant evolutionary changes of plants or their environmental tolerances and there do not appear to have been, at least in California, extinction of plant species during aboriginal times. While many plants were extirpated from some areas of California, virtually all taxa known from the proxy records continue to exist and they probably have the same or very similar climatic relationships to those that were extirpated. Undoubtedly some evolution has occurred, but the degree of change has yet to be determined and is probably a minor concern at the landscape scale, albeit one that should not be overlooked. In contrast to plants, there have been major extinctions of mammals, with the demise of most of California's megafauna during the Late Pleistocene (LP), including mammoths, horses, bison, and ground sloths. Once extinct, the megafauna were never fully replaced and their effect on their former habitats ended (Martin 1967). How this change affected ecosystems and the plant communities within these ecosystems warrants further study.

Marine Fossil/Isotopic Record

Micro- and macrofossils and their associated isotopic records contained in anoxic to suboxic sediments from a number of deep sea basins off the California coast provide high resolution proxy records of marine conditions that span 150,000 years or more. For the

Late Pleistocene/Holocene the most significant are the foraminifera oxygen isotope records from the Santa Barbara basin (Kennett and Ingram 1995; Kennett and Kennett 2000), which have the longest and highest resolution of all the proxy records of the Southern California Bight. Mussel shells taken from archaeological contexts have provided a discontinuous 2,000-year isotopic record of sea temperatures for the central California coast (Jones and Kennett 1999).

Tree Rings, Climate, and Fire Regimes

Tree rings provide high-resolution records of climate (Hughes et al. 1982) and fire (Arno and Sneck 1977). Since tree rings are formed annually, their width, density, and isotopic composition can provide a precise record of the conditions under which they were formed with short lag times. Fire scars can be dated and provide a record of fire recurrence. Transfer functions have allowed for the reconstruction of past precipitation as well as temperature (by cross dating the upper and lower limits of trees' ranges, isotopic compositions, and frost rings) and river runoff for a number of locations in California. To be an effective tool, a network of trees for a given area needs to be developed. Dating of inundated tree stumps has been used to reconstruct past lake levels as well (Stine 1990). The time depth for tree ring records extends back some 8,700 years for bristlecone pine *(Pinus longaeva)* in the White Mountains near the border with Nevada (LaMarche 1973), but most records for other California trees are less than 2,500 years old. Blue oak *(Quercus douglasii)* tree ring chronologies, with their strong correlation to precipitation and runoff, provide a >400-year high-resolution record for central California (Stahle et al. 2001).

Sedimentary charcoal records from lakes and marine basins provide fire histories that extend well into the Pleistocene (Byrne 1978; Byrne et al. 1977; Mohr et al. 2000). Based on charcoal concentration values of two lakes in the eastern Klamath Mountains, for example, Mohr et al. (2000) found high fire-event frequencies around 6400 and 2000 cal B.C. and cal A.D. 1000, and low values around 2800 cal B.C. Such fire-event frequencies may have been related to climate since fire occurrences in this region appear to increase during dry periods.

Neotoma (Pack Rat) Nests

Pack rats have a behavioral pattern that has proved valuable in the interpretation of past plant distributions. They collect items within ~100 meters, mainly plant parts, and incorporate them into their nests in dry caves and crevices. The nests are then preserved by the pack rats' urine, which cements them together. The crystallized urine (amberat) can preserve these remains for tens of thousands of years in the absence of moisture. The preservation of plant remains in pack rat middens often is excellent, and it allows for the identification of species and for a variety of morphological, geochemical, and genetic analysis (Betancourt et al. 1990).

Pollen and Microfossil Records

Palynology has proven very useful for reconstructing past vegetation since pollen grains are abundant, and their outside shell (or exine) can remain preserved for many millennia. Because of their relative abundance, stratigraphic frequencies of pollen grains and spores can provide diachronic records of vegetation over long periods. Synchronic contemporary pollen rain can provide a representative index of modern vegetation types that can be used for comparative purposes as well as for determining the presence or absence of individual plant taxa in Quaternary pollen analysis. Chronological control has generally been achieved by radiocarbon dating sediments from which pollen grains are obtained or from associated plant macrofossils (e.g., seeds), but new efforts are being made to date the pollen grains themselves in order to achieve greater chronological precision. For California, Quaternary palynology has been constrained by an uneven distribution of favorable depositional environments, an extremely complex flora, limited funding, and few researchers.

The Multiproxy Record

SPATIAL AND TEMPORAL SCALE The scale at which we examine environmental change in this chapter is, to the degree possible, at the landscape level—relatively contiguous regions with similar topographic characteristics, climate, vegetation types, and substrate. The temporal scale (Figure 2.2) is primarily millennial because of the resolution of most of the records. A finer temporal scale is used in landscapes where higher resolution data are available.

The earliest human occupation of California is generally agreed to have occurred 12,000 to 13,000 years ago. Examining antecedent conditions during the extremely cold glacial conditions of the LGM helps us understand the environments that humans eventually encountered. Many ecosystem processes and changes that shape patterns of the effective human environment occur at timescales long enough for existing conditions to incorporate the persistence of past effects

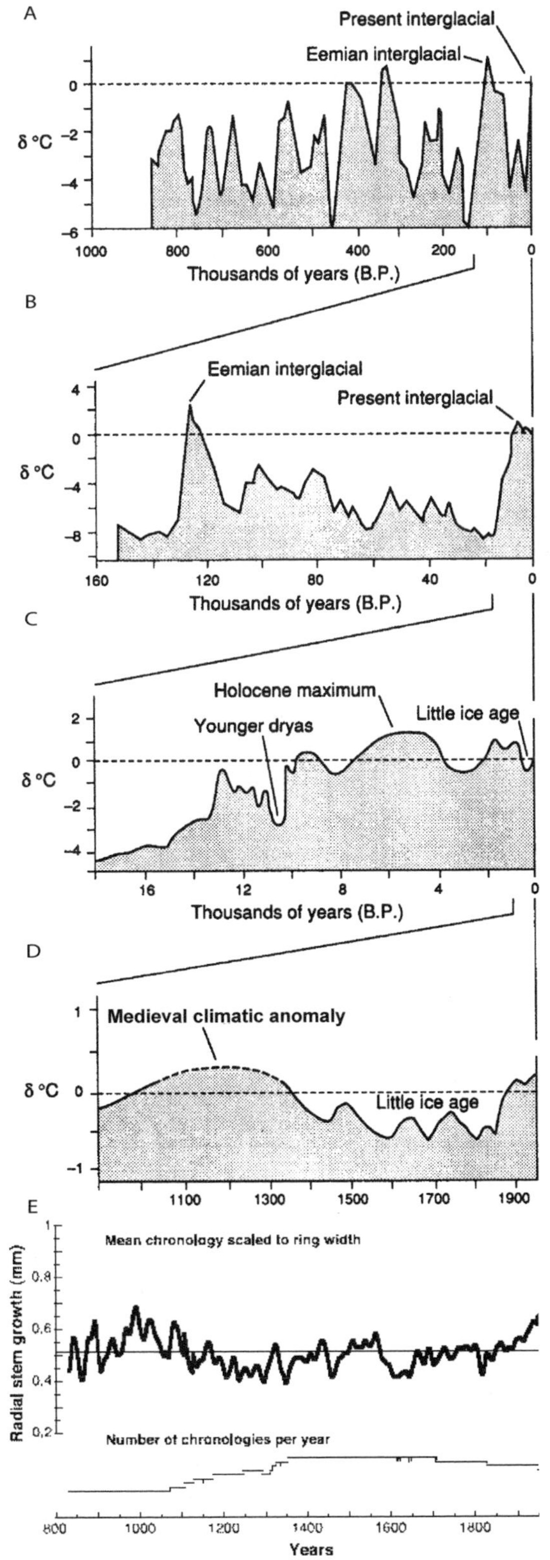

Figure 2.2. Generalized global surface temperatures at four (A – D) timescales (modified from Woolfenden 1996; original from Tausch et al. 1993); (E) Reconstructed northern hemisphere temperature variability during the past 1,800 years based on tree-ring series (Esper et al. 2002).

(Magnuson 1990; Scholes 1990). In addition, humans had to adapt to the high-magnitude change of the Pleistocene/Holocene Transition, which was unusually rapid relative to subsequent changes.

The dating of the Pleistocene/Holocene at 10,000 years ago is based on the geological convention for establishing chronological boundaries by the International Commission on Stratigraphy (ICS). There have been major vegetation changes across the boundary but those changes are time transgressive. The Holocene is a continuation of the global warming trend that began several thousand years earlier and peaked about 9,000 years ago with maximum summer insolation in the Northern Hemisphere. Temperatures cooled after about 6,000 years ago, reaching a minimum during the Neoglacial around 2,500 years ago. The two latest temperature cycles were the Medieval Climatic Anomaly (MCA) from about cal A.D. 800 to 1300 (Meese et al. 1994; Stine 1994) and the following Little Ice Age (LIA), which ended in the mid-nineteenth century. These Holocene climatic fluctuations have not been of the same magnitude as the shift from the Pleistocene to the Holocene, and the timing and duration of the Holocene events have been quite variable. For example, in the past the LIA was viewed as a single sustained cold period with dates ranging from A.D. 1200 to 1800 to A.D. 1350 to 1900. More recently, however, the LIA has been characterized by major and sudden fluctuations in climate often lasting only decades and affecting some regions more than others (Grove 1988).

LANDSCAPES Landscape-scale geographical regions similar to those in the Jepson manual (Hickman 1993) and Baumhoff (1978) will be used for our discussion (Figure 2.3). California can be divided into two major regions—Cismontane and Transmontane—each with distinct subregions based on topography, climate, and flora. Cismontane California includes lands west of the Cascade–Sierra Nevada–Peninsular range crest and is comparable to the California Floristic Province in the Jepson manual. We have placed the entire Sierra Nevada and Cascades within the Cismontane region, since the majority of those ranges falls west of the crests. The area to the east, the Transmontane, is equivalent to the Great Basin, Modoc Plateau, and desert provinces in the Jepson manual.

CISMONTANE CALIFORNIA

Northwest

Unlike most of the populations in Cismontane California, the ethnographic cultures of northwestern Cal-

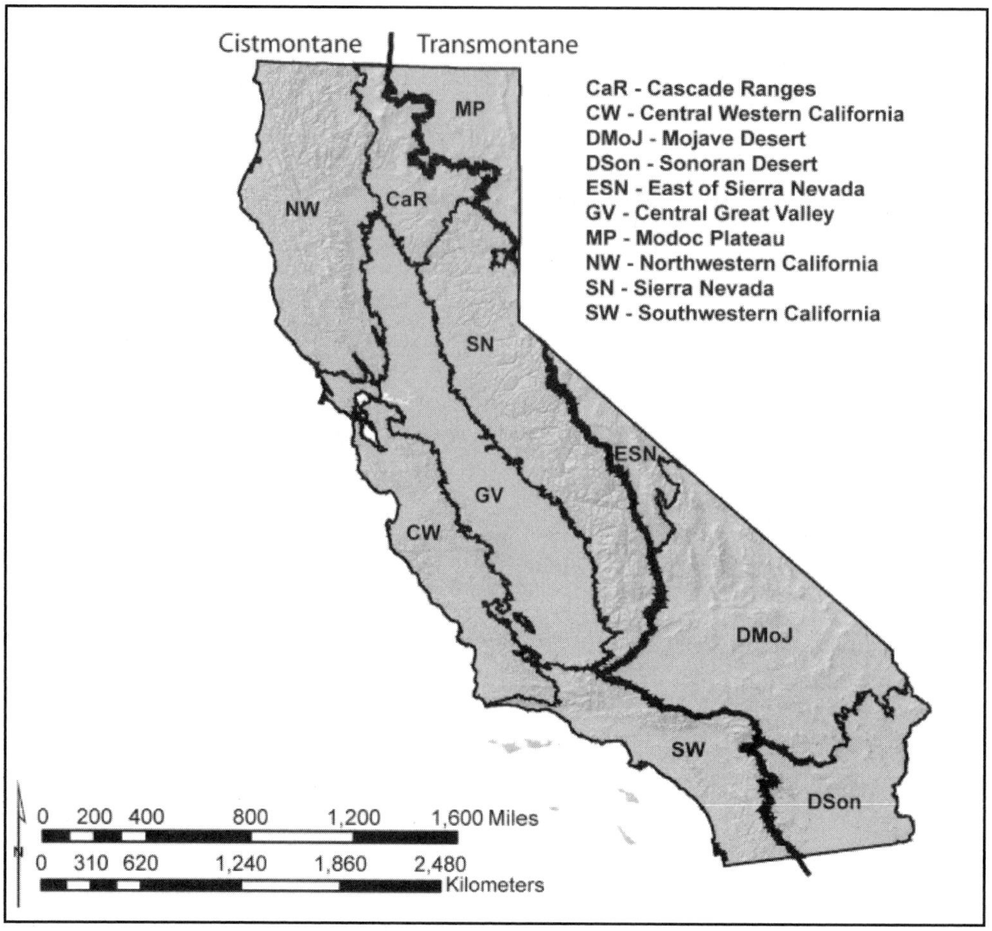

Figure 2.3. Jepson regions (Hickman 1993) by cismontane and transmontane division.

ifornia were more like those of the Northwest Coast culture area (Baumhoff 1978). This is also true of the environment that represents the southernmost extension of the midlatitude temperate rain forest. This mountainous region is characterized by long, wet winters and, along the coast, foggy, cool summers. Its streams support abundant anadromous fish runs.

The landscape of northwestern California is dominated by the physiographically and geologically distinct Klamath Mountains, which extend northward into southwestern Oregon and comprise a high-elevation hub between the California Coast Ranges, Southern Cascade/Sierra Nevada, Northern Cascades, and Oregon/Washington Coast Ranges. Locally, the Klamath Mountains are topographically complex, with major subranges divided by deep, narrow river canyons, bounded to the west by the Pacific coast and the east by the Sacramento, Shasta, and Rogue Valleys. The Klamath River, with headwaters in southern Oregon, cuts a low-elevation swath through the region; although it divides mountains exceeding 2,700 meters, it enters the province at only 650 meters elevation and then flows 290 kilometers to the Pacific. Geologically, the region is underlain by a mosaic of rock types that creates a spatially diverse set of edaphic influences on plant communities. Large bodies of serpentine and other ultramafic rocks found throughout the region exert profound controls on plant distributions, excluding some otherwise common species while allowing others tolerant of the low-calcium, high-metal soils to persist under greatly reduced competition. More benign bodies of granitic and sedimentary rocks are also scattered throughout the region, and the rich soils that develop on them typically support dense forests.

Superimposed on the structural complexity of northwestern California are two strong climatic gradients. A range of elevations from sea level to over 2,700 meters produces a climatic continuum from hot-summer, mild-winter river valleys to cool-summer, frigid-winter mountain summits. At the same time, a profound maritime-to-continental gradient exists from the coast to the eastern edge of the region. This latter gradient produces a shift in climate from the relatively wet, equable coast to the relatively dry, seasonal interior. The immediate coastline is typically cool and damp even in summer due to persistent advection fog from the Pacific Ocean.

The layers of topographic, geologic, and climatic complexity in northwestern California support an equally complex vegetation mosaic. The region is the meeting place of forest types of diverse geographic affinities. Temperate rain forests of redwood and Douglas fir occupy the coastal strip and lower river valleys of the region. The mid-elevation interior of the Klamath Mountains supports mixed evergreen forests with varying mixtures of Douglas fir, pine, oak, tanoak, and Port Orford and incense cedars. The eastern edge of the region finds forests of drought-adapted pine, juniper, oak, and mountain mahogany, which share some floristic similarities with the western Great Basin. Diverse montane forests of fir, hemlock, pine, and spruce occupy the higher elevations of northwestern California. These coniferous forests are extremely species rich, with 16 or more conifer species per square mile in several locations throughout the area (Sawyer and Keeler-Wolf 1995; Sawyer and Thornburgh 1970).

In recent years several studies of pollen in lakes and marine cores have begun to shed light on the temporal variability of the region's forests. Taken together, the studies show that the forests of northwestern California have undergone major changes in composition and structure consistent in timing with the known mechanisms of regional climate change. In some cases, the magnitude of change is inconsistent with the long-standing view of the area as a Quaternary forest refuge.

LATE GLACIAL MAXIMUM The vast majority of high-elevation depositional basins in northwestern California are glacial in origin and therefore contain records of montane vegetation that postdate the last glacial maximum. Bolan Lake (1,638 meters) in the Siskiyou Mountains provides a record of sedimentary pollen and charcoal back to 17,000 years ago (Briles et al. 2005). From 17,000 to 15,000 years ago, vegetation at the site was dominated by sagebrush, pine, spruce, and cedar (Cupressaceae). This assemblage is typical of much colder and drier conditions than currently exist in the region. Taxa typical of more temperate conditions, such as Douglas fir and true fir, became important at the site between 15,000 and 10,500 years ago. Slow charcoal accumulation indicates that fires were infrequent, while low sedimentary organic content indicates that lake productivity was low, likely due to cold temperatures. Records of similar age from Bluff Lake (1,921 meters) and Mumbo Lake (1,860 meters) in the eastern Klamath region show that the area was open subalpine parkland vegetation dominated by sagebrush and grasses prior to 11,000 cal B.C. (Daniels et al. 2005; Mohr et al. 2000).

Twin Lakes (1,200 meters) in the southern Siskiyou Mountains is a slump basin that yielded a 50,000-year record of vegetation changes (Figure 2.4) at an elevation now at the upper limit of mixed evergreen forest (Wanket 2002). Throughout the Late Pleistocene and including the LGM, forests around Twin Lakes were dominated by taxa more typical of the present-day northern Cascade Mountains. An open forest of mountain hemlock, western hemlock, spruce, pine, and fir persisted until 11,000 cal B.C. at Twin Lakes, indicating colder conditions, abundant snowpack, and greatly reduced summer drought relative to today. Conditions at Twin Lakes appear to have been more maritime than at Bolan and Bluff Lakes, implying a strong east-west climatic gradient. Absent from the record of this period is pollen from Douglas fir, oak, and tanoak, the primary constituents of mixed evergreen forests today. Sedimentary charcoal is rare in the record before about 12,000 cal B.C., when a sudden increase in charcoal influx coincides with an increase in herbaceous pollen relative to the dominant mountain hemlock.

PLEISTOCENE/HOLOCENE TRANSITION The period from 11,000 to 8000 cal B.C. was one of dramatic changes in vegetation in northwestern California. At Twin Lakes, a subalpine forest dominated by mountain hemlock was replaced by a closed forest of pine and fir within a few hundred years at 11,000 cal B.C. (Wanket 2002). Temperate taxa such as alder, Douglas fir, oak, and tanoak appeared as minor components of the vegetation at this time, suggesting a higher temperature. A second major change in vegetation occurred about 1,000 years later, when montane and subalpine taxa such as fir, mountain and western hemlock, and spruce abruptly disappeared. This second vegetation shift, which corresponds with the end of the Younger Dryas interval as recorded in Santa Barbara basin sediments (Hendy et al. 2002), was accompanied by large-scale fire disturbance as evidenced by increased sedimentary charcoal and a large spike in alder pollen. After 9000 cal B.C. the Twin Lakes forest was dominated by pine and cedar, with minor components of Douglas fir and tanoak. At Bolan Lake in the Siskiyous, the transition from cold-adapted subalpine/montane forest to temperate forest of pine, cedar, Douglas fir, and huckleberry oak occurred at about the same time as the second vegetation shift at Twin Lakes (Briles et al. 2005).

At Mumbo and Bluff Lakes in the eastern Klamath Mountains, increased pollen frequencies of pine

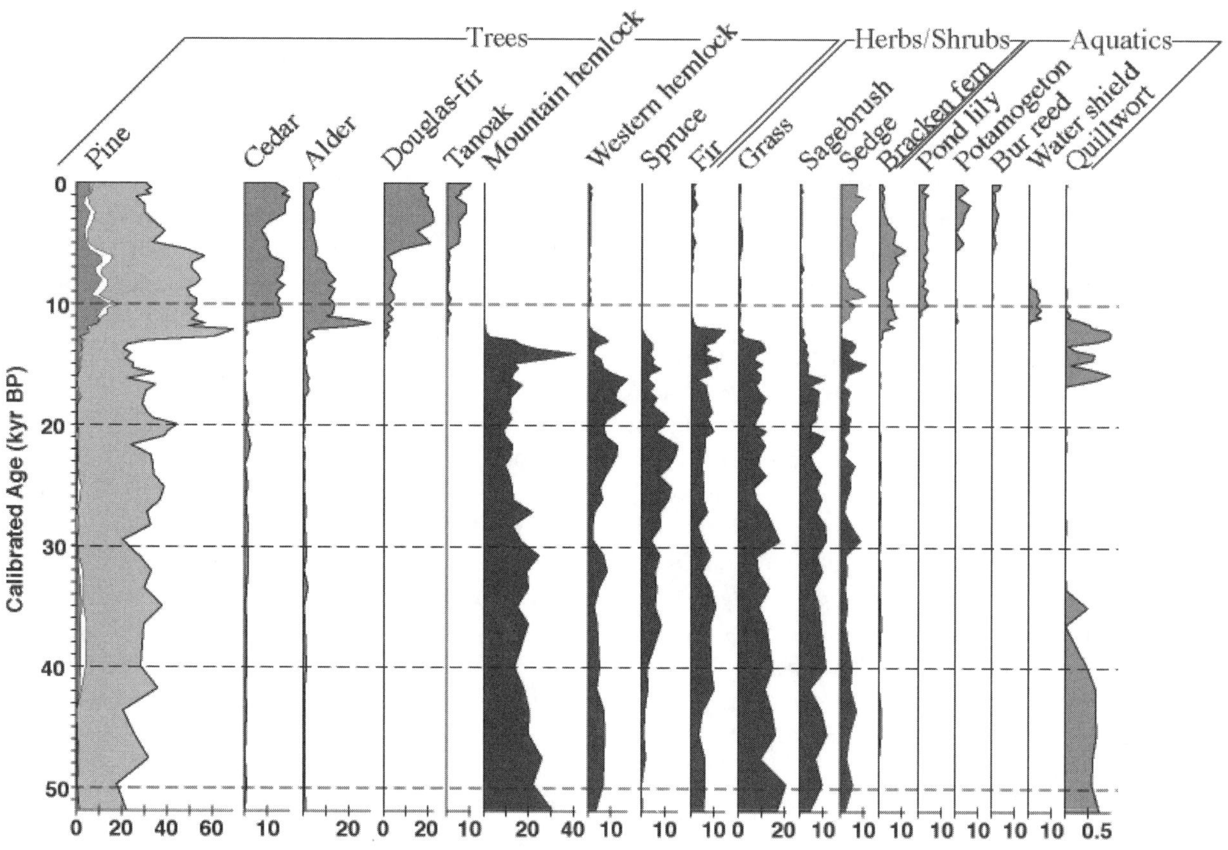

Figure 2.4. Pollen percentage diagram for major taxa from Twin Lake, Klamath Mountains (Wanket 2002).

and fir and decreased herb pollen values between 11,000 and 9100 cal B.C. indicate the development of an open forest with relatively warmer and wetter conditions than before but cooler by about 3°C (Smith and Anderson 1992) and wetter than today. Similar conditions are present at Cedar Lake (1,743 meters) located at the headwaters of the Sacramento River at this time (West 1989). The frequency of fire events in this period ranges from five to eight per 1,000 years, which is low relative to the Holocene average (Mohr et al. 2000). After 9000 cal B.C., forests at both sites were dominated by pine, huckleberry oak, and cedar. From seven marine and coastal northern California pollen records, Heusser and Barron (2002) interpreted early Holocene forests as being composed of remnants of full-glacial age open pine woodlands, chaparral, and grasslands with isolates of communities that later developed into the present-day associations.

EARLY/MIDDLE HOLOCENE Between 11,000 and 4,500 years ago, vegetation records from throughout northwestern California indicate conditions that were effectively drier than today. In Middle Holocene marine assemblages, pines, herbs, and oak increase as redwood and cedar decline, implying enhanced seasonality, particularly warm, dry summers (Heusser and Barron 2002). A stronger summer drought may also be reflected in the drying out of wetlands and significant amounts of charcoal in sediments deposited between 9,000 and 4,000 years ago. At Bolan Lake and Twin Lakes in the Siskiyou Mountains, the dominance of pine and cedar (probably incense cedar) and relatively minor components of Douglas fir, fir, and tanoak/chinquapin indicate that during the Middle Holocene conditions were more similar to those of today's eastern Klamath Mountains (Briles et al. 2005; Wanket 2002). Summer drought appears to have been well established in the Siskiyous by 8000 cal B.C. At Bolan Lake, fire event frequency peaked at 10 events per thousand years at about 5000 cal B.C.

A pollen record from Frog Pond, a low-elevation (600 meters) slide-impounded lake above the central Klamath River canyon, provides a record of changing composition of a mixed evergreen forest (Wanket and Bills 2005). Before approximately 5,000 years ago, pine and oak were the primary forest constituents while tanoak and alder were uncommon. This situation is found today upriver in the eastern Klamath Mountains, where conditions are considerably drier and more continental.

Early and Middle Holocene forests surrounding Mumbo, Bluff, and Cedar Lakes are dominated by pine and Cupressaceae (most likely Port Orford cedar at Cedar Lake) with significant amounts of shrub oak *(Quercus vaccinifolia)* and members of the rose family (Daniels et al. 2005; Mohr et al. 2000; West 1989). At higher elevations pine, scrub oak, Oregon oak, and sagebrush characterize the vegetation surrounding the higher-elevation Crater Lake (2,288 meters) at 6500 to 3700 cal B.C. (Mohr et al. 2000). These Early and Middle Holocene forests imply increased temperatures and decreased effective precipitation. For Bluff Lake the charcoal-peak frequency fluctuates from 6 to 10 events per 1,000 years; whereas at Crater Lake the frequency of fire events is 11 to 17 fire events per 1,000 years. Fires were frequent at both sites at ca. 6300 and 2000 cal B.C.

LATE HOLOCENE Essentially modern forests developed after 6,000 years ago in northwestern California. Beginning ca. 4,000 years ago, marine pollen records show millennial- and submillennial-scale oscillations with an overall rise in conifer-dominated assemblages, especially redwood (Heusser and Barron 2002). This overall increase in effective moisture is punctuated by a decline between about 1,300 to 700 years ago, when a decrease in redwood and alder, along with an increase in pine, suggests warmer, drier summers. Similar transitions to more maritime forests occurred later at Bolan Lake (2500 cal B.C.) and Twin Lakes (3500 cal B.C.) in the Siskiyous, where decreases in pine corresponded to increases in fir, Douglas fir, and tanoak/chinquapin (Briles et al. 2005; Wanket 2002). At Twin Lakes this transition was a single step, while at Bolan Lake the transition occurred in two stages, the latter at about 300 cal B.C.

In the eastern Klamaths, slight increases in fir and pine suggest that conditions at Mumbo and Bluff Lakes became cooler after about 2000 cal B.C. (Daniels et al. 2005; Mohr et al. 2000). Decreases in oak beginning about 1000 cal B.C. suggest a relatively closed canopy forest and by cal A.D. 1, the modern forest of fir, pine and incense cedar was established. Modern forests of fir, mountain hemlock, and pine were well developed by ca. cal A.D. 800 during a period of increased fire-event frequency. At lower elevation Cedar Lake, the establishment of modern forests of pine, fir, Douglas fir, and manzanita occurred after 2100 cal B.C. (3,450 ± 90 B.P.) when conditions became cooler and wetter than before (West 1989).

Multiproxy records from offshore marine sediments provide a generalized reflection of the coastal environments (Heusser and Barron 2002). Some of the marine records correspond with the terrestrial records in that they show a similar sequence but include a record of redwoods that may reflect the degree of coastal upwelling that is so critical in supporting a maritime economy. The present distribution of redwoods is within a narrow coastal strip from just over the Oregon border to the northwestern edge of San Luis Obispo County and thus overlaps two other landscapes—the North Coast and South Coast Ranges. While the Late Pleistocene/Holocene record for redwood is sketchy and uneven, there is sufficient data to suggest that redwood has shifted its range in response to climate shifts (Noss 2000).

North Coast Range

Baumhoff (1978) considered the North Coast Range as probably California's richest environment for nonagricultural populations. It is an area of great topographic, edaphic, and climatic diversity ranging from high-elevation red fir forests to large areas of oak woodland and forests to dense riparian redwood groves. The topographic complexity and edaphic diversity resulted from a geologic history which gave rise to a juxtaposition of strikingly different rock types. These substrate contrasts, particularly ultramafic rocks such as serpentine, contribute to the juxtaposition of vegetation types and species of widely different geographic relations. There is a strong climatic gradient from the maritime climate of the coast to the more continental interior. Like northwestern California, the rivers and streams supported anadromous fish runs. The prehistory and paleoenvironmental history are equally complex, and have been documented by a number of records.

For the higher elevations of this landscape, West (1989, 1990, 1993) examined the sediments of small landslide lakes and spring deposits located in a number of different vegetation types. Some of the records are >10,000 years long, but most are confined to the Middle to Late Holocene. Some of the radiocarbon dates used for temporal control are derived from sediments that probably include several hundred years of deposition and, therefore, the resolution for shifts in the pollen record is less specific. Using an indicator species model for the region, more continental, possibly cooler conditions were indicated for the earliest Holocene Period (>8500 years ago), when pine pollen was dominant (West 1993). Pollen concentration values suggest open pine parkland at higher elevations in the LP, while at Lily Pond (1,244 meters) the possible appearance of lodgepole pine occurred some 9,000 to 10,000 years ago. Oak pollen values reach their highest percentages during the Middle Holocene at most localities as the result of oaks expanding their overall range and moving upslope. Declining oak pollen values and increasing values for Douglas fir and tan oak, most evident after 3,800 to 2,300 years ago at most localities, indicate cooler maritime conditions with wet winters and more moderate temperatures throughout the year. Douglas fir pollen values show a time transgressive increase from north to south beginning about 6,000 years ago (Figure 2.5) with a sharp increase about 2,500 to 3,000 years ago, suggesting a shift in mean storm tracks southward (West 1990) and greater effective moisture. The pattern of Douglas fir pollen in the profiles is consistent with the Klamath Mountains record at Twin Lakes (Wanket 2002).

In the lowlands, Adam (1988), Adam and West (1983), Adam et al. (1981), and West (2001) have presented the most coherent pollen analysis of Clear Lake sediments that include the LP and Holocene. Taking a long-term perspective, Adam presented two pollen records from lake sediments that cover more than an estimated 150,000 years. In LP sediments, pine, fir, and TCT pollen grains are relatively most abundant and imply that a conifer forest surrounded Clear Lake. Inter- and intraglacial sediments, including the Holocene, are characterized by abundant pollen grains from oak and chaparral taxa. A higher-resolution pollen record from the same series of United States Geological Survey cores is presented in West (2001) extending back to the LGM that may provide a record of the Younger Dryas (YD) cold period (Figure 2.6). Pines, fir, and TCT taxa (cypress and incense cedar) were rapidly replaced by oaks during the transition from the LP to the Holocene, but there appears to be a relatively short, steplike pattern reversal in the pollen record suggesting that pines increased with a return to colder temperatures. This short-term reversal (ca. 500 to 800 years) ended as abruptly as it began, and oaks once again replaced pines as the dominant arboreal

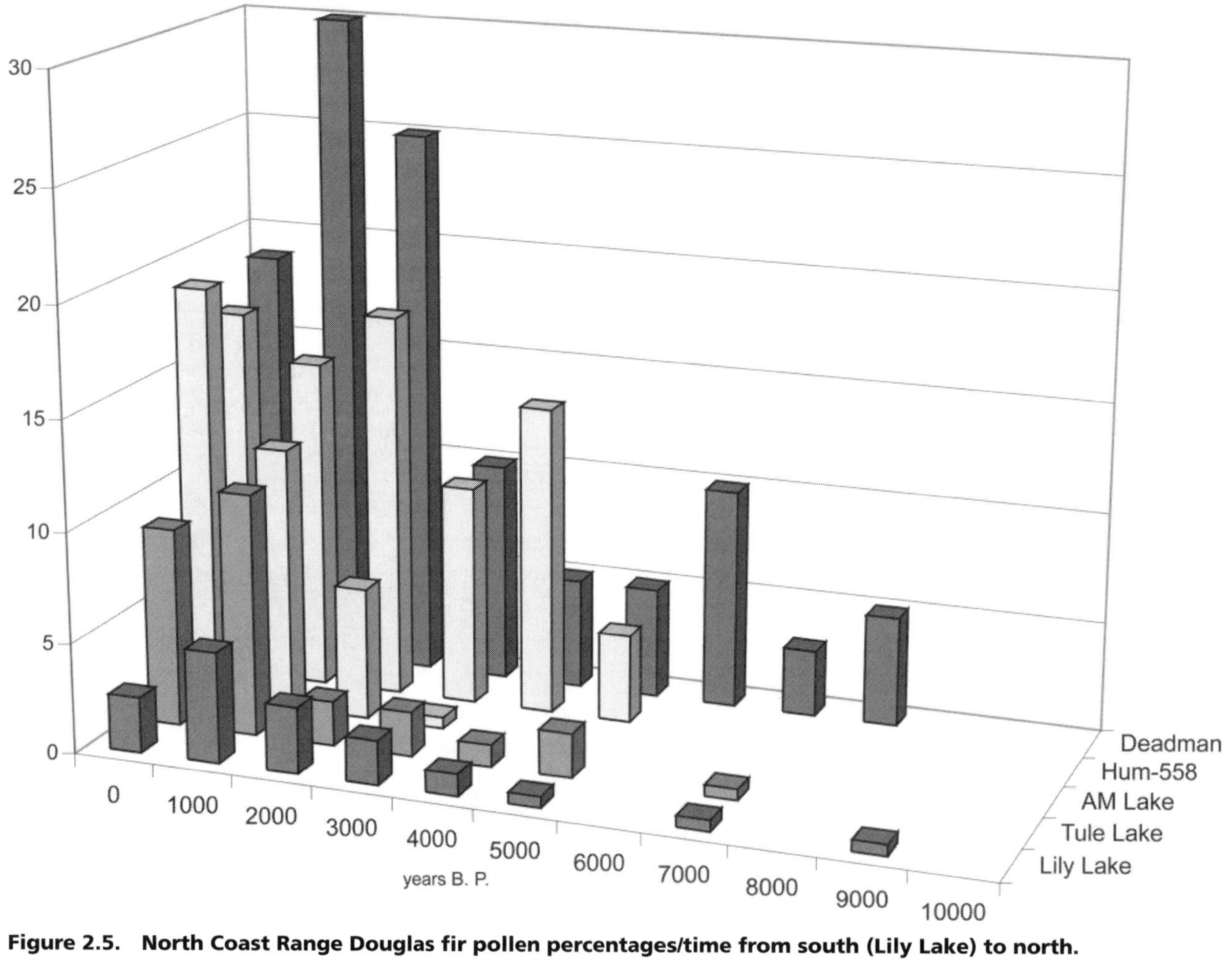

Figure 2.5. North Coast Range Douglas fir pollen percentages/time from south (Lily Lake) to north.

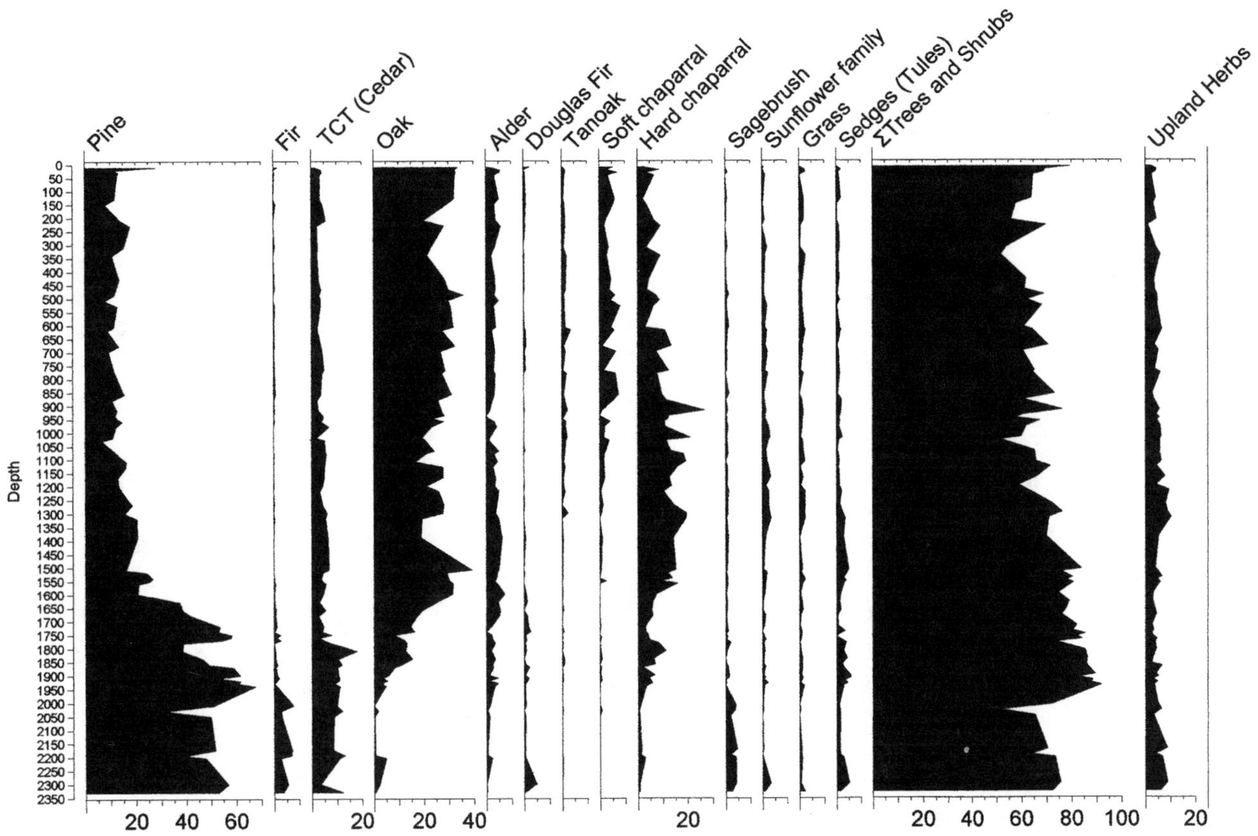

Figure 2.6. Pollen percentage diagram for major taxa from Core CL-73-5 Clear Lake, Lake County, California (West

species in the Clear Lake basin. Shifting patterns of pollen values from chaparral taxa suggest a transition from hard chaparral communities to soft chaparral communities by the Late Holocene. Mean LGM temperatures were estimated to be 7–8°C cooler than today while Middle Holocene temperatures may have been 1–2°C warmer (Adam and West 1983).

Near the coast at Olema Marsh north of San Francisco Late Pleistocene/Early Holocene pollen assemblages suggest a forest cover of Douglas and other fir (Generaux et al. 2003). A similar forest can be found today 33 kilometers to the northwest at Willow Creek just south of the mouth of the Russian River where grand fir *(Abies grandis)* mixes with Douglas fir. Temperate conditions are inferred and, as today, there was a climatic gradient from the maritime coast to the more continental inland.

In contrast to Heusser and Barron's (2002) findings from farther north, Bergquist (1977, 1978) found spruce *(Picea)* pollen in sediments from Bodega Bay that are probably LP in age and would imply cool, moist conditions. However, on the coast near Bodega Bay, Rypins et al. (1989) did not recover any spruce pollen from sediments dating 12,000 to 7,500 years ago, implying that spruce must be from an earlier time period, possibly the LGM.

Sacramento Valley

The Sacramento Valley is the northern half of California's Great Valley. It is generally a large trough that, with little exception, is filled with alluvium and drained by the Sacramento River. The most notable exception is the Sutter Butte, a striking volcanic plug that juts some 600 meters above the valley floor. Baumhoff (1963:225–226) concluded that the Sacramento Valley was the richest in acorn and deer staples of any area in the state, further enhanced by linear fish resources, the Sacramento River and its tributaries, producing an acorn-fish-game adaptation that was distinctly Californian.

The Sacramento River basin floodplains once supported extensive riparian woodlands along the major rivers. Historical accounts and maps indicate the existence of continuous forests up to eight kilometers wide along the Sacramento River, plus extensive forests on higher terraces even farther from the river. Presettlement estimates of riparian vegetation along the Sacramento River range from 320,000 to 4,000,000 hectares

(800,000 to 1,000,000 acres). Flanking the riparian forests on higher surfaces were grasslands and on lowlands were seasonal wetlands. Today the entire landscape has been reworked by agriculture and other forms of development, making it difficult to determine the extent and diversity of precontact ecosystems (White 2003a). A pollen and macrofossil record from beneath Sacramento suggests that pines and red fir extended farther down the American River canyon during the LGM and that oaks had a very restricted distribution (West 1997). Only temporally short Holocene pollen records exist for the entire valley and results have not been published; other paleoenvironmental data of a greater temporal span have been derived primarily from geomorphic/soil studies, vertebrate fossil finds, and archaeological investigations (White 2003a).

TREE RINGS Flows of the Sacramento and Feather Rivers have been reconstructed back to A.D. 869 from tree ring data (Meko 2001; Meko et al. 2001). These high-resolution reconstructions provide a detailed account of runoff unparalleled for most of cismontane California. Low-flow years and periods were identified; only six were lower than the lowest flow year of record, the 1977 drought year. Two of the dates for drought fall within the Medieval Climatic Anomaly (MCA), but according to Meko's findings, the MCA was not the most significant drought affecting the Sacramento River watershed in the last 1,000 years. In fact, the watershed may have experienced a climatic amelioration during the time when severe drought was still impacting the Southwest (Cook et al. 2004), thus suggesting a possible north/south phase shift in drought severity and timing.

Sacramento–San Joaquin Delta

The Sacramento–San Joaquin Delta is located at the confluence of the Sacramento and San Joaquin Rivers in central California and covers approximately 294,000 hectares (735,000 acres). Prior to 1850 the delta was a vast tule marsh with riparian forests along the natural levees of the major rivers. Fossil evidence indicates that this vegetation was present for at least 6,000 years (West 1977). In the late prehistoric period most of the settlements were located on the tops of partly drowned dunes (so-called sand mounds) and the higher natural levees.

Unlike true deltas such as the Nile, this delta is a large tidal wetland and floodplain of one-third of the state's runoff. The current delta is primarily the result of post-Pleistocene sea level rise, aggradation of fine-grained sediments, and the bioaccumulation of organics (Atwater 1980; Shlemon and Begg 1975). While there is some evidence for tectonic subsidence, the amount has not been clearly determined for the Holocene but is probably minor. At the end of the Pleistocene, sea level was more than 55 meters lower than today (Atwater et al. 1977) and the shoreline was situated some distance west of San Francisco. As the result of worldwide glacial ice melting, sea levels rose rapidly until about 8,000 years ago and then slowed considerably (see Chapter 3). By ~6,000 years ago the current delta began to form. Consequently the aggradation of fine-grained sediments and bioaccumulation of organics, mostly derived from aquatic-emergent plants, were the primary factors in the evolution of the delta. As sea level rose, aeolian dunes derived from river-transported sands were totally or partially inundated forming isolated, sandy islands surrounded by marshland. These relict dunes were favored by prehistoric populations for settlements and other activities (West et al. 2001).

Delta proxy records include Gorman and Wells's (2000) study of stream flow based on sediments and plant macrofossils for the past 7,000 years, Stahle et al.'s (2001) >400-year blue oak *(Quercus douglasii)* tree ring–based runoff and salinity record, and Starratt's (2002) 3,000-year diatom-based freshwater flow variation study for the Suisun Bay. During the Holocene, discharge from the Sacramento and San Joaquin Rivers was broadly comparable to modern flows; however, an extended period of higher flow began 3,800 years ago and continued for almost two millennia (Gorman and Wells 2000). At the northern margins of Suisun Bay in the western delta, Starratt (2002) found two intervals dominated by freshwater diatoms (550 cal B.C. to cal A.D. 230 and approximately cal A.D. 750 to 1850) and two intervals dominated by brackish water and marine diatoms (1050 to 550 cal B.C and cal A.D. 200 to 1200). He equated these cycles with variations in runoff and suggested that they reflect contemporaneous precipitation on both sides of the Sierra Nevada as they are compatible with the pattern of lake levels at Mono and Pyramid Lakes. A tree ring chronology from blue oak, with its strong correlation to precipitation and hence runoff, provides a >400-year high-resolution record for San Francisco Bay salinity (Stahle et al. 2001) and shows that low salinity occurred during very strong El Niño events and that the California drought of 1976–1977 was one of the worst of the past 400 years.

San Joaquin Valley

The San Joaquin Valley receives considerably less rain than the Sacramento Valley, less than 25 centimeters annually at its southern end. Moisture in the San Joaquin Valley is primarily derived from Sierra snowmelt runoff that begins in the spring and ends, under natural conditions, in the summer. As a result the San Joaquin Valley was marked by extensive but shallow lakes, the largest being Tulare Lake (which at times covered more than 2,070 square kilometers) and permanent and seasonal wetlands that supported large expanses of aquatic-emergent vegetation that provided important resources for prehistoric populations. Riparian vegetation was not as well developed as that of the Sacramento Valley and was far less diverse.

Davis's (1999a) pollen study of Tulare Lake sediments provides a record of local and regional vegetation for the Late Pleistocene and Holocene in the southern San Joaquin Valley. The Early Holocene pollen spectra prior to 8,000 years ago are dominated by Cupressaceae (most likely juniper), pine, oak, sagebrush, and greasewood, suggesting a pinyon-juniper-oak woodland in the uplands, with greasewood on the salt flats near the lake. By 8,000 years ago juniper and sagebrush pollen values decline to background levels whereas oak pollen values peak for the Holocene between 8,500 and 7,500 years ago. Giant sequoia was widespread along the Sierra streams draining into Tulare Lake prior to 9,000 years ago.

Some 7,000 years ago greasewood disappears from the record, and between 7,000 and 4,000 years ago, major increases in shrub-herb pollen suggest expansion of xerophythic shrub steppe. Higher values for pollen grains from littoral plants such as tules and decreases in abundances of pelagic algae suggest lower water levels. Pollen data further suggest that the late Holocene began with a cold, wet period 3,500 to 2,500 years ago with higher lake levels followed by progressively lower lake levels. Davis (1999a:254–255) inferred from these trends that the Early Holocene was cold and wet, and that maximum temperature and drought occurred between 7,000 and 4,000 years ago. Cool, moist climate from ca. 4,000 to 2,000 years ago was followed by a return to aridity and high temperature ca. 1,000 years ago. Of particular interest is the abundance of charcoal in the record, which shows increased frequencies after ca. 7,000 years ago, implying greater fire frequency in Holocene woodlands and grasslands.

South Coast Range, Southern Coastal/Islands

PROXY RECORDS FROM MARINE BASINS Pollen records recovered from anoxic marine basins off southern California by Heusser (1995, 1998) have provided the longest and most continuous millennial-scale vegetation record for the region. LGM pollen spectra are characterized by maximum values of conifers (pine and juniper-cypress) and minimal values for oak and chaparral taxa. At the transition from the Pleistocene to the Holocene (14,000 to 10,000 years ago) there is a rapid increase in oak, herbs, and chaparral taxa and a corresponding decrease in conifers, signaling the initial development of Holocene-type plant communities (e.g., oak woodland, chaparral, and coastal sage scrub). During the Holocene there is an overall increase in oak, chaparral, and herbs and a decrease in pine. Brief shifts in oak, pine, and juniper-cypress occur at ~1,000-year intervals (Heusser and Sirocko 1997). Heusser believes that the absence of pollen from northern conifers such as western hemlock or coast redwood in records south of ~35° N implies that the southern limit of these Pacific Northwestern forests was never farther south of its present extension. The presence of undated wood attributed to coast redwood found at Rancho la Brea tar pits in the Los Angeles basin (Warter 1976) requires further examination.

Using a relatively high-resolution (ca. 25-year intervals in the past 3,000 years and ca. 50-year intervals from 11,000 to 3,000 years ago) record of changes in the oxygen isotopes of southern California marine foraminifera, Kennett and Kennett (2000) demonstrated that sea surface temperatures (SST) oscillated from warm to cold and back on a millennial timescale. Distinct SST cooling episodes were found to vary in length, but generally occurred at intervals of 1,500 years. Early and Middle Holocene conditions were more stable, with inferred SST varying up to 3°C. In contrast, they found that the Late Holocene SST exhibited much greater instability, with average temperature variation up to 5°C, a Holocene temperature range much greater than that observed from terrestrial records (Adam and West 1983). For the past 3,000 years, three general climatic phases were discerned: 1050 cal B.C. to cal A.D. 450 when SST were relatively warm and stable, cal A.D. 450 to 1300 when SST were cold and unstable, and cal A.D. 1300 to present when SST were warmer and more stable. Their study also included a nonlinear proxy measure of marine productivity based on inferred upwelling, where periods of greater upwelling were interpreted as representing higher marine productivity. The largely cold SST interval between cal A.D. 450 and 950 was not matched by an increase in the upwelling proxy, whereas there was a relatively strong relationship between cold SST and inferred intense upwelling from cal A.D. 950–1550. Relatively warm SST periods with inferred low upwelling occurred from 1050 cal B.C. to cal A.D. 450 and after cal A.D. 1550. The most favorable interval for marine productivity was from cal A.D. 950 to 1300. Terrestrial records of precipitation appear to have an inverse correlation with cold SST, where low terrestrial precipitation correlates with especially low SST in the Santa Barbara basin (Graumlich 1993; Larson and Michaelson 1989; Stine 1994). This may be partly due to a stronger thermal gradient from land to sea.

A number of Holocene pollen records from mainland and island coastal estuaries have provided lower-resolution vegetation histories at local and landscape scales (Anderson 2002; Cole and Liu 1994; Cole and Wahl 2000, Davis 1992; Shelley et al. 2003; West 1988). These records reflect the effects of sea level change, runoff, climate, and land-use changes on vegetation patterns that have occurred in their respective catchments. Based on a series of paleoenvironmental records from floodplains and lagoons along the San Diego County shore, Pope et al. (2004) argued that the Early Holocene (ca. 10,000 to 7,000 years ago) was a period of vigorous upwelling and frequent coastal fog. The Middle Holocene (ca. 7,000 to 3,000 years ago) was a period of mild, stable climate (with less upwelling and few if any El Niño events), and the Late Holocene (ca. 3,000 years ago to present) was characterized by a highly variable climate with frequent El Niño events and droughts.

From a tightly dated sequence of deposits at Daisy Cave on San Miguel Island (Erlandson et al. 1996), pollen values suggest that pine trees were abundant in the vicinity of the cave when sea levels were lower prior to ca. 10,000 cal B.C. After this time, pine pollen values decline dramatically and pollen from members of the sunflower and rose families and oak pollen increase significantly. Today no trees are found on San Miguel Island. Similar high pine as well as high cypress pollen values have been recorded for LP sediments on Santa Rosa Island, suggesting that pine and cypress forests were more extensive >10,000 years ago on the Northern Channel Islands than they are today.

From Santa Ynez River alluvium, a climatically driven paleoflood/geomorphic record has been reconstructed that covers the LP and Holocene (Ostenaa et al. 1996). Two prominent Holocene surfaces and the channel of the Santa Ynez River are inset in an extensive LP terrace that is 20,000 to 15,000 years old. The Holocene terrace stabilized about 2,900 years ago, while the upper floodplain stabilized about 700 years ago. The relationship between the timing of the stabilization of the geomorphic surfaces with vegetation and SST shifts noted for the region is significant since the older Millingstone sites are confined to the LP terrace while late sites are found on all surfaces.

Sierra Nevada

The Sierra Nevada extends north to south for 650 kilometers along the eastern boundary of California. It has been uplifted to elevations of over 4,300 meters along a mountain front fault system and tilted to the west. To a large extent the mountain range has been shaped by glacial and fluvial erosion over the past 2.6 million years, which has widened and deepened the canyons of the major drainages. The immense latitudinal and elevational extent of the range and the contrast in moisture regimes on both sides produces very diverse habitats.

On the mesic west slope, vegetation grades from foothill associations of grass, chaparral, pine, and oak through several montane conifer forest types to alpine shrub on the crest (Miles and Goudey 2005; Sawyer and Keeler-Wolf 1995). Major rivers lined by riparian woodlands flow westward in deeply incised canyons with bedrock-controlled channels to the Great Valley.

Natural vegetation along the steep eastern escarpment ranges from desert shrub and singleleaf pinyon woodland to subalpine conifer woodland and alpine cushion plants, shared with the west side, at the higher elevations. Alluvial fans and glacial moraines emanating from the canyons provide habitat for several shrub associations. The gently rolling Kern Plateau on the southernmost part of the range provides habitat for singleleaf pinyon on lower elevations, above which are found Jeffrey pine and mixed conifer forest. Extensive sedge meadows are distributed over the plateau (Sawyer and Keeler-Wolf 1995; Woolfenden 2003).

WESTERN SLOPE Proxy records for the western slope of the Sierra Nevada are sparse for the late glacial period as a consequence of the scarcity of natural lakes and wetlands at elevations below the glacial termini and conditions arid enough for the preservation of pack rat middens. According to macrofossils in pack rat middens, in the lower Kings Canyon between 920 and 1,270 meters, where an oak–pinyon pine/chaparral woodland now grows, a unique forest of Utah juniper and associated red fir, incense cedar, sugar pine, and ponderosa pine, including nearby expanded groves of giant sequoia, was present during the last glaciation (Cole 1983). This association remained intact until about 14,600 years ago when different species began to depart. Composition of this Pleistocene forest is typical of the east side at higher elevations and west slope mesic habitat. Cole attributes this to either the marble substrate of the sites, a cold, dry continental late glacial climate, or a combination of both with an uneven snow accumulation. Farther north, around Nichols Meadow at an elevation of 1,510 meters, pollen findings indicate that around 18,500 years ago a cold and dry climate maintained an open conifer woodland of pine and juniper and sagebrush-grass associations resembling those now growing in subalpine habitat east of the crest. This assemblage persisted until 12,500 years ago (Koehler and Anderson 1994b). Other pollen sites on the west slope and in the Tahoe basin above 1,500 meters, dating to the late glaciation between 16,000 and 11,000 years ago, also record sagebrush steppe–woodland where there is now montane or upper montane forest. This vegetation association persisted until 13,000 to 10,000 years ago, depending on elevation and latitude, and at an anomalous 7,000 years ago in the San Joaquin River drainage basin (Adam 1967; Anderson 1990; Davis and Moratto 1988; Davis et al. 1985; Mackey and Sullivan 1991; Power 1998). Giant sequoia in the southern Sierra Nevada apparently had a broad distribution during the late glacial period from low elevations around Nichols Meadow at 1,510 meters to high elevations of 2,863 meters around East Lake shortly after deglaciation. Giant sequoias were briefly present at Exchequer Meadow 10,680 years ago and became established in their modern range between 9,000 and 6,000 years ago, but were rare until about 4,500 years ago (Anderson and Smith 1994).

As climate warmed, the ice cap that formerly covered the Sierra Nevada thinned and glaciers retreated until both likely disappeared from the crest and valleys about 12,000 to 13,000 years ago. There was a reversal at about 14,200 years ago when a small glacial advance (Recess Peak) occurred subsequent to the retreat of the Tioga glaciers (Clark and Gillespie 1996) after which the warming trend resumed, accompanied by less seasonality and more effective moisture. The sagebrush steppe and woodland were replaced relatively rapidly by a closed mixed conifer forest. As highlighted at Swamp Lake in Yosemite National Park, some late glacial forests at intermediate elevations consisted of a diverse association of lower and upper montane and subalpine species that included lodgepole pine, western white pine, ponderosa pine, white and red fir, incense cedar, mountain hemlock, and western juniper, unlike any modern assemblage (Smith and Anderson 1992). Also, between 16,000 and 11,000 years ago a change in the glacially dominated hydrology is seen in the transition of the basal sediments from gravels, sands, silts, and glacial flour to organic silts, muds, and peat. This allowed for the first development of meadows.

With the intensification of warming and decrease in effective moisture after 10,000 years ago, postglacial montane forests began to change rapidly with a decrease in pine and an increase in incense cedar and oak (Figure 2.7). Ponderosa pine moved upslope and the more mesic species of western white pine, sugar pine, red fir, mountain hemlock, western juniper, and lodgepole pine temporarily disappeared at intermediate elevations centered around 2,000 meters and moved to higher elevations. At higher elevations in the southern Sierra Nevada (2,863 meters), pine rapidly increased to maximum abundances while juniper and sagebrush decreased about 9,000 years ago and oak significantly increased (Power 1998). Farther north, deglaciated subalpine sites were still occupied by sagebrush steppe and scattered trees by 9,000 years ago, as indicated by the record from Tioga Pass Pond at 3,018 meters (Anderson 1990). During the Early Holocene warm period, a dry open coniferous forest with a montane shrub understory was growing throughout the range. This period was also marked by a maximal frequency of oaks and a dramatic increase in fires as indicated by high concentrations of charcoal in sediments. Obviously both aridity and intensification of the fire regime were opening up the denser Late Pleistocene forest canopy and changing its composition. At several sites, lake levels dropped and meadows dried and were invaded by conifers (Anderson 1990; Koehler and Anderson 1995; Wood 1975).

Climate began to cool with an increase of effective moisture after about 6,000 years ago, resulting in a decrease in oak and alder from their Early Holocene maxima, an increase in fir and incense cedar, and a canopy closure of montane forests. Charcoal concentrations also decrease, indicating a less intense fire regime. There were differences in the timing of vegetation. In some areas, oaks continued to increase, from a maximum abundance at about 4,500 years ago in the Lake Moran area to a late 2,800 years ago at Osgood Swamp (Adam 1967; Edlund 1991). At Balsam Meadow in the southern Sierra Nevada, the synchronous rise in abundances of fir, incense cedar, and oak, along with the decrease in pine during the past 3,000 years, has been explained as a downslope shift of the species that comprise the present community (Davis et al. 1985). The climatically sensitive montane and subalpine vegetation around the high-altitude sites in the Yosemite National Park area of Starkweather (2,438 meters), Tioga Pass Ponds, and

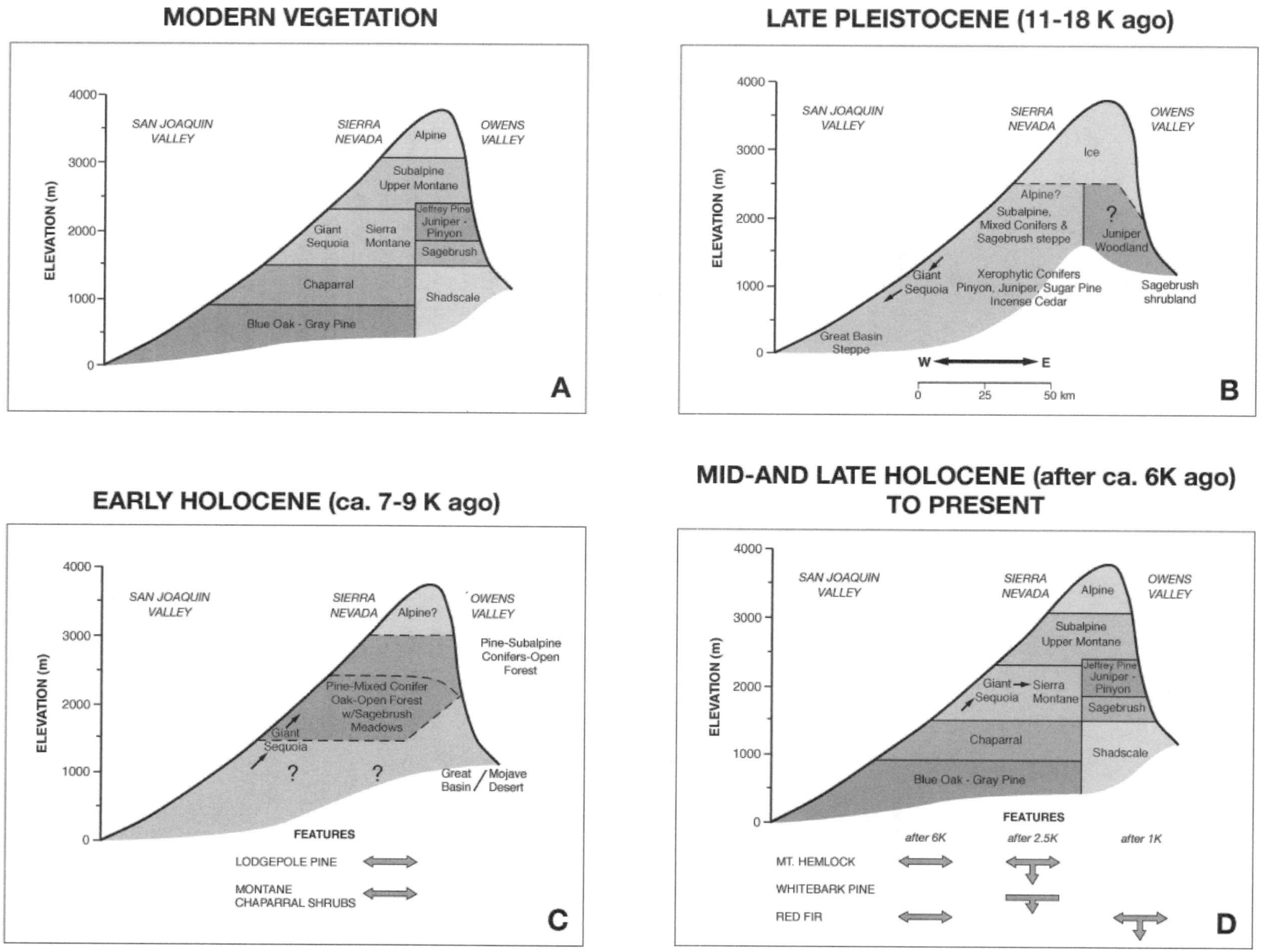

Figure 2.7. Synthetic diagram of vegetation change since the LGM for the Sierra Nevada (R. S. Anderson).

Ten Lakes (2,743 meters) document variation in the upper altitudinal limits of red fir and mountain hemlock and the lower range of whitebark pine after 6,000 years ago. Following an increase in subalpine conifer populations, the upper altitudinal limits of mountain hemlock and red fir and the lower limits of whitebark pine were depressed between about 3,000 and 2,500 years ago. The collective pattern from these sites can be interpreted as a response to cooler conditions with increased winter snow depths beginning about 3,000 to 2,500 years ago leading to the formation of the modern forests (Anderson 1990). Sampling intervals of lake and wetland sediments are usually too wide to resolve the Medieval Climatic Anomaly (MCA) or Little Ice Age (LIA), but there are indications of the MCA at East Lake, in the upper Kings River drainage basin where there was a rapid decrease in fir beginning at about cal A.D. 670 followed by increases in more xeric taxa such as sagebrush after 1,000 years ago (Power 1998).

EASTERN SLOPE The only pollen record for the late glaciation in the eastern escarpment is from Barrett Lake in the Mammoth Lakes basin at 2,816 meters. The lake is now surrounded by an upper montane mixed mountain hemlock–red fir–lodgepole pine–limber pine forest, but during the interval of 11,730 to 10,000 years ago a nearly treeless, newly deglaciated landscape was present (Anderson 1987).

Lodgepole–limber pine forest is thought to have been established by 10,000 years ago, followed by local individuals of mountain hemlock 1000 years later, and an increase in eastside montane and Great Basin shrubs. After this, there was no discernible trend in forest composition and abundance until 5,500 years ago when conifers increased with the addition of red fir until a peak was reached around 1,000 years ago, followed by a decline. Similarly, below the crest in the lodgepole pine forest of the upper Rush Creek drainage basin at 2,900 meters, an Early Holocene dry conifer forest with a shrub understory of sagebrush and grass became more mesic after about 5,000 years ago as marked by an increase in fir (Dull and Edlund 1997). Farther north, at the base of the Sierra Nevada below Sonora Pass, a rise in pine pollen at the expense of sagebrush has been recorded (Byrne et al. 1979). There was also a large increase in Cyperaceae, signifying the establishment of a wetland.

The dynamics of climate and vegetation have been detailed for the past 2,000 years by tree ring analysis. A decreased interval of precipitation for the period of cal A.D. 900–1300 was identified in the reconstructed annual June–July precipitation from the long-term bristlecone pine chronology in the White Mountains, where major droughts occurred between A.D. 900 and 1100 and A.D. 1200 and 1300 (Hughes and Graumlich 1996). These have been correlated with low stands of Mono Lake, Owens Lake, Tenaya Lake, lakes around the Tahoe basin, and low flows of the West Walker River (Stine 1994, 2001). Related droughts in the western United States have also been reconstructed from a spatially extensive grid of tree ring series for the past 1,200 years (Cook et al. 2004). The period A.D. 900–1300 was one of elevated warmth concurrent with the Medieval Climatic Anomaly (Bradley et al. 2003). Four extreme droughts centered on A.D. 936, 1034, 1150, and 1253 have been identified. According to climatic models, they probably were produced by La Niña–like conditions that induce drought in the western United States.

The tree line, defined by foxtail pine at the crest of the southern Sierra Nevada, was influenced by variations in temperature and water availability (Lloyd and Graumlich 1997). Pines migrated upslope above their present limits during warm temperatures between 100 cal B.C. and cal A.D. 900, and downslope to the current tree line during periods of major droughts from cal A.D. 1000 to 1400. The droughts killed adult trees and the cool temperatures during the LIA inhibited seedling recruitment between cal A.D. 1500 and 1900.

The recent dynamics of climate and vegetation since cal A.D. 1850 on both slopes of the Sierra Nevada are unique because the transition from the Little Ice Age to a warmer climatic regime co-occurred with the post–Gold Rush settlement and land use of the Sierra Nevada that altered fire regimes and vegetation patterns. It is thus difficult to tease out cultural and natural effects.

FIRE In the Sierra Nevada, climate, fire regimes, and vegetation form an interacting system. Highly diverse soil types, climates, topography, and plant species have created a heterogeneous vegetation mosaic structured by repeat entries of fire of varying intensity, size, and interval, and by climate change. Instead of "resetting" succession, fire has been an ongoing architect of the mosaic of vegetation patch types (Millar and Woolfenden 1999). Historic fire regimes reconstructed from tree rings and sedimentary charcoal analysis have been linked to climate variability, especially effective moisture, at decadal to millennial scales (Anderson and Smith 1994; Brunelle and Anderson 2003; Edlund 1994; Edlund and Byrne 1991; Smith and Anderson 1992; Swetnam 1993; Swetnam and Betancourt 1998).

Cascades

The volcanic Cascade Ranges extend north from the Sierra Nevada and generally above 500 meters support ponderosa pine, montane fir/pine, and lodgepole pine forests with treeless alpine communities on Mount Shasta and Lassen Peak. The interface between the southern Cascades and the Sierra Nevada is defined geologically and topographically but there is no vegetational break; rather, the forests of the Cascade-Sierran axis change gradually with latitude (Hickman 1993).

Proxy records from the Cascades are similar to those of the Sierra Nevada, but there are fewer records. At the southern end of the Cascade Range, Little Willow Lake (located within Lassen Volcanic National Park) has provided one of the most detailed vegetation records of the past 13,500 years for the region (West 2004). The pollen record of vegetation succession covers the transition from late glacial climates of the Pleistocene to postglacial climates of the Holocene: initially a sagebrush steppe prior to 12,500 years ago, then a pine-dominated forest from 12,500 to 3,100 years ago, and finally the fir forest of today. Abrupt transitions from sagebrush steppe to pine forest and the shift to fir forest took place in <500 years. Between 13,500 and 12,500 years ago, the climate was more seasonal and colder, analogous to the climates of high elevations within the Great Basin today. Conditions were warmer than today between 9,000 and 3,100 years ago, with the warmest period between 9,000 and 7,500 years ago. The expansion or increase in density of fir beginning ca. 3,100 years ago appears congruent with that observed in the central and southern Sierra and eastern Klamath Ranges (Mohr et al. 2000), indicating that the climate cooled and effective moisture levels increased, particularly winter snow depths.

From Medicine Lake northeast of Mount Shasta, a sediment core yielded a pollen and diatom record representing the past 11,400 years (Starratt et al. 2003). Although the pollen record is dominated by pine (probably lodgepole) throughout the Holocene, shifts in aquatic and secondary terrestrial taxa reflect changes in effective moisture. Before 4500 cal B.C., sagebrush pollen was an important component, suggesting that the lower tree line was located at a higher elevation, and thus closer to the lake, than today. Since 4500 cal B.C. sagebrush has become less common while fir pollen has increased, indicating a trend toward higher moisture availability and greater snow pack in the late Holocene. Fluctuations in aquatic taxa such as quillwort and sedge suggest periodic oscillations in lake level in the Late Holocene. Periods of increased aquatic pollen 5,000 to 4,000 and 3,000 to 2,000 years ago may reflect lower effective moisture which allowed the lake shelf to be colonized by aquatic plants. The ratio of the diatoms *Cyclotella* and *Navicula* is low during these periods, supporting the idea of low lake stands with a broad lake shelf.

TRANSMONTANE CALIFORNIA

Western Great Basin and Southern Deserts

The Sierra Nevada and the Transverse and Peninsular Ranges of southern California bound the series of block-faulted mountains and broad valleys that often contain playas, termed the Basin and Range Province, which includes the northern cold Great Basin Desert and the southern warm Mojave and Sonoran Deserts. The boundary between the Mojave and Sonoran Deserts in California differs slightly among scientists but is approximately centered at 34° N latitude. The Mojave Desert extends north into Owens and Eureka Valleys centered at about 37° N latitude.

The Great Basin vegetation associations that ascend from the bottom of the basins to the mountain crests are saltbush associations, shadscale, big sagebrush and bitterbrush shrub, singleleaf pinyon, Utah juniper woodland, Jeffrey pine and white fir forest, low sagebrush, and subalpine bristlecone pine and limber pine forest. The highest mountains of the region are the White and Inyo Ranges that parallel the Sierra Nevada.

Mojave Desert vegetation grades from creosote bush and white bursage associations to a variety of mixed saltbush and other warm desert shrubs, Joshua tree woodland, sagebrush-bitterbrush associations, California juniper and singleleaf pinyon–Utah juniper woodland, blackbush scrub, and white fir woodland on the highest peaks. The more summer–wet climate of the Sonoran Desert also supports such trees as blue and foothill palo verde, ironwood, smoke trees; and ocotillo, and arborescent cacti. An area of low basins and a delta plain associated with the Gulf of California is often differentiated as the Colorado Desert.

During the last glaciation, higher winter precipitation and runoff from glaciers and permanent snowfields in the mountains fed lakes that were impounded in many of the desert valleys and persisted from the runoff and lower evaporation induced by cooler temperatures (Anderson and Wells 2003; Smith and Street-Perrott 1983; Wells et al. 2003).

WESTERN GREAT BASIN In the California section of the western Great Basin, pollen sequences and plant macrofossils in pack rat middens from Tule Lake,

Mono Lake, Black Lake, the White Mountains, Owens Valley, and Owens Lake (Batchelder 1970; Byrne et al. 1979; Davis 1999b; Jennings and Elliot-Fisk 1993; Koehler and Anderson 1994a, 1995; Mensing 2001; Woolfenden 2003) provide evidence that the characteristic lowland vegetation type of the last glaciation was sagebrush steppe or Utah juniper woodland with an understory of sagebrush and bitterbrush. Singleleaf pinyon was also present in the southern Owens Valley. During the last glacial maximum in Owens Valley, the lower forest border of juniper and pinyon-juniper woodland was depressed about 500 to 600 meters. Evidence for glacial-age montane vegetation in the White-Inyo Range is lacking except for a pack rat midden on Cerro Gordo at the southern end of the Inyo Mountains that contains bristlecone pine. A downslope expansion of limber pine and bristlecone pine woodland can be extrapolated from known records on the higher peaks in the Mojave Desert (Spaulding 1990). Between about 19,000 and 9,500 years ago xeric shrub species appeared, followed by the upslope retreat of woodland and the establishment of modern desert vegetation.

During the Holocene in the White Mountains, the minimum altitude of the upper tree line was 150 meters above present tree line prior to 3,700 years ago due primarily to higher temperatures (LaMarche 1973). Similarly, pinyon-juniper woodland inhabited the subalpine elevation at 3,048 meters by 5,640 years ago, which is now occupied by bristlecone pine–limber pine woodland (Jennings and Elliott-Fisk 1993). On the northwest slope at 1,830 meters, however, pinyon woodland with a sagebrush understory, lacking more xeric species, existed between 8,790 and 7,810 years ago. By 4,510 to 2,130 years ago in the southern end of the White Mountains, vegetation was little different from modern flora. With cooling climate after 6,000 years ago, bristlecone pine retreated downslope in a steplike fashion until about cal A.D. 1700 and cal A.D. 1860, when the species reached its lowest elevation of the past 7,000 years. With post-LIA warming, this pine has been reestablishing itself at nearly Middle Holocene elevations (LaMarche 1973).

After 10,000 years ago in the southern Owens Valley, juniper continued to decrease as xeric shrubs such as mountain mahogany, white bursage, winter fat, wolfberry, wishbone plant, and salt bush species increased. Juniper finally departed completely from Owens Valley (Alabama Hills) between 9,500 and 7,650 years ago (Koehler and Anderson 1994a, 1995). Only small changes are evident subsequent to 2,830 years ago.

At this point the northern migration of singleleaf pinyon, an important component of the Great Basin and Mojave Desert uplands, can be mentioned. Pollen data from Owens Lake indicate that this tree was in the area since the last interglacial (130,000 years ago). According to pack rat midden macrofossils, it has been positively identified during the LGM, between 22,900 and 17,680 years ago at 1,155 meters at the western base of the southern Inyo Mountains (Koehler and Anderson 1994a) and at a higher-elevation site in the northern Inyo Mountains (2,609 meters) by 7,880 years ago (Reynolds 1996). Pinyon has also migrated west into the eastern escarpment of the Sierra Nevada since the late nineteenth century. Photographs taken in the 1880s show the absence of pinyon in areas where there is now extensive woodland. Additional, albeit indirect, evidence for the absence of this species is the lack of prehistoric and historic pine nut gathering camps in the eastern escarpment woodland. Such camps are numerous in the pinyon-juniper woodland in the Great Basin hills and mountains immediately to the east.

SOUTHERN DESERTS Between 18,000 and 12,000 years ago the expansive and now very arid Mojave Desert was occupied by Utah juniper woodland below 1,000 meters, grading to juniper and pinyon-juniper woodland between 1,000 and 1,800 meters, and subalpine woodland of limber pine and bristlecone pine at the highest sites on some mountain ranges (Figure 2.8) (Spaulding 1990). The pinyon-juniper understory in the central Mojave Desert consisted of bitterbrush, mountain mahogany, and desert almond (Koehler et al. 2005). Treeless vegetation associations, composed of cool desert shrubs such as Mormon tea, shadscale, rubber rabbitbrush, and snowberry occurred on southwest-facing slopes at lower elevations. Chaparral yucca (also found in the Whipple Mountains of the Sonoran Desert) is an unusual occurrence since the species now grows in the inner coast ranges of southern California with arid climates moderated by marine air and so implies an equable climate of cool summers and moderated winters during the last glaciation.

Late glacial woodland is also documented at the southern end of the Sierra Nevada from pack rat middens dated at 13,800 to 12,820 years ago in the Scodie Mountains at 1,125 meters. This woodland is singleleaf pinyon–California juniper with an understory of sagebrush, bitterbrush, and desert scrub oak, which is the only known late glacial occurrence of desert scrub oak or any other oak in the Mojave Desert (McCarten and Van Devender 1988) and may signal the

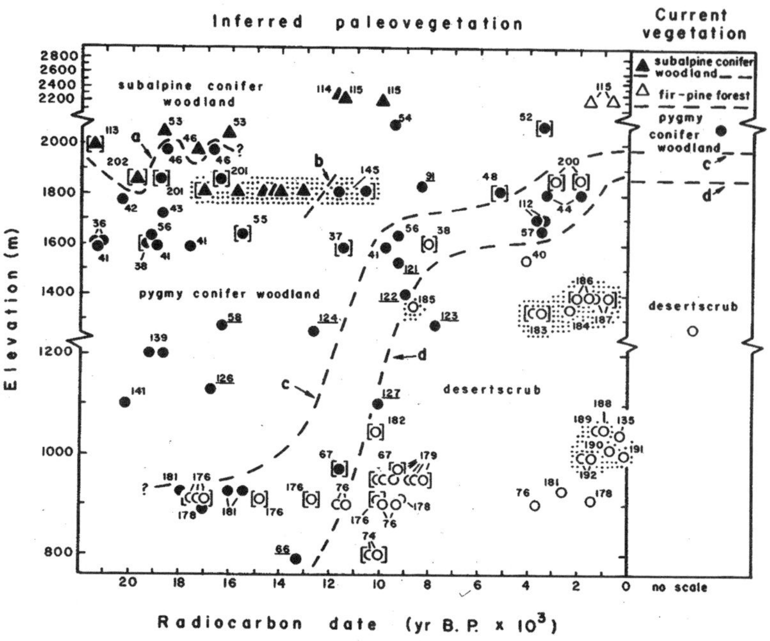

Figure 2.8. Inferred Mojave Desert vegetation history. (From Packrat Middens: The Last 40,000 Years of Biotic Change, edited by Julio L. Betancourt, Thomas R. Van Devender, and Paul S. Martin © 1990 The Arizona Board of Regents. Reprinted by permission of the University of Arizona Press.)

northward dispersal of oak or its spread from relict populations (Spaulding 1990). Surprisingly, the best analog for the macrofossil assemblage is singleleaf pinyon–California juniper woodland on the north slope of the San Bernadino Mountains.

The vegetation history of the Sonoran Desert in California is represented by only three pack rat midden localities adjacent to the Colorado River, which provide late glacial dates beginning from the earliest date of 16,900 years ago (Van Devender 1990). On the northern edge of the Sonoran Desert, in the Whipple and Chemehuevi Mountains, late glacial vegetation is primarily single leaf pinyon–California juniper (Utah juniper in the Chemehuevi Mountains) woodland with an understory of chaparral yucca, Bigelow beargrass, and Mojave sage. The Picacho Peak site, near the California-Arizona border, is in one of the hottest and driest areas in North America. The earliest dates of the vegetation chronology from 10,780 to 10,050 cal B.C. indicate a late glacial hot desert association of creosote bush, Joshua tree, blackbush, rabbitbrush, Mojave sage, and cactus species that is similar to mesic areas of the present Mojave Desert except for the lack of white bursage.

The general trend of late glacial to Holocene vegetation change in the Mojave and Sonoran Deserts is a replacement of the extensive conifer woodland by desert scrub at lower elevations as woodland elements dispersed upslope. This vegetation transition involved a shift in the relative composition of shrub species from cooler desert species such as sagebrush, rabbitbrush, and shadscale to the more arid adapted Mormon tea, matchweed, desert thorn, cactuses, and Joshua tree, and a final replacement by white bursage, creosote bush, and other desert thermophiles (Spaulding 1990). The modern Mojave Desert species migrated at different rates. Juniper had disappeared from the northern slopes of Eureka Valley by ~8,300 years ago as desert scrub such as indigo bush and holly goldenbush colonized the area (Spaulding 1990). Bursage arrived by 6,800 years ago, followed by creosote bush between 5,600 and 3,900 years ago. In Death Valley, juniper was gone by 11,210 years ago, followed by chaparral yucca and shadscale after 10,000 years ago (Wells and Woodcock 1985; Woodcock 1986). Hot desert began to develop 10,230 years ago as indicated by the arrival of white bursage. Between then and 1,990 years ago, creosote bush became fully established. The Little Ice Age may have been recorded on the east side of Death Valley by a downslope shift in blackbrush between 290 and 270 years ago, where creosote bush is today (Cole and Webb 1985; Spaulding 1995a). This occurred about 100 years after a shallow lake formed in the Silver Lake playa around 390 years ago (Enzel et al. 1992) during the coldest period of the Little Ice Age (Graumlich 1993; Moberg et al. 2005).

In the central Mojave Desert a warming climate is marked by the disappearance of pinyon after ca. 11,500 years ago, followed by juniper, Joshua tree, and bitterbrush after 9,910 years ago (Koehler et al. 2005). Woodland seemed to prevail in the southwestern end of the desert until about 7,800 years ago when desert scrub species arrived. The earliest appearance of creosote bush in the central Mojave Desert is dated 6,910 years ago north of Silver Lake and at a higher elevation in the Granite Mountains 5,960 years ago. Creosote bush migrated to sites north and west by 4,760 to 4,580 years ago slowly expanding throughout the central Mojave Desert. By about 5,000 years ago the vegetation had elements similar to that of today but modern associations developed only several thousand years later.

To the south on the xeric southeast to southwest-facing slopes of the Marble Mountains, a creosote bush–white bursage association was already established by 8,000 years ago. An increase in moisture between 3,490 and 3,160 years ago that persisted until after ca. 2,640 years ago is indicated by the presence of the more mesic blackbrush, Mojave sage, and goldenbush at the upper elevations of the Little Granite Mountains. This may reflect the cool-moist climatic episode that occurred throughout the southwest between 4,000 and 2,500 years ago (Neopluvial), which includes the existence of another lake stand in the Silver Lake playa around 3,620 years ago (Enzel et al. 1992).

At the north end of the Sonoran Desert, pinyon dropped out of the record after 11,000 years ago while California juniper lingered until 2,100 years later (Van Devender 1990). Hot desert vegetation began to migrate into the area as early as 11,500 years ago, beginning with the arrival of pygmy cedar and catclaw acacia. Creosote bush sporadically appeared from about 10,400 years ago but did not dominate the record until 2,300 years later. Contrary to the migration pattern farther north, bursage lagged creosote bush and did not become part of the full association until about 5,000 years ago. In the lower Colorado River Valley the more mesic associates began to drop out by 11,000 years ago, beginning with the extralocal Joshua tree and blackbush, and were mostly gone about 10,000 years later. Vegetation transitional between the late glaciation and Holocene lingered until about 7,000 years ago, after which a creosote bush–brittle bush–pygmy cedar association dominated until about 4,800 years ago when ironwood, ocotillo, and a surprisingly late white bursage arrived after 600 years ago to complete the modern association.

NORTHEAST (MODOC PLATEAU) The volcanic tablelands east of the Cascade Range comprise the Modoc Plateau. Besides the major volcanic centers there are hundreds of short-lived, small- to moderate-volume volcanoes throughout the region. Eruptive activity since the LGM has been episodic and mainly along the Cascade margin. Where they have not been drained for agriculture the large intermountain basins still contain the remnants of shallow lakes and marshes—Tule, Lower Klamath, Clear, and Goose Lakes—but perennial streams are relatively uncommon because of the fractured volcanic rock which acts like a sponge to surface runoff. In contrast to the Cascades which support montane pine and fir forests, the arid Modoc Plateau primarily supports Great Basin (cold desert) vegetation dominated by low sagebrush, sagebrush, rabbitbrush, bitterbrush, and bunchgrasses. Western junipers are scattered in various densities on the better drained rocky surfaces. The isolated Warner Mountains form a distinct floristic subregion (Odion et al. 1998). Unlike the Great Basin and desert mountains to the south, pinyon pine is entirely absent.

The environment and cultures of northeastern California are more typical of the plateau and Great Basin. Many of the winter settlements were along or nearby the region's lakes and there was a heavy dependence on lacustrine resources. Models of Late Pleistocene and Holocene paleoclimates suggest considerable regional variation and no comparable counterparts in the paleorecord (Bryson et al. 1997).

Paleoenvironmental proxy records dating to the LGM and Holocene are relatively scarce for the region since the initial study by Hansen (1942). Hansen's pollen record from Klamath Lake postdates the Mazama ash fall about 7,000 years ago and indicates a shift from ponderosa and white pines to lodgepole pine implying a cooling tend in the upper levels. From wood rat middens at Lava Beds National Monument, Mehringer and Wigand (1987) found western juniper (*Juniperus occidentalis* var. *occidentalis*), sagebrush, and mountain mahogany *(Cercocarpus ledifolius)* present over the past 5,300 years. It is likely, though unknown, except for the historic period, that the density and elevation distribution of juniper woodlands may have varied during this time. At the southern margins of the Modoc Plateau, West and McGuire (2004) have presented a record of marsh burning (at least 22 events) and vegetation change for the past 9,500 years. Based on the fluctuations of pollen values of aquatic-emergent plants there may have been periods of more effective moisture between 4,000 and 3,000 years ago and the past 1,500 years. Prior to 5,000 years ago there may have been a couple of periods of more effective moisture, but these were short-lived and the marsh was generally more alkaline with lower water levels. However, because of the gaps in the pollen record as the result of burning, establishing accurate time constraints for high-resolution climatic interpretation is not possible.

DISCUSSION

One of the most important lessons from the proxy record of the past 20,000 years is that change in the structure, composition, and landscape patterns of vegetation, along with other components of the environment, is more typical than is stability, and those changes have been frequent and have occurred with a greater magnitude and duration than is provided by direct observation. The record also exhibits as much past regional variation in California as that of today, and it is apparent that the different regions have distinct histories. Although contrasting regional vegetation types have their unique historical trajectories, they have similar trends since vegetation has generally tracked climate variation from decadal, centennial, to millennial scales. This continuous alteration of vegetation over the long term goes beyond the widely held equilibrium concept of relatively stable associations of plant species for which the only dynamic is a cycle of disturbance and recovery of a shifting mosaic through one or more pathways. The successional cycle is embedded in a hierarchy of climate variability at differing timescales, which forces both long-term trends and rapid transitions in vegetation and disturbance regimes. Although climate has an effect on the recruitment, establishment, and mortality of local plant populations, it is apparently most influential at regional to continental scales, whereas at small spatial scales internal biotic processes, substrate, and topography dominate.

Low frequency glacial-interglacial cycles and higher frequency climate shifts such as the Medieval Climatic Anomaly and Little Ice Age have obvious effects on the environment, but the smaller cycles occurring yearly and over decades and centuries such as the Pacific (inter-) Decadal Oscillation (PDO) and El Niño–Southern Oscillation (ENSO) can also significantly affect California terrestrial and marine environments. For example, climatic conditions associated with ENSO during the El Niño phase in general have a strong correspondence with high winter rainfall in southwestern California. Conditions are reversed during La Niña (Southern Oscillation) antiphase. The effects on coastal upwelling and marine resources as the result of ENSO are known, but the time depth of ENSO phenomenon is unclear (Quinn 1999; Rosenthal and Broccoli 2004). From Santa Barbara basin sediments, Heusser and Sirocko (1997) suggest that centennial scale fluxes in pine pollen correspond with ENSO-related conditions extending back to the LP, but temporally corresponding terrestrial records are less specific. On the other hand, the low frequency shift from the LGM to the Holocene is readily apparent in all California marine and terrestrial paleoproxy records spanning that period.

CHAPTER 3

Postglacial Evolution of Coastal Environments

PATRICIA M. MASTERS AND IVANO W. AIELLO

IN 1984 RECOGNITION OF THE EFFECTS AND RATE OF postglacial sea level rise on the evolution of coastal and nearshore environments in California was relatively new. A tentative chronology for Terminal Pleistocene/Early Holocene sea level rise had only been available since 1968 (Milliman and Emery 1968), and its implications for California archaeology had been considered systematically for the first time only in 1978. Bickel (1978) and later Moratto (1984) both discussed the vast amounts of land inundated by sea level rise over the past 20,000 years or so as representing a significant problem for the identification and study of early coastal adaptations. Broad coastal terraces, submerged now but exposed during the Terminal Pleistocene/Early Holocene, would have provided attractive locations for human settlement, and possibly even a corridor for migration.

Also important was an understanding of the paleoenvironmental history of California's estuaries. At the end of the Pleistocene, San Francisco Bay was one section of a deeply incised river channel that emptied into the Pacific 40 to 50 kilometers west of the present-day Golden Gate. As with most of California's estuaries, the mudflats and marshlands that provide habitat for a rich assortment of intertidal bivalves and waterfowl only appeared later during the Holocene when sea level rise slowed and sediments accumulated. In 1984 consideration of the effects of estuary evolution of prehistoric humans was focused largely on San Francisco Bay, although earlier studies in the San Diego area (e.g., Warren 1964) suggested a similar chronology. Since that time, marine scientists and archaeologists have continued to study a multitude of processes involved with the postglacial evolution of coastal and nearshore environments. Many of the trends identified before 1984 have been corroborated by more recent studies, but greater variety and complexity of coastal processes have been recognized as well.

In 1985, for example, Erlandson identified shellfish assemblages in archaeological sites on the Santa Barbara coast that indicated the presence of an Early Holocene estuarine system that has since been completely obliterated by sea level rise. Radiocarbon findings have also established that some small estuaries were present as early as 10,000 years ago on the central coast. Other marine and nearshore processes, including the effects of the El Niño–Southern Oscillation (ENSO) and the accumulation of sediments on outer shores at Middle Holocene, have also been identified as significant influences on the availability of resources and habitats to early forager populations. Overall, continued research on the regional consequences of sea level rise, climate controls on coastal processes, and geology in the past 20 years has extended paleogeographic interpretations to most of the central and southern California coast.

This chapter will summarize findings for the period from the last glacial maximum (LGM) to the end of the prehistoric era in 1769. Because a great deal of information has accumulated in the past two decades, the chapter has two sections. It begins with a treatment of southern California and concludes with consideration of portions of the central and northern coastlines. Unfortunately, detailed paleogeographic reconstructions are still unavailable for the California coastline north of Bodega Bay.

SOUTHERN CALIFORNIA, BY PATRICIA M. MASTERS

How the dynamic interface between the sea and the land of southern California has evolved during the past 20,000 years and the diverse resources it may have offered to early people are key issues in California prehistory. There are two complementary approaches to reconstructing past coastlines. A descriptive approach is based on geological or environmental information that is specific to the localities where remote sensing, coring, or archaeological data are available. A process-based approach, on the other hand, applies the physics of waves, currents, and sediment transport to known geology over regional areas. A process-based analysis of paleocoastlines that has proven widely useful to California archaeologists and ecologists was published over 20 years ago (Inman 1983). Inman reconstructed the coastline in the vicinity of La Jolla, California,

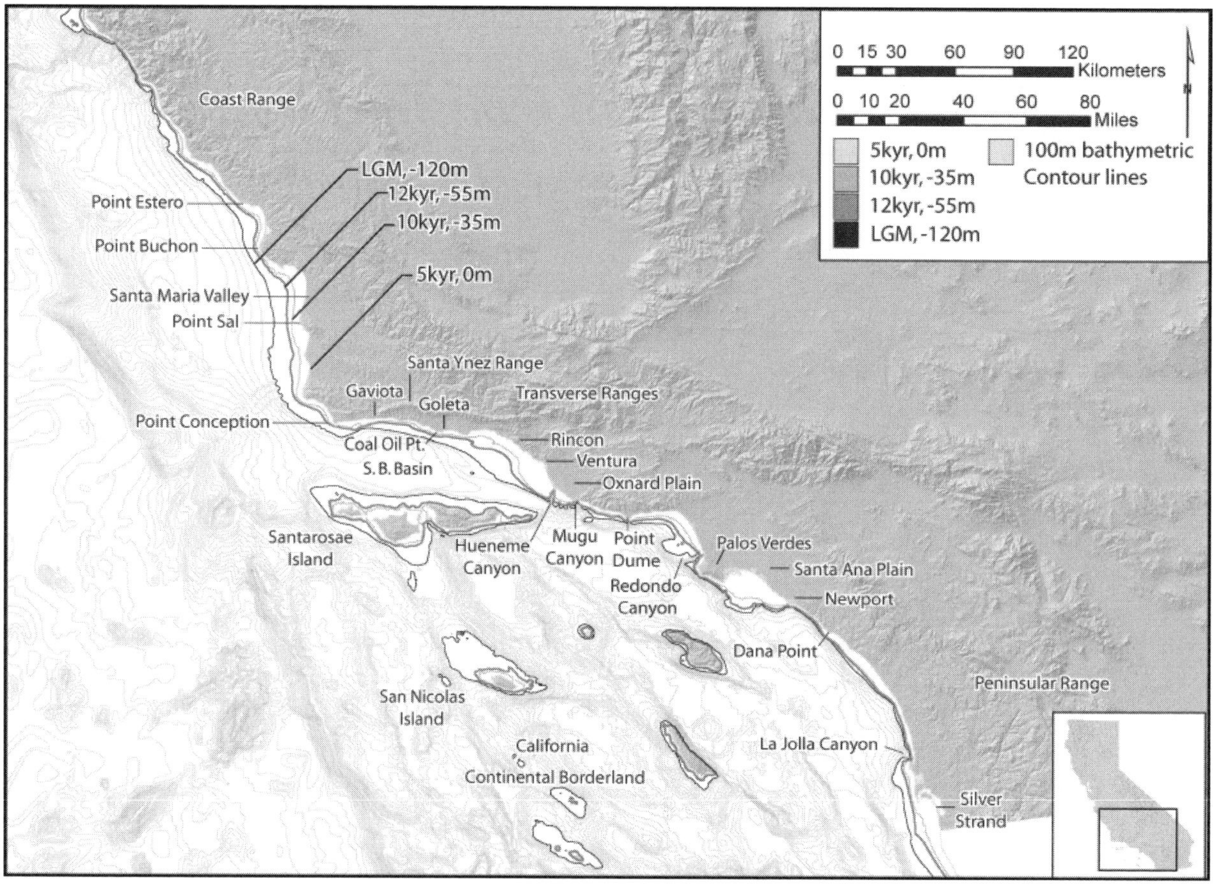

Figure 3.1. Approximate shoreline locations for the LGM, 12,000 years ago, 10,000 years ago, and 5,000 years ago for southern California.

over an entire glacial-interglacial cycle, and his study has become the prototype for applying the coastal processes to regional geomorphology under changing sea levels.

Since it appeared, more recent work has linked climate forcing to coastal processes, new information documents paleoclimate variability, and sea level history is better constrained. We now understand the major role of the El Niño–Southern Oscillation in driving the wave energy that erodes the coast and in bringing sediments to the coast. The paleoclimate record of ENSO variability and its effects on coastal processes are providing new insights into the interpretation of California's ancient coastlines. In addition, higher-resolution chronologies for the transitions in coastal morphology and associated ecosystems come from archaeological investigations of the past two decades.

This section focuses on the evolution of the California coast between Point Estero and the U.S.-Mexican border. The 480-kilometer coastline includes the south-central coast extending from Morro Bay to Point Conception and the entire coast of the Southern California Bight (Figure 3.1). Starting from the geological setting, which exerts a primary control on the landforms of California's Pacific margin, the coastal processes responsible for erosion and deposition are applied to a well-documented sea level history in order to reconstruct coastlines for the last glacial maximum (LGM) ca. 20,000 years ago, the Younger Dryas (YD) stillstand 12,000 years ago, the Early Holocene 10,000 years ago, and the present stillstand starting 6,000 to 5,000 years ago. Coastal processes operating at those times are inferred from paleoclimate indicators with multidecadal to millennial scales. Whether the coast is rocky with deep embayments or blanketed with sandy beaches has important implications with regard to biological productivity and the marine resources sought by hunter-gatherer-fisher populations. The timing of this rocky-sandy transition for specific reaches of the southern coast is estimated from the local archaeological record, which is limited by some caveats but remains a valuable indicator of the types of coastal ecosystems encountered by early people. In order to correlate chronologies based on different dating methods and materials, all dates discussed here are in calendar years before present.

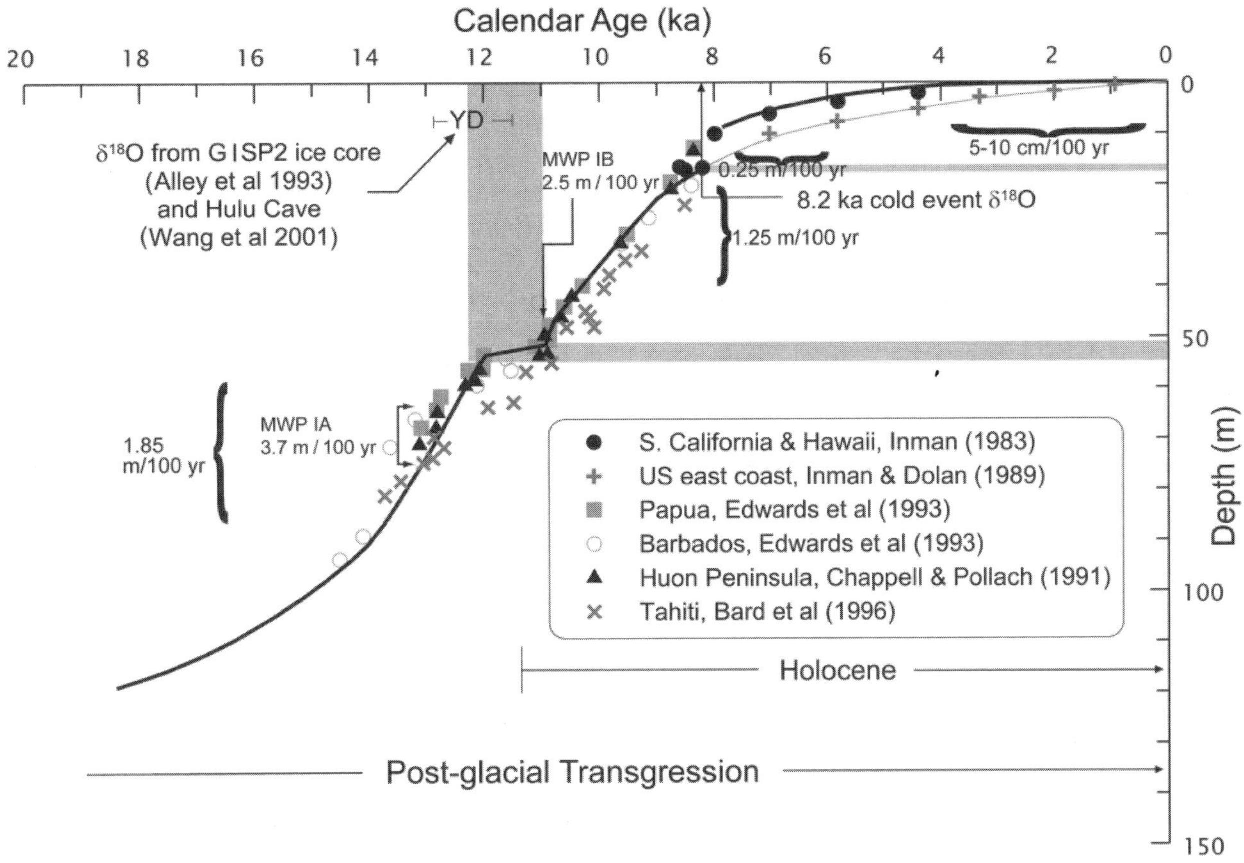

Figure 3.2. Sea level during postglacial transgression with stillstands associated with the Younger Dryas, the cold event at 8,200 years ago, and the past 6,000 years (after Inman et al. 2005). Shaded areas indicate shore platform cutting. Meltwater pulses after Fairbanks (1989) and Bard et al. (1990). The heavy black line is a curve fitted to the California/Hawaii and Huon data and extrapolated to the LGM at 120+/-10 mbpsl (Lambeck et al. 2002).

Geological Setting

Tectonic processes shaped the ocean basins and adjacent land masses, and the large-scale features of the California coast are related to its position on the plate boundaries. A collision or active margin coast such as California occurs where two plates impinge on each other (Inman and Nordstrom 1971), and it contrasts with the passive or trailing edge margin of the eastern United States. As the Pacific plate is subducted beneath the North American plate, the leading edge of the plate boundary has been folded and fractured by lateral transform motions. These processes have created a rugged coastline backed by sea cliffs and mountain ranges. North of Point Conception, the narrow continental shelf and slope descend to deep trenches and ocean basins, but to the south, the continental borderland features a complex northwest-southeast trending structure of islands, banks, and basins shaped by faults with marked lateral motion and block rotation (Legg 1991). Submarine canyons, also structurally controlled, are incised into the shelves and debouch to the deep basins. A few coastal plains formed by regional tectonics bring the major rivers to the ocean from the coastal basins of the Santa Maria, Santa Ynez, Ventura, and Santa Clara Valleys, the Oxnard Plain, and the Santa Ana River Gorge and Plain. Intermittent streams follow steep-sided canyons as they emerge from the coastal ranges, and all but a few drainages are relatively small with high gradients. Paleovalleys and channels cut into the shelf off major streams during low seastands.

The narrow (average width ~10 kilometers), steep continental shelf is of particular interest because it was the coastal plain during the LGM when sea level stood at 120 ± 10 mbpsl (meters below present sea level) (Figure 3.2). The shelf break, where the gradient steepens into the slope, occurs at ca. 120 mbpsl north of Point Conception due in part to higher wave energy on that exposed coast. South of Point Conception, headlands and islands shelter the coast from high waves and the break is near 80 mbpsl. Seismic profiling shows large areas of bare, wave-cut shelf off headlands or down drift of the prevailing northwesterly swell where there are few sediment sources (Slater et al. 2002). This wave-cut surface underlies the Holocene sediment cover brought to the shelf by the rivers following sea level rise. Sands stored on mainland shelves during high seastands are eroded and carried to the slopes during regressions (Gorsline and Teng 1989). In consequence, the continental shelf was largely denuded of sediment during the LGM, and Pleistocene sediments occur only in a depositional basin such as the Santa Clara–Ventura River depocenter, which has experienced significant subsidence since the LGM (Dahlen et al. 1990). It is therefore unlikely that paleoenvironmental information is retrievable from shelf deposits outside of depocenters.

Coastal Processes

The evolution of the coast since the LGM has been determined by rising sea level and the flow of energy and sediment through coastal areas. This interaction between climate and sea level created coastal ecosystems that have fluctuated between rocky kelp forest environments at lower seastands and sandy environments during interglacial periods (Graham et al. 2003; Inman 1983). Differences in productivity between the two dominant ecosystems would be expected to influence the relationship of early human settlers to the coast.

Since the LGM, rates of sea level rise have varied widely but with no apparent reversals in regions like California that are distant from crustal warping by ice sheets or deep ocean waters (Figure 3.2). During the meltwater pulses (MWP) ~13,500 (11,500 cal B.C.) and ~11,000 (9000 cal B.C.) years ago, the rate of rise was in the range of two to four meters per century bringing rapid inundation of the shelf and erosion of surficial sediments. At stillstands during the YD and the past 6,000 years, waves cut a nearly flat platform at the shore where riverine sediment, if available, could accumulate.

The coastal processes driven by changes in sea level are outlined in Inman's (1983) paleocoastline reconstruction for the steep, narrow shelf near La Jolla (Figure 3.3). Valley cutting during lowered sea level ($t_2 - t_3$) entrenched stream channels across the shelf. The higher gradient between the upland portions of the watersheds and the lower sea level increased the power of streams to transport coarser materials to the coast. The model delineates a Late Pleistocene/Early Holocene period of rocky, exposed coasts intersected by deeply incised valleys cut over 80,000 years of lowered sea level since the last interglacial (t_1). As sea levels rose following the LGM, the valleys flooded (t_4), and these estuaries trapped sediment at their heads so the outer coast remained sand starved and rocky. During the Middle Holocene, the sea level rise slowed, waves cut the shore platform, and cobble spits formed at the mouths of the estuaries. Stream-borne sediments were infilling and shoaling the estuaries (t_5), and fine sandy sediments could be brought to the coast by floods. Spits periodically closed the remaining tidal lagoons, and the rocky coastline was buried by sand beaches. A long interval of interglacial high seastand returned the coastal valleys to the broad floodplains that exist today (t_5).

Much of the Holocene evolution of the southern California coast was governed by sediment supply. Recent studies have shown the dependence of rainfall, stream flow, and sediment flux on decadal variability in ENSO. In the instrumental record, dry periods (predominantly La Niña conditions) and wet periods (dominated by El Niño events) persist for 20 to 30 years (Inman and Jenkins 1999). These wet/dry cycles appear to be linked to the Pacific Decadal Oscillation (Mantua and Hare 2002) and differ in characteristic wave climates (Graham and Diaz 2001; Inman and Jenkins 1997). During dry periods, winter storm fronts from Aleutian lows make landfall in Washington and Oregon so that California receives less rainfall and wave direction is from the northwest. Sediment transport is mainly to the south, and lower stream flow means decreased sediment flux to the coast. During wet periods, winter storms come from the west and strike California directly with strong winds, high waves, and heavy rainfall. El Niño–dominated periods see the greatest erosion on the California coast (Inman and Jenkins 1997, 1999; Storlazzi and Griggs 2000). Sea cliffs retreat, the littoral sand transport system is disrupted, and floods discharge high volumes of sediment at river mouths.

The relationship of sediment flux to wet/dry climate periods varies with regional geology of the southern California coast (Inman and Jenkins 1999; Masters 2006). The Santa Maria and Santa Barbara regions experience the greatest increase in sediment flux during the wet period, due to the highly erodible Cenozoic formations of the Transverse Ranges. Estero Bay in the Coast Range province is least affected because precipitation is higher and more consistent in either climate cycle. However, in the San Diego region with its granitic ranges, sediment is supplied to the coast only during the wet periods. In consequence, multidecadal or longer wet/dry cycles determine the

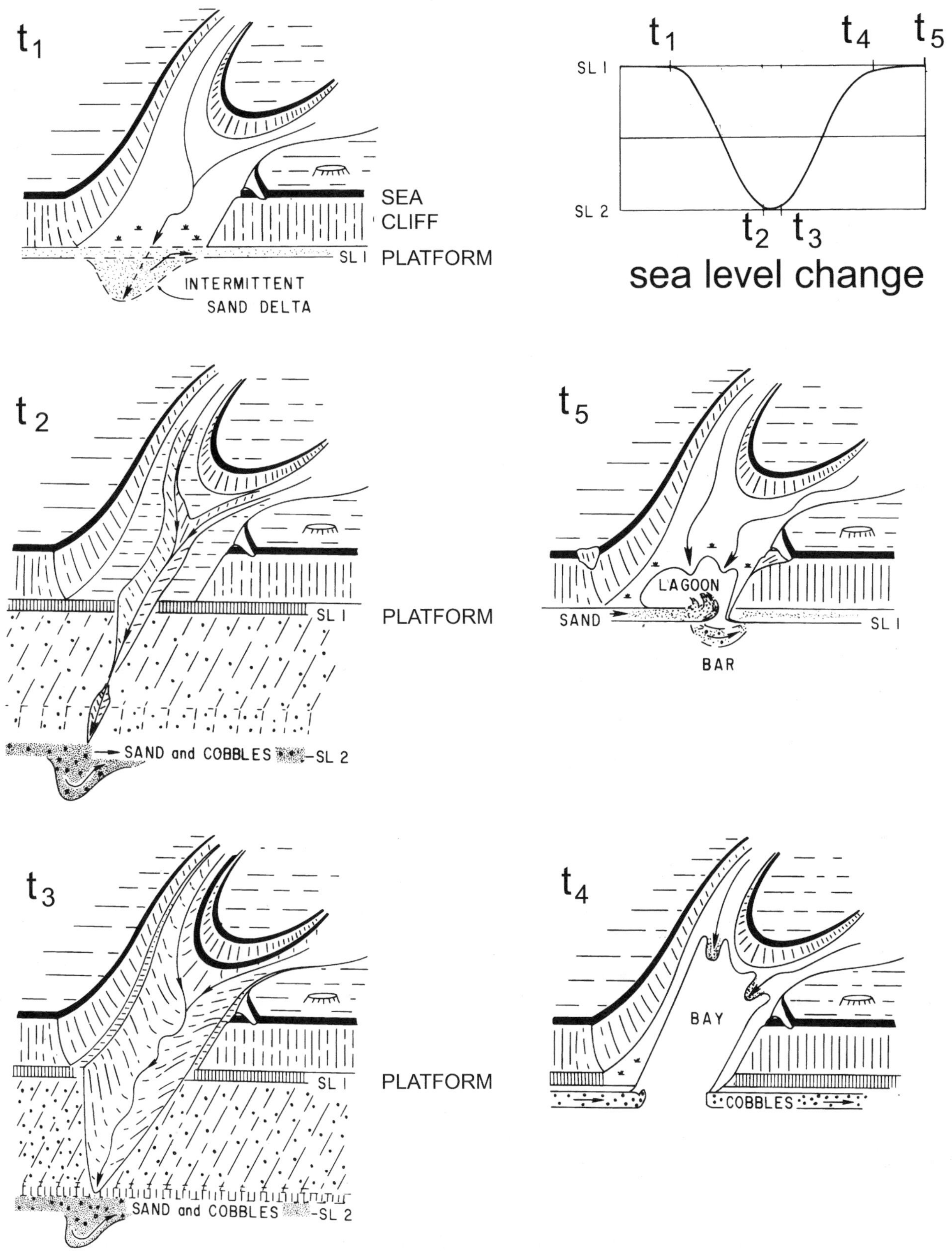

Figure 3.3. Diagram of valley cutting during lowered sea level (t_2-t_3) and trapping of sediment in bays during sea level rise (t_4-t_5) with a generalized sea level curve for times t_1-t_5. Modified from Inman (1983).

sediment regimes along these different lengths of the California coast. Paleoclimate research indicates these cycles influenced coastal processes during the LGM and YD, as well as the Holocene.

The wet winter/dry summer climate characteristic of southern California appears to have persisted over the past 160,000 years, and there were 10 large multidecadal wet events between ca. 20,000 years ago and the YD (Heusser and Sirocko 1997). With a precipitation anomaly of up to 700 millimeters per year, these wet periods produced high stream flow that accelerated valley cutting across the continental shelf between 20,000 and 12,000 years ago. However, at the LGM sea level, riverine sediment was discharged to the steep continental slope and was lost to deep water until the rocky shelf north of Point Conception began to flood following the LGM (Figure 3.2). For much of the borderland to the south, the mainland LGM coast stood at an elevation below the shelf break, which formed 30- to 50-meter-high sea cliffs backing the narrow rocky shore. The continental slope drops off steeply (>10 percent gradient) to great depths, and kelp forests grew on narrow fringing reefs to a depth of 90 meters within the photic zone. The shore zone was very energetic because the steep slope allowed the larger waves to break at the coast.

As sea level rose with sustained melting, the transgressing seas brought wave energy up onto the shelf of the bight around 14,000 to 13,000 years ago and eroded unconsolidated sediments along with any environmental record they contained. The incised stream valleys flooded (Figure 3.3), and estuarine habitats most attractive to early foragers expanded rapidly with the meltwater pulses (MWP) at 13,500 and 11,000 years ago. Little platform cutting took place as the surf zone moved rapidly up the shelf, and sediment from streams was deposited in the heads of the estuaries and did not reach the coastline. In general, the coastline remained rocky with little sediment cover, while the submerged shelf area increased and kelp forests expanded.

The brief return to glacial conditions during the Younger Dryas (YD; 12,800 to 11,400 years ago or ca. 10,800 to 9400 cal B.C.) was accompanied by a still-stand in sea level at ~55 mbpsl, resulting in a wave-cut platform. Kelp beds probably flourished on the YD platform (Figure 3.2) following the rapid sea level rise 11,000 years ago (MWP IB). The habitats dominated by rocky kelp forest would have provided a resource-rich environment that may have outranked terrestrial resources for early people during this cold, predominantly dry climate.

With sea level at ~35 mbpsl between 10,000 and the cold event 8,200 years ago, embayments offered quiet-water marine habitats. These deep, well-circulated estuaries supported fish nurseries, shellfish, shorebirds, and marine mammals. With little evidence of El Niño activity at that time (Cane 2005; Friddell et al. 2003; Moy et al. 2002), sediment supply to the coast was limited, especially in the San Diego region. The wave-swept outer coast was devoid of fine sediments, and steep cobble beaches would have been prevalent during the latter part of this period. Nearshore areas also lacked sand cover, and shallow rocky reefs with abundant fish communities were widespread.

As sea level rise slowed 6,000 to 5,000 years ago, the rocky-sandy transition began to reshape wide regions into modern coastal landforms (Figure 3.4). Throughout southern California, sediment flux increased markedly with intensification of ENSO. As the estuaries shoaled, productive estuarine habitats declined, and the expansion of sand and mudflats marked the transition to infaunal ecosystems (Graham et al. 2003). During El Niño floods, fine sediment was moved to the open coast where the near-stillstand was cutting the shore platform that allowed sand beaches to accrete. The littoral "river of sand" gradually reduced the productive rocky intertidal and shallow reef habitats.

In the Late Holocene, large estuaries were replaced by shallow wetlands and lagoons that periodically closed due to spit formation. During the past 2,000 years, megadroughts that lasted 200 years (Stine 1994) likely closed the lagoons (resulting in hypersaline conditions and loss of productivity) while megafloods with return periods of 200 to 400 years (Schimmelmann et al. 2003) reopened lagoons in southern California. Kelp forests were limited to the wave-cut platforms off rocky headlands, and shallow rocky reefs were smothered by sand accumulation on the inner shelf. Sand beaches accreted within the littoral cells, at least during the low wave energy of the summer season.

Archaeological Evidence for the Transition to Littoral Cells

The archaeological record largely corroborates the paleocoastline reconstructions, but there are intriguing differences in date of onset for the rocky-sandy coast transition among the littoral cells. In the first half of the Holocene, that estuaries were an economic and settlement focus in the Morro, Santa Maria, western

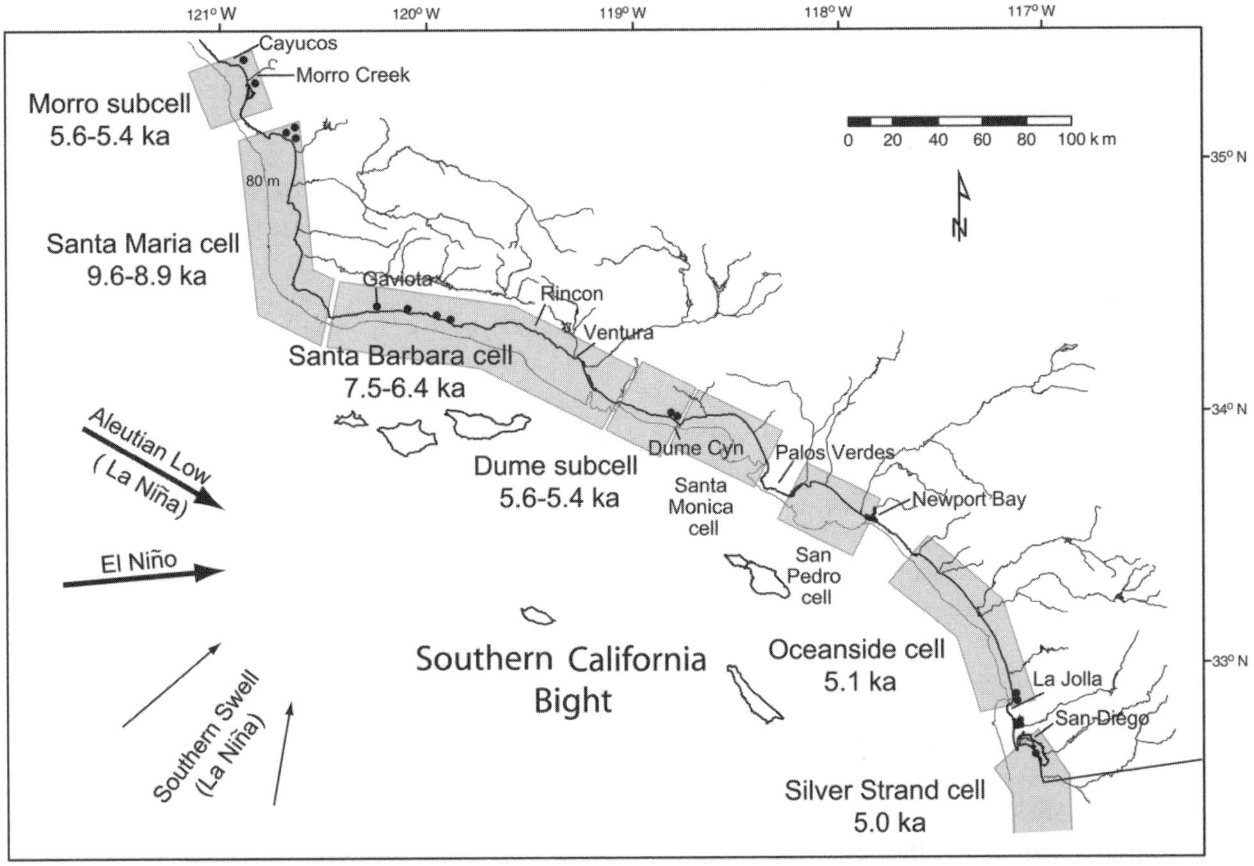

Figure 3.4. Earliest Pismo clam dates from archaeological sites (•) within southern California littoral cells and characteristic wave directions (after Masters 2006). A littoral cell is a coastal compartment that contains the sources (rivers), transport paths (beaches), and sinks (submarine canyons) of sediment (Inman and Frautschy 1965).

Santa Barbara, and San Diego regions is well documented (Carrico and Ainsworth 1980, Erlandson 1994; Fitzgerald 2004; Gallegos 1991; Jones et al. 1994; Mikkelsen et al. 2000; Pigniolo et al. 2001; Warren 1968), yet the transition to the modern littoral cells may have occurred 3,000 to 5,000 years earlier in the Santa Barbara and Santa Maria cells than in the Oceanside and Silver Strand cells (Masters 2006). The interplay of sea level, regional geomorphology, and ENSO controls on wave climate and sediment flux apparently produced this range of coastal response times.

Indeed, estuaries and sand beaches may have evolved together on the Santa Maria coast. The first perennial sand beaches appeared in the Santa Maria cell between 10,000 and 9,000 years ago based on radiocarbon-dated Pismo clam shell from archaeological sites (Breschini and Haversat 1991a; Fitzgerald 2000; Jones, Fitzgerald et al. 2002). Pismo clams (*Tivela stultorum*) require wide, fine-grained sand beaches that are not lost during winter storms. Thus dates on Pismo clams infer minimum ages for perennial sand beaches (Masters 2006), and these sites offer evidence of the first sand beach habitats recorded for southern California since the last interglacial 125,000 years ago. However, estuarine taxa are more plentiful in these early sites, indicating the presence of estuaries as well as sand beach habitats. Interestingly, the Pismo dates provide evidence of sand beaches here during a period of relatively rapid sea level rise of more than a meter per century (Figure 3.2).

The unique geomorphology of the Santa Maria cell permitted wave sheltering by the massive headland of Point Buchon to the north and sediment trapping by Point Sal to the south (Bowen and Inman 1966). Following the YD, sea level rise pushed the shoreline into the wave shadow of Point Buchon for northwesterly approaching waves, and the now submerged headland of the present-day Point Sal began to act as a groin. The abundant sediment supply from the Transverse Ranges was confined to the wide, gently sloping shelf where no submarine canyon sink could divert sand to deeper water, and the sediment built into dunes and formed barrier beaches. Even the relatively rapid rate of sea level rise 10,000 to 9,000 years ago (Figure 3.2) was no impediment to littoral sand transport and beach deposition, perhaps aided by strong but infrequent El Niño activity (Keefer et al. 2003) that occurred between ~12,000 and ~8,000 years ago which would have built beaches at the northern end of the cell. Point Buchon sheltered these beaches from the northwest storms during the La Niña–dominated climate of 8,000 to 5,000 years ago (Friddell et al. 2003; Keefer et al. 2003; Koutavas et al. 2002; Moy et al. 2002). Kelp forests were absent on the sandy shelf but well established around the rocky headlands to the north and south.

Although deeply incised stream valleys may not have formed during glacial seastands on this shelf due to its low gradient, estuarine habitats developed in the back dune areas of the coastal plain where drainages excavated channels and supplied fresh water. Analogous to the U.S. east coast, where sediment is supplied from the wide shelf, barrier rollover protected these low-lying areas from wave energy (Inman and Dolan 1989). By the Early Holocene, Halcyon Bay (Dills 1981) and the paleo-Santa Maria (Knott and Eley 2006) were the largest estuarine systems in this cell. Since barrier formation required wave sheltering from Point Buchon, the Santa Maria shelf likely did not develop estuaries before the YD sea level. By ~10,000 years ago, cultural deposits in the vicinity of Halcyon Bay (SLO-801, SLO-832, and SLO-1797) attest to estuarine habitat (Breschini and Haversat 1991a; Fitzgerald 2000; Jones, Fitzgerald et al. 2002).

The coastal evolution of the Santa Barbara region also was determined by a large headland and copious sediment supply from the Transverse Ranges. The east-west trending coast of the Santa Barbara cell is protected by Point Conception (Figure 3.4). West of Gaviota, archaeological deposits dated to 9,000 to 7,000 years ago contain predominantly estuarine species of shellfish indicating a rocky coast intersected by numerous small embayments (Erlandson 1994). After 7,000 years ago, estuarine taxa were replaced by rocky coast and sand beach shellfish remains (Erlandson 1997a). High sand yield from the steep watersheds of the Santa Ynez Range was delivered directly to the coast and protected from the oblique wave approach by the small valley headlands as well as wave sheltering by Point Conception and the Channel Islands. Between Goleta and Ventura, the most rapid uplift rates in the continental United States of ~2 millimeters per year (Keller and Gurrola 2000) kept pace with sea level rise of ~2.5 millimeters per year (Figure 3.2) and facilitated beach accretion near Goleta. The earliest dates for sand beach taxa range between 7,500 and 6,400 years ago on the western Santa Barbara coast (Figure 3.4), and sand beaches continued to build between 5,800 and 5,600 years ago resulting in several additional sites with 80–99 percent Pismo clam remains. However, between 4,000 and 3,000 years ago a shift to predominantly rocky coast shellfish occurred along the western coast (Erlandson 1997b). The apparent loss of sand beaches may be related to increased El Niño activity ~5,000 years ago (Cane 2005; Friddell et al. 2003; Moy et al. 2002). El Niño storms generate high waves in the channel that rapidly erode sand from the western beaches and transport it to the eastern portion of the cell.

East of Coal Oil Point, the wide shelf and coastal plain allowed formation of larger estuaries (Colten 1989; Erlandson 1997b). Settlements on the western margin of Goleta lagoon dating to 6,000 to 5,000 years ago contain a mixture of rocky and sandy habitat species, particularly in the early components of the sites. These deposits reflect the proximity of the western drainage basins with their signature of rocky and sandy coastal habitats. Possibly due to declining productivity in the western cell, the Goleta lagoon sites show the proportions of bay species increasing from Early to Late Period components (Colten 1989; Erlandson 1997b).

In the eastern part of the cell between Ventura and Point Hueneme, the beaches and shelf are wide and trend southeast with large rivers as the major sediment sources. While less is known of the prehistory of the coast east of Rincon, shellfish generally were a minor component after ca. 4,000 years ago in sites along the Santa Barbara coast (Erlandson and Rick 2002a). Plentiful sediment brought to the coast by the Ventura and Santa Clara Rivers caused pro-grading of the Oxnard Plain and may have buried or eroded earlier sites. However, Pismo clam dates appear after 4,000 years ago in this region of the cell (Masters 2006), perhaps as a result of extensive erosion in the western part of the cell following the increase in El Niño activity after ~5,000 years ago.

Finally, the modern configuration of southern California's littoral cells developed 6,000 to 5,000 years ago as would be expected with slowing in the rate of marine transgression. In the northern half of the study area between Estero Bay and Santa Monica Bay, sand beaches were most widespread in that time range (Masters 2006). The Morro and Dume subcells accreted sand beaches when sea level rise caused Morro Rock and Point Dume to act as sand retention features. Wave sheltering by Point Estero, Point Conception, and the Northern Channel Islands favored accretion over erosion in these localities.

Along most of the Santa Monica cell, however, the thin sediment cover on the shelf indicates that the cell has been sand starved since the end of the Pleistocene (Slater et al. 2002) and that wave energy reaching the earlier (lower) coastlines transported available sediment toward Redondo submarine canyon. Although these conditions should have supported productive rocky intertidal habitats, shellfish were a minor resource to people inhabiting the coast of Santa Monica Bay and the Santa Monica Mountains during the Middle Holocene (Gamble and King 1997). Fishing and hunting were more important, and this trend continued with an emphasis on fishing into the Late Holocene (Gamble and Russell 2002).

To the south, the San Pedro littoral cell and Newport coast extend from the Palos Verdes headland to Laguna Beach along a generally north-south trending coastline. The shelf is wide from Palos Verdes to the submarine canyon off Newport Bay, where it becomes very narrow along the pocket beaches to Dana Point. As was the situation with the coastal plains of the eastern Santa Barbara and central Santa Monica cells, little is known of prehistoric coastal sites from the San Pedro area, perhaps owing to the wide shelf and greater distance to cliffed terrain where sites would not be drowned by sea level rise. However, Newport coast sites reveal collecting from rocky coast habitats between 5,700 and 5,100 years ago (Mason et al. 1997). At small summer encampments on the Newport coast, remains of kelp bed fish are another indication of predominantly rocky shorelines. No Pismo clam dates are reported for this section of the southern coast (Masters 2006). Therefore, down drift of Newport submarine canyon, low sediment supply to the narrow shelf, and direct wave attack probably prevented accretion of sand beaches between 6,000 and 5,000 years ago when they were already prevalent in the northern cells. However, kelp bed–rocky intertidal habitats apparently were not as productive by the end of the middle Holocene. The period between 3,000 and 1,300 years ago saw abandonment of the Newport coast and little occupation even at Newport Bay (Mason et al. 1997). Interestingly, this period coincides with intensified El Niño activity inferred from a number of studies (Benson et al. 2002; Enzel et al. 1992; Ingram 1998; Keefer et al. 2003; Moy et al. 2002; Sandweiss 2003; Stine 1990). On this exposed coast, higher-energy El Niño storms erode beaches and disrupt kelp beds. The Late Holocene shift in settlement pattern to the San Joaquin Hills (Mason et al. 1997) shows that interior resources outranked coastal resources during a period of great climate variability.

The southernmost Oceanside and Silver Strand cells are the last to show archaeological evidence of lagoon closure and sand beaches ~5,000 years ago (Masters and Gallegos 1997). In these far southern cells, the strong dependence of sediment flux on El Niño–dominated climate periods may have delayed the onset of littoral sand transport and deposition of perennial beaches (Masters 2006). The six large lagoons in the Oceanside cell also served as sediment traps for stream-borne material. Without major headlands along the 84 kilometers of its north-south trending coast, the Oceanside cell is exposed to southerly transport that rapidly denudes the platform and delivers sand into the submarine canyon sink at La Jolla. The sand-starved shelf also reflects a deficit of sediment supply since the end of the Pleistocene (Slater et al. 2002). Around 5,000 years ago, Pismo clam dates confirm that the intercanyon shelf at La Jolla had accumulated sand (Figure 3.4). In the Silver Strand cell, there was probably little sand yield from the vast Tijuana River watershed before ~5,000 years ago, and climatic and geological constraints starved the cell, resulting in the relatively late deposition of the Silver Strand tombolo and enclosure of San Diego Bay (Elliott 1987; Masters 2006).

Thus the estuaries of the Early Holocene as well as the resource-rich rocky coast habitats extending from the intertidal to the kelp forests on the shelf provided the opportunity for maritime adaptations. In the Northern Bight, the longer coastlines of Santarosae and San Nicolas islands as well as the narrower straits between the islands and the mainland coast increased access to marine resources. In the Santa Maria region, rocky coasts were probably confined to the major headlands, and the estuaries were protected by barrier beaches. Until oak woodlands expanded after ~8,000 years ago, coastal resources may have outranked the terrestrial resources available in the conifer communities of the mainland. When sand beaches began to accrete and estuarine and rocky coast habitats declined, the loss of benthic ecosystems was important to foraging populations. This transition occurred around 7,000 years ago in the western Santa Barbara cell and about 5,000 years ago in the San Diego region. By the Late Holocene, sand beaches and tidally flushed lagoon environments fluctuated with ENSO cycles. During La Niña–dominated periods, the lagoons shoaled, and during El Niño–dominated periods, floods reopened lagoons to tidal flushing and restored productivity. But overall, the late Holocene appears to have been a period of reduced coastal resources except for groups able to access offshore fisheries and island resources.

CENTRAL AND NORTHERN CALIFORNIA, BY IVANO W. AIELLO

Paleogeographic reconstructions of the coastal landscape of central California between Point Sur and Bodega Bay for the Late Pleistocene and Holocene are considered here. Based on a synthesis of the geologic and paleo-oceanographic data, these reconstructions indicate that initial human settlement of coastal central California occurred during a crucial period of reorganization of coastal environments characterized by dramatic and rapid changes that marked the transition from the postglacial landscape to modern Holocene conditions. The coast in this region is characterized by steep (as many as 100 meters high), actively eroding coastal bluffs often incised into uplifted marine terraces and commonly fronted by low, wave-cut shore platforms, or very small pocket beaches. These sea cliffs are interrupted at irregular intervals by larger pocket beaches that form at the mouths of coastal streams and by infrequent continuous beaches in sheltered bays. Most of the terrestrial sediment is supplied to the coast by rivers and streams during large discharge events. High precipitation generally enhances coastal erosion along cliffed shorelines, and it has been suggested that ENSO events exert principal control on the evolution of the central coast of California (Storlazzi and Griggs 2000).

Tectonic activity of the faulted transform margin of central California has exerted a primary control on coastal geomorphology which has also been modified by secondary erosion, deposition, and sea level history, as well as by the tertiary physical processes of wave and current activity (Inman and Nordstrom 1971). Tectonic uplift of the active margin of central California has produced a rugged coastline characterized by high sea cliffs cut into coastal mountain ranges, steep-sided river valleys, small pocket beaches backed by cliffs, marine terraces, and a narrow modern wave-cut bench. Conversely, estuaries and embayments formed in flat-lying areas of tectonic subsidence commonly characterized by a relatively broad shelf. Harder, weather-resistant, and poorly fractured rocks tend to form promontories and headlands, while easily eroded and highly faulted and fractured rocks are characterized by greater sea cliff retreat and indentations and embayments. Tectonics are also largely responsible for controlling the shape of the continental shelf and continental slope and the geometry and location of submarine canyons (Aiello 2005).

Post-LGM Climate in Central and Northern California

Waters off the coasts of northern California and southern Oregon lie near the modern-day boundary between the subarctic and subtropical gyres of the North Pacific, where they are influenced by the strength and character of the California Current (Huyer 1983). The California Current begins at the divergence of the North Pacific Drift, which lies off the coast of Oregon and Washington. During much of the spring and summer, juxtaposition of the North Pacific High and the North American Low results in strong, persistent northwesterly winds which induce coastal upwelling and lead to high biologic productivity. Winters are influenced by a weakened North American Low, the migration of the North Pacific High to south of 35° N, and the migration of the jet stream and associated Aleutian low pressure cells to an average position of 38° N. Winters are typically mild, wet, and stormy, with southwesterly winds and a noticeable lack of upwelling (Huyer 1983).

Studies of modern conditions, such as those by Strub et al. (1987), emphasize the major regional differences in seasonal cycles of currents, SST, winds, and sea level between southern and central California (between 33° N and 38° N). They stress that magnitudes of the seasonal cycles of all variables are at a maximum between about 38° N and 43° N (northern California to southern Oregon), implying a stronger sensitivity to climatic cycles such as ENSO.

Recent paleo-oceanographic studies demonstrate that sediments deposited beneath northeastern Pacific waters off the coasts of northern California and southern Oregon represent the latest Quaternary climatic changes. Detailed comparisons of marine microfossil and pollen assemblages also demonstrate a strong link between oceanic and continental climate change for the region (Barron et al. 2003; Pisias et al. 2001). Sabin and Pisias (1996) presented radiolarian-based sea surface temperature (SST) suggesting that the regional pattern of oceanic circulation reached its present configuration ca. 13,000 years ago. They argued that prior to 13,000 years ago, the North Pacific Drift lay farther south in response to a more southerly position of the North Pacific high pressure cell. The Late Glacial (16,000 to 14,700 years ago) was marked by reduced biologic productivity (Lyle et al. 2000). Core studies

(Barron et al. 2003) highlight the domination of pine and prominence of sagebrush (a remnant of glacial vegetation), suggesting a dry, cool environment for the first part of the deglaciation.

The Bølling-Allerod (14,600 to 12,900 years ago) stands out clearly by alkenone SSTs that are >10°C, and it is characterized by increased biogenic productivity off northern California and southern Oregon. This warming event marks the beginning of the replacement of glacial open pine woodland by Holocene oak and coastal redwood assemblages. The high variability in SSTs recorded in marine sediments is similar to the high-amplitude variations in pine and alder, suggesting alternating cool, dry and warm, wet environments. A distinctive interval of lower alkenone SSTs (<8°C, or 3–4°C cooler than surrounding intervals) correlates remarkably well with the Younger Dryas (12,900 to 11,600 years ago), a period of reduced biologic productivity. Increased pine pollen during the early part of the Younger Dryas suggests cooler, drier climates, whereas increasing alder during its latter half signals a trend toward warmer, wetter climates (Barron et al. 2003). These paleo-oceanographic data suggest that high climatic variability marked by alternating dry and wet periods characterized maritime and land climate in northern California between the end of the LGM and the beginning of the Holocene. The shift to warmer and wetter climates at the end of the Younger Dryas corresponds to the establishment of ENSO conditions that lasted through the Holocene. During ENSO conditions, northern California beaches typically experience higher sediment yields from both river sources and cliff erosion. Storm tracks and waves hit the coast directly from the west, causing complex longshore transport patterns that redistribute the beach sand both northward and southward from the river mouths (Figure 3.5a).

Holocene SST reconstructions indicate that temperatures were at a maximum about 10,000 years ago in both the northern and southern regions (Sabin and Pisias 1996), but the middle part of the Holocene (ca. 8,000 to 5,000 years ago) stands out as the coolest period (by 1–2°C) of the Holocene in the northern region (Santa Cruz to the Oregon border). This cooler Middle Holocene period was dominated by drier La Niña conditions, reduced river runoff, southward directed longshore transport, and generally starved beaches (Figure 3.5b). The Early and Late Holocene, in contrast, were distinguished by increased biologic productivity. However, the Early Holocene was a time of generally warm conditions due to weaker flow of the California Current (Barron et al. 2003). A cooler middle Holocene SST could indicate increased coastal upwelling off much of California and southern Oregon (Van Geen et al. 1992), but an increasing contribution of redwood pollen after 5,200 years ago in cores from northern California (Barron et al. 2003) might reflect increasing coastal upwelling during the latter part of the Holocene. Redwood signals the establishment of modern mesic coastal communities and the transition to a more maritime climate characterized by mild winters and cool summers dominated by fog. Forests of coastal redwood are best developed where fog associated with cold upwelling waters moderates summer temperatures (mean July temperature of 17°C) and ameliorates drought.

Atmospheric modeling studies by Clement et al. (2000) argue that El Niño events were suppressed during the middle part of the Holocene. A Late Holocene intensification of ENSO cycles documented in coastal Peru after 3,200 to 2,800 years ago (Sandweiss et al. 2001) may be responsible for the high variability of terrestrial and marine climate cycles seen in the paleo-oceanographic record off central California (Barron et al. 2003). At the same time, Late Holocene warming of winter SSTs off northern California, as suggested by the alkenone data, could have been encouraged by increasing wintertime insolation. The relative increase in coastal redwood pollen (Barron et al. 2003) after ca. 5,200 years ago may be evidence of warmer winters in adjacent coastal regions.

Late Quaternary Paleogeography

The most extensive onshore geologic record of coastal deposition during the Quaternary in central California is preserved in the relatively stable and/or subsiding areas of the coast and continental shelf. Conversely, the regional Quaternary record characterized by uplifted coastal terraces and cliffed shorelines is only fragmentary. High-resolution explorations of the seafloor with acoustic imagery of the continental shelf, including air gun, high-resolution seismic reflection data, digitally processed side-scan sonar, and multibeam bathymetric surveys have significantly increased our knowledge of the offshore region of central California and allowed for the building of mosaics of seafloor images and seafloor geologic interpretation of unprecedented detail (Eittreim et al. 2002). Moreover, interpretation of both onshore and offshore geologic data in combination with the paleo-oceanographic and paleoclimatic reconstructions from core sediments allow detailed paleogeographic reconstructions of the

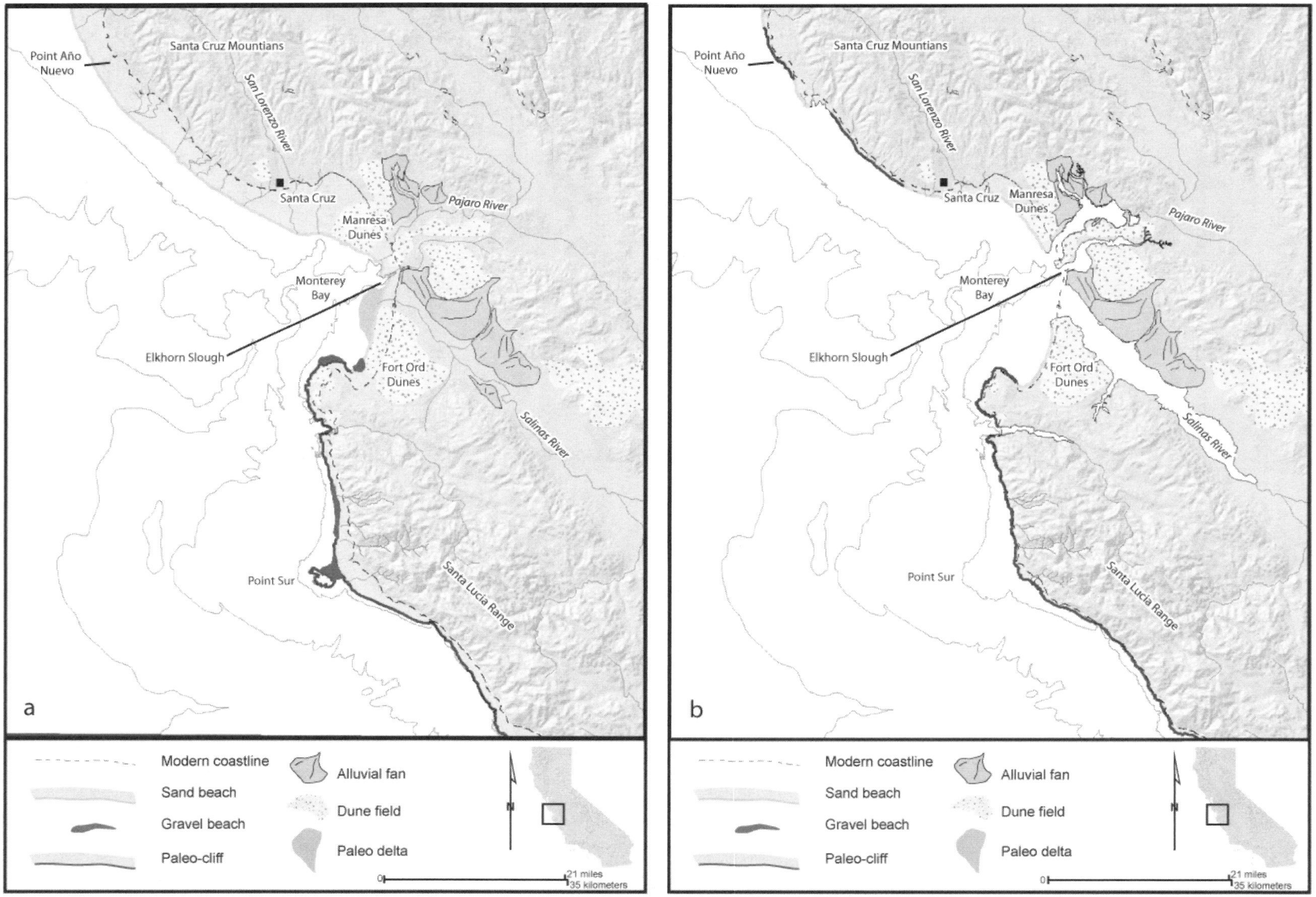

Figure 3.5. Paleogeographic reconstructions of the Monterey Bay region (a) at the end of the Younger Dryas (ca. 12,000 years ago) and (b) during the Early Middle Holocene (ca. 8,000 years ago).

post-LGM coastal environments for the region with detail not possible in previous years.

Late Quaternary reconstructions for the northern portion of the central coast (Figure 3.5) and southern portion of the north coast (Figure 3.6) show two key periods of postglacial climate and sea level history: the end of the Younger Dryas (ca. 12,000 year ago) when sea level was about 60 meters lower (Figures 3.5a, 3.6a), and the Early/Middle Holocene (ca. 8,000 years ago; Figures 3.5b, 3.6b) when sea level was about 10 to 15 meters below its present. Both periods followed prolonged sea level stillstand conditions, accompanied by formation of relatively stable coastlines. The probable distribution of beaches, coastal cliffs, estuaries, deltas, and the other different types of coastal environments that developed during the two key periods has been based on direct geologic evidence, when available. Coastal paleogeography has also been reconstructed on the basis of relationships between the particular climatic and oceanographic regimes that characterized the two key periods, the tectonic setting of the area, the morphology of the paleocoastlines, and their relationships with the onshore hydrographic network as the primary source of terrigenous material to the coast.

Analogous to modern coastlines, the paleocoastline was characterized by a variety of adjacent coastal environments that reflect the geologic and climatic complexity of the region. However, the geologic record indicates that the paleogeographic evolution of the region since the LGM was characterized by common large-scale events that formed mainly in response to rising sea level conditions and changing climatic regimes. During the LGM the shoreline was located just beyond the shelf break, and under such lowstand conditions most of the rivers became entrenched, forming incised valleys. Late Pleistocene to Early Holocene dune sand deposits formed during low sea level stands and subsequent transgression, during which large volumes of fluvial and glacially derived sediment were blown into dunes (Atwater et al. 1977). The post-LGM rise in sea level also caused erosional transgression of the shoreline; the continental shelf off central California is thought to coincide with an erosional wave-cut platform developed during the Holocene transgression. In particular, modern midshelf areas are the sites of the thickest deposits of Holocene sediment, above the prominent widespread erosional unconformity that has been recently dated to the base of the Holocene (Eittreim et al. 2002).

CENTRAL AND SOUTHERN MONTEREY BAY REGION The record of late Quaternary history in central Monterey Bay is preserved primarily in coastal terrace deposits, fluvial terraces, valley fills of the Pajaro River, Elkhorn Slough, and Salinas River, in coastal dunes, and in the largely undifferentiated Pleistocene Aromas sand (Figure 3.5a; Chin et al. 1988; Dupré 1990). The Salinas Valley's Quaternary record consists of a series of fluvial terraces and associated alluvial fans, locally overlain by aeolian deposits near the coast (Aromas red sand). The latter also occur in the southern margin of Monterey Bay, including the Early Pleistocene fluvial and alluvial fan deposits of the Paso Robles formation and the coastal dune complex of Fort Ord, correlative to the Manresa and Sunset dunes in the central Monterey Bay. Most of these dune deposits formed during the LGM, when marine sands were extensively exposed and reworked to form an extensive coastal dune field that migrated as far as 10 kilometers inland of the present shoreline, covering much of the central and southern parts of the Monterey Bay coastal plain.

All of the rivers entering the Monterey Bay region (San Lorenzo, Pajaro, Elkhorn Slough, Salinas, and Carmel) became entrenched during the LGM, forming incised valleys as much as 85 meters deep at the present-day coastline. The subsequent rise in sea level was accompanied by deposition of gravel-rich sediment in the lower parts of the valley fill. This was followed by flooding of the coastal portion of the valley and deposition of estuarine mud, locally up to 30 meters thick and extending up to 35 kilometers inland of the present shoreline. The upper part of the valley fill consists mainly of meandering stream deposits and flood basin clay. Aggradation of the trunk streams dammed many of the smaller entrenched tributaries. This caused deposition of thick sequences of lacustrine and flood basin clay which underlies many of the lakes and sloughs adjacent to the main courses of the Pajaro and Salinas Rivers (Figure 3.5b).

During pre-Holocene times, the location of Elkhorn Slough was the site of the much larger Elkhorn Valley, an old river valley that forms the landward extension of the Monterey Canyon. Holocene core sediments collected in Elkhorn Slough (Schwartz et al. 1986) reveal nonmarine gravelly sands at depths of 29 mbsl at the mouth of the slough, suggesting that local drainage in Elkhorn Valley was sufficient to incise a stream channel to these depths, probably during the LGM. Chin et al. (1988) estimate that during the LGM, the Salinas River entrenched valleys, and subsequent Early Holocene embayment may have been as deep as

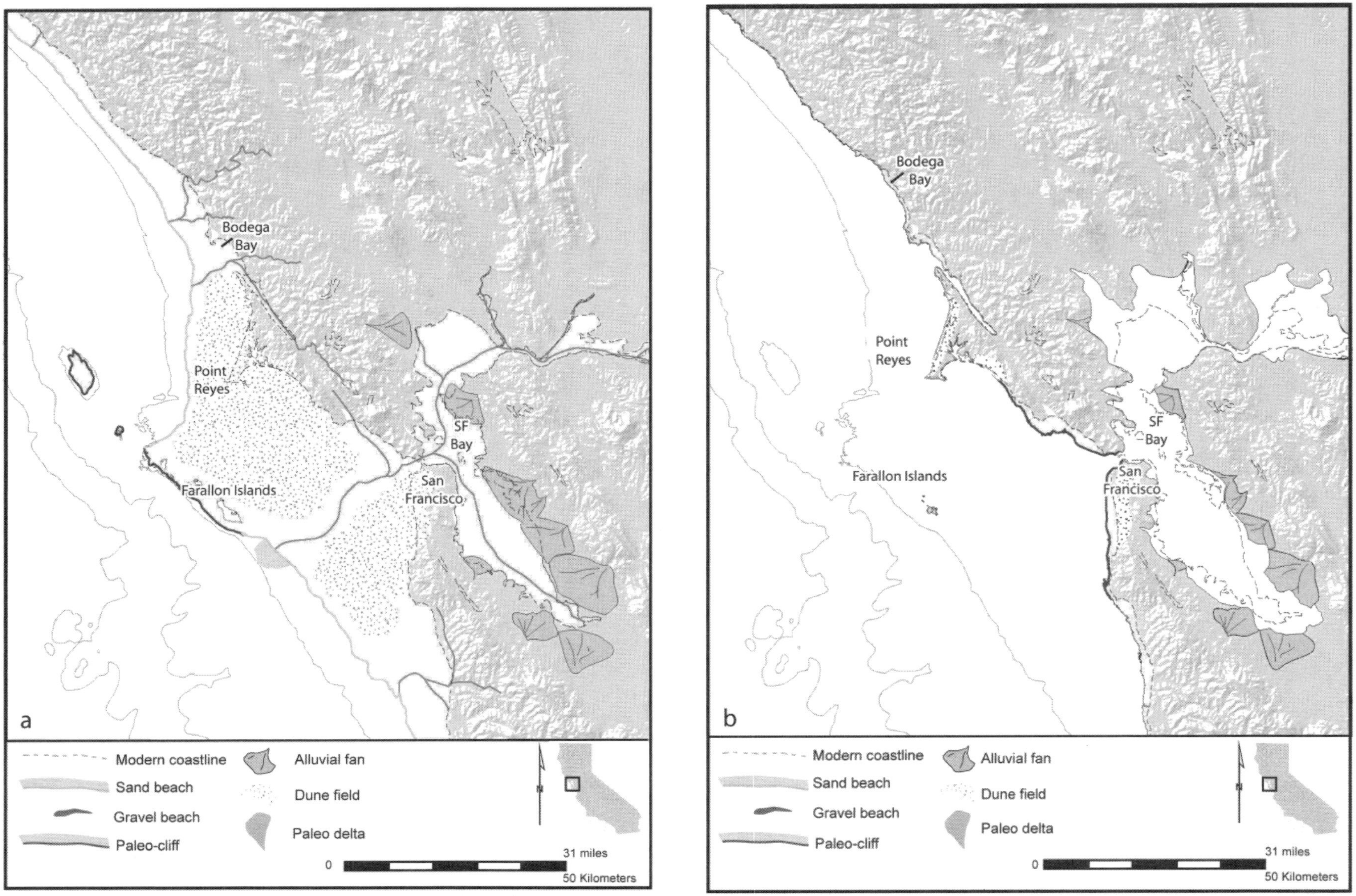

Figure 3.6. Paleogeographic reconstructions of the San Francisco Bay and Point Reyes areas (a) at the end of the Younger Dryas (ca. 12,000 years ago) and (b) during the Early Middle Holocene (ca. 8,000 years ago).

60 to 90 meters and may have extended up to 40 kilometers inland from the present coastline. It thus may have been comparable in size to modern South San Francisco Bay (Figure 3.5b). Considering the depth and extent of the Early/Middle Holocene Salinas embayment and the sediment-trapping capabilities of embayments (Atwater et al. 1977; Dupré 1975), it is conceivable that little sediment has reached the shelf from this drainage since the LGM (Chin et al. 1988).

The post-LGM rise in sea level caused erosional transgression of the Monterey Bay shoreline, which, according to Mullins et al. (1985), formed a submerged marine terrace at ~55 mbpsl during the Younger Dryas stillstand (Figure 3.5a). The subsequent continued rise in sea level and resultant shoreline erosion was accompanied by the development of a series of parabolic coastal dunes which now form a belt 200 to 700 meters wide and up to 45 meters high along much of the Monterey Bay shoreline. As sea level continued to rise, marine waters gradually invaded Elkhorn Valley resulting in the deposition of a fining upward sequence similar to those described by Dupré (1975) from other areas in the central Monterey Bay region. This fining upward sequence depicts a gradual shoaling and decrease in depositional energy at the mouth of Elkhorn Slough during the Holocene sea level rise (Schwartz et al. 1986). At about 8,000 years ago, when relative sea level was ~ 15 meters lower than present, a high-energy tidal inlet existed at the mouth of Elkhorn Slough (Figure 3.5b). Energy within the depositional environment of Elkhorn Slough gradually decreased with shoaling. Estuarine clays on top of the sequence indicate a quiet-water estuary at about 2,000 years ago. Similar estuarine clays have been reported from the subsurface of the nearby Pajaro and Salinas River valleys (Dupré 1975). However, rates of Holocene sediment accumulation in the Salinas Valley were greater, by a factor of two to three, than those in Elkhorn Slough, which resulted in a complete infilling of the Salinas Valley, whereas Elkhorn Slough remains today as an open estuary. The reconstruction of Schwartz et al. (1986) also showed that at about 4,500 years ago, salt marshes in Elkhorn Slough were approximately half of their present size, and intertidal mudbanks lined the margins of the slough's main channel.

The shelf subbottom off the Salinas River mouth consists of a thick plano-convex lens of sediment (up to 35 meters; Salinas River lobe) overlying the early Holocene shelf-wide unconformity (Chin et al. 1988). The deposits comprising this lobe have been interpreted as representing a progradational marine-to-nonmarine depositional sequence created by a delta formed during shoreline transgression (Figure 3.5a).

Around Monterey Bay and over large areas of the seafloor surrounding the granitic rock outcrops of the Monterey Peninsula, coarse sand deposits occur on the inner shelf, between 60 meters and 10 meters below the surface. Cliff erosion and/or deposition of coarse sands characterized the postglacial coastal environments over large sectors of the southern Monterey Bay region. This region is exposed to large ocean swells, with limited sources of fine sediment and perhaps a relatively rich source of coarse sand eroding from the granitic rocks of the area (Figure 3.5a).

South of the Monterey Bay, the bedrock of the Sur platform forms a submerged promontory located southwest of the San Gregorio Fault. This promontory was visible until the beginning of the Holocene. The same coarse-sand facies found in the Monterey Bay is also observed on the Sur platform.

NORTHERN MONTEREY BAY AND SANTA CRUZ SHELF The northern area of the Monterey Bay region is characterized by young tectonic uplift of the Santa Cruz Mountains where the Quaternary record of Pleistocene glacio-eustatic variations is preserved in a series of uplifted coastal terraces. Offshore, in the northeastern Monterey Bay, on the shelf between Aptos and Capitola, the Pleistocene Aromas sand formation overlies the Purisima formation and forms the pre-Holocene surface (McCulloch and Greene 1989). This aeolian sand unit is covered on the shelf by a thin veneer of Holocene sediment but is exposed on the upper continental slope on the north side of Monterey Canyon (Eittreim et al. 2002).

As Mullins et al. (1985) and Greene (1977) have shown, the mid-Santa Cruz shelf region has a cover of sediment up to 30 meters thick. Geophysical studies along the continental shelf between Año Nuevo and Soquel Cove showed traces of offshore extensions of headlands, and sediment-filled low areas in the nearshore rock exposures associated with correlative onshore coastal streams (Figure 3.5a; Eittreim et al. 2000, 2002). Anima et al. (2002) showed that during the LGM, streams flowed across the exposed Santa Cruz shelf cutting channels through the bedrock. Based on seismic reflection data, the paleovalleys are covered with more than 20 meters of sediment and have depths as much as 95 meters below present sea level, although the sediment-filled channels are not visible beneath 70 meters below sea level. The erosional unconformity that occurred during the last marine transgression may have eroded and widened the previously subaerally exposed stream channels. The mouths of many of these streams were inundated during the Holocene transgression, forming low-gradient floodplains, coastal lagoons, and marshes in their lower reaches, many of which are backed by dune fields (Figure 3.5b).

Side-scan sonar data from offshore Point Año Nuevo show an intricate network of paleochannels, mainly oriented northeast to southwest, that appear to lie along the trend of faults mapped onshore, suggesting the channels formed along shear zones in bedrock (Anima et al. 2002). Recently northeast-trending faults and fractures cross-setting both offshore and onshore strands of the San Andreas Fault system have been recognized by Aiello (2005) as possible tectonic lineations that have controlled many similarly trending geologic features in the region and the orientation of the coastal paleovalleys. South of Año Nuevo, each of the six coastal streams from San Vicente Creek to Wilder Creek have offshore channels that have eroded across the bedrock outcrop (Anima et al. 2002; Figure 3.5b).

A broad low area referred to by Anima et al. (2002) as the San Lorenzo paleovalley occupies an area from southeast of Point Santa Cruz to Schwan Lagoon. The paleochannels of these topographic low areas are traceable out to approximately 39 meters water depth and 3.25 kilometers offshore. The paleochannel of the San Lorenzo River trends along the west side of the area traceable to approximately 12 meters of water and 2 kilometers from the mouth of the San Lorenzo River. However, geophysical data collected beyond these distances and depths do not show remnants of paleochannels. Seismic profiles collected in Soquel Cove show the remnants of three large paleochannels that trend northeast to southwest and trend toward Soquel submarine canyon. The paleochannels widen offshore and were mapped to 28 meters water depth and 3.6 kilometers offshore (Anima et al. 2002).

SAN FRANCISCO BAY AND GULF OF THE FARALLONES As reported in Atwater (1979), pioneer geologist Andrew C. Lawson in 1894 interpreted the numerous islands, peninsulas, and small embayments near San Francisco as former hills, ridges, and stream valleys drowned by the sea. Inferring that San Francisco Bay did not exist before this submergence, Lawson proposed that the ancestral drainage of the San Joaquin and Sacramento Rivers must have flowed through the Golden Gate to a coastline located to the west. Later geologic studies of the San Francisco Bay region confirmed the early reconstruction and described a complex paleogeography for the post-LGM period characterized by deep and shallow seas, stream valleys, and hills, as well as estuarine embayments such as exist today. Eustatic sea level fluctuations, crustal deformation, and tectonic subsidence during the past few million years have caused episodic submergence and emergence of low-lying valleys and thereby created such ephemeral embayments as the present San Francisco Bay estuary (Atwater et al. 1977; Atwater 1979 and references therein). Core samples collected to assist in the design of footings for bridges and buildings (Atwater et al. 1977) have shown that estuaries and stream valleys have alternately occupied the site of the bay during the past million years. However, they also show that no fewer than three cycles of submergence and emergence preceded the episode of inundation that created the present estuary (Atwater 1979).

The recent maps of Quaternary deposits, including stream and marine terraces, alluvial fans and levees, beaches, dunes, and marshes proposed for the nine-county San Francisco Bay region (Knudsen et al. 2000) and the southern San Francisco Bay (Hitchcock and Helley 2003), offer a picture of unprecedented detail of the Pleistocene landscape, characterized by broad alluvial plains incised by stream channels, similar to the modern landscape (Figure 3.6). Also the recent exploration of the seafloor off San Francisco, mainly from marine geophysical and aeromagnetic surveys, added new information about offshore geology and the location of submarine strands of the San Andreas Fault system. The continental shelf west of San Francisco is characterized by the Farallon platform lying beneath the Gulf of the Farallons west of the San Gregorio Fault. During the last glacial period, fluvial and aeolian sediments covered valleys that occupied the San Francisco Bay basin. These nonmarine Pleistocene deposits experienced a sustained period of subaerial exposure, weathering, and consolidation during this period of lower sea level (Helley et al. 1979). The continental shelf was more broadly exposed above sea level, with the coastline as much as 35 kilometers west of the present one. The Farallon Islands were then rugged hills rising above a broad, gently sloping plain, with a rocky coastline lying to the west. The lowland that now forms the San Francisco Bay was a broad, forested valley. Local tributary rivers and streams converged near the center of the modern Bay Area to join the river that rushed from eastern California past the present location of San Francisco and out onto the broad alluvial plain (now the continental shelf covered by the ocean). This huge river was carrying the runoff water from about 40 percent of California's land area during a time that was cooler and wetter than the present. Once the river met the broad, flat plain west of San Francisco, it meandered to the coast, just south of the Farallon Hills (Figure 3.6a; Lajoie 1986). Horses, bison, camels, and mammoths roamed the Bay valley, while smaller vertebrates lived in the brush and grass. Specimens of all of these fossils have been found in sediment exposed in deep pits northwest of San Jose near Mountain View, excavated for San Francisco's garbage in the early 1970s. Fossil wood found in these deposits has yielded radiocarbon ages of 21,000 to 23,000 RCYBP (Helley et al. 1979), just prior to the LGM. The episode of submergence that created San Francisco Bay began about 15,000 to 18,000 years ago (Figure 3.6a; Atwater 1979). At the onset of the glacial retreat, the shoreline was located near the Farallon Islands. In order to meet this shoreline, the combined Sacramento and San Joaquin Rivers must have flowed through the Golden Gate and traversed an exposed continental shelf. Some of the sand that reached floodplains and beaches on the shelf was probably swept by westerly winds into the ancient dunes that covered much of the site of San Francisco and extended across the site of the Bay to Oakland (Figure 3.6a; Atwater et al. 1977). The Holocene sand dunes of the San Francisco Bay formed one of the most extensive coastal dune systems on the west coast of North America, underlying about one-third of San Francisco. A long stillstand of sea level at about 12,000 years ago is indicated by widespread, thick, nearshore deposits of gravel and sand presently at ~55 meters depth (Figure 3.6a). The early paleogeographic reconstruction of Atwater (1979) suggests that ephemeral estuaries probably occupied low-lying areas at or near the site of the Bay each time the sea approached its present level during the past 500,000 to 1 million years. Sediment from at least four of these estuaries has been found beneath the site of the Bay (Ross 1977). The sea level rose high enough by about 9,000 years ago to extend into the valley of San Francisco Bay (Figure 3.6b). By 5,000 years ago, the sea level reached nearly its present position, then ceased rising. Ages of shell middens around the Bay date to about 5000 RCYBP, but no older (see Chapter 8). This suggests that older habitation sites are now below sea level, corresponding to earlier, lower stands of the ocean.

Future studies need to develop detailed paleogeographic reconstructions for the coast north of San Francisco Bay. While the southern and central coasts have been extensively researched over the past two decades, this region remains less studied and less well-known. The location of former shorelines can be approximated based on the rate of sea level rise and known bathymetry, but such a reconstruction does not take into account complex sequences of erosion and fill that would have been associated with the lower courses of the Klamath, Russian, Eel, Mattole, and Smith Rivers. More research needs to be completed in order to develop an accurate, empirically based paleogeography for this area.

CHAPTER 4

One If by Land, Two If by Sea: Who Were the First Californians?

Jon M. Erlandson, Torben C. Rick, Terry L. Jones, and Judith F. Porcasi

Understanding how and when humans first settled California is intimately linked to theories of the initial colonization of the Americas. Questions about the timing of the earliest migrations and the origins of the first Americans have been central to American archaeology for more than a century, and there is a vast scientific and popular literature on the topic. A variety of disciplines contribute to the data and debates that frame our current knowledge of the subject, but archaeology continues to play a central role in understanding the origins, antiquity, and lifeways of the earliest Californians and Americans.

A decade ago, most archaeologists probably would have argued that we knew with reasonable certainty when and how humans first entered the New World. For much of the past century, the peopling of the Americas was seen as a wholly terrestrial enterprise, where hunters marched out of northeastern Asia and across the frigid plains of Beringia, through the fabled ice-free corridor, and into the heartland of North America. In this scenario, these first Americans arrived about 13,000 years ago and spread rapidly through uninhabited interior regions leaving scattered Clovis points, kill sites, and campsites to mark their presence. According to this story, American coastlines (including California's) were not systematically settled until at least 5,000 to 4,000 years later, as large game animals were hunted out of interior regions and people were forced to adapt to the supposedly less productive habitats and resources (shellfish, etc.) of coastal zones. Thus coastlines were largely irrelevant to questions related to the initial colonization of the New World and the early stages of cultural development in North America. This story fit comfortably in a larger body of anthropological theory that argued that seafaring and maritime adaptations developed relatively late in human history (Erlandson 2001, 2002).

Recent data from Africa and the Pacific Rim challenge these models, showing that anatomically modern humans *(Homo sapiens sapiens)* settled some African coastlines at least 125,000 years ago, reached Australia by boat roughly 50,000 years ago, and colonized several island archipelagoes of the eastern Pacific between about 40,000 and 15,000 years ago. Such discoveries, along with new doubts about the availability of the ice-free corridor route at key times, have pushed a coastal migration theory to the forefront of the debate about how and when the Americas were first colonized. The coastal migration theory has also gained credibility in recent years because of new evidence from early sites along the Pacific coast of the Americas, including sites on islands off Alta and Baja California roughly contemporary with Clovis and Folsom sites in the interior (Des Lauriers 2005b; Erlandson et al. 1996; Johnson et al. 2002).

Although fluted Paleo-Indian points have been found in both interior and coastal areas of the state (see Chapter 5), the focus of most scholars on the ice-free corridor and the conservative Clovis-first scenario left California and the broader Pacific coast relatively peripheral to discussions of the peopling of the New World. This was very different from the important role coastal California played in scientific debates about New World colonization in the 1960s, 1970s, and 1980s. It also differs from the current situation, where archaeological discoveries from coastal California are again contributing to the debate about the origins and antiquity of the first Americans. Then and now, such debates have been framed by competing colonization models based on long versus short chronologies. These debates have also been strongly influenced by the dynamic geography of Beringia, the "ice-free corridor," and the Pacific Northwest through the last glacial-interglacial cycle.

In the past 20 years, there have been major shifts in anthropological perspectives on the initial colonization of the Americas. Here we review some theoretical, methodological, and evidentiary changes of the past two decades, focusing on how these developments have affected our notions of when and how California was first settled. Our goal is not a comprehensive review of the history of knowledge related to the peopling of the Americas, which is beyond the scope of this chapter, but a summary of the current status of scientific knowledge in light of some of the major discoveries in California over the past 20 years.

COLONIZATION CHRONOLOGIES: THE LONG AND THE SHORT OF IT

The "discovery" and conquest of the New World by people of European ancestry triggered a wave of speculation and research about the origins of the indigenous peoples of North and South America. If Christopher Columbus's mistaken characterization of these diverse cultures as Indians proves he was more lost than not, it also provided the first connection between Native Americans and Asia. To Columbus and many other European explorers, the people they encountered after sailing across the Atlantic Ocean were clearly of Asian origin. This Asian connection has dominated scholarly thought about the peopling of the Americas ever since and is supported by an overwhelming body of scientific data (Fagan 1987; Madsen 2004).

From the very beginning, scholarly views of the antiquity of human settlement in the Americas have also been characterized by competition between long versus short chronologies. Even as the relatively conservative Clovis-first model came to dominate American archaeology, a vocal minority has argued that the human history of North and South America extended back beyond the last glacial maximum, to 25,000 years, 50,000 years, or more (Bada et al. 1974; Carter 1980a; Davis 1978; Guidon and Delibrias 1986; Leakey et al. 1972; MacNeish 1971; Orr 1968). Late in 2004, the popular media widely reported an age of 50,000 years for another pre-Clovis candidate, the Topper site in South Carolina, but little scientific evidence has been released to support such claims.

California has produced more than its share of pre-Clovis sites: from Orr and Berger's "fire areas" on Santa Rosa Island (Berger 1982; Berger and Orr 1966; Orr 1968), Carter's (1980a, 1980b) claims for last Interglacial humans at Texas Street and Tecolote Canyon, Davis's (1975, 1978) China Lake finds, the Calico site in the Mojave Desert (Leakey et al. 1972), and numerous human skeletons purportedly dating to the Pleistocene (Bada et al. 1974; Berger et al. 1971). None of these pre-Clovis localities has withstood rigorous scientific scrutiny or attracted widespread scholarly acceptance (see Chartkoff and Chartkoff 1984; Erlandson 1994; Fagan 2003; Moratto 1984), although some continue to be investigated (Basgall 2003; Erlandson 2000; Vellanoweth and Erlandson 2000).

California's "Pleistocene" skeletons were widely cited by proponents of a long chronology for the peopling of the Americas, but skepticism was also widespread (Chartkoff and Chartkoff 1984:33–35; Moratto 1984:52). They included the Sunnyvale skeleton estimated to be up to 70,000 years old; the Angeles Mesa (Haverty) remains thought by some to be over 50,000 years old; Del Mar man dated from 48,000 to 41,000 years; the San Jacinto (Riverside) remains to roughly 37,000 years; La Jolla Man to about 28,000 years; Los Angeles Man to 26,000 years; the Yuha burial to about 22,000 years (Bischoff et al. 1976); and the Laguna Woman skull between about 17,000 and 15,000 RYBP. Most of these were dated via the amino acid racemization technique, calibrated with an early ^{14}C date for Laguna Woman (Erlandson 1994:216–217; Taylor 1991:90). In a setback for the long chronology, several papers published in the 1980s (Bada 1985; Bada et al. 1984; Stafford et al. 1987; Taylor 1983; Taylor et al. 1985, 1987) reported that all these "Pleistocene" skeletons were Holocene in age, including a date of 5100 ± 500 RYBP for the Laguna Woman skull. The revised dates for these skeletons—along with studies of other "Pleistocene" bone samples such as the Old Crow flesher from the Yukon redated by Nelson et al. (1986) from about 28,000 RYBP to 1800 RYBP—contributed to the skepticism and conservatism of proponents of the short chronology and Clovis-first models during the 1980s and 1990s. Such short chronologies held that people first entered the Americas around 11,500 RYBP, the equivalent of about 11,300 cal B.C.

PALEOGEOGRAPHY OF BERINGIA AND THE PACIFIC NORTHWEST

For both the long and short chronologies, understanding the dynamic paleogeography of North America during and since the last glacial is crucial. The vast majority of scientists believe the initial colonization of the Americas came from northeast Asia, a view supported by overwhelming evidence from archaeology, linguistics, biological anthropology, and genetics. Except for the Bering Strait area, North and South America are isolated by the vast expanses of the Atlantic and Pacific Oceans—major barriers for early human migration. During glacial periods when world sea levels were lower, however, Siberia and Alaska were joined by the lowland plain of Beringia, 1,000 kilometers or more wide. Using boats or walking across sea ice in winter, humans could also have crossed from northeast Asia into Alaska virtually anytime during the past 50,000 years.

Human migrations deeper into North America were more constrained by the glacial and sea level histories of northwestern North America. For decades, the existence of a human migration route through a long, narrow ice-free corridor between Laurentide and Cordilleran ice sheets was assumed by archaeologists, despite the fact that no Clovis-age sites had been found in the area. At the same time, a coastal migration route was long believed to have been impossible, based on the assumption that much of the northern northwest coast was blocked by massive walls of glacial ice extending to the edge of the continental shelf. Recent data suggest, however, that the ice-free corridor was blocked from about 21,000 to as late as 11,000 cal B.C. and may have remained a relatively bleak and barren proglacial landscape for centuries after that (Clague et al. 2004). This raises significant questions about the use of the ice-free corridor by pre-Clovis peoples to colonize the subarctic areas of North and South America.

In contrast, outer coast areas of the Pacific Northwest now appear to have been largely deglaciated by about 14,000 cal B.C., and they supported a relatively diverse and productive array of marine and terrestrial resources, including grizzly bears and other mammals (see Heaton and Grady 1993; Mann and Hamilton 1995). Brigham-Grette et al. (2004:59) suggested that the south coast of Beringia may have been "geomorphically complex during the late glacial, with hundreds of islands located just off a coast riddled with bays and inlets. Even covered with sea ice much of the year, the south coast of Beringia would have provided rich habitat for seals, walrus, and other marine organisms" (Brigham-Grette et al. 2004:59). Recognizing that maritime peoples had adapted to the relatively cool waters of the eastern Pacific during the last glacial, Erlandson et al. (2004) suggested that the widespread distribution of kelp forests along northern Pacific coastlines may have provided a "kelp highway" for maritime peoples, offering a similar suite of marine resources, reduced wave energy, and holdfasts for boats. There is still much to be learned about the nature of Beringia's south coast, but recent data suggest that a coastal migration route was much more feasible than previously believed.

OPENING PANDORA'S BOX: BREAKING THE CLOVIS BARRIER

Even as new data on the feasibility of interior and coastal migration routes were emerging, widespread support for the conservative Clovis-first model collapsed. The Monte Verde site in Chile is often given credit for breaking the Clovis barrier, but the first widely accepted evidence for a pre-Clovis occupation of the Americas came from the Nenana complex in central Alaska (Powers and Hoffecker 1989; Hoffecker et al. 1993). Dated as early as 11,800 RYBP (~11,600 cal B.C.), Nenana assemblages lack fluted points but share many technological similarities with Clovis (Goebel et al. 1991). Found near the northern entrance to the ice-free corridor, the definition of the Nenana complex had little impact on Clovis-first models because it involved a movement of interior peoples out of northeastern Asia, a migration through the ice-free corridor, and a logical technological precursor for an American invention of the fluted point technologies emblematic of Clovis and Folsom.

Until the publication of a detailed site report for Monte Verde (Dillehay 1997) and the "certification" of the site by a panel of distinguished experts (Meltzer et al. 1997), the intellectual climate of the late 1980s and 1990s was relatively conservative. Widespread (if not unanimous) scholarly acceptance of Monte Verde reshaped the debate about the peopling of the Americas. Dated to about 12,500 RYBP (~12,600 cal B.C.), Monte Verde cannot be absorbed by Clovis-first models because it appears to be about a millennium older than Clovis and is located thousands of kilometers to the south near the Chilean coast. If humans reached coastal Chile as much as 14,500 years ago, their ancestors could not have traveled through an ice-free corridor far to the north that did not open until about 1,500 years later. These findings dramatically revived debate and research related to the origin of the first Americans and elevated the coastal migration theory and the Pacific coast of North America from the margins of American archaeology to center stage. When combined with other research on the antiquity of boats, maritime migrations, and coastal adaptations—including the discovery of Terminal Pleistocene sites on California's Channel Islands (see below) and the coast of Peru (deFrance et al. 2001; Keefer et al. 1998; Sandweiss et al. 1998)—the acceptance of Monte Verde has strengthened scholarly and popular support for a coastal migration of maritime peoples around the North Pacific during the Late Pleistocene (Dixon 1999; Erlandson 1991a, 1994, 2002; Fedje et al. 2004; Fladmark 1979; Gruhn 1994; Jones, Fitzgerald et al. 2002).

The breaking of the Clovis barrier also gave new life to those who believe the New World may have been colonized before the last glacial maximum (Madsen 2004). In the process, it also raised the lid of a proverbial Pandora's box, spawning more radical proposals and media coverage. One theory suggests that humans colonized the Americas in the Pleistocene by crossing the North Atlantic (Bradley and Stanford 2004; Stanford and Bradley 2002), an idea given little credence by most scientists (see Clark 2000; Straus 2000).

In our view, such proposals are not required to account for the available data, which can be explained by multiple migrations into the New World shortly after the end of the last glacial. At present, it seems most likely that the peopling of the Americas included both coastal and interior migrations of peoples from northeastern Asia and Beringia, with an earlier migration possibly following the northern Pacific coast. If such an early coastal migration took place—which has yet to be proven—the evidence for early maritime exploration will be difficult to identify due to postglacial sea level rise and coastal erosion. One way or another, the pre-Clovis occupation of the Americas remains poorly defined, in part because initial populations must have been small and mobile, moving across American landscapes and seascapes relatively rapidly.

TERMINAL PLEISTOCENE AND EARLY HOLOCENE OCCUPATIONS

We know of no serious candidates for pre-Clovis occupations in California that have not already been proposed, vetted, and rejected by most scholars. Clovis-like fluted points have been found on the coast and in the interior, but most are isolated finds without stratigraphic, artifactual, or faunal associations (see Chapter 5). The fluted points from coastal sites (Bertrando 2004b; Erlandson et al. 1987; Mills et al. 2005; Simons et al. 1985) show that some Paleo-Indians were familiar with California's coastal landscapes. None of the fluted point localities are well dated, but they likely were left by Paleo-Indians between about 11,500 and 9000 cal B.C. In the absence of good chronological data for California's fluted points, Clovis peoples conceivably originated along the Pacific coast and then moved into the continental interior (Erlandson 1994:268). It seems more likely, however, that Clovis-like points in California were left by later Paleo-Indians spreading westward from the interior of North America.

Along with uncertainties about the origin of Clovis (or closely related) peoples in California, we know little about their economies, technologies, or lifeways. A possible exception is a deeply buried cultural horizon identified by Beaton (1991b) at an interior rock shelter located near the shore of Tule Lake near the California-Oregon border (Figure 4.1). At SIS-218, near the base of a 2.4 meter cultural sequence, Beaton found a hearth associated with artifacts and the bones of freshwater fish, waterfowl, and mammals. Charcoal from the hearth was dated to 11,450 ± 340 RYBP (ca. 11,300 cal B.C.), a date essentially contemporary with Clovis. Only limited excavations were completed at SIS-218 and no detailed report has been published. A brief preliminary report described a small assemblage of artifacts from the basal levels, however, including an

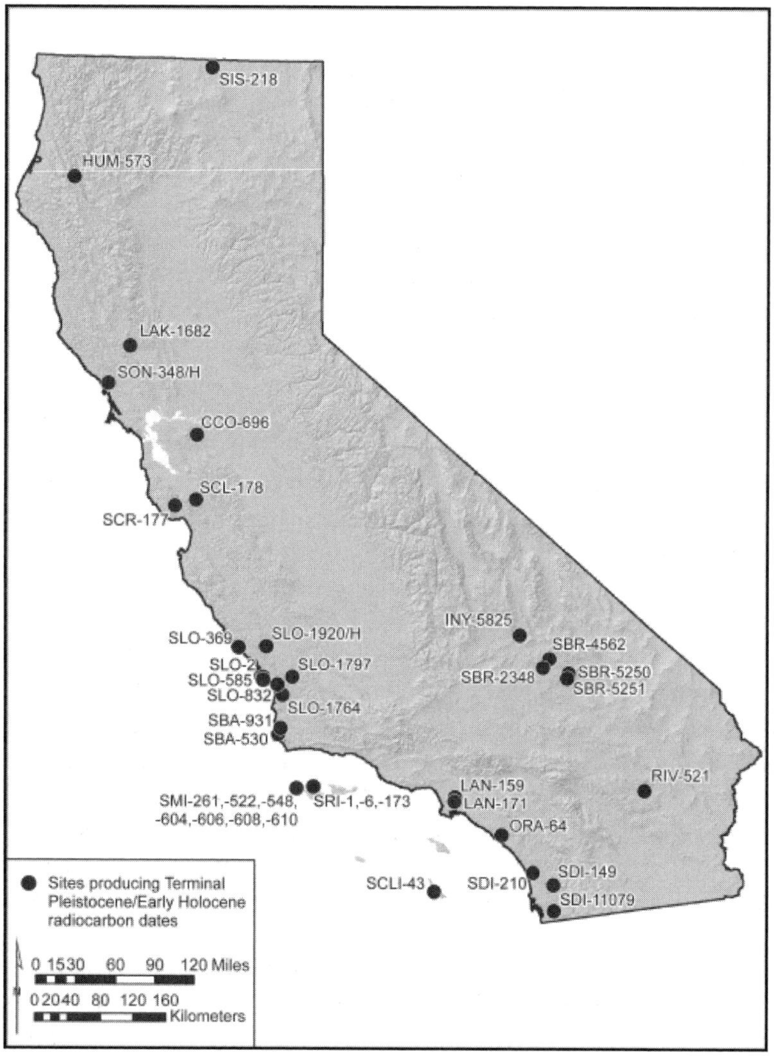

Figure 4.1. California sites with Terminal Pleistocene/Early Holocene radiocarbon dates.

undiagnostic biface fragment, a unifacial tool, and obsidian and cryptocrystalline debitage (Beaton 1991b). Beaton concluded that the early levels at SIS-218 were occupied "by small lakeshore-focused groups which employed economic strategies primarily directed toward the taking of fish and waterfowl."

Several other interior sites located adjacent to lakes or marshes have produced radiocarbon dates suggesting that they were occupied between about 8000 and 7000 cal B.C. (Table 4.1). Many of these sites are discussed in later chapters; here we note that several sites in the desert of southeastern California have produced spire-removed *Olivella* beads directly dated via accelerator mass spectrometry (AMS) to between 9000 and 7000 cal B.C. (Fitzgerald et al. 2005). These marine shell beads indicate that trade networks existed between California's Paleo-Coastal peoples and their interior neighbors as the Pleistocene came to a close.

On the coast itself, other than a few fluted point localities, the earliest widely accepted sites come from the Northern Channel Islands, including Arlington Springs (SRI-173) on Santa Rosa Island and Daisy Cave (SMI-261) on San Miguel Island (Erlandson et al. 1996; Johnson et al. 2002; Rick et al. 2001). SRI-173 was discovered in 1959, when Orr (1962, 1968) found human bones eroding from a thin paleosol exposed in the walls of Arlington Canyon near a spring on the northwestern coast of Santa Rosa Island. The paleosol that the bones were embedded in was found in a stratified sequence of arroyo fill sediments 11 meters (37 feet) below the surface. Radiocarbon (^{14}C) dating of charcoal found near the bones suggested that the individual died approximately 10,000 RYBP, an age confirmed through dating of a sample of the bone itself to 10,080 ± 810 RYBP (Berger and Protsch 1989:59). Calibration of the original ^{14}C dates from the site suggest that Arlington Man died about 12,000 years ago (ca. 10,000 cal B.C.). More recently, AMS dating of human bone samples curated at the Santa Barbara Museum of Natural History produced a wide range of dates for Arlington Man, with uncalibrated ages ranging from about 11,000 to 6600 RYBP (Johnson et al. 2002:543). Further fieldwork at the site found no additional archaeological remains in the Terminal Pleistocene strata, but they shed greater light on the stratigraphy and paleoecology of the locality, and provided a suite of additional ^{14}C dates on organic materials from the strata believed to have bracketed the human bones. Johnson et al. (2002) argued that the oldest of several dates (ca. 11,000 cal B.C.) on human bone provide the most likely age of Arlington Man, but a more conservative interpretation is that she died sometime between 11,000 and 10,000 cal B.C. Even these dates may be several centuries too old if Arlington Man regularly consumed marine resources (likely for an occupant of the Channel Islands), as no marine reservoir effect appears to have been applied in calibrating the dates from bone collagen. Nonetheless, the dating of Arlington Man demonstrates that Paleo-Indian peoples colonized the Northern Channel Islands at least 12,000 years ago, which required the use of seaworthy boats (Erlandson 2002).

The presence of maritime Paleo-Indians on the Northern Channel Islands during the Terminal Pleistocene is confirmed by archaeological evidence from Daisy Cave, located on the northeastern coast of San Miguel Island (Erlandson 2007; Erlandson et al. 1996; Rick et al. 2001). Daisy Cave has produced evidence for multiple occupations by Paleo-Coastal peoples between about 9500 and 6600 cal B.C. Terminal Pleistocene occupation of the cave was limited, but the lowest well-defined cultural horizon—a thin soil horizon known as Stratum G—produced a few Monterey chert and siliceous shale artifacts associated with a small assemblage of shellfish remains from rocky intertidal habitats (Erlandson et al. 1996). The earliest Daisy Cave assemblage is probably derived from a single brief occupation, but its significance is magnified by the fact that it comes from an island that required seaworthy boats to reach. San Miguel also contains almost no terrestrial resources that would have attracted early peoples, who must have come to the island primarily for its wealth of marine resources.

Between about 8000 and 6600 cal B.C., Paleo-Coastal peoples visited Daisy Cave repeatedly, leaving a much broader range of materials. Strata E and F contain a series of well-preserved occupation layers containing a variety of artifacts made from stone, bone, shell, and plant remains. The chipped stone assemblage consists primarily of expedient tools and debitage, and the few projectile points or bifaces recovered (mostly leaf-shaped specimens and an eccentric crescent) suggest that hunting was not a major activity. Numerous spire-removed *Olivella biplicata* beads were also found in Strata E and F, similar to those from other early coastal and interior sites in California (Erlandson et al. 2005; Fitzgerald et al. 2005). Another extraordinary aspect of the early maritime technology at Daisy Cave is an assemblage of small bone bipoints or fish gorges—the oldest known fishhooks in the Americas. Also recovered were more than 1,500 pieces of twisted sea grass cordage, along with a few woven items and

Table 4.1. ^{14}C Dates from Well-Documented Terminal Pleistocene and Early Holocene Sites in California

Site Number and Name	*Material Dated*	*Lab Number*	*Provenience Unit:depth (cm)*	*Measured Age (RYBA)*	*$^{13}C/^{12}C$ Adj. Age (RYBA)*	*Calibrated Age (BC)*	*References*
			COASTAL and NEAR-COASTAL SITES				
LAN-159 La Brea	Human bone collagen	UCLA-1292BB	Pit 10	9000 ± 80	9080 ± 80	8520 (8270) 7980	Berger at al. 1971
LAN-171 Haverty**							Brooks et al. 1990
ORA-64 Irvine	*Olivella* bead	CAMS-43524	14:70-80	-	8840 ± 50	7420 (7070) 7010	Koerper 1981;
	Olivella bead	CAMS-43532	1650:10-50	-	8850 ± 60	7430 (7080) 7010	Macko 1998;
	Olivella bead	CAMS-42591	1856:0-20	-	8870 ± 50	7440 (7090) 7030	Erlandson et al.
	Olivella bead	CAMS-43526	268:0-50	-	8950 + 50	7470 (7130) 7080	2005
SBA-530 Honda	*Mytilus* (multiple pieces)	Beta-17260	Near base	8430 ± 120	8840 ± 120	7800 (7070) 6910	Glassow 1996a
	Mytilus	Beta-31172	7N/2W:0-10	8280 ± 90	8690 ± 90	7360 (6990) 6850	Woodman et al. 1995
SBA-931	*Mytilus*	Beta-17002	5:100-120	9440 ± 150	9850 ± 150	9170 (8360) 7880	Glassow 1991
Surf	*Mytilus*	Beta-15671	1:150-160	9150 ± 160	9560 ± 160	8630 (8030) 7590*	
SCL-178 Blood Alley	*Olivella* bead	Beta-186022	13:500	8110 ± 50	8520 ± 50	6940 (6780) 6630[a] 7000 (6840) 6670[b]	Fitzgerald and Porcasi 2003
	Sylvilagus auduboni	Beta-183408	731:460-490	8390 ± 50	8370 ± 50	7570 (7450) 7210	
SCLI-43	Charcoal	Beta-76021	C:Basal	8120 ± 310	8110 ± 300	7730 (7070) 6400	Cassidy et al.
Eel Point	Marine shell	Beta-76152	2N/35E:Str. 11	7720 ± 130	8140 ± 130	6700 (6400) 6150	2004; Porcasi et al. 2000
SCR-177	Charcoal	Beta-7713	Rock feature B26	6970±150	-	6110 (5780)5530	Cartier 1993a
	Charcoal	Beta-7714	40-60				Fitzgerald and
			Rock feature B29 60-80	7050±110	-	6110 (5940, 5910, 5980) 5670	Jones 1999
SDI-149 Harris	Charcoal	A-722A	-	-	9030 ± 350	9200 (8260) 7380	Warren 1966, 1967
SDI-210	*Mytilus*	LJ-967	1:160-170	9020 ± 500	9430 ± 500	9210 (7880) 6740	Moriarty 1967
SDI-11079 Remington	*Olivella* bead	Beta-118072	-	-	9400 ± 60	8330 (7870) 7310[a]	Kyle et al. 1998
SLO-2 Diablo	*H. rufescens*	GAK-2044	N1/W5:290	-	9780 ± 260	9180 (8320) 7540	Greenwood
Canyon	Human bone	UCLA-1686A	S4/W9:20-330	-	9480 ± 175	9240 (8770) 8330*	1972
SLO-369	Mixed shell	Beta-167229	-	-	8980 ± 80	7630 (7030) 6910	Parker 2004
	Mixed shell	Beta-165338			8830 ± 70	7800 (7110) 6990	
SLO-585	*H. rufescens*	GAK-2040	N12-W6	8410 ± 260	8820 ± 260	7460 (7030) 6850	Greenwood 1972
SLO-832/	*S. nuttalli*	Beta-146602	S32/W19:120-30	8490 ± 70	8950 ± 70	7490 (7360) 7090	D. Jones et al.
1420	*P. staminea*	Beta-141922	S9/E4:130-140	9120 ± 170	9540 ± 180	8370 (7960) 7530	2002;
	Macoma	UCR-1342	M-1:130-150	8520 ± 140	8930 ± 140	7570 (7310) 6980	Gibson 1996
SLO-1764	*S. nuttallii*	Beta-93199	-	8300 ± 60	8720 ± 60	7260 (7030) 6860	Lebow et al. 2001
SLO-1797	*S. nuttallii*	Beta-104767	10:80-100	9500 ± 260	9900 ± 270	9050 (8350) 7730	Fitzgerald 2000; T.
Cross Creek	*S. nuttallii*	Beta-104769	2:90	9230 ± 100	9640 ± 100	8320 (8030) 7880	Jones et al. 2002
SLO-1920/H Bunkhouse	*Olivella* bead	Beta-151613	3:110-120	8400 ± 40	8830 ± 40	7630 (7050) 6910[a] 7640 (7120) 6950[b]	Stevens et al. 2004
	S. nuttallii	Beta-147055	1:64	8090 ± 70	8520 ± 70	6960 (6780) 6590[a] 7010 (6840) 6640[b]	
SMI-261	*Tegula*	Beta-52360	E-6:Stratum G	10,180 ± 70	10,600 ± 70	9670 (9170) 8910	Erlandson et al.
Daisy Cave	*H. rufescens*	Beta-14660	E-6:Stratum G	10,260 ± 90	10,700 ± 90	9950 (9550) 8930	1996; Rick et al.
	Charred twig	CAMS-33369	94-E6: Str. G	-	9580 ± 60	9160 (8920) 8760	2001
SMI-522	*M. californianus*	OS-27943	Base of midden	-	9450 ± 70	8330 (7880) 7590	Erlandson and
	H. cracherodii	Beta-151616	Base of midden	-	9220 ± 120	8300 (7660) 7120	Rick 2002b
SMI-548	*Mytilus californianus*	OS-31684	Area A:0-5	-	9070 ± 55	7870 (7480) 7090	Erlandson et al.
		Beta-130893	Area A:Surface	8940 ± 140	9380 ± 140	8340 (7870) 7180	2004
SMI-604	*Mytilus*	Beta-171120	Probe: 0-10	8610 ± 90	9030 ± 100	7170 (7260) 7460	Rick et al. 2003
Seal Cave	*californianus*	OS-34804	Probe: 25	-	9440 ± 50	8240 (7880) 7870	
SMI-606	*Mytilus*	Beta-145307	Unit 1	-	8760 ± 80	7630 (7030) 6890	Erlandson, Rick,
Busted Balls	*californianus*	Beta-145308	East Locus		8920 ± 90	7800 (7120) 6980	and Batterson 2005

SMI-608	*M. californianus*	OS-44638	-	-	9200 ± 50	7890 (7660) 7160	Erlandson, Braje, Rick, and Peterson 2005; Braje et al. 2005a
	H. cracherodii	OS-48348	-	-	9270 ± 50	8300 (7730) 7190	
SMI-610 RS Cliffs	*Mytilus californianus*	OS-27940	Sea cliff:0-10	-	8940 ± 60	7470 (7130) 7070	Erlandson work in progress
		OS-28282		-	9080 ± 60	7800 (7490) 7140	
SON-348/H Duncans Point Cave	*Mytilus californianus*	CAMS-82844	Column:250-260	-	8715 ± 35	7030 (6980) 6930	Kennedy et al. 2005;
	Charcoal	CAMS-86877	Column:230-240	-	7890 ± 35	6980 (6690)	Schwaderer
	Charcoal	Beta-35229	Unit 2:222	-	8620 ± 420	8270 (7600) 7140	1992
SRI-1 Garanon	*Mytilus californianus*	Beta-34922	Sea cliff: Basal midden	8320 ± 105	8730 ± 105	7310 (7010) 6940	Erlandson and Morris 1992
SRI-6	*Haliotis rufescens*	Beta-47625	Component 1		8800 ± 80	7330 (7050) 6990	Erlandson et al. 1999
SRI-173 Arlington	Human bone collagen	CAMS-16814	Arlington Man	-	9180 ± 70	8610 (8370) 8300*	Johnson et al. 2002
	Human bone collagen	CAMS-16810	Arlington Man	-	10,960 ± 80	11,210(11,040) 10,700	
	Charcoal	CAMS-13036	-	-	10,090 ± 70	10,320(9690)9310*	
				INTERIOR SITES			
CAL-629/630 Skyrocket	Charcoal	WSU-4614	Hearth in stone platform feature	8550 ± 150	-	8170 (7580) 7190	Bieling et al. 1996
CCO-696	Charcoal	Beta-93715	Trench 7-27-1: 320-375	-	8440 ± 100	7590 (7490) 7270	Meyer and Rosenthal 1997
	Charcoal	Beta-85993	NW1:390-415	-	8810 ± 60	7990 (7920) 7670	
HUM-573	Bulk soil: house floor	Beta-13757	Feature 1:30-40	-	7120 ±_50	6160 (5990, 5940, 5930) 8840	Fitzgerald and Hildebrandt 2002
INY-182 Stahl	*Olivella* bead	AA-8620	4:70-80	8670 ± 85	9080 ± 85	7840 (7270) 7040[a] 7830 (7440) 7100[b]	Schroth 1994: 314-332
	Olivella bead	AA-8621	9:110-120	8625 ± 110	9035 ± 110	7820 (7300) 6990[a] 7830 (7380) 7050[b]	
INY-5825	Peat	Beta-170208	S48/W30.5: 2-6	-	10,110 ± 110	10,380 (9740, 9720, 9700) 9280	Basgall 2004b
LAK-1682 Crazy Creek	Charcoal	Beta-71636	3:20-24	7320 ± 270	-	6440 (6210, 6190, 6180, 6170, 6160, 6130, 6100) 5980	Rosenthal et al. 1995
RIV-521	*Olivella* bead	AA-8613	8:25-30	9330 ± 90	9740 ± 90	8630 (8310) 7770[a] 9090 (8220) 7860[b]	Schroth 1994: 314-332
	Olivella bead	AA-8614	4:40-50	7920 ± 85	8330 ± 85	6870 (6530) 6380[a] 6890 (6630) 6430[b]	
SBR-2348 Goldstone	*Olivella* bead	AA-12403	1:30-40	9125 ± 80	9535 ± 85	8340 (7890) 7600[a] 8350 (8050) 7640[b]	Basgall and Hall 1994: 26-27
SBR-4562 Awl Site	*Olivella* bead	AA-12404	S60/W72:130-140	9450 ± 110	9860 ± 110	9160 (8340) 7880[a] 9160 (8420) 7920[b]	Basgall and Hall 1994: 26-27;
	Charcoal	Beta-16100	S50/W65:90-100	-	9410 ± 115	9160 (8690) 8300*	Fitzgerald et
	Charcoal	Beta-16313	S49/W64:80-90	-	9470 ± 115	9220 (8740) 8350	al. 2005
SBR-5250 Rodgers Ridge	*Olivella* bead	AA-12405	S122/W2:0-5	10,085 ± 85	10495 ± 85	9640 (9010) 8690[a] 9950 (9250) 8880[b]	Basgall and Hall 1994: 26-27;
	Bulk soil	Beta-12840	N42.5/W60:50-70	-	8410 ± 140	7730 (7500) 7080	Fitzgerald et
	Bulk soil	Beta-12844	S84/W35:20-30	-	8410 ± 210	7690 (7500) 6860	al. 2005
SBR-5251 Flood Pond	*Olivella* bead	AA-12406	N0/W15: Surface	8930 ± 85	9340 ± 85	8310 (7720) 7170 8320 (7780) 7200	Fitzgerald et al. 2005
SIS-218 Tule Lake	Charcoal	Beta-39545	Fire pit:215-220	11,450 ± 340		13,140 (11,490) 10,730	Beaton 1991b

*Multiple pieces

**17 ^{14}C dates on human bones from five individuals. RCYBP range from 15,900 ± 250 (HA-104B) to 2730 ± 190 (UCR-3084/CAMS-438). No agreement on actual ages of specimens.

Notes: Rounded calendar dates include intercept (in parentheses), with age range at two sigma using established regional marine reservoir correction rates of 225±35[a] and 290±35[b]. All *Olivella* beads are spire-removed types. Calibrated dates marked with an * have multiple intercepts. Non-shell samples (charcoal, bone, bulk soil, peat) calibrated as terrestrial samples.

See also Table 15.3, Chapter 15 this volume.

bundles or clumps of unwoven sea grass (Connolly et al. 1995). The hundreds of small pieces of cordage appear to be the cutoffs and other leftovers from the manufacture of cordage, maintenance of fishing nets, and other activities.

Several other Paleo-Coastal sites dated between about 8000 and 7000 cal B.C. have been identified on San Miguel and Santa Rosa Islands (Braje et al. 2005a; Erlandson 1994; Erlandson and Morris 1992; Erlandson et al. 1999, 2004; Erlandson, Braje et al. 2005; Erlandson, Rick et al. 2005; Rick et al. 2003, 2005a, b). Most are situated near springs located some distance from the Early Holocene coast and may represent dry season campsites. Several of these shell middens have produced bone gorges and *Olivella* beads similar to those found at Daisy Cave. Population densities are traditionally thought to have been very low during the Early Holocene, but the growing number of early island and mainland sites suggests that more people were present in the area than previously believed. This seems consistent with the 3,000 to 2,000 years of demographic expansion expected given the presence of fluted points near the coast and the Terminal Pleistocene occupations of Arlington Springs and Daisy Cave. With shorelines dating to this time period heavily impacted by rising seas and coastal erosion, moreover, the known Paleo-Coastal sites probably represent just a fraction of the sites that once existed in the area. An 8,500-year-old maritime occupation at Eel Point (SCLI-43) on San Clemente Island, located more than 60 kilometers off the San Diego coast, also reflects a relatively sophisticated boat and maritime technology (Cassidy et al. 2004).

Along with these island sites, numerous shell middens from the central and southern California coast have been dated between 8000 and 7000 cal B.C. (Table 4.1). These include mainland sites such as Duncans Point Cave (SON-348/H; Schwaderer 1992) on the northern coast, SLO-2 at Diablo Canyon (Greenwood 1972), Cross Creek (SLO-1797; Jones, Fitzgerald et al. 2002), SBA-931 on Vandenberg Air Force Base (Glassow 1996a), ORA-64 on Newport Bay (Koerper 1981; Macko 1998), Agua Hedionda (SDI-210; Moriarty 1967), and many others. Impressive clusters of early sites have been documented along the mainland coast in the San Diego, Santa Barbara, and San Luis Obispo areas (see Bertrando and Levulett 2004; Erlandson 1994; Erlandson and Moss 1996; Jones 1991), but early coastal shell middens continue to be poorly represented in the San Francisco Bay Area and the northern California coast. Spire-removed *Olivella* shell beads have been found in many of these early coastal sites (see Erlandson, Macko et al. 2005; Fitzgerald et al. 2005). Eccentric crescents have also been found in some mainland Paleo-Coastal sites, as have leaf-shaped bifaces, manos, and metates (Erlandson 1994; Jones, Fitzgerald et al. 2002; Koerper 1981; Macko 1998). The presence of multiple components (or lengthy occupations) and heavy soil mixing by gophers and other burrowing animals at most mainland sites limits the chronological resolution with which their assemblages can be interpreted, but it seems likely that bone gorges, boats, and other maritime technologies were also used by mainland Paleo-Coastal peoples.

The southern and central California coast contains one of the earliest, most extensive, and best documented records of maritime activity in the Americas. By 10,000 years ago, these Paleo-Coastal peoples had used seaworthy boats for at least two millennia and developed the earliest fishhooks in the New World, early cordage and basketry made from sea grass and probably other materials, beads made from marine shell, and trade networks with interior peoples—a more sophisticated maritime adaptation than most scholars would have guessed possible a decade ago.

DIVERSITY IN PALEO-INDIAN ECONOMIES

Early California sites have also contributed to a reassessment of the nature of Paleo-Indian subsistence strategies. Earlier views of Paleo-Indian lifeways were heavily influenced by the discovery of Clovis and Folsom sites in the American Southwest and Plains regions, where fluted points and other artifacts were associated with the remains of large game animals. This led many to argue that Paleo-Indians were relatively specialized hunters who swept across the continent in search of Pleistocene megafauna which were rapidly hunted to extinction (see Martin 1967). Where large game animals were abundant and accessible, the view of some Paleo-Indians as big-game hunters may be correct, just as bison hunting dominated the economy of many Plains Indian peoples historically. Recent research suggests, however, that extending such analogies to a continent-wide Paleo-Indian focus on large game is deeply problematic.

Recent studies suggest that Paleo-Indian economies were relatively diverse and that humans played a limited role in the extinction of large Pleistocene mammals (Grayson and Meltzer 2002, 2003). Across much of the continent, large game was probably less abundant and smaller animals and plant foods were probably more dependable staples for Paleo-Indian peoples. Research in Alaska (Yesner 1996), coastal California (Erlandson et al. 1996; Rick et al. 2001), Amazonia (Roosevelt et al. 1996, 2002), and the Andean region (Dillehay and Rosen 2002; Keefer et al. 1998; Richardson 1998; Sandweiss et al. 1998) shows that many Paleo-Indians harvested a variety of plant and animal foods, including smaller species once thought to be marginal. In a survey of Paleo-Indian foraging in North America, Cannon and Meltzer (2004) also documented considerable variation in subsistence strategies across the continent, including only limited evidence for big-game hunting.

Data on human subsistence in California during the Terminal Pleistocene are limited, but a number of coastal middens provide quantitative data on the fauna taken by Paleo-Coastal peoples from about 8000 to 6500 cal B.C. One of the largest and best preserved faunal assemblages comes from the Early Holocene strata at Daisy Cave, which were rich in marine shellfish and fish remains, and also produced bones of sea otter, pinnipeds, and sea birds. The shellfish were dominated by California mussels, black abalones, turban snails, and other rocky intertidal taxa. Over 27,000 fish bones from at least 18 types of fish were also found in these early levels (Rick et al. 2001), but they are dominated by smaller species (i.e., surfperch, rockfish, cabezon, sheephead) found near shore in rocky coast and kelp forest habitats. Dietary reconstructions for the Early Holocene strata suggest that shellfish and fish made up roughly equal amounts of the meat consumed by the site occupants, with marine mammals and birds being supplemental resources (Rick et al. 2001). Nonetheless, the relatively eclectic nature of coastal foraging at Daisy Cave suggests that its Paleo-Coastal occupants were capable of taking a variety of marine resources and that their economy was fully maritime by at least 8000 to 7000 cal B.C.

A variety of quantitative measures (MNI, weight method, allometry) have been used to estimate the amount of edible meat provided by various faunal classes at other Paleo-Coastal sites from the Channel Islands, the mainland coast, and pericoastal settings (Erlandson 1994; Erlandson et al. 1999, 2004; Erlandson, Rick et al. 2005; Rick et al. 2001, 2005a). Except for Daisy Cave, the available data suggest that shellfish were extremely important in Paleo-Coastal economies on the islands and along the mainland coast. Allometric analysis of Paleo-Coastal subsistence supports the dietary significance of marine shellfish in coastal settings, but also documents considerable diversity in Paleo-Coastal lifeways (Porcasi 2007). The economic importance of shellfish declines from an average of more than 90 percent in island sites, to 73 percent in sites located along the mainland coast, and about 25 percent for pericoastal sites. The significance of marine mammals and fish also declines along this gradient from islands to interior settings. Unfortunately we still know relatively little about Paleo-Coastal plant use. Given the heavy reliance on lean shellfish meats in coastal areas, however, plant foods must have been a crucial source of carbohydrates, fats, and calories (Erlandson 1988, 1991a). An increase in the number of milling tools in mainland sites from 8000 to 6500 cal B.C. suggests that small seeds were more important through time.

CURRENTS AND COUNTERCURRENTS

The initial peopling of California almost certainly involved multiple migrations from northeastern Asia to the Americas. We still have much to learn about the timing of these migrations and the routes these first Americans followed. Recent theories related to the development of anatomically modern humans in Africa and the subsequent spread of our species to the farthest reaches of the earth provide a unified concept with which to understand the peopling of California and the New World. Maritime peoples used boats and substantial sea crossings to move through island Southeast Asia into Australia, western Melanesia, and the Ryukyu Islands before the height of the last glacial. By the last glacial maximum, maritime peoples on islands off Japan had adapted to coastal waters with temperatures comparable to those of the Gulf of Alaska today. Early maritime peoples could have followed the coasts of northeastern Asia and Beringia into the Americas shortly after the end of the last glacial maximum, but more research must be done before we know whether such a migration actually took place.

Based on current evidence, it seems unlikely that humans reached the New World prior to the last glacial maximum—by land or by sea. If they had, the archaeological record in North America should be more similar to that of Australia, which appears to have first been settled about 50,000 years ago. The initial peopling of these two previously unoccupied continents provides fertile ground for analogy (see Beaton 1991a; Jelinek 1992), despite the very different environments the initial colonists of the two regions encountered. In our view, comparing the archaeological records of Australia and the Americas raises fundamental questions for those who propose that the New World was colonized more than 30,000 years ago. Today Australia is considerably smaller than North America, but during the last glacial maximum vast ice sheets covered much of northern North America and Australia was approximately 15 percent larger than today. Yet a relatively small number of Australian archaeologists has found dozens of stratified and well-dated sites older than 35,000 to 25,000 years. If the Americas were first colonized 50,000 or even 30,000 years ago, we should have little difficulty finding unequivocal sites dated to at least 20,000 to 15,000 years ago. Instead, despite more than a century of careful research by thousands of scientists, not one unequivocal site older than 15,000 years has been documented in California or North America.

CONCLUSION

> It is conceivable but highly improbable, that America was populated in the remote past more than 50,000 years ago. . . .The case for humans in California between 50,000 and 30,000 years B.P. is also far from compelling. . . .The testimony on behalf of California's settlement 30,000 to 15,000 years ago is more promising but still inconclusive. . . .There can be little doubt that California was inhabited, albeit sparsely, between 15,000 and 10,000 years ago. (Moratto 1984:70–71)

More than 20 years after these words were published, the situation has changed little. Claims for a very early settlement of the Americas continue to be made, but the case for an occupation prior to 50,000 or 25,000 years ago is poorly documented and far from compelling. With the redating of several "Pleistocene" skeletons from California to the Holocene (Taylor et al. 1985), the case for a human occupation of California or the Americas between 30,000 and 15,000 years ago is now considerably less promising than it was in 1984. The case for an occupation of California between 15,000 and 11,000 years ago has been established beyond any reasonable doubt, but the date of first settlement remains very much in question.

What has changed in the past two decades is the nature of the debate about when, how, and from where California and the Americas were first settled. In the mid-1980s, the study of Paleo-Indian origins was moving into a conservative phase as numerous purportedly Pleistocene sites in California and beyond were found to be Holocene in age and the Clovis-first model was gaining credibility. The Monte Verde site remains controversial, but its widespread acceptance rejuvenated archaeological, geological, genetic, and other scientific studies related to the peopling of the Americas. When combined with new archaeological and paleoecological data, the collapse of the Clovis barrier has elevated a marginal coastal migration theory to a prominent position in American archaeology. In the process, it has moved California and the broader Pacific coast back to center stage in the search for the origins of the first Americans.

In the past 20 years, our knowledge of the lifeways of these early peoples has also changed significantly. Archaeological data suggest that Paleo-Indian subsistence varied across the Americas, including the use of a variety of marine resources on the California coast. By about 10,000 years ago, California's Paleo-Coastal peoples were traveling in seaworthy boats, using fishhooks and other fishing tackle, hunting marine mammals and sea birds, weaving cordage and basketry from sea grass, and making shell beads for ornamental use and exchange with interior peoples. Such variability in the adaptations of these early peoples testifies to the diversity and resilience of California's first inhabitants. This assortment of early coastal lifeways and the possibility of multiple migrations into the New World add to the complexity of the debate over when and where the first Americans came from.

CHAPTER 5

Colonization Technologies: Fluted Projectile Points and the San Clemente Island Woodworking/Microblade Complex

Michael F. Rondeau, Jim Cassidy, and Terry L. Jones

Of considerable if not paramount importance to alternative interpretations of the colonization of California are the technological and stylistic attributes of artifacts employed by the earliest inhabitants to make their way into western North America, either by sea or by land. As the preceding chapter showed, increasing evidence for very early occupation of the California coast was a significant trend in research discoveries over the past two decades. Most of this evidence has come in the form of radiocarbon-dated faunal remains. Because such remains tend to be abundant and well preserved in coastal settings, establishing the absolute age of early coastal occupations has been relatively easy. Faunal preservation is generally more problematic in the interior, but even there, findings from the past two decades include reasonably secure radiocarbon determinations from charcoal and marine shell beads that indicate human occupation between 9,000 and 8,000 cal B.C. In some instances, tool assemblages associated with Terminal Pleistocene and Early Holocene occupations have been relatively well defined (e.g., the stemmed point complexes of southeastern California and the Millingstone expression on the central coast), but it is generally assumed that these do not represent the earliest habitation of California. This distinction still belongs to fluted projectile points, which are most commonly recovered as isolates. At the same time that radiocarbon evidence for Terminal Pleistocene/Early Holocene occupation has accumulated, new discoveries of fluted projectile points have been made throughout the state in nearly every possible environmental setting except the Channel Islands.

In the first half of this chapter we review the accumulated record of fluted projectile point finds as of 2005, and we address issues related to the classification and chronology of this important artifact type. While there remain certain complications in the definition of fluted point variants in California, the type as a whole has reasonably secure temporal if not adaptive implications. In the second half of the chapter we describe a more tentatively defined artifact complex proposed as an alternative to Clovis on the California Channel Islands. In over a century of intensive archaeological research, not a single fluted specimen has been recovered from the islands, yet there is increasing radiocarbon evidence for Terminal Pleistocene habitation (e.g., Daisy Cave and Arlington Woman) coeval with the generally accepted time range of Clovis.

In many cases this evidence indicates unequivocal human presence and use of watercraft as early as ca. 12,000 years ago (see Erlandson et al. 1996; Chapter 4 in this volume), but findings are less certain with respect to the tools and technology associated with the earliest insular occupations. The Arlington Woman site, for example, consisted entirely of human skeletal remains, while finds from Daisy Cave are relatively limited because much of the deposit was removed by an early researcher. One Early Holocene site, Eel Point (SCLI-43) on San Clemente Island, has witnessed more extensive excavation, and has produced a more substantial collection of formal tools. While the basal levels at Eel Point date only to ca. 7100–6400 cal B.C. (see Chapter 4), the site is currently the oldest on San Clemente Island and seems to represent the initial settlement of this fairly remote, insular setting. In 2004 Cassidy et al. suggested that that tool assemblage revealed in the site's oldest levels was different from that of mainland Paleo-Indian and may instead correlate with microlithic or microblade technologies of northeastern Asia and Alaska. This proposal, while not universally accepted (Des Lauriers 2005a), is advanced in the second half of this chapter.

CALIFORNIA FLUTED PROJECTILE POINTS, BY MICHAEL F. RONDEAU

Over the past two decades, reports of fluted projectile points have continued to increase across California

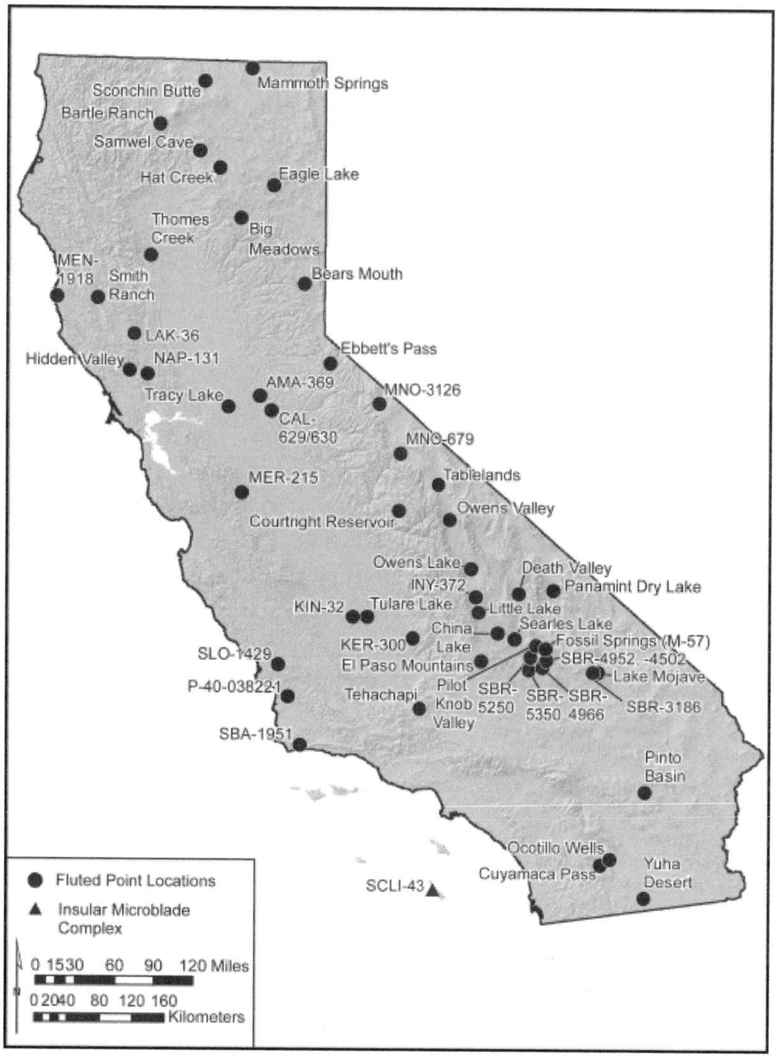

Figure 5.1. Fluted projectile point locations and the Eel Point site (SCLI-43).

so that the number of specimens is thought to stand at more than 400 (Dillon 2002). In truth, the actual number of fluted points recovered from within the state is very approximate, since the majority are from private collections, not all of which include reliable provenience records. Nonetheless, fluted projectile points have been found in the Central and North Coast Ranges, the Central Valley, the northern interior, the Sierra Nevada, the southern deserts, and the coasts of northern and southern California (Figure 5.1, Table 5.1). The following is a summary of attributes of California fluted projectile points based on a review of the majority of the specimens made by the author over the past two decades. Issues of how the fluted point designation has been assigned to early point specimens in California will also be considered. This review builds on the recent and important synthesis by Dillon (2002).

Definition

Fluted projectile points in California exhibit a high degree of variability, and there has been some discussion of the precise definition of the type (Dillon 2002). California fluted points are defined here as lanceolate bifaces, usually with an edge-ground concave base, that exhibit a large central flake scar running from the basal end up the middle of at least one face toward the tip. More than one flute may be present on a single face. The lanceolate form can be elongate to stubby due to manufacturing factors or damage and repair events (Figure 5.1). Common repairs that tend to modify the lanceolate outline include the flaking of a new base and reshaping of broken tips. The shape of the concave base may vary from slightly indented, to curved, to V-shaped, to a deep, almost bell-shaped curve. Basal edge grinding or smoothing of the lower edges is common on both lateral margins and the basal margin, but there are cases where not all three edges exhibit grinding or the same degree of smoothing.

The most important element used in identification of fluted points is the channel or flute scar. This is also the most difficult attribute to define, which has complicated determinations of exactly which points should properly be classified as fluted. Various definitions have been proposed (Bradley 1993; Crabtree 1972; Warren and Phagan 1988). Sollenberger defined the flute scar as "any basal thinning flake(s) that travel past the area of the hafting element" (Bradley 1993:254), but this definition does not provide any guidance as to how the hafting element is distinguished or how this should be applied to points with rebuilt bases where the hafting element has been moved closer to the base. Crabtree (1972:66) described the flute scar as having parallel sides and being the result of "special preparation of the surface and platform area to accomplish the fluting." The consideration of specialized platform preparation is clearly important to the fluting process. A partially proportional definition requiring the flute to be at least a quarter of the length of the point and at least a third of its width was proposed by Warren and Phagan (1988).

Table 5.1. Fluted Point Locations in California

Trinomial/Primary Number	*Location*	*Site Name*	*Reference*
AMA-369	Ione		Delacorte et al. 2000
CAL-629/630	Copperopolis	Skyrocket	Bieling et al. 1996
INY-372		Rose Springs	Yohe 1992a
KER-300			Zimmerman et al. 1989
KIN-32		Witt	Riddell and Olsen 1969
LAK-36		Borax Lake	Meighan and Haynes 1970
MEN-1918	Caspar		Simons et al. 1985
MER-215		Woolfsen Mound	Dillon 2002:113
MNO-679			Basgall 1988
MNO-3126	Bridgeport		Halford 2001
NAP-131			Dillon 2002:113
SBA-1951			Erlandson et al. 1987
SBR-3186	Silurian Valley		Taylor et al. 1987
SBR-5350	Tiefort Basin (M-130)		Sutton and Wilke 1984
SBR-5250			Jenkins 1985
SBR-4952-4502		Bow Willow	Warren and Phagan 1988
SBR-4966		Henwood	Warren and Phagan 1988
SLO-1429	Santa Margarita		Gibson 1996
P-40-038221	Nipomo		Bertrando 2004b; Mills et. al 2005
	Bartle Ranch		Jenkins 2005
	Big Meadows		Kowta 1988
	China Lake		Dillon 2002:113
	Cuyamaca Pass		Dillon 2002:113
	Death Valley		Dillon 2002:113
	Eagle Lake		Dillon 2002:113
	Ebbett's Pass		Dillon 2002:113
	El Paso Mountains		Glennan 1987a;
	Fossil Spring (M-57)		Dillon 2002:113
	Hat Creek		Dillon 2002:113
	Hidden Valley		Dillon 2002:113
	Lake Mojave		Dillon 2002:113
	Little Lake		Warren and Phagan 1988
	Mammoth Springs		Dillon 2002:113
	Ocotillo Wells		Fritz Riddell, personal communication 2001
	Owens Valley		Campbell et al. 1937
	Owens Lake		Campbell et al. 1937
	Panamint Dry Lake		Dillon 2002:113
	Pilot Knob Valley		Glennan 1987a
	Pinto Basin		Dillon 2002:113
	Samwel Cave		Treganza 1964
	Sconchin Butte		Moratto 1984:87
	Searles Lake		Warren and Ranere 1968
	Sierra National Forest	Courtright Reservoir	Johnston and Price 2002
	Sierra Valley	Bear's Mouth	Foster and Betts 1995
	Smith Ranch	Smith Ranch #6	Hamilton 1994
22B-1	Tablelands		Giambastiani 2004
	Tehachapi		Glennan 1987b
	Thomes Creek		Dillon 2002:113
	Tracy Lake		Heizer 1938
	Tulare Lake	Trico	Dillon 2002:113
	Yuha Desert		Davis et al. 1980

This definition also includes the requirement that the flute scar is directed from the base toward the tip and "truncate[s] at least some lateral edge-producing flake scars" (1988:121). This definition also has merit and the proportional elements, especially, deserve testing because they have received some support elsewhere in southern California (Basgall and Hall 1991).

For the current discussion, the flute is defined as an end-thinning flake scar originating from the base of the point of sufficient size to create a pronounced concavity in the basal cross-section. If both faces are fluted, then the basal cross-section will be biconcave as illustrated by the specimen from MEN-1918 (Simons et al. 1985:265). The flute scar will have generally parallel sides and can truncate or be overlapped by horizontal pressure flakes from the sides of the point. Basal grinding will usually be more recent than any of the horizontal pressure scars. A flute scar may also be identified by evidence of prior preparation for its removal, including an isolated platform remnant, an inverted narrow "bottle neck" at the proximal end of the flake scar, or occasional remnants of prior pressure flake scars.

Fluted points from California are made from a wide variety of materials, including high-quality cryptocrystalline silicates, obsidian, and quartz crystal. The cryptocrystalline silicates include commonly recognized varieties such as Franciscan and Monterey cherts, with a variety of other sources, including Jacalitos Canyon in Kern County, the Tehachapi Mountains, and the southern deserts. Obsidian comes from a range of sources spread across California, including Borax Lake, Napa Valley, Buck Mountain, Bodie Hills, Casa Diablo, Queen, Saline Valley 1, and Coso.

California Fluted Points in Historical Context

Fluted projectile points are generally accepted as the oldest cultural artifacts in North America. They are dated outside of California to nearly 13,500 calendar years based on radiocarbon assays (Haynes 1964; Roosevelt et al. 2002; Taylor et al. 1996). Unfortunately no fluted point specimens from California have been associated with radiocarbon dates, nor have any been found in unequivocal association with Pleistocene fauna. There has also been a long tradition of variable, if not confusing, terminology being used in reference to fluted points.

In the 1920s, findings from the Folsom site in New Mexico proved the long-standing hypothesis that humans were present in North America during the Pleistocene (Cook 1927; Figgins 1927). The most impressive finds from Folsom were finely made projectile points found in association with the remains of an extinct Ice Age bison (Wormington 1965:fig. 1). These artifacts, with very pronounced flutes that usually covered a large portion of both faces, came to be known as Folsom points. Their recovery led to the recognition that flute scars on projectile points are a diagnostic feature of considerable antiquity. Fluted specimens were subsequently found across North America, both in existing collections and during later fieldwork. In California the earliest finds were from LAK-36 (Figure 5.2a) in the North Coast Range (Harrington 1938) and an isolate from the Sacramento Valley (Heizer 1938). Many of the early fluted point finds were equated with and essentially described as Folsom points, and California was no exception with terms such as Folsom, Folsom-like, and Folsomoid (Campbell and Campbell 1940; Campbell 1949; Graham 1951; Harrington 1938, 1948; Heizer 1938; Simpson 1947) commonly applied.

In the 1930s, the findings from Blackwater Draw, New Mexico, led to the definition of a different variant of fluted point (associated with mammoth bones) that would come to be known as Clovis. This type was larger and not as finely flaked, and it exhibited flute scars that extended a shorter distance up from the base. In addition, examples of this variant were found below Folsom points that were again associated with bones of Ice Age bison (Boldurian and Cotter 1999; Hester 1972). The Clovis discovery led to a growing recognition that there were other fluted point types in North America that varied in time and by region as well as by morphology and technology. Acceptance of different fluted point types, however, was sometimes slow, as typified by these comments: "A second type, called Generalized Folsom, is larger, without ears, and imperfectly grooved. Though a terminology has been set up by which the first type is called simply Folsom, and the second Clovis Fluted, Ohio Fluted, etc., depending on where it is found, I shall, for convenience, adhere to the older names" (Macgowan 1950:112).

Macgowan's use of "older names" included Generalized Folsom for what is now called Clovis (1950:113). A sorting out of Paleo-Indian point types was nevertheless in progress. Wormington (1965) recognized that although the Borax Lake points had been reported as Folsom they did not fit the classic form. She argued that these points should be named after the type site as Borax Lake fluted points. A basic problem in establishing fluted point types across

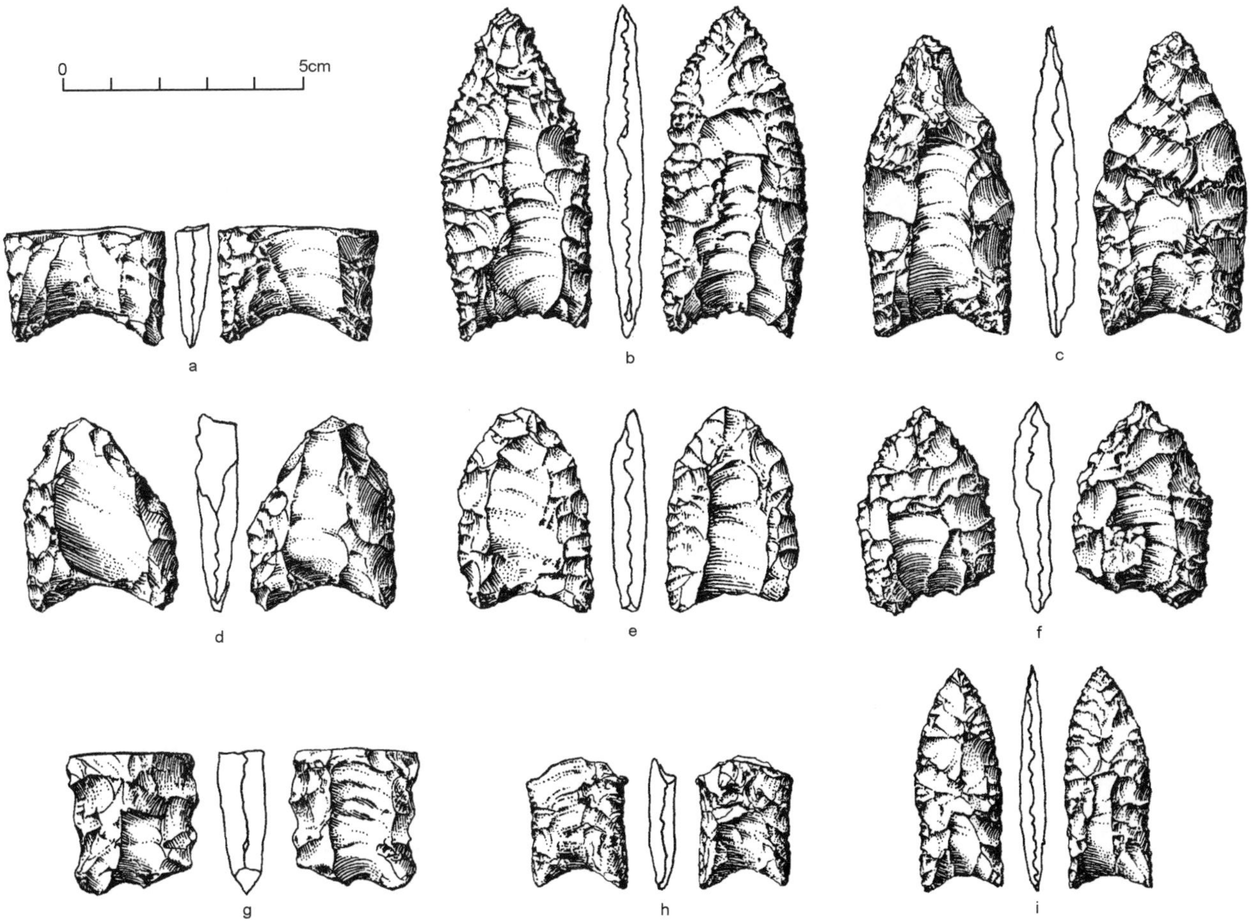

Figure 5.2. California fluted projectile points.
(a) Bartle Ranch (Jenkins 2005); (b) LAK-36 (Borax Lake) (Harrington 1948); (c) Sierra National Forest (Johnston and Price 2002); (d) Skyrocket (Bieling et al. 1996); (e) Nipomo (Mills et al. 2005); (f) Thomas Creek (Dillon 2002); (g) Santa Margarita (Gibson 1996); (h) Tulare Lake (Hopkins Collection); (i) Tulare Lake (Hopkins Collection) (by Rusty van Rossmann).

North America that still persists today was articulated as early as the 1960s:

> Some archaeologists interpret variations between Clovis fluted points of the High Plains and Southwest and fluted points of the eastern United States as indications of temporal as well as typological differences, and argue that the eastern specimens are ancestral to Clovis points, because of the latter's late position in an *inferred* developmental sequence. Other archaeologists recognize minor differences but do not consider Clovis points typologically different from eastern fluted points . . . they argue that, without supporting geochronological evidence, temporal differentiation is not justified. (Haynes 1964:1408)

In California, the use of the Folsom label persisted to some extent (Davis 1963), but the greater formal variability recognized for Clovis eventually resulted in many fluted points from California and elsewhere being reclassified from Folsom to Clovis. As this change in thinking occurred, a wide array of fluted point variants were all assigned to the Clovis type across North America. Haynes (1964:1408) noted that "variations within individual collections are as great as variations between collections." Widespread claims of Clovis finds made it seem that they were spread all across North America south of the ice sheets. California was not immune to this, as Haynes (1964) included the Borax Lake site (LAK-36) as an example of an undated Clovis site in spite of Wormington's recommendation (1965).

Later publications in California came to recognize points as Clovis or Clovis-like (Riddell and Olsen 1969). Also in 1969, Davis and Shutler reviewed fluted points from California and Nevada, noting that several appeared similar to Clovis and one to Folsom, but concluded that "morphologically there were great variations in form and size" (1969:159). By 1971 Glennan, writing on fluted points in California, stated that "these western fluted points fall generally into a Clovis classification typologically" (1971:25). In 1978 Davis claimed to have found proto-Clovis in undated desert contexts and proposed that Clovis subsequently spread eastward from California (1978:xi).

Today a range of fluted point types has been proposed for some of the eastern regions of North America. Most of these are assumed to follow Clovis in time, although most have not been securely dated. These types involve different fluting methods and are thought to represent different time periods (Haynes 1993). In the southeastern United States, for example, five different fluted point types have been identified (Meltzer 1988), and three types are known for the Great Lakes region, one of which, the Gainey type, is seen by some as analogous to the Clovis type (Strock 1991).

In California, the situation remains somewhat different. With some important exceptions (Rondeau 1985; Wallace and Riddell 1988; Warren and Phagan 1988; Wilke 1991), fluted point studies in California continue to be dominated by reports of single isolated specimens from surfaces contexts (Table 5.1). A notable exception is MNO-679, the Komodo site, where Basgall (1988) argued for the presence of a single Paleo-Indian component that produced 45 projectile points, nearly all concave base fragments with pronounced basal thinning. Typological affiliation of the points, however, is somewhat ambiguous owing to vagaries and overlaps in type definitions. Basgall (1988:111) described the collection as "morphologically similar to forms variously designated Clovis-like, Western Clovis, Folsomoid, Black Rock Concave Base, and Great Basin Concave Base by different authors." Subsequent analysis in one case resulted in classification of a few of these projectile points as fluted (Dillon 2002) while in another, the entire point collection was designated as nonfluted (Justice 2002). Unfortunately this ambiguity is not surprising, since it reflects a lack of agreement on type parameters and more importantly the complete dearth of well-dated Paleo-Indian components in California.

The Komodo site is one of only four locations to produce a significant sample of concave base, basally thinned (arguably fluted) projectile points in California, the others being LAK-36, the Borax Lake site, China Lake, and Tulare Lake. The Komodo site, like LAK-36, was dated solely on the basis of obsidian hydration owing to the lack of any other dateable material. Hydration results from both Komodo and LAK-36 indicate significant antiquity, but vagaries in the conversion of hydration readings to calendric time preclude a reliable estimate for absolute age in both cases. What can be stated with certainty is that both sites date to sometime during the Terminal Pleistocene–Early Holocene. At LAK-36 Meighan and Haynes (1970) used hydration results to distinguish earlier true fluted points (those with extended flute scars) from later concave-based points with short flutes and/or simple basal thinning. Examples of the latter are common in Middle and Late Holocene contexts in central California. The hydration results from LAK-36 clearly reflect the typological and temporal distinction between fluted and basally thinned concave base points. Hydration results from the Komodo site suggest greater antiquity overall for basally thinned concave base points from that location, but provide no clear basis for distinguishing fluted versus nonfluted types.

Another important sample of fluted points is from Tulare Lake, where collections have been generated by private collectors over at least the past half century. My analysis of the specimens in these collections, as well as those by others (Wilke 1991), suggest that a significant number of points from Tulare Lake referred to as Clovis are neither Clovis nor fluted. While there clearly are fluted points from Tulare Lake, their number apparently needs to be substantially revised downward. A major research effort is needed to actually substantiate the number of fluted points found in the Tulare Lake vicinity and to define the range of their morphological variability.

Discussion

The dating of fluted points in California continues to be a significant issue. While it is reasonable to assume that the California examples are generally coeval with fluted points found and dated elsewhere in North America (ca. 11,500 to 9000 cal B.C.), this assumption remains unproven. Whether California fluted points represent an early or later portion of this overall chronological range has important implications for models of California's initial settlement. Likewise, the lack of faunal remains (megafauna or other) associated with any of the fluted point discoveries remains a significant problem that will only be resolved with future discoveries. Despite such complications it is clear that a rather varied set of projectile points has been correctly identified as fluted in California. A statewide inventory is needed not only to verify what have been called fluted points in California, but to also document (at least in a preliminary sense) the extant range of variation. Ultimately such defined variation may set the stage for the identification of discrete types or subtypes and refined chronological assessments.

THE SAN CLEMENTE ISLAND WOODWORKING/ MICROBLADE COMPLEX, BY JIM CASSIDY

The spread of maritime sites in the New World has been associated with the Paleoarctic Tradition of western Alaska, including the Denali Complex, and the origin of these New World traditions has been directly traced to the Diuktai and subsequent Sumnagin Traditions of eastern Siberia (Goebel 2002). North American archaeologists familiar with the prehistory of Beringia, Alaska, and the northwest coast have a deep appreciation for processes relating to the migration and diffusion of maritime societies across the North Pacific. The defining technologies associated with Early Holocene North Pacific maritime traditions include wedge-shaped and frontally fluted microblade cores, platform tablets, burins, cobble choppers, scrapers, notching tools, and occasionally bifaces. While many archaeologists have developed sophistication in the analysis of bifacial stone tool production, a corresponding awareness of the significance of other traditions of tool production, including microblade and flake-core technology, has been less forthcoming (Steffen et al. 1999).

If California archaeologists are to recognize the existence of an Early Holocene maritime presence, they may need to employ technological models that correspond to nonbifacial modes of stone tool production. The techniques involved in microcore and blade production are as distinctive and purposive as bifacial core-reduction techniques (Elston and Kuhn 2002; Imamura 1996). Production of microblades for slotted bone or wood implements yields considerably different patterns than many California archaeologists are accustomed to. While microblade cores, discarded microblades, and burins may be found in work areas where production activities took place, the end product of slotted hafting devices and usable microblades have usually been removed to locations where hunting activities were carried out (Fisher 2002).

Microlithic technology afforded lightweight, easily maintainable tools and weapons for people who had limited access to high-quality lithic raw materials, owing to high mobility and/or resource scarcity (Bleed 2002). Such tools have been widely employed by highly mobile hunter-gatherers on a worldwide basis, and are commonly associated with seafaring populations. While direct evidence of watercraft construction and use is not likely to be found in archaeological contexts, research strategies can be pursued that technologically model stone tool assemblages associated with these activities.

Among the insular sites dating to the Early Holocene off the southern California coast, only Eel Point (SCLI-43) has yielded a substantial collection of lithic tools. Among the tools recovered from the Early Holocene component at Eel Point are items representing an extensive woodworking tool kit recovered from a localized work area. The tools recovered from the floor of this work area include flake drills, reamers, scraper planes, a wood-splitting wedge, sandstone abraders, an asphalt-smeared sea mammal rib with a blunted end from abrasion, cobble choppers, utilized flakes, a notching tool, and a large biface blank. This tool kit is fully consistent with the Paleoarctic Tradition and contains all of the technological elements required for watercraft construction and maintenance.

Although the remains of prehistoric watercraft are unlikely to be recovered, it seems reasonable to assume that the most important woodworking activities that would take place in an island site would include the care of the only possible means of transport onto and off the island (however, see Cassidy 2006). Also, in direct association with the woodworking tools were a burin and a number of wedge-shaped microcores (Figure 5.3j, k) (Cassidy et al. 2004:121). To date, this is the only site in coastal California that has reported evidence of Early Holocene microblade technology. The similarities between the Early Holocene microblade assemblage at Eel Point and those found contemporaneously among sites of the northwest coast, western Alaska, and eastern Siberia are striking. Further, a shared reliance on watercraft as a means of transport and a clear dependence on highly abundant, predictable, and aggregated pelagic resources, such as dolphin, pinnipeds, and mussels (*Mytillus spp.*), provide strong lines of evidence that connect these widely separated geographic regions.

Further, the tool kit recovered from the floor of the Early Holocene component at Eel Point contrasts sharply with the three stratigraphically distinct subsequent occupations (Cassidy et al. 2004:Table 2). Unique to the Early Holocene woodworking tool kit are microcores, a burin, a notched (spokeshave) tool (Figure 5.3h), blunt-nosed reamers (Figure 5.3e, f), sandstone abraders, scraper planes (Figure 5.3a, b), a wood-splitting wedge (Figure 5.3d), and a blunted, fossilized sea mammal rib smeared with asphaltum (Fagan 2004:119). Such tools are not found in the subsequent Middle Holocene occupation, nor in contemporaneous mainland deposits. In contrast, the

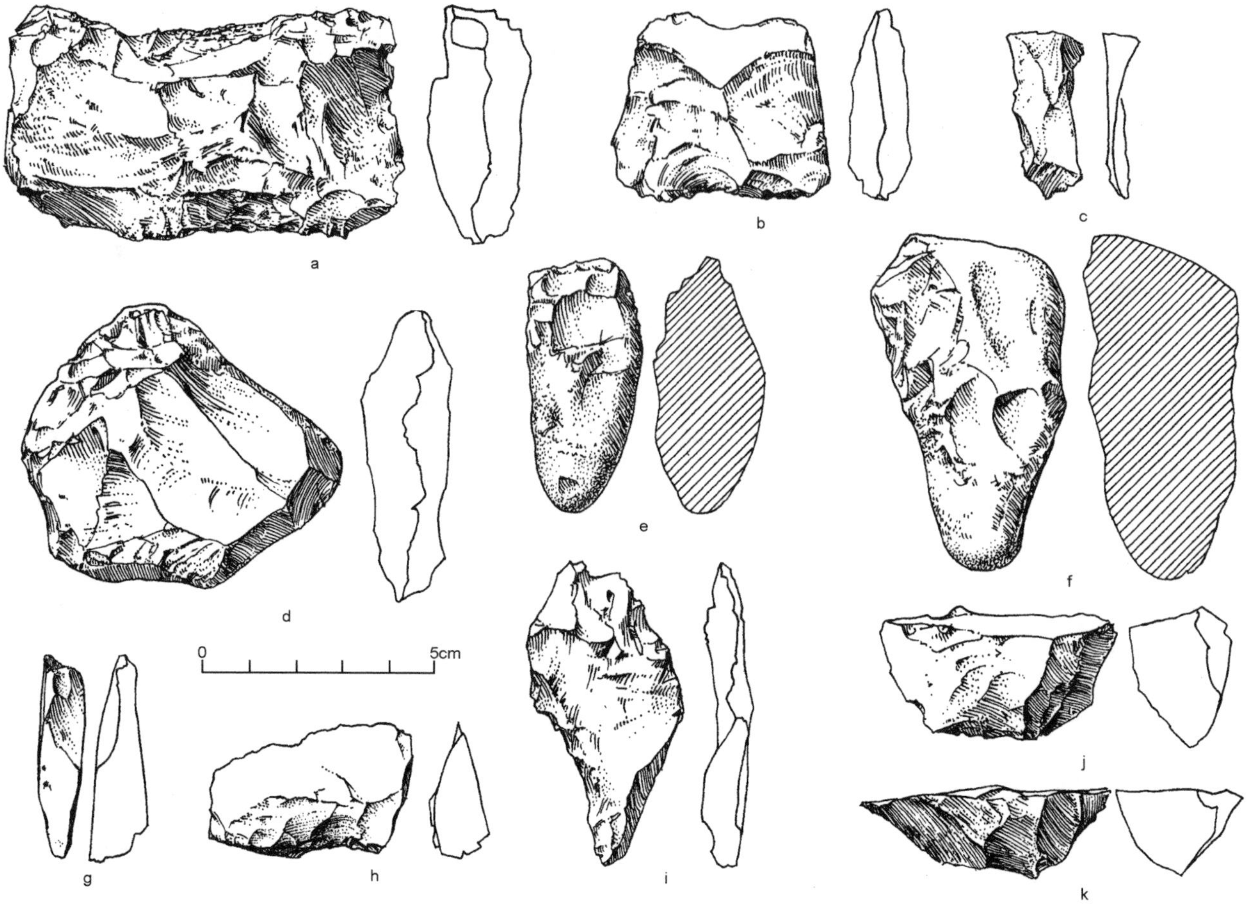

Figure 5.3. Assorted tools from the Early Holocene component at Eel Point.
(a) large scraper plane, specimen 3931, Unit 29N/15E, level 4; (b) small scraper plane, specimen 3815, Unit 29N/15E, level 3; (c) blade, specimen 4074, Unit 28N/14E, level 3; (d) wood splitting wedge, specimen 3931, Unit H, level 4; (e) blunt nosed reamer, specimen 3227, Unit H, level 4; (f) blunt nosed reamer specimen 2185 Unit 28-29N/16, 120 cm; (g) burin, specimen 3973, Unit H, level 4; (h) spokeshave, specimen 4138, Unit 30N/12E, level 4; (i) flake drill, specimen 3930, Unit H, level 4; (j) microcore, specimen 2695, Unit 30N/15E, level 4; (k) microcore (bifaced), specimen 2185, Unit 28-29N/16, 120 cm; (by Rusty van Rossmann).

Middle Holocene occupation is high in numbers of flake cores, hammerstones, pitted anvil stones, grinding slabs, handstones, retouched flakes, and bifacial points. The Middle Holocene tool technology is consistent with changes reflected in the associated faunal assemblage that show emphasis on shellfish collection and increased nearshore fishing. Unlike the Early Holocene assemblage at Eel Point, the later assemblages directly reflect contemporaneous changes found on the southern California mainland coast.

The Early Holocene occupation at Eel Point lasted over 500 years and was separated by a hiatus of 1,500 years from the Middle Holocene occupation (Cassidy et al. 2004:Table 1). The remarkable contrast between these two occupations and their tools strongly indicates different technological orientations. Also, associated faunal remains indicate subsistence practices shifted from a concentration on the hunting of dolphin and pinniped to a more generalized foraging lifestyle (Ames 2002; Porcasi and Fujita 2000; Raab et al. 1994). The contrasts between these two occupations not only highlight different subsistence-related technologies, but also may represent the intrusion of different ethnic groups to this remote site 80 kilometers from the mainland (Yesner and Pearson 2002).

Evidence accumulated over the past two decades has clearly established the presence of Early Holocene maritime traditions along the southern California coast and has provided significant support to Michael Moratto's (1984) proposed Paleo-Coastal Tradition. Emerging evidence from the Eel Point site suggests the possibility of a connection between the northern Paleoarctic Tradition and at least one component of the California Paleo-Coastal Tradition.

CHAPTER 6

Linguistic Prehistory

VICTOR GOLLA

IN 1984 MICHAEL MORATTO DEVOTED THE CONCLUDING chapter of his influential textbook to the presentation of a comprehensive model of the linguistic prehistory of California. While admittedly a "working model, subject to verification and change as more and better data are brought to bear" (1984:530), this was the first general synthesis since the days of Dixon and Kroeber (1919) of the findings of California Indian historical linguistics, and as such it has had an enduring impact on the thinking of archaeologists and linguists, including my own. Moratto makes the following key points:

- The geolinguistic mosaic of the ethnographic period, with its startling diversity of languages and language families, surely implies that "repeated population shifts" have occurred in this region (Moratto 1984:531). Migrations into, out of, and within the California culture province must play a significant role in California prehistory; in situ developments can account for only a small part of the observed linguistic diversity.
- The primary evidence for these prehistoric movements consists of language family relationships, and in particular the deepest of these relationships: the Uto-Aztecan family, the Algic superfamily, the Penutian stock, and the Hokan stock. (To this I would add the residuum of languages not affiliated with any of the preceding, specifically the Yukian and Chumash languages.)
- The absolute chronology of the internal diversification within language family relationships is to some extent retrievable from the degree of diversity shown, either by formal methods such as glottochronology or by informal comparisons to known historical cases. While calibrating linguistic dates with archaeological dates is fraught with multiple difficulties, some correlations are clearly more probable than others, and where there is a congruence of linguistic and archaeological dates the correlation may be considered firm.
- The linguistic prehistory of California must be viewed in the broader context of the known or probable historical relationships among the languages of North America, and possibly of the entire hemisphere. As Moratto succinctly puts it, "California was neither an island nor a cul de sac, and its linguistic configurations can be understood only with reference to a larger sweep of prehistory" (1984:543).

To these points I would add one more:

- In addition to the inferences we can draw from comparative data, the evidence of interinfluence between languages and language families is often of crucial importance in understanding the linguistic prehistory of a region. This evidence includes both borrowed words and borrowed phonological and grammatical structures, and it occurs both between adjacent languages and—most important for historical purposes—between a language formerly spoken in some territory (the "substrate" language in the jargon of historical linguistics) and the language that has replaced it.

I review below the six primary language family relationships represented in aboriginal California and propose a reconstruction of prehistoric events and developments that would account for the observed linguistic situation. In some cases my proposals do not noticeably differ from those put forward by Moratto. Where they diverge to some degree or another, this largely reflects perspectives derived from more recent linguistic studies.[1]

ATHABASKAN

The languages of the Athabaskan family (Figure 6.1), although widely dispersed in western North America, are only shallowly differentiated. The family apparently has a time depth of little more than two millennia (Krauss and Golla 1981). The most widely accepted reconstruction situates the proto-Athabaskan homeland along the upper Yukon River in the interior of northern British Columbia and the southern Yukon. Adjacent groups on the coast to the west and south spoke related languages, ancestral to modern Eyak, Tlingit, and Haida, reflecting the diversification of a Na-Dene speech community that probably entered North America about 6,000 years ago (Fortescue 1998).

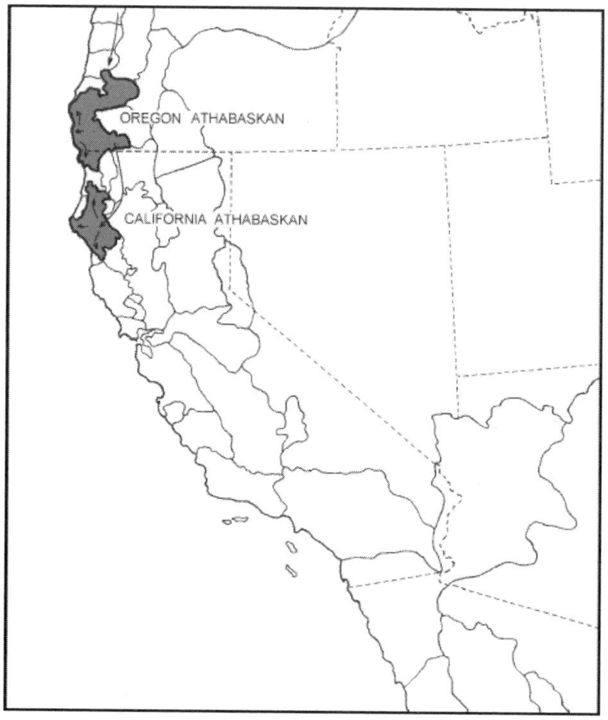

Figure 6.1. Oregon and California Athabaskan subfamilies.

At some date subsequent to 2,000 years ago groups of Athabaskan speakers—small bands of boreal forest hunters and riverine fishermen—began moving south from central British Columbia, eventually following the Columbia River to the Pacific.[2] This movement was roughly coincident with the spread of a microblade tradition in this area that can be associated with innovative bow and arrow technology, and lexical evidence within Athabaskan indicates that these migrants were familiar with the sinew-backed bow. Either as part of this Columbia River migration or soon thereafter, Athabaskan-speaking groups moved south along the coastal mountains into southwestern Oregon and northwestern California, where dialects ancestral to the Oregon and California Athabaskan subfamilies appear to have become separated about 1,300 years ago.

In southwestern Oregon, the Athabaskans rapidly infiltrated the eastern side of the coastal mountains from the Umpqua Valley south to the Illinois Valley, displacing earlier Kalapuyan, Takelma, and possibly Wintuan and Algic inhabitants. A largely in situ differentiation into a dialect chain then followed, with the Upper Umpqua, Upper Coquille, and Galice-Applegate languages representing the continuation of this core area into the historical period. Occupation of the Curry and Del Norte County coastline resulted from a slow, secondary expansion downstream along the Coquille, Rogue, and Smith Rivers, which probably absorbed Coosan-speaking populations in the north and Algic speakers farther south. The Chetco-Tolowa language at the southern end of this coastal strip has numerous distinctive traits, probably reflecting the rapid transformation of a Rogue River dialect in a multilingual setting where the majority of speakers were non-Athabaskans.

In northwestern California, after an initial occupation of the area between the Van Duzen River and the upper Eel River, a largely in situ differentiation seems to have occurred, resulting in a dialect chain in which the Nongatl, Lassik, Sinkyone, and Wailaki "languages" (more accurately, local dialects) are the ethnographically attested variants. Secondary expansions resulted in three clearly marked-off languages: Hupa-Chilula to the northeast along the middle and lower Trinity River, Mattole and Bear River in the windswept coastal valleys near Cape Mendocino, and Kato in Cahto Valley at the head of the South Fork of the Eel.

The pattern of diversification suggests an early split between the Hupa-Chilula language and the rest, but since at least one important grammatical innovation links Hupa-Chilula specifically to Kato, the dialectal groups may have had a different geographical relationship during early stages of differentiation. A Chimariko substratum is likely for the dialects of Hupa-Chilula spoken along the Trinity River, reflecting an expansion of Hupa eastward into Chimariko territory that was still under way at the beginning of the historical period. However, at least some of the distinctive phonological traits of Hupa-Chilula are better explained by Karuk or Wiyot influence. A Yukian substratum beneath both Wailaki and Kato is likely on cultural and other nonlinguistic grounds, but specific linguistic influences from Yukian are not easy to identify in either language, other than a few Yuki loanwords in Kato.

ALGIC

Yurok and Wiyot were spoken in adjacent territories on the heavily forested northwestern coast of California from the Klamath River to the Eel River (Figure 6.2). The relationship of Yurok and Wiyot was recognized by Dixon and Kroeber (1913), who called it the Ritwan family, a coinage based on the cognate stems for "two" in both languages (Dixon and Kroeber 1919:54). The proposal first made by Sapir (1913) that the two languages are distantly related to the Algonquian family, although controversial at first, is now considered to be proven (Goddard 1975). Yurok, Wiyot, and Algonquian are assigned to a superfamily or stock variously called Algic, Algonquian-Ritwan, or Wiyot-Yurok-Algonquian; I will use "Algic" here. The Algic stock was assumed at first to be a binary relationship between the Ritwan languages and Algonquian, but this has become less certain with the accumulation of more accurate descriptive data. While some continue to believe a Ritwan branch is justified (Berman 1984, 1990), Proulx, the linguist who has given the matter the most sustained attention, finds the evidence unconvincing and treats Wiyot, Yurok and Algonquian as three equally old branches of Algic (Proulx 1994:152–153).

Estimates of the time depth of Algonquian generally place the dispersal of the family around 3,000 years ago (Proulx 1981:14). The time depth of Algic must be greater, although not dramatically so; 4,000 years ago seems reasonable. If Algonquian, Wiyot, and Yurok are separate branches of Algic, this would of course also be the date of the Yurok-Wiyot split. If Ritwan is a valid subgroup, the time depth of the Yurok-Wiyot split could be shallower, perhaps around the 2,300 years indicated by Swadesh's lexicostatistical calculation (1959).

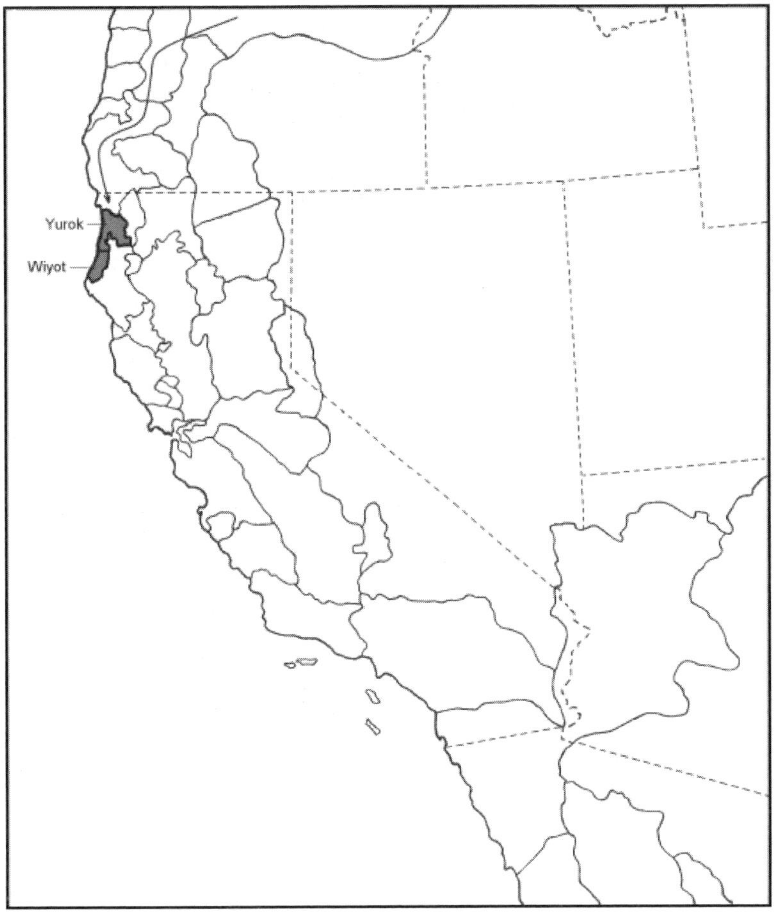

Figure 6.2. California Algic languages (Ritwan).

The hypothetical proto-Algic homeland that best fits the linguistic facts is on the Columbia Plateau, somewhere in the region historically occupied by the Sahaptians and the Interior Salish.[3] From here, the proto-Algonquians could have expanded east to the Plains and beyond, while the early "Ritwans" could have moved south and west. Algic speakers might well have occupied large portions of western Oregon for several hundred years before the Athabaskans entered the area around 1,300 years ago. In this location they would have been on the southern periphery of northwest coast cultural developments, helping to explain, among other cultural parallels, the unusual congruence in kin term systems between the Yuroks and Wiyots and the Coast Salish, Chimakuan-, and Wakashan-speaking peoples of Puget Sound and Vancouver Island (Kroeber 1934).

Archaeologists have frequently speculated that the appearance of the sophisticated fishing technology of the Gunther Complex in northwestern California between 1,500 and 1,100 years ago must somehow be correlated with the intrusion of Algic- and Athabaskan-speaking groups into the area from the north. One possibility is that Athabaskan incursions into California and Oregon around 1,300 years ago triggered a southward movement of Algic speakers along the coast, bringing them and the Athabaskans into northwestern California roughly simultaneously.

For this scenario to be correct, however, either the ancestors of the Wiyots and Yuroks would have had to enter their historic areas already speaking well-differentiated languages, or the processes of linguistic change would have had to work on these languages with unprecedented speed. A more likely reconstruction would have speakers of early Wiyot arriving in the Humboldt Bay area considerably earlier than ancestral Yurok speakers in the Klamath River area. Historic Wiyot would be the surviving segment of a continuum of Algic speech that stretched from the central Oregon coast to Cape Mendocino in pre–Gunther Complex times. Yurok, on the other hand, would represent the speech of a group originally located much farther north in the Algic language chain, displaced to the Klamath River after 1,300 years ago as a consequence of the Athabaskan invasion. The appearance of the

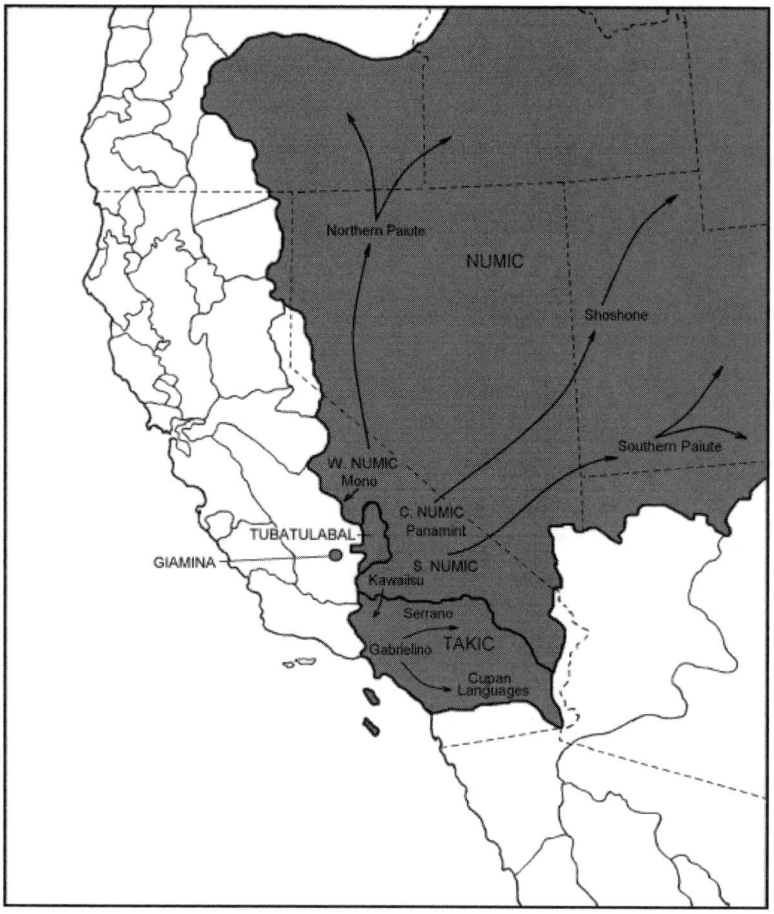

Figure 6.3. California Uto-Aztecan groups (Numic, Takic, Tubatulabal).

Gunther Complex in northwestern California could thus be linked to the arrival of Yurok speakers in particular, not of the Algic languages in general.

This reconstruction is in essential agreement with the one proposed by Whistler (1979) and summarized in Moratto (1984:481–484). However, Whistler puts the Wiyot arrival around 1,100 years ago, the Yurok about 900 years ago, and Athabaskan entry as late as 700 years ago. However, these dates are too recent to explain the existing linguistic differences, particularly between California and Oregon Athabaskan. I would propose cal A.D. 100 or earlier for the original Algic spread down the coast and the settlement of early Wiyots on Humboldt Bay, cal A.D. 700 to 800 for the arrival of the Yuroks on the Klamath River, and no later than cal A.D. 800 to 900 for the intrusion of Athabaskans into the Trinity-Eel drainage.

UTO-AZTECAN

The Uto-Aztecan (UA) language family (Figure 6.3) is one of the geographically most extensive in the Americas and probably has a time depth of about 5,000 years (Campbell 1997:133). The deepest internal division is between the northern branch, comprising the languages in California, the Great Basin, and the Pueblo Southwest, and the southern branch, extending from O'odham in southern Arizona to Pipil in Central America. The origin of the northern-southern UA split (as well as its implications for early migrations either from north to south or south to north) is not fully understood.[4] However, most specialists agree that by 3,500 to 2,500 years ago, dialects of the northern UA branch were probably spoken in a continuous band across the southern basin from the Colorado River to the Sierra Nevada, with a distinction slowly emerging between an eastern group ancestral to Hopi and the Numic subfamily and a western group ancestral to Tubatulabal and the Takic subfamily (Hale and Harris 1979:175). It is not unlikely that this east-west split was correlated with the northward expansion of Yuman along the Colorado River after 2,500 years ago.

Tubatulabal is a single language spoken ethnographically along the upper Kern River northeast of Bakersfield. While Tubatulabal has a closer affinity to the Takic languages than to Numic or Hopi, the distinctive features of Tubatulabal seem best explained as representing the in situ development of a local variety of Northern UA. The Takic languages appear to stem from another variety of Northern UA that was originally spoken close by, most likely in the region around Tehachapi Pass occupied by Kitanemuk speakers in the historic period. A third Californian variety of Northern UA is possibly attested in Giamina or Omomil, the poorly attested language of a small group that lived west of Tubatulabal territory near the Poso Creek Yokuts (Kroeber 1907:126–128).

Most of Takic territory in southern California appears to have been occupied by Uto-Aztecan speakers in a series of relatively late expansions from the northeast. Moratto's proposal (1984:165) that the end of the Early Period in the Serrano and Gabrielino area, ca. 3,500 to 3,200 years ago, correlates with the beginning of the Takic expansion seems somewhat early. Although Miller has calculated deeper glottochronological dates (1983:119), the internal diversity of the attested Takic subfamily strikes most linguists as roughly comparable to that of the Romance languages, or approximately 2,000 years (Jacobs 1975:5). The differences are somewhat greater among the languages in the northern half of Takic territory (Gabrielino, Serrano-Kitanemuk, and perhaps Tataviam) than in the south (Luiseño, Cupeño, and Cahuilla—the "Cupan" languages), making it likely that ethnographic Cupan territory reflects a fairly recent Uto-Aztecan intrusion, probably within the last millennium. Since the Cupan languages show closer affinities with Gabrielino than with Serrano, this subgroup probably originated on the southern and eastern borders of Gabrielino territory and expanded southward along the coast and eastward through San Gorgonio Pass. Yuman traits in the phonologies of the Cupan languages suggest that at least part of the territory into which Cupan expanded was previously occupied by speakers of Diegueño or other Yuman languages (Hinton 1991), although lexical evidence for a Yuman substratum is sparse (Bright and Bright 1969).

The internal diversity of the Numic subfamily is more shallow than Takic, with a maximum time depth of between 1,500 and 2,000 years. There are three branches—Western, Central, and Southern Numic—each consisting of a dialect chain in which at least two languages are generally identified. These chains converge geographically—and their internal differences are greatest—on the eastern slope of the Sierra Nevada between Mono Lake and Tehachapi Pass, indicating a recent southwest to northeast expansion across the Great Basin (Lamb 1958). An estimate of 1,000 years for the time depth of the split between the Numic dialect chains correlates well with archaeological indications of a change of subsistence strategies and social structures in the Great Basin beginning about 800 years ago (Bettinger and Baumhoff 1982). Expanding Western (and possibly Central) Numic probably replaced Plateau Penutian languages (ancestral Maiduan, Klamath, Modoc, Molala, and Sahaptian). Southern Numic, on the other hand, expanded into territory in which Anasazi Pueblo influence had been strong, and possibly replaced either a Kiowa-Tanoan language or a variety of Hopi.

An alternative hypothesis, identifying the proto-Numic community with the Virgin River Anasazi in southern Nevada and southwestern Utah, has had its adherents, notably Gunnerson (1962). A variant of this proposal has recently been put forward by Hill (2002). In her reconstruction, the Numic pioneers of the central and northern parts of the Great Basin would have expanded north from the historical Southern Numic area on the Colorado Plateau as the result of "devolution" from Anasazi maize farming to a dispersed foraging subsistence strategy. The reconstructability in proto-Numic of a number of words that point to a former acquaintance with horticulture seems to support her argument. Hill explains the dialectal complexity of the Mono-Panamint-Kawaiisu area as the result of rapid innovation as Numic dialects were incorporated into the communicational matrix of the California area.

While linguistic evidence indicates that Numic is closer to Hopi than to either Tubatulabal or Takic (Manaster Ramer 1992), there is evidence that a secondary period of contact between Hopi and both the Numic and Takic languages may have begun around cal A.D. 500. At this time the archaeology of the eastern Mojave Desert shows a major discontinuity that appears to be linked to the expansion of the Western Anasazi from the Virgin River area of southern Nevada as far west as Halloran Spring and Soda Lake (Warren and Crabtree 1986:189–191). Since the Western Anasazi were closely connected to the ancestral Hopi, some of the distinctly "Puebloid" features of Takic religion and ceremony, possibly including complex ritual speech patterns, might have found their way into California at this time.

PENUTIAN

Languages belonging to the Penutian stock are spoken as far north as southeastern Alaska (Tsimshianic). The majority are in Oregon, both east and west of the Cascades (Figure 6.4). The Penutian languages of the California culture area are the southernmost whose relationship to the stock is clearly established, although proposals of varying degrees of likelihood have been made to include Zuni and several Mesoamerican languages in the Penutian relationship. These potential outliers excluded, the time depth of the stock strikes most specialists as comparable to Indo-European (ca. 6,500 years ago).[5]

The Penutian languages historically spoken in California appear to represent at least two (and probably three) separate branches of the stock. Maiduan is probably best included in the Plateau Penutian branch, together with Klamath-Modoc, Molala, and Sahaptian (Berman 1996). Wintuan also shows strong structural connections to Plateau Penutian but shares considerable vocabulary with the Western Oregon Penutian languages, particularly Alsea (Golla 1997). The remaining California Penutian languages, those belonging to the Miwok, Costanoan (or "Ohlonean"),

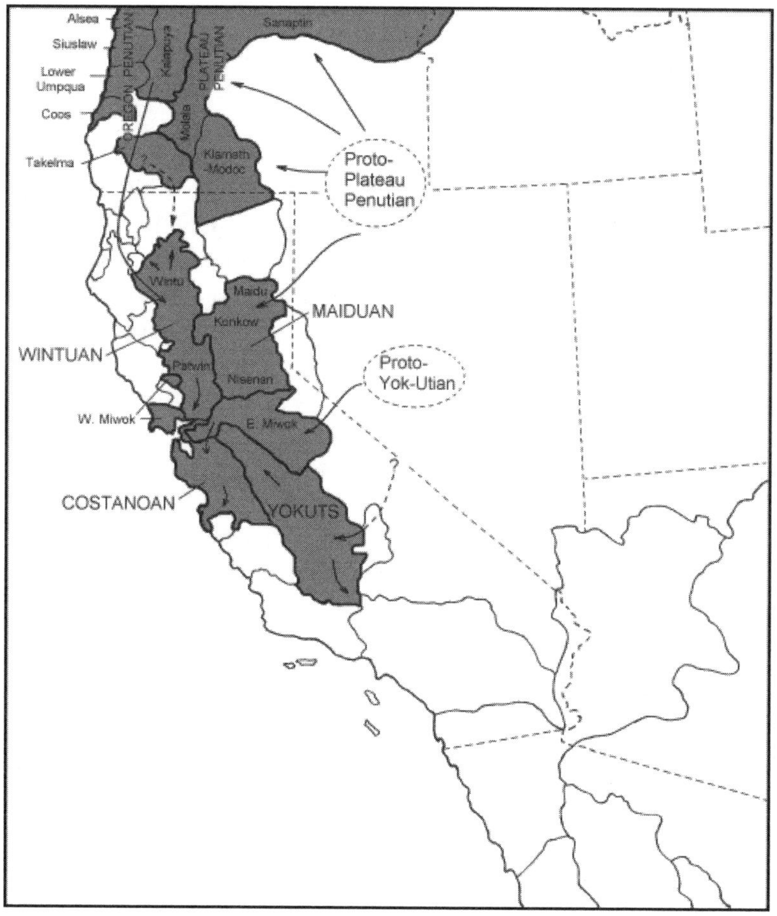

Figure 6.4. Probable origins and movements of California Penutian groups.

and Yokuts subfamilies, constitute a separate branch of Penutian ("Yok-Utian") that appears to have no other members (Callaghan 1997, 2001).

The geographical distribution of the Penutian languages in western North America is best explained by hypothesizing an ancient continuity of Penutian dialects on the Columbia Plateau and northern portions of the Great Basin with a series of coastward migrations bringing Penutian speakers west of the Cascades and Sierra Nevada at various times. In such a scenario, Yok-Utian speakers would have entered central California across the Sierra Nevada, Maiduan would be a displaced remnant of a Penutian speech area in the basin-plateau, and Wintuan, with its roots in the same area, would reflect a complex migration, first west into central Oregon and later south into California. Needless to say, such a reconstruction is highly speculative.

Yok-Utian

Yok-Utian has two distinct subbranches, Miwok-Costanoan (or "Utian") and Yokuts. The time depth of the Miwok-Costanoan split appears to be on the order of 4,000 to 4,500 years. The reconstructed plant and animal lexicon of proto-Utian indicates that it was spoken in or around the Sacramento–San Joaquin Delta, suggesting a correlation between the proto-Utian community and the Windmiller Pattern, which developed in the delta area after 4,400 years ago. The well-established archaeological connection between the Windmiller Pattern and northern Great Basin and plateau traditions, most notably the Lovelock Culture of northwestern Nevada, is also consistent with a Yok-Utian correlation.

The expansion of the Windmiller Pattern into the Coast Range and the San Francisco Bay area after 4,000 years ago can be taken as tracking the westward expansion of Utian speech at this period. Moratto's suggestion that the emergence of the Berkeley Pattern "represents a fusion of older Hokan . . . and intrusive Utian cultural elements in the Bay Area" (1984:553) remains the most plausible scenario. The split between Miwok and Costanoan apparently dates to this period.

The time depth of Yokuts is difficult to estimate, but the small number of significant phonological and morphological differences among Yokuts subgroups (despite often considerable differences in vocabulary) indicates a relatively recent date for proto-Yokuts, probably between 1,500 and 1,000 years ago. The geographical patterning of internal diversity indicates a likely homeland in the foothills of the southern San Joaquin Valley. We thus lack direct evidence on which to reconstruct the deeper prehistory of Yokuts, and a three-millennia gap yawns between the proto-Yokuts period and the most likely date of the split between pre-proto-Yokuts and Utian, around 4,500 years ago. Since a Salinan-like Hokan language apparently formed the substratum for proto-Yokuts, it is reasonable to assume that for much of the pre-proto-Yokuts period a significant part of the speech community was located elsewhere. This could well have included the northern San Joaquin Valley adjacent to early Utian territory, and Whistler (1984) has proposed that the vocabulary distinctive of some of the Delta Yokuts dialects may reflect substratal influence from pre-proto-Yokuts or from an extinct Yok-

Utian language. Equally plausible, however, is that pre-proto-Yokuts was spoken in the Great Basin. Callaghan has recently noted that the plant and animal vocabulary shared by Yokuts and Utian is compatible with a homeland in a much drier environment than central California, and that the two Yok-Utian subgroups may have separated before the Utian migration across the Sierra Nevada. In which case, the speakers of pre-proto-Yokuts may have lingered in the Great Basin until comparatively recent times, eventually moving into California across the southern Sierra Nevada via the routes used in the historic period by the Western Mono. A close connection between Yokuts culture and the prehistoric cultures of the Great Basin has been independently proposed by Dawson on the basis of basketry styles (Fowler and Dawson 1986:728–729).

Maiduan

Maiduan is a family of four closely related languages: Konkow (Northwestern Maidu), Chico Maidu, Mountain (Northeastern) Maidu (often referred to simply as "Maidu"), and Nisenan. Their relationship is a historically shallow one, comparable perhaps to West Germanic, and the northern three—Konkow, Chico, and Mountain Maidu—form a closely knit subgroup, Northern Maidu, vis-à-vis Nisenan (Southern Maidu). That three of the four Maiduan languages were located in the northern third of Maiduan territory indicates a southward spread from a proto-Maiduan homeland. Phonological and morphological features shared by all Maiduan languages suggest that a Hokan language was substratal in this area, most likely Washo.

The presence in Nisenan (but not in the three other Maiduan languages) of a significant number of widespread central California loanwords suggests a recent spread into non-Maiduan—most likely Miwok—territory. Given the shallow differences among the languages, this spread could not have begun before 1,200 to 1,000 years ago and was probably still under way at the beginning of the historic period. The ethnographically salient boundary between foothill and valley cultures (cf. Kroeber 1929) cuts across both the Konkow and Nisenan languages and is reflected only by low-order dialectal differences. This contrasts with the sharp discontinuity of language (or even language family) that is found elsewhere along the eastern edge of the Central Valley—the boundary between the Wintu and the Yana, between the Plains and Sierra Miwok, between the Northern Valley and Delta Yokuts and the Sierra Miwok; and between the Southern Valley and Foothill Yokuts. All of these linguistic boundaries are at least as old as the beginning of Late Period cultural elaborations ca. cal A.D. 1400. Nisenan and Konkow, however, seem to have spread west only in the past few centuries, long after the large villages along the Sacramento and lower Feather Rivers had developed a society distinct from that of the foothills.

There is evidence, both lexical and grammatical, that Maiduan is to be grouped with Klamath, Molala, and Sahaptian in the Plateau Penutian branch of the Penutian stock (DeLancey 1996; DeLancey and Golla 1997:181). The Plateau Penutian languages, however, are related at a time depth of at least three millennia, indicating that the attested Maiduan languages reflect a diversification that occurred long after the Maiduan branch separated from the other Plateau Penutian languages. The most likely scenario is that the proto-Maiduan speech community is the only surviving portion of a more widespread pre-proto-Maiduan community in the northwestern Great Basin and adjacent Sierra Nevada California that was displaced by the expansion of Western Numic after cal A.D. 1000.

Wintuan

An estimated time depth of 1,500 years for the split between the two branches of Wintuan—Northern (Wintu-Nomlaki) and Southern (Patwin)—correlates well with the inception of the Augustine Pattern in the southern Sacramento Valley around cal A.D. 500 to 600. The most likely scenario is that Wintuan-speaking invaders, armed with the bow and arrow (which makes its first appearance in the central California archaeological record at about this time), began entering parts of the Sacramento Valley sometime before cal A.D. 500. The area they first occupied—probably north of Colusa County—was largely Hokan territory, most likely Pomo. When Wintuans later expanded into the southern half of the valley, they would have encountered Miwok speakers, explaining the numerous Miwok loanwords in Patwin, particularly for the distinctive flora and fauna of the region (Whistler 1977).

Expansion also took place at the northern end of Wintuan territory. The absence of well-marked dialects in most of Wintu territory, contrasting with relatively salient dialect boundaries in Nomlaki and Patwin, argues for the recent expansion of Wintu beyond a core area south and east of Redding. This seems likely to have been correlated with the northward spread of the Augustine Pattern into Shasta County beginning around 1,200 years ago. This process appears to have moved slowly, reaching the more north-

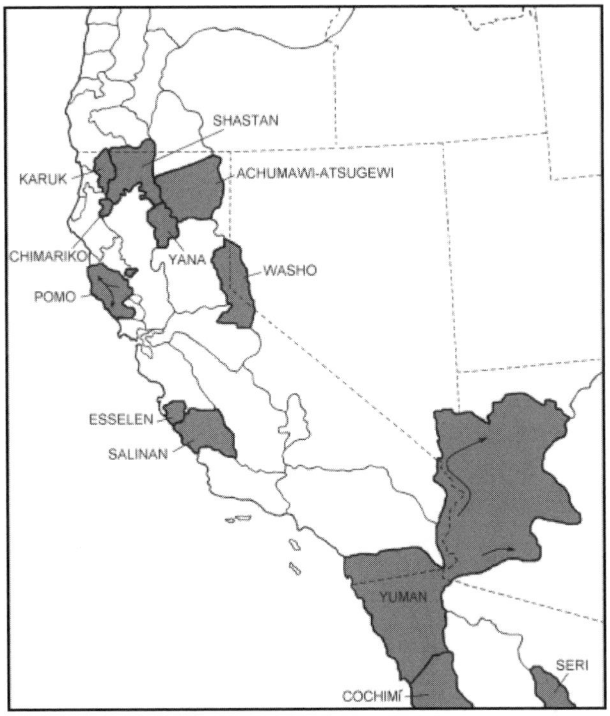

Figure 6.5. Hokan families and isolates of the California area.

erly and westerly areas no earlier than 700 years ago, and could be seen continuing at the time of contact in the eastern part of Trinity River Chimariko territory and along the lower Pit River.

That the original Wintuan homeland was in western Oregon is indicated by the nature of the plant and animal vocabulary that can be reconstructed in proto-Wintuan, which includes no terms for California species that are not found also in western Oregon and many terms for species common to both areas (Whistler 1977). In addition, Wintuan and Alsea, on the central Oregon coast, share a substantial number of lexical resemblances that are best explained as borrowings from Alsea (Golla 1997). These are, however, almost entirely confined to Northern Wintuan (Wintu and Nomlaki), suggesting that there were two Wintuan migrations, one group speaking a dialect with Alsea influences (pre-Northern Wintuan), the other speaking a dialect without such influences (pre-Southern Wintuan).

One possible scenario is that the Wintuans followed two routes into California, possibly at separate times. The pre-Northern Wintuan group might have moved through the Rogue River Valley and Shasta Valley, and then down the Sacramento River, while the pre-Southern Wintuan group might have taken a more westerly route that followed the Coast Range trails, entering the Sacramento Valley in the vicinity of Cottonwood Creek. It seems unlikely that the migrating Wintuans could have brought with them complex riverine fishing technology or most of the other features of the Augustine Pattern. They probably came in small parties of warlike nomads, not unlike the Athabaskans. Indeed, it seems a plausible hypothesis that most or all of the rugged territory historically occupied by the Oregon and California Athabaskans, from the Umpqua Valley to the Eel River, was at some point occupied by the early Wintuans, and that the Wintuan and Athabaskan migrations were components of a general southward displacement of peoples in California and Oregon in the middle of the first millennium A.D.

HOKAN

The Hokan phylum is the oldest linguistic relationship among western North American languages that can be established by normal comparative linguistic methods. The time depth of the relationship is on the order of 8,000 years ago, making it comparable to the Afro-Asiatic relationship in North Africa and the Near East, which includes Semitic, Ancient Egyptian, Berber, and a number of Sudanic languages. Hokan has no clear high-level subgrouping, and the languages are scattered as classificatory isolates or in subfamily clusters of closely related languages from the California-Oregon border to southern Mexico. The restricted territories of the California Hokan isolates (Chimariko, Karuk, Yana, Esselen, Salinan, Washo) suggest that they are the eroded remnants of formerly widespread language groups (Figure 6.5). This is bolstered by the fact that many Athabaskan, Algic, Uto-Aztecan, and Penutian languages show evidence of substratal influence from one or more Hokan languages. Only two Hokan subfamilies, Pomo and Yuman, exhibit sufficient internal diversity to allow some linguistic perspective on recent prehistory.

Pomo

There are seven historically attested Pomo languages, generally classified into four branches: one for each of the two languages spoken around Clear Lake (Southeastern and Eastern Pomo); a third for Northeastern Pomo, spoken in an isolated location in the western Sacramento Valley; and Western Pomo, which includes the four languages spoken along the Russian River (Northern, Central, Southern, and Southwestern Pomo). The shallower time depth (apparently not much more than 1,500 years) of the Western Pomo branch as compared with the relatively deep split (2,000 years or more) between Eastern and Southeastern Pomo, has led most researchers to assume that the Pomo occupation of the Clear Lake basin is older than that of the Russian River. Oswalt, whose interpretation is the most widely accepted, sees Clear Lake as the proto-Pomo homeland, with subsequent dispersions to the northeast (Northeastern Pomo) and to the west, and with the Russian River valley first occupied by Pomo-speaking people around cal A.D. 500 (Oswalt 1964).

Whistler (1988), noting the unbroken continuity of the Late Borax Lake Pattern in the Clear Lake basin, proposes that proto-Pomo was spoken there as early as 5,000 years ago, and that "pre-proto-Pomo" can be traced back to the arrival of the (Early) Borax Lake Pattern at Clear Lake around 7,000 years ago. Whistler correlates the first movement of the Pomo into the Russian River drainage with the expansion of the Borax Lake Pattern into that area around 4,000 years ago. Although this scenario makes an interesting fit with the archaeological record, the dates are difficult to reconcile with observed Pomo linguistic diversity, which indicates that proto-Pomo was spoken not much earlier than 2,250 to 2,500 years ago.[6]

The Pomo languages have been in contact with Yukian for a long period, and borrowing has taken place in both directions. There are numerous Yukian loanwords in Pomo, some apparently borrowed into proto-Pomo at an early date, others more recently into individual languages (Elmendorf, personal communication, 1984). The earlier borrowings are consistent with the view held by many archaeologists that a Yukian occupation preceded all others in the North Coast Ranges (Fredrickson 1984:509). Pomo influence on (southern) Yukian, on the other hand, may have been an important factor in the development of Wappo.

Miwok influence on Pomo is not extensive, largely confined to lexical borrowing between Lake Miwok and Southeastern Pomo. On the other hand, phonological and grammatical similarities indicate an old and important relationship between Pomo and Wintuan that is not well understood. Among other convergences, Pomo and Wintuan are the only language families in western North America to have a four-way contrast in stop phonemes: plain, aspirated, glottalized, and voiced. Such structural parallels usually reflect sustained contact, but the circumstances under which the southward migrating proto-Wintuan speakers would have had such contact with one or more Pomo languages are not clear.

Yuman

Yuman is a family of eight closely related languages spoken along the Colorado River from the Grand Canyon to the Gulf of California, on the plateau of northwestern Arizona, and along the Pacific coast of far southern California and far northern Baja California. Kiliwa in Baja California is the most divergent language in the family, and it constitutes an independent subgroup. The other seven languages are divided into four subgroups from south to north: Paipai, Delta-California (Cocopa and Diegueño), River (Quechan, Maricopa, and Mojave), and Upland Yuman or Pai (a cluster of dialects usually referred to individually as Havasupai, Hualapai, and Yavapai). The time depth of Yuman diversification is shallow, certainly no greater than 2,000 years (Hale and Harris 1979), but the family as a whole has a distant but well-established relationship to the Cochimí family of the Baja California peninsula, and Cochimí-Yuman has a time depth at least twice as great.

The River and Delta-California subgroups stand apart from the rest of Yuman in many phonological and grammatical features. Joël speculates that much of this specialization is linked to the rapid cultural changes that followed the adoption of agriculture along the Colorado River, which she dates as late as cal A.D. 800 to 1000 (1964:103–105). Even with these developments discounted, however, it is clear that the greatest differentiation within Yuman lies in the south, and that there was a late expansion of the Pai languages northward.

Since both Yuman and Cochimí are relatively shallowly differentiated and the area in which they adjoin is the most linguistically complex in their combined territories, it is a reasonable speculation that the proto-Cochimí-Yuman homeland was situated in the highlands of northern Baja California and the adjacent Colorado River delta to the east. If it could be shown that some the languages of the southern tip of Baja California were part of a wider Cochimí-Yuman, a long-term association of the stock with the peninsula would be all but certain. As it stands, however, the only language of this region for which data exists, Waikuri, can only be shown to be of probable Hokan affiliation (Gursky 1966). It is just as likely that the deeper connections of proto-Cochimí-Yuman are to be found in Hokan languages to the north or east.

A link between Yuman-Cochimí and Seri, a Hokan isolate on the eastern shore of the Gulf of California, is suggested by geography. Seri was included in a wider Yuman family by Powell in his general classification (1891), and Kroeber further explored the connection as part of a wider grouping that included Chontal of Oaxaca, or Tequistlateco (Kroeber 1915),

Figure 6.6. Unaffiliated language families of California.

and as a bilateral relationship (1931). The accumulation in recent decades of extensive and accurate data on Seri and the Yuman languages, however, has made it abundantly clear that whatever relationship exists between Seri and Yuman, it is not a close one (Crawford 1976; Hale and Harris 1979:173). Sapir, in his general comparative work on Hokan, saw evidence for grouping Yuman with Esselen, but he put Seri with Salinan (Sapir 1925:525). Although this classification has received some substantiation from lexicostatistics (Bright 1956), it has not been widely accepted.

CHUMASH AND YUKIAN

The Chumash and Yukian language families belong to none of the above groups and have no demonstrated relationship to each other (Figure 6.6).

Chumash

The Chumash (or Chumashan) languages form a close-knit independent family. At one time linguists believed them to be of Hokan affiliation but now most treat them as a classificatory isolate.[7] Three branches of the family are usually recognized: Obispeño, or Northern Chumash, a single language with at least two dialects (Klar 1992:18); Central Chumash, a group of at least four distinct languages (Purísimeño, Ineseño, Barbareño, and Ventureño); and Island Chumash, the language that was spoken on the three inhabited islands in the Santa Barbara Channel, Santa Cruz, Santa Rosa, and San Miguel. Obispeño and Central Chumash are distinct phonologically, lexically, and grammatically. Island and Central Chumash resemble each other more closely, but the relationship is obscured by a recent layer of borrowings into Island Chumash from Ventureño and Barbareño.

The artifactual and skeletal evidence that has been analyzed to date indicates an extraordinary demographic and cultural stability in the Northern Channel Islands and adjacent mainland from the Terminal Pleistocene/Early Holocene (12,500 to 10,000 years ago) to the historic period (Arnold 2001b:13–14). However, the internal diversity within Chumash is no greater than that of Germanic or Romance, implying a time depth of not much more than two millennia. This suggests that the historic boundaries of Chumash linguistic territory may be the result of the relatively recent expansion of a language originally localized in only one part of that territory, overlying an earlier, much greater linguistic diversity.

It could be hypothesized that this expansion occurred in two waves. An initial expansion early in the first millennium A.D. (if not before) would have brought the language into at least two areas that were originally non-Chumash speaking—in the northwest, where Obispeño shows evidence of having replaced Salinan, or a similar Hokan language, in much of its territory, and on the Channel Islands, where the influence of a substratal language of unknown provenience may be seen in the numerous words that are not cognate with other Chumash languages (Klar 2002:657).

The relative homogeneity of Central Chumash could be accounted for by a second expansion, probably from Ventureño territory, which would have overlaid the earlier Chumash spread with innovative Central Chumash dialects in all but the Obispeño and Island areas. The diversity within Central Chumash is consistent with a time depth of between 1,000 and 1,200 years, suggesting that the spread of the Central Chumash languages may have been an element in the development of medium-distance trading networks marked by the introduction of plank-canoe technology around cal A.D. 700 to 1000 (Arnold 2001b).

Yukian

The Yukian family consists of two quite distinct languages, Northern Yukian and Wappo, with Northern Yukian divided into three distinct dialects or emergent languages, Yuki, Huchnom, and Coast Yuki. The differentiation within Northern Yukian does not appear to be older than 1,000 years. The dialectal divisions within Wappo are even shallower.

Elmendorf's glottochronological calculations put the date of separation between Northern Yukian and Wappo at approximately 3,000 years ago (1968:178). Although this gives the split a much greater time depth than earlier estimates, such as Kroeber's 500 years ago (1925:218), it fits well with recent syntheses of North Coast Range archaeology. Thus Fredrickson, on the basis of archaeological correlations, dates the expansion of Pomo groups into the Russian River Valley to the Middle Archaic Period between 5,000 years and 3,000 years ago (1984b:510). If the pre-Pomo language of this area was Yukian, as seems likely, this expansion could have been the catalyst that separated early Wappo from the rest of Yukian around the date that Elmendorf's calculations suggest. However, a 1500 cal B.C. date for Western Pomo expansion is difficult to reconcile with linguistic estimates of the age of the Pomo family, which are on the order of 2,000 to 2,500 years ago.

Whenever and wherever Wappo diverged from Northern Yukian, it probably involved substantial influence from Pomo, since a number of the phonological and grammatical differences between Northern Yukian and Wappo are best explained as a "Pomoization" of the latter. Miwok influence on Wappo, by contrast, is largely confined to superficial lexical borrowing. This is consistent with a late date for the Wappo occupation of the Napa Valley, where an older Miwok population appears to have been absorbed. A correlation of a Wappo intrusion with the beginning of the St. Helena Aspect of the Augustine Pattern, around 1500 years ago, is generally accepted (Fredrickson 1984:511).

PREHISTORIC IMPLICATIONS

The earlier history of the Chumash and Yukian languages is highly speculative. Physical and archaeological associations point to the possibility that both speech communities represent the survival of very old linguistic traditions along the California coast.

The physical characteristics of the (Northern) Yukians and their immediate Athabaskan neighbors—long-headedness and very short stature—indicate an isolated gene pool that could well be, as Kroeber proposed (1925:159), a relict population from the earliest peopling of California. Their well-attested hostile relationships with neighboring groups could be seen as a social adaptation that has promoted long-term ethnic survival; they are the Basques of northern California. If this view is correct, an early form of Yukian could well have been the basal linguistic stratum in a significant part of California. There is indeed some evidence of this. In an unpublished paper, Elmendorf (1984) compiled a list of words shared by Yukian with other California languages—most of them likely to be borrowings in one direction or the other. He found 30 or more words shared with adjacent Wintuan, Pomo (many with proto-Pomo), and Miwok (many with proto-Miwok). Among nonadjacent languages, the largest number of sharings was with Wiyot (23), Yokuts ("a fair number"), Chumashan (25 to 30), and Uto-Aztecan (35 or more). Smaller numbers were shared with Chimariko (14) and Maiduan (12). Few or none were shared with Karuk, Shasta, Palaihnihan, Salinan, and Esselen.

Substantial numbers of lexical resemblances have also been adduced between Yukian and Siouan, Yuchi, and the Gulf languages (Elmendorf 1963; Munro 1994). These are not easily dismissed, but the geographical discontinuity is enormous. It is highly unlikely that the linguistic similarities reflect direct connections more recent than the Archaic, although proposals for an improbable Yukian hegira to California from the Southeast (or vice versa) have been made (Swadesh 1954:324). A more plausible hypothesis would be that certain languages of the Gulf Coast and Mississippi Valley share a remote common parentage with what could be argued is the earliest stratum of languages along the Pacific coast—Yukian, Chumash, the language substratal to Island Chumash, and possibly one or more of the languages at the southern tip of Baja California—and reflect an early coastal pattern of settlement of the continent during the Terminal Pleistocene and Early Holocene.

NOTES

1. The classification of California Indian languages at the language family and phylum level is admittedly not cut-and-dried. With Athabaskan (the focus of my own primary research), Algic, and Uto-Aztecan there is a firm consensus

among linguists regarding what languages belong to the family and how they should be subgrouped. There is much less agreement, however, regarding the Penutian and Hokan relationships, and some methodologically conservative historical linguists (e.g., Campbell 1997) consider them to be unproven hypotheses. My position, which I believe is shared by the majority of my colleagues, is that such extreme skepticism is unwarranted, and that while future research will undoubtedly alter the details, both relationships are historically valid in broad outline.

2. The outline of Athabaskan settlement and diversification in Oregon and California presented in the remainder of this section represents the author's own research.

3. The Columbia Plateau appears to be a "spread area" (Nichols 1992) in which languages replace one another with relative frequency. The shallow dialect diversity within Shuswap, Okanagan, and Kalispel suggests a very late spread of these languages, possibly within the past 500 years. Similarly, the dialect divisions and the large area covered by Sahaptin and Nez Perce suggests that they also have expanded into much of their present territory very recently (Kinkade et al. 1998:68–69).

4. The prevailing view is that the proto-Uto-Aztecan speech community was located in the northern portion of the area historically occupied by the family. Fowler (1983), on the basis of reconstructed plant and animal terms, considers the most likely PUA homeland to have been in central and southern Arizona and adjacent parts of northern Sonora and Chihuahua, possibly extending west into southern California. Hill (2001) has recently argued that terms connected with maize cultivation can be reconstructed in PUA; consequently the homeland must have been located much further south.

5. For a survey of recent work on comparative Penutian linguistics, see DeLancey and Golla (1997).

6. Whistler's scheme of Pomo linguistic prehistory is also summarized in McCarthy (1985). For a critical assessment, see Olmsted (1985).

7. Dixon and Kroeber's (1913) proposal that Chumash and Salinan were related, and that this group ("Iskoman") formed a branch of Hokan, was based on very little Chumash data. When Harrington's massive documentation of several varieties of Chumash finally became available after his death in 1961, it soon became clear that Iskoman was not a valid grouping. While Salinan is demonstrably an isolate within Hokan, the Hokan status of the Chumash family has become increasingly doubtful (Campbell 1997:125–126; Kaufman 1988).

CHAPTER 7

Northwest California: Ancient Lifeways among Forested Mountains, Flowing Rivers, and Rocky Ocean Shores

William R. Hildebrandt

Northwest California covers lands from Bodega Bay to the Oregon border and from the Pacific coast to the east slope of the North Coast Ranges and Klamath Mountains. This region encompasses seven modern counties, including Sonoma, Lake, Mendocino, Humboldt, Trinity, Del Norte, and Siskiyou. At the time of historic contact, this was a land of great environmental and ethnographic diversity which helped foster a rich, complex archaeological record. Evidence of prehistoric peoples begins at the Pleistocene/Holocene Transition with fluted point assemblages from the Clear Lake basin. Moving forward through the Holocene, archaeological data reveal a high degree of geographic variability in economic adaptations and culture, no doubt linked to some of the highest linguistic diversity ever recorded on earth.

Much of the archaeological information available from northwest California has been produced after the publication of Fredrickson's chapter, "North Coastal Region," in Moratto (1984). Along the northernmost coast (Del Norte and Humboldt Counties), for example, little had been accomplished since the work of scholars like Loud (1918), Bennyhoff (1950), Elsasser and Heizer (1964, 1966), Gould (1966), and Milburn et al. (1979). Since 1984, the area has seen multiple synthetic publications derived from graduate student research and smaller-scale cultural resource management projects (Hildebrandt 1984; Hildebrandt and Levulett 1997, 2002). Archaeological data were also very sparse along the Mendocino and Sonoma coasts at the time of Fredrickson's writing, but thanks to the multiyear studies by Dowdall (2002), Kennedy (2005), Layton (1990), Lightfoot et al. (1991), Schwaderer (1992), and White (1991), we now have a good understanding of the settlement histories of these areas.

Although work by Eidsness (1986), Hildebrandt and Hayes (1993), and Sundahl and Henn (1993) in the Pilot Ridge–Trinity River area contributed data on the northern interior, research has slowed during the past decade and much remains to be learned from this area. Ongoing work by Tushingham (2005) on the Smith River in Del Norte County is a refreshing change to this trend, and promises to provide important data and interpretations in the near future. Interior Mendocino County, which was a center for numerous settlement pattern studies prior to 1984 (see Fredrickson 1984:Eel River Subregion), has seen only a few large-scale studies since that time (Huberland 1989; Keter 1995). Fortunately this is not the case for interior Sonoma and Lake Counties, as the research efforts by scholars from UC Davis, Sonoma State University, and Chico State University have taken giant strides forward. Basgall and Bouey's (1991) work at Warm Springs, for example, has provided an important synthesis for the Russian River area, while White's multiyear studies in the Clear Lake basin culminated in one of the finest monographs ever published on California prehistory (White et al. 2002).

THE ECONOMIC POTENTIAL OF NORTHWEST CALIFORNIA

Terrestrial habitats of northwest California are largely conditioned by local geomorphology, topography, and rainfall. The North Coast Ranges and Klamath Mountains are composed of an intricate pattern of ridgelines that are interspersed by numerous valleys of varying sizes. Moving east from the coast, elevations typically reach 500 to 1,500 feet along the seaboard and summit heights of 6,500 to 8,000 feet just west of the Sacramento Valley. Elevations also vary with latitude, with the tallest peaks and ridgelines occurring in the north (e.g., Siskiyou and Trinity Counties) and relatively more gentle terrain in the south (e.g., Lake and Sonoma Counties). Rainfall also follows a latitudinal gradient, as annual precipitation ranges from 70 to 100 inches per year in several portions of the northern counties, and averages around 40 inches farther south.

The above geographic patterns in elevation and rainfall result in significant north-south differences in terrestrial vegetation, hydrology, and subsistence resource productivity. Although redwood forest occurs along the near-coastal mountains throughout the region, the northern counties (Del Norte, Siskiyou, Humboldt, and Trinity) are dominated by mixed evergreen forest, montane forest, and grand fir–Sitka spruce forest, while the southern areas (Mendocino, Lake, and Sonoma Counties) have a more diversified combination of mixed evergreen, mixed hardwood, and blue oak–gray pine forest, as well as communities of chaparral and valley oak savanna; many of these southern habitats contained an abundance of high-quality, acorn-producing species including tan oak, black oak, and valley oak. Lagoons and estuaries occur up and down the coast, but most are found north of Cape Mendocino (e.g., Humboldt Bay, Big Lagoon, Stone Lagoon, Lake Earl), while coastal and interior prairies occur sporadically throughout the region.

Due to latitudinal differences in rainfall, anadromous fish runs were most productive in the northernmost areas, where the Smith, Klamath, and Trinity Rivers had king salmon runs during fall and spring. Fall king salmon runs occurred in all major streams down to the Mattole River, but were rare or absent farther south. Silver salmon had a more extensive distribution, occurring in all but a few of the smaller streams in Mendocino and Sonoma Counties, while steelhead trout occurred in all the coastal streams of northwest California (Baumhoff 1963). Other important fish included the lamprey eel and sturgeon, found in highest densities to the north, and a variety of resident fishes like suckers and hitch, which were abundant in Clear Lake and its adjacent tributaries (White et al. 2002).

Marine mammals were present up and down the coast, but major sea lion rookeries were only present in Humboldt and Del Norte Counties where offshore rocks were plentiful. Deer and elk were important game animals throughout northwest California, and a variety of smaller animals were also used (e.g., rabbits, rodents, insects), particularly in the more southerly latitudes. Plant food diversity also varies along a north-south dimension, with the northernmost areas producing a rather narrow range of edible resources dominated by acorns, tubers, and berries, while acorns, berries, buckeye, manzanita, clover, small seeds, pine nuts, tubers, and pepperwood nuts were commonly used foods in the south.

Nonfood commodities were important for residential structures, basketry, and various tools and ceremonial items. Many of these implements and facilities were made from perishable materials and usually don't preserve in the archaeological record. An important exception to this rule is obsidian, which figures heavily in prehistoric studies throughout the region. Major obsidian sources occur in the Napa Valley area, along the shores of Clear Lake (Borax Lake, Mount Konocti), and near Santa Rosa (Annadel); obsidian from northeastern California (e.g., Medicine Lake Highlands, Warner Mountains) was also transported into the northern reaches of northwest California.

NATIVE PEOPLES AT HISTORIC CONTACT

As discussed by Golla (see Chapter 6 in this volume), over 20 distinct languages representing five linguistic families were present in northwest California at historic contact (Figure 7.1). This diverse array of tribal entities can be divided into two major groups based on a series of shared cultural traits—the Northwest Coast and the California Culture areas.

The Northwest Coast Culture area extends from Alaska and Canada (e.g., Tlingit, Kwakiutl) south to Cape Mendocino, where the Tolowa, Yurok, Wiyot, Karok, and Hupa represent a peripheral expression of the adaptation. The latter groups lived in relatively high densities, and occupied permanent coastal and interior riverine settlements. Many of these settlements were supported by the storage of acorns and the use of large communal fish weirs, river canoes, large oceangoing canoes, composite harpoons, and redwood smoke houses that facilitated the harvest and storage of fish and marine mammals (Figure 7.2). Wealthy families owned many of these capital-intensive technologies, as well as important resource areas such as acorn groves, river eddies for obtaining fish, and portions of offshore sea lion rookeries (Goddard 1903; Goldschmidt 1951a; Kroeber 1925; Waterman 1920). Individual households possessing superior pools of labor could generate substantial food surpluses and other items of wealth, ultimately separating themselves from the less successful family units. Unlike most populations elsewhere in California, these northern groups lacked the tribelet organization originally defined by Kroeber (1925). Instead, Goldschmidt (1951a) argued that the concept of village and tribe was essentially nonexistent, as the individual or immediate family took precedence. "Though persons were identified by their village of residence and their tribe of origin, neither of these groups had any direct claim upon the action of the individual" (Goldschmidt 1951a:507). There was a universal concept of privately owned property, including money (e.g., dentalium), which was linked to differential wealth and power within the population, and stratified community organization (Fredrickson 1984; Gould 1975; Kroeber 1925).

The California Culture area includes most of the southern Athabaskan peoples (Chilula-Whilkut, Mattole, Nongatl, Lassik, Sinkyone, and Wailaki), as well as the Yuki, Miwok, Wappo, and multiple Pomoan groups. Rather than focusing on maritime and riverine resources, they relied on a broader array of terrestrial foods, especially acorns. Unlike the Yurok and Tolowa, groups living along the coast did not venture out to sea. Instead, they practiced a littoral adaptation where marine resources like shellfish and small schooling fish were obtained on a seasonal basis from the shore or nearshore locations. This economic system often resulted in a higher level of residential mobility than observed farther north, as many people followed a seasonal round that encompassed both coastal and interior habitats.

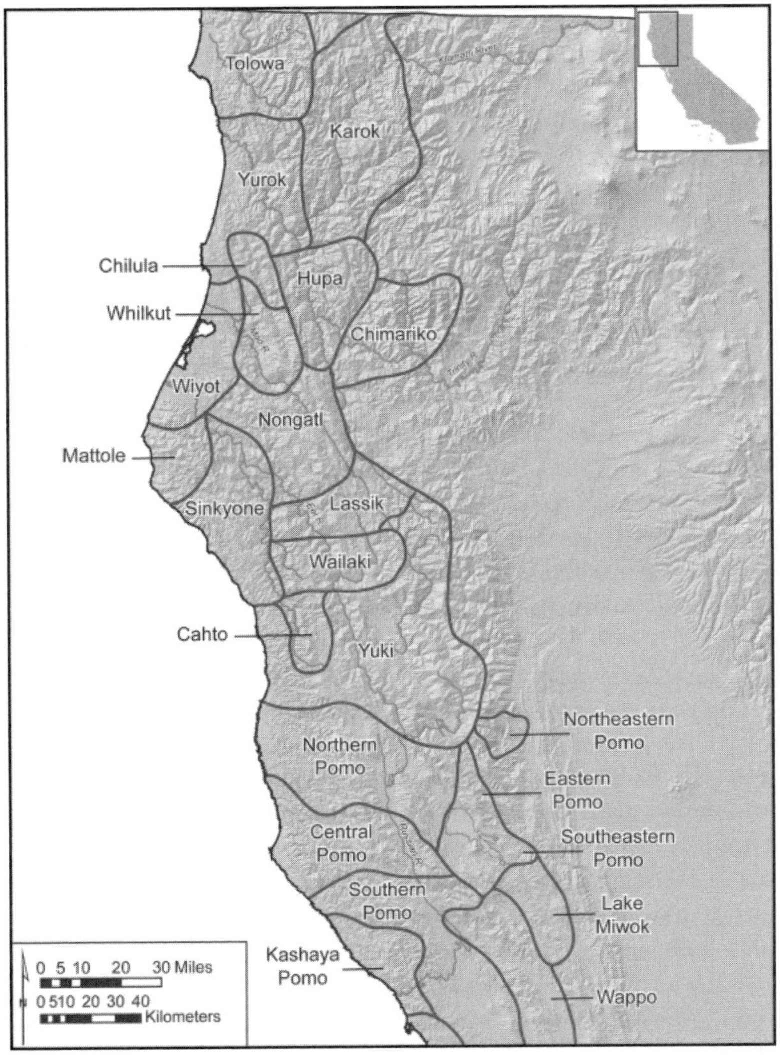

Figure 7.1. Approximate location of tribal groups, northwest California.

Groups within the California Culture area living along major interior drainages made use of anadromous fishes, but the reduced productivity of the runs (with regard to both frequency and size) also led to a more diversified adaptation. In addition to hunting large and small game, people like the Yuki used multiple kinds of acorns, including the tan oak, valley oak, and black oak. Pine nuts, buckeyes, pepperwood nuts, and various other plant foods were also important subsistence resources. The primary political unit was the tribelet, not the family household of the more northerly groups. Each tribelet typically had a main village center composed of multiple family dwellings and a dance house; it was also the residence of the tribelet chief. A variable number of satellite villages were tied to the main tribelet center, but the relationship was changeable depending on the popularity of the chief. Duties and responsibilities of chiefs were also fluid, but these individuals usually decided when festivals and rituals were held, arbitrated disputes, and maintained traditional forms of behavior (McCarthy et al. 1985).

People spent winter in the villages, living on stored foods. With the advent of spring, they collected and consumed clovers, greens, and tubers. Many interior groups moved into the mountains in the summer to collect and hunt for food, often changing settlements five or six times during a season. Seeds from small grasses and flowers were collected and became important storage items. Various berries were eaten, with some dried and stored for winter use. By the fall, the ripening of acorns and pine nuts, as well as arrival of anadromous fish, made for a busy time as the collection, processing, and storage of these resources ensured survival through the upcoming winter.

Pomoan peoples living around the margins of Clear Lake represent a significant departure from the aforementioned pattern. Although the tribelet was also the primary sociopolitical unit, some of the centralized villages were larger than was typical elsewhere in the

Figure 7.2. Karok fisherman using a lift net from a scaffold built at Shanamkarak. (Courtesy of the Phoebe Apperson Hearst Museum of Anthropology and the Regents of the University of California. Photographed by Alfred L. Kroeber, cat. no. 15-1383.)

North Coast Ranges. Moreover, they did not use the common settlement system of fall-winter aggregation in multifamily villages, followed by population dispersals in the spring and summer. Instead, cyprinid fish runs (e.g., suckers, hitch) into the feeder streams of Clear Lake during spring and early summer not only held the local people in their villages for an extended period of time, but also brought in people from adjoining areas who established temporary camps to participate in the harvest (White et al. 2002).

CULTURAL HISTORICAL DEVELOPMENTS: CHANGING PATTERNS OF SUBSISTENCE, SETTLEMENT, AND SOCIOPOLITICAL ORGANIZATION

Several different strategies have been used to help organize and understand the archaeological record of northwest California. These strategies vary along a continuum of detail, ranging from focusing on high-resolution culture histories on a local level, to identifying only the broadest general archaeological trends observed on a regional or interregional level. While the former approach is appropriate for studies of stylistic traits associated with local population replacements, the more generalized end of the continuum is applied here, since the goal of this chapter is to organize the archaeological record in a way that is relatively easy to understand and conducive to comparisons with other parts of California and beyond.

Two organizational schemes are used to interpret the prehistory of northwest California, one chronological and the other cultural. The chronological scheme is derived from the study of North American geology and paleoecology, and is purely an organizational tool (i.e., it is independent of prehistoric cultural developments). Four time periods are recognized: Pleistocene/Holocene Transition (11,500 to 8000 cal B.C.), Early Holocene (8000 to 5000 cal B.C.), Middle Holocene (5000 to 2000 cal B.C.), and Late Holocene (post-2000 cal B.C.). Organization of archaeological findings will follow the original work of Fredrickson (1974a, 1984), relying on two basic units: *pattern* and *aspect*. The most general unit is the *pattern*, which is a "configuration of basic traits [representing] a basic adaptation generally shared by a number of separate cultures over an appreciable period of time within an appreciable space" (Bennyhoff and Fredrickson 1994). An *aspect* is a local variant of a *pattern* that typically has a time-space dimension, and unique artifact styles that could reflect more discrete cultural groups. *Phases* are subgroupings of the aspect, but represent the most detailed, local units of analysis and are used only selectively here.

Six basic patterns are recognized: Post, Borax Lake, Berkeley, Mendocino, Gunther, and Augustine. As outlined by Figure 7.3, these patterns span different lengths of time in different areas, and also vary with regard to their internal differentiation (i.e., the number of aspects they include). The following discussion describes each of these patterns, focusing on their respective artifact assemblages, adaptive pose, sociopolitical organization, and time-space distributions. These relationships will then be used to identify some of the most important research issues and themes of the region, which will hopefully provide some direction and inspiration for future researchers.

Finally, due to the large size of northwest California and some of the latitudinal gradients in environment and culture outlined above, it will be useful to compare archaeological findings from the north to those of the south. When such comparisons are appropriate, the northern areas will include Del Norte, Siskiyou, Humboldt, and Trinity Counties, while the southern areas include Mendocino, Lake, and Sonoma Counties (Figure 7.4).

Pleistocene-Holocene Transition (11,500 to 8000 cal B.C.)

The Post Pattern is the earliest cultural manifestation in northwest California and is best illustrated by the fluted (Clovis-like) projectile points and chipped stone crescents from the Borax Lake site near Clear Lake (LAK-36; Figure 7.5). Unfortunately, multiple excavations and surface collections at the site have failed to discover clear, single-component areas (either vertically or horizontally), so an associated assemblage has never been identified or securely dated with radiocarbon. Nevertheless, obsidian hydration readings from the artifacts themselves range between 8.5 and 10.0 microns on Borax Lake obsidian. These are the earliest obsidian hydration readings in the Clear Lake basin and probably correspond to the Pliestocene/Holocene Transition (see Fredrickson and Origer 2002:156; White et al. 2002:427).

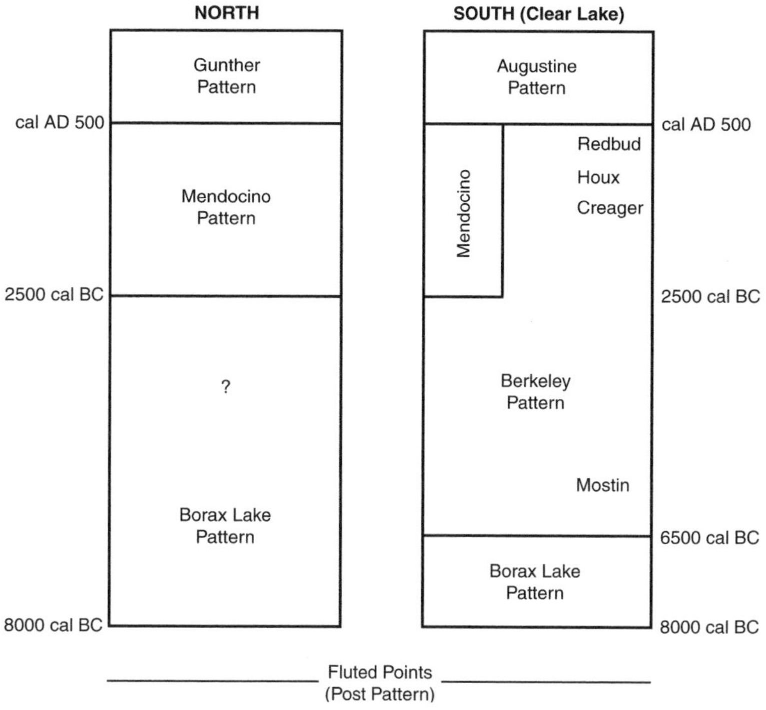

Figure 7.3. Northwest California chronological sequences.

Well-defined Post Pattern assemblages have not been found elsewhere in northwest California. A fluted point was discovered near the coast in Mendocino County (Simons et al. 1985), while crescents have been found at Bodega Head (Moratto 1984) and near Santa Rosa (Origer and Fredrickson 1980). Regrettably, however, all these artifacts were in isolated contexts or lacked strong association with well-dated strata or other artifacts. Finally, very old materials have also been found in excavations at a site near Clear Lake (LAK-510; White et al. 2002) and at Cache Creek (LAK-1581; DeGeorgey 2004), but both components are dated with obsidian hydration and lack diagnostic items.

Given that none of the Post Pattern materials have been found in good stratigraphic context, we currently know little about the adaptive system they represent. The presence or absence of other important artifact types (e.g., milling gear) remains unknown, and there are no known associations with faunal remains (including extinct Pleistocene species). The latter association has never been established elsewhere in California or the Great Basin, so the subsistence pursuits of these early peoples remains an important research topic for future archaeologists.

Early Holocene (8000 to 5000 cal B.C.)

Much more is known about the Early Holocene, as archaeological manifestations of the Borax Lake Pattern have been discovered and studied throughout the interior of northwest California. The earliest evidence of the Berkeley Pattern at Clear Lake also occurs during this interval, as well as a series of coastal components in Sonoma County lacking clear cultural affiliation.

BORAX LAKE PATTERN Along its northern distribution in Humboldt and Trinity Counties, the Borax Lake Pattern is represented by large wide-stemmed projectile points with indented bases (Figure 7.5), serrated bifaces, ovoid flake tools, handstones, millingslabs, and edge-flaked spalls. This diversified assemblage is commonly found in sites located across a wide range of environmental contexts, including ridge tops between 4,500 and 6,000 feet along Pilot Ridge and South Fork Mountain (HUM-573, HUM-367), and along terraces adjacent to the Trinity River (TRI-1008; Hildebrandt and Hayes 1993; Sundahl and Henn 1993). Excavations at one of the ridge-top sites (HUM-573) discovered a hard-packed house floor associated with the aforementioned assemblage and three possible post holes. A soil sample from the floor produced a radiocarbon date of 5995 cal B.C., making it one of the oldest houses ever excavated in California (Fitzgerald and Hildebrandt 2002). Obsidian hydration data collected from both upland and lowland settings indicate that the pattern may have persisted in Humboldt and Trinity Counties until roughly 3000 cal B.C., but this is far from certain as we have a limited understanding of obsidian hydration rates in this area.

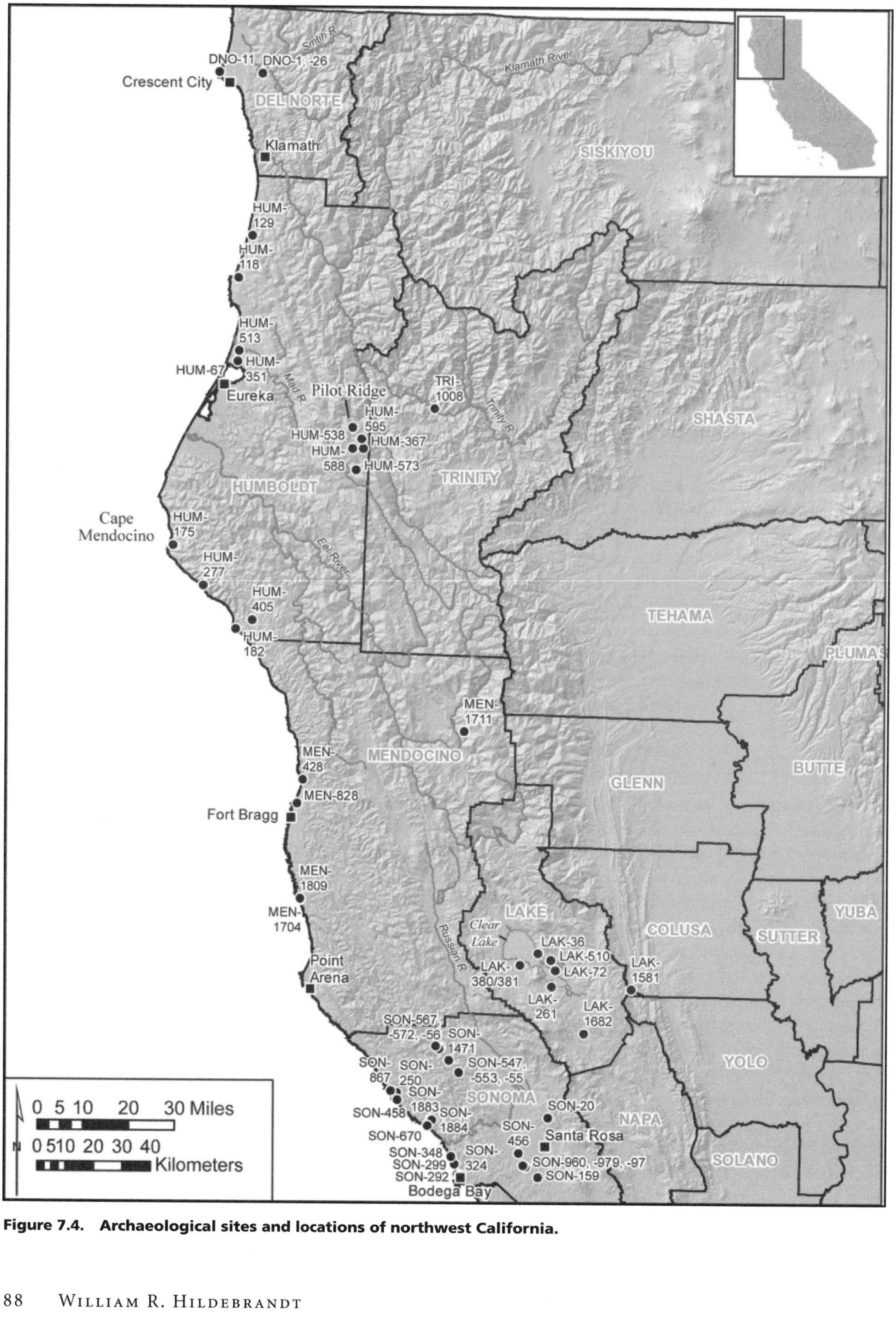

Figure 7.4. Archaeological sites and locations of northwest California.

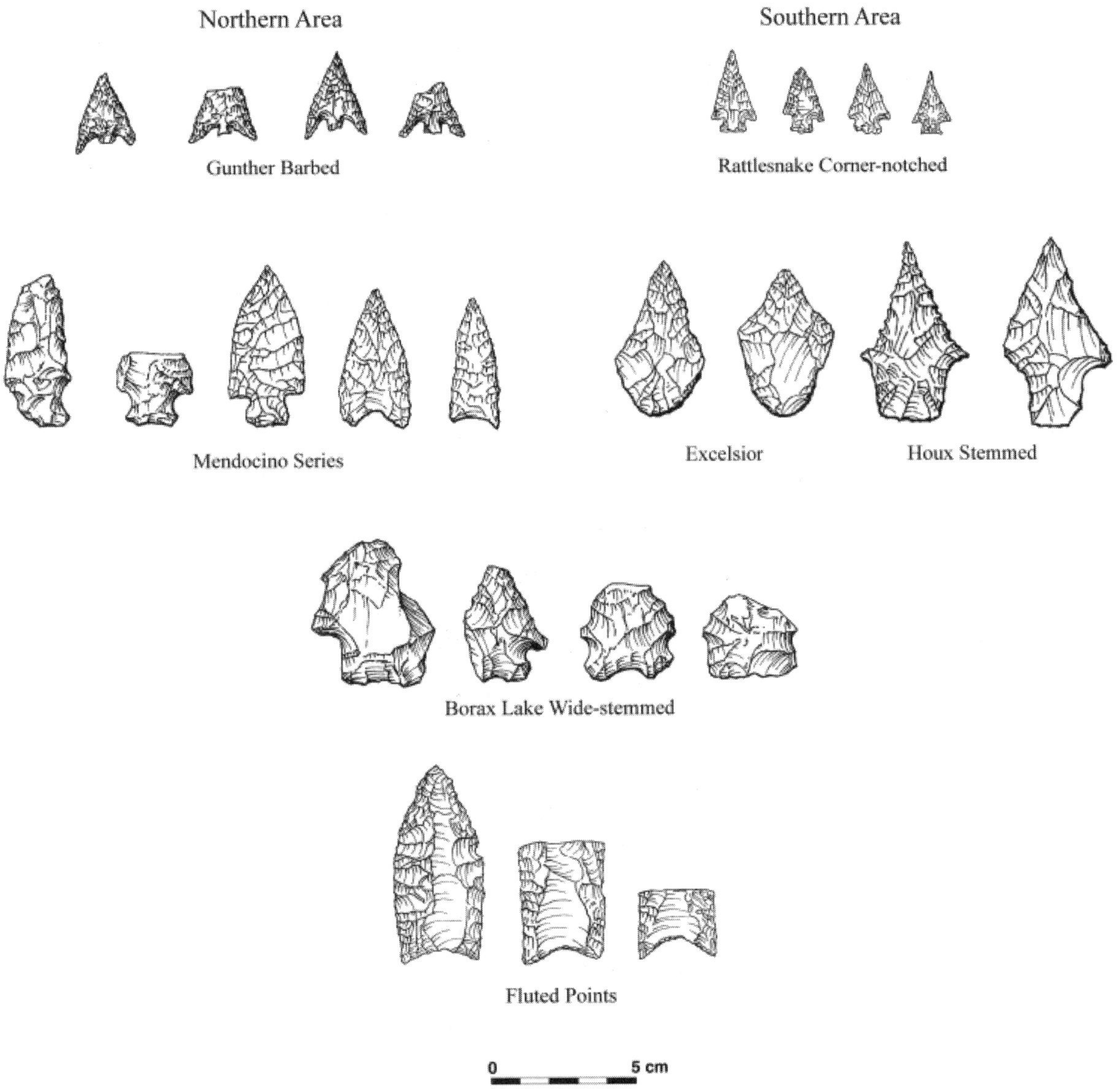

Figure 7.5. Projectile point sequence for northwest California.

Faunal and floral remains have not been discovered in these northern sites, largely because conifer leaf litter and heavy rainfall compromise the preservation of subsistence remains. The composition and homogeneity of the Borax Lake artifact assemblages, however, appear to represent a "forager" approach to subsistence-settlement organization. With this strategy, little emphasis is placed on storage, and incongruities in the distribution of resources over time and space are solved by moving people from places of declining productivity to areas where foraging opportunities are enhanced. This approach requires frequent residential moves by the entire social unit, resulting in the generalized assemblages and homogeneous settlement structure observed in the archaeological record.

The Borax Lake Pattern is also well represented farther south in the Clear Lake basin (White et al. 2002), the mountains of Mendocino County (MEN-1711; Huberland 1989), and the Santa Rosa Plain (SON-20; Origer and Fredrickson 1980). Unlike the northern sites, Clear Lake assemblages are represented by flaked stone only, including large wide-stemmed points (square bases, some with fluting), ovoid flake tools, and thin bladelet flakes. Obsidian hydration data indicate these materials might be older than those to the north, as they appear to range between 8500 and 6000 cal B.C. It remains an open question as to whether the narrow, flaked stone–dominated artifact assemblages found in the Clear Lake area reflect an earlier pre-Archaic hunting focus, or whether more complete assemblages actually exist but have not yet been discovered. It is also possible that the older flaked stone–dominated assemblages occur in the north but have not been recognized.

A robust assemblage of milling gear dating to the Early Holocene has been discovered about 20 kilometers southeast of Clear Lake at LAK-1682 (Rosenthal et al. 1995), but its cultural affiliation has been extensively debated. The site produced several handstones, millingslabs, core tools, and rock features, as well as a lesser number of bifaces and projectile points (including one Borax Lake wide-stemmed point). A radiocarbon date of 6160 cal B.C. was obtained from one of the rock features, but obsidian hydration data from the shallow site produced readings spanning much of the Holocene. Based on these findings, Rosenthal et al. (1995) concluded that some of the assemblage reflects an early Borax Lake Pattern occupation, but the site was reused on multiple occasions later in the Holocene, probably to process the gray pine nuts abundant in the local area.

Fitzgerald and Jones (1999) have proposed a different view, arguing that the site represents a northern California variant of the Millingstone Horizon. Following the lead of D. L. True et al. (True and Baumhoff 1985), who have attributed undated scatters of milling gear and cobble tools near Lake Berryessa to the Millingstone Horizon, Fitzgerald and Jones (1999) discount the accuracy of the obsidian hydration data provided by Rosenthal et al. (1995) and propose that LAK-1682 is a single component representation of a cultural group that was different from the early Berkeley or Borax Lake patterns observed at Clear Lake. Given that handstones and millingslabs were used throughout much of the occupational sequences of northwest California, particularly among mobile peoples (e.g., Mendocino Pattern, below), Rosenthal et al. (1995) feel that assigning cultural historical status to such material is highly problematic. Unless one chooses to accept the obsidian hydration data from LAK-1682, however, the ultimate solution to the debate will require additional radiocarbon dates from the multiple features existing at the site (i.e., do they span much of the Holocene or cluster around 6000 cal B.C.?).

EARLY BERKELEY PATTERN: MOSTIN PHASE Several important changes take place in the Clear Lake area at around 6500 cal B.C. with the beginning of the Berkeley Pattern. Unlike the more northerly areas, where the residentially mobile Borax Lake Pattern adaptation continued for thousands of years, the Berkeley Pattern at Clear Lake (also known as the Houx Aspect of the Berkeley Pattern) provides the first evidence of more stable, long-term settlements (Fredrickson 1974a, 1984; White et al. 2002). The initial Mostin Phase (ca. 6500 to 4300 cal B.C.) is defined by Houx contracting-stemmed and square-stemmed points (Figure 7.5), formalized burial patterns (including extended burial posture), the use of pestles, and a relatively abundant presence of acorn macrofossils. The presence of pestles and acorns at this time depth is important, as it represents some of the earliest evidence for acorn use in California (Wohlgemuth 2004). White and King's (1993) analysis of site structure and composition at the type site (LAK-380/381) also indicates a possible separation between occupation areas and places used for burial, which is a pattern often associated with permanent settlements; however, they concluded that the site was probably occupied on an intermittent basis due to the patchy and dispersed nature of the midden deposits.

COASTAL MANIFESTATIONS Archaeological materials dating to the Early Holocene are rare along the coast. Only one well-defined Borax Lake Pattern site has been found near the ocean (HUM-513/H). It lies on a coastal prairie about two kilometers from the coast in Humboldt County but lacks shellfish or any other marine indicators and appears to be a short-term hunting camp, perhaps focused on the acquisition of Roosevelt elk.

Additional evidence comes from farther south in Sonoma County at the Duncan's Landing site (SON-348/H), where excavation of a rock shelter located on the coastal bluff produced a deeply buried component dating to about 6600 cal B.C. The artifact assemblage is limited to a few formed tools, but the subsistence remains include significant quantities of shellfish (mostly outer coast mussel but some estuary species), as well as a relatively diverse mix of marine and terrestrial mammals (Schwaderer 1992; Wake and Simons 2000). Although little is known about the overall subsistence-settlement organization of these early people at Duncan's Landing, they clearly used both marine and terrestrial resources and probably practiced a relatively mobile settlement system, the latter confirmed by stable isotope analyses on shellfish indicating only fall and winter occupations of the coast (Kennedy 2005; Kennedy et al. 2005). The relationship of these materials to the Borax Lake, Early Berkeley, or some other cultural pattern is unknown and remains a major research question for the region.

Middle Holocene (5000 to 2000 cal B.C.)

Little is known about the earliest part of the Middle Holocene (ca. 5000 to 3000 cal B.C.). At Clear Lake, for example, archaeological data are essentially absent between 4300 and 1200 cal B.C., largely due to the unstable nature of geomorphic processes during this interval (sporadic periods of intense erosion and deposition appear to have obliterated the record; White et al. 2002). Farther north in the Pilot Ridge area, Hildebrandt and Hayes (1993) could not identify archaeological assemblages falling between the Borax Lake and Mendocino Patterns, so they (probably incorrectly) pushed the age of the Borax Lake Pattern forward in time. Clear evidence for Middle Holocene archaeology is also lacking in the river valleys (Basgall and Bouey 1991; Hildebrandt and Levulett 1997; Meighan 1955) and on the coast north of Cape Mendocino (Eidsness 1993; Gould 1966; Hildebrandt and Levulett 2002), where occupations don't begin until after 3000 cal B.C. when the Mendocino Pattern emerges.

Archaeological materials dating between 3100 and 2300 cal B.C. have been discovered near Bodega Bay (e.g., SON-2378, SON-1735), but they are ephemeral (Kennedy 2005). Excavations at a series of small shell middens produced shellfish but little else. Similar to the Early Holocene component at Duncan's Landing, staple isotope analyses from shell indicate only short-term fall and winter occupations.

Although Kennedy's (2005) and Schwaderer's (1992) findings from the Sonoma coast lack robust artifact assemblages with obvious cultural affiliations, these data are extremely important because they demonstrate that an archaeological record exists during a significant portion of the Middle Holocene. While White et al.'s (2002) explanation for the Clear Lake hiatus is reasonable and supported by a strong corpus of geomorphological data, not all contexts in northwest California should have suffered the same fate. This is particularly the case for places like Pilot Ridge, where earlier Borax Lake Pattern materials are found in near-surface contexts and would have also been stripped or buried by Middle Holocene erosional forces, had such forces been significant in this location; this is also the case along the ancient coastal prairies where deposits have remained intact throughout the Holocene. It seems probable, therefore, that a Middle Holocene archaeological record actually exists but is not being recognized. On the coast, where datable material (shellfish) is available, we see it. On the interior, however, where sites lack datable shellfish and we have no recognizable artifact types (e.g., a well-known, time-sensitive projectile point form), it goes largely unnoticed. According to Weigel (1993), some of the problem may stem from the xeric climatic conditions of the Middle Holocene (see West 1993; Chapter 2 in this volume) which may have negatively impacted the anadromous fishery and other important resources, perhaps causing a dispersal of human populations and a less visible archaeological record during this interval.

The following discussion focuses on the archaeological record that has been recognized so far: the Mendocino Pattern (3000 cal B.C. to cal A.D. 500). Although it cross-cuts the Middle/Late Holocene boundary, with much of it falling in the latter interval, it represents an archaic adaptation that contrasts sharply with archaeological patterns that come later.

MENDOCINO PATTERN (3000 CAL B.C. TO CAL A.D. 500) The Mendocino Pattern first appears around 5,000 years ago in a variety of places in northwest California. Common artifacts include side-notched, corner-notched, and concave-base dart points (of the Willits and Mendocino series; Figure 7.5), handstones and millingslabs, various types of flake tools, cobble tools, and, in some cases, a limited number of cobble mortars and pestles. McKee unifaces are also an important part of the assemblage north of Sonoma County, while leaf-shaped dart points can also occur in the more southerly sites. Based on some of these differences, White et al. (2002) have assigned northern assemblages to the Mendocino Aspect and southern expressions to the Hultman Aspect.

Dowdall (2002), Layton (1990), and Kennedy (2005) have excavated Mendocino Pattern components along the Mendocino and Sonoma coasts, where they estimate the pattern persists between about 3000 cal B.C. and cal A.D. 500 (MEN-1704, SON-458, SON-299, SON-867). Most sites represent either temporary hunting camps or short-term forager residential bases occupied by people with a largely terrestrial subsistence orientation. Moving to the southern interior, Basgall and Bouey (1991) found several Mendocino Pattern sites (known as the Skaggs Phase) at Warm Springs along tributaries of the Russian River, and also emphasize the high degree of residential mobility associated with the adaptation (SON-572, SON-568, SON-547). Similar findings have been made along the Santa Rosa Plain (SON-456, SON-960; Jones and Hayes 1993) and on lands in and around the Clear

Lake basin (LAK-72, LAK-261, LAK-510; White et al. 2002). In the latter area, it appears that Mendocino people practiced a mobile system of settlement using the lake and adjacent uplands, visiting the lake during spring fish runs and coexisting with Berkeley Pattern people (see below).

The earliest manifestations of the Mendocino Pattern in the more northerly areas are not well defined, nor is there a clear picture of the adaptation. Coastal evidence is available from Point St. George (DNO-11; Gould 1966), Humboldt Bay (HUM-351; Eidsness 1993), and the King Range of southern Humboldt County (HUM-277; Hildebrandt and Levulett 2002; Levulett 1985), but none of these sites predate 500 cal B.C. Similar to the Sonoma and Mendocino coasts, the sites appear to represent temporary hunting camps or seasonal encampments by people with a terrestrial orientation.

Up in the northern mountains, most of the sites are specialized hunting camps (HUM-538, HUM-588, HUM-595), which is significantly different from the earlier Borax Lake Pattern where the uplands were dominated by residential sites. This finding led Hildebrandt and Hayes (1993) to hypothesize that the Mendocino hunting camps represented logistical forays from more substantial residential sites in the lowlands. Rather than representing a mobile system of settlement as the more southerly areas did, they argue that a sedentary settlement system, supported by the intensive harvest and storage of salmon and acorns, emerged at about 1500 cal B.C. Unfortunately, riverine excavations have been limited to a few sites. One of these, the McKee Flat site (HUM-405), yielded a diversified assemblage of both flaked and ground stone artifacts (including some mortars and pestles) as well as dark midden soils, but lacked the preservation of bone. Tushingham (2005) is currently excavating sites on the Smith River to investigate this issue (DNO-26, DNO-1). Preliminary findings from the site complex located seven miles from the coast show evidence of two components. The earliest predates 500 cal B.C. and includes redwood plank houses associated with a small amount of salmon bone and acorn macrofossils, providing some support for a more settled, riverine adaptation. A more intensified use of the local landscape is also supported by a study of prehistoric fire ecology in the Pilot Ridge area, where an analysis of upland pollen spectra generated by West (1993) led Weigel (1993) to conclude that large upland prairie habitats were created and maintained by human intervention after circa 500 cal B.C.

Late Holocene (Post-2000 cal B.C.)

The earliest part of the Late Holocene is marked by the continuation of the Mendocino Pattern in many northern areas, and the development and expansion of the Berkeley Pattern in the south. By cal A.D. 500, major change occurs throughout northwest California, as the precursors of the ethnographic cultures emerge, represented by the Gunther Pattern in the north and the Augustine Pattern in the south.

BERKELEY PATTERN As outlined above, the Berkeley Pattern is first recognized early in the Holocene at Clear Lake (Mostin Phase; 6500 to 4300 cal B.C.). After a hiatus in the archaeological record, it reappears again at about 1200 cal B.C. and continues until about cal A.D. 800 (LAK-72, LAK-261, LAK-510). White et al. (2002) recognize three phases (Creager, 1200 to 600 cal B.C.; Houx, 600 cal B.C. to cal A.D. 100; Redbud, cal A.D. 100 to 800), with an ultimate climax postdating 600 cal B.C. Artifact assemblages are elaborate and include leaf-shaped (Excelsior) and stemmed projectile points (Figure 7.5), a highly developed bone tool industry, many fishing-related implements (spears, harpoons, hooks, net sinkers), baked clay objects (including a few fragments of pottery), and a relatively high frequency of mortars and pestles. Basketry impressions obtained from baked clay, combined with changes in bone awl technology, appear to be linked to production of more varied types of baskets ranging from tightly woven "show baskets" to the loose-weave burden forms. Site structure is also quite formalized and includes black midden deposits, well-defined house floors, and a variety of other residential features. This higher degree of sedentism appears to be based on a subsistence economy built around the intensive use of acorns, large terrestrial game, and fish. Use of the local fishery was extremely important, as multiple runs of cyprinids occurred from February through July, allowing local populations to remain settled during this interval (White et al. 2002).

The local fishery also contributed to the subsistence system of surrounding groups, including the upland people associated with the Mendocino Pattern. According to White et al. (2002), the more sedentary Berkeley Pattern people controlled access to this superabundant resource and allowed the more mobile upland people to participate in the fish harvest, probably requiring exchange of some other valuable commodity. This relationship was discovered by careful chronological analyses of Berkeley and Mendocino pattern sites located along the lakeshore, where White found that they were both occupied at the same time, but with most Mendocino deposits situated in discrete places lacking the well-developed midden deposits common to the Berkeley Pattern.

Intergroup exchange relationships are also evidenced along several other dimensions. Production of obsidian bifaces from the Borax Lake source reached maximum intensity during this interval (1200 cal B.C. to cal A.D. 800) and were distributed far and wide throughout the region. Shell beads, including disks, saucers (G series), and saddles (F series) also became important, providing additional evidence for a greater reliance on exchange.

At about 500 cal B.C. there appears to have been an out-migration of Berkeley Pattern peoples to the west, crossing through the Santa Rosa Plain (SON-978, SON-979, SON-456; Jones and Hayes 1993) and the Warm Springs area (SON-556, SON-568; Basgall 1993c; Basgall and Bouey 1991), and ultimately reaching the coast (SON-292, SON-324; Dowdall 2002; Kennedy 2005). Most researchers attribute these changes to the expansion of Pomoan populations from their Clear Lake homeland, presumably replacing earlier Yukian-speaking peoples who occupied these outlying areas (Basgall 1982; Baumhoff 1980; Fredrickson 1984; Golla, Chapter 6 in this volume; White et al. 2002). Basgall and Bouey (1991) obtained large samples of Berkeley Pattern material at Warm Springs (called the Dry Creek Phase), where artifact assemblages include Excelsior projectile points, mortars and pestles, and high frequencies of Clear Lake obsidian; a higher degree of residential stability is also indicated by the formation of rich midden deposits. In contrast to the earlier Mendocino Pattern, where residential mobility was the primary adaptive strategy, the Berkeley Pattern apparently placed a greater emphasis on the storage and intensive use of acorns (Basgall 1987). Similarly to the Clear Lake area, the Berkeley and Mendocino Patterns apparently co-occurred in time in the Warm Springs Locality, with Berkeley people dominating the river valleys while the Mendocino folk were widely dispersed in the uplands (SON-1471; Stewart 1993).

Berkeley Pattern indicators are also common on the Sonoma and Mendocino coasts, but the intensity of occupation varies from place to place. Large residential bases are established in southern Sonoma County near Bodega Bay between 300 cal B.C. and cal A.D. 1, and include Excelsior points, shellfish hooks, notched net sinkers, bone tools, and mortars and pestles (Dowdall 2002; Kennedy 2005). These data, combined with stable isotope analyses on shellfish by Kennedy (2005), indicate year-round occupations during this interval. Similar findings have been made in Mendocino County north of Fort Bragg (MacKerricher State Park), where White (1991) excavated large house structures with multiple storage pits associated with artifacts dominated by Clear Lake obsidian and other Berkeley Pattern indicators (e.g., Excelsior points, bone and antler tools, mortars and pestles), as well as rich faunal assemblages composed of sea lion, elk, and salmon (MEN-828).

A different situation is encountered at intervening areas along the coast, where the Berkeley Pattern is represented by a brief interval or not at all. The former is the case near Albion, where Layton (1990) found a series of short-term hunting camps with Clear Lake obsidian and Excelsior points dating to around cal A.D. 500 (MEN-1809), while no evidence of the Berkeley Pattern has been found along the northern Sonoma County coast (Dowdall 2002; Lightfoot et al. 1991).

GUNTHER PATTERN (POST CAL A.D. 500) The Berkeley Pattern does not spread north of central Mendocino County, as Mendocino Pattern indicators appear to have persisted until about 1,500 years ago in the northern counties. Although it remains unclear whether or not the Mendocino Pattern developed the same degree of sedentism and cultural elaboration as the Berkeley Pattern along the northern river valleys, a high degree of sedentism is clearly evidenced by the later Gunther Pattern, particularly along the northern coast. Excavations at multiple sites north of Cape Mendocino, where offshore rocks and islands are plentiful (Elsasser and Heizer 1964, 1966; Gould 1966; Milburn et al. 1979), have yielded high frequencies of Gunther barbed projectile points (Figure 7.5) and concave-based points used to tip composite harpoons used for taking marine mammals and fish (DNO-11, HUM-129, HUM-118, HUM-67). Ground and polished stone artifacts are also abundant, some exhibiting impressive artistic elaboration. Flanged pestles, well-made mauls (used with antler wedges), and notched net sinkers are common, while significant frequencies of steatite bowls, zoöform clubs, and polished stone adze handles have also been found. Fishing gear is common, represented by various bone and antler spears, harpoons, and hooks (Bennyhoff 1950). The emphasis on implements geared toward the marine environment is complemented by faunal assemblages dominated by seals, sea lions, and marine fish. Many of these resources were obtained with the use of oceangoing canoes, either from distant offshore rocks or on the open water (Hildebrandt 1984).

All northern coastal sites are structurally complex, as they typically have well-defined houses, cemeteries, artifact caches, and midden/refuse areas. Redwood houses have been discovered on multiple occasions and often have stone patios and prepared clay floors. In addition to the zoöform clubs, ceremonial items include large obsidian blades (used ethnographically in the White Deerskin dance) and dentalia, most recovered from burial contexts in the early twentieth century. These items are buried with only a limited number of people in the population (including some children), and probably reflect the high level of social stratification known among the local peoples at historic contact (Hildebrandt and Levulett 2002). According to Golla (Chapter 6 in this volume), the Gunther Pattern probably relates to the arrivals of people speaking Algic languages, beginning with the Wiyot at about cal A.D. 100 and the Yurok at cal A.D. 700 to 800, and a later wave of Athabaskans around cal A.D. 800 to 900, who ultimately diverged into several distinct languages and dialects.

South of Cape Mendocino, along the southern Humboldt County coast, offshore rocks are rare and the adaptation appears to be more terrestrial in its orientation (HUM-175, HUM-277, HUM-182). Although Gunther barbed projectile points are still used, harpoons, woodworking tools, plank houses, and ceremonial objects are quite rare. Archaeofaunal remains also lack the maritime focus of the more northern areas, as they are typically dominated by deer and a lesser frequency of nearshore marine mammals. Most of these sites represent a seasonal littoral adaptation, with a large portion of the subsistence economy geared toward the interior.

An interesting exception to this rule is a brief intrusion of Gunther Pattern people identified farther south by White (1991) in Mendocino County just north of Fort Bragg. The site (MEN-428B) is located next to a lagoon (Inglenook Fen) and was occupied between cal A.D. 270 and 500. It contained many northern artifact types including Gunther barbed projectile points, small concave-based harpoon tips, elk bone chisels, and stone mauls. Almost all the obsidian in the site came from the northern Medicine Lake Highlands source area (as opposed to Clear Lake), and the faunal assemblage was dominated by elk and offshore birds, a pattern also similar to findings from northern sites at places like Stone Lagoon (except for the absence of seal and sea lion bone). This discovery led White (1991) to conclude that the initial colonization of northwest California by Gunther Pattern people (probably Algic speakers) extended well south of their ultimate range but retracted to the more northerly areas (e.g., north of Cape Mendocino), where the presence of offshore rocks and islands allowed the more maritime-oriented subsistence economy to develop and flourish up to historic contact.

The interior record of the northern counties is less clear due to the absence of large-scale excavations. Tushingham's (2005) late period components on the Smith River revealed a riverine village including plank houses (DNO-26, DNO-1), Gunther barbed projectile points, net sinkers, fishing gear, mortars and pestles, and a wide range of other residential materials (e.g., steatite pipes) postdating cal A.D. 1000. The small sample of faunal remains from the site included salmon as well as sea mammal and marine shellfish, showing economic connections to the coast.

AUGUSTINE PATTERN (POST CAL A.D. 500) A contrasting archaeological pattern is revealed in the southern counties. Known as the Augustine Pattern, it includes rattlesnake corner-notched projectile points (Figure 7.5) that extend up to the Sonoma-Mendocino County line, where they overlap with the Gunther series points (see Jaffke 1997). In the vicinity of its homeland in the Sacramento–San Joaquin Delta region, the Augustine Pattern is associated with a large-scale ceremonial complex including *Olivella* and clamshell disk beads, magnesite cylinder, and "banjo" *Haliotis* ornaments, bird bone whistles and tubes, and flanged steatite pipes. Preinterment burning with tightly flexed burials was relatively common, while cremation of high-status individuals has also been observed (Bennyhoff 1994b).

The full complement of Augustine Pattern traits has not been found in northwest California, and there appears to be a great deal of socioeconomic variability across the region, even within the Pomoan linguistic area (Jones and Hayes 1993). Some places reveal a continuance of the sedentary systems initiated by the Berkeley Pattern (SON-159; Keswick 1990), while others show mobile adaptations, sometimes even more mobile and dispersed than the Berkeley adaptation that preceded it. Dowdall (2002) has encountered the latter situation on the Sonoma County coast, where the Augustine Pattern is represented only by seasonal occupation (SON-458, SON-250/H, SON-670/H), as opposed to the more sedentary system reflected by the earlier Berkeley Pattern archaeological record. Work at Fort Ross by Lightfoot et al. (1991) also found short-term use of the outer coast, which appears to have been linked to a series of centralized villages located on the nearby ridgelines (SON-1883, SON-1884). More permanent occupations have also been observed at the open air component at Duncan's Landing (SON-348/H), where Kennedy's (2005) stable isotope analyses reveal multiple seasons of use.

A high degree of variability is also seen on the interior. Basgall and Bouey's (1991) work at Warm Springs reveals an increased number of sites in habitats that were not used before. Many of these sites are small and were occupied for short periods of time, and produced both mortar-pestle and handstone-millingslab technology (SON-553, SON-556, SON-567, SON-568). The diversification of habitat use and ground stone technology appears to represent a more intensive use of the local resource base. Rather than representing a more mobile adaptation like that seen by Dowdall (2002) on the coast, Basgall and Bouey (1991) think most of the small sites were linked to centralized villages found in a limited number of places along the major drainages (but none have been excavated). Most researchers have also argued for a centralized village pattern at Clear Lake, but large-scale excavations have yet to be accomplished at Augustine Pattern sites in this area either, as clearly illustrated by White et al.'s (2002) findings, which do not postdate cal A.D. 800.

RESEARCH THEMES IN NORTHWEST CALIFORNIA

The foregoing review identifies numerous subsistence, settlement, and socioeconomic changes in prehistoric northwest California. Some of these changes are clearly defined within certain parts of the region, but in other areas we know very little. In the latter situations, our lack of knowledge is often due to the absence of a well-defined archaeological record. There are also cases where a record exists but goes unnoticed or is misunderstood because it does not conform to currently recognized artifact typologies or our preconceived notions of unilinear evolutionism. With these considerations in mind, this chapter concludes with a discussion of four major research themes. Each theme highlights important breakthroughs in the study of prehistoric northwest California, but also identifies where research efforts should be focused in the future.

The first theme focuses on the origin of intensive coastal adaptations in northwest California, and why the relatively late emergence of this ocean-dominated subsistence strategy differs from central and southern California, where marine resource use originates deep in the prehistoric past. The origin of the salmon-acorn economies observed along the great northern river valleys is then addressed, emphasizing uncertainties as to when and how this important adaptation began. A third important theme comes from recent findings in the Clear Lake area that have led us to reevaluate traditional views regarding the antiquity of acorn use, the relationship between acorn processing and mortar and pestle technology, and how these activities are linked to storage and the origin of sedentary settlement systems in prehistoric California. Finally, the socioeconomic florescence of the Berkeley Pattern is addressed, giving specific attention to why it developed in some places and not others, and why it was replaced in certain areas by a more mobile adaptation later in time. The latter situation is particularly significant as there are numerous places elsewhere in California, the Great Basin, and the Southwest where similar shifts have occurred, but these shifts have rarely been recognized in northwest California.

Origin of Intensive Coastal Use: Does It Really Postdate 1000 cal B.C. in Northwest California?

A substantial Early Holocene archaeological record exists along the southern and central coasts of California, including many Millingstone sites clustered around ancient estuary habitats (see Chapters 4, 14–15 in this volume). This is not the case in northwest California. There are hints of an Early and Middle Holocene record at Duncan's Landing and Bodega Bay, and some terrestrially focused Mendocino Pattern sites farther north, but there is no evidence of long-term habitation or focused marine resource use until the Late Holocene. Some have argued that the north coast should have the same settlement chronology as southern and central California, suggesting that the absence of early sites is due to a higher degree of destruction from Holocene sea level rise, fluvial erosion during periods of high rainfall, or insufficient archaeological investigation (i.e., the sites exist but haven't been found yet; see Jones 1991). An alternative view is that the higher productivity of interior habitats—dense concentrations of salmon, elk, and deer—resulted in a much later use of coastal resources such as shellfish, particularly when compared to the south coast where salmon and elk are completely absent, and interior habitats are much more desert-like in character (Hildebrandt and Carpenter 2006; Hildebrandt and Levulett 1997).

Ultimate resolution of this debate will require a more systematic approach to survey and excavation. Some of this work has already been accomplished along the King Range coast where early materials have not been found despite the fact that its coastal terraces have been uplifting at a rate greater than the sea

(Hildebrandt and Levulett 1997; Levulett 1985). The next step is to continue to focus on old landforms (i.e., Pleistocene or older terraces), particularly near estuary habitats that either are extant (e.g., Humboldt Bay, Lake Earl) or may have existed in the past (e.g., at the mouths of major streams). With regard to the latter settings, researchers should attempt to find shell midden sites containing a mix of species that differ from what is available from current intertidal settings, as nonindigenous species could reflect different, more ancient ecological conditions. Some headway has been made in the Bodega Bay area, but much work remains to be done along the estuary and lagoon habitats north of Cape Mendocino.

Origin of the Intensive Salmon-Acorn Economy Along the Northern River Valleys: Did It Emerge at 1500 cal B.C. or After cal A.D. 500 with the Arrival of the Gunther Pattern?

A similar but more localized debate surrounds the origins of the salmon-acorn complex observed at historic contact among the interior Tolowa, Yurok, Wiyot, Hupa, and Karuk. Early work by Bennyhoff (1950) indicated that long-term storage of these important resources occurred quite late and was associated with the arrival of the Gunther Pattern after cal A.D. 500. Hildebrandt and Hayes (1993) predicted that the more sedentary adaptation must have happened at about 1500 cal B.C. based on a shift in the uplands from residential use (represented by the Borax Lake Pattern) to specialized hunting at Mendocino Pattern sites. They supported their position with a limited amount of lowland data not directly associated with the major northern rivers (e.g., the McKee Flat site on the Mattole River).

Until quite recently, contributions to this debate have been silent, as no excavations have occurred on the interior. Tushingham's work on the Smith River has been an important exception to this situation. In addition to documenting a post cal A.D. 1000 Gunther Pattern village, her discovery of a component with plank houses and trace amounts of acorn and salmon bone predating 500 cal B.C. may indicate the beginnings of the sedentary adaptation. If this turns out to be the case, then the origins of the salmon-acorn complex conform with the Hildebrandt-Hayes hypothesis, making it necessary to define a new pattern for these findings, as they contrast significantly with the Mendocino Pattern with its high degree of residential mobility, relatively sparse assemblages of artifacts and features, and lack of well-developed midden soils.

Plant Macrofossils, Mortars and Pestles, and the Origin of Intensive Acorn Use

Basgall's outstanding (1987) work on northern California's acorn economies proposed that high processing costs associated with tannic acid leaching made acorns an expensive resource that was not intensively used until after 500 cal B.C. in northwest California. This conclusion, however, is based on the assumed association between mortars and pestles and the use of acorns. More recent investigations at Clear Lake and elsewhere in California have produced data supporting an alternative view of prehistoric acorn use. Plant macrofossil data from early Holocene components at Clear Lake, Los Vaqueros (Contra Costa County), and the Sky Rocket site (Calaveras County) show that acorns were a primary resource at this early time, but associated with handstone-millingslab technology, not mortars and pestles. Rather than the handstone-millingslab complex being associated with small seeds, and mortars/pestles with acorns, plant macrofossil data indicate that small seeded plants are actually added to the diet late in time (similar to many other places in North America) and that different types of milling gear are more highly linked to settlement organization (Rosenthal and McGuire 2004; Wohlgemuth 2004). Although some have suggested that the earliest uses of acorn could have depended on passive leaching in wetland settings and not have required sophisticated milling gear (White et al. 2002; Wohlgemuth 2004), it seems more likely that people operating within a mobile system of settlement who could not carry their milling gear (e.g., Borax Lake and Mendocino Pattern) would have used the more expedient handstone and millingslab, which could be produced on demand with little investment. Mortars and pestles, in contrast, are more costly to produce but more efficient at processing food resources, and should only occur among more sedentary peoples who could rely on the regular use of their tools (Rosenthal and McGuire 2004).

This is a very important breakthrough, as it helps explain why (1) mortars and pestles were not accepted and used simultaneously throughout northwest California, (2) mortars and pestles are not typically found in Early Holocene contexts even though acorn plant macrofossils are, and (3) mobile peoples (e.g., the Mendocino Pattern) didn't use mortars and pestles but often occupied areas containing multiple species of acorns.

The Rise and Fall of the Berkeley Pattern: Where, When, and Why?

The Berkeley Pattern represents a cultural climax within the southern portion of northwest California between 600 cal B.C. and cal A.D. 800. It differs from the surrounding Mendocino Pattern by having higher degrees of sedentism evidenced by well-defined house floors, rich midden deposits, and seasonal indicators spanning most of the year. According to White et al. (2002), control and administration of superabundant resources like the spring fish runs allowed certain people to develop increasing amounts of wealth and power by participating in large-scale exchange systems. As these exchange relationships developed and local commodities were moved greater distances to outlying areas, they helped fuel a more intensified use of the local resource base. Ultimately it appears that colonizing populations moved out of the Clear Lake core, spreading west through Warm Springs and out to the coast, bringing with them archaeological indicators we recognize as the Berkeley Pattern.

By roughly cal A.D. 800 the Berkeley Pattern came to a close and was replaced by the Augustine Pattern. Many researchers have assumed or expected that the sociopolitical complexity and high levels of intergroup exchange continued forward or even intensified over time, reaching peak intensity just before historic contact. But where is the archaeological record supporting this presumed outcome of unilinear evolutionism? It doesn't exist on the coast where Dowdall (2002) finds more ephemeral occupations and a decline in the use of obsidian. Warm Springs also sees a decline in obsidian from Clear Lake, and a shift to the use of numerous small sites, although these are assumed to have been tied to large village hubs that have not yet been excavated (Basgall and Bouey 1991). Even at Clear Lake, obsidian production at the quarries and adjacent sites essentially collapses after cal A.D. 800 (see White et al. 2002:449), and little is known about the Augustine Pattern. While it is true that increasing levels of complexity occur in many places late in time (e.g., the Gunther Pattern north of Cape Mendocino or the Augustine Pattern in the delta region), this is not necessarily the case in many parts of California, where there appears to be a decentralization of population, with people converting to smaller groups and more mobile settlement systems. This settlement shift has been noted on San Francisco Bay, where large Middle Period settlements (like the Berkeley Pattern) appear to be replaced by a dispersion of much smaller sites (Lightfoot and Luby 2002).

This is also the case in the Great Basin, where Numic family bands expanded throughout the region after cal A.D. 1000, sometimes replacing sedentary horticulturists like the Fremont and western Anasazi (Bettinger and Baumhoff 1982; McGuire and Hildebrandt 2005). Rather than assuming increasing levels of sociopolitical complexity over time and presuming that the ethnographic record reflects a cultural climax, California archaeologists should carefully (and objectively) compare the post cal A.D. 1000 records to those that came before. Such an analysis may reveal that, similar to the Great Basin and many parts of the Southwest, cultural expressions like the Berkeley Pattern are unique and significantly different from the late prehistoric and ethnographic patterns. Just as archaeologists studying Anasazi and Fremont would balk at using Paiute-Shoshone ethnographies to explain their prehistoric records, it is critical for California archaeologists to consider these same constraints when attempting to understand the deep and varied archaeological record of our state.

CHAPTER 8

Punctuated Culture Change in the San Francisco Bay Area

Randall Milliken, Richard T. Fitzgerald, Mark G. Hylkema, Randy Groza, Tom Origer, David G. Bieling, Alan Leventhal, Randy S. Wiberg, Andrew Gottsfield, Donna Gillette, Viviana Bellifemine, Eric Strother, Robert Cartier, and David A. Fredrickson

The San Francisco Bay Area supported a dense hunter-gatherer population over thousands of years, a population that has left a rich and varied archaeological record. When Spanish settlements were established in 1776, the Bay Area was a place of incredible language diversity. Seven languages were spoken—Southern Pomo, Wappo, Patwin, Coast Miwok, Bay Miwok, Karkin Costanoan, and San Francisco Bay Costanoan (Figures 8.1, 8.2). The diverse ecosystem of the bay and surrounding lands supported an average of three to five persons per square mile, but reached over six persons per square mile in the Los Altos–Palo Alto vicinity in the South Bay and 11 persons per square mile in the Petaluma River basin in the North Bay (Milliken 1995a:19–21).

At Spanish contact, the Bay Area people were organized into local tribelets that defended fixed territories under independent leaders (Kroeber 1932). Typically, individual Bay Area tribelets included 200 to 400 people distributed among three to five semipermanent villages, within territories approximately 10 to 12 miles in diameter (Milliken 1995a). Bean and Lawton (1973) describe aspects of contact period regional organization as follows:

> Within the aboriginal social-religious institutions . . . smoothly articulated intergroup relationships were regulated by . . . secret societies or cults, confirming and demonstrating who had economic and political privileges, always supported in a ritual and cosmological referent of some sort. These institutions were responsible for distributing energy within the various subsystems, so that temporal or spatially related inequities in food and other economic goods could both be alleviated or maintained, depending on the particular needs of the corporate group. (Bean and Lawton 1973)

The distribution of artifacts in protohistoric sites—clamshell disk beads, distinctive *Haliotis* pendants, flanged steatite pipes, chevron-etched bone whistles and tubes, elaborately finished stone "flower pot" mortars, and needle-sharp coiled basketry awls—reflects the relative complexity of the native world at the Spanish arrival.

In 1984 both Moratto and the Chartkoffs dated the appearance of complex hunter-gatherer societies in the Bay Area to about 4,000 years ago, and both argued that complexity increased from that time forward. Both authors looked to population growth as a stimulus for resource intensification, increased cooperation, and social stratification (Chartkoff and Chartkoff 1984:227–237; Moratto 1984:276, 281–283). Moratto (1984) differed from the Chartkoffs (1984) by incorporating "language group migration" into his explanatory model. He posited that proto-Utians (ancestors of all Costanoan and Miwok-speaking groups) entered the East Bay about 4,500 years ago and then expanded throughout the Bay Area at the expense of forager groups who spoke Hokan languages. Subsequent development took place, he suggested, through internal change within the Utian population, with final Augustine Period development driven by indirect influence from Wintuan populations expanding into the North Bay (Moratto 1984:283). Chartkoff and Chartkoff (1984:205) rejected the importance of language group migration as an explanation, and instead asserted that new kinship systems were the innovation that freed people to increase status differentiation and develop rational regional institutions (Chartkoff and Chartkoff 1984:149–150).

The San Francisco Bay Area archaeological record as of the early 1980s has been summarized by Moratto (1984:227–237, 252–283). As ground disturbance has continued in the Bay Area since then, so too has archaeological fieldwork. Large-area survey, common in rural California, seldom takes place in the urban Bay Area. Instead, sites are usually encountered prior to or during

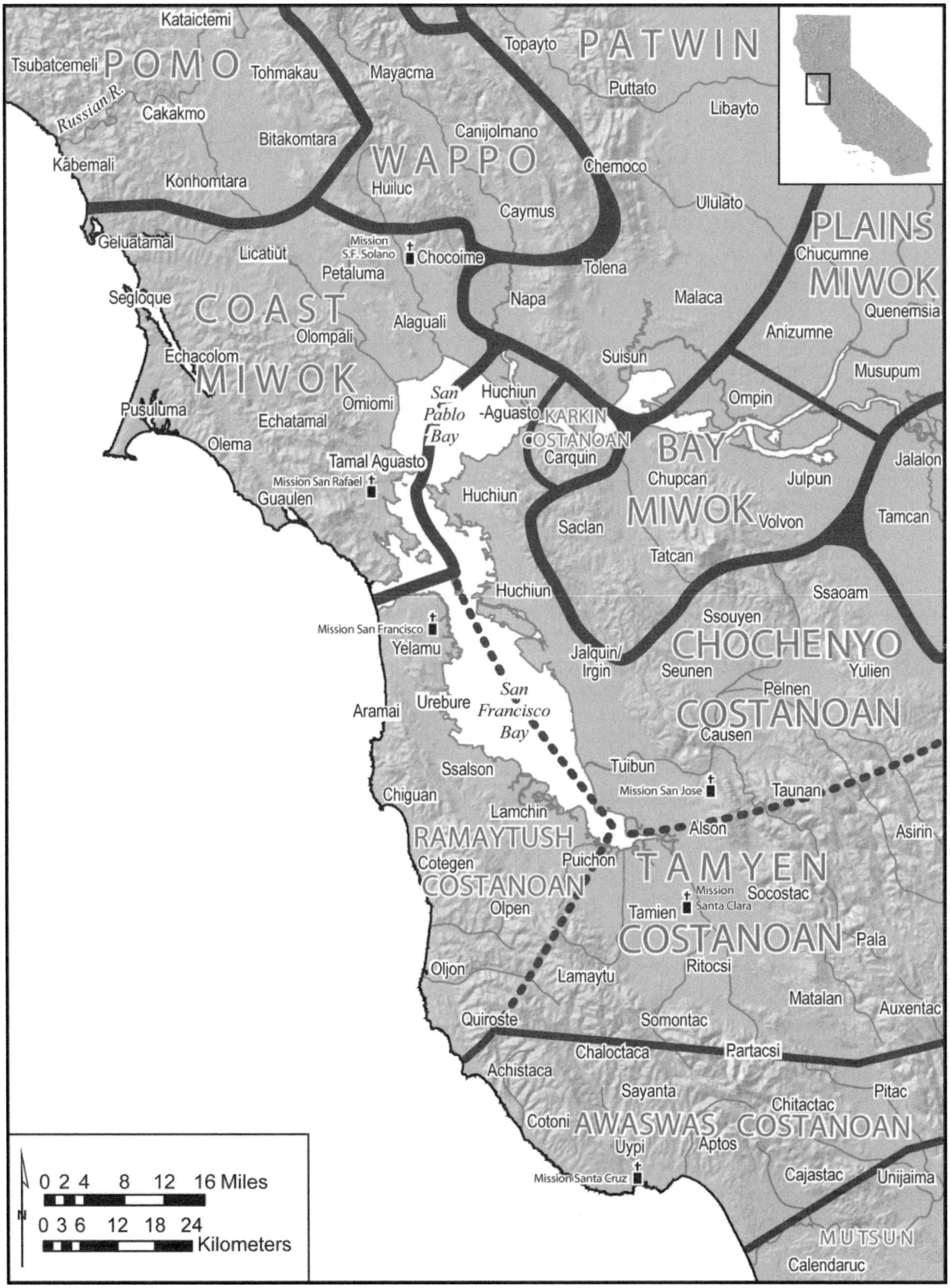

Figure 8.1. San Francisco Bay Area language groups and local, multivillage tribal communities.

Figure 8.2. Dancers and audience in the plaza of Mission Delores (San Francisco) in October 1816, by L. Choris. (Courtesy of the Bancroft Library, University of California–Berkeley.)

land alteration for new home and industrial park development, urban redevelopment, highway construction, or linear underground utility installation. Figure 8.3 shows the locations of 200 prehistoric Bay Area sites with dated components critical to the interpretation of San Francisco Bay Area prehistory. Of the 200 sites, 93 (46 percent) were first studied prior to January 1, 1983, while the other 107 (54 percent) have been reported since that date. Santa Clara and San Francisco Counties have seen the greatest relative amount of post-1982 study, while Marin and Contra Costa Counties have seen relatively little (Table 8.1).

The initial sections of this chapter update topical themes—chronological and taxonomic issues, settlement systems, subsistence patterns, mortuary patterns, and physical anthropology. The final section takes a sequential approach. It describes cycles of change in Bay Area prehistory—population growth, economic intensification, symbolic integration, conflict, then crash—along a trajectory of generally increasing cultural complexity.

CHRONOLOGICAL AND TAXONOMIC ISSUES

A Hybrid Cultural Taxonomy

The San Francisco Bay Area is the meeting ground of two different systems for organizing the archaeological record into coherent units of observation and comparison.

- The Early-Middle-Late Period nomenclature of Beardsley (1954), dubbed the Central California Taxonomic System (CCTS) by Gerow (1968), is used by South Bay archaeologists (Bellifemine 1997; Cartier et al. 1993; Hylkema 2002) and some Central Bay archaeologists (Broughton 1999; Lightfoot and Luby 2002).
- The *Archaic-Emergent* temporal structure of Fredrickson (1973, 1994a), with specific cultural configurations identified by economic patterns, stylistic aspects, and temporally constricted regional phases, is used by North Bay archaeologists (Stewart 2003; White et al. 2002) and some Central Bay archaeologists (Meyer and Rosenthal 1997).
- A hybrid system, marking large blocks of time with the Early-Middle-Late Period structure and differentiating units of culture with Fredrickson's pattern, aspect, and phase concepts, is used by some Central Bay archaeologists (cf. Banks and Orlins 1985:28–51; Wiberg 1996a:123–128, 1997:9–17).

The third alternative, the hybrid system using the Early-Middle-Late Period *temporal sequence* (with all earlier post-Pleistocene times lumped as the Early Holocene) and the pattern-aspect-phase *cultural sequence*, is used in this chapter (Figure 8.4). The hybrid

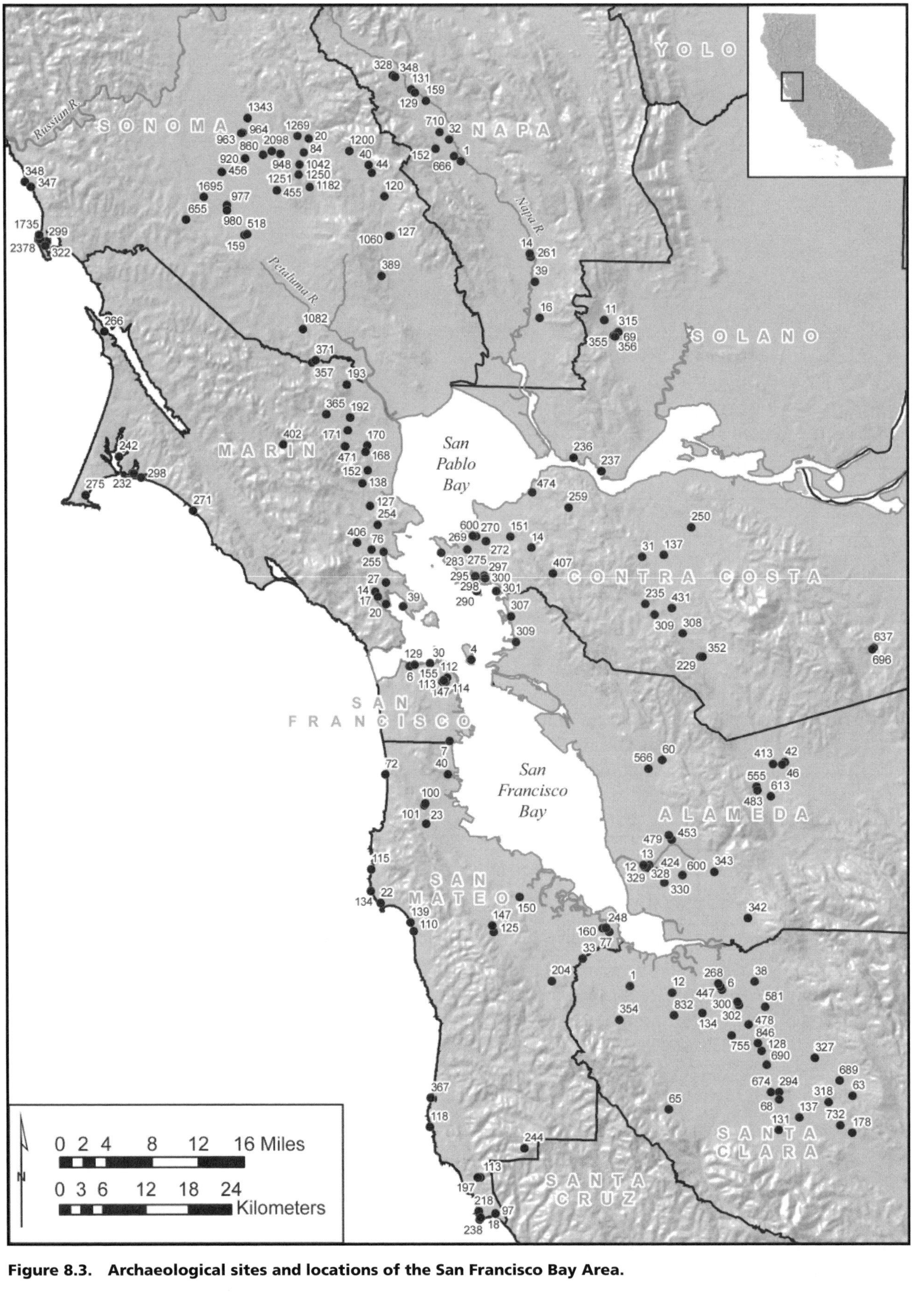

Figure 8.3. Archaeological sites and locations of the San Francisco Bay Area.

Table 8.1. Counts of Sites Mapped on Figure 8.3 by County, Differentiating Pre- and Post-January 1, 1983, Reports and Noting Density of Reported Sites

County	*Sites Mapped on Figure 8.3*	*Pre-Jan. 1983 Reports*	*Post-Jan. 1983 Reports*	*Bay Area Land (square miles)*	*Square Miles per Mapped Site*
Alameda	21	12 (57%)	11 (43%)	780	37
Contra Costa	28	21 (75%)	7 (25%)	580	21
Marin	28	21 (75%)	7 (25%)	588	21
Napa	14	6 (43%)	8 (57%)	500	36
San Francisco	10	2 (20%)	8 (80%)	91	9
San Mateo	26	9 (35%)	17 (65%)	531	20
Santa Clara	30	6 (20%)	24 (80%)	760	25
Solano	7	3 (43%)	4 (57%)	170	24
Sonoma	36	13 (36%)	23 (64%)	740	20
Total	200	93 (46%)	107 (54%)	4,740	24

taxonomic system has the advantage of allowing the identification of regional aspects within larger cultural patterns, as well as allowing subdivision of cultural patterns into short sequential phases of 200- to 300-year duration, when data are available. In deference to North Bay nomenclature, however, Archaic-Emergent equivalents to the Early, Middle, and Late Periods are selectively added below in parentheses.

Patterns, Phases, Aspects, and Localities

Definitions for the concepts of pattern, phase, and aspect are explained here as we use them in this chapter, following Fredrickson (1973, 1994a). The term *locality* is explained both as Fredrickson (1973, 1994a) used it and in the different way we use it in this chapter.

Patterns are units of culture marked by distinct underlying economic modes, technological adaptations, and ceremonial practices (Fredrickson 1994a:39–47). Separate patterns could co-occur in restricted geographical areas. For instance, during the Early Period (Middle Archaic) the range of Mendocino Pattern mobile foragers overlapped the territories of Lower Berkeley Pattern sedentary villagers in the northernmost portions of the San Francisco Bay Area.

Phases, following terminology developed by Willey and Phillips (1958), are the smallest units of related site components "spatially limited to the order of magnitude of a locality or region and chronologically limited to a relatively brief interval of time" (Fredrickson 1994a:34). Phases in most parts of California, and most areas of the world, tend to be anywhere from 500 to many thousands of years long. But Bennyhoff (1994c:74) isolated sequences of short cultural phases of 200- to 300-year duration for many parts of the Late Holocene San Francisco Bay Area. Names of the local phases, such as Castro and River Glenn, derive from type sites (Bennyhoff 1986; Fredrickson 1973, 1994a). We consider documentation of such named phases crucial for future comparative research, but beyond the scope of the current overview (for phase seriation of artifacts, see Moore [1982]).

Aspect is the term Fredrickson coined to identify a local variation of one of his major economic patterns. "A sequence of phases within a single district is referred to herein as an *aspect.* Both phases (during a single time interval) and aspects (usually covering several time intervals) are district representatives of a pattern, a generalized cultural configuration usually encompassing one or more regions" (Fredrickson 1994a:35). Under the hybrid taxonomic system, Beardsley's (1954) Bay Area Stege, Ellis Landing, and Fernandez facies are considered to be San Francisco Bay Aspects of the more widely distributed Lower Berkeley, Upper Berkeley, and Augustine Patterns. Also under the hybrid system, the long phases of the South Bay chronology, such as Metcalf Creek and Sandhill Bluff, become aspects of a pertinent pattern (Figure 8.4).

Locality, according to Fredrickson (1973), is a "geographical space which exhibits complete cultural homogeneity at any given time." For purposes of inquiry, research, and comparison, the Bay Area has been divided into 18 localities in this chapter. Fredrickson's locality could change shape over time. In contrast, the localities of this chapter, such as "the San Mateo Coast," the "Santa Rosa Plain," and "the Livermore Valley," are fixed geographic areas, approximately 16 miles in diameter. We can be fairly certain that before the Spanish arrival, contemporaneous archaeological sites within each locality would have been created by people who interacted directly with one another, whether or not they shared a specific culture.

Shell Bead Horizons and Dating Scheme D

The cultural patterns, aspects, and phases of the Bay Area are anchored in time by Dating Scheme D, a pan-

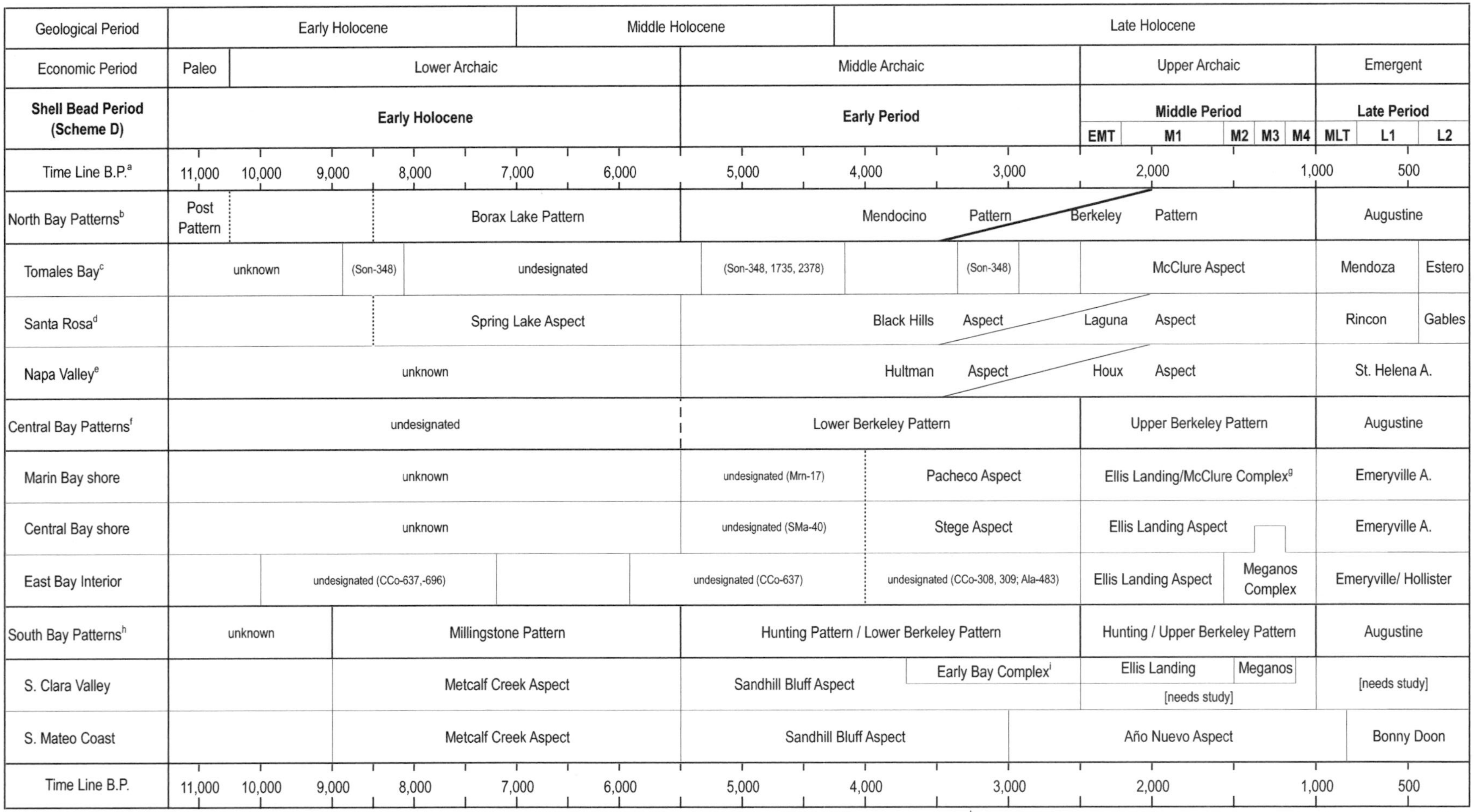
Geological Period
Early Holocene
Middle Holocene
Late Holocene
Economic Period
Paleo
Lower Archaic
Middle Archaic
Upper Archaic
Emergent
Shell Bead Period (Scheme D)
Early Holocene
Early Period
Middle Period
Late Period
EMT
M1
M2
M3
M4
MLT
L1
L2
Time Line B.P.[a]
11,000
10,000
9,000
8,000
7,000
6,000
5,000
4,000
3,000
2,000
1,000
500
North Bay Patterns[b]
Post Pattern
Borax Lake Pattern
Mendocino Pattern
Berkeley Pattern
Augustine
Tomales Bay[c]
unknown
(Son-348)
undesignated
(Son-348, 1735, 2378)
(Son-348)
McClure Aspect
Mendoza
Estero
Santa Rosa[d]
Spring Lake Aspect
Black Hills Aspect
Laguna Aspect
Rincon
Gables
Napa Valley[e]
unknown
Hultman Aspect
Houx Aspect
St. Helena A.
Central Bay Patterns[f]
undesignated
Lower Berkeley Pattern
Upper Berkeley Pattern
Augustine
Marin Bay shore
unknown
undesignated (Mrn-17)
Pacheco Aspect
Ellis Landing/McClure Complex[g]
Emeryville A.
Central Bay shore
unknown
undesignated (SMa-40)
Stege Aspect
Ellis Landing Aspect
Emeryville A.
East Bay Interior
undesignated (CCo-637,-696)
undesignated (CCo-637)
undesignated (CCo-308, 309; Ala-483)
Ellis Landing Aspect
Meganos Complex
Emeryville/ Hollister
South Bay Patterns[h]
unknown
Millingstone Pattern
Hunting Pattern / Lower Berkeley Pattern
Hunting / Upper Berkeley Pattern
Augustine
S. Clara Valley
Metcalf Creek Aspect
Sandhill Bluff Aspect
Early Bay Complex[i]
Ellis Landing
Meganos
[needs study]
[needs study]
S. Mateo Coast
Metcalf Creek Aspect
Sandhill Bluff Aspect
Año Nuevo Aspect
Bonny Doon
Time Line B.P.
11,000
10,000
9,000
8,000
7,000
6,000
5,000
4,000
3,000
2,000
1,000
500

Note: [a] Time periods here are based on calibrated radiocarbon dates and absolute time, causing the Pleistocene/Holocene divide to shift from 10,000 to 11,500 B.P.; [b] North Bay patterns follow White et al. (2002), who has modified Fredrickson (1973); [c] Tomales Bay aspects follow Beardsley (1954) with components at Duncans Landing noted (Kennedy 2005); [d] Santa Rosa aspects follow Fredrickson (1989); [e] Napa Valley aspects follow Fredrickson (1984:515); [f] Central Bay aspects follow Bennyhoff (1994c:74); [g] Marin bayshore Upper Berkeley Pattern components suggest a complex of Ellis Landing and McClure Aspect elements (Goerke and Cowan 1983:63); [h] Patterns and aspects in the South Bay, encompassing San Jose, Santa Teresa, and Point Año Nuevo localities, are from Hylkema (2002); [i] Early Bay Complex is distinguished at University Village site (SMa-77) because it mixes central bay Stege Aspect (Ala-307) ornaments and tools with a flaked tool assemblage typical of the south bay Sandhill Bluffs Aspect.

Figure 8.4. Concordance of archaeological time periods, patterns, and aspects in the San Francisco Bay Area.

central California sequence of directly dated *Olivella* shell bead horizons. Scheme D is the fourth radiocarbon-based sequence available for central California. The first such scheme, here called Scheme A, was introduced in 1958 by R. F. Heizer on the basis of 17 radiocarbon dates. In 1984, central California archaeologists, including the Chartkoffs and authors in the Moratto volume, relied on Dating Scheme A. It is a "long" chronology, placing the beginning of the Late Horizon (Late Period) at A.D. 300 to 500 (uncalibrated radiocarbon years).

Dating Scheme B was introduced by Bennyhoff and Hughes in their 1987 *Olivella* shell bead monograph. It was based on 180 central California radiocarbon dates from charcoal, collagen, and shell; the dates were neither calibrated nor corrected for the marine reservoir effect. Scheme B moved the Middle/Late Period Transition (MLT) forward to A.D. 700 to 900. Elsasser (1978:41) proposed a compromise between Schemes A and B that was labeled Scheme C by Bennyhoff and Hughes (1987:147).

Dating Scheme D was developed by Groza (2002) in consultation with a consortium of archaeologists and in cooperation with the Indian community. It was initially based on 103 AMS radiocarbon dates on well-provenienced *Olivella* beads representing 10 of Bennyhoff's 11 bead horizons (Early/Middle Transition beads were not sampled). The new radiocarbon dates shift many shell bead horizons forward in time as much as 200 years. (See Chapter 17, Figure 17.2 for a representation of the Scheme D Late Holocene time periods in relation to the southern California temporal sequence.)

The notation used in this chapter for the Scheme D shell bead horizons is new. Bennyhoff and Hughes (1987) labeled 11 Scheme B shell bead horizons within the Early, Middle, and Late Periods as *phases,* the same term Bennyhoff (1986) elsewhere applied to regionally restricted cultural units. We use the term *bead horizon* instead of *phase* for the short time periods marked by trade of particular bead types across wide areas of central California, in order to clearly separate units of time and units of culture. In our nomenclature, the Early Period/Middle Period Transition bead horizon (marked by split-beveled *Olivella* beads) can be noted as the EMT. Bead horizons of the subsequent Middle Period are labeled M1, M2, M3, and M4; each has its own signature shell bead array. The MLT (Middle Period/Late Period Transition) and Late Period bead horizons L1 and L2 follow. (No shorthand is used for the Early Period, since it has yet to be divided into shorter bead horizons.) We reiterate that the bead horizons are units of *time*, with no cultural implications other than the fact that they are defined by widely traded shell bead types.

Summary: A Complex Taxonomy for a Complex Prehistory

The large number of separate prehistoric Bay Area cultural aspects are shown in Figure 8.4. The figure is a nightmare of detail to novices and archaeologists with "lumper" predilections, yet it represents real and significant variation in time and space. Aspect-defining artifacts for three localities in or near the San Francisco Bay Area are illustrated in Figures 8.5 (Santa Rosa Locality), 8.6 (San Mateo Coast Locality), and 8.7 (Los Vaqueros Locality, east edge of the Central Bay Area). See pages 119–123.

SETTLEMENT SYSTEMS

Since the 1980s Bay Area researchers have sought to interpret settlement systems within Binford's (1980) forager-collector model, which posits two extremes of hunter-gatherer behavior: mobile small bands versus storage-oriented central place villagers (cf. Polansky 1998). T. F. King (1974b) suggested synchronic variations along the forager-collector cline in the Bay Area during the Middle Period, with inhabitants of bay shore Marin County living in sedentary villages nestled in rich heterogeneous environments, in contrast with inhabitants of the Fremont Plain, who moved seasonally between marsh edge villages and camps in upland oak groves.

Years earlier, Beardsley (1955:138–139) contrasted the *central-based wandering model*, in which a community "spends part of each year wandering and the rest at a settlement or central base to which it may or may not consistently return in subsequent years" with the *semipermanent sedentary model*, in which a community "can be identified with a village that establishes itself in successive locations, occupying each for several years." More recently, Banks and Orlins (1981) presented a version of the central-based wandering model on the basis of historic evidence for San Francisco Peninsula tribelets at the time of the Spanish arrival. Tribelet populations on that landscape were divided among three to five specific villages, some or all of which relocated more than once a year. Because the system was used by territorially restricted groups in a densely populated landscape, it should not be confused with a mobile forager strategy. Banks and Orlins (1981) called it a *periodically mobile home base* model.

North Bay

In the North Bay, a concept of concurrent landscape use by settled collectors and wide-ranging mobile foragers was introduced by Wickstrom (1986) for part of the Late Holocene in the Santa Rosa Locality. Jones and Hayes (1989:16–18; 1993) refined the Santa Rosa Locality land-use sequence. They classified site components into site types (task-specific locations, residential camps, and semipermanent villages), then stratified them by time (primarily using obsidian hydration) and environmental zones (Jones and Hayes 1989:229). The pattern that emerged suggested Paleo-Indian forager use of lacustrine zones, followed by Lower Archaic (Early Holocene) and Middle Archaic (Middle Holocene and Early Period) forager residential camps along marshes and on grasslands, succeeded by Upper Archaic (Middle Period, i.e., after 500 cal B.C.) "concurrent use" by people using forager residential camps and people using semipermanent collector villages, finally leading to Emergent (Late Period, i.e., post cal A.D. 1000) semipermanent collector villages in oak woodlands, with residential camps along marshes.

Fredrickson (1989a) offered an analysis of changing North Bay settlement and chronology similar to that of Jones and Hayes (1989), but specific to the Laguna de Santa Rosa area along the west side of the Santa Rosa Plain. He proposed that overlapping use of the Laguna area by foragers (Black Hills Phase of the Mendocino Pattern) and collectors (Laguna Phase of the Berkeley Pattern) occurred between 1500 cal B.C. and cal A.D. 1. Later, Jones and Hayes (1993) redated the period of forager-collector overlap to cal A.D. 500 to 1000.

South Bay

In the 1970s King and Hickman (1973) proposed that Late Period settlement in the Gilroy-Hollister area (south of the San Francisco Bay Area) utilized valley-edge logistical centers, with special task locations in the higher uplands and along marsh edges. In the 1980s prehistorians tested the applicability of the model to the San Jose Locality at the south end of San Francisco Bay and the inland Santa Teresa Locality between San Jose and Gilroy (see Elsasser 1986). Bergthold (1982) showed that the large residential villages of the northern Santa Clara Valley were typically out in the center of the valley along perennial streams, but she lacked the temporal evidence necessary for documenting change or continuity of settlement pattern over time. Cartier et al. (1993:54) revisited Bergthold's model with new temporal evidence, suggesting that some settlement shifts occurred in the Santa Teresa Locality about 2,000 years ago and arguing for a population drop in the San Jose Locality at the end of the Middle Period.

Early mobile forager land use gave way to semisedentary collector land use in the South Bay by the outset of the Middle Period (Upper Archaic) at about 500 cal B.C., according to a recent synthesis by Hylkema (2002:233, 250). By cal A.D. 700 that collector pattern was trending toward the more complex social organization that would lead to the rich midden central sites of the Late Period. Meanwhile the forager system persisted through the Middle Period on the nearby San Mateo coast to the west; it did not change to the collector mode until the Late Period, after cal A.D. 1200. When coastal area people did shift to a collector economy (with mortar and pestle predominance at central sites), they developed a specialized transhumance pattern between upland meadows and coastal terrace—summer hunting for juvenile deer in the uplands, then winter otter and harbor seal hunting on the coast (Hylkema 2002:255).

Central Bay

Central Bay settlement pattern studies have been time stratified and locality based. Banks and Orlins (1981) used the "periodically mobile home base" model that we mentioned above to explain how so many Middle Period residential sites could have been generated in the Richmond Locality of the East Bay. They documented 28 residential sites within a 10 kilometer circle, each containing at least two meters of cultural deposit, and inferred that they were generated by people who utilized only two or three of the sites as semipermanent villages at any one time. The problem for archaeologists, they pointed out, is that sites used as residences during one generation may have been used as special activity locations by other generations, making locality-wide settlement patterns nearly impossible to interpret.

Parkman (1994:45) built a model of "the semisedentary and seasonal nature of the settlement of the southern Alameda County bay shore, an area that is characterized by a broad plain separating the bay shore and bay hills." He pointed out an increase in deer (found in the hills) relative to elk at bay shore sites during the Late Period (citing Hildebrandt et al. 1984; Watts 1984) and argued that Middle Period elk hunters were not as logistically oriented as the Late Period people, who brought deer and processed vegetal foods back from inland foothills to bay shore residential villages during the spring and fall.

Wilson (1999) presented a more complex settlement pattern analysis for the Fremont Plain, modeling differing land use over five time periods—Early, EMT, Middle, MLT, and Late—broken into components using obsidian hydration, radiocarbon dates, and seriated artifacts from eight residential/cemetery sites. He posited light initial residential occupation at the end of the Early Period at ALA-343, six kilometers inland from the bay marshes. He inferred that the bay marsh edge was first settled at the Patterson Mound (ALA-328) at the end of the Early Period, around 600 cal B.C. (Wilson 1999:5). He viewed the Middle Period as a time of competition between two unrelated groups, a marsh-oriented people at ALA-328 and an inland people at ALA-343 who "began challenging ALA-328 for area dominance" (Wilson 1999:6). He inferred that the Late Period was a time of peace and locality-wide integration, on the basis of an increase in identified site components along the bay shore marsh and farther inland. Wilson's study could be strengthened by tracking possible settlement shifts through the four phases of the Middle Period. Nevertheless, the study provides a rare, time-sensitive analysis of site distributions and discusses sites in terms of human communities.

Late Period population and settlement increase around San Francisco Bay has generally been accepted (see Elsasser 1978:43), but some scholars have argued that it actually decreased (Beardsley 1954:84–86; Banks and Orlins 1981; Jones 1992:12–15; Hildebrandt and Jones 1992:378; Holson et al. 2000:24–28). Lightfoot and Luby (2002) examined settlement patterns within a 15 by 15 kilometer area of the Richmond Locality. Most of the sites in their sample were bay shore sites with Middle Period components. Late Period components, on the other hand, were fewer in number and more evenly distributed between bay shore locations and locations three to five kilometers inland. "Some sites that served as mounded villages in the Middle Period were apparently deserted and then later re-used as special-purpose places in the Late Period where individuals continued to be buried and where occasional gatherings and ceremonies took place" (Lightfoot and Luby 2002:277). They concluded that the Middle Period was a golden age of shell mound communities and that population dropped during the Late Period, concurrent with the shift of central sites away from the bay shore (Lightfoot and Luby 2002:276–277).

In order to see if a general shift inland occurred everywhere around the bay, we collated evidence for bay shore and inland habitation at four localities. Our results support a view of decreased bay shore strand occupation in the Richmond Locality. But the decrease occurred after Bead Horizon M1 within the Middle Period rather than at the beginning of the Late Period (Table 8.2). Elsewhere, increased Late Period bay shore occupation is indicated in the San Rafael and Fremont Localities, while Middle to Late Period stability is suggested in the San Jose Locality. All in all, data on settlement shifts are inconclusive due to (1) small sample sizes, (2) geographic bias in past archaeological testing programs, and (3) varying geomorphic processes of site burial.

SUBSISTENCE PATTERNS

Late-twentieth-century research interest in subsistence behavior—from least effort modeling to patch utilization theory to optimal foraging theory—has generated new studies and new insights about Bay Area prehistory. In this section we review selected studies on mammal, shellfish, and plant harvest.

Mammal Harvesting Patterns

Late Holocene faunal exploitation in the South Bay over the past 4,000 years has been characterized as a deer economy by Hildebrandt et al. (1984), utilizing the principles of optimal foraging theory (see Broughton 1999:5–12 for theoretical considerations). Since 1990 numerous faunal studies have been undertaken using intensification theory. Hildebrandt and Jones (1992) studied 11 bay shore sites to document a shift from large-bodied pinniped, especially northern fur seal, dominance in the Early Period (2500 to 500 cal B.C.), to terrestrial large mammal dominance in their Middle Period (500 cal B.C. to cal A.D. 1 [actually the EMT]), to an increase in sea otter and harbor seal in their Late Period (post cal A.D. 1, encompassing most of the Middle and Late Periods). Hylkema (2002:254) noted a shift from large sea mammal exploitation to sea otter exploitation along the San Mateo coast at a later date, the onset of the Late Period.

The concept of the broad-spectrum coharvesting exploitative strategy—short-term local shifts from one resource to another as a flexible adaptive response to resource explosions and crashes—was offered by Simons (1992:73–103) as a description of the central California mode of animal harvest for the entire late Holocene. He documented an increase in the harvest of sea otters, relative to large artiodactyls, on the bay shore during the Middle Period, followed by a rebound of deer exploitation during the Late Period.

Table 8.2. Counts of Site Components (Stratified by Distance from the Bay Shore) at Four Example Localities, Together with Total Count of All Documented Components at the 200 Sites Mapped on Figure 8.3

Locality	*Bead Horizon Phase*									
Distance from Bay	Early 3,000 yrs	EMT 300 yrs	M1 600 yrs	M2 200 yrs	M3 200 yrs	M4 250 yrs	MLT 200 yrs	L1 300 yrs	L2 250 yrs	Total
San Rafael Locality (25 sites)										
0–2 km	2	1	6	1	1	4	4	7	6	32
2–10 km	1	1	0	0	0	1	0	0	2	5
10–16 km	0	0	0	0	0	0	0	0	0	0
% for locality	8	5	16	3	3	14	11	19	22	*100*
Richmond Locality (29 sites)										
0–2 km	5	9	10	7	4	3	3	4	6	51
2–10 km	0	0	1	4	4	3	1	3	3	19
10–16 km	0	0	0	0	0	0	0	0	0	0
% for locality	7	13	16	16	11	9	6	10	13	*100*
Fremont Locality (16 sites)										
0–2 km	0	2	3	3	2	2	2	5	4	23
2–10 km	0	0	1	0	3	1	2	0	1	8
10–16 km	0	0	0	0	0	0	0	0	0	0
% for locality	0	6	13	10	16	10	13	16	16	*100*
San Jose Locality (20 sites)										
0–2 km	1	0	1	0	2	1	3	4	2	14
2–10 km	2	3	4	4	6	4	1	3	1	28
10–16 km	1	0	1	0	0	0	1	2	0	5
% for locality	9	6	13	9	17	11	11	19	6	*100*
Total Bay Area (200 sites)										
Components	61	56	86	60	67	64	67	105	101	667
% of Total	9	8	13	9	10	10	10	16	15	*100*

Hylkema (1991:377; 2002:257) suggested that otters were harvested for their pelts rather than their meat, based on the relative completeness of sea otter skeletal remains at Late Period site SMA-115 on the coast just south of San Francisco. Broughton (1994b) argued that foraging efficiency declined through the Late Holocene on the basis of increasing ratios of otter to deer in 18 temporally discrete Middle and Late Period site components from three localities around the bay. He interpreted the increase of sea otter bone as evidence of deer population decline that may have been partially related to human-deer competition for acorns. When sorted by time, Broughton's components reveal that the shift to otter predominance took place suddenly at the M1/M2 divide, about cal A.D. 425 to 475, when a new cultural pattern, the Meganos Aspect, was spreading into the East Bay. The suddenness of the otter bone increase leads us to suggest a cultural interpretation, that the new group may have desired sea otter pelts for cloaks or vests.

A buffer zone patch exploitation model was offered by Broughton (1999) to explain an artiodactyl rebound at the Emeryville shell mound (ALA-309) following many years of relative increase in small mammal remains at the site. Broughton dated the beginning of the rebound at cal A.D. 1, and he noted a gradual increase in the deer-to-small mammal ratio up to cal A.D. 1250. He posited the existence of buffer zones between the habitation areas of neighboring tribal communities, zones where deer could thrive and be available for people willing to travel great distances to hunt them and carry them back to their core tribal areas (Broughton 1999:64–65). Broughton's conclusion is based on the study of a trench sample from a single site. Valente (1998b:212), in a single site study at MRN-254, found the opposite type of faunal assemblage change, from a Middle Period cervid economy to a more diversified Late Period economy that included waterfowl, deer, and carnivores. Future studies of change and continuity in faunal exploitation patterns will have to rely on comparative study of multiple sites within localities, in order to overcome the problems of limited and anomalous component samples.

Differences in faunal assemblages over the past 2,500 years are attributable to geography and habitat, not intensification over time, concludes a recent comparative study by Simons (2004:408–422). He compared the faunal assemblages of the inland Santa Clara Valley, the East Bay, and western Solano County. He found that intensive cottontail rabbit harvesting was important throughout the Middle and Late Periods everywhere but in Solano County. He noted that fractions of deer, elk, and pronghorn varied with geography but not time, a pattern that supports his 1992 broad-spectrum coharvesting model.

Intensification of Shellfish Harvesting

A shift from oyster harvesting to mussel harvesting and then clam digging was noted on the central and northern bay shore very early (Gifford 1916). Bennyhoff (in Elsasser 1978:39; in Moratto 1984:262) seriated the shifts to the Middle Period, oyster giving way to mussel at the M1/M2 break (about cal A.D. 430), and mussel giving way to clam at the M3/M4 break (about cal A.D. 800). Moratto (1984:259) favored sedimentation as the explanation for the shifts. Jones (1992:4) reopened the possibility that the shifts reflected oyster overexploitation. Broughton (1999:71) too argued that oysters and mussels were overharvested, forcing people to dig clams out of the mud. Story et al. (1966:48) suggested that an oyster bed near San Mateo had been smothered by sedimentation at about cal A.D. 250–350, just prior to Bennyhoff's suggested oyster-mussel shift. Gottsfield (in Pastron et al. 2004:79–80) documented a sudden shift from mussel exploitation to clam exploitation at the Mission Bay site cluster (SFR-112, 113, 114, 147, 155) on the northern San Francisco Peninsula at approximately cal A.D. 100–160. A possible correlation between this foraging shift, the bay sedimentation event, and a cultural disruption at the M1/M2 boundary (the Meganos intrusion discussed below) deserves future study.

In the South Bay, clams were never an important dietary element; mussel and oyster harvesting persisted through the Late Period (Bickel 1976:37; Cartier 1996; Rosenthal 2001). Roop et al. (1982) and later Cartier et al. (1993:168–171) have noted large amounts of coastal shellfish (relative to bay shellfish) in sites of the Santa Teresa Locality, more than 16 kilometers south of the bay, in contrast to the preponderance of bay shore shellfish in sites of the bay shore San Jose Locality.

A sudden intensification of tiny horn snail (*Cerithidea* spp.) harvest, relative to the oyster and mussel harvest, occurred along the South Bay shore at the outset of the Late Period. Hylkema (2002:252) suggested that increasing populations began to gather horn snails during off-months when mussels were inedible. An alternative social intensification model might suggest that surplus labor was being spent in the Late Period to gather the snails as luxury food items, regardless of high collection costs.

Plant Harvesting Intensification

The accepted paradigm of plant harvesting—that acorns were not added to small seeds as important carbohydrates until 4,000 years ago—has been called into question in the past 10 years with the aid of macrobotanical recovery from midden and features. Wohlgemuth (2004:144–145) synthesized recent macrobotanical studies to present a comparative view of plant harvesting intensification in central California. Acorn use is well documented in the Early Holocene (Lower Archaic), but small seed use is not. Millingslabs and handstones, the original paradigm infers, were used to process small hard seeds and nuts, whereas mortars and pestles were used to make flour from acorns (Fredrickson 1973; Moratto 1984:264; see also Basgall 1987). We now know that mortars were in use at least 5,700 years ago in the Bay Area (Rosenthal and Meyer 2004a:34–35; Wohlgemuth 2004:143).

Passive acorn leaching is evidenced during the Early Period (Middle Archaic), along with peak use of bulbs and some use of small seeds, in pits at SOL-391 near Fairfield. Pounding acorns for flour increased during the Middle Period (Upper Archaic). Use of small seeds, including green-phase seeds, increased greatly in the Late Period (Emergent Period) at the Fairfield site and at most other sampled localities in west-central California. At a few sites on the immediate shore of San Francisco Bay (ALA-309, 310, 604), however, sparse amounts of acorn and small seeds were recovered from Middle Period components, and neither acorn nor small seeds were recovered from Late Period components (Wohlgemuth 2004:114–120).

Wohlgemuth's (2004:70) bay shore data were strongly weighted to the EMT and M1 basal levels of one site, ALA-309 (Emeryville). Popper and Martin (Wiberg 2002:9–11) report remarkably high amounts of goosefoot, along with acorn and several other seeds, at EMT site SCl-478 (Skyport Plaza), only four kilometers south of the bay shore in the San Jose Locality (see also Legare 1998 for MRN-254). Obviously a larger comparative sample is needed, as is a rigorous study of burned small seed preservation problems, in order to refine our understanding of plant food resource use in the past.

MORTUARY PATTERNS AND SYMBOLIC EXPRESSIONS

Evidence of ritual treatment of the dead is one of the few archaeological windows for viewing the emergence of social complexity in the past. Despite the fact that professional archaeologists avoid excavating burials in the Bay Area whenever possible, more burials have been scientifically removed over the 25 years since 1982 (approximately 3,750) than were removed over the previous 100 years (approximately 3,570), due to ongoing urban development. In this section we discuss the themes pertinent to social complexity—mortuary contents, mortuary structure, relative grave wealth, and interpretation of change in mortuary structure and wealth over time.

Status Goods and Surplus Labor

The full array of artifacts that prehistoric Californians placed in the graves of their deceased is too extensive to recount here (Beardsley 1954:80–101; Bickel 1976; Fredrickson 1974b; Moratto 1984:264–265, 275–276; Leventhal 1993). Ornamentally shaped stone mortars may be the most expensive items found as grave offerings. Fully shaped examples appear after cal A.D. 1200 (Bellifemine 1997; Leventhal 1993:222; Wilson 1993). Beardsley (1954:31) found that some ornamental mortars weighed 80 pounds and had been carried over 30 miles to their final disposition site. Transportation is the least of the costs for the creation of a fully shaped show or flower pot mortar, however. Leventhal and Seitz (1989:156–165) determined that it took 17.2 hours and 46,000 blows just to create a small five centimeter mortar cup on a granodiorite boulder. Leventhal (1993:225–226) writes, "The energy output . . . must have made these large, finely made objects highly desirable commodities, especially for wealthy families."

Shaped marine shell beads are another category of items placed with burials that were costly to manufacture or obtain. Thousands of beads went into the ground as mortuary offerings each year during most time periods. Raw material was obtainable only along the coast. Each shaped bead, cut from the hard wall of *Olivella, Haliotis,* or clamshell, represented almost an hour of production activity. C. King (1974b:84) argued that high-labor beads circulated in centralized political systems where it was important to control flows of subsistence goods from community food stores; less expensive decorative beads (of larger diameter, less careful edge finish, or made from softer materials such as steatite), on the other hand, circulated in economic systems where centralized control was not an issue (see Chapter 17 for discussions of recent studies on Santa Barbara Channel shell bead manufacture and trade and the implications for the Bay Area).

Beautifully manufactured blades of obsidian and chert or carefully shaped elongate elk femur artifacts distinguished occasional burials during some bead horizons of the Middle Period. Late Period mortuaries contain steatite pipes with elaborate flanges, elongated flanged stone pestles, stone plummets (charmstones), and a wide array of distinctive *Haliotis* ornaments. Destruction and burial of wealth items in Middle and Late Period mortuaries intentionally or unintentionally prevented the depreciation of wealth item values that would have accompanied their accumulation among the living. Wealth destruction also indicates that surplus time and specialized labor were available to replenish the supply.

Cemeteries versus Dispersed Graves

Four modes of mortuary location and organization have been described in the Bay Area. The first, and seemingly most common, is the noncemetery pattern, where people were buried in a dispersed informal way under house floors and at other places in or adjacent to a village. The other three are dedicated cemeteries where interments were placed in some formal structure: (1) cemeteries in rich midden adjacent to villages, (2) cemeteries away from villages in sterile or near-sterile sediments, and (3) possible dedicated cemetery mounds with formal burials and some dietary residue from feasting.

Both dispersed and compact mortuaries in rich midden sites were well documented prior to 1984 (T. King 1970, 1974b:38; Fredrickson 1974b:62–63). Since then, many off-village cemeteries have been documented in East Bay and Santa Clara Valley Middle Period and MLT sites. One example is the multicomponent Rubino site (SCL-674) in the Santa Clara Valley, regarding which Pastron (1999:iv) stated, "The intensity of occupation at the site was at no time commensurate with the extensive number of burials interred there." The Mazzoni site (SCL-131), another nonvillage cemetery in the Santa Clara Valley, is remarkable for its lack of grave offerings. A cache of obsidian blades at the cemetery may "represent a conspicuous, highly valued commodity, offered, not cached . . . [in] homage to a sacred plot" (Pastron and Walsh 1989:86); obsidian hydration rims suggest the cache was buried during poorly documented Bead Horizon M4. In the East Bay, a number of nonmidden cemeteries, each representing one or two upper Middle Period bead horizons (M2, M3, M4), have now been recognized (Bennyhoff 1994c:66).

Leventhal (1993) proposed that bay shore mounds were dedicated burial and funerary sites. He argued that the Ryan Mound (ALA-329) in the Fremont Locality had been created by "large groups of people purposefully engaged in mound-building activities as part of the commemoration, ritual obligation and specialized treatment for mostly a distinctive class of people" (Leventhal 1993:259). The mound, occupied continually during Bead Horizons M4 through L2, contained little shell, but typically large amounts of waterfowl bone. Leventhal (1993:251–252) interpreted the dietary remains as the product of feasts and cemetery offerings left after groups gathered to honor the elite dead. Lightfoot (1997) summarized the more commonly accepted view that the bay shore mounds are multipurpose sites, used repeatedly as residential locales, ceremonial centers, and long-term repositories for the dead.

Luby and Gruber (1999:101) incorporated part of Leventhal's thesis, that bay shore mounds were places where feasting occurred as part of mortuary ritual. Luby (1992) described a shift of mortuary patterning at the Patterson Mound (ALA-328) in the Fremont Locality, from an organized submound cemetery (presumably off-village) to a midden mound village with dispersed inhumation. That shift occurred over a short period of time, between the beginning and end of the EMT (500 to 200 cal B.C.). Luby (2004) recently interpreted the shift as a reflection of cultural change, from explicit social inequality to public expression of an egalitarian ideal.

Statistical Analysis of Mortuaries

Only three mortuary studies have been carried out since 1984 that take a quantitative approach to the structure of a Bay Area cemetery. Cartier et al. (1993) developed a statistical method to quantify social inequality on the basis of the range of wealth within a given mortuary component. This methodology attempted to score the value of each type of item found in grave lots; uncommon and exotic items and those representing large investments of production time were given high scores. The total score for a given grave was called the grave association (GA) score. Using GA score distributions, they highlighted distinctions along a cline from the poorest mortuary (SCL-128, Holiday Inn) to the richest mortuary (SCL-690, Tamien Station) in their study area. Wealth was most evenly distributed in the richest cemetery, Tamien Station (SCL-690, predominately an MLT site). Inequality was highest in the poorest site, the Holiday Inn site (SCL-128, mixed M2, M3, L1, L2 components).

Bellifemine (1997) utilized multivariate analysis to demonstrate a high degree of spatial organization in the largely L1 cemetery at SCL-38 (Yukisma site), a dark midden site where 244 individuals were recovered with 32,000 beads and other associated artifacts. She made the following observations about the cemetery:

> The central cluster is strongly associated with males and cremations, while four of the other clusters (two in the middle ring, two in the outer) have a balanced sex ratio. This last could indicate lineal groups, clans, or moieties, and later DNA analysis could verify this patterning. Furthermore, there are preferential areas for youths, elders, and infants in the intermediate and peripheral regions. . . . There is also a correlation between the artifact frequency sets and the spatial clustering. (Bellifemine 1997:260)

Mortars and pestles in the SCL-38 mortuary tended to co-occur in burials with beads, whereas utilitarian bone artifacts tended to co-occur with bone tubes and whistles (Bellifemine 1997:260). Four artifact types were restricted to the rich central cemetery area: charmstones, stone beads, type K *Olivella* beads, and type M *Olivella* beads. If this pattern holds at other sites, it could be used to refine the GA scoring system proposed by Cartier et al. (1993).

The third statistical approach to a Bay Area mortuary was that of Luby (1992, 2004), as part of his study of the submound and midden mortuaries of the Patterson Mound (ALA-328) during the EMT. Of 100 graves in the basal strata of the site that included both mortuaries, 30 were randomly selected and scored for burial attributes. Cluster analysis, specifically unweighted pair–group cluster analysis, was applied to the sample, illuminating two distinct groups of similar burials: (1) a statistical cluster containing a small but diverse array of accompaniments, primary inhumation, and cremation, that included most of the sterile sediment submound burials, and (2) a statistical cluster of dispersed interments in the midden just above the submound burials, with very few accompaniments and no cremations. Based on this study, Luby (2004) argued for the decline in publicly expressed social inequality at the beginning of the Middle Period.

The Meaning of Mortuary Wealth

By 1984 most scholars agreed that formal cemeteries with differential grave wealth, reflecting the emergence of status ascription and hierarchical social control, appeared late in Bay Area prehistory. But disagreement existed regarding the precise time of that emergence. T. F. King (1974b:38) argued for status ascription's first appearance at the beginning of the Middle Period (Upper Archaic), while Fredrickson (1974b:62–63) did not see it until the beginning of the Late Period (Emergent). Recent studies indicate that cemetery wealth differentiation did not develop steadily over time and space. Milliken and Bennyhoff (1993) illustrated an increase in mortuary wealth and wealth differentiation, expressed by shell bead numbers and concentration, from the Early Period to the Middle Period, followed by a marked increase during the MLT, then a steady decline through Bead Horizons L1 and L2 of the Late Period (Hylkema 2002:258–261; Wiberg 1996a:376–380). They offered two alternative explanations for the Late Period drop in mortuary bead counts and concentration: (1) bead inflation as certain bead types became accessible to most families in a culture (cf. King 1990:95, 118 for the Santa Barbara Channel) or (2) a shift from show-off behavior (conspicuous destruction of wealth through funerary offering by a limited numbers of rich families) to conspicuous gifting behavior (redistribution of beads by rich families to poorer families at funerary or mourning ceremonies).

A mortuary pattern that seems on the surface to suggest social equality may mask more subtle aspects of social control, writes Luby (2004). A simple and undifferentiated mortuary pattern, such as the terminal EMT midden inhumations at ALA-328, may mask the presence of a strong aggrandizer leadership if that leadership accepts an egalitarian ideal. A decrease in mortuary inequality over time may reflect emergence of a corporate mode of inequality, where collective ritual, kinship affiliation, public mound construction, and suppressed display of economic differences are emphasized (Luby 2004:18).

With the new concepts of conspicuous gifting and egalitarian ideal in mind, we are reminded of Fredrickson's (1974b:65) argument that the people who brought the Late Period Augustine Pattern into the Walnut Creek Locality had an incipient social ranking system. Status and prestige were obtained and controlled through membership in a new regional ceremonial system that was marked in graves by unique status markers, especially "banjo" *Haliotis* ornaments (Fredrickson 1974b:65–66, see also Chartkoff and Chartkoff 1984:237; Leventhal 1993:230–236).

We conclude the review of mortuary studies with a caution that there may have been periods, as yet undocumented, when access to symbols of wealth and power was impeded. Mortuaries lacking grave associations are difficult to place in time. In large, multicomponent bay shore mounds, such as the Emeryville shell mound, any short time periods of burial without any grave associations would be impossible to recognize. Inability to recognize and study the temporal patterning of wealthy-poor mortuary assemblages may be inhibiting us from recognizing evidence of punctuated change in the past.

PHYSICAL ANTHROPOLOGY

Physical anthropology research in the Bay Area prior to the 1980s focused on biological distance between populations (Breschini 1983:52–55). More recent bioarchaeological studies have explored additional research issues, including skeletal evidence for dietary stress and signs of interpersonal violence and warfare.

Physical Types and Genetic Populations

As proposed by Gerow (1968), a single physical type prevailed among all central California peoples throughout the Late Holocene, with the exception of the divergent Windmiller people of the delta. The central California type was characterized by a broad-headed (mesocephalic) cranium in combination with relatively small postcranial morphology (Wallace and Lathrop 1975). The Early Period Windmiller people, on the other hand, were longheaded (dolichocephalic) and taller. Gerow (1993) later suggested that the Windmiller people were migrants into California with affiliation to archaic populations of the eastern United States and lowland eastern Mexico. Whatever their origin, the Delta people became smaller and wider-faced over time. By the Late Period they were morphologically similar to other central California peoples, including Bay Area groups (Gerow 1968:96–98).

Breschini (1983:56–61) distinguished a Penutian (Wintuan and Miwok) cranial type from a Hokan (Shasta and Salinan) type using discriminate analysis on small samples from geographically discrete areas. He argued that Bay Area Costanoan speakers exhibited metric cranial characteristics intermediate between Hokan and Penutian extremes, concluding that the Costanoan speakers are a genetic mix of the two. This conclusion is controversial in light of ongoing debate among linguists regarding the reality of either the Hokan or Penutian language stocks (Chapter 6 in this volume). The differences Breschini found may track the effects of genetic drift rather than migration events (Cartier 1993:90; Suchey 1975). It is also important to recognize that Breschini's interpretations were based on an extremely small sample of metric data.

Despite concerns about overinterpretation, osteologists have continued to measure skeletal attributes that may illustrate population differentiation and mixing. In an intriguing study in the Green Valley area of the Napa Locality, Wiberg (1992:236) contrasts the 2600 to 500 cal B.C. cemetery population at SOL-315 with the cal A.D. 600 to 1900 population at adjacent site SOL-355: "Osteometric data indicate earlier site inhabitants were more narrow-headed and postcranially smaller than later [ones]" suggesting to Wiberg a shift from Yukian or Hokan people to Penutian people at 500 cal B.C.

Stark shifts in physical type have also been noted in the East Bay. Early Period Livermore Valley people were significantly larger than subsequent Middle Period and Late Period people (Wiberg 1996a:377–379). On the Fremont Plain, Hall et al. (1988) reported that the individuals of the Meganos extended burial population at ALA-343 (M3 Bead Horizon) were larger and higher-vaulted than typical Bay Area people, but somewhat smaller than Windmiller populations. That pattern supports Bennyhoff's (1994d:83) hypothesis that the Meganos culture carriers were intermarried Berkeley and Windmiller Pattern people. Given all these findings, a new regional comparative study of cranial and postcranial attributes, by bead horizon and locality, seems warranted.

Osteology and Health

Bay Area mortuary populations have not been studied for evidence of progressive dietary stress over time to the extent that Santa Barbara Channel and Sacramento Valley populations have. Relevant data are scattered in site reports and local overviews (cf. Holson et al. 2000:524–535; Jurmain 1993; Roop et al. 1982). In a synchronic comparative study of Livermore Valley skeletal populations, Wiberg (1996a:267–284, 383) found evidence for increased upper respiratory tract infections among Late Period women, perhaps reflecting work activity in aggregated groups and exposure to fire smoke. Almost twice as many women as men exhibited carious dental lesions (during all time periods), and Late Period women showed increased cribra orbitalia, a skeletal pathology thought to result from iron-deficiency anemia (Wiberg 1996a:383). In a recent study Bartelink (2006) used stable isotope data from human bone collagen to document significant regional differences in diet and health between three different prehistoric Bay Area populations.

Evidence for Warfare

Osteological evidence for warfare and other expressions of interpersonal violence occur in four forms: (1) healed bone fractures and puncture wounds, (2) direct evidence of violent death (e.g., embedded projectile points), (3) postmortem modification of skeletal material, and (4) the haphazard disposal of the dead on burned house floors or in nonformal burial pits. Hylkema (2002:260) discussed evidence for violent death at many East and South Bay sites. Strother (2003) presented a detailed summary of evidence for violent death at nine East and South Bay sites with components dating to the Middle and Late Periods.

Well-documented evidence of violence has been reported at the EMT/M1 Skyport Plaza site (SCL-478) in northern San Jose, where Wiberg (2002) documented extended burials that "appear to be linked with evidence of violence and special mortuary treatment, i.e. partial dismemberment (trophy taking) and interment in multiple graves." Pesnichak and Evans (2005:14), reporting on a subsequent excavation in a different part of SCL-478, noted victims of violent death lying on house floors, perhaps with burned roofs; they concluded that the distribution of the skeletons and their demographic mix clearly showed that the inhabitants of SCL-478 had been attacked. At the Rubino site (SCL-674), polished forearm elements were recovered that exhibited cut marks along the shaft; it was another EMT/M1 mortuary (Grady et al. 1999).

The burial population of the Late Period Hillsdale site (SCL-294) in the Santa Teresa Locality of San Jose exhibited higher rates of healed fractures and penetration wounds, 17 percent of the total population, than reported anywhere else in North America; healed wounds were 50 percent higher in females than males (Richards 1988:120-122). Elsewhere, at several Middle Period and Late Period sites in the Fremont and San Jose Localities, Jurmain (1990) reported numerous examples of forearm trauma (usually on the left arm), interpreted as the result of parry fractures. Additionally, multicomponent Early, Middle, and Late Period sites CCO-474 in the Richmond Locality and ALA-613 in the Livermore Locality yielded a catalog list of evidence for violent interactions, including scalping, sharp-force trauma to the neck, embedded projectile points, parry fractures, and modified human bone artifacts (Strother et al. 2005; Estes et al. 2002).

Taken as a whole, reports seem to support Chartkoff and Chartkoff's (1984:236) prediction of increased violence over time, corresponding with increased resource stress and territoriality. However, some Bay Area mortuary assemblages show little or no evidence of violent death. For instance, the mortuary population of 131 skeletons at the Kenwood II site (SCL-689) in the Santa Teresa Locality south of San Jose exhibited no signs of interpersonal violence (Clark and Reynolds 2003:8). A comprehensive study is needed, quantifying amounts of violence on a horizon-by-horizon and locality-by-locality basis, in order to reconstruct and explain changing patterns of intergroup conflict.

THE BAY AREA CULTURAL SEQUENCE IN BRIEF

This section describes a series of cultural changes in the San Francisco Bay Area over the past 10,000 years. We skip discussion of occupation during the 11,500 to 8000 cal B.C. time frame, when Clovis big-game hunters, then initial Holocene gatherers, presumably lived in the area. Evidence for those periods has not yet been discovered, presumably because it has been washed away by stream action, buried under more recent alluvium, or submerged on the continental shelf (Rosenthal and Meyer 2004a:1). We do have enough evidence to document an in-place forager economic pattern beginning at 8000 cal B.C., followed by a series of five cycles of change that began at approximately 3500 cal B.C., all described in subsections below.

The Early Holocene (Lower Archaic), cal 8000–3500 B.C.

An opaque portrait of a generalized mobile forager pattern, characterized by the millingslab and handstone and by a variety of large wide-stemmed and leaf-shaped projectile points, emerges around the edges of the San Francisco Bay Area during the Early Holocene Period (including part of the geological Middle Holocene). The earliest Bay Area date for a millingstone component is 7920 cal B.C., obtained in the mid-1990s from a discrete charcoal concentration beneath an inverted millingslab at CCO-696 at Los Vaqueros Reservoir in the hills east of Mount Diablo (Meyer and Rosenthal 1997). The date came from the deepest component at CCO-696 (390–415 centimeters), which also contained a wide-stemmed projectile point of Napa Valley obsidian with a mean hydration band of 6.9 microns. Archaeobotanical remains from CCO-696 suggested an economy focused on acorns and wild cucumbers (Wohlgemuth 1997).

The earliest documented grave in west-central California was recovered in the 1990s at CCO-637 (within a few hundred meters of CCO-696 at Los Vaqueros Reservoir), where a single radiocarbon date of 6570 cal B.C. was returned from a loosely flexed burial (Meyer and Rosenthal 1998). A 325-centimeter-deep component at CCO-696 yielded a tightly flexed burial that returned a date of 5490 cal B.C. The millingstone assemblage at Los Vaqueros reservoir has yet to be assigned a phase or aspect name (Figure 8.4).

In the South Bay, SCL-178, the Metcalf Creek site, gives its name to the Metcalf Creek Aspect (or Phase), the millingstone pattern cultural expression in the Santa Clara Valley and adjacent coast. Findings from Metcalf are discussed in more detail in Chapter 9. Another Metcalf Creek Aspect millingstone site, SCL-65 (the Saratoga site), produced two flexed burials beneath cairns of millingstones dating between 5400 and 4900 cal B.C. (Fitzgerald 1993). Local Franciscan chert dominates the Early Holocene Santa Clara Valley components (Hylkema 2002:235).

The earliest radiocarbon dates in the North Bay come from the Duncan's Landing site (SON-348/H), a rock shelter that has produced a basal date of ca. 7000 cal B.C. (see Chapter 4 in this volume; Kennedy et al. 2005). The deposit was predominately mussel shell, with limited quantities of fish, bird, and pinniped, with limited numbers of obsidian flake tools and no milling equipment (Schwaderer 1992). A wide-stemmed projectile point from the site produced a hydration reading of 7.5 microns (Borax Lake obsidian), suggesting manufacture about 8,000 years ago. Farther inland, the Spring Lake site (SON-20) in a small valley just east of Santa Rosa has yielded stone millingslabs as well as large wide-stemmed projectile points and other flaked stone tools, a large proportion made from Borax Lake obsidian from distant Lake County. SON-20 is the type site of the Spring Lake Aspect of the Borax Lake Pattern, again thought to represent a mobile forager economic pattern (Fredrickson 1989a:22-23).

The Early Period (Middle Archaic), 3500 to 500 cal B.C.

New ground stone technology and the first cut shell beads in mortuaries signal sedentism, regional symbolic integration, and increased regional trade in the Bay Area, beginning at 3500 cal B.C. The earliest cut bead horizon—the *Olivella* grooved rectangle (Vellanoweth 2001), bracketed 3400 to 2500 cal B.C.; in the Bay Area it is represented so far by a single bead from the San Bruno Mound (Clark 1998:127, 156). Double-perforated *Haliotis* rectangle beads are first documented in the Bay Area in the 5,590-year-old Sunnyvale Red Burial (SCL-832), which also contained red ocher and exhibited preinterment burning (Cartier 2002). The earliest known *Olivella* rectangle beads with drilled perforations date to 4,800 years ago in a burial that contained red ocher and also exhibited preinterment burning from CCO-637 at Los Vaqueros reservoir (Rosenthal and Meyer 2000). Rectangular *Haliotis* and *Olivella* beads are the markers of the Early Period bead horizon; they continued in use at least until 2,800 years ago (Ingram 1998; Wallace and Lathrop 1975:19 for ALA-307; Gerow 1968 for SMA-77).

The mortar and pestle are first documented in the Bay Area shortly after 4000 cal B.C. Pestles utilized with wooden mortars have been dated to 3800 cal B.C. in the Los Vaqueros reservoir area (CCO-637; Meyer and Rosenthal 1997). By 1500 cal B.C. cobble mortars and pestles were used to the exclusion of millingslabs and handstones at the West Berkeley site on the east shore of San Francisco Bay (Wallace and Lathrop 1975:19) and in deeply buried components at CCO-308 in the San Ramon Valley (Fredrickson 1966) and ALA-483 in the Livermore Valley (Wiberg 1996a:373). Millingstone and mortar assemblages may or may not have been contemporary at two East Bay sites with poor component differentiation (CCO-474 [Estes et al. 2002]; ALA-613).

In the central Bay Area, the Lower Berkeley Pattern, marked by mortars and pestles and a burial complex with ornamental grave associations, represents a movement from forager to semisedentary land use at shell mounds like West Berkeley (ALA-307), Ellis Landing (CCO-295), and Pacheco (MRN-152). Elliptical house floors with postholes, dating to 1500 cal B.C., were discovered in 2005 at the Rossmoor site (CCO-309) in the Walnut Creek Locality; they clearly suggest sedentism or semisedentism in the interior East Bay (Price et al. 2006).

At the north end of San Francisco Bay, variations of mobile band (forager) economies persisted for much of the Early Period (Middle Archaic). The generalized Early Holocene Borax Lake Forager Pattern (rich in obsidian flaked stone) gave way to more localized forager lifeways of the Mendocino Pattern, the chert-using Black Hills aspect of the Santa Rosa Locality, and the obsidian-using Hultman Aspect in the Upper Napa Valley. The collector-oriented Lower Berkeley Pattern, with its cobble mortars and flexed burials in residential midden sites, spread into the Napa Valley at about 1500 cal B.C. and to the Santa Rosa Locality by 1000 cal B.C. (Bennyhoff 1994b:52). For much of the Early Period, the lowland sedentary collectors lived side by side with the upland mobile foragers who occasionally visited lowland marshes.

Lower Middle Period (Initial Upper Archaic), 500 cal B.C. to cal A.D. 430

A major disruption in symbolic integration systems is clear in the record by about 500 cal B.C., the end of the Early Period (although disruption may have begun a few hundred years earlier). The ubiquitous rectangular shell beads, in use for 3,000 years, disappeared from not only the Bay Area but the Central Valley and southern California as well. Split-beveled and tiny saucer *Olivella* beads, the first examples of a whole new suite of decorative and presumed religious objects, appeared during the EMT (Elsasser 1978:39). However, EMT mortuaries around the Bay contained few accompaniments, and spire-lopped *Olivella* beads were more common than the cut beads (Luby 2004). The first rich black midden sites are noted in the Napa Valley in EMT sites (Bennyhoff 1994b:52). New sites were occupied at Bodega Bay (Kennedy 2005). Cobble mortars and Excelsier leaf-shaped projectile points appeared on the Santa Rosa Plain (Figure 8.5).

Bead Horizon M1 of the Middle Period (Upper Archaic, 200 cal B.C. to cal A.D. 430), developing out of the EMT, marks a cultural climax on San Francisco Bay. *Olivella* saucer beads became common and new circular *Haliotis* ornaments appeared. New bone tools and ornaments also appeared, among them barbless fish spears, elk femur spatulae, tubes, and whistles (Elsasser 1978:39). Basketry awls (split cannon bones) with shouldered tips, indicating coiled basketry manufacture, appeared in the Central and North Bay (Bennyhoff 1986:70; Bieling 1998:218).

Mortars and pestles continued to be the sole grinding tools during Bead Horizon M1 in the Central Bay, while mixed mortars and millingslabs continued in use around the peripheries. Net sinkers, a typical Early Period marker all around the bay, disappeared at most sites but continued in use well into the Middle Period at SFR-112 (Pastron and Walsh 1988a:90). The pure millingslab/handstone-oriented forager economy, however, continued along the Pacific coast of San Mateo County (Hylkema 2002:261).

Upper Middle Period (Late Upper Archaic), cal A.D. 430 to 1050

A dramatic cultural disruption occurred in central California at about cal A.D. 430. The *Olivella* saucer bead trade network suddenly collapsed, 53 of 103 known M1 sites were abandoned, sea otter bones spiked in the remaining sites, and the Meganos extended burial mortuary pattern began to spread in the interior East Bay (Bennyhoff 1994a, 1994d). These changes co-occurred with the inception of a series of *Olivella* saddle bead horizons—M2, M3, and M4—that would mark central California bead trade until cal A.D. 1000 (Groza 2002). "A Castro phase inhabitant, decked out in Saucer beads and black *Haliotis* ornaments, would have seen a Sherwood phase inhabitant, wearing ear spools, saddle bead appliqué, and red *Haliotis* rectangles, as different, even if few past archaeologists did," wrote Bennyhoff (1986:69), contrasting people of specific lower Middle Period (M1 Bead Horizon) and upper Middle Period (M3 Bead Horizon) cultural phases of his Alameda district.

The first sign of the Meganos complex, characterized by dorsal extended burials, appeared at ALA-413, the Santa Rita village site in the Livermore Valley. There, a 30-year-old man was buried at the end of Bead Horizon M1 with approximately 30,000 *Olivella* saucer beads (the largest documented California bead lot), quartz crystals, and bead appliquéd bone spatulae (Wiberg 1988). Unlike the deeper flexed interments at the site, this individual was buried in dorsally extended Meganos style. One associated saucer bead provided a median AMS intercept of cal A.D. 388 ($\Delta R = 225 \pm 35$; Groza 2002:158). Within a few years the saucer beads disappeared as burial accompaniments, replaced by rough-edged full saddle *Olivella* beads with remarkably small perforations, markers of Bead Horizon M2a. Six full saddle *Olivella* beads have been directly dated so far, from flexed burials at ALA-329 and CCO-269 along the bay shore, and from extended burials at ALA-413 and CCO-151 farther inland. All six have calibrated median intercepts in the narrow cal A.D. 420–450 time range (Groza 2002).

Bead Horizon M2b is marked by mixed *Olivella* saddle beads with tiny 1.0- to 1.5-millimeter perforations that date to cal A.D. 430–600. The Meganos mortuary style continued to spread westward during M2b. A number of new items appeared in Central Bay sites during the M2a and M2b horizons, including beautifully fashioned show blades, fishtail charmstones, new *Haliotis* ornament forms, and mica ornaments (Elsasser 1978:39:Fig. 3). The earliest evidence for inland manufacture of *Olivella* wall beads is found on the Santa Rosa Plain (Tamez 1978).

The climax of upper Middle Period stylistic refinement occurred during Bead Horizon M3 (cal A.D. 600 to 800). It is marked by small, delicate square saddle *Olivella* beads in burials, occasionally with small, poorly shaped *Olivella* saucer beads, often in off-village single component cemeteries. Single-barbed bone fish spears, ear spools, and large mortars first appear during M3. Wohlgemuth (2004:146) notes an increase in seed recovery from middens dated to this time. The Meganos mortuary complex spread during M3 from the interior almost to the Bay at the Fremont BART site (ALA-343), and into the Santa Clara Valley at Wade Ranch (SCL-302). It did not, however, reach the West Bay or the North Bay.

Bead Horizon M4 (cal A.D. 800 to 1050) may be a period of postclimax culture in parts of the Bay Area. It is marked by a devolution of the *Olivella* saddle bead template into a variety of wide and tall bisymmetrical forms, and by the appearance of distinctive *Haliotis* ornament styles (unperforated rectangles and horizontally perforated half ovals). Grave accompaniments are completely lacking at the Santa Teresa Locality Mazzoni site (SCL-131) in the South Bay, and few other mortuaries can even be dated to this time period.

Initial Late Period (Lower Emergent), cal A.D. 1050 to 1550

The lifeways in place at the Spanish entry emerged during the time of the Late Period shell bead horizons. Culture moved up a notch in complexity, from that of collectors who buried their dead with diverse, numerous, but fairly simple ornaments to collectors who invested large amounts of time in the creation of finely wrought wealth objects. The Late Period was called the Emergent Period by Fredrickson (1973, 1994c:100–101), in recognition of the appearance of a new level of sedentism, status ascription, and ceremonial integration in lowland central California. Scheme A dated the beginning of the Late Period to cal A.D. 300, but it is now clear that the Middle/Late Transition (MLT) bead horizon, marking the beginning of the Late Period, began at cal A.D. 1000. During the MLT, fully shaped show mortars, new *Olivella* bead types, and a new array of multiperforated and bar-scored *Haliotis* ornaments appeared at such sites as CCO-308

(Fredrickson 1973), ALA-42 (Wiberg 1997), and SCL-690 (Hylkema 2006). These items are initial markers of the Augustine Pattern. The classic Augustine Pattern markers appeared in Bead Horizon L1 (after cal A.D. 1250); among them were the arrow, the flanged pipe, the *Olivella* callus cup bead, and the banjo effigy ornament (Bennyhoff 1994c).

The first arrow-sized projectile point types in the Bay Area were the Stockton serrated series, a unique central California type (Bennyhoff 1994b:54; Hylkema 2002:49; Justice 2002:352). Surprisingly, they did not appear until after cal A.D. 1250. Biface and debitage production dropped significantly at Napa Valley Glass Mountain quarries with the appearance of the bow and arrow (Gilreath and Wohlgemuth 2004:14). At the same time, Napa Valley obsidian manufacturing debris increased dramatically in the interior East Bay. "Technological organization is defined by acquisition of large Napa Valley flakes that were treated as cores to produce small points, preforms, and miscellaneous simple flake tools," wrote Bieling (1997:76). In the San Jose and Point Año Nuevo Localities of the South Bay, however, debitage and casual tools continued to be derived from local Franciscan chert, and finished projectile points of Napa Valley obsidian continued to be imported from the north (Bellifemine 1997:124–136; Clark and Reynolds 2003:8; Hylkema 2002:250). Jackson and Ericson (1994) argue that Late Period North Bay obsidian exchange was regulated by social elites.

More evidence of increasing social stratification is provided by mortuary evidence. Partial cremation, often associated with the wealthiest grave offerings, appeared, or in some places reappeared. Although numbers of shell beads with burials actually dropped (Milliken and Bennyhoff 1993:392), the overall array of uncommon wealth items increased in high-status burials and cremations (Fredrickson 1994b:62). Fredrickson (1974b:66) and Bennyhoff (1994b:70, 72) suggested that the mortuary pattern, including signature *Haliotis* "banjo" effigy ornaments, reflected a new regional ceremonial system that was the precursor of the ethnographic Kuksu cult, a ceremonial system that unified the many language groups around the Bay during Bead Horizon L1.

Terminal Late Period: Protohistoric Ambiguities

The signature *Olivella* sequin and cup beads of the central California L1 Bead Horizon abruptly disappeared at around cal A.D. 1500 to 1550. Clamshell disk beads, markers of the L2 Bead Horizon, began to spread across the North Bay at that time, but were not initially traded south of Carquinez Strait. From cal A.D. 1500 to cal A.D. 1600 or 1650, the only shell beads in South Bay and Central Bay mortuaries were *Olivella* lipped and spire-lopped beads, and they occurred in far smaller numbers than the bead offerings of the L1 Horizon (Milliken and Bennyhoff 1993:392). While site distributions did not change remarkably, L2 components often seem to be thin signatures on the surface of rich L1 middens.

The North Bay was the seat of innovation during the L2 Horizon in the Bay Area. The toggle harpoon, hopper mortar, plain corner-notched arrow-sized projectile point, clamshell disk beads, magnesite tube beads, and secondary cremation all appeared in the north first. The toggle harpoon, known earlier in northwest California, replaced the multibarbed fish spear. The hopper mortar appeared on the Santa Rosa Plain and the Napa Valley for the first time, but did not spread to the Central or South Bay (Bennyhoff 1994b:54; Wickstrom 1986). Simple corner-notched points replaced Stockton serrated points in the North Bay and began to appear in the Central Bay, while Desert side-notched points spread into the South Bay from the Central Coast (see Hylkema 2002; Jackson 1986, 1989a; Jurmain 1983).

Clam beads were not manufactured in volume on the coast. Some manufacture did occur at Point Reyes (King and Upson 1970:131), but at Bodega Bay, known ethnographically as a collecting point for clamshells, only one bead blank and several drills were recovered during controlled-volume sampling at five separate sites (Kennedy 2005). Evidence of a thriving clam disk manufacturing industry does appear on the Santa Rosa Plain some 30 kilometers inland (Keswick 1990; Wickstrom 1986), as well as at NAP-539, 80 kilometers inland in the Berryessa Valley (Hartzell 1991), and YOL-69 (Wiberg 2005), 115 kilometers inland in the lower Sacramento Valley. The earliest date for clam disks south of Carquinez Strait, cal A.D. 1670, was obtained from a charcoal lens at CCO-309 (V. M. Fredrickson 1968).

Why did shell bead types, mortuary wealth distributions, and some technological artifact types change after cal A.D. 1500? Had population shot past carrying capacity due to success of regional organization during the L1 Horizon, spawning conflict and wealth contraction? Were populations on the move, forcing or marrying their way into neighboring lands? Did European-introduced epidemics spread across the continent following Spanish explorations in Mexico, causing population crashes and cultural disturbances (Erlandson and Bartoy 1995; Preston 1996)? Whatever the cause, indications are that another upward cycle of regional integration was commencing when it was interrupted by Spanish settlement in the Bay Area in 1776.

CONCLUSION: WHAT DROVE CHANGE IN BAY AREA PREHISTORY?

In conclusion, some brief comments are offered regarded two common explanatory themes for past change in Bay Area prehistory: linguistic group migration and population pressure. Gerow (1968:98) and Breschini (1983:64–70, 98–101) posit an east-to-west spread of the mortar-based collector economy into the Bay Area during the Early Period, carried by proto-Penutian speaking peoples from the delta. Moratto (1984:207, 280, 550–557) agrees, but suggests that the invading Penutian groups were proto-Utians (ancestral Miwok-Costanoans), already differentiated from other Penutian groups. Bennyhoff (1994c:83) argues, alternatively, that the proto-Utians had come into the central San Francisco Bay Area somewhat earlier and developed the Early Period Berkeley Pattern in place (Bennyhoff 1986:67, 1994b:66). Fredrickson (1989a) concurs with Bennyhoff, positing a Lower Berkeley Pattern spread from the Central Bay into the North Bay after 1500 cal B.C. and tying it to a proto-Miwok separation from proto-Costanoan (Ohlone). An alternative argument can be made for a later arrival of the Utians, with a proto-Costanoan entry into the Bay Area during the Early Period, and the Miwokans remaining on the Sierran side of Sacramento Valley until a later date.

It was the general consensus in 1984 that Miwokan speakers expanded eastward from the North Bay into the Sacramento Valley at the EMT (500 to 200 cal B.C.), forcing the Windmiller Pattern people south into the San Joaquin Valley (Bennyhoff 1994c:66; Fredrickson 1984:511; Moratto 1984:210; Wiberg 1993:265). Under the alternative model, the Miwokans actually moved westward into the North Bay during or just prior to the EMT.

The Meganos extended burial practice in the East Bay, also found in the Stockton vicinity, seems to have its antecedent in the Early Period Windmiller Pattern of the Sacramento–San Joaquin Delta. The language of the people who carried the Windmiller and Meganos cultures has been suggested as an extinct subgroup of Utian (Moratto 1984:201–211) or as proto-Yokutsan (James Bennyhoff, personal communication to Randall Milliken, 1980). Whatever their language, their cultural pattern was pushed from the East Bay to the San Joaquin Valley at the end of the Middle Period, probably by speakers of proto-San Francisco Bay Costanoan. But what change stimulated such an expansion-retraction?

No change was more dramatic than the appearance of the Augustine Pattern, beginning in the MLT and consolidating in the L1 Bead Horizon. Bennyhoff (1994c:66–67) argues that it arose through stimulation from Patwin speakers newly arrived into the Sacramento Valley from Oregon, bringing with them the bow, the flanged pipe, preinterment grave pit burning, and other new traits. It is a challenge to linguistic group–based explanation that the key traits of the Augustine Pattern were shared by Plains Miwoks, Patwins, Bay Miwoks, San Francisco Bay Costanoans, Coast Miwoks, Wappos, and southern Pomos at the time of Spanish settlement. Perhaps the Augustine Pattern, with its inferred shared regional religious and ceremonial organization, was developed as a means of overcoming insularity, not in the core area of one language group but in an area where many neighboring language groups were in contact.

Finally we turn to the question of population pressure, often offered as an explanation for the rise of cultural complexity in the past. Under hunting and gathering conditions, human populations have an "intrinsic rate of natural growth" in the general range of 1 percent to 3 percent per year, which allows them to double in size within a century, unless the growth rate is somehow checked (Richardson et al. 2001:396–397). Bay Area population pressure must have been incessant in all times in the past, with the exception of the initial centuries of colonization during the Terminal Pleistocene. We presume that Bay Area populations cyclically approached and overran their carrying capacity, crashed (probably through warfare, since humans have only one important predator), and quickly rebounded. Only technological or social innovations allowed the carrying capacity to be raised, and such innovations, we suggest, did not always occur.

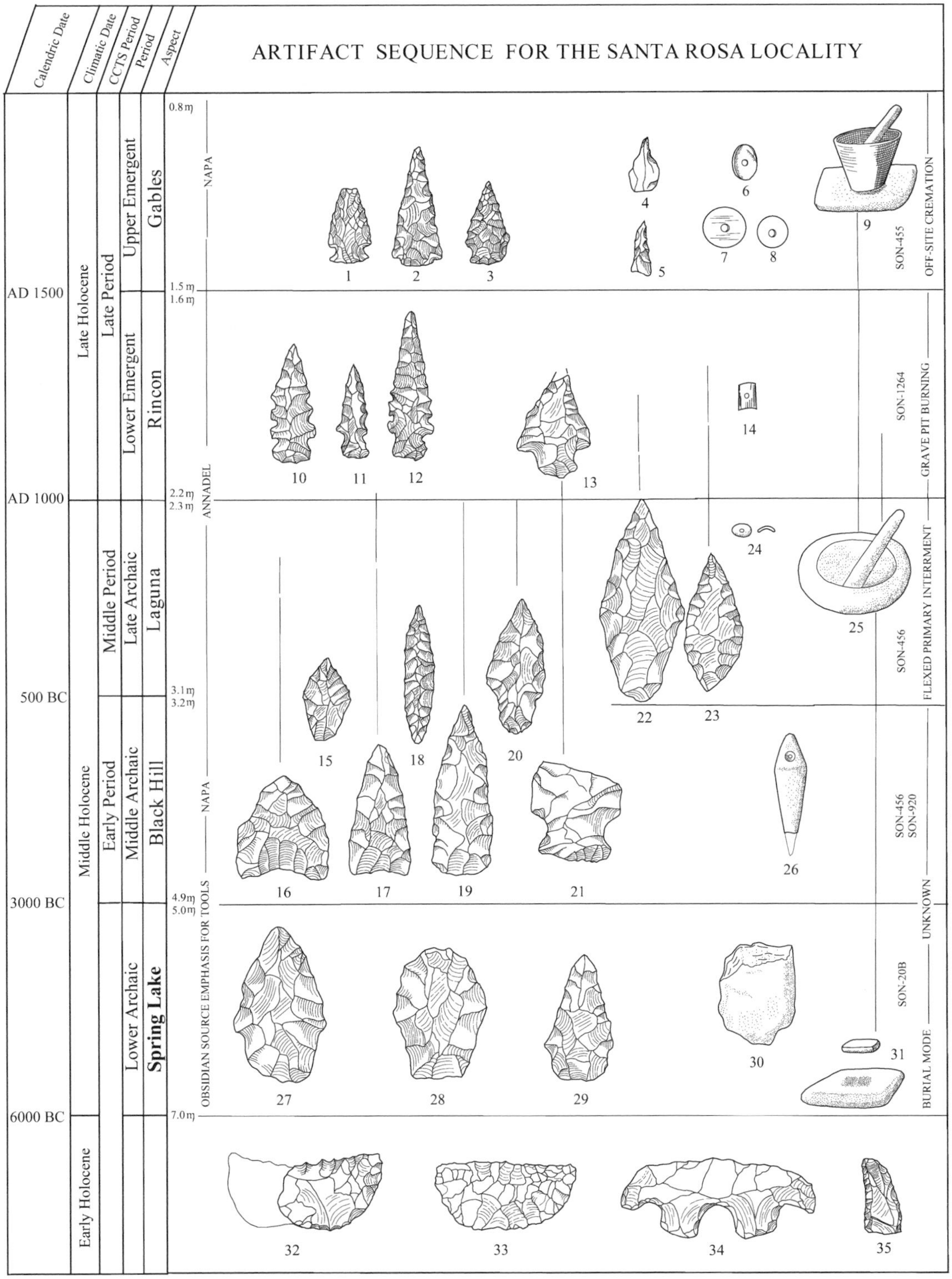

Figure 8.5. Artifact sequence for the Santa Rosa Locality. Key: (1–3) obsidian corner-notched arrow points; (4–5) chert bead drills; (6) *Olivella* lipped bead; (7–8) clamshell disk beads; (9) hopper mortar and pestle; (10–12) obsidian serrated, corner-notched projectile points; (13) side-notched spear point or hafted knife; (14) *Olivella* rectangular bead; (15) obsidian small, diamond-shaped projectile point; (16–17) obsidian (or chert) concave-based projectile points; (18) obsidian (or chert) narrow, leaf-shaped projectile point; (19-20) chert stemmed projectile points; (21) chert side-notched spear point or hafted knife (chert earlier, obsidian later); (22–23) obsidian shouldered, lanceolate projectile points; (24) *Olivella* saddle-shaped bead; (25) bowl mortar and pestle; (26) blue schist charmstone (biconically drilled); (27–28) obsidian wide-stemmed projectile points; (29) obsidian small-stemmed projectile point; (30) basalt unifacial cobble tool; (31) millingslab and handstone; (32) obsidian (Napa) butterfly form crescent; (33) chert lunate form crescent; (34) chert zoomorphic form crescent; (35) high-quality chert unifacial tool. (Only projectile points drawn to relative scale. Drawings by Nelson Thompson.)

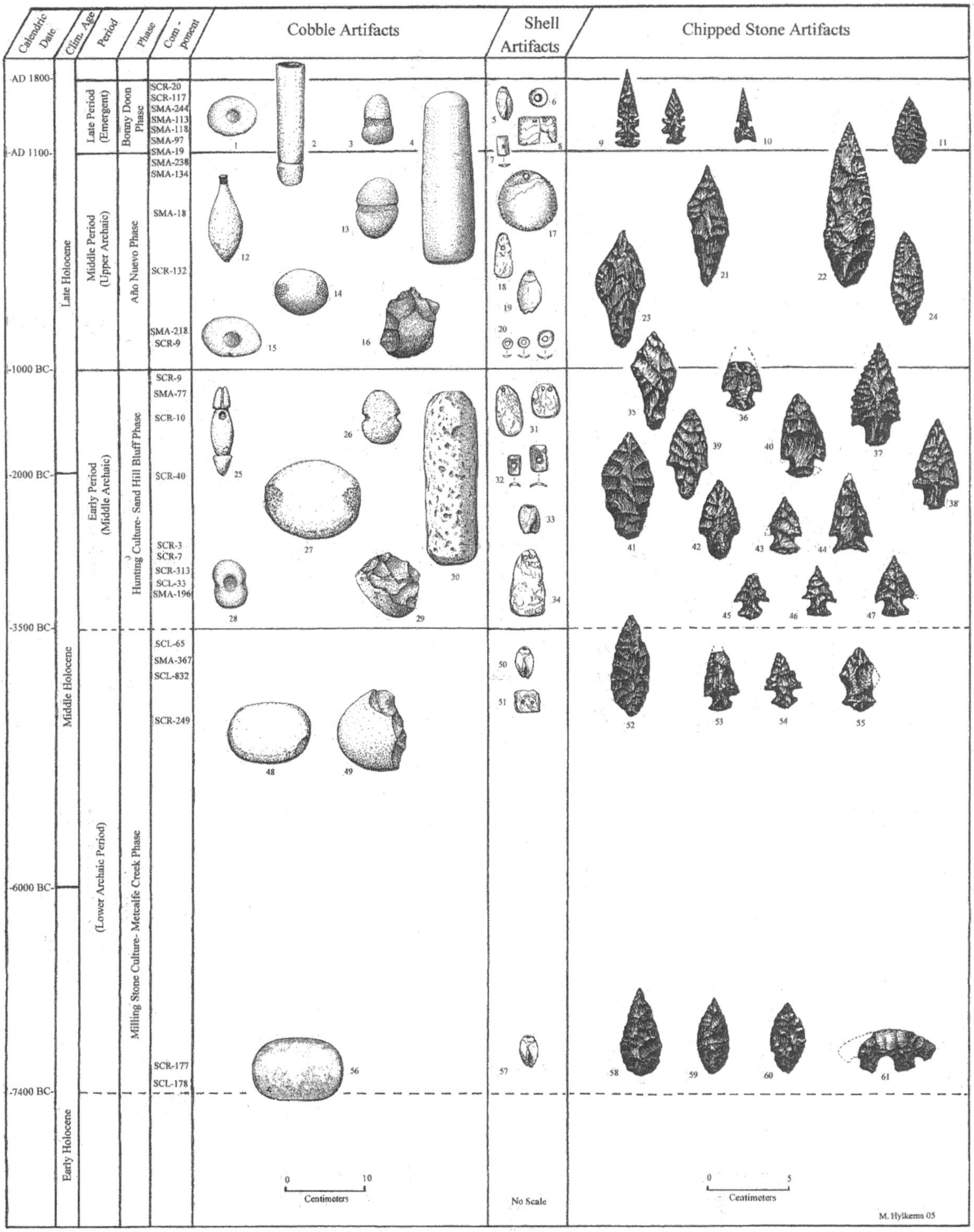

Figure 8.6. Artifact sequence for the San Mateo coast and Santa Cruz Localities.

Key: (1) sandstone bi-pitted cobble, SMA-134;
(2) chlorite schist tobacco pipe, SCR-117;
(3) Andesitic grooved sinker, SMA-238;
(4) sandstone pestle, SCR-20;
(5) *Olivella biplicata* type A1 series bead, SMA-244;
(6) steatite disk bead, SMA-244;
(7) *Olivella* M1a thin rectangle bead, SCR-20;
(8) *Haliotis* type RC5e ornament SMA-238;
(9) Napa obsidian Stockton-serrated points, SMA-244;
(10) Monterey chert desert side-notched point, SCR-20;
(11) Napa obsidian lanceolate point, SMA134;
(12) Andestic piled charmstone, SCR-132;
(13) sandstone grooved sinker, SCR-132;
(14) granitic shaped handstone, SCR-132;
(15) sandstone bi-pitted cobble, SCR-132;
(16) basaltic cobble chopper, SMA-218;
(17) *Haliotis* type CA3h ornament, SCR-10;
(18) *Haliotis* type OB3 ornament, SCR-9;
(19) *Olivella biplicata* type A1 series bead, SMA-18;
(20) *Olivella biplicata* type G series beads, SMA-218;
(21) Monterey chert Año Nuevo long-stemmed point, SCR-9;
(22) Napa obsidian lanceolate point, SMA-97;
(23) Monterey chert Año Nuevo long-stemmed point, SMA-218;
(24) Napa obsidian lanceolate point, SMA-18;
(25) serpentine perforate charmstone, SCR-93;
(26) sandstone edge-notched sinker, SMA-77;
(27) granitic handstone SCR-9;
(28) granitic bi-pitted cobble, SCR-7;
(29) quartzitic cobble chopper, SCR-7;
(30) sandstone pestle, SCR-40;
(31) *Haliotis* type SC3 and FA5 ornaments, SMA-77;
(32) *Olivella biplicata* L series rectangle beads, SMA-77;
(33) *Olivella biplicata* type B series barrel bead, SCR-38;
(34) *Haliotis* type OK5 ornament, SMA-77;
(35) Monterey chert Año Nuevo long-stemmed point, SMA-218;
(36) Monterey chert notched point, SCR-9;
(37) Franciscan chert Rossi square-stemmed point, SCR-9;
(38) Monterey chert Rossi square-stemmed point, SCR-7;
(39) Monterey chert shouldered contracting-stemmed point, SCR-40;
(40) chalcedony notched point, SCR-7;
(41) Monterey chert contracting-stemmed biface, SCR-7;
(42) Monterey chert shouldered contracting-stemmed point, SCR-7;
(43-47) Franciscan chert notched points SCR-7;
(48) sandstone handstone, SCL-65;
(49) quartzitic cobble chopper, SCR-177;
(50) *Olivella biplicata* A1 series bead, SCL-832;
(51) *Haliotis* type H2a bead, SCL-832;
(52) Monterey chert biface, SMA-196;
(53) Monterey chert notched point, SCR-249;
(54) Monterey chert notched point, SCR-313;
(55) Monterey chert notched point, SCL-65;
(56) sandstone handstone, SCL-178;
(57) *Olivella biplicata* type A1 series bead, SCL-178;
(58-60) Monterey chert lanceolate points, SCR-177;
(61) Monterey chert eccentric crescent, SCR-177.
(Some artifacts not drawn to scale. Artifacts depicted are represented at multiple sites. Drawings by Mark G. Hylkema.)

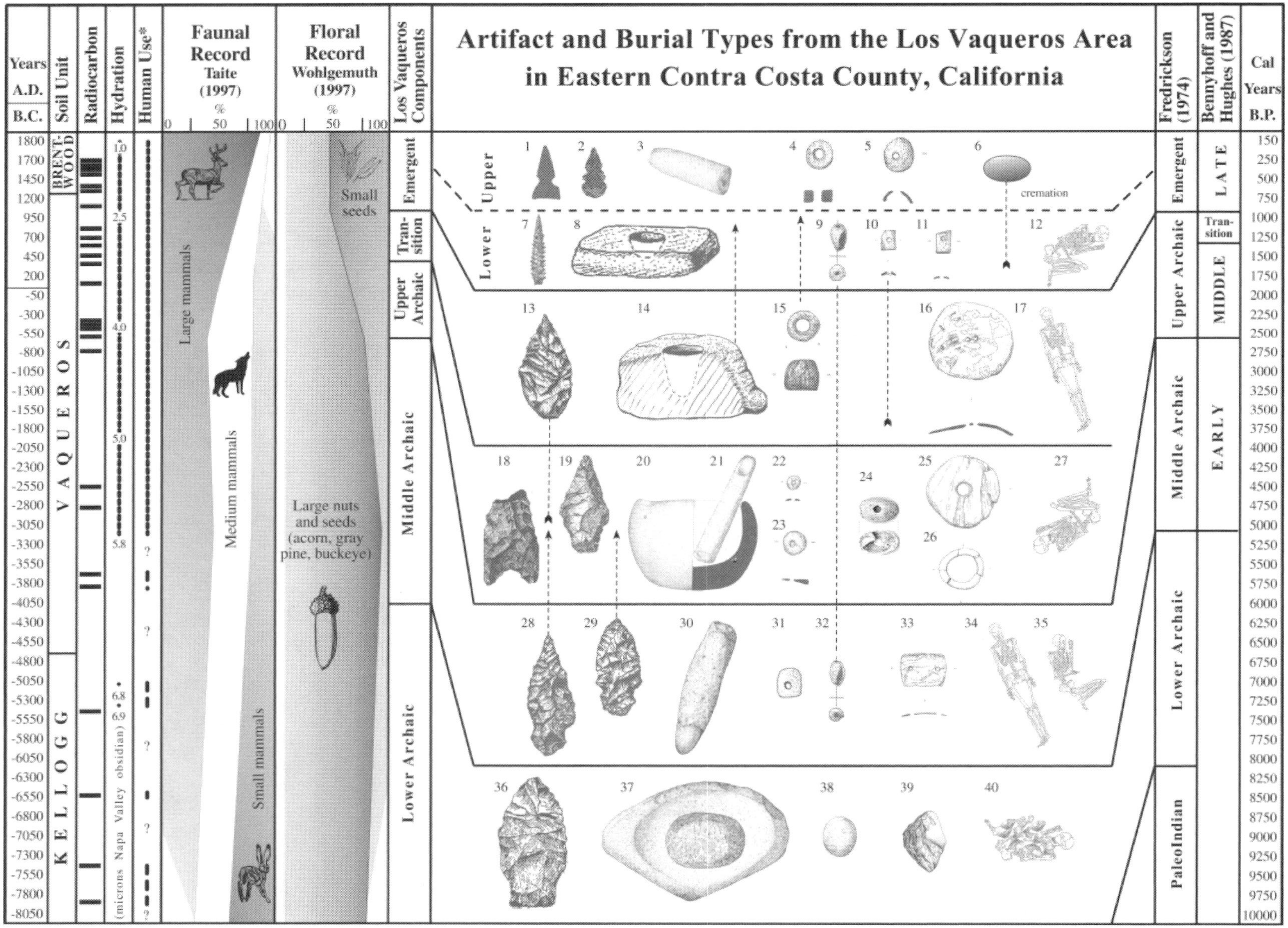

Figure 8.7. Artifact sequence for the border area between the Livermore Locality and the San Joaquin Valley.

Key: (1) Panoche side-notched and desert side-notched projectile points (mainly cryptocrystalline rock);
(2) Stockton side-notched and corner-notched projectile points made only of obsidian;
(3) small cylindrical pestles;
(4) clamshell disk beads;
(5) lipped *Olivella* beads, Type E;
(6) cremation of human remains;
(7) Stockton stemmed projectile points made only of obsidian;
(8) small block mortars;
(9) spire-lopped *Olivella* beads, Type A1b;
(10) thin rectangular *Olivella* beads, Type M1;
(11) thin rectangular *Olivella* beads, Type M2;
(12) tightly flexed burials with variable orientations;
(13) shouldered lanceolate projectile point made of obsidian;
(14) bedrock mortars (Upper Archaic Period cups larger than Emergent Period cups;
(15) steatite beads;
(16) *Haliotis* ornaments, Type CA4fm;
(17) ventrally extended burials primarily with northern orientations;
(18) concave-base projectile points made of chert and obsidian;
(19) contracting-stemmed projectile point made of chert;
(20) shaped and cobble bowl mortars;
(21) shaped and cobble pestles;
(22) saucer *Olivella* beads, Type G1 and G2;
(23) *Macoma* clam disk beads;
(24) split *Olivella* beads, Type C;
(25) *Haliotis* ornaments, Type C1C;
(26) *Haliotis* ornaments, Type C2C;
(27) tightly flexed burials, primarily with southwest orientation;
(28) side-notched projectile point made of chert (CCO-637, Burial 7, 3850 cal B.C.);
(29) side-notched projectile point made of chert (CCO-637, Burial 5, 3720 cal B.C.);
(30) cobble pestles with convex parabolic end wear;
(31) thick rectangular *Olivella* beads;
(32) spire-lopped *Olivella* beads, Type A1a;
(33) *Haliotis* ornament, Type uBA7;
(34) fully extended and semiextended burials, primarily with northwest orientations;
(35) loosely flexed burials, primarily with northwest orientations;
(36) wide-stemmed projectile point made of obsidian (CCO-696, 6.9 microns Napa Valley);
(37) millingslabs and oval bifacial handstones;
(38) small round handstones;
(39) cobble-core tools;
(40) cairn burial (CCO-696, Burial 160, 5540 cal B.C.).
Approximate timing and duration of human use in the project area based on combined radiocarbon and obsidian hydration evidence. Courtesy of Jack Meyer.

The Central Coast: A Midlatitude Milieu

Terry L. Jones, Nathan E. Stevens, Deborah A. Jones, Richard T. Fitzgerald, and Mark G. Hylkema

The Central Coast is defined as the region south of San Francisco Bay and north of the Southern California Bight, encompassing the South or Central Coast Ranges west of the Great Valley. While distinguished by remarkable biotic diversity, the region is internally cohesive in terms of environment and prehistoric culture. Ethnographically, it was marked by numerous small, autonomous polities defined by Alfred Kroeber (1955) as tribelets, while environmentally it is outside the influence of San Francisco Bay (the largest California estuary and the last to mature) and north of Point Conception. The latter marks a major division between the ocean currents, climate, flora, and fauna of southern versus northern California. The distinctive midlatitude climatic regime and associated biota of the Central Coast correspond relatively well with the contemporary political divisions of southern Santa Clara, San Benito, Santa Cruz, Monterey, and San Luis Obispo Counties and the western fringes of Kings, Merced, and western Fresno counties.

Twenty years ago the Central Coast was a seriously understudied region whose cultural and environmental diversity had yet to be fully documented. Findings from three major projects dominated interpretations: Breschini and Haversat's (1980) testing at MNT-170 on Pescadero Point in Carmel (Figure 9.1), Dietz and Jackson's (1981) investigation of 19 coastal sites in Pacific Grove, and Greenwood's (1972) analysis of six coastal middens at Diablo Canyon in San Luis Obispo County. A handful of earlier studies including Clemmer's (1962) report of a house floor from Morro Bay, excavations at Pico and Little Pico Creeks on the northern San Luis Obispo County coast (Abrams 1968; Leonard 1968), work in the interior ranges by the California Department of Parks and Recreation (Olsen and Payen 1968, 1969, 1983; Pritchard 1970, 1983; Riddell 1968), and Pohorecky's dissertation on the Big Sur coast (1976) also produced important, albeit largely descriptive and chronological findings.

Preliminary testing results from the Scotts Valley site (SCR-177) also loomed large in interpretations of Central Coast prehistory in 1984, since preliminary radiocarbon dates suggested the possibility of a Terminal Pleistocene/Early Holocene pericoastal occupation. Radiocarbon dates from Diablo Canyon also suggested Early Holocene coastal occupation, but uncertainties over both of these projects were palpable in 1984. The Scotts Valley findings were limited to preliminary testing results whereas the Diablo Canyon dates seemed anomalously older than any other coastal site in western North America. There was also long-standing and lingering mistrust of radiocarbon determinations from marine shells which provided most of the dates from Diablo Canyon. As recently as 1988, old dates from marine shells were dismissed by many Central Coast researchers, including one of us (see Dietz et al. 1988), despite the misgivings of others (Breschini and Haversat 1991a). Overall, fewer than 100 radiocarbon dates were available from the Central Coast region in 1984 (Breschini and Haversat 2005b), and there were precious few instances where individual components or constituent assemblages were adequately defined or bracketed in time. Subsurface data, in most cases largely descriptive, were available from no more than 50 sites. There was no regional culture history, and substantial faunal data were available from no more than four or five sites, mostly in the Monterey area.

While questions continue to abound, many of the most glaring gaps in Central Coast archaeology have been filled in the past two decades. Subsurface data, including more than 1,200 radiocarbon dates, are available from nearly 300 sites (Breschini and Haversat 2005b). Problems in the calibration of marine shell–derived radiocarbon dates have been reduced to relatively minor issues (e.g., exact reservoir effect correction),[1] and major studies have been completed in nearly every locality, particularly along the coastline. An integrated regional culture history documents variability and continuity in human coastal and nearshore adaptations over the past 10,000 years with hints of occupation as early as 12,000 to 13,000 years ago. For the most part, present-day conceptualizations of the region's prehistory were foreshadowed by the seminal

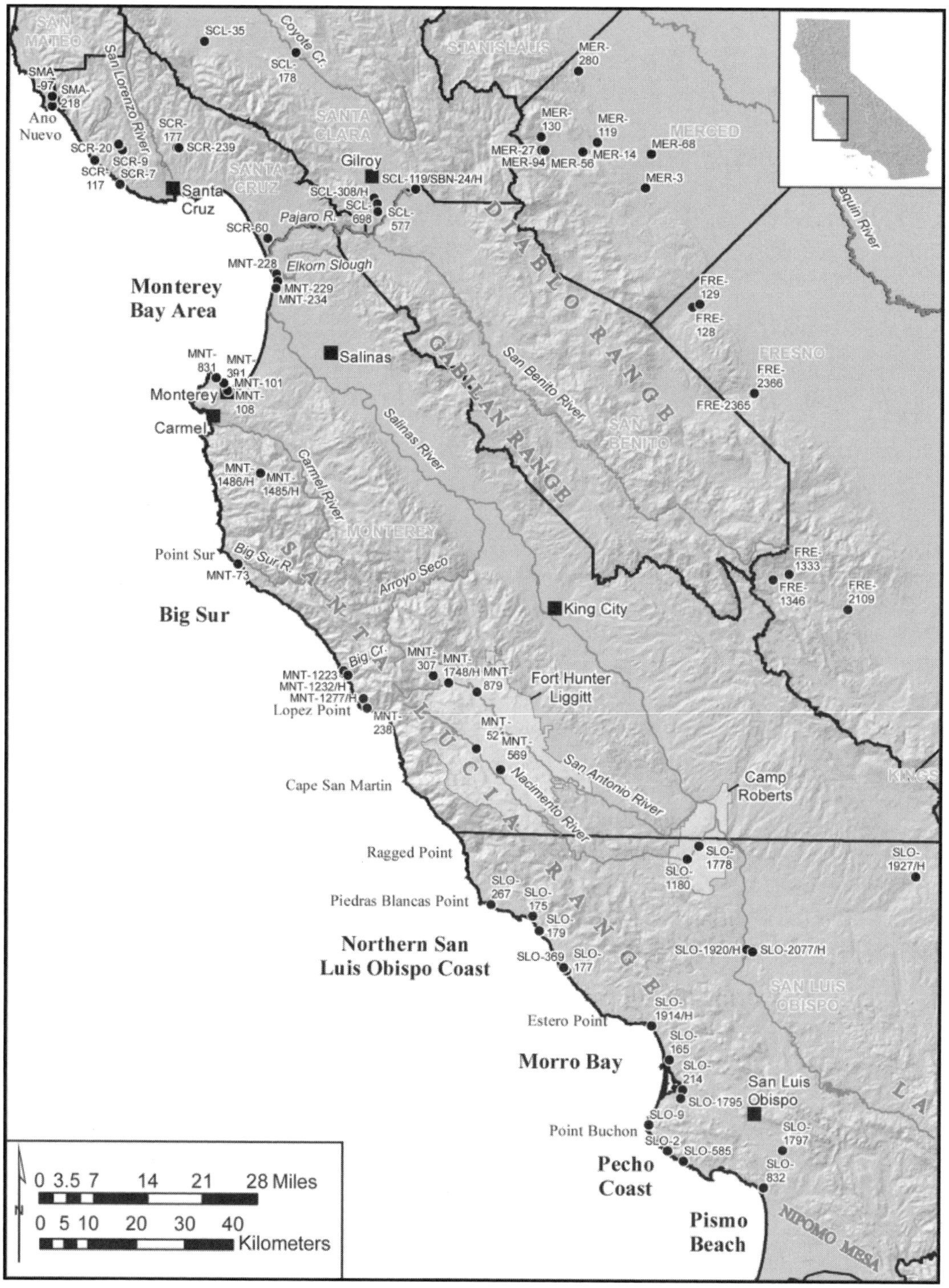

Figure 9.1. Archaeological sites and localities of the central California coast.

research at Pescadero Point, Pacific Grove, and Diablo Canyon. In recent years all of these projects have been supplanted by larger excavations and/or enhanced radiocarbon dating, but many of the interpretations in these insightful early investigations provide the basis for the broader outline of the region's prehistory that we draw here.

ENVIRONMENT

Two distinct types of coastline are found along the shores of Santa Cruz, Monterey, and San Luis Obispo Counties: open coast (unprotected surf-swept beaches or rocky headlands) and lagoons/estuaries. As discussed in Chapter 3, the latter are the products of sea level rise and the drowning of river valleys during the

Late Pleistocene through Middle Holocene that provide significant shelter from the open ocean. The Central Coast is dominated by an exposed shoreline with a mixture of rocky and sandy substrates that shifted in expanse through the Holocene. Major estuaries and lagoons are found at Elkhorn Slough and Morro Bay, although archaeological findings from southern San Luis Obispo County indicate the presence of an extensive paleoestuary that had largely disappeared by Late Holocene as a result of rising sea levels and infilling of sediments (Dills 1981; Fitzgerald 2000; D. Jones et al. 2002; T. Jones et al. 2002).

The terrestrial environment of the Central Coast is marked by a series of relatively low (600–1,500 meters) northwest-southeast trending mountain ranges with the precipitous Santa Lucia Range causing a rain shadow effect on the interior ranges (Gabilan, Diablo, La Panza, and Temblor) and making them progressively more xeric to the east. Climate is solidly Mediterranean with rainfall coming almost exclusively between late fall and spring. Regional rainfall totals are heavily influenced by the El Niño–Southern Oscillation. El Niño events of moderate, strong, and very strong intensity occur every five to fifteen years and are generally associated with warm sea surface temperatures and increased storm activity. The largest river in the region, the Salinas, flows northward between the Santa Lucia and Gabilan Ranges, but was a magnet for prehistoric habitation only along its upper tributaries, the San Antonio and Nacimiento Rivers. For the most part, Central Coast rivers provided little in the way of important aquatic resources.

Owing to its midlatitude location, the Central Coast is marked by a complex mosaic of hardwood and relict closed-cone pine forests near the coast, blue oak–gray pine forest, valley oak savanna and chaparral in the interior valleys, and California prairie in the most xeric areas. Grassland and coastal sagebrush are more abundant in the south while resource-poor redwood forest occurs at moderate elevations in the north. Overall, the vegetative mosaic is slightly less complex than that to the south because of the linear patterning caused by parallel mountain ranges. Marshes comprised a significant proportion of the precontact landscape in the vicinity of estuaries and small inland lakes.

NATIVE SOCIETIES AT CONTACT

While Spanish seafarers made brief stops on the Central Coast as early as 1542, long-term contact was initiated in 1769 by the Portolá overland expedition. At that time most of the central California coast was occupied by a large number of small, autonomous tribelets (Kroeber 1955). Actual ethnographic observations of these societies were afforded only to the earliest Spanish explorers and missionaries, and the documentation resulting from these early contacts is woefully incomplete. Attempts at more systematic anthropological description were not initiated until early in the twentieth century following at least 150 years of precipitous population decline.[2] Speakers of Native languages were still present in the early 1900s, and the earliest salvage ethnographies emphasized documentation of dying languages (Figure 9.2). In the case of at least one language (Esselen), this effort was too late to recover much information, but for others, such as Salinan, the linguistic record is better documented. Because the remaining speakers had forgotten the actual native names for their tribelets, language has been used as a means of aggregating the small autonomous native societies into groups ("tribes") under a false premise that tribelets speaking related dialects and/or languages shared ethnic identities (Kroeber 1955).

Four language groups are represented on the Central Coast: the Costanoan subfamily of Utian in the Monterey Bay area, the Esselen language of the Hokan stock in the upper drainage of the Carmel River and northern Santa Lucia Range, the Salinan languages (a group of related dialects of the Hokan stock) along the Big Sur coast, and Obispeño (Northern Chumash), of the Chumashan isolate family along the coast of San Luis Obispo County. It has been suggested that a fifth unknown but distinct "Playano" language may have been spoken in the Cambria area. Some modern descendants in the Monterey Bay area prefer the term "Ohlone," based on the name of a village on the San Francisco Peninsula.[3] Analysis of records from the Spanish missions has provided the names of tribelets and other communities for the areas in which the Costanoan, Esselen, Salinan, and Northern Chumash (Obispeño) languages were spoken (Gibson 1983; C. King 1974a, 1994; Milliken 1981, 1988; Milliken and Johnson 2005) (Figure 9.3). Actual village locations and tribelet boundaries remain poorly documented, and there are remarkably few firm associations between named villages and archaeological sites, and even fewer cases where village sites have been excavated.

The manner in which subsistence was accomplished within tribelet communities vis-à-vis systems of seasonality and settlement is frustratingly unclear, but the accounts of the earliest Spanish explorers consistently allude to relatively small groups that moved seasonally and exploited a wide range of terrestrial and marine

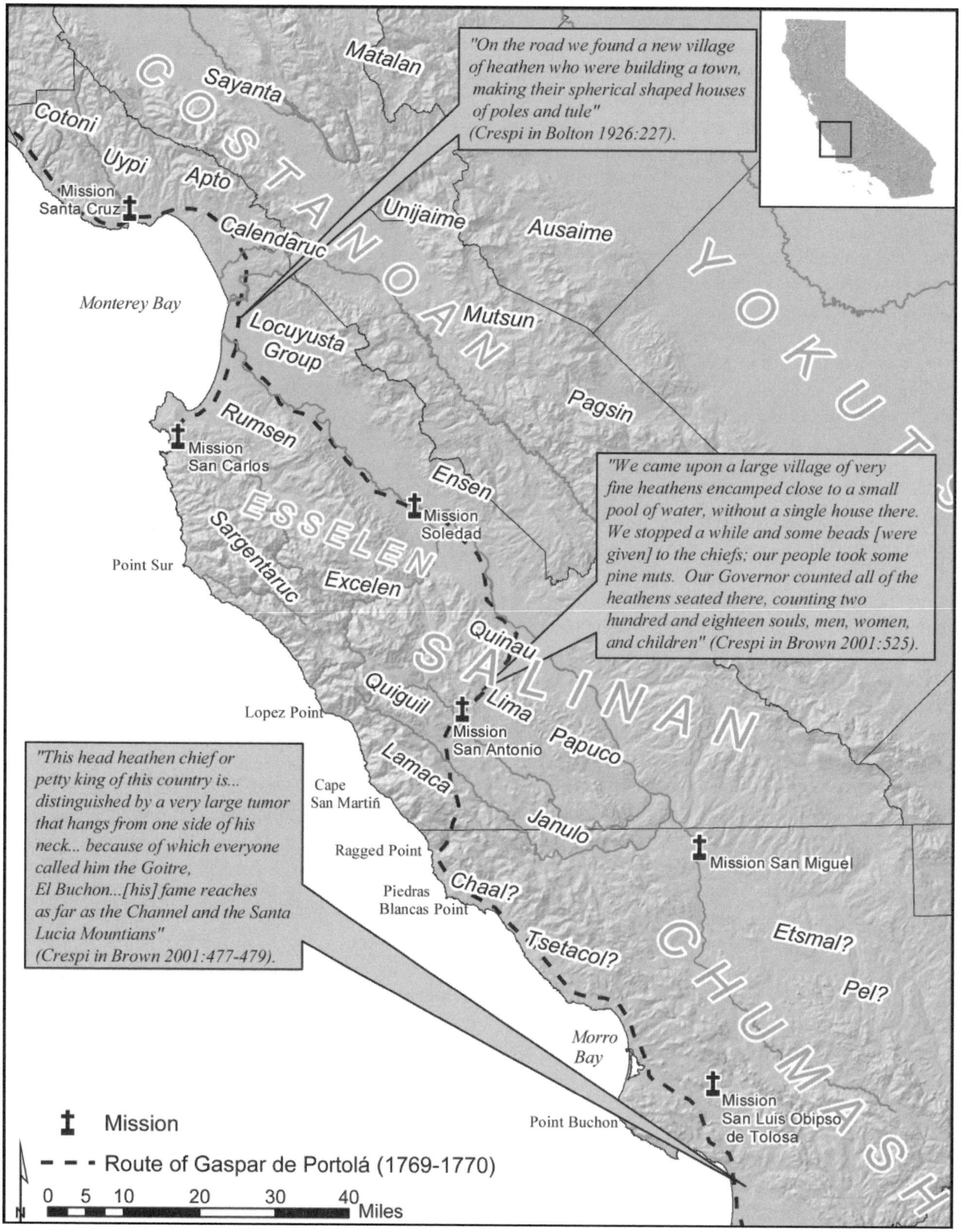

Figure 9.2. Approximate location of tribal groups, central California coast (based on Spanish mission records [Milliken 1981, 1988; Milliken and Johnson 2005], route of the Portolá expedition, and key passages from the Crespi diaries [Brown 2001]).

Figure 9.3. John Peabody Harrington with Rosario Cooper (far left), last known speaker of Obispeño Chumash ca. 1916 in Arroyo Grande, California. (National Anthropological Archives, Smithsonian Institution [91-31415].)

resources. In 1769 Fages (1937:67) noted that the local inhabitants "do not have fixed places for their villages, but wander here and there wherever they can find provisions at hand." This type of description is common in early Spanish accounts throughout the region. These sources repeatedly mention the use of tule balsas and bows and arrows, and the exploitation of acorns, pine nuts, buckeye nuts, seeds, strawberries, blackberries, sardines and other fish, shellfish, deer, antelope, rabbits, and quail (Broadbent 1972; Fages 1937; Menzies 1924). Early accounts also refer to regular controlled burning (Anderson 2005; Gordon 1979).

While the early historic accounts imply bandlike mobility and subsistence, certain aspects of the ethnohistoric record suggest a higher level of sociopolitical complexity. The greatest conundrum in Central Coast ethnohistory is reconciling apparent bandlike subsistence practices with early accounts of ascribed political power, highly formalized leadership statuses, economic redistribution, and widespread warfare. Most historic accounts allude to groups of 40 to 60 people, which is a typical size for mobile bands. However, one early encounter at Avila Beach near San Luis Obispo suggested as many as 300 people aggregated in one place (Wagner 1929:161), while another in the Nacimiento Valley by the Portolá expedition suggested as many as 600 people harvesting pine nuts (Brown 2001:515). A large structure that reportedly held as many as 200 people was noted near Point Año Nuevo. The Nacimiento Valley account probably represents a brief aggregation of multiple groups focused on heavy exploitation of one seasonally abundant resource, while the others still represent congregations of people considerably smaller than in the Santa Barbara Channel, where early accounts refer to permanent communities of as many as 800 to 1,000 people (King 1990).

More intriguing signs of complexity include suggestions of significant concentrations of political power and prestige especially among the Obispeño (Northern Chumash), where early accounts repeatedly describe one exceptionally prestigious chief, Buchon, who traveled with an entourage, directed attacks on other groups, and was able to command tribute even after his death (Brown 2001:463–465, 475–479, 713–717, 721–723; Bolton 1930:268). The repeated references to Buchon's power and influence have been commonly interpreted (Gibson 1991; Milliken and Johnson 2005) as an ethnically based (Chumash) sociopolitical system more complex than that of the Salinan, Esselen, or Ohlone tribelets. There are, however, clear suggestions of formal leadership status (Levy 1978a:487), hereditary chiefly power, and accumulation of wealth by chiefs (Harrington 1942:33) among the Ohlone and Salinan as well. Most evidence suggests that authority in those areas was limited to individual villages, village clusters, and/or lineages, but one account from the Monterey Bay area clearly suggests a hierarchical political structure (Fages 1937:73–74). Often overlooked, this account more closely approximates a chiefdom-type political structure than any attributed to the Buchon polity. Other hallmarks of significant complexity represented in the Santa Barbara Channel (e.g., craft specialization in the form of bead and canoe manufacture, full sedentism, and an intensive maritime economy) were absent from the Central Coast.

HISTORY OF ARCHAEOLOGICAL RESEARCH AND KEY COMPONENTS

With some notable exceptions, the Central Coast was generally passed over by the earliest generation of California archaeologists, who tended to focus heavily on the more visible records of San Francisco Bay and the Santa Barbara Channel. It was not until the advent of cultural resources management (CRM) in the 1970s that the region witnessed a sustained research effort, much of this in the past 20 to 25 years. Unlike many other areas of California, the vast majority of land in this region is privately owned including many of the areas most amenable to prehistoric occupation (e.g., the Monterey Peninsula). Survey of these lands has progressed slowly if not episodically in response to seemingly relentless land development.

Although surface finds have contributed insights into settlement-subsistence practices (Baldwin 1971; Jones and Haney 2005; Jones et al. 1989; Mikkelsen and Hildebrandt 1990; Sickler-Hylkema 2005; Whitley et al. 2004), the most valuable research findings of the past two decades have come from subsurface investigations. While many of these are best characterized as small-scale testing projects, major excavations producing well-dated and well-defined components have also been completed. In general, Central Coast deposits do not exhibit good cultural stratigraphy owing to, among other things, prolific populations of burrowing animals. In the 1980s much was written about the serious mixing that can result from the activities of these animals (Bocek 1986; Johnson 1989). With a few important exceptions (e.g., Willow Creek and Diablo Canyon) vertical superposition of components is uncommon, and the value of some sites (e.g., SCR-177, the Scotts Valley site) has been compromised by the presence of materials from multiple, vertically mixed components. Fortunately the midlatitude diversity of the Central Coast seems to have encouraged a situation where single sites were not continuously occupied for extremely long periods of time. As a result, single-component and horizontally stratified multicomponent sites (with significant temporal gaps between components) are relatively abundant. Findings from these sites and the less common vertically stratified deposits have contributed most to an enhanced regional prehistory.

Findings from 284 subsurface investigations were examined for this chapter, although sites with well-dated, well-sampled, and thoroughly analyzed components are far fewer in number. The following is a description of components that have been especially important in developing this improved conceptualization. The review begins in the north and progresses southward and inland. In general, the region can be broken into localities based on the types of shoreline environments that foster distinctive shell assemblages in nearshore middens.

Santa Cruz/Southern Santa Clara Valley

The most important syntheses for this area are by Hylkema (1991, 2002) for the coast and Hildebrandt (1983) and Hildebrandt and Mikkelsen (1993) for the interior. The Scotts Valley site (SCR-177), which produced promising test data in the late 1970s (Cartier 1982), proved somewhat disappointing when larger-scale excavations were completed in the 1980s (Cartier 1993a). The site has produced radiocarbon dates representing every millennium from 13,000 years ago to the present, but deposits were not stratified and there are serious questions about the cultural origin of most of the charcoal used for dating. Lightning fires are regular, natural occurrences in central California (many native species require fire for germination), and charcoal from nonfeature contexts is unreliable for dating. Two feature-related charcoal dates in close proximity to milling tools suggest the presence of a local expression of the Millingstone Culture dating ca. 6000 to 5800 cal B.C. (Fitzgerald and Jones 1999). These dates provide a minimal age for the earliest site occupations, but it is likely that use of SCR-177 began earlier. Unfortunately there is nothing in the chronometric or other findings from the site that allows us to determine the actual age of this site use with any degree of confidence.

A slightly less problematic Millingstone expression was identified at the Metcalf site (SCL-178), a deeply stratified deposit in the southern Santa Clara Valley where extensive excavations in the early 1980s revealed cultural materials as deep as nine meters below the surface (Hildebrandt 1983). Radiocarbon determinations from a feature and an *Olivella biplicata* spire-lopped bead indicate the presence of cultural materials dating as early as 7500 cal B.C. (Fitzgerald and Porcasi 2003; Fitzgerald et al. 2005). Like Scotts Valley, SCL-178 also produced a series of much older charcoal-derived radiocarbon dates that have little if any verifiable association with cultural materials. An occupation nearly contemporaneous with the early use of SCL-178 was identified at SCR-38 on the Santa Cruz coast, where radiocarbon results indicate ephemeral habitation dating ca. 6900 cal B.C. (Bryne 2002).

More recent Middle and Late Holocene coastal and near-coastal components have been reported from SCR-7 (the Sand Hill Bluff site), SCR-40, and SCR-9 (Hylkema 1991). A modest data recovery project completed by Jones and Hildebrandt (1990) at SCR-7 suggests that part of the site was occupied from 4100 to 1500 cal B.C. A nearly contemporaneous (ca. 3000 cal B.C.) deeply buried component was identified by Cartier (1992) at SCR-239 in Scotts Valley. Evidence for more recent occupation comes from SCR-9 and SMA-218 with well-sampled components dating 900 cal B.C. to cal A.D. 800. Important post cal A.D. 1000 occupations have been identified at SMA-244, SCR-20 (Hylkema 1991; Roop 1976), and SCR-117 (Fitzgerald and Ruby 1997). In the southern Santa Clara Valley, Hildebrandt and Mikkelsen (1993) described a series of components from SCL-119/SBN-24/H, SCL-308/H, SCL-577/H, SCL-639/H, and SCL-698, dating 2000 cal B.C. to cal A.D. 1300. Also important are findings from SCL-35 near Gilroy which include a small number of burials dating 700 cal B.C. to cal A.D. 400, unusual rock art (cupules and concentric ring petroglyphs), and dietary debris from an occupation dating cal A.D. 1500 (Cartier 1995).

Elkhorn Slough

Middens in the Elkhorn Slough Locality are distinguished by the remains of estuarine shellfish from the former mouths of the Pajaro and Salinas Rivers. Nearly unknown in 1984, this area has witnessed a series of major excavations that document occupation between 6300 cal B.C. and cal A.D. 1500 (Jones 2002). Initially the antiquity of human presence in the area was not recognized because of mistrust of radiocarbon dates from marine shell, but once this mistrust was proven unfounded, occupations dating ca. 6000 to 5000 cal B.C. have been recognized at nearly every site excavated in the area (Fitzgerald 2004), including MNT-228 (Jones et al. 1996), MNT-229 (Dietz et al. 1988; Jones and Jones 1992), MNT-234 (Breschini and Haversat 1995a; Milliken et al. 1999), and SCR-60 (Newsome et al. 2004). Substantial components representing occupation between ca. 1000 cal B.C. and cal A.D. 1200 were also identified at MNT-228, MNT-229, and MNT-234. A large burial population and meager nonmortuary assemblage were identified at SCR-44, which was used between 1000 cal B.C. and cal A.D. 300 and also ca. cal A.D. 1500 (Breschini and Haversat 2000). Modest evidence for occupation post cal A.D. 1000 is also available from MNT-234 along with a slightly more robust sample from MNT-1765 (Fitzgerald et al. 1995).

Monterey Peninsula

Midden deposits on the Monterey Peninsula are dominated by abalone and mussel shells that reflect a highly productive exposed rocky shoreline. This was one of the few areas discussed at length in 1984 based on the findings from Pacific Grove (Dietz and Jackson 1981) and Pescadero Point (Breschini and Haversat 1980). Since then, at least a dozen significant excavations have been completed mostly by Gary Breschini and Trudy Haversat who have been consistently tenacious in their attempts to obtain meaningful data from important sites, often in the face of significant resistance from developers and private landholders. Since 1984 the antiquity of human use of the peninsula has been extended back several millennia. The oldest occupations are now known from MNT-170 (ca. 3900 cal B.C.) (Dietz 1991) and MNT-831 (5000 cal B.C.), although material marking the earliest use of these sites is very limited. More substantive findings are from slightly later components at MNT-108 (2400 to 1000 cal B.C.) (Breschini and Haversat 1989a), MNT-170 (3700 to 3300 and 2400 to 1400 cal B.C.) (Dietz 1991), MNT-391 (3400 cal B.C. to cal A.D. 1) (Cartier 1993b; D. Jones 1992), and MNT-831 (3600 to 1400 cal B.C.) (Breschini and Haversat 2002). Of these, the most important by far is MNT-391, which produced the most substantial Early Period mortuary, tool, and faunal assemblages in the region. Substantial evidence representing the period between 1000 cal B.C. and cal A.D. 1000 has been less forthcoming, although an important exception was at MNT-101 (2000 cal B.C. to cal A.D.700) reported by Dietz (1987). Also of some importance during this period is an apparent gap in radiocarbon distributions between cal A.D. 600 and 700 identified by Breschini and Haversat (2005b). Occupations postdating cal A.D. 900–1000 include a number of coastal processing stations (MNT-170; Dietz 1991, MNT-1084; Breschini and Haversat 1991b, MNT-1935; Breschini and Haversat 2003c) and extremely important, albeit slightly mixed, components from MNT-1485/H, MNT-1486/H, and MNT-1601 in the upper Carmel Valley (Breschini and Haversat 1992, 1995b).

Big Sur

The Big Sur coast is marked by rocky shore middens that front a precipitous coastline with only small and occasional terraces. Until the 1980s, subsurface data were limited to findings from MNT-44, MNT-281, and MNT-282 at Willow Creek, Isabella Meadows Cave (MNT-250), and preliminary findings from MNT-238 (Moratto 1984). Since then, a substantial amount of research has documented human occupation from 4400 cal B.C. to historic times. The oldest component (4400 cal B.C.) identified so far was found at MNT-1232/H on the coast within Landels Hill Big Creek Reserve, where it was associated with a modest assemblage of tools and faunal remains (Jones 2003; Fitzgerald and Jones 1999). A comparable date was obtained from MNT-521 in the interior albeit with no clear associations (Jones and Haney 1997). Substantial components marking the period between 3500 cal B.C. and cal A.D. 1000 are known from the coast at MNT-1228 (3700 to 3100 cal B.C.), MNT-73 (2300 to 1700 cal B.C.), MNT-185/H (Motz et al. 1989), and MNT-238 (Mikkelsen et al. 2004), and from the interior at MNT-569, MNT-521, and MNT-1918. Components postdating cal A.D. 1250 are extremely common both on the coast (MNT-1223, MNT-1227; Jones 1995, 2003, MNT-1942; Wohlgemuth et al. 2002) and in the interior (MNT-323; Swernoff 1982, MNT-879; Haney et al. 2002, MNT-910, and MNT-1748/H; Jones and Haney 2005). MNT-307 (Breschini and Haversat 2005a) and MNT-1277/H (Jones 2003), associated with Salinan place-names, produced relatively recent prehistoric and contact-era materials.

San Simeon Reef (Northern San Luis Obispo Coast) and Adjacent Interior

The coastline south of Big Sur is distinguished by more expansive coastal terraces and a mix of exposed and sheltered rocky shores. San Simeon Point, an erosion-resistant headland, is a major feature. Middens commonly exhibit shellfish assemblages dominated by mussels, abalone, and unusually high frequencies of turban snails (*Tegula* spp.). Important excavations in this locality described in 1984 (Pico and Little Pico Creeks) have in the subsequent two decades been reanalyzed, including additional excavation and enhanced chronometric analyses (Ferneau 1998; Jones and Ferneau 2002a; Jones and Waugh 1995; Waugh 1992). Important studies were also completed early on by Bouey and Basgall (1991), Gibson (1979a, b), and Hines (1986).

As elsewhere, indications of early human occupation from shell-derived radiocarbon dates, initially dismissed (see Pierce 1979:42), have been clearly validated in the past decade (Bertrando and Levulett 2004; Fitzgerald 2004). Radiocarbon results from SLO-177 and especially SLO-369 indicate occupation ca. 7000 cal B.C., including an apparent house floor at the latter (Parker 2004). Components marking these earliest occupations are not well segregated, however. Important Early Holocene components have also been identified inland, including a buried component dating ca. 5000 cal B.C. at SLO-1756 (Fitzgerald 1997). Unfortunately a more recent date of 950 cal B.C. was also recovered from the same stratigraphic context, reflecting ever-present problems with mixing. Another interior site with substantial evidence of Early Holocene occupation is SLO-1920/H, reported by Stevens et al. (2004). This multicomponent site yielded four radiocarbon dates between 7100 and 6600 cal B.C. associated with small tool and faunal assemblages.

Evidence for more recent use of the San Simeon Reef area is slightly more abundant with important components identified at SLO-175 (3500 to 2800 cal B.C.) (Jones and Waugh 1995), SLO-179 (Jones and Ferneau 2002a), SLO-273 (1600 to 800 cal B.C. and cal A.D. 1000 to 1300), SLO-274 (3600 to 800 cal B.C.) (Hildebrandt et al. 2002), SLO-1622 (2900 to 1900 cal B.C.), and SLO-1677 (3100 to 1800 cal B.C.) (Joslin 2006). The most intensively sampled site is SLO-267, dating 1400 cal B.C. to cal A.D. 1000. Post cal A.D. 1000 components have been identified in the Cambria area at SLO-71 and SLO-115 (Joslin 2006) at San Simeon State Park (Hines 1986) and at SLO-1914/H near Cayucos (Farrell et al. 2004), although samples from these locations are extremely limited. Findings from the adjacent interior appear to mark a range of time periods (Basgall 2003a; Carpenter et al. 2004), but chronological control is imprecise owing to poor preservation and limited radiocarbon analysis. Exceptions are a well-delineated post cal A.D. 1200 component at SLO-1180 and a large floor feature at SLO-1778 dating ca. 400 cal B.C. (Basgall 2003a).

Morro Bay

The second most important estuary on the Central Coast, Morro Bay, was known in 1984 only by the materials from SLO-239, a midden deposit with a large, well-preserved house floor near Morro Rock (Clemmer 1962). Unfortunately this site has never been dated by radiocarbon, and the antiquity of estuarine adaptations in this locality was not recognized until later in the 1980s. As in other portions of the San Luis Obispo district, important early studies were done by Robert Gibson (Gibson 1981a), and important research summaries have been presented by Bertrando (2004a), Mikkelsen et al. (2000), and Jones et al. (2002).

Three sites testify to exploitation of the bay 7,000 to 8000 years ago: SLO-165 (basal date 6100 cal B.C.) (Mikkelsen et al. 2000), SLO-215 (5800 cal B.C.) (T. Jones et al. 2004), and SLO-812 (6000 cal B.C.), although samples associated with these dates are small. Limited radiocarbon results from SLO-877, slightly north of the bay, suggest human presence as early as 6700 cal B.C. The most important, best-defined component in the area is at SLO-165, dating 3600 to 1000 cal B.C. Other sites producing more limited suites of dates and tools within this same span include SLO-14 (Parker 1996), SLO-1795 (Bertrando 2004a), SLO-1212 (Bertrando 2000), and SLO-977 (Dallas 1992). Substantial components representing the period between 1000 cal B.C. and cal A.D. 1000 have yet to be identified, although minor occupations in this range are evident at SLO-165 and SLO-812. Sites showing evidence for post cal A.D. 1000 occupation include SLO-214, SLO-463, and SLO-1385 (Parker 2000), but samples from all of these deposits are limited.

Pecho Coast

While the rocky coast between Morro Bay and Pismo Beach has previously been subsumed within the Morro Bay area, it is in fact marked by a distinctive stretch of exposed shoreline that harbors several of the oldest archaeological sites in central California. Greenwood's (1972) monumental study of six sites at Diablo Canyon still stands as the seminal work for this area, and her original study has been supplemented by more detailed study of flaked stone (Farqhuar 2003) and faunal remains. Both SLO-2 and SLO-585 produced substantial components dating between 8000 and 3000 cal B.C. Newly available chronometric data show that both sites were largely unoccupied from 3000 to 500 cal B.C. Both have substantial components dating cal A.D. 1500 to contact, while SLO-2 was also occupied from 500 cal B.C. to cal A.D. 1000. An extremely cohesive component was recently identified at Coon Creek (SLO-9) north of Diablo Canyon dating cal A.D. 1000 to 1250, while a more recent occupation was identified at SLO-7 (cal A.D. 1250 to 1700) (Breschini and Haversat 1988). SLO-2 produced the oldest human remains in the region, a flexed burial dating ca. 8000 cal B.C.

Pismo Beach/Nipomo Mesa

The Pismo Beach area is marked by extensive dunes including the Pleistocene Nipomo Mesa and nearshore deposits of Holocene age. Exposed sandy shores provide habitat for Pismo clams which are abundant in some sites, but estuarine shells from the extinct Halcyon Bay estuary are common at many locations. Important early research was completed by Gibson (1981b), and summaries of research in this locality have recently been presented by D. Jones et al. (2002), Jones and Darcangelo (2004), and Fitzgerald (2000). By far the most important sites investigated in the locality are SLO-1797 (Cross Creek) and SLO-832/1420, which produced radiocarbon evidence for initial occupation dating 8300 to 7900 cal B.C. Only slightly younger was SLO-1764 with an estuarine shellfish assemblage dating 7200 to 7000 cal B.C. (Lebow et al. 2001). Occupations postdating 3000 cal B.C. are known from Avila Beach (Moriarity and Burns 1962), and SLO-393 and SLO-406 on the Nipomo Mesa (Conway 2000). Many other sites on the Mesa away from water sources have proven difficult to date because cultural residues commonly lack organic debris (Fitzgerald et al. 2000). An important Late Period component was identified in the Arroyo Grande area at SLO-372 (Baker 1977).

Interior

Owing to the remote and rugged nature of the interior coast ranges, archaeological research has tended to be sporadic and largely overshadowed by developments in adjacent areas. The most substantial projects were completed in the 1960s in anticipation of reservoir construction (Olsen and Payen 1968, 1969, 1983; Pritchard 1983). Since then, research has included a series of smaller test excavations that have yielded important albeit limited findings from a variety of areas. In 1987 Breschini and Haversat investigated a series of small rock shelters at FRE-1333, one of the only upland sites (elevation 2,360 feet) in the Diablo Range yet investigated. A small but diverse assemblage and two human burials suggest more than ephemeral site use (Breschini and Haversat 1987) between cal A.D. 500 and 1500.

Between 1988 and 1994, a group of dedicated archaeologists and private citizens known as the Coalinga Archaeological Research Group (COALARG) was active throughout the southern Diablo Range in western Fresno County (Betts and Foster 2001). COALARG recorded or otherwise investigated nearly 100 sites in the Coalinga backcountry, many on private land. This group also completed test excavations at FRE-1346 (Jenkins 2001).

In 1990, an extensive survey and site evaluation project was undertaken in the Los Banos Creek area upstream from previous excavation work in the late 1960s (Mikkelsen and Hildebrandt 1990). Among important aspects of this work were the refining of chronology through reanalysis of shell bead and ornament data from the Pacheco Pass cultural sequence and one of the first attempts to describe archaeological sites in the region with reference to prehistoric subsistence-settlement patterns. Hylkema's (1993) study of settlement in the Diablo Range suggested that the upland areas of it were intensively occupied by groups representative of Olsen and Payen's (1969) Pacheco Complex (i.e., Early and Middle Periods) while later (i.e., post cal A.D. 1000) occupations were concentrated around larger habitation sites in lower elevation settings.

Renewed investigation of sites in the Panoche Creek drainage occurred during the 1990s. Work at three sites was conducted by a field class from California State University–Fresno in 1993 and 1994, including surface inspection and excavation of approximately three cubic meters of deposits from FRE-2366 (LaJeunesse et al. 1996). Though small, the collection from FRE-2366 provides useful data including time-sensitive *Olivella* beads, obsidian hydration readings, and identified faunal remains. In 1997 another site in this drainage (FRE-2365) was excavated as mitigation for damage suffered during a wildfire (Milliken and Meyer 1997). A sample of 3.2 cubic meters produced an assemblage similar to that from FRE-2366. Despite being buried almost two meters below the surface, a radiocarbon sample from the midden dated to only 1440 +/– 60 years BP. More recently Basgall and Giambastiani (1999) reported testing results from five sites near the Kern/San Luis Obispo County border. Three of these, KER-1304, KER-4620, and KER-4623/H, revealed substantial subsurface deposits spanning the Early through Late Periods, with the bulk of occupation attributable to the Middle Period. Just to the south near Polonio Pass, an additional site (SLO-1355) produced obsidian hydration readings and bead data suggesting occupation during the Early and Middle Periods (Tiley 2001). Stevens et al. (2004) reported a group of sites near Paso Robles, including SLO-1920/H and SLO-2077/H, with occupations spanning the Millingstone through Late periods. Most recently, Sickler-Hylkema (2005) completed an ambitious evaluation of prehistoric land-use patterns in the Diablo Range incorporating surface data from over 400 sites. Whitley et al. (2004) completed an equally important survey in the Carrizo Plain area.

CULTURE HISTORY, SETTLEMENT, AND SUBSISTENCE

Among the three seminal investigations that defined Central Coast prehistory in 1984, only Greenwood's (1972) study combined ecological interpretations with a traditional, artifact-defined cultural chronology. Both Breschini and Haversat (1980) and Dietz and Jackson (1981) passed over traditional culture history and focused almost exclusively on issues of subsistence, settlement, and ecology, relying on radiocarbon dates for temporal control. While issues of subsistence and ecology still represent the most interesting aspects of the region's prehistory, much work in the past two decades by several of us has also sought to establish a traditional cultural sequence history at the same time that these other issues have been advanced.

One of the reasons researchers in the early 1980s avoided a traditional cultural sequence was that normative archaeology by that time had produced a quagmire of unresolved issues about terms and their meanings. On the Central Coast, research was further complicated by the existence of well-established cultural schema for the San Francisco Bay to the north and the Santa Barbara area to the south that relied on alternate conceptual underpinnings and different archaeological evidence. One of us has discussed this situation at length on a number of occasions (see Jones 1993; Jones and Waugh 1995). The fact remains that time can be divided by any number of criteria and it is possible to ignore cultural divisions and rely strictly on a calendric scale, as is done in some parts of California. Nonetheless, there is significant variability in artifact assemblages over time on the Central Coast, and several stylistic/typological transitions are so striking that it seems unwise to overlook them. The chronological system employed here incorporates six *periods*, locally defined *phases*, and regional *cultures*, similar to Fredrickson's (1974a) *patterns*. Periods are as follow:

Late (cal A.D. to 1250–1769)
Middle/Late Transition (cal A.D. 1000 to 1250)
Middle (600 cal B.C. to cal A.D. 1000)
Early (3500 to 600 cal B.C.)
Millingstone (or Early Archaic) (8000 to 3500 cal B.C.)
Paleo-Indian (pre-8000 cal B.C.)

The Early, Middle, and Late Periods reflect longstanding perceptions of central California prehistory that extend back to the 1930s, when three superimposed archaeological cultures were identified in the lower Sacramento Valley/Delta (Lillard and Purves 1936; Lillard et al. 1939). Since then, Early, Middle, and Late Periods have been defined largely on the basis of distinctive bead types. Owing to wide-ranging cultural interactions, these types occurred contemporaneously over large portions of California and were originally referred to in terms of horizons. Unfortunately many other traits co-occurring with the beads in the lower Sacramento Valley (but not found elsewhere) were incorrectly included within the original horizon definitions, so that the concept of horizon was eventually dropped from California archaeology despite the fact that the bead style–defined periods are in fact classic examples of horizon phenomena. On the Central Coast, the Early Period is marked by thick rectangular (Class L) *Olivella* beads, the Middle Period is marked by normal saucer (G2) *Olivella* beads, and the Late Period is marked by lipped (Class E) and cupped (Class K) *Olivella* beads (Bennyhoff and Hughes 1987) and steatite disks. Thin rectangular (Class M) *Olivella* beads are known in the Monterey Bay area but not to the south. The Middle/Late Transition is here regarded as a distinctive period during which tiny saucer (G1), G2, and K beads co-occurred, but this definition is not accepted by all. Hylkema (2002) sees no such transition in the Santa Cruz area, and dates the onset of the Late Period to cal A.D.1000, whereas Breschini and Haversat (2002) date the onset of the Late Period to cal A.D. 900 or earlier on the Monterey Peninsula. Hughes and Milliken (Chapter 17 in this volume) date a Middle/Late Transition at cal A.D. 1050 to 1250 in central California, although they subsume the transition within the Late Period and correlate it with split-punched (Class D) *Olivella* beads. Perhaps as an artifact of sampling, split-punched beads have not been found in appreciable quantities on the Central Coast and it is difficult to employ them as important temporal markers in this area.

Broader patterns in the regional prehistory, first recognized by Greenwood (1972) at Diablo Canyon, are reflected in three major cultural divisions marked by highly distinctive tool assemblages: the Millingstone Culture, the Hunting Culture, and Late Period. Although some may view the first two terms as old-fashioned conventions that oversimplify complex relationships between material and nonmaterial culture, the fact remains that a progression of three distinctive complexes can be readily detected over the whole Central Coast region. Earlier human presence in the area is suggested only by isolated fluted projectile points from Nipomo (Bertrando 2004b; Mills et al. 2005) and at SLO-1429 near Santa Margarita (Gibson 1996), probably reflecting habitation sometime between 13,000 and 10,000 years ago. No substantive components of this age have yet been identified, however. A long-standing suggestion that pre-Holocene antiquity is represented by eccentric crescents is not matched by the temporal contexts of crescents recovered from MNT-229 (Jones and Jones 1992) and SMA-134 (Hylkema 1998), which suggest ages only in the range of 6000 to 4500 cal B.C. An eccentric crescent from SCR-177 can be dated with no more certainty than other materials from that site.

Millingstone Culture, 8000 to 3500/3000 cal B.C.

While the Millingstone Culture was discovered in southern California as early as 1929 (D. B. Rogers 1929) and defined more precisely in 1955 (Wallace 1955), its existence on the Central Coast was only recognized in 1972 by Roberta Greenwood. Its occurrence throughout the region during the Early Holocene or Early Archaic has been proposed more recently by Fitzgerald and Jones (1999), although Hildebrandt (1983) earlier recognized a northern manifestation at SCL-178. In both its northern and southern expressions, Millingstone is consistently marked by large numbers of well-made handstones and/or millingslabs, crude core and cobble-core tools, and less abundant flake tools and large side-notched projectile points (Figure 9.4). Pitted stones also occur in some Millingstone contexts (e.g., SLO-2 and SLO-585), although they were absent from SLO-1797. Contracting stemmed points, while more common in later contexts, were recovered from the Millingstone levels at SLO-2 as well. The oldest expressions of the pattern are known from SLO-2 and SLO-1797 (8000 cal B.C.), while slightly younger components have been identified at MNT-1232/H, SCL-178, SCR-177, SLO-177, SLO-585, SLO-832, SLO-1756, and SLO-1920/H. An undated component was recently identified at SLO-1842 within Camp Roberts (Carpenter et al. 2004) while another, at MNT-831 on the Monterey Peninsula, suggests that Millingstone may have persisted to 3000 cal B.C. Findings at MNT-1232/H, SCR-177, and SLO-832 suggest that lanceolate points occur within Millingstone components, as do crescents, based on examples from MNT-229 and SCR-177. Three human burials from the deepest Millingstone levels at SLO-2 are among the oldest human remains in California. One highly deteriorated skeleton appeared to be in a flexed position while another had a flat, oval, unmodified stone over the skull (Greenwood 1972:8). Three phases are considered local variants of the same general pattern: Metcalf in the north, Interpretive in the Big Sur area, and Diablo in the south (Figure 9.5).

Millingstone occupations have been recognized at no fewer than 42 sites in a range of settings, including the open rocky coasts (e.g., SCR-38, SLO-2, SLO-585, and SLO-177), the Morro Bay and Elkhorn Slough

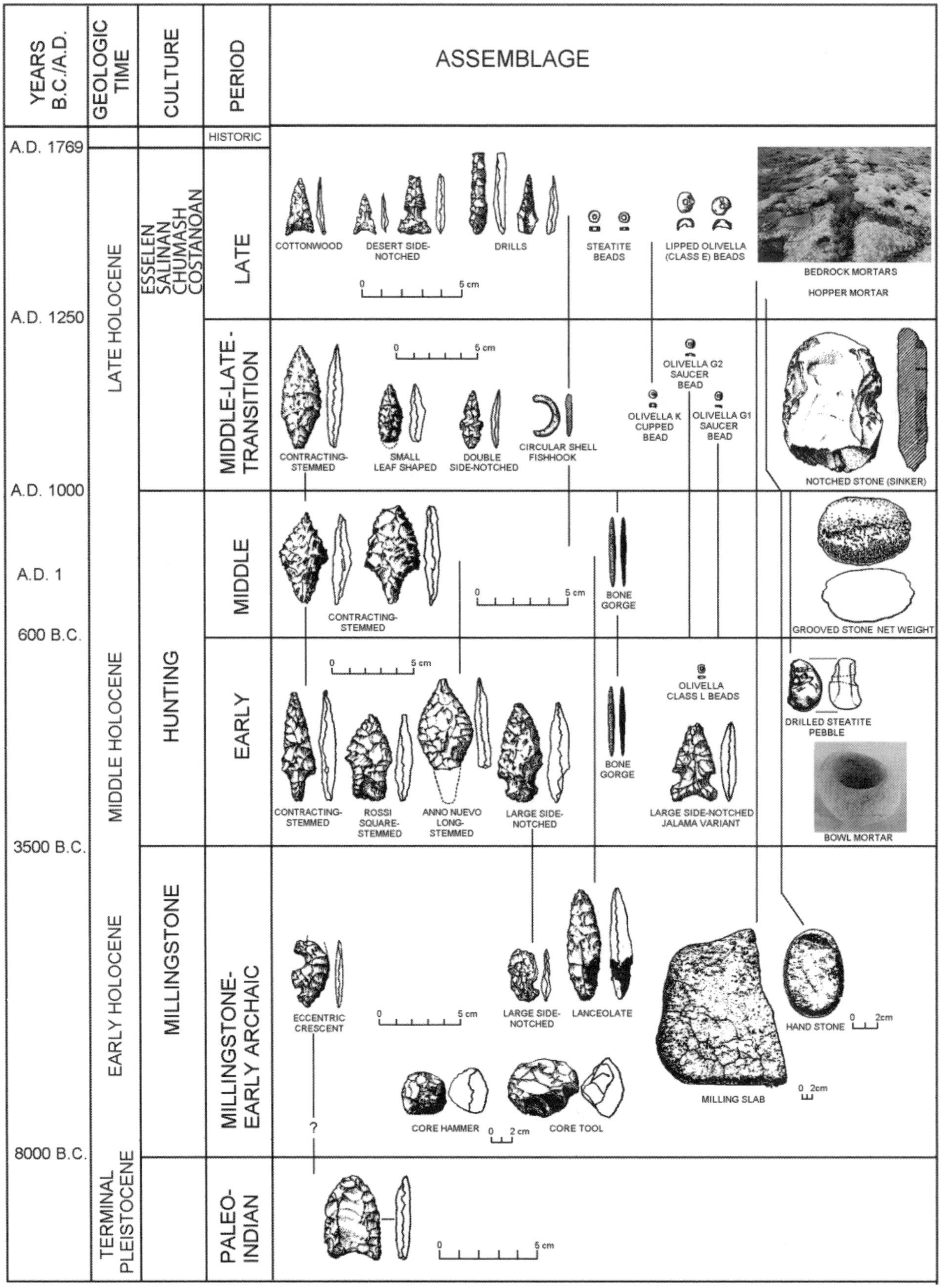

Figure 9.4. Generalized culture history for the Central Coast region.

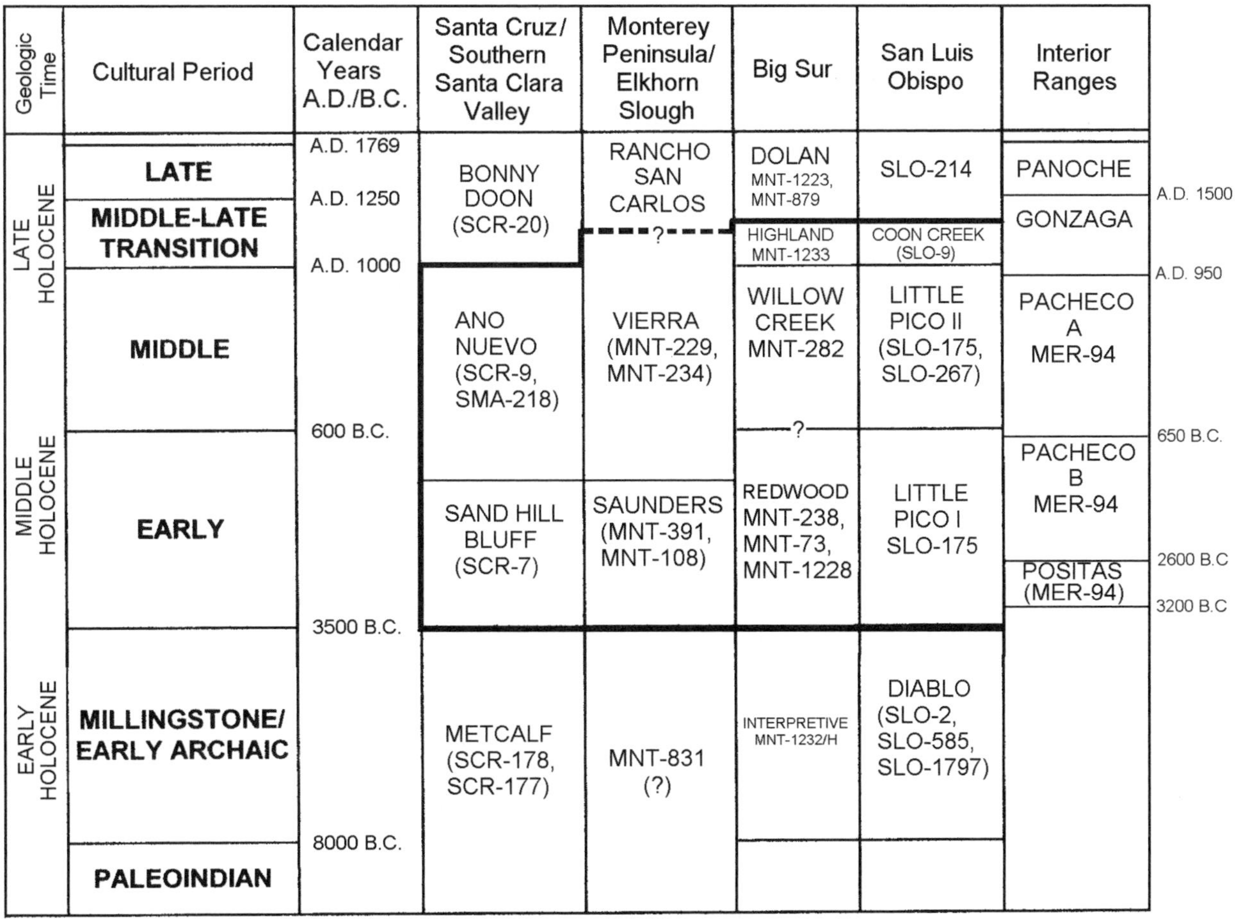
Geologic Time
Cultural Period
Calendar Years A.D./B.C.
Santa Cruz/ Southern Santa Clara Valley
Monterey Peninsula/ Elkhorn Slough
Big Sur
San Luis Obispo
Interior Ranges
LATE HOLOCENE
MIDDLE HOLOCENE
EARLY HOLOCENE
LATE
MIDDLE-LATE TRANSITION
MIDDLE
EARLY
MILLINGSTONE/ EARLY ARCHAIC
PALEOINDIAN
A.D. 1769
A.D. 1250
A.D. 1000
600 B.C.
3500 B.C.
8000 B.C.
BONNY DOON (SCR-20)
ANO NUEVO (SCR-9, SMA-218)
SAND HILL BLUFF (SCR-7)
METCALF (SCR-178, SCR-177)
RANCHO SAN CARLOS
?
VIERRA (MNT-229, MNT-234)
SAUNDERS (MNT-391, MNT-108)
MNT-831 (?)
DOLAN MNT-1223, MNT-879
HIGHLAND MNT-1233
WILLOW CREEK MNT-282
?
REDWOOD MNT-238, MNT-73, MNT-1228
INTERPRETIVE MNT-1232/H
SLO-214
COON CREEK (SLO-9)
LITTLE PICO II (SLO-175, SLO-267)
LITTLE PICO I SLO-175
DIABLO (SLO-2, SLO-585, SLO-1797)
PANOCHE
GONZAGA
PACHECO A MER-94
PACHECO B MER-94
POSITAS (MER-94)
A.D. 1500
A.D. 950
650 B.C.
2600 B.C
3200 B.C

Figure 9.5. Archaeological phases of the Central Coast. The bold lines indicate phases associated with the Hunting Culture.

estuaries, the paleoestuary of Halcyon Bay, and the nearshore interior valleys (SCL-178, SLO-1842, SLO-1920/H). In the Central Coast region few Millingstone components have been found farther than 25 kilometers inland from the shore,[4] and most interior Millingstone sites have produced marine shells indicating that site inhabitants also exploited coastal environments. At least for now, the available record suggests that many Millingstone groups maintained a connection to the coast, including the oldest Millingstone expressions at Cross Creek and Diablo Canyon. The broader Millingstone Culture, however, is associated with a bewildering array of habitats, ranging from the Sierran foothills (Bieling et al. 1996) to paleolakeshores in the southern Santa Clara Valley. The importance of lacustrine habitats during the Millingstone Period inland is debated (Hildebrandt 1997a, b; Jones 1997).

Faunal remains indicate that Millingstone peoples practiced broad-spectrum hunting and gathering, exploiting shellfish, fish, birds, and mammals, although robust faunal assemblages are not common. This is particularly true inland where faunal preservation is poor (Carpenter et al. 2004). As discussed in Chapter 4 of this volume, the oldest vertebrate remains from SLO-2 show a dominance of deer, pelagic birds, and rabbits. Rocky coast fish were caught, and shellfish represented a significant if not dominant portion of the diet. Faunal remains from the oldest inland expression of Millingstone at SLO-1797 (Cross Creek) showed almost no use of vertebrates and heavy exploitation of shellfish and (inferentially) seeds and other vegetal foods. Several other Millingstone components at SLO-215, SLO-232, and SCL-178 are dominated by rabbits, but larger Millingstone assemblages from SLO-2 and SLO-585 show a strong preference for deer. Shellfish assemblages are dominated by estuarine species at some locations (Elkhorn Slough, Cross Creek, Pismo Beach) and rocky coast taxa (e.g., mussels) at others (MNT-1232/H, SLO-2). Fish bone in Millingstone sites is considerably less abundant than in later deposits, with densities ranging from only 3 to 129 NISP/m^3.

In an extremely important study of Millingstone age burials from SCR-60, Newsome et al. (2004) inferred from stable isotope analysis a diet composed of 70–84 percent marine food. Given the low frequency of fish and pinniped bones in most Millingstone assemblages, this suggests heavy use of shellfish, which is supported by dense concentrations of shells in many deposits and dietary reconstructions based on these and other faunal remains. The oldest residential feature in the region, dating to the early Millingstone Period, was identified by Parker (2004) at SLO-369 in Cambria, where he interpreted a dish-shaped depression at the base of a midden as a likely house floor.

Hunting Culture, 3500/3000 cal B.C. *to cal* A.D. *1000/1250*

In 1929 David Banks Rogers coined the term "Hunting Culture" to define a distinctive complex in the Santa Barbara area that, in contrast with Millingstone (Roger's Oak Grove), was marked by large quantities of stemmed and notched projectile points. Components exhibiting such artifacts tended to overlay Millingstone expressions. In 1972 Greenwood confirmed this trend at Diablo Canyon and dated its appearance at ca. 3500 to 3000 cal B.C. Since then, it has become clear that many sites up and down the Central Coast show the same basic yet striking pattern in which large projectile points become extremely abundant after ca. 3500/3000 cal B.C. In interior sites where soil acidity destroys faunal remains, Hunting Culture middens are marked almost exclusively by dense accumulations of points and other large bifaces (e.g., MNT-1918) (Jones and Haney 2005). In most cases, Hunting Culture assemblages are associated with the establishment of new settlements ca. 3500 to 3000 cal B.C., including MNT-108, MNT-391, MNT-1228, SCR-7, SLO-165, and SLO-175. The Hunting Culture can be considered synonymous with the Sur Pattern defined by Breschini and Haversat (1980), Dietz and Jackson (1981), and Moratto (1984), although the artifact-based definition used here differs from the earlier emphasis on midden characteristics (e.g., middens with shell).

Hunting Culture typologies have been refined in recent years to include projectile points and other formal artifacts as markers of discrete phases. Early attempts (Dietz et al. 1988; Jones 1993) emphasizing a "splitting" approach have proven less useful than a "lumping" system preferred here. The Early Period is marked by co-occurrence of contracting-stemmed and Rossi square-stemmed (Central Coast Stemmed Series) points (Figure 9.4), and large side-notched variants (as a holdover from Millingstone). This pattern is well represented at MNT-238, MNT-391, and MNT-1918. A distinctive Año Nuevo long-stemmed point occurs in the Santa Cruz and Monterey areas. Ground stone assemblages show retention of the earlier handstone/slab dyad along with pitted stones. Portable mortars and pestles appear for the first time in low frequencies. Cobble-core tools occur in lower frequencies than earlier. Line fishing implements are limited to bipointed bone gorges. Early Period phases of the Hunting Culture include Sand Hill Bluff in the Santa Cruz area, Saunders on the Monterey Peninsula, Redwood in Big Sur, and Little Pico I in San Luis Obispo. The southern phases show more use of steatite while the Sand Hill Bluff is distinguished by a distinctive serrated side-notched point. The San Luis Obispo area is marked by a subtype of large side-notched point sometimes referred to as Jalama.[5] Breschini and Haversat (2002) believe that the Early Period should be extended back to 4000 cal B.C. and divided into two subphases (I and II) in which Phase I shows retention of Millingstone traits while Phase II, postdating ca. 2000 cal B.C., is marked by high frequencies of stemmed points and the first appearance of mortars and pestles and Class L rectangular *Olivella* beads. This proposal is supported by findings from some locations (e.g., MNT-73, 238, 521, and 831) and should be further considered as more components dating 3000 to 2000 cal B.C. are discovered.

The most important Early Period burial population is from MNT-391; it shows a preference for flexed position and grave associations that commonly included Rossi square-stemmed projectile points, fish gorges, and Class L beads (Cartier 1993b). Three burials were directly dated between 2300 and 1300 cal B.C., making them contemporary with a smaller burial group from SCR-60.

Middle Period expressions of the Hunting Culture are well represented at SCR-9, SMA-218 (defining the Año Nuevo Phase), MNT-101, MNT-282 (defining the Willow Creek Phase), MNT-229 (defining the Vierra Phase), MNT-234, MNT-521, SLO-175 (defining the Little Pico II Phase), and SLO-267, which show retention of contracting-stemmed points and disappearance of square-stemmed and large side-notched variants. The Año Nuevo Phase includes a distinctive long-stemmed variant well represented at SCR-9 and SMA-218. Beads are dominated by G2 saucers replacing L2 thick rectangles, and ground stone assemblages show continued use of both slabs/handstones and portable mortars/pestles. The latter dominates assemblages at some places (e.g., MNT-229) while the former is more important at others (e.g., MNT-521). Circular shell fishhooks appear for the first time but bone gorges persist. Pitted stones are often the most abundant artifact in Middle Period sites although they were absent from MNT-229. Grooved stone net sinkers are common as well. Well-made bone flutes are occasionally found as burial accompaniments (e.g., at SLO-2, SLO-175, and MNT-229). Graves from all of these sites show continued preference for the flexed burial position. Other common Middle Period burial accompaniments include bone tubes and large quantities of *Olivella* G2 beads. Toward the end of the Middle Period the appearance of small leaf-shaped projectile points at sites such as SLO-179 marks the arrival of bows and arrows, although this new weapon seems to have been relatively unimportant at first.

The terminal phases of the Hunting Culture and their dating are important if not contentious topics. There is no question that the Central Coast was witness to dramatic changes in assemblages and settlement sometime after ca. cal A.D. 1000, highlighted by the appearance of large numbers of arrow points, disappearance of most stemmed points, and changes in bead types. This vigorous transition seems to date slightly differently in different areas, although the imprecision of radiocarbon dating and the poor resolution of some components complicate perceptions of the timing and nature of changes. In the Santa Cruz area, Hylkema (2002) argues that an abrupt, highly visible transition took place at cal A.D. 1100. In Big Sur, findings from MNT-1233 suggest that the Hunting Culture persisted until cal A.D. 1200–1300. An exceptionally discrete component at SLO-9 on the Pecho Coast marks a Coon Creek Phase, proposed here for the first time, that clearly delineates the Middle/Late Transition in the San Luis Obispo district. Excavated by field class students from Cal Poly–San Luis Obispo in 2004 and 2005, this site produced an exceptionally discrete component dated with seven radiocarbon assays (derived from marines shells) that fall between cal A.D. 900 (1720 + 40 years B.P.; Beta 199103) and cal A.D. 1280 (1470 + 40 years B.P.; Beta 198050). The assemblage associated with the occupation reflects a clear affiliation with the Hunting Culture. It was dominated by contracting-stemmed projectile points, small leaf-shaped arrow points, expedient, notched line sinkers, circular shell fishhooks, and G2 *Olivella* saucer beads (Figure 9.4). The unique and peculiar double side-notched point was represented by a single example. This type is more common in Middle/Late contexts in the Cambria area (Figure 9.4), where multiple examples were recovered from an unusual mass grave at SLO-175 (Jones and Waugh 1995).

To date, 157 sites have produced evidence of occupation during the era of the Hunting Culture. A preference for coastal habitation is still fairly apparent, but large Hunting Culture middens also occur in pericoastal valleys. Within the drainages of the Nacimiento and San Antonio Rivers at Fort Hunter Liggett, the Hunting Culture is extremely visible with large sites concentrated in valley oak savanna. There is also strong evidence for occupation even farther inland at such sites as MER-94, SLO-1355, and KER-4623/H, although precise dating is problematic in the interior. Assemblages from the inland area also need to be further evaluated vis-à-vis their affiliation with the Hunting Culture. Hunting Culture sites are often marked by highly visible accumulations of biface-derived debitage, and a range of site types has been recognized including middens, flaked and ground stone scatters, and scatters of flaked stone that only include lithic procurement stations/quarries. Identified within Fort Hunter Liggett, the Los Osos area (Bertrando 2004a), the Nipomo Mesa, and the Diablo Range (Hylkema 1993; Sickler-Hylkema 2005), this assortment of site types suggests a measure of logistical hunting. But more than anything else it reflects heavy reliance on large projectile points and other large bifacial implements by Hunting Culture peoples. Known residential features are limited to two fairly large (approximately 10 meters in diameter), circular house floors, one at SLO-1778 on the Nacimiento River dating to the Middle Period (Basgall 2003a), and another identified by Clemmer (1962) at SLO-239 on Morro Bay, tentatively dated to the Middle/Late Transition (Mikkelsen et al. 2000).

Hunting Culture faunal assemblages show variability, but most Early Period components emphasize deer (SCR-7, MNT-1228, MNT-238), while SLO-165 at Morro Bay showed continued focus on rabbits, and MNT-391 on the Monterey Peninsula was dominated by sea otters. Fish remains from Early Period components show increases over the Millingstone Culture as reflected by findings from MNT-108 and SLO-165, but Middle Period expressions show significantly greater concentrations. MNT-228 and 234 at Elkhorn Slough, for example, produced 3,416 and 5,100 fish NISP/m^3 respectively from Middle Period deposits processed with three millimeter (1/8 inch) mesh. SLO-267, on the open coast, however, only produced 459 NISP/m^3. Middle Period bird and mammal assemblages show a common emphasis on deer as represented at SCR-9, MNT-228, MNT-229, MNT-521, SLO-2, and SLO-267. Northern fur seals, however, dominated the remains from SMA-218 at Año Nuevo, and sea otters were the most abundant taxon at MNT-101 on the Monterey Peninsula. Some Middle Period (e.g., MNT-63) and Middle/Late Period components (MNT-3) still show dominance of rabbits while others produced an abundance of deer bones (e.g., MNT-1233 on the Big Sur coast). Shellfish were part of the diet at all coastal sites, but they seem to have decreased in importance relative to vertebrates. Radiocarbon-dated acorn remains from SLO-165 suggest that this important resource was exploited to some unknown degree by Hunting Culture people (Mikkelsen et al. 2000).

Late Period, cal A.D. 1250 to 1769

Late Period assemblages are easily distinguished from the Hunting Culture throughout the region by profusions of Desert side-notched and Cottonwood arrow points, small bifacial bead drills, bedrock mortars, hopper mortars, Class E (lipped) and K (cupped) *Olivella* beads, and steatite disk beads (Figure 9.4). Thin rectangular (Class M) beads and small serrated arrow points are known from the Santa Cruz area and the Monterey Peninsula. Most Late Period sites, when adequately sampled, produce a few bead drills and small amounts of *Olivella* bead manufacturing debris (e.g. MNT-879), suggesting that low-level bead production was common and widespread. This contrasts significantly with the Santa Barbara Channel, where bead industries were profuse. Circular shell fishhooks were still used and there is some evidence for persistence of contracting-stemmed points in low frequencies. Breschini and Haversat (2002) believe that Desert side-notched arrow points were strictly postcontact or protohistoric in the Monterey Peninsula area.

The Late Period is marked by a profusion of single-component sites in the interior and on the coast with a decided focus on the former. A suggestion by one of us (T. Jones 1992) for wholesale abandonment of the coast during the Late Period has been proven somewhat exaggerated by the discovery of Late Period middens at Big Sur (Breschini and Haversat 2005a; Hildebrandt and Jones 1998; Wohlgemuth et al. 2002), San Simeon Reef (Joslin 2006), and Morro Bay (SLO-23). Nonetheless, Late Period sites are most abundant away from the shoreline in a variety of settings including the interior ranges, and Late occupation has been recognized at no fewer than 157 sites. Typical Late Period occupations are marked by small middens with associated or nearby bedrock mortars. As with earlier periods, residential features are uncommon, but circular house floors roughly three to four meters in diameter are known from Big Sur on the coast at MNT-1227 (Jones 2003) and in the interior at MNT-1748/H (Jones and Haney 2005). While expansive sites have been documented at some locations (e.g., MNT-1277/H in Big Sur; Jones 2003; SLO-214 in Los Osos; Hoover and Sawyer 1977), Late Period middens are often fairly small (30 to 40 meters in diameter) with several discrete deposits clustered in one area. For the most part, the Late Period shows strong if not remarkable consistency in assemblages, site types, and settlement patterns across the region despite linguistic variability. Unique to the Monterey Peninsula are dense deposits of whole abalone shells, commonly interpreted as abalone collecting stations used by task-specific groups of inland-based collectors (Breschini and Haversat 1980; Dietz and Jackson 1981). Recognition and dating of these important sites was a major contribution of Breschini and Haversat's (1980) and Dietz and Jackson's (1981) research on the Peninsula. Referred to as markers of a provisional Monterey Pattern in the early work, these sites are now classified as coastal shellfish processing locations (Breschini and Haversat 1991b).

ALTERNATIVE INTERPRETATIONS

While interpretations of the regional culture history have focused on a number of developments at the local level (some out of sync with the broader regional patterns), most explanatory efforts have focused on the process of initial human colonization and the major intervals of transition at 3500/3000 cal B.C., 600 cal B.C., and cal A.D. 1250. Interregional variability makes it challenging to generalize about the changes apparent at these points of time, and it is abundantly clear that no single model or theory can accommodate all of the archaeological and ethnohistoric evidence. Principles derived from behavioral and cultural ecology, including optimization, intensification, extensification, and deintensification, have proven useful for characterizing certain trends at certain times and places, but other developments seem best viewed as products of historic contingencies. Specific variables that almost certainly influenced human behavior in the region that can be tracked in the prehistoric record include regional and local environmental variability, and population growth, declines, and migrations.

Issues of Colonization

Understanding the process of the initial peopling of central coastal California is complicated by uncertainties about timing, route(s), and means of arrival. With no substantive evidence for occupation before ca. 8000 cal B.C. yet recovered from the region itself, perceptions continue to be influenced by finds from elsewhere in the state, specifically the fluted projectile points from Tulare Lake (see Chapter 5 in this volume) and the evidence for use of Daisy Cave on San Miguel Island as early as ca. 12,000 years ago (see Chapter 4 in this volume). Neither of the alternative routes of entry suggested by these findings—an interior route or travel along the coast with the aid of watercraft—can be ruled out. Nonetheless, nearly every aspect of the Central Coast archaeological record suggests a process of colonization that began on the coast and gradually spread inland. Virtually all of the earliest known sites have been identified on the shore or in pericoastal valleys, and most dietary reconstructions suggest heavy reliance on shellfish by the earliest inhabitants. It is not unreasonable to envision a scenario in which initial colonization was accomplished by people with boats who slowly became more terrestrially focused over time. While such a scenario seems plausible, the isolated fluted projectile points from Nipomo and Santa Margarita probably predate the coastal Millingstone expressions and further suggest that colonization from the interior cannot be ruled out. Central California could well have been colonized from either or both directions. People likely passed by and through the Central Coast on their way to points farther south. If North America was witness to a series of coastal migrations—which it almost certainly was—the Central Coast was a point along the journey for any number of different groups.

The Millingstone Enigma

Fluted points aside, the oldest substantial human occupations in the region are 10,000-year-old expressions of the California Millingstone Culture. Lingering objections (Glassow 2004a) to this characterization fly in the face of clear patterns first identified by Greenwood (1972) at Diablo Canyon and subsequently corroborated at Cross Creek (Fitzgerald 2000; Fitzgerald and Jones 2003; Jones et al. 2002). These earliest occupations represent a basic pattern that persisted for roughly 5,000 years, marked by distinctive concentrations of millingslabs, handstones, and crude core tools. As early as 1955 (Wallace 1955) this complex was seen as a somewhat peculiar manifestation of societies that relied more on gathering than hunting. In the past decade, faunal and floral assemblages have generally supported the notion of a de-emphasis on hunting by Millingstone people, and the adaptation has been viewed less as peculiar and more as rational (Erlandson 1991b; Jones 1996; McGuire and Hildebrant 1994; Hildebrandt and McGuire 2002). As faunal assemblages dominated by rabbits and shellfish have been documented at places like SCL-178 in the Santa Clara Valley and SLO-832 in Pismo Beach, Millingstone has increasingly been viewed as an optimal gathering/trapping strategy for midlatitude coastal North America (Erlandson 1991b; D. Jones et al. 2004; McGuire and Hildebrandt 1994). Recently documented deer-dominated assemblages in Millingstone components at SLO-2 and SLO-585, however, suggest that a parsimonious explanation for the seemingly peculiar Millingstone adaptation still eludes us. Hildebrandt and McGuire (2002) suggest that Millingstone may represent an optimal solution to reduced environmental richness during the warmer climate of the Early to Middle Holocene. In the Great Basin, Byers and Broughton (2004) demonstrated that artiodactyl populations were suppressed during Early to Middle Holocene due to warm, arid climatic conditions, and it is likely that California may have experienced similar effects which could help explain the low frequency of deer remains in some Millingstone sites. The persistence of Millingstone for thousands of years after the middle Holocene in parts of southern California, however, seems to conflict with any ecological interpretation, which led two of us (Fitzgerald and Jones 1999) to fall back on a largely cultural explanation for the Millingstone tradition.

Middle Holocene Change: The 3500 cal B.C. Transition

While the Millingstone-Hunting shift may ultimately prove to be more gradual, it is currently envisioned as a fairly vigorous transition marked by the establishment of new settlements up and down the coast (e.g., MNT-108, MNT-391, SLO-165, SLO-175, SCR-7, and SCR-239) as well as the earliest well-documented occupation in the interior ranges (MER-94). Regionwide occupation patterns show a marked upward trend at this juncture (Figure 9.6). Interregional trade marked by obsidian from eastern and northern California increases, projectile points become more numerous, and an important new technology—the mortar and pestle—appears for the first time. Much about the Hunting Culture suggests a more labor-intensive adaptation than that of Millingstone. But patterns are

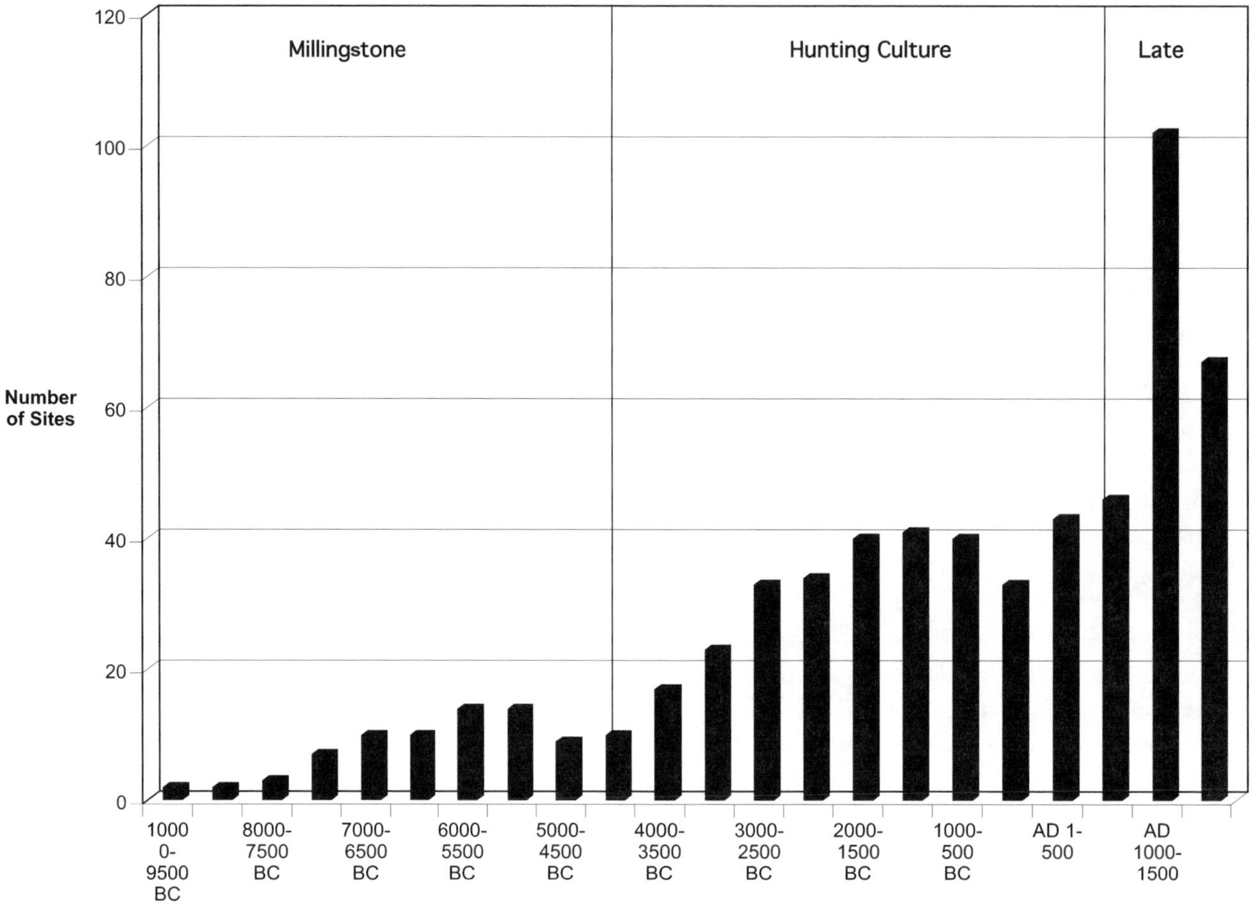

Figure 9.6. Number of sites occupied every five centuries based on calibrated radiocarbon dates (oldest occupations based on isolated fluted projectile points).

not entirely uniform, and more controlled comparisons are needed in light of the broad array of foods represented in the Millingstone components at places like Diablo Canyon. Site locations and faunal assemblages suggest that Hunting Culture people hunted deer and elk heavily, but they also exploited marine mammals, rabbits, fish, and shellfish. Bone isotope findings from SCR-60 show a noticeable reduction in reliance on marine foods across the Millingstone-Hunting transition. The degree to which such trends reflect developments across the entire region remains to be determined.

Factors thought to have influenced the timing and character of changes at this juncture include population circumscription (Jones 1996), the amelioration of climate (Hildebrandt and McGuire 2002), stabilization of sea levels, and possible intrusions of populations from the interior to the coast (Mikkelsen et al. 2000). Dense accumulations of fish bone in Middle Period middens, increased representation of mortar/pestle technology, and greater accumulations of obsidian suggest intensification of the basic Hunting Culture adaptation during the 4,500 years when the pattern was present. Continuity in the Hunting Culture lifeway is well represented at places like MNT-238 on the Big Sur coast (which shows the same basic adaptation from 2000 cal B.C. to cal A.D. 800) and at CA-SLO-175, where Little Pico Phases I and II were defined.

Settlement disruption and/or abandonment is evident as well. Breschini and Haversat (2005b) emphasize the common occurrence of sites on the Monterey Peninsula with Early and Late Period components but no Middle Period occupation. This pattern is also seen at some places on the northern San Luis Obispo coast (Hildebrandt et al. 2002; Joslin 2006). Regional site occupation trends show near stasis between 3000 cal B.C. and cal A.D. 1000 (Figure 9.6). Localized environmental changes, however, seem to have influenced settlement in the Elkhorn Slough area, which was temporarily abandoned early during the Hunting Culture era in response to hydrographic shifts. Not surprisingly, dates from the adjacent Pajaro River estuary (Newsome et al. 2004) show exploitation of that resource base during the time when Elkhorn Slough was apparently nonproductive. Isotope findings from burials at SCR-60 suggest a shift toward more terrestrial emphasis in diet, which Newsome et al. (2004) attribute to the limitations of the marine resource base for intensified subsistence. Logical as this case may seem, it belies the subsistence potential of the Pajaro River and Elkhorn Slough fisheries.

While a case has been made by one of us (Jones) (Hildebrandt and Jones 1992) that impact to marine mammal populations began with the earliest settlement of the coast, the low numbers of pinniped bones in Millingstone assemblages at locations like SLO-2 and MNT-229 suggest that impacts were probably moderate before the advent of the Hunting Culture. Clear evidence for hypothesized onshore rookeries has not been forthcoming except for the island-like setting of MNT-234. Greater frequencies of marine mammal bones mark the Hunting Culture, and it is likely that northern fur seal populations at Año Nuevo and Moss Landing were heavily exploited from this time onward. Exploitation of sea otters also seems to have increased to the point that population impacts would have become inevitable.

An extremely important burial from MNT-391, an infant interred with thousands of grave goods, suggests that positions of prestige and/or power may have been ascribed during all or parts of the Early Period (Cartier 1993b). Similar burials from SLO-406 suggest ascription during the Middle Period as well (Tainter 1971b), but such burials are not common enough to infer a rigid, firmly established, long-lasting power structure. Obsidian from Hunting Culture sites reflects long-distance exchange relationships extending to sources in eastern and northern California, although hydration results from Diablo Canyon and Scotts Valley indicate that such relationships were already established during the Millingstone Period on an apparently more limited basis. Increased exploitation of the sea otter as represented at MNT-391 and SLO-165, as well as localized production of beads at sites like MNT-391 and MNT-229, may reflect activities related to participation in trade with interior groups. Jones (1996) further suggested that population circumscription, regular intergroup trade, and increased importance of processing labor signaled lineal descent groups, not bands. The Hunting Culture seems to mark societies with incipient cultural complexity during a period of relative cultural stasis that came to a rather abrupt end between cal A.D. 1000 and 1250. Breschini and Haversat (2005b) do not agree with this characterization, however, and think, based on patterning in radiocarbon dates, that the interval of cal A.D. 600–700 was a time of major change in the Monterey Bay area. They note (personal communication 2005) that sites on the Monterey Peninsula occupied prior to cal A.D. 660 were abandoned for several hundred years while dozens of new sites were established shortly after that date. According to their analysis of date distribution frequencies, no site currently known on the peninsula was occupied both immediately before and immediately after cal A.D. 660.

The Late Period Revolution and the Archaeology of Tribelets

While the transition from Millingstone to Hunting seems to be marked by relatively distinct diachronic patterns, the changes transpiring on the Central Coast after cal A.D. 1000 can be described as nothing less than revolutionary in comparison with the fairly static situation that preceded them. Late Period assemblages, with abundant arrow points, bead-manufacturing drills, shell and stone beads, and bedrock mortars, differ dramatically from those of the Hunting Culture. A distinctive disruption in settlement is also evident, and sites showing continuity across the Middle/Late Transition (e.g., FRE-1333) are rare. The period between cal A.D. 1000 and 1500 shows more sites occupied than during any other time in the region's prehistory with a 100 percent increase over the previous half millennium, but there is also a marked increase in site abandonment beginning at cal A.D. 1250 (Figure 9.7). Commonly, settlements that were initially established ca. cal A.D.1250 were occupied into the 1700s, and it can be argued fairly strongly that the ethnographic patterns observed at contact, including the tribelet form of political organization, date back to ca. cal A.D. 1250.

The Late Period developments can be viewed in two ways. First, signs of economic intensification include an apparent explosion in bedrock mortar sites in the interior (implying greater use of labor-intensive nut crops), increased use of lower-ranked woodland communities (Jones and Haney 2005) and other interior habitats, faunal assemblages dominated by cottontail rabbits (Carpenter et al. 2004), and an increased use of turban snails on the north coast of San Luis Obispo (Rudolph 1985). The Santa Cruz/Santa Clara area shows signs of heightened territoriality with marine shells becoming less common in the interior (Hildebrandt 1997a) and Franciscan cherts from interior sources disappearing from the coast and being replaced by the locally available Monterey chert (Hylkema 1991). Such developments are all seemingly

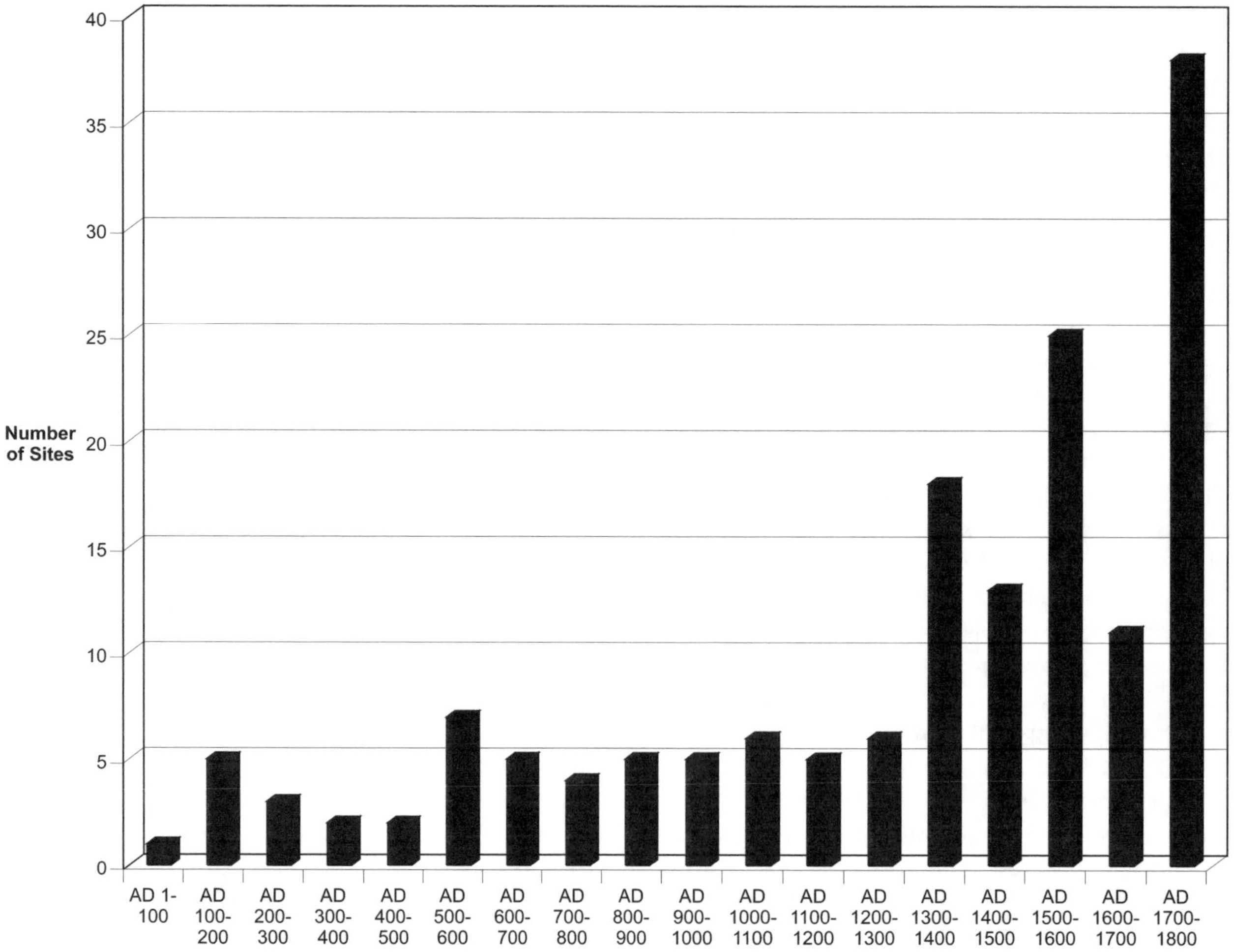

Figure 9.7. Site abandonments cal A.D. 1–1800.

consistent with population growth and an increasingly intensive terrestrial adaptation. One of us has suggested (Hildebrandt and Jones 1992; T. Jones 1992: 15–16) that such changes may reflect limitations of the Central Coast marine resource base, which could only sustain certain levels of human population, although Newsome et al. (2004) made the same case for changes ca. 3000 cal B.C.

An alternative and more recent view attributes developments across the Middle/Late Transition to demographic problems associated with Medieval droughts (Jones et al. 1999; Jones and Ferneau 2002b; Jones and Kennett 1999), and the widespread movement of people throughout central California (some to the coast) in response to altered hydrographic situations. Paleoenvironmental data from the Sierra Nevada and elsewhere (Graumlich 1993; Stine 1994) provide fairly strong evidence that these droughts occurred, but more corroborating evidence from the immediate area is still needed. Survey findings by Whitley et al. (2004) from the Carrizo Plain in the southeastern interior of the Central Coast region, while preliminary, suggest widespread abandonment of that area immediately preceding the population increase on the coast. In general, the Medieval droughts hypothesis emphasizes the abrupt character of Late Period settlement and assemblage changes, and the fact that many developments, including decreased interregional exchange (marked by lower frequencies of obsidian), do not seem consistent with linear adaptive progress or progressive social evolution. Further, ethnohistoric accounts suggest that Late Period and contact-era populations consisted of small, mobile groups with some measure of sociopolitical complexity, although not necessarily greater than that of the societies that came before. The notion of deintensification has been used to characterize the Late Period relative to the terminal Middle Period (Jones and Ferneau 2002b) and to counter a widespread assumption that the Late Period represented the pinnacle of prehistoric population density, sociopolitical complexity, and subsistence intensity. Greenwood (1978) and Preston (1996) suggest that deintensification may have been caused not by prehistoric droughts but by catastrophic contact with European diseases that may have arrived centuries before the establishment of actual Spanish settlements.

The widespread use and production of beads during the Late Period (coincident with a decline in obsidian and long-distance trade) is another strong pattern that requires serious attention. Bead production on the Central Coast was neither as intensive nor centralized as in the Santa Barbara Channel (see Arnold 2001a), but Late Period deposits consistently produce more shell and stone beads than middens from earlier periods. Beads almost certainly became a more standardized and common medium of exchange during the Late Period than they had been previously. Their increased abundance may also represent production for use as tribute in new and qualitatively different political systems that featured individuals like Buchon with significant amounts of power. This system, which also featured intergroup violence, may have emerged either in the face of drought-related subsistence problems or the protohistoric plagues. In either case, developments during the Late Period are seen as partially related to demographics but more to historic events—particularly arrival of the bow and arrow, European diseases, anomalously severe droughts, and/or the emergence of powerful leaders who benefited from the state of flux associated with the end of the Hunting Culture. Considerably more fine-grained data are needed from Late Period contexts to evaluate the relative importance of these various factors.

The uniformity of the regional material record for the Late Period seemingly conflicts with the presence of multiple unrelated language stocks, particularly the speakers of Costanoan languages in the north, the Hokan affiliates Salinan and Esselen in the central area, and the Northern Chumash isolate in the south. These linguistic categories reflect very different histories of human migration yet they exhibit a nearly identical material culture. In the Monterey Bay area, serrated arrow points, occasional banjo pendants of abalone shell, and Class M *Olivella* rectangular beads may distinguish Costanoan speakers from groups speaking languages of the Hokan stock, although serrated points occur no farther south than Gilroy and seem to distinguish northern from southern Ohlone groups. The appearance of Class M beads and other artifacts after cal A.D. 1000 may represent the Utian intrusion, but Breschini and Haversat (2005b) are convinced, based on patterns in radiocarbon dates, that speakers of Utian languages (presumably proto-Costanoan) arrived on the Monterey Peninsula during the Middle Period ca. 500 cal B.C.

While this seems hard to reconcile with the material record, the Late Period patterns show that simple correlations between material and nonmaterial culture are not to be expected. There are also some traits of the Vierra Phase at Elkhorn Slough (high frequency of bone tools, large number of mortars and pestles) that seem consistent with the Berkeley Pattern in the San Francisco Bay/Delta area, the presumed homeland of the Costanoan speakers. The Salinan and Chumashan areas, on the other hand, seem virtually indistinguishable in terms of their Late Period records. Late and contact sites in the Salinan area uniformly date back to no earlier than ca. cal A.D. 1250, which suggests a likely date of entrance for speakers of those languages, but the timing of their appearance may reflect adaptive responses not necessarily tied to ethnolinguistic identities. Such a late entrance is also inconsistent with most estimates for the antiquity of Hokan languages in California (see Chapter 6 in this volume). Furthermore, the same pattern is apparent in the Obispeño area, where Chumash speakers are assumed to have had a long presence. Also complicating such patterns is the occurrence of double side-notched arrow points and mass graves on the northern San Luis Obispo coast, which are so unlike patterns in the surrounding areas that they seem to reflect a wholly different, intrusive group (Jones and Waugh 1995).

Difficulties in distinguishing ethnic migrations versus adaptive responses highlight two general themes that permeate the archaeology and prehistory of midlatitude coastal California: diversity and instability. Marked by a rich, linear concentration of resources, the Central Coast was a constant magnet for human occupation. The pattern of occupation related to this resource base is not one of permanence but rather of intermittent use on both seasonal and longer timescales. Radiocarbon dates continue to illuminate situations where seemingly homogeneous midden deposits actually reflect multiple occupations separated by prolonged periods of abandonment, often of a millennium or more. This pattern, perhaps first recognized at Elkhorn Slough (Dietz et al. 1988; Dondero et al. 1984), is increasingly evident in the Santa Cruz area (e.g., SCR-20), the Monterey Peninsula (see discussion by Breschini and Haversat 2005b), the northern San Luis Obispo coast (Hildebrandt et al. 2002; Joslin 2006), the Los Osos area, and at Diablo Canyon. It is tempting to surmise that the diversity and flux of Central Coast environments fostered a certain degree of instability in cultural adaptations over time. Shifts toward complexity represented by burials at MNT-391 and SLO-406 and toward sedentism as reflected by large Middle and Middle/Late Transition house floors cannot be linked with any clear, linear trajectories of population or technological development at the regional or local level. Trends of incremental sociological and technical evolution seem to have always been truncated or interrupted for one reason or another. Consequently future research will need to focus more on the pattern of intermittent occupation and multiscaled site abandonment that seems to characterize this midlatitude milieu.

Overall, the complex relationships between material culture, group history, and linguistics on the Central Coast are a microcosm of California prehistory. It is possible that mitochondrial and nuclear DNA studies may resolve some of these issues, but it is more likely they will continue to illuminate complicated patterns related to a highly diverse natural environment, growing human populations, varied cultural traditions, historical migrations, and other events, along with a full range of intergroup and human-environment relationships.

NOTES

1. Several alternative reservoir correction values have been used on the Central Coast, including 225+35 (Stuiver et al. 1986), 250+35 (Newsome et al. 2004), 290+35 (Ingram and Southon 1996), and 325+35 (Jones and Jones 1992), each supported by various data, including dates from shell/charcoal pairs. No single correction factor accommodates all of the available findings, consistent with year-to-year variability in upwelling intensity. All dates in this chapter were corrected with a value of 290+35.
2. Several scholars (Erlandson and Bartoy 1995, 1996; Preston 1996) have suggested that population decline began not long after the Spanish appearance in Mexico in 1519 as a result of rapidly spreading diseases in advance of the Spanish themselves.
3. There is also a suggestion that the term "Ohlone" is derived from the Miwok, *'olo·-win,* which means "westerners."
4. This generalization applies only to the coastal region, as Millingstone sites are known in the San Joaquin Valley farther inland (see Chapter 10 in this volume).
5. The Jalama large side-notched variant was vaguely defined by Lathrap and Troike (1984) on the basis of specimens with bifurcated as opposed to convex bases. Both Greenwood (1972) and Dietz and Jackson (1981) distinguished two variants of large side-notched points, but they each emphasized different morphological traits. Clearly this typology needs improvement, but for now, we defer to the rather loose definitions of Lathrap and Troike.

CHAPTER 10

The Central Valley: A View from the Catbird's Seat

JEFFREY S. ROSENTHAL, GREGORY G. WHITE, AND MARK Q. SUTTON

THE CENTRAL VALLEY OF CALIFORNIA IS ONE OF THE world's largest intermontane basins (Dupre et al. 1991), extending 650 kilometers between the Siskiyou Mountains on the north and the Tehachapis on the south. The Coast Ranges lie to the west and the high peaks of the Sierra Nevada and Cascade Ranges are to the east (Figure 10.1). The region is warm and well watered, one of the most diverse and productive environmental zones in California. Early in prehistory, people of the Central Valley settled in villages where they created a sophisticated material culture, became the nexus of an extensive trade system involving a wide range of manufactured goods from distant and neighboring regions, and developed population densities and village sizes equaled only by agricultural societies in the southwestern and southeastern United States. As reflections of these developments, the archaeological record of the Central Valley is among the most fascinating in western North America, spanning the full sweep of hunter-gatherer adaptations; from the earliest, technologically conservative, low-density colonizers to the most recent, technologically elaborate, and densely packed populations present at historic contact.

Professional archaeologists and avocationalists alike have been drawn to the extensive mound sites of the valley for more than a century. Unlike other places in California, however, archaeological research in the region has waned over the past 20 years. Since Moratto's (1984) summary of Central Valley archaeology, basic understanding of culture history in the region has progressed very little, and we continue to lack well-grounded chronologies for large segments of the valley. Extant collections reveal a diverse and complex archaeological record, yet few modern studies have redressed past errors in interpretation or synthesized the considerable archaeological information available for this region.

Despite these problems, archaeological research conducted in the Central Valley remains among the most important in the state. Over the past two decades, the region's archaeological record has been a proving ground for theories that have advanced a new understanding of prehistoric California. This research has been at the highest order—the causes and consequences of prehistoric culture change (Basgall 1987; Beaton 1991c; Cohen 1981).

ENVIRONMENTAL CONTEXT

The Central Valley is divided into two major physiographic provinces separated by the expansive Sacramento–San Joaquin Delta. To the north lies the Sacramento Valley, drained by the southward-flowing Sacramento River, and to the south lies the San Joaquin Valley, drained by the northward-flowing San Joaquin River. Near the central outlet, the principal waterways merge with the westward-flowing drainages of the Mokelumne and Cosumnes Rivers. Around this confluence, the vast marshes and sloughs of the Sacramento–San Joaquin Delta developed over the past 7,000 years in response to worldwide advances in sea level (Atwater 1980; Goman and Wells 2000; Shlemon and Begg 1975). The extreme southern end of the Central Valley is separated from the northern outlet by prominent Late Pleistocene alluvial fans formed by the Kings River and Los Gatos Creek (Atwater et al. 1986). South of this divide, all drainages empty into the shallow basins formed by ancient Tulare, Buena Vista, and Kern Lakes. In the past, these now dry lake basins frequently overflowed northward, feeding the San Joaquin River.

Quaternary landscapes are fairly uniform throughout the Great Valley, descending in age from a fringe of weathered and rolling piedmonts to the active basins and floodplains of the valley bottom. The piedmonts are composed of a combination of early Tertiary fluvial sediments forming benchlike deposits, as well as incised Pleistocene fans associated with stream and river debouches at the base of the foothills. The valley bottom is made up of younger, active alluvial fans, alkali basins composed of deep beds of clay and silt, and river floodplains consisting of well-sorted silt, sand, and gravel. The floodplains contain elevated natural levees that were favored as prehistoric habitation areas.

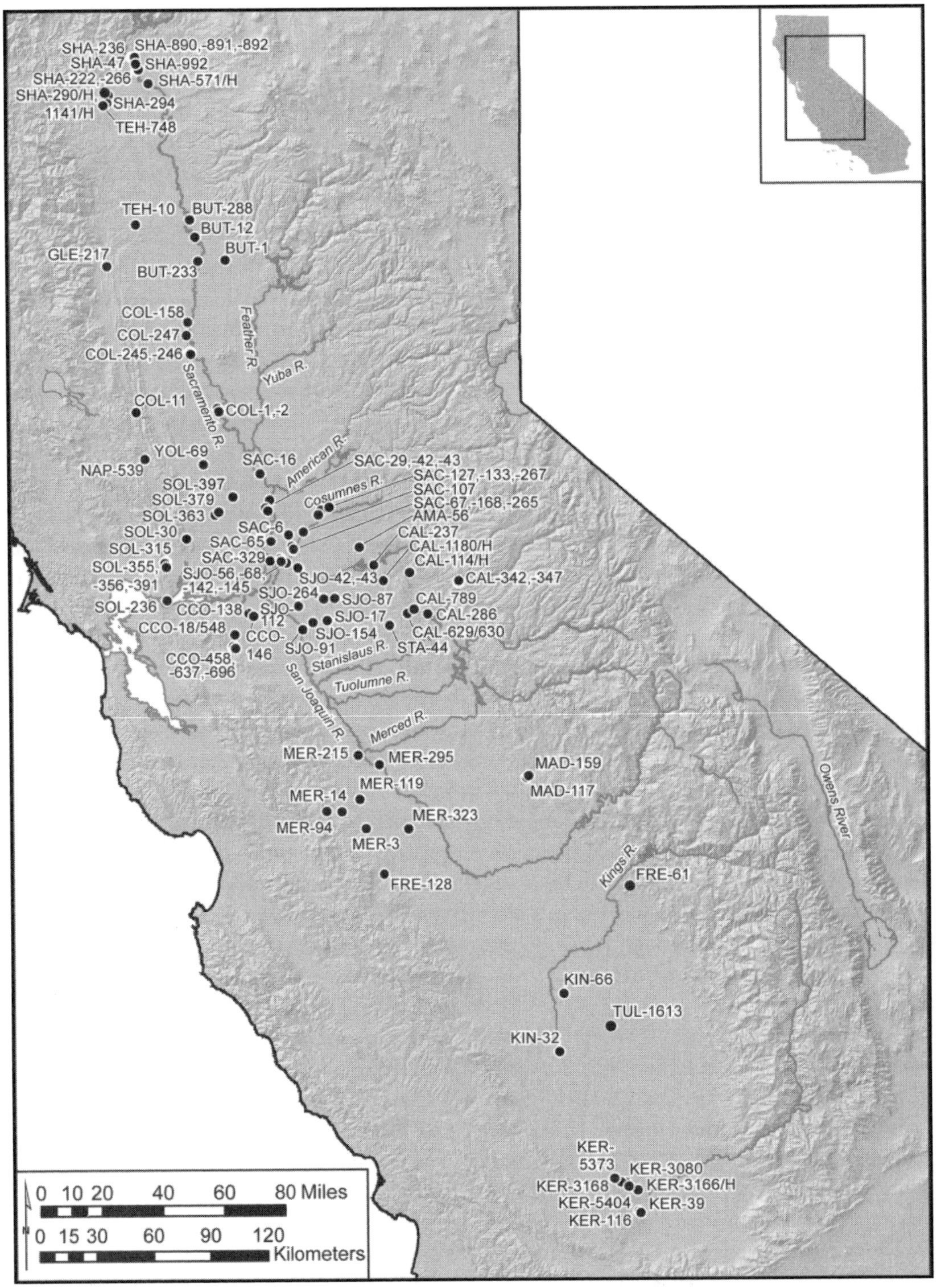

Figure 10.1. Archaeological sites and locations of the Central Valley.

The axial Sacramento and San Joaquin Rivers drain a combined watershed of over 122,000 square kilometers, accounting for 40 percent of the state's freshwater runoff. There is a significant latitudinal gradient in precipitation, with increasingly arid conditions prevailing to the south. Thus the Sacramento Valley is comparatively well watered while the San Joaquin Valley is a semiarid steppe. Due to the rain shadow effect of the Coast Ranges, there is also a significant longitudinal precipitation gradient. Most of the region's freshwater originates from the Sierra and Cascade slopes, emptying into the east side of the valley. Drainages on the west side are comparatively small and widely dispersed.

Central Valley habitats included riparian forest, marsh, alkali basins, oak savanna, and foothill woodland communities. Because the valley is narrow along its entire length, and vegetation communities are arranged longitudinally along soil, elevational, and hydrological gradients, at least some of each habitat is accessible within a day's walk from anywhere in the basin. In the Sacramento and northern San Joaquin Valleys, wide swaths of multitiered riparian forest lined the deep floodplain soils bracketing major waterways (Burcham 1957; Kuchler 1977). In the central Sacramento Valley and portions of the San Joaquin, extensive seasonal wetlands and alkali basins flanked the active floodplains. In the delta, marshlands covered more than 200,000 hectares (500,000 acres), including open water and dense stands of tule and bulrush. The shallow lakes of Tulare basin also supported a comparable area of marshland. Broad piedmonts rimming the valley floor supported bunch grass prairie and dispersed oaks in the Sacramento Valley, and a treeless plain with patchy, alkali-tolerant annual forbs and grasses in the San Joaquin Valley.

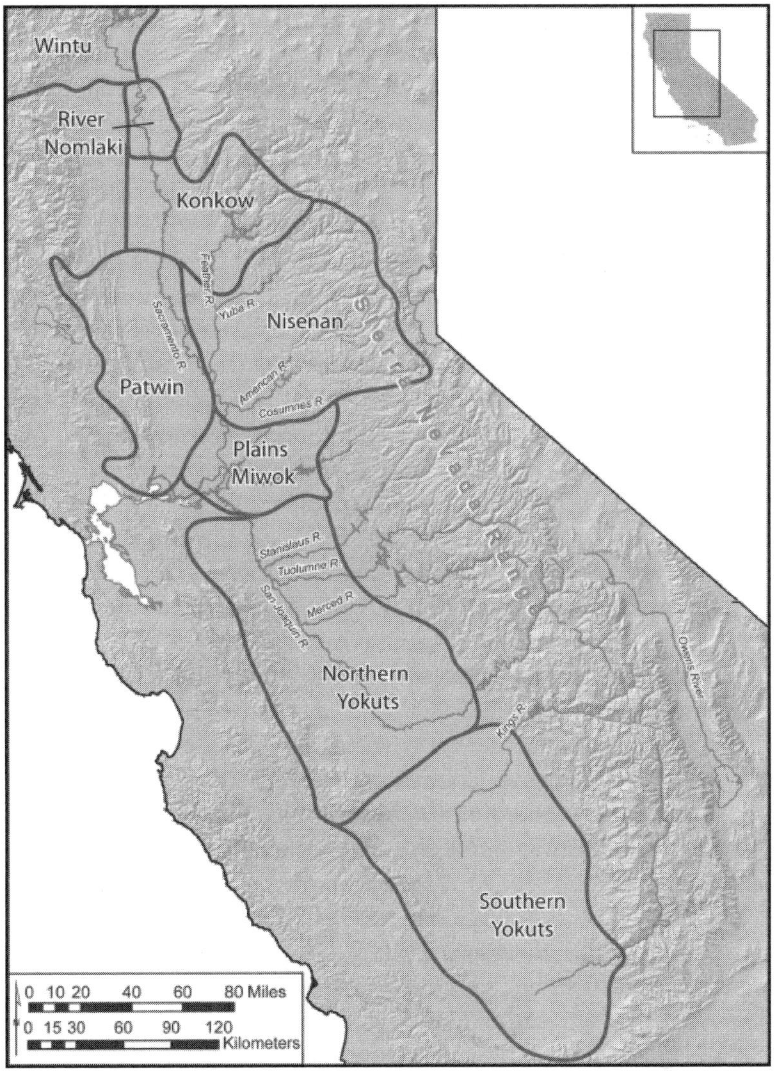

Figure 10.2. Approximate location of tribal groups, Central Valley.

NATIVE PEOPLES AT CONTACT

An estimated 100,000 people, about one-third of the state's native population, lived in the Central Valley when Europeans first ventured into the region between A.D. 1772 and 1821 (Cook 1955, 1976, 1978; Moratto 1984:171). These people spoke seven distinct languages of the Penutian stock (Figure 10.2), five in the Sacramento Valley (Wintu, Nomlaki, Konkow, River Patwin, and Nisenan) and two in the San Joaquin Valley (Miwok and Yokuts). Common linguistic roots indicate these groups had a related history and regular interaction (see Chapter 6 in this volume). A shared heritage is also indicated by common technological, economic, ceremonial, and sociopolitical characteristics described by twentieth-century anthropologists who identified the Central Valley as the core of the California Culture area (Figure 10.3) (Goldschmidt 1951b; Klimek 1935; Kroeber 1936, 1939).

THE CENTRAL VALLEY ARCHAEOLOGICAL RECORD

Persistent problems have hindered Central Valley archaeological research over the past two decades. There have been few opportunities for new investigation, as most surface sites have been destroyed. Early-twentieth-century records indicate a density of one mound site for every two to three miles of major waterway (Schenck and Dawson 1929; White 2003b). Most, and in some areas all, of these mounds have been destroyed by agricultural development, levee construction, and river erosion. At the same time, over the past 20 years, most new information has come from a handful of small-scale investigations. There have been few large cultural resource management–sponsored projects, and only two Ph.D. dissertations have focused on Central Valley archaeology (Hartzell 1992; White 2003a). Published studies have mostly re-

Figure 10.3. Big Head dancer and round house, Grindstone Rancheria, May 1923. (Courtesy of the Bancroft Library, University of California–Berkeley, photograph by C. Hart Merriam, cat. no. 1978.008T/195/Pl no. 35.)

worked old data or stayed on a traditional theoretical plane (Basgall 1987; Beaton 1991c).

Further, existing collections are rife with sampling biases. In the early twentieth century, teams of mostly untrained but energetic investigators explored numerous mound sites (Lillard et al. 1939; Schenck and Dawson 1929). These initial explorations culminated in professional investigations, including Depression-era salvage efforts at several key sites, and publication of synthetic studies on major artifact types, features, and cultural sequences (Gifford 1940, 1947; Heizer 1941b, 1949; Lillard et al. 1939; Wedel 1941). All this early fieldwork, however, was marked by a focus on artifact and burial recovery and a frank indifference to dietary remains and technological features, thus hampering modern attempts at reanalysis (Bouey 1995; Hartzell 1992).

Last, the Central Valley's archaeological record, as we know it today, is biased by natural processes of landscape evolution. Surface sites are embedded in young sediments set within a massive and dynamic alluvial basin, while most older archaeological deposits have been obliterated or buried by ongoing alluvial processes. Consequently archaeologists have had to struggle to identify and explain long-term culture change in portions of the Central Valley where available evidence spans only the past 2,500 years or in rare cases 5,500 years.

Chronological Framework

As it stands, there is no single cultural-historical framework that accommodates the entire prehistoric record of the Central Valley. Detailed cultural chronologies exist for some portions of the basin (e.g., the lower Sacramento Delta region), while the timing and nature of cultural succession in other regions remains poorly defined (e.g., the northern Sacramento and San Joaquin Valleys). In many cases, local sequences were built on few (if any) radiocarbon dates (Kowta 1988; Olsen and Payen 1969; Sundahl 1992; Warren and McKusick 1959), relying instead on the cross-dating of stylistically distinct artifact types and other cultural patterns (e.g., burial mode). To this time, however, there have been few attempts to update and evaluate the relevance of these chronologies, although the ages of many diagnostic artifacts have been significantly refined (e.g., shell beads) (Bennyhoff and Hughes 1987; Groza 2002).

Moratto's (1984) synthesis of Central Valley archaeology relied heavily on the taxonomic framework developed in a series of mostly unpublished papers by Bennyhoff and Fredrickson (Elsasser 1978; Fredrickson 1973, 1974a). Hughes (editor, 1994) compiled these important manuscripts, making them widely available. While the comparative framework established by Bennyhoff and Fredrickson (1994) and Fredrickson (1973, 1974a) is designed to incorporate a wide range of local and regional traditions, it has not been systematically applied outside the Sacramento Valley. As a result, the following discussion uses a simple classification based on Fredrickson's (1973, 1974a) California adaptation of the Willey and Phillips (1958) period and stage integrative scheme.

Fredrickson (1973, 1974a) proposed three basic periods: the Paleo-Indian, Archaic, and Emergent. New radiocarbon determinations (Groza 2002; LaJeunesse and Pryor 1996; Meyer and Rosenthal 1997), adjusted with modern calibration curves, are used here to make the following divisions: Paleo-Indian (11,550 to 8550 cal B.C.), Lower Archaic (8550 to 5550 cal B.C.), Middle Archaic (5550 to 550 cal B.C.), Upper Archaic (550 cal B.C. to cal A.D. 1100), and Emergent (cal A.D. 1100 to Historic).[1]

Paleo-Indian (11,550 to 8550 cal B.C.)

Recent geoarchaeological studies have shown that periodic episodes of erosion and deposition during the Holocene have removed or buried large segments of the Late Pleistocene landscape (Rosenthal and Meyer 2004a, b; White 2003b). Archaeological deposits associated with these ancient landforms either have been destroyed or lie buried beneath more recent alluvial deposits. In certain zones, Late Pleistocene landforms are common near the surface, but these are generally associated with landscapes that would have attracted only limited human use (e.g., the arid piedmonts on the valley margin).

Most claims for very ancient human occupation in California had effectively been dismissed through radiocarbon dating when Moratto (1984) published his chapter on the first Californians. One exception is the Farmington Complex from the lower Calaveras River (Treganza 1952; Treganza and Heizer 1953) and adjacent drainages (Johnson 1967:283–284), thought to be evidence of a pre–projectile point occupation in California (Krieger 1964). The Farmington Complex remained undated (but see Ritter et al. 1976) until geoarchaeological investigations in the vicinity of type site STA-44 (Dalldorf and Meyer 2004) demonstrated that this assemblage of cobble cores, biface rough-outs, and stone-working debris is contained in Holocene alluvial terraces and not Pleistocene glacial outwash (Dalldorf and Meyer 2004; Moratto 1984:63; Rosenthal and Meyer 2004b:96).

Currently the earliest accepted evidence of human occupation in the Central Valley comes from the basally thinned and fluted projectile points found at scattered surface locations, primarily in the southern portion of the basin. Often compared to Clovis points, these distinctive projectiles are well dated elsewhere in North America to a brief interval between about 11,550 and 9550 cal B.C. (Fiedel 1999). To date, only three localities in the San Joaquin Valley have produced early concave base points (see Chapter 5 in this volume), including Tracy Lake, the Woolfsen mound (MER-215), and the Tulare Lake basin (Heizer 1938; Moratto 1984; Peak and Weber 1978). A single possible fluted point was reported from the Sacramento Valley near Thomes Creek (Dillon and Murphy 1994). All of these artifacts were recovered from remnant features of the Pleistocene landscape.

At the Witt site (KIN-32) in the southern San Joaquin Valley, hundreds of early concave base points have been discovered along a remnant shoreline occupied during a Late Pleistocene lowstand of Tulare Lake (a local expression of the "Clovis drought") (Davis 1999a; Haynes 1991; Willig 1991). Uranium series (^{230}Th) dates were obtained on human bone fragments and extinct fauna from this shoreline, providing some preliminary evidence for the maximum age of human occupation in the Central Valley. The human bone from KIN-32 produced uncalibrated dates of 11,379, 11,380, and 15,802 RCYBP, while the fauna returned dates of 10,788, 15,696, and 17,745 years RCYBP (West et al. 1991). Unfortunately there is no clear association between the extinct fauna, human bone, and projectile points from Tulare Lake (Fenenga 1992; West et al. 1991).

Lower Archaic (8550 to 5550 cal B.C.)

As a result of climate changes at the end of the Pleistocene, alluvial fans and floodplains throughout the lowlands of central California responded with a significant period of deposition beginning about 9050 cal B.C. This episode of landscape evolution covered many Late Pleistocene alluvial landforms and resulted in a clear stratigraphic boundary between sediments from the Late Pleistocene and Holocene (Rosenthal and Meyer 2004a). Another period of climate change at the beginning of the Middle Holocene, around 5550 cal B.C., initiated a second cycle of widespread fan and floodplain deposition. This latter episode buried many of the earliest archaeological deposits known from central California (Meyer and Rosenthal 1997; Rosenthal and Meyer 2004a, b).

Like the Paleo-Indian Period, Lower Archaic occupation of the Central Valley is mostly represented by isolated finds. Stemmed points, chipped stone crescents, and other distinctive flaked stone artifacts are commonly found on the ancient shore of Tulare Lake, alongside early concave base points (Fenenga 1992; Wallace and Riddell 1991). In the Sacramento Valley, an isolated flaked stone crescent was found on an ancient alluvial fan west of Orland (Johnson et al. 1984:65). Only one Lower Archaic archaeological deposit (KER-116) has been identified in the Central Valley proper, associated with a deeply buried soil uncovered on the ancient shoreline of Buena Vista Lake (Fredrickson and Grossman 1977; Hartzell 1992).

KER-116 produced radiocarbon dates on freshwater mussel shell ranging between 7175 and 6450 cal B.C. (Fredrickson and Grossman 1977; Hartzell 1992). Salvage investigations at KER-116 produced a small artifact assemblage including three chipped stone crescents, a stemmed projectile point fragment, a carved stone atlatl spur, and a few small flaked stone implements. The deposit also yielded a human skull fragment and a small yet diverse faunal assemblage that included freshwater fish, waterfowl, freshwater mussels, and a few fragments of artiodactyl bone (Hartzell 1992). No milling tools or plant remains were identified at KER-116, so the nature of plant use during the Early Archaic remains unknown. Thick Coso obsidian hydration rims from KER-5373/H and Early Holocene radiocarbon dates of 6360 cal B.C. and 5650 cal B.C. on *Tivela* disk beads from KER-3168 (Jackson et al. 1998) indicate Lower Archaic occupation in the Elk Hills, just west of Buena Vista Lake.

Lower Archaic artifacts from Tulare Lake basin include stemmed points similar to Borax Lake wide-stemmed points from the North Coast Ranges, as well as Lake Mojave, Silver Lake, and Pinto points similar to those found in the Great Basin. Chipped stone crescents are also a common element of Lower Archaic components (Fenenga 1992). The three crescents from KER-116 are among the only examples from dated stratigraphic contexts in California (Fenenga 1992; Fredrickson and Grossman 1977; Hartzell 1992). Bipointed "humpies" are another common flaked stone tool found alongside crescents and early wide-stem points on the southwestern shores of Tulare Lake (Sampson 1991).

Despite the dearth of large mammal remains from the lone sampled site (KER-116), the common occurrence of large, heavily reworked projectile points has led to the interpretation that hunting artiodactyls was a focus of Early Archaic economies (Wallace 1991). While milling implements, subsidiary processing tools, and other direct evidence of plant foods are largely absent from valley floor assemblages, recent investigations in the adjoining Sierra Nevada and Coast Range foothills have documented Lower Archaic sites with abundant milling equipment and other indications of a reliance on plant foods (Meyer and Rosenthal 1997). Contrary to earlier studies, which have argued for the use of small seeds (Basgall 1987; McGuire and Hildebrandt 1994), nut crops associated with expanding woodlands may have been the primary target of seasonal plant exploitation (LaJeunesse and Pryor 1996; Rosenthal and McGuire 2004), based on the dominance of acorn and pine nutshell in Early Holocene strata at the Skyrocket site (CAL-629/630; Rosenthal and McGuire 2004) and at Los Vaqueros (CCO-696; Meyer and Rosenthal 1997). These foothill sites, often marked by dense accumulations of handstones, millingslabs, and various cobble-core tools, appear to represent frequently visited camps in a seasonally structured settlement system (Basgall and True 1985; Hale 2001; LaJeunesse and Pryor 1996; McGuire and Hildebrandt 1994; Meyer and Rosenthal 1997; Moratto 2002; Rosenthal and McGuire 2004; Sundahl 1992).

Relationships between foothill and valley floor adaptations are relatively unknown and can only be solved by discovery and investigation of additional valley sites. Distinctly divergent valley floor and foothill adaptations and cultural traditions are evident in the Middle Archaic record, and it is possible that these distinctions first emerged in the Lower Archaic. On the other hand, large stemmed projectile points found at Lower Archaic sites CAL-342 and CAL-629/630 in the Sierra foothills are similar to those recovered from the Witt site in the Tulare basin, suggesting that valley and foothill sites could be seasonal expressions of the same adaptation.

Regional interaction spheres appear to have been well established in the Lower Archaic. Marine shell beads from California are found in Early Holocene deposits in the western and central Great Basin (Bennyhoff and Hughes 1987; Fitzgerald et al. 2005), and obsidian from the eastern Sierra makes up a large proportion of nonlocal flaked stone tools and toolmaking debris from Lower Archaic sites on both sides of the Central Valley (e.g., CAL-629/630 and CCO-696). Obsidian was not reported, however, from the basal stratum at KER-116 in the Buena Vista Lake basin and appears to be rare among the many stemmed points from Tulare Lake (Wallace and Riddell, eds. 1991).

Middle Archaic (5550 to 550 cal B.C.)

The beginning of the Middle Archaic was characterized by a substantial change in climate, with warmer, drier conditions prevailing throughout central California. Tulare Lake shrank in size and eventually desiccated, matching similar declines in other western lakes (Benson et al. 2002; Davis 1999a; White et al. 2002). At the same time, an important new wetland habitat formed in the Central Valley as rising sea levels pushed inland and led to the development of the Sacramento–San Joaquin Delta (Atwater and Belknap 1980; Goman and Wells 2000). The wider Central Valley landscape also changed significantly. Following an initial period of deposition (about 5550 cal B.C.), fans and floodplains stabilized. This period of landscape stability is represented by Middle Holocene buried soils found in alluvial landforms throughout central California (Meyer 1996; Meyer and Rosenthal 1997; Rosenthal and Meyer 2004a, b). Many of the best documented Middle Archaic deposits (5550 to 550 cal B.C.) are associated with these buried land surfaces, including CCO-18/548, CCO-637, COL-247, CAL-342, CAL-286, CAL-347, CAL-789, CAL-629/630 (Atwater et al. 1990; LaJeunesse and Pryor 1996; Meyer 2005; Meyer and Rosenthal 1998; Morattto and Arguelles 1984; O'Brien 1984; Peak and Crew 1990; Rosenthal and McGuire 2004; Rosenthal and Meyer 2004b; White 2003b).

A growing body of evidence indicates there were two distinct settlement-subsistence adaptations operating in central California beginning in the Middle Archaic, one centering on the foothills and the other on the valley floor (Fredrickson 1994c:102–103; Rosenthal and McGuire 2004:161–163).

FOOTHILL TRADITIONS In contrast to the paucity of evidence from the valley floor, Middle Archaic sites dating between about 4050 and 2050 cal B.C. are comparatively common in the foothills, particularly in buried contexts (Basgall and Hildebrandt 1989; LaJeunesse and Pryor 1996; Meyer and Rosenthal 1997; Milliken et al. 1997; Peak and Crew 1990; Rosenthal and McGuire 2004; Rosenthal and Meyer 2004b; Sundahl 1992). These deposits are characterized by an abundance of expedient cobble-based pounding, chopping, scraping, and mulling tools, continuing a pattern first observed in the Early Holocene. Archaeobotanical assemblages from foothill sites CAL-789, CAL-629/630, and FRE-61 confirm that acorn and pine nuts were targeted plant foods (McGuire 1995; Rosenthal and McGuire 2004; Wohlgemuth 2004).

Closely similar functional assemblages have been identified as far north as SHA-1169 in the Sacramento River canyon (Basgall and Hildebrandt 1989) and as far south as FRE-61 on the Kings River fan in the southern San Joaquin Valley (McGuire 1995). Examples from the North Coast Ranges foothills, such as SOL-315 and GLE-217, are associated with the Mendocino Pattern, an upland adaptive strategy featuring high residential mobility that persisted well into the Upper Archaic (Fredrickson 1974a; White and Weigel 2006; White et al. 2002; Wiberg 1992).

Foothill tradition artifact assemblages are composed almost exclusively of flaked and ground stone tools used in food procurement and processing. Few bone or shell artifacts, beads, or ornaments have been encountered. Tabular pendants, incised slate, and perforated stone plummets are uncommon but widespread (Basgall and Hildebrandt 1989; Rosenthal and McGuire 2004; Sundahl 1992; White and Weigel 2006; Wiberg 1992). Projectile points include notched, stemmed, thick-leaf, and narrow concave base darts, with a high degree of local and regional morphological variability. Source materials are also variable, owing primarily to a reliance on local toolstone supplemented by a small percentage of obsidian derived from the nearest quarries in the North Coast Ranges, Cascades, and eastern Sierra. Rock-filled hearths and ovens are common (White and Weigel 2006; Wiberg 1992), while several graves have been identified capped by cairns of unmodified rock and milling equipment, including examples at CAL-1180/H, FRE-61, GLE-217, MRP-181, and SOL-315 (Fitzwater 1962; McGuire 1995; Milliken et al. 1997; White and Weigel 2006; Wiberg 1992).

VALLEY TRADITIONS Cultural deposits associated with the early Middle Archaic (ca. 5550 to 2050 cal B.C.) are rare in the Central Valley, due in part to geomorphic changes described above. Only four dated components and a few isolated artifacts are associated with this time period, primarily found in buried contexts. In the Sacramento Valley, augers dug at the Reservation Road site, COL-247, encountered a buried midden at 3.0 to 3.5 meters below surface dating to 4020 cal B.C. The component was not excavated (White 2003a, 2003b). In the San Joaquin Valley, the stratigraphically deepest occupation at SJO-68 dates to a minimum of 3050 cal B.C. (Lillard et al. 1939:31–32; Ragir 1972:27, 39), and two buried sites in the northern Diablo Range (CCO-637 and CCO-18/548) have been dated between 4950 and 3050 cal B.C. (Meyer 2005; Meyer and Rosenthal 1998).

Sites and site components associated with later portions of the Middle Archaic (post-2550 cal B.C.) are comparatively well represented in the Sacramento Valley (Figure 10.4) and Delta, and northern San Joaquin Valley. Sites of this age have produced elaborate material culture and diverse technological and dietary assemblages, including BUT-233, CAL-237, CCO-18/548, CCO-637, COL-247, SJO-68, SJO-112, SJO-142, SJO-145, and SAC-107 (Heizer 1949; Meacham 1979; Meyer and Rosenthal 1998; Olsen and Wilson 1964; Ragir 1972; Schulz 1981; Welden 1990; White 2003a, b; Wiberg and Clark 2004).

The late Middle Archaic record reveals a distinct adaptive pattern reflecting the emergence of logistically organized subsistence practices and increasing residential stability along river corridors of the Sacramento and San Joaquin Valleys. This riverine adaptation appears to have been fully in place by perhaps 6,000 years ago; however, the origins, spatial extent, and regional variability of the pattern are as

Figure 10.4. Late Middle Archaic assemblage from the Colusa Reach of the Sacramento River COL-247, Stratum 2. (a) contracting-stemmed points; (b) leaf-shaped points; (c) Martis corner-notched point; (d) notched pebble net-sinker; (e) pebble hammer; (f) ceramic egg shape; (g) *Olivella* L2 rectangle, *Haliotis* disk, *Macoma* disk, and spirelopped *Olivella*; (h) *Haliotis cracherodii* disk ornament; (i) disk-shaped handstone; (j) perforated plummet; (k) elk antler "shoehorn"; (l) meta-sedimentary core tool; (m) elk cannon bone dagger (after White 2003a: Figs. 112–113).

yet poorly known. Extended residential settlement at these sites is indicated by refined and specialized tool assemblages and features, a wide range of nonutilitarian artifacts, abundant trade objects, and plant and animal remains indicative of year-round occupation (Moratto 1984; Ragir 1972; Schulz 1970, 1981; White 2003a, b).

The archetypical Middle Archaic expression, identified as the Windmiller Pattern (Fredrickson 1973, 1974a; Moratto 1984), was first recognized at a handful of sites found on old levee ridges adjacent to freshwater marshes and well-watered riparian settings near the confluence of the Mokelumne and Cosumnes Rivers in the delta region (Heizer 1949; Lillard et al. 1939; Olsen and Wilson 1964; Ragir 1972). With the exception of an early component at SJO-68, Windmiller sites in the Central Valley date between 1850 and 750 cal B.C. (Olsen and Wilson 1964; Ragir 1972; Rosenthal and Meyer 2004b; Schulz 1981).

Windmiller settlements are unique in their prevalence of westerly oriented, ventrally and dorsally extended burials, along with sophisticated material culture found primarily as grave offerings (Heizer 1949; Olsen and Wilson 1964; Ragir 1972). New finds show that Windmiller sites were widespread in the San Joaquin Valley during the Middle Archaic and did not necessarily spread from the delta region, as previously assumed by Beardsley (1954) and Heizer (1958:7). Several sites, including CCO-18/548, CCO-637, CAL-237, and CAL-629/630, found on the margins of the northern Diablo Range and Sierra Nevada, contain ventrally and dorsally extended burials contemporaneous with Windmiller settlements in the eastern delta (Farris et al. 1988; Johnson 1967; LaJeunesse and Pryor 1996; Meyer and Rosenthal 1997; Wiberg and Clark 2004). In fact, the earliest extended burials found in the northern Diablo Range at CCO-637 are 700 to 800 years older than those reported from SJO-68 (Meyer and Rosenthal 1998; Ragir 1972), suggesting this lowland tradition has an origin considerably earlier than previously demonstrated. Further, a tradition of extended burial posture can now be recognized throughout the San Joaquin Valley as far south as Buena Vista Lake, at sites dating from the Middle through Upper Archaic Periods (Bennyhoff 1994c, 1994d; Delacorte 2001; Dougherty and Werner 1993; Fenenga 1973; Fredrickson and Grossman 1977; Moratto 1984:210–211; Peak and Weber 1978; Pritchard 1970, Warren and McKusick 1959; Wedel 1941).

In the Sacramento Valley, a general absence of Middle Archaic sites makes it difficult to identify a dominant mode of interment. However, flexed and extended burials were identified in Middle Archaic strata at Reservation Road (COL-247; White 2003a, 2003b), and only flexed burials were found farther north at Llano Seco (BUT-233; Welden 1990).

As early as 4050 cal B.C., mortars and pestles were used at sites in the lowlands of central California, particularly in marsh side and riparian settings in the northern San Joaquin and southern Sacramento valleys, at sites such as COL-247 and SJO-68, and in the northern Diablo Ranges at CCO-637 (Basgall 1987; Meyer and Rosenthal 1998; Ragir 1972; Rosenthal and McGuire 2004; Schulz 1981; White 2003b). Various lines of evidence suggest that the shift to mortar and pestle accompanied more intensive subsistence practices and greater residential stability (Basgall 1987). However, the adoption of this technology does not track with changes in the types of plant foods processed. Acorn and pine nut shells are common in virtually all Middle Archaic archaeobotanical assemblages at sites with and without the mortar and pestle (e.g., BUT-233, CCO-18/548, COL-247; FRE-61; SOL-391; CCO-637, CCO-18/548, CAL-789; Basgall 1987; McGuire 1995; Meyer 2005; Meyer and Rosenthal 1997; Rosenthal and McGuire 2004; White 2003b; Wiberg and Clark 2004; Wohlgemuth 2004).

Fishing may have also taken on new importance to Central Valley groups during the Middle Archaic, as new fishing technologies such as gorge hooks, composite bone hooks, and spears, along with abundant fish remains, are represented in Middle Archaic lowland assemblages from such sites as CCO-18/548, CCO-637, COL-247, SAC-107, SJO-56, and SJO-68 (Broughton 1988; Heizer 1949; Meyer 2005; Meyer and Rosenthal 1997; Ragir 1972; Schulz 1981; White 2003a; Wiberg and Clark 2004).

Several other technologies common in later time periods are first apparent in the archaeological record of the northern San Joaquin Valley and the southern Sacramento Valley during the Middle Archaic. These include baked-clay impressions of fine twisted cordage and twined basketry, basketry awls, simple pottery and other baked clay objects found at sites such as COL-247 and SJO-68. A variety of finely made stone plummets and perforated "pencils," bird bone tubes, shell beads, and other personal adornments have also been recovered from Middle Archaic deposits (Olsen and Wilson 1964; Ragir 1972; White 2003a, b; Wiberg and Clark 2004).

Faunal assemblages recovered from CCO-18/548, CCO-637, COL-247, SJO-68, and SJO-112 reflect a heavy reliance on the emerging mosaic of marshes, riparian forests, and grasslands in central California. Tule elk, mule deer, and pronghorn are all represented, as are small and large fish, rabbits and hares, waterbirds, other terrestrial carnivores, raptors, and rodents (Broughton 1994a; Meyer 2005; Meyer and Rosenthal 1997, 1998; Olsen and Wilson 1964; Ragir 1972:159; Taite 1999; White 2003a, b).

Exchange of commodities such as obsidian, shell beads and ornaments, as well as perhaps other perishable items, was widespread during the Middle Archaic. People living in the Central Valley became important consumers of obsidian quarried on the east side of the Sierra Nevada at Bodie Hills, Casa Diablo, Coso, and Mount Hicks; from the North Coast Ranges at Napa Valley and Borax Lake; and from the southern Cascades at the Tuscan source (Bouey 1995; Ericson 1981; Jackson 1974; Meyer and Rosenthal 1998; Sundahl 1992; White 2003a; Wiberg and Clark 2004). Two types of individually made wall beads cut from the shell of *Olivella biplicata* are first found in Middle Archaic contexts, marking the beginning of a manufacturing industry and exchange network that would develop through the Late Holocene (Bennyhoff and Hughes 1987; Groza 2002; Milliken and Bennyhoff 1993). Grooved-rectangle beads found at KER-3166/H and KER-5404 in the southern San Joaquin Valley are the earliest of these wall beads, consistently dating older than 3050 cal B.C. (Jackson et al. 1998:144; Siefken 1999:55; Vellanoweth 2001). Early *Olivella* rectangle beads found at CCO-637 and CCO-18/548 are slightly younger, dating between 2520 and 1630 cal B.C.

Upper Archaic (550 cal B.C. to cal A.D. 1100)

The beginning of the Upper Archaic Period corresponds roughly with the onset of Late Holocene environmental conditions, marked by an abrupt turn to cooler, wetter, and more stable climate. Western lakes that dried or diminished during later parts of the Middle Holocene returned to spill levels by 1050 cal B.C. (Benson et al. 2002; Sims et al. 1988). Decreased salinity and bayward migration of alkaline-adapted plants in the delta indicate greater freshwater flows in the Sacramento/San Joaquin watershed during this period (Goman and Wells 2000). Climatic changes also resulted in renewed fan and floodplain deposition and soil formation in the Central Valley. In most regions, the current surface soils formed in deep Late Holocene alluvium capping the erratic, heavily weathered Middle Holocene landscape (Rosenthal and Meyer 2004a:29; Waters 2002; White 2003a, b).

The Upper Archaic archaeological record is better represented and understood than previous time periods. Cultural diversity was more pronounced and is clearly reflected in a geographically complex mosaic of distinct sociopolitical entities marked by contrasting burial postures, artifact styles, and other elements of material culture (Bennyhoff 1977; Bennyhoff and Fredrickson 1994; Kowta 1988; Rosenthal 1996; Sundahl 1992).

The Upper Archaic witnessed the development and proliferation of many specialized technologies, including new types of bone tools and other bone implements (e.g., wands, tubes, ornaments), as well as widespread manufactured goods like saucer and saddle-shaped *Olivella* beads, *Haliotis* ornaments, obsidian bifacial rough-outs, and well-made ceremonial blades (Bennyhoff and Fredrickson 1994; Fredrickson 1974a; Moratto 1984). Polished and ground stone plummets are common in regions surrounding the rivers and marshlands of the delta and southern San Joaquin Valley, and are occasionally found in arranged caches (Seals 1993; Shapiro and Tremaine 1995; Sutton 1996b).

Economies varied regionally, focused on seasonally structured resources that could be harvested and processed in bulk, such as acorns, salmon, shellfish, rabbits, and deer. In the delta region and adjacent portions of the Sacramento and San Joaquin Valleys, use of mortars and pestles along with a rich archaeobotanical record reflect a heavy reliance on acorns (Basgall 1987; Fredrickson 1974a:125; Moratto 1984:209; White 2003a, b; Wohlgemuth 1996, 2004). On the margins of the valley, handstones and millingslabs are dominant in Upper Archaic assemblages (Basgall and Hildebrandt 1989; Kowta 1988; Moratto 1972; Siefken 1999; Sundahl 1982, 1992), along with acorn hulls and pine nut shells (Wohlgemuth 1996, 2004).

Beginning after 2,700 years ago, large mounded villages developed in the delta region of the lower Sacramento Valley (e.g., Bouey 1995; Lillard et al. 1939; Ragir 1972; Schenck and Dawson 1929; Schulz 1981) related to a cultural tradition originally termed the Middle Horizon and identified by Fredrickson (1973, 1974a) as the Berkeley Pattern. Berkeley Pattern sites of the lower Sacramento Delta region contain extensive accumulations of habitation debris and features, especially fire-cracked rock heaps, shallow hearths, rock-lined ovens, house floors, and flexed burials—all reflecting long-term residential occupation (Bouey 1995:348–349). Although the most significant Berkeley Pattern deposits were excavated long ago, more recent analysis of sites in the lower Sacramento Valley (e.g., COL-247, SAC-42, SAC-43, SAC-133, SAC-265, SOL-355, SOL-363, SOL-379) has added important information, particularly on economic aspects of the pattern (Bouey 1995; Bouey and Waechter 1992; Milliken 1995b; Peak et al. 1984; Peak and Associates 1984; Rosenthal and White 1994; Shapiro and Tremaine 1995; Sheeders 1982; Wiberg 1993; Wohlgemuth 2004).

Only in the eastern delta at SAC-107 does stratigraphic succession indicate that the Berkeley Pattern replaced an earlier Windmiller tradition. Descendants of the Windmiller culture continued to occupy the San Joaquin Valley during the Upper Archaic (Bennyhoff 1994c, d). Their sites, distinguished by a common extended burial posture, are found along the western and southern edges of the delta (e.g., CCO-146, SJO-91) and along the side streams and axial marshes of San Joaquin and Merced Counties (e.g., SJO-17, SJO-87, SJO-106, SJO-154, SJO-264, MER-3, MER-215, MER-323) until sometime between 1,000 and 800 years ago (Bennyhoff 1994c, d; Delacorte 2001; Dougherty and Werner 1993; Fenenga 1973; Milliken et al. 1997:35; Moratto 1984:210–211; Peak and Weber 1978; Pritchard 1970).

The lower foothill woodlands of the San Joaquin Valley appear to have been a boundary area. Judging by clusters of extended Upper Archaic burials found at sites as far east as San Andreas (CAL-114/H; Stewart and Gerike 1994), Copperopolis (CAL-629/630; LaJeunesse and Pryor 1996), and Buchannan reservoir (Chowchilla Phase; MAD-117, MAD-159; Moratto 1972, 1984), valley people may have periodically colonized riparian and other well-watered foothill habitats along the base of the Sierra. On the western margins of the San Joaquin Valley, discrete cemeteries of either extended (e.g., CCO-696 East, MER-3) or flexed burials (e.g., CCO-696 West, MER-94) date to the Upper Archaic (Meyer and Rosenthal 1997; Olsen and Payen 1969; Pritchard 1970) and probably represent alternating occupation by groups originating in the valley and adjacent coast ranges.

Little is known about Upper Archaic cultures in the southern San Joaquin Valley (Siefken 1999:56–57). Hartzell (1992) reports year-round villages at KER-116 and KER-39 on Buena Vista Lake. These deposits incorporate a variety of residential features, including house floors, and extensive accumulations of dietary debris that reflect exploitation of both aquatic and terrestrial environments (Hartzell 1992:304–305).

In the far northern part of the Sacramento Valley, few Upper Archaic sites have been investigated. All appear to be related to the Whiskeytown Pattern (e.g., SHA-47, SHA-571/H, SHA-890, SHA-891, SHA-892, SHA-992), a technologically conservative and mobile adaptation found throughout the adjoining foothills (Sundahl 1982, 1992). In contrast to later Shasta Complex sites, Upper Archaic deposits associated with the Whiskeytown Pattern lack developed middens and residential features, and fish bone and other riverine resources are rare or absent (Hildebrandt et al. 2005:50–52). Although it was once thought that substantial Upper Archaic villages should be located along the northern Sacramento River (Basgall and Hildebrandt 1989:450), such sites have not yet been identified (Hildebrandt et al. 2005:50–52).

In the northeastern Sacramento Valley, Upper Archaic sites appear to be more substantial village settlements (Deal 1987). The lower component at mound site BUT-288 produced several domestic and processing features, human graves, and a variety of bone implements and marine shell beads and ornaments. The faunal assemblage reflects spring through winter occupation (Deal 1987). Similar features and artifact and dietary assemblages are reported from BUT-233, BUT-294, and GLE-101 (Welden 1990; White 2003a; Zancanella 1987).

People living in the San Joaquin Valley during the Upper Archaic remained important consumers of obsidian obtained from the east side of the Sierra. Stone workers at three main quarries—Bodie Hills, Casa Diablo, and Coso—manufactured bifacial blanks that were transported over the mountains along well-defined, east-west travel corridors (Bouey and Basgall 1984; Ericson 1981; Jackson et al. 1994). In the southern Sacramento Valley, obsidian was obtained primarily from quarries to the west in the North Coast Ranges, at Borax Lake and the upper end of Napa Valley. Specialist stone workers living near these quarries manufactured lanceolate-shaped bifaces that were widely traded throughout the Central Valley (Carpenter and Mikkelsen 2005; White 2003a; White et al. 2002). In the northern and eastern valley, obsidian was obtained primarily from Tuscan and Medicine Lake Highlands quarries, with the former becoming more important over time (Deal 1987; Sundahl 1992; Zancanella 1987).

Emergent Occupation (cal A.D. 1000 to Historic)

The relatively stable climatic regimes established at the outset of the Late Holocene appear to have prevailed throughout much of the Emergent Period, but several flood and drought events have been identified locally. These include pulses of floodplain deposition between cal A.D. 950 and 650 and again at about cal A.D. 1350 (Meyer and Rosenthal 1997; Rosenthal and Meyer 2004a, b; White 2003a, b), a major delta flood dating to cal A.D. 1420 (Goman and Wells 2000), and a significant drought in the Sacramento River watershed between cal A.D. 1585 and 1575 (Meko 2001; Meko et al. 2001). It isn't clear, however, if these were unusual events or simply products of the comparatively profound resolution of more recent paleoenvironmental evidence.

The Emergent Period is associated with the Augustine Pattern (Fredrickson 1994c) in the lower Sacramento Valley/Delta region (previously known as the Late Horizon), and the Sweetwater and Shasta Complexes in northern Sacramento Valley (Fredrickson 1973, 1974a; Kowta 1988; Sundahl 1982). Sporadic research in the San Joaquin Valley has resulted in few named Emergent Period components or phases. Only the Pacheco Complex from the western edge of the valley has been formally defined (Olsen and Payen 1968, 1969, 1983; Pritchard 1970).

The Emergent Period archaeological record is the most substantial and comprehensive available for any period, and the assemblages and adaptations represented are the most diverse (Bennyhoff 1977; Fredrickson 1974a, Kowta 1988; Sundahl 1982, 1992). After cal A.D. 1000, many archaic technologies and cultural traditions disappeared throughout the Central Valley. Each region witnessed the onset of cultural traditions similar to those existing at the time of European-American contact. The Emergent Period is marked by the introduction of the bow and arrow, which replaced the dart and atlatl as the favored hunting implement between about cal A.D. 1000 and 1300 (Bennyhoff 1994a). A change from less to more complex social forms is indicated by increased variation in burial type and furnishings (Atchley 1994; Bennyhoff and Fredrickson 1994; Milliken and Bennyhoff 1993). In the Sacramento Valley, large, populous towns developed at points along the river where fish weirs were constructed (e.g., COL-1, COL-2, SHA-222, SHA-266; Sundahl 1982; White 2003a). Similar mound villages and smaller hamlets were established in the delta region and along major tributaries (e.g., BUT-1, BUT-12, BUT-288, CCO-138, COL-11, SAC-16, SAC-127, SAC-267, SAC-29, SOL-397, TEH-10, YOL-69; Atchley 1994; Derr 1983; Eugster 1990; Johnson 1976; Johnson and Dondero 1990; Olsen 1963; Peak et al. 1984; Schenck and Dawson 1929; Shapiro and Tremaine 1995; White 2003a; Wulf 1997). In the San Joaquin Valley, villages and smaller residential communities developed along the many sidestreams of the foothills and along the river channels and sloughs of the valley bottom (e.g., FRE-128, MER-3, MER-119, KIN-66, TUL-1613; Dillon et al. 1991; Olsen and Payen 1968; Pritchard 1970, 1983; Siefken 1999).

Two broad phases are widely recognized during the Emergent Period: the Lower and Upper. The Lower Emergent is marked by the first appearance of banjo-type *Haliotis* ornaments in the southern Sacramento Valley/Delta region, as well as elaborately incised bird bone whistles and tubes, flanged soapstone pipes, and rectangular *Olivella* sequin beads. Upper Emergent artifacts include small corner-notched and desert series arrow points, *Olivella* lipped and clam disk beads and bead drills, magnesite cylinders, hopper mortars, and village sites with house pits often attributable to known ethnographic settlements (Beardsley 1954:77–79; Bennyhoff, in Elsasser 1978:44; Fredrickson 1984; Moratto 1984:213; Pritchard 1970, 1983). Other new traits that distinguish the Augustine Pattern in the delta region include preinterment grave pit burning with tightly flexed burials. Cremation was apparently reserved for high-status individuals during the Lower Emergent but was widespread during the Upper Emergent (Fredrickson 1974a:127; Moratto 1984:211).

Grave offerings such as shell beads and ornaments regularly occur with utilitarian items including pestles and mortars often "killed" before burial. In the Sacramento Valley area, fishing equipment is more common, elaborate, and diverse than in earlier phases and includes several types of harpoons, bone fish hooks, and gorge hooks (Beardsley 1954:78; Bennyhoff, in Elsasser 1978:44; Moratto 1984:211; Sundahl 1982). Twined and coiled basketry, netting, and other perishables were preserved at MER-3, SAC-29, SOL-236, TEH-10, and YOL-69 (Johnson and Dondero 1990; Pritchard 1970; Polanich 2005), while house floors and other structural remains are commonly preserved at Emergent Period sites throughout the valley and adjoining foothills (e.g., CAL-1180/H, CCO-458, COL-11, KER-39, MER-3, MER-113, MER-215, MER-295, SAC-29, SAC-267, SHA-222, SHA-266, SHA-294, SHA-1141/H; Dondero and Johnson 1988; Hartzell 1992; Johnson 1976; Meyer and Rosenthal 1997; Milliken et al. 1997; Olsen 1963; Maniery and Brown 1994; Peak and Weber 1978; Pritchard 1970, 1983; Sundahl 1982; White 2003a). A local form of pottery known as Cosumnes brownware was made in the lower Sacramento Valley, represented at several sites including SAC-6, SAC-67, SAC-107, SAC-127, SAC-265, SAC-267, and SAC-329 (Johnson 1990; Kielusiak 1982). In the Tulare basin, pottery was obtained through trade from groups living in the foothills to the east (Wallace 1990). Baked clay balls, probably used for cooking, are a common constituent in Central Valley sites where stone is absent (e.g., SAC-16, SAC-265, SAC-267) (Derr 1983:92; Johnson 1976:301–319; Moratto 1984:213; Sheeders 1982:81–94). Human and animal effigies of baked clay are known from several sites in the lower Sacramento Valley and Delta regions (e.g., SAC-6, SAC-16, SAC-29, SAC-267, SJO-42, SJO-43) (Johnson 1976:301–319; Kielusiak 1982; Schenck and Dawson 1929).

During the Lower Emergent Period, the most unique arrow point style in California was developed in the delta or adjacent regions to the west, known as the Stockton serrated point (Dougherty 1990). While other arrow point styles found in the Central Valley have morphological similarities to widespread types found in adjacent regions and may have been adopted from neighboring groups, the Stockton serrate is clearly an independently developed point type. This may be taken as evidence that changes in other aspects of culture in the southern delta represent internal developments and not the in-migration of new people. South of the delta in Merced, Stanislaus, and Fresno Counties, there is little evidence for the first arrow point styles, but by perhaps 500 years ago, the Panoche side-notched point, a variant of the Desert side-notched, was in use on the western side of the San Joaquin Valley, and cottonwood points are found in the Tulare and Buena Vista basins (Hartzell 1992:173; Moratto 2002; Olsen and Payen 1983; Pritchard 1970; Siefken 1999:152–154). In the northern Sacramento Valley, Gunther-barbed points were introduced as early as cal A.D. 770 (Basgall and Hildebrandt 1989:123; Jaffke 1997). By the end of the local sequence, Desert side-notched points were in use, just as they were in many places in the Central Valley, often alongside other local arrow point types (Baumhoff and Byrne 1959; Dougherty 1990; White 2003b).

The emphasis of Emergent Period economies was regionally variable, although fishing and plant harvesting appear to have increased in importance over time throughout the Central Valley. Most residential sites dating to the Emergent Period include large quantities of fish bone and a diverse assortment of mammal and bird remains evidenced by collections from numerous sites (e.g., AMA-56, BUT-1, COL-158, COL-245/H, KIN-66, MER-215, SAC-133, SAC-329, SHA-266, SHA-290/H, SHA-294) (Bouey and Waechter 1992; Broughton 1988; Dondero and Johnson 1988; Furlong 2004; Schulz et al. 1976; Siefken 1999; Simons 1978; Soule 1976; Valente 1998a; White 2003a). Throughout the Central Valley, mortars and pestles predominate after 1,000 years ago. Small seeds became increasingly important in deposits from the lower Sacramento Valley/Delta region (e.g., CCO-458, COL-245, SOL-356, SOL-397, SUT-17, YOL-69) while the greater size of certain grass seeds may indicate incipient horticulture (Miksicek 1999; Wohlgemuth 2004). Acorn, pine nut, and manzanita are abundant throughout the Emergent Period in the large village middens of the northern Sacramento Valley, including SHA-47, SHA-236, SHA-222, SHA-290/H, and TEH-748 (Dondero and Johnson 1988; Wohlgemuth 2004:104–106), while little is known about plant use in the San Joaquin Valley (Wohlgemuth 2004).

Sometime during the past 800 years, there was a significant change in the nature of obsidian production in central California. Bifaces were no longer commonly manufactured at centralized quarry workshops or nearby villages. Instead, raw obsidian cobbles and flake blanks were moved out of the Napa Valley to consumers in neighboring regions. This resulted in substantial changes in manufacturing residues at Emergent Period sites in the lower Sacramento Valley (e.g., CCO-138, YOL-69) and Diablo Ranges (CCO-458) (Bieling 1996; Bloomer 2005; Fredrickson 1968, 1969; Meyer and Rosenthal 1997).

Decentralization in the production of shell beads is also evident in Emergent Period sites. During the past 800 to 500 years, *Olivella* bead blanks and manufacturing refuse from interior central California sites, such as CCO-458, KIN-66, NAP-539, and SOL-356 (Hartzell 1992; Meyer and Rosenthal 1997; Siefken 1999; Wiberg 1996b), marks the beginning of local bead-making industries. By about 300 years ago, clam shell disk beads became widely used and clam shell manufacturing waste and bead blanks are found throughout Upper Emergent sites exclusively in the lower Sacramento Valley west of the Sacramento River (e.g., SOL-30, SOL-397, YOL-69). This tradition of bead manufacture may be related to the adoption of a monetized system of exchange (Chagnon 1970; C. King 1978).

CULTURE CHANGE IN THE CENTRAL VALLEY

In the years leading up to publication of *California Archaeology* (Moratto 1984), most researchers had arrived at the view that native people in the Central Valley had achieved high population densities and cultural elaboration as the result of a relatively affluent environment stocked with abundant and predictable foodstuffs (Baumhoff 1963; Moratto 1984:171). This view began to change in the early 1980s, as a growing radiocarbon database demonstrated that sites more than 2,500 years old were rare in the Central Valley, which was interpreted as evidence for a sharp increase in human population during the Upper Archaic (Breschini 1983; Schulz 1981). Several studies also concluded that the devices associated with pursuit and processing of ethnographic staples (e.g., the mortar and pestle related to acorn processing, and net weights, spears, and hooks needed for fishing) were relatively recent innovations that came into widespread use only after 2,500 years ago (Fredrickson 1973, 1974a; Gould 1964; Ragir 1972; Schulz 1981). To explain these developments, archaeologists started thinking about the record in new ways, first exploring causal relationships between population density and the emergence of social stratification (Fredrickson 1974b; T. King 1970, 1974b, 1978; Moratto 1972) and later turning to the broader concepts of late prehistoric *intensification*, demographic forcing, and optimality theory.

Intensification

Cohen (1981) introduced the new concept of intensification, arguing that California's late prehistoric diets were not efficient and balanced but were encumbered by higher processing costs when compared to earlier diets, and that reliance on these costly foods (such as acorns) had actually been forced by late prehistoric population increase. Basgall (1987) built on the notion of demographic forcing, arguing that imbalances between human population and available resources might result from a variety of different kinds of events, such as local population growth, in-migration of new populations, resource depletion due to human overharvest, or declines in productivity due to climate change. Basgall (1987) proposed that regional variation in central California was a product of differences in the rate at which these various demographic thresholds were breached. Beaton (1991c) also sought to strengthen the intensification model by introducing a distinction between intensification as "the sum of additional labor and material devoted to increasing the yield of currently exploited resources within the residential estate" versus extensification as "the sum of additional labor and material devoted to the capture of new resources either within or without the estate" (Beaton 1991c:951).

Despite the predictive and synthetic potential demonstrated by initial efforts to develop intensification theory, during the 1990s it became clear that the theory had progressed well beyond the existing archaeological record. First, the theory relied on claims of population increase but no quantitative evidence was forthcoming. Second, the theory claimed that certain foods were inefficient but no one provided actual data on nutritional returns versus processing costs. Third, the proponents of demographic forcing claimed that prehistoric diets had changed, but they provided little evidence in support of this position. Fortunately a new generation of studies has addressed these shortcomings.

Demographic Forcing

With the goal of developing an indirect measure of population pressure, researchers have begun to study the enormous collections of human skeletal remains from the Central Valley to identify changes in health status. These studies consistently show that pathologies associated with poor nutrition and interpersonal violence are more frequent and age/sex dependent over time, implying that Central Valley groups were often stressed (Dickel 1985; Dickel et al. 1984; Ivanhoe 1995; Jurmain 2001; Nelson 1991; Schulz 1981; Tenney 1986). Mortality profiles from Central Valley sites also indicate that population increased steadily from the late Middle Archaic through the Emergent Periods (Bouey 1995:353; Doran 1980).

To directly measure prehistoric population growth over the past 4,000 years, White (2003b) studied ethnographic River Patwin and Valley Konkow territory, where the distinctive demographic, social, and economic extremes of the Central Valley had reached their apex (Baumhoff 1963; Kroeber 1922, 1936, 1939). Ethnographic and historical sources were consulted for information about village and population size, and records of all known surveys, sites, and excavations were examined. There were 29 excavated village sites with 39 separate occupation components which were assigned an age based on time-marker artifacts and radiocarbon dates. White (2003b) estimated population at around 625 persons by the end of the Middle Archaic (2550 cal B.C.), doubling and redoubling to 3,424 persons near the end of the Upper Archaic (cal A.D. 750), and tripling again to 12,555 persons by the end of the Emergent (cal A.D. 1820; Figure 10.5), findings consistent with predictions from intensification theory.

Optimality and Resource Depression

Through the 1980s, the California intensification literature relied on simple claims of relative efficiency rather than actual measurement of food value. New research on optimality theory addresses this shortcoming. Optimality theory assumes that human adaptations were conditioned by the fundamental goal of energetic efficiency, and thus diet tended to be composed of the most profitable resources involving the highest gain for the least expenditure. Of particular interest to intensification theory are the implications about demographic forcing. For example, optimality models predict that hunter-gatherers will often overharvest favored prey species like deer and elk, which are easy to diminish because they take a long time to reach reproductive maturity, gestate slowly, and have few offspring. Thus human demographic forcing is likely to result in local depletion of these species, with ensuing resource depression leading to diet and technological change.

Broughton (1988) introduced these concepts to Central Valley archaeology with a study of prehistoric Sacramento River fisheries. He created a diet-breadth model for the Sacramento Valley and predicted that early diets should concentrate on large game (tule elk, deer, pronghorn antelope), with ensuing resource depression resulting in a shift to small game (rabbits, squirrels, waterfowl), and then to fish (salmon, perch, minnows). He examined a number of Sacramento Valley archaeological assemblages and found that Upper Archaic Period diets were characterized by a low ratio of fish to terrestrial game, while Emergent Period diets had a high ratio of fish to terrestrial game, indicating a decline in foraging efficiency over time, consistent with predictions from intensification theory. Broughton (1994a) also conducted a more general study based on examination of faunal assemblages ranging in age from the Middle Archaic to the Terminal Prehistoric Period. He found that over time, anadromous and resident fish made up a progressively larger part of the diet relative to mammals. These studies implied that increasing reliance on local fisheries in part facilitated late prehistoric human population growth.

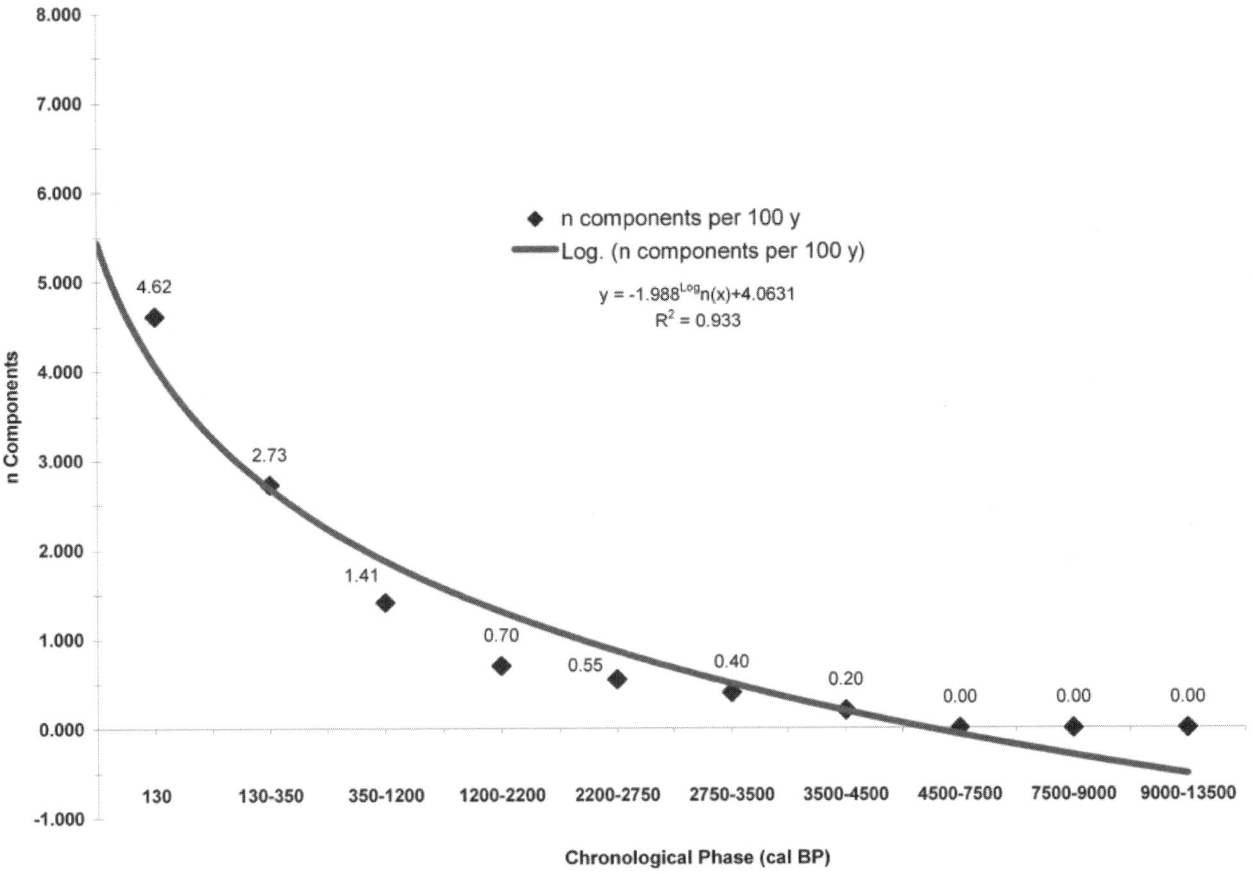

Figure 10.5. Lower Sacramento Valley population curve.

The Trouble with Acorns

Despite the early success of optimality theory, recent evidence pertaining to acorn exploitation provides a striking example of counterintuitive results. Based on changes in the types of stone grinding tools, Basgall (1987) argued that California's distinctive acorn economy developed relatively late in time—just 2,500 years ago in the Central Valley and substantially later in perimeter territories. Like Cohen (1981), Basgall (1987) concluded that the acorn was a high-cost vegetal food forced by late prehistoric population/resource imbalances. Wohlgemuth (1996) studied plant macrofossil assemblages recovered by flotation from a series of sites in Central California spanning the Middle Archaic through Emergent Periods (5500 cal B.C. to historic), and found a pattern of increasing density and diversity of seeds, and a greater proportion of large nut crops (especially acorn) during the Upper Archaic, consistent with Basgall's (1987) intensification argument. In addition, however, his research has also found widespread evidence for extensive use of acorns at a much earlier time depth and the increasing importance of small seeds relative to acorns during the Emergent Period, the latter especially acute in areas with the highest population densities (Wohlgemuth 2004).

With a new appreciation for the antiquity of acorn use, White (2003b) argues that either demographic thresholds were reached at an earlier time depth than previously predicted, or the food was more profitable than currently credited and therefore diet breadth models need to be recast. White suggests that we dispense with the assumption that acorns always required multistage processing, or that the end product was necessarily a fine, leached flour. Alternative products and processing probably characterized the Lower and Middle Archaic, involving methods that minimized handling costs. Whole or mulled acorns may have been treated with clay (White et al. 2002:536; White 2003b:26), a strategy that can reduce tannic acid content by more than 75 percent without the need for high-cost leaching (see Johns and Duquette 1991).

The Trouble with Small and Large Game

While Broughton's (1988, 1994a) analysis of Central Valley faunal assemblages focused on sites dating almost entirely to the Upper Archaic, most researchers took his model to unequivocally predict a prevailing pattern of large game harvest during the Archaic, replaced by small game harvest in the Emergent. In sharp contrast to this expectation, recent investigations at sites throughout the Central Valley have consistently found evidence for a high ratio of small to large game for over 7,000 years, between 7850 and 550 cal B.C. (Hartzell 1992; Meyer and Rosenthal 1997; Taite 1999; White 2003a), and a rise in the rate of large game harvest late in the prehistoric record (Furlong 2004; Taite 1999; Valente 1998a; White 2003a, 2003b). This is a phenomenon that has come to be identified by many researchers as the "artiodactyl spike."

These latter analyses show a substantial increase in the proportion of large game relative to small game, especially after 550 cal B.C., when other parts of the archaeological record clearly indicate that the rate of culture change was on the rise, and intensification phenomena were increasingly pronounced. Several explanations have been advanced, including the notion that later in time, people harvested in previously untouched environmental and cultural buffer zones (Broughton 1999; Holanda 2000; Taite 1999), that populations increasingly practiced mass capture methods, like deer drives and fences (White et al. 2002), that males began to hunt for prestige and not solely caloric gain (Hildebrandt and McGuire 2002), or simply that deer populations rebounded with the onset of Late Holocene environmental conditions (Broughton and Bayham 2003). The debate is ongoing (Furlong 2004; White 2005).

The Problem of the Whole Diet

While it is tempting to regard shortcomings in predictions about acorns, small game, and large game as evidence of a weakness in intensification theory itself, we may be missing the big picture and will only understand the fluctuations evident in game harvest and plant use once they are compared to each other and to important technological factors. White (2003b) attempted to synthesize the economic data from the same zone where he studied population, with the ultimate goal of correlating population expansion with economic change. He found a sharp increase in the rate of plant food production and sharp decline in the rate of animal food production after cal A.D. 770.

Notably, fish bone assemblages showed that more and smaller fish were taken after cal A.D. 770. Further, there was a steady decrease in the quantity and diversity of stone tools in village sites throughout this span, suggesting that plant food production and fish harvest involved off-site fixtures or soft technologies, probably including weirs, dip nets, seines, textile seed beaters, winnowing trays, and cooking vessels, as well as wooden mortars and perhaps wooden pestles, all technologies that are difficult to find and track in the archaeological record, and whose absence may have biased earlier studies (White 2003b).

White's (2003b) results show that the real story in the Central Valley is not in plant foods on the one hand or animal foods on the other, but the relationship between them. Plotting plant food and fish harvest curves against the Sacramento River population curve (Figure 10.6) shows that population had a direct causal relationship with plant food intensification (see also Wohlgemuth 2004).

QUESTIONS FOR FUTURE RESEARCH

While these results give us a renewed appreciation for intensification theory, the precise relationship between population change and culture change is still at issue. Even though we currently lack a common currency to measure the relative value of plant and animal foods, it is plain that the overall efficiency of the diet must have plummeted dramatically during the Emergent Period. Further, we currently have no means of relating economic change to sociocultural developments. However, the issue is central to determining if intensification was the unembellished product of resource depression and population growth, as current models require. Social complexity and instability clearly increased over time in the Central Valley, but because there is little or no attention to this issue the potential causal relationships are not part of the current debate. While it is possible that environmental productivity increased in the Late Holocene, it is also likely that any increase in food density would have rapidly created more densely packed populations facing the same problems with the same adaptation—the same ratio of people to resources that existed before the change in productivity. Thus intensification could only be related to a diminished ratio of resources to people, with proximate causes that might include environmental degradation or resource depression resulting from inexorable population growth.

We are convinced that resource intensification in the Central Valley was also marked by changes in human organization in response to changes in resource density. Intensification was manifested in the development of an administrative elite able to plan and manage mass capture (White et al. 2002) and in changes

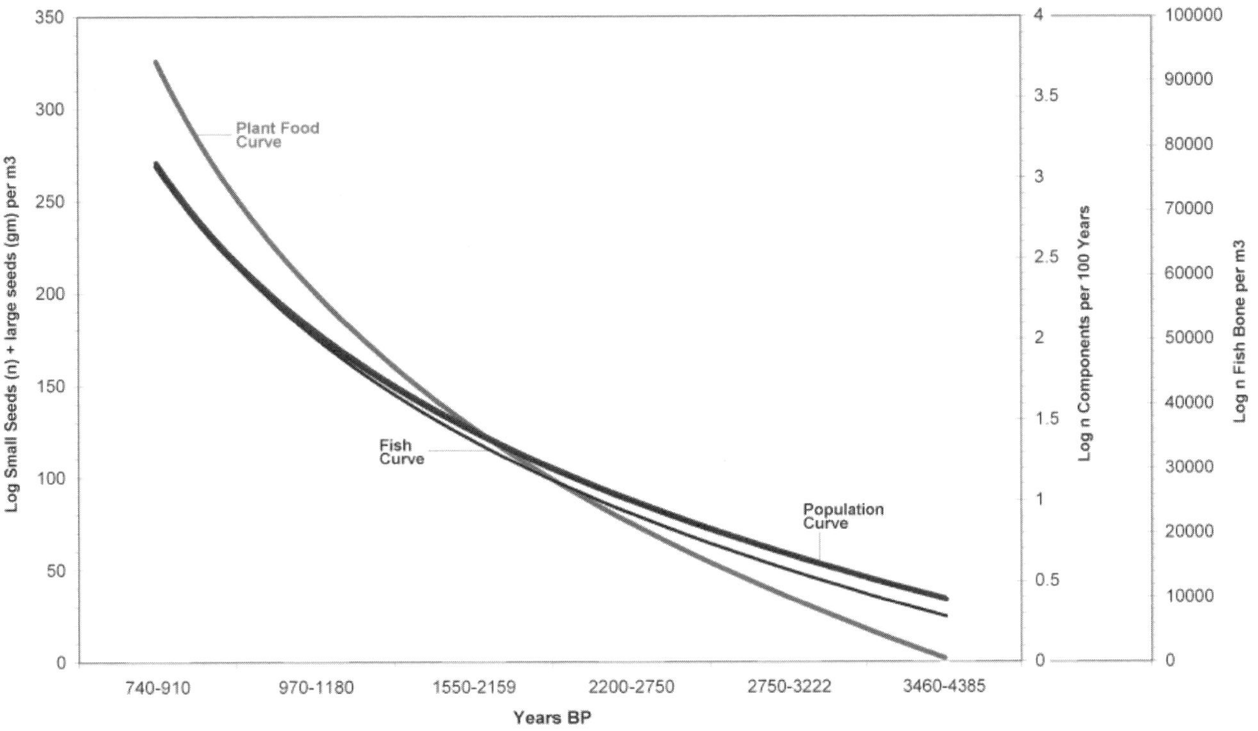

Figure 10.6. Lower Sacramento Valley plant, fish, and population curves, showing increases in plant and fish production closely linked to demographic change.

in the labor investment of women toward provisioning and men toward prestige-seeking activity (Hildebrandt and McGuire 2002). In fact an important body of new research is beginning to address gender-based differences in sociopolitical roles (Atchley 1994), work habits (Cordero 2001), and health status (Hollimon 1995; Schulz 1981). These studies have found widespread evidence for differences over time between men and women in the organization of labor and access to subsistence resources and positions of authority.

Aside from the vital issues described above, two areas are poorly treated in current research. First, the problem of social change in relation to economic change is not well understood. Unfortunately, an extensive and valuable literature on the evolution of prehistoric Central Valley social structure (Fredrickson 1974b; T. King 1970, 1974a, 1978; Milliken and Bennyhoff 1993) and culture history (Bennyhoff and Fredrickson 1994) is underused if not commonly ignored. Renewed attention to these studies could contribute significantly to the present limited frame of reference. Second, the proper role of regional trade in intensification theory is now poorly understood and difficult to judge because intensification models focus on endogenous processes and seek triggering conditions in the dynamics of local population-resource relationships. Beaton's (1991c) model argues that intensification preceded extensification. However, new studies have shown that transregional trade appeared in the Central Valley during the Lower Archaic and was well established in the Middle Archaic, far in advance of the Emergent Period demographic thrust (Jackson et al. 1998; Rosenthal and Meyer 2004b; Vellanoweth 2001). A new theory incorporating exchange as a dimension of intensification is clearly in order.

The exciting thing about working in the field of Central Valley prehistory is that the basic terms of the argument are truly at issue with each shovel turned. We expect the next 20 years of research to supply a variety of new evidence pertinent to exploration of the causes and consequences of culture change in California's Great Valley.

NOTE

1. Unless otherwise noted, ^{14}C dates appearing here have been calibrated using CALIB v. 4.3 (Stuiver and Reimer 1993).

CHAPTER 11

Models Made of Glass: A Prehistory of Northeast California

KELLY R. MCGUIRE

NORTHEAST CALIFORNIA REPRESENTS A VAST borderland that separates biogeographic, ethnographic, and prehistoric California from the Great Basin. The northern tier of this region includes a series of juniper-covered volcanic uplands, sagebrush valleys, pine forests, and lake country known as the Modoc Plateau. The Pit River and its tributaries comprise the major hydrological feature of this area; it bisects the Modoc Plateau and is part of the westward-draining Sacramento River hydrological system. To the southeast, near the Madeline Plains and Secret Valley, is the most northwestern extent of the Lahontan basin—a vast depression that once contained Pleistocene Lake Lahontan, of which Honey Lake is the remaining vestige. This area is typically Great Basin in character, consisting of a series of sagebrush- and saltbush-covered fans and basins, barren playa margins, and isolated uplands. It is also within eyeshot of the snow-capped peaks and yellow pine forests of the Cascade and Sierra Nevada Ranges. No fewer than four ethnographic groups inhabited this region at the beginning of the nineteenth century, some desert oriented (Northern Paiute), others more typically Californian (Maidu, Pit River, and Modoc). The prehistoric record of northeast California extends back at least 12,000 to 13,000 years and suggests that the divisions that mark the California and Great Basin culture zones are of long standing.[1]

NATURAL SETTING

Northeast California encompasses parts of three major physiographic provinces, including the Modoc Plateau, the Cascade Range, and the western Great Basin. The region as a whole is characterized by cool, dry summers, with annual precipitation ranging from less than 13 centimeters in low-lying desert basins to up to 100 centimeters in higher montane settings. The varied distribution of natural resources in these environments provided markedly different opportunities for the prehistoric and historic period occupants of the region. These primary physiographic regions are described below, with particular attention given to the abundance and distribution of water, plants, and animal foods that may have influenced prehistoric lifeways.

Northeast California is flanked on the west by the Cascade Range, which in this region extends from the Medicine Lake Highlands, southeast toward Fall River Valley and Lassen Volcanic National Park, to just north of Lake Almanor in Plumas County (Figure 11.1). This area spans a broad expanse of relatively young volcanic tablelands punctuated by numerous cones and flows. The Quaternary volcanic rocks with well-preserved, sometimes historically active volcanic cones and vents, such as Mount Lassen, distinguish the Cascade region from the Tertiary tablelands of the Modoc Plateau to the east and the complex, ancient lithologies of the Sierra Nevada to the south. The larger watersheds are drained by river systems that meander along these fault and joint lines and, at their lower reaches near the Sacramento Valley, are confined to steep, incised canyons.

Because the Cascades in this region lack a well-defined, high-elevation crest and thus no orographic barrier to prevailing westerly airflow, there is no sharp east-west zonation in climatic regimes. As a result, a more complex mosaic of California cismontane and Great Basin vegetation types is found in this region (Bryson and Hare 1974; Spaulding 1995b). On the west face of the Cascades, chaparral and oak–gray pine woodland occupy the lowest elevations, while higher elevations contain large tracts of ponderosa pine and fir. More interior zones are characterized by sagebrush steppe and juniper shrub savanna.

The Modoc Plateau covers most of northeast California, extending from Lower Klamath, Tule, Clear, and Goose Lakes along the Oregon-California border, south to the Madeline Plains. It consists of a broad volcanic tableland that has been broken in places by isolated volcanic cones, numerous rimrock benches, deeply incised canyons, river valleys, lakes, and playas. Elevations over most of the Modoc Plateau exceed 1,820 meters, providing substantially cooler and wetter conditions than in desert areas to the east.

Dominant vegetation in all but the mountainous uplands consists of a sagebrush-grassland association,

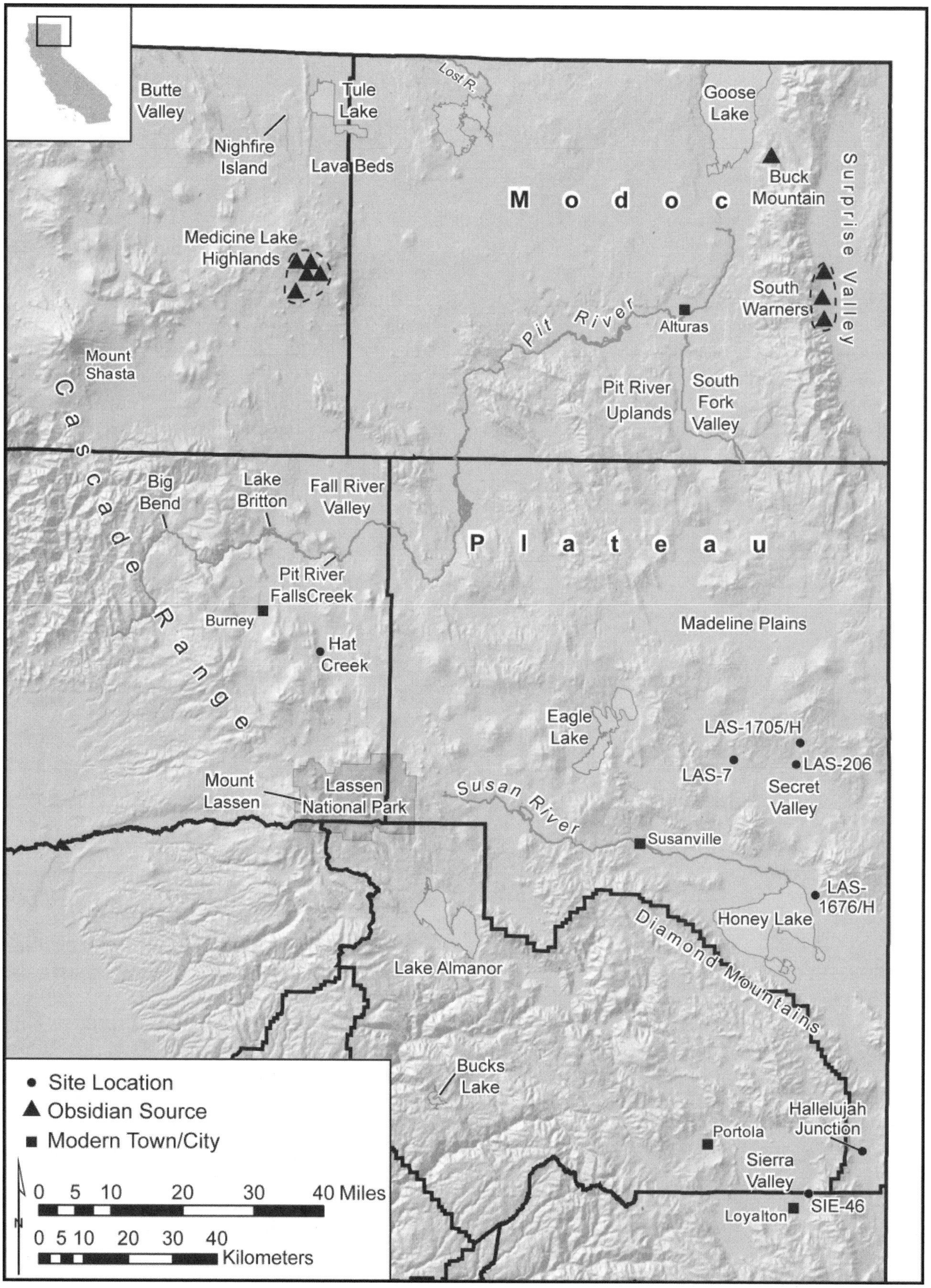

Figure 11.1. Archaeological sites and locations of northeast California.

with sometimes dense stands of juniper growing on rockier substrates and hillsides. In montane settings such as the Cascade and Warner Mountains, ponderosa pine dominates. Well-developed marsh communities border the major water courses that bisect this region, including the Pit River and its many tributaries, sloughs, and backwaters. Plants of aboriginal significance as food in these habitats included a variety of seeds and, more importantly, roots such as camas and epos.

Antelope and deer once abounded on the Modoc Plateau, and the Pit River is said to have been named by early settlers after the numerous pits that local Indians excavated to trap deer (Olmsted and Stewart 1978). Despite the importance of terrestrial game, it was in many places eclipsed by the resident and migratory waterfowl and fish that inhabited the many lakes, streams, and marshes of the region. The falls of the Pit River, between Hat Creek and Burney, mark the upstream limit of anadromous salmonid runs, and thus serves as a biogeographic break in prehistoric lifeways represented to the east (upstream) and west (downstream) of this point.

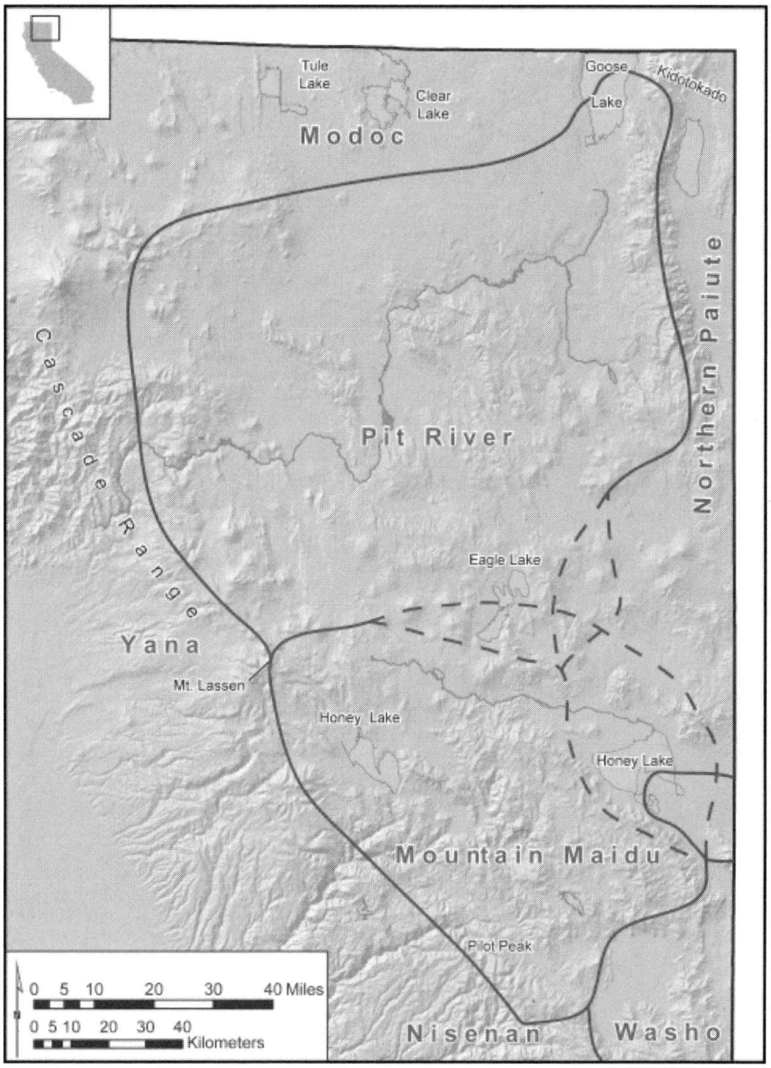

Figure 11.2. Approximate location of tribal groups, northeast California.

The Great Basin zones of northeast California are located along a narrow strip east of the Warner Mountains, encompassing to the south the Madeline Plains, Secret Valley, and Honey Lake basin. Elevations over most of the province range from 1,450 to 2,200 meters, though they reach as high as 3,635 meters atop the Warner Mountains. This northeastern fringe of the Great Basin consists of extensive, southeast-to-northwest trending fault-block ranges with broad graben valleys separating the low mountains. Many of the large valleys of this area, such as Honey Lake, Madeline Plains, and Surprise Valley, show evidence of Pleistocene pluvial lakes. Strand lines and beaches are common along these basin margins and provide evidence of deep lakes formed during a wetter and cooler climate. With the drier conditions of the Holocene, these basins typically contained smaller, fluctuating lakes marked by dunes and isolated wetlands.

Dominant plant associations found within the Great Basin region of northeast California include the shadscale-greasewood community, which occupies most of the alluvial plains, alkaline sinks, and lower mountain slopes of this region. At various times in the past, the alkaline soils supported vast tracts of inkweed or *wada*, after which the Honey Lake Paiute or Wadatkuht ("Wada eaters") were named. At slightly higher elevations along the Sierran front is a sagebrush-scrub community. Seed-bearing plants are generally less abundant in these habitats, but edible roots such as wild onion, epos, balsamroot, and biscuitroot are more numerous. At still higher elevations in the sagebrush community are open stands of western and Utah juniper.

ETHNOGRAPHIC PEOPLES

At the time of European contact, northeast California was home to four major tribal groups, including the Modoc, Pit River, Mountain Maidu, and Northern Paiute (Figure 11.2). For the most part, the Modoc,

Figure 11.3. WA-WÁ-WOK-GEE-NAY-GEÉ (Big Pete). This Pit River man was with his father at the Battle of Infernal Caverns in 1867. His father was killed in the attack. Big Pete died in 1929. (Photo printed with permission from the Modoc County Historical Society.)

Pit River (Figure 11.3), and Maidu were more typically Californian with regard to language, settlement-subsistence, and material culture, whereas the Northern Paiute practiced a more desert-oriented lifeway similar to other Numic-speaking peoples of the Great Basin.

The Modoc lived on both sides of what is now the California-Oregon border and immediately east of the Cascade Range, and spoke a dialect of a language that is a member of the Plateau Penutian family (Stern 1998:446). Modoc territory centered around Lower Klamath, Tule, and Clear Lakes, and along the Lost River, which flows between Clear and Tule Lakes (Kroeber 1925:318; Merriam and Talbot 1974:14; Ray 1963:xi–xii). The Pit River Indians are traditionally associated with a vast area of northeastern California that encompasses the mountainous Pit River drainage from southern Goose Lake all the way to Big Bend in Shasta County. Pit River tribes are composed of two groups: the Achumawi, consisting of nine bands, and the Atsugewi, with two bands (Kniffen 1928:303; Olmsted and Stewart 1978). The Achumawi language and its relative, Atsugewi, together form the Palaihnihan family, a member of the Hokan stock; each language contains dialects that correspond to the band divisions (Olmsted 1966; Shipley 1978). The Mountain Maidu are one of three Maidu tribal groups that make up the Maiduan language family, a member of the Penutian language stock. The Mountain Maidu once held a large territory that reached on the northwest from Mount Lassen east to beyond Honey Lake, turning southwest to the Sierra Buttes, and then northwest across Pilot Peak and back to Mount Lassen.

The Northern Paiute are composed of 22 bands (Stewart 1939; Fowler and Liljeblad 1986:Fig.1). These peoples speak dialects of the Northern Paiute language, one of the several closely related Numic languages spoken across the Great Basin (Fowler and Liljeblad 1986:435). Northeast California is home to two of the 22 Northern Paiute bands, including the Wadatkuht or Honey Lake Paiute, and the Kidutokado of the Surprise Valley area.

Traditional lifeways associated with the California groups—Modoc, Pit River, and Mountain Maidu—represent variations on a theme for these upland hunter-gatherers. Women gathered plant foods as they became available. In contrast to seed resources so important to desert populations located to the east, a number of root crops, particularly epos and camas, were of critical importance for all three groups. Epos was dried in the sun and stored for the following winter, as well as eaten in season. Camas roots and other bulbs were gathered from the marshy lowlands, and later in the season, salmon berries, bear berries, juniper berries, wild plum, and wild buckwheat were available in upland areas. Dried and ground supplies of these resources were stored for winter use (Kniffen 1928:305). Acorns were available in those areas of northeast California located mainly to the west, as well as in more limited areas, such as the Diamond Mountains near Honey Lake, to the east.

Hunting and fishing were important to all three groups. With respect to the former, small game appears to have been important whenever available, and was actively pursued by men and occasionally by women and children. Larger game such as antelope was hunted on the plains, and mountain sheep were hunted in the higher crags and lava beds (Ray 1963:182). Hunting activities associated with deer and elk intensified in the fall before the first snows. Maidu men were skillful hunters who often took bears for meat and hides, which were used in rituals (Dixon 1905:193–194; Riddell 1978:375; Voegelin 1942:58). With respect to fishing, spring and summer found the Modoc on the Upper Klamath Lake and Lost River taking advantage of sucker runs. Salmon were available to many Pit River bands to the west of Fall River, where the seasonal run ended at natural obstructions on the Pit River (Kniffen 1928:Map 1). Upstream bands concentrated their efforts on the many fish in the local streams. Similarly the Mountain Maidu took advantage of fish runs in the sloughs and tributaries of the Susan River and Willow Creek. Almost all of the major water sources in northeast California are associated with extensive marsh zones and bottomlands rich in resident and migratory waterfowl that were also important food resources.

In contrast to the California tribal groups, the Northern Paiute traditionally practiced a more dispersed subsistence-settlement system similar to that described by Julian Steward (1938) for Great Basin family band foragers. Northern Paiute bands foraged throughout their home territory, and many used resources in neighboring districts as well (Fowler and Liljeblad 1986:437). Settlement and subsistence patterns were closely tuned to fluctuations in the seasonal availability and distribution of wild food resources. The Wadatkuht caught suckers in great numbers with nets as the fish ran up Long Valley Creek in the spring to spawn (Riddell 1960a:34). By summer the seed products became available, and the women gathered them in abundance. Pinyon nuts and later acorns were gathered in the fall. Importantly, the Diamond Mountains provided the Wadatkuht access to acorns (Riddell 1960a:37). They are one of only a few of the basin bands who had access to this valuable resource within their own territory. The more arid regions produced jackrabbits, while the higher, timbered regions yielded deer. Supplies of these foods were stored for use during the winter months, when resources were limited.

THE PREHISTORIC PAST

Over the course of 60 years, archaeological research in northeast California has resulted in any number of local and regional chronological schemes (Basgall and Hildebrandt 1989; Baumhoff 1955; Cressman 1977; Hildebrandt and Mikkelsen 1995; Hughes 1986a; Johnson and Theodoratus 1984; Kowta 1988; O'Connell 1975; Pippin et al. 1979; Raven 1984; Riddell 1960b; Sampson 1985; Sundahl 1992; White et al. 2005). More recent syntheses have attempted to bring some order to this confusion through a standardized chronology that allows comparisons over the disparate cultural and environmental zones that characterize this region (Delacorte 1997a; McGuire 2002). This chronology, summarized in Table 11.1, is used throughout the present discussion.

Early Holocene

The earliest Paleo-Indian occupation of northeast California is reflected in Clovis-like projectile points, as well as suggestively large hydration readings on obsidian tools and flakes. Although rare, Clovis points have been recovered from Samwel Cave (Treganza 1964), Mammoth Springs, Eagle Lake, Hat Creek (Dillon 2002:113), and Sconchin Butte (Moratto 1984:87). These tools have not been directly dated but are assumed to date in the range of Clovis points found elsewhere in North America (ca. 11,500 to 9500 cal B.C.). In addition, several Paleo-Indian sites have been identified along the margins of Honey Lake and other major basins, recognized primarily by exceedingly large obsidian hydration rim values. The earliest radiocarbon date in northeast California is 11,450 ± 340 RCYBP (see Chapter 4) and comes from a fire pit located in a rock shelter on the western shore of Tule Lake (Beaton 1991b:64). The hearth contained ash and fragments of burned wood and fish bone, suggesting the shelter was used by "Paleoindian foragers

Table 11.1. Cultural Periods for Northeast California

Period	*Dates*
Early Holocene	5000+ cal B.C.
Post-Mazama	5000–3000 cal B.C.
Early Archaic	3000–1500 cal B.C.
Middle Archaic	1500 cal B.C.–cal A.D. 700
Late Archaic	cal A.D. 700–1400
Terminal Prehistoric	cal A.D. 1400–Contact

who were exploiting the lakeshore/marsh resources of Tule Lake" (Beaton 1991b:64).

Elsewhere in western North America but not in northeast California, Clovis points have been found in association with the bones of extinct megafauna (e.g., mammoth and large bison), suggesting that early populations were focused on large game hunting. In northeast California, as with the Great Basin (Willig and Aikens 1988), Paleo-Indian assemblages generally do not occur with milling equipment. Most archaeologists agree that early populations were highly mobile, traveling in small groups and settling around lakes and along rivers where game also tended to aggregate.

Prehistoric occupation of northeast California toward the latter part of the Early Holocene (<9500 cal B.C.) is documented by various large lanceolate and stemmed projectile points that typically occur with a variety of heavy core tools, bifaces, patterned and unpatterned flake tools, and chipped stone crescents, around the former shores of extinct pluvial lakes and other ancient landforms. Wide-stemmed projectile points tend to be more common along the western parts of this region (Clewett and Sundahl 1983; Sundahl 1992; White et al. 2005), whereas Great Basin stemmed series points typify Early Holocene components in desert areas to the east. Important Early Holocene sites containing stemmed points have been reported in the Fort Rock and Lower Klamath Lake basins (Bedwell 1970, 1973; Cressman 1942; Cressman et al. 1940); Surprise Valley (O'Connell 1975); near the shores of Goose, Clear, and Tule Lakes (Beaton 1991b; West and Welch 2001); in Butte Valley (Jensen and Farber 1982); along the bottomlands of the Madeline Plains and Honey Lake Basin (Delacorte 1997b; McGuire 2000; Milliken and Hildebrandt 1997); and at Eagle and Bucks Lakes (Kowta 1988). More sporadic occurrences of Early Holocene material are also reported from various localities in the Modoc National Forest (Delacorte 1997b:11), and in any number of contexts across the western Great Basin (Willig and Aikens 1988).

While there has been some tendency to view Early Holocene adaptations in general as mostly directed at large game, sites along the shores of Honey Lake have a high degree of assemblage diversity that includes both flaked stone *and* ground stone. These tools, as well as significant concentrations of small game (mostly rabbits), fish, and shellfish remains, make up the Early Holocene assemblages in this area. This diversified set of resources clearly reflects some level of intensification, contrary to the view of Early Holocene peoples as primarily big-game hunters (Milliken and Hildebrandt 1997:159). There is no question, however, that Early Holocene populations were highly mobile and territorially expansive in their wanderings. Evidence for this is provided by obsidian source profiles of projectile points and other tools, which consistently exhibit the highest source variation observed for any prehistoric period. This pattern has been recognized elsewhere in the western Great Basin (Basgall and McGuire 1988; Delacorte 1997b; Delacorte and McGuire 1993) and is usually ascribed to high residential mobility encompassing a comparatively large geographic area.

Post-Mazama

The best-known Post-Mazama manifestation in northeast California is found in Surprise Valley, in the form of highly formalized, semisubterranean house structures. O'Connell (1971, 1975) included these features in his Menlo Phase, dating between 4500 and 2500 cal B.C. Morphologically distinctive artifacts found in these components include large side-notched projectile points, antler wedges, mortars with V-shaped bowls and pointed pestles, T-shaped drills, tanged blades, and flaked stone pendants. All of these artifacts and features appear to be of northern derivation, with comparable forms identified at numerous sites on the Columbia Plateau but rarely at more southern Great Basin localities. Subsistence remains at sites in Surprise Valley, the Klamath basin, and other places attest to the regular (if infrequent) hunting of bison and elk; these remains disappear altogether in the record of later occupations from more southern areas (O'Connell 1971, 1975; Sampson 1985). Menlo Phase sites are normally found near marshes or permanent water sources; components of the same age and manifesting much the same lakeshore adaptation have been identified at Nightfire Island on Lower Klamath Lake (Sampson 1985).

The most unambiguous evidence of Post-Mazama occupation in archaeological assemblages across this region is the presence of Northern side-notched projectile points, the same variant found in Menlo Phase components in Surprise Valley. Where they occur in good stratigraphic contexts, Northern side-notched points generally appear to postdate the 5000 cal B.C. Mount Mazama ash fall (Leonhardy and Rice 1970; Wilde 1985), with terminal dates for the type at around 2500 to 3000 cal B.C. (Layton 1985; O'Connell 1971, 1975; Sampson 1985). As nearly as can be reconstructed, these points are distributed in a fanlike pattern across the Columbia Plateau and northern reaches of the Great Basin, again suggestive of plateau influences during this time period (Delacorte 1997b). Their southernmost extent within northeast California and western Nevada is the South Fork Valley/Madeline Plains area and the Smoke Creek Desert. Northern side-notched points, as well as obsidian hydration values on other tools and debitage of corresponding age, have been documented in upland assemblages from the Modoc Plateau (Hildebrandt and Mikkelsen 1995). This appears to be the first substantial occupation of the upland zones in northeast California and suggests that settlement systems dating to this time were not wholly confined to valley bottoms and lakeshore contexts. Hildebrandt and Mikkelsen (1995) characterize upland foraging strategies at this time as highly mobile with no systematic dependence on storage.

South of the Madeline Plains, Northern side-notched points are comparatively rare, replaced by a disparate series of possible Middle Holocene time markers including Gatecliff, Fish Slough, as well as large contracting-stemmed and other Martis-like variants (Hildebrandt and King 2002:18–21). Post-Mazama components are relatively rare and, given the uncertain dating of these markers, the sites tend to be recognized primarily on the basis of obsidian hydration dating. Noting the diversity of projectile point types with hydration values indicative of Post-Mazama vintage, Milliken and Hildebrandt (1997) speculate that well-watered areas along the Sierran front (including the Honey Lake basin) may have offered refuge to populations from adjacent desert areas that were affected by Middle Holocene warming and decreased resource productivity.

At least in the southern part of northeast California, the effects of Middle Holocene warming can also be seen in land-use shifts dating to this time. Most Early Holocene sites in the Honey Lake region occur along the featureless landscape at the edge of the Honey Lake playa, presumably along the former lake shore or marsh boundary. Most Middle Holocene (Post-Mazama and Early Archaic) sites, on the other hand, occur almost exclusively upslope on the alluvial fans and adjacent to what can still be recognized as prominent sources of freshwater (Milliken and Hildebrandt 1997; Rosenthal 2000). A similar land-use change appears to have occurred on the Madeline Plains, where most of the Early Holocene sites are associated with the lake or marsh-edge features. Conversely, virtually all of the Middle Holocene components are found along major drainages or adjacent to springs (Rosenthal 2000). Pond-edge sites and riparian habitats appear to have taken on new importance in this period, as once productive wetlands and lakes disappeared.

While the relative frequencies of various stone tools remain constant in Early and Middle Holocene assemblages from these lake basins, there is a threefold increase in the frequency of milling equipment corresponding to the latter period that has been attributed to the rising importance of plant resource exploitation (Rosenthal 2000). Along these same lines, Kowta (1988:193–194) speculated on the existence of a Millingstone Horizon similar to that described for southern California and dating to roughly the same time period, which he sees as a generalized hunting and gathering tradition geared toward the intensive exploitation of plant resources.

Early Archaic

The Early Archaic, at least in comparison to the two preceding periods, marks the beginning of major increases in archaeological visibility across northeast California (see Kowta 1988). Any number of excavations and large-scale surveys have yielded some evidence, either in the form of diagnostic artifacts or appropriately large obsidian rim values, characteristic of Early Archaic occupation. It is at this time, for example, that we see the first sustained occupations marked by components containing millingstones, mortars and pestles, and a variety of dart forms in Lassen Volcanic National Park (White et al. 2005) and the Bucks Lake region (Johnson 1980).

Recognition of Early Archaic components, however, depends in part on a reasonably reliable projectile point chronology. Unfortunately, there is a high degree of regional and temporal variation in key Early Archaic time markers. On the Modoc Plateau, the Gatecliff Split Stem point, the classic Great Basin Early Archaic indicator, is essentially absent, replaced by Elko and Siskiyou side-notched forms, which can date to as early as 2500 cal B.C. (Hildebrandt and King 2002; see also Mack 1991). To the south, where Gatecliff series points are more common, they also tend to occur with Elko points and other large, Martis-like dart points (Bennyhoff and Hughes 1987:163; Hildebrandt and King 2002; McGuire 1997a:223; Milliken and Hildebrandt 1997).

Perhaps the best example of increased archaeological visibility during this time is the Martis Complex (or Martis Tradition), which has been identified primarily in upland contexts along the eastern and western flanks of the Sierra Nevada north of Lake Tahoe.

From its earliest formulation (Heizer and Elsasser 1953) and notwithstanding any number of periodic reconceptualizations over the past 45 years (Elsasser 1960; Elston et al. 1977; Jackson et al. 1994; Kowta 1988; McGuire and Bloomer 1997; Waechter 2002a, b), the Martis Complex has been synonymous with the heavy use of basalt in the manufacture of large bifacial tools. The production of basalt bifaces from material emanating from a series of upland quarries (Jackson et al. 1994; McGuire and Bloomer 1997; Waechter 2002c), coupled with the vast amount of reduction debris generated by on- and off-site reduction activities, is responsible for the high visibility of Martis components in upland contexts in the north-central Sierra Nevada. McGuire and Bloomer (1997) cite a variety of evidence, including both basalt and obsidian chemical sourcing studies, to suggest that much of the Sierran basalt was being exploited by population centers located in the central valley and foothill areas to the west (e.g., the Windmiller and Mesilla Complexes). Settlement systems were thus oriented along major east-west trending drainages extending from lowland villages to quarry zones located near the crest of the Sierra Nevada.

Early Archaic components elsewhere in northeast California, and particularly in Great Basin contexts, typically occur with numerous flake tools, bifacial knives, heavy core implements, and, importantly, a wide array of ground stone milling equipment. In Surprise Valley, mortars with V-shaped bowls and pointed pestles appear to be replaced in the Early Archaic period by U-shaped grinding bowls and flat- or round-ended pestles, and perhaps greater use of millingstones (O'Connell 1975). In Sierra Valley, several large, rock-lined processing features, inferred to have functioned as roasting ovens, have been identified, and they appear to be contemporaneous with a Martis occupation in this area (Waechter and Mikesell 2002). Similar Early Archaic processing features have been reported from Secret Valley, along with the increased use of basalt core tools tied to the processing of tubers, stalks, and other fibrous vegetal matter (McGuire 1997a).

At Nightfire Island on Lower Klamath Lake, the existence of a semipermanent village indicates that the island had become a focus of the annual subsistence round, rather than a peripheral component (Sampson 1985). This period is characterized by clay-lined pit houses, an increasingly diversified assemblage, and a substantial increase in the frequency of milling equipment. Settlement elaboration and pit house construction have also been documented along the Middle Pit River drainage at this time, with base camps tending to be concentrated on the higher terraces and benches above the river (Cleland 1995:5–10).

Middle Archaic

As a general characterization, the increases in archaeological visibility and settlement differentiation observed during the preceding Early Archaic accelerated during the Middle Archaic. Along the northern part of the Modoc Plateau, evidence of Middle Archaic Period occupations is widespread, with important sites and components at Nightfire Island and other locations in the Klamath and Tule Lake basins (Cressman 1942; Sampson 1985), Lava Beds National Monument (Squire and Grosscup 1952; Swartz 1964), Surprise Valley (O'Connell 1971, 1975), and virtually every valley system and section of the Modoc Plateau where significant investigations have been conducted (Delacorte 1997a; Gates 1983; Hildebrandt and Mikkelsen 1995; McGuire 2000; Nilsson et al. 2000; Raven 1984; Theodoratus et al. 1979).

To the south, the most dramatic example of this increased visibility is found in Secret Valley and manifested at such sites as LAS-7 (the Karlo site), LAS-206, and LAS-1705/H (McGuire 1997a). This is represented by a proliferation of house structures, midden deposits, hearths, ovens, and burials, as well as by the richest and most diverse assemblage of artifacts and subsistence remains identified in the region. Similar elaborations in settlement activity have been identified in adjacent desert areas (Leach 1988; Seck 1980), the Middle Pit River (Bayham and Valente 1995; Broughton 1994a; Chatters and Cleland 1995; Cleland 1995), the Feather River drainage (Kowta 1988), and the Eagle Lake area (Pippin et al. 1979). Most of this elaboration appears to date to the latter end of the Middle Archaic Period, perhaps extending into the early part of the Late Archaic.

In the Lake Tahoe and Truckee Meadows areas, much of the Martis phenomenon that began during the Early Archaic along the crest zones of the Sierra Nevada continued unabated through the Middle Archaic Period. Major Middle Archaic settlements, similar to those identified in Secret Valley, are reported at Hallelujah Junction and Sierra Valley (Elston 1979; Waechter and Mikesell 2002). Middle Archaic hunting components and feature complexes are described at Loyalton rock shelter in eastern Plumas County (Wilson 1963), as well as in the Long Valley area (Pendleton and Thomas 1983).

Elsewhere in California, the Middle Archaic is seen as a cultural fluorescence or golden age, the most dramatic development being the occupation of large semisedentary villages, but also including elaborations in material culture, house construction, obsidian production, and ceremonial activity, particularly directed at big game hunting (Hildebrandt and McGuire 2002). To a large extent, this characterization holds for northeast California; many of the most elaborate villages and base camps documented date to this period. Residential stability appears to have increased during this time, but logistical mobility, particularly that employed by male hunting parties in pursuit of large game, appears to have been greater than in earlier periods (McGuire 2002). This would explain the ubiquity of hunting camps and features, as well as basalt and obsidian flake scatters in upland contexts throughout the region.

Perhaps tied to this increase in long-range logistical mobility were increases in obsidian quarry production. Findings from the PGT pipeline project (Hildebrandt and Mikkelsen 1995) indicate a Middle Archaic peak in obsidian biface production, similar to those noted for South Warners, Bordwell Spring, and Buffalo Hills obsidians in Secret Valley (McGuire 2002). The ubiquity of basalt quarry activity and biface reduction debris in upland Sierran contexts likely results from similar quarry production processes.

Obsidian source profiles for the Middle Archaic period diverge from trends observed elsewhere in the western Great Basin. For most areas, source diversity actually reached its lowest levels at this time. The focus seems to have shifted to more regularized acquisition of a few key glasses procured during logistical forays from larger villages and base camps. For example, in the Madeline Plains/Secret Valley region a reduction in the representation of minor sources is seen, with a corresponding increase in Buffalo Hills (formerly Unknown B) obsidian, and continuing use of South Warners and Bordwell Spring glass. On the northern fringe of the Modoc Plateau, archaeological assemblages contain almost exclusively high-quality glass from the Medicine Lake Highlands. Buck Mountain obsidian dominates sites in the Upper Pit River basin (McGuire 2002). It seems that populations were now regularly targeting a few key quarry localities, as contrasted with more ad hoc toolstone procurement conducted during the course of the seasonal subsistence round. This systematic and regular use of a few favored toolstone sources over a broad sweep of time resulted in greater homogeneity of obsidian source profiles.

Much of this obsidian was making its way to distant regions, particularly coastal areas to the west, suggesting a period of increased trade and exchange (Hughes 1986a). Along these lines, Bennyhoff and Hughes (1987:161) noted that trade of marine-shell beads into the Great Basin from California reached its peak in the first part of the Middle Archaic, roughly between 1500 and 1200 cal B.C. The fluorescence of settlement activity associated with Middle Archaic occupations may have been accompanied by a robust trade and exchange network.

Late Archaic

For northeast California, the transition from the Middle to the Late Archaic produced major changes in assemblage structure, subsistence, and settlement organization. Some of these changes may have resulted from climatic instability. The most significant event in this regard, referred to as the Medieval Climatic Anomaly, was a warm, dry interval from cal A.D. 900 to 1400 (Stine 1994; Jones et al. 1999). This drought period had major effects on prehistoric populations, although the exact relationships between climatic change and certain cultural shifts observed in the archaeological record is not well understood. Whether or not induced by climatic change, increases in population density, or other factors, cal A.D. 1000 marks a time of instability and upheaval in much of California and the western Great Basin.

The cal A.D. 1000 date neatly divides the Late Archaic Period. The early part (ca. cal A.D. 200 to 1000) appears to share greater affinities with the previous Middle Archaic Period, while the latter part (ca. cal A.D. 1000 to 1400) is perhaps more representative of the final phase of prehistoric use. This dichotomy serves as a caution for lifeway reconstructions and other models that attempt to lump Late Archaic assemblages into a single analytical unit.

Archaeological deposits attributable to the Late Archaic interval are ubiquitous in northeast California, with important sites reported in the Klamath, Tule, and Goose Lake basins (Cressman et al. 1940; Hughes 1977; Rodeffer and Galm 1985; Sampson 1985; Squire and Grosscup 1954; Swartz 1964), the Modoc uplands (Gates 1983), Surprise Valley (O'Connell 1971, 1975), and the central Pit River drainages (Baumhoff and Olmsted 1963, 1964; Cleland 1995; Manuel 1989). There are also important Late Archaic sites in Lassen Volcanic National Park (White et al. 2005), the Honey and Eagle Lake basins, and Secret Valley (Pippin et al. 1979; Riddell 1956, 1960b; Wohlgemuth 1978). Numerous Late Archaic components are recognized from excavations conducted for transmission line and natural gas pipeline archaeological programs (Delacorte 1997a; McGuire 1997a, b, 2000, 2002; Milliken and Hildebrandt 1997; Nilsson et al. 2000). In the Tahoe/Truckee region, Late Archaic components are known as Early Kings Beach (Elston et al. 1977, Elston et al. 1994; Heizer and Elsasser 1953; Jackson et al. 1994).

From an assemblage standpoint, the Late Archaic is typically marked by the occurrence of Rose Spring and Gunther barbed arrow points, which reflect the advent of bow and arrow technology in the region. This technology may have been introduced into the region several hundred years earlier than elsewhere in the Great Basin and California, thus accounting for the slightly greater antiquity (ca. cal A.D. 200 versus 650) of these point forms in this area. Technological changes accompanying the introduction of the bow and arrow include a shift to generally smaller, flake-based implements. Beginning around cal A.D. 950, brownware ceramics also occur in Late Archaic and Terminal Prehistoric components in the northern part of the region (Mack 1991:130).

With respect to house and community structure in the southern parts of the study area, those Late and Middle Archaic houses that predate cal A.D. 1000 often appear in small clusters rather than as isolated features, and are structurally more formal with elaborate superstructures, central hearths, caches, storage pits, and perimeter rock, perhaps reflecting prolonged seasonal occupations (McGuire 2002). Houses postdating cal A.D. 1000 generally lack this complexity and can occur as more ephemeral domestic features, rock rings, or living surfaces. But this period also marks the appearance of some of the largest contemporaneous social aggregations (villages) documented in the western Great Basin during the Late Holocene, such as Amadee Village located on the north shore of Honey Lake (Clay 1996; McGuire 2002; Rosenthal 2000). These villages, however, appear to have been occupied for only short durations and lack the semisedentary quality of their Middle Archaic counterparts. The aggregation of people into these large Late Archaic villages may have been a defense response to the perceived threat of warfare, raiding, or other forms of social conflict that seem to have been prevalent at this time (McGuire 2002:38–39).

From a settlement-subsistence perspective, this appears to have been a time of expanding resource intensification. Faunal remains from regional sites show a dramatic decline in the use of large game (Carpenter 2002). In Sierra Valley, Waechter and Andolina (2005) report a massive camas root processing complex, with multiple oven and hearth features, dating to the latter half of the Late Archaic (see also Waechter 2005). Similar concentrations of processing features dating to this time have been documented in the Truckee Meadows at Reno (Turner 1993). In the Middle Pit River region at this time, Chatters and Cleland (1995:27–29) document escalating population densities coupled with expanding resource intensification, the latter indicated by intensive exploitation of freshwater mussels and increased use of seeds and manzanita berries. Also tied to resource intensification during the Late Archaic, White et al. (2005) identified dramatic increases in populations occupying alpine zones at Lassen Volcanic National Park that mirror similar developments in the Central Valley to the west (White et al. 2005:180). On the Madeline Plains and in South Fork Valley (Delacorte 1997b, 2002), there was a dramatically expanded use of upland habitats on the Modoc Plateau after cal A.D. 1000. This expanded use appears to have depended heavily on the seasonal exploitation of epos and possibly other roots. Although some of these root crops may have been exploited to a limited extent in earlier times, their intensive use and storage in the late period reflects a fundamental shift in land-use patterns that may have developed in response to widespread population and resource imbalances.

On the Modoc Plateau, these changes were accompanied by major shifts in toolstone production. Whereas Middle Archaic populations may have been targeting a few key quarry zones for the purpose of biface production, by about cal A.D. 1000 this form of production had ceased, giving way to a more disparate pattern of toolstone procurement by more locally based populations that perhaps featured increased reliance on exchange networks, as well as scavenging and reuse of older archaeological materials. Such a pattern seems to be reflected in a greater diversity of raw material sources at sites dated to this time (McGuire 2002; see also Chatters and Cleland 1995:27–26). Greater source diversity may have also been the result of increased use of obsidian pebble and cobble materials, often originating from disparate source locations, found in secondary alluvial contexts (see Young 2002).

Terminal Prehistoric

From an assemblage standpoint, the hallmarks for the Terminal Prehistoric period are Desert side-notched and cottonwood projectile points. Gunther series points continue from the previous period, although in smaller numbers and geographically confined to the northern and western portions of northeast California. Rose Spring and Desert side-notched points have been used throughout the Great Basin to distinguish the Late Archaic and Terminal Prehistoric Periods, respectively. However, numerous radiocarbon dates and obsidian hydration values from the Pit River uplands indicate that the use of Rose Spring points in some areas may have extended throughout the Terminal Prehistoric period—well past the cal A.D. 1400 cutoff normally defined for the type (Hildebrandt and King 2000:221–252).

Although there is no necessary correlation between language, lifeways, and material culture (see Hughes 1992a), throughout much of the central and eastern parts of northeast California, the Terminal Prehistoric period is marked by wholesale shifts in populations, centering on the arrival of desert-oriented Numic groups (Northern Paiute) from southeastern California (see Bettinger and Baumhoff 1982; Fowler 1972; Lamb 1958; Madsen and Rhode 1994; Sutton 1986). Numic groups perhaps made their appearance along the eastern Sierran front in the Reno area around 500 years ago, and the northern reaches of the study area near the Oregon border as late as 200 to 300 years ago.

In essence, large seasonal or semipermanent Late Archaic settlements were abandoned by this time and replaced by substantially smaller sites inhabited by one or a few independent households (Delacorte 1997c:154). Coinciding with the shift to smaller settlements was a significant reduction in the logistical procurement of resources, most of which were now exploited on a daily basis from residential encampments. Much the same pattern is reflected in a lack of specialized implements or functionally specific tool kits, with the artifact assemblages from one site to the next being extremely similar and comprised predominantly of expedient implements that required little effort to make and could easily be discarded.

At least in Great Basin contexts of northeast California, Numic settlements have almost a stand-alone domestic quality about them, as might be expected from a series of dispersed, short-term occupations by small family units. This may explain why several large, multicomponent village localities, such as those described for Surprise Valley (O'Connell 1975; O'Connell and Inoway 1994), the Humboldt lakebed (Livingston 1986), and Secret Valley (McGuire 1997a; Riddell 1960b), which contain a large numbers of house structures that appear to have been constructed at various intervals throughout the Late Holocene, abruptly show a sharply reduced presence of Terminal Prehistoric residential activity (McGuire 2002:29–39). The spatial requisites of work, domestic, and residential activities appear to be much less segregated during this time period, often contracted around a small apron surrounding a single house structure. This is not unlike the ethnographic descriptions of Numic family bands provided by Steward (1938) and others, and appears qualitatively different from the pattern that immediately preceded it.

This settlement dispersion is exemplified in Secret Valley (McGuire 1997a) and no doubt other desert areas to the east, where site components are much more ephemeral, usually represented by isolated ground stone/rock concentrations or hearths that are occasionally accompanied by limited debris scatters and/or small pockets of organically stained soil. Milling and processing activities therefore appear to be ubiquitous. Actual millingstones, however, tend to be large, usually unshaped blocks, and are thought to be stationary elements associated with more widely scattered field camps and stations, as opposed to an aspect of the recurrent residential behavior characterizing the earlier period.

The exception to the Numic settlement pattern described above occurs in northern and western portions of the study area. In these areas, the final phase of prehistoric occupation may have been accompanied by a stronger village pattern. In the Middle Pit River area, Cleland (1995:5–11) reports more intensified use of habitation sites centered on major river margins. This pattern appears to have continued up to about cal A.D. 1700–1750, when a series of European disease epidemics may have had profound effects on native populations (Chatters and Cleland 1995:27–15). Near Crooks Canyon, on the South Fork drainage of the Pit River and adjacent uplands, the settlement system also differed from the Numic lifeway. Here house structures and other residential features appear suddenly at about cal A.D. 1450. These are both single- and multi-family residential camps containing a variety of stone and bone tools, roasting features, hearths, work areas, and storage pits, reflecting a full range of residential activities, including plant and animal processing and tool maintenance and production (Delacorte 2002; Waechter 2002d).

While this village pattern may relate to the intensification of upland root crops that began during the Late Archaic period, an equally plausible explanation for the appearance of these remote upland villages is the threat of conflict and warfare (see LeBlanc 1999).

According to this thesis, a major settlement shift to a more remote location like the Pit River uplands may well reflect mounting intergroup hostilities perhaps related to the arrival of Numic-speaking populations. In essence, the rugged canyon and rimrock country of the Modoc and Pit River uplands may have served as a safe refuge during times of conflict, and this conflict may have been the driving force behind these Late Prehistoric settlement shifts. Interestingly, faunal remains from this period show a marked rebound in the use of large game animals, a phenomenon that seems to be associated with increased periods of conflict (Carpenter 2002).

Future Prospects

Northeast California is obsidian country; almost all flaked stone assemblages from all time periods are dominated by this volcanic glass. Providing a trace chemical fingerprint of origin, combined with a built-in chronometer in the form of the hydration process, obsidian expands the analytical arsenal for understanding the past. Indeed, the utility of obsidian in this regard has long been recognized in northeast California and is exemplified by the pioneering efforts of Richard Hughes (1982, 1985, 1986a; see also Chesterman 1955). All things being equal, then, archaeologists working in northeast California will always have the advantage of obtaining some level of temporal control over the materials they find in archaeological sites, as well as the ability to identify the geographic source of origin of many of these implements.

Finally, northeast California will remain a laboratory for understanding the nature of boundary lands, in this case the division between the California and Great Basin culture spheres. Whereas this boundary to the south is separated and perhaps buffered by the Sierran cordillera and sparsely populated desert areas, this interface in northeast California is much more intimate. Typically Californian prehistoric lifeways existed side by side with those more oriented to the Great Basin. Thus in the vast sagebrush tracts of the northwestern Great Basin represented in northeast California, we find well-developed middens, cemetery lots, hopper mortars, elaborate pit houses, and the occasional Gunther barbed projectile point—all suggestive of prehistoric lifeways usually associated with peoples to the west. And from the other direction, and throughout northeast California, the ubiquitous and late-dating Desert side-notched point is thought to have been introduced into the area by Great Basin Numic-speaking immigrants. The proximity of these ancient lifeways continues to be reflected in contemporary native society among the Maidu, Pit River, and Northern Paiute peoples of this region, all of whom consider large (and occasionally overlapping) tracts of northeast California to be their ancestral homeland.

NOTE

1. Portions of this presentation are based on previous syntheses produced by Far Western Anthropological Research Group. I acknowledge and thank the many colleagues who participated in these studies. The ethnographic discussion is adapted from a recent overview by Helen McCarthy and Heather Scotten (2004).

CHAPTER 12

The Sierra Nevada: Archaeology in the Range of Light

KATHLEEN L. HULL

LOOKING EAST ACROSS THE FLOWERED PLAIN OF California's Central Valley in the late 1800s, conservationist John Muir beheld the Sierra Nevada in the distance and later described the range as "miles in height . . . and so gloriously colored, and so luminous, it seems to be not clothed with light but wholly composed of it, like the wall of some celestial city" (Muir 1894:2). For Muir, this "range of light" was a place of beauty, contentment, and introspection, drawing him to contemplate nature and the place of humankind within it. The Sierra Nevada continues to fascinate archaeologists, in part because this was one of the last regions in the state to witness systematic archaeological research. Much remains to be learned about prehistoric use of the area, and the nature of the archaeological record poses many challenges to interpretation.

Our modern sensibilities may find this area less hospitable than the temperate coast and plains of California and therefore an unexpected place for native occupation. Despite the fact that the mountains encompass often rugged terrain between the rich wetlands of California's Central Valley and the high desert of the Great Basin, the archaeological record of the Sierra Nevada documents use for thousands of years and has connections to the cultural history of both the east and the west. After more than 50 years of archaeological investigation, however, many questions remain regarding basic research issues such as cultural chronology and the subsistence strategies of the native inhabitants. The past 25 years of research have also witnessed significant synthetic studies and the development of regional research designs that have provided focus for ongoing investigations. Such guidance, as well as the innovative thinking of researchers, has resulted in exemplary studies of technology, exchange, gender relations, and population movements, with the promise of future contributions to understanding the past in this region and the role of Sierra people in shaping California's cultural landscape.

THE ENVIRONMENT AND THE PEOPLE OF THE SIERRA NEVADA

The Sierra Nevada Range in eastern California is 640 kilometers (400 miles) long and approximately 80 kilometers (50 miles) wide. It abuts the southern end of the Cascade Range on the north and adjoins the central Transverse Ranges of southern California in the south. The crest of the Sierra attains a maximum of elevation of approximately 2,740 meters (9,000 feet) in the north, but gradually increases in elevation to the south. The highest peaks and passes rise to more than 3,960 meters (13,000 feet) in elevation and include Mount Whitney, the highest point in the contiguous 48 states at 4,418 meters (14,496 feet). The slope of the Sierra Nevada also varies from west to east, as the western slope rises gradually over the width of the range. In contrast, the eastern slope exhibits an often dramatic, relatively steep escarpment, particularly in the southern half of the range.

The topographic relief of the Sierra Nevada reflects its unique geologic history. The mountains are composed primarily of a large batholith of granitic rock that has been subject to uplift for millions of years and has undergone more recent glaciation. Uplift of the eastern side has been dominant, resulting in the westward tilt of the range and the steeper slopes characteristic of the eastern side. Likewise, uplift has been greater in the south than in the north. As a result, somewhat older prebatholithic metamorphic rocks occur as roof pendants on the highest peaks of the southern range, but are more abundant and continuous in lower elevations of the western front of the northern range. These older formations include metavolcanic rocks, as well as metasediments such as quartzite, marble, slate, and schist. Younger volcanic rocks including basalt are also found in the Sierra north of Lake Tahoe, evidently related to volcanism of the adjoining Cascade Range (Schoenherr 1992). For the native people of the Sierra Nevada, the distribution of these various rock types had direct bearing on stone procurement and production technology, while the presence of gold-bearing deposits in the foothills of the northern and central Sierra also had a significant impact on native people and culture after 1849 as a result of the Gold Rush.

Several major river watersheds—from the Feather River in the north to the Kern River in the south—

occur along the western slope of the Sierra Nevada (Figure 12.1). These rivers originate as streams in the snowmelt and proglacial lake basins of the Sierra crest, and drain into the Central Valley. Conversely, the Truckee River originates at Lake Tahoe in the northern Sierra and flows east into the Great Basin. Multiple tributaries of the Carson and Walker Rivers also originate on the east slope south of Lake Tahoe and flow into the Great Basin. Smaller streams that drain the remainder of the steep east slope primarily contribute to the Owens River watershed. As discussed below, the watersheds of the west slope in particular served to define traditional territories of native people in the area, and the often deep and rugged canyons formed by the rivers hampered north-south travel by native occupants of the region, with the intervening ridges instead facilitating travel east and west.

The snowpack of the high Sierra that feeds this hydrological system is due to the prevailing west to east movement of storms from the Pacific Ocean, which contributes substantial precipitation in the form of rain and snow during the winter months, as moisture is lost as the storms rise over the mountains. The amount of rain and snow varies with elevation, and the snowline also varies from year to year between 900 and 1,500 meters (3,000 and 5,000 feet) in elevation. There is an approximate 0.55°C (1°F) decrease in temperature for each 90-meter (300-foot) increase in elevation (Schoenherr 1992:71; Storer et al. 2004:12), with a concomitant increase in annual precipitation of 5 to 10 centimeters (2 to 4 inches) for this same interval. Snowfall accounts for more than 85 percent of the total precipitation in the higher elevations of the Sierra (Storer et al. 2004:15) and would have made much of the high Sierra inhospitable for winter use in the past.

Since precipitation and growing season vary with elevation, these factors, as well as slope and latitude, result in diverse biotic communities in the mountains. Schoenherr (1992; see also Munz and Keck 1959:14–18) identifies six major vegetation communities along the western slope of the Sierra Nevada today (although numerous vegetation series and diverse habitats occur within these broad communities) (Sawyer and Keeler-Wolf 1995), which include, from lowest to highest, chaparral, foothill woodland, yellow pine forest, lodgepole–red fir forest, subalpine forest, and the alpine zone. The latter four communities also occur on the east slope, although in generally higher and narrower elevation zones. The east side also supports pinyon-juniper woodland in the mid elevations, while small, relict groves of Big Trees *(Sequoia gigantea)* are also present midslope on the western side as far north as the Stanislaus River. These groves are most abundant, however, in the Kings and Kaweah River watersheds of the southern Sierra.

As temperatures rise and snow melts during the spring and summer, different vegetal resources become available to people and other animals within each biotic community, prompting upslope movement in the spring and return to lower elevation zones in the late fall in most areas of the range. The current structure of modern vegetation communities, however, is due at least in part to fire suppression activities, historic mining, logging, and cattle grazing, as well as global warming that began sometime between A.D. 1850 and 1900 (Sierra Nevada Ecosystem Project 1996). Human action also shaped past vegetation communities in many areas of the Sierra Nevada, with cultural modification of the landscape by native inhabitants through use of fire and other means (Anderson 2005; Anderson and Carpenter 1991; Anderson and Moratto 1996; Reynolds 1959).

In addition to the elevation-related biotic variation apparent today, significant climatic shifts and concomitant vegetation change occurred in the Sierra Nevada during the Holocene (Spaulding 1999; Woolfenden 1996). Pollen stratigraphic records indicate that the current pattern of climate and the primary constituents of vegetation communities were apparently in place by the Middle Holocene (ca. 1000 cal B.C.). Plant species frequency within various biotic communities and habitats, however, has continued to change since that time on scales of decades or centuries. Other paleoenvironmental data also suggest that severe droughts affected the Sierra Nevada at ca. A.D. 892 to 1112 and A.D. 1210 to 1350 (Lindström 1990; Stine 1994), while earlier periods of drought or drier conditions are also evident in the northern Sierra (Lindström 2000). Reflecting persistent low precipitation during these periods, evidence for these droughts comes in the form of tree stumps currently submerged in high-country lakes and rivers of the eastern Sierra, including Lake Tahoe, Fallen Leaf Lake, Donner Lake, Independence Lake, the Walker River, Mono Lake, and Tenaya Lake. Radiocarbon dates on the outer growth ring of these stumps document commencement of vegetation growth in former lake and stream beds following dramatic decreases in water levels during these arid periods.

Given the geographic position of the Sierra Nevada within California, the culture and history of the native people of the region are connected to that of both California and the Great Basin. Ethnographic data indicate that these people were traditionally organized in

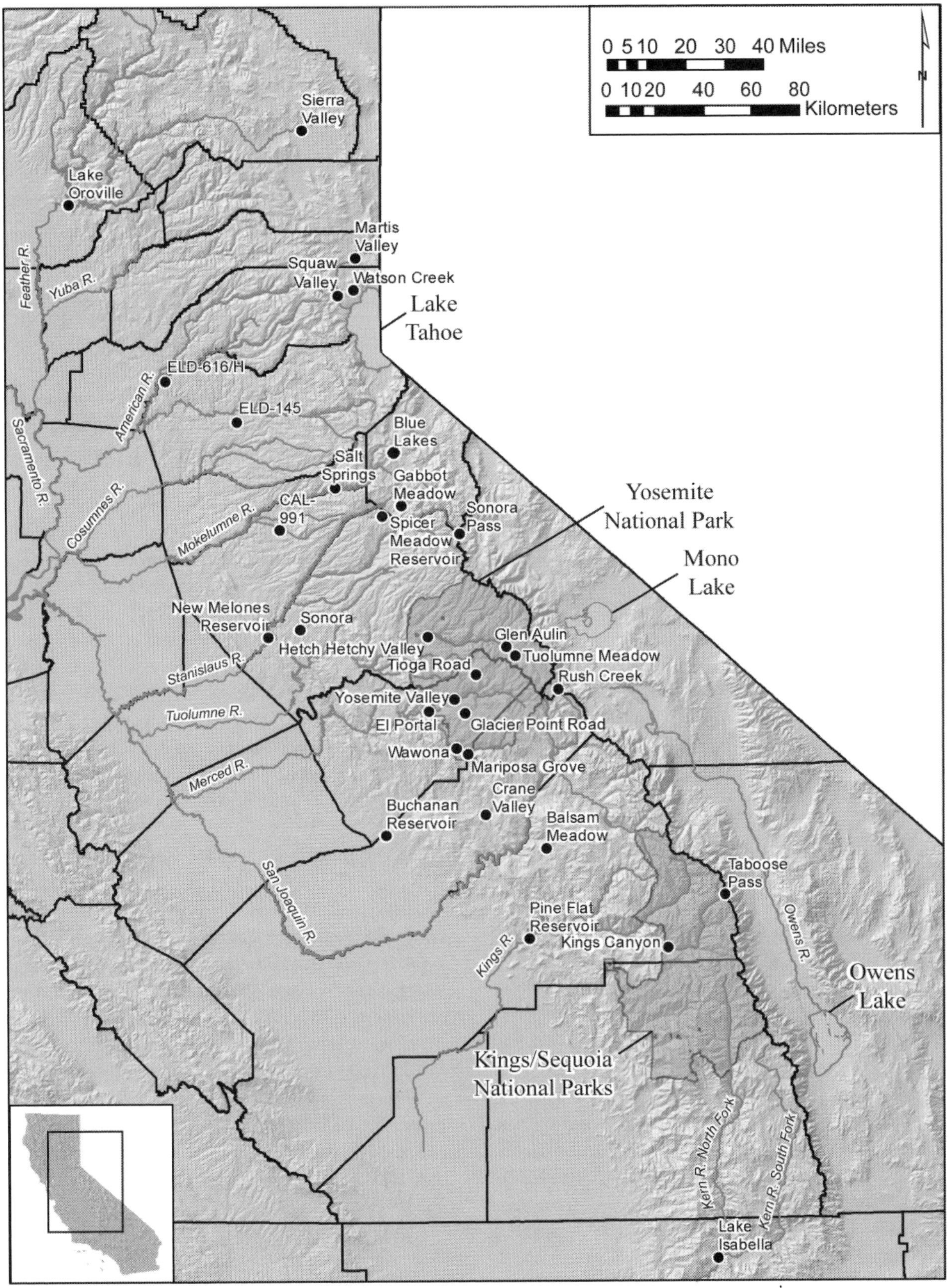

Figure 12.1. Archaeological sites and locations of the Sierra Nevada.

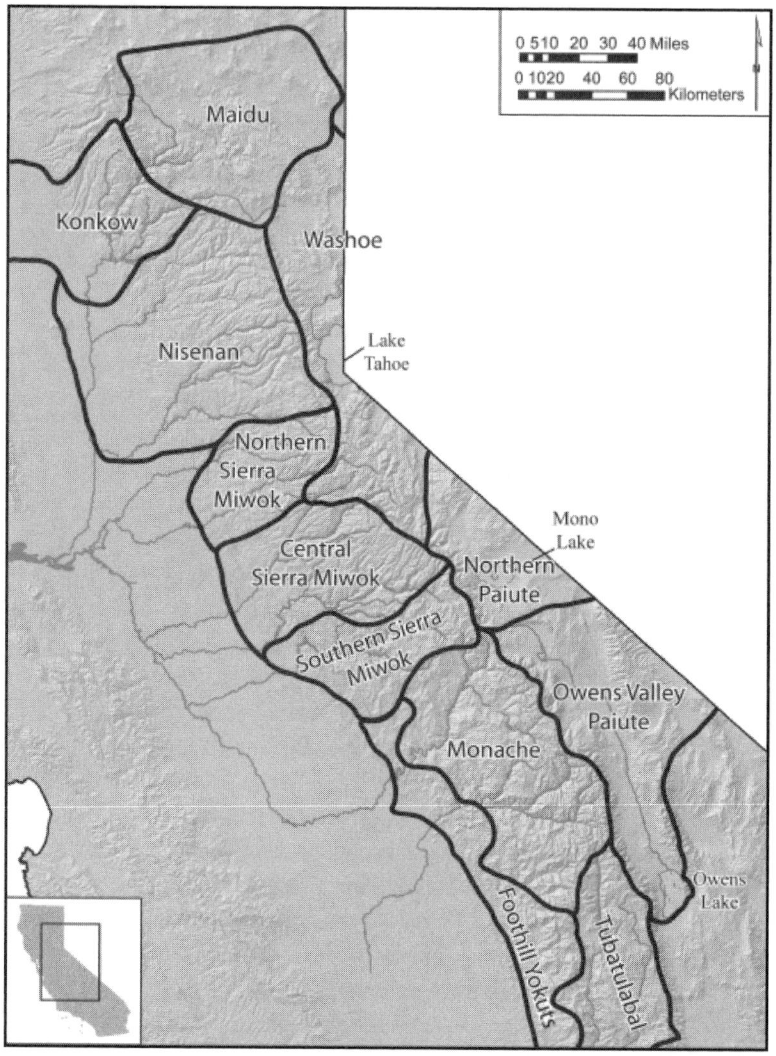

Figure 12.2. Approximate location of tribal groups, Sierra Nevada.

small village tribelets rather than the large, politically unified tribes common in many other areas of North America. Therefore, consideration of native cultural groups within the Sierra, as elsewhere in California, is facilitated by considering ethnolinguistic affiliation (Figure 12.2). At historic contact, the native people of the northern Sierra included the Maidu and Konkow of the Feather River drainage (Riddell 1978), the Nisenan of the Yuba and American River watersheds (Wilson and Towne 1978), and the Washoe of the Lake Tahoe region (d'Azevedo 1986). The Washoe territory was permeable, however, as d'Azevedo (1986:467) notes, allowing negotiated joint use of much of this area by neighboring peoples. The Washoe speak a language in the Hokan stock (Jacobsen 1986), and the other three groups speak Maidu dialects of the Penutian family.

The northern, central, and southern Miwok (or Me'wuk) inhabited the west slope of central Sierra Nevada, including the Cosumnes, Mokelumne, Stanislaus, Tuolumne, and Merced River drainages (Levy 1978b). The languages of these three groups also belong to the Penutian family. East of the crest in the central Sierra was the territory of the Northern Paiute (Fowler and Liljeblad 1986), a Numic-speaking people in the Uto-Aztecan language family. While maps of ethnolinguistic "territories" (Kroeber 1925) tend to depict the Sierra crest as a boundary between the Paiute and their western neighbors, people who wintered in lower elevations of either the eastern or western slopes both likely used the high country within and south of Washoe territory on a seasonal basis (Steward 1933:325, 329). There was no "boundary" in any fixed sense.

Finally, in the southern Sierra, the Monache (Western Mono) occupied the midslope of the San Joaquin, Kings, and Kaweah Rivers (Spier 1978b). Foothill Yokuts lived on the lower slopes of these same drainages (Spier 1978a), and the Tubatulabal inhabited the watershed of the Kern River (C. R. Smith 1978). The Owens Valley Paiute and Western Shoshone were located on the east side of the southern Sierra (Liljeblad and Fowler 1986; Thomas et al. 1986). Linguistic data suggest that the Monache, speakers of a Numic language of the Uto-Aztecan linguistic family like their Paiute and Shoshone neighbors, are a relatively recent arrival to the west slope from the east ca. 500 years ago (Theodoratus Cultural Research and Archaeological Consulting and Research Services 1984:135). Their seasonal use of the area, however, may have had much deeper roots. Tubatulabal is also a Uto-Aztecan language, but Yokuts languages are within the Penutian linguistic family. Once again, the high Sierra was likely an area of joint use by western and eastern peoples; for example, the Paiute and other occupants east of the mountains used areas west of the Sierra crest, including the Kern Plateau.

Despite this linguistic diversity, some general similarities in material culture and cultural practices of these Sierra people can be drawn from ethnography. Such similarities largely reflect adaptation to the mountainous environment and its biotic zonation. For example, all western slope groups spent the winter in larger villages at lower elevations at or below the snowline. During the summer and fall families dispersed to higher elevation zones, following the seasonal migration of game and the appearance of greens, bulbs, fruits, and nuts. With the exception of the Washoe, people of the eastern slope also used the area only on a seasonal basis, although the steeper slope of the eastern Sierra provided access to diverse biotic zones without requiring relocation of residential sites for extended periods. High Sierra environments and resources such as pinyon nuts were within a day's walk of the base of the mountains. Dwellings at seasonal camps in the high country were likely ephemeral brush shelters, while more substantial structures of bark slabs were constructed for use in the fall and winter.

Deer and acorns were particularly important subsistence resources to the people of the Sierra Nevada, although the mountains would have afforded a great diversity of game and plant foods given the multiple biotic zones. Processing of vegetal resources such as acorns was facilitated by the large granite or basalt outcrops present. Mortars were created in these outcrops for pounding foodstuffs such as acorns, manzanita berries, and small game; abundant water-worn cobbles served as expedient pestles. Sierra people traded with neighboring groups to the east and west for resources not locally available, including foodstuffs and stone for the manufacture of tools. Arguably one of the most important items acquired through trade in the central and southern Sierra was obsidian, since local granite is unsuitable for flaked stone tool manufacture. Baskets served for cooking and storage (Figure 12.3), and granaries were often built to store acorns over winter. The construction of such granaries, however, varied among the different ethnolinguistic groups.

Figure 12.3. Yosemite Indians, Yosemite Valley, ca. 1865. (Courtesy of the J. Paul Getty Museum, Los Angeles; John P. Soule [photographer] about 1865, albumen silver.)

ARCHAEOLOGICAL STUDY PRIOR TO 1980

Excellent summaries of archaeological investigations in the Sierra Nevada prior to 1980 are provided by Chartkoff and Chartkoff (1984) and Moratto (1984). Therefore, only a brief review will be provided here, and the reader is directed to the bibliography of the latter book for citations for the investigations discussed. Systematic archaeological survey and excavation in the Sierra Nevada was initiated by University of California–Berkeley, faculty and students in late 1940s and early 1950s. These investigations included work in the Lake Tahoe basin, Yosemite National Park, Kings Canyon, and various reservoirs in the southern Sierra Nevada (see Figure 12.1). Investigations primarily by those affiliated with or trained at the University of California continued during the early 1960s, but there was a substantial increase (and perhaps equally important, sustained work by a diverse cadre of researchers) with the rise of cultural resource management projects beginning in the early 1970s. Notable among these projects were archaeological investigations for reservoir developments in the lower foothills at Lake Oroville on the Feather River, New Melones reservoir on the Stanislaus River, Buchanan reservoir on the Chowchilla River, and Lake Isabella on the Kern River. In addition, work continued in the Lake Tahoe region, and investigations for hydroelectric projects in the middle San Joaquin drainage and portions of the Pacific Crest Trail in the southern Sierra were undertaken at this time.

Most studies during the first two decades of work focused on sites and areas along major rivers, often in low- to middle-elevation settings. Work at Lake Tahoe was a notable exception, as it provided data for a higher-elevation zone. In addition, as was common for archaeological research of this era (particularly in an area subject to relatively little investigation), these efforts focused on providing a general picture of changes in material culture through time. Numerous local chronological sequences based primarily on projectile points, milling tools, ground stone ornaments, and the use of specific lithic materials were proposed. Absolute dating of suggested temporal complexes or phases was problematic, however, given the poor preservation of radiocarbon-datable features. Many of these sequences relied instead on temporal information from the Central Valley or western Great Basin to infer the time of phase transitions, and the initial time of occupation remained largely undetermined.

In general, these sequences documented initial use of large stemmed or corner-notched dart points and portable millingstones prior to about cal A.D. 500. Basalt served as the dominant lithic material in the northern Sierra, where such stone was locally available. Use of obsidian imported from east of the Sierra was prevalent in most other areas except in the low elevation zones of the west, where use of chert was common. Dart technology gave way to the bow and arrow after about cal A.D. 500, as indicated by use of smaller corner-notched points. Introduction of bedrock mortars also occurred sometime between cal A.D. 500 and 1250, with this technology taking advantage of the large rock outcrops common in the mountains. Occupants of the northern Sierra discontinued their reliance on basalt, but both chert and (to a lesser extent) obsidian found favor in this area after ca. A.D. 500. In the central and southern Sierra, use of obsidian continued, and geochemical studies by Jackson (1974) documented a geographic pattern of reliance on the nearest high-quality material. Bodie Hills obsidian was commonly used in the north-central Sierra, Casa Diablo obsidian was prevalent in the central and south-central Sierra, and glass from the Coso volcanic field was common in the southernmost areas (see Chapter 17). After ca. cal A.D. 1250, use of small side-notched or (in the northern Sierra) contracting stem arrow points, ground stone ornaments, and bedrock mortar technology was dominant.

As of 1980, then, a general outline of the culture history of the Sierra Nevada had emerged and the primary constituents of the archaeological record had been recognized. Assemblages were dominated by flaked and, to a lesser extent, ground stone artifacts. The former included projectile points, other bifacial tools such as drills, expedient flake scrapers, and debitage, while the latter included both portable and stationary milling implements. Stationary milling features with mortars were common throughout the range, but other features such as house floors and hearths were relatively rare due to bioturbation of deposits or ephemeral use in upper elevation zones, or both. Organic materials including faunal bone, botanical remains, and shell beads were also infrequent, likely due to the coarse, acidic soils typical of the region. Preservation of such remains was enhanced, however, if deposits were in rock shelters, which were rare but present in various areas of the Sierra.

A BRIEF HISTORY AND MAJOR PROJECTS SINCE 1980

Since 1980, cultural resource management investigations have contributed significantly to our knowledge of Sierra Nevada archaeology. These efforts include the completed reports for the New Melones project (Moratto et al. 1988), excavation at Early Holocene sites in the central Sierra foothills and northern uplands, and increased work in mid- to upper-elevation areas. For example, important studies for cultural resource compliance have been undertaken in the northeastern area at Sierra Valley (Waechter and Andolina 2005), the Tahoe-Truckee region (Ataman et al. 1999; Bloomer et al. 1997; Elston et al. 1994; Lindström 1982), the American River watershed (Jackson and Ballard 1999; Rosenthal and Waechter 2002), the Mokelumne River drainage (Wirth Environmental Services 1985), the headwaters of the Stanislaus River (Peak and Neuenschwander 1991), Yosemite National Park (Hull and Moratto 1999), the Rush Creek watershed of the east-central Sierra (Jackson and Morgan 1999), and Crane Valley (Goldberg and Skinner 1990; Goldberg et al. 1986) and Balsam Meadow (Jackson and Dietz 1984; Goldberg and Moratto 1984) of the San Joaquin River watershed. In addition, some graduate student research projects have been undertaken in various areas, including studies of fishing in the Truckee River region (Lindström 1992), Early Holocene occupation at Lake Tahoe (Martin 1998), contact-era culture change in the central Sierra (Hull 2002; Van Bueren 1983), and alpine land use in the southern Sierra (Roper-Wickstrom 1992; Stevens 2005).

Examination of archaeological contributions since 1980 benefits from several important synthetic studies of Sierra Nevada archaeology completed in the past two decades. The *Cultural Resources Overview of the Southern Sierra Nevada* (Theodoratus Cultural Research and Archaeological Consulting and Research Services 1984) considered the archaeology of portions of the San Joaquin, Kings, Kaweah, and Kern River watersheds, and Kowta's (1988) model of native land use in the Feather River area provided an overview for the northernmost area of the Sierra Nevada. The *Framework for Archaeological Research and Management for North-central Sierra Nevada* (Jackson et al. 1994), also known as FARM, encompassed the area from the American to the Tuolumne River on the west slope, well as the Lake Tahoe basin. Finally, the *Archaeological Synthesis and Research Design, Yosemite National Park, California* (Hull and Moratto 1999) summarized data for the central Sierra and updated the previous research design for this region (Moratto 1981). This volume fit the Merced and upper Tuolumne River watersheds into the chain of synthetic work for the Sierra Nevada, effectively completing coverage of the entire range.

As these documents indicate, issues of chronology have continued to occupy an important place in Sierra Nevada archaeology. New sequences have been proposed for previously unstudied areas such as the Mokelumne River drainage (Cleland 1988), and researchers have continued to refine existing temporal sequences (Figure 12.4). In particular, this latter work has witnessed the incorporation of subsistence-settlement adaptive strategies into temporal schemes for the Tahoe-Truckee area (Elston et al. 1994) and lower Stanislaus River (Moratto et al. 1988). Such interpretations often rely on ethnographic data and postulated population movements based on linguistic data, however, rather than unequivocal archaeological evidence, casting some doubt on their applicability to more ancient time periods. Conversely, the routine use of obsidian hydration dating has significantly improved the prospects for independent dating of assemblages, decreasing the reliance on temporal data from the east or west. Obsidian hydration studies have not necessarily realized this full potential, however, as data have often been tied to projectile point sequences of the Great Basin, in particular, rather than radiocarbon dates specific to Sierra archaeological sites (see Rosenthal 2002; Theodoratus Cultural Research and Archaeological Consulting and Research Services 1984). Likewise, many radiocarbon dates derive from nonfeature contexts, undermining confidence in the finer details of nearly all existing chronological sequences. As noted in recent syntheses (Jackson et al. 1994; Moratto 1999), this methodological issue is crucial in light of ongoing attempts to understand adaptive shifts and the proximate cause(s) of apparent culture change.

While generally affirming earlier observations, studies since 1980 have incrementally advanced our understanding of changes in material culture through time, particularly with respect to lithic procurement and technology. Poor preservation of organic materials in mid- to high-elevation zones remains a significant problem, however, and hampers full understanding of subsistence and related settlement shifts. Likewise, the evident reoccupation of sites over hundreds or thousands of years has been amply demonstrated by obsidian hydration studies and, coupled with factors undermining depositional integrity, continues to challenge archaeologists working in this region. Dwelling, storage, and processing features other than the ubiquitous bedrock mortar continue to be rare, especially in mid-elevation zones. New types of features have been recognized, however, including stone granary bases in the low-elevation areas of the southern Sierra, rock ring dwellings and possible stone game drive features in the alpine zone of the central and southern Sierra Nevada (Roper-Wickstrom 1992; Stevens 2005), and stone-lined vegetable processing features in the northern Sierra (Bloomer et al. 2002; Waechter and Andolina 2005).

SIGNIFICANT DEVELOPMENTS SINCE 1980

Both the FARM and the *Yosemite Synthesis* identify broad research themes that structure the discussion of significant archaeological interpretations since 1980. These documents also note the contribution of Sierra studies to paleoenvironmental research over the past two decades, particularly with respect to documenting prolonged droughts (Lindström 1990, 2000; Stine 1994), considering the potential effect of Inyo-Mono volcanic activity on the occupants of the west slope (Jackson and Morgan 1999; Spaulding 1999), and the use of fire as a vegetation management tool (Anderson and Moratto 1996). Since Woolfenden (1996; Spaulding 1999) provides a detailed review of such research, the current summary will focus on the remaining research domains of chronology, economy, settlement, social organization, and demography. Only a few issues and case studies in each of these domains can be considered in the limited space here.

Chronology

Two important contributions have been made within the realm of chronology in the Sierra Nevada—one related to knowledge of past peoples and land use, and the other methodological. In the first case, archaeological investigations since 1980 have added significantly to our appreciation for Early Holocene use in the Sierra Nevada and California more generally. Although still largely confined to isolated projectile points or modest assemblages in the higher elevation zones, work in the Stanislaus River watershed and elsewhere in the northeastern Sierra has documented earlier initial use of both lower and upper elevation settings than previously known (Martin 1998; Peak and Neuenschwander 1991). Extending the record of human use into the more distant past (ca. 8000 cal B.C.), these finds often reveal the use of large stemmed points similar to those associated with this time period in the Great Basin or, less frequently, possible fluted

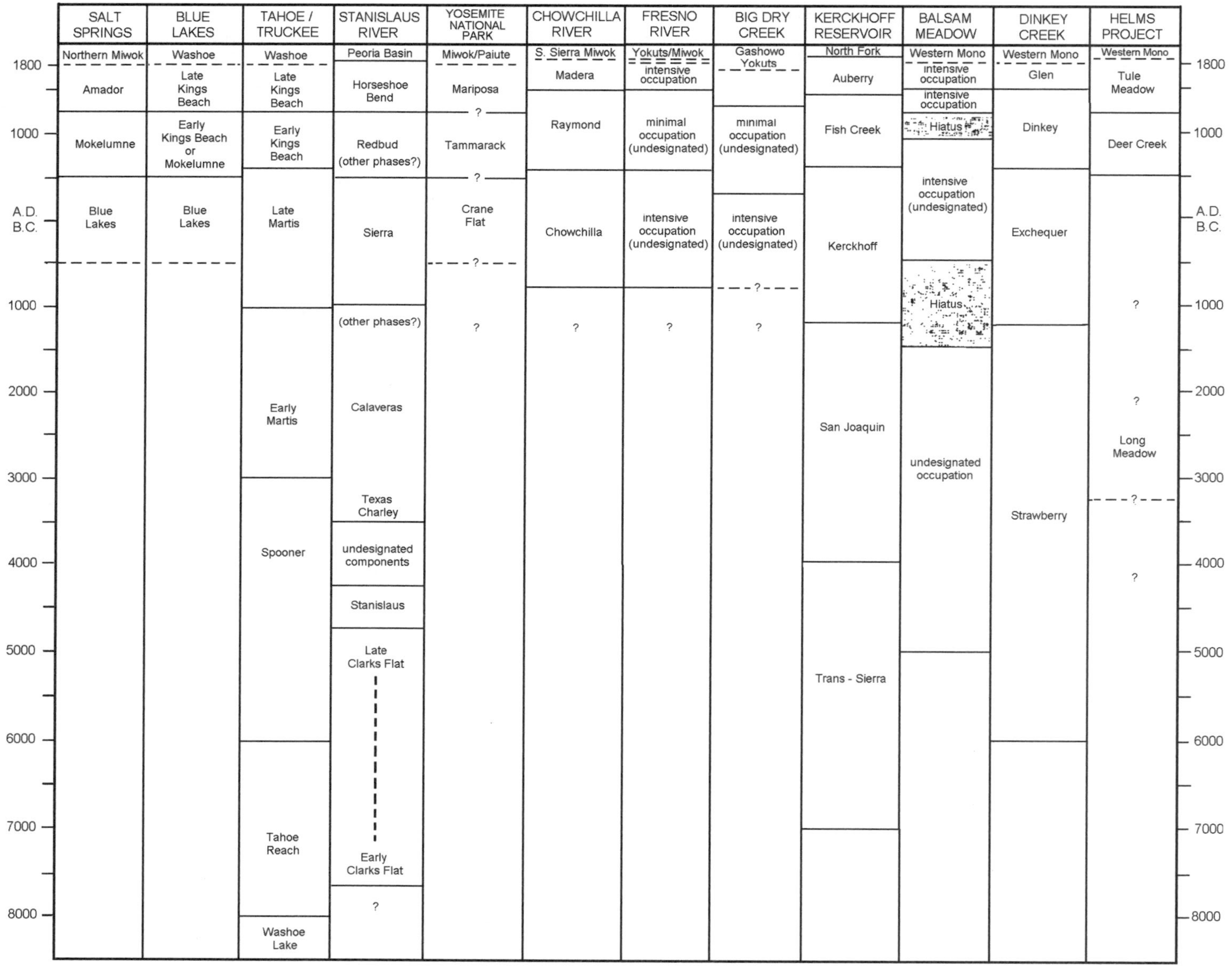

Figure 12.4. Chronological sequences of the Sierra Nevada (after Moratto 1999).

points like those in related Late Pleistocene and Early Holocene occupation in areas to the east and west. Reviewing the evidence amassed thus far, Moratto (1999) suggests that such early use may be recognized elsewhere in the Sierra as well, and he stresses that future studies must consider geomorphic context to ensure that such early use is not overlooked.

With respect to methods, the routine use of obsidian hydration analysis since the mid-1980s has provided for both relative dating of deposits and studies of site formation, as well as new approaches to absolute dating with hydration results. Recent research has sought to establish temperature-dependent obsidian hydration rates for major obsidian sources used by Sierra peoples through the application of mathematical models of the hydration process (Hull 2001, 2002; Stevens 2002, 2005). While such models continue to be refined in laboratory research of obsidian from elsewhere in the world (Anovitz et al. 1999, 2004) and these studies may necessitate further refinement of hydration applications in the Sierra, such absolute dating methods may ultimately provide for assessment of culture change disentangled from the "total packages" of phase constructs common to more traditional cultural chronology in the Sierra and elsewhere in California. Instead, individual traits can be examined independently, as is necessary for analyses seeking cause and effect. Recognizing the potential of this approach may require a reevaluation of obsidian hydration sampling methods, however, including a move away from the common practice of simple column sampling based on an arbitrary number of flakes from every or alternate 10 centimeter excavation levels. Such a strategy may tell us more about rates of sediment deposition or geomorphic processes than intensity of cultural activity, contrary to the assumptions that often underlie such sampling.

Economy

FLAKED STONE TECHNOLOGY As highlighted above, the northern Sierra and lower western flank differ from the remainder of the Sierra in the local availability of toolstone, which may contribute to differences in lithic technology between these areas. In regions of both local and distant material acquisition, however, Sierra archaeologists have traditionally focused on bifacial reduction. This perspective was fostered in part by the predominant mode of production at major obsidian quarries of eastern California investigated by Ericson (1981, 1982) and others (Jackson 1984) in the late 1970s and early 1980s. Ongoing archaeological research on the western slope since the mid-1980s, however, has shifted the focus of reduction technology studies to direct assessment of west slope lithic assemblages rather than consideration of only quarry production. Although evidence of biface production and even biface caches in the northern portion of Yosemite National Park (Humphreys 1994) consistent with the traditional model of lithic material acquisition is common in the Sierra, a more diverse picture of obsidian acquisition has begun to emerge.

For example, Jackson's (1988) report of a large core on the western slope in the San Joaquin River drainage suggests transport of some material in relatively unworked form. West slope technological analysis in recent years highlights evidence of scavenging as a means of material acquisition. Rather than acquisition of obsidian via trans-Sierra travel or trade, Goldberg and Skinner (1990) documented bipolar reduction of scavenged Sierra concave base projectile points late in time to produce flakes of sufficient size for production of arrow points at Crane Valley. This production strategy was confirmed here and in subsequent studies elsewhere through the use of multiple obsidian hydration samples from a single artifact. As both the bipolar fracture and the original worked surface were sampled, hydration data indicated that bipolar reduction occurred significantly later than original manufacture of the large concave base point.

Such rethinking of obsidian procurement and use in the western Sierra has led to even greater focus on technology, highlighting a research area in which Sierra archaeology has played a particularly significant role in California archaeology rather than representing an inordinate fixation on technology for its own sake. Lithic tools and debris are the one constant (and common) element of the archaeological record of this region, while the prevalence of obsidian in central and southern Sierra assemblages provides for obsidian hydration dating that can identify temporal trends. Investigation of bipolar reduction, final projectile point manufacture in the form of notching, regularized biface production indicated by transverse parallel pressure flakes, and examination of scavenging through hydration sampling of bulb removal flakes, among other technological traits, all promise to provide a fuller understanding of resource acquisition through time in light of factors such as territoriality or seasonally restricted access. The results of these analyses may ultimately enhance interpretation elsewhere in California where direct temporal data are lacking but similar technological trends have been observed.

GROUND STONE TECHNOLOGY Understanding of ground stone technology in the Sierra has also witnessed significant change in the past 20 years, due to an influential functional study of bedrock mortars (McCarthy, Blount, and Hicks 1985). Working from information provided by native consultants and existing ethnography, this research suggested that the depth of mortars was related to function rather than duration of use, as previously supposed. That is, mortars were actually carved, pecked, and shaped to specific depths for particular purposes. Based on ethnographic research among the Monache, who focused on the processing of black oak acorns, three functional types were identified. Shallow starter mortars were used for initial acorn processing, somewhat deeper finishing mortars were used for final acorn processing, and deep seed mortars were used to process seeds.

This model was subsequently applied to archaeological data from various areas in the central and southern Sierra, including Crane Valley (McCarthy, Blount, and Hicks 1985) and Yosemite National Park (Hull et al. 1999). In Crane Valley, the archaeological data indicated that these functional types were recognized in prehistory as well, since the relative representation of mortars within the three classes was consistent with that identified in the ethnographic sample. However, the researchers warned that the model might only apply to the Monache and the processing of black oak acorns.

In Yosemite, stationary milling feature data were considered in light of this model and another based on Miwok ethnography, with data in some areas very similar to those observed in Crane Valley. Comparison of milling technologies in mid-elevation valleys in the watersheds of the Tuolumne and main Merced Rivers (e.g., El Portal, Glacier Point Road, Tioga Road, Yosemite Valley) with those at sites in drainage of the south fork of the Merced River (e.g., Mariposa Grove, Wawona), however, seemed to demonstrate distinct geographic preferences in vegetal processing (Hull et al. 1999). Although starter and finishing mortar cups occur in roughly equal proportions in both areas (Table 12.1), deeper seed cups tend to be more common in the south than in the north. In the latter area, milling slicks are more common, suggesting two alternate means of processing smaller seeds in these two regions. Jackson et al. (1994) cautioned against ascribing ethnicity based on milling technologies, as factors such as local resource exploitation may affect processing decisions made by people in the past. The differences in stationary milling feature assemblages between the main and south forks of the Merced River, however, cannot be attributed to environmental characteristics. Therefore these data may suggest the potential to explore regional (if not ethnic) preferences in processing technologies.

One of the most difficult problems still facing Sierra Nevada archaeologists with respect to ground stone tools is determining when the shift from millingstones to mortars occurred in this region. Here, as elsewhere in California, such a shift has generally been taken to represent an increasing emphasis on acorns in the diet, although ethnographic data from throughout California document the use of mortars to process a variety of vegetal and animal products, as well as minerals (Rucks 1995; Schroth 1996). If mortars were primarily used to process acorns, however, the shift from millingstones (i.e., small seed processing) to mortars would represent a significant subsistence shift. Viewed within optimal foraging models, acorn processing requires a substantial time investment. This subsistence intensification would not occur unless necessitated by an imbalance between subsistence resources and population. As discussed by Basgall (1987), such an imbalance could have occurred due to increasing population size and

Table 12.1. Relative Representation of Mortars and Milling Slicks in Various Areas of the Central Sierra Nevada

Region	*Starter Mortars (%)*	*Finishing Mortars (%)*	*Seed Mortars (%)*	*Milling Slicks (%)*
Crane Valley	52.3	18.9	28.9	
Mariposa Grove	59	13	28	
Wawona	37	15	44	
El Portal	50	15	26	10
Glacier Point Road	57	13	22	8
Yosemite Valley	75	10	8	7
Hetch Hetchy Reservoir	86	7	6	1
Lower Tioga Road	69	17	13	1
Upper Tioga Road	83	7	3	7

Source: After Hull et al. 1999.

concomitant territorial circumscription preventing expansion into other areas. Thus, determining when this technology was adopted in the Sierra is crucial to inferring subsistence intensification, particularly since other sources of data on these issues are unlikely to be developed given poor preservation of organic materials. In addition, the shift to bedrock mortars could have further implications with respect to the role of women's work, gender relations, concepts of ownership, and attachment to place (see below).

Timing of the introduction of bedrock mortars has been difficult to establish because these features cannot be directly dated. Rather, dates must derive from associated cultural deposits, and obsidian hydration dating of artifacts from such sites often reveals multiple components spanning hundreds or thousands of years. Stevens (2002) made an initial attempt to address this issue through an innovative study that brought together data from a large area of the southern Sierra Nevada. He argued that a regional approach can overcome potential idiosyncrasies of individual site dates and provide the broad picture of mortar use through time. Relying on temperature-corrected obsidian hydration dates from associated deposits, this study suggests that mortars may have been introduced more than 2,500 years ago, with use peaking in low and mid-elevation zones after cal A.D. 500. In contrast, use of mortars in higher elevation zones did not become prevalent until after cal A.D. 1000 and is especially indicated in the past 500 years. These results suggest possible increased use of more marginal high Sierra locales late in time, perhaps related to population growth, the migration of Monache to the west slope of the Sierra, or both.

EXCHANGE As noted previously, the general geographic distributions of obsidian quarry source materials in western Sierra archaeological sites were established in the 1970s. Continuing work provides more detail, however, particularly with respect to recognizing intrasource patterns and use of lesser quarry sources such as Fish Springs and Mono Craters by Sierra people. In addition, as noted previously, technological studies have significantly altered our view of how lithic material was acquired, with potential implications for how archaeological sites should be sampled to recognize possible source-specific patterns of material use.

Identification of intersource geochemical variability at Casa Diablo and the Coso volcanic field by Hughes (1989, 1994b) has provided for finer distinctions in defining regional obsidian use, with initial results from Sierra archaeological studies suggesting acquisition of material from the nearest available flow. With respect to lesser quarry sources, ongoing research suggests that use of Mono Craters obsidian became more common after the formation of Panum Dome ca. cal A.D. 1350, and this material may have supplanted Casa Diablo obsidian as the predominant material in the areas closest to this new source (see Hull 2002). Likewise, work in Sequoia National Park indicates likely direct acquisition of Fish Springs glass and the significance of this material in proximate areas of the high Sierra such as Taboose Pass (Roper-Wickstrom 1992; Stevens 2005). Farther north, work in the Feather, American, and Yuba River watersheds has documented use of northern rather than eastern California obsidian source materials, including Tuscan, Kelly Mountain, East Medicine Lake, and South Warners.

Understanding the source of basaltic materials for tools in the northern Sierra and potential geographic patterns of use has been a more difficult problem until recently. Particularly significant advances have been made in the past 15 years, with the initiation of basalt and vitric tuff geochemical source studies (Bloomer et al. 1997; Jackson et al. 1994; Lindström and Bloomer 1994; Northrup et al. 1999). Such studies distinguish more than a dozen quarry source materials, including major sources at Alder Hill and Watson Creek in the Tahoe-Truckee region and the Gold Lake group to the northwest in Sierra County. McGuire and Bloomer (1997; see also Northrup et al. 1999) document both local use and east-to-west transport of Sierra basalt in the Yuba and American River watersheds. These patterns mirror east-west transport or exchange of obsidian observed in the central and southern Sierra, and underscore the dearth of north-south exchange or transport in this rugged terrain.

Settlement

As elsewhere in California, Binford's (1980) model of forager and collector subsistence-settlement strategies has become the dominant means by which regional researchers consider settlement in the Sierra Nevada. Again, making broad characterizations for the Sierra as a whole, it appears that initial sustained occupation of the Sierra after ca. 3000 cal B.C. represents relatively large residential sites occupied (or reoccupied) for substantial periods of time. Such a pattern is consistent with the collector mode of organization, and some researchers suggest that this use represents a primary hunting focus in many mid- to high-elevation areas. This conclusion is based primarily on artifact assemblages, however, rather than faunal or floral remains. After ca. cal A.D. 500, the settlement pattern clearly shifts, with residential sites both smaller in size and more ephemeral in terms of quantity of cultural debris. Rather than sustained occupation, this use seems more consistent with short-term residential bases and possible limited subsistence resource acquisition of foragers rather than collectors. In the northeastern Sierra, Elston and his colleagues (Intermountain Research 1995:17) suggested that this may reflect an accommodation to the arrival of pinyon to the area, while on the west slope there is some speculation that this change may be related to the incorporation of acorn into the diet. After ca. cal A.D. 1250, there is a return to large, substantial residential sites and concomitant subsistence resource diversification. In the alpine areas of the southern Sierra (Stevens 2005), such use is even represented by sites with rock-based dwellings, evidently reflecting occupation by people spending winter months on the eastern rather than western slope of the Sierra. This late use represents a return to a collector strategy.

Social Organization

Social organization remains a relatively enigmatic archaeological research domain in the Sierra because the types of data often considered in such studies—including burials and ornamental objects—are rare in all but the lowest elevation zones. One exception is Jackson's (1991) study of bedrock mortars in the southern Sierra, in which he argued for the importance of female activities in dictating habitation location. Prior to the introduction of bedrock mortar technology to the Sierra, all technology associated with hunting and gathering was portable. Jackson therefore concluded that decisions about where to establish camps or villages were based on factors such as availability of and access to subsistence resources, particularly game. With the increasing importance of acorn and the stationary milling technology associated with it, however, the location of camps and villages became dictated in part by the availability of suitable rock outcrops, as well as oaks. Jackson suggested that this shift—presumably associated with women's work—meant that the influence of women in residential location decisions may have increased, representing a potential shift in power and gender relations within households or groups.

Although several assumptions regarding decision making and subsistence resource distributions necessarily underlie this argument, this research challenges Sierra archaeologists—and California archaeologists in general—to consider issues of gender and social organization from data other than burials or similar sources traditionally invoked in such research. Recent ethnographic research among the Washoe (Rucks 1995) also highlights the significance of portable and stationary milling implements to concepts of property, sharing, social relations, and worldview. Such observations have potential application to future archaeological research on milling artifacts (and perhaps other tools) in the Sierra Nevada, pushing archaeological research of material culture beyond technology.

Demography

Apparent shifts in population size through time were recognized in the archaeological record of the Sierra and adjoining foothills more than three decades ago. This was demonstrated most dramatically at Buchanan reservoir (Moratto 1972), and subsequent studies throughout the range (Goldberg et al. 1986; Hull and Moratto 1999; Stevens 2002; Wirth Environmental Services 1985) have suggested that populations may have suffered significant declines between ca. cal A.D. 500 and 1200 or, alternately, may have adopted a settlement system that resulted in more dispersed and ephemeral occupation sites that can be mistaken for regional population decline. Assessing the validity of one or the other of these perspectives is difficult, as this topic requires a regional (rather than site-specific) approach to analysis. In addition, random sampling and the collection of data with the specific intent of demographic reconstruction is necessary. These requirements have not been met in most demographic analyses, although recent research in Yosemite Valley based on more than 2,200 obsidian hydration dates was so structured (Hull 2002). Significantly, this study also documented significant population decline—likely unattributable simply to settlement reorganization—between approximately cal A.D. 500 and 1350.

As indicated by recent work in the Rush Meadow area (Jackson and Morgan 1999), any interpretation of population size and movements in the Sierra will likely require a detailed and holistic approach. In this region, for example, it appears that there were local responses to periodic volcanic activity in the Inyo-Mono chain, including possible local abandonments on the order of 100 to 300 years. The potential for local events of either natural or cultural origin to influence regional demography argues for careful assessment of the variety of possible factors contributing to patterns we observe in the archaeological record of the Sierra Nevada and elsewhere in California.

CONCLUSION

In general, the emerging picture for the Sierra Nevada is one of initial use or occupation in the Tahoe-Truckee region and lower western foothill areas by small, relatively mobile groups by at least 7500 cal B.C. Significant occupation of the Sierra foothills, and especially use of mid- to upper-elevation areas of the central and southern Sierra, did not become prevalent until after ca. 3000 cal B.C. There may have been a hunting focus at this time in upper-elevation areas, but the presence of portable milling equipment argues for a more diverse subsistence base in low- to mid-elevation occupation sites, at least. Between ca. cal A.D. 500 and 1250, a significant shift in human use of the Sierra Nevada is evident. Substantial changes occurred with respect to technology, trade, subsistence, settlement, and population. The potential interplay of these factors and concomitant environmental change in the form of long-term climatic trends and shorter-term natural events such as prolonged droughts and volcanic activity in the Inyo-Mono region hamper attempts to reach definitive conclusions regarding proximate, or even ultimate, cause.

At a minimum, it appears that there was a substantial population decline along the entire length of the western slope of the Sierra at this time. Such decline is indicated throughout the northern Sierra, the lower elevation zones of the central and southern Sierra, and in mid-elevation zones of Yosemite National Park. Population decline may also have occurred elsewhere. This phenomenon may in part represent a shift in settlement to other areas; for example, some researchers have suggested that there may have been more activity in Sierra Valley (Waechter and Andolina 2005). Other similarly affected areas of the northeastern Sierra include the Blue Lakes region on the Mokelumne River (Wirth Environmental Services 1985) and mid-elevation locales in the central and southern Sierra such as Crane Valley (Goldberg et al. 1986) and Balsam Meadow (Jackson and Dietz 1984). The recent data from Yosemite Valley (Hull 2002), however, do not support the posited upslope shift of population for the central and southern Sierra as a whole, and data from the Mokelumne drainage (Wirth Environmental Services 1985) may be too limited to argue unequivocally for population dispersal (as opposed to decline) at this time. In other words, the Yosemite Valley study suggests that apparent population decline is not simply a function of more dispersed land use on the western slope of the Sierra related to adoption of the bedrock mortar and acorn intensification.

The record of latest use of the Sierra after ca. cal A.D. 1250 to 1500 reflects a return to a more densely settled region, with more intensive use of vegetal foods such as acorns (in the west) and pinyon nuts (in the east). Although distinctions between the northern and central/southern Sierra are evident throughout the sequence in terms of lithic material use and perhaps flaked stone tool assemblages, this latest occupation marks an even greater delineation. There is a clear affinity in the northwestern zone to areas farther north and west in terms of lithic materials and projectile point types, while the central and southern Sierra continue a "blended" pattern of traits common to both the east and west.

Avoiding the question of ethnicity or interpretations based on linguistic data for any of these broad periods of use after 3000 cal B.C., at a minimum the archaeological record of the Sierra Nevada appears to document significant population movements or dispersal coincident with or beginning somewhat prior to a period of environmental stress between cal A.D. 500 and 1250 (Waechter and Andolina 2005). Providing well-reasoned interpretations and defensible arguments regarding the cause of this or other patterns, however, will necessarily depend on placing the Sierra data in the larger context of archaeology to both the west and east. Initial steps have already been taken in this direction, including Kowta's (1988) model for the northern Sierra, work in the Truckee River area (Elston et al. 1994), and investigations in Tuolumne Meadows (Hull et al. 1995) and the alpine southern Sierra Nevada (Stevens 2005).

FUTURE DIRECTIONS

As with archaeology anywhere, researchers in the Sierra Nevada must cope with the limitations and embrace the strengths of the regional record. Two major limitations overshadow Sierra archaeology. The first is the complexity of site formation due to evident reoccupation and bioturbation. The second is poor preservation of features and organic remains. In the former case, new micromorphology techniques recently employed in Yosemite National Park (Hicks et al. 2006) may hold promise, or at least thoroughly and critically document the obstacles researchers face when attempting to base interpretations on stratigraphy. With respect to the issue of preservation, advancements in recovery and analysis of organic residues or soil chemistry may ultimately provide a better view of that part of the archaeological record underrepresented in the Sierra Nevada. Currently, however, it appears that we will never be able to make the quantitative—as opposed to qualitative—statements relevant to subsistence and other related research domains that are possible in areas to the east and west. The one exception, as highlighted by Hull and Moratto (1999), is rock shelter deposits that foster better preservation, although recent research has suggested that these sites may have witnessed significant use only in the past 300 years (Hull 2002; White 1988).

The archaeological record of the Sierra Nevada also has some significant strengths, primarily the capacity to date artifacts via obsidian hydration dating, which can offset some of the problems created by site formation issues. With this tool, central and southern Sierra archaeologists have the capacity to break free of the dependency on the Great Basin chronology. They can also begin to move away from a reliance on categories such as phases and periods to absolute dating, which is critical to assessing potential cause and effect in short- and long-term culture change in the region. Issues such as the timing of the introduction of bedrock mortars and the bow and arrow, the decline in trans-Sierra exchange (Bennyhoff and Hughes 1987), and possible population decline can be explored. Answers to these questions, in turn, are significant to a host of other issues, such as subsistence intensification and potential changes in social organization.

Sierra Nevada archaeology benefits from the fact that much of this area is federal land that continues to be the focus of ongoing archaeological survey and is less developed than many other areas of the state. As the above review highlights, these characteristics facilitate a broad regional approach to a variety of issues and suggest that the archaeological record of the Sierra has significant contributions to make to California archaeology. A regional perspective and site preservation enhance understanding settlement patterns in light of foraging models, although the lack of direct subsistence data tempers enthusiasm somewhat in the Sierra. In all but the lowest elevation zones of this region, subsistence and its relevance to settlement must be inferred instead from artifact assemblages and features. Likewise, while changes in human population size and movements made possible by a regional perspective may be of particular interest to Sierra archaeologists, the patterns and possible causes for such shifts have potential significance to areas to the west, as well, and may be related to long-term climatic trends observed throughout western North America (Jones et al. 1999; Woolfenden 1996). Ongoing studies of flaked and ground stone tool technology in the Sierra may provide interesting case studies of use to researchers elsewhere in California and the Great Basin, while also providing a fuller understanding of regional trends of embedded versus logistic procurement, exchange, and ethnic identity. Geochemical studies of basaltic materials in the north, intersource differences in eastern California obsidians, and perhaps similar advancements with respect to cryptocrystalline silicates will also contribute important information to these research topics. The archaeological record of the Sierra also documents the effects of Euro-American incursion on native peoples at some distance from nonnative settlements on the coast, and provides a view of short- and long-term culture change in such contexts that can contribute to our understanding of contact-era culture change in both California and North America as a whole.

Finally, the continued integration of ethnography and the traditional knowledge of Indian people of the Sierra into archaeological research holds great promise. Thus far, such work has primarily focused on milling technology (McCarthy et al. 1985; Rucks 1995) and land-use practices (Anderson 2005; Anderson and Moratto 1996). These topics and others, including documentation of past events in native oral tradition and myth (Hull 2002) and the influence of nonnative incursion on traditional lifeways (Davis-King 1998; Rucks 1995), are prospects for future research. In addition, archaeologists and native people who have collaborated on projects in this region have found that this experience enriches their sense of participation and the connection of past and present, while also expanding the relevance of archaeological investigations.

Whatever avenues of future research are taken in the Sierra, we must bear in mind that the record can only be understood in terms of the processes and events that were taking place to both the east and west. The archaeological record of this region—rather than representing a marginal area in either the past or present—has relevance to not only Sierra archaeologists but also to those working throughout California and the Great Basin. The "light" of Sierra Nevada archaeology is the contribution it can make to a wide array of theoretical, methodological, and anthropological issues both within the Sierra and beyond.

CHAPTER 13

Prehistory of the Northern California Bight and the Adjacent Transverse Ranges

MICHAEL A. GLASSOW, LYNN H. GAMBLE, JENNIFER E. PERRY, AND GLENN S. RUSSELL

THIS CHAPTER PRESENTS THE PREHISTORY OF THE Northern section of the California Bight and the adjacent transverse ranges, which for convenience we shall refer to as the Northern Bight. This geographic area includes the coastline from Vandenberg Air Force Base to the vicinity of Palos Verdes, as well as the Santa Ynez Range, the Santa Ynez Valley, the Santa Monica Mountains, and the Los Angeles basin. Lands at the northern margins of Ventura and Santa Barbara Counties are included as well, but archaeological data are scant for these interior lands. Also included are the Northern Channel Islands. At the time of Spanish colonization, most of these lands were occupied by the Central Chumash, and the eastern portion of this area, within the Los Angeles basin, were occupied by the Tongva (Gabrielino). Chumash descendants are numerous in the area today and have been involved in cultural revitalization throughout the twentieth century (Figure 13.1).

Research over the past 20 years, as well as the application of theoretical perspectives that have come to the fore over this period, have resulted in the acquisition of a substantially increased knowledge base for Northern Bight prehistory. Articles in prominent journals and books published by well-known presses have brought national and international visibility to the region. Underlying this significant expansion of knowledge is an increase in both the quantity and quality of data derived from the archaeological record, the dramatic increase in the number of radiocarbon dates being arguably the most important. King's (1990) chronological scheme, which is still is widely used, has been refined based on patterning in the distribution of radiocarbon dates. Other important developments are more prevalent use of eighth-inch mesh water screening, laboratory sorting of all material caught by screens, and flotation. As a result, systematic recovery of small objects such as fish bones, beads, and floral remains has opened new analytical vistas. As is true throughout California, much of this expansion and refinement of the database is a result of cultural resource management (CRM). Indeed, the bulk of research accomplished during the past 20 years, including much in academic contexts, has been driven by the objectives of CRM.

Three broad realms of theory have characterized archaeology in the Northern Bight over the past 20 years. One of these, with roots extending back to the 1950s, consists of various ecological approaches, including optimal foraging theory, related economic theories, and evolutionary ecological theory; all of these have been concerned mainly with aspects of subsistence change. The second realm of theory includes various social evolutionary perspectives on the development of sociopolitical and economic complexity. Archaeologists interested in both categories have also been interested in the role of paleoenvironmental change in altering the resource base of the prehistory of the Northern Bight. Although they are still sketchy, paleoenvironmental records coming into existence over the past 20 years have been actively applied to models of adaptive change, and there has been a good deal of lively debate concerning the nature and magnitude of the impact of environmental variability on human cultural systems. A third theoretical approach that has been slower to develop concerns the role of technological change in cultural evolution, even though technological developments have often been highlighted in arguments concerning subsistence change.

THE BEGINNINGS OF PREHISTORY

The Northern Bight has yielded some of the earliest evidence of human occupation in California, which is considered in detail in Chapter 4 of this volume. Arlington Springs Woman from Santa Rosa Island (SRI-173) is one of the earliest finds of human remains in North America (Figure 13.2). Radiocarbon dates derived from human bones as well as rodent bones from the deposits in the immediate vicinity of the human remains have yielded dates of approximately 11,000 cal B.C. (Johnson et al. 2002). On the coastal

Figure 13.1. Chumash house constructed for the 1923 Ventura county fair by Chumash descendants. Identities of men in the photograph are unknown. (Printed with permission of the Department of Anthropology, Santa Barbara Museum of Natural History, photo no. (P)NA-CA-CH-71.)

mainland opposite Santa Rosa Island, archaeological site SBA-1951 yielded a basal corner of a Clovis point (Erlandson et al. 1987), which may indicate mainland occupation of comparable age (see Chapter 5). Evidence of occupation approximately 1,500 years later has come from excavation at Daisy Cave (SMI-261) on San Miguel Island (Erlandson et al. 1996). The earliest deposits at the site appear to date as early as 9500 cal B.C. (see Table 4.1, Chapter 4), and shallower strata date between 7000 and 8000 cal B.C. (and younger). On Santa Rosa Island a buried midden exposed along the face of a sea cliff dates to 7300 cal B.C. (Erlandson et al. 1999). These finds hint at occupation of the Northern Bight coeval with the Paleo-Indian manifestations elsewhere in North America, but their scarcity and limited cultural context indicate that a good deal more work must be accomplished before this stage of prehistory can be properly understood.

On the mainland, the Surf site (SBA-931) overlooking the mouth of the Santa Ynez River has a basal stratum associated with a suite of radiocarbon dates indicating occupation between ca. 8000 and 7500 cal B.C. (Glassow 1996a:71–85). Despite deposits of this age being mixed with later deposits, the data show that inhabitants of the site collected shellfish 10,000 years ago, but the importance of other kinds of food sources, such as terrestrial mammals, is still unknown. The kinds of tools used at this time are also unknown, but the recovery of debitage indicates that they included flaked tools made of the local chert. A number of archaeologists have proposed that the lowest level (Level 1) of the Malaga Cove site (LAN-138) near Palos Verdes on the southern edge of the Los Angeles basin also is very early, perhaps coeval with the San Dieguito Complex in San Diego County (Moratto 1984:132; Wallace 1986:26). However, as Erlandson (1994:224) points out, the dating of the earliest deposits at the Malaga Cove site is unclear. They could be as early as 8000 cal B.C., but it seems just as likely that they date after 7000 cal B.C.

Coastal sites of the California Bight dating earlier than 7000 cal B.C. have been included in the Paleo-Coastal Tradition (Glassow 1996a:50), tentatively defined by Moratto (1984:104). However, sites of this age are too few and their contents too scanty to provide a meaningful regional picture of human activities. It is apparent, nonetheless, that shellfish were acquired as food resources, and data from Daisy Cave on San Miguel Island indicate that fishing with gorge and line was practiced by about 7800 cal B.C. (Rick et al. 2001). Milling implements were not used in the Northern Bight during these early times. Because population probably was at very low density and quite mobile, most or all sites would be expected to be small and to have minimal archaeological deposits (Erlandson 2000:22). Furthermore, sites of this antiquity would be most subject to the ravages of time, including destruction by coastal erosion as sea level continued to rise relatively rapidly at the end of the last Ice Age and burial under alluvial or aeolian deposits. Because the archaeological record for this earliest period is so minimal at present, little can be concluded regarding continuity between these early cultures and those after 7000 cal B.C., which are much better documented.

THE EARLIEST WELL-ESTABLISHED OCCUPATION: THE MILLINGSTONE HORIZON

Sometime between about 7000 and 6500 cal B.C. the population of the Northern Bight, as well as of the whole southern California coast, began expanding. Because sites of this age typically contain abundant metates and manos, Wallace (1954) named this period the Millingstone Horizon, which includes manifestations from San Diego through the Santa Barbara Channel. Wallace's original term has endured, with many archaeologists referring to these manifestations

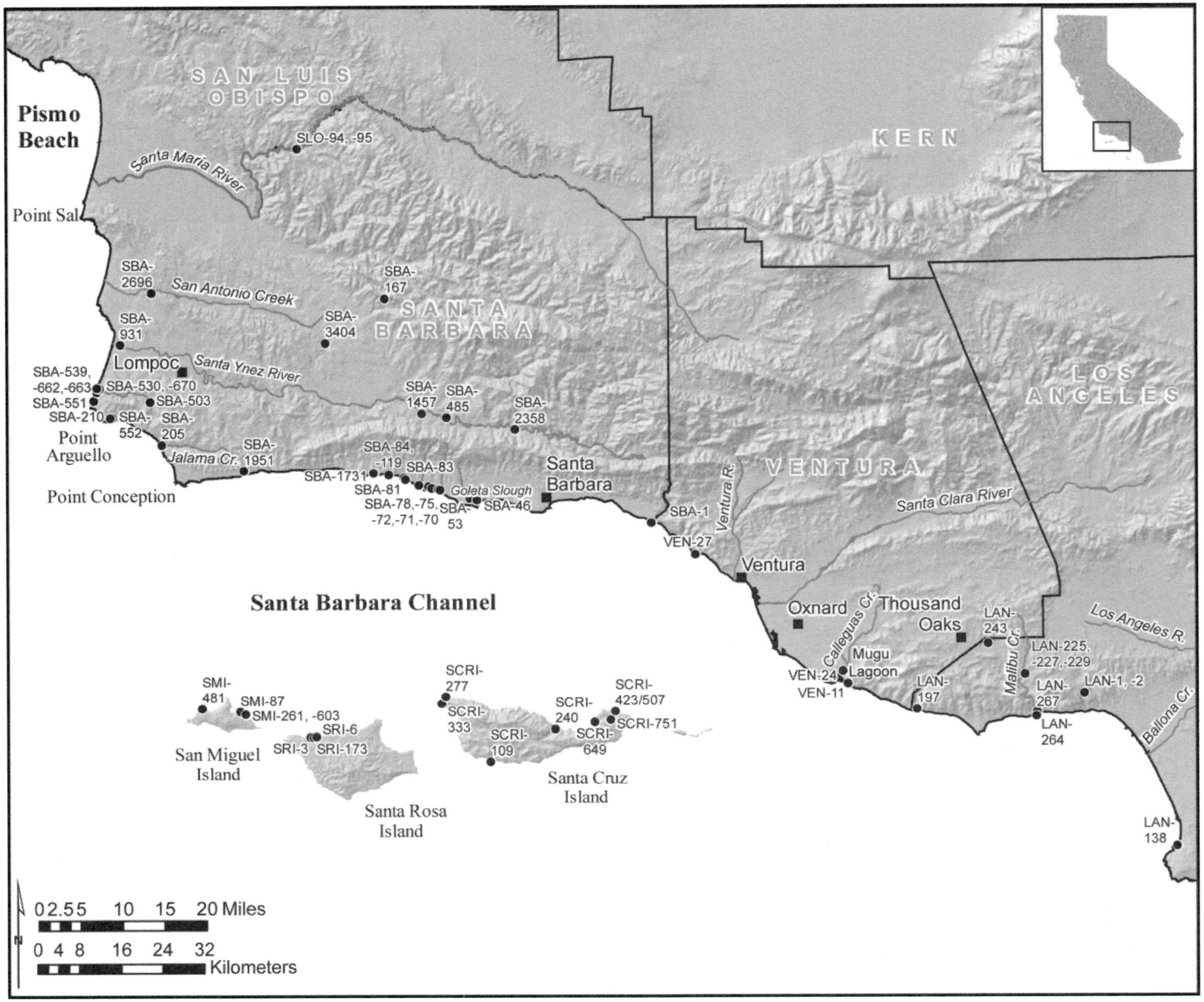

Figure 13.2. Archaeological sites and locations of the Northern Bight region.

as either the Millingstone Horizon or the Millingstone Period. Various end dates are given for the Millingstone Horizon, often as late as 3500 cal B.C. However, for several reasons, we use an end date of approximately 5000 cal B.C., which is somewhat earlier than King's end date for his Early period, Phase Ex.

Most sites known through radiocarbon dating to be of this antiquity are at or near the coast. Although the coastal zone probably supported higher population density than the interior, the smaller number of sites known to have existed in the interior undoubtedly is due to their decreased visibility and lack of easily recoverable organic remains from which radiocarbon dates can be obtained. Sites of this age adjacent to watercourses are also likely to be buried under alluvium, a result of the larger watershed sizes of interior drainages.

Only limited information is available regarding environment during this period, and some of the available data are conflicting (Glassow et al. 1988; Heusser 1978; Kowta 1969:36, 55; Pisias 1978; Warren 1968:5). A record of Holocene seawater temperature fluctuation, based on oxygen isotope data derived from a marine sediment core, indicates that water temperature was cooler and marine productivity higher than present through most of the period (Kennett 2005:66). A definitive record of vegetation characteristics during this period is yet to be developed, although some pollen data imply that vegetation communities were much as they are today (Erlandson 1994:32–33). Sea level was still rising, albeit at a much slower rate than earlier, and Early Holocene transgression into canyon mouths would have created conditions for significantly more widespread lagoons, estuaries, and tidal wetlands than was the case in later prehistory (Erlandson 1994:34; Warren 1968:6).

Despite factors that frustrate archaeologists' efforts to identify and date sites of the Millingstone Horizon, approximately 40 are known through radiocarbon dating to pertain to this time period, many more than for the period preceding 7000 cal B.C. Many sites contain substantial volumes of deposits and many hundreds of artifacts, implying regular use and longer intervals of residence annually even if populations remained relatively mobile. The site with the thickest deposits known to date to this period is located on southern Vandenberg Air Force Base (SBA-552). The lower 3.5 meters of deposits, possibly extending over an area about two hectares in size, date before 5500 cal B.C. (Glassow 1996a:87–88).

One of the difficulties with investigating sites of this age is the considerable disturbance caused by bioturbation, particularly gopher or ground squirrel burrowing. Not taking this into account has led to a number of misinterpretations of a site's archaeological record, some of which have been identified (Erlandson et al. 1988; Erlandson 1994:179–180; King 1967:62).

The most distinctive characteristic of sites dating between 7000 and 5000 cal B.C. is an abundance of metates and manos, many fragmentary. Manos are probably more abundant in site deposits than metates as a result of the former wearing out faster than the latter (Glassow et al. 1991:7,19). Hammerstones that appear to have been originally cores or core tools also are abundant in the sites and were probably used to shape metates and manos and to keep their working surfaces pitted in order to maintain milling efficacy. Substantial quantities of fist-size and larger rocks also occur, often as dense sheets in which metates and manos are mixed. Many of these rocks are fire affected, implying that they were heated stones used in baking food products, perhaps in pit ovens.

Artifact assemblages from sites of this time period also include a variety of flaked stone tools. Sites in the Santa Monica Mountains typically contain abundant fist-size plano-convex cores and core tools (often called scraper planes) of quartzite, basalt, and other volcanic stone materials as well as flake tools of the same materials (King 1967). Sites along the mainland coast of the Santa Barbara Channel and Vandenberg Air Force Base have yielded similar tools, but because of the availability of chert, many smaller flaked stone tools are also present (Erlandson 1994; Glassow et al. 1991:12.72; Owen et al. 1964). Flaked stone tools were used for cutting and scraping, but the particular kinds of material processed with them is unknown. Kowta (1969:52–53) proposed that so-called scraper planes were used to process agave and yucca leaves to extract fiber, although some probably are simply unifacial cores (Treganza and Bierman 1958:73). The abraded edges on some scraper planes and other core tools imply heavy-duty scraping, and use-wear analysis and experimentation with replicated scraper planes support Kowta's proposal (Salls 1985b). Curiously, sites of this age contain few or no projectile points, those present typically being of a leaf-shaped form reminiscent of earlier projectile points, and little evidence of biface manufacture (Glassow et al. 1991:12.71–12.73).

Artifacts and faunal remains provide information about diet, although available data have obvious biases due to differential preservation and recovery. Metates and manos indicate that various kinds of seeds and perhaps nuts were collected and milled into flour from which food products were made. Because of better preservation, much more is known about relative importance of various types of fauna to the diet. Open coast sites frequently contain a high density of mussel shells, and often scattered Pismo clam shells as well. Shells from estuarine clams and cockles at many sites close to the mouths of canyons indicate the existence of estuaries during this period, which later became filled with alluvial deposits (Erlandson 1994:255). Bones from sites of this age are often highly fragmented. For example, deer leg bone fragments may be only a few centimeters long. Although fish bones may be underrepresented, it seems clear that fishing was not a significant enterprise (Rick and Erlandson 2000:628). Coastal dwellers may have captured fish by hand in tidal pools, but the presence of bone gorges indicates that they also practiced line fishing. Despite the problems with differential preservation of faunal remains pertaining to different taxa, Erlandson's (1994:166) analysis of subsistence practices during this time period suggests that Millingstone Horizon peoples, at least while they occupied coastal sites, depended mainly on shellfish as a source of protein, with hunting and fishing contributing relatively small amounts to the diet.

Interior areas were occupied as well, though their dating has been problematic. A substantial number of sites dating to this time period probably exist in the interior of the Santa Monica Mountains and the valleys immediately to the north. Known examples that date earlier than 5000 cal B.C. include LAN-1 (the lower component) (Treganza and Bierman 1958); LAN-225, overlooking Las Virgenes Creek (King et al. 1968); and VEN-536 (lower stratum) (Clewlow et al. 1979). In the Santa Ynez Valley, West and Slaymaker (1987) located a series of sites along the edge of Lake Cachuma (a reservoir along the Santa Ynez River) that contain milling implements and may date earlier than 5000 cal B.C. Recent test excavations at two of these sites unfortunately did not yield organic samples adequate for radiocarbon dating (Bever et al. 2004:113–115). Conway (1995) obtained a radiocarbon date of 6900 cal B.C. from charcoal associated with a stratum bearing manos at site SBA-1457, located in a tributary canyon south of Lake Cachuma. However, the charcoal for this date may be of natural origin. At SBA-485, a site overlooking the upper end of Lake Cachuma, a radiocarbon date of 5100 cal B.C. was associated with a lower stratum yielding abundant metates and manos (Otte 2001:5). Few faunal data are available from interior sites dating prior to 5000 cal B.C., but rabbits and deer were presumably important. Interior sites generally contain no shell, as would be expected, but if shellfish had been imported from the coast, their shells may have disappeared due to chemical weathering.

Sites falling into the time period between 7000 and 5000 cal B.C. also exist on the Northern Channel Islands, but the few documented so far differ from their mainland counterparts in that they contain no milling artifacts. On San Miguel Island, Daisy Cave (SMI-261) contains deposits dating within this time interval (Erlandson et al. 1996), and on Santa Rosa Island, Orr (1968:115–129; Erlandson 1991a:106–107) excavated a cemetery at which some burials date to 5900 cal B.C. (SRI-3). On both islands several other archaeological deposits have been dated to this time period (Erlandson 1991a). On Santa Cruz Island, the lowermost strata at the Punta Arena site (SCRI-109) date between 6700 and 5500 cal B.C. (Glassow 2002b), and another site on the northern coast (SCRI-277) has basal deposits dating to 5300 cal B.C. (Glassow 1980:82–83). All of these sites yielded evidence of dependence on marine resources, mainly shellfish, but including pinnipeds, fish, and marine birds. Both Daisy Cave and the Punta Arena site have yielded bone gorges dating to this period. Apparently utilization of seeds that were milled into flour was not practiced by the islanders at this time, perhaps because appropriate seed-bearing plants were not as abundant on the islands.

Sometime during this period people began to make beads from olive shells *(Olivella biplicata)* (King 1990:106–107). The most prevalent bead form is an olive shell from which the spire had been removed by either abrasion or chipping. Beads from burials show their use as personal adornment. They may be indicative of the beginnings of a regional exchange system that became increasingly more important during later periods of prehistory. King (1990:117) proposes that the comparatively few types of beads and their distribution among individual burials in cemeteries dating to the Early Period (which ended about 600 cal B.C.) generally indicate that political, economic, and religious institutions were not clearly differentiated. In other words, social differentiation was apparently minimal, and political leadership was probably weak and depended on individuals with exceptional leadership skills. Little may be added to these tentative interpretations about social organization during the Millingstone Horizon other than to propose that the group of people that occupied a residential base, perhaps not exceeding 50 individuals, probably was an extended family that was for the most part economically independent.

An issue of special significance in attempting to understand subsistence during the Millingstone Horizon is the degree to which food storage was practiced. The evidence for seed utilization is suggestive of storage because seeds may be stored for months or years if kept dry and protected from pests. The presence of storage containers or granaries would be a definitive indication of storage, but evidence of these is not likely to be preserved. Evidence of houses used by Millingstone Horizon peoples is also nonexistent except for D. B. Rogers's (1929:344) reference to settlements of "five to twenty semi-subterranean dirt-banked huts," each consisting of "a circular pit, from thirteen to fifteen feet in diameter, with perpendicular walls . . . put down to a depth of approximately thirty inches" (D. B. Rogers 1929:180; Gamble 1991:132, 153, 171).

Another fundamental issue confronting archaeologists trying to understand ecological adaptation of Millingstone Horizon peoples is the nature of settlement systems. Some archaeologists assume, at least implicitly, that the known sites of the time period are essentially a representative sample of residential bases. McGuire and Hildebrandt (1994:43), for instance, have argued that Millingstone Horizon people moved periodically from one residential base to another, each being characterized by the presence of metates and manos. They go on to argue that these sites reflect minimal gender differentiation: men and women worked together in acquiring food resources rather than men specializing in hunting and women in collecting plant food. In contrast, Glassow (1996a:130–131) argues that Millingstone Horizon sites may be a biased sample of those used through the course of an annual round of movement between resource areas. He suggests that males produced sites that are difficult to recognize or date in that they would have been hunting camps occupied for short periods of time at which little organic material usable for radiocarbon dating would have been left behind. Currently available data do not allow these two opposing hypotheses to be evaluated. Indeed, settlement systems during this time period were likely more complex than prevailing models suggest.

The Millingstone Horizon in the Northern Bight is the earliest widespread occupation that archaeological research has revealed so far, and it is a local manifestation of coastal and near-coastal occupation throughout central and southern California. The advent of a subsistence system focused on seed collecting and milling with metates and manos was most likely a revolutionary change from the past, and it appears to have allowed a much larger population to exist in the Northern Bight than previously, even though density undoubtedly was much lower than later in prehistory. Yet the origins of the Millingstone Horizon remain obscure. It may have arisen from a coastal variant of the San Dieguito Complex in San Diego County, but again, evidence is still too meager to evaluate this hypothesis.

FOUNDATIONS OF A MARITIME LIFEWAY: 4500 TO 2000 CAL B.C.

The frequency of radiocarbon-dated sites declines beginning about 6500 cal B.C. in the Northern Bight, which probably signals a decline in population due to environmental conditions that affected either terrestrial or marine resources or both. At about 4500 cal B.C., the frequency of dated sites begins to rise again, and by 4000 cal B.C. or a bit later, frequencies are at least as high as they were around 6000 cal B.C. The period of relatively lower frequencies of dated sites correlates roughly with a period of warm seawater temperatures and intermittently low marine productivity (Kennett 2005:66). Human settlement along the coast probably would have been depressed during the periods of lower productivity.

Date frequencies for the Northern Bight begin to decline again around 3000 cal B.C. or somewhat earlier, a pattern particularly apparent on the Channel Islands. As a result, the period between 4500 and 3000 cal B.C. may be seen as a relatively discrete period of prehistory during which population density apparently was higher than before or after. There is reason to suspect, however, that many of the cultural characteristics manifest between 4500 and 3000 cal B.C. persisted until 2000 cal B.C. or even later. Because few sites are known to date between 3000 and 2000 cal B.C., little archaeological information exists to clarify the nature of this continuity.

In this chapter we place the end the Millingstone Horizon at about 5500 to 5000 cal B.C. in the Northern Bight in recognition of the depressed frequencies of radiocarbon-dated sites between 5500 and 4500 cal B.C. and some significant changes in subsistence and technology, and probably also social organization evident after 4500 cal B.C. In King's (1990:28) chronological scheme, phase Eya is dated to the time interval between 4000 and 3000 cal B.C., but radiocarbon dates from Santa Cruz Island sites imply that the beginning of the phase is probably closer to 4500 cal B.C. King dated his subsequent phase, Eyb, to 3000 to 1000 cal B.C., but he had no radiocarbon dates to confirm this time interval. Indeed, the nature of phase Eyb is poorly defined, and temporal differences will likely be discovered as more site assemblages are dated to this time interval. For current purposes, a date of 2000 cal B.C. seems reasonable as a chronological division, given that a number of sites date between 2000 and 1000 cal B.C. and are best considered in the context of later cultural development.

Although metates and manos continued in use during this time period, Gamble and King (1997:63–64) propose that both kinds of artifacts changed form, metates becoming thicker and heavier, and manos acquiring diverse shapes. It is significant, however, that mortars and pestles were added to the milling repertoire sometime around 4000 cal B.C. A few isolated instances of the use of mortars and pestles may date prior to 4500 cal B.C., the best case for which is their presence at the Sweetwater Mesa site (LAN-267). Mortars in the collection from this site have small, shallow depressions (King 1967:37–39), quite different from the large, deep depressions of later examples. The association between grinding implements (metates and manos) and pounding implements (mortars and pestles) is most evident at the Aerophysics site (SBA-53; Harrison and Harrison 1966).

We have yet to understand the use of these early mortars and pestles. Based on ethnographic data from many parts of California, some archaeologists have proposed that they were used to pound acorns and large seeds into flour, thus signaling the advent of acorns as an important food product (e.g., Gamble and King 1997:67). However, the earliest mortars and pestles may have been used to process starchy tubers or other underground plant parts, such as bulrush roots (Glassow 1996b). Regardless of the particular kinds of products processed with mortars and pestles, they undoubtedly indicate an expansion of the diet to include newly important food resources. Many sites dating to this time period contain few or no mortars and pestles and thus closely resemble sites of the preceding period in containing an abundance of metates and manos. If mortars and pestles were used at this time for processing foods present only in particular habitats, they would not be expected to occur at sites where these habitats were absent.

Another change occurring sometime around 4000 cal B.C. is a significant increase in the quantity of projectile points in site deposits. The 1956–1957 excavation at the Aerophysics site, for instance, yielded 88 projectile points (Harrison and Harrison 1966:17). The form of the projectile point is new. Instead of being leaf-shaped, it is side-notched (Figure 13.3), a form that appears to be unique to the period between 4500 and 3000 cal B.C. in the Northern Bight. The greater prevalence of projectile points may be an indication that hunting, particularly of large game animals such as deer, became more important. However, animal bones are not significantly more abundant at sites of this age than at earlier sites. If hunting was not significantly more important than it was earlier, then the greater prevalence of projectile points is likely to be related to a change in where the points were made and discarded. For instance, men may have made or discarded points at campsites during Millingstone Horizon times and then shifted these activities to residential bases beginning about 4500 cal B.C. (Glassow 1997:86–87).

More complicated settlement systems appear beginning about 4500 cal B.C. or somewhat later. The Aerophysics site is arguably the largest mainland site in the Northern Bight known to date within the 4500 to 3000 cal B.C. time period. Other sites occupied during this time period are much smaller, with a lower density of artifacts and faunal remains (e.g., SBA-75; Erlandson 1988). This distinction in site size and complexity may indicate that the Aerophysics site was a principal residential base for people living in the central Santa Barbara Channel region, perhaps occupied for relatively long periods of time during the year (Glassow 1997). The smaller sites, on the other hand, would have been occupied for much shorter periods. Nonetheless, this distinction may be due largely to variation in the diversity and abundance of resources. The immediate vicinity of the Aerophysics site offered an unusually wide variety of marshland and estuarine resources as well as diverse dry land resources, and so may have been a more popular location than others where resources were less abundant. However, the 1956–1957 collection from the Aerophysics site contains many formally shaped flaked stone tools, including bifacial drills, apparent lance points, and unifacial points (Figure 13.3) that are rare or absent from contemporaneous sites. These imply that a variety of relatively specialized activities took place at this site but not at others, thus reinforcing the idea that Aerophysics site had a special place in the settlement system.

The formal flaked stone tools from the Aerophysics site are also intriguing in that little evidence of their manufacture is present in a small sample of systematically screened deposits excavated by a University of California–Santa Barbara field class in 1985. The prevalence of small flakes less than 10 millimeters in

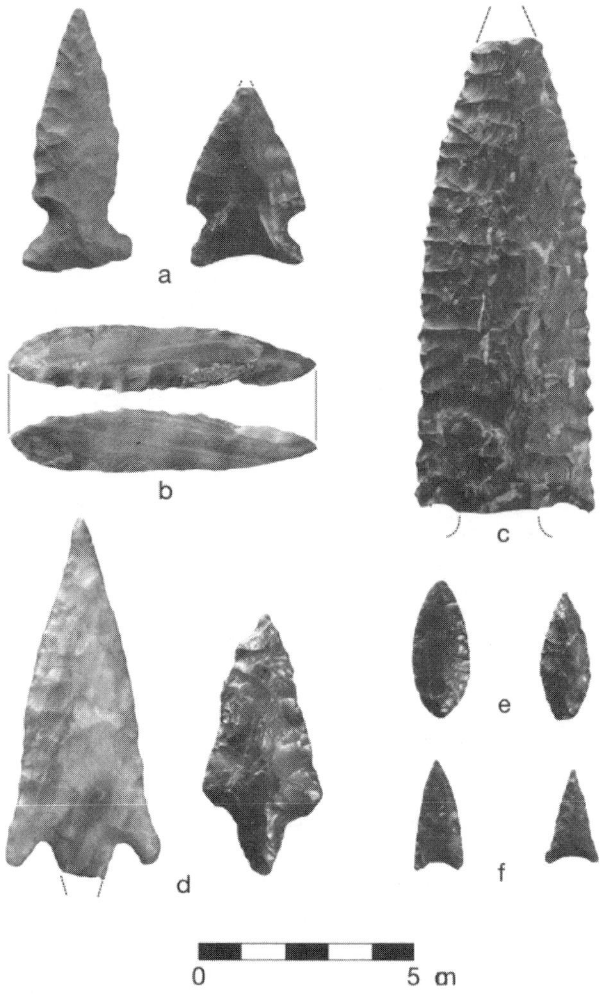

Figure 13.3. Projectile points in Northern Bight site collections. (a) Side-notched points from CA-SBA-53; (b) unifacial point from CA-SBA-53; (c) lance point from CA-SBA-53; (d) contracting-stemmed points from various sites; (e) leaf-shaped arrow points from various sites; (f) concave base (cottonwood triangular) points from various sites.

length implies that projectile points and other formal flaked stone tools were manufactured elsewhere and brought to the Aerophysics site for use. A likely possibility is the Santa Ynez Valley. Collections from site SBA-485, overlooking the upper end of Lake Cachuma, contain the same side-notched projectile points found at the Aerophysics site (Macko 1983). The two sites were probably occupied at the same time, although SBA-485 was also occupied during earlier and later periods. SBA-485 contains abundant flaked stone tool manufacturing waste and is a good candidate for a site occupied by people who also occupied the Aerophysics site. It is possible that the settlement system of the people who occupied the Aerophysics site included various coastal campsites as well as one or more residential bases in the Santa Ynez Valley.

Sites on the Northern Channel Islands occupied between 4500 and 3000 cal B.C. are distinctive in that the majority of those dated to this time period contain abundant red abalone shells. This is especially evident on Santa Cruz Island, where red abalone shells are rare at earlier and later sites. Most island sites of this time period are small, with deposits usually less than 0.5 meter thick. Typical of most Channel Island sites, mussel shell accounts for most of the shellfish remains, but the large red abalone shells are highly visible because so many are whole or nearly so. The prevalence of red abalone shells appears related to ocean waters being cooler than before or after the period when the middens were formed (Glassow 1993b; Glassow et al. 1994).

As earlier, the ecological adaptation of the islanders was clearly different from that of their coastal mainland contemporaries. One indication of this is the rarity (or even absence) at island sites of the distinctive side-notched projectile points found in contemporaneous mainland sites. Stone mortars and pestles also are typically rare or absent on the islands. Both the points and the milling implements probably were used mainly for nonmarine resources that were either absent or not abundant on the islands. For obvious reasons island populations placed a good deal more emphasis on marine resources, including fish, sea mammals, and particularly shellfish. People living at the Punta Arena site (SCRI-109) on Santa Cruz Island focused subsistence efforts on hunting dolphins, whose bones are abundant in the site's deposits (Glassow 2005). The emphasis on dolphin hunting is probably related to the proximity of a deep, steep-sided submarine canyon, a situation that does not occur elsewhere around the Northern Channel Islands. Dolphins were (and still are) attracted to this locality because of the highly productive marine life at the canyon edge due to upwelling.

Punta Arena and another site near the western extreme of the island (the El Montón site, SCRI-333; Wilcoxon 1993) are larger and have thicker deposits compared to the other Santa Cruz Island sites dated to this period. Both are situated in localities with rich and diverse marine resources, so their volume and contents may simply reflect this. However, the El Montón site is associated with a cemetery (King 1990:269–275), which implies more stable, longer-term occupation. People may have been relatively sedentary while residing at this site for part of the year but highly mobile during the remainder of the year.

A few island sites of this age have yielded digging-stick weights, attesting to the acquisition of corms, bulbs, and/or tubers. The blue dicks corm *(Dichelostemma capitatum)* was important on the islands at the time of European colonization (Timbrook 1993:56), and most likely was utilized throughout much of the islands' prehistory.

In the only cemetery known to date to the 4500–3000 cal B.C. period, the El Montón site (Olson 1930; King 1990), increased numbers and diversity of shell beads and ornaments found with the dead suggest greater social complexity than during the Millingstone Horizon (Glassow 2004b). The nature of this complexity, however, is difficult to adduce. King (1990:95) notes that "wealth" artifacts (beads and ornaments, decorated hairpins) and ritual objects tended to be relatively more dispersed among the burials than was typical later in time (after about 600 cal B.C.), from which he infers that positions of higher status were associated with seniority and leadership ability even though society was essentially egalitarian. Some of the social complexity of this time period may be related to increased commerce between the islands and the mainland. Some of the more common objects associated with burials are hairpins, each made from a longitudinally split section of a deer metatarsal, with the bone derived from the mainland due to the absence of deer on the islands (King 1990:270–275). Increased commerce across the channel (and perhaps also between the islands), as well as the dolphin hunting undertaken by occupants of the Punta Arena site, imply that watercraft were used more intensively than before. This more intensive use may have been facilitated by technological improvements in watercraft, but no archaeological evidence yet indicates this (Glassow 2004b).

Cultural development on the islands between 3000 and 2000 cal B.C. is still poorly documented. The emphasis on collecting red abalone on Santa Cruz Island ended by about 3000 cal B.C., and none of the 13 sites with abundant red abalone shells has evidence of occupation continuing after this date (although a few have overlying deposits dating much later in time). Most likely coastal mainland settlement underwent a similar disruption, but rodent burrowing and other types of disturbance to sites have so far prevented assessment of this possibility. King's (1990) analysis of Channel Islands cemetery collections indicates a good deal of continuity in such items as shell beads and ornaments, hairpins, and ritual objects from the period before 3000 cal B.C. to possibly as late as 1000 cal B.C. (the end of his phase Eyb). This implies that despite environmental changes affecting the availability of red abalone, craft production and social and economic organization remained unchanged. As mentioned above, however, the side-notched projectile point was no longer made after about 3000 cal B.C.

Beyond the Santa Barbara Channel mainland coast and the islands, comparatively few sites in the Northern Bight are associated with radiocarbon dates falling within the 4500 to 2000 cal B.C. time period. Nonetheless, many sites have yielded large side-notched points of the type in the Aerophysics site collections, indicative of occupation between 4500 and 3000 cal B.C., although most have deposits in which artifacts of this time period are mixed with earlier or later deposits or both. Indeed, some sites were probably occupied at different times beginning as early as 7000 cal B.C. and extending as late as 2000 cal B.C. or even later. Examples include SBA-485 in the Santa Ynez Valley and the Tank site (LAN-1) in Topanga Canyon. In the case of the latter site, however, there is a stratigraphic distinction between deposits that date earlier than 5000 cal B.C. and those that date later.

Along the coast north of Point Conception, side-notched points came from excavation at a site at Jalama Beach (SBA-205) (Lathrap and Hoover 1975), but they occur in a stratum of deposits that contains evidence of later occupation as well. To the north, on Vandenberg Air Force Base and in the vicinity of Lompoc, occupation during this time period is represented by radiocarbon dates and finds of the distinctive side-notched projectile points at several sites (Glenn 1991). However, collections from deposits of this age are not large and in some cases are not clearly differentiated from earlier or later deposits and/or are not well dated (e.g., basal deposits at SBA-210). An exception is two side-notched points from a recent investigation at SBA-530, overlooking the mouth of Honda Canyon. These were found in deposits clearly dating between 4200 and 3000 cal B.C.

Overall, the period between 4500 and 2000 cal B.C. is pivotal in many respects in that a number of changes that took place presaged later cultural development, particularly before 3000 cal B.C. Mortars and pestles, for example, were used for the first time, indicating that diet included a greater variety of plant foods. Higher frequency of projectile points implies either a greater emphasis on terrestrial hunting, a major shift in gender-based division of labor, a shift in the nature of settlement systems, or some combination thereof. Increased use of watercraft and perhaps design improvements are implied by the emphasis on dolphin hunting at one island location, expansion of fishing practices to include offshore species, and the presence in island sites of various artifacts made of deer bone from the mainland. Finally, mortuary practices suggest greater emphasis on status differentiation, perhaps associated with larger leadership roles. A decline in population after 3000 cal B.C. is apparently associated with an environmental shift not yet well understood.

MARINE AND TERRESTRIAL TRANSITIONS FROM THE MIDDLE TO LATE HOLOCENE, 2000 CAL B.C. TO CAL A.D. 1

Spanning the transition from the Middle to Late Holocene (1500 cal B.C.), this time period follows the adoption of mortars and pestles, includes the transition to circular shell fishhooks around 500 cal B.C., but precedes the introduction of the plank canoe and bow and arrow around cal A.D. 500 (Erlandson 1997a; Glassow 1996a). In addition to significant shifts in subsistence and increased coastal settlement around 2000 to 1000 cal B.C., artifact analysis from habitation and burial sites reflects cultural elaboration, indicating a transition from egalitarianism to achieved differences in wealth and status (Erlandson and Rick 2002a; Hollimon 1990; King 1990; Lambert 1994; Lambert and Walker 1991). Changes in technology, subsistence, and settlement from 2000 to 1000 cal B.C. reflect an increasingly maritime orientation, with intensified fishing and regional exchange arguably providing the basis for subsequent socioeconomic and political complexity in the region.

Over the past 20 years, the archaeological record for the period between 2000 and 1000 cal B.C. has been augmented substantially by survey and excavation on the Northern Channel Islands and along the mainland coast. Fifty-four sites have components radiocarbon dated to this time period. Relevant archaeological data for the western extreme of the Northern Bight are limited primarily to Vandenberg Air Force Base, and studies in the Santa Ynez Valley and elsewhere in the interior are limited for many of the reasons mentioned earlier. Despite growing contributions from mainland excavations, the majority of sites with components dating between 2000 cal B.C. and cal A.D. 1 have been identified on the Northern Channel Islands. Relative to the other islands, Santa Cruz Island has the largest number of relevant sites (23) because of its larger size and more protracted history of archaeological investigations by a greater number of researchers. Most of these sites are located in coastal settings west of the narrow neck (isthmus) of the island, but 10 sites have been identified on eastern Santa Cruz Island through investigations beginning in the early 1990s.

Based on faunal data from sites throughout the Northern Bight, one of the most significant shifts in subsistence between 2000 cal B.C. and cal A.D. 1 is the well-documented broadening of diet to emphasize a diverse array of marine and terrestrial habitats and species (Erlandson 1997a, b; Erlandson and Rick 2002a; Glassow 1996b, 1997; Kennett 1998, 2005; Perry 2003; Vellanoweth et al. 2000). Coastal and island populations diversified their technologies and subsistence practices substantially to emphasize pulpy plant foods such as acorns, islay, and roots (tubers, corms, and bulbs), as well as fish and sea mammals (Glassow 1996b, 1997). As processing implements for a variety of plants and small fauna (e.g., rabbits, shellfish), mortars and pestles, of more refined forms than earlier, were among the tools that made such diversification and subsequent resource intensification possible.

Technological innovations appearing in the archaeological record of the Northern Bight between 2000 cal B.C. and cal A.D. 1 include contracting stem points (Figure 13.3), notched stone sinkers or net weights, and circular shell fishhooks, all of which directly transformed hunting, fishing, and possibly dimensions of violence (Erlandson 1997a; Glassow 1997). The transition from side-notched dart points to contracting stemmed points around 2000 cal B.C. may reflect shifts in hunting and/or warfare strategies, with Glassow (1997) emphasizing the advantages of attachment between the point and shaft through the application of asphaltum. Concurrent with this development are some of the earliest examples of asphaltum basketry impressions and tarring pebbles, indicating that asphaltum was used for a range of tool manufacturing purposes for at least 4,000 years (Erlandson 1997b; Erlandson and Rick 2002a:170). Artifacts from SBA-1900, a site occupied between 1500 and 1000 cal B.C., reflect the range of technologies available at this time, including metates and manos, mortars and a pestle, charmstones, a notched cobble net sinker, contracting stem points, tarring pebbles, and asphaltum-stained cobbles (Erlandson 1997b:99).

Notched stone sinkers or net weights around 2000 to 1000 cal B.C. and circular shell fishhooks around 500 cal B.C. provided opportunities to diversify marine resource use from the overwhelming emphasis on shellfish that characterized the Early and Middle Holocene (Erlandson 1997a, b; Glassow 1993a, 1996a; Kennett 1998). Late Holocene subsistence appears to be much broader as fishing efforts were expanded (e.g., kelp bed and midchannel fishing) and intensified (e.g., nearshore netting) to varying degrees throughout the Northern Bight (Erlandson and Rick 2002a; Glassow 1993a, 2002a). Such changes are well represented in the mixed diet of Middle to Late Holocene deposits at Cave of the Chimneys (SMI-603) on San Miguel Island (Vellanoweth et al. 2000:612). At this site, faunal remains from three strata dating to 4000, 3800, and 2500 RCYBP reflect the diminished importance of shellfish from 83 percent to 25 percent and a concomitant increase in fish from 17 percent to 52 percent of the meat yield. Relevant faunal data have also been obtained from Daisy Cave (SMI-261) in deposits dating between 800 and 3000 RCYBP (Vellanoweth et al. 2000) as well as more recently from SMI-87 and 481 (Rick 2004a, b).

Similar trends have been identified in Middle to Late Holocene deposits at sites throughout Santa Cruz Island and Santa Rosa Island, where Glassow (1993a), Kennett (1998), Perry (2003), and others have documented a significant increase in fishing after about 1000 cal B.C. The most comprehensive subsistence data for this transition are presented by Glassow (1993a) with respect to Santa Cruz Island and by Kennett (1998, 2005) based on sites located there and on Santa Rosa Island. Of the 12 sites discussed by Glassow (1993a), six have subsistence data for components dating between 2000 cal B.C. and cal A.D. 1. Deposits dating between 2000 and 500 cal B.C. are dominated by shellfish, which represents between 70 percent and 96 percent of the protein yield, with fish contributing between 1 percent and 30 percent. In contrast, for those dating after 500 cal B.C., shellfish represents between 9 percent and 70 percent (primarily under 45 percent) of the protein yield and fish between 18 percent and 80 percent (Glassow 1993a:79). Kennett (1998:277, 327; 2005:189–192) also documents intensified fishing through time with similar variability with respect to the relative contributions of shellfish and fish at different sites.

Along the coastal mainland south of Point Conception, Erlandson (1994, 1997b), Glassow (1997), and Erlandson and Rick (2002a) have observed a similar shift in the relative importance of fishing. Erlandson (1997b) discusses the distribution of sites dating between 2300 and 1100 cal B.C. along the coastline south of Point Conception, such as SBA-1808, 1900, and 2067 along or near Gaviota Creek, which have yielded evidence for shellfish comprising 50 to 70 percent of the edible meat represented by faunal remains. Meat contributions from fish (including nearshore sandy bottom species) and sea mammals are variable, ranging to as much as 30 percent and 50 percent respectively, with land mammals such as deer and rabbit also represented in the diet. At these sites there is also evidence for plant exploitation, based partly on the identification of abundant ground stone implements but also 17 burned rock features at SBA-2067, which Erlandson (1997b:99) suggests may have been used for cooking *Yucca whipplei*. In contrast, Late Holocene deposits at four coastal sites, SBA-72S, 1491, 1731, and 2149, indicate the diminished importance of shellfish, representing no more than 13 percent of the protein yield, whereas fish contributions vary between 17 percent and 75 percent and sea mammals between 4 percent and 47 percent (Erlandson and Rick 2002a:176). In sum, faunal data from Middle to Late Holocene deposits at these and other sites south of Point Conception, such as SBA-84 at El Capitan State Beach (Glassow 1992), have been interpreted similarly to island data, in that fishing and sea mammal hunting were intensified after 1000 cal B.C. to varying degrees depending on site location among other factors.

Based on extensive survey and excavation on Vandenberg Air Force Base, subsistence patterns north of Point Conception differ from both the islands and mainland to the south, especially with respect to the role of fishing (Glassow 1996a, 2002a). At sites throughout the region through time, shellfish were an essential component of the diet, with California mussel *(Mytilus californianus)* representing 80 percent or more of the protein yield at SBA-210, 530, 539, 551, 552, 663, and 670 (Glassow 1996a:124). Excluding SBA-552 and 663, the rest of the sites have components dating between 2000 cal B.C. and cal A.D. 1, in which California mussel is the dominant species (Glassow 1996a:125). Although fishing was intensified, particularly after cal A.D. 500, it was never comparable to that conducted south of Point Conception. At five of the sites (SBA-210, 530, 539, 551, and 670), fish contributed no more than 14 percent of the dietary protein regardless of time period (Glassow 1996a:125). Sea mammal hunting fluctuated in importance through time, but was apparently intensified from about 200 cal B.C. to cal A.D. 1100 based on the relatively higher proportions of sea mammal bone from upper deposits at the same sites (Glassow 2002a:189). Terrestrial resources were more limited along the coastline of Vandenberg Air Force Base, with plants such as oaks being extremely rare within 10 kilometers of the coast due to the strong winds and fog that characterize this region (Glassow 1996a:6).

Alongside changes in subsistence is evidence for increased sedentism and cultural elaboration around

2000 to 1000 cal B.C. throughout the Northern Bight (Erlandson 1997a, b; Erlandson and Rick 2002a; Glassow 1997; King 1990). On the Northern Channel Islands and coastal mainland, increased sedentism is associated with an intensified marine-oriented economy as larger settlements were established directly on the coast to access increasingly maritime opportunities (Gamble and King 1997; Gamble and Russell 2002; Kennett 1998, 2005; Kennett and Conlee 2002; Munns and Arnold 2002; Perry 2003, 2004). Gamble and Russell (2002:107) summarize King's (1990) assessment of changes in settlement from 3500 to 600 cal B.C., which he interprets as trending toward a greater emphasis on boats and ocean resources, increased regional organization and larger populations, and less emphasis on defensive locations by 600 cal B.C. (Kennett 1998). This pattern is well documented on eastern Santa Cruz Island where spatial distribution of 90 temporal components at 66 sites representing occupation from 6000 cal B.C. to historic times indicates that the shift to coastal residential bases occurred after 500 cal B.C. (Perry 2003, 2004).

Increased sedentism between 2000 cal B.C. and cal A.D. 1 is evident at coastal sites throughout the region based on their increased size and/or high density of faunal remains and artifacts, floral assemblages indicative of year-round habitation, formal architecture including large clusters of semisubterranean houses and ceremonial structures at sites such as SBA-81 in Las Llagas Canyon, and formal cemeteries (LAN-2, 197; SBA-1, 71, 81, 119; SCRI-333; and SRI-41) (Erlandson 1997b; Erlandson and Rick 2002a:179; Gamble and Russell 2002:108; Glassow 2002a). Several coastal sites were occupied, at least seasonally, from 2000 cal B.C. to cal A.D. 1 through historic times, such as Xaxas (SCRI-240) at Prisoner's Harbor and Swaxɨl (SCRI-423/507) at Scorpion Anchorage on Santa Cruz Island as well as at Noqto (SBA-210) south of Point Arguello and SBA-72 in Tecolote Canyon on the mainland (Arnold 1987, 2001c; Erlandson and Rick 2002a; Glassow 1996a; Kennett 1998). Seemingly continuous occupation from 1200 cal B.C. into historic times of the historic village and major trade port of Xaxas on the north side of the island is based on more than 20 radiocarbon dates and temporally diagnostic artifacts (i.e., beads and microdrills), highlighting the ongoing role this location played in the increasingly maritime economy (Arnold 1987, 2001c:48; Arnold and Graesch 2001; Arnold et al. 2001; Kennett 1998, 2005; Preziosi 2001).

Settlement trends north of Point Conception differ from those evident to the south and on the Northern Channel Islands in at least two significant respects. First, inhabitants of the Vandenberg region engaged a much higher degree of residential mobility through time (Glassow 2002a). Second, of the known residential bases, most are in the interior with few situated directly on or near the coast because of the strong northwest-prevailing winds, fog, cool temperatures, severe winter storms, and intense wave action that characterize the Vandenberg coastline (de Barros et al. 1994:2–1). The exceptions are sites located along south- to southwest-facing expanses of coastline, particularly those adjacent to Point Sal and Point Arguello, which provide protection from the strong northwesterly winds and heavy surf (Glassow 1996a). Along a stretch of south-facing coastline east of Point Arguello is the historically documented village of Noqto (SBA-210), which also contains Middle Holocene deposits dating to about 5,000 years ago, this long span of occupation highlighting its ongoing importance in the regional settlement-subsistence system (Glassow 2002a:192). However, the most substantial residential bases during the Late Holocene are found in the most hospitable interior locations along drainages that were convenient access routes between these sites and the coast, such as SBA-2696 situated 15 kilometers inland along San Antonio Creek (Colten et al. 1997; Glassow 2002a).

Regardless of such regional differences, it is apparent that resource diversification, including intensified fishing and coastal sedentism, are associated with changes in social organization and ideology between 2000 cal B.C. and cal A.D. 1. Coastal sites throughout the Northern Bight have yielded substantial evidence for status differentiation and ritual behavior, including ceremonial enclosures and formal cemeteries with a wide range and abundance of beads, ornaments, and ritual items (Erlandson and Rick 2002a; Lambert 1994; Lambert and Walker 1991). Furthermore, artifacts similar to those ethnographically associated with ritual behavior have been recovered from the mainland and Santa Cruz Island, including "eagle or bear claws, charmstones, pipes, bone tubes, whistles, and quartz crystals" at the cemeteries at SBA-81 and SBA-119 (Erlandson and Rick 2002a); deer tibia whistles, quartz crystals, and turtle shell rattles recovered from burials at SCRI-83 assigned to the period between 1400 cal B.C. and cal A.D. 300 (Hollimon 1990, 2004; Corbett 2004); and incised stones at SBA-210, SCRI-649, and SCRI-751 (Bury et al. 2004; Perry 2003). In addition, at least one rock art site, Swordfish Cave (SBA-503) in Honda Canyon on Vandenberg Air Force Base, is associated with this period, based on the presence of red ochre in deposits dating between about 1600 and 1450 cal B.C. (Lebow and Onken 1997).

Noting the correlation between artifacts dating to this time and those historically documented as being associated with high-status individuals, including ritual items, Erlandson and Rick (2002a:181) observe that "these parallels with ethnographic Chumash practices, along with clear evidence of an elaborate and diversified material culture, suggest that fundamental aspects of Chumash society emerged near the end of the Middle Holocene or early in the Late Holocene." The abundance of social and ideology-related features and artifacts, along with the production of rock art, implies that changes in status and power were occurring in Santa Barbara Channel region. King (1990:162) interprets such evidence as power being concentrated in informal ritual and political organization in contrast to the ascribed status, formalized political leadership, and rise of secular power through exchange interaction that characterized the past 1,000 years (Arnold and Green 2002; Gamble et al. 2001, 2002).

When accounting for such transformations, researchers have tended to invoke fluctuating environmental conditions and increasing population density as factors related to technological innovation and shifts in settlement and subsistence strategies. Based on paleoenvironmental data, oak woodlands and other plant resources were distributed extensively between 2500 and 1300 cal B.C., when the "warmest and most climatically variable intervals during the Holocene occurred" (Kennett 1998:245; Kennett and Kennett 2000). Following the earlier introduction of mortars and pestles, technological innovations between 2000 cal B.C. and cal A.D. 1, such as contracting stemmed points and the more intensive and diverse use of asphaltum, broadened opportunities to exploit changing terrestrial and marine habitats, resulting in the inclusion of lower-ranked resources in the diet (Glassow 1997). Furthermore, net weights, fishhooks, and later plank canoes promoted development of a maritime-oriented economy, with intensified fishing and trade underwriting coastal and island sedentism and specialization (Arnold 1995, 2001a, b; Arnold and Bernard 2005; Colten 2001; Erlandson and Rick 2002a; Hudson et al. 1978; Kennett 1998, 2005; Pletka 2001).

Erlandson and Rick (2002a:180) suggest that resource diversification, sedentism, and cultural elaboration between 2000 cal B.C. and cal A.D. 1 correspond with slightly increased population densities, although substantial population growth probably did not occur until after cal A.D. 500 (Glassow 1999). With recent radiocarbon dates adding to the number of sites representing this time frame, it appears that increasingly dense and permanent settlements along the coast, and resulting territorial circumscription, likely contributed to further resource intensification, increased socioeconomic interaction and differentiation, and competition and violence, all of which are evident in sites dating between 2000 cal B.C. and cal A.D. 1 (Erlandson 1997a; Erlandson and Rick 2002a; King 1990; Lambert 1994; Lambert and Walker 1991; Walker 1989). In sum, recent archaeological research has contributed significantly to the understanding that the hallmarks of historically documented complexity are rooted in significant technological and demographic transformations beginning 4,000 years ago along the coastlines of the Northern Bight.

IMPORTANT TECHNOLOGICAL AND SOCIAL DEVELOPMENTS, CAL A.D. 1 TO 1000

Several additional significant cultural changes occurred during the period between cal A.D. 1 to 1000, the full contexts of which are not yet well understood. Other changes are best characterized as continuations of development beginning during earlier periods. According to Kennett's seawater temperature curve (Kennett 2005:66), this period is transitional between moderately warm conditions to increasingly colder conditions, along with increasingly variable marine productivity during the second half of the period. Cultural responses to these changing conditions are not yet apparent, nor are the climatic conditions that may be associated with these water temperature fluctuations (Gamble 2005).

As was the case during the latter part of the preceding period, the substantial accumulation of midden deposits at some coastal sites indicates increasing sedentism. This is also reflected in the presence of well-developed cemeteries, some being relatively large. Examples are SBA-81 with 364 burials, SBA-71 with 75 burials, and SRI-6 with 221 burials. According to King (1990:34–35), these cemeteries date between cal A.D. 1 and 700. It also seems that population was growing substantially through this period, especially after about cal A.D. 500, as indicated by increasing frequencies of radiocarbon-dated site components (Glassow 1999).

Arguably the most significant change during this time interval is the introduction of the plank canoe, or *tomol* as it was known on the mainland at the time of European colonization. King (1990:85) proposed that the plank canoe began to be manufactured sometime around cal A.D. 500, basing his argument on the earliest available dates for a distinctive type of flaked chert drill. He proposed that these were appropriate for drilling the holes in the wood planks of which the canoes were constructed. On the basis of available archaeological evidence of plank canoe manufacture, Gamble (2002b) concluded that the earliest evidence may be a few hundred years later. However, Arnold (1995:736; Arnold and Bernard 2005) suggested that the plank canoe was developed at a somewhat later date on the basis of other kinds of evidence, such as the temporal occurrence of swordfish bones and trade goods. Gamble (2002b:313) points out that sewn-plank watercraft technology existed in Polynesia and that Polynesian contact with the people of the Northern Bight is possible, although she states there is little archaeological evidence to support this. The idea that the Chumash plank canoe may be a result of contact with Polynesians has recently been taken up by Jones and Klar (2005; Klar and Jones 2005).

The immediate impact of the development of the plank canoe is not completely apparent, although a noticeable increase in the acquisition of large deep-sea fish such as tuna and swordfish appears to be one result (Arnold and Bernard 2005; Bernard 2004; Davenport et al. 1993; Gamble 2002b). King (1990:85) notes that within a few hundred years after the introduction of the plank canoe, harpoons began to be made, and he proposes that their use would have required such a watercraft.

As discussed later, the plank canoe became important in commerce between the mainland coast and the Channel Islands, and it also became important in fishing. It is possible that moderate expansion in these activities did take place once the plank canoe began to be used, but it seems that the full potential of the plank canoe was not realized until later in prehistory. King (1990:85) suspects that the tule balsa was used prior to the plank canoe, but if so it was of a type reasonably well adapted for channel crossings. It is also possible that some sort of more sophisticated watercraft was in use immediately prior to the introduction of the plank canoe.

Another technological change with important implications is the introduction of the bow and arrow, which replaced the throwing stick (atlatl) and dart sometime around cal A.D. 500 or shortly thereafter, as it did in other parts of California (Moratto 1984:283, 338, 420). Evidence for the introduction of the bow and arrow is a marked decrease in the size of projectile points. The earliest well-documented arrow points are leaf shaped (convex base) in form (Figure 13.3), and it is the dominant form at SBA-117, the basal deposits of which have yielded a radiocarbon date of about cal A.D. 500 (Glassow 1992:113). A square-stemmed form of arrow point possibly also was made in some parts of the Northern Bight (e.g., at VEN-61 near the city of Ojai) (Susia 1962:168), but its temporal placement relative to the much more prevalent leaf-shaped form remains uncertain. Asphaltum was used in attaching leaf-shaped points to arrow shafts, as was the case with the earlier dart points.

As Bradbury (1997:210) points out, the bow and arrow would have been superior in warfare to the throwing stick and dart, and as discussed later, the role of the bow and arrow in intergroup competition within the Santa Barbara Channel region became apparent after cal A.D. 1000. This new weaponry also was used in hunting large game, but it is not yet clear whether subsistence was affected by this technological shift.

King's (1990:99, 228–229) analysis of shell beads from Santa Barbara Channel sites revealed that the production of *Olivella* wall beads, most being a type known as saucers, expanded dramatically near the beginning of this period. Another expansion in the intensity of bead making occurred near the beginning of the next period, considered below, although Kennett (2005:202) proposes that it began as early as cal A.D. 700. King also documents an elaboration in various kinds of bone and stone ornaments and ritual items at the beginning of the period. He (1990:99) proposes that the distribution of beads and ritual objects among burials and within particular localities within a cemetery indicates social differentiation among elite individuals within a village society. He suggests that control of political and economic decision making was in the hands of one group of elite individuals and control of ritual activities was in the hands of another. Regardless of whether this proposal is ultimately supported by additional data, it seems likely that social differentiation increased significantly at the beginning of this period. Other manufactured items, such as stone mortars and pestles, are carefully made but do not appear to be significantly more elaborate than those of the preceding period.

The period between cal A.D. 1 to 1000 was one of significant changes in technology, society, and economy. It is a period in which regional populations apparently grew to much higher levels and several important steps were taken along the road to increasing social and economic complexity. The period clearly deserves more attention than it has received up to now in order to understand the contexts of these changes and their implications for future cultural development.

COMPLEXITY AND CLIMATIC CHANGE, CAL A.D. 1000 TO MISSIONIZATION

At the time of European colonization, the western portion of the Northern Bight was occupied by the Chumash and the eastern portion by the Tongva, who spoke one of the southern California Takic languages. Tongva territory included the Los Angeles basin, the eastern Santa Monica Mountains, and the San Fernando Valley and the hills immediately to the north (Figure 13.4). The Chumashan and Takic language groups are unrelated, yet similarities in their material culture (Hudson and Blackburn 1979:17-41) are testimony to the social and economic relations that linked the Chumash and Tongva. The largest villages and the zone of highest population density existed along the mainland coast of the Santa Barbara Channel between the cities of Carpinteria and Goleta, with village populations reaching as high as 500 to 800 individuals. Interior villages varied considerably in size, the largest being in the Santa Ynez Valley with populations of 150 to 250, and the smallest in remote corners of the interior with populations of 15 to 30 (Applegate 1975; Brown 1967).

All major aspects of Chumash and Tongva cultural systems as they were at the time of European contact were in place by cal A.D. 1300, and considerable research over the past 20 years in the Northern Bight has been concerned with clarifying the nature of cultural complexity during the post cal A.D. 1300 period and the various factors that led to this complexity during the preceding few hundred years. Much of this research has been focused on the effects of climatic and environmental change on the development of complex sociopolitical and economic systems, particularly among coastal populations of the Santa Barbara Channel (Arnold 1992a, 2001c; Gamble 2005; Glassow 1996a; Johnson 2000; Kennett 1998; Kennett and Kennett 2000; Lambert 1994; Raab et al. 1995; Raab and Larson 1997).

Arnold (1987, 1992a; 2001c) was among the first to propose that climatic conditions had a deleterious effect on Santa Barbara Channel populations, suggesting that an unfavorable warm water period between cal A.D. 1150 and 1250 on the Northern Channel Islands created adverse environmental conditions. As a result, sometime between cal A.D. 1200 and 1300 a ranked society emerged. Arnold proposed a new chronological period, the Middle/Late Transition (cal A.D. 1150–1300), which encompassed the changes that occurred during this time interval. In contrast to Arnold, Raab and his colleagues (Raab and Larson 1997; Raab et al. 1995) proposed that droughts, some severe, occurred intermittently during the longer period known as the Medieval Climatic Anomaly (Jones et al. 1999; Stine 1994) between cal A.D. 800 and 1400, these affecting terrestrial resource productivity and freshwater availability. On the basis of seawater temperature and marine productivity records, Kennett and Kennett (2000) proposed that high marine productivity and sustained terrestrial drought occurred between cal A.D. 450 and 1300. It is significant that the Medieval Climatic Anomaly began over 300 years before the Middle/Late Transition and may have played a significant role in the development of social complexity before the Middle/Late Transition. These scholars, as well as others including Walker and Lambert (1989), Colten (1993, 1995), Lambert (1994), Johnson (2000), and Glassow (1996a), hypothesized that socioeconomic complexity arose at least in part as a result of environmental stress that led to social hierarchy and greater complexity.

Gamble (2005) has suggested that solid chronological evidence for long-term climatic change followed by punctuated cultural adjustments is lacking. She has countered the environmentally based arguments by pointing out that hunter-gatherer societies such as the Chumash developed a multitude of adaptive strategies to cope with periodic droughts, El Niño events, and other environmental perturbations. She concurs with King (1990), who has suggested that cultural change was more gradual. An understanding of the basis for these varying viewpoints requires consideration of the results of archeological research accomplished over the past few decades that has focused on the latter part of the Middle Period, the Late Period, and the nature of Chumash sociopolitical organization at the beginning of European colonization.

An important key to understanding social complexity is the nature and scope of craft specialization. The archaeology and ethnohistory of Santa Cruz Island provided some of the first evidence of this. King (1976) compiled evidence of craft specialization on the island in his elucidation of intervillage exchange networks within regions occupied by the Chumash people, which King defined as three major ecological zones, the Northern Channel Islands, the mainland coast, and the interior (or inland area). Later research by Arnold and her colleagues yielded details of the nature of craft specialization (Arnold 1987, 1992a;

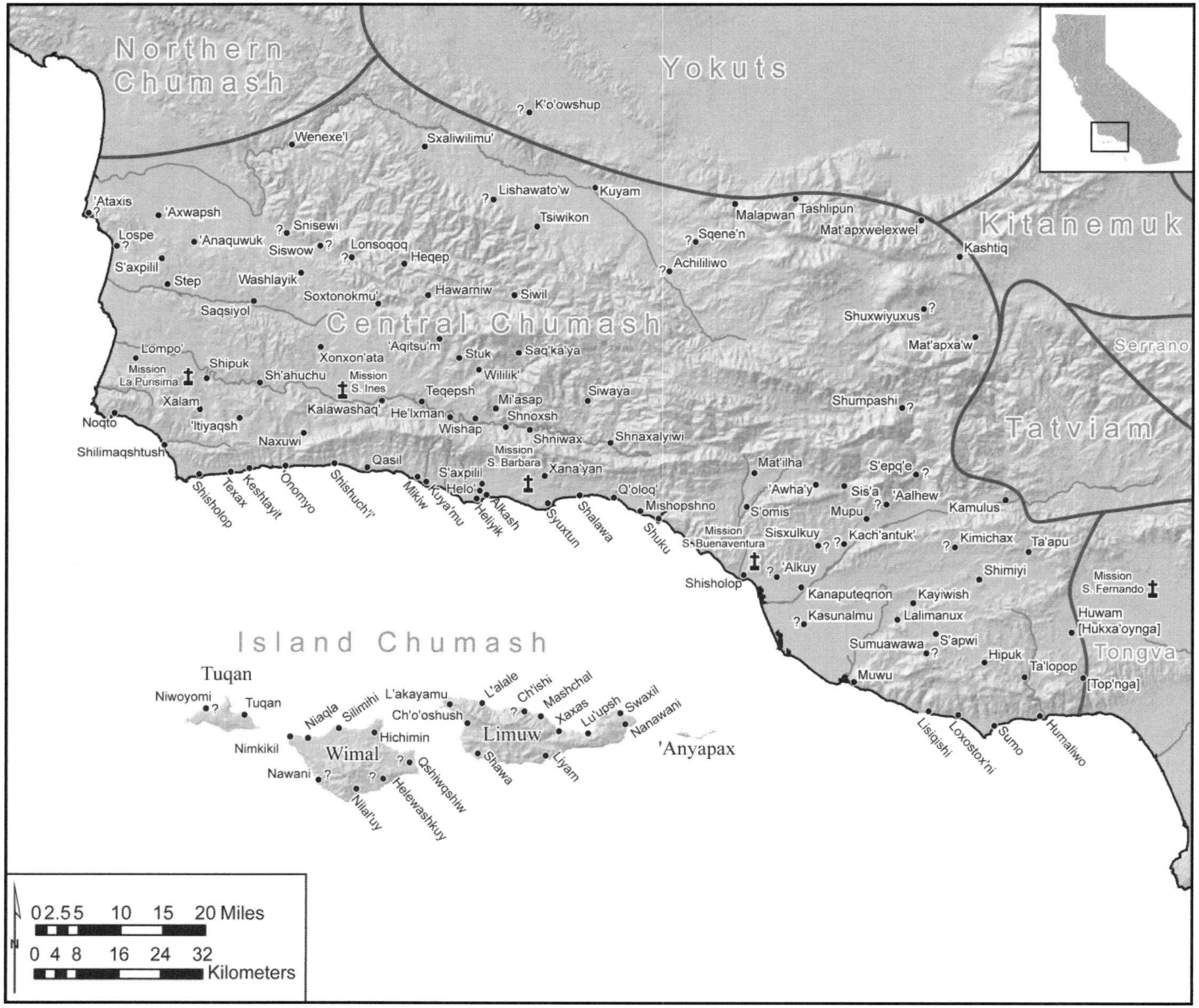

Figure 13.4. Approximate location of tribal groups, Northern Bight region (after McLendon and Johnson 1999).

Arnold and Graesch 2001; Arnold and Munns 1994; Arnold et al. 2001; Preziosi 2001) through analysis of large collections of microblades, microblade drills, bead manufacturing detritus, and beads. As a result of this research, it is now apparent that from about cal A.D. 1200 until missionization, island populations were the exclusive manufacturers of literally millions of shell beads. The beads were perforated by drill tips made from chert microblades, most of which were manufactured in large quantities at villages in the eastern sector of Santa Cruz Island. The exchange of the beads for mainland products, and the intensive use of the beads in exchange relationships throughout mainland Chumash territory and beyond, resulted in one of the most developed regional economic exchange systems in North America.

Arnold and her colleagues (Arnold and Graesch 2001; Arnold and Munns 1994) suggested that the manufacturers of shell beads and microblades became specialized during the Middle/Late Period Transition, cal A.D. 1150 to 1200, although a smaller-scale expansion appears to have occurred about 200 to 400 years earlier, perhaps coeval with the advent of microblade drill manufacture (Kennett 2005:202–206). Beginning about cal A.D. 1200 the more costly and time-consuming *Olivella biplicata* callus beads began to be made, a type that has been identified as a monetary currency at the time of European contact (Arnold and Munns 1994; Arnold and Graesch 2001:80; King 1976). Arnold (1987:220; Preziosi 2001:157–161) also noted a shift at this time in microblade production, from trapezoidal forms produced in the later Middle Period to prepared triangular forms manufactured in the Late Period. In conjunction with this shift, Arnold suggests that the centers of microblade production were reorganized, with centralization of the industry on Santa Cruz Island.

Arnold (1992a, 2001c) and Munns and Arnold (2002) also examined settlement patterns at this time and noted that relatively few sites on Santa Cruz Island have been securely dated to the Middle/Late Transition Period. Arnold (1992a:76) proposed that several Middle Period settlements on Santa Cruz Island were suddenly abandoned about cal A.D. 1200–1300. Furthermore, Munns and Arnold (2002) suggest that fish supplanted shellfish as a dietary mainstay at about this time. As well, osteological evidence indicates an overall decline in health and an increase in violence (Lambert 1994). This lasted until about cal A.D. 1300, when Munns and Arnold (2002) suggest that violence decreased and the health of inhabitants improved.

Significant archaeological work also has occurred on Santa Rosa and San Miguel Islands. Kennett (1998) and Kennett and Conlee (2002) stated that the earliest evidence for settled villages on these islands occurs at about cal A.D. 650. Kennett (1998, 2005; Kennett and Conlee 2002) noted that some settlement locations on these islands were disrupted between cal A.D. 1150 and 1300, perhaps because of drought (Kennett and Conlee 2002). However, after this period, many of these same settlement locations were reoccupied. The dietary importance of fish increased after cal A.D. 950 and remained important thereafter. As well, evidence of bead making dates to this time on eastern Santa Rosa Island. On San Miguel Island, the production of mortars and pestles at 16 sites increased in importance after cal A.D. 650. A greater emphasis on territoriality appears to have begun around cal A.D. 650, seemingly related to competition for terrestrial resources, especially freshwater (Kennett 1998; Kennett and Conlee 2002; Kennett and Kennett 2000).

Evidence for climatically induced change along the Santa Barbara Channel mainland coast is not as definitive as appears to be the case on the Northern Channel Islands. Part of the reason is the lack of systematic, focused attention on the post cal A.D. 1000 period on the mainland, but the inability to distinguish between Terminal Middle Period and Late Period deposits due to rodent disturbance is another obvious reason. The Corral Canyon site (SBA-1731), one of the few with intact stratified deposits, dates between cal A.D. 500 and 1600, therefore spanning the Middle/Late Transition (Erlandson and Rick 2002a). Erlandson found that the faunal and floral assemblages at the site were diverse, including an abundance of fish and sea mammal remains, and that the site shows "little evidence of unusually warm water temperatures or any serious degradation of the marine environment" (Erlandson and Rick 2002a:175–176). The faunal assemblage at the Pitas Point site (VEN-27), a mainland coastal site in the Ventureño Chumash region occupied between approximately cal A.D. 1000 and 1500 (Gamble 1983), provides additional evidence of subsistence during the Middle/Late Transition. Ongoing analysis of the fish remains (Shalom 2005) indicates a diverse assemblage of fish, with numerous pelagic species. The assemblage indicates that there was no shortage of fish during this time interval. In addition, Walker's analysis of sea mammal remains from the site (personal communication, 1997) revealed that forelimb bones of fur seal were much more common in deposits dating between cal A.D. 1000 and 1150 than in deposits dating to the later years of occupation. He suggested that these cuts of meat were traded from the Channel Island rookeries to the site during the late Middle Period.

There is also evidence for the specialized manufacture of artifacts at both sites. At Corral Canyon, 1,460 fragments of *Olivella biplicata* shell indicate that the inhabitants were making cup beads from the callus portion of the shell (Erlandson and Rick 2002a). The density of bead detritus from this site is higher than that from any other mainland channel site and overlaps the lower range of densities in sites on the Northern Channel Islands (Arnold and Graesch 2001). At the Pitas Point site, over 650 tarring pebbles used to line the interior of water bottles with asphaltum were collected. In addition, a basket-making activity area was found in a probable Middle/Late Transitional period level in one of the houses (Gamble 1983). Water bottles may have been produced for export in response to drought-induced water scarcity in other areas of the Santa Barbara Channel (Gamble 2005:100). Also, Wake (2001:196) noted evidence for the manufacture of deer bone tools at the Pitas Point site and suggested that awls and other bone implements may have been produced there and then traded to Santa Cruz Island.

The presence of several large Late Period settlements along the Santa Barbara mainland coast indicates that regional population probably reached its peak during this period, although accurate population estimates are not available. This larger population size may be related to the earlier development of important subsistence technologies (discussed earlier) and economic exchange networks that allowed villages not only to cope more effectively with hard times but also to grow (King 1990; Erlandson and Rick 2002a; Glassow 1996a). Arrow points also changed in form around the beginning of the Late Period or slightly before. The leaf-shaped form was replaced with a concave base form typical of many regions of California and the Great Basin (typically called the cottonwood triangular type, Figure 13.3). This change in point form correlates with the abandonment of the use of asphaltum in hafting.

At the time of European contact, the Chumash of the Vandenberg region were not as complex as those living along the Santa Barbara Channel. Glassow (1996a, 2002a) proposes that this was due in part to the absence of plank canoes north of Point Conception. As was the case along the Santa Barbara Channel, populations in the Vandenberg region probably grew during the course of the Late Period. The population in this region abruptly began to rise after cal A.D. 600 and peaked during the Late Period (Glassow 1996a:101, 2002a:200–203). Associated with population growth was a refinement of technology and intensification of subsistence, although the use of maritime resources in the Vandenberg region was rather conservative in comparison to the channel region (Glassow 2002a:191). Shellfish remained the principal food (70 percent of the protein) throughout the Late Holocene. Nonetheless, fishing from shore, probably using hooks and nets, became relatively more important after cal A.D. 1200, as did intensive hunting of aquatic birds from lagoon habitats.

Changes in subsistence in the Vandenberg region also correlated with changes in settlement patterns, with more sites situated in a greater diversity of environmental situations during the Late Period. The high density of sites and diversity of locations indicates a high degree of mobility (Glassow 2002a:192), but this period is also characterized by longer-term principal residential bases, such as at the village site of Noqto (SBA-210) (Glassow 2002a:194).

Population growth in the Vandenberg region also may be related to more intensive economic exchange (Glassow 2002a). The increased density of shell beads and ornaments imported from the Santa Barbara Channel area, including *Olivella* callus cups, in sites occupied after cal A.D. 1200 indicates that Vandenberg populations participated in the regional money-based economic system concentrated along the central Santa Barbara Channel coast, but did not manufacture the beads on which the system was based. Archaeological evidence does suggest that large, high-quality Monterey chert bifacial preforms (Arnold 1992b) were manufactured at Vandenberg sites for exchange to adjacent regions, where they may have been used to make the knife and harpoon points that are common in Late Period sites (Glassow 1996a:142, 2002a:198). In summary, Glassow (2002a:203) suggested that the changes in Late Period society in the Vandenberg region may be linked to local population growth, possible immigration (Glassow 1996a:138), and external processes and events that took place along the adjacent Santa Barbara Channel.

As was the case in the Vandenberg region, population in the inland area of Santa Barbara County, including the central Santa Ynez Valley watershed and the mountain ranges and canyons northward to the margins of the Carrizo Plain, was not as dense as along the Santa Barbara Channel coast. An important question addressed by archaeologists who have investigated sites in this region is the relations between occupants of these inland areas with populations along the channel coast. Spanne (1975) suggested that populations from the coast migrated to the interior during the winter to take advantage of steelhead trout run on the Santa Ynez River. During the summer inland groups migrated to the coast to fish in the Santa Barbara Channel. Others (Glassow 1979; Tainter 1971a, 1972, 1975) have also considered implications of the inland-coastal seasonal variation in resource availability, but have suggested instead that the strategy employed was exchange of subsistence resources, not movement of people (Horne 1981; Macko 1983; McRae 1999).

Horne (1981) proposed that by the Middle Period, occupation of the inland region was based on a seasonal round centered on larger residential bases. Population likely expanded during the Middle Period, probably in association with increasing differentiation in social and economic roles, as was the case along the Santa Barbara Channel. Exchange with coastal villages and intervillage social and political ties based on marriage, which ethnohistorical studies have documented, probably had its origin sometime during the Middle Period (Horne 1981:194–195). Horne (1981:56) noted the increasing complexity of exchange during the Late Period, with the development of regional craft specialization and religious practices analogous to those along the channel coast.

Several sites provide subsistence and other data that can be used to evaluate Horne's propositions. The site of Xonxon'ata (SBA-3404; Hildebrandt 2004) has provided critical data for understanding not only subsistence but also exchange relationships with the coast. The fish assemblage is dominated by species well suited for exchange, such as sardines and anchovies (83 percent). The shellfish assemblage is dominated by mussels (70.4 percent), which were probably transported whole and alive from the coast, a distance of 27–33 kilometers. Other inland sites, such as SBA-485 (Macko 1983) and SBA-2358 (Anderson 1997), show a similar pattern of abundant remains of small schooling or other fish and shellfish.

Other items derived from the coast at Xonxon'ata include stone bowl fragments of steatite probably from Santa Catalina Island and numerous shell beads, many of which are *Olivella* cupped beads. Hildebrandt (2004:80) suggested that the coastal-interior exchange network during the Late Period may have become more important when interior population densities increased to a point at which local deer herds became depleted and the need arose for nonlocal sources of meat. The faunal assemblages from the Xonxon'ata site and other inland sites, such as SBA-485 (Macko 1983), are consistent with this proposal in that lagomorph bones are far in excess of artiodactyl bones. Collections from another inland Chumash village site provides a contrasting picture. The site of Soxtonokmu' (SBA-167), occupied from the Late through Historic Periods (cal A.D. 1500 to 1804), has a relatively high frequency of deer bone and low frequency of shellfish remains and fish bone (McRae 1999:129). Unlike other inland sites that may not have had enough deer meat available, it is possible that the inhabitants of Soxtonokmu' did not need as much coastally derived fish and shellfish to supplement their diet. Basketry and deer bone tools may have been produced at the site for trade with other villages, including coastal settlements.

The available evidence from inland sites, although still sparse, indicates that the area had relatively dense population by the end of the Middle Period, as well as exchange relationships with the coast that apparently expanded during the Late Period. The goods traded between inland and coastal villages probably included such items as toolstone, basketry, bone tools, and pine nuts, but the commodities traded undoubtedly varied, reflecting the environmental diversity that characterized the inland area. Based on the size and internal organization of Late Period sites and limited mortuary data, it is likely that ranked social organization existed in the inland communities, similar to that seen in coastal villages.

The Santa Monica Mountains and interior valleys within and immediately to the north are separated from the Santa Barbara Channel and the inland areas north of the channel by the broad, low-lying lands on either side of the Santa Clara River mouth. Although Late Period coastal villages in this region were not as large as those along the Santa Barbara Channel mainland coast, patterns of settlement, subsistence, and social organization were generally similar (Gamble and Russell 2002). Population size peaked during the period after cal A.D. 1000, and settlements were integrated into regional sociopolitical organizations based on hereditary ranking (Gamble et al. 2001), specialization, and exchange. Sedentary coastal settlements were linked through exchange of fish and other resources with smaller settlements located in the interior valleys (King 1990; Gamble and Russell 2002).

There is some disagreement over the nature and degree of sedentism among late prehistoric inland populations of the Santa Monica Mountains. King (2000:75) identifies the presence of permanent prehistoric inland villages and notes that botanical evidence from the inland village of Talepop (LAN-229) is indicative of year-round occupation. In contrast, Van Horn (1987:63–74) suggests that there were no large, permanently occupied settlements in the interior; rather, population centers were located on the coast with only a few scattered semipermanent villages in the interior. Dillon and Boxt (1989:152–159) suggest a shifting village or rancheria model of settlements in the Santa Monica Mountains and interior valleys. They propose that permanent inland villages did not exist and that population congregated into larger settlements during winter months and dispersed as small family groups during the late spring and summer months.

At the time of European contact, the Tongva occupied the Los Angeles basin and lands immediately north. Takic-speaking people apparently expanded into the Los Angeles basin relatively late in prehistory, although archaeologists' opinions differ with regard to the timing of this expansion (see Chapter 6 in this volume). A recent analysis of skeletal collections from the Southern Channel Islands indicates that Takic-speaking people likely replaced earlier populations who spoke an unrelated language sometime around 500 cal B.C. (Kerr 2004:139), although the replacement surely would have been earlier on the mainland.

It has often been assumed that the Tongva had settlement systems, subsistence strategies, and social organizations similar to but not as complex as their northerly Chumash neighbors. This argument is based largely on the projection of ethnohistoric and ethnographic data into the past (Bean and Smith 1978; Hudson 1969, 1971; McCawley 1996). Following this logic, scholars have argued that the Tongva lived in politically autonomous, socially stratified villages with populations of approximately 150 people. Systematically recovered archaeological data that support such a conclusion are minimal, possibly due in part to the destruction of village sites by urban development. Recent archaeological research (Grenda and Altschul 2002a) provides a somewhat different picture: habitation sites were hierarchically organized around estuaries (Grenda and Altschul 2002a:128) but settlement sizes were highly variable across the basin, reflecting resource availability. Grenda and Altschul (2002a:129) suggest that some estuaries supported large habitation sites, while others were characterized by a rancheria pattern of linked but dispersed small habitation sites. Grenda and Altschul (2002b:166) also maintain that populations at smaller estuaries practiced a strategy of mobility, with at least part of the population dispersing to forage in other areas during periods of resource stress. Research on subsistence remains from the Playa Vista/Ballona Creek area (Altschul et al. 1992; Becker 2003; Grenda et al. 1994; Maxwell 2003) supports the idea that subsistence practices focused primarily on local estuarine, coastal, and near-coast resources. This research identifies a generalized subsistence base of a broad mix of terrestrial and marine resources with a shift from lagoon to sandy shoreline shellfish species as lagoon environments silted in. Fishing concentrated on nearshore environments with relatively little exploitation of deep-sea resources (Maxwell 2003; Salls 1985a, 1987; Salls and Cairns 1994).

Based on the distribution of similar stone effigies (Gamble and Russell 2002), it appears that the prehistoric Tongva shared at least some aspects of ritual with the Santa Monica Mountains Chumash to the north. In contrast, the presence of some cremations at Tongva sites during this period, which are essentially absent at Chumash sites, indicates a degree of social separation from the Chumash, despite interaction with other Takic-speaking groups to the east and south (Gamble and Russell 2002).

As the Spanish began to explore and eventually colonize the Northern Bight, the Chumash and their Tongva neighbors had the most complex political and economic organization in California, and, for that matter, in all of western North America. Johnson (2000) was able to elucidate important aspects of this complexity through his extensive analysis of mission register data, particularly through consideration of geographic patterns in intervillage marriages. His analysis indicated that politically independent households and villages in different environmental zones were linked through marriages and matrilocal residence, which would have served as the basis for an exchange system that distributed goods throughout the Northern Bight and beyond. As King (1976) had argued, this exchange system minimized localized subsistence stress resulting from climatic fluctuation through distribution of resources from one area to another.

WHEN DID COMPLEX SOCIOPOLITICAL, RELIGIOUS, AND ECONOMIC SYSTEMS DEVELOP IN THE NORTHERN BIGHT?

Although important changes in economic organization occurred during the Middle/Late Transition, particularly with regard to the production and use of shell bead money, there is clear evidence of social and political complexity prior to the transition. This evidence is manifest in mortuary practices, religious artifacts, sweat lodges and houses, and the nature of the plank canoe. Compelling evidence from mortuary contexts for the existence of a ranked society with a hereditary elite is apparent at least by the late Middle Period in the Santa Barbara Channel area (Gamble et al. 2001, 2002). Bioarchaeological data from a cemetery at the coastal site of Malibu (LAN-264) dating to Middle Period Phase 5 (cal A.D. 900 to 1150) indicate that ranking and hereditary leadership had emerged at least by this time.

Evidence from other sites with mortuary data point to ranking and hereditary leadership prior to the Late Period. A burial from Mescalitan Island (SBA-46) that dates to Middle Period Phase 5c (cal A.D. 1050 to 1150; Glassow et al. 1986) is indicative of significant social complexity. The burial was originally found in a flexed position face down on the surface of a whalebone scapula that was elaborately decorated with hundreds of inlaid shell beads and ornaments. Other elaborate grave offerings included hundreds more shell beads, a wide-mouth sandstone bowl mortar with inlaid beads, a large stone tubular bead with inlaid shell disk beads, other tubular stone beads, and abalone ornaments (Orr 1943).

It is also of interest that subterranean sweat lodges were used throughout the region at least by the Middle Period and eventually became standardized in their shape and appearance (Gamble 1991, 1995). By the Historic Period, sweat lodges in the interior and coastal areas of the Chumash region were almost identical in appearance, as can be seen in examples at H'elexman (SBA-485) in the Santa Ynez Valley, Mikiw (SBA-78) on the mainland coast, Wenexe'l (SLO-94/95) in the Cuyama River valley, and the Mathews site (excavated by W. D. Strong in the 1930s), also in the Cuyama River valley.

The plank canoe *(tomol)* was a complex watercraft, entailing sewn-plank technology, by 1500 years ago, if not centuries earlier (Gamble 2002b). The *tomol* was not only important in the intensification of maritime subsistence, but was also central to an interregional system of exchange. Significant items exchanged throughout southern California and even farther by the end of the Middle Period included not only shell beads and ornaments but also steatite artifacts, chipped stone materials, mortars, pestles, and red ochre.

In summary, a great deal of sociopolitical, economic, and religious complexity clearly existed during the latter part of the Middle Period, and significant elements of this complexity originated centuries earlier. Much of the disagreement regarding the nature of this complexity revolves around when hereditary leadership originated. It seems likely that differences in interpretation of the existing data will be resolved once models of hereditary leadership and its development become more diverse and incorporate greater detail about how it operated over the course of time.

CONCLUSION

Compared to other regions of California, prehistoric cultural systems of the Northern Bight are distinctive in certain respects. As many have pointed out over the years, the relatively quiet waters of the Northern Bight, particularly in the Santa Barbara Channel, allowed for the use of watercraft for marine fishing and commerce between the mainland coast and the Channel Islands. It is also significant that nowhere else in California were islands inhabited by populations that articulated socially and economically with the mainland. This juxtaposition of islands (including the Northern Channel Islands and Santa Catalina Island) and the mainland gave a distinctive flavor to the prehistory of the Northern Bight, particularly later in prehistory as islanders began to manufacture quantities of craft items of interest to mainlanders.

The prehistory of the Northern Bight also extends farther back in time than is the case in most other regions of California, and prehistoric cultural systems span an unusually wide spectrum between simple and complex. The earliest peoples of the Northern Bight appear not to have had sociopolitical or economic organizations any more complex than found elsewhere in California, although they may have been living at higher densities. Beginning around 4,000 years ago or shortly afterward, the first strong hints of social and economic complexity are manifest, although on a moderate scale. From then on, signs of complexity become more obvious and diverse, and by the time of European contact, the Chumash and their coastal Tongva neighbors had hereditary political offices and a social elite, different sorts of regional organization, and a well-developed shell bead currency that facilitated intervillage and cross-channel commerce. With regard to the latter characteristic, nowhere else in California was a regional economy as monetized as in the Northern Bight, even though shell bead money was used throughout California.

Northern Bight prehistory also witnessed significant technological changes that affected many aspects of ecological adaptation, society, and economy. These include the mortar and pestle, shell fishhook, harpoon, plank canoe, bow and arrow, and microblades.

Of these, the plank canoe and microblades are not shared by other California groups, and both are intimately associated with the rise of complex sociopolitical organization, microblades being used in the manufacture of shell beads on a relatively large scale and plank canoes requiring considerable investments of time and expertise in their manufacture, let alone their facilitation of cross-channel commerce. Both reflect the importance of offshore island populations in the development of complexity.

It is not surprising that archaeologists working in the Northern Bight over the past 20 years have been concentrating their attention on the evolution of complex sociopolitical and economic organization. Moreover, it is not surprising that most of this attention has been focused on the developments over the last millennium, when different archaeological manifestations of complexity are most apparent. As we have emphasized, however, complexity has deep roots in the region's prehistory, and it is certainly worth considering its earlier forms in order to develop a fuller picture of its evolution and to explore the various determinants of this evolution. One of the variables underlying the evolution of complexity in the Northern Bight is population growth. We have pointed out that population growth becomes obvious beginning sometime around 1,500 years ago, and it seems likely that relatively high levels were reached by 1,000 years ago. The development of new subsistence technology, including particularly the mortar and pestle, shell fishhook, and plank canoe, allowed expansion of the resource base to include new foods and greater access to foods already part of the diet. Although archaeological evidence is circumstantial, food storage, particularly of acorns and dried fish, undoubtedly had become important as well. Consequently, increasing numbers of people could be supported within the Northern Bight. The expansion of regional economic systems involving various manufactured items such as shell beads, which could be exchanged for food resources, may also have played a role in supporting population growth.

Another focus of interest developing over the past 20 years has been the role of environmental change in fostering or triggering cultural change. A fundamental problem in attempting to explore the relationship between these two realms of change has been the specificity of paleoenvironmental records. The water temperature and marine productivity records produced by Kennett and Kennett (2000; Kennett 2005) are impressive in their detail and the trend patterns they display. However, they are not direct records of the distribution and abundance of specific kinds of food resources on which prehistoric people depended. Models that make the translation between the records and food resources are still rudimentary, and as a result the arguments made by archaeologists regarding the effects of environmental change on subsistence are necessarily simplistic (Gamble 2005). A related problem is that paleoenvironmental records do not inform on all relevant aspects of the environment. For instance, the Kennett and Kennett (2000) records pertain to marine productivity but not necessarily to terrestrial productivity. The controversies over the past two decades surrounding the role of environmental change discussed above generally revolve around interpretation of paleoenvironmental records and the kind of impact, if any, that environmental change had on cultural systems, particularly in the realm of subsistence. The resolution of these controversies probably will not be forthcoming until new or refined paleoenvironmental records become available and archaeologists develop more explicit models of resource utilization and its effect on different realms of cultural behavior.

Looking to the future, archaeology will continue to make progress in understanding the prehistory of the Northern Bight, but the rate of progress depends on whether several important issues are addressed. First, as is true of regional archaeological programs elsewhere in California, attention must be given to reevaluating and refining chronology. Many conclusions about the chronology of a site's occupation are based on a few radiocarbon dates, which may mean that some interpretations about the course of prehistory are simply wrong. The difficulty with chronology is particularly acute with regard to drawing conclusions about relatively short time spans such as the Middle/Late Transition and the time intervals immediately before and after.

Second, inland areas of the Bight, particularly the larger valleys that contain many sites, need substantially more attention. The number of investigated sites is very low in most inland watersheds, and knowledge of their prehistory is meager. Considering the exchange relationships that existed between inland and coastal areas throughout prehistory, and the possibility that coastal and inland areas were joined in one settlement system during earlier periods of prehistory, knowledge of regional prehistory will remain skewed without more knowledge derived from inland sites. However, such sites offer archaeologists some difficult challenges in that many lack obvious organic materials that may serve as radiocarbon samples. This is especially the case with sites dating to the Early and Middle Holocene. More intensive recovery techniques than have been typical may need to be applied to obtain datable material.

Third, it makes sense to continue the relatively high level of archaeological activity on the Channel Islands, which began about 20 years ago. Much of the recent focus on the Channel Islands is a result of significantly greater access in comparison to mainland areas, but the needs of CRM programs have also driven much of this research. Nonetheless, this island focus has important implications for elucidating the prehistory of the Northern Bight as a whole. Because sites have not been disturbed by land development and there are no rodent burrowing problems, the prospect for building high-resolution chronologies is substantially greater than on the mainland. As a consequence, knowledge of prehistory on the Channel Islands will provide a basis for a better understanding of the relatively more blurred prehistory on the mainland.

We can also expect future archaeologists to devote greater attention to some of the theoretical arguments prevalent within archaeology today. Currently theories derived from evolutionary and behavioral ecology and others concerned with social and political organization are commonly employed in developing explanations for cultural change and diversity in the Northern Bight. As more control is gained over chronology and as new or refined measures of human behavior are developed, applications of these theories will become more explicit. The region's archaeology will likely allow new theoretical constructions to be developed, particularly because the Northern Bight's archaeological record is so rich and diverse and spans such a long period of prehistory.

CHAPTER 14

Prehistory of the Southern Bight: Models for a New Millennium

BRIAN F. BYRD AND L. MARK RAAB

THE GEOGRAPHICAL FOCUS OF THIS CHAPTER IS California's Southern Bight, roughly the southern half of the arc extending from the Mexican border to Point Conception. As defined here, this region encompasses Orange and San Diego Counties, western Riverside County, and the offshore islands of Santa Catalina, San Clemente, and San Nicolas (the Southern Channel Islands). At the time of Spanish contact this region was occupied by native groups (Figures 14.1, 14.2) most commonly referred to as the Tongva (Gabrielino), Juaneño (Ajachemen), Luiseño, and Kumeyaay (Bean and Shipek 1978; Bean and Smith 1978; Kroeber 1925; Luomala 1978; McCawley 1996). Our objective in this chapter is to present a regional summary of research on California prehistory since the appearance of Moratto's (1984) *California Archaeology* and Chartkoff and Chartkoff's (1984) *The Archaeology of California*.

The Southern Bight is remarkably well suited to such a retrospective analysis. This region illustrates a number of important research advances that have been made since the appearance of those two volumes. Data from this area allow us to assess in considerable detail some of the ideas advanced by Moratto and the Chartkoffs. At the same time, however, these studies have generated data that provoke fundamentally different understandings of California prehistory than those in the decades leading up to publication of the two 1984 books. These advances, outlined below, seem likely to propel archaeological research in new directions in the new millennium.

Though they expressed differing perspectives, *California Archaeology* and the *Archaeology of California* were the most comprehensive and also the first statewide syntheses of California prehistory. Both appeared at a time when California archaeology was on the cusp of enormous changes. Following the 1970s, the field experienced an explosive proliferation of archaeological information under the aegis of contract archaeology, the "radiocarbon revolution," and the appearance of a large cadre of archaeologists holding diverse theoretical viewpoints. The result, signaled by the appearance of the two books, was the rise of California archaeology as an intellectual force in its own right. They not only reflected the transformation of California archaeology but also sketched pathways along which research would develop over the following two decades, posing interesting questions about the nature and timing of prehistoric culture change. Chartkoff and Chartkoff (1984), for example, emphasized broad patterns of progressive cultural development, culminating in Late Holocene cultural climaxes characterized by high degrees of adaptive success. By contrast, Moratto (1984:460–464) suggested that culture change may have been more regionally and temporally variable than previously thought, and included episodes of culture change caused by such factors as climatic stresses. One of the most prescient questions posed by Moratto (1984:104–113) was whether a Paleo-Coastal Tradition actually had existed along the California coastline during the Early Holocene, breaking sharply with traditional views of seafaring and intensive maritime adaptations as Late Holocene developments. In the discussion that follows, we point out the ways in which researchers working in the Southern Bight have made significant progress in addressing the following questions:

- Was prehistoric culture change relatively gradual and developmental or more punctuated and multidirectional?
- Did trans-Holocene culture change stem essentially from terrestrial cultural adaptations or did the coastlines play an important early role?
- Did prehistoric culture change result in Late Holocene cultural climaxes characterized by high levels of adaptive success or was change induced by resource scarcity?
- Did environmental stresses play an important role in prehistoric culture change or was change driven by essentially intracultural forces?
- Can California prehistory be explained best in terms of broad developmental stages or regional cultural variability?

Creating a coherent picture of these research advances in the study area inevitably forces certain com-

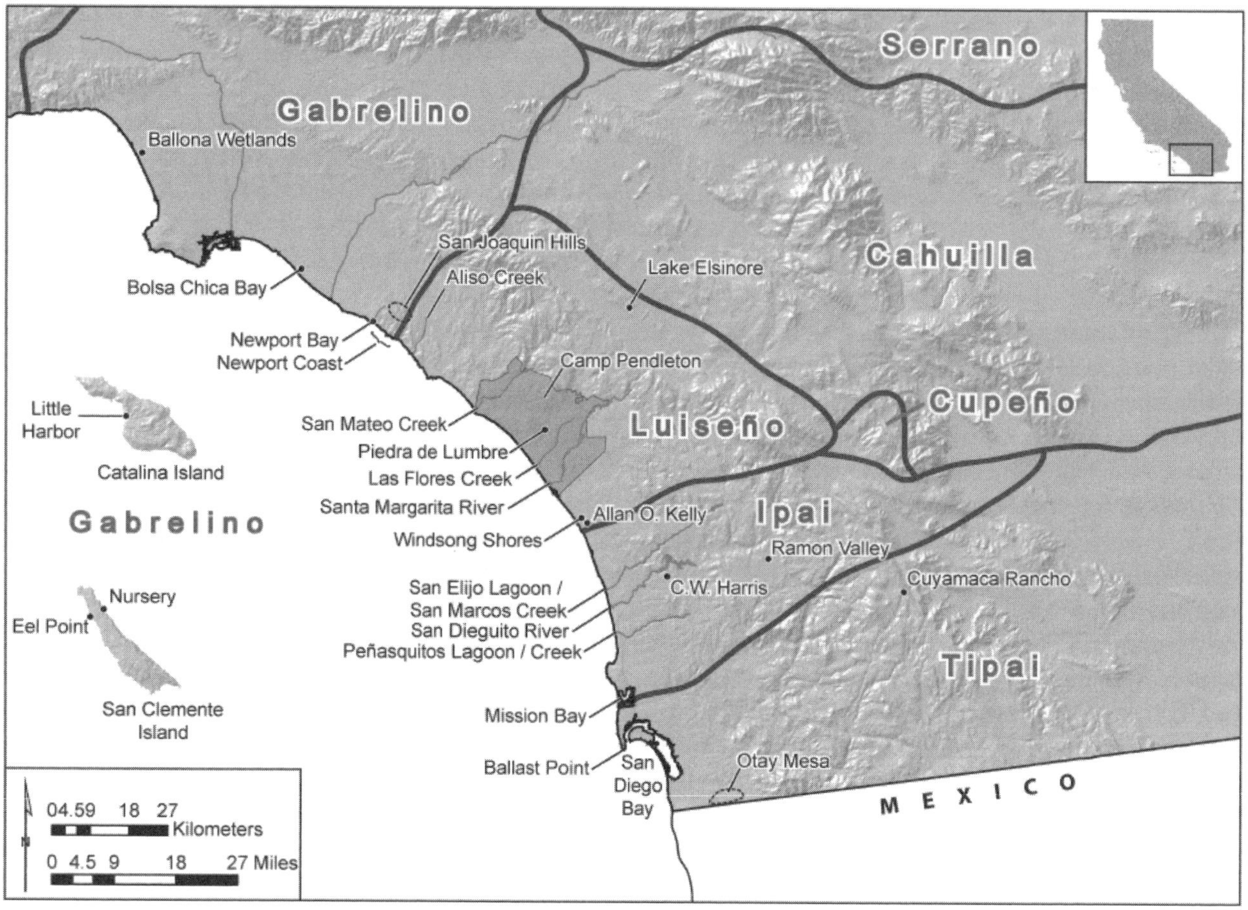

Figure 14.1. Ethnographic divisions, archaeological sites, and locations of the Southern Bight.

promises, one of which is our exclusive focus on the prehistoric era. Although historic-era archaeology has made great strides during the past two decades, space limitations do not allow us to treat this topic here. Literally thousands of reports dealing with the prehistory of the study area have appeared during the past two decades—far too many to cite let alone synthesize here. Instead, we summarize what we consider to be important advances on key research topics. This is partly a subjective decision, but it also reflects the research topics that have dominated peer-reviewed publications from the study area. These research themes largely draw on results from the mainland coastal area and the Southern Channel Islands, and to a much lesser extent on results from the more inland parts of the study area. In taking this approach, we emphasize topics that link this large and varied region together and reflect subject matter largely unexplored in the seminal 1984 books. There is no question that the perspectives presented in this chapter are heavily influenced by our own research experiences in the study region; however, we try to acknowledge divergent theoretical viewpoints and interpretations. We may also be able to bring some useful perspectives to this discussion, since both of us have had the good fortune to be involved in long-term, multifaceted research projects in the region. Moreover, this experience encompasses both mainland and insular (Southern Channel Islands) settings.

Our overall approach in this summary is to highlight selected projects and publications that best illustrate the changing research context of the Southern Bight, including the Ballona wetlands, Marine Corps Base Camp Pendleton, Lake Elsinore, Newport coast and bay projects, San Joaquin Hills projects, San Clemente Island, and San Nicolas Island (Altschul and Grenda 2002; Altschul et al. 1992; Byrd and Berryman 2006; Gamble and Russell 2002; Grenda 1997; Grenda et al. 1994; Koerper et al. 2002; Mason et al. 1997; Raab 1997; Raab et al. 2002; Reddy and Berryman 1999a, b;Vellanoweth et al. 2002) (Figure 14.1; Table 14.1).

THE RADIOCARBON REVOLUTION: HOW OLD IS THE PAST?

Modern archaeology has been aided by many technical advances but none more important than the radiocar-

Figure 14.2. Native Luiseño woman, Pi-yum'ko, Coronacion Pauvel, San Diego September 1901. (Courtesy of the Bancroft Library, University of California–Berkeley, photograph by C. Hart Merriam, cat. no. 1978.008/2300/p4 no. 1.)

bon revolution. Archaeological progress depends directly on accurately determining the age of objects and events from the past. Yet during most of the twentieth century, archaeologists were often forced to work with only a relative sense of time, usually as a result of observing changes in the style of artifacts they excavated from the layers of archaeological sites (Trigger 1989). It was not until the 1970s and 1980s that radiocarbon dating was routinely employed in California archaeology, and the increased levels of research funding afforded by cultural resources management (CRM) archaeology played a major role in this trend. During the past two decades, detailed chronologies of prehistoric cultural development have become available for the first time in many regions of California (Breschini et al. 2004). For example, Koerper et al. (2002:67) note that almost 1,300 radiocarbon dates are now available for Orange County alone. San Clemente Island is currently represented by about 400 radiocarbon dates, San Nicolas Island may rival this number, and Camp Pendleton has more than 200 radiocarbon dates (Byrd and Reddy 2002; Vellanoweth et al. 2002). This rich database is allowing researchers to move away from coarse-grained cultural sequences (Early, Middle, Late; Paleo-Indian, Archaic, Late Prehistoric) and really track the tempo of change, note the precise point in time for key developments, and provide a coherent approach to correlating the timing of external variables and internal social change. Much more rigorous use of radiocarbon data is needed (beyond simple comparisons of aggregate number of dates per century), along with consistent reporting, calibration, and use of the reservoir correction (Byrd et al. 2004).

CHRONOLOGY OF PREHISTORY: EARLY, MIDDLE, AND LATE HOLOCENE

California archaeologists advanced many different prehistoric cultural chronologies during the twentieth century (Moratto 1984:xxxii–xxxiii). While these chronologies were constructed to serve various research objectives, we have essentially adopted Erlandson and Colten's (1991:1–2) division of the Holocene into Early, Middle, and Late subdivisions. This approach offers an intuitive and consistent alternative to the disparate and sometimes confusing chronologies found in the archaeological literature. For our purposes we have broken the Holocene into the following three-part chronology: Early Holocene, 9600 cal B.C. to 5600 cal B.C.; Middle Holocene, 5600 to 1650 cal B.C.; and Late Holocene, 1650 cal B.C. to cal A.D. 1769 (Spanish colonization of California with first mission constructed at San Diego).

The Early Holocene

TRADITIONAL MODELS OF EARLY HUMAN SETTLEMENT As discussed in Chapter 4, traditional models of California prehistory postulate that the state's first inhabitants were Paleo-Indian big-game hunters who ranged across North America during the closing phases of the last Ice Age (Fagan 2003; Moratto 1984; Wallace 1978). Evidence for Paleo-Indian occupation of southern California, particularly the coastal areas, remains scanty at best (Erlandson 1991b), and there is still wide-ranging support for scenarios that derive California's first coastal populations from the interior of western North America, perhaps as a result of the impact of post-Pleistocene climate change (Erlandson 1994:269–272). As the (Wisconsin) Ice Age began to wane, warming and drying conditions between about 10,000 and 8000 cal B.C. are thought to have triggered far-reaching cultural responses in California. In the desert interior, lakes and streams that were once fed by moist Pleistocene climatic conditions began to shrink. Cultures dependent on these lacustrine environments, subsumed under the heading of a Western Pluvial Lakes Tradition (WPLT), responded by exploiting a wider range of plant and animal species and by mi-

Table 14.1. Prominent Archaeological Sites and Projects in the Southern Bight Region

Site / Project Area	*Description*	*Recent Major Reference*
Allan O. Kelly Site (SDI-9649)	Key early La Jollan site	Koerper et al. 1991
Ballast Point Site (SDI-48)	Major Middle Holocene maritime site	Gallegos and Kyle 1998
Eel Point site (SCLI-43)	Major multicomponent (Early Holocene onward) habitation site	Raab et al. 2002
C.W. Harris Site (SDI-149)	Type site of San Dieguito, Early Holocene	Warren et al. 1998
Little Harbor (SCAI-17)	Major Middle Holocene rockshelter	Raab et al. 1995
Nursery Site (SCLI-1215)	Middle Holocene village site	Raab et al. 1994
Piedra de Lumbre Quarry (SDI-10,008)	Unique chert quarry	Pigniolo 1994
Windsong Shores (SDI-10,965)	Early Holocene La Jollan site	Gallegos 1991
Lake Elsinore site (RIV-2798)	Major trans-Holocene site	Grenda 1997
Ballona Wetlands	Major locus of trans-Holocene occupation	Altschul et al. 2005
Bolsa Chica Bay	Major Middle Holocene onward excavations	Koerper et al. 2002
Camp Pendleton	Major survey and excavations, trans-Holocene	Reddy and Berryman 1999a, 1999b; Byrd and Berryman 2006
Cuyamaca Rancho State Park	Late Holocene upland settlement system	Gamble 2004; Gross and Sampson 1990
Newport Coast Project	Major survey and excavations, trans-Holocene	Mason et al. 1997; Koerper et al. 2002
Otay Mesa	Numerous surveys and excavations, trans-Holocene	Kyle et al. 1990, Robbins-Wade 1992
Ramon Valley Project	Cluster of Late Prehistoric inland sites	Cooley and Barrie 2004
San Joaquin Hills Projects	Major survey and excavations, dominated by Late Prehistoric	Koerper et al. 2002, Strudwick 2005
San Clemente Island	Numerous surveys and excavations, trans-Holocene	Yatsko 2000
San Elijo Lagoon Project	Early – Middle Holocene shell middens	Byrd et al. 2004
San Nicolas Island	Surveys and excavations, trans-Holocene	Martz and Rosenthal 2001

grating to regions with more favorable moisture conditions, including the southern California coast.

Some archaeologists see developments of this kind at the C. W. Harris site (SDI-149) in San Diego County (Carrico et al. 1991; Warren et al. 1998). Leaf-shaped and large-stemmed projectile points, scrapers, and other stone tools from the Harris site define the San Dieguito Complex (Warren 1968), which is considered to be technologically similar to interior WPLT sites. Radiocarbon dates of only ca. 8000 to 6500 cal B.C. from the Harris site, the low number of similar sites of comparable age in the region (Pigniolo 2005; Chapter 4 in this volume), and an ongoing debate on the relationship between the Harris site and sites of similar age with different lithic technologies along the coast (e.g., the Windsong Shore and the Allan O. Kelly [SDI-9649] sites; see Table 14.1, Figure 14.1) suggest that this problem needs additional research and new data (Gallegos 1991; Koerper et al. 1991; Moratto 1984:97–99; Warren et al. 1998).

After this initial settlement, traditional models suggest, coastal groups gradually adopted marine foods such as shellfish and fish, particularly after post-Pleistocene sea level rise created estuaries and bays, the remnants of which dot the San Diego and Orange County coastlines today. In this context, the La Jolla Complex of the Archaic Period flourished along the coast (Gallegos 1992; Moratto 1984; Rogers 1966; Warren et al. 1998). These shell middens are generally characterized by flaked cobble tools, basin metates, manos, discoids, and flexed burials. Initial Archaic exploitation of the San Diego area littoral zone is generally considered to have entailed sizable semisedentary populations focused around resource-rich bays and estuaries (Crabtree et al. 1963; Gallegos 1992; Moriarty et al. 1959; Shumway et al. 1961; Warren 1964, 1968; Warren and Pavesic 1963; Warren et al. 1961). Shellfish were interpreted as a dietary staple; plant resources (both nuts and grasses) were also important contributors to the diet, while hunting and fishing were less important.

EARLY HUMAN SETTLEMENT: CALIFORNIA PALEOCOASTAL TRADITION Archaeological findings from the past two decades challenge these traditional scenarios. Current evidence suggests that the initial human settlement of California, including the Southern Bight, was a more complex phenomenon than envisioned in traditional models. Perhaps the most dramatic change in our understanding of this process comes from the coast. At present, the oldest reliably established coastal occupation in California—perhaps the oldest archeological site in the state—is Daisy Cave (SMI-261) on San Miguel Island, about 40 kilometers off the Santa Barbara coast (see Chapters 4, 13 this volume). The oldest cultural layer at Daisy Cave is dated to between 9600 and 9000 cal B.C., making it one of the oldest archaeological sites currently known in California (Erlandson et al. 1996). Orange and San Diego Counties and the Southern Channel Islands have not yet produced equally early dates, but radiocarbon evidence shows occupation of the coastal region between ca. 8000 and 7000 cal B.C. (Byrd 2003; Byrd et al. 2004; Gallegos 1991; Koerper et al. 1991, 2002:Fig. 5.2).

EARLY SETTLEMENT OF THE SOUTHERN CHANNEL ISLANDS Some of the most detailed evidence of early maritime cultural development comes from the Southern Channel Islands, particularly San Clemente Island. During the past 20 years, San Clemente Island has emerged as a major natural laboratory for the study of coastal prehistory. Like the other Channel Islands, archaeological preservation on San Clemente is exceptional owing to many factors, including a lack of both burrowing animals and urban industrial development. Although San Clemente Island has been the scene of numerous archaeological investigations during the past 20 years by university and CRM-based researchers, the Eel Point archaeological site (SCLI-43) is the oldest and most extensively documented site on the island (Cassidy et al. 2004; Raab and Yatsko 1992; Raab et al. 2002; Yatsko 2000). With occupation beginning between 6500 and 6000 cal B.C. and ending about the time of European contact, Eel Point offers important insights about the cultural characteristics of Early Holocene coastal dwellers.

EARLY BOATS, SEA TRAVEL, AND A MARITIME ECONOMY Located about 40 kilometers from the other nearest island (Santa Catalina) and 77 kilometers from the mainland coast, San Clemente Island, even during lowered sea levels of the last Ice Age, could only be reached by water. The occupation of San Clemente and other Channel Islands during the Early Holocene affords circumstantial yet unequivocal evidence of some of the earliest sea travel in North America. However, recent discoveries at Eel Point provide intriguing evidence of early maritime technology, including stone tools capable of fabricating boats. Cassidy et al. (2004) show that this tool kit, dating to 6000 cal B.C., was technologically comparable to tools used by historic Chumash Indians to make wooden seagoing canoes (see Chapter 5 in this volume).

Early settlement of the Channel Islands is significant because these islands offered few land-based foods, resulting in obligatory maritime economies. Studies at Eel Point show that during the Early Holocene, site inhabitants enjoyed a highly productive marine economy, based to a large extent on hunting seals, sea lions, and dolphins and collecting shellfish (Garlinghouse 2000; Porcasi and Fujita 2000; Porcasi et al. 2000). Based on these data, coastal locations, including the Channel Islands, offered attractive settlement locations to early human settlers. These data help explain why paleocoastal cultural traditions appeared in southern California and vindicate Moratto's hypothesis regarding the existence of this tradition.

The Middle Holocene

Traditional models of California prehistory view the Middle Holocene as a time of cultural transition, during which Early Holocene cultural adaptations were gradually modified into forms recognizable during the Late Holocene. For example, across much of central and southern California, millingstone cultures appeared around 6000–5000 cal B.C. featuring an adaptation focused on collection and processing of small plant seeds and the hunting of a variety of medium and small game animals. In the Southern Bight, environmental factors are thought to have played a major role in altering these early, generalized hunting and gathering adaptations.

Traditional reconstruction of Middle Holocene occupation on the mainland has emphasized sizable, semisedentary populations focused around the resource-rich bays and estuaries of San Diego and Orange Counties (Crabtree et al. 1963; Gallegos 1992;

Moriarty et al. 1959; Shumway et al. 1961; Warren 1964, 1968; Warren and Pavesic 1963; Warren et al. 1961). Shellfish have been interpreted as dietary staples; plant resources (both nuts and grasses) were also an important dietary component, while hunting and fishing were thought to be less important.

This adaptive strategy, often referred to as the La Jolla Culture in the San Diego area or the Millingstone Horizon in Orange County, was viewed as remaining largely unchanged for several thousand years. According to Warren et al. (1961:25), "the La Jolla Complex reached its population and cultural climax between 7000 and 4000 years ago when there was a plentiful supply of shellfish in the lagoons along the coast." This reconstruction went on to posit major changes in human adaptations after 4,000 years ago when estuarine silting was considered to have become so extensive that it caused a decline in associated shellfish populations. This in turn was considered to have caused a major depopulation of the coastal zone, with settlements shifting inland to a river valley orientation, intensifying exploitation of terrestrial small game and plant resources, possibly including acorns (Christenson 1992; Crabtree et al. 1963; Gallegos 1985, 1987, 1992; Masters and Gallegos 1997; Rogers 1929:467; Warren 1964, 1968; Warren and Pavesic 1963; Warren et al. 1961). The coast was thought to have been abandoned or only seasonally occupied, with a possible slight increase in coastal occupation after 1,600 to 1,200 years ago.

Today Middle Holocene occupation of the mainland region is recognized as considerably more diverse than initially posited. Important Middle Holocene sites have been documented in inland settings, while considerable variability is recognized in adaptive strategies along the length of the Southern Bight littoral zone (Byrd and Reddy 2002; Mason et al. 1997; Masters and Gallegos 1997). In addition, there are many localities along the coastline where continuity in occupation from the Middle to the Late Holocene is now well documented. For example, San Diego Bay, Mission Bay, the Peñasquitos Lagoon/Sorrento Valley area, San Elijo Lagoon/Escondido Creek, the Santa Margarita River drainage, Las Flores Creek, and San Mateo Creek in the San Diego area all include settlements that were occupied from the later part of the Middle Holocene into the Late Holocene (Byrd et al. 2004; Byrd and Reddy 2002; and references therein). Thus initial impressions of uniform coastal settlement changes near the end of the Middle Holocene have not been widely verified by subsequent archaeological research.

Moreover, independent paleoenvironmental data collected recently from a series of drainages reveals that the exact timing and magnitude of coastal habitat changes varied considerably within the region (Altschul et al. 2005; Anderson and Byrd 1998; Byrd 2003; Byrd et al. 2004; Davis 1992; Pope 1997; Waters et al. 1999). Well-dated, continuous sequences of Holocene geologic deposits extending back prior to 9000 cal B.C. in the three drainage systems (Las Flores Creek, San Elijo Lagoon/ Escondido Creek, and the lower Santa Margarita River valley) reveal complex physiographic histories. Notably, the larger drainage systems were more likely than smaller systems to remain tidally flushed and maintain rich estuarine habitats during climatic downturns. Overall, new data clearly demonstrate that patterns of environmental changes and cultural response along the Southern Bight mainland were quite different and much more diverse than previously suspected.

CULTURAL INTERACTION AND MIGRATION The Middle Holocene has rarely been viewed as a time of large-scale cultural interaction by groups living across California or between California and the rest of the American West. Archaeologists have generally theorized that regional cultural interaction spheres arose during the Late Holocene, as regional trade networks sprang up as an adjunct to increasing techno-economic efficiency and the desires of social elites to acquire social power and wealth through the control of these networks (Arnold, ed. 2001; Gamble and Russell 2002). Intriguing evidence has emerged, however, of geographically expansive trade networks and spheres of culture interaction linking the Southern Bight with a vast region of the American West during the Middle Holocene.

Based initially on excavations on Santa Catalina and San Clemente Islands, Howard and Raab (1993), Raab and Howard (2000), and Raab et al. (1994) proposed that *Olivella* grooved rectangle (OGR) beads, a rare type manufactured from the marine purple olive shell *(Olivella biplicata)*, may mark a 5,000-year-old OGR corridor—a trade network extending from the Southern Channel Islands across southern California through the Mojave Desert, along the western fringes of the Great Basin to Oregon. Additional OGR beads were identified on San Nicolas Island, placing these beads on each of the three largest Southern Channel Islands. Yet despite more than a century of archaeological investigations, including considerable attention to marine shell beads, no examples of the OGR type are reported from the Northern Channel Islands. Based on this evidence, Howard and Raab (1993) proposed that OGR beads might mark a discrete Middle Holocene sphere of trade and interaction that included the Southern Channel Islands and portions of the adjacent mainland; a sphere that, remarkably, excluded the Northern Channel Islands, only 80 kilometers distant.

Vellanoweth (1995) subsequently recovered OGR beads on San Nicolas Island from a stratigraphic context dated ca. 3500–2900 cal B.C.; one OGR specimen produced a direct date of 3500–3300 cal B.C. (Vellanoweth 1995:17). Jenkins and Erlandson (1996) also demonstrated the existence of OGR beads at the DJ Ranch site in the Fort Rock Valley of central Oregon. These specimens, the most distant from the southern California coast recorded to date, are close to the younger end of the age spectrum for California OGR beads; they were recovered from context dated ca. 2900–1500 cal B.C. (Jenkins and Erlandson 1996). This discovery added a dramatically greater spatial dimension to the OGR distributional pattern:

> As suggested by Howard and Raab (1993) and others, the distribution of OGR beads along the southern California coast and their presence in Middle Holocene sites in the western and northern Great Basin may support the existence of an early cultural interaction sphere, possibly linking Uto-Aztecan peoples of the southern California coast and the western Great Basin. Remarkably, more OGR beads have now been found at the DJ Ranch site in central Oregon, up to 1,200 km from their probable point of origin on the southern Channel Islands, than have been found in the heavily studied Santa Barbara Channel region immediately to the north of the proposed cultural interaction sphere. (Jenkins and Erlandson 1996:301)

This evidence opened up another intriguing possibility. Based on linguistic evidence, California anthropologists have long hypothesized that, at some time or times during prehistory, speakers of Uto-Aztecan languages migrated from the Great Basin across southern California, and eventually colonized the Southern Channel Islands. The movement of these peoples across southern California is thought to have displaced resident groups, creating a distinctive "Shoshonean wedge" of speakers of Uto-Aztecan languages across southern California (Kroeber 1925; Moratto 1984; see also Chapters 6, 19 this volume). Noting that the distribution of ORG beads closely corresponds to this Shoshonean wedge, some researchers have suggested that they may mark an ancient migration route or alignment of linguistically linked population about 5,000 years ago (Raab and Howard 2000; Vellanoweth 1995). Other researchers point to Middle Holocene human skeletal evidence from the Southern Channel Islands as possible evidence of such a migration, arguing that genetically distinct group of islanders appears in the islands in a time frame that is compatible for Middle Holocene migrations of new populations into California and the Southern Channel Islands, including San Clemente and San Nicolas (Kerr and Hawley 2002; Titus 1987).

MARITIME SEDENTISM Traditionally, Middle Holocene groups have been viewed as Archaic-style hunter-gatherers, with seasonally mobile settlement patterns. According to these scenarios, groups such as Millingstone folk moved their camps with the changing seasons in order to better obtain various food resources. Dynamics of this kind were thought to have provided little incentive to invest large amounts of labor in substantial houses or permanently occupied villages. Recent evidence shows, however, that small maritime villages consisting of substantial house structures appeared on San Clemente Island at least as early as the Middle Holocene.

Some of the most detailed information about house construction on prehistoric San Clemente Island comes from the Nursery site (SCLI-1215) and the Eel Point archaeological site (SCLI-43). At the Nursery site, named after a nearby native plant nursery, UCLA investigators initially discovered saucer-shaped house floors about 0.5 meter deep and 4.0 to 5.0 meters in diameter, with evidence of collapsed whale bone roof structures (Rigby 1985). A charcoal sample from one these structures yielded a radiocarbon date of ca. 2000 cal B.C. (Rigby 1985). Subsequent work at the site exposed a complete house structure (House Pit 2), described by Salls et al. (1993). Like the UCLA discovery, this house was constructed in a circular pit 4.5 meters in diameter and about 0.5 meter deep. This work showed that whale bone roof members had once been set in holes between 10 and 30 centimeters in diameter at the floor perimeter. The stub of a whale rib was still in place in one of these holes. Large quantities of whale bone were found on the house floor, including masses of whale bone at the east and west periphery of the floor (Salls et al. 1993:186–188). This house yielded a date of ca. 2800 cal B.C. (Raab et al. 1994; Figure 14.3). Research at the site suggests that these houses were part of a Middle Holocene village containing at least 18 dwellings (Raab et al. 1994). The Nursery site is not alone in producing evidence of early house construc-

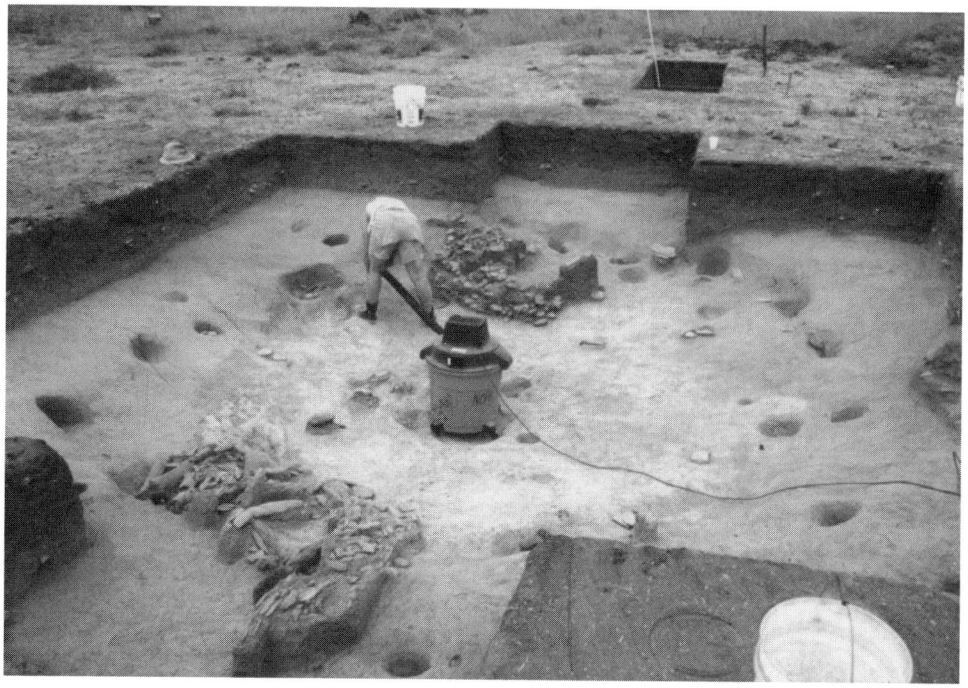

Figure 14.3. House structure at the Nursery site, San Clemente Island.

tion. Fiore (1998) described Middle Holocene house features at SCLI-43, the Eel Point site that produced radiocarbon dates comparable to the oldest house remains from Nursery (Fiore 1998:31).

These data may point to some of the earliest residential structures in coastal California, if not the state. Salls et al. (1993) argue that structures of this kind indicate a substantial degree of residential permanence, and that these structures were part of communities occupied for more than one season each year, if not on a year-round basis. Currently the seasons during which sites such as Nursery and Eel Point were occupied are not known in detail, making it difficult to determine the longevity of annual occupation of the domestic structures. However, middens adjacent to the San Clemente Island houses rival deposits associated with mainland sites that were occupied for multiple seasons during the latter portion of the Late Holocene (Byrd 1998; Byrd and Reddy 2002). In the study region, house structures have been only infrequently encountered in mainland settings (Grenda et al. 1998; Winterbourne 1967), in large part due to more extensive bioturbation and modern development. The presence of daub on some mainland sites does indicate that structures were present (Strudwick 2005). Based on this evidence, the appearance of sedentary communities appears to reflect a more temporally and spatially complex pattern than traditional models of cultural development suggest. It might also be noted that two of the Middle Holocene houses at the Nursery site produced OGR beads from their floors, linking this community to the OGR bead pattern (Howard and Raab 1993; Raab et al. 1994).

The Late Holocene

According to traditional models, the Late Holocene was the time period during which cultural patterns and tribal groups observable by early Euro-American explorers and settlers emerged. Sometime after cal A.D. 500, the bow and arrow appeared, with ceramics adopted after cal A.D. 1000 at the start of (or during) the Late Prehistoric Period (Meighan 1954; Rogers 1945; True 1966; Warren 1964, 1968). Many also supposed that this was a time when migrations created the historic linguistic landscape and new forms of social expression, including mortuary practices with cremations, replaced inhumations. This period was typically characterized as resource rich, and climatic instability not discussed. Surpluses of food, especially acorns, were thought to have sustained the social arrangements documented by anthropologists in the twentieth century. These ideas were in accord with the notions of Kroeber (1925) and other early authorities, who characterized aboriginal California, particularly coastal areas, in terms of virtually assured natural food supplies and some of the world's most benign climatic regimes. Subsequent theorizing and synthetic accounts of coastal adaptations have often elaborated on this perspective, emphasizing highly successful cultural adaptations and high levels of social complexity. The utopian character of these theories has been characterized as benign environmental determinism by some observers (Raab and Jones 2004).

In contrast, an extensive body of research during the past two decades has revealed more complex and dynamic regional and local patterns of change. The empirical patterns that have emerged from these studies stand in marked contrast to the scenarios described above. The timing of the adoption of new technologies (such as the bow and arrow and ceramics) and social expressions (particularly cremations) vary greatly within the region, typically earlier in the east than the west and occurring very late and minimally in some coastal and insular contexts (Byrd 2003; Christenson 1990; Gallegos 2002; Gamble and Russell 2002; Griset 1996; Koerper et al. 1996, 2002; McDonald and Eighmey 1998). Dynamic patterns of intergroup trade and interaction, as well as intragroup dynamics, played major roles in these trends.

These studies also suggest that culture change was sometimes rapid rather than gradual; stressful times were not limited to postcontact times but occurred periodically during the prehistoric era; littoral and marine resources remained extremely important; and major shifts took place in subsistence practices, settlement patterns, and the organization of labor (Byrd and Reddy 2002; Gallegos 2002; Koerper et al. 2002; Raab et al. 2002; Vellanoweth et al. 2002). In particular, recent research has explored the impact of resource intensification dynamics and paleoenvironmental fluctuations on culture change (Jones et al. 1999).

SUBSISTENCE CHANGE Contrary to the glowing assessments offered by traditional models of Late Holocene coastal adaptation, the long-term trajectory of many California foraging adaptations appears to be marked by overexploitation of high-ranked food items, leading to resource depression and shifts to more costly resources. Dynamics of this kind have been identified for many of the food resources used by the region's prehistoric coastal populations, including shellfish, fish, sea mammals, terrestrial mammals, and plant remains (Byrd 1996; Byrd and Reddy 2002; Koerper et al. 2002; Raab 1992; Raab and Yatsko 1992; Raab et al. 2002; Salls 1988; Vellanoweth et al. 2002). Thus during the Late Holocene, hunter-gatherers throughout the Southern Bight region increasingly focused on smaller resources that generally occurred in greater amounts.

For example, on San Clemente Island, where trans-Holocene maritime hunting-fishing-gathering practices have been studied in detail at the Eel Point and other archaeological sites, the hunting of large sea mammals and relatively productive shellfish gave way during the Late Holocene to enormously intensified fishing, small sea mammal hunting, and collecting of the smallest species of shellfish. These trends appear to reflect a marked decrease in foraging efficiency over time (Broughton and O'Connell 1999; Garlinghouse 2000; Glassow 1996a:36–39; Hildebrandt and Jones 1992; Kelly 1995; Porcasi et al. 2000). Although resource intensification of this kind is currently viewed in various ways, Broughton (1997: 846) defines it as "a process by which the total productivity or yield per areal unit of land is increased at the expense of declines in overall caloric return rates or foraging efficiency." Thus resource intensification is the result of consuming increasing quantities of lower-ranked, less-productive food species.

Turning to a mainland example, an extensive body of data from Camp Pendleton has demonstrated that Late Holocene subsistence practices emphasized the most abundant nearby resources, notably smaller, labor-intensive shellfish, fish, small terrestrial mammals, and small-seeded plants (Byrd 1996; Byrd and Reddy 1999, 2002). Smaller shellfish, most notably *Donax gouldii* but also *Tegula,* became key elements of this subsistence strategy (Byrd 1996; Reddy 1996a, 1999a). The dietary importance of large mammals declined during the Late Holocene, while small terrestrial mammals increasingly dominated the terrestrial meat diet. Fish resources were focused primarily on smaller, nearshore schooling species, and entailed a decrease in diversity (Wake 1999). Similar trends have been noted along the Newport coast and the San Joaquin Hills (Koerper et al. 2002:70–72).

At the same time, a wide range of local plant resources (over four dozen genera) were exploited along the northern San Diego coast during the Late Holocene (Klug and Popper 1995; Martin and Popper 1998, 1999; Reddy 1996b, 1997a, b, 1999a, b, 2001, 2003). Plant resource exploitation was focused on species requiring higher handling costs, particularly grasses (Poaceae) (Reddy 1999b). Grass seeds belonging to *Bromus/Stipa* spp., *Hordeum* sp., *Phalaris* sp., and *Sporobulus* sp. occurred in the highest frequencies. Direct macrobotanical evidence of acorn exploitation is minimal, a trend also noted at more inland Late Holocene sites (Reddy 1997b, 2004). It remains uncertain whether this pattern reflects dietary emphasis, acorn processing methods, or both. "Fire followers" (plants that thrive in open areas created by regular fires) are represented to varying degrees at Late Holocene coastal sites. These include *Callandria, Lotus, Marah,* corms/bulbs from wild flowers, *Hordeum, Trifolium, Chenopodium,* and *Poaceae.* These patterns may indicate that intentional burning took place to varying degrees along the coast (Blackburn and Anderson 1993).

Bean and Lawton's (1976) publication on protoagriculture (drawing on ethnohistoric and ethnographic observations) argued that when the Spanish first entered the San Diego region, grasses were intensively manipulated, seasonal burning was an important aspect of this process, and in all probability it entailed cultivation in a variety of coastal settings (Shipek 1989). Recently this topic has been explicitly addressed by research examining morphological changes in wild barley in coastal Orange County (Klug and Koerper 1991) and the modeling of crop processing stages and the documentation of intensive exploitation of small-seeded plants near the end of the Holocene on coastal Camp Pendleton (Reddy 1999a, 2001, 2003).

These important studies show the tremendous potential for such research but also highlight how we lag behind our colleagues elsewhere in the United States. For example, systematic and intensive paleoethnobotanical investigations in eastern North America (where literally thousands of liters of sediment have been floated and studied) have revolutionized perspectives on early agriculture and revealed an indigenous pristine hearth for agriculture that entailed small seed resources such as *Chenopodium* (Smith 2001). Only by conducting intensive archaeological research and investing substantial research funds on this topic will researchers in California make comparable advances. Until that time, the alluring possibility of indigenous cultivation in the Southern Bight will remain in the murky realm of conjecture.

SETTLEMENT PATTERN RECONFIGURATION Both mainland and Channel Island locations witnessed the emergence of similarly structured settlement patterns during the Late Holocene (Byrd and Reddy 1999, 2002; Koerper et al. 2002; Raab et al. 2002), suggesting that the study area may reflect robust, widespread shifts in regional land use. Regional settlement organization was powerfully conditioned by techno-economic adaptations and provides another line of evidence to examine intensification dynamics. Late Holocene coastal southern California was dramatically affected by several correlates of resource intensification. A key aspect was the emergence of a distinctive type of Late Holocene settlement pattern characterized by comparatively large residential camps linked to numerous ephemeral satellite sites. The smaller sites were nonrandomly distributed, short-term encampments, some of which were dedicated to relatively specialized subsistence tasks. Such patterns are now documented on San Clemente Island (Raab et al. 2002) and on the mainland coast in the San Joaquin Hills and on Camp Pendleton (Brewster et al. 2003; Byrd and Reddy 1999, 2002; Koerper et al. 2002). Site types in each area include major residential bases, short-term residential camps, and limited activity sites (Rosenthal et al. 2001).

These trends are undoubtedly tied to changes in subsistence practices. As subsistence strategies increasingly focused on smaller resources that required more time and effort to procure and process, their exploitation entailed more complex settlement configurations that included both targeting and encounter strategies. These trends accelerated during the Late Holocene, particularly after about cal A.D. 1300.

RELATED CHANGES IN HUNTER-GATHERER SOCIETIES These changes in settlement and subsistence strategies were undoubtedly tied to broader changes in social interaction. Associated changes in social discourse may have included increasing community size, greater lengths of stay at major residences, and shifts in intracommunity organization. The latter may have entailed major social reorganization (with political and economic leaders emerging), more need for structured decision making with respect to the assignment of economic tasks, and formal mechanisms for dealing with scheduling conflicts. A particularly intriguing aspect of this issue entails whether the gender-based division of labor noted ethnohistorically emerged with the shift to intensive mass collection and harvesting of shellfish and grasses (Jones 1996; McGuire and Hildebrandt 1994).

CAUSAL FACTORS The key question arises, What were the causal factors underlying these changes in subsistence practices, settlement organization, and other related activities? Recent years have seen arguments linking critical changes in economy and settlement patterning with paleoenvironmental fluctuations, which in turn initiated productive debates over periodic overexploitation as a factor in structuring Late Holocene island adaptations based largely on fishing and the nature of mainland littoral adaptations (Laylander and Christenson 1988; Rosenthal et al. 2001). Despite the research advances engendered by these models and related debates, a number of important questions remain unresolved. One of the most important of these involves unraveling the potential causal interrelationship between paleoenvironmental fluctuations and social factors in bringing about Late Holocene cultural patterns.

Research of the past several decades has emphasized the high population density of the region's hunter-gatherers, their intensified economies, and their relatively complex sociopolitical systems. Depending on a few ubiquitous but low-ranked, labor-intensive, and storable resources put Late Holocene people in ecological jeopardy, since few alternative foodstuffs were available in times of resource stress. While much of the Holocene archaeological record may reflect a process of intensification and population growth, it is also probable that this long-term trend toward intensification put coastal populations at increasing risk in the event of severe fluctuations in the climate. With the Late Holocene emphasis on low-ranked resources and mass harvesting, more limited options were available to increase production, and these economies may have been more vulnerable to high-intensity environmental change (Jones et al. 1999:155).

Recent evidence derived from a series of problem-oriented projects along the coast in this region reveal that the settlement and subsistence responses to paleoenvironmental changes were dynamic and locally innovative as well as nonenvironmentally deterministic, and did not entail coastal abandonment (Altschul et al. 2005; Byrd and Reddy 2002; Gallegos 2002; Gamble and Russell 2002; Koerper et al. 2002). These new results demonstrate intensification in the exploitation of littoral resources and coastal occupation. Those who championed the traditional interpretations of southern California coastal prehistory noted earlier viewed this pattern as evidence of an extraordinary degree of adaptive continuity across time. This seems simplistic at best; however, since profound differences in settlement and subsistence patterns that emerged during the Late Holocene have been revealed by recent research.

A particularly important aspect of this discussion has been the impact of unusually severe and persistent medieval-era droughts (often referred to as the Medieval Climatic Anomaly, MCA) on longer-term adaptive trends (Jones et al. 1999). An important part of this argument has been that long-term shifts in foraging efficiency prior to the MCA positioned Late Holocene hunter-gatherers for disaster (Jones et al. 1999). Studies of the MCA anomaly have been productively pursued in mainland and insular settings. For example, Yatsko's (2000) research on San Clemente Island shows that this semiarid island, acutely sensitive to changes in moisture, reflects dramatic changes in settlement patterning between about cal A.D. 1100 to 1300, shifts that appear to reflect the reorganization of settlement around areas with a greater geological potential for surface water.

We do not mean to imply that all Late Holocene adaptive changes were caused by negative environmental change, but rather that rapid external changes may have served as catalysts for internal changes within hunter-gatherer communities. Indeed it is possible that recent discussion has on occasion overemphasized negative external change as a driver of social change. At Camp Pendleton, the proliferation of more specialized sites occurs immediately after the end of the Medieval Climatic Anomaly around cal A.D. 1300, and this is the time frame after which most small sites flourish on San Clemente as well. These post-MCA changes imply that rapid improvement in the environment may have released some of the environmental pressures on population levels and their spatial distribution, and fostered an increased presence of hunter-gatherers on the landscape.

Overall, two major points have emerged from recent Late Holocene research. First, external change was rapid and often negative, and communities in the Southern Bight reacted in a variety of novel ways to these fluxes in external conditions. Second, casual relationships between shifts in social organization and external variables were extremely complex, and will require high-resolution data to fully resolve. We suspect that these trends toward greater intensification imply that potentially profound changes occurred with respect to the social institutions of these hunter-gatherer communities. Although new types of gear and equipment were also needed, we do not consider that these social changes required major technological breakthroughs. From our perspective, the crucial changes in intracommunity socioeconomic organization were related to the greater investment in time necessary to collect, process, and store smaller food resources, and the impact of changes in the organization of labor on settlement structure.

PREHISTORY UPSIDE DOWN

Based on recent research in the Southern Bight, prehistory turns out to be much different than once thought. Once accepted notions about prehistoric cultural development have been turned upside down. Intensively maritime economies, seafaring, residential sedentism, and large-scale trade networks were viewed traditionally as hallmarks of a Late Holocene cultural climax in southern California, culminating millennia of incremental cultural improvements. A large body of evidence now shows that these traits were all present thousands of years earlier than once supposed, and culture change was highly variable across time and space. Substantial evidence shows that sea travel and distinctively maritime cultural adaptations were well established during the Early Holocene, if not the Terminal Pleistocene. Residential sedentism and large cultural interaction spheres, including trade, appeared at least as early as the Middle Holocene. Our understanding of the Late Holocene is also shifting. This time period was often conceptualized as a time of paramount socioeconomic elaboration, based on studies of the Chumash Indians of the Santa Barbara coastal region. This picture has given way to appreciation of much greater variation in social complexity and settlement patterns across southern California, including groups such as the Kumeyaay of southern San Diego County. Where monolithic reconstructions of cultural elaboration once held sway, we now have competing theoretical models, some of which view Late Holocene culture change as far more punctuated than once imagined and far more driven by stresses such as climate change and resource depression than adaptive optimality.

These data suggest that a fundamental rethinking is under way about California prehistory and the ways it is studied. We are learning that the prehistoric past contained complex and varied cultural patterns that do not necessarily have analogs in the ethnohistoric present and cannot be explained on the basis of traditional reconstructions of California prehistory.

MODELS FOR A NEW MILLENNIUM

Since the 1984 publication of *California Archaeology* and the *Archaeology of California*, perhaps the most profound change we have witnessed is not simply the dramatic increase in archaeological data, but rather how these data force us to model the past. Earlier we alluded to the fashion in which California archaeology was overshadowed during much of the twentieth century by an anthropological establishment focused to a large extent on ethnohistory. Particularly in an era when archaeological practitioners lacked a detailed sense of prehistoric time, ethnohistoric analogies afforded attractive analogies for reconstructing prehistoric cultural arrangements. Given that Late Holocene archaeological records were frequently the best preserved and most visible, and therefore the most intensively studied, it should come as no surprise that theorizing about culture change across the whole of prehistory frequently revealed the heavy impression of Late Holocene cultural arrangements. While many recognized in the abstract that different kinds of cultural arrangements probably existed in the past, reconstructions of prehistory often reflected a reverse engineering of the Late Holocene—theorizing about the long-term changes that would have been necessary to produce the Late Holocene/Early Historic archaeological/ethnohistoric record. Until the past two decades, this theorizing had to be undertaken with modest stocks of archaeological data, particularly from Middle and Early Holocene time periods. Given the information available to archaeologists during the first three-quarters of the twentieth century, the results are impressive. Whatever questions may now be raised about these reconstructions, these efforts did afford a logical and coherent basis for theory development and analysis of archaeological data.

We increasingly understand, however, that California's prehistoric past was complex, multidirectional, and multicausal. As the data on Early Holocene seafaring, maritime adaptations, Middle Holocene sedentism and trade, and Late Holocene climatic flux and resource scarcity suggest, we can only be misled by imagining the native cultural patterns of the early historic era as analogous to much older time periods. The rich ethnohistoric data on native Californians and ethnographic reconstructions based on early-twentieth-century interviews (rather than participant-observer data) is the envy of archaeologists working on hunter-gatherers in other areas of the world. This information is unquestionably important in understanding how historic native groups adapted to the study region. On the other hand, research of the past two decades demonstrates with increasing clarity that this information has very real limitations. Above we noted increasing agreement that prehistoric culture change was much more variable across time and space than was once suspected. The prehistoric past contained cultural patterns that have no historic analogs. To continue to model large expanses of prehistoric time and space largely on the basis of historical ethnographic analogies is an increasingly questioned practice. However, we are not suggesting that archaeologists ought to ignore ethnohistoric information, since historical patterns tell us how particular groups adapted to cultural and physical environments.

A good approach for the future is the use of modern ethnohistoric research techniques to better understand immediate precontact patterns of social interaction. For example, mission period baptismal, death, marriage, and census registers provide new insight into the size of Native American coastal villages and intervillage relationships. Recent research along these lines suggests, for example, that eight villages of at least 100 individuals existed within the area of modern-day Camp Pendleton and that there was strong patterning in village intermarriage (Johnson and Crawford 1999). These results are inconsistent with the long-held view that settlement patterning in the study region was seasonally bipolar, with only temporary or seasonal camps along the coast (Quintero 1987; Rosenthal et al. 2001; Waugh 1986). Similar techniques are also yielding new insights in the Southern Channel Islands (Johnson 1989).

In contrast to the studies above, we have seen countless reports and publications that first describe alleged native cultural patterns in the Late Prehistoric/Early Historic time frame, then go on to offer opinions about how far back in time these patterns can be recognized in the archaeological data. Many of these reports do not seem to recognize that inferring patterns of behavior from ethnohistoric accounts is as theory-laden an exercise as archaeological inferences drawn from material culture. Through assertion and repetition, popular interpretations of ethnohistory are represented as objectively established facts. We are all entitled to our own opinions, but we are not entitled to our own facts. Ethnohistoric accounts tend to depend on the theoretical assumptions they are paired with. In our view, California research could benefit from a far more open and rigorous discussion of this problem.

Whatever the fate of such a debate, research of the past twenty years confronts us with cultural patterns that cannot be accounted for by reference to historic Indian groups. This is where archaeology can make powerful new contributions. Archaeologists are in a position to understand how the past was different from the ethnohistoric present, and why. To achieve this purpose we need to expand on a couple of trends that have emerged during the past two decades. One of these is the diversification of theoretical models. An examination of the literature cited above shows the deployment of a spectrum of theoretical approaches to the study area, ranging from foraging optimization models to neo-Darwinian selectionist perspectives to culture-historical orientations. The application of a wide range of modern theories of hunter-gatherer behavior (Bettinger 1991; Kelly 1995) is a trend that should be encouraged.

A second major change forced by new data is growing debate among researchers. As theoretical models increasingly compete to explain the past, debate is not only inevitable but highly desirable, for example, questions about whether Early Holocene coastal dwellers were effective seafarers, whether Middle Holocene groups moved away from the mainland coast after bays silted in, whether climatic stress played a role in Late Holocene cultural patterning, whether Late Holocene economic patterns reflect resource depression or abundance, and others. This is a trend that should also be encouraged.

Finally, those who may have worried that archaeological progress would be hampered by the lack of formal regional research designs, the split of archaeology into "academic" and "contract" branches and other ostensible problems, can take heart. The past two decades suggest that archaeologists of all kinds continue to seek explanations of the past in more creative and productive ways. Moratto (1984) and Chartkoff and Chartkoff (1984) helped us gather our thoughts for this task. Their books distilled what many were thinking as California archaeology approached the end of the twentieth century. With these works as reference points, we can now see that California's ancient peoples achieved complex and interesting cultures earlier than we might have imagined. Just as importantly, the Moratto and Chartkoff and Chartkoff volumes signaled the rise of an increasingly sophisticated and intellectually autonomous California archaeology. As these trends continue into the new millennium, archaeology is forging new research models that will undoubtedly transform our understanding of California prehistory yet again.

CHAPTER 15

Advances in Understanding Mojave Desert Prehistory

MARK Q. SUTTON, MARK E. BASGALL, JILL K. GARDNER, AND MARK W. ALLEN

IT HAS BEEN TWO DECADES SINCE CLAUDE WARREN (1984) put forth an outline of the prehistory of the California deserts, and that work has withstood the test of time, although subsequent studies have provided greater detail (Tables 15.1, 15.2). Much of the more recent work has been conducted through cultural resource management (CRM) projects, primarily on military reservations, other federal lands, and public works projects. For example, large-scale surveys and excavations at hundreds of sites at Fort Irwin in the central Mojave Desert have made it the most thoroughly investigated archaeological region of comparable size in western North America. Along with some academic efforts, this work continues to frame much of the research in the Mojave Desert.

Several general updates of the archaeology of the Mojave Desert (or parts of it) have been published since Warren's overview (Basgall 2000a, b; Sutton 1988, 1996a), and it is not our intent to provide yet another update, as research generated in the past two decades is simply too vast to cover here. Instead, we have chosen to discuss a few topics of current interest, including paleoenvironment, dating and nomenclature, the evolution of cultural systems, and linguistic prehistory.

BACKGROUND

The Mojave Desert occupies much of southeastern California and extends into Arizona and Nevada (Figure 15.1). It is a warm temperature desert (Rowlands et al. 1982) with the Joshua tree *(Yucca brevifolia)* as the standard vegetative marker. For the purposes of this chapter, the Mojave Desert is divided into three geographic regions: western, central, and eastern.

The Mojave Desert was occupied by a number of ethnographically distinct groups, all of which spoke languages of either the Northern Uto-Aztecan or Yuman families. In general, Uto-Aztecan groups speaking Southern Numic languages (Kawaiisu, Koso [Panamint], and Southern Paiute [Ute]) occupied the northern half of the Mojave, while Takic groups (Kitanemuk and Serrano) occupied the southern half. Yuman-speaking groups, such as the Mojave, lived along the California-Arizona border (Figure 15.2). These societies were mobile hunter-gatherers, although some horticulture was conducted by a few groups in the far eastern Mojave. Each had broad, flexible territories and joint use rights to many areas, a less structured pattern than in the rest of the Great Basin.

A GREATER UNDERSTANDING OF PALEOENVIRONMENT

The past 20 years have witnessed profound advances in our understanding of paleoclimatic conditions in the Mojave Desert. The basic structure of Mojave Desert environments set important constraints on how regional landscapes could be used by native populations (MacMahon and Wagner 1985). Unlike the rest of the Great Basin, which shows strong vertical zonation in plant communities, more regular water sources, and greater uniformity in the spatial and temporal distri-

Table 15.1. Summary of Major Archaeological Research in the Mojave Desert Since 1982: Large-Scale Inventories

General Location	*Approximate Acres Surveyed*	*Recorded Prehistoric Sites*	*Most Recent Inclusive Reference*
China Lake Naval Weapons Center	125,000	1,200	None
Edwards Air Force Base	150,000	1,690	Loechl et al. 2004
Fort Irwin	220,000	1,030	Basgall 2000b
Twentynine Palms Marine Corps Center	150,000	1,373	MCAGCC 2002
Bureau of Land Management (BLM)	2,500,000	~15,000	Various BLM overviews

Table 15.2. Summary of Major Archaeological Research in the Mojave Desert Since 1982: Excavations

Site/Locality (date excavated)	*Site Type(s)*	*General Time Period(s)*	*Investigators/ Comments*	*Most Recent Inclusive Reference*
		WESTERN MOJAVE DESERT		
China Lake (ongoing)	Full range	Paleoindian to historic	Various, many reports	Basgall et al. 2003
Coso Junction Ranch (INY-2284; 1970s)	Large habitation	Gypsum to Late Prehistoric	UCLA, no site report	Whitley et al. 1988
Coso Volcanic Field (ongoing)	Quarries, camps	Paleo-Indian to Late Prehistoric	Far Western, many reports	Gilreath and Hildebrandt 1997
Edwards Air Force Base (ongoing)	Nearly full range	Paleo-Indian to historic	Various, many reports	Loechl et al. 2004
Cantil (KER-2211) and Koehn Lake (KER-875) (1984–1997)	Large habitation, camps	Gypsum to Late Prehistoric	CSU Bakersfield, no site report on KER-875	Sutton 1996a
Red Mountain (1978–present)	Camps	Gypsum to Late Prehistoric	BLM, CSU Pomona	Allen 2004
Red Rock Canyon area (1972–1999)	Nearly full range	Gypsum to historic	Various, few reports	Gardner 2002
Rose Spring (INY-372; 1987–1989)	Large habitation	Pinto to historic	UC Riverside, no site report	Yohe 1992b, 2000
Stahl (INY-182; 1987)	Large camp	Pinto	UC Riverside	Schroth 1994
		CENTRAL MOJAVE DESERT		
Afton Canyon (SBR-85; 1985)	Large habitation	Gypsum to Late Prehistoric	UC Riverside	Schneider 1989
Fort Irwin (ongoing)	Full range	Paleo-Indian to historic	Various, many reports	Basgall 2000b
Lake Mojave (ongoing)	Camps	Paleo-Indian	UNLV	Warren 2004
Soda Spring (1970s and 1980s)	Camps	Paleo-Indian to historic	CSU Fullerton, few reports	Sutton 1996a
Summit Valley (1990–1995)	Large habitation, camps	Gypsum to Late Prehistoric	CSU Bakersfield	Sutton 1996a
		EASTERN MOJAVE DESERT		
Clark Mountain (1984–1987)	Many camps	Lake Mojave to Historic	UC Riverside, UNLV	Rafferty 1994
Death Valley (ongoing)	Full range	Paleo-Indian to historic	Various, many reports	Schneider et al. 2000
Joshua Tree (ongoing)	Full range	Paleo-Indian to historic	UC Riverside, UNLV	Warren and Schneider 2000
Rustler Rockshelter (SBR-288) and Providence Mountain area (1992–2000)	Camps and shelters	Gypsum to Late Prehistoric	CSU Bakersfield	Sutton 2005
Twentynine Palms (ongoing)	Full range	Paleo-Indian to historic	Various, most recently CSU Sacramento, many reports	Basgall 2003

bution of subsistence resources, much of the Mojave Desert is characterized by broad swaths of relatively unproductive habitat punctuated by resource patches of uncertain value. As such, particular subregions can vary significantly across not only seasons but between years and longer intervals. Modern climatic data suggest that periods of reduced rainfall in one sector of the desert may have been balanced by enhanced conditions in another area.

The basic climatic scheme developed decades ago for western North America (Antevs 1948) continues to be used to define major climatic periods in the Mojave Desert. During the Late Pleistocene (ca. 18,000 to 8000 cal B.C.), conditions in the Mojave Desert were gener-

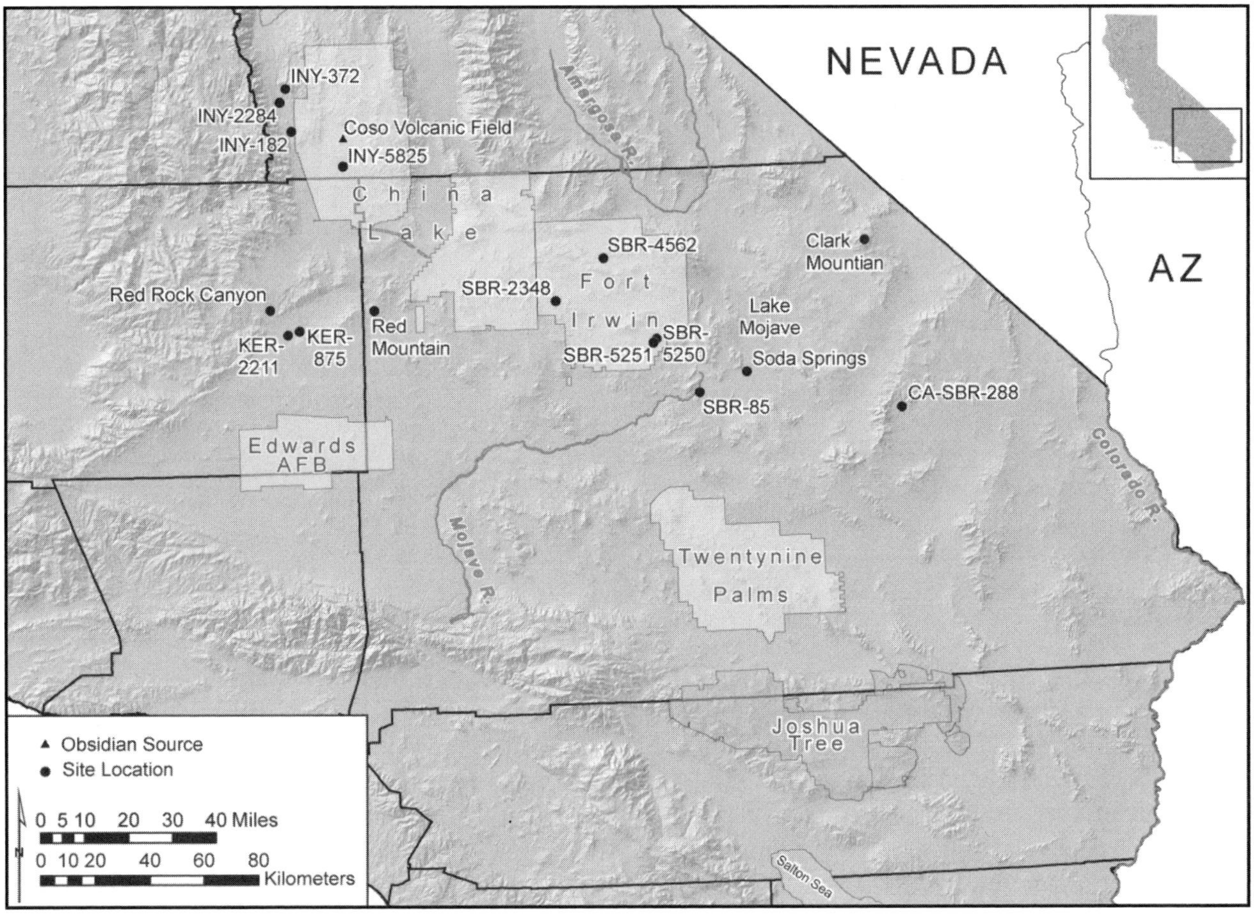

Figure 15.1. Archaeological sites and locations in the Mojave Desert.

ally cool and wet. During the Early Holocene (ca. 8000 to 6000 cal B.C.), conditions were somewhat cooler and moister than today. The Middle Holocene (ca. 6000 to 3000 cal B.C.) witnessed a much warmer and drier climate than modern times. Finally, the climate became moderately cooler and wetter again during the Late Holocene (ca. 3000 cal B.C. to present), punctuated with periods of drought.

In the past few decades, more detailed paleoenvironmental data have been obtained from the Mojave Desert. Many of these data have been derived from lake level studies and woodrat middens (Benson et al. 1990, 2002; Enzel et al. 1989, 1992; Koehler et al. 2005; Kuehn 2002; Rhode 2001; Spaulding 1990, 1995a). The recent summary of the Owens Lake record (Benson 2004) portrayed a general drying trend beginning by 9600 cal B.C., with relatively wet conditions and regular lake recharge between 8000 and 6000 cal B.C.; shallow, rapidly oscillating lake levels between 6000 and 4500 cal B.C.; a persistently dry lake bed between 4500 and 1900 cal B.C.; and periodic, often short-term filling events during and after the Little Ice Age. Similar evidence for oscillating lakestands persisting into the Middle Holocene was obtained from Rosamond Lake in the western Mojave Desert (4800 cal B.C.; Orme 2004) and Emerson Lake in the eastern Mojave Desert (5400 to 4900 cal B.C.; Kuehn 2002).

Woodrat middens from the north-central and southern Mojave are broadly consistent with these hydrologic records, suggesting that creosote biotic communities first became established ca. 4900 cal B.C. or soon thereafter (Koehler et al. 2005). These paleoclimatic data have important implications for early occupation in the region, suggesting at least two possibilities: (1) that patterns of enhanced precipitation may have persisted later than was previously believed, and (2) that the warm period during the Middle Holocene may have had profound effects on the distribution of water and biotic resources.

Short- and long-term trends in environmental productivity must have had strong influences on the mode and tempo of occupation strategies, affecting the intensity and cycling of local and regional land-use patterns (Basgall 2000b). To the extent that prehistoric

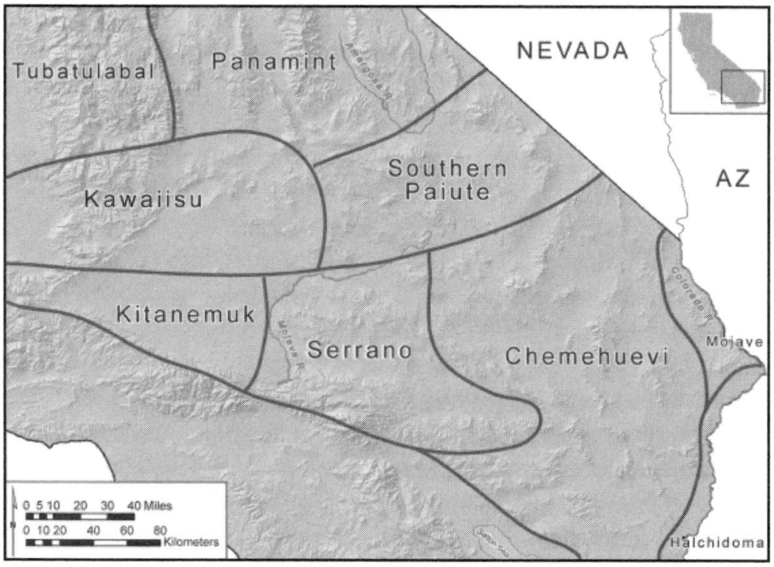

Figure 15.2. Approximate locations of ethnographic groups in the Mojave Desert.

populations could monitor the location and magnitude of storm tracks or precipitation levels, they must have been able to predict which habitats and resources would produce the highest net foraging returns during any one period. It is possible that large tracts of the desert were effectively abandoned or rarely visited during particular periods of time (e.g., Gardner 2006).

In some cases, these climatic changes are thought to have been coincident with major technological or subsistence adjustments, although the nature and extent of the correlation between climate and culture change in this region are unclear. New data suggest that some portions of the Middle Holocene were not as bleak as once portrayed; this fact has implications for arguments about both an occupational hiatus during Gypsum times (see below) as well as the factors that prompted the adoption of milling-dominant technologies.

These environmental findings have allowed archaeologists to make broad generalizations about the impact of these variations on human populations, although there is certainly no consensus about such postulated impacts (Basgall and Hall 1992, 1993a; Cleland and Spaulding 1992, 1993). There has been much debate about the effects of climatic fluctuations on prehistoric populations in the western Mojave Desert, as this region has often been perceived as having minor environmental variation throughout most of the Holocene (Basgall and Hall 1992:6).

Climate Change during the Late Holocene

Most of the paleoenvironmental data that have accumulated in the past few decades for the Mojave Desert, as well as the Great Basin as a whole, relate to the Late Holocene. Recent evidence for climatic change during the Late Holocene comes from dendrochronological reconstructions, pollen studies, skeletal data, archaeological assemblages, paleohydrologic data, geomorphological studies, and other sources. It is now possible to detect climate variation on as little as an annual basis and also to make broad generalizations regarding climate, at least for the Late Holocene (Anderson and Smith 1991; Lloyd and Graumlich 1997).

In particular, the Late Holocene was witness to two significant climatic episodes: the Medieval Climatic Anomaly (MCA) and the Little Ice Age (LIA). How dramatic these impacts were remains unclear, although data for the former indicate striking correlations between drought and changes in subsistence, population demographics, exchange systems, and health (Jones et al. 1999; Gardner 2006). The following is a brief discussion of these two episodes, including their potential impact on prehistoric cultures.

THE MEDIEVAL CLIMATIC ANOMALY Scholars have been investigating the scope and impact of the MCA since the mid-1960s (Lamb 1965; Jones et al. 1999; Gardner 2006). How widespread this climatic event was and how it may have impacted human populations have been debated ever since. While Lamb (1965:13) placed the MCA between about A.D. 1000 and 1200, most researchers now bracket it between about cal A.D. 800 and 1350. The timing and intensity of the climatic changes during the MCA vary regionally, although the warmest phases appear to have taken place during the mid-twelfth century (Anderson and Smith 1991:40; Graumlich 1993:253).

In the western Mojave Desert, the MCA was coincident with a number of culture changes. It was a time that witnessed the decline of large villages that had been established about cal A.D. 1 (Sutton 1996a; Whitley et al. 1988). Apparently conditions became so unfavorable that few people remained in much of the Mojave Desert (Basgall et al. 1988; McGuire and Hall 1988). On the other hand, rather than abandonment, there may have been merely a population shift to a different settlement pattern, with people aggregating into more compact settlement units to take better advantage of diminishing resources due to environmental deterioration (Gardner 2006).

THE LITTLE ICE AGE One of the most significant global climatic events of the past millennium, the LIA is generally dated between about cal A.D. 1400 and 1875 (Wigand and Rhode 2002). A variety of evidence suggests that during the LIA in the Great Basin, there were cooler temperatures and greater winter precipitation that signaled the end of the drought episodes of the MCA and the beginning of a gradual re-expansion of juniper woodland (Wigand and Rhode 2002:331).

During the LIA, temperatures fell about 0.5°C below modern levels (Graumlich 1993:253). These severe cold conditions are believed to have generated major global crises, including crop failures, virtual elimination of some fish populations, social and political conflict, and increased incidence of disease (Fagan 1999, 2000). How the LIA affected the Mojave Desert specifically is unclear at this time, but evidence from the Great Basin in general suggests that it may have had a substantial impact.

DATING AND NOMENCLATURE

As a result of archaeological investigations during the past two decades, we are gaining a better understanding of the chronological sequences in the Mojave Desert, although several gaps continue to create interpretive difficulties and radiometric dates remain uncommon (Table 15.3). In part, these advances stem from continuing field research in the region, but they are also related to different applications of radiocarbon methods, such as those on sediment units and marine shell artifacts. Obsidian hydration has been more widely employed, although obsidian occurs in low frequencies in many contexts. Our understanding of hydration rates continues to improve, making the technique increasingly useful. Also, the use of flaked stone technological profiles has been applied as a way to relatively order archaeological assemblages (Basgall 1993a).

A continuing distraction in Mojave Desert archaeology is nomenclature. A major issue is the interchangeable use of the terms "period" and "complex" to define both time spans and cultural entities. We propose the use of climatic periods (e.g., Early Holocene) to specify spans of calendric time and cultural complexes (e.g., Lake Mojave Complex) to denote specific archaeological manifestations that existed during (and across) those periods (Table 15.4).

A further complication is the fact that early researchers applied a number of terms to assemblages across the Mojave Desert, often with little consideration for the labels used by others, resulting in an abundance of terms being applied to similar materials within the desert. Here we propose a simplified nomenclature for Mojave Desert cultural complexes (Table 15.4), which is not to suggest that cultural systems were homogeneous and neatly sequential across the region. We fully expect that chronological periods will continue to be refined, and that the discovery of new cultural complexes will eventually compel us to revise this nomenclature.

The use of certain artifacts as temporal markers, especially projectile points, has continued mostly unchanged over the past 20 years (Figure 15.3, Table 15.4). The dating of such artifacts has improved and the temporal spans are generally tighter, although some scholars (Flenniken and Wilke 1989; Schroth 1994) have argued that dart points are poor temporal markers due to changing morphologies as the result of rejuvenation. While this issue has ignited some debate, at least as it relates to dart points, most archaeologists still use the standard point types as temporal markers.

THE EVOLUTION OF CULTURAL SYSTEMS

Our understanding of prehistoric cultural systems in the Mojave Desert, at least for the Holocene, has greatly expanded over the past two decades. With that in mind, within the broad temporal periods defined below are a number of cultural complexes, some of which span the transition between periods.

The Pleistocene

The only cultural complex dating to the Pleistocene that has been confidently identified in the Mojave Desert is Clovis (ca. 10,000 to 8000 cal B.C.). Proponents of a pre-Clovis occupation of the Mojave Desert continue to argue their case, but most of the primary data are unpublished and the broader archaeological community remains largely unconvinced. That said, with the growing corpus of evidence for a pre-Clovis occupation of the Americas (Dillehay 1997; Madsen 2004), the possibility of a pre-Clovis presence in the Mojave Desert cannot be discounted. For example, Basgall (2000b) raised the possibility that clusters of exceptionally large hydration measurements from some sites in the Mojave Desert may constitute evidence of a pre-Clovis occupation.

Various terms have been employed to designate the earliest human occupation in the Mojave Desert and other parts of western North America during the Terminal Pleistocene, the most common being Paleo-Indian. As stated above, in the Mojave Desert, the only Paleo-Indian complex so far identified is Clovis,

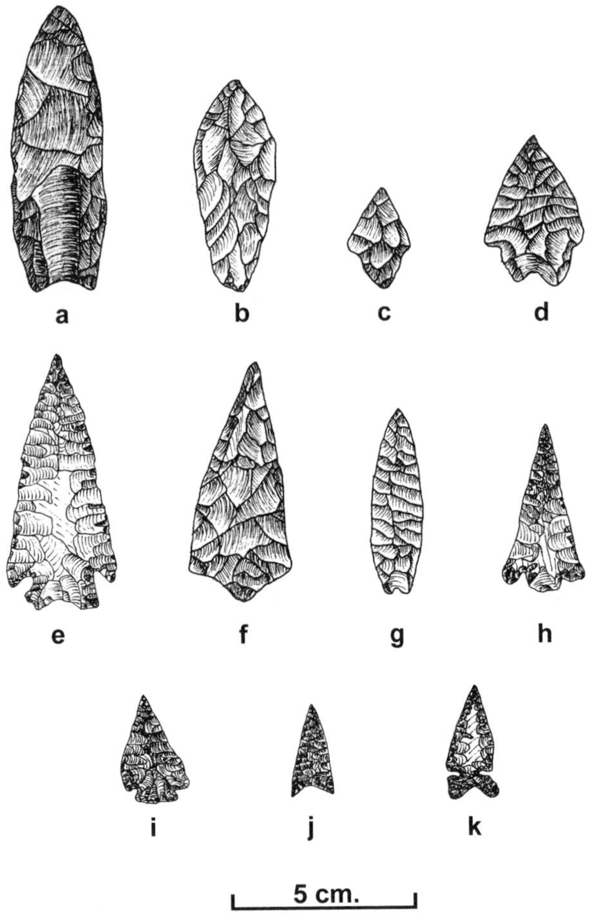

Figure 15.3. Major projectile point types in the Mojave Desert.
(a) Clovis; (b) Lake Mojave; (c) Silver Lake; (d) Pinto; (e) Elko; (f) Gypsum; (g) Humboldt concave base; (h) Eastgate; (i) Rose Spring; (j) Cottonwood triangular; (k) Desert Side-notched.

marked by the characteristic fluted projectile point of the same name. Fluted points appear more often in the north and west than in other sectors of the Mojave, with concentrations reported in the drainage basins of Pleistocene lakes China (Basgall 2005a, b; Davis 1978; Dillon 2002; Rosenthal et al. 2001; Warren and Phagan 1988) and Thompson (Rosamond, Rogers, and Koehn playas) (Basgall and Overly 2004). These are areas of substantial external stream runoff that would have been well watered into the Early Holocene.

It is not clear, however, whether all of the identified "Clovis" points from the Mojave Desert actually represent the Clovis complex or a later cultural complex that also used some form of fluted or basally thinned, concave base projectile points (see Chapter 5 in this volume). The cultural relationship between fluted points and the later Great Basin stemmed (GBS) series points is also a consideration. Such artifacts have been recovered from an increasing but still small number of locales across the Mojave Desert, although rarely in buried contexts and frequently associated with stemmed points.

It is now clear that fluted and stemmed points have significant differences in distribution, material profiles, and manufacturing techniques (Basgall and Hall 1991) and often occur in separate site contexts or as part of discrete clusters within larger surface accumulations (Basgall 2004a, 2005a, b). Less clear is the precise chronological position of fluted point forms in the Mojave Desert due to a lack of reliable radiocarbon dates. Temporal data derived from obsidian hydration measurements indicate, on average, that fluted/basally thinned points in the southwestern Great Basin are older than their stemmed counterparts (Basgall 1988; Gilreath and Hildebrandt 1997).

Warren (2000) attempted to date fluted points based on their topographic position within the Lake China basin (see also Rosenthal et al. 2001). With the Searles/Lake China hydrologic record serving as a clock, an observed propensity for fluted points to cluster below the Searles Lake overflow sill (795 meters) led Warren to infer deposition during the so-called Clovis drought at ca. 9200 cal B.C. Subsequent research in the Lake China basin (Basgall 2004b, 2005a, b) has not refuted this idea, but has shown that fluted points are also abundant above this elevation, while stemmed forms occur in some frequency below it. While little progress has been made in resolving the absolute age of fluted points, they do appear to represent distinct, probably sequential technologies that overlap temporally with stemmed points, at least in some areas.

The nature of Paleo-Indian cultural systems remains poorly defined. Evidence from this period is limited to a few isolated finds of fluted points and a single presumed occupation site at Lake China (Davis 1978). Based on this very sparse evidence, all we can say about Paleo-Indian groups is that they probably had small populations and were highly mobile, living in small, temporary camps located near (then) permanent water sources.

The Early Holocene

The only truly coherent and integrated archaeological pattern in this region during this time is the Lake Mojave Complex (Amsden 1937; Campbell et al. 1937), generally dating between 8000 and 6000 cal B.C. This complex is characterized by projectile points of the GBS series (Lake Mojave and Silver Lake) and abundant bifaces, as well as steep-edged unifaces, crescents, and occasional cobble-core tools and ground stone implements. In-

Table 15.3. Recent Radiocarbon Assays from Selected Early Sites in the Mojave Desert

Site	*Region*	*Complex*	*Material Dated*	*Measured Age* (RCYBP)	*$^{13}C/^{12}C$ Adj. Age* (RCYBP)	*Calibrated Age* B.C.*	*Laboratory Number*	*Reference*
SBR-5250	Ft. Irwin	Lake Mojave	*Olivella* bead	10,085 ± 85	10,495 ± 85	9640 (9010) 8690	AA-12405	Basgall and Hall 1994
INY-5825	Lake China	Lake Mojave	Peat	--	10,010 ± 110	10,380 (9740, 9720, 9700) 9280	Beta-170208	Basgall 2004b
INY-5825	Lake China	Lake Mojave	Soil	9870 ± 50	--	9450-9250	Beta-170210	Basgall 2004b
INY-5825	Lake China	Lake Mojave	Soil	8390 ± 130	--	7610 (7500) 7070	Beta-170209	Basgall 2004b
INY-182	Stahl	Pinto	Carbonized organic matter	8900 ± 65	--	8060 (7960) 7870	AA-10536	Schroth 1994
INY-182	Stahl	Pinto	*Olivella* bead	8670 ± 85	9080 ± 85	7840 (7270) 7040	AA-8620	Schroth 1994
INY-182	Stahl	Pinto	Carbonized organic matter	8625 ± 60	--	9680 (9530) 9450	AA-10535	Schroth 1994
INY-182	Stahl	Pinto	*Olivella* bead	8625 ± 110	9035 ± 110	7820 (7300) 6990	AA-8621	Schroth 1994
INY-182	Stahl	Pinto	*Olivella* bead	8400 ± 85	8810 ± 85	7670 (7120) 6910	AA-8622	Schroth 1994
INY-182	Stahl	Pinto	Carbonized organic matter	7060 ± 60	--	5940 (5910) 5880	AA-10537	Schroth 1994
RIV-521	Pinto Basin	Pinto	*Olivella* bead	9330 ± 90	9740 ± 90	8630 (8310) 7770	AA-8613	Schroth 1994
RIV-521	Pinto Basin	Pinto	*Olivella* bead	7920 ± 85	8330 ± 85	6870 (6530) 6380	AA-8614	Schroth 1994
RIV-521	Pinto Basin	Pinto	*Olivella* bead	7730 ± 85	8140 ± 85	6620 (6420) 6220	AA-8616	Schroth 1994
RIV-521	Pinto Basin	Pinto	Hearth charcoal	7520 ± 120	--	6510 (6370) 6120	UCR-2621	Schroth 1994
RIV-521	Pinto Basin	Pinto	*Olivella* bead	7225 ± 85	7635 ± 85	6080 (5910) 5720	AA-8615	Schroth 1994
RIV-522	Pinto Basin	Pinto	Bone point	7820 ± 80	--	6790 (6600) 6460	AA-8618	Schroth 1994
KER-3939	Garlock Fault	Pinto	Hearth charcoal	7170 ± 140	7980	6340 (6030) 5730	Beta-74108	Gardner et al. 2002
KER-3939	Garlock Fault	Pinto	Hearth charcoal	6968 ± 109	7800	6020 (5850) 5660	AA-14553	Gardner et al. 2002
KER-3939	Garlock Fault	Pinto	Hearth charcoal	5602 ± 71	6390	4600 (4440) 4260	AA-14548	Gardner et al. 2002
KER-3939	Garlock Fault	Pinto	Hearth charcoal	5600 ± 50	--	6430-4350	Beta-112551	Gardner et al. 2002
SBR-2348	Ft. Irwin	Pinto	*Olivella* bead	9125 ± 80	9535 ± 85	8340 (7890) 7600	AA-12403	Basgall and Hall 1994
SBR-2348	Ft. Irwin	Pinto	Charcoal	5540 ± 90	--	4600-4080	Beta-55691	Basgall and Hall 1994
SBR-4562	Ft. Irwin	Pinto	*Olivella* bead	9450 ± 110	9860 ± 110	9160 (8340) 7880	AA-12404	Basgall and Hall 1994
SBR-5251	Ft. Irwin	Pinto	Charcoal	6640 ± 65	--	5660-5480	Beta-45611	Hall 1993
SBR-5251	Ft. Irwin	Pinto	*Olivella* bead	8930 ± 85	9340 ± 85	8310 (7720) 7170	AA-12406	Basgall and Hall 1994
SBR-3632	Twentynine Palms	Pinto	Charcoal	8030 ± 50	--	7080-6710	Beta-103975	Basgall and Giambastiani 2000
SBR-9415	Twentynine Palms	Pinto	Charcoal	8570 ± 50	--	7710-7530	Beta-175147	Basgall and Pierce 2004
SBR-3632	Twentynine Palms	Deadman Lake	Charcoal	7970 ± 70	--	7060-6660	Beta-136533	Basgall 2003
SBR-3632	Twentynine Palms	Deadman Lake	Charcoal	6760 ± 80	--	5830-5530	Beta-136534	Basgall 2003
SBR-3632	Twentynine Palms	Deadman Lake	Charcoal	7560 ± 40	--	6480-6280	Beta-183170	Basgall and Pierce 2004
SBR-8959	Twentynine Palms	Deadman Lake	Charcoal	6410 ± 80	--	5510-5220	Beta-183171	Basgall and Pierce 2004
SBR-9727	Twentynine Palms	Deadman Lake	Charcoal	7620 ± 40	--	6590-6420	Beta-183173	Basgall and Pierce 2004

*Rounded calendar dates include midpoint (in parentheses) (calibrated with CALIB 4.3), and/or with age range at two sigma (CALIB 5.0.2), using an established regional marine reservoir correction rate of 225±35 for shell samples.

Table 15.4. Proposed Concordance of Terms for Temporal Periods and Complexes in the Mojave Desert

<table>
<tr><th>Temporal Period</th><th>Cultural Complex</th><th>Approximate Dating</th><th>Previously Known As</th><th>Marker Artifacts</th></tr>
<tr><td rowspan="2">Pleistocene</td><td>Pre-Clovis (hypothetical)</td><td>Pre-10,000 cal B.C.</td><td>Early Man
Early Humans
Pre-Projectile Point</td><td>Unclear</td></tr>
<tr><td>Paleo-Indian</td><td>10,000–8000 cal B.C.</td><td>Clovis
Early Systems
Big Game Hunting Tradition
Malpais</td><td>Fluted points (Clovis)</td></tr>
<tr><td rowspan="2">Early Holocene</td><td>Lake Mojave</td><td rowspan="2">8000–6000 cal B.C.</td><td rowspan="2">Western Pluvial Lakes Tradition
Western Lithic Co-tradition
Western Stemmed Tradition
Playa Complex
San Dieguito Complex
Lake Mohave Complex
Early Archaic
Death Valley I
Period I</td><td rowspan="2">Stemmed points (e.g., Lake Mojave, Silver Lake)</td></tr>
<tr><td rowspan="2">Pinto</td></tr>
<tr><td rowspan="2">Middle Holocene</td><td rowspan="2">7000–3000 cal B.C.</td><td>Little Lake
Amargosa I
Period II
Death Valley II</td><td>Pinto Series points</td></tr>
<tr><td>Deadman Lake</td><td>N/A</td><td>Contracting stemmed and leaf-shaped points</td></tr>
<tr><td rowspan="3">Late Holocene</td><td>Gypsum</td><td>2000 cal B.C.–cal A.D. 200</td><td>Newberry
Elko
Amargosa II
Period II
Death Valley II</td><td>Gypsum and Elko Series points</td></tr>
<tr><td>Rose Spring</td><td>cal A.D. 200–1100</td><td>Saratoga Springs I
Period III, Phase II
Late Rose Spring
Haiwee
Death Valley III
Period III
Saratoga
Amargosa I
Amargosa III</td><td>Rose Spring and Eastgate Series points</td></tr>
<tr><td>Late Prehistoric</td><td>cal A.D. 1100–Contact</td><td>Yuman
Hakataya
Patayan
Period IV
Prehistoric Shoshonean
Protohistoric
Shoshonean
Marana
Cottonwood</td><td>Desert Series points, ceramics</td></tr>
</table>

creasing numbers of Lake Mojave Complex artifacts and assemblages have been identified, but most frequently as surface finds lacking reliable radiometric associations. Material residues attributable to the Lake Mojave Complex have now been reported in some density from Lake Mojave, Fort Irwin (see Basgall 2000b), Twentynine Palms (Basgall 2004b; Basgall and Giambastiani 2000), Rosamond Lake (Basgall and Overly 2004), and Lake China (Basgall 2004b, 2005a, b; Gilreath and Hildebrandt 1997). The largest suite of regional dates has been derived from Fort Irwin, where nine radiocarbon assays from five components range between ca. 9000 and 6000 cal B.C. (Basgall and Hall 1994; Table 15.3). Most recently, a significant Lake Mojave assemblage was documented at Lake China (INY-5825), in association with fossil spring organics dating between ca. 9700 and 9300 cal B.C., along with an artifact-bearing paleosol dated to 7500 cal B.C. (Table 15.3). Chronological estimates for the Lake Mojave Complex remain broadly consistent with data for GBS assemblages elsewhere in western North America (Basgall 1993a; Beck and Jones 1997; Willig and Aikens 1988).

Flaked stone artifacts in Lake Mojave assemblages include tools that are consistent with long-term curation and transport, frequently bearing evidence of multiple use trajectories. Extralocal materials are common, suggesting extensive annual foraging ranges; marine shell beads likewise imply wide spheres of interaction. Small numbers of ground stone implements occur regularly within these components, although wear on these tools is often ephemeral and inconsistent with heavy hard seed milling, suggesting there was little reliance on vegetal resources. Heavily battered cobble tools also occur sporadically in these assemblages, but it is unclear whether these relate to plant and/or animal processing; future protein residue studies may clarify the role of these implements in the technology of Mojave Desert populations.

In terms of settlement organization, Lake Mojave components include extensive residential accumulations, such as those reported at Fort Irwin (Basgall 1993a, 2000b; Hall 1993) and Lake China (Basgall 2004b; Davis 1978), as well as workshops (Basgall 2004a) and small camps containing a handful of formed tools (Basgall 2005a, b; Rosenthal et al. 2001). The largest of these site manifestations appears to be functionally redundant with the smaller ones, which are thought to represent locations of recurrent use rather than different settlement types. Thus, the Lake Mojave pattern appears to reflect a forager-like strategy organized around relatively small social units.

Still to be resolved are the nature of Lake Mojave Complex hunting patterns and the value of lacustrine habitats within these systems. Substantial archaeofaunal data from this complex have only been recovered from deposits at Fort Irwin (Basgall 1993a; Douglas et al. 1988), where taxonomic profiles and protein residue analyses suggest reliance on smaller taxa (lagomorphs, rodents, and certain reptiles) and only occasional use of large game. This focus on smaller taxa has been difficult to reconcile with flaked stone assemblages dominated by heavy projectile points, bifaces, and formalized scrapers that appear geared toward large game (Elston and Zeanah 2002; Warren 1991, 2002). With regard to the reality of lacustrine adaptations in the Mojave Desert, available settlement data suggest it was not extensive lakeside marshes that attracted human occupation, but rich resource patches in a host of environmental situations.

In accounting for the structure of the Lake Mojave cultural system, it is perhaps informative to consider the dynamic nature of environments at the Pleistocene/Holocene transition. Pluvial lake basins were rapidly drying, new biotic associations were becoming established, and rapid climatic oscillations would surely have led to unpredictability in resource distribution and abundance (Basgall 2000b; Madsen 1999). This would have encouraged intensive environmental monitoring, wherein groups would have employed high levels of residential mobility in an effort to track the mode and tempo of resource productivity. Some parts of the Mojave Desert were evidently more attractive on a regular basis than others (e.g., the Lake China basin), but individual occupation events were short-term and sporadic everywhere. Regular recharge of catchments along the eastern front of the Sierra Nevada and Transverse Ranges likely provided mosaics of rich distribution drainages containing diverse subsistence products, while internally drained basins of the interior desert provided less frequent settlement draws.

Data from a number of sites in the central and northern Mojave Desert indicate a temporal overlap between Lake Mojave and Pinto complexes, with the inception of the Pinto Complex occurring sometime during the later part of the Early Holocene. Overlapping radiometric dates and hydration profiles, as well as the periodic co-occurrence of GBS and Pinto series projectile points at some locations, support this assertion. Nevertheless, the two complexes appear to be distinct, with statistically divergent hydration ranges and consistently different site distributions (Basgall 1995; Warren 2002).

The Middle Holocene

Chronologies for the Middle Holocene are more complex and regionally heterogeneous than was envisioned 20 years ago. At that time, archaeologists were concerned mainly with the temporal position of Pinto assemblages; when they first appeared and how long they persisted. Researchers today confront the prospect of multiple culturally and technologically distinct populations inhabiting and exploiting the Mojave Desert during this period.

THE PINTO COMPLEX The primary cultural complex heretofore associated with the Middle Holocene is called Pinto, commonly assumed to have neatly followed the Lake Mojave Complex and to have lasted until ca. 3000 cal B.C. Information obtained in the past two decades, however, suggests that the inception of the Pinto Complex was during the Early Holocene, overlapping the Lake Mojave Complex. Radiometric assays obtained by Schroth (1994) from Pinto Basin and the Stahl (Little Lake) locality range between 8310 and 5910 cal B.C. (Table 15.3). There has been some reluctance to accept such early dates for the Pinto Complex, a response to the embedded notion that Pinto was more recent (cf. Warren 1984; but see Jenkins 1987) and to uncertainties regarding the depositional context of some radiocarbon samples (Basgall and Hall 2000). On the other hand, assays from three Pinto components at Fort Irwin range between 8340 and 3590 cal B.C. (Table 15.3; Basgall 2000b; Basgall and Hall 1994; Hall 1993), four new assays from the Garlock Fault site (KER-3939) fall between ca. 6300 and 4200 cal B.C. (Gardner et al. 2002), and a newly acquired assay from Twentynine Palms calibrates to 6870 cal B.C. (Table 15.3; Basgall and Pierce 2004). Thus, with an ever-growing body of ancient dates from additional Mojave Desert localities, it becomes increasingly difficult to deny the possibility that the beginning of the Pinto Complex dates sometime during the Early Holocene.

The Pinto Complex has the most widespread expression of any of the early manifestations in the Mojave Desert, with substantial components now reported from Fort Irwin (Basgall and Hall 1993b, 1994; Hall 1993; Jenkins 1987; Laylander and Victorino 2001), Silurian Valley (Byrd, ed. 1998), Twentynine Palms (Basgall and Giambastiani 2000; Basgall et al. 2003), and various other places in the Mojave Desert (Basgall and Overly 2004; Giambastiani and Basgall 2000). There appears to be broad continuity in the flaked stone technologies of the Lake Mojave and Pinto complexes, both of which are characterized by extensive use of toolstones other than obsidian and cryptocrystalline silica, and by regular use of bifacial and unifacial core/tool forms. The signature stemmed, indented-base Pinto series projectile points show high levels of blade reworking and appear to have frequently served as tips for thrusting spears rather than darts. Reduced toolstone source diversity among Pinto assemblages implies a reduction in foraging ranges from the Lake Mojave Complex, although the presence of *Olivella* shell beads indicates regular regional interaction with coastal groups. Patterns of faunal exploitation remain similar to those of the Lake Mojave Complex, although artiodactyl frequencies drop and the reliance on small fauna increases slightly.

The most important distinction between the Lake Mojave and Pinto assemblages relates to the prevalence of ground stone implements. Milling tools are moderately abundant in nearly all known Pinto deposits and occur in great frequencies in some places. Proportional representations of milling tools in the composite Fort Irwin collection, for example, suggest levels of ground stone artifact abundance as high as anytime during the Holocene (Basgall 2000b). Not only do these data resolve questions about the importance of milling equipment to Pinto populations, but revised dating estimates demonstrate that intensive levels of plant processing began by ca. 7000 cal B.C., roughly coincident with comparable patterns on the California coast (Fitzgerald 2000; Jones, Fitzgerald et al. 2002). Broad-spectrum economies appear to have emerged at roughly the same time in both coastal and interior settings. Further, the Mojave Desert data indicate that the emergence of intensive plant exploitation occurred before the onset of severe Middle Holocene dessication.

Sites of the Pinto Complex occur in a diverse range of topographic and environmental zones; within remnant pluvial lake basins, adjacent to fossil stream channels and spring/seep locations, and in upland contexts. Larger sites, which appear to correlate with well-watered locations, contain substantial middens and a breadth of cultural debris not present at smaller sites. These data are consistent with expectations of residential bases that were occupied for prolonged periods by moderate to large numbers of people. Such groups probably consisted of multiple families or macrobands, inferring a collector-like settlement strategy with centralized site complexes in favorable locations in order to stage logistical forays into surrounding resource patches (cf. Basgall 2000b; Warren 2002). Judging by the high frequencies of milling tools at many of these bases, access to plant resources must have been a key determinant for site placement. It may be significant that the Pinto Complex emerged subsequent to the most dramatic climatic fluctuations of the Early Holocene, after which biotic conditions presumably became more predictable.

Warren (1991) suggested that the Lake Mojave and Pinto complexes formed a single cultural tradition, arguing that the subsistence focus of the Pinto Complex remained similar to that of Lake Mojave, at least initially, and that the pursuit of artiodactyls remained a major focus. Warren (1991) hypothesized that as game populations declined, the effort to hunt them may have intensified with a decreasing rate of success, eventually leading to collapse of the system and a shift to a more broad-based economy. This interesting model remains to be tested.

THE DEADMAN LAKE COMPLEX The Deadman Lake Complex, proposed here for the first time, appears to have been a separate cultural complex within the Middle Holocene. In contrast to the Pinto Complex, which was a pan-desert expression, sites attributable to the Deadman Lake Complex have thus far been identified solely at Twentynine Palms in the southeastern Mojave Desert (Basgall and Giambastiani 2000; Basgall and Pierce 2004). While this geographic range will likely be expanded in the future as more work is conducted in adjacent areas or as older data are reassessed, the Deadman Lake Complex may reflect close cultural connections to the Southwest Archaic that become increasingly weak to the north and west.

Assemblages attributable to the Deadman Lake Complex are characterized by small- to medium-size contracting-stemmed or lozenge-shaped points, extensive concentrations of battered cobbles and core tools, abundant bifaces, simple flake tools, and milling implements (Figure 15.4). Toolstone profiles demonstrate considerable quantities of nonsilicate material, including coarse- to fine-grained igneous rock and modest amounts of obsidian (local and exotic). Simple spire-lopped *Olivella* shell beads are frequently present in Deadman Lake deposits, with specimens attributed to both the Pacific coast (*O. biplicata*) and the Sea of Cortez (*O. dama*). Five radiocarbon dates from three separate components range between ca. 7500 and 5200 cal B.C. (Table 15.3). These assays are consistent with data from Ventana Cave in southwestern Arizona, where similar points were recovered from strata dating to about 6000 cal B.C. (Haury 1950; Huckell and Haynes 2003).

Comparable assemblages are yet to be reported from other regions of the Mojave Desert, although this may reflect a bias in identification rather than an actual absence. Contracting-stemmed point morphologies are routinely placed within the Gypsum Complex (see below) and considered coterminous with Elko series points. Basgall (1993b) and Basgall and Hall (1994), for example, reported contracting-stemmed points from sites at Fort Irwin made from igneous toolstones that are all but absent from typical Gypsum Complex assemblages.

The small sample of known Deadman Lake Complex sites and assemblages means that any characterization of the broader cultural system must be provisional at best. Two of the known components occur along the margins of Deadman and Emerson lakes, but most such sites are situated on old alluvial piedmonts above these basins. Emerson Lake assemblages are characterized by thin, heavily eroded, and oxidized sediments and essentially surface deposits. Flaked stone is generally similar to that of the Pinto Complex, although marked by more extensive use of local igneous materials, core tools, and simple flake implements. Deadman Lake assemblages contain moderate amounts of ground stone, but the most prevalent processing tools are flaked and battered cobbles, many that are extensively worn. While the artifact assemblages demonstrate an apparent emphasis on vegetal-related activities, the specific nature of plant exploitation appears to have been more generalized than in Pinto contexts. Extraction clearly involved intensive crushing or pulping activities, although flotation efforts have yet to recover identifiable botanical remains from intact deposits. Faunal recovery is rare from these largely surface deposits, but excavation of a deeply buried component at Deadman Lake yielded a sample dominated by small fauna (lagomorphs, rodents, reptiles) that is not unlike those retrieved from Pinto components at Twentynine Palms (Basgall 2003b; Basgall and Giambastiani 2000; Basgall et al. 2003).

Few other details are known at this time, although differences in the distribution and composition of Pinto and Deadman Lake components at Twentynine Palms may reflect somewhat divergent subsistence focuses. The former occur mainly within remnant pluvial lake basins, the latter primarily at higher elevations that would have supported quite different resource constellations. This potential niche differentiation would have facilitated occupation of the same area by two distinct populations, possibly following divergent seasonal or annual schedules. It is also possible that the Deadman Lake Complex simply reflects a segment of the tactical inventory of the Pinto Complex, rather than a separate cultural entity.

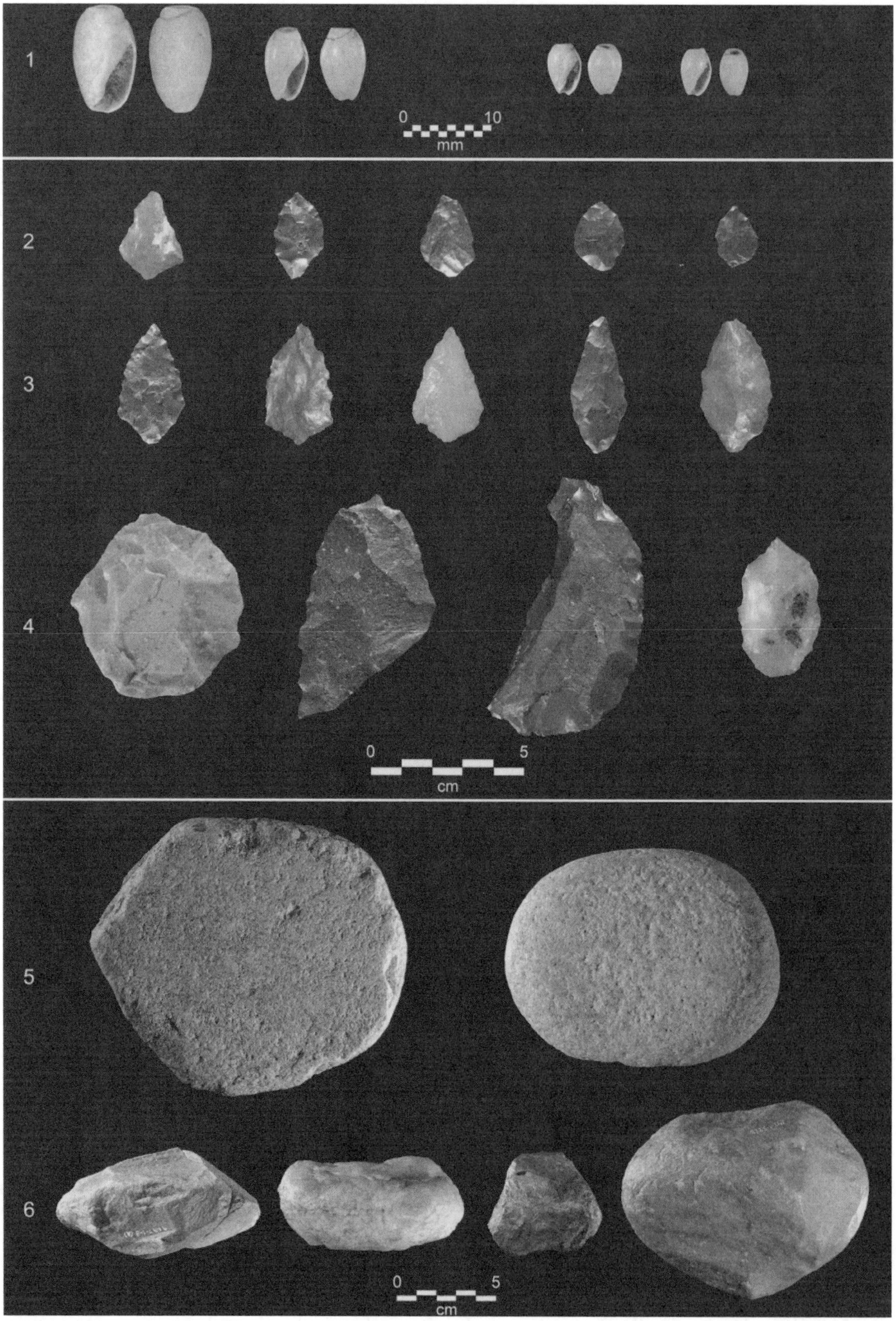

Figure 15.4. Artifacts of the Deadman Lake Complex (Row 1, shell beads; Rows 2–3, projectile points; Row 4, bifaces; Row 5, handstones; Row 6, cobble implements) (by David Nicholson and assembled by Bridget Wall).

AN OCCUPATIONAL HIATUS? Toward the end of the Middle Holocene, environmental conditions became hotter and drier in the Mojave Desert and there are few sites that date between ca. 3000 and 2000 cal B.C. This suggests that population densities were very low in the Mojave Desert and it is possible that some areas were largely abandoned. This roughly 1,000-year "hiatus" between the Pinto (and Deadman Lake?) Complex and the later Gypsum Complex may have been of even longer duration, as most known Pinto components date prior to 4500 cal B.C.

The Late Holocene

The chronological sequence for the Late Holocene has been well documented. In some parts of the Great Basin, the beginning of this period witnessed a time of greater precipitation and elevated lake levels (Rhode 2001; Wigand and Rhode 2002). While such data are relatively sparse for the Mojave Desert, it appears as if similar fluctuations were occurring there.

THE GYPSUM COMPLEX The earliest Late Holocene complex is called Gypsum, defined by the presence of a range of corner-notched (Elko series), concave base (Humboldt series), and well-shouldered contracting-stemmed (Gypsum series) point forms. The Gypsum Complex dates roughly between 2000 cal B.C. and cal A.D. 200, a temporal span corroborated by numerous radiocarbon dates since the late 1980s (Basgall et al. 1988; Gilreath and Hildebrandt 1997; Sutton et al. 1993). Gypsum Complex data from the northern Mojave Desert, in particular, appear congruent with temporal parameters of adjacent areas of the Great Basin (Warren 1984).

Perhaps the most confounding aspect of the Gypsum Complex relates to its evident scarcity in the southern and eastern reaches of the desert. Despite intensive survey and excavation programs in places such as Fort Irwin and Twentynine Palms, relatively few large or deep deposits of this age have been encountered (Basgall 2003b). This evident paucity of major Gypsum-era components no doubt relates to their ephemeral character and thus problems of identification.

The Gypsum Complex emerged during a time when conditions were somewhat wetter and cooler than during the Middle Holocene. During the early part of this complex, it is thought that settlement and subsistence were centered near streams. At the same time, it appears that there were increases in trade and social complexity. Gypsum components tend to be smaller but somewhat more numerous than those of preceding occupations and are found over a more diverse array of locations. Along with the marker projectile point types, artifact assemblages include evidence of ritual activities, such as quartz crystals, paint, and rock art (Davis and Smith 1981; Warren and Crabtree 1986), as well as numerous bifaces. Exploitation of artiodactyls, lagomorphs, and rodents is evident from a number of Gypsum Complex sites. The proposed Pinto/Gypsum hiatus noted above is one that needs to be viewed across the region. The Fort Irwin data suggest that the gap may be more apparent than real, reflecting changes in settlement organization more than anything, although this may not be true in other areas of the Mojave.

THE ROSE SPRING COMPLEX Beginning about cal A.D. 200 (or perhaps a little earlier) (Gardner 2006:364–365), cultural systems changed dramatically across the Mojave Desert, most notably in the western part of the region. The bow and arrow diffused into the area at this time, with the marker projectile points for this complex presumably used as arrow points. In the western Mojave, there is strong circumstantial evidence that lake levels (at least at Koehn Lake) increased after about cal A.D. 1, indicating a more mesic environment (Gardner 2006; Sutton 1996). While it is possible that the rainfall that fed the rise of Koehn Lake was limited to the southern Sierra Nevada and did not significantly influence the biotic communities of the desert proper, the presence of a large quantity of burned juniper from the Koehn Lake site (KER-875) suggests the presence of a juniper woodland in the immediate area.

Archaeological evidence for the Rose Spring Complex indicates a major population increase, dramatic changes in artifact assemblages, and well-developed middens, at least in the western Mojave Desert (Gardner 2002, 2006; Sutton 1988, 1996a). The general dating of the Rose Spring Complex remains roughly as it was in 1984 (ca. cal A.D. 200 to 1100), reinforced by additional radiocarbon assays (Gardner 2002; McGuire et al. 1982; Sutton and Jackson 1993; Yohe 1992b). Common artifacts of the Rose Spring Complex include Eastgate and Rose Spring series projectile points, stone knives, drills, pipes, bone awls, various milling implements, marine shell ornaments, and after large quantities of obsidian (Sutton 1996a; Warren and Crabtree 1986).

Rose Spring sites are commonly found near springs, along washes, and sometimes along lakeshores. Evidence of architecture includes wickiups, pit houses, and other types of structures, suggesting intensive occupations. Populations appear to have reached their peak during this time, judging from the sheer number of known sites. The combination of a more productive environment and a more efficient hunting technology (bow and arrow) may have contributed to the population increase at this time.

The frequency of obsidian in Rose Spring components indicates that the procurement and processing of obsidian were essential aspects of the settlement and subsistence practices of the inhabitants of this region. The fact that all but a few of the obsidian specimens from Rose Spring components in the western Mojave Desert have been chemically traced to the Coso Volcanic Field demonstrates that people were involved in trading activities with populations near the Coso Locality and/or traveled there to obtain obsidian themselves (Gardner 2006). The resource emphasis was clearly on medium to small game, predominately lagomorphs and rodents.

The MCA began roughly during the middle of Rose Spring Complex times and then intensified for several hundred years. As lakes began to desiccate during this time, it seems that settlement patterns (at least in the western Mojave Desert) changed from associations with permanent water sources to more ephemeral ones. The increased hunting efficiency of the bow and arrow may have taken a toll on resource availability as the new technology initially fostered an increase in human carrying capacity (Yohe and Sutton 1999). If demand on particular resources (e.g., artiodactyls) was heightened, the MCA may have stressed an already overtaxed resource base. Coupled with a steadily declining environment and less water, this may have resulted in changes that led to the end of the Rose Spring Complex by about cal A.D. 1100.

AGRICULTURAL INFLUENCES IN THE EASTERN MOJAVE DESERT Beginning just before cal A.D. 1, agricultural peoples appear to have been present in portions of the eastern Mojave Desert, including the region just north of the Providence Mountains. By about cal A.D. 700, Anasazi populations were well established in the Muddy and Virgin river areas and controlled or influenced a considerable portion of the northeastern Mojave Desert (Lyneis 1995). Anasazi influence persisted into the early Late Prehistoric complexes.

LATE PREHISTORIC COMPLEXES After about cal A.D. 1100, the environment continued to deteriorate as a result of the MCA, new technologies were introduced, populations appear to have declined, and a number of separate cultural complexes emerged that are believed to represent the prehistoric aspects of known ethnographic groups. Warren (1984:420) noted "strong regional developments" across the Mojave Desert during this time, including Anasazi interests in turquoise mining in the Mojave Trough, Hakatayan influence from the Colorado River, and the Numic Paiute and Shoshone culture that likely spread eastward (the Numic expansion; see below) from the western Mojave Desert about cal A.D. 1000.

Late Prehistoric occupation sites in the Mojave Desert represent a variety of types, including a few major villages with associated cemeteries, as well as special purpose and seasonal sites (Gardner 2006). Artifact assemblages consist of Desert series projectile points, buffware and brownware ceramics, shell and steatite beads, slate pendants, incised stones, and a variety of milling tools (Warren and Crabtree 1986). Faunal remains typically consist of lagomorphs, deer, rodents, and some reptiles. Obsidian use dropped off significantly, and flaked stone tool manufacture shifted to silicate stone. Our understanding of the time frame for the Late Prehistoric complexes (ca. cal A.D. 1100 to contact) has remained largely unchanged over the past 20 years.

In an analysis of various aspects of the archaeological record of Late Prehistoric complexes, Sutton (1989) proposed a number of interaction spheres across the Mojave Desert at this time, with boundaries that generally match the geographic distribution of groups of the ethnographic period. The northern sphere is characterized by both Desert side-notched and Cottonwood projectile points, brownware ceramics, some buffware near the Mojave River, and the use of obsidian obtained mostly from northern sources (primarily Coso). The eastern sphere is characterized by the presence of both brownware and buffware ceramics, a dominance of Cottonwood projectile points, and the exclusive use of local obsidian sources. For some reason, groups in the eastern Mojave were not participating in the Coso obsidian trade. The area just north of the Mojave River seems to have been the boundary between the two spheres (Warren 1984:Fig. 8.26).

In contrast, Basgall (2000b) and Basgall and Hall (1992, 1994) pointed to the lack of obvious Late Prehistoric cultural boundaries or major transitions at Fort Irwin to the north of the Mojave River. Eerkens (1999) argued that Fort Irwin was essentially a buffer zone or area of jointly controlled resources shared by bordering ethnic groups. However, Allen (1998:74) posited that this "buffer" may have been a product of competition rather than cooperative sharing. Farther north, a clear shift to Shoshone culture during the

Late Prehistoric is evident in Death Valley (Wallace 1977, 1988). The eastern Mojave Desert is not as well understood and needs both additional fieldwork and synthesis (Sutton 1996a:239–240, 2005).

A Model of Culture Change

Over the past two decades, Sutton and colleagues (Sutton 1996a:243–244; Gardner 2002, 2006) have articulated an elaborate model of culture change for the past several thousand years of western Mojave Desert prehistory. This model incorporates environmental data, linguistic prehistory, changing settlement patterns, and stylistic markers to argue for significant shifts in economic practices, mobility, and the distribution of cultural (i.e., linguistic) groups across the western Mojave between Late Gypsum and Late Prehistoric times.

Simply stated, the model proposes that during later Gypsum times, the western Mojave Desert was relatively warm and dry and human populations based themselves in the southern Sierra Nevada/Tehachapi Mountains, using the desert on an ephemeral basis. This changed during the wetter and cooler Rose Spring era, with people moving out into the desert on a permanent basis and using the highlands on a transitory basis. Beginning about cal A.D. 1000, the climate became warmer and drier once again (the MCA), and the settlement-subsistence patterns changed back to the basic pattern of the Gypsum Complex. As a result, the presumed large populations during Rose Spring times may have had no place to go, which may have played a role in the Numic expansion.

A variant of this model may offer an explanatory framework suitable for the entire Mojave Desert in order to assist in understanding how various regions of the Mojave underwent similar processes or events, as well as how they may have differed. Ongoing research by Mark Allen in the Red Mountain Archaeological District in the west-central Mojave Desert suggests patterns that conform to most of the predictions of the Sutton model for the western Mojave, although the intensity of occupation is less at Red Mountain spring locations than at the lake environments studied by Sutton. At Red Mountain, the cultural transition from Gypsum to Rose Spring times was apparently a smooth one, with the same camp locations used during both periods. However, in contrast to the valley village sites in the western Mojave Desert, Red Mountain continued to be used after cal A.D. 1000. It should likewise prove useful to apply this explanatory framework to the central and eastern Mojave Desert.

LINGUISTIC PREHISTORY

The linguistic prehistory of California in general is highly complex (see Chapter 6 in this volume), as is that of the Mojave Desert specifically. Little is known of the linguistic situation in the Mojave until about 3000 cal B.C., when it is believed that Northern Uto-Aztecan (NUA) occupied at least the western part of the Mojave Desert, presumably moving north from Mexico. By about 1000 cal B.C., NUA appears to have differentiated into its major family groups (Tubatulabalic, Hopic, Numic, and Takic). Tubatulabalic remained in place in the southern Sierra Nevada while Hopic apparently moved eastward, eventually ending up in the northern part of the Southwest sometime before cal A.D. 1 (Sutton 2000).

The history of Numic is fairly well understood, at least in general outline (see Madsen and Rhode 1994). From a homeland in the western Mojave Desert/southern Sierra Nevada, Numic diverged into three languages that later (ca. cal A.D. 1000) expanded north and east. The southernmost Numic group, the Southern Paiute, expanded across much of the Mojave Desert north of the Mojave River, while the Shoshone occupied the far northern portion (see Sutton 1994). The impetus of the Numic expansion is not clear, but it may have been related to environmental changes (e.g., the MCA). The mechanism for the expansion continues to be debated (see Sutton and Rhode 1994), although warfare may have been involved (Sutton 1986).

The history of Takic is not as well understood. Takic groups probably originated in the southwestern Mojave Desert, then diverged and expanded south and east sometime around 500 cal B.C. At contact, Takic groups occupied the Mojave Desert south of the Mojave River and much of southern California. The impetus and mechanism for this expansion are unknown. If the southwestern Mojave Desert was the homeland for Takic, this event should be reflected in the archaeological record. Although few archaeological data are available to clarify this issue, it does seem clear that a number of major settlements were established in the Antelope Valley (within ethnographically documented Takic territory) beginning around 500 cal B.C., presumably in conjunction with an increase in population and trade (Sutton 1988). It is unclear if these developments reflect the divergence of Takic, the expansion of Takic, both, or neither. The only links between these events and the Takic is geography and timing which at best constitute circumstantial evidence.

The Mojave River seems to have been an important boundary between Numic and Takic groups during prehistoric times. An analysis of Late Prehistoric artifact assemblages across the Mojave Desert suggests that regional interaction spheres closely match the ethnographic situation (Sutton 1989), reflecting the differences in artifacts and other traits between Numic and Takic groups, as well as Yuman groups to the east (Sutton 1989:110). These include a combination of both Desert side-notched and Cottonwood triangular points (Numic); Cottonwood triangular but no Desert side-notched points (Takic); and differences in brownware (Numic and Takic) and buffware (Yuman) ceramics. Other differences, such as toolstone use, are also apparent.

It is believed that the Yuman Desert Mojave occupied much of the eastern Mojave Desert (Lerch 1985) during late prehistory. There seems to have been an influx of Puebloan groups into the eastern Mojave after ca. cal A.D. 500. Subsequent to ca. cal A.D. 1200, the Numic Chemehuevi replaced the Desert Mojave and Puebloan groups across the eastern Mojave, even occupying a portion of the Colorado River valley in the nineteenth century.

OTHER RESEARCH ISSUES

Consequences of Bow and Arrow Technology

Another important issue addressed in the past 20 years is the timing of the introduction of the bow and arrow into the Mojave Desert. Rose Spring projectile points are presumed to be arrow points, so the use of such points as chronological markers is thought to be related to the entry of bow and arrow technology during this time. This new technology may have altered subsistence systems, as faunal assemblages in the northeastern Mojave Desert appear to indicate a shift from artiodactyls to smaller game, mostly lagomorphs. This apparent shift in subsistence focus away from artiodactyls may have led to decreased residential mobility, as people no longer pursued large mammals (Sutton 1996a). The same pattern is not evident in the southwestern Mojave, where large residential sites are evident earlier than the bow and arrow. This scenario led Yohe and Sutton (2000) to suggest that the Rose Spring Complex originated somewhat earlier (ca. cal A.D. 200) than previously thought.

Toolstone Procurement and Use

Although involving specific areas and influenced by the nature of local toolstone sources, recurrent shifts occurred in material use profiles and manufacturing technologies after the Middle/Late Holocene transition. Early assemblages in all parts of the desert are characterized by extensive use of fine-grained igneous stone, especially for bifacial implements, a preference that virtually disappears after 2000 cal B.C. These tendencies are particularly strong in areas with abundant igneous toolstone (Basgall 1993a, b, 2000b), and less so where coarse-grained volcanics are more limited (Basgall and Giambastiani 2000; Basgall and Overly 2004).

By Gypsum times, obsidian trade and use was common, although obsidian rarely dominates flaked stone assemblages of this age. At the end of Rose Spring times, obsidian trade over much of the Mojave Desert dramatically declined, suggesting a major sociopolitical shift (coincidentally about the time of the MCA and the Numic expansion). A better understanding of other major items traded across the Mojave, including marine shell ornaments, pottery, and turquoise, will serve to highlight changes in sociocultural interaction as well as levels of residential mobility and range.

WHAT NEXT? THE FUTURE OF MOJAVE DESERT ARCHAEOLOGY

In addition to the many site/locality-specific studies that are conducted, research should begin to consider larger scale patterns that might highlight important differences between far-flung areas. This will not only clarify variations in such things as basic assemblage composition but will help resolve larger issues such as how environments influence cultural adjustments. These issues need to be integrated with better landscape studies that articulate how surface age and other factors shape the archaeological record. It is only in this way that we will be able to track occupation intensity (and other measures) across space and time.

A major direction for future research regarding the late prehistory of the Mojave Desert is further examination of the traveler-processor model (Bettinger 1999a; Bettinger and Baumhoff 1982) in which rising sedentism late in the prehistoric sequence is argued to have precipitated increased population size, territoriality, plant food processing (particularly seeds), and logistical subsistence organization (Arnold et al. 2004; Basgall 2000b; Bettinger 1999a). One recent approach to settlement-subsistence shifts has been to focus on the sourcing of ceramics to identify changes in mobility (Eerkens 2003; Eerkens et al. 2002b). It will likely prove fruitful to combine this parsimonious theoretical orientation with further studies of environmental change (Gardner 2006), social roles (Walsh 2000), ethnicity (Earle 2004), competition (Lambert 2002), cooperation (Eerkens 1999), and ideology (Hildebrandt and McGuire 2002; Whitley 2000a).

The past two decades have witnessed monumental growth in the amount of information regarding the prehistory of the Mojave Desert, due largely to CRM projects along with some academic research. The tremendous escalation in survey and excavation efforts has contributed much new information, particularly within military installations that have long-term, well-funded compliance programs. On the other hand, some of the work has been of poor quality, has been inadequately disseminated, and/or has been conducted with insufficient attention to regional issues. To move the discussion in a more positive direction requires comparisons at broader spatial scales that can highlight important variations across different sectors of the Mojave Desert and adjacent areas. Neither cultural nor environmental parameters were likely uniform across the entire region at any time in the past, and there were undoubtedly profound differences in the intensity of local occupation and the range of activities in which populations were engaged from place to place and through time.

CHAPTER 16

The Colorado Desert: Ancient Adaptations to Wetlands and Wastelands

Jerry Schaefer and Don Laylander

The Colorado Desert is a geographical region with its own unique natural and cultural history. The archaeology is distinctive, yet it is embedded in a larger context that includes the Mojave Desert to the north, the Sonoran Desert to the east, and the mountains and coastlines of southern California and northern Baja California to the west and south. Since Warren's 1984 summary of California desert archaeology, a steady stream of studies has enhanced our understanding of this region's past. Schaefer (1994a, b) summarized some of these advances and continuing issues 10 years after Warren's synthesis. This current summary brings our understanding up to the twentieth anniversary of Warren's (1984) contribution to Moratto's *California Archaeology*. Space limits us to references that best lead the reader to the substantial body of recent reports and articles. Tables 16.1 and 16.2 provide more inclusive lists of major contributing archaeological projects.

Before the late 1970s there were few well-reported, large-scale data recovery projects or regional surveys. Since then, however, substantial advances in our understanding of Colorado Desert culture history, settlement patterns, and cultural processes have come from cultural resource management (CRM) projects and a few academic endeavors. Most earlier surface surveys were opportunistic or purposive in nature, providing partial or tentative interpretations of the relative age and cultural contexts of features such as trails, cleared circles, rock rings, and surface artifact scatters. Cultural histories have been strengthened with a greater corpus of radiocarbon-dated archaeological contexts, and where those have not been forthcoming for earlier sites or undatable surface components, greater meaning has been obtained by application of forager theory and more sophisticated lithic technology studies.

LATE PLEISTOCENE THROUGH HOLOCENE

Solid evidence for a human presence in the Colorado Desert during the Late Pleistocene or Early Holocene is still scarce. This situation stands in marked contrast to the well-documented Early Holocene occupations in surrounding regions, including the Mojave Desert and coastal southern California. Rather than reflecting an absence of any early occupation, the geographical gap is probably the result of other circumstances, including highly mobile early settlement strategies, instability of landforms in the Salton basin and Colorado River valley, and the limited amount of archaeological investigation carried out between the river and the basin and farther west within Anza-Borrego Desert State Park.

The Yuha burial (IMP-108), which 30 years ago was proposed to date back into the Pleistocene, has now been assigned a Late Holocene age, based on AMS radiocarbon dating (Taylor et al. 1985), as has the Truckhaven burial (Figure 16.1). Geologically based claims for very early archaeological deposits in the Yuha basin remain inconclusive. Proposals for an extensive presence of the Terminal Pleistocene/Early Holocene San Dieguito Complex in the Colorado Desert, based on heavily patinated scrapers or cores and "sleeping circle" features, still lack any solid chronological confirmation.

Archaeological evidence predating the Late Prehistoric advent of ceramics and the bow and arrow also continues to be meager but with some improvements. Scattered occurrences of large projectile points similar to Pinto and Elko forms have been reported. One substantial study comes from the region's western margin at Indian Hill rock shelter (SDI-2537), where Wilke, McDonald, and others greatly expanded on the earlier investigations by William J. Wallace and his associates (McDonald 1992; Wilke et al. 1986). Indian Hill documents an occupation extending back more than 4,000 years and seems to represent a relatively stable habitation base. Floral remains suggest a human presence during several different seasons, and subsurface cache pits indicate that resources were stored in anticipation of regular return visits. Similar slab-lined pits were documented in a Tahquitz Canyon (RIV-45) rock shelter in Palm Springs, where cached milling equipment, a very low artifact frequency, and the absence of any midden accumulation suggests logistical foraging by mobile groups (Bean et al. 1995). Colorado Desert

Table 16.1. Summary of Archaeological Research in the Colorado Desert Since 1984: Major Inventories

General Location	*Approximate Acres Surveyed (Recorded Prehistoric Sites)*	*Latest Inclusive Reference*
Lower Colorado River (Pilot Knob, Senator Wash, Palo Verde Point, Ripley)	6057 (64)	Ezzo and Altschul 1993
Lower Colorado River (Big Maria/Quien Sabe terraces)	3100 (56)	Ezzo 1994
San Sebastian Marsh	3200 (77)	Schaefer and Moslak 2001
Pilot Knob to Palo Verde Valley Pipeline	3000 (80 linear miles) (99)	Cleland and Apple 2003
Salton Sea Test Base	6400 (166)	Apple et al. 1997
Yuma Proving Ground	85,000 (750)	Oxendine 2000
Chocolate Mountains Gunnery Range	6300 (recent) and 11,000 (pre-1982) (250)	Apple and Shaver 2005
West Mesa, NAF El Centro	25,455 (170)	Zepeda-Herman and Underwood 2005
East Mesa, Mesquite Mine and Imperial Mines	17,000 (250)	Pigniolo et al. 1997 Schaefer and Pallette 2003
IID Transmission Lines	3500 (240 linear miles) (250)	various IID consultants
Santa Rosa/San Jacinto National Monument	8000 (103)	ASM Affiliates and Jones & Stokes 2005

Table 16.2. Summary of Archaeological Research in the Colorado Desert Since 1984: Excavation Projects

Site/Locality (Date Excavated)	*Site Type(s)*	*Period*	*Investigators*	*Latest Inclusive Reference*
Barrel Springs (1976)	Camps	Late Prehistoric	CA Parks and Rec.	Oxendine 2002
West Mesa, Superstition Mtn (1987)	Camps	Late Prehistoric	Mooney and Associates	Schaefer 1988
East Mesa, Mesquite Mine (1987)	Lithic procurement	no date	Mooney and Associates	Shackley 1988
Stollard Site et al., Colorado River (2001–2002)	Camps, quarries, pot drops	Late Prehistoric	EDAW	Cleland and Apple 2003
Indian Hill Rockshelter (1958, 1984–1987)	Camps, shelters	Archaic-Late Prehistoric	UC Riverside	McDonald 1992
Salton Sea Complex, Lake Cahuilla (1996–1997)	Camps, fish traps	Late Prehistoric	EDAW	Apple et al. 1997
Tahquitz Canyon (1988–1990)	Habitation, camps, shelter	Archaic-historic	CSRI	Bean et al. 1995
West Mesa, Lake Cahuilla (1991–1992)	Camps, cremations	Late Prehistoric	Recon	Eighmey and Cheever 1992
Trigo Mtns. (1984, 1988)	Pot caches	Late Prehistoric-historic	Various institutions, Statistical Research	Bayman et al. 1996, Shelly and Altshul 1989
Dunaway Road, Lake Cahuilla (1985)	Camp	Late Prehistoric	Mooney and Associates	Schaefer 1986
East Mesa, Lake Cahuilla (1985)	Camps	Late Prehistoric	Westec	Gallegos 1986
Elmore Site, Salton Sink (1992, 1997)	Camp	Late Prehistoric	Caltrans District 11, ASM Affiliates	Laylander 1997 Schaefer 2000a
Heritage Palms, Indio, Lake Cahuilla (1994–1995)	Camps	Archaic-Late Prehistoric	CRM Tech	Love 1996
Salton Basin, Lake Cahuilla (1999)	Camp	Late Prehistoric	ASM Affiliates	Schaefer 2000b

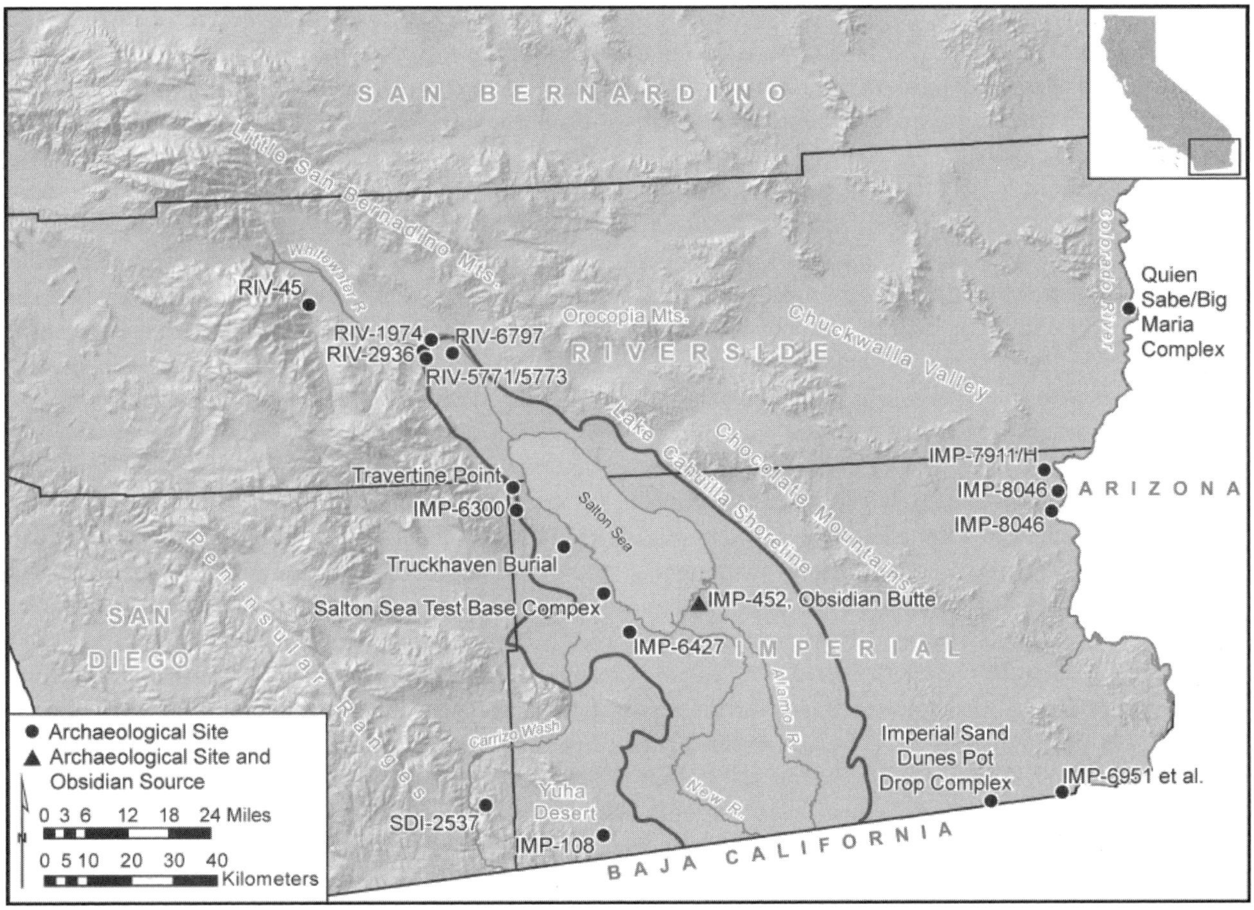

Figure 16.1. Archaeological sites and locations of the Colorado Desert.

rock art studies have pointed to Archaic Period roots for the art, with a continuous progression toward distinctive Patayan symbolic systems (Hedges 2005; McCarthy 1993).

Several important late Archaic sites are now documented from the northern Coachella Valley (Love and Dahdul 2002). Deeply buried midden deposits with clay-lined features and living surfaces, cremations, hearths, and a rock shelter deposit have been found at sites radiocarbon dated from before 1000 cal B.C. to cal A.D. 700. Faunal assemblages are dominated by lagomorphs. The larger sites suggest a more sustained settlement type than previously known for the Archaic Period in this area. Among the most impressive is RIV-2936, located well above the Lake Cahuilla shoreline, which contained multiple living surfaces with clay-lined hearths, milling equipment, shell beads, Coso obsidian bifaces and debitage, and wonderstone debitage (see below under "Lithic Procurement"). Radiocarbon dates indicate a range of occupation between cal A.D. 135 and 645. A similarly dated assemblage at RIV-6797 found beneath 50 centimeters of lake sediments suggests a Late Archaic occupation during a recessional or interlacustral phase of Lake Cahuilla.

Two first millennium B.C. temporary camps, RIV-1974 and RIV-5771/5773, were found deeply buried in dunes near the maximum shoreline of Lake Cahuilla (Love and Dahdul 2002). Remains of fish, shellfish, and migratory waterfowl confirm a lacustrine adaptation, but with a substantial dietary contribution from lagomorphs. While some of the other Late Archaic Period sites without fish bone or shellfish might have had Lake Cahuilla associations, these sites provide some of the best evidence for human adaptation to Lake Cahuilla prior to cal A.D. 700, and hint at what we may be missing because of sedimentation and extensive agricultural development within the Salton basin.

In most cases, early projectile points have been reported only as isolates on desert pavements, but a recent inventory within the Salton Sea Test Base produced a cluster of early points including Lake Mojave, Pinto/Gatecliff, and Elko forms, as well as two eccentric crescents, scattered among protohistoric sites on the relic bed of Lake Cahuilla, 30 meters below sea level (Apple et al. 1997; Wahoff 1999). If these points were indeed found in situ, as the investigators suggest, they must have escaped burial by lake sediments by specific hydrological conditions. Alternatively, they could have been collected from elsewhere for reuse by protohistoric occupants.

LAKE CAHUILLA

The Colorado Desert's most remarkable prehistoric geographical feature was the extensive freshwater lake periodically created in the Salton basin by the wayward Colorado River. When its waters were present, they brought with them several species of freshwater fish, shellfish, migratory aquatic birds, and a riparian flora and fauna. During the lake's intermittent absence, most of the basin was extremely arid, with useful resource zones limited to a few alkali flats and seasonal overflow inlets. If the lake was a magnet for human use when it was present, it may also have functioned to some degree as a barrier to travel between eastern and western portions of the Colorado Desert.

Considerable advances have been made during the past two decades toward refining the Late Prehistoric chronology of Lake Cahuilla (see Schaefer 2002), but many major uncertainties persist. An earlier view held that the lake had come and gone in a single, centuries-long episode between about cal A.D. 1000 and 1500. This scenario has now been eliminated on the basis of radiocarbon, stratigraphic, and early historical evidence, which in concert indicates the existence of no fewer than three separate cycles of inundation and desiccation between about cal A.D. 1200 and the late 1600s (Laylander 1997). As previously discussed, a Late Archaic phase has also now been well established from investigations at a dozen sites on the northern end of Lake Cahuilla (Love and Dahdul 2002). The lake's presence or absence during earlier portions of the Holocene is essentially unknown, but until there is evidence to the contrary, the apparent lack of any substantial Early or Middle Holocene archaeological sites associated with lake shorelines may suggest that the basin was generally dry.

Even during the final two millennia of prehistory, it is not yet known whether the lake was full most of the time, with brief interruptions by episodes of desiccation; whether the basin was usually dry, with short-lived fillings; or whether lake levels were typically in a state of flux. Hydrological modeling has suggested some chronological constraints on the sequence of Lake Cahuilla's rises and falls (Laylander 1997; Waters 1983; D. Weide 1976; Wilke 1978). Based on modern parameters for water flow in the lower Colorado River and the rate of evaporation in the Salton basin, it would have taken a minimum of about 18 years for the river to completely fill the basin, and a minimum of about 56 years for the lake, once it was isolated from the Colorado River, to finally disappear. In other words the minimum time span for a complete lacustrine cycle is about three-quarters of a century.

An issue hotly debated two decades ago was whether the shoreline of Lake Cahuilla was a major focus for permanent or semipermanent aboriginal settlement, or whether its use was more sporadic and incidental within the wider regional settlement systems (M. Weide 1976; Wilke 1978). The picture that seems to be emerging is that there was substantial variability in settlement and subsistence orientation along different segments of the lake's shoreline (Gallegos 1980; von Werlhof 2004a). Settlement appears to have been most intensive in the northwest, in the Coachella Valley, where evidence suggests the presence of fairly large-scale, multiseasonal occupations in some locations and markedly seasonal temporary encampment in others (Sutton 1993, 1998). On the lake's eastern shoreline, there are long stretches where sites are generally smaller with a lower density and diversity of materials, perhaps reflecting the relative sterility of the deserts that lay immediately to the east and the long distances that had to be crossed by lakeshore visitors coming from the Colorado River. A few larger and more complex sites with cremations occur in locations where washes emptied into the lake or around embayments that developed behind sand spits. Occupations on the western shore may have been intermediate in their range of variability, thanks to the variety of resources that were accessible from the lake in the Peninsular Ranges and along that ranges' eastern margin. Larger temporary camp complexes also occur where major drainages entered the lake or where seasonal alkali pans and mesquite dunes occurred adjacent to the shoreline (Schaefer 1988). Seriously understudied are the fish traps and associated fish camps that occur on recessional beach lines in the northwest quadrant of Lake Cahuilla (Apple et al. 1997; Collins and Collins 2004; Gruver 2004; Hines 2004). Excavations of well preserved slab-lined house pits indicate seasonal camps of from one to a dozen domestic units. Some camps appear to represent very short-lived and specialized fishing enterprises. Others indicate more sustained household subsistence activities, with an effort to balance high-protein fish diets with carbohydrates from the seeds of alkali-tolerant plants that grew along receding shorelines (Schaefer 2000b).

Unfortunately, little evidence is available concerning the areas around Lake Cahuilla's southern shore, where the effects of the lake's comings and goings may have been particularly dramatic. Hypothetically, if the Colorado River's waters were completely diverted to feed the rising lake for a span of up to two decades, the Colorado delta—which was otherwise a relatively resource-rich zone—may have become nearly uninhabitable, resulting in severe population stresses that would have had repercussions throughout a wider region.

OBSIDIAN BUTTE

Closely linked with Lake Cahuilla in the archaeological record is Obsidian Butte, the Colorado Desert's major source of volcanic glass, located near the southern edge of the present-day Salton Sea. When the waters of Lake Cahuilla stood higher than 40 meters below sea level, the obsidian quarry was entirely submerged and its material could only be acquired through scavenging at earlier archaeological sites. Consequently, the cycles of obsidian exploitation and lacustrine resource use were directly out of phase with each other.

X-ray fluorescence chemical characterization of Obsidian Butte glass now permits its definitive identification in archaeological contexts (Hughes 1986b). Present evidence, both in the Colorado Desert and in coastal southern California, points to the use of the material primarily, perhaps even exclusively, during the final millennium of prehistory. Obsidian Butte was coastal southern California's main source of obsidian, supplanting an earlier predominance of glass from the more distant Coso volcanic field in the northern Mojave Desert. Why this chronological contrast existed in the two sources is not yet clear. The late flowering of the Obsidian Butte source may reflect such factors as its possible inaccessibility during early periods, environmental or social impediments to earlier travel or trade, or limitations of the usefulness of this particular material within the earlier technology. Even at the zenith of its use, obsidian represented no more than a supplementary toolstone, rarely accounting for as much as 10 percent of the debitage in assemblages from montane and coastal southern California (Hughes and True 1985; Laylander and Christenson 1988; Schaefer 1988).

Hydration measurement on Obsidian Butte glass continues to be comparatively neglected as a chronometric tool. During the past 20 years, a few hundred hydration measurements have been taken and at least seven tentative rates for calibrating the observed microns of hydration with elapsed calendar years have been proposed, but there is no consensus on their validity (Laylander 1997). Several of the proposed rates were based in part on now-superceded ideas about the chronology of Lake Cahuilla, as well as uncertain assumptions about the termination of aboriginal obsidian in the historic period. The development of hydration studies has probably been slowed by the comparatively minor use of this material throughout most of the region and by the availability of several alternative chronological indicators.

LITHIC PROCUREMENT

The types of lithic material exploited prehistorically in the Colorado Desert included cryptocrystalline silica (chert, chalcedony), obsidian, crystalline volcanics (basalt, rhyolite, etc.), quartz, and various plutonic, metamorphic, and sedimentary rocks. The Colorado Desert's varied geology provided multiple sources for most of these materials. Crystalline volcanic rock was probably the most extensively used material, and many potential primary sources for it existed on the eastern margins of the Peninsular Range and in the Chocolate Mountains and other ranges. Cryptocrystalline silica cobbles from the Plio-Pleistocene terraces along the Colorado River were also extensively quarried (Ezzo and Altschul 1993).

Identifying the specific source locations for archaeological lithic specimens has not generally been attempted, with two notable exceptions. The first, of course, is obsidian, which has been traced to the Obsidian Butte source, as discussed above. A second instance is the material known as "wonderstone," produced by hydrothermal infusion of silica into sedimentary rock. The Wonderstone West Rainbow Rock Locality (IMP-6300) near Travertine Point on the western margin of the Salton basin has been described as one of the largest and most extensively exploited bedrock lithic procurement areas in the Colorado Desert (Pigniolo 1995:123). Another source of wonderstone, reported to be macroscopically distinctive from the Rainbow Rock material, is located at Cerro Colorado, located west of Mexicali just south of the U.S.-Mexican border.

Some of the lithic artifacts in the Colorado Desert reflect considerable effort and skill in manufacture. Most notable are the small projectile points of the Late Prehistoric Period, some of which are unusually long and narrow, and resemble points from the Hohokam area of southern Arizona. Other small points were carefully serrated, such as the Dos Cabezas serrated type defined at the Indian Hill rock shelter (Wilke and McDonald 1986). However, for the most part the prehistoric lithic technology of the Colorado Desert seems to be aptly characterized as "expedient" (Ludwig 2005). The tools used for cutting, scraping, pounding, and milling functions seem to have often been produced rapidly from locally available toolstone, and were just as rapidly discarded. More specialized industries have been associated with production of sandstone metates on the western side of the desert, arrowmaker workshops at seasonal encampments around alkali pans (Schaefer 1988), and large quarries for the production of pestles and metates from volcanic outcrops along the lower Colorado and Gila River valleys (Pendleton et al. 1986; Schneider 1993, 1994).

PATAYAN CERAMICS

Patayan ceramic studies were in their infancy 20 years ago. It was too soon after Michael Waters's (1982a, b, c) reworking of Malcolm Rogers's unpublished lower Colorado buffware ceramic typology and his critique of Schroeder's (1958) Hakataya ceramic series to permit a systematic appraisal of the efficacy of various ceramic typologies for dating or understanding geographical factors in ceramic manufacture, use, and exchange. Both Waters's and Schroeder's systems were based on surface collections with little information from stratigraphic excavations or associated radiocarbon dates. Waters gave primacy to rim form as the first step in classifying buffware types, while Schroeder focused on temper, inclusions, and surface treatment. Both attempted to define geographical limits of production for each type, and Schroeder (1979) went so far as to assign specific tribal affiliations. May's (1978) effort to organize Rogers's unpublished ceramic notes and type collection into a larger number of types, including many discrete brownware types, has received only limited application but has been recently applied to surface-collected rims from Lake Cahuilla (May 2001).

Researchers applying Waters's system to large excavated assemblages have experienced difficulty (Seymour 1997). Some ceramicists make use of the typology as best they can but include descriptions of variants or "hybrids" to account for variability beyond the normative descriptions (Apple et al. 1997; Schaefer 1994c, 2000). In the absence of diagnostic rims, others have lumped types together to discriminate untempered types (Black Mesa Buff, Tumco Buff) from mineral-tempered types (Colorado Beige, Palomas Buff, Parker Buff, Topoc Buff), or have moved in the direction of site-specific classification systems. As a result, Patayan ceramic classification schemes still fall short of the acuity needed to provide more than gross chronological estimates or to allow for identification of manufacturing regions.

Dates for the introduction of ceramics into the Salton basin can now be more firmly fixed. Several aceramic sites in the Coachella Valley date between cal A.D. 340 and 1200 (Love and Dahdul 2002). While investigators consider that some of the later-dated sites in this group may not be truly preceramic, the preponderance of evidence suggests that ceramics were not introduced or were rarely used prior to cal A.D. 1000. Somewhat older dates of cal A.D. 870 to 1010 have been associated with what are conventionally identified as Patayan I ceramic types (Colorado Beige, Colorado Red, Black Mesa Buff) on the northeastern shoreline of Lake Cahuilla, not far from where the Cocomaricopa trail enters the Coachella Valley from the Colorado River (Schaefer et al. 2003). Lake Cahuilla may have attracted Colorado River peoples (and with them, ceramic technology) to the Coachella Valley, and a shared interest in the lakeshore may have facilitated cultural exchange between Yuman and Takic peoples. The early ceramic dates in the Colorado Desert agree well with the beginning of widespread use of Tizon brownware in the Peninsular Ranges and on the Pacific coast, although there are a few western dates from ceramic carbon residues that may suggest an initial introduction of ceramics by cal A.D. 800, if not earlier (Griset 1996).

A serious contradiction to Waters's ceramic chronology was reported from the North Baja pipeline project (Hildebrand 2003). Deep mechanical trenches on elevated alluvial terraces of the Colorado River at the Stollard site localities in the southern Palo Verde Valley (IMP-7911/H, IMP-8046) revealed ceramic-associated cultural features and occupational levels extending to depths of 60 centimeters at one site and 139–200 centimeters at another. Some questions of stratigraphic integrity and archaeological contexts for the ceramics still remain to be resolved. Nevertheless, this is the first time that Patayan ceramics have been found on the lower reaches of the Colorado River in association with stratigraphically sealed charcoal concentrations and hearth features. At both sites the distribution of Black Mesa Buff and Colorado Beige sherds, some with the distinctive rims attributed to Patayan I (cal A.D. 700–1000), were found in association with cal A.D. 1300–1600 radiocarbon dates. Parker Buff also appeared to occur in Patayan I associations earlier than expected. Other apparent anomalies included the absence of more commonly known Patayan

II and III types such as Tumco Buff and Colorado Buff, as well as recurved rims that would be expected at sites postdating cal A.D. 1000. Elsewhere, ceramic types with recurved rims generally accepted as Patayan II and III dominate ethnohistoric period collections from the Colorado River and from sites on the western side of the Coachella and Imperial Valleys, although they show greater variability of mineral inclusions and temper than previously realized (Schaefer 1994b, c).

Technical analysis is beginning to demonstrate potential to improve the interpretive value of Colorado Desert ceramics. Rogers defined Salton Brown as a desert brownware associated with the western side of the Colorado Desert including the Lake Cahuilla shoreline (May 1978). Instrumental neutron activation analysis (INAA) and petrographic studies have shown Salton Brown to be transitional in paste chemistry between desert buff- and mountain brownware. One source of the ware's sedimentary clay was the Brawley Formation. When examined under high magnification, the ware can be discriminated from Tizon Brown on the basis of mineral inclusions (Hildebrand et al. 2002). Applying the improved typing methods to a site in the eastern Peninsular Range, Gallucci (2001) identified many more desert-derived brownware sherds in addition to the small number of buffware sherds. Similarly, brownwares in desert collections that were previously assumed to be Tizon are now being retyped as Salton Brown based on INAA and petrographic tests. If confirmed by additional studies, earlier interpretations of mobility between upland and lowland areas based on brownware frequencies will require revision in light of what appears to be a pattern of desert resources being transported in ceramic vessels to upland areas in the southwestern portion of the Colorado Desert, while the opposite pattern seems to characterize the northwestern Colorado Desert (Schaefer 1994b, c).

AGRICULTURE

The Colorado Desert is notable for the extension of agriculture into prehistoric California. At contact, the Colorado River and delta Yumans were growing a wide variety of domesticates and wild grasses, which contributed from 30 to 50 percent of their subsistence economy (Castetter and Bell 1951). Large-scale artificial irrigation was out of the question because of the Colorado River's meanderings and destructive seasonal flooding, thus precluding the development of more sedentary agriculture-based societies like the Hohokam. Sadly, archaeological evidence for the prehistory of Colorado River agriculture is buried or plowed into river valley sediments. One of the few recent empirical finds is corn pollen in the adhesives used to seal a cached olla in the Trigo Mountains, Arizona, overlooking the southern Palo Verde Valley (Shelley and Altschul 1989).

Agriculture is presumed to have roots in the earliest Patayan Phase dating from at least cal A.D. 700, most likely having spread from the Hohokam area or from northern Mexico (McGuire and Schiffer 1982). Every early explorer on the lower Colorado River, beginning with Alarcón in A.D. 1540, described aboriginal cultigens. The early introduction of Old World species such as wheat and watermelons is also attested in the ethnohistoric record. Desert Tipai (i.e., Kamia) lineages of Imperial Valley practiced floodplain agriculture along the New and Alamo Rivers, presumably having learned the techniques through their close association with the Quechan on the Colorado River. The Desert Tipai also constructed small dams and ditches to divert water onto adjacent terraces (Gifford 1931). People in the Jacumba Valley on the eastern edge of the Peninsular Ranges practiced something akin to irrigation agriculture with small dams and ditches at least as early as the first half of the nineteenth century (Gifford 1931). Tipai migration legends seem to place them on the shores of Lake Cahuilla at the time of the final recession, and no doubt horticulture reached the Imperial Valley soon after the final recession had ended, around A.D. 1700, although the first written accounts date to the 1840s (Forbes 1963). Someday archaeological research may ascertain when agriculture was practiced in the western Colorado Desert.

The Cahuilla were observed growing corn, pumpkins, melons, and watermelons at the time of the first recorded Mexican incursions into the Coachella Valley in 1823–1824 (Bean and Mason 1962:46, 104). The accounts noted walk-in wells from which pot irrigation could presumably have been practiced. Wheat and barley, which require more efficient forms of irrigation (including small dams, reservoirs, and irrigation ditches), may also have been grown, but were not observed by American scientists until the 1850s (Wilke and Lawton 1975:28). Small dams, reservoirs, and irrigation ditches were also observed at this time.

The antiquity and origins of agriculture and irrigation methods among the Cahuilla and other southern California desert tribes remains the subject of continuing inquiry, as is the question of whether prehistoric agriculture extended west of the Peninsular Ranges in southern California (Laylander 1995; Schaefer and Huckleberry 1995). References to cultigens in mythology (Lawton and Bean 1968) and ethnohistoric period Tipai domestic seed caches (Treganza 1946, 1947) have been used to hypothesize prehistoric period acquisition. While both myths and caches included Old World cultigens in addition to native Southwest crops, the possibility remains that the Cahuilla adopted agriculture long before direct mission influence. Likewise Cahuilla use of dams and ditches may have been invented locally, acquired from the Tipai (Wilke and Lawton 1975), or adopted as a result of mission influence from Baja or Alta California or from Sonora (Forbes 1963).

There is archaeological evidence that cultigens at least reached the western Colorado Desert through trade, if not by local production. Field pumpkin *(Cucurbita pepo)* seeds are reported from coprolite residues at Myoma Dunes on the northern shoreline of Lake Cahuilla and were also found cached in an olla on the west shoreline north of the Fish Creek Mountains (Wilke 1978; Wilke et al. 1977). The Myoma Dunes seeds were radiocarbon dated to cal A.D. 1420–1660, placing them in the last or next-to-last stand of Lake Cahuilla.

Carbonized maize (*Zea mays*) and tepary beans (*Phaseolus acutifolius*), as well as uncarbonized gourds, have been recovered from early- to mid-nineteenth-century Cahuilla middens that also contain glass beads, flaked glass, and other Euro-American items, including domesticated animal bones from one site (Tahquitz Canyon; RIV-45) in Palm Springs. A few tepary beans have also been recovered from possible eighteenth-century contexts, but the poor resolution of radiocarbon dates precludes use of such evidence to confirm early Cahuilla agriculture. A Cahuilla dam and reservoir still exist near Andreas Canyon, and substantial evidence of mid- to late-nineteenth-century irrigation has been archaeologically documented throughout the area (Schaefer and Huckleberry 1995; Schaefer et al. 2002). Ethnohistoric documentation and archaeological findings place all of these irrigation systems in the early to middle nineteenth century, although these features indicate the independent application of substantial Cahuilla expertise, probably acquired from exposure to Euro-American irrigation methods. The paucity of evidence for cultigens in flotation samples and its absence in pollen samples from prehistoric components at RIV-45 and other desert Cahuilla sites suggests that agriculture did not play a significant role in the Cahuilla economy until after the beginning of the nineteenth century. It is possible that cultigens were introduced several centuries earlier, possibly as a Spanish-influenced complex, which would explain the presence of Old World species in Cahuilla mythology. Intensification of agriculture evidently was stimulated by a number of possible historical and environmental factors, including the final desiccation of Lake Cahuilla, regional population growth, decreased potential for mobility, and the acculturative process, including the introduction of Euro-American irrigation methods.

TRADE, TRAVEL, SYMBOLISM, AND CULTURAL EXCHANGE

Several lines of evidence also hint at the web of connections that linked locations in the Colorado Desert with areas within and beyond the region. The high level of mobility that characterized much of Patayan settlement and subsistence appears to have been an important factor in promoting a substantial amount of cross-cultural integration and interaction through time, despite shifting patterns of enmity. Alternative models of interaction between mobile Patayan hunter-gatherers and sedentary mixed-horticultural peoples (Patayan and Hohokam) have been articulated through the study of the spatial distribution of site types, rock art, ceramics, shell, obsidian sources, and other indicators.

Important advances have been made in interpreting the complex of trails, cairns, geoglyphs, cleared circles, rock rings, other desert pavement features, and artifact scatters as an integrated group within the context of cultural landscapes. They include the Pilot Knob Complex (IMP-6951 and other sites), Palo Verde Point (IMP-6905), Ripley (AZ:R:10:1), and the extensive Quien Sabe/Big Maria Complex. The well-inventoried corpus of major Colorado River geoglyph and rock art sites is now interpreted by some researchers as a series of integrative ceremonial centers along a route between sacred places, and as expressions of Yuman cosmology and iconography (Altschul and Ezzo 1994; Cleland 2005; Ezzo and Altschul 1993; Hedges 2005; Johnson 1985; Woods et al. 1986). Most recently, von Werlhof (2004b) applied River Yuman ethnographic sources and consultation with elders to find direct referents to the creation story in some of the best-known Colorado Desert geoglyphs. Various functions suggested for these sites include shamanic practice, vision questing, curing, and communal ceremonialism. Other expressions of symbolic activity are indicated by nonrandom pot drop distributions along trails approaching springs and tanks. These widely spaced water sources were crucial to practical survival during long-distance travel or seasonal rounds and held important spiritual values as well, as evidenced by their frequent association with major rock art complexes (McCarthy 1993; Schaefer 1992). A similar phenomenon may explain the substantial number of pot drops along a posited travel corridor through the Imperial Sand Dunes (Underwood 2004).

Lithic materials attest to links that stretched both within and beyond the region. As noted above, Obsidian Butte glass occurs fairly commonly in montane and coastal southern California. Wonderstone attributed to the Rainbow Rock source has been identified in western San Diego County and the northern Coachella Valley (Bean et al. 1995; Pigniolo 1995). Obsidian from sources in northeastern Baja California near San Felipe has been found in coastal southern California, and this material may have passed through the Colorado Desert (McFarland 2000). Steatite artifacts occasionally found in Colorado Desert sites evidently represent links with the Peninsular Ranges. Argillite has been attributed to a source in central Arizona (Bean et al. 1995).

Shell beads and ornaments provide another set of indicators for extraregional connections. Artifacts manufactured from shellfish species that inhabit the northern Gulf of California but not the opposite Pacific coast, particularly *Olivella dama*, have been found in coastal southern California and the Great Basin (Bennyhoff and Hughes 1987). Like San Felipe obsidian, these materials may have passed through the Colorado Desert. A similar observation applies to shells from coastal southern California species that have been found in archaeological contexts in the American Southwest as well as the Colorado Desert (Ahlstrom 2000). Shell artifacts found at sites in the Colorado Desert may reflect direct procurement by desert inhabitants traveling to coastal areas to the west or south, or they may indicate exchange with other groups residing in those areas. The Elmore site (IMP-6427), a protohistoric recessional Lake Cahuilla site in western Imperial County, contained shell debitage that attests to the local manufacturing of *Olivella* beads and other shell artifacts (Rosen 1995). Notably, the patterns of shell artifact use in the Coachella Valley, which during ethnohistoric times was inhabited by Takic speakers, seem to reflect close ties with the sophisticated Santa Barbara Channel Bead Complex, while areas farther south inhabited ethnohistorically by Yuman speakers do not match this pattern. This suggests a significant late prehistoric cultural divide that may have coincided approximately with the linguistic divide of ethnohistoric times. Ceramics also testify to interregional connections. An example is a cache of lower Colorado buffware anthropomorphic figurines that was recovered in Orange County (Koerper and Hedges 1996).

With research focusing for the past two decades on reconstructing localized cultural histories and adaptive patterns, there has been little effort to apply or refine the Patayan (Hakataya) cultural construct. This is in part due to the huge diversity of cultural patterns that have been subsumed under the label Patayan. On the Colorado River and delta it applies to a mixed horticultural, hunting, and gathering pattern focused on the lowland desert riparian habitats. Most archaeological information comes from spatially peripheral sites to such an extent that Patayan along the river is largely defined by extrapolating the ethnographic record back into the Late Prehistoric past. To examine eastern Patayan residential sites, or at least temporary fishing and hunting/gathering camps, it is necessary to turn to the Imperial and Coachella Valleys, where the river people had crossed inhospitable desert to reach the eastern shore of Lake Cahuilla (Schaefer et al. 2003; von Werlhof 2004a). On the western side of the Salton Trough, the Patayan pattern was expressed quite differently by hunters and gatherers who practiced seasonal transhumance across an elevation-stratified series of upland and lowland habitats. The Cahuilla to the north and the Tipai to the south (Figure 16.2) shared similar adaptive strategies, cultural practices, and material culture despite their linguistic and sociopolitical differences. Archaeological evidence points increasingly to influences of cultural exchange between people of Takic, Numic, and Yuman ancestry in shaping Patayan cultural history and technology in the Colorado Desert. This likely involved coresidence in boundary areas and perhaps intermarriage, as suggested by Quechan (Figure 16.3) identification of some apparently non-Yuman clan origins (Forbes 1965:36). Shaul and Hill (1998) also argue from historical linguistics that proto-River Yuman speakers participated in a multiethnic Hohokam complex that included proto-Tepiman and probably Zuni speakers.

To the extent that ceramic traditions correlate with ethnic or cultural affiliations, these spheres of interaction are suggested by the co-occurrence of Great Basin and Colorado River Yuman ceramic figurine styles in the Coachella Valley (Bean et al. 1995); the possible co-occurrence of Patayan, Southern Paiute, and Ancestral Puebloan pottery types in the Las Vegas Valley (Seymour 1997); and the gradient in the co-occurrence

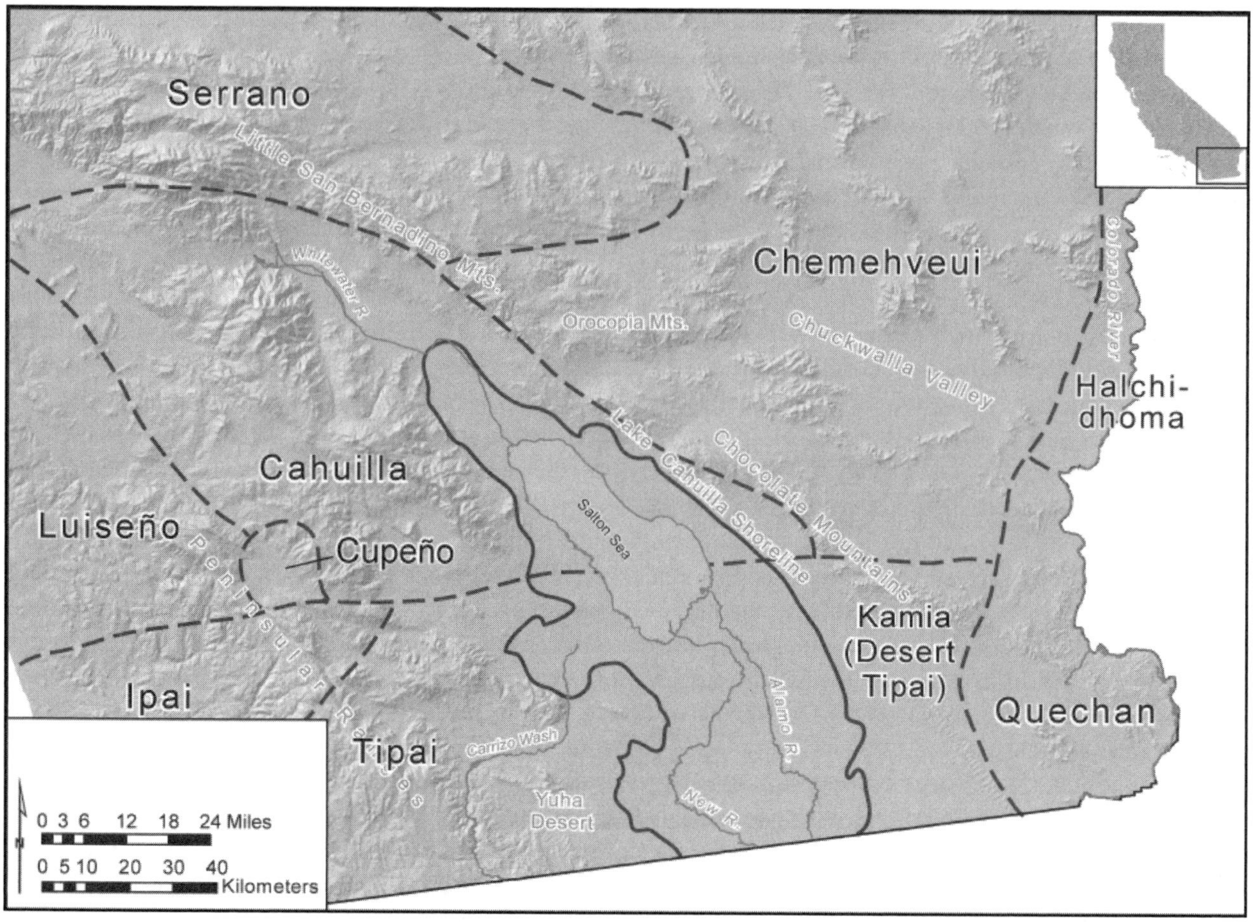

Figure 16.2. Approximate location of tribal groups, Colorado Desert.

of Patayan and Hohokam ceramics across the lower and middle Gila River and in western Papagueria, including a Patayan enclave at a major Hohokam site (Ahlstrom 2000; Shaul and Andresen 1989).

NATIVE AMERICANS, ARCHAEOLOGISTS, AND THE PUBLIC AS PARTNERS IN INTERPRETING THE PAST

Recent decades have witnessed a greater inclusion of descendant peoples in the interpretation and management of cultural resources in the Colorado Desert. Principal partners include the Tipai (Kumeyaay), Paipai, Cocopah, Quechan (Yuma), Halchidhoma, Ahamakav (Mojave), Chemehuevi, Serrrano, and Cahuilla. While Native American paradigms of the past differ greatly from those of anthropological archaeology, there has been substantial ground for mutually rewarding exchange of ideas and preservation efforts, including the application of cultural landscape concepts.

The Malki Museum, founded in 1965, as the first Indian inspired and managed museum on a California reservation, encouraged collaboration between Native communities, anthropologists, and ethnohistorians. Museums or CRM programs can now be found on the Cocopah, Fort Yuma-Quechan, Fort Mojave, Colorado River Indian Tribes, and Agua Caliente reservations, among others. Among the newest, the Agua Caliente Band of Cahuilla Indians maintains the nonprofit Agua Caliente Cultural Museum in downtown Palm Springs and is soon to break ground on an ambitious facility that will include exhibit space, curation facilities, archives, a research library, and classrooms. The Agua Caliente Band has also developed a comprehensive cultural resources program, including professionally trained monitors and a federally recognized Tribal Historic Preservation Office (THPO).

Other expressions of public support for Colorado Desert archaeology include Imperial Valley Desert Museum's efforts to complete its new facility in Ocotillo and the Colorado Desert Archaeology Society's collaboration with the Anza-Borrego Institute to open the Begole Archaeological Center in Anza-Borrego Desert State Park and to begin a research grant program. Imperial Valley College continues to train students in field methods, and by so doing has contributed substantially to the inventory of such features as Lake Cahuilla fish camps, geoglyphs, and trails. Most archaeological research in the region is being conducted by CRM firms for projects on public lands of the Bureau of Land Management, Bureau of Reclamation, Department of Defense, Caltrans, Imperial Irrigation District, and Coachella Valley Water District. An explosion of private land development in the Coachella Valley has also spurred numerous investigations.

PROSPECTS

While substantive advances have been made in Colorado Desert archaeology during the past two decades, the potential for further significant advances continues to be high. Although the final period of prehistory is now coming into focus, the chronology and lifeways of the region across the long millennia prior to cal A.D. 1000 are still no more than dimly understood. A nagging challenge is whether effective strategies can be developed to discover and study the surviving archaeological traces that may lie deeply buried under fluvial and lacustrine sediments in the floodplain and two deltas of the Colorado River. Improved techniques are needed to date and glean more information from the ubiquitous surface features on desert pavements, perhaps through optically stimulated luminescence or thermoluminescence dating. The unmatched dynamism of the natural environment manifested by Lake Cahuilla and its dramatic effects on settlement patterns offer important opportunities for fine-tuning late prehistoric chronologies based on radiocarbon, ceramics, projectile points, shell beads, and obsidian, and for applying the results to foraging theory, questions of short-term adaptive flexibility, and a better understanding of the mechanisms of cultural change. Given the region's geographical position as a nexus between agricultural societies of the Southwest, complex hunter-gatherer communities of coastal southern California, classic desert cultures of the Great Basin and Mojave, and the separate world of peninsular Baja California, we are virtually guaranteed that new insights into the prehistory of this region will also shed light on wider anthropological problems.

Figure 16.3. Two Quechan men photographed by Elias A. Bonine, 1870s. (National Anthropological Archives, Smithsonian Institution, Washington, D.C.)

CHAPTER 17

Prehistoric Material Conveyance

RICHARD E. HUGHES AND RANDALL MILLIKEN

BOTH *CALIFORNIA ARCHAEOLOGY* (MORATTO 1984) AND *The Archaeology of California* (Chartkoff and Chartkoff 1984) deal with trade and exchange (material conveyance) to varying degrees, but neither devotes a full chapter to the topic. This is not to say that the authors considered the topic unimportant; on the contrary they were clearly aware, as were other contributors to *California Archaeology* (e.g., Fredrickson 1984:487, 504–505, 519–520, 527; Warren 1984:390–391, 423–424, 430) that trade and exchange studies are integral to understanding development and change in prehistoric California societies (Moratto 1984:4–5; Chartkoff and Chartkoff 1984:134–136, 231–234; see also Chartkoff 1989; 2001:127–128). But both were published too late to include the obsidian studies wave, which crested dramatically in the state after 1982. Major studies involving obsidian and shell beads have appeared since that time. Studies of other materials such as basalt (Day 2002; Latham et al. 1992; Waechter 2002c), pottery (Eerkens et al. 1999, 2002b; Hurd et al. 1990), and turquoise (Leonard and Drover 1980) will no doubt provide important complementary information in the future but, as Jackson and Ericson (1994:388) observed over a decade ago, most of what we know about prehistoric material conveyance in prehistoric times still comes from analysis of obsidian and shell beads and ornaments.

The two 1984 books took on the impossible task of synthesizing all of California archaeology. In the decades since they were written, the body of information related to trade and exchange has increased by orders of magnitude. In light of this, we have attempted in this chapter to present a compromise overview highlighting some results while placing major emphasis on dating and methodological issues that underlie and influence archaeological approaches to trade and exchange studies in the state. We refer the reader to Jackson and Ericson's (1994) outstanding summary of much of the work published before 1994.

INTERPRETING OBSIDIAN DISPERSAL

As others have pointed out (Earle and Ericson 1977; Earle 1982), the basic data in trade and exchange studies are (1) point source of origin, (2) deposition context, and (3) dating. In the case of obsidian, the geologic origin of an artifact is established by documenting a chemical correspondence between the trace element composition of the artifact and that of a parent geologic/geochemical entity (generically referred to as obsidian "source").[1] We can reach firm probabilistic conclusions about where the raw material originated, where and in what archaeological context the artifact was recovered, and, using typological affinities and/or ^{14}C associations or obsidian hydration rim readings, estimate how old the specimen is. Beyond this, however, our inferences less secure. Accounting for the actual behavioral mechanisms responsible for the observed archaeological distributions involves invoking inferential arguments that must take into account a variety of contextual factors (Hughes 1988). There is nothing wrong with this; without sound, reasoned inferences we would have no archaeological interpretations. But what we wish to make clear is that automatic appeals to distance, whether near or far, as proxies for either direct access or trade/exchange may do a profound injustice to the record we hope to understand (cf. Basgall 1979; Jackson 1988).

Recent studies, particularly those by Jackson (1986, 1989a), show the importance of studying the movement of materials at the community level (Hughes and Bettinger 1984; Fredrickson 1989b, 1996). Unlike early work, current studies are more attuned to the material consequences of the actions of smaller interest groups with differing social, economic, and religious ties which frequently crosscut ethnic and linguistic boundaries. For example, based on his research in north-central California, Jackson (1986:122) concluded that during the late prehistoric period,

> (1) Obsidian was exchanged across some ethnic boundaries but not others; (2) proportions of represented obsidian sources changed across some ethnic and tribelet boundaries but not across others; (3) obsidian projectile points and raw material were imported by groups who otherwise had suitable lithic raw materials; (4) obsidian exchange represents at

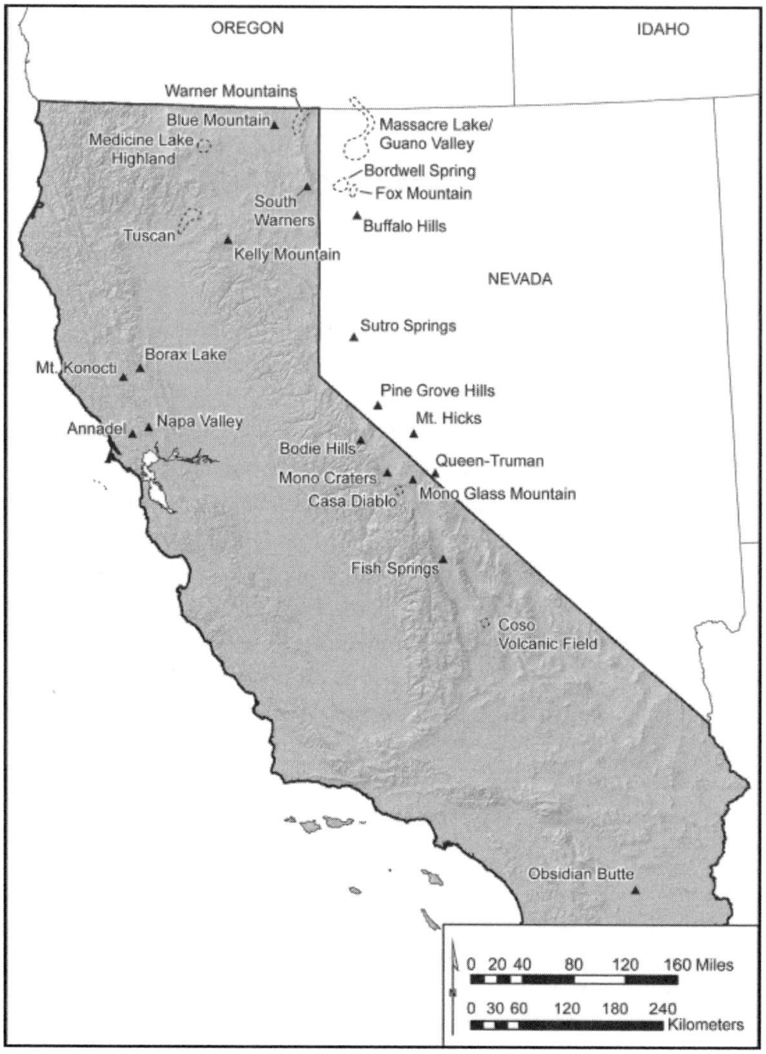

Figure 17.1. Archaeologically significant obsidian sources in California and western Nevada. (Dashed lines around California sources specify areas containing more than one chemically distinct variety of obsidian, while those around northern Nevada sources demarcate the general areal limits of each glass type.)

least two different modes of production—one characterized by tribelets who imported obsidian although they controlled their own productive obsidian sources (e.g. Gualomi Pomo); another mode of production is distinguished by groups who did not import "coals to Newcastle" (e.g. Napa Valley Wappo); (6) intertribelet obsidian exchange is apparently coincidental with marriage ties between tribelet elites; (7) commodities recognized as wealth items (e.g., clam disk beads) penetrated all territorial boundaries, but were used principally by the elite, while obsidian raw material and artifacts were impeded by some territorial boundaries, and were used by all classes (Stockton curves are an exception).

Jackson's work carries profound implications for obsidian studies of earlier periods. Other studies have informed on dimensions of prehistoric social ranking (Dillian 2002; Hughes 1978, 1990; Hughes and Bettinger 1984), territoriality (Bettinger 1982; Fredrickson 1989b), and craft specialization (Arnold 1987, 1990).

Progress in studying issues of obsidian conveyance depends on placing site assemblages in a secure temporal context and on an understanding of the primary and secondary spatial distribution of chemically characterized material (Hughes and Smith 1993; Young 2002). Obsidian hydration has been both useful and controversial as a dating technique, depending on whether it is viewed in an absolute or a relative sense. Those committed to the former perspective (Stevenson et al. 2000) continue investigating the effects of different variables (currently intrinsic water content), improvements in empirical rate formulation (Dominici 1984; Hall and Jackson 1984; Hull 2001), effective hydration temperature (J. King 2004), and the precision and accuracy of derived hydration dates (Laylander 2002). Other researchers (Anovitz et al. 1999) have declared the technique an outright failure as a chronometric tool. As noted elsewhere, some of these problems involve difficulties in translating closed system (i.e., controlled laboratory) experiments into the open system realm of archaeology, where a host of depositional and postdepositional factors come into play (Hughes 1992b). In contrast with the checkered results of attempts at absolute dating, the relative dating approach has enjoyed widespread success, particularly in the North Coast Ranges of California (DeGeorgey 2004; Fredrickson 1989b; Fredrickson and White 1988; Hildebrandt and Levulett 1997; Huberland 1989; Origer 1982; Origer and Wickstrom 1982; Parker 1993; Tremaine 1993; White 2002) and the Great Basin (Beck and Jones 1994; Jones and Beck 1990, 1992; Jones et al. 2003).

From an archaeological standpoint, California is blessed with numerous high-quality obsidian deposits that served as sources for prehistoric artifact material (Figure 17.1). A major development in obsidian studies over the past 20 years, based on the important pioneering studies of Ericson (1981, 1982), Jack (1976), and Jackson (1974), is the coalescence of improved instrumentation, increased geological sophistication, and more thoroughgoing reconnaissance that allowed obsidian sources to be chemically partitioned. In an attempt to replicate the results of the U.S. Geological Survey (Bacon et al. 1981), obsidian from the Coso volcanic field was subjected to sampling and geochemical analysis (Hughes 1988). The results showed that distinctive varieties of obsidian recognized by the USGS can be identified using a nondestructive quantitative technique within an area previously considered a single source (Jack 1976). Intrasource chemical contrasts were later identified between Mono Craters and Mono Glass Mountain (Hughes 1989) in the Casa Diablo area (Hughes 1994b) of central eastern California, in the southern Cascades (Hamusek-McGann 1995), and in the interior desert portion of southern California (Shackley 1994).

One implication of these findings is that since specific chemical types within a volcanic field could be identified, it would be possible investigate whether or not the obsidians had different use-life histories, whether or not they were exploited by prehistoric peoples at different times, conveyed in different directions at different points in time, and/or used to manufacture different classes of artifacts at different points in time (Hughes 1988:263; 1994b:268). For many years this remained only a tantalizing possibility, partly because few artifacts had been partitioned by appropriate chemical type. But recently, based on a large sample of specimens from the China Lake area, Eerkens and Rosenthal (2004) have provided empirical support for use of different varieties of Coso obsidian through time. Whether or not these distinctions apply only to local assemblages or more widely in the region awaits further research, but they are sufficiently encouraging to prompt similar studies at other sources where intrasource chemical distinctions have been documented.

Advances in instrumentation now allow analysis of obsidian specimens of smaller physical size. The use of partially destructive neutron activation analysis (Eerkens et al. 2002a) and nondestructive x-ray fluorescence has reduced the size range of materials amenable to analysis, making it possible to analyze artifacts (like trimming, finishing, and notching flakes) that were previously too small for quantitative analysis.

Recent studies have documented variability in the prehistoric production, use, and distribution of material from obsidian quarries. Gilreath and Hildebrandt (1997) have identified a series of shifts in obsidian production in the Coso volcanic field. They observed that despite earlier high production levels between ca. 3,300 and 1,350 years ago, there was a significant drop in obsidian use beginning around 1,300 years ago and that "obsidian exploitation at Coso was at its lowest level ever in the late period" (Gilreath and Hildebrandt 1997:183). Similarly shaped production curves for Bodie Hills (Singer and Ericson 1977:Fig. 8), Casa Diablo (Bouey and Basgall 1984; Hall 1983), and Borax Lake (Fredrickson and Origer 2002) suggest that these quarries also experienced marked production declines after 1,300 years ago, although other work at Bodie Hills (Jackson 1984; Halford 2001) suggests more intensive use of this source earlier and later than previously believed (see also Ramos 2000 for research on the Queen source).

Extensive research projects in northeastern California have been summarized by McGuire (2002) and Hildebrandt and King (2002), who identified changes in the numbers of obsidian sources used in projectile point manufacture over several thousand years. Early period (pre–Middle Archaic forms; including Gatecliff, northern side-notched, Humboldt, and Great Basin stemmed) points were manufactured from a relatively large number of sources, the Middle Period sample (consisting of Elko and Siskiyou side-notched) was represented by many fewer sources, while the Late Period (Rose Spring, Cottonwood, small stemmed) contained the greatest number of sources. In addition to these changes, long-term stability in obsidian acquisition/production spheres was identified, suggesting the long-standing existence of socioeconomic boundaries in the area, which contrasts with source use changes in projectile point assemblages from the Klamath Lakes area and Surprise Valley (Hughes 1986a). Hildebrandt and King's (2002) research combining source-specific obsidian hydration rim readings and radiocarbon dating supports significant refinement in the age ranges attributed to a number of time-sensitive projectile points types in the Modoc Plateau area. While stability in obsidian projectile point source profiles also characterizes the 5,000-year history of sites in the Sacramento River canyon (Basgall and Hildebrandt 1989), Bevill's (2004) analysis of material from the Squaw Creek site indicates discrepancies in the hydration ages for pre-2000 cal B.C. materials in the area. Hutchins and Simons (2000) found no source-use patterning in a sample of projectile points from Truckee Meadows spanning the past 5,000 years.

Along the northwest California coast, Hildebrandt and Levulett (1997) documented a fascinating interior/coastal source use disjunction, with interior sites containing mainly North Coast Ranges obsidians while sites along the coast contained mostly obsidian from the Medicine Lake Highland in northern California. Using source-specific obsidian hydration rim readings, Hamusek-McGann et al. (1998) completed an important study of use and occupation in the nearby Shasta Valley.

Along the south-central California coast, Jones and Waugh (1995, 1997:124–126) proposed an increase in obsidian exchange ca. 3500 cal B.C., culminating in a peak toward the end of their Middle Period (ca. 600 cal B.C. to cal A.D. 1000) with a significant reduction in imported obsidian beginning during the Middle/Late Transition (ca. cal A.D. 1000–1250).

In central eastern California variability in obsidian source use has also been documented. Earlier periods are characterized by a greater diversity of sources, and then a reduction through time culminates in the predominant use of local sources during the later periods (Basgall 1989). This same pattern appears to hold for the northern Mojave Desert area (Basgall 2000b; Basgall and Hall 1992). Sites in northern Owens Valley (Zeanah and Leigh 2003) provide evidence for diachronic change in source use, with waxing and waning use of local obsidian (Fish Springs) and noteworthy use of eastern source materials between ca. 1,300 and 1,400 years ago. Data from sites to the south near Independence show a variable but comparatively high (50 percent and greater) use of nonlocal obsidians from ca. 3,200 to 1,350 years ago, a marked increase in eastern source materials around 1,300 to 1,400 years ago, then a return to dominant use of local glass from ca. 1,350 to 650 years ago (Basgall and Delacorte 2003).

In the Sierra Nevada, Moratto (2002) reports fluctuations in the use of different obsidian sources and changing debitage frequencies through time in the New Melones area, while Roper-Wickstrom's (1993) studies at high altitude sites in the southern Sierra showed long-term use of the area and revised the previously proposed distribution of Fish Springs obsidian. Hull (2002, 2005) employed hydration data from obsidian debitage to posit changes in population density in the Yosemite Valley beginning with a gradual increase between ca. 3500 cal B.C. and cal A.D. 600, a marked decline from ca. cal A.D. 600 to 1400, followed by a slight increase in population after cal A.D. 1400. In southern California, despite the greater distance involved, obsidians from the Coso volcanic field appear to have been conveyed to archaeological sites in coastal southern California earlier in time than nearby glass from Obsidian Butte (Hughes and True 1985; Koerper et al. 1986). Macko et al. (2005) recently reported the remarkable occurrence of northeastern California obsidian at a coastal site in Orange County but were properly cautious about inferring a specific behavioral mechanism for this conveyance.

Promising studies using neutron activation analysis may allow pottery to be "sourced" in some parts of California and the Great Basin. Studies conducted to date suggest most pottery was manufactured for local consumption and not widely exchanged, at least in the Owens Valley and other parts of the southwestern Great Basin (Eerkens et al. 1999, 2002b). Neutron activation analysis of ceramics from California missions and presidios also has been initiated (Skowronek et al. 2003), opening an exciting new area for conveyance studies during the Historic Period.

INTERPRETING SHELL BEAD DISPERSAL

Prehistoric California peoples manufactured a great variety of marine shell beads. Specific forms (types) or groups of distinct forms were produced and widely distributed during restricted periods of time (Beardsley 1948, 1954; Bennyhoff and Heizer 1958; Elsasser 1978; C. King 1978; Lillard et al. 1939). Although *California Archaeology* and *The Archaeology of California* both refer to shell beads as trade items, currency, and dating tools, neither work discusses prehistoric coast-to-interior shell bead conveyance networks in detail. Since 1984, shell bead studies have moved forward on three fronts:(1) determining the temporal spans of specific bead forms, (2) documenting spreads and disruptions of specific exchange networks, and (3) accumulating mortuary and production location data to provide insight on the emergence of socioeconomic complexity. We discuss all three of these areas here, with special emphasis on chronological revisions for specific bead forms derived from direct AMS dates on suites of *Olivella* beads, as well as recent efforts to source *Olivella* beads to specific locations along the California coast.

Regional Interaction Spheres and Shell Bead Horizons

Marine shell beads are among the most common artifacts recovered in Late Holocene archaeological habitation sites in lowland cismontane California. These common beads, made from the shells of *Haliotis*, *Olivella*, *Mytilus*, *Saxidomus*, and *Tivela* species, were conveyed far inland from the Pacific coast. Late Holocene shell beads were manufactured in such large numbers and with such morphological uniformity that we would expect they were manufactured by cadres of specialists residing proximate to their supply source. Furthermore, the vast majority of inland sites contain only small amounts of shell bead manufacturing refuse, amounts not at all commensurate with the numbers of finished beads recovered. Thus indirect trade rather than direct access is often presumed. Authors refer to shell bead interaction areas (C. King 1978:60), interaction spheres (Siefkin 1999:347), and trade and exchange networks (Bennyhoff and Hughes 1987; Hughes and Bennyhoff 1986). Bennyhoff and Hughes (1987:154–156) have delineated four shell bead exchange spheres in California (northern California, central California, southern California, Gulf of California), each marked by a particular sequence of bead forms.

Distinguishing between trade and direct access is clearly important to shell bead conveyance studies and is complicated by uncertainty about past population densities and the conditions under which population density influenced or encouraged the formation of exclusive bounded territories. Some prehistorians believe that population densities were comparatively low in the Early and Middle Holocene, which would have allowed people direct access to materials that would later be available only through indirect means. If this were the case, then at certain times inland groups might have traveled to the coast to gather shells. Fitzgerald et al. disagree with that view:

> There remains the possibility that the presence of *O. biplicata* spire-lopped beads in the interior of southeastern California represents the activities of widely ranging, highly mobile terminal Pleistocene/early Holocene foragers (i.e., the beads represent direct acquisition not long-distance trade).... Nonetheless, we feel there is little point in considering the specimens reported here as anything other than products of trade.... Archaeological studies have shown that the inland and coastal areas exhibit different cultural patterns during the interval indicated by the radiocarbon results: the Milling Stone Culture or Horizon on the coast and Lake Mojave/early Pinto complexes in the interior. Recent investigations have provided strong evidence that each of these complexes was associated with distinctive settlement patterns and subsistence practices which suggests they represent at least two different resident populations—not a single highly mobile people. (Fitzgerald et al. 2005:431)

Given the interior-to-coast distances involved, Fitzgerald et al. (2005) may be correct that Early Holocene people in the Mojave Desert obtained their marine shells through trade. We caution, however, that distinctive settlement patterns and subsistence practices need not be impediments to occasional direct access.[2] Long-distance conveyance aside, the question of shell bead trade versus direct acquisition remains open for inland areas adjacent to the Pacific coast, even during protohistoric times.

Problems involving identification, dating, and tracing continuity and disruption of shell bead conveyance networks require comment. Detailed sequences of Late Holocene shell bead assemblage horizons were proposed by King (1982) for southern California and by Bennyhoff and Hughes (1987) for central California using an "early-middle-late" period time–artifact sequence derived from an artifact horizon scheme that emerged in central California prior to World War II (Heizer and Fenenga 1939). Richard Beardsley (1948, 1954) added phases within the sequences but was unable to determine, in many cases, whether the phases represented synchronic or diachronic variation. Beardsley's artifact horizon scheme came to be known as the Central California Taxonomic System (CCTS). By the late 1960s, CCTS was being challenged by many archaeologists in part because mistaken assumptions about contemporaneity of certain mortuary practices impeded recognition of parallel cultural successions in different parts of central California (Gerow 1954, 1968; Moratto 1984:199; Fredrickson 1994a; Hughes 1994c:1–3). Nevertheless, Bennyhoff (1994b:68–72; Elsasser 1978:38–44) resolved most CCTS sequence problems for major artifact classes, including marine shell beads. The bead assemblage horizons proposed by Bennyhoff and Hughes (1987) for central California and by King (1982, 1990) for southern California consist of phases of less than 300 years duration within the Early, Middle, and Late Periods.

Although many time-sensitive marine shell bead forms occurred in identical sequence in southern and central California, portions of dating schemes by King (1990) and Bennyhoff and Hughes (1987) were not in temporal alignment. *Olivella* and *Haliotis* rectangles mark the Early Period in both areas, and these rectangular templates gave way to circular forms in both areas during the first part of the Middle Period. King's (1990) and Bennyhoff and Hughes's (1987) dates for the Early and initial Middle Periods match, but the temporal discrepancy between the two chronologies begins at the Middle/Late Transition (MLT), marked in both areas by the appearance of the *Olivella* split-punched bead. Bennyhoff and Hughes (1987:149) proposed dating between 1,250 and 1,050 years ago for the bead assemblage in central California MLT, while King (1990:28, 237) proposed a 900–800 years ago bracket for Phase M5, marked by the equivalent bead assemblage, in southern California. Was the unique split-punched bead really accepted and then replaced in central California before it appeared in southern California? The answer to this question carries implications for the interpretation of source and timing of innovation in bead forms and associated artifact assemblages at the MLT.

Approaching Absolute Dating for Bead Horizons

A new understanding of Early Holocene and Middle Holocene shell bead conveyance horizons has emerged from recent accelerator mass spectrometry (AMS) dating of *Olivella* shell beads (Fitzgerald et al. 2005; Vellanoweth 2001). Groza (2002) recently used direct AMS dating to address chronological problems by building a new dating scheme for the Late Holocene central California bead horizons. Supported by a grant from the Lawrence Livermore Lab, and with the support of local Ohlone/Costanoan Indian groups, Groza (2002) obtained 103 AMS radiocarbon dates on well-provenienced *Olivella* beads. She produced entire suites of dates for marker beads of each hypothesized sequential bead assemblage in the Bennyhoff and Hughes (1987) chronology. Her results generally confirm the sequential order proposed by Bennyhoff and Hughes (1987), but the derived AMS dates shift many important bead assemblage horizons as far as 200 years forward in time, beginning with the second phase of the Middle Period (the *Olivella* Type F2a Full Saddle Horizon). That shift reconciles temporal incongruities between the central and southern California chronologies. Groza refers to the new central California chronology as Dating Scheme D.[3]

Direct AMS dating has also provided support for King's (1990) southern California shell bead horizon dating sequence, through 11 shell bead dates (eight *Olivella*, two *Megathura*, one *Mytilus*) from site ORA-378 in Orange County (Gibson and Koerper 2000). We look forward to an extensive direct AMS dating program of shell beads from the Santa Barbara Channel to directly date the chronology that currently relies on bead–charcoal date pairings and cross-dating with beads recovered from the Southwest. However, AMS data already at hand (Gibson and Koerper 2000; Groza 2002) point to a unified chronology for Late Holocene shell bead forms in both southern and central California (Figure 17.2).

Unfortunately, direct AMS dates still do not provide an absolute chronometric scale for prehistoric central California bead assemblages, due to the problem of the marine reservoir effect. Marine mollusks create their shells from calcium carbonate suspended in ocean water. At any given time, calcium carbonate in ocean water has a lower ^{14}C percentage than carbon in the terrestrial cycle because old carbon, which has lost radioactivity, is moved upward from deep ocean waters by changing currents. As a result, marine shells produce raw and corrected radiocarbon readings that are more divergent from calendar age than do terrestrial charcoal samples. Calibration programs adjust marine shell dates to calendar age (Stuiver and Reimer 1993, 2000), but these programs depend on a ΔR variable that compensates for local variability in deep ocean carbonate upwelling.

Until 2002, following Stuiver et al. (1986), most studies reporting AMS shell dates in California utilized a ΔR of 225 ± 35 years for beads thought derived from California *Olivella biplicata* shells (Breschini and Haversat 2003b; Breschini et al. 2003; Groza 2002; Schroth 1994; Vellanoweth 2001). But studies on historic shells gathered in the years prior to 1949 (when nuclear testing greatly increased atmospheric ^{14}C) revealed differences in marine reservoir effect along a gradient from southern to northern California. Recognizing this, Ingram and Southon (1996) proposed a ΔR of 220 ± 40 years for the most southerly portion of the California coast, 233 ± 60 years for the Santa Barbara Channel, 290 ± 35 years for central California, and still higher values for areas farther north. Most of the dates derived from *Mytilus* shell, but Prior et al. (1999) recently dated a historic *Olivella* shell from San Nicolas Island that supports a reservoir correction of 225 ± 60 years. In a new study based on 140 direct *Olivella* shell dates, Randy Groza (personal communication, 2005) suggests a ΔR of 260 ± 35 for *Olivella* beads recovered in both the Santa Barbara Channel and central California sites, based on empirical adjustments to dates returned from needle-drilled *Olivella* rough disk beads contextually dated to the A.D. 1790s. The ambiguity of ΔR has led Fitzgerald et al. (2005) and Hylkema (2004) to report tables of shell bead AMS dates with calibration results for both ΔR 225 ± 35 and ΔR 290 ± 35.

The marine reservoir effect appears to vary temporally and spatially due to changes in upwelling along the California coast. Kennett et al. (1997) offer evidence indicating that the ΔR for the Channel Islands dropped to 210 ± 80 during the 8440–4310 RCYBP

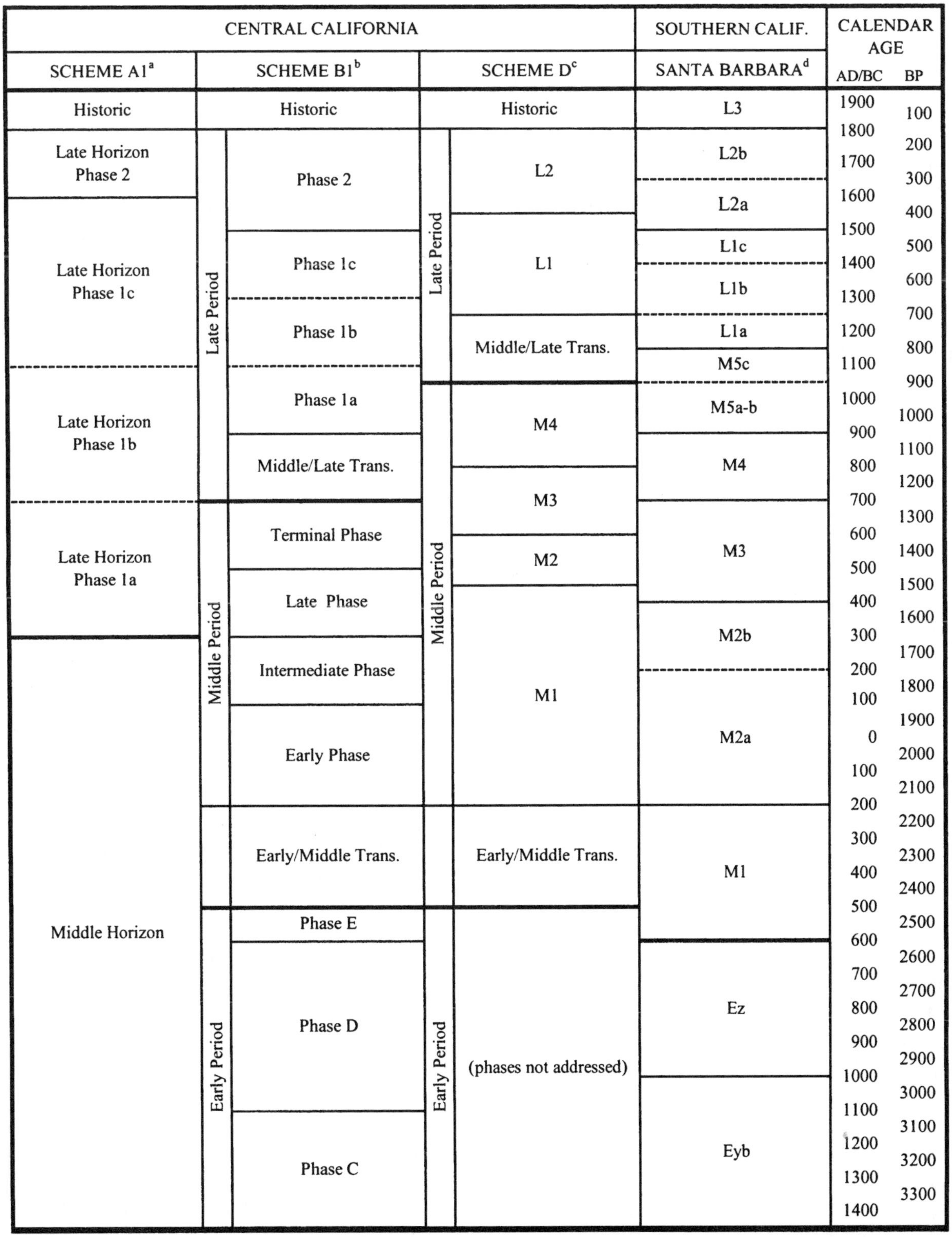
CENTRAL CALIFORNIA
SOUTHERN CALIF.
CALENDAR AGE
SCHEME A1[a]
SCHEME B1[b]
SCHEME D[c]
SANTA BARBARA[d]
AD/BC
BP
Historic
Late Horizon Phase 2
Late Horizon Phase 1c
Late Horizon Phase 1b
Late Horizon Phase 1a
Middle Horizon
Historic
Late Period
Phase 2
Phase 1c
Phase 1b
Phase 1a
Middle/Late Trans.
Middle Period
Terminal Phase
Late Phase
Intermediate Phase
Early Phase
Early/Middle Trans.
Early Period
Phase E
Phase D
Phase C
Historic
Late Period
L2
L1
Middle/Late Trans.
Middle Period
M4
M3
M2
M1
Early/Middle Trans.
Early Period
(phases not addressed)
L3
L2b
L2a
L1c
L1b
L1a
M5c
M5a-b
M4
M3
M2b
M2a
M1
Ez
Eyb
1900
1800
1700
1600
1500
1400
1300
1200
1100
1000
900
800
700
600
500
400
300
200
100
0
100
200
300
400
500
600
700
800
900
1000
1100
1200
1300
1400
100
200
300
400
500
600
700
800
900
1000
1100
1200
1300
1400
1500
1600
1700
1800
1900
2000
2100
2200
2300
2400
2500
2600
2700
2800
2900
3000
3100
3200
3300

Figure 17.2. Concordance of recent central and southern California dating schemes.
[a]Scheme A1 derived from uncorrected terrestrial dates on archaeological assemblages from the early 1950s (Heizer 1958); [b]Scheme B1 reflects uncorrected charcoal, bone collagen, and shell dates on seriated assemblages collected from the 1950s to the 1970s (Bennyhoff and Hughes 1987); [c]Scheme D derives from direct dates on seriated *Olivella* shell beads, calibrated with on-line CALIB 4.4 using Delta R = 260 ± 35 (Groza et al. n.d.); [d]Santa Barbara Channel sequence derived from terrestrial dates on seriated assemblages, calibrated in the late 1980s (King 1990:20–22).

period. More disturbing, these authors also found that AMS dates from different growth bands on a single *Mytilus* shell can vary as much as 200 years, suggesting a strong effect of differential upwelling during the life of an individual marine organism. Instability in upwelling is now recognized as a key inhibiting factor in constructing radiocarbon–calendar year calibration curves (Guilderson et al. 2005).

To put the ΔR problem in perspective, slight differences are not particularly important to discussions of 9,000–11,000-year-old *Olivella* spire-lopped beads, nor are they critical to reports on 4,400- to 5,400-year-old *Olivella* grooved rectangles. Amid attempts to document fine-grained shifts in bead trade horizons during the past 2,000 years, even 50-year disagreements about ΔR become a significant problem. Temporal boundaries between bead assemblages of short duration, even those established by large suites of beads, may be clouded if the assemblage changes occurred during time periods of major change in offshore upwelling. Thus Dating Scheme D and other dating schemes based on direct AMS shell dates cannot be considered absolute dating frameworks.

New Views on Specific Bead Horizons

Recent AMS direct dating has provided greater time depth for the earliest shell bead distribution horizon (for *Olivella* spire-lopped beads) in western North America. The first direct AMS date on a spire-lopped bead was obtained from a specimen recovered from Fort Rock Cave, Oregon, which returned a date of 6630 cal B.C. (Jenkins 1986). Fitzgerald et al. (2005) cite 13 recently obtained AMS dates to conclude that *Olivella* spire-lopped beads "were being transported from the coast to locations 250–365 km inland by 8300 to 8000 cal B.C."

The earliest *Olivella* wall bead (a shell bead cut and shaped from the wall of a marine mollusk shell) distribution horizon also has recently been identified through direct AMS dating. The type was the grooved rectangles, labeled Class N by Bennyhoff and Hughes (1987:141–142). The ambiguous context of Class N bead recovery led Bennyhoff and Hughes (1987:142) to assign the type via seriation to a number of discontinuous time periods, all in the Late Holocene. Later, Jenkins and Erlandson (1996) marshaled charcoal-dating evidence for Middle Holocene Class N *Olivella* beads in the Fort Rock Valley, Oregon. Vellanoweth (2001) reports direct AMS dates on Class N beads from sites in the Great Basin and southern California to document that they were manufactured and widely distributed between 3450 and 2450 cal B.C.

Nearly two decades ago, Bennyhoff and Hughes (1987) concluded that marine shell bead conveyance into the Great Basin from California reached its peak during the Early Period:

> Our interpretation of the evidence is that shell bead and ornament trade between the Great Basin and California was at its peak during the Early period (ca. 2000–200 B.C.) and that it declined sharply during the subsequent Middle period (ca. 200 B.C.–A.D. 700). To judge from the absolute frequency of specimens, shell trade appears to have increased somewhat during the Late Prehistoric period (A.D. 700–1500), but again declined to reach a marked low in the Protohistoric period (A.D. 1500–1800). (Bennyhoff and Hughes 1987:161)

No subsequent studies have contradicted their evidence for a peak of shell bead trade from California into the Great Basin during the Early Period. In fact, recent work in Oregon (Jenkins et al. 2004:259, 265), including new AMS bead dates, lends support to this conclusion.

The overall bead assemblages of central and southern California were very different in the Early Period, despite the fact that the same *Olivella* bead forms (Class L rectangles and Class B barrels) were used in both areas. While *Olivella* Class L beads dominated central California assemblages, they were not nearly as common in the south as *Tivela* clam disks. During the first part of the following Middle Period (600 cal B.C. to cal A.D. 1050), complete template replacement occurred in both southern and central California bead assemblages, as round *Olivella* saucers and *Haliotis* nacreous disks became the marker beads in both areas (Bennyhoff and Hughes 1987; King 1990:229). It is presently unclear whether that convergence of bead forms during the initial Middle Period was the result of a new level of trade integration, cultural convergence, or some combination of the two.

Synchrony between southern and central California Middle Period shell bead horizon was disrupted abruptly sometime between cal A.D. 430 (ΔR 225 ±3 5) and cal A.D. 510 (ΔR 290 ± 35), as indicated by five direct AMS dates on *Olivella* Type F2a full saddle beads from four different central California sites (Groza 2002). Full saddle beads are diagonally cut *Olivella* wall beads with chipped outer edges and very small (0.9–1.4 mm) perforations (Bennyhoff and Hughes 1987:130–132). They occur in pure bead lots with burials stratigraphically above burials with pure lots of saucer beads at central California sites ALA-309 (Emeryville shell mound) (Bennyhoff 1986), ALA-413 (Santa Rita Village) (Wiberg 1984), and SOL-270 (Cook site) (McGonagle 1966; Rosenthal 1996), and in the basal components at ALA-329 (Ryan mound) (Leventhal 1993) and CCO-151 (El Sobrante; Phoebe A. Hearst Museum of Anthropology, Archaeological Archives, Manuscript no. 119). This sudden complete replacement of the dominant bead form in the central California exchange network, without equivalent change in the southern California exchange network, was coincident with the spread of the Meganos Aspect (marked by extended mortuary posture) from the delta into portions of the San Francisco Bay Area (Bennyhoff 1994a, b).

Over the latter portion of the Middle Period, from approximately cal A.D. 500 to 1050, succeeding central California *Olivella* saddle beads (types F2c, F2d, F3a, F3b) became bisymmetrical with well-ground edges but retained very small perforations and four-sided shouldered silhouettes. Groza's (2002) direct AMS results show that the *Olivella* saddle template shift during that time did not follow the full saddle (Type F2a, F2b) to mixed saddle (Types F2a, F2b, F3a) to square saddle (Types F3a, F3b) progression that Bennyhoff and Hughes (1987) hypothesized. Instead, the Full Saddle Horizon gave way to a short period of mixed wide saddles (Type F2c)/square saddles (Type F3a), then to square saddles (Types F3a, F3b), and then, surprisingly, back to a 200-year horizon of mixed wide saddles/square saddles (Groza 2002; Milliken 2004). During this latter part of the Middle Period, *Olivella* saucers continued to be the predominant bead class in the southern California exchange network, and occasional *Olivella* saucer lots appeared in central California assemblages otherwise dominated by *Olivella* saddles.

The abrupt split between southern and central California bead exchange networks midway through what the CCTS nomenclature portrays as a single unified period (the Middle Period) calls for explanation. Who started making an entirely new wall bead form, the saddle bead, in central California? Where are the production locations for the new saddle bead? Why were the saddle beads apparently not accepted south of Monterey Bay? The answer to these questions may reflect regional turmoil and population disruption in central California at approximately cal A.D. 500.

The transition from the Middle to the Late Period, termed the Middle/Late Transition (MLT) in the CCTS and phases M5c/L1a in King's southern California sequence, was dated to 1,250–1,050 years ago in central California by Bennyhoff and Hughes (1987) and to 900–700 years ago in southern California by King (1990). Although the two exchange networks remained divergent through this time period, Dating Scheme D reconciles the two chronologies by bringing the central California MLT forward to cal A.D. 1050–1250 (Figure 17.2). Despite the presence of the unique *Olivella* split-punched bead (Class D) and massive numbers of tiny *Olivella* saucers (Type G1) in both southern and central California, the predominate MLT bead of central California—the *Olivella* M1a sequin rectangle—was not conveyed south of Big Sur on the coast and the Merced River in the interior.

During the succeeding Late Period, the southern and central California bead exchange horizons remained divergent. During Phase 1 the *Olivella* callus cupped (Type K1) beads were characteristic of both networks but the various types of central California *Olivella* Class M rectangles did not appear in southern California, while the medium-size *Olivella* saucers, *Mytilus* disks, and *Tivela* disks of southern California never appeared in the central part of the state. The pattern was similar in Phase 2, when the *Olivella* lipped series (Class E) marked both the south and the center of California, but the array of *Olivella* callus cupped beads, *Tivela* disks and cylinders, *Mytilus* disks and cylinders, and *Haliotis* disks common in southern California did not appear in central California (Bennyhoff and Hughes 1987; King 1990:237). Finally, there is currently no evidence that the signature *Saxidomus* clamshell disk beads diagnostic of Phase 2 in central California ever spread as far south as Monterey Bay, suggesting a retraction north of the central California exchange network after ca. cal A.D. 1550 (King 1978:60–62; Siefkin 1999:347–350).

For the Santa Barbara Channel area, the dual themes of increased shell bead manufacture and increased social complexity have become important topics since 1984. King (1990) used cemetery data to argue for successive waves of development in regional trade and sociopolitical complexity, suggesting one pulse at the end of the Early Period and another at the beginning of the Late Period. Arnold (1992a, 1992c, 2001a) rejected the importance of Early Period social development on the Santa Barbara Channel, concluding instead that the first important increase in bead production, trade, and social complexity occurred at the end of the Middle Period and then accelerated as a response to environmental stress during the MLT (Arnold et al. 1997; Arnold and Graesch 2001). Her evidence indicates that a few plank canoe owners controlled island to mainland bead-for-food trade during the Late Period (Arnold 1997). Graesch (2004) and Rick (2004c) have recently provided evidence for red abalone bead production in the Northern Channel Islands that culminated during the Historic Period.

Most central California studies addressing trade and the rise of social complexity were written prior to 1984 (Fredrickson 1974b, 1994b; T. King 1974b, 1978; C. King 1978), appealing to models of a monetized economic structure in ethnographic times (Chagnon 1970; Vayda 1967). Only one quantitative regional study has been carried out to investigate changes in bead distribution over space and time in central California in recent years. In it, Milliken and Bennyhoff (1993) presented evidence that shell bead manufacture and trade increased dramatically in central California during the MLT, then gradually declined through the phases of the Late Period. Over that time, bead wealth appeared with increasing frequency as a funerary offering in mortuary populations, leading the authors to suggest that the shifting distribution of beads in burials through the Late Period reflected a wider access to beads in the population at large and a corresponding decrease in the importance of beads as exclusive prestige symbols (Milliken and Bennyhoff 1993:388).

Olivella Bead Sources and Manufacturing Locations

Discussions of shell bead conveyance network expansion and contraction necessarily involve questions about source locations and production centers, as do related discussions of exchange network coalescences and divergences over time. Some recent studies begin with the premise that the Santa Barbara Channel Islands are the source of all inland shell beads north of the Gulf of Mexico exchange network area and inland from cismontane California. Jenkins et al. (2004), for example, interpret the presence of marine shell beads in Middle Holocene/Early Period (4150–3650 cal. B.C.) contexts in the Fort Rock region of central Oregon as indicative of an extensive western North American trading network:

> We believe a need-driven market for shell items in the northern Great Basin may well have stimulated both southern and northern trade networks to greater and more reliable production. Thus, we view the Fort Rock Region as a distant—though thoroughly integrated—component of long-distance Middle Holocene trade networks extending from southern California and northern Mexico to Oregon and possibly to Idaho. (Jenkins et al. 2004:266–267)

The authors include a map showing a hypothetical trade route from southern California to central Oregon by way of the east side of the Sierra, report a small amount of *Olivella* bead production detritus in Oregon, and suggest transport of raw material and blanks indicating "a relatively sophisticated trade system which may have involved mass production and long distance marketing between population centers" (Jenkins et al. 2004:264). Vellanoweth (2001) also proposes a southern California source for Middle Holocene shell bead trade in western North America. He suggests a Channel Island source for the *Olivella* grooved rectangle (Type N) beads that appeared in Nevada and Oregon between 3450 and 2450 cal B.C., noting that the largest numbers of Type N beads have been recovered on the Southern Channel Islands (Vellanoweth 2001:946). Although the proponents of a southern California center for most Early and Middle Holocene *Olivella* beads in the West may be correct, the Early and Middle Holocene archaeological record in central California is still remarkably limited, so the importance of central and northern California *Olivella* shell sources prior to the Late Holocene cannot yet be fully evaluated.

Arnold and Graesch (2001) hold a view opposite from King (1990) regarding shell bead conveyance inland from the Santa Barbara Channel during the Late Period. They argue that beads were not moved inland in great numbers:

> Literally millions of beads were made on the Channel Islands during the final 600 years of occupation, and the greatest percentages were consumed in island and mainland Chumash households, burial rites, and ceremonies. That is, the bulk of Chumash trade was "middle-distance" trade within their own territories. (Arnold and Graesch 2001:111)

King (1990:111, 122, 129), on the other hand, found evidence that Santa Barbara Channel shell beads were traded throughout southern California and surrounding areas, citing recovery of Early, Middle, and Late Period shell beads similar to those of the channel in Los Angeles, Orange, San Bernardino, and Riverside Counties. Others have noted that large numbers of Late Period beads of typical Santa Barbara Channel form have been recovered inland to the east of protohistoric Chumash linguistic territory. Siefkin (1999:349), for example, reports on the large numbers of Santa Barbara Channel–style shell beads at Late Period sites in the southern San Joaquin Valley. Farther inland in the Owens Valley of transmontane

California, small numbers of *Olivella* lipped (Class E) and cupped (Class K) are found at many Late Period sites, although central California Late Period *Olivella* sequin rectangles (Class M) and *Saxidomus* clam disks are absent (Bettinger 1989; Milliken 1999:107).

In central California, no coastal *Olivella* bead "mints" have yet been discovered comparable to those of the Channel Islands. While few coastal sites have more than 100 pieces of *Olivella* detritus per cubic meter (Dietz 1987:144), small-scale *Olivella* bead manufacturing workshops have been documented on the Marin coast (King and Upson 1970), a few dozen miles inland in Sonoma County; one *Olivella* bead workshop has been described almost 50 miles inland in eastern Napa County (Hartzell 1991). Inland manufacture is a hallmark of *Saxidomus* clam shell bead dispersal during Phase 2 of the Late Period. Thousands of broken pieces of *Saxidomus* shell, along with shell bead blanks in various stages of manufacture, have been recovered from site components as far inland as the Sacramento River (Schulz 1994; Stromberg 1992; Wiberg 2005).

Another controversy that requires further study is the degree to which the southern California and Gulf of Mexico exchange networks overlapped, diverged, or were completely separate from one another at various times in the past. Rosen (1995) argued that *Olivella* shell beads recovered from site IMP-6427 do not cross-date to King's southern California chronology and that the predominance of *O. dama* points to a stronger tie to the Gulf of California than to the southern California coast. This is not surprising, having been anticipated by earlier authors cited by Bennyhoff and Hughes (1987:155). What is important here is that a growing body of evidence suggests that the boundary between the Gulf of California and southern California exchange networks shifted through time. Gibson and Koerper (2000) report such a change, arguing that longtime reliance on Santa Barbara Channel barrel beads in Orange County was interrupted at the end of the Middle Period, after which time *O. dama* shell was imported and barrel beads were manufactured locally. By historic contact times, however, Santa Barbara Channel beads were again predominant as far south as San Diego according to Zepeda (2004:127), who also reports a dearth of evidence for shell bead manufacturing in San Diego County.

There may be special significance to the remarkably widespread areal distribution of needle-drilled *Olivella* disk beads (Class H in Bennyhoff and Hughes 1987), a precise historic time marker thought to have been manufactured on the Channel Islands as late as 1816, 46 years after Spanish settlement of southern California (Johnson 1982; McLendon and Johnson 1999). A refined time sequence based on changes in outer bead diameter was developed, and cross-dating was based on presence or absence of certain associated historic artifacts augmented by knowledge of the times of village abandonment as people moved to the local Franciscan missions (King 1995). King's size sequence, illustrated as a series of overlapping bell-shaped size curves, extends from the 1770s to the 1850s. Zepeda (2004:139) reports large numbers of *Olivella* H Class needle-drilled disks recovered from San Diego County, and postulates that they "were manufactured by the Chumash during the historic period and traded down to the Kumeyaay, either directly or indirectly" (see also King 2004). Historic *Olivella* H disks have also been recovered from sites located a considerable distance north of Santa Barbara; they have been found in large numbers at a historic contact-period site in the southern Santa Clara Valley south of San Francisco Bay (Hildebrandt et al. 1995), at the Mission Santa Clara cemetery (Hylkema 1995), and at a site dated to A.D.1790–1810 on Cache Creek in the lower Sacramento Valley (Wiberg 2005). We presume that needle-drilled *Olivella* disks in historic central California sites derive from the Channel Islands, but this requires independent verification of the geographic source of the *Olivella* shell.

A potential method for sourcing *Olivella* shell, with positive preliminary results, is described by Eerkens et al. (2005). The authors studied the $^{12/13}C$ and $^{16/18}O$ ratios of *Olivella* shells collected up and down the California coast and report finding patterned differences in oxygen $^{16/18}O$ ratios that seem to reflect ocean temperature gradients, allowing *Olivella* shells from southern and northern California to be differentiated by oxygen isotope values alone. Because of the complex local variation in upwelling events, carbon signatures alone cannot be used to discriminate northern from southern California shells, but when combined with $^{16/18}O$ data, the carbon data can help distinguish between nearby sites on different Channel Islands and the nearby mainland. Eerkens et al. tested three *Olivella* H Class needle-drilled disks recently recovered from the lower Sacramento Valley YOL-69 and one *Olivella* needle-drilled disk from a historic cemetery at Mission Santa Clara. Shell isotope fingerprints indicate that all four of the beads derived from *Olivella* shell that had grown in the warm waters south of Point Conception, tentatively supporting long-distance shell bead trade in California during the initial Mission Period. We hope that this new method will help resolve a number of the shell bead source area questions discussed above and that shell sourcing will become a tool for identifying more precisely the localized marine environments from which archaeologically significant shells could have been obtained. Such an advance will greatly aid in tracking development, disruption, and change in regional California bead trade networks.

SHELL AND OBSIDIAN

In this chapter we have offered only general summaries of some of the important research conducted over the past 20 years. We have emphasized recent refinements in shell bead dating because improved precision and accuracy allow for finer temporal resolution of the duration and demise of different types, and because such refinements allow temporal reconciliation of southern and central bead conveyance networks requisite for evaluating proposed correlations between major environmental shifts and cultural change in California prehistory. Refinements notwithstanding, it still may be difficult to decide whether some temporal discrepancies are real, and if others are masked by difficulties in converting from radiocarbon dates to calendar years at the centennial level (Guilderson et al. 2005).

To the extent that calibration issues can be eliminated, observed discrepancies may represent (in certain areas during different time periods) fluctuations in the influence or pervasiveness of trade/exchange media reflexive of population densities sufficient for the development of social institutions and status for which certain beads were emblematic (influencing demand). Given the variety of social contexts in which beads functioned, they probably were conveyed via different networks at different times, perhaps for different reasons, irrespective of typological similarities. Temporal resolution via typological and hydration dating for obsidian is, by shell bead standards, comparatively crude, introducing a dating mismatch between these materials that influences correlation efforts and interpretation. Nonetheless, there appears to be an important and widespread concordance between shell and obsidian data indicating rather abrupt change at around cal A.D. 500–700 in the central parts of the state, characterized by obsidian quarry production declines, source use shifts, and bead network disruption. The meanings of these changes are presently unclear, but their geographic expression implies that they represent local responses to more widespread social and/or environmental change during this time interval.

CONCLUSION

Dramatic improvements have been made over the past 20 years in specifying the time and space distributions of materials in California's past. We have learned much more about where materials were procured, where they went, when, and the variable deposition contexts in which they were recovered. Yet the broader archaeological significance of such information is still far from self-evident.

One might assume that we know much more about prehistoric trade and exchange in California, but there are reasons to remain skeptical of studies purporting to demonstrate the existence of trade or exchange networks in the absence of strong supporting evidence and argumentation. Archaeological inferences (or conjectures) about trade/exchange relationships are based primarily on knowledge of the source of the material and its archaeological context (including its age). In a strict sense we are attempting to understand the ways in which material was *conveyed* from its point of origin to its archaeological recovery context (Hughes 1994a:376). Conveyance, rather than trade and/or exchange, is perhaps a more realistic term for what actually can be supported from distribution data alone, whereas other contextual information (that derived from analysis of grave offerings, from domestic architecture associations, caches, lithic reduction studies and experiments, large comparable data sets from different classes of artifacts, etc.) might be mustered to support more refined arguments about whether exchange/trade or direct access was more likely in any specific case (Jackson 1988; Kuhn 2004; Rick and Jackson 1992). We currently know a lot about distribution, but considerably less about trade and exchange. It is perhaps another consequence of archaeology's continuing "loss of innocence" (Clarke 1973) that distance, which once seemed clear evidence for prehistoric trade/exchange to earlier generations of archaeologists, appears a far less obvious proxy for such activity today.

Finally, it is abundantly clear that we cannot treat prehistoric commodity exchange, or conveyance, in prehistoric California as a unitary phenomenon. Twenty years ago there was only dim appreciation of this, but today it is apparent that prehistoric shell bead and ornament distributions, peaks and declines, are not isomorphic with those of obsidian, and that the mechanisms responsible for observed distributions varied depending on a variety of contextual factors. As discussed with respect to California and Great Basin studies (Hughes 1994a), conveyances no doubt varied by material type, artifact class, physiographic location, and time. Isolating and identifying these factors and conjoining them with other archaeological evidence will be one of the more daunting and rewarding challenges for those seeking an integrated understanding of California's past.

NOTES

1. Because of the summary nature of this review we have purposefully avoided addressing issues of incorrect obsidian source assignments or erroneous shell bead type identifications. But we can't help commenting on the disturbing tendency toward minimalism, or avoiding primary data altogether (e.g., Bailey 2006). Spiraling costs associated with publishing reams of data tables that few (if any) will ever use serve as a strong incentive to eliminate or seriously eviscerate raw data, but inspection of primary data is usually the only way to verify, correct, or refine chemical type/source assignments (Hughes 1984). With regard to shell beads, sample measurements are critical, but they cannot replace high-quality photographs or drawings.

2. Examples of long-distance direct access pertain to the Historic Period, after the horse had been introduced to California and the greater West (see Heizer 1942b; Pilling 1950).

3. The term "Dating Scheme D" for Groza's central California bead horizon chronology follows Bennyhoff and Hughes (1987:147), who labeled Heizer's (1958) long chronology Dating Scheme A, their own chronology Dating Scheme B, and Elsasser's (1978) seldom cited chronology Dating Scheme C.

CHAPTER 18

Rock Art in the Golden State: Pictographs and Petroglyphs, Portable and Panoramic

AMY J. GILREATH

WHILE THE TWO 1984 ARCHAEOLOGICAL OVERVIEWS OF California were in many respects exceptional, neither dealt extensively with prehistoric art. Because chronological placement of rock art was uncertain then (and remains tenuous today), Moratto (1984) and Chartkoff and Chartkoff (1984) could not associate artistic renderings with the other diachronic and regional archaeological patterns they discussed. Consequently they deferred to an earlier overview by William Clewlow (1978). His summary chapter in the California volume of the *Handbook of North American Indians* series reflected an interest in California rock art inherited from Robert Heizer, who had long been involved in California rock art studies (Heizer 1953b; Heizer and Baumhoff 1962; Heizer and Clewlow 1973). Heizer was preceded by Julian Steward (1929), who had followed in the path of Alfred Kroeber (1925). This long tradition of rock art study, carried on initially by scholars from the University of California, Berkeley, has been continued by a resurgence of interest in the mid-1990s, centered at the University of California, Los Angeles. Largely due to the influence of Clement Meighan, this renewed interest is reflected by the volume of research completed by David Whitley (1987, 1992, 1994b, 1997, 1998, 2000a; Whitley and Dorn 1987).

In comparison to "dirt" archaeology, rock art has also been advanced by the efforts of devoted nonarchaeological professionals. Such avocationalists deserve great recognition for advancing rock art preservation as well as public awareness and education. Active rock art avocational groups exist in all parts of the state where appreciable quantities of rock art can be found. Despite this public interest and enthusiasm, there has been "a reluctance of . . . mainstream anthropologists to fully accept the inherent cultural heritage values of rock art investigation" (Clewlow 1998:20). Many career archaeologists avoid rock art. This reluctance may be linked to the sensational and popular rock art theories spun out by "cranks" who "see rock art as the result of visits from aliens, prophetic fulfillment of oracles, Nordic conquests, and a variety of other nonsensical reveries" (Clewlow 1998:20). Regardless of the cause, it is both peculiar and regrettable that so many scholarly archaeologists avoid this part of the archaeological record: peculiar, because it sets archaeologists apart from the general public, which commonly regards rock art as the most fascinating and readily appreciated part of the prehistoric record; regrettable, because it is beautiful and provides much direct evidence of prehistoric artistic expression, spirituality, values, and emotions. By persistently failing to incorporate rock art into characterizations of prehistoric California Indians, archaeologists are often guilty of portraying prehistoric native peoples as "uncultured" and driven only by short-term economic decision making.

This chapter has three objectives. As a starting point, it underscores how integral rock was to human existence in premodern times. Aside from the Central Valley, California is a rock-filled, mountainous environment. In times past, when all travel was by foot, California native people had to walk on rock or around it when moving from one place to another. They often chose to live under natural rock shelters or inside caves, or were forced to clear rock to make comfortable living areas. Out of necessity, everyone fashioned rock into everyday tools—the hand-shaped milling gear of women and the hunting gear of men. The extraordinarily worn condition of molar teeth in prehistoric skulls results from the rocky grit that they routinely ingested as an unavoidable component in food. Grit was forever working through native people's digestive tracts, was blown into their eyes, and was trapped under their fingernails. Ethnographies describe, and contemporary traditional California native people know of, a world where the rock itself is inhabited by spirits, powers, or forces that can cause harm or can be helpful. The second objective of this chapter is to cultivate the reader's appreciation for the rich and varied rock art record made by California Indians of the recent and distant past. This is done with illustrations of artifacts, features, and rock art panels from different regions within the state, making it possible

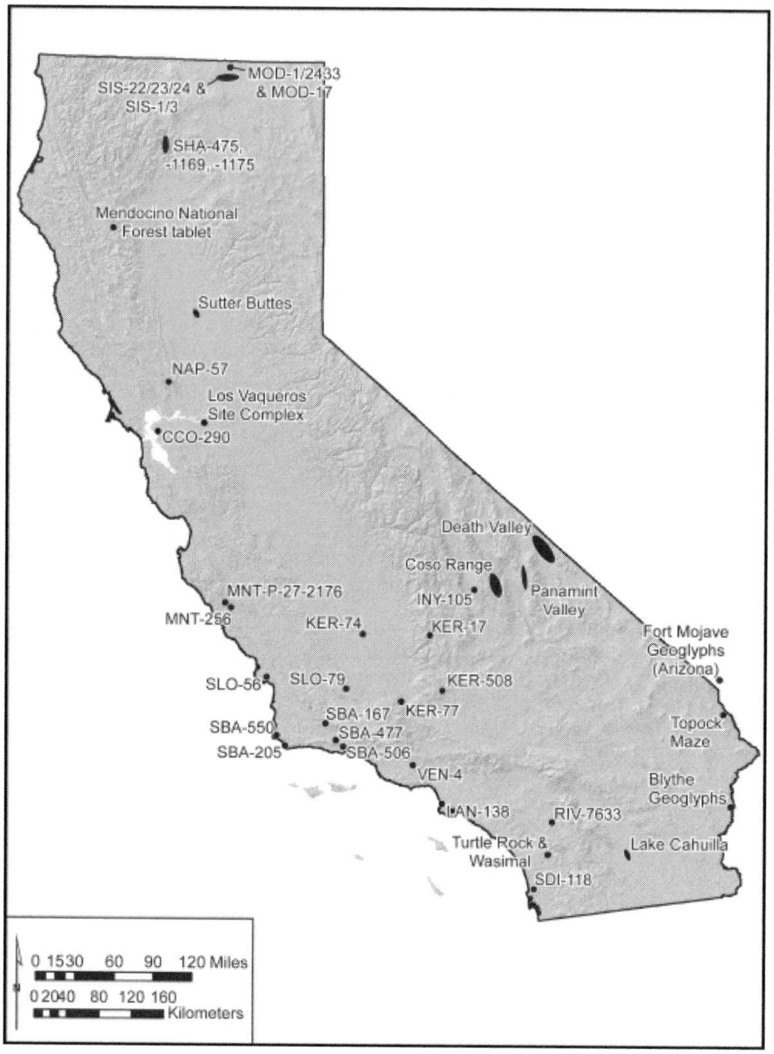

Figure 18.1. Selected California rock art sites and localities.

for the casual reader to glance at the work; temporal and distributional information are provided for the more serious reader. The final objective is to stimulate greater research interest in rock art, so that decorated rock and significant rocky landscapes are increasingly incorporated into archaeological characterizations of prehistoric peoples and their lifeways.

ROCK ART

The discussion in this chapter begins with small decorated pebbles and slates no bigger than one's hand. Stationary pictographs (painted designs) and petroglyphs (pecked, carved, or incised designs) on boulders and bedrock, often achieving a monumental scale, are considered next. Moving to an even larger scale, we then review geoglyphs and intaglios, earth works and rock alignments that take on a perceived pattern when viewed from a distance of several hundred feet. The discussion ends with examples of rock formations and outcrops that are imbued with power, are associated with myths, or serve as a touchstone for a group's identity. While the first three categories of rock art are physically made (although governed by behaviors dictated partly by metaphysical beliefs), this last category encompasses rocky landmarks that are understood or valued purely for their metaphysical properties. For many native California tribes, the boundary between a physical and metaphysical world is permeable and negotiable. As such, it is appropriate for this review of rock art to give at least passing consideration to rock art as a bridge between the two worlds.

Small, Decorated Rocks

Different regions within the state have evidence for a tradition of pebbles or small natural platy tablets of stone that were painted or incised. These are sometimes referred to as mobiliary art because of their portability. Typical designs were incised or cut into one or both faces of slate or schist tablets, or painted on pebbles.

INCISED SLATES Incised slates occur with some frequency in three areas of the state (Carpenter 1988), but they have been found in abundance only in Shasta County. Three sites (SHA-475, SHA-1169, and SHA-1175; Figure 18.1) clustered on the upper Sacramento River produced nearly 1,500 incised slates, with only a handful found at other sites nearby. The upper Sacramento River collection (McGuire 1989) is one of the most extensive assemblages of portable prehistoric art in North America. It is also one of the best dated bodies of prehistoric rock art in the New World, a benefit of the fact that it was recovered from rich midden deposits that also yielded considerable charcoal and obsidian. Chronometric assays from these associated materials indicate dating between 3000 and 1500 cal B.C. The incised slates are made of local metasedimentary siltstone and schist, green to gray in hue, with complete items averaging about 45 by 30 by 6 millimeters (18 grams). The most common designs are parallel bands in-filled with a series of straight lines and X's, or more complex cross-hatching often using triangle or diamond shapes (Figure 18.2a). Three-quarters of them have designs cut into only one face. They seem to have been worn or carried by their owners, and their frequency and distribution throughout the site deposits suggest that they commonly broke or were lost during everyday activities. McGuire (1989: D43) convincingly argues that these amulets were group markers that provided "stylistic reinforcement of group affiliation and social integration."

The second area with an incised stone tradition is coastal southwestern California. In Monterey, San Luis Obispo, Santa Barbara, Ventura, Los Angeles, and Orange Counties, one or two but no more than a few dozen pieces are occasionally found in sites. Regional literature sometimes refers to them as plaques or tablets. Nearly all are in Chumash sites, and most are in deposits younger than 1,000 years, e.g., SBA-477/Cachuma Dam; SBA-205/Jalama (Lathrap and Hoover 1975); SLO-56/Port Hartford (Pilling 1952), and various sites on Santa Cruz and other Channel Islands (Lee 1981a; D. B. Rogers 1929) (Figure 18.1). Comparatively few examples are from earlier contexts, but among these are a handful from the upper levels at the Tank site (LAN-2; Greenwood 1979:276) and from various levels at Malaga Cove (LAN-138; Figure 18.1; Walker 1951; see also painted pebbles, below). Cameron (1990) collated information on incised stones found in Orange County, and noted that nearly all are from coastal (not inland) sites, and that there are some indications they came into use a bit earlier than in Santa Barbara County. Nonetheless, she considers them late and places them between cal A.D. 500 and 1500 (Cameron 1990:72). Near the northern perimeter of the Chumash area, several have been recovered at sites on and near Willow Creek on the Monterey County coast (MNT-281 and MNT-471, Pohorecky 1976). These latter items are north of Chumash territory but still tend to come from relatively late contexts.

Comparison of the numerous illustrations of the incised stones from Jalama (Figure 18.2b; Lathrap and Hoover 1975) to those from Orange County (Cameron 1990) and from the Channel Islands and nearby mainland (Lee 1981a) indicates they are similar in size, simplicity, and design. Some from the latter context are distinguished by a simple, graceful representational design, such as a stick-figure anthropomorph (Lee 1981a), rather than the more common angular cross-hatched or zonal geometric designs. Throughout this region, a fair number of examples have been found with burials, but this is not an exclusive association.

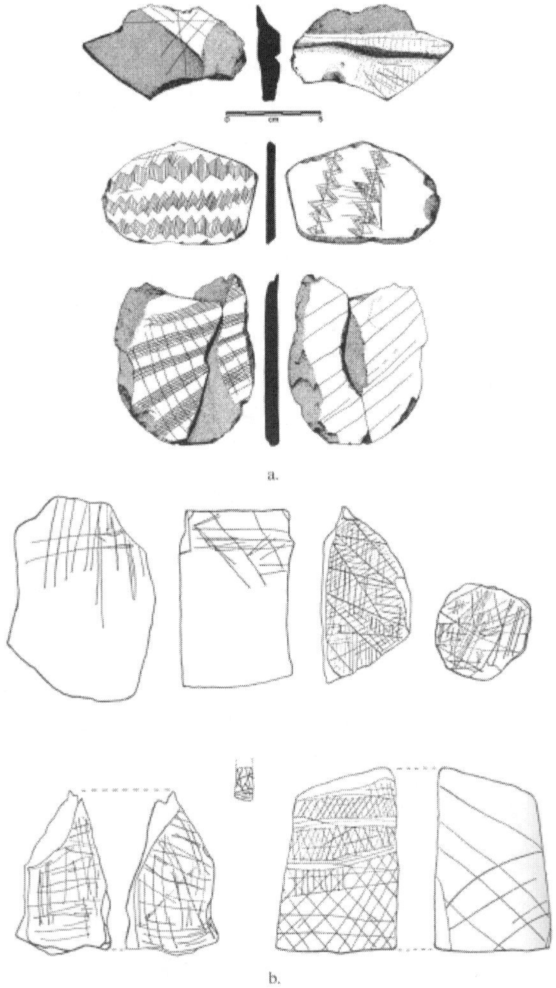

Figure 18.2. (a) Incised slates from Shasta County (McGuire 1989), reproduced courtesy of Kelly McGuire and the Center for Archaeological Research at Davis. (b) Incised slates from Jalama (SBA-205) (Lathrap and Hoover 1975:98), reproduced courtesy of Robert Hoover and the San Luis Obispo County Archaeological Society.

The third area with an incised stone tradition is the Mojave Desert, with lovely, pale green incised slates recovered fairly frequently from Death Valley, northeastern San Bernardino County, and Inyo County (Bettinger 1989:77–78; Harrington 1957; Hunt 1960:169–170; Lanning 1963; Warren 1984). Their distribution also extends farther east across southern Nevada, where they fall within the southern style of the Great Basin incising tradition defined by Thomas (1983a, b, c). The 400-plus pieces considered in her study came from Gatecliff Shelter, central Nevada, from deposits dating between 1260 cal B.C. and cal A.D. 1300. In southeastern California, however, this tradition is comparatively late, with examples usually found at sites dating between cal A.D. 500 and 1500. Bits and pieces are found in and among occupational debris, suggesting that they, like those from the upper Sacramento River canyon, were personal adornment items in fairly common use, broken or lost during everyday activities. Ritter (1980) and Thomas (1983c:351) offer an alternative explanation, perceiving a relationship between pinyon-reliant subsistence practices and incised mobiliary rock art.

One other instance in the state where incised stones had a specific use, albeit a confined distribution, should be mentioned. Several sites in San Diego County have produced "warming stones." These are large, shaped soapstone items, weighing on the order of 35 pounds, with angular, geometric designs engraved on them (Parkman 1983), and sometimes smeared with ochre (Polk 1972). Kroeber (1925:716), drawing from Waterman (1910:286–287), describes them as "a large crescentic stone, heated and placed between the girls' legs to soften the abdominal tissues and render motherhood easy and safe. These stones have been spoken of as sacred." This ritual was part of a female puberty ceremony among the Diegueno and Kumeyaay (Luomala 1978:603). This practice was in use into the late 1800s, but its level of antiquity is unknown.

Finally there is the possibility of a "big tablet" custom, but data are sketchy. Four large slabs on the order of 40 to 50 centimeters long and about 25 centimeters wide (about the size of a millingstone) have been found singly in interior Coast Range areas in the central part of the state. Individual specimens have been described from Merced, Alameda, and Sonoma Counties, and the Mendocino National Forest (Meacham 1984; Parkman 1981). One from Mendocino (Figure 18.1) appears to be the most elaborate, with one band of connected diamonds and a line connecting a series of evenly spaced circles.

PAINTED PEBBLES Evidence for a tradition of painting water-worn pebbles or shaped pieces of slate exists primarily from a few small areas. A handful of Chumash sites in Santa Barbara, Ventura, and Los Angeles Counties each have produced one or a few painted pebbles (Curtis 1959; Hudson and Blackburn 1986; Lathrap and Hoover 1975; Lee 1981a, b; Meighan 1969; Walker 1951). Similar items have been found at one site in the Cajon Pass area, between the Mojave Desert and the Transverse Ranges (Smith and Mosely 1962). Nearly a dozen are known from the eastern shoreline of prehistoric Lake Cahuilla (Hedges 1981), while a handful of sites in Napa County have produced a few dozen painted pebbles (Heizer 1953a). Others seem to be isolates: two from a Late Period cemetery in Kern County (KER-74; Figure 18.1; Riddell 1951); two from a San Francisco Bay shell mound (CCO-290, Figure 18.1; Fredrickson 1977); two from Shasta County (Sundahl 1984); one from Lassen County (Pilling 1957), and so forth. They nearly always occur in late contexts, certainly less than 1,000 years old, but probably more on the order of less than 500 years, regardless of where they are in the state. Most items retain lines or patches of red, white, black, or dark brown pigment.

Chumash painted pebbles tend to be of simple design, typically with red pigment near one end or in a few lines. One atypically intricate painted slate was recovered from a named Chumash village (Soxtonocmu) in interior Santa Barbara County (Lee 1981b). No more than 200 years old, it has red centipedes (a common motif in Chumash cave art), and X's, and was partly covered with asphaltum (Figure 18.3b). Lee links it to Chumash shamanic practices, giving an account of a Chumash shaman who painted a design to avert a storm, and another account of one who caused a famine by painting people bleeding out of the mouth. A Chumash rock art classification scheme proposed by Hyder and Oliver (1986) that integrates portable styles and motifs with those painted in fixed places points to this item as an example of Chumash Style B rock art (monochromatic and linear).

The most elaborate group of painted slates in the state is from the Napa region, described by Meighan et al. (1953). These items are 4 to 8 centimeters long, 2 to 4 centimeters wide, and about 0.5 centimeter thick, and they have red, white, and black lines or nested arches painted usually on one face (Figure 18.3b). Many were associated with a single cremation from Wooden Valley that is less than 700 years old.

Conceding that painted pebbles and slates are primarily a Late Period phenomenon, ethnographic information is particularly relevant when considering their likely function. Kroeber (1925:197–199) quotes at length from an autobiographical account of a Yuki rattlesnake shaman north of Napa, describing one of his curings: "When we laid the wounded man down he was nearly dead. I painted a flat stone red and white. Then I addressed the sun." The man's narrative continues, saying that a rattlesnake shaman "paints wavy lines . . . on a flat stone, warms the wounded part with hot ashes, lays the stone on for a time and begins to suck." Yuki territory is about 80 kilometers north of Napa in interior Mendocino County, but no such items have been reported from archaeological sites there, suggesting that they were uncommon, do not preserve (e.g., the paint washes off quickly), or have

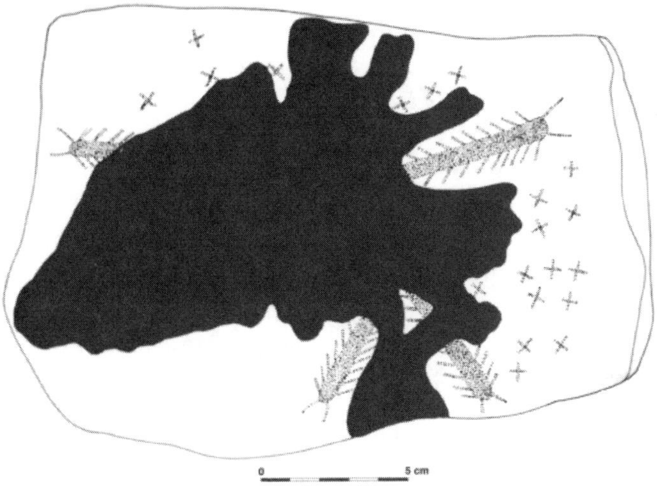

a.

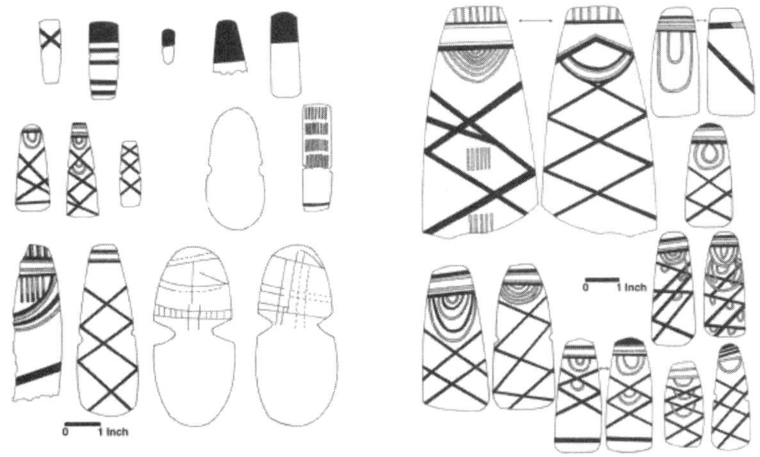

b.

Figure 18.3. (a) Painted slate from SBA-167, *Soxtonocmu* (Lee 1981a:117), reproduced courtesy the Malki Press. (b) Painted slates from the Napa region (Heizer 1953a:Fig. 2, 334).

some other equally indefinite explanation. Frank Day, a well-known contemporary Maidu artist, shows and describes a stone being put to a similar use in the western Sierra Nevada foothills, roughly 80 kilometers east of Yuki territory (Dobkins 1997:45). When he was a small child shortly after the turn of the century, he and his father encountered Ishi ministering to an injured friend. In describing his painting of this, Day recalls that Ishi was using the reflections from an abalone shell to warm water that in turn heated the stone.

In summary, small decorated rocks date variably according to type. Painted pebbles tend to be quite late, and there is compelling ethnographic evidence that some were used in healing practices and others in girls' puberty rituals. Archaeological evidence further suggests that some had a role in burial practices. Incised slates, on the other hand, date to different periods based on geographical location. In Shasta County they are Middle Archaic; in southwestern coastal California and in the interior Mojave Desert they tend to be less than 1,500 or 1,000 years old. Many of them may have been items of personal adornment and tokens of group identity.

Pictographs

Pictographs tend to occur in appreciable quantities in regions where sandstone and granite formations prevail: coastal and southern California, including the desert, and the southern Sierra Nevada. Far less commonly, pictographs were applied to basalt or other volcanic formations. There is strong evidence of a pictograph tradition in four different regions, which Grant (1965:111) refers to as Chumash (roughly Los Angeles, Ventura, Santa Barbara, and San Luis Obispo Counties), southwestern California (roughly San Diego and Riverside Counties), Tulare (roughly the southern Sierra Nevada), and northeast California (e.g., the lava caves within the Modoc Plateau).[1] Most pictographs are probably less than 1,000 years old due to the rock's susceptibility to natural erosion.

Chumash cave and rock shelter painting is the most famous (and perhaps the most studied) rock art in California. This is largely due to its beauty and to Campbell Grant's widely circulated and beautifully illustrated studies, the product of three decades of work before he died in 1992. Distinguishing elements of Chumash rock art include the sun wheel or mandala; an aquatic motif (elongated forms ending with split fin tails); bilaterally symmetrical representational designs that include anthropomorphic figures, with a split head and arms and legs bent at a 45 degree angle (Figure 18.4a); and use of dot patterns or outlines, with meticulous detail and delicately painted fine-line precision (Hudson and Conti 1981, 1984; Hudson and Lee 1984:28; Hyder 1989; Hyder and Oliver 1986; Lee 1977:2, 1984). Both monochrome and polychrome panels are common throughout the Chumash rock art area. Red is the most common color, followed by black, then white. The paintings rarely are composed murals; instead, designs tend to be "placed by themselves, free-floating in space" (Lee 1984:14). In terms of placement on the landscape, there seems to be a preference for high, small alcoves and overhangs. Again, because of the pictographs' relatively young age, it is reasonable to expect some correlations with the ethnographic record. In this regard, Grant notes stylistic variation coinciding with Kroeber's (1925) Chumash dialect areas.

Grant proposes that shamans made these paintings for religious purposes, yet begins his section entitled "Religion and Shamanism" by noting that "we know almost nothing of the Chumash religion" (Grant 1965:61). In the years since, we have come to know much about this subject thanks primarily to Blackburn's (1975) and Hudson and Blackburn's (1985, 1986, 1987) reporting of John P. Harrington's ethnographic notes. Subsequent publications such as Hudson and Underhay (1978) abound with information on Chumash material culture, mythology, and cosmology.

After studying Chumash rock art and ethnographic information for many years, Hudson and Lee (1984; Hudson and Conti 1984:78) argue that specific symbols functioned "(1) to maintain the sacred; (2) to maintain cosmic equilibrium; and (3) to acquire or manipulate power as an individual." A group of spiritual specialists in Chumash culture, the *'antap*, were responsible for handling supernatural power and symbols used in art, poetry, music, and so on, and played a key role in manipulating that power. From this interpretive context, Lee (1977:2) notes that for Chumash rock art, "one design may represent an entire myth," which provides a partial explanation for the widespread distribution of a repeated but limited suite of symbols throughout the area influenced or occupied by the Chumash.

A considerable amount of Chumash rock art was made to influence cosmic or heavenly imbalances such as the equinox, solstice, eclipse, as well as earthly instability such as earthquakes and storms. A number of Chumash rock art sites have been interpreted from the context of archaeoastronomy, functioning as cosmic observatories and depicting constellations and other celestial bodies. Such sites include Burro Flats (VEN-4; Figure 18.1; Romani et al. 1985), Lizard Cave in the San Emigdio Mountains (KER-5525; Sprague and Grasse 2001), Indian Creek in the San Rafael Range (Bracher 1984), Montgomery Potrero on the Sierra Madre Ridge (SBA-502/526; Lee 1984), and Honda Ridge (SBA-550; Figure 18.1; Sehgal 2003), among others. Hyder (1989), however, comparing the Chumash archaeological record on Sierra Madre Ridge to the San Marcos Pass area, points out the difficulty in establishing genuine associations between rock art, site location, and celestial rhythms, and the lack of rigorous methodology in many such studies.

California state parks provide public access to Chumash rock art at Painted Cave in San Marcos Pass (SBA-506; Figures 18.1 and 18.4b). The Bureau of Land Management seasonally provides guided tours of Painted Rock (SLO-79, La Piedra Pintada; Figure 18.1) in the Carrizo Plain. To help facilitate protection, the Los Padres National Forest recently closed Pleito Creek (KER-77) in the San Emigdio Mountains to the public.

Pictographs are uncommon north of Chumash territory in Monterey County. The most impressive are at MNT-44 in the rugged Santa Lucia Mountains near Tassajara and are dominated by elongated white

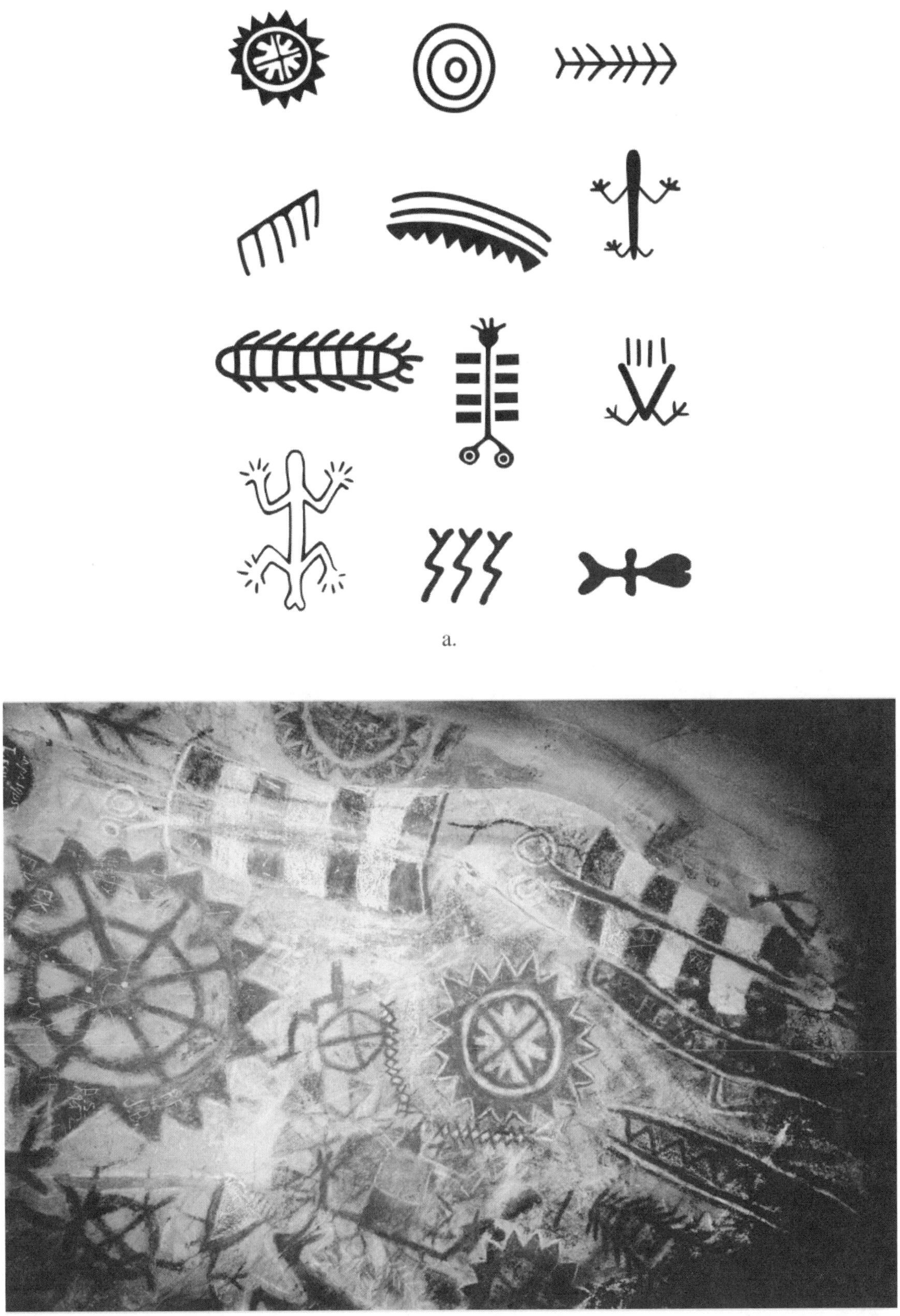

a.

b.

Figure 18.4. (a) Common motifs in Chumash pictographs (based on Hudson and Lee 1984:28; Hyder 1989:23). Drawings by Wendy Masarweh. (b) Chumash polychrome panel from SBA-506, Painted Cave (Bury 1999:152). Photograph by Rick Bury.

handprints (see photographs in Breschini and Haversat 2004) and at MNT-256 (Figure 18.1; La Cueva Pintada), 32 kilometers to the east. J. A. Mason offers the following early-twentieth-century description of MNT-256:

> The walls . . . are well covered with paintings in different colors and designs. Most of them are merely outlined in a red ochre or paint. A yellowish-white material like a clay, and a black, probably of charcoal or soot is evident. Some . . . are entirely filled in with color, while others are made of lines and dots. . . . The figures themselves are in many cases truly pictographic, the human figure, turtle, and sun being among those recognized. (1912:154–155)

Farther south in coastal areas and in the southwestern desert, pictograph styles are quite distinct from those of the Chumash, although they are still highly variable. Much of the detailed information on rock art throughout San Diego and Riverside Counties is the result of Ken Hedges's work since 1970. Over the years, various style names have been proposed, and Hedges recently synthesized much of his work, defining three pictograph styles for the region south of the Transverse Ranges: San Luis Rey, Rancho Bernardo Rectilinear Abstract, and La Rumorosa (Hedges 2002). San Luis Rey–style paintings (Hedges 1973; Smith and Freers 1994) are characterized by vertical red lines of linked diamonds and parallel zigzag lines (Figure 18.5a), and can be associated with Luiseno female puberty ceremonies, other ritual functions, and the Mission Period Chinigchinish cult. (An earlier, nearly equivalent term was Southern California Rectilinear Abstract.) Rancho Bernardo Rectilinear Abstract–style paintings are distinctive, with their red, mazelike designs (SDI-118; Figure 18.1; Hedges 1973, 2002). La Rumorosa–style paintings (formerly termed Peninsular Range Representational) are recognizable from their use of digitate anthropomorphs and geometric designs. This style is associated with Kumeyaay rock shelters (see also painted pebbles above and *yonis* discussed below) on the east slope of the Peninsular Range and into Baja California.

In the southern Sierra Nevada (eastern Kern, Tulare, and Fresno Counties), pictographs tend to be widely dispersed in comparison to the preceding areas, typically with a few panels co-occurring on the underside of a granite boulder, overhang, or cliff face (Figure 18.5b). Sites here generally do not have the quantities or the elaborate panel compositions found in southern California. Southern Sierra Painted (also termed Tulare)–style pictographs are usually polychromatic, with curvilinear (circles, dots) and angular (Y- and T-shapes, rakes, etc.) elements, as well as human (anthropomorphic) and animal (zoomorphic) elements. Tomo-Kahni State Park in the Tehachapi Mountains, established in 1993, provides the public with guided tours of the Kawaiisu ethnographic village, Nuooah, and the polychrome rock art found in this area. KER-508, Teddy Bear or Creation Cave (Figure 18.1), named for a dominant burly bearlike design, is the best studied of these sites (Sutton 1982). According to oral tradition, this is where the Nuooah world was created. Polychrome designs in red, yellow, black, and white occur, with a number of anthropomorphic and zoomorphic elements. Pictographs in the Colorado Desert, western Mojave Desert, and San Bernardino County bear superficial similarity to Tulare and southwestern California styles.

The central and northern Sierra Nevada is largely devoid of pictographs except for two small areas identified by Payen (1966). These include a pocket of mostly monochrome designs (and a few polychrome) along the Mokelumne River at the mountain-valley juncture, and a few polychrome sites in Yosemite Valley along the Merced River. Pictographs are even more uncommon in the San Francisco Bay Area, essentially limited to a few simple (birdlike) designs in about half a dozen of the Vasco caves in the vicinity of Los Vaqueros (Figure 18.1), painted in red or black (Fentress 1992).

Lava Beds National Monument on the Modoc Plateau (Siskiyou and Modoc Counties) encompasses many of the known northeast California pictograph sites (SIS-22/23/24, SIS-1/3; Figure 18.1), and certainly some of the best documented ones (Lee et al. 1988; Loubser and Whitley 1999). In contrast to the foregoing areas, this is a basalt flow landscape, with the pictographs placed near the mouth of lava tubes, sinks, and caves. Motifs are heavily dominated by geometric patterns, mostly zigzags, circles, and dots, usually made with black paint. Occasionally red elements co-occur, and less frequently white pigment is also present.

Though not common anywhere, there are examples throughout the state where pigment has been applied to petroglyphs. Since pigments applied to a surface are far more susceptible to erosion than pecked or deeply incised designs, the actual frequency of this practice cannot be known.

Pictograph studies in California each tend to focus on an individual valley or mountain range, and as a

a.

b.

Figure 18.5. (a) San Luis Rey–style pictograph, RIV-7633. Photograph by John Berg. (b) Southern Sierra pictograph, KER-17, Palakuch. Photograph by Amy Gilreath.

consequence, they often "split" rather than "lump" documented patterns. California is a large state, the archaeology has great time depth and complexity, and, as alluded to earlier, rock art tends to receive only secondary attention. In instances where focused studies have been completed, they tend to give detailed consideration to the art itself but comparatively little to the larger prehistoric archaeological context in which it occurs. Ethnographic (rather than archaeological) information usually provides the contextual interpretation for pictographs. This is not necessarily objectionable, since most of the pictographs are less than 1,000 years old. It does, however, mean that the interpretations are constrained by the ethnographic record, which is patchy for most areas in the state and nonexistent in others.

DATING As radiocarbon dating techniques are increasingly refined, ever smaller samples of organic material can be dated absolutely. Accelerator mass spectrometry (AMS) radiocarbon dating is a methodological breakthrough in dating pictographs. With this technique, an unnoticeably small area from a pictograph can serve as an adequate sample. As Watchman (1992) relates, oils, waxes, and organic compounds in dyes, paints, and surface varnishes lend themselves to this dating technique. At this early juncture, radiocarbon dates on pictographs seldom parallel regional radiocarbon date profiles compiled from habitation sites, with the rock art dates usually falling at the early end of the occupational date sequence. It is possible that rock art is older than most habitation sites, but this seems unlikely. The offset may reflect limitations of the currently available sample, since the few directly dated pictographs cannot yet be considered representative. One might also suspect that contamination is more of a problem with rock art paint than with subsurface organic samples. Sources of error might include ancient wood charcoal being used as the "crayon," or contamination from waterborne minerals (e.g., calcium carbonate). At present, it seems best to consider direct dating of pictographs to be in a preliminary phase in which a substantial number of additional data points need to accumulate before meaningful interpretations can be drawn.

Cupules

Cupule-covered rocks exist throughout the state (Fentress 1992; Fleschman1975; Gorden 1990; Nissen and Ritter 1986; Payen 1966; Workman 2003), not to mention throughout the world. North of San Francisco Bay, the Pomo have "baby rocks," which are boulders covered with cupules (Figure 18.6a) known from ethnographic information to be associated with fertility (Barrett 1952; Heizer 1953b). An individual cupule, shaped like half of a sphere or orb, is usually 3 to 5 centimeters across and about half as deep. While they may occur singly or with several pecked into a boulder, more often several dozen co-occur and cover a considerable area of a boulder. To the annoyance of True and Baumhoff (1981) and Hedges (1983), the northern California fertility functional ascription was uncritically applied to cupule rocks throughout southern California. They did not question a nearly universal ceremonial function, but True and Baumhoff (1981:265) regarded cupules as "part of a widespread cultural pattern in California and the Great Basin" of considerable antiquity, and convincingly associated with early Hokan peoples. Consequently borrowing from a comparatively recent ethnographically based interpretation for cupules for one Hokan group, and applying it to superficially similar cupules in a geographically removed area inhabited by culturally distant non-Hokan groups, was, in their view, unsound. True and Baumhoff's criticism helped prompt Smith and Lerch (1984) to compile distributional and ethnographic information on cupules for southern California. Those researchers found ethnographic information that documented a variety of uses for cupules ranging from weather control to women's fertility, as trail markers, tests of boys' strength, and paint cups; in short, any number of functions. The conclusion that Smith and Lerch drew from their study, one that seems to best characterize this type of petroglyph element, is that the only thing cupule rocks hold in common is "the idea that there is some power embodied in the rock which can be tapped by making cupules" (Smith and Lerch 1984:7).

Three styles have been defined within the pit-and-groove tradition in the central and northern Sierra Nevada (Payen 1966): pitted boulders, simply with cupules; pit-and-groove, commonly "two pits connected by a groove or a groove terminated by a pit" (Payen 1966:58); and complex pit-and-groove. The last is sometimes an extensive composition of hundreds of cupules; elsewhere it consists of elaborations on the more simply constructed pit-and-grooves, but also includes elliptical to rounded grooves partially or entirely bifurcated with a line. The latter he interprets as female genital designs and sometimes refers to as "vulvaforms" (Payen 1966:58). Cupules and variations on cupules heavily dominate the rock art in the central and northern Sierra Nevada, the North Coast Ranges,

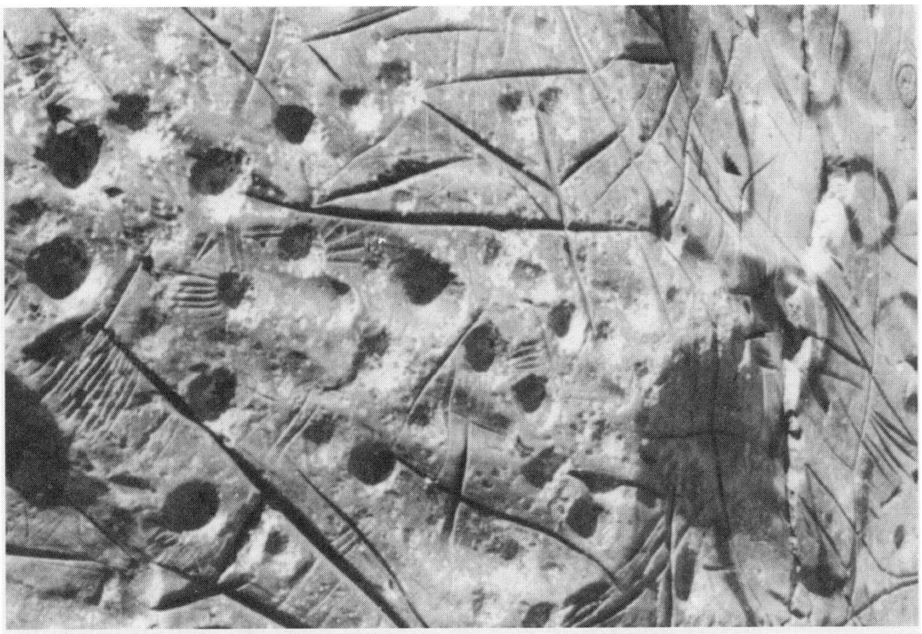

a.

b.

Figure 18.6. (a) Complex pit-and-groove petroglyph, MEN-1800, Baby Rocks. Photograph by Tammara Norton. (b) Bighorn sheep petroglyph, Coso Rock Art National Historic Landmark, INY-14-5375. Photograph by Amy Gilreath.

and the San Francisco Bay Area (Fentress 1992), but in low frequencies, whereas they are commonly encountered everywhere else in the state (e.g., Fleschman 1975; Lee 1981a; Workman 2003).

In terms of the chronological placement of cupules, in many places they appear more eroded or worn than other types of rock art, and are therefore generally thought to be old. It is not unreasonable to suspect that temporally they are a basal form of rock art. Given their extraordinarily wide distribution, however, and the considerable ethnographic information that exists about them, it must be concluded that the tradition persisted for a long time in certain places, often in locations where Hokan languages were spoken. In fact, cupules continue to be made or repecked by the Karuk in northwestern California. Payen (1966) considered pitted boulders and pit-and-groove designs to be the most ancient, but thought that the complex pit-and-groove compositions dated to the Late Prehistoric or Early Historic Period. The most famous of these is available to the public at Indian Grinding Rock State Park in Volcano, Amador County, known to the Miwok as *Chaw'se*.

Petroglyphs

Pecking, carving, chiseling, or abrading designs into boulders and bedrock—petroglyph manufacture—is also a deep tradition. It is reasonable to assume that the first Californians of 12,000 to 15,000 years ago made the earliest designs. There is more convincing archaeological contextual evidence that the tradition was well established by 7,000 or 8,000 years ago. Designs carved into stone by pecking or scratching are particularly abundant in the Great Basin areas of the state, northeast and east of the Sierra Nevada; by comparison, they are lightly sprinkled throughout the Sierra Nevada, the Coast Ranges, and the Transverse Ranges.

Clewlow (1978) depicts five zones within California where petroglyph traditions are well represented, suggesting that much of the state lacks petroglyph sites. Three areas are each associated with a distinctive style: the southwest coast, the Central Sierra, and the north coast. The two remaining areas have a single Great Basin style and include northeastern California and a vast zone covering the east half of southern California (east of the Sierra Nevada, as well as most of San Bernardino and Imperial Counties, and the east half of Riverside County). Extensive survey of public lands has since established that petroglyphs exist outside of these five zones, although they are uncommon. Benefiting from this added information, Whitley (2000a) sketches only three zones that blanket the state: the Great Basin Tradition, running the length of California, east of the crests of the dominant ranges; the Plateau Tradition, covering a small area that extends south from the Oregon state line to take in much of the Modoc Plateau; and the California Tradition, overlying the rest of the state except for the far northwest corner, where petroglyphs are rare. His three-zone scheme has been criticized as too reductionist, obscuring variability that exists and masking regional and local styles (Hedges 2002). But again, the tension between "lumpers" and "splitters" is unending. This chapter will rely on Whitley's scheme.

GREAT BASIN TRADITION The relative chronology that Heizer and Baumhoff (1962) sketched from eastern California and Nevada sites still is a useful construct. Abstract curvilinear designs dominate the early end of the timescale, followed by rectilinear and then representational. Scratched designs are quite young. This sequence does not hold true everywhere, nor is the timing of these trend shifts constant across the state. But still it serves well as a broad-scale, interpretive guide. In the Coso Range (Figure 18.1), the abstract to representational to scratched progression has been clearly demonstrated by superpositioning, subjective consideration of degrees of weathering and repatination, and the archaeological context of the rock art (Gilreath 1999a, b, 2003). Coso petroglyphs are often considered the most impressive in the West (Younkin 1998), an impression reinforced by their quantity, estimated to be in the hundreds of thousands. In this setting, abstract designs like circles and lines can range from simple to elaborate compositions. Representational designs start as simple sheep and stickmen-like figures, and evolve into elaborate and highly stylized sheep and anthropomorphs (Figures 18.6b, 18.7a; Grant et al. 1968). Nonrepresentational scratched designs can overlie both (Figure 18.7b). At Coso, archaeological contexts indicate that the highly stylized representational sheep and patterned-bodied anthropomorphs were made during a brief period prior to 1,000 years ago, after which the manufacture of pecked designs abruptly stopped (Gilreath 1999b). It is not widely known, but scratched designs are also common in parts of the Coso Range (Gilreath 2003) and seem to fill the late (precontact) end of the sequence, when they were often used to deface earlier pecked designs. As Hedges (2002:36–38) warns, however, the Coso Range "is tightly constrained in a geographical area and stylistic content." The archaeologist who imposes

a.

b.

Figure 18.7. (a) Patterned-body anthropomorphic petroglyph, Coso Rock Art National Historic Landmark, INY-283. Photograph by Amy Gilreath. (b) Scratched design overlaying earlier petroglyph, Coso Rock Art National Historic Landmark, INY-5501. Photograph by Amy Gilreath.

the "Coso scheme" onto the rock art variability found throughout the western Great Basin risks "totally misrepresenting the nature of rock art in the California deserts."

Whitley (1987, 1992, 1994a, b, c, 1997, 1998, 2000a) has developed an interpretation of rock art—especially that of Coso—that builds on the three stages of trance (TST) neuropsychological model of Lewis-Williams (1986) and Lewis-Williams and Dowson (1988). This approach places great importance on the different mental images that one experiences while transitioning into a deep, altered state of consciousness (Whitley 1998:150–156). Whitley explains Coso rock art as the work of shamans drawing both natural symbols (those visible in the mind's eye at different states of altered consciousness) and images that are culturally determined and have traditional meaning or use. The former take in a variety of geometric motifs (dots, spirals, parallel lines, cross-hatching, etc.) that are entoptic or phosphenetic phenomena. Entoptic (literally, within the eyes) phenomena are luminous images generated by the optical system when affected by mind-altering drugs, fatigue, trance, and so on; phosphenes are the visual images seen when the eyeballs are pressed. The traditional images are a product of a particular culture, and one method for understanding the significance of these culturally determined motifs is to analyze the ethnographic record. Specifically, Whitley attributes Coso rock art to Numic rain shamans from throughout the Great Basin, who came to this locality on spiritual-religious quests. He contends that Numic peoples consider the Coso area a "particularly likely place to acquire the power to control weather," and that the bighorn sheep motif is prevalent because the animal is the "special spirit helper of rain shamans" (Whitley 1996:49).

Consistent with the TST or neuropsychological model, Whitley has argued that variability along the abstract-representational continuum has little to do with time (e.g., Whitley 1994c:10–14), but reflects differences in the psychological condition of the producer (invariably a shaman) as well as the overall purpose of the ceremony during which the rock art was made. He advances a theory that ties rock art to shamans and ritual initiates, and holds that careful study of the ethnographic record and information from knowledgeable contemporary Native Americans will best inform us of rock art's meaning.

Shamanistic interpretations are now commonplace in rock art literature. It is the prevailing paradigm, and Whitley is "one of the most vocal and well-known proponents of the Three Stages of Trace model" (Helvenston and Bahn 2005:80). This approach and Whitley's research in particular have been critiqued, and the criticisms have tended to excite as much interest as the original assertions. Hedges (2001), for example, takes strong exception to Whitley's interpretation of the ethnographic record, specifically his characterization of adolescence ceremonies in southern California and the purported linkage between rain shamans and bighorn sheep. He feels that Whitley has inaccurately interpreted the primary ethnographic sources. The same sentiment is echoed by Quinlan (2000a), to whom Whitley (2000b) offers a response, which is followed in turn by a rebuttal from Quinlan (2000b). Most recently Helvenston and Bahn (2005:80–110) "refute the shamanic or neuropsychological model that Lewis-Williams and Dowson proposed" and "challenge many of [Whitley's] assertions, as well as his interpretations of older ethnographic sources." Regarding the TST model, Helvenston and Bahn note that there are 70 different forms of altered states of consciousness, and only mescaline, psilocybin, and LSD "produce a pattern of images consistent with the TST model" (Helvenston and Bahn 2005:58). Furthermore, they see no reason to "assume that the artists required a trance experience in order to produce the rock art" (Helvenston and Bahn 2005:59). This high-energy debate and the sometimes personal attacks will likely continue until an improved theoretical paradigm is embraced.

Hildebrandt and McGuire (2002) and McGuire and Hildebrandt (2005) have provided the most recent explanation for the florescence of Coso rock art, one that has little to do with shamanic practices and much to do with symbolic communication and status. Applying costly signaling theory, they interpret Coso rock art as part of prestige hunting behavior, and as one of a number of cultural elaborations that characterize the Middle Archaic in California. In their analysis,

> the rise of prestige hunting is accompanied by a highly visible symbolic expression depicting the animals, weaponry, and participants of the hunt. Although the meaning and purpose of this signaling behavior is not entirely clear (possibilities include network and alliance building among elite males; advertisement of individual hunting prowess; individual artistic technical skill; warnings to other males and groups), it all appears to be a very expensive effort to build upon and enhance the theme of the successful hunt and hunter. (McGuire and Hildebrandt 2005:707)

Where rock art is known to be late and there is reasonable evidence of cultural continuity from earlier times to the recent past, ethnographic information is an obvious interpretive reference. Some petroglyphs may be of fairly recent manufacture, but that cannot be said for most. When they are recent, careful and conscientious use of the ethnographic record clearly informs us about their role and function. When the art is of considerable antiquity, the relevance of the ethnographic record should be questioned.

PLATEAU TRADITION Petroglyphs associated with this tradition generally occur spatially with pictographs. Drawing from James Keyser's extensive rock art work in the Plateau and Columbia River gorge, Whitley offers the following:

> Plateau Tradition rock art is characterized by simple stick-figure humans, block-bodied animals, rayed circles or arcs, concentric circles, and 'tally' marks (or sets of short parallel lines), along with a variety of other but less common geometric designs. The art includes engravings, usually pecked, and paintings, which tend to be thick lined and crudely rendered. (Whitley 2000a:68)

Some of the examples at Petroglyph Point (MOD-1/2433; Figure 18.1; Lee et al. 1988) occur on wave-cut notches high up on the face of the cliff, a location accessible by boat or raft only during ancient high-water stands. Their placement on the cliff face and their spatial relationship to pictographs elsewhere in this vicinity suggest that the petroglyphs are much older than the pictographs.

CALIFORNIA TRADITION Petroglyph sites are not common throughout this vast zone, with a few in the north and central Sierra (Payen 1966) and the western part of the Transverse Ranges (Whitley 2000a:56–57). As discussed above, cupule rocks have a wide distribution, occurring throughout and beyond the California Tradition area. Ongoing research by Gillette (Gillette and Saltzman 2003; see also Fentress 1992) increasingly suggests that pecked curvilinear nucleate (PCN) elements are somewhat comparable to cupules. Chronologically they seem to be a basal form of rock art: the design is simple, rarely deviating from an oval groove around a raised center; multiple elements co-occur, covering a considerable area of a boulder; and they have a wide distribution, occurring throughout the Coast Ranges (north and south). Earlier concerns that these elements were bowl or vessel blanks not yet detached from the talcy rock on which they occur have since been laid to rest. In addition to cupules and PCNs, pecked abstract curvilinear design elements are common to the California Tradition. In a few instances, deep but finely incised lines of abstract rectilinear elements (e.g., grids, diamond chains, ladders) and curvilinear elements (e.g., sun rays, concentric circles) have been documented, mostly in the western part of the Transverse Ranges (Whitley 2000a:57), but also in the North Coast Ranges (Clewlow 1978:622).

In the central and northern parts of the state, a recurring research objective has been to associate particular rock art styles with particular ethnographic or language groups. Payen (1966), for example, looks for such correlations in the ethnographic territories of the Maidu, Miwok, and Washo. Ritter and Parkman (1992), following Payen's work, explore such correlations in the adjoining Konkow and Nisenan territories as well. Looking deeper into the past, True and Baumhoff (1981) consider the possibility that rock art, especially cupules and pit-and-groove petroglyphs, might provide some clarity on the chronological and spatial relationship between Hokan-speaking people and subsequent immigrations. Fentress (1992) continues in this vein, looking at the petroglyphs in Alameda and Contra Costa Counties as a possible source of information for differentiating proto-Hokan, Hokan, and Penutian influences.

In comparison to pictographs, comparatively subtle traits may differentiate one petroglyph style from another. As such, there is some concern that the California Tradition may be so broadly defined and inclusive as to mask regional variability. Two examples suggest this may be the case. Payen (1966) identifies the Valley Sierra Abstract petroglyph style as widespread throughout the Sierra Nevada, distributed along the lower elevations near the edge of the valley floor, but with a particularly well-developed complex north of the Cosumnes River in the low foothills around Sierra Valley. He differentiates this from High Sierra Abstract/Representational petroglyphs, which occur only in the northern portion of the Sierra Nevada and at high elevations. Sites with this rock art style display complex and dense panels placed on expanses of glacially polished bedrock.

DATING The past 20 years have seen considerable research on dating petroglyphs through determination of the absolute age of desert varnish that has accumulated on them. Desert varnish is common on rock surfaces in arid environments as an orange to blue-black patina made up primarily of accumulated clay minerals and iron and manganese oxides. Much of this progress is due to research by Ronald Dorn on cation ratios (Dorn 1983, 1989, Dorn et al. 1990), the formation of varnish layers (Dorn 1992a, b, 1994), and accelerator (AMS) radiocarbon dating of organic matter trapped in the accreted varnish (Dorn et al. 1989, 1992). Samples gathered from Coso rock art petroglyphs have provided much of the data used in these studies and have even been cited as "compelling evidence for occupation of the western hemisphere as early as 20,000 years BP" (Whitley and Dorn 1988:4).

Cation-ratio analysis as a technique for dating desert varnish was first presented by Dorn (1983). In short, the technique is based on the premise that the ratio of more mobile or leachable cations (e.g., potassium and calcium) to less mobile ones (e.g., titanium) decreases with time. The first cation-ratio leaching curve was calculated for the Coso region, and came from Dorn's (1983) pairing of cation-ratio results with potassium-argon (K/Ar) dates obtained by Duffield and Bacon (1981) for about 15 sample localities of basalt formations in the Coso volcanic field. Dorn and Whitley's (1983) first results on five Coso rock art elements suggested that Great Basin Curvilinear Abstract designs began at least as early as 3600 cal B.C. and were still being made as recently as 50 cal B.C., substantially different from the 100 cal B.C. to cal A.D. 1500 range suggested by Heizer and Baumhoff (1962:234). This provided some support for the standing stylistic chronology, with Curvilinear Abstract occurring first, and Abstract Rectilinear and Representational designs coming somewhat later (cal A.D. 1 to 1500). In 1988, however, Whitley and Dorn reported 23 cation-ratio results from the Coso Range that led them to significantly different conclusions (see also Whitley and Dorn 1987). They discarded the standing stylistic sequence, since the oldest date they obtained (approximately 16,000 cal B.C.) was for a Representational design. This date, combined with comparably old cation-ratio age determinations on several basalt tools from deeper in the Mojave Desert, is tendered by them as evidence for occupation of the area some 7,000 years earlier than is conventionally accepted. On the recent end of the timescale, cation-ratio results indicated that Coso rock art manufacture continued up to cal A.D. 1550.

Geoglyphs

Geoglyphs and intaglios are made by changing the distribution of rocks and pebbles on the ground surface, resulting in an alignment or clearing on desert pavement. "Gravel pictographs," a term used by Harner (1953), remains a good descriptive expression. These designs are distributed in desert areas throughout southeastern California. Alignments are widely distributed, while representational figures are found close to the Colorado River only. Many of these designs are so large that they were first identified from the air. Some of the earliest discoveries were made in the 1930s by pilots flying small aircraft along the lower Colorado River. Low-altitude flight continues to be an effective reconnaissance method for finding these features.

ALIGNMENTS Large-scale rock alignments in and around Panamint and Death Valleys (Figure 18.1) are particularly well-known, thanks to the early work of Davis and Winslow (1965), with more recent and considerable study by Jay von Werlhof, Harry Casey, and Christopher Raven. The northern extent of these alignments falls in Eureka Valley, a short distance north of Death Valley. A few in Owens Valley and Red Rock Canyon at the eastern base of the southern Sierra Nevada mark their western limit. Several are described here to provide a sense of their structure, size, and variability. Near the mouth of Wildrose Canyon in Panamint Valley is a geoglyph that is a single-course alignment of fist-size cobbles and pebbles, 45 meters long. Colorful rocks in a series that are part of the design cross over the presumptively earlier Wildrose Trail. That short strand of colorful rocks may have "served as a spirit break to [misguide] malfeasant forces plying the sacred path" (von Werlhof 1987:75). One in Death Valley is even larger, 70 by 50 meters, forming a rectangular design with circular elements appended. Some sections were made by pouring cobbles along the course, though others are a single-course alignment. On close examination, von Werlhof (1987:190) determined that the geoglyph was "put together over a long period of time and under the supervision of various persons," using different construction techniques. Others are smaller in scale, such as one in Panamint Valley that is 8 by 7 meters, roughly circular, containing an amorphous design and a cairn. It is described as having associated "well-tamped" pavement areas that "formed a compact and uninterrupted surface" (von Werlhof 1987:40). Others in Death Valley demonstrate yet another construction technique, with gravel removed and not just raked aside.

Von Werlhof (1987) considers these alignments as products of group ritual, based on how frequently adjacent areas were tamped down, probably due to dancing. He also considers that many of these resulted from multiple-use episodes, with pieces or segments added over the years; some he judged complete and others incomplete. He reminds us that "as with other archaeological remains, we see earthen art as only a product, whereas its probable intent was essentially as a process" (von Werlhof 1987:13), meaning that they are better appreciated as an event or an experience, rather than as static, inert marks on the ground.

The famous earthen figures near the Colorado River consist of the mystic maze and the few dozen giant desert figures (Harner 1953; Setzler and Marshall 1952). The latter were discovered by a pilot flying between Las Vegas and Blythe in 1932, and were publicly reported by Woodward (1932). M. J. Rogers (1929) describes the Topock Maze (Figure 18.1) as parallel windrows about five feet apart, covering 18 acres. Harner (1953) quotes from an unpublished, undated manuscript by Albert Schroeder (on file, Bureau of Reclamation, Boulder City) of secondhand ethnographic information that, prior to 1900, the "Mohave used to put some of their men in the center of the area of alignment and then left them to find their way out of the maze without crossing the gravel alignments. By doing this they would leave the devil behind them." Whitley (2000a:95) relates a similar account by Edward Curtis (1908): "It is believed that by running in and out through one of these immense labyrinths, one haunted with a dread [ghost] may bewilder the spirit occasioning it, and thus elude them." Both accounts indicate that the maze was used in a spiritual cleansing act by Yuman peoples who occupied the lower Colorado River. Given the long-distance travel and trade networks that the Yuma groups maintained, the idea of a need for runners to cleanse or purify themselves after contact with strangers is not surprising.

In spite of the anecdotal accounts concerning the Topock Maze, there is no hard ethnographic information on groups making gravel pictographs. Skeptics existed then, as now, concerning the maze's origin. The unpublished Schroeder account continues, "This informant became very angry when Mrs. Brown remarked that some thought the maze was the result of railroad labor raking the desert gravels into long rows to simplify gathering for use as aggregate in the construction of the railroad bridge piers" (Harner 1953:10–11).

Concerning the giant figures, considerable reliance is placed on Boma Johnson's work (1985, 2003) and Whitley's (2000a) description, which place the figures in the context of Yuman cosmology, origin myths, and religion. These figures portray mythic characters and often are found where mythic events are thought to have occurred. Like the comparatively unstructured alignments described above, these too are understood to be group ceremony phenomena:

> Led by shamans . . . participants walked along a ritual pathway or circuit, scraped into the desert pavement . . . stopping at certain marked spots corresponding to locations or events described in myth. These pathways and other site features . . . were positioned to illustrate the cosmologic model of the Yuman universe, the main axis of which was the Milky Way. Since the ritual use of the site consisted of a series of creation events traced along this cosmologic model, the ritual was in essence a reenactment. (Whitley 2000a:94–96)

The Blythe geoglyphs have a 20- to 25-meter-long humanlike figure and a smaller mountain lion–like quadruped, while those 160 kilometers north at Fort Mojave in Arizona (Figure 18.1) are the best example of the "hero twins of the creation myth" (Johnson 1985:35). There are nearly 60 sites that contain humanlike earth figures, "nearly all . . . made with the torso part of the body deeply entrenched . . . while the limbs are usually only tamped into the surface with little or no gravel removal. The most common trait . . . is the apparent purposeful omission of the head and/or one or both arms from the figure. . . . The dual or twin figures often are primarily the only features at a [geoglyph] site" (Johnson 1985:10–11). The famous geoglyphs at Fort Mojave have been thought to represent the twin brother deities: one (Mastamho) created, the other (Kataar) opposed creation. Each is about 18 meters tall. Co-occurring animals such as the mountain lion are the good brother's helpers.

The Colorado River geoglyphs are perhaps 1,000 years old. No one has much confidence in placing an age on the abstract alignments that are more broadly distributed. The lack of associated time-sensitive artifacts and charcoal-bearing features leave us guessing at their antiquity based on grossly inexact natural indications, such as the amount of patina redeveloped on hand-placed cobbles, and their embeddedness in the desert pavement.

Mythic Landscapes

Where decent ethnogeographies exist for the state, they document a landscape rich in places of power, creatures, and mythic beings, and often they correspond to a recognizable rock formation. Examples from the southern, central, and northern parts of the state are provided here to demonstrate the integrated role that rocks play for a great number of native California groups.

For San Diego County, DuBois (1908:149) describes Turtle Rock and nearby Wasimal (Figure 18.1) as "an unmodified rock which represents a small ground-hawk who gave up in the mythical race between the mountain people and the west." True and Waugh (1986) share the account of a Luiseño elder, telling of the peril of looking at a particular cave in this area, a mistake that "would lead to sure death, and it was possible that one would be turned to stone (there being several large upright boulders along the margin of the same canyon which were described as 'ancestors')" (True and Waugh 1986:271). One other interesting type of rock formation, the *yoni*, is well documented in Kumeyaay territory, in the southeast corner of San Diego County and extending south into Baja California. These "natural features, which strikingly resemble the human vulva" (McGowan 1982:1), occur infrequently on large granite boulders, rounded and cracked from weathering. Considerable ethnographic information exists that led McGowan (1982:20) to conclude that here such features "represent vaginal openings into the uterus of Mother Earth and that spirits associated with them were called upon to increase the fertility of Kumeyaay women." Late Period occupational debris, in addition to pictographs, is often found associated with these uncommon natural features.

In Monterey County there is *hoy*, described by Mason (1918:92–93) as the place where Salinan people knew of a rock monster that murdered people; he would "kill them by throwing them over the hill where some little black birds would eat them." Using a photograph that J. P. Harrington took of this rock formation in 1931, Jones et al. (2000) were able to relocate *hoy* and recorded it as MNT-P-27-002176 (Figure 18.1). More often there are no old photographs of these legendary places, and the links that would make it possible to map the mythical landscape of the past are broken.

To the north, in the Sacramento Valley, Dixon's (1905:260) ethnography reports that for the Maidu, the soul or ghost of a dead person leaves the physical world through the Sutter Buttes (Figure 18.1), never to return; in this place, by some accounts, the Creator (Kodomyeponi) had lived for a time. In anthropological literature, Riddell (1978:383–384) tells us that "the Maidu and Konkow environs were occupied by mysterious powers and spirits. These lived in natural geographic sites such as rocky peaks, cliffs, rapids, waterfalls, and mountain lakes, and also in the sky." Jewell (1987:21) uses the term "petromythology" to refer to the Konkow Maidu's "use of rock formations to illustrate traditional stories." Frank Day, through his paintings of mythical creatures being transformed into the landscape, and through descriptions of his works, allows a novice to gain a deeper appreciation of the Maidu world and of the Native "California [of] many 1000s of years ago." Day relays that "Indians are directed by detailed guidance to where one today finds these great creeping and crawling animals in petrified stages or in the granite hills above Oroville" (Dobkins 1997:72).

CONCLUSION

The rich and varied rock art in California profoundly enhances the prehistoric and ethnographic records. It ranges from a simple daub of red paint and a pecked cupule, to delicately etched pendants or designs on bedrock, to elaborate polychrome pictograph and elaborate petroglyph panels. On a grander scale, native people rearranged rocks on expanses of desert pavement and developed a spiritual regard for isolated bedrock exposures, solitary buttes, and mountains. Whatever its form, rock art was intimately related to its natural setting and its spiritual or cosmological context. We, like the first Californians, form reverent attachments to particular rocky landscapes that serve as our touchstones. Many of these—Half Dome, the Big Sur coastline, and Mount Shasta—continue to be destination locations. With the mere thought or sight of them, we are renewed, enriched, and deeply connected to California.

NOTE

1. Grant counts Monterey as a fifth group, considering a cluster of sites in the Santa Lucia Mountains that bear similarity to Obispeño Chumash rock art, although there is little information that supports this distinction. Instead, as Hyder and Lee (2003:25) state in the recent overview they developed for California state parks, "The Central Coast Range remains a relative mystery . . . Little formal work . . . has entered the rock art literature."

CHAPTER 19

Prehistoric Mitochondrial DNA and Population Movements

JASON A. ESHLEMAN AND DAVID GLENN SMITH

NO OTHER AREA OF PREHISTORIC RESEARCH HAS expanded more in the past 20 years than the study of DNA. Mitochondrial DNA (mtDNA) data did not exist in 1984, as sequencing of the human mitochondrion was only completed in 1981 and the methods of extraction and preliminary ordering of Native American mitochondrial lineages were not perfected until the 1990s. The coming of age of mtDNA research by human biologists has provided an important new means of examining past migrations in many parts of North America. Mitochondrial DNA is inherited only maternally, so over many centuries mutations gradually accumulate in daughter lineages, making it possible to reconstruct ancestral types and derived lineages and relate them to each other.

Over the past decade, studies of mtDNA have focused on two alternative sources: living California Indians whose genealogies can be traced (through an unbroken female line of descent) to the time of historic contact and prehistoric skeletal remains. Mitochondrial DNA from these two sources has been used as a powerful tool for unraveling the complicated history of group migrations that underlies the California linguistic mosaic. A summary of findings and implications of mtDNA from living California Indians was recently published by Johnson and Lorenz (2006), and in this chapter we will consider findings from prehistoric human skeletons.

The analysis of ancient DNA in the New World has largely confirmed the findings of studies of modern DNA and other genetic polymorphisms. Haplogroups A, B, C, and D have been identified through both restriction fragment length polymorphisms (RFLP) and mtDNA control region (CR) sequencing analysis in many prehistoric samples throughout the Americas (Carlyle et al. 2000; Kaestle and Smith 2001; Lalueza-Fox et al. 1997; Malhi 2001; Malhi et al. 2002; Parr et al. 1996; Ribeiro-Dos-Santos et al. 1996; Stone and Stoneking 1998). Studies of ancient mtDNA diversity in most regions of North America reveal that Native American haplogroup frequency distributions often exhibit temporal as well as regional continuity (Carlyle et al. 2000; O'Rourke et al. 2000). At present, ancient mtDNA in the Americas has confirmed the presence of five haplogroups, but additional lineages may be found in skeletal remains representing populations that have subsequently gone extinct. In many studies of ancient Native American populations, some samples have been discovered that apparently do not belong to one of the five known Native American haplogroups. Some (if not all) of these data likely result from external contamination in the analysis. However, the discovery of additional haplogroups from ancient or modern populations could shed light on questions concerning the number of migrations to the Americas and population dynamics since colonization.

In addition to regional studies, mtDNA analysis has been used to directly test specific hypotheses of population movement proposed by earlier North American prehistorians (archaeologists and linguists). Carlyle et al. (2000) demonstrate that the haplogroup frequency distribution of an ancient population that practiced the Anasazi cultural tradition in the American Southwest is not significantly different from that of modern Pueblo populations. This study provides biological as well as cultural evidence for unbroken ancestor/descendant relationships in the American Southwest during the past two millennia. Malhi et al. (2004) have shown that high frequencies of Haplogroups B and D have been characteristic of populations of the Columbia Plateau for a least eight millennia. Hayes and O'Rourke (2001) demonstrate long-term continuity of high frequencies of Haplogroups A and D in the Aleutian Islands. In contrast, Kaestle and Smith (2001) demonstrated that ancient western Great Basin populations differ genetically from modern Native American inhabitants of the region, probably due to a population spread of Numic speakers into the Great Basin from southern California approximately 1,000 years ago (Bettinger and Baumhoff 1982). While boundaries based on language and/or culture do not always coincide with those based on the distribution of genetic traits, they provide hypotheses about prehistory that can be tested by comparing the mtDNA of modern and prehistoric populations.

Though the samples from the Americas analyzed to date are limited in both geographic scope and raw numbers of samples, ancient DNA analysis indicates that distribution of mtDNA lineages also appears to be relatively stable over time (O'Rourke et al. 2000), indicating that in many cases, genetic drift has not altered their distributions sufficiently to preclude the detection of ancestor/descendant relationships between prehistoric and modern populations.

While useful, ancient DNA analysis is not without significant obstacles in analysis. Ancient DNA is typically highly degraded and survives in much lower copy numbers than modern DNA. Consequently ancient DNA is highly vulnerable to contamination from modern sources, and specific precautions against contamination (Kelman and Kelman 1999) should always be employed. These measures serve to minimize contamination and actually identify contamination when present so that it does not lead to false inferences. Success rates for the recovery of ancient DNA vary widely from site to site and even among individual samples at a particular site. Not all material is equally likely to yield results. Evidence from a number of studies, although sometimes anecdotal, indicates that DNA extracts from teeth are far more likely to yield amplifiable DNA than are extractions from bone from the same individual. Sample sizes are generally small and statistical analyses may inaccurately identify true populations in any biological sense because of proximity at a recovery site.

ANCIENT DNA IN PREHISTORIC CALIFORNIA

Prior to European contact, the western edge of North America exhibited an exceptionally high level of linguistic diversity (Campbell 1997), with over 80 separate languages spoken in California alone (Golla, Chapter 6 in this volume; Moratto 1984). This great diversity has been cited as evidence for a greater antiquity of human occupation in these regions than in the rest of the Americas (Nichols 1990; Nettle 1998). Particular patterns of this diversity, assessed by shared cognates and grammatical similarities between mutually unintelligible languages, have also been used to formulate hypotheses of human migration and expansions in western North America as well as higher-level subgroupings that are presumed to reflect closer relationships among certain group of Native American populations. Among these higher-level groupings are the Penutian and Hokan language stocks, first proposed by Dixon and Kroeber (1913). The presence of similar languages over large geographic areas has been used to infer a common source population for speakers of these languages. Both the Hokan and Penutian language stocks are widely distributed throughout western North America, and their particular distributions have long been interpreted as evidence of prehistoric migrations and population expansions that brought speakers of these languages to their historic distribution (Moratto 1984). If valid, these groups reflect quite ancient language stocks, but the application of traditional historical-comparative methodology has produced no consensus on this point.

The "Hokan-Penutian" Model

The distribution of the Hokan and Penutian language stocks (as proposed by Dixon and Kroeber 1913), has suggested to some linguists that there were one or more migrations of Penutian speakers into the Central Valley at some time in prehistory. Historical comparative linguistics has had considerable influence on archaeological interpretations of the region, and some hypothesize that a shift in the population of the Central Valley approximately 4,500 years ago is visible with the appearance of the Windmiller Culture (Breschini 1983; Moratto 1984). The notable nonrandom distribution of Penutian and Hokan languages has long suggested that Penutian migrations displaced older Hokan-speaking populations in the Central Valley. Based principally on linguistic evidence, specific archaeological patterns in the Central Valley and Sacramento River delta region have been hypothesized to reflect entry of Penutian speakers into the area and their subsequent spread throughout the entire Central Valley (Breschini 1983; Fredrickson 1973; Hattori 1982; Moratto 1984; Ragir 1972). The ring of Hokan-speaking populations surrounding a contiguous body of Penutian-speaking tribes suggests that at one time most of California was occupied by Hokan speakers who were later displaced by an expansion of Penutian (Kroeber 1935). Glottochronological estimates for the age of the Utian branch of the Penutian stock (the Miwok and Costanoan language families) in California date to 4,500 to 5,200 years ago (Callaghan 1997; Moratto 1984), which coincides closely with the appearance of the Windmiller Culture in the Central Valley (Fredrickson 1973; Ragir 1972). Characteristics of Windmiller mortuary practices (see Chapter 10 in this volume) include extended burials, the presence of *Haliotis* and *Olivella* beads, characteristic charmstones, red ochre, and large projectile points (Ragir 1972).

Similar elements at the Kramer Cave site in western Nevada suggest cultural contact between Great Basin peoples and the coeval Windmiller Cultures. Red ochre, charmstones, and large contracting-stemmed and leaf-shaped projectile points link Windmiller with the Dalles sites in Oregon (9,800 to 6,000 years ago; Hattori 1982), the homeland of other peoples whose languages are hypothesized to be related to California Penutian. Foster (1996) associates Windmiller with a proto-Utian group and suggests a Penutian homeland in the northwestern Great Basin or on the Columbia Plateau, localities displaying similarities in Early/Middle Holocene (Altithermal) culture.

The degree to which Penutian itself is a valid linguistic unit, however, remains contentious (Campbell 1997). While many argue for the existence of the Penutian stock, it seems increasingly unlikely that California Penutian represents a single genetic unit within Penutian (DeLancey and Golla 1997). For example, ties between Wintuan and coastal Oregon languages suggest that Wintuan speakers might have reached California in a separate and more recent migration from that which brought Utians to the Central Valley (Delancey 1987; Golla 1997; Whistler 1977). Likewise, cognates for plant and animal terms in Maidu languages might be recent innovations indicating a migration from the Great Basin more recent than the one that brought the Utians to California (Moratto 1984). Consequently Whistler (1977) argues for the possibility of as many as four migrations bringing Penutian speakers into California, corresponding with the four linguistic families of Penutian found in California. Callaghan (1997) has argued that the Utian and Yokuts languages share closer ties than other branches within the hypothesized Penutian stock. The Yok-Utians would in this case represent the oldest presence of Penutian in California. While linguistic evidence points to a California home of proto-Utian, attempts to reconstruct a proto-Yok-Utian homeland in California have not been successful.

There is, however, evidence of genetic ties between Penutian populations (Eshleman et al. 2004). Unlike Hokan, in which populations are argued to have diversified largely in situ, the distribution of the Penutian languages is thought to have resulted from multiple interregional migrations and demic spreads encompassing populations in California, the Great Basin, the Columbia Plateau, and perhaps beyond (DeLancey and Golla 1997). Languages as far north as British Columbia and as far south as southern Mexico have at one time or another been argued to belong to the Penutian stock (Sapir 1929). While measures of genetic distances based on mtDNA frequencies between Central Valley Yok-Utians and the Yakima of the Columbia Plateau alone do not offer overwhelming support for a Penutian hypothesis, and the small genetic distance between the Wishram and Yakima (languages of neighboring tribes assigned to the Plateau group of Penutian) could easily be explained by gene flow due to their geographic proximity, the California and Columbia Plateau groups are more closely related than geography alone would predict. The haplogroup frequency distribution of the Plateau Wishram and the Central Valley Yok-Utians, both of which have high frequencies of Haplogroup D, are not statistically different at the 0.05 level of probability, and the genetic distances between the two are relatively small. As high frequencies of Haplogroup D are not common in any alleged Hokan group, and Haplogroup D is relatively rare throughout North America, its presence in Wishram and Yakima of the plateau might reflect a distant genetic relationship consistent with the Penutian language hypothesis. Curiously, this high frequency of D is also shared with the Northern Paiute, speakers of a Numic language in the Uto-Aztecan language family with no close connection with Penutian. Kaestle and Smith (2001) have suggested that this group may have admixed with an older Penutian population. While the mtDNA haplogroup frequencies of the ancient inhabitants of the western Great Basin do not resemble those of the modern inhabitants of the western Great Basin, they are statistically indistinguishable from a California Penutian population (Kaestle and Smith 2001).

A study of ancient DNA from California's Central Valley has recovered mtDNA from three sites: Windmiller burials at SJO-112 and Middle Horizon burials at SOL-270 and AMA-56 (Eshleman 2002). In total, mtDNA was recovered, typed, and confirmed from 16, 23, and 6 individuals respectively, representing a success rate of roughly 50 percent for bone from burials at these sites. This may be atypical for the region, however, as additional sites assayed were abandoned when pilot studies failed to regularly recover DNA.

Statistical analysis of the haplogroup frequencies revealed that the distributions of haplogroups from the three Central Valley sites were not significantly different from each other (Eshleman 2002). Composite Middle Horizon (SOL-270, AMA-56) haplogroup frequency distributions do not differ from the Windmiller burials at SJO-112. Both populations are characterized by high frequencies of Haplogroups C and

D, which seems to indicate continuity of mtDNA lineages among the female residents of the Central Valley during the transition from Windmiller to the Middle Horizon. Such continuity over time has been demonstrated elsewhere, although most studies have compared mtDNA from prehistoric sites to that found among modern Native American populations.

Statistical dissimilarity between the haplogroup frequency distributions of the Windmiller site and modern Yok-Utians (California Penutian) (Eshleman 2002; Eshleman et al. 2004; Johnson and Lorenz 2006; Lorenz and Smith 1996) provides no immediate support for the hypothesis that Windmiller marks the earliest arrival of Penutians into California. The high frequency of Haplogroup C among all the ancient California populations stands in marked contrast to the haplogroup frequencies of the modern Yokuts and Costanoan who, like Penutian-speaking tribes on the Columbia Plateau, exhibit high frequencies of Haplogroups B and D.

There is some evidence that the Middle Horizon does show continuity with modern California Penutian groups. SOL-270 site burials are not significantly different from modern Yokuts and Costanoan in their haplogroup frequencies. It is possible, then, that the Middle Horizon, but not Windmiller, represents the earliest influx of Penutian peoples into the region. However, if both Windmiller and Middle Horizon California burials represent a single population, as seems likely given the regional and temporal continuity observed in other adjacent regions, then their combined mtDNA haplogroup frequencies do not closely resemble that of Penutian populations in California or on the Columbia Plateau, where other allegedly Penutian languages were spoken. Moratto (1984) hypothesized that the development of the Berkeley Pattern of the Middle Horizon represents an expanding Penutian population, beginning with Windmiller, spreading beyond the Central Valley and perhaps mixing with older Hokan-speaking populations. This does not seem likely in light of the lack of statistical homogeneity between Windmiller burial haplogroup frequency distributions and that of modern native populations in the area. Likewise, genetic distances between ancient California populations and modern populations do not support particularly close ties or continuity between the ancient and modern groups. Because of the apparent continuity between Windmiller and the Middle Horizon, it seems unlikely that greater similarities between the Middle Horizon and modern groups than between Windmiller and modern groups represent a real population replacement during the Middle Horizon, although new migrants admixing with indigenous populations could certainly have contributed to the apparent differences over time.

Curiously, the distribution of haplogroups among the ancient Californians is also dissimilar to that of the ancient populations of the western Great Basin, which is statistically indistinguishable from that of both modern Penutian populations in California and the California cultural region as a whole (Eshleman 2002; Kaestle and Smith 2001). The observed similarity between burials at Pyramid Lake and Stillwater Marsh in the western Great Basin has been used to argue an ancestor/descendant relationship between the ancient population of the western Great Basin and modern Native Americans in California. However, the overall dissimilarity in haplogroup frequencies between prehistoric California and the prehistoric western Great Basin suggests that if female lineages migrated from the Great Basin into California, this migration and subsequent expansion in California was initially limited in number or occurred more recently in prehistory than has been suggested by comparative linguistics. Haplogroup frequency distributions provide no evidence for a Penutian replacement of older Hokan-speaking populations in either the Middle Horizon or Windmiller burials.

Although the ancient populations do not appear statistically similar to modern Yokuts, Costanoan groups, or individuals from sites in the western Great Basin, neither do they appear greatly similar to either of the allegedly Hokan speaking groups, the Washo and the Yuman (Eshleman 2002). While both of these populations exhibit relatively high (>35 percent) frequencies of Haplogroup C, Haplogroup B (which is scarce among the ancient California burials) is the most common haplogroup in both the Yuman and Washo. The very limited sample of Northern Hokan known likewise does not exhibit the dearth of Haplogroup B seen in the ancient Californians, though the sample ($N = 8$) is too small for valid statistical analysis. On balance, this indicates more complex population dynamics than a simple Penutian replacement of an older Hokan population, calling into question the presence of a pre-Penutian Hokan-speaking population in the region.

Of populations surveyed for mtDNA diversity in western North America, the sites analyzed from ancient California most closely resemble the Takic speakers from southern California. While the present-day homeland of people who speak Takic languages, a subbranch of the Uto-Aztecan language family (Campbell 1997), lies south of California's Central Valley, Nichols (1988) has noted linguistic evidence indicative of a proto-Uto-Aztecan presence in the Central Valley. If the similarity in haplogroup frequency distribution is indicative of recent shared ancestry or an ancestor-descendant relationship, the present study lends support to the hypothesis that speakers of a Uto-Aztecan language were living in the Central Valley at least between about 4,000 and 2,000 years ago. Similarly, Klar (1980) gives evidence from Northern Chumash numerals that early Chumashan speakers were in contact with Uto-Aztecan speakers before Yokuts arrived in the Central Valley.

Alternatively, because the Takic show some resemblance to Washo and Yuman populations (Eshleman et al. 2004), this similarity may be part of a larger regional pattern of mtDNA diversity that once extended farther north into California's Central Valley. A similar pattern has also been demonstrated in ancient burials from San Clemente Island dating to perhaps 3,000 years ago (Potter 2004). Takic speakers do not show many similarities in mtDNA with other Uto-Aztecan populations. As members of a language family, Uto-Aztecan populations exhibit extreme plasticity in mtDNA (Malhi et al. 2003). If a Uto-Aztecan migration into the region as part of a hypothesized Shoshonean wedge into the region (Kroeber 1925; Moratto 1984) involved wholesale admixture with earlier indigenous females, the mtDNA signatures from Takic speakers today may not be an accurate indicator of linguistic affinities to prehistoric peoples. If indeed Yuman and Washo are related to each other as part of the Hokan language stock, and if Hokan-speaking peoples once populated the Central Valley of California, admixture between the Hokan and Takic might account for the similarities between ancient populations in the valley and in the Takic region. However, this by itself does not explain why the Takic population appears much more similar to the ancient Central Valley Californians than to any of the alleged Hokan populations.

It is possible that haplogroup frequencies shifted due to genetic drift, and if so, similarity or dissimilarity would not be indicative of genetic relatedness. Evidence of continuity of haplogroup frequency distributions over time (Carlyle et al. 2000; Malhi 2001; Malhi et al. 2001; O'Rourke et al. 2000; Stone and Stoneking 1998) has been largely derived from studies probing shallower time depths between the ancient and modern populations. It is also possible that the sample of California Penutians does not represent a valid population for comparison. The sample of modern Yok-Utian is small (N = 24) and is based on the still unconfirmed linguistic hypothesis that Yokuts and Utian are related at some meaningful time depth and are more closely related to each other than to any other groups (Callaghan 1997; DeLancey and Golla 1997). Both the Yokuts and Utian samples are predominantly Haplogroups B and D, although on their own neither is large enough for valid statistical comparisons (Johnson and Lorenz 2006).

None of these cases, however, effectively accounts for the dissimilarity between Windmiller burials and either the ancient peoples of the Great Basin or any of the modern Penutian-speaking peoples. If the archaeological ties between Windmiller Culture and the coeval Great Basin are indicative of a population movement or spread, this movement must have been largely devoid of females through whom mtDNA lineages travel and spread. While continuity between some Middle Horizon peoples and historic indigenous residents of the region, strongly influenced by admixture, cannot be ruled out, it seems likely that if a migration from either the Columbia Plateau or western Great Basin brought Penutian speakers into California, at least some of these migrations occurred in recent prehistory. Also possible is that all three prehistoric Central Valley sites represent only part of a heterogeneous landscape in the past that may have included still unsampled populations more closely related to the historic inhabitants of the region.

The sequences obtained from the first hypervariable segment of the mitochondrial control region (HVSI, a noncoding portion of the mtDNA molecule) from the three prehistoric valley sites confirms continuity between peoples of the Early (Windmiller) Horizon and the later Middle Horizon peoples based solely on mtDNA haplogroup frequencies (Eshleman 2002). This continuity is expressed by shared sequences between sites and is again consistent with archaeological interpretations that ascribe change from Early to Middle Horizon cultures to in situ development. One derived haplogroup, C, was found at all three ancient Central Valley sites while other haplotypes were shared between pairs of sites. In general, these findings confirm the conclusions drawn from haplogroup frequencies that failed to indicate strong ties between the prehistoric Central Valley mtDNA and that from modern individuals.

These data further confirm ties with sequences obtained from Takic speakers. More than half of the Haplogroup C HVSI sequences obtained from the prehistoric sites showed a transition at np16311, which has also been observed among Takic speakers (Johnson and Lorenz 2006), Late Period burials from a prehistoric cemetery near Palmdale (Kemp et al. 2005), and Northern Paiute and the Washo (Kaestle 1998). It has not been observed among California or other Penutian speakers, or in the prehistoric Great Basin. Elsewhere, this particular marker is rare, though it has been identified among Algonquian and Siouan speakers (Malhi et al. 2001), a Piman individual from the Southwest (Malhi et al. 2003), and among aboriginal Chilean populations (Horai et al. 1993).

Though widely spread among ancient and modern groups, the lone shared haplotype of Haplogroup D (Eshleman 2002) is a widespread type present in populations throughout North and South America. The lack of derived types among the ancient California samples might indicate that Haplogroup D is a more recent arrival to the region relative to the more diverse, more widely shared haplotypes of Haplogroup C, a conclusion that is echoed by lower levels of molecular diversity among members of Haplogroup D than members of Haplogroup C in the prehistoric samples (Eshleman 2002). The HVSI diversity (θs) for Haplogroup D (1.8397) was also significantly lower in prehistoric California than in either the prehistoric Great Basin (3.504: Kaestle 1998) or the protohistoric Columbia Plateau (3.266: Malhi 2001).

Haplotypes of Haplogroup B from any of the Central Valley burials were not shared between ancient samples from California and any other populations presently surveyed, though Haplogroup B is common among modern Native Americans in the western United States (Malhi et al. 2002). Whistler (1977) and Golla (1997) have speculated that Wintuan peoples migrated southward from Oregon into the northern Central Valley in a migration separate from those that brought other Penutian peoples (Maiduan, Yokutsan, and Utian) into central California. This haplotype is closely related to other haplotypes discovered in the protohistoric Wishram (Malhi et al. 2004) and modern Yakima individuals from the Columbia Plateau (Shields et al. 1993). Thus the sharing of this haplotype between populations in California and the Columbia Plateau suggests an ancient common ancestry or contact between the two. This does not appear to be related to any earlier Penutian migration into central California. At the very least, this derived type has yet to be discovered in any prehistoric burial in the region.

In general, mtDNA reveals that the Windmiller Culture probably does not represent Penutian-speaking peoples arriving in California and replacing an older Hokan population. Rather, the lack of continuity between the ancient populations and modern Penutians in California indicates that if Penutian-speaking peoples migrated to the region, they probably entered California at some recent time after Middle Horizon archaeological sites were formed. While HVSI sequence data generally support these findings, they also suggest that some migrants may have migrated to the Central Valley beginning with Windmiller and, even more likely, with Middle Horizon, though the most significant changes to the mtDNA landscape appear to have occurred more recently.

The Channel Islands and the Shoshonean Wedge

While regional continuity dominates the mtDNA landscape in western North America, there is a sharp contrast between coastal and interior populations (Eshleman et al. 2004). Haplogroup A is rare or absent in all populations of western North America save for those who have historically resided along the coast, among whom it is the predominant haplogroup. Inland neighbors of the Chumash possess little or no Haplogroup A. It is rare or absent among both modern and ancient samples from the Southwest (Carlyle et al. 2000; Malhi et al. 2003), the Great Basin (Kaestle and Smith 2001), and California's Central Valley (Eshleman 2002; Eshleman et al. 2004). In contrast, Haplogroup A is found in high frequencies among the Salinan and Esselen along the coast to the north of the Chumash (Lorenz and Smith 1996) and has been identified in three of three ancient skeletal samples from Monterey County (Eshleman 2002).

One notable exception to this coastal pattern is the mtDNA from Takic speakers, in whom Haplogroup A is rare or nonexistent. Although Takic speakers historically inhabited coastal territories directly south of Chumash tribes (including the Southern Channel Islands), their mtDNA differs in both haplogroup frequencies and predominant sequences. Despite close geographic proximity, the Chumash and Takic are quite distinct in their mtDNA (see above).

The Chumash languages were once considered part of the larger Hokan stock or superstock that included Yuman speakers living south of the Takic (Kroeber 1925; Sapir 1929). The presence of the Uto-Aztecan Takic populations between Chumash and Yuman speakers was interpreted as evidence of Uto-Aztecan peoples migrating into the area displacing earlier Hokan groups (Moratto 1984). Though Chumash languages are no longer widely regarded as part of a larger Hokan grouping (Mithun 1999), the presence of the Uto-Aztecan Takic languages along the southern California coast is still often interpreted as evidence of migration into the region. The rather abrupt discontinuity in mtDNA between Chumash- and Takic-speaking populations also speaks to an intrusion at some point in prehistory.

Data collected by Potter (2004) from burial sites on San Clemente Island indicate that as early as the Middle Holocene, inhabitants of the island exhibited haplogroup frequencies similar to those seen among modern Takic speakers. Burials from the Eel Point site (SCLI-43), dating to ca. 3,000 years ago, indicate that half of eight individuals from whom DNA could be extracted belonged to Haplogroup C, while two more were found to be members of Haplogroup B; a single individual was a member of Haplogroup A (Potter 2004). This distribution is broadly characteristic of modern Takic speakers as well. Potter notes that statistically, the Eel Point samples are most similar to modern southern California Uto-Aztecan, and are unlike modern Chumash speakers.

The Late Holocene Nursery site (SCLI-1215) on San Clemente Island also produced mtDNA patterns distinct from modern Chumash, although the haplogroups from 13 burials differed as well from those obtained from Eel Point (Potter 2004). A lower incidence of Haplogroup C from the Nursery site (15 percent; 2 of 13 individuals definitively typed) stands in contrast to not only the Eel Point burials but also modern southern California Uto-Aztecan populations (Eshleman et al. 2004; Lorenz and Smith 1996) and other Holocene populations from California (Eshleman 2002). The presence of Haplogroup B in high frequency (46 percent) at the Nursery site is more generally characteristic of many modern populations in western North America, including Uto-Aztecan-speaking Akima O'odham (Piman) and Taano O'odham (Papago) of the Southwest (Malhi et al. 2003) and Numic peoples of the Great Basin (Kaestle and Smith 2001), though also of many non-Uto-Aztecan groups.

The observation that Uto-Aztecan speakers, unlike many other linguistic groups (Eshleman et al. 2004; Lorenz and Smith 1996), differ greatly in their mtDNA haplogroup frequencies and share few haplotypes between populations (Malhi et al. 2003) significantly clouds both the origins and timing of any prehistoric migration into the region. Indeed modern southern California Uto-Aztecan groups appear more closely related to nearby Yuman speakers than to other Uto-Aztecan populations in the Southwest, Great Basin, or central Mexico (Johnson and Lorenz 2006; Kaestle and Smith 2001; Malhi et al. 2003). Although the Eel Point burials do indicate genetic continuity with contemporary Uto-Aztecan populations in southern California, the actual linguistic affinities are still questionable if, as appears to be the case elsewhere, Uto-Aztecan languages spread without an accompanying pronounced spread of mtDNA types.

Whether or not the two San Clemente Island sites are closely related is debatable. It is possible that differences in haplogroup frequencies represent different populations. Alternatively, the difference may be the result of small sample size or evidence of genetic drift in a small population, both of which make it difficult to use mtDNA to link these sites to particular modern populations.

Nonetheless, neither the Eel Point nor the Nursery site burials appears closely related to modern Chumash speakers. Both San Clemente burial sites did possess individuals belonging to Haplogroup A, indicating the possibility of limited admixture with Chumash populations among whom this haplogroup is common. As both Chumash- and Takic-speaking populations exhibited similar methods of subsistence in the Channel Islands, some admixture is not unexpected, but such evidence has not been uncovered in modern populations, where Chumash and Takic speakers differ most dramatically. This sharp division among modern populations is also seen in prehistoric burials from LAN-2233, where all five burials that produced mtDNA were members of Haplogroup C, with no Haplogroup A (Eshleman 2003). It is possible, especially considering the uniformity of mtDNA haplogroups analyzed, that the LAN-2233 samples are not representative of the population as a whole. While the burials do not show affinities with modern Chumash individuals, it is not possible to draw firm conclusions about the degree of admixture at this time from such a sample.

Potter's study also found individuals that could not be typed as members of Haplogroup A, B, C, D, or X on the Channel Islands. Though possibly indicative of additional pre-Columbian lineages once present in the Americas, further studies are necessary to confirm this finding. While several studies of ancient DNA in the Americas have produced a limited number of "other" haplotypes inconsistent with any known modern Native American haplogroup (Hauswirth et al. 1994; Lalueza-Fox et al. 1997; Ribeiro-Dos-Santos et al. 1996), considerable skepticism is warranted as errant results from contamination can appear as real, especially when the source of the contamination is not readily recognizable.

CONCLUSION

While studies of ancient DNA have not set to rest unconfirmed hypotheses in California prehistory, they have provided data suggestive of complex population movements over thousands of years that continued until at least the past millennium. This is particularly true in the Central Valley, where linguistic models of a Penutian intrusion associated with the Windmiller Pattern ca. 4,000 years ago do not seem to be supported. Rather, when assessed through prehistoric mtDNA, the Penutian spread into California seems to have been a more recent Late Period phenomenon (Eshleman 2002). Although modern DNA supports the existence of a Penutian grouping that included ethnographic populations of the Central Valley (Eshleman et al. 2004), it is possible that the valley was inhabited prehistorically by populations more closely related to modern Takic speakers than to any ancestors of modern Hokan speakers. Limited data from both ancient and modern populations make these conclusions tentative, however.

In southern California, ancient DNA has verified a deeper presence of individuals sharing mtDNA types with modern Takic speakers, sites on San Clemente Island (Potter 2004), and burials in present-day Palmdale (Kemp et al. 2005). While discontinuity of mtDNA types between Uto-Aztecan populations over a wider geographic area makes it difficult to assess linguistic affiliations within the language family using mtDNA (Malhi et al. 2003), there does not appear to be a recent infusion of peoples into the region. Further, the division between Chumashan and Uto-Aztecan mtDNA appears to have existed prior to 3,000 years ago.

As a tool for archaeological investigation, ancient DNA does show utility. While best used in conjunction with other archaeological, linguistic, and cultural data, it provides a direct means of identifying biological relationships between peoples over time. As more data are collected, ancient DNA will serve as a tool to both assess existing hypotheses and provide hypotheses of its own that are not suggested from other sources.

CHAPTER 20

Colonization, Culture, and Complexity

Terry L. Jones and Kathryn A. Klar

With expanded theoretical horizons, an arsenal of powerful and sophisticated analytical techniques, and a massive, CRM-generated database, what concrete improvements in our understanding of California's past have emerged over the past 20 years? In 1984 Michael Moratto and Joseph and Kerry Chartkoff developed portraits of California's prehistory that were fundamentally perceptive and accurate, and yet decidedly different. Moratto (1984) emphasized linguistic prehistory, correctly recognizing that California's highly complex linguistic mosaic can only be explained as the end product of a long, complex series of group migrations, intrusions, and replacements. In attempting to reconstruct these population movements, Moratto integrated historic linguistic analysis with paleoenvironmental information to develop a masterful, highly plausible prehistory in which climatic flux was seen as an important agent of cultural change.

Chartkoff and Chartkoff (1984), on the other hand, were less concerned with linguistic groups and focused instead on incremental economic and adaptive changes associated with gradual population growth. As California's native population grew over the past 12,000 or 13,000 years, people gradually became more sedentary, increased their participation in trade, and became more sociopolitically complex. While different from Moratto's historical ecology, the Chartkoffs' work presents an equally insightful portrait of California's prehistoric past. These two alternative models represent the starting point for any synthetic consideration of California prehistory, and the theoretical elements they incorporate—linguistic history, population-induced economic and sociopolitical adjustment, and climate-driven cultural change—are emphasized in the following attempt to summarize more recent interpretations of California prehistory. We will accomplish this by discussing three topics: colonization—the process of humans spreading into and adjusting to California and its environments; culture—the binding force of ideas, values, and shared history that shaped the ethnolinguistic diversity of native California, and its reflection in complex, regionally varied archaeological chronologies; and complexity—the nonmobile, economically intensive adaptations and elaborate forms of sociopolitical organization present throughout most of contact-era native California that emerged at various times as a result of alternative stimuli and historical trajectories.

COLONIZATION

Intensive paleoenvironmental research completed over the past two decades has enhanced our understanding of the process of humans first entering California and adjusting to its environments. This explosion in contextual data from both marine and terrestrial contexts is well represented in Chapters 2 and 3, which show richer and more concrete reconstructions of California's past environments than were possible in 1984. Not surprisingly, these reconstructions show patterns far more complex than previously recognized, but as a general observation, California's paleoenvironments are now best viewed as both reflections of varied regional responses to global climatic trends and as strictly localized or stochastic events. In 1984, teleconnections between California and global circulation patterns had not yet been fully appreciated nor were the complex relationships between localized events and global trends clearly understood. Important long-term developments in California's environmental past related to larger-scale global trends have been summarized below based on findings outlined in Chapters 2 and 3.

Context: Global, Local, Marine, Terrestrial

LAST GLACIAL MAXIMUM, 21,000 TO 18,000 YEARS AGO Any consideration of western North American prehistory must begin at a minimum with the last glacial maximum, the period of maximal extent of ice during the last Pleistocene glacial advance. While this phenomenon was understood in 1984, the term last glacial maximum (LGM) was not yet in use. It is now clear that during the LGM, sea level was ca. 120 meters below its present position, ice sheets covered the higher elevations of the Sierra Nevada and Klamath Ranges, extensive lake systems existed in the southeastern part of the state, present-day estuaries were marked by deeply incised river valleys, five of the Northern Channel Islands made up a single island, and the coastline of northern California was as much as 30 to 40 kilometers west of its present location. Pollen studies, summarized in Chapter 2, suggest that mean LGM temperatures were at least 7°C to 8°C cooler than today and that conifers were more widespread and occurred at lower elevations, although plant association series (Sawyer and Keeler-Wolf 1995) from the period have no modern analogs. Because of the extent of glacial ice, California would have been nearly impossible to reach from northeastern Asia, and initial human settlement could only have taken place either before or after this interval. While the possibility of pre-LGM human colonization has been discussed (see Madsen 2004), the archaeology of California so far supports only a post-LGM date.

YOUNGER DRYAS, 12,900 TO 11,400 YEARS AGO The LGM was followed by a general trend of climatic amelioration and postglacial ocean transgression as the Pleistocene gradually gave way to the Holocene interglacial. Post-LGM melting of the glaciers opened up the New World for migration from Asia, but the overall warming trend was also marked by stadial-interstadial oscillations, including at least one relatively brief return to cold, near-glacial climate during the Younger Dryas (YD). Hendy et al. (2002) have recently reported synchronicity between the Santa Barbara Channel and the Greenland ice cores for several post-LGM climatic events, originally detected in Europe (e.g., the Bølling [14,700 to 14,000 years ago] and Ållerød [14,000 to 12,700 years ago] interstadials bisected by the Older Dryas stadial [14,000 years ago]). Only the YD, however, was pronounced enough to be clearly detected in both the Santa Barbara Channel and terrestrial pollen sequences. Pre-YD (13,500 years ago) and post-YD (11,000 years ago) meltwater pulses influenced the pace of sea level rise along the California coast, where they contributed to rapid expansion of estuarine habitats. The YD itself was first identified in Europe and the North Atlantic, and has been recognized as a global phenomenon since at least 1991 (Kudras 1991). It is generally characterized as cold, abrupt, and dry. Findings from the Greenland ice cores suggest that it may have ended with a 7°C increase in mean temperatures in a mere 50 years (Alley et al. 1993). In the North Coast Range, West (2001) identified a brief but dramatic increase in pine at the expense of oaks (which had been increasing since the LGM) that appears synchronous with the YD. In southern Arizona, Haynes (1991) reported evidence for what he calls "Clovis droughts" coincident with the Younger Dryas, dating ca. 11,000 to 10,700 cal B.C.; however, this event is only modestly supported in California at Tulare Lake (Riddell and Olsen 1969). The YD is also reflected by a stillstand in sea level rise at ca. 50–55 meters (Figure 3.2) that was likely accompanied by some florescence in kelp forests. Dating of manifestations of the YD in California varies somewhat, but globally it is bracketed between approximately 12,900 and 11,500 years ago (11,000–9600 cal B.C.) (Alley et al. 1993; Hendy et al. 2002; Kudras 1991). This abrupt event would have affected human populations differently than gradual climatic amelioration, which could have been accommodated by slow, almost imperceptible cultural adjustment. Abrupt changes associated with the beginning and end of the YD may well have provoked other types of responses.

TERMINAL PLEISTOCENE/EARLY HOLOCENE WARMING With the termination of the Younger Dryas, global climate continued the warming trend that began after the LGM. The response of vegetation to the Pleistocene/Holocene Transition was complex (see Figure 2.7) as individual taxa and entire communities were reshuffled in response to the shift from Pleistocene to present-day climatic regimes. Pollen sequences throughout the state document highly localized responses generally consistent with warming and/or drying. In some locations (e.g., the Northwest and the South Coast Ranges, Northern Channel Islands) the most dramatic changes occurred during the Pleistocene/Holocene Transition (ca. 13,000 to 10,000 years ago) including expansion of oaks at the expense of conifers. The complexity of localized responses, however, is reflected by findings from Medicine Lake, northeast of Mount Shasta, where the pollen record is dominated by pine throughout the Holocene. In the Mojave and Sonoran Deserts, conifer woodland was replaced by desert scrub, while the Sierra Nevada witnessed the development of high-elevation meadows. Vegetation communities similar to those of the present were established in most locations by ca. 6,000 years ago. Pleistocene megafauna were gone early in this interval, as were many large pluvial lakes. Estuaries and wide sandy beaches were established in selected areas of southern California as early as 10,000 to 9,000 years ago; these habitats would appear slightly later in other localities (e.g., archaeological evidence shows no signs of the presence of estuarine shellfish habitat in San Francisco Bay before 6,000 years ago). Following the YD stillstand, sea levels continued to rise fairly rapidly until an apparent cold water event ca. 8,200 years ago

(Figure 3.2), after which the rate of rise was slower. On the San Diego coast, Pope et al. (2004) argued that the Early Holocene (10,000 to 7,000 years ago) was marked by vigorous upwelling. When the present sea level stillstand began about 6,000 to 5,000 years ago, sediment accumulation began to outpace the rise of the sea, and most modern coastal landforms began to develop. By the beginning of the Holocene, California had been transformed into an environment relatively similar to that of the present, but profoundly different from the Pleistocene. In one way or another, Terminal Pleistocene human populations had to adjust to this transformation.

MID-HOLOCENE OPTIMUM, 8,000 TO 4,000 YEARS AGO Most local pollen sequences exhibit a peak in the expansion of oaks and/or other xeric taxa sometime during the Early to Middle Holocene, although the timing of this optimum and its specific effects vary regionally. In the Klamath Mountains, pines and oaks expanded at the expense of redwood and cedar, whereas fire frequencies at Bolan Lake show a peak at ca. 7,000 years ago (Wanket 2002). Several locations in the North Coast Ranges exhibit peak percentages of oak pollen around mid-Holocene, suggesting mean temperatures 1–2°C warmer than today (Adam and West 1983). In the Tulare Lake basin, Davis (1999b) interprets the period from 7,000 to 4,000 years ago as a time of maximum temperatures and drought, while the San Diego coast was marked by mild, stable climate with less upwelling and few El Niño events. In the central Mojave Desert by mid-Holocene the gradual replacement of conifers and woodland by desert scrub species was essentially complete, although fully modern associations were not established until several thousand years later (Spaulding 1990). As Moratto (1984:544, 547) and others before him (Antevs 1948) recognized, the disappearance of formerly productive lakes and the decrease in productivity associated with replacement of woodland by scrub would have had negative effects on resident populations, albeit of a more gradual character than during the YD.

On the coast, with the end of sea level rise ca. 5,000 years ago, many estuaries were transformed into tidally flushed lagoons that periodically closed due to spit formation during dry periods. Productivity of many of the smaller southern California estuarine systems began to decline (Graham et al. 2003) at the same time that abundant shellfish habitat was established for the first time in San Francisco Bay. Finally, the modern configuration of southern California's littoral cells developed 6,000 to 5,000 years ago.

NEOGLACIAL/NEOPLUVIAL, 2000 TO 4000 YEARS AGO Most local pollen sequences show a return to slightly cooler and/or moister conditions after the mid-Holocene peak. These trends include an increase in redwood pollen in the northwest reflecting increased moisture, higher flow in the Sacramento and San Joaquin Rivers from ca. 3,800 to 2,000 years ago (Goman and Wells 2000), signs of cooler moister climate in the Tulare basin, and increased winter snow depths beginning about 3,000 to 2,500 years ago on the western slope of the Sierra Nevada (Anderson 1990). In the Mojave Desert, vegetation remains suggest an increase in moisture between ca. 2,600 and 3,500 years ago while a lake stand in the Silver Lake playa around 3,620 years ago (Enzel et al. 1992) is also consistent with the Neopluvial. On the San Diego coast, Pope et al. (2004) suggested on the basis of pollen and other studies from estuarine deposits, that climate became more variable with frequent El Niño events and droughts after 3,000 years ago. In general, the Late Holocene appears to have witnessed an overall reduction in coastal resources except in areas where people had the technology and proximity to exploit offshore fish populations, sea mammals, and island resources.

MEDIEVAL CLIMATIC ANOMALY, 700 TO 1,300 YEARS AGO The occurrence of unusually warmer and/or drier climate during the centuries of ca. cal A.D. 1000 to 1250 was first recognized in Europe primarily on the basis of historic written sources (Lamb 1965). In subsequent decades, all or varying parts of the period between cal A.D. 400 and 1400 have been referred to as the Medieval Warm Period or Little Climatic Optimum (Moratto et al. 1978). Moratto (1984:566) referred to the period from cal A.D. 400 to 1400 as the Little Altithermal and associated it with warm, dry conditions and rapid change in native societies. Recent research suggests a more restricted time span and the occurrence of anomalously severe droughts rather than uniformly warm temperatures. Stine (1994) argued for a Medieval Climatic Anomaly (MCA) rather than a simple warm period on the basis of evidence for severe droughts at Mono Lake in eastern California and Patagonia. Graumlich (1993) found evidence for nearly identical droughts in tree rings from the southern Sierra Nevada. The bristlecone chronology from the White Mountains shows major droughts between cal A.D. 900 and 1100 and A.D. 1200 and 1300 (Hughes and Graumlich 1996) that coincide with lowstands of Mono Lake, Owens Lake, Tenaya Lake, low flow in the West Walker River (Stine 1994, 2001), and other droughts elsewhere in the western United States (Cook et al. 2004). In northwest California, pollen sequences show that a general trend toward increased effective moisture was punctuated 1,300 to 700 years ago by a decline in redwood and alder. In the Tulare basin, Davis (1999b:254–255) reported a return to arid conditions after the cooler moist Neopluvial. In the Sierra Nevada, sampling intervals are usually too coarse-grained to identify the MCA, but at East Lake in the upper Kings River drainage, there was a rapid decrease in xeric taxa including sagebrush after 1,000 years ago (Power 1998). Flows of the Sacramento and Feather Rivers reconstructed from tree ring data (Meko 2001; Meko et al. 2001) indicate that of six periods with flow lower than the lowest flow year of 1977, two occurred during the MCA, although these were not the most severe of the past 1,100 years. Most characterizations suggest that the droughts during the MCA were severe enough to cause problems for residents of poorly watered areas of native California.

LITTLE ICE AGE, 600 TO 150 YEARS AGO As the most recent prehistoric climatic interval, the Little Ice Age (LIA) is relatively well attested to in California as a time of colder climate marked by greater snowpack (incipient glacier formation) in the Sierra Nevada. As West et al. point out in Chapter 2, however, the LIA was not one sustained cold period but was actually marked by major and very sudden fluctuations in climate that often lasted only decades and affected some regions more than others (Grove 1988). The LIA may have fostered both opportunities and challenges for native populations, as high elevations of the Sierra Nevada and Cascade Ranges would have been frequently impassable, but snowmelt would have kept lowland rivers and lakes full.

CYCLICAL AND OTHER SHORT-TERM VARIABILITY Perhaps no aspect of our understanding of California's past environments has increased as much since 1984 as our appreciation of short-term cyclical variation, particularly the influence of the El Niño–Southern Oscillation (ENSO). The effects of El Niño on California were not generally recognized until the severe El Niño of 1982 forced scientists to realize that the phenomenon was not restricted to the Southern Hemisphere. This discovery and recognition of the Pacific Decadal Oscillation came too late for mention in the 1984 books, but as Patricia Masters points out in Chapter 3, today we recognize three major roles of ENSO: (1) it drives wave energy that erodes the coast and influences sediment flux; (2) it influences alternate cycles of dry and wet climate, some lasting multiple decades; and (3) it affects major variability in the productivity of nearshore and littoral environments. Not long after El Niño's influence on coastal productivity was recognized, several authors (Arnold 1992b; Simons 1992) discussed its likely effects on prehistoric populations, suggesting that sudden, dramatic decreases in marine productivity would have had serious effects on coastal populations who relied heavily on fish, shellfish, and pinnipeds. Others have pointed out that increased terrestrial productivity associated with increased rainfall during El Niños would offset the coastal problems (Jones and Kennett 1999). In either case the ability to recognize such short-term events in the coarse-grained California archaeological record remains poor. Findings from pollen cores and marine sequences suggest Late Holocene intensification in El Niño events beginning either 5,000 years ago (Masters, Chapter 3) or 3,000 years ago (Pope et al. 2004).

Initial Settlement

Perceptions of the chronology and processes involved in the initial settlement of California have changed dramatically in the past 20 years due largely to empirical findings that have led archaeologists to acknowledge a situation more complicated than previously thought. Nonetheless, today's perceptions of California's first settlement were foreshadowed by alternative scenarios developed in the Chartkoff and Moratto texts. The Chartkoffs generally endorsed a version of what is today commonly referred to as the Clovis-first model in which California is thought to have been initially settled by big-game hunters with fluted projectile points who arrived via the ice-free corridor around 15,000 years ago. These specialized Paleo-Indian hunters adapted to climatic warming and the disappearance of megafauna by developing broader Archaic economies as early as 11,000 years ago. Moratto, on the other hand, while recognizing that California's fluted projectile point record provides some support for the traditional Clovis model, also acknowledged small but growing evidence for early use of coastal environments, and proposed a tentative Paleo-Coastal Tradition as a marker of coastal migration into California.

While a certain murkiness remains in the empirical record of the first Californians, some patterns have been strengthened over the past 20 years, particularly the evidence for early use of the California coast. Radiocarbon dates of 9170 and 9550 cal B.C. from Stratum G in Daisy Cave on San Miguel Island (see Chapter 4), two of the three oldest ^{14}C determinations from California, testify to people using watercraft at a very early time. Faunal remains from this and other sites also indicate that people were fishing and collecting shellfish. As Rondeau et al. point out in Chapter 5, the absence of fluted points and culturally associated megafauna remains from the island sites suggests that the earliest coastal dwellers may have had cultural origins and affiliations different from that of mainland Paleo-Indians. Jones and Fitzgerald et al. (2002) suggested that Paleo-Coastal was perhaps synonymous with the Millingstone Culture, but the earliest island sites are not classic Millingstone expressions. Based on the unusual tool assemblage from the Eel Point site on San Clemente Island, Jim Cassidy suggests in Chapter 5 that the earliest coastal inhabitants may have had ties with microblade cultures of coastal Alaska and northeast Asia. From a nearly contemporaneous site on San Miguel Island (SMI-608, dating ca. 7500 cal B.C.) Erlandson, Braje et al. (2005) recently defined a small biface-oriented assemblage startlingly similar to mainland collections from Diablo Canyon and later coastal sites on the Central Coast (MNT-391; Cartier 1993b). Both SMI-608 and Eel Point are 2,000 years younger than the earliest occupation at Daisy Cave, and both suffer from small sample size (e.g., there is no significant sample of actual microblades, as opposed to microblade cores, from Eel Point while there are only two complete projectile points from SMI-608). Nonetheless, these two modest assemblages appear radically different from each other and suggest the possibility of different cultural origins for the first settlers of the Northern and Southern Channel Islands.

As summarized by Rondeau et al. in Chapter 5, fluted points have also continued to be found in California over the past 20 years. The lack of clarity regarding California Paleo-Indians is largely due to the fact that these artifacts are generally found as isolates or at sites with no possibility for radiocarbon dating. The oldest cultural radiocarbon date in the state (11,490 cal B.C.) from SIS-218 in northeastern California suggests human presence in the interior during the window now commonly attributed to fluted points (11,500 to 9000 cal B.C.), but the date provides few additional insights, as no projectile points or other cultural markers were recovered in association. Beyond the simple observation that we are still missing the long-sought, well-dated Paleo-Indian deposit with faunal associations, it seems prudent, based on the currently available record, to conclude that California must have been colonized by both land and sea between 13,500 and 10,000 years ago by people with different adaptations and cultural backgrounds. The cultural and linguistic diversity that distinguishes Native California almost certainly began to develop during the Paleo-Indian Period. Such a conclusion does not differ appreciably from that of Moratto (1984) except that, owing to the sparse empirical record available in 1984, he was more cautious regarding the likelihood of a coastal migration. While the coastal corridor seems to date slightly later than the interior route associated with fluted points, there is little reason to think that the former was derived from the latter, but rather that the two represent temporally and culturally distinct colonization events. Since the oldest coastal occupation (Daisy Cave) correlates strongly with the terminal date for the YD, coastal colonization may have been a post-YD phenomenon unrelated to earlier mainland Paleo-Indian events. Of course, it must be assumed that most evidence for late Pleistocene use of coastal environments has been lost to post-LGM sea level rise and the attendant destruction of old coastal sites.

Relations with Environment

CLIMATE FORCING From the time of initial colonization onward, California prehistory can be viewed at least partially as a process of human adjustment to environmental conditions, at first to those encountered by the founding populations and later to changes over time. This theme was well developed in both the Moratto and Chartkoffs texts, although more strongly in the former. In both of the earlier studies, the founding populations were thought to have adjusted slowly and gradually to climatic warming associated with the Pleistocene/Holocene Transition. At some level, such gradual adjustment makes sense, but an increasingly resolute paleoenviromental record suggests that abrupt climatic changes were also an important factor in California's past, often precipitating punctuated cultural responses (Arnold 1992a; Jones et al. 1999; Moratto 1984; Hull and Moratto 1999; Moratto et al. 1978; Raab and Larson 1997). In this regard, the Younger Dryas is increasingly recognized as a dramatic and rapid climatic event, and the noticeable disconnect between the fluted point record and the rest of California archaeology, or between Terminal Pleistocene and Holocene California, may reflect an early example of punctuated equilibrium. Clovis in California could represent an adaptive/migratory thrust that failed owing to negative effects of the YD, and subsequently provided little if any adaptive or population foundation for later cultural expressions. Of course, the empirical record for the Terminal Pleistocene is so depauperate that any number of alternative scenarios are plausible.

Following the Pleistocene/Holocene Transition, the climatic interval that has historically attracted the most attention in California and the rest of western North America is the mid-Holocene optimum, referred to by Antevs (1948) as the Altithermal. The degree to which arid and/or warmer conditions during the early Middle Holocene were severe enough to force cultural adjustments is a long-standing issue in western archaeology that was being actively debated in 1984. Perhaps disappointingly, this issue remains unresolved in 2007. Pollen and other paleoenvironmental findings indeed show the interval was generally warmer and/or dryer. Unlike the YD, however, this does not seem to have been an abrupt or short-lived event but rather a gradual temperature increase that culminated in a peak followed by a gradual amelioration. Pollen sequences show that lakes like Owens in eastern California and Tulare in the Central Valley were essentially dry during all or part of the period from ca. 1900 to 5000 cal B.C.

In the North Coast Ranges, an occupational hiatus is suggested between ca. 4300 and 1200 cal B.C. possibly related to aridity and erosion. In the Mojave Desert, the effects of mid-Holocene warming have been fiercely debated (Basgall and Hall 1992, 1993a; Cleland and Spaulding 1992, 1993), but there is some evidence for an occupational hiatus between 3000 and 2000 cal B.C. On the Central Coast, some researchers (Mikkelsen et al. 2000) have suggested there was a population intrusion from the interior ca. 3500 cal B.C. caused by increasingly intolerable conditions in the interior deserts. This possibility was suggested years ago by Warren (1968) for the southern coast, but today's prevailing interpretation of the Santa Barbara Channel (presented by Glassow et al. in Chapter 13) emphasizes population declines at ca. 6500, 4500, and 3000 cal B.C., apparently due to environmental stresses. In 1984 Moratto (1984:549) also envisioned the coast not as a potential refugium but as an area where populations were also negatively affected by mid-Holocene aridity. In the Southern Bight region, there were significant populations of coastal hunter-gatherers on the mainland, and sedentary or semisedentary house dwellers on San Clemente Island who exhibit no obvious signs of the effects of mid-Holocene aridity. The Sierra Nevada shows an increasingly visible archaeological record after 3000 cal B.C., but Hull in Chapter 12 is hesitant to attribute this to climatic events (although see Hull and Moratto 1999). In northeast California, a distinctive settlement shift is seen at mid-Holocene with the disappearance of wetlands and lakes, when pond-edge sites and riparian habitats became more important. In the San Francisco Bay Area, Central Valley, and Colorado Desert, records are all somewhat mute on the issue of early mid-Holocene climate forcing since these regions have very incomplete early Holocene records. The San Francisco Bay Area however, does show an increasingly visible record after 2000 cal B.C. coeval with the maturation of the state's largest estuarine system.

While climatic amelioration after the end of the mid-Holocene optimum must have provided new opportunities and challenges for California populations (Moratto 1984:552–553), the postoptimum interval that has received the most attention in the past 20 years with respect to climatically induced cultural change is the Medieval Climatic Anomaly. The MCA spans major transitions in nearly all regional cultural chronologies in California, including Middle/Late in the San Francisco Bay, Central Coast, and Northern Bight regions, Upper Archaic/Emergent in the Central Valley, Late Archaic/Terminal Prehistoric in northeast California, and Rose Springs/Late Prehistoric in the Mojave Desert. Like the Altithermal, the degree to which climatic perturbations effected typological and other cultural changes has been an issue of much debate. In 1984 Moratto (1984:560) suggested that a rapid shift to warm, dry conditions after ca. A.D. 400 caused "population movements, changes in settlement patterns, economic adjustments, disruption of exchange systems, and other cultural changes." The MCA is now dated more tightly to cal A.D. 800–1350. Many of these apparent responses have been supported by subsequent research, but ambiguities still abound. Major settlement shifts, migrations, and/or breakdowns in exchange are seen in the southern North Coast Ranges, the Central Coast, the western Mojave Desert, northeast California, and especially in the Sierra Nevada, where Hull suggests there was a significant population decline between cal A.D. 500 and 1250. The former date, however, is too early to reflect the Medieval Climatic Anomaly, and it must therefore represent either the chronological imprecision of obsidian hydration dating used to anchor Sierran chronologies, or some phenomenon other than the MCA. In the San Francisco Bay Area, there has been some argument for movement away from the bayshore at the end of the Middle Period (Lightfoot and Luby 2002:276–277), but Milliken et al. in Chapter 8 now date this shift to pre-MCA times. Data do show a significant increase in sites beginning ca. cal A.D. 1250, a trend that is also apparent on the Central Coast (see

Chapter 9). For the Central Valley, Rosenthal et al. in Chapter 10 report few obvious signs of drought or its cultural effects.

In the Northern Bight, increased shell bead production during the MCA was originally attributed by Arnold (1992a, b) to a dramatic decline in marine productivity. Subsequent paleoenvironmental research has shown that seas were generally cold and productive off southern California during the MCA and that weather was probably dry (Kennett 1998, 2005; Kennett and Kennett 2000). Gamble (2005), however, suggests that the Chumash were technologically capable of coping with an arid climate during the MCA. Little evidence for MCA-induced cultural change is apparent in the western Mojave or Colorado Deserts, while the Southern Bight shows an increase in specialized sites on the mainland after ca. cal A.D. 1300 at the same time that San Clemente Island was witness to major abandonments (Yatsko 2000). Overall, there is growing evidence for punctuated cultural response to the MCA in California, albeit of widely varying character. Some researchers (Basgall 1999, 2006; Bettinger 1999b) think that the influence of environmental change during this interval needs further substantiation, and there can be little doubt that the MCA will continue to be a focus of research and debate in the future.

RESOURCES, TECHNOLOGY, AND DEMOGRAPHIC CONSEQUENCES While models of climatically induced cultural change ultimately rely on premises of demographic imbalance, much thinking about California prehistory in 1984 and since has focused more directly on population-driven changes exclusive of climatic variability. Such models, including that of the Chartkoffs in 1984, tend to focus on technological innovations as part of broader economic progressions as well as on the subsistence potential of particular habitats and resources. The Chartkoffs' 1984 model generally linked population growth with economic progress in three stages or periods: Paleo-Indian (15,000 to 11,000 years ago), marked by widely separated, highly mobile microbands pursuing a focal (big-game) economy; Archaic (11,000 to 4,000 years ago), marked by a broader diet, a diffuse economy, proliferation of specialized tools, and colonization of new ecological niches; and Pacific (4,000 years ago to contact), marked by focal economies that included a wide range of foods with specialized focus on a few. This is similar to Fredrickson's (1974a) influential evolutionary model for the North Coast Ranges, which included three major periods: Paleo-Indian (12,000 to 8,000 years ago), Archaic (8,000 to 1,500 years ago), and Emergent (1,500 years ago to contact). The Archaic was further subdivided into Lower (8,000 to 5,000 years ago) marked by little hunting and heavy use of plant foods; Middle (5,000 to 3,000 years ago) marked by initial use of mortars and pestles (acorns inferred), population growth, and more diversified economies; and Upper (3,000 to 1,500 years ago) marked by increasing sociopolitical complexity including sustained exchange between groups. The Emergent was divided into Lower (1,500 to 500 years ago) distinguished by the bow and arrow (replacing the atlatl), well-established group territories, florescence of maritime economies in southern California, and increasingly regularized intergroup exchange with more materials entering the exchange networks, and Upper (500 years ago to contact) marked the appearance of the clam shell bead money economy and interconnection of previously separate south and Central Coast exchange networks.

The Chartkoff and Fredrickson models constitute the frame of reference for the more detailed regional considerations of subsistence completed in subsequent years. Much recent research has focused on clarifying the relative importance and chronologies of key resources (e.g., seeds, acorns, deer, rabbits, shellfish, anadromous fish, marine fish, and to a lesser extent marine mammals) and on the technologies used to pursue and process them (handstones/millingslabs [manos/metates], mortar/pestles, bow and arrow points, atlatl and darts, fishhooks, fishing nets and weights, baskets, ceramics, watercraft, and specialized maritime technologies like the harpoon). Progress in the past 20 years has benefited from both empirical findings and new theoretical perspectives that have changed the way these foods and associated technologies are viewed. The latter include optimal foraging, economic intensification, costly signaling, and other applications of behavioral ecology. The combination of theory and data has in some cases resulted in significant revisions to previous assessments of the antiquity and relative importance of certain resources. Research from the southern California islands and mainland, for example, has shown that some marine foods (e.g., shellfish and fish) were exploited as early as the Terminal Pleistocene/Early Holocene by people who used fish gorges, basketry, and watercraft (Connolly et al. 1995; Erlandson et al. 1996; Rick et al. 2001). The importance of shellfish to these early coastal economies has been demonstrated repeatedly (Erlandson 1991b, 1994; Erlandson et al. 1999, 2004; Jones and Richman 1995). Pinniped rookeries have also been linked to early coastal adaptations

(Hildebrandt and Jones 1992), but their exploitation was more localized than that of shellfish. Remains of marine fish, on the other hand, are present in virtually all of the earliest coastal midden deposits, and generally increase through the Holocene. The archaeology of anadromous fisheries contradicts the importance of this resource in ethnographic accounts, however, as archaeological findings show that salmonoids were insignificant prehistorically in the San Francisco Bay Area and Central Valley (Gobalet et al. 2004). The only place in California where their importance is still assumed is in the northwest, where the timing of the emergence of intensive salmon-acorn economies observed historically among the Tolowa, Yurok, Wiyot, Hupa, and Karuk remains uncertain. Traditionally this economy has been associated with the appearance of the Gunther Pattern (cal A.D. 500), but new findings from the Smith River may push it back to at least 1000 cal B.C., supporting a proposal first advanced by Hildebrandt and Hayes (1993).

Although economies emphasizing elk, mountain sheep, and pinnipeds can be identified locally in prehistoric California, deer and rabbits typically were the most important vertebrate resources other than fish, and the past decade has featured considerable discussion about the relative value of these two prey items (Broughton 1999; McClure 2004; Hildebrandt and McGuire 2002). McGuire and Hildebrandt (1994) suggested that rabbit trapping was more efficient than deer hunting, and argued that an apparent emphasis on the latter by Millingstone people represented an optimal subsistence strategy for midlatitude native California during the Early Holocene. This proposal also advanced thinking about changing gender roles in Native California over time, a topic that has received considerable attention in its own right (Hollimon 1990; Jackson 1991; Jones 1996). Subsequently Hildebrandt and McGuire (2002) and McGuire and Hildebrandt (2005) attempted to explain greater reliance on deer and elk during the Middle and Late Holocene in some parts of California as the result of males increasing their participation in costly signaling. While the low frequency of deer remains in some Early Holocene contexts does demand attention, many researchers do not see this resource as energetically inferior to rabbits (Codding and Jones 2007; Jones 1991; McClure 2004:223; Simms 1985; Ugan 2005). Byers and Broughton's (2004) demonstration that deer were absent from much of the Great Basin during the mid-Holocene may prove applicable to California, but debate over this issue will go on.

The past 20 years have also seen increased focus on the causes and consequences of emergent acorn economies, a topic with a long history of study in California (Gifford 1936). Recent reconsideration of the issue was encouraged by Basgall's influential (1987) paper in which he portrayed acorns as expensive and labor-intensive. Accepting the traditional association between acorn exploitation and mortars/pestles, Basgall suggested that intensive acorn economies began ca. 500 cal B.C. in northwest California when mortars became more abundant than millingslabs/handstones (presumably used to process small seeds). Following Basgall's lead, much research in the past two decades has sought to define the first appearance of mortars and pestles in other regions, and this technological dyad is now dated to 6500 cal B.C. in northwest California, 3700 cal B.C. in the San Francisco Bay Area, 3500 cal B.C. on the Central Coast, 2000 cal B.C. in the Sierra Nevada, and 4000 cal B.C. in the Northern Bight. Other research has sought to identify acorn use directly using plant macrofossils recovered through flotation (see Wohlgemuth 2004). Based on finds of charred acorns, Hildebrandt in Chapter 7 of this volume portrays subsistence intensification differently than Basgall, suggesting that acorns were probably exploited earlier and small seeds later. Such proposals will again be a focus of research and debate in the future, but it seems likely that California's myriad habitats may not have fostered a uniform statewide pattern of intensification.

Two other technologies of crucial importance to native California were the bow and watercraft. In 2006 the ultimate points of origin and paths of diffusion associated with these technologies remain unclear. The earliest evidence for the bow and arrow comes from eastern California, where Rose Springs points are dated to cal A.D. 200 in northeast California and the Mojave Desert. Dates of cal A.D. 500 are assigned in northwest California (Gunther barbed) and in the Sierra Nevada. Arrow points appear more recently in the Central Valley and the San Francisco Bay Area where Stockton serrated points date no earlier than cal A.D. 1000. On the Central Coast and Northern Bight, small leaf-shaped points appear between ca. cal. A.D. 500 and 1000, but their arrival is nearly synchronous with that of harpoon barbs, and the points may represent that weapon, not the bow. Unequivocal arrow points in the form of Cottonwood and Desert side-notched types appear only ca. cal A.D. 1250 on the Central Coast, and, it seems that arrow points arrived earlier in the interior than on the coast.

Watercraft, on the other hand, have been a topic of a considerable research and debate in the past 20 years, beginning with discussions about the relative importance of the sewn-plank canoe *(tomolo)* versus oceangoing dugouts (Jobson and Hildebrandt 1980; Hudson 1981), which served to heighten awareness of the importance of these craft to the maritime economies in Northwest California and on the Channel Islands. Issues that arose subsequently include the chronology and causes underlying watercraft innovation, although finds from the islands, discussed above, demonstrate use of some type of boats much earlier (ca. 9500 cal B.C.) than imagined in 1984. The type of vessel used during the Terminal Pleistocene remains an issue, as many assume it was a dugout or tule canoe; however, Cassidy et al. (2004) suggested it may have been some type of composite craft (see Chapter 5 in this volume). Hildebrandt (1984) suggested that dugouts were important in the Northwest for their value in pursuing low-ranked marine mammals, an argument that he later extended to the Central Coast and Southern Bight (Hildebrandt and Jones 1992).

Most Channel archaeologists see the value of the *tomolo* in its use for exchange between the Channel Islands and mainland (Arnold 1992a, 1995, 2001a; Gamble 2002b), and for occasional pursuit of pelagic species (Arnold and Bernard 2005; Bernard 2001, 2004; Davenport et al. 1993). Most envision the *tomolo* as a relatively recent indigenous innovation, although Fagan (2004) suggested it was developed early in the Holocene in response to sea level rise. Jones and Klar (2005) and Klar and Jones (2005) have suggested that sewn-plank boat technology was introduced into California by Polynesians sometime between cal A.D. 400 and 800, but Glassow et al. in Chapter 13 show little interest in this hypothesis. Overall, recognition of the importance of watercraft and their antiquity in native California has increased significantly as a result of research completed in the past two decades, and the range of opinion on key issues suggests that this technology will continue to be a focus of intense interest in coming years. In Polynesia, the idea of devolution in watercraft sophistication and use is associated with the later part of the prehistoric period (see Kirch 2000), and this concept may have some utility in California. The settlement patterns exhibited around California's estuaries and islands reflect the regular use of boats, but watercraft may have become less useful in some areas over time as territories were more rigidly established and water travel was more constrained.

HUMAN IMPACTS Another example of wider horizons in perceptions of human-environmental relations involves the negative effects of prehistoric predation on native fauna. In 1984, considerations of human influences on California's natural environment were generally limited to positive effects, particularly those associated with controlled burning (see Lewis 1973), which some see as a form of sophisticated environmental stewardship (Anderson 2005; Blackburn and Anderson 1993; Stewart 2002). Negative impacts were largely limited to Martin's Pleistocene overkill hypothesis (Martin 1967). In the intervening 20 years, California has still failed to produce a single piece of evidence to support the overkill hypothesis, and there is increasing recognition that the number and range of species that went extinct at the close of the Pleistocene are more consistent with an environmental event than with overhunting (Grayson and Meltzer 2003). Nonetheless, now as then, some aspects of the North American extinctions are consistent with a human role, and the hypothesis is still viable (Barnosky et al. 2004; Koch and Barnosky 2006), especially in California.

Megafauna aside, the past 20 years have seen cases for suppression and/or extirpation of faunal populations as a consequence of population growth and economic intensification rather than outright extinction. Foremost among these are arguments for overpredation of large pinnipeds, first suggested by Hildebrandt and Jones (1992) and subsequently supported by a number of authors (Burton 2000; Burton et al. 2001, 2002; Hildebrandt and Jones 2002; Lyman 2003; Walker et al. 2002), but challenged by others (Arnold and Colten 1998; Lyman 1995). Arguments have also been made for prehistoric overexploitation of artiodactyls (Broughton 1994b) and fish (Broughton 1997, sturgeon; Salls 1992, cabezon), although the latter are poorly supported. A stronger case for human suppression of shellfish populations has been made (Jones 1996; Jones and Richman 1995; White 1989). Overall, the past 20 years have seen remarkable progress in recognition of a wide range of relationships and more complicated interconnections between humans and the prehistoric California landscape.

CULTURE

The past 20 years have also seen improvements, changes, and additions to the basic artifact chronologies that frame California prehistory. Of course, the Terminal Pleistocene remains unclear, owing to our inability to locate components of that age, many of which were either deeply buried (Rosenthal and Meyer 2004a) or destroyed by sea level rise. Some significant gaps remain for the Holocene (e.g., in the Central Valley and Colorado Desert), and chronological resolution is not as good for some areas as for others. In certain regions (e.g., the San Francisco Bay), accelerator mass spectrometry (AMS) technology has improved chronological precision on a revolutionary level, allowing for the direct dating of individual shell beads. As discussed by Milliken et al. in Chapter 8, AMS dates have effectively resolved long-standing questions about the absolute dating of bead horizons. Overall, reasonably secure cultural sequences are now available for most of California. These reflect a complicated record with a great deal of regional variation. As discussed above, much of the diachronic variability in these chronologies can be related to changes in environment and economy, but California's regionally varied culture histories also reflect a complicated linguistic mosaic that resulted from a long history of in-migrations by speakers of different language stocks.

In 1984 Moratto based his masterful linguistic prehistory on comparisons between regional cultural sequences and historical linguistic studies, supplemented with limited osteometric data (Gerow 1968). Then as now, the complex nature of the relationships between language, material culture, and physical type was recognized, although some (Hughes 1992a) have argued that such complexity was not sufficiently acknowledged in 1984. Golla's interpretations of California's ethnolinguistic prehistory in Chapter 6 benefit from 20 additional years of research on California's native languages, which have resulted in an exceptionally thorough new synthesis.

The most significant developments related to California's prehistoric ethnic diversity are recognition of the Chumashan family as a linguistic isolate and the availability of mtDNA data as a significant new form of empirical information. This new line of evidence also increases by an order of magnitude the complications involved in reconstructing past population movements in California, since we cannot assume that genetic populations corresponded with linguistic stocks, material cultures, or adaptations.[1] Also, the mtDNA sample is at present very limited. Some of the preliminary findings from modern California Indians (Johnson and Lorenz 2006) exhibit reasonable correlations with the linguistic classifications discussed by Golla in Chapter 6. Modern mtDNA, for example, supports the distinctiveness of Chumashan with an absence of Haplogroup B (which is well represented in all other California linguistic stocks), along with a high frequency of Haplogroup A (Table 20.1). The Penutian stock and Uto-Aztecan family, on the other hand, both show high frequencies of Haplogroup B and almost no representation of Haplogroup A. Haplogroup C dominates the Uto-Aztecan family but is underrepresented in Penutian. More importantly, as discussed by Eshleman and Smith in Chapter 19, mtDNA findings from prehistoric skeletons generally indicate significant genetic distance between ancient and modern California populations and do not support close ties or continuity between the ancient and modern groups.

The matrix of historical linguistic reconstructions, osteometric data, and mitochondrial DNA (mtDNA) findings that is now available for comparison with archaeological culture histories is highly complex. Integrating these various lines of evidence into a single, unified portrait of California prehistory is a daunting task that will require significant intellectual effort in the coming decades. The following is only a summary of a few of the key findings and issues in California's linguistic archaeology.

First Peoples

Mitochondrial DNA is relatively mute on the identity of the earliest Californians, since the oldest successful mtDNA extractions date only to the mid-Holocene. Increasingly refined assessments of the ethnolinguistic identities of the first Californians continue to rely on historical-comparative linguistics and archaeology. As summarized by Golla, the former suggests that the earliest stratum of languages along the Pacific coast may have included Yukian, Chumashan, the language substratal to Island Chumash, and/or one or more of the languages at the southern tip of Baja California. Golla feels this is consistent with coastal settlement during the Terminal Pleistocene/Early Holocene. The latter shows a fluted point complex restricted to the mainland, and at least two distinctive complexes on the Channel Islands: the tentatively defined San Clemente Island woodworking/microblade complex, and an Early Holocene stemmed point complex on the Northern Islands. Correlations between ancient languages and specific artifact complexes are not straightforward and cannot be automatically assumed, but recent recognition of a closely related mtDNA haplotype among the Cayapa Indians of coastal Ecuador, the Chumash, and an Early Holocene skeleton from Alaska (Johnson and Lorenz 2006) suggests that groups speaking pre-proto-Chumashan were among those who arrived in the New World via a coastal route. Linguistic evidence for a language substratal to Chumashan on the

Table 20.1. Modern and Archaeological Mitochondrial DNA Lineages in California by Haplogroup

Linguistic Group/ Archaeological Culture	*Haplogroup A*	*Haplogroup B*	*Haplogroup C*	*Haplogroup D*	*Totals*
LINGUISTIC GROUPS					
Algic Stock					
Yurok	0	0	1	0	1
Subtotals	0	0	1	0	1
Uto-Aztecan Family					
Tubatulabal	0	2	1	1	4
Numic Branch					
Kawaiisu	0	3	1	1	5
Mono	0	3	0	1	3
Takic Branch					
Gabrielino	0	1	0	1	2
Kitanemuk	0	0	2	1	3
Serrano/Vanyumé	0	2	1	1	4
Cahuilla	0	2	3	1	6
Cupeño	0	1	1	0	2
Luiseño	1	4	13	0	18
Subtotals	1	18	21	7	47
Penutian Stock					
Wintuan Branch					
Wintu	0	2	0	0	2
Southern Patwin	0	1	0	0	1
Yok-Utian Branch					
Utian Family					
Miwok	0	3	0	1	4
Costanoan	0	1	2	1	4
Yokuts	1	8	1	6	15
Subtotals	1	15	3	8	26
Hokan Stock					
Achumawi/Atsugewi	0	1	0	0	1
Esselen	1	0	0	0	1
Salinan	3	2	0	1	6
Yuman Family					
Ipai	0	2	5	0	7
Tipai	0	0	1	0	1
Yuma	0	1	0	0	1
Subtotal	4	6	6	1	17
Chumashan Family					
Obispeño	0	0	0	3	3
Purisimeño	1	0	0	1	2
Ineseño	3	0	0	2	5
Barbareño	1	0	1	2	4
Ventureño	5	0	1	0	6
Island	1	0	0	0	1
Subtotal	11	0	2	8	21
ARCHAEOLOGICAL CULTURES					
Windmiller	0	1	9	6	16
Berkeley	1	4	14	10	29

Sources: Eshleman and Smith, Chapter 19, this volume; Eshleman 2002; Johnson and Lorenz 2006.

Channel Islands (Klar 2002) is intriguing in this regard, as is Potter's (2004) identification of a possible unknown haplogroup on San Clemente Island. Both findings provide tiny hints of populations that settled in California temporarily and then moved on or were replaced by later migrants. Notably, stemmed/side-notched point complexes on the Kamchatka Peninsula dating 11,400 cal B.C. show some resemblance to assemblages dating 8000 to 7000 cal B.C. from southern California (Goebel et al. 2003:504). While the Siberian assemblages are too late and too dissimilar to be ancestral to Clovis, they could correlate with a slightly later, post-YD coastal colonization of the New World.

Early Holocene Migrations

Both Moratto in 1984 and Golla in the present volume think that the Hokan stock of language families has considerable time depth in California and that it was probably more widespread earlier than it was at the time of contact. The isolation of Hokan families within California has long been seen as a product of intrusions by speakers of other languages. Moratto (1984:543) speculates that speakers of Hokan languages entered California from the interior and may be represented by the Western Pluvial Lakes Tradition (WPLT). In Chapter 15 of the current volume, the WPLT is subsumed within a broader rubric of Early Holocene stemmed point complexes represented in the Mojave, the Sierra Nevada, and northeast California. On the Central Coast, Northern Bight, Southern Bight,[2] and in southern Central Valley, and San Francisco Bay Area, the Early Holocene (ca. 8000 to 6000 cal B.C.) is marked by the Millingstone Culture. In northwest California, the Borax Lake Pattern marks this period.

Although specific linguistic-archaeological correlations remain challenging at this time depth, the stemmed point complexes hold together reasonably well and exhibit a spatial distribution consistent with a widespread early Hokan substratum. Archaeological findings also suggest that speakers of the Salinan languages of the Hokan stock were relatively recent arrivals to the Central Coast region, not long-term residents. The Borax Lake Pattern has been associated by some (Whistler 1988; discussed by Golla in Chapter 6) with Hokan, specifically pre-proto-Pomoan, but others associate it with Yukian. Moratto (1984:544) suggests that Borax Lake might represent an adaptive outgrowth from earlier Paleo-Coastal settlement by pre-proto-Yukian speakers, basing his interpretation on the presumed Terminal Pleistocene age of the Mostin site near Clear Lake. In Chapter 7, Hildebrandt, following White et al. (2002), has repositioned Mostin as an aspect of the Berkeley Pattern, dating ca. 6500 to 4300 cal. B.C., and associates it with proto-Pomoan (Hokan) speakers who occupied a Clear Lake homeland as early as ca. 6500 cal B.C. and later expanded south and west. It is tempting to speculate that the Millingstone Culture also represents an adaptive outgrowth in southern and central California by Paleo-Coastal speakers of a pre-proto-Chumashan language. This possibility contrasts with Moratto's (1984:547) suggestion that milling tools came to the south coast from the interior deserts through diffusion and population migration. Neither of these alternatives should be rejected, but the coastal mtDNA pattern associated with Chumashan languages, the recognition of Chumashan as a linguistic isolate, and the antiquity (ca. 8000 cal B.C.) of millingstones on the coast (e.g., Cross Creek and Diablo Canyon) provide some support for the other possibility.

Middle and Late Holocene Intrusions

With the possible exception of the northwest coast and the high elevations of the White Mountains, virtually all of California was settled by mid-Holocene, so that more recent population movements might be classified more as intrusions rather than as simple migrations, although in-migration was probably facilitated in some instances by the departure of earlier peoples. Languages that made their way into California after the mid-Holocene include those in the Penutian and Algic stocks, and the Uto-Aztecan and Athabaskan families.

Golla suggests that the Penutian homeland stretched between the Columbia Plateau and northern portions of the Great Basin, and that Yok-Utian speakers entered central California across the Sierra Nevada, Maiduan speakers arrived from the basin-plateau, and Wintuan speakers moved first westward into central Oregon and then southward into California. The discovery by Malhi et al. (2004) that high frequencies of Haplogroups B and D have been characteristic of populations of the Columbia Plateau for a least eight millennia is consistent with high frequency of those haplogroups among modern descendants of speakers of Penutian languages in California (Table 20.1). Golla in Chapter 6 continues to support Moratto's 1984 idea that the Windmiller Pattern represents establishment of a proto-Utian community in the Sacramento–San Joaquin Delta. Both are convinced that similarities between Windmiller and the Lovelock Culture of northwestern Nevada probably reflect the Yok-Utian connection. This is supported by mtDNA haplogroup frequencies that show that the ancient inhabitants of the western Great Basin are statistically indistinguishable from California Penutian populations (Kaestle and Smith 2001), but do not resemble the modern inhabitants of the Western Great Basin, as described by Eshleman and Smith (Chapter 19).

The Berkeley and Windmiller Patterns have long been the primary foci of discussions concerning Penutian entry into California. Both Moratto (1984) and Golla (Chapter 6) support the idea that Windmiller intrusion into the San Francisco Bay area resulted in the Berkeley Pattern as a " a fusion of older Hokan . . . and intrusive Utian cultural elements" (Moratto 1984:553). This proposal was generally consistent with the ideas of Gerow (1968:98) and later Breschini (1983:64–70, 98–101), who argued for east-to-west spread of proto-Penutian speaking peoples from the delta into the Bay Area during the Early Period, with the older Hokan population represented at University Village, and speakers of proto-Penutian languages represented by the Early Berkeley Pattern in the East Bay. Bennyhoff (1994c:83), however, objected to classification of Berkeley as a mere variant of Windmiller, and argued that the two patterns represented culturally and physically distinct populations. He thought that proto-Utians entered the central San Francisco Bay Area earlier, and developed the Early Period Berkeley pattern in place (Bennyhoff 1986:67, 1994b:66). Fredrickson (1989a) concurred with Bennyhoff, positing a Lower Berkeley Pattern spread from the Central Bay into the North Bay after 1500 cal B.C., tying it to a proto-Miwok separation from proto-Costanoan. In 1984 there was a general consensus that Miwokan speakers expanded eastward from the North Bay into the Sacramento Valley during the Early/Middle Transition (ca. 500 to 200 cal B.C.), forcing the Windmiller Pattern people south into the San Joaquin Valley (Bennyhoff 1994c:66; Fredrickson 1984:511; Moratto 1984:210).

New findings that bear on the issue of the ethnolinguistic affiliation of Berkeley Pattern peoples include those of White et al. (2002), who identified an early Berkeley Aspect in the Clear Lake area (Chapter 7), and Eschelman and Smith's (Chapter 19) finding of mtDNA continuity between Windmiller and Berkeley in the Sacramento Valley. In Chapter 10, Rosenthal et al. present archaeological findings showing that a key Windmiller trait, ventral-extended burials, can be recognized throughout the San Joaquin Valley as far south as Buena Vista Lake as early as ca. 4000 cal B.C. Windmiller sites appear to have been occupied until 800–1000 years ago in the San Joaquin Valley, whereas in the Sacramento Valley, the Berkeley Pattern replaced Windmiller at ca. 700 cal B.C.

As discussed by Milliken et al. in Chapter 8, the Meganos Culture in the East Bay and Stockton areas has also been implicated in Late Holocene movements of speakers of proto-Penutian languages. Generally thought to be an outgrowth from Windmiller, Meganos is alternately associated with Utian (Moratto 1984:201–211) or proto-Yokutsan and seems to mark an intrusion first into the East Bay and then into the Central Valley at the end of the Middle Period, probably in response to the movement of proto-Costanoan speakers. Rosenthal et al. in Chapter 10 also argue for archaeological correlation between Windmiller, Meganos, and Yokuts.

Complicating this picture considerably, however, is strong contrast between all of the ancient California populations that exhibit high frequencies of Haplogroup C and modern Yokuts and Costanoan who exhibit high frequencies of Haplogroups B and D. While some ambiguity remains, Eschelman and Smith (Chapter 19) see little support from mtDNA for a Penutian replacement of older Hokan-speaking populations in either Berkeley (Middle Horizon) or Windmiller Pattern burials. While more mtDNA samples are needed, such findings are likely to serve as catalysts for new thinking about the Utian intrusion. One alternative is that the dramatic cultural changes accompanying the appearance of the Augustine Pattern in the San Francisco Bay Area could represent the initial Utian entrance, but Milliken et al. in Chapter 8 envision Augustine as more of a shared regional religious and ceremonial organization rather than a marker of ethnic identity.

The Algic and Athabaskan intrusions are as yet uncomplicated by mtDNA findings and show reasonable correlations between the archaeological and linguistic records, although the Algic/Athbaskan distinction cannot yet be recognized archaeologically. Both Golla (Chapter 6) and Hildebrandt (Chapter 7) suggest that the Gunther Pattern probably relates to the arrival of people speaking Algic languages, beginning with the Wiyot at about cal A.D. 100 and followed by Yurok settlement along the Klamath River ca. cal A.D. 700–800. A later intrusion of Athabaskans around cal A.D. 800–900 into the Trinity-Eel drainage ultimately diverged into several distinct languages and dialects. Discovery of a Gunther component at MEN-428B, dating cal A.D. 270–500, led White (1991) to conclude that the initial colonization of northwest California by Algic-speaking peoples extended well south of their ultimate range, with a later retraction to the more northerly areas (e.g., north of Cape Mendocino).

The situation with Uto-Aztecan languages in California is complicated, perhaps more so now than in 1984, as a result of new findings. Moratto (1984) thought that proto-Uto-Aztecan made its appearance in southeastern California by 3000 cal B.C., whereas Golla (Chapter 6) suggests that northern Uto-Aztecan languages were being spoken in a continuous band across the southern Great Basin from the Colorado River to the Sierra Nevada by 1500 cal B.C. Differences of opinion exist on the timing of western expansion of Takic speakers, with Moratto (1984:560) suggesting this took place as early as 3,500 years ago, whereas Golla, based on research from the past 20 years, suggests this took place only 2,000 years ago. In the Antelope Valley, Sutton et al. (Chapter 15) note an increase in settlement ca. 500 cal B.C., which they think may represent the arrival of speakers of Takic languages. Numic expansion north and east from a southeastern California homeland is seen by most as occurring ca. 1,000 years ago, although the Numic speakers intruded into northeast California only 300 years ago. Hill's (2002) hypothesis that Numic settlers in the central and northern parts of the Great Basin arrived via a northward expansion from the Colorado Plateau and a "devolution" from Anasazi maize farming is not backed by most archaeologists, but, as Golla outlines in Chapter 6, it does have some substantive linguistic support. Mitochondrial DNA findings complicate the Uto-Aztecan situation considerably as Eshleman and Smith show that ancient Californian mtDNA most closely resembles that of modern Takic speakers from southern California. They further suggest that speakers of a Uto-Aztecan language were living in the Central Valley at least between 2,000 and 4,000 years ago, supporting a case made earlier by Nichols (1988) on the basis of linguistics. As with the other findings from mtDNA, this is likely to encourage discussion, debate, and a demand for further studies in the future.

COMPLEXITY

California's native past is also a story of complex hunter-gatherers, people who survived by foraging but also had some degree of sedentism, population density, permanent social inequality, craft specialization, nonband forms of political organization, lineal descent reckoning, wide-ranging and intensive exchange relationships, developed concepts of wealth and usury, and warfare. However, the distribution of these traits was highly varied across space as well as time. Unraveling the evolution of native Californian complexity has been a singular focus of research both before and after 1984, and the most influential proposals have relied on cultural evolutionary frameworks represented in models by the Chartkoffs (1984) and Fredrickson (1974a), whose ideas were discussed earlier in reference to the emergence of intensive economies. In both of these, complexity is seen as evolving gradually, hand in hand with increasingly intensified subsistence.

Most of the authors of the regional chapters in the current volume discuss archaeological evidence for the appearance of one or more traits of complexity, although sociopolitical developments are considerably easier to recognize in the ethnographic record. In this light it should not be surprising that many researchers continue to envision sociopolitical developments as evolving gradually, paralleling population growth and trends of subsistence intensification. Nonetheless, the single most influential model of sociopolitical evolution in the past two decades was created by Arnold (1992a), who argued not for incremental evolution but for the punctuated emergence of a chiefdom and craft specialization in the Santa Barbara Channel very late in the region's prehistory (ca. cal A.D. 1150). This proposal fostered some of the most heated debate in the history of California archaeology (Arnold 1992a, 1997, 2001; Gamble and Russell 2002; Raab and Larson 1997; Raab et al. 1995), and while most southern Californianists still support a gradual, incremental evolution that began earlier (see Erlandson and Rick 2002a; King 1990), this model clarified issues related to emergent complexity in an unprecedented way. It also invoked historical and ecological causes for sociopolitical progress, as Arnold argued that concentrated political power and craft specialization emerged in the face of a subsistence crisis. Historical explanations have also been suggested elsewhere, particularly in northwest California, where the establishment of sedentary economies is associated with emigration of ethnolinguistic groups (e.g., the Pomoan/Berkeley expansion out of Clear Lake and the Algic/Athabaskan/Gunther settlements along the north coast). In the San Francisco Bay Area, Fredrickson (1974b:65) posits a historic dimension to his evolutionary scheme suggesting that incipient social ranking was introduced by the people who brought the Augustine Pattern into the Walnut Creek Locality during the Late (Emergent) Period. Fredrickson's model differs significantly from the Chartkoffs' in that he explicitly recognizes the likelihood of historically based variation in the timing and spread of political complexity.

Cases of in-migration of complex systems are generally compatible with cultural evolutionary models (e.g., they posit relatively recent appearances of sociopolitical sophistication), but research from the past two decades has revealed patterns that contradict some aspects of unilineal cultural evolution. In these instances, the earlier models have proven most valuable as frames of reference that illuminate nonlinear developments, particularly with respect to the three most heavily studied traits of complex foraging: warfare, sedentism, and trade.

Intergroup conflict and warfare, while not ignored prior to 1984 (see Pastron 1973), have been more extensively researched in recent decades. One of the most influential studies was by Lambert (1994), who showed that osteological signs of violence peaked prior to the Late Period in the Santa Barbara Channel. Raab and Larson (1997) and Jones et al. (1999) subsequently attributed this peak to demographic imbalance caused by medieval droughts. More recent studies in the San Francisco Bay Area (Pilloud 2005), however, show that links between violence, health, and drought are not as strong as previously thought (Weiss 2002). Sutton et al. and McGuire in the present volume report evidence for violence associated with the Numic expansion in the Mojave Desert and Northeast respectively. In the San Francisco Bay Area, strong evidence for violence has been reported as early as ca. 500 cal B.C. (Early/Middle Transition/Middle Period Phase 1) at SCL-478, where Wiberg (2002) documented partial dismemberment (trophy taking) and interment in multiple graves, and Pesnichak and Evans (2005:14), reported victims of violent death lying on house floors, indicating that they had been attacked. At a contemporary site in the South Bay, Rubino (SCL-674), Grady et al. (1999) recovered polished human forearm elements with cut marks. Greater frequencies of healed fractures and penetration wounds (17 percent of the total population) were reported from Late Period contexts at SCL-294 in the Santa Teresa Locality in the South Bay (Richards 1988:120–122), which provides some support for Chartkoff and Chartkoff's (1984:236) prediction of increased violence over time, related to increased resource stress and territoriality. As Milliken et al. point out in Chapter 8, however, some Bay Area mortuary assemblages show little or no evidence of violent death.

Sedentism and relative mobility have been subjects of intense research over the past two decades, resulting in some instances (e.g., the San Francisco Bay Area) in a wide range of opinions. In general, many regions are now suspected of supporting relatively nonmobile or "semi-sedentary" forager populations earlier than previously thought. Residential stability and signs of logistical organization are suggested by at least mid-Holocene on the Central Coast, the Northern Bight, Southern Bight, Northeast, and along the Sacramento and San Joaquin Rivers. In several regions (e.g., the Northwest and Central Valley), sedentary systems were thought to have coexisted alongside more mobile lifeways by mid-Holocene. More importantly, with respect to unilinear social evolution, in several areas, peak levels of sedentism seem to have been reached well before the last millennium of prehistory. The strongest statement on this phenomenon is made by Hildebrandt in Chapter 7 where, in the southern North Coast Ranges, he notes evidence for ephemeral occupation and declines in the use of obsidian after ca. cal A.D. 800. Similar patterns are seen in the Sierra Nevada, the Central Coast, and Northeast. As Hildebrandt suggests, these signs of population decentralization, smaller social groups, and higher mobility during the Late Period confound the predictions of unilinear models. As Gilreath notes in Chapter 18, even artistic expression seems to have reached a peak prior to the Late Prehistoric Period, as Coso petroglyphs, which include highly stylized representational sheep and patterned-bodied anthropomorphs, were replaced 1,000 years ago by unimpressive scratched designs. Such trends demand further recognition and attempts at explanation.

Similar patterns are apparent in the production and exchange of obsidian, although as Hughes and Milliken discuss in Chapter 17, much research in the past two decades has shown how difficult it can be to evaluate the latter. Nonetheless, peaks in production at major obsidian quarries including Coso (Gilreath and Hildebrandt 1997), Bodie Hills (Singer and Ericson 1977:Fig. 8), Casa Diablo (Bouey and Basgall 1984; Hall 1983), and Borax Lake (Fredrickson and Origer 2002) seem to have been reached around 1,300 years ago with declines thereafter. On the basis of continuity in obsidian source frequencies, many regions (e.g., the Northeast and Central Coast) show long periods of stable intergroup relations during mid-Holocene that changed or deteriorated after ca. 1,500 to 1,000 years ago.

Patterns in shell bead production and exchange contrast with patterns in obsidian production, probably because beads, unlike obsidian, had no strictly utilitarian function. Long-distance conveyance of shell beads into the Great Basin seems to have peaked considerably earlier (ca. 500 cal B.C.) than production of bifaces at obsidian quarries. More significantly, bead production did not decrease but instead increased dramatically throughout central and southern California (e.g., the San Francisco Bay Area, Central Coast, Central Valley, and Northern Bight) after ca. cal A.D. 1000. Types varied within regional stylistic spheres, and beads were not frequently exchanged across long distances. Rather, as Rosenthal et al. recognize in Chapter 10, bead production seems to have become decentralized after ca. cal A.D. 1000, with greater numbers of individuals participating in manufacture. This pattern is well represented on the Central Coast, where Jones et al. in Chapter 9 refer to a Late Period revolution marked by ubiquitous evidence for low-level bead production. Concerning the San Francisco Bay Area, Milliken and Bennyhoff (1993:388) argue that after ca. cal A.D. 1000, bead wealth appeared increasingly as a mortuary offering, reflecting wider access to beads in the population at large and the declining importance of beads as prestige symbols. Rosenthal et al. in Chapter 10 suggest this pattern reflects the emergence of a monetized system of exchange (Chagnon 1970; King 1978), whereas Jones et al. in Chapter 9 relate it to the rise of qualitatively different political systems that featured individuals with significant amounts of power. In the Santa Barbara Channel, Arnold (1992a) attributed increased bead production to the emergence of craft specialization coordinated by elites. Increased bead production during the Late Period also seems to conform with Jackson and Ericson's (1994) model of increasing exchange across shorter distances over time in California.

A common theme in earlier research on California sociopolitical evolution was the notion that Late Period prehistoric and ethnographic political systems represented significant progress in integrating communities and distributing resources within and between communities. This notion was most strongly developed by C. King (1976), who suggested that monetized intervillage exchange among the ethnographic Chumash served to reallocate resources throughout the Chumash interaction sphere. Fredrickson (1974b), however, suggested that central California tribelets represented an important political achievement in which sharing of resources across territorial boundaries was institutionalized. Gamble (2005) suggested that the presence of such institutions and traditions provided Native Californians with significant buffers against the impacts of extreme climatic variability. Viewed in this light, the increased bead production of the Late Period in central and southern California is consistent with the predictions of linear cultural evolution.

As with so many other aspects of California prehistory, emergent complexity defies explanation via any single theoretical perspective. Some regions conform with the expectations of linear cultural evolution, whereas in others, devolution, decentralization, and deintensification seem to have occurred late in time. Alternative explanations for these developments invoke historical contingencies (e.g., in-migration of new groups, protohistoric plagues; Preston 1996), demographic imbalances, climatic perturbations (climate forcing and punctuated cultural response), inefficiencies inherent in archaic economies (McGuire and Hildebrandt 2005), or some combination thereof. While this range of opinions is interesting and should fuel further discussion, near unanimity on the basic description of many phenomena and their dating is extremely encouraging with regard to prospects for future research.

EPILOGUE: THE FUTURE OF A CHAOTIC PAST

California's prehistory was complicated, and attempts to generalize about the region's past reveal a certain disorderliness. It should not be surprising that 20 years ago, it took two books with different perspectives to fully characterize California archaeology. In the intervening years, theoretical perspectives have continued to broaden, at the same time that powerful new methods have been developed, and an enormous data base has been created—one that continues to grow at a remarkable rate. Some methodological advances (e.g., mtDNA, AMS dating, and isotope analysis) are already providing powerful new forms of empirical evidence with which to evaluate a wide range of alternative models and hypotheses. Unanticipated discoveries in the archaeological record have also fueled significant progress although overemphasis on the deductive method in some instances has prevented progress from taking place more quickly, as has increasing politicization of the research process and its findings. Progress in the future will come from continued theoretical and methodological advances, the application of both deductive and inductive approaches, and continued collaboration between Native Americans and archaeologists (some of whom are now also archaeologists). In the next 20 years, California's past will become even more complicated, but the efforts represented by the contributors to this volume suggest that archaeologists will be up for the intellectual and practical challenges that lie ahead.

NOTES

1. To date, only mtDNA studies have been published for California. The mtDNA molecule is a small one, simply structured by molecular standards, and easy to work with in comparison with nuclear DNA. The technically more difficult process of Y chromosome analysis is beginning to reveal unsuspected prehistoric patterns in other parts of the world, and will soon be applied to California. Until we have equal documentation of both sides, we are only talking about the movement of women, and of those particular women whose lineages survived to whatever date we access their mtDNA. We know nothing about the analogous situations of earlier generations of men in prehistory. Further, it is dangerous in this matter, as in any cultural analysis, to rely too heavily on historically attested practices or on post-European written records to illuminate prehistory. We must be sure that the picture we paint is not a projection of our own ideas and expectations about human relations. We have little idea of whether ancient Californians were matrilocal or patrilocal at any give time or place; whether they took captives in wars, or slaves in raids; what limitations and opportunities endogamy and exogamy presented; how monogamous either men or women were; how much "the kindness of strangers" in taking in orphans and disabled persons influenced gene pools; or about ancient epidemics and other cataclysmic events such as earthquakes and tsunamis which may have caused rapid breakdowns in family structures (as we see in post-European contact situations) with attendant social disruptions.

2. Whether the Millingstone Culture was preceded by San Dieguito Complex in San Diego County is a matter of debate and remains unresolved.

References

Abrams, D. M.
1968 Salvage Investigations at the Little Pico Creek Site: 4-SLO-175. *Robert E. Schenk Archives of California Archaeology* 4:1–40.

Ackerman, R. E.
1996 Ground Hog Bay, Site 2. In *American Beginnings: The Prehistory and Palaeoecology of Beringa*, edited by F. H. West, pp. 424–430. University of Chicago Press, Chicago.

Adam, D. P.
1967 Late Pleistocene and Recent Palynology in the Central Sierra Nevada, California. In *Quaternary Paleoecology,* edited by E. J. Cushing and H. E. Wright Jr., pp. 275–302. Yale University Press, New Haven, Connecticut.
1988 *Palynology of Two Upper Quaternary Cores from Clear Lake, Lake County, California.* U.S. Geological Survey Professional Paper 1363.

Adam, D. P., and G. J. West
1983 Temperature and Precipitation Estimates Through the Last Glacial Cycle from Clear Lake, California, Pollen Data. *Science* 219:168–170.

Adam, D. P., J. D. Sims, and C. K. Throckmorton
1981 130,000-yr Continuous Pollen Record from Clear Lake, Lake County, California. *Geology* 9:373.

Adeny, T. E., and H. I. Chapelle
1983 *The Bark Canoes and Skin Boats of North America.* Smithsonian Institution, Washington, D.C.

Adovasio, J. M.
1986 Prehistoric Basketry. In *Great Basin*, edited by Warren d'Azevedo, pp. 194–205. Handbook of North American Indians. Vol. 11. W. G. Sturtevant, general editor. Smithsonian Institution, Washington, D.C.

Ahlstrom, R. V. N.
2000 *Living in the Western Papaguería: An Archaeological Overview of the Barry M. Goldwater Air Force Range in Southwestern Arizona.* Prepared by SWCA for the 56th Range Management Office, Luke Air Force Base, Arizona.

Aiello, I. W.
2005 Fossil Seep Structures of the Monterey Bay Region and Tectonic/Structural Controls on Fluid Flow in an Active Transform Margin. Palaeogeography, Palaeoclimatology, *Palaeoecology* 227:124–142.

Aikens, C. M., and S. N. Rhee
1992 *Pacific Northeast Asia in Prehistory.* Washington State University Press, Pullman.

Allen, M. W.
1998 Fort Irwin Archaeology: A Preserved Past for the Mojave Desert. *San Bernardino County Museum Association Quarterly* 45 (1–2):71–75.
2004 *Late Prehistoric Culture Change in the West-Central Mojave Desert: Perspectives from Red Mountain.* Report on file, Department of Geography and Anthropology, California State Polytechnic University, Pomona.

Alley, R. B., D. A. Meese, C. A. Shuman, A. J. Gow, K. C. Taylor, P. M. Gootes, J. W. C. White, M. Ram, E. D. Waddington, P. A. Mayewski, and G. A. Zielinski
1993 Abrupt Increase in Greenland Snow Accumulation at the End of the Younger Dryas Event. *Nature* 362:527–529.

Alley, R. B., J. Marotzke, W. D. Nordhaus, J. T. Overpeck, D. M. Peteet, R. A. Pielke Jr., R. T. Pierrehumbert, P. B. Rhines, T. F. Stocker, L. D. Talley, and J. M. Wallace
2003 Abrupt Climate Change. *Science* 299:2005–2010.

Altschul, J. H., and J. A. Ezzo
1994 The Expression of Ceremonial Space Along the Lower Colorado River. In *Recent Research Along the Lower Colorado River*, edited by J. A. Ezzo, pp. 51–68. Statistical Research Technical Series no. 51. Prepared for USDI Bureau of Reclamation, Lower Colorado Regional Office, Boulder City, Nevada.

Altschul, J. H., and D. R. Grenda (editors)
2002 *Islanders and Mainlanders: Prehistoric Context for the Southern California Bight.* SRI Press, Tucson.

Altschul, J. H., J. A. Homburg, and R. Ciolek-Torrello
1992 *Life in the Ballona: Archaeological Investigations at the Admiralty Site (CA-LAN-47) and the Channel Gateway Site (CA-LAN-1596-H).* Statistical Research Technical Series 33.

Altschul, J. H., R. Ciolek-Torrello, D. R. Grenda, J. A. Homburg, S. Benaron, and A. Q. Stoll
2005 Ballona Archaeology: A Decade of Multidisciplinary Research. *Proceedings of the Society for California Archaeology* 18:283–301.

Ames, K. M.
2002 Going by Boat: The Forager-Collector Continuum at Sea. In *Beyond Foraging and Collecting: Evolutionary Change in Hunter-Gatherer Settlement Systems,* edited by B. Fitzhugh and J. Habu, pp. 19–52. Kluwer Academic/Plenum, New York.

Ames, K. M., and H. D. G. Maschner
1999 *Peoples of the Northwest Coast: Their Archaeology and Prehistory.* Thames & Hudson, London.

Amsden, C. A.
1937 The Lake Mojave Artifacts. In *The Archaeology of Pleistocene Lake Mojave*, edited by E. W. C. Campbell, W. H. Campbell, E. Antevs, C. A. Amsden, J. A. Barbieri, and F. D. Bode, pp. 51–97. Southwest Museum Papers no. 11.

Anderson, D. E., and S. G. Wells
2003 Latest Pleistocene Lake Highstands in Death Valley, California. In *Paleoenvironments and Paleohydrology of the Mojave and Southern Great Basin Deserts,* edited by Y. Enzel, S. G. Wells, and N. Lancaster, pp. 115–128. Special Paper 368. Geological Society of America, Boulder.

Anderson, K. A.
1997 Lithic Analysis of CA-SBA-2358: A Middle-to-Late Period Prehistoric Site Located in the Middle Santa Ynez River Valley. Master's thesis, Department of Anthropology, University of California, Santa Barbara.

Anderson, M. K.
2005 *Tending the Wild: Native American Knowledge and Management of California's Natural Resources.* University of California Press, Berkeley.

Anderson, M. K., and M. J. Moratto
1996 Native American Land-Use Practices and Ecological Impacts. In *Sierra Nevada Ecosystem Project: Final Report to Congress.*

Vol. 2, pp. 187–206. University of California, Centers for Water and Wildland Resources, Davis.

Anderson, R. S.

1987 Late-Quaternary Environments of the Sierra Nevada, California. Ph.D. dissertation, University of Arizona.

1990 Holocene Forest Development and Paleoclimates within the Central Sierra Nevada, California. *Journal of Ecology* 78:470–489.

2002 *Fire and Vegetation History of Santa Rosa Island, Channel Islands National Park, California.* Final Report for a Cooperative Agreement (1443CA8000-8-0002) Between Channel Islands National Park and Northern Arizona University.

Anderson, R. S., and B. F. Byrd

1998 Late-Holocene Vegetation Changes from the Las Flores Creek Coastal Lowlands, San Diego County, California. *Madrono* 45:171–182.

Anderson, R. S., and S. L. Carpenter

1991 Vegetation Change in Yosemite Valley, Yosemite National Park, California, During the Protohistoric Period. *Madrono* 38:1–13.

Anderson, R. S., and S. J. Smith

1991 Climatic Extremes of the Last 4,000 Years as Reflected in the Pollen Records from the Southern Sierra Nevada, California. In *Proceedings of the Southern California Climate Symposium, 25 October 1991, Trends and Extremes of the Past 2000 Years,* edited by M. R. Rose and P. E. Wigand, pp. 27–43. Technical Report no. 11. Natural History Museum of Los Angeles County.

1994 Paleoclimatic Interpretations of Meadow Sediment and Pollen Stratigraphies from California. *Geology* 22:723–726.

Anderson, S., A. T. Bankier, B. G. Barrell, M. H. L. de Bruijn, A. R. Coulson, J. Drouin, I. C. Eperon, B. Nierlich, A. Roe, F. Sanger, P. H. Schrier, A. J. H. Smith, R. Staden, and C. Young

1981 Sequence and Organization of the Human Mitochondrial Genome. *Nature* 290:457–465.

Anima, R. J., S. L. Eittreim, B. D. Edwards, and A. J. Stevenson

2002 Nearshore Morphology and Late Quaternary Geologic Framework of the Northern Monterey Bay Marine Sanctuary, California. *Marine Geology* 181:35–54.

Anovitz, L. M., J. M. Elam, L. R. Riciputi, and D. R. Cole

1999 The Failure of Obsidian Hydration Dating: Sources, Implications, and New Directions. *Journal of Archaeological Science* 26:735–752.

2004 Isothermal Time-series Determination of the Rate of Diffusion of Water in Pachuca Obsidian. *Archaeometry* 46:301–326.

Antevs, E.

1948 Climatic Changes and Pre-White Man. *University of Utah Bulletin* 38:168–191.

1953 On Division of the Last 20,000 Years. *University of California Archaeological Survey Reports* 22:5–8.

1955 Geologic-Climatic Dating in the West. *American Antiquity* 20:317–335.

Apple, R. M.

1982 *Western Salt Industrial Park Archaeological Report.* New Horizons Planning Consultants, San Diego. Report on file, South Coast Information Center, San Diego State University.

Apple, R. M., and C. L. Shaver

2005 *Chocolate Mountain Aerial Gunnery Range: Cultural Resources Survey of 12 Targets and Monitoring of 14 Archaeological Sites.* Prepared by EDAW, San Diego, for Navy Facilities Engineering Command, Southwest, San Diego. Report on file, South Coast Information Center, San Diego State University.

Apple, R. M., A. York, A. Pigniolo, J. H. Cleland, and S. Van Wormer

1997 *Archaeological Survey and Evaluation Program for the Salton Sea Test Base, Imperial County, California.* Prepared by KEA Environmental for U.S. Department of the Navy, Southwest Division, Naval Facilities Engineering Command, San Diego. Report on file, South Coast Information Center, San Diego State University.

Applegate, R.

1975 An Index of Chumash Placenames. In *Papers on the Chumash,* pp. 19–46. San Luis Obispo County Archaeological Society Occasional Papers no. 9.

Arno, S. F., and K. M. Sneck

1977 *A Method for Determining Fire History in the Coniferous Forests of the Mountain West.* USDA Forest Service General Technical Report INT-42, Intermountain Forest and Range Experiment Station, Ogden, Utah.

Arnold, J. E.

1987 *Craft Specialization in the Prehistoric Channel Island, California.* University of California Press, Berkeley.

1990 Lithic Resource Control and Economic Change in the Santa Barbara Channel Region. *Journal of California and Great Basin Anthropology* 12:158–172.

1992a Complex Hunter-Gatherer-Fishers of Prehistoric California: Chiefs, Specialists, and Maritime Adaptations of the Channel Islands. *American Antiquity* 57:60–84.

1992b Early-Stage Biface Production Industries in Coastal Southern California. In *Stone Tool Procurement, Production, and Distribution in California Prehistory,* edited by J. E. Arnold, pp. 67–129. Cotsen Institute of Archaeology, University of California, Los Angeles.

1992c Cultural Disruption and the Political Economy in Channel Islands Prehistory. In *Essays on the Prehistory of Maritime California,* edited by T. L. Jones, pp. 129–146. Center for Archaeological Research at Davis no. 10. University of California, Davis.

1995 Transportation Innovation and Social Complexity Among Maritime Hunter-Gatherer Societies. *American Anthropologist* 97:733–747.

1997 Bigger Boats, Crowded Creekbanks: Environmental Stresses in Perspective. *American Antiquity* 62:337–339.

2001a Social Evolution and the Political Economy in the Northern Channel Islands. In *The Origins of a Pacific Coast Chiefdom: The Chumash of the Channel Islands,* edited by J. E. Arnold, pp. 287–296. University of Utah Press, Salt Lake City.

2001b The Chumash in World and Regional Perspectives. In *The Origins of a Pacific Coast Chiefdom: The Chumash of the Channel Islands,* edited by J. E. Arnold, pp. 1–19. University of Utah Press, Salt Lake City.

2001c The Channel Islands Project: History, Objectives, and Methods. In *The Origins of a Pacific Coast Chiefdom: The Chumash of the Channel Islands,* edited by J. E. Arnold, pp. 21–52. University of Utah Press, Salt Lake City.

Arnold, J. E. (editor)

2001 *The Origins of a Pacific Coast Chiefdom: The Chumash of the Channel Islands.* University of Utah Press, Salt Lake City.

2004 *Foundations of Chumash Complexity.* Cotsen Institute of Archaeology, University of California, Los Angeles.

Arnold, J. E., and J. Bernard

2005 Negotiating the Coasts: Status and the Evolution of Boat Technology in California. *World Archaeology* 37:109–131.

Arnold, J. E., and R. H. Colten

1998 Prehistoric Marine Mammal Hunting on California's Northern Channel Islands. *American Antiquity* 63:679–701.

Arnold, J. E., and A. P. Graesch

2001 The Evolution of Specialized Shellworking Among the Island Chumash. In *The Origins of a Pacific Coast Chiefdom: The Chumash of the Channel Islands,* edited by J. E. Arnold, pp. 71–112. University of Utah Press, Salt Lake City.

Arnold, J. E., and T. M. Green

2002 Mortuary Ambiguity: The Ventureño Chumash Case. *American Antiquity* 67:760–771.

Arnold, J. E., and A. Munns
1994 Independent or Attached Specialization: The Organization of Shell Bead Production in California. *Journal of Field Archaeology* 21:473–489.

Arnold, J. E., and B. Tissot
1993 Measurement of Significant Marine Paleotemperature Variation Using Black Abalone Shells from Middens. *Quaternary Research* 39:390–394.

Arnold, J. E., R. H. Colten, and S. Pletka
1997 Contexts of Cultural Change in Insular California. *American Antiquity* 62:300–318.

Arnold, J. E., A. M. Preziosi, and P. Shattuck
2001 Flaked Stone Craft Production and Exchange in Island Chumash Territory. In *The Origins of a Pacific Coast Chiefdom: The Chumash of the Channel Islands*, edited by J. E. Arnold, pp. 113–132. University of Utah Press, Salt Lake City.

Arnold, J. E., M. R. Walsh, and S. E. Hollimon
2004 The Archaeology of California. *Journal of Archaeological Research* 12:1–73.

ASM Affiliates and Jones & Stokes
2005 *Santa Rosa and San Jacinto Mountians National Monument Inventory.* Prepared by ASM Affiliates and Jones & Stokes for the USDI Bureau of Land Management, Palm Springs, California. Copies available from ASM Affiliates, Carlsbad, California.

Ataman, K., M. R. Harmon, C. M. Hodges, R. J. Jackson, A. T. Leigh, K. C. Long, J. Nadolski, J. J. Northrup, W. Broadhead, and C. Skinner
1999 *Post Modern Martis: New Archaeological Investigations in Martis Valley.* Summit Envirosolutions, Reno, Nevada, and Pacific Legacy, Cameron Park, California. Submitted to U.S. Army Corps of Engineers, Sacramento, California, and California Department of Transportation, Marysville, California.

Atchley, S. M.
1994 A Burial Analysis of the Hotchkiss Site (CA-CCO-138). Master's thesis, Department of Anthropology, California State University, Sonoma.

Atwater, B. F.
1979 Ancient Processes at the Site of Southern San Francisco Bay: Movement of the Crust and Changes in Sea Level. In *San Francisco Bay: The Urbanized Estuary, Investigations into the Natural History of San Francisco Bay and Delta with Reference to the Influence of Man*, edited by T. J. Conomos, pp. 31–45. Pacific Division of the American Association for the Advancement of Science, San Francisco.
1980 *Attempts to Correlate Late Quaternary Climate Records Between San Francisco Bay, the Sacramento-San Joaquin Delta, and the Mokelumne River, California.* University Microfilms International.

Atwater, B. F., and D. F. Belknap
1980 Tidal-Wetland Deposits of the Sacramento-San Joaquin Delta, California. In *Quaternary Depositional Environments of the Pacific Coast.* Pacific Coast Paleogeography Symposium 4, edited by M. E. Field, R. G. Douglas, A. H. Bouma, J. C. Ingle, and I. P. Colburn, pp. 89–103. The Pacific Section of the Society of Economic Paleontologists and Mineralogists, Los Angeles.

Atwater, B. F., C. Hedel, and E. Helley
1977 *Late Quaternary Depositional History, Holocene Sea Level Changes, and Vertical Crustal Movement, Southern San Francisco Bay, California.* U.S. Geological Survey Professional Paper 1014. U.S. Government Printing Office, Washington, D.C.

Atwater, B. F., D. P. Adam, J. P. Bradbury, R. M. Forester, R. K. Mark, W. R. Lettis, G. R. Fisher, K. W. Gobalet, and S. W. Robinson
1986 A Fan Dam for Tulare Lake, California, and Implications for the Wisconsin Glacial History of the Sierra Nevada. *Geological Society of America Bulletin* 97:97–109.

Atwater, B. F., D. A. Trumm, J. C. Tinsley III, R. S. Stein, A. B. Tucker, D. J. Donahue, A. J. T. Jull, and L. A. Payen
1990 Alluvial Plains and Earthquake Recurrence at the Coalinga Anticline. In *The Coalinga, California, Earthquake of May, 1983*, edited by M. J. Rymer and W. Ellsworth, pp. 273–297. U.S. Geological Survey Professional Paper 1487.

Bacon, C. R., R. Macdonald, R. L. Smith, and P. A. Baedecker
1981 Pleistocene High-Silica Rhyolites of the Coso Volcanic Field, Inyo County, California. *Journal of Geophysical Research* 86:10,223–10,241.

Bada, J. L.
1985 Aspartic Acid Racemization Ages of California Paleoindian Skeletons. *American Antiquity* 50:645–647.

Bada, J. L., R. A. Schroeder, and G. F. Carter
1974 New Evidence for the Antiquity of Man in North America Deduced from Aspartic Acid Racemization. *Science* 184:791–793.

Bada, J. L., R. Gillespie, J. A. J. Gowlett, and R. E. M. Hedges
1984 Accelerator Mass Spectrometry Radiocarbon Ages of Amino Acid Extracts from Californian Paleoindian Skeletons. *Nature* 312:442–444.

Bailey, J.
2006 X-ray Flourescence Characterization of Volcanic Glass Artifacts from Wilson Butte Cave. In *New Excavations at Wilson Butte Cave, South-Central Idaho*, edited by R. Gruhn, pp. 119–138. Occasional Papers of the Idaho Museum of Natural History no. 38.

Baker, B.
1977 Madonna Ranch, CA-SLO-372: An Interpretation of an Inland Chumash Site. Master's thesis, Department of Anthropology, California State University, Long Beach.

Baldwin, M. A.
1971 *Archaeological Evidence of Cultural Continuity from Chumash to Salinan Indians in California.* San Luis Obispo County Archaeological Society Occasional Papers no. 6.

Banks, P. M., and R. I. Orlins
1981 *Investigation of Cultural Resources Within the Richmond Harbor Redevelopment Project 11-A, Richmond, Contra Costa County, California.* California Archaeological Consultants, Oakland. Submitted to the City of Richmond, California. Copies available from Northwest Archaeological Information Center, Department of Anthropology, Sonoma State University, Rohnert Park, California.
1985 *Limited Archaeological Excavations at CA-CCO-299, A Stege Mound, Richmond, Contra Costa County, California.* California Archaeological Consultants, Oakland. Submitted to the Pacific Gas and Electric Company, San Francisco. Copies available from Northwest Archaeological Information Center, Department of Anthropology, Sonoma State University, Rohnert Park, California.

Bard, E., B. Hamelin, and R. G. Fairbanks
1990 U-Th Ages Obtained by Mass Spectrometry in Corals from Barbados: Sea Level During the Past 130,000 Years. *Nature* 346:456–458.

Bard, E., B. Hamelin, M. Arnold, L. Montaggioni, G. Cabioch, G. Faure, and F. Fougerie
1996 Deglacial Sea-Level Record from Tahiti Corals and the Timing of Global Meltwater Discharge. *Nature* 382:241–244.

Barnosky, A. D., P. L. Koch, R. S. Feranec, S. L. Wing, and A. B. Shabel
2004 Assessing the Causes of Late Pleistocene Extinctions on the Continents. *Science* 306: 70–75.

Barrett, S. A.
1952 Material Aspects of Pomo Culture. *Bulletin of the Public Museum of the City of Milwaukee* 20(1–2).

Barron, J. A., L. Heusser, T. Herbert, and M. Lyle
2003 High-Resolution Climatic Evolution of Coastal Northern California During the Past 16,000 Years. *Paleoceanography* 18:(1), 1020, doi:10.1029/2002 PA000768.

Bartelink, E. J.
2006 Resource Intensification in Pre-Contact Central California: A Bioarchaeological Perspective on Diet and Health Patterns Among Hunter-Gatherers from the Lower Sacramento Valley and San Francisco Bay. Ph.D. dissertation, Department of Anthropology, Texas A&M University.

Basgall, M. E.
1979 To Trade or Not to Trade: A Pomo Example. *Journal of California and Great Basin Anthropology* 1:178–182.
1982 Archaeology and Linguistics: Pomoan Prehistory as Viewed from Northern Sonoma County, California. *Journal of California and Great Basin Anthropology* 4:3–22.
1987 Resource Intensification Among Hunter-Gatherers: Acorn Economies in Prehistoric California. *Research in Economic Anthropology* 9:21–52.
1988 Archaeology of the Komodo Site, An Early Holocene Occupation in Central-Eastern California (The Archaeology of CA-MNO-679: A Pre-Archaic Site in Long Valley Caldera, Mono County, California). In *Early Human Occupation in Far Western North America: The Clovis Archaic Interface*, edited by J. A. Willig, C. M. Akins, and J. L. Fagan, pp. 103–119. Nevada State Museum Anthropological Papers no. 21.
1989 Obsidian Acquisition and Use in Prehistoric Central Eastern California: A Preliminary Assessment. In *Current Directions in California Obsidian Studies*, edited by R. E. Hughes, pp. 111–124. Contributions of the University of California Archaeological Research Facility 48.
1993a Early Holocene Prehistory of the North-Central Mojave Desert. Ph.D. dissertation, Department of Anthropology, University of California, Davis.
1993b *The Archaeology of Nelson Basin and Adjacent Areas, Fort Irwin, San Bernardino County, California.* Report submitted to the Department of the Army, Corps of Engineers, Los Angeles.
1993c Chronological Sequences in the Southern North Coast Ranges, California. In *There Grows a Green Tree: Papers in Honor of David A. Fredrickson*, edited by G. White, P. Mikkelsen, W. R. Hildebrandt and M. E. Basgall, pp. 167–196. Center for Archaeological Research at Davis no. 11. University of California, Davis.
1995 Obsidian Hydration Dating of Early Holocene Assemblages in the Mojave Desert. *Current Research in the Pleistocene* 12:57–60.
1999 Comment on *Environmental Imperatives Reconsidered: Demographic Crises in Western North America During the Medieval Climatic Anomaly,* by T. L. Jones, G. M. Brown, L. M. Raab, J. L. McVickar, W. G. Spaulding, D. J. Kennett, A. York, and P. L. Walker. *Current Anthropology* 40:157–158.
2000a Patterns of Toolstone Use in Late-Pleistocene/Early-Holocene Assemblages of the Mojave Desert. *Current Research in the Pleistocene* 17:4–6.
2000b The Structure of Archaeological Landscapes in the North-Central Mojave Desert. In *Archaeological Passages: A Volume in Honor of Claude Nelson Warren*, edited by J. S. Schneider, R. M. Yohe II, and J. K. Gardner, pp. 123–138. Western Center for Archaeology and Paleontology Publications in Archaeology 1.
2003a *Eligibility Assessments for Eight Prehistoric Archaeological Sites at Camp Roberts, Camp San Luis Obispo, and Monterey Counties, California.* Archaeological Research Center, California State University, Sacramento. Copies available from South Central Archaeological Information Center, Department of Anthropology, University of California, Santa Barbara.
2003b *Further Archaeological Assessments in Deadman Lake Basin, Marine Corps Air Ground Combat Center, Twentynine Palms, California.* Report submitted to the Department of the Army, Corps on Engineers, Sacramento.
2004a *Archaeological Assessment of Two Early Holocene Sites in the Noble Pass Training Area, Marine Corps Air Ground Combat Center, Twentynine Palms, California: Evaluation of CA-SBR-9577 and SBR-9578.* Report submitted to the Department of the Army, Corps of Engineers, Sacramento.
2004b *The Archaeology of Charlie Range Basalt Ridge: An Initial Assessment of the CA-INY-5825 Locality, Naval Air Weapons Station, Inyo County, California.* Report submitted to the Naval Air Weapons Station, China Lake.
2005a *Another Look at the Ancient Californians: Resurvey of the Emma Lou Davis Stake Areas and Reassessment of Collections, Naval Air Weapons Station, China Lake, Kern County, California.* Report submitted to the Naval Air Weapons Station, China Lake.
2005b *Further Archaeological Survey of the Lake China Basin, Naval Air Weapons Station, China Lake, California.* Report submitted to the Naval Air Weapons Station, China Lake.
2006 An Environmental Assessment of Late-Holocene Environmental Change in the Southwestern Great Basin. In *From Avocados to Millingstones: Papers in Honor of Delbert L. True,* edited by M. E. Basgall and G. Waugh. Monographs in California and Great Basin Anthropology. California State University, Sacramento. In press.

Basgall, M. E., and P. B. Bouey
1991 *The Prehistory of North-Central Sonoma County: Archaeology of the Warm Springs, Dam-Lake Sonoma Locality.* Vol. 1. U.S. Army Corps of Engineers, Sacramento. Report on file, Northwest Information Center, Department of Anthropology, Sonoma State University, Rohnert Park, California.

Basgall, M. E., and M. G. Delacorte
2003 *Phase II Evaluations at Nine Archaeological Sites Near Independence, Inyo County, California.* ARC Technical Report 02-59. Archaeological Research Center, Department of Anthropology, California State University, Sacramento.

Basgall, M. E., and M. A. Giambastiani
1999 *Draft Report Muddle in the Middle: Phase II Test Excavations of Five Sites (CA-KER-1304, KER-4620, KER-4621, KER-4622, and KER-4623/H): Kern County, California.* Archaeological Research Center, Department of Anthropology, California State University, Sacramento. Copies available from California Department of Transportation, San Luis Obispo.
2000 *An Archaeological Evaluation of 13 Locations in the Deadman Lake Basin, Marine Corps Air Ground Combat Center, Twentynine Palms, California.* Report submitted to the Department of the Army, Corps of Engineers, Los Angeles.

Basgall, M. E., and M. C. Hall
1991 Relationships Between Fluted and Stemmed Points in the Mojave Desert. *Current Research in the Pleistocene* 8:61–64.
1992 Fort Irwin Archaeology: Emerging Perspectives on Mojave Desert Prehistory. *Society for California Archaeology Newsletter* 26(5):1–7.
1993a Conventional Wisdom as "Alternative Perspective" on Mojave Desert Prehistory? *Society for California Archaeology Newsletter* 27(6):4–8.
1993b *Archaeology of the Awl Site, CA-SBR-4562, Fort Irwin, San Bernardino County, California.* Report submitted to the Department of the Army, Corps of Engineers, Los Angeles.
1994 *Archaeological Investigations at Goldstone (CA-SBR-2348): A Middle Holocene Occupation Complex in the North-central Mojave Desert, California.* Report submitted to the Department of the Army, National Training Center, Fort Irwin.
2000 Morphological and Temporal Variation in Bifurcate-Stemmed Dart Points of the Western Great Basin. *Journal of California and Great Basin Anthropology* 22:237–276.

Basgall, M. E., and W. Hildebrandt
1989 *Prehistory of the Sacramento River Canyon, Shasta County, California, at CA-SHA-1176, SHA-1175, SHA-476.* Center

for Archaeological Research at Davis no. 9. University of California, Davis.

Basgall, M. E., and K. R. McGuire
1988 *The Archaeology of CA-INY-30: Prehistoric Culture Change in the Southern Owens Valley, California.* Report submitted to the California Department of Transportation, Sacramento.

Basgall, M. E., and S. A. Overly
2004 *Prehistoric Archaeology of the Rosamond Lake Basin: Phase II Cultural Resource Evaluations at 41 Sites in Management Region 2, Edwards Air Force Base, California.* Report submitted to the Department of the Army, Corps of Engineers, Sacramento.

Basgall, M. E., and W. Pierce
2004 *Archeological Assessment of Four Prehistoric Sites in the Acorn Training Area, Marine Corps Air Ground Combat Center, Twentynine Palms, California.* Report submitted to the Department of the Army, Corps of Engineers, Fort Worth.

Basgall, M. E., and D. L. True
1985 *Archaeological Investigations in Crowder Canyon, 1973–1984: Excavations at sites SBR-421B, SBR-421C, SBR-421D, and SBR-713, San Bernardino County California.* Report prepared for the California Department of Transportation, District 8, San Bernardino.

Basgall, M. E., M. C. Hall, and K. R. McGuire
1988 *The Late Holocene Archaeology of Drinkwater Basin, Fort Irwin, San Bernardino, California.* Report on file, San Bernardino County Archaeological Information Center, San Bernardino County Museum, Redlands.

Basgall, M. E., L. Johnson, and M. Hale
2003 *An Evaluation of Four Archeological Sites in the Lead Mountain Training Area, Marine Corps Air Ground Combat Center, Twentynine Palms, California.* Report submitted to the Department of the Army, Corps of Engineers, Sacramento.

Batchelder, G.
1970 Post-glacial Ecology at Black Lake, Mono County. Ph.D. dissertation, Arizona State University.

Baumhoff, M. A.
1955 Excavations at Site TEH-1 (Kingsley Cave). *University of California Archaeological Survey Reports* 30:40–73.
1963 Ecological Determinants of Aboriginal California Populations. *University of California Publications in American Archaeology and Ethnology* 49:155–336.
1978 Environmental Background. In *California*, edited by R. F. Heizer, pp. 16–24. Handbook of North American Indians. Vol. 8. William C. Sturtevant, general editor. Smithsonian Institution, Washington, D.C.
1980 The Evolution of Pomo Society. *Journal of California and Great Basin Anthropology* 2:175–185.

Baumhoff, M. A., and J. S. Byrne
1959 Desert Side-notched Points as a Time Marker in California. *University of California Archaeological Survey Reports* 48:32–65. University of California, Berkeley.

Baumhoff, M. A., and D. L. Olmsted
1963 Palaihnihan: Radiocarbon Support for Glottochronology. *American Anthropologist* 65:278–284.
1964 Notes on Palaihnihan Culture History: Glottochronology and Archaeology. *University of California Publications in Linguistics* 34:1–12. Berkeley, California.

Bayham, F. E., and N. Valente
1995 The Vertebrate Archaeofauna: Prehistoric Animal Use in the Pit River Drainage. In *Prehistory of the Middle Pit River, Northeastern California: Archaeological Investigations at Lake Britton, Pit 3, 4 & 5 Project.* Vol. 1, edited by J. H. Cleland. Report submitted to Pacific Gas and Electric Company, San Francisco.

Bayman, J. M., R. H. Hevly, B. Johnson, K. J. Reinhard, and R. Ryan
1996 Analytical Perspectives on a Protohistoric Cache of Ceramic Jars from the Lower Colorado Desert. *Journal of California and Great Basin Anthropology* 18:131–154.

Bean, L. J., and H. W. Lawton
1973 Some Explanations for the Rise of Cultural Complexity in Native California with Comments on Proto-Agriculture and Agriculture. In *Patterns of Indian Burning in California: Ecology and Ethno-history*, edited by H. Lewis, pp. v–xvii. Ballena Press Anthropological Papers 1. Ramona, California.
1976 Some Explanations for the Rise of Cultural Complexity in Native California with Comments on Proto-Agriculture and Agriculture. In *Native Californians: A Theoretical Retrospective,* edited by L. J. Bean and T. C. Blackburn, pp. 7–30. Ballena Press, Ramona, California.

Bean, L. J., and W. M. Mason
1962 *The Romero Expeditions, 1823–1826.* Ward Ritchie Press, Los Angeles.

Bean, L. J., and F. C. Shipek
1978 Luiseño. In *California*, edited by Robert F. Heizer, pp 550–563. Handbook of North American Indians. Vol. 8. W. C. Sturtevant, general editor. Smithsonian Institution, Washington, D.C.

Bean, L. J., and C. R. Smith
1978 Gabrielino. In *California*, edited by R. F. Heizer, pp. 538–549. Handbook of North American Indians. Vol. 8. W. C. Sturtevant, general editor. Smithsonian Institution, Washington, D.C.

Bean, L. J., J. Schaefer, and S. Brakke Vane
1995 *Archaeological, Ethnographic, and Ethnohistoric Investigations at Tahquitz Canyon, Palm Springs, California.* Prepared by Cultural Systems Research, Menlo Park, California, for Riverside County Flood Control and Water Conservation District.

Beardsley, R. K.
1948 Culture Sequences in Central California Archaeology. *American Antiquity* 14:1–28.
1954 Temporal and Areal Relationships in Central California Archaeology. *University of California Archaeological Survey Reports* 24:1–62; 25:63–131.
1955 Functional and Evolutionary Implications of Community Patterning. *Memoirs of the Society for American Archaeology* 2:131–151.

Beaton, J. M.
1991a Colonizing Continents: Some Problems from Australia and the Americas. In *The First Americans: Search and Research*, edited by D. Meltzer and T. Dillehay, pp. 209–230. CRC Press, Boca Raton.
1991b Paleoindian Occupation Greater than 11,000 years BP at Tule Lake, Northern California. *Current Research in the Pleistocene* 8:5–7.
1991c Extensification and Intensification in Central California Prehistory. *Antiquity* 65:946–952.

Beck, C., and G. T. Jones
1994 Dating Surface Assemblages Using Obsidian Hydration. In *Dating in Exposed and Surface Contexts*, edited by C. Beck, pp. 47–76. University of New Mexico Press, Albuquerque.
1997 The Terminal Pleistocene/Early Holocene Archaeology of the Great Basin. *Journal of World Prehistory* 11:161–236.

Becker, K. M.
2003 Invertebrate Faunal Remains. In *At the Base of the Bluff, Archaeological Inventory and Evaluation Along Lower Centinela Creek, Marina del Rey, California*, edited by J. H. Altschul, A. Q. Stoll, D. R. Grenda, and R. Ciolek-Torello, pp. 179–200. Playa Vista Monograph Series Test Excavation Report 4. Statistical Research, Tucson.

Bedwell, S.
1970 Prehistory and Environment of the Pluvial Fort Rock Lake Area of Southcentral Oregon. Ph.D. dissertation, Department of Anthropology, University of Oregon, Eugene.
1973 *Fort Rock Basin: Prehistory and Environment.* University of Oregon Books, Eugene, Oregon.

Bellifemine, V.
1997 Mortuary Variability in Prehistoric Central California: A Statistical Study of the Yukisma Site, CA-SCL-38. Master's thesis, Department of Interdisciplinary Studies, San Jose State University, California.

Bennyhoff, J. A.
1950 Californian Fish Spears and Harpoons. *University of California Anthropological Records* 9:295–338.
1977 *Ethnogeography of the Plains Miwok.* Center for Archaeological Research at Davis Publication no. 5. University of California, Davis.
1986 The Emeryville Site, Viewed 93 Years Later. In *Symposium: A New Look at Some Old Sites,* edited by G. S. Breschini and T. Haversat, pp. 65–75. Archives of California Prehistory 6. Coyote Press, Salinas.
1994a The Napa District and Wappo Prehistory. In *Toward a New Taxonomic Framework for Central California Archaeology: Essays by James A. Bennyhoff and David A. Fredrickson,* edited by R. E. Hughes, pp. 49–56. Contributions to the University of California Archaeological Research Facility 52, Berkeley.
1994b Central California Augustine: Implications for Northern California Archaeology. In *Toward a New Taxonomic Framework for Central California Archaeology: Essays by James A. Bennyhoff and David A. Fredrickson*, edited by R. E. Hughes, pp. 65–74. Contributions of the University of California Archaeological Research Facility 52, Berkeley.
1994c A Delta Intrusion to the Bay in the Late Middle Period in Central California. In *Toward a New Taxonomic Framework for Central California Archaeology: Essays by James A. Bennyhoff and David A. Fredrickson*, edited by R. E. Hughes, pp. 7–13. Contributions of the University of California Archaeological Research Facility no. 52.
1994d Variation Within the Meganos Culture. In *Toward a New Taxonomic Framework for Central California Archaeology: Essays by James A. Bennyhoff and David A. Fredrickson*, edited by R. E. Hughes, pp. 81–89. Contributions of the University of California Archaeological Research Facility no. 52.

Bennyhoff, J. A., and D. Fredrickson
1994 A Proposed Integrative Taxonomic System for Central California Archaeology. In *Toward a New Taxonomic Framework for Central California Archaeology: Essays by James A. Bennyhoff and David A. Fredrickson*, edited by R. E. Hughes, pp. 15–24. Contributions of the University of California Archaeological Research Facility 52, Berkeley.

Bennyhoff, J. A., and R. F. Heizer
1958 Cross-Dating Great Basin Sites by Californian Shell Beads. *University of California Archaeological Survey Reports* 42:60–92.

Bennyhoff, J. A., and R. E. Hughes
1987 Shell Bead and Ornament Exchange Networks Between California and the Western Great Basin. *Anthropological Papers of the American Museum of Natural History* 64:79–175.

Benson, L. V.
2004 Western Lakes. In *The Quaternary Period of the United States*, edited by A. Gillespie, S. Porter and N. Atwater, pp. 185–204. Elsevier, Amsterdam.

Benson, L. V., D. R. Curry, R. I. Dorn, K. R. Lajoie, C. G. Oviatt, S. W. Robinson, G. I. Smith, and S. Stine
1990 Chronology of Expansion and Contraction of Four Great Basin Lake Systems During the Past 35,000 years. *Paleogeography, Paleoclimatology, Paleoecology* 78:241–286.

Benson, L. V., M. Kashgarian, R. Rye, S. Lund, F. Paillet, J. Smoot, C. Kester, S. Mensing, D. Meko, and S. Lindström
2002 Holocene Multidecadal and Multicentennial Droughts Affecting Northern California and Nevada. *Quaternary Science Reviews* 21:659–682.

Berger, A. L., J. Imbrie, J. Hays, G. Kukla, and B. Saltzman (editors)
1984 *Milankovitch and Climate, Part 1.* D. Reidel Publishers, Dordrecht.

Berger, R.
1982 The Wooley Mammoth Site, Santa Rosa Island, California. In *Peopling of the New World*, edited by J. E. Ericson, R. E. Taylor, and R. Berger, pp. 163–170. Anthropological Papers 23, Ballena Press.

Berger, R., and P. C. Orr
1966 The Fire Areas on Santa Rosa Island, California, II. *Proceedings of the National Academy of Sciences* 56:1678–1682.

Berger, R., and R. Protsch
1989 UCLA Radiocarbon Dates XI. *Radiocarbon* 31:55–67.

Berger, R., R. Protsch, R. Reynolds, C. Rozaire, and J. R. Sackett
1971 New Radiocarbon Dates Based on Bone Collagen of California Indians. *Contributions of the University of California Archaeological Research Facility* 12:43–49. Los Angeles.

Bergquist, J. R.
1977 Depositional History and Fault-related Studies, Bolinas Lagoon, California. Ph.D. dissertation, Department of Geology, Stanford University.
1978 Depositional History and Fault-related Studies, Bolinas Lagoon, California. *U.S. Geological Survey Open-File Reports* 78–802:164.

Bergthold, J. C.
1982 The Prehistoric Settlements and Trade Models in the Santa Clara Valley, California. Masters thesis, Department of Anthropology, California State University, San Francisco.

Berman, H.
1984 Proto-Algonquian-Ritwan Verbal Roots. *International Journal of American Linguistics* 50:335–342.
1990 New Algonquian-Ritwan Cognate Sets. *International Journal of American Linguistics* 56:431–434.
1996 The Position of Molala in Plateau Penutian. *International Journal of American Linguistics* 62:1–30.

Bernard, J. L.
2001 The Origins of Open-Ocean and Large Species Fishing in the Chumash Region of Southern California. Master's thesis, Department of Anthropology, University of California, Los Angeles.
2004 Status and the Swordfish, the Origins of Large-Species Fishing Among the Chumash. In *Foundations of Chumash Complexity*, edited by J. E. Arnold, pp. 25–51. Cotsen Institute of Archaeology, University of California, Los Angeles.

Bertrando, E. B.
2000 *Phase 3 Cultural Resource Mitigation (Data Recovery, Capping, and Monitoring)(CA-SLO-1212), APN:074-302-016; 02021; 022, Los Osos Valley Road, Los Osos.* Bertrando and Bertrando Research Consultants, San Luis Obispo. Copies available from South Central Archaeological Information Center, Department of Anthropology, University of California, Santa Barbara.
2004a *Phase 3 Data Recovery and Mitigation of CA-SLO-1795, 1319 Los Osos Valley Road, Los Osos, California.* Bertrando and Bertrando Research Consultants, San Luis Obispo. Copies available from South Central Archaeological Information Center, Department of Anthropology, University of California, Santa Barbara.
2004b Evidence and Models for Late Pleistocene Chronology and Settlement Along California's Central Coast. In *Emerging from the Ice Age: Early Holocene Occupations on the California Central Coast*, edited by Ethan Betrando and Valerie A. Levulett, pp. 93–105. San Luis Obispo County Archaeological Society Occasional Papers no. 17.

Bertrando, E. B., and V. A. Levulett (editors)
2004 Emerging from the Ice Age—Early Holocene Occupations on Californi's Central Coast: A *Compilation of Research in Honor*

of Roberta S. Greenwood. San Luis Obispo County Archaeological Society Occasional Papers no. 17.

Betancourt, J. L., T. R. Van Devender, and P. S. Martin
1990 *Packrat Middens: The Last 40,000 Years of Biotic Change*. University of Arizona Press, Tucson.

Bettinger, R. L.
1982 Aboriginal Exchange and Territoriality in Owens Valley, California. In *Contexts for Prehistoric Exchange*, edited by J. E. Ericson and T. K. Earle, pp. 103-127. Academic Press, New York.
1989 The Archaeology of Pinyon House, Two Eagles, and Crater Middens: Three Residential Sites in Owens Valley, Eastern California. *Anthropological Papers of the American Museum of Natural History* 67.
1991 *Hunter-Gatherers: Archaeological and Evolutionary Theory*. Plenum Press, New York.
1999a From Traveler to Processor: Regional Trajectories of Hunter-Gatherer Sedentism in the Inyo-Mono Region, California. In *Settlement Pattern Studies in the Americas: Fifty Years Since Virú*, edited by B. R. Billman and G. M. Feinman, pp. 39–55. Smithsonian Institution, Washington, D.C.
1999b Comment on *Environmental Imperatives Reconsidered: Demographic Crises in Western North America During the Medieval Climatic Anomaly*, by T. L. Jones, G. M. Brown, L. M. Raab, J. L. McVickar, W. G. Spaulding, D. J. Kennett, A. York, and P. L. Walker. *Current Anthropology* 40:158–159.

Bettinger, R. L., and M. A. Baumhoff
1982 The Numic Spread: Great Basin Cultures in Competition. *American Antiquity* 47:485–503.

Betts, J., and D. G. Foster
2001 *Investigations of the Coalinga Archaeological Research Group 1988 to 1994*. California Department of Forestry Archaeological Reports no.29. Sacramento.

Bever, M., J. Holson, K. Killackey, W. Allen, and K. Bartoy
2004 *Data Recovery Excavation at Two Prehistoric Archaeological Sites on Cachuma Reservoir, Santa Barbara County, California*. Report on file, South Central Information Center, Department of Anthropology, University of California, Santa Barbara.

Bevill, R. W.
2004 Obsidian Hydration: The Squaw Creek Site Revisited. *Proceedings of the Society for California Archaeology* 17:133–138.

Bickel, P. M.
1976 Toward a Prehistory of the San Francisco Bay Area: The Archaeology of Sites Ala-328, Ala-13, and Ala-12. Ph.D. dissertation, Department of Anthropology, Harvard University. University Microfilms, Ann Arbor.
1978 Changing Sea Levels Along the California Coast: Anthropological Implications. *Journal of California Anthropology* 5:6–20.

Bieling, D. G.
1996 "Obsidian Studies." In *Archaeological Excavations and Burial Removal at Sites CA-ALA-483, CA-ALA-483 Extension, and CA-ALA-555, Alameda County, California*, edited by Randy S. Wiberg. Holman and Associates, San Francisco. Submitted to David Homes, Walnut Creek. Copies available from Northwest Information Center, Sonoma State University, Rohnert Park.
1997 "Obsidian Studies." In *Archaeological Investigations at Site CA-ALA-42 Alameda County, California: Final Report*, edited by Randy S. Wiberg, pp. 67–82. Holman and Associates, San Francisco. Submitted to Standard Pacific of Northern California, Pleasanton. Copies available from Northwest Information Center, Sonoma State University, Rohnert Park.
1998 *Archaeological Investigations at CA-MRN-254, the Dominican College Site, San Rafael, Marin County, California*. Holman and Associates, San Francisco. Submitted to Dominican College, San Rafael, California. Submitted to Davidon Homes, Walnut Creek, California. Copies available from Northwest Information Center, Department of Anthropology, Sonoma State University, Rohnert Park, California.

Bieling, D. G., R. M. LaJeunesse, and J. H. Pryor
1996 Skyrocket: A Central Sierran Paleoindian Archaic Transition Site. *Current Research in the Pleistocene* 13:4–6.

Binford, L. R.
1980 Willow Smoke and Dogs' Tails: Hunter-Gatherer Settlement Systems and Archaeological Site Formation. *American Antiquity* 45:4–20.

Bischoff, J. L., R. Merriam, W. M. Childers, and R. Protsch
1976 Antiquity of Man in America Indicated by Radiometric Dates on the Yuha Burial Site. *Nature* 261:128–129.

Blackburn, T. C.
1975 *December's Child: A Book of Chumash Oral Narratives Collected by J. P. Harrington*. University of California Press, Berkeley.

Blackburn, T. C., and K. Anderson
1993 *Before the Wilderness: Environmental Management by Native Californians*. Ballena Press, Menlo Park, CA.

Bleed, P.
2002 Cheap, Regular, and Reliable: Implications of Design Variation in Late Pleistocene Japanese Microblade Technology. In *Thinking Small: Global Perspectives on Microlithization*, edited by R. G. Elston and S. L. Kuhn, pp. 95–102. Archaeological Papers of the American Anthropological Association no. 12.

Bloom, A. L.
1983 Sea Level and Coastal Changes. In *The Holocene*, edited by H. E. Wright Jr., pp. 42–51. Late Quaternary Environments of the United States. Vol. 2. University of Minnesota Press, Minneapolis.

Bloomer, W. W.
2005 Flaked Stone. In *Final Report: Archaeological Evaluation and Mitigative Data Recovery at CA-YOL-69, Madison Aggregate Plant, Yolo County, California*, edited by R. S. Wiberg, pp. 10–27. Holman and Associates Archaeological Consultants, San Francisco. Submitted to Solano Concrete Company, Fairfield. Copies available from Northwest Information Center, Department of Anthropology, Sonoma State University, Rohnert Park, California.

Bloomer, W. W., J. Betts, and S. Lindström
2002 *'itdiyu* (ovens) in the Wašiw Sierra. *Proceedings of the Society for California Archaeology* 15:94–101.

Bloomer, W. W., S. A. Waechter, and S. Lindström
1997 *Basalt Quarrying on Watson Creek: An Archaeological and Ethnographic Study in the Northern Lake Tahoe Basin*. Vol. 1. Prepared for the U.S. Forest Service, Lake Tahoe Basin Management Unit, South Lake Tahoe, California.

Blytt, A.
1876 Essay on the Immigration of the Norwegian Flora During Alternating Rainy and Dry Periods. Cammermeyer, Christiania (Oslo).

Bocek, B.
1986 Rodent Ecology and Burrowing Behavior: Predicted Effects on Archaeological Site Formation. *American Antiquity* 51:589–603.
1990 Prehistoric Settlement Pattern and Social Organization on the San Francisco Peninsula, California. In *Between Bands and States*, edited by S. Gregg, pp. 58–88. Southern Illinois University Center for Archaeological Investigations, Carbondale.
1992 Subsistence, Settlement, and Tribelet Territories on the Eastern San Francisco Peninsula. *Proceedings of the Society for California Archaeology* 5:269–298.

Boldurian, A. T., and J. L. Cotter
1999 *Clovis Revisited: New Perspectives on Paleoindian Adaptations from Blackwater Draw, New Mexico*. University Museum Monograph 103. University of Pennsylvania Museum.

Bolton, H. E.
1930 *Anza's California Expeditions.* Vols. 1–5. University of California Press, Berkeley.
Bonnichsen, R., B. T. Lepper, D. Stanford, and M. R. Waters (editors)
2005 *Paleoamerican Origins: Beyond Clovis.* Center for the Study of the First Americans. Texas A&M University. College Station, Texas.
Bouey, P. D.
1995 *Final Report on the Archaeological Analysis of CA-SAC-43, Cultural Resources Mitigation for the Sacramento Urban Area Levee Reconstruction Project, Sacramento County, California.* Far Western Anthropological Research Group, Davis. Report on file, North Central Information Center, Department of Anthropology, California State University, Sacramento.
Bouey, P. D., and M. E. Basgall
1984 Trans-Sierran Exchange in Prehistoric California: The Concept of Economic Articulation. In *Obsidian Studies in the Great Basin*, edited by R. E. Hughes, pp. 135–172. Contributions of the University of California Archaeological Research Facility 45.
1991 *Archaeological Patterns Along the South Coast, Point Piedras Blancas, San Luis Obispo, California: Archaeological Test Evaluations of Sites CA-SLO-264, SLO-266, SLO-267, SLO-268, SLO-1226, and SLO-1227.* Far Western Anthropological Research Group, Davis, California. Copies available from California Department of Transportation, San Luis Obispo.
Bouey, P. D., and S. A. Waechter
1992 Final Report on Phase II Test Excavations at CA-SAC-133 Near Sloughhouse, Sacramento County, California. Far Western Anthropological Research Group, Davis. Submitted to the California Department of Transportation, District 3, Marysville.
Bowen, A. J., and D. L. Inman
1966 *Budget of Littoral Sands in the Vicinity of Point Arguello, California.* U.S. Army Corps of Engineers, Technical Memorandum 19, Coastal Engineering Research Center, Washington, D.C.
Brace, C. L., A. R. Nelson, and P. Qifeng
2004 Peopling of the New World: A Comparative Craniofacial View. In *The Settlement of the American Continents*, edited by C. Michael Barton, Geoffrey A. Clark, David R. Yesner, and Georges A. Pearson, pp. 28–38. University of Arizona Press, Tucson.
Bracher, K.
1984 Appendix B: Comments on Celestial Representations in Rock Art at Indian Creek. Papers on Chumash Rock Art. San Luis Obispo County Archaeological Society Occasional Papers no. 12.
Bradbury, A.
1997 The Bow and Arrow in the Eastern Woodlands: Evidence for an Archaic Origin. *North American Archaeologist* 18:207–233.
Bradbury, J. P., and R. M. Forester
2002 Environment and Paleolimnology of Owens Lake, California: A Record of Climate and Hydrology for the Past 50,000 Years. In *Great Basin Aquatic Systems History: Smithsonian Contributions to the Earth Sciences* no. 33, edited by R. Hershler, D. B. Madsen, and D. R. Currey, pp. 145–174. Smithsonian Institute, Washington, D.C.
Bradley, B. A.
1993 Paleo-Indian Flaked Stone Technology in the North American High Plains. In *from Kostenki to Clovis, Upper Paleolithic–Paleo-Indian Adaptations*, edited by O. Soffer and N. D. Parslov, pp. 251–262. Plenum Press, New York.
Bradley, B. A., and D. Stanford
2004 The North Atlantic Ice-edge Corridor: A Possible Palaeolithic Route to the New World. *World Archaeology* 36:459–478.
Bradley, R. S., M. K. Hughes, and H. F. Diaz
2003 Climate in Medieval Time. *Science* 302:404–405.
Braje, T., J. M. Erlandson, and T. C. Rick
2005a Reassessing Human Settlement on the South Coast of San Miguel Island, California: The Use of ^{14}C Dating as a Reconnaissance Tool. *Radiocarbon. In press.*
2005b An 8700 Year Old Shell Midden from the South Coast of San Miguel Island, California. *Current Research in the Pleistocene. In press.*
Breschini, G. S.
1983 *Models of Population Movements in Central California Prehistory.* Coyote Press, Salinas.
Breschini, G. S., and T. Haversat
1980 *Preliminary Archaeological Report and Archaeological Management Recommendations for CA-MNT-170, on Pescadero Point, Monterey County, California.* Archaeological Consulting, Salinas, California. Copies available from Northwest Information Center, Department of Anthropology, Sonoma State University, Rohnert Park, California.
1987 Archaeological Investigations at CA-FRE-1333. In the White Creek Drainage, Western Fresno County, California. *Archives of California Prehistory* 12:1–101. Coyote Press, Salinas.
1988 *Archaeological Investigations at CA-SLO-7 and CA-SLO-8, Diablo Canyon, San Luis Obispo County, California.* Archives of California Prehistory 28. Coyote Press, Salinas.
1989a *Archaeological Investigations at CA-MNT-108 at Fisherman's Wharf, Monterey, Monterey County, California.* Archives of California Prehistory 29. Coyote Press, Salinas.
1989b *Preliminary Archaeological Report and Archaeological Management Recommendations for CA-SLO-129, Cayucos, San Luis Obispo County, California.* Copies available from South Central Archaeological Information Center, Department of Anthropology, University of California, Santa Barbara.
1991a Early Holocene Occupation of the Central California Coast. In *Hunter-Gatherers of Early Holocene Coastal California*, edited by J. M. Erlandson and R. H. Colten, pp. 125–132. Cotsen Institute of Archaeology, University of California, Los Angeles.
1991b Archaeological Investigations at Three Late Period Coastal Abalone Processing Sites on the Monterey Peninsula, California. *Archives of California Prehistory* 33:31–62. Coyote Press, Salinas.
1992 *Baseline Archaeological Studies at Rancho San Carlos, Carmel Valley, Monterey County, California.* Archaeological Consulting, Salinas, California. Copies available from Northwest Information Center, Department of Anthropology, Sonoma State University, Rohnert Park, California.
1994 Rumsen Seasonality and Population Dynamics. In *The Ohlone Past and Present: Native Americans of the San Francisco Bay Region*, edited by L. J. Bean, 193–202. Ballena Press, Menlo Park.
1995a *Archaeological Evaluation of CA-MNT-234, at the site of the proposed Moss Landing Marine Laboratory, Moss Landing, Monterey County, California.* Archaeological Consulting, Salinas, California. Copies available from Northwest Information Center, Department of Anthropology, Sonoma State University, Rohnert Park, California.
1995b *Additional Archaeological Investigations Prepared as a Supplement to Phase II Cultural Resources Investigations for the New Los Padres Dam and Reservoir Project, Carmel Valley, Monterey County, California.* Archaeological Consulting, Salinas, California. Copies available from Northwest Information Center, Department of Anthropology, Sonoma State University, Rohnert Park, California.
2000 *Archaeological Data Recovery at CA-SCR-44 at the Site of the Lakeview Middle School, Watsonville, Santa Cruz County, California.* Archives of California Prehistory 49. Coyote Press, Salinas.
2002 *Report on Archaeological Monitoring for a Portion of CA-MNT-831, Pacific Grove, Monterey County, California.*

Archaeological Consulting, Salinas, California. Copies available from Northwest Information Center, Department of Anthropology, Sonoma State University, Rohnert Park, California.
2003a *Report on Archaeological Investigations for Portions of CA-MNT-1612, Pacific Grove, Monterey County, California.* Archaeological Consulting, Salinas, California. Copies available from Northwest Archaeological Information Center, Department of Anthropology, Sonoma State University, Rohnert Park, California.
2003b *Archaeological Test Excavation of CA-SCR-151 on Assessor's Parcel 034-046-001, Capitola, Santa Cruz County, California.* Limited distribution technical paper prepared by Archaeological Consulting, Salinas, California.
2003c *Archaeological Evaluation of a Portion of CA-MNT-1935, on Assessor's Parcel 007-031-016, Pacific Grove, Monterey County California.* Archaeological Consulting, Salinas, California. Copies available from Northwest Archaeological Information Center, Department of Anthropology, Sonoma State University, Rohnert Park, California.
2004 *The Esselen Indians of the Big Sur Country: The Land and the People.* Coyote Press, Salinas.
2005a *Draft Report Exploring Coast Interior Relationships in the Monterey Ranger District Los Padres National Forest.* Archaeological Consulting, Salinas. Prepared for the Los Padres National Forest, Goleta. Copies available from Archaeological Consulting, Salinas.
2005b Radiocarbon Dating and Cultural Models on the Monterey Peninsula, California. *Pacific Coast Archaeological Society Quarterly.* In press.

Breschini, G. S., T. Haversat, and K. Carlisle
2003 *Report on Archaeological Investigations for Portions of CA-MNT-1612, Pacific Grove, Monterey County, California.* Limited distribution technical paper prepared by Archaeological Consulting, Salinas, California.

Breschini, G. S., T. Haversat, and J. M. Erlandson (compilers and editors)
2004 *California Radiocarbon Dates: An Online Data Base.* Coyote Press, Salinas. www.californiaprehistory.com/radiodb1.html.

Brewster, A., B. F. Byrd, and S. N. Reddy
2003 Cultural Landscapes of Coastal Foragers: An example of GIS and Drainage Catchment Analysis from Southern California. *Journal of GIS in Archaeology* 1:48–60.

Brigham-Grette, J., A. V. Lozhkin, P. M. Anderson, and O. Y. Glushkova
2004 Paleoenvironmental Conditions in Western Beringia Before and During the Last Glacial Maximum. In *Entering America,* edited by D. B. Madsen, pp. 29–61. University of Utah Press, Salt Lake City.

Bright, W.
1956 Glottochronologic Counts of Hokaltecan Material. *Language* 32:42–48.
1976 *Variation and Change in Language: Essays by William Bright.* Stanford University Press, Palo Alto.

Bright, W. (editor)
1964 *Studies in Californian Linguistics.* University of California Publications in Linguistics 34.

Bright, W., and M. Bright
1969 Archaeology and Linguistics in Prehistoric Southern California. *University of Hawaii Working Papers in Linguistics* 1(10).
1976 Archaeology and Linguistics in Prehistoric Southern California. In *Variation and Change in Language: Essays by William Bright,* edited by A. S. Dil, pp. 189–205. Stanford University Press, Stanford.

Briles, C., C. Whitlock, and P. Bartlein
2005 Postglacial Vegetation, Fire, and Climate History of the Siskiyou Mountains, Oregon, U.S.A. *Quaternary Research* 64:44–56.

Broadbent, S. M.
1972 The Rumsen of Monterey: An Ethnography from Historical Sources. *Contributions of the University of California Archaeological Research Facility* 14:45–94.

Brooks, S. R., R. H. Brooks, G. E. Kennedy, J. Austin, J. R. Firby, L. A. Payen, P. J. Slota Jr., C. A. Prior, and R. E. Taylor
1990 The Haverty Human Skeletons: Morphological, Depositional, and Geochronological Characteristics. *Journal of California and Great Basin Anthropology* 12:60–83.

Broughton, J. M.
1988 Archaeological Patterns of Prehistoric Fish Exploitation in the Sacramento Valley. Master's thesis, Department of Anthropology, California State University, Chico.
1994a Late Holocene Resource Intensification in the Sacramento River Valley, California: The Vertebrate Evidence. *Journal of Archaeological Science* 21:501–514.
1994b Declines in Mammalian Foraging Efficiency During the Late Holocene, San Francisco Bay. *Journal of Anthropological Archaeology* 13:371–401.
1997 Widening Diet Breadth, Declining Foraging Efficiency, and Prehistoric Harvest Pressure: Ichthyofaunal Evidence from the Emeryville Shellmound, California. *Antiquity* 71:845–862.
1999 Resource Depression and Intensification During the Late Holocene, San Francisco Bay: Evidence from the Emeryville Shellmound Vertebrate Fauna. *University of California Anthropological Records* 32.

Broughton, J. M., and F. E. Bayham
2003 Showing Off, Foraging Models, and the Ascendance of Large-Game Hunting in the California Middle Archaic. *American Antiquity* 68:783–789.

Broughton, J. M., and J. F. O'Connell
1999 On Evolutionary Ecology, Selectionist Archaeology, and Behavioral Archaeology. *American Antiquity* 64:153–165.

Brown, A. K.
1967 The Aboriginal Population of the Santa Barbara Channel. *University of California Archaeological Survey Reports* 69:1–99.
2001 *A Description of Distant Roads: Original Journals of the First Expedition into California 1769–1770 by Juan Crespi.* San Diego State University Press.

Brown, W. M., M. J. George, and A. C. Wilson
1979 Rapid Evolution of Animal Mitochondrial DNA. *Proceedings of the National Academy of Sciences of the United States of America* 76:1967–1971.

Bruenelle A., and R. S. Anderson
2003 Sedimentary Charcoal as an Indicator of Late-Holocene Drought in the Sierra Nevada, California, and Its Relevance to the Future. *Holocene* 13:21–28.

Bryne, S.
2002 *Archaeological Monitoring of the Wilder Ranch Bike Path Construction and Mitigation Related to Archaeological Site CA-SCR-38/123/H.* Garcia and Associates, San Anselmo, California. Copies available from Northwest Archaeological Information Center, Department of Anthropology, Sonoma State University, Rohnert Park, California.

Bryson, R. A., and F. K. Hare (editors)
1974 *Climates of North America.* Scientific Publishing, New York.

Bryson, R. U., R. A. Bryson, and L. M. Ramirez
1997 *Paleoclimates of the Northwestern Great Basin: Northeast California and Western Nevada. Tuscarora Natural Gas Pipeline Project.* Report prepared for Far Western Anthropological Research Group, Davis, California.

Budinger, F. E., Jr.
2004 The Calico Project at 40 Years: Questions Answered and Questions Still Unanswered. Paper presented at the Great Basin Anthropological Conference, Sparks, Nevada.

Burcham, L. T.
1957 *California Range Land*. California Division of Forestry, Sacramento.
Burton, R. K.
2000 Ecology of the Northern Fur Seal (*Callorhinus ursinus*) from the Middle and Late Holocene of California. Ph.D. dissertation, Department of Anthropology, University of California, Santa Cruz.
Burton, R. K., D. Gifford-Gonzalez, J. J. Snodgrass, and P. L. Koch
2002 Isotope Tracking of Prehistoric Pinniped Foraging and Distribution Along the Central California Coast: Preliminary Results. *International Journal of Osteoarchaeology* 12:4–11.
Burton, R. K., J. J. Snodgrass, D. Gifford-Gonzalez, T. Guilderson, T. Brown, and P. L. Koch
2001 Holocene Changes in the Ecology of Northern Fur Seals: Insights from Stable Isotopes and Archaeofauna. *Oecologia* 128:107–115.
Bury, R.
1999 Too Many Shamans: Ethics and Politics of Rock Art Interpretation. *American Indian Rock Art* 25:149–154.
Bury, R., A. Padgett, D. Reeves, and D. Robinson
2004 Incised Stone. In *Vandenberg Air Force Base Rock Art Survey and Inventory*, edited by R. Bury, A. Padgett, D. Reeves, and D. Robinson, pp. 7-1–7-58. Report on file, 30CES/CEVPC, Vandenberg Air Force Base, California.
Byers, D. A., and J. M. Broughton
2004 Holocene Environmental Change, Artiodactyl Abundances, and Human Hunting Strategies in the Great Basin. *American Antiquity* 69:235–256.
Byrd, B. F.
1998 Harvesting the Littoral Landscape During the Late Holocene: New Perspectives from Northern San Diego County. *Journal of California and Great Basin Anthropology* 20:195–218.
Byrd, B. F. (editor)
1996 *Coastal Archaeology of Las Flores Creek and Horno Canyon, Camp Pendleton, California*. ASM Affiliates, Carlsbad, California. Report on file, South Coast Information Center, San Diego State University.
1998 *Springs and Lakes in a Desert Landscape: Archaeological and Paleoenvironmental Investigations in the Silurian Valley and Adjacent Areas of Southeastern California*. ASM Affiliates, Carlsbad, California. Report submitted to Department of the Army, Corps of Engineers, Los Angeles.
2003 *Coastal Views of Prehistoric Middens: Archaeological Investigations and Paleoecological Reconstructions Along Las Flores Creek, Camp Pendleton, California*. ASM Affiliates, Carlsbad, California. Report on file, South Coast Information Center, San Diego State University.
Byrd, B. F., and S. Berryman
2006 Approaching Prehistory in the Future on Camp Pendleton, Southern California. *Proceedings of the Society for California Archaeology* 19. In press.
Byrd, B. F., and S. N. Reddy
1999 Collecting and Residing Near the Shore: The Role of Small and Large Sites in Settlement Reconstruction. *Pacific Coast Archaeological Society Quarterly* 35(1):33–56.
2002 Late Holocene Adaptations Along the Northern San Diego Coastline: New Perspectives on Old Paradigms. In *Catalysts to Complexity: Late Holocene of the California Coast*, edited by J. Erlandson and T. L. Jones, pp. 41–62. Cotsen Institute of Archaeology, University of California, Los Angeles.
Byrd, B. F., K. O. Pope, and S. N. Reddy
2004 *Results of NSF-Funded Archaeological and Paleoenvironmental Investigation at San Elijo Lagoon, San Diego County, California*. ASM Affiliates, Carlsbad, California. Report on file, South Coastal Information Center, San Diego State University.
Byrne, R.
1978 Fossil Record Discloses Wildfire History. *California Agriculture* 10:13–14.
Byrne, R., D. Araki, and S. Peterson
1979 Report on Pollen Analysis of the Core from Tule Lake, Mono County, California. Report on file, Geography Department, University of California, Berkeley.
Byrne, R., J. Michaelsen, and A. Soutar
1977 Fossil Charcoal as a Measure of Wildfire Frequency in Southern California: A Preliminary Analysis. In *Proceedings of the Symposium on the Environmental Consequences of Fire and Fuel Management in Mediterranean Ecosystems*, pp. 361–367. General Technical Report WO-3, U.S. Department of Agriculture, Forest Service, Washington, D.C.
Callaghan, C. A.
1997 Evidence for Yok-Utian. *International Journal of American Linguistics* 63:18–64.
2001 More Evidence for Yok-Utian: A Reanalysis of the Dixon and Kroeber Sets. *International Journal of American Linguistics* 67:313–345.
Cameron, C.
1990 Engraved Stones of Orange County. *Proceedings of the Society for California Archaeology* 3:59–74.
Campbell, E. W. C.
1949 Two Ancient Archaeological Sites in the Great Basin. *Science* 109:340.
Campbell, E. W. C., and W. H. Campbell
1940 A Folsom Complex in the Great Basin. *Southwest Museum Masterkey* 14:7–11.
Campbell, E. W. C., W. H. Campbell, E. Antevs, C. E. Amsden, J. A. Barbieri, and F. D. Bode
1937 *The Archaeology of Pleistocene Lake Mojave*. Southwest Museum Papers no. 11.
Campbell, L.
1997 *American Indian Languages: The Historical Linguistics of Native America*. Oxford University Press, New York.
Campbell, L., and M. Mithun
1979 *The Languages of Native America: Historical and Comparative Assessment*. University of Texas Press, Austin.
Cane, M. A.
2005 The Evoluton of El Niño, Past and Future. *Earth and Planetary Science Letters* 230:227–240.
Cannon, M. D., and D. Meltzer
2004 Early Paleoindian Foraging: Examining the Faunal Evidence for Large Mammal Specialization and Regional Variability in Prey Choice. *Quaternary Science Reviews* 23:1955–1987.
Carlyle, S. W., R. L. Parr, M. G. Hayes, and D. H. O'Rourke
2000 Context of Maternal Lineages in the Greater Southwest. *American Journal of Physical Anthropology* 113:85–101.
Carpenter, D., D. Nicholson, and D. W. Zeanah
2004 *Draft Report Archaeological Evaluations of Twelve Prehistoric Properties on Camp San Luis Obispo and Camp Roberts, San Luis Obispo County, California*. Archaeological Research Center, Department of Anthropology, California State University, Sacramento. Copies available from Camp Roberts, California.
Carpenter, E.
1988 *Materials for the Study of Social Symbolism in Ancient and Tribal Art: A Record of Tradition and Continuity*. Vol. 2. Rock Foundation, New York.
Carpenter, K. L.
2002 Reversing the Trend: Late Holocene Subsistence Change in Northeastern California. In *Boundary Lands: Archaeological Investigations Along the California–Great Basin Interface*, edited by K. R. McGuire. Nevada State Museum Anthropological Papers no. 24. Carson City, Nevada.

Carpenter, K. L., and P. Mikkelsen
2005 *Lithic Production and Craft Specialization in the Middle Period: Data Recovery Excavations at CA-NAP-172.* Far Western Anthropological Research Group, Davis. Submitted to the State Water Resource Control Board, Sacramento, and the City of Calistoga. Copies available from Northwest Archaeological Information Center, Department of Anthropology, Sonoma State University, Rohnert Park, California.

Carrico, R. L., and P. Ainsworth
1980 *Archaeological Salvage at W-192A, Imperial Beach, California.* Westec Services, San Diego, California. Report on file, South Coast Information Center, San Diego State University.

Carrico, R. L., T. G. Cooley, and R. P. Case
2004 *Draft Final Archaeological Data Recovery Report for a Portion of CA-SDI-48 at Buildings 139 and 158, Naval Submarine Base, San Diego.* Mooney and Associates, San Diego. Report on file, South Coast Information Center, San Diego State University.

Carrico, R., T. G. Cooley, and J. M. Clevenger
1991 *Final Archaeological Excavations at the Harris Site Complex, San Diego County.* Report on file, South Coastal Information Center, San Diego, California.

Carter, G. F.
1980a *Earlier Than You Think.* University of Texas A&M Press, College Station.
1980b The Metate: An Early Grain-Grinding Implement in the New World. In *Early Native Americans: Prehistoric Demography, Economy, and Technology*, edited by D. L. Browman, pp. 21–40, Moutoun, The Hague.

Cartier, R. R.
1982 Current Research. *American Antiquity* 47:229.
1992 *Data Recovery Report of the Borland Property on Santa's Village Road in the City of Scotts Valley, County of Santa Cruz.* Archaeological Resource Management, 496 N. 5th Street, San Jose. Copies available from Northwest Information Center, Sonoma State University, Rohnert Park.
1993a *The Scotts Valley Site: CA-SCR-177.* Santa Cruz Archaeological Society. Santa Cruz.
1993b *The Saunders Site: MNT-391, a Littoral Site of the Early Period.* Scotts Valley Historical Society Monograph 1. Scotts Valley, California.
1995 Phase II Archaeological Testing Report and Determination of Eligibility Chitactac-Adams Heritage County Park Improvement. Archaeological Resource Management, 496 N. 5th Street, San Jose. Copies available from Northwest Information Center, Sonoma State University, Rohnert Park.
2002 The Sunnyvale Red Burial, CA-SCL-832. *Proceedings of the Society for California Archaeology* 15:49–52.

Cartier, R. (editor)
1996 *The Hiller Site: CA-SMA-160.* Archaeological Resource Management, San Jose. Submitted to Lincoln Property Company, Foster City, California. Copies available from Northwest Information Center, Department of Anthropology, Sonoma State University, Rohnert Park, California.

Cartier, R., J. Bass, and S. Ortman
1993 *The Archaeology of the Guadalupe Corridor.* Santa Clara County Archaeological Society, Santa Clara, California, and Archaeological Resource Management, San Jose, California.

Cassidy, J.
2006 A Possible Chipped Stone Boat Effigy from the Early Holocene Component of the Eel Point Site (CA-SCLI-43), San Clemente Island, California. *Current Research in the Pleistocene* 23:82–83.

Cassidy, J., L. M. Raab, and N. A. Kononenko
2004 Boats, Bones, and Biface Bias: The Early Holocene Mariners of Eel Point, San Clemente Island, California. *American Antiquity* 69:109–130.

Castetter, E., and W. Bell
1951 *Yuman Indian Agriculture.* The University of New Mexico Press, Albuquerque.

Chagnon, N. A.
1970 Ecological and Adaptive Aspects of California Shell Money. *University of California Archaeological Survey Reports* 12:1–25. Los Angeles.

Chappell, J., and H. Pollach
1991 Post-Glacial Sea-Level Rise from a Coral Record at Huon Peninsula, Papua New Guinea. *Nature* 349:147–149.

Chartkoff, J. L.
1987 Bleak and the Grey: Critical Issues of Publication and Scholarship in California Archaeology. *Society for California Archaeology Newsletter* 20(3):2–4.
1989 Exchange Systems in the Archaic of Coastal Southern California. *Proceedings of the Society for California Archaeology* 2:167–186.
1992 Development of Theory in California Archaeology, 1966–1991. *Proceedings of the Society for California Archaeology* 5:1–25.
1997 The Bleak and the Grey Revisited. *Archives of California Prehistory* 45:41–66. Coyote Press, Salinas, California.
2001 Exchange Systems and Sociopolitical Complexity in the Central Sierra Nevada: Perspectives on the Impact of Coastal Colonialism on Inland Communities. *Journal of California and Great Basin Anthropology* 23:125–138.

Chartkoff, J. L., and K. K. Chartkoff
1984 *The Archaeology of California.* Stanford University Press, Stanford.

Chatters, J. C., and J. E. Cleland
1995 Conclusions: Environment, Population, and Human Adaptation on the Middle Pit River. In *Prehistory of the Middle Pit River, Northeastern California: Archaeological Investigations at Lake Britton, Pit 3, 4 & 5 Project.* Vol. 1, edited by J. H. Cleland. Report submitted to Pacific Gas and Electric Company, San Francisco.

Chesterman, C. W.
1955 Age of the Obsidian Flow at Glass Mountain, Siskiyou County, California. *American Journal of Science* 253:418–424.

Chin, J. L., H. E. Clifton, and H. T. Mullins
1988 Seismic Stratigraphy and Late Quaternary Shelf History, South-Central Monterey Bay, California. *Marine Geology* 81:137–157.

Christenson, L. E.
1990 The Late Prehistoric Yuman People of San Diego County, California: Their Settlement and Subsistence System. Ph.D. dissertation, Department of Anthropology, Arizona State University, Tempe. University Microfilms, Ann Arbor.
1992 The Late Prehistoric Yuman Settlement and Subsistence System: Coastal Adaptation. In *Essays on the Prehistory of Maritime California*, edited by T. Jones, pp. 217–230. Center for Archaeological Research at Davis no. 10. University of California, Davis.

Clague, J. J., R. W. Mathewes, and T. A. Ager
2004 Environments of Northwestern North America Before the Last Glacial Maximum. In *Entering America*, edited by D. B. Madsen, pp. 63–94. University of Utah Press, Salt Lake City.

Clark, D. H., and A. R. Gillespie
1996 Timing and Significance of Late-Glacial and Holocene Cirque Glaciation in the Sierra Nevada, California. *Quaternary International* 38/39:21–38.

Clark, G. A.
2000 Deconstructing the North Atlantic Connection. *Current Research in the Pleistocene* 17:11–14.

Clark, M.
1998 *Evaluative Archaeological Investigations at the San Bruno Mountain Mound Site, CA-SMA-40, South San Francisco,*

California. Holman and Associates, San Francisco. Submitted to Terrabay Development. Copies available from Northwest Information Center, Department of Anthropology, Sonoma State University, Rohnert Park, California.

Clark, M., and A. L. Reynolds
2003 *Archaeological Investigations and Mitigative Data Recovery at CA-SCL-689 on Pulte Homes' Kenwood II Project Area, San Jose, California*. Holman and Associates, San Francisco. Submitted to Pulte Home Corporation, Pleasanton, California. Copies available from Northwest Information Center, Department of Anthropology, Sonoma State University, Rohnert Park, California.

Clarke, D. L.
1973 Archaeology: The Loss of Innocence. *Antiquity* 77:6–18.

Clay, V. L.
1996 *Sagebrush Smoke and Rabbit Tales: The Archaeology of Eagle Valley Village (26Or214, Area J.), Carson City, Nevada*. Report submitted to Carson Community Development and Nevada State Historic Preservation Office, Carson City.

Cleland, J. H.
1988 A Tentative Culture-Historical Sequence for the Mokelumne River Canyon. *Proceedings of the Society for California Archaeology* 1:217–223.
1995 *Prehistory of the Middle Pit River, Northeastern, California: Archaeological Investigations at Lake Britton, Pit 3, 4 and 5 Project*. Vol. 1. KEA Environmental. Report on file, North Central Information Center, California State University, Sacramento.
2005 The Sacred and the Mundane: Cultural Landscape Concepts and Archaeological Interpretation in the Colorado Desert. *Proceedings of the Society for California Archaeology* 18:130–135.

Cleland, J. H., and R. M. Apple
2003 *A View Across the Cultural Landscape of the Lower Colorado Desert. Cultural Resource Investigations for the North Baja Pipeline Project*. Prepared by EDAW, Inc., for Tetra Tech FW, Santa Ana, California and North Baja Pipeline LLC, Portland, Oregon.

Cleland, J. H., and W. G. Spaulding
1992 An Alternative Perspective on Mojave Desert Prehistory. *Society for California Archaeology Newsletter* 26(6):1–6.
1993 Conventional or Not, the Wisdom Regarding Paleoenvironmental Change in the Mojave Desert. *Society for California Archaeology Newsletter* 27(6):8–9.

Clement, A. C., R. Seager, and M. A. Cane
2000 Suppression of El Niño During the Mid-Holocene by Changes in the Earth's Orbit. *Paleoceanography* 15:731–737.

Clemmer, J. S.
1962 *Archaeological Notes on a Chumash House Floor at Morro Bay*. Report on file, California Department of Parks and Recreation, Sacramento.

Clewett, S. E., and E. Sundahl
1983 *Archaeological Excavations at Squaw Creek, Shasta County, California*. Shasta College Archaeology Laboratory, Redding, California. Submitted to Shasta-Trinity National Forest. On file, Northeast California Information Center, California State University, Chico.

Clewlow, C. W., Jr.
1978 Prehistoric Rock Art. In *California*, edited by R. F. Heizer, pp. 619–625. Handbook of North American Indians. Vol. 8. W. C. Sturtevant, general editor. Smithsonian Institution, Washington, D.C.
1998 The History of California Rock Art Studies: A View from the Coso Range. In *Coso Rock Art: A New Perspective*, edited by Elva Younkin, pp. 11–26. Maturango Museum Publication no. 12. Banning, California.

Clewlow, C. W., D. S. Whitley, and E. L. McCann (editors)
1979 *Archaeological Investigations at the Ring Brothers Site Complex, Thousand Oaks, California*. Monograph 13. Cotsen Institute of Archaeology, University of California, Los Angeles.

Codding, B. F., and T. L. Jones
2007 Man the Showoff? Or the Ascendance of a Just-So Story: A Comment on Recent Applications of Costly Signaling in American Archaeology. *American Antiquity*, in press.

Cohen, M. N.
1981 *Pacific Coast Foragers: Affluent or Overcrowded?* Seri Ethnological Studies no. 9. Osaka.

COHMAP Members
1988 Climate Changes of the Last 18,000 Years: Observations and Model Simulations. *Science* 241:1043–1052.

Cole, K. L.
1983 Late Pleistocene Vegetation of the Kings Canyon, Sierra Nevada, California. *Quaternary Research* 19:117–127.

Cole, K. L., and G. W. Liu
1994 Holocene Paleoecology of an Estuary on Santa Rosa Island, California. *Quaternary Research* 41:326–335.

Cole, K. L., and E. Wahl
2000 A Late Holocene Paleoecological Record from Torrey Pines State Reserve, California. *Quaternary Research* 53:341–351.

Cole, K. L., and R. H. Webb
1985 Late Holocene Vegetation Changes in Greenwater Valley, Mojave Desert, California. *Quaternary Research* 23:227–235.

Collins, G. E., and K. M. Collins
2004 A Preliminary Overview of a Kumeyaay Fish Camp. In *The Human Journey and Ancient Life in California's Deserts: Proceedings from the 2001 Millennium Conference*, edited by M. W. Allen and J. Reed, pp. 143–147. Maturango Museum Publication no. 15. Ridgecrest, California.

Colten, R. H.
1989 Prehistoric Shellfish Exploitation around the Goleta Lagoon, California. *Journal of California and Great Basin Anthropology* 11:203–214.
1993 Prehistoric Subsistence, Specialization, and Economy in a Southern California Chiefdom. Ph.D. dissertation, Department of Anthropology, University of California, Los Angeles.
1995 Faunal Exploitation During the Middle to Late Period Transition on Santa Cruz Island, California. *Journal of California and Great Basin Anthropology* 17:93–120.
2001 Ecological and Economic Analysis of Faunal Remains from Santa Cruz Island. In *The Origins of a Pacific Coast Chiefdom: The Chumash of the Channel Islands*, edited by J. E. Arnold, pp. 199–220. University of Utah Press, Salt Lake City.

Colten, R. H., C. G. Lebow, C. Denardo, R. L. McKim, D. R. Harro, C. H. Miksicek, and B. Bowser
1997 *Hunter-Gatherer Land Use in the San Antonio Creek Drainage*. Report on file, South Central Archaeological Information Center, Department of Anthropology, University of California, Santa Barbara.

Connolly, T., J. M. Erlandson, and S. E. Norris
1995 Early Holocene Basketry from Daisy Cave, San Miguel Island, California. *American Antiquity* 60:309–318.

Conway, T.
1995 *Camping in the Canyon—Phase 2 Archaeological Testing of Four Archaeological Sites at the Circle V Ranch (Campo Cielo), Tequepis Canyon, Los Padres National Forest, Santa Barbara County, California*. Report on file, Heritage Resource Center, Santa Barbara Ranger District, Los Padres National Forest.
2000 *An Archaeological Records Search and Cultural Resource Constraints Analysis, Highway 1, Nipomo Mesa Area, San Luis Obispo County, California*. Copies available from South Central Information Center, Department of Anthropology, University of California, Santa Barbara.

Cook, E. R., C. A. Woodhouse, C. M. Eakin, D. M. Meko, and D. Stahle
2004 Long-Term Aridity Changes in the Western United States. *Science* 306:1015–1018.
Cook, H. J.
1927 New Geological and Palaeontological Evidence Bearing on the Antiquity of Mankind in America. *Natural History* 27:240–247
Cook, S. F.
1955 The Aboriginal Population of the San Joaquin Valley, California. *University of California Anthropological Records* 16:16–80.
1976 *The Population of the California Indians, 1769–1970*. University of California Press, Berkeley.
1978 Historical Demography. In *California*, edited by R. F. Heizer, pp. 91–98. Handbook of North American Indians. Vol. 8. W. G. Sturtevant, general editor. Smithsonian Institution, Washington, D.C.
Cooley, T. G., and L. J. Barrie
2004 Archaeological Excavation at the Village of Pa'mu, Ramona Valley, California. *Proceedings of the Society for California Archaeology* 17:43–56.
Cooper, W. S.
1967 *Coastal Dunes of California*. Geological Society of America Memoir 104. Boulder, Colorado.
Copland, J. M., and R. E. Fike
1988 Fluted Projectile Points in Utah. *Utah Archaeology* 1988:5–28.
Corbett, R.
1999 Chumash Bone Whistles: The Development and Elaboration of Ritual Activity and Ceremonial Integration in Chumash Society. Master's thesis, Department of Anthropology, University of California, Los Angeles.
2004 Chumash Bone Whistles: The Development of Ceremonial Integration in Chumash Society. In *Foundations of Chumash Complexity*, edited by J. E. Arnold, pp. 65–74. Cotsen Institute of Archaeology, University of California, Los Angeles.
Cordero, R. M.
2001 The Daily Grind: Activity Patterns, Sexual Division of Labor, and Central California Prehistory. Master's thesis, Department of Anthropology, California State University, Chico.
Court, A.
1974 The Climate of Coterminous United States. In *Climates of North America,* edited by R. A. Bryson and F. K. Hare, pp. 193–344. World Survey of Climatology. Vol. 11. Elsevier Scientific Publishing Company, Amsterdam.
Crabtree, D. S.
1972 *An Introduction to Flintworking*. Occasional Papers of the Idaho State University Museum no. 28, pt. 2, edited by E. H. Swanson Jr., and B. R. Butler. Pacatello, Idaho.
Crabtree, R. H., C. N. Warren, and D. L. True
1963 Archaeological Investigations at Batiquitos Lagoon, San Diego County, California. *University of California Archaeological Survey Annual Report 1962–1963*, pp. 243–278. Los Angeles.
Crawford, J. G.
1976 Seri and Yuman. In *Hokan Studies*, edited by M. Langdon and S. Silver, pp. 305–324. The Hague, Mouton.
Creger, C. C.
1991 Completing the Circle: The Archaeology of Duck Flat, Nevada. Master's thesis, Department of Anthropology, University of Nevada, Reno.
Cressman, L. S.
1942 *Archaeological Researches in the Northern Great Basin.* Carnegie Institution of Washington Publications 538. Washington, D.C.
1977 *Prehistory of the Far West: Homes of Vanished Peoples.* University of Utah Press, Salt Lake City.
Cressman, L. S., H. Williams, and A. Krieger
1940 *Early Man in Oregon: Archaeological Studies in the Northern Great Basin.* University of Oregon Monographs, Studies in Anthropology no. 3. Eugene.
Crowell, A. L.
1999 Maritime Cultures of the Gulf of Alaska. *Revista de Arqueologia Americana* 17–19:177–216.
Curtis, E. S.
1908 *Mohave.* The North American Indian. Vol. 2, edited by F. W. Hodge. Plimpton Press, Norwood, Massachusetts.
Curtis, F.
1959 *Arroyo Sequit: Archaeological Investigation of a Late Coastal Site in Los Angeles County, California.* Archaeological Survey Association of Southern California 4.
Dahlen, M. Z., R. H. Osborne, and D. S. Gorsline
1990 Late Quaternary History of the Ventura Mainland Shelf, California. *Marine Geology* 94:317–340.
Dallas, H., Jr.
1992 Hunters and Gatherers at CA-SLO-977, San Luis Obispo County. In *Archaeological Investigations of Some Significant Sites on the Central Coast of California*, edited by H. Dallas Jr. and G. S. Breschini, pp. 1–37. Archives of California Prehistory 37. Coyote Press, Salinas.
Dalldorf, G., and J. Meyer
2004 *Extended Phase I Geoarchaeological Investigations for the Rock Creek Bridge Scour Project, CA-STA-69, State Route 4, Stanislaus County, California.* Anthropological Studies Center, Sonoma State University, Rohnert Park. Submitted to the California Department of Transportation, District 10, Stockton.
Daniels, M. L., R. S. Anderson, and C. Whitlock
2005 Vegetation and Fire History since the Late Pleistocene from the Trinity Mountains, Northwestern California, U.S.A. *Holocene* 15:1062–1071.
Darigo, N. J., and R. H. Osborne
1986 Quaternary Stratigraphy and Sedimentation of the Inner Continental Shelf, San Diego County, California. In *Shelf Sands and Sandstones*, edited by R. J. Knight and J. R. McLean, pp. 73–98. Canadian Society of Petroleum Geologists Memoir 11. Calgary, Alberta.
Davenport, D., J. R. Johnson, and J. Timbrook
1993 The Chumash and the Swordfish. *Antiquity* 67:257–272.
Davis, C. A., and G. A. Smith
1981 *Newberry Cave.* San Bernardino County Museum Association, Redlands, California.
Davis, E. L.
1963 The Desert Culture of the Western Great Basin: A Lifeway of Seasonal Transhumance. *American Antiquity* 29:202–212.
1975 The "Exposed Archaeology" of China Lake, California. *American Antiquity* 40:39–53.
Davis, E. L. (editor)
1978 *The Ancient Californians: Rancholabrean Hunters of the Mojave Lakes Country.* Natural History Museum of Los Angeles County Science Series no. 29.
Davis, E. L., and R. Shutler Jr.
1969 Recent Discoveries of Fluted Points in California and Nevada. *Nevada State Museum Anthropological Papers* 14:154–169.
Davis, E. L., and S. Winslow
1965 Giant Grand Figures of the Prehistoric Desert. *American Philosophical Society* 109:8–21. Philadelphia.
Davis, E. L., K. H. Brown, and J. Nichols
1980 *Evaluation of Early Human Activities and Remains in the California Desert.* Bureau of Land Management, Cultural Resources Publications, Anthropology-History, Barstow.
Davis, O. K.
1992 Rapid Climatic Change in Coastal Southern California Inferred from Pollen Analysis of San Joaquin Marsh. *Quaternary Research* 37:89–100.

1999a Pollen Analysis of Tulare Lake, California: Great Basin-like Vegetation in Central California During the Full-Glacial and Early Holocene. *Review of Palaeobotany and Palynology* 107:249–257.

1999b Pollen Analysis of a Holocene-Late Glacial Sediment Core from Mono Lake, Mono County, California. *Quaternary Research* 52:243–249.

Davis, O. K., and M. J. Moratto

1988 Evidence for a Warm Dry Early Holocene in the Western Sierra Nevada of California: Pollen and Plant Macrofossil Analysis of Dinkey and Exchequer Meadows. *Madroño* 35:132–149.

Davis, O. K., R. S. Anderson, P. L. Fall, M. K. O'Rourke, and R. S. Thompson

1985 Palynological Evidence for Early Holocene Aridity in the Southern Sierra Nevada, California. *Quaternary Research* 24:322–332.

Davis, S. D.

1996 Hidden Falls. In *American Beginnings: The Prehistory and Palaeoecology of Beringia*, edited by F. H. West, pp. 413–424. University of Chicago Press, Chicago.

Davis-King, S.

1998 *Johnny Wilson's Place: Investigations at CA-MRP-362/H and CA-MRP-363H Within the El Portal Archaeological District, Mariposa County, Yosemite National Park, California.* Davis-King & Associates, Standard, California. Submitted to USDI Yosemite National Park.

Day, D.

2002 Basalt Distribution Findings on the Tahoe National Forest. *Society for California Archaeology Newsletter* 36(3):39–42.

d'Azevedo, W. L.

1986 Washoe. In *Great Basin*, edited by W. L. d'Azevedo, pp. 466–498. Handbook of North American Indians. Vol. 11. William C. Sturtevant, general editor. Smithsonian Institution, Washington, D.C.

Deal, K. K.

1987 The Archaeology of the Cana Highway Site, CA-BUT-288, Butte County, California. Master's thesis, Department of Anthropology, California State University, Chico.

De Barros, P., C. F. Woodman, and T. P. Rudolph

1994 *Archaeological Survey and Evaluation, Purisima Point Sites SBA-224 and SBA-225, Vandenberg Air Force Base, Santa Barbara County, California.* Report on file, South Central Archaeological Information Center, Department of Anthropology, University of California, Santa Barbara.

DeFrance, S. D., D. Keefer, J. Richardson, and A. U. Almarez

2001 Late Paleo-Indian Coastal Foragers: Specialized Extractive Behavior at Quebrada Tacahuay, Peru. *Latin American Antiquity* 12:413–426.

DeGeorgey, A.

2004 A Single Component Paleo-Indian Site in Northern California. In *Proceedings of the Society for California Archaeology* 17:35–42.

Delacorte, M. G.

1997a *Culture Change Along the Eastern Sierra Nevada/Cascade Front: History of Investigations and Summary of Findings.* Vol. 1. Submitted to the Tuscarora Gas Transmission Company, Reno.

1997b *Culture Change Along the Eastern Sierra Nevada/Cascade Front. South Fork Valley and Madeline Plains.* Vol. 3. Submitted to the Tuscarora Gas Transmission Company, Reno.

1997c *Culture Change Along the Eastern Sierra Nevada/Cascade Front. Pah Rah Uplands.* Vol. 7. Submitted to the Tuscarora Gas Transmission Company, Reno.

2001 *Phase II Test Excavations of Three Prehistoric Sites (CA-SJO-93,CA-SJO-264,CA-SJO-265) Along State Route 88, San Joaquin County, California.* Report prepared for the California Department of Transportation, District 10, Stockton.

2002 Late Prehistoric Resource Intensification in the Northwestern Great Basin. In *Boundary Lands: Archaeological Investigations Along the California–Great Basin Interface*, edited by K. R. McGuire. Nevada State Museum Anthropological Papers no. 24, Carson City, Nevada.

Delacorte, M. G., and K. R. McGuire

1993 *Report of Archaeological Test Evaluations at Twenty-Three Sites in Owens Valley, California.* Far Western Anthropological Research Group, Davis, California, Contel of California, Bureau of Land Management, California Desert District. Submitted to California Department of Transportation. Report on file, North Central Information Center, California State University, Sacramento.

Delacorte, M. G., J. Berg, and J. Meyer

2000 *Test Excavations and Evaluations at CA-AMA-569. Amador County, California, State Route 88.* Submitted to the California Department of Transportation, Stockton. Report on file, North Central Information Center, California State University, Sacramento.

DeLancey, S.

1987 Klamath and Wintu Pronouns. *International Journal of American Linguistics* 53:461–464.

1996 Penutian in the Bipartite Stem Belt: Disentangling Areal and Genetic Correspondences. *Proceedings of the 22nd Annual Meeting of the Berkeley Linguistics Society.* Department of Linguistics, University of California, Berkeley.

DeLancey, S., and V. Golla

1997 The Penutian Hypothesis: Retrospect and Prospect. *International Journal of American Linguistics* 63:171–202.

Derr, E. H.

1983 Archaeological Investigations of a Middle/Late Horizon Village in the Lower Sacramento Valley of California. Master's thesis, Department of Anthropology, California State University, Sacramento.

Des Lauriers, M.

2005a The Watercraft of Isla Cedros, Baja, California: Variability and Capabilities of Indigenous Seafaring Technology Along the Pacific Coast of North America. *American Antiquity* 70:342–360.

2005b Terminal Pleistocene and Early Holocene Occupations of Isla Cedros, Baja California. *Journal of Island and Coastal Archaeology*, in press.

Dickel, D. N.

1985 Growth Stress and Central California Pre-Historic Subsistence Shifts. *American Journal of Physical Anthropology* 63:152.

Dickel, D. N., P. D. Schulz, and H. M. McHenry

1984 Central California: Prehistoric Subsistence Changes and Health. In *Paleopathology at the Origins of Agriculture*, edited by M. N. Cohen and G. J. Armelagos, pp. 439–461. Academic Press, Orlando.

Dietz, S. A.

1987 *Archaeological Test Excavations at CA-MNT-101, CA-MNT-298, CA-MNT-929, and El Castillo at the Presidio and City of Monterey, California.* Archaeological Consulting and Research Services, Santa Cruz. Copies available from Northwest Archaeological Information Center, Department of Anthropology, Sonoma State University, Rohnert Park, California.

1991 *Final Report of Archaeological Investigations at Pescadero Point, Data Recovery Excavations and Monitoring of CA-MNT-170.* Archaeological Consulting and Research Services, Santa Cruz. Copies available from Northwest Archaeological Information Center, Department of Anthropology, Sonoma State University, Rohnert Park, California.

Dietz, S. A., and T. L. Jackson
1981 *Report of Archaeological Excavations at Nineteen Archaeological Sites for the Stage 1 Pacific Grove-Monterey Consolidation Project of the Regional Sewerage System.* Archaeological Consulting and Research Services, Santa Cruz. Copies available from Northwest Archaeological Information Center, Department of Anthropology, Sonoma State University, Rohnert Park, California.

Dietz, S. A., W. R. Hildebrandt, and T. L. Jones
1988 *Archaeological Investigations at Elkhorn Slough: CA-MNT-229, a Middle Period Site on the Central California Coast.* Papers in Northern California Anthropology 3. Northern California Anthropological Research Group, Berkeley.

Diffenbaugh, N. S., and L. A Sloan
2004 Mid-Holocene Orbital Forcing of Region-Scale Climate: A Case Study of Western North America Using a High Resolution RCM. *Journal of Climate* 17:2927–2937.

Dillehay, T. D. (editor)
1989 *Monte Verde, a Late Pleistocene Settlement in Chile: Paleoenvironment and Site Context.* Vol. 1. Smithsonian Institution, Washington, D.C.
1997 *Monte Verde, a Late Pleistocene Settlement in Chile: The Archaeological Context and Interpretation.* Vol. 2. Smithsonian Institution, Washington, D.C.

Dillehay, T. D., and J. Rosen
2002 Plant Food and Its Implications for the Peopling of the New World: A View from South America. In *The First Americans: The Pleistocene Colonization of the New World*, edited by N. G. Jablonski, pp. 237–253. Memoirs of the California Academy of Sciences 27.

Dillian, C. D.
2002 More Than Toolstone: Differential Utilization of Glass Mountain Obsidian. Ph.D. dissertation, Department of Anthropology, University of California, Berkeley.

Dillon, B. D.
2002 California Paleoindians: Lack of Evidence, or Evidence of Lack? In *Essays in California Archaeology: A Memorial to Franklin Fenenga*, edited by W. J. Wallace and F. A. Riddell, pp. 110–128. Contributions of the University of California Archaeological Research Facility no.60.

Dillon, B. D., and M. A. Boxt
1989 Comparisons and Conclusions. In *Archaeology of the Three Springs Valley, California*, edited by B. D. Dillon and M. A. Boxt, pp. 138–169. Monograph 30. Cotsen Institute of Archaeology, University of California, Los Angeles.

Dillon, B. D., and J. A. Hamilton
1994 Fluted Projectile Points from Eden Valley, Mendocino County, California. *Tularg Newsletter* 7(4):2–9.

Dillon, B. D., and D. W. Murphy
1994 A Fluted Point from Thomes Creek, Tehama County, California. *Tularg Newsletter* 7(3):2–6.

Dillon, B. D., J. Porcasi, T. Gutman, P. Porcasi, and F. Wood
1991 Preliminary Report on Excavations at the Creighton Ranch Site (CA-TUL-1613), Tulare County, California. In *Contributions to Tulare Lake Archaeology I: Background to the Study of Tulare Lake's Archaeological Past*, edited by W. J. Wallace and F. A. Riddell, pp. 61–70. Tulare Lake Archaeological Research Group, Redondo Beach.

Dills, C. E.
1981 *Halcyon Bay: An Ancient Estuary.* Society for California Archaeology Occasional Papers 3:43–48. California State University, Fullerton.

Dixon, E. J.
1993 *Quest for the Origins of the First Americans.* University of New Mexico Press, Albuquerque.
1999 *Bones, Boats, and Bison: Archeology and the First Colonization of Western North America.* University of New Mexico Press, Albuquerque.

Dixon, R.
1905 The Northern Maidu. *American Museum of Natural History Bulletin* 17:119–345.

Dixon, R. B., and A. L. Kroeber
1913 New Linguistic Families in California. *American Anthropologist* 15(3):647–655.
1919 Linguistic Families of California. *University of California Publications in American Archaeology and Ethnology* 16:647–655.

Dobkins, R. J.
1997 *Memory and Imagination: The Legacy of Maidu Indian Artist Frank Day.* Oakland Museum of California.

Dominici, D. A.
1984 Calibration of the Obsidian Butte Hydration Rate and Its Implications Regarding Late Prehistoric Exchange. Master's thesis, Department of Anthropology, San Diego State University.

Dondero, S. B., and J. J. Johnson
1988 *Dutch Gulch Lake, Excavations at Six Prehistoric Sites, Cottonwod Creek Project, Shasta and Tehama Counties, California (Draft).* Hornet Foundation of California State University, Sacramento. Submitted to the Army Corps of Engineers, Sacramento. Copies available from the Northeast Archaeological Information Center, Department of Anthropology, California State University, Chico.

Dondero, S., D. Noble, J. Offerman, and T. Schuster
1984 *A Preliminary Report on Archaeological Testing of CA-MNT-229.* California Department of Transportation, Sacramento. Copies available from Northwest Archaeological Information Center, Sonoma State University, Rohnert Park, California.

Doran, G. H.
1980 Paleodemography of the Plains Miwok Ethnolinguistic Area, Central California. Ph.D. dissertation, Department of Anthropology, University of California, Davis.

Dorn, R. I.
1983 Cation-ratio Dating: A New Rock Varnish Age Determination Technique. *Quaternary Research* 20:49–73.
1989 Cation-ratio Dating of Rock Varnish: A Geographical Perspective. *Progress in Physical Geography* 13:559–596.
1992a Rock Varnish. *American Scientist* 779:542–553.
1992b Paleoenvironmental Signals in Rock Varnish on Petroglyphs. *American Indian Rock Art* 13:1–18.
1994 Dating Petroglyphs with a Three-Tier Rock Varnish Approach. In *New Light on Old Art: Recent Advances in Hunter-Gatherer Rock Art Research*, edited by D. S. Whitley and L. L. Loendorf, pp. 13–36. Institute of Archaeology, University of California, Los Angeles.

Dorn, R. I., and D. S. Whitley
1983 Cation-ratio Dating of Petroglyphs from the Western Great Basin. *Nature* 302:816–818.

Dorn, R. I., A. J. T. Jull, D. J. Donahue, T. W. Linick, and L. J. Toolin
1989 Accelerator Mass Spectrometry Radiocarbon Dating of Rock Varnish. *Geological Society of America Bulletin* 101:1363–1372.

Dorn, R. I., P. B. Clarkson, M. F. Nobbs, L. L. Loendorf, and D. S. Whitley
1992 New Approach to Radiocarbon Dating of Organic Matter Encapsulated by Rock Varnish, with Examples from Archeology and Geomorphology. *Annals of the Association of American Geographers* 82:136–151.

Dorn, R. I., T. A. Cahill, R. A. Eldred, T. E. Gill, B. H. Kusko, A. J. Bach, and D. L. Elliott-Fisk
1990 Dating Rock Varnishes by the Cation Ratio Method with PIXE, ICP, and the Electron Microprobe. *International Journal of PIXE* 1:157–195.

Dougherty, J. W.
1990 The Obsidian Projectile Points of the King Brown Site: CA-SAC-29, Sacramento County, California. Master's thesis,

Department of Anthropology, California State University, Sacramento.

Dougherty, J. W., and R. H. Werner
1993 *Final Report: Archaeological Testing, Data Salvage and Burial Rescue at CA-MER-323, An Archaeological Site Near South Dos Palos, Merced County, California.* Report prepared for Joint Powers Authority, Dos Palos and South Dos Palos, Merced.

Douglas, C. L., D. L. Jenkins, and C. N. Warren
1988 Spatial and Temporal Variability in Faunal Remains from Four Lake Mojave-Pinto Period Sites in the Mojave Desert. In *Early Human Occupation in Far Western North America: The Clovis-Archaic Interface*, edited by J. A. Willig, C. Melvin Aikens, and J. L. Fagan, pp. 131–144. Nevada State Museum Anthropological Papers no. 21.

Dowdall, K. M.
2002 Late Holocene Cultural Diversity on the Sonoma Coast. In *Catalysts to Complexity: Late Holocene Societies of the California Coast*, edited by J. M. Erlandson and T. L. Jones, pp. 282–302. Cotsen Institute of Archaeology, University of California, Los Angeles.

DuBois, C. G.
1908 Religion of the Luiseno and Diegueno Indians of Southern California. *University of California Publications in American Archaeology and Ethnology* 8(3).

Duffield, W. A., and C. R. Bacon
1981 Geological Map of the Coso Volcanic Field and Adjacent Areas, Inyo County, California. *U.S. Geological Survey Miscellaneous Investigations* (Series Map 1-1200, Scale 1:50,000).

Dull, R., and E. Edlund
1997 Paleoenvironmental Analysis of Waugh Lake and Lower Rush Meadow, Investigations at CA-MNO-2440/H, Mono-2459, MNO-2460, MNO-2461 and MNO-2463. In *Archaeological Data Recovery Program-Rush Meadow,* edited by T. L. Jackson, Appendix I, pp. 1–20. Pacific Legacy, Aptos. Report on file, Supervisor's Office, Inyo National Forest, Bishop, California.

Dupré, W. R.
1975 Quaternary history of the Watsonville lowlands, North-central Monterey Bay region, California. Ph.D. dissertation, Department of Geology, Stanford University.
1990 Quaternary Geology of the Monterey Bay Region, California. In *Guidebook: Pacific Section, American Association of Petroleum Geologists* 67:185–191.

Dupré, W. R., R. B. Morrison, H. E. Clifton, K. R. Lajoie, D. J. Ponti, C. L. Powell II, S. A. Methieson, A. Sarna-Wojcicki, E. L. Leithold, W. R. Lettis, P. F. McDowell, T. K. Rockwell, J. R. Unruh, and R. S. Yeats
1991 Quaternary Geology of the Pacific Margin. In *Quaternary Nonglacial Geology: Conterminous U.S.*, edited by R. B. Morrison, pp. 141–214. The Geology of North America. Vol. K-2, Chapter 7. The Geological Society of America, Boulder, Colorado.

Earle, D. D.
2004 Native Population and Settlement in the Western Mojave Desert in the 18th and 19th Centuries. In *The Human Journey and Ancient Life in California's Deserts: Proceedings from the 2001 Millennium Conference*, edited by M. W. Allen and J. Reed, pp. 173–186. Maturango Museum Publication no. 15, Ridgecrest.

Earle, T. K.
1982 Prehistoric Economies and the Archaeology of Exchange. In *Contexts for Prehistoric Exchange*, edited by J. E. Ericson and T. K. Earle, pp. 1–12. Academic Press, New York.

Earle, T. K., and J. E. Ericson
1977 Exchange Systems in Archaeological Perspective. In *Exchange Systems in Prehistory*, edited by T. K. Earle and J. E. Ericson, pp. 3–12. Academic Press, New York.

Edlund, E. G.
1991 Reconstruction of Late Quaternary Vegetation and Climate at Lake Moran, Central Sierra Nevada, California. Master's thesis, Department of Geography, University of California, Berkeley.
1994 Bunker Lake Paleoecological Analyis. In *Framework for Archaeological Research and Management: National Forests of the Northcentral Sierra Nevada*, edited by R. J. Jackson. U.S. Forest Service, Placerville.

Edlund, E. G., and R. Byrne
1991 Climate, Fire, and Late Quaternary Vegetation Change in the Central Sierra Nevada. In *Fire and the Environment: Ecological and Cultural Perspectives*, edited by S. S. Nodvin and T. A. Waldrop, pp. 390–396. General Technical Report SE-69. U.S. Forest Service, Southeastern Forest Experiment Station, Asheville, N.C.

Edwards, R. L., J. W. Beck, G. S. Burr, D. J. Donahue, J. M. A.Chappell, A. L. Bloom, E. R. M. Druffel, and F. W. Taylor
1993 A Large Drop in Atmospheric $^{14}C/^{12}C$ and Reduced Melting in the Younger Dryas, Documented with ^{230}Th Ages of Corals. *Science* 260:962–968.

Eerkens, J. W.
1999 Common Pool Resources, Buffer Zones, and Jointly Owned Territories: Hunter-Gatherer Land and Resource Tenure in Fort Irwin, Southeastern California. *Human Ecology* 27:297–318.
2003 Residential Mobility and Pottery Use in the Western Great Basin. *Current Anthropology* 44:728–738.

Eerkens, J. W., and J. S. Rosenthal
2004 Are Obsidian Subsources Meaningful Units of Analysis? Temporal and Spatial Patterning of Subsources in the Coso Volcanic Field, Southeastern California. *Journal of Archaeological Science* 31:21–29.

Eerkens, J. W., G. S. Herbert, J. S. Rosenthal, and H. J. Spero
2005 Provenance Analysis of *Olivella biplicata* Shell Beads from the California and Oregon Coast by Stable Isotope Fingerprinting. *Journal of Archaeological Science* 32:1501–1514.

Eerkens, J. W., J. King, and M. D. Glascock
1999 Early Pottery from Sunga'va and Implications for the Development of Ceramic Technology in Owens Valley, California. *Journal of California and Great Basin Anthropology* 21:275–285.
2002a Artifact Size and Chemical Sourcing: Studying the Potential Biases of Selecting Large Artifacts for Analysis. *Society for California Archaeology Newsletter* 36(3):25–29.
2002b Ceramic Production Among Small-Scale and Mobile Hunters and Gatherers: A Case Study from the Southwestern Great Basin. *Journal of Anthropological Archaeology* 21:200–229.

Eidsness, J. P.
1986 Prehistoric Archaeology Within Chimariko Territory, Northwest California. Master's thesis, Department of Anthropology, Sonoma State University, Rohnert Park.
1993 *Archaeological Investigations at CA-HUM-351/H on Humboldt Bay, California.* Report on file, Northwest Information Center, Department of Anthropology, Sonoma State University, Rohnert Park.

Eidsness, J., and T. L. Jackson
1994 *Historic Preservation Plan: Fort Hunter Liggett Military Installation, California.* Biosystems, Inc. Prepared for the U.S. Army Corps of Engineers, Contract no. DACA05-90-C-0175. Copies available from Cultural Resources Office, Fort Hunter-Liggett.

Eighmey, J., and D. Cheever
1992 *Excavations at Dry Lake, Sites 4-IMP-5260, 4-IMP-5261, and 4-IMP-5262, Imperial County, California.* Prepared by Regional Environmental Consultants (RECON) for USDI Bureau of Land Management, El Centro.

Eittreim, S. L., R. J. Anima, and A. J. Stevenson
2002 Seafloor Geology of the Monterey Bay Area Continental Shelf. *Marine Geology* 181:3–34.

Eittreim, S. L., R. J. Anima, A. J. Stevenson, and F. L. Wong
2000 Seafloor Geology of Monterey Bay to Point Sur Continental Shelf, California. *United States Geological Survey Miscellaneous Field Studies.* Map, 1:100,000 scale.

Elliott, W. J.
1987 The Silver Strand: A Unique Tombolo, San Diego, California. In *Centennial Field Guide*, edited by M. L. Hill, pp. 169–170. Cordilleran Section of the Geological Society of America. Vol. 1. Boulder, Colorado.

Elmendorf, W. W.
1963 Yukian-Siouan Lexical Similarities. *International Journal of American Linguistics* 29:300–309.
1968 Lexical and Cultural Change in Yukian. *Anthropological Linguistics* 10:1–41.
1984 Yukian Sharings. Paper presented at the 1984 Hokan-Penutian Workshop, U.C. Berkeley, June 22–24, 1984.

Elsasser, A. B.
1960 The Archaeology of the Sierra Nevada in California and Nevada. *University of California Archaeological Survey Reports* 51:1-93.
1978 Development of Regional Prehistoric Cultures. In *California*, edited by R. F. Heizer, pp. 37–57, Handbook of North American Indians. Vol. 8. W. G. Sturtevant, general editor. Smithsonian Institution, Washington, D.C.
1986 *Review of the Prehistory of the Santa Clara Valley Region.* Archives of California Prehistory 7. Coyote Press, Salinas.

Elsasser, A. B., and W. A. Gortner
1991 The Martis Complex Revisited. *North American Archaeologist* 12:361–376.

Elsasser, A. B., and R. F. Heizer
1964 Archaeology of HUM-67, the Gunter Island Site in Humboldt Bay, California. *University of California Archaeological Survey Reports* 62:5–122.
1966 Excavation of Two Northwestern California Coastal Sites. *University of California Archaeological Survey Reports* 67:1–149.

Elston, R. G.
1979 *The Archaeology of U.S. 395 Right-of-Way Between Stead, Nevada, and Hallelujah Junction, California.* Archaeological Survey/Anthropology Department, University of Nevada. Report on file, North Central Information Center, California State University, Sacramento.

Elston, R. G., and S. L. Kuhn
2002. *Thinking Small: Global Perspectives on Microlithization.* Archaeological Papers of the American Anthropological Association no. 12.

Elston, R. G., and D. W. Zeanah
2002 Thinking Outside the Box: A New Perspective on Diet Breadth and Sexual Division of Labor in the Pre-Archaic Great Basin. *World Archaeology* 34:103–130.

Elston, R., J. O. Davis, A. Leventhal, and C. Covington
1977 *The Archaeology of the Tahoe Reach of the Truckee River.* Prepared for the Tahoe-Truckee Sanitation Agency. Report on file, Cultural Resources Office, Tahoe National Forest, Nevada City, California.

Elston, R., S. Stornetta, D. P. Dugas, and P. Mires
1994 *Beyond the Blue Roof: Archaeological Survey on Mt. Rose Fan and Northern Steamboat Hills.* Intermountain Research, Silver City, Nevada. Submitted to Toiyabe National Forest on behalf of the American Land Conservancy, San Francisco.

Enzel, Y., D. R. Cayan, R. Y. Anderson, and S. G. Wells
1989 Atmospheric Circulation During Holocene Lake Stands in the Mojave Desert: Evidence of Regional Climate Change. *Nature* 341:44–48.

Enzel, Y., W. J. Brown, R. Y. Anderson, L. D. McFadden, and S. G. Wells
1992 Short-Duration Holocene Lakes in the Mojave River Drainage Basin, Southern California. *Quaternary Research* 38:60–73.

Ericson, J. E.
1981 *Exchange and Production Systems in Californian Prehistory: The Results of Hydration Dating and Chemical Characterization of Obsidian Sources.* British Archaeological Reports, International Series no. 110.
1982 Production for Obsidian Exchange in California. In *Contexts for Prehistoric Exchange*, edited by J. E. Ericson and T. K. Earle, pp. 129–148. Academic Press, New York.

Erlandson, J. M.
1985 Early Holocene Settlement and Subsistence in Relation to Coastal Paleogeography: Evidence from CA-SBA-1807. *Journal of California and Great Basin Anthropology* 7:103–109.
1988 *Cultural Ecology on the Southern California Coast at 5000 B.P.: A Comparative Analysis of CA-SBA-75.* Archives of California Prehistory 15. Coyote Press, Salinas.
1991a Early Maritime Adaptations on the Northern Channel Islands. In *Hunter-Gatherers of Early Holocene Coastal California*, edited by J. M. Erlandson and R. H. Colten, pp. 101–111. Cotsen Institute of Archaeology, University of California, Los Angeles.
1991b Shellfish and Seeds as Optimal Resources: Early Holocene Subsistence on the Santa Barbara Coast. In *Hunter-Gatherers of Early Holocene Coastal California*, edited by J. M. Erlandson and R. H. Colten, pp. 89–100. Institute of Archaeology, University of California, Los Angeles.
1994 *Early Hunter-Gatherers of the California Coast.* Plenum Press, New York.
1997a The Middle Holocene Along the California Coast. In *Archaeology of the California Coast During the Middle Holocene*, edited by J. M. Erlandson and M. A. Glassow, pp. 1–10. Cotsen Institute of Archaeology, University of California, Los Angeles.
1997b The Middle Holocene on the Western Santa Barbara Coast. In *Archaeology of the California Coast During the Middle Holocene*, edited by J. M. Erlandson and M. A. Glassow, pp. 91–110. Cotsen Institute of Archaeology, University of California, Los Angeles.
2000 A Stratified Association of Mammoth Remains and Archaeological Materials at Running Springs, San Miguel Island, California. *Current Research in the Pleistocene* 17:22–24.
2001 The Archaeology of Aquatic Adaptations: Paradigms for a New Millennium. *Journal of Archaeological Research* 9:287–350.
2002 Anatomically Modern Humans, Maritime Voyaging, and the Pleistocene Colonization of the Americas. In *The First Americans: The Pleistocene Colonization of the New World*, edited by N. G. Jablonski, pp. 59–92. Memoirs of the California Academy of Sciences no. 27.
2007 Sea Change: The Paleocoastal Occupations of Daisy Cave. In *Seeking Our Past: An Introduction to North American Archaeology*, edited by S. W. Neusius and G. T. Gross. Oxford University Press, Oxford.

Erlandson, J. M., and K. Bartoy
1995 Cabrillo, the Chumash, and Old World Diseases. *Journal of California and Great Basin Anthropology* 17:153–173.
1996 Protohistoric California: Paradise or Pandemic? *Proceedings of the Society for California Archaeology* 9:304–309.

Erlandson, J. M., and R. H. Colten
1991 An Archaeological Context for Early Holocene Studies on the California Coast. In *Hunter-Gatherers of Early Holocene Coastal California*, edited by J. M Erlandson and R. H. Colten, pp. 1–10. Cotsen Institute of Archaeology, University of California, Los Angeles.

Erlandson, J. M., and D. Morris
1992 CA-SRI-1: A 'Pleistocene' Shell Midden on Santa Rosa Island, California. *Current Research in the Pleistocene* 9:7–10.

Erlandson, J. M., and M. L. Moss
1996 The Pleistocene-Holocene Transition Along the Pacific Coast of North America. In *Humans at the End of the Ice Age*, edited

by L. G. Straus, B. V. Eriksen, J. M. Erlandson, and D. R. Yesner, pp. 277–301.

Erlandson, J. M., and T. C. Rick

2002a Late Holocene Cultural Developments Along the Santa Barbara Coast. In *Catalysts to Complexity: Late Holocene Societies of the California Coast,* edited by J. M. Erlandson and T. L. Jones, pp. 166–182. Cotsen Institute of Archaeology, University of California, Los Angeles.

2002b A 9,700-year-old Shell Midden on San Miguel Island, California. *Antiquity* 76:315–316.

Erlandson, J. M., R. H. Colten, and M. A. Glassow

1988 Reassessing Owen's 'Early Horizon' of the Southern California Coast: New Data on the Chronology of the Glen Annie Canyon Site (CA-SBA-142). *Journal of California and Great Basin Anthropology* 10:237–245.

Erlandson, J. M., T. G. Cooley, and R. Carrico

1987 A Fluted Projectile Point Fragment from the Southern California Coast: Chronology and Context at CA-SBA-1951. *Journal of California and Great Basin Anthropology* 9:120–128.

Erlandson, J. M., T. C. Rick, and M. R. Batterson

2005 Busted Balls Shell Midden: An Early Coastal Site on San Miguel Island, California. *North American Archaeologist.* In press.

Erlandson, J. M., T. J. Braje, T. C. Rick, and J. Peterson

2005 Beads, Bifaces, and Boats: An Early Maritime Adaptation on the South Coast of San Miguel Island, California. *American Anthropologist* 107:677–683.

Erlandson, J. M., M. E. Macko, H.Koerper, and J. Southon

2005 The Antiquity of *Olivella* Shell Beads at CA-ORA-64: AMS Radiocarbon Dated Between 9420 and 7780 Cal BP. *Journal of Archaeological Science* 32:393–398.

Erlandson, J. M., T. C. Rick, R. L. Vellanoweth, and D. J. Kennett

1999 Maritime Subsistence at a 9300 Year Old Shell Midden on Santa Rosa Island, California. *Journal of Field Archaeology* 26:255–265.

Erlandson, J. M., T. C. Rick, R. L. Vellanoweth, and T. Largaespada

2004 CA-SMI-548: A 9500 Year Old Shell Midden at Running Springs, San Miguel Island, California. In *Emerging from the Ice Age—Early Holocene Occupations on California's Central Coast: A Compilation of Research in Honor of Roberta S. Greenwood,* edited by E. Bertrando and V. Levulett, pp.81–92. San Luis Obispo County Archaeological Society Occasional Papers no. 17.

Erlandson, J. M., D. J. Kennett, B. L. Ingram, D. A. Guthrie, D. P. Morris, M. A. Tveskov, G. J. West, and P. L. Walker

1996 An Archaeological and Paleontological Chronology for Daisy Cave (CA-SMI-261), San Miguel Island, California. *Radiocarbon* 38:355–373.

Eshleman, J. A.

2002 Mitochondrial DNA and Prehistoric Population Movements in Western North America. Ph.D. dissertation, Department of Anthropology, University of California, Davis.

2003 Molecular Analysis for the Burial Population at CA-LAN-2233. In *Prehistory in the Transverse Ranges of California: An Archaeological Investigation in the Santa Clara River Valley.* Vol. 4. Edited by G. Waugh. Archaeological Research Center, Department of Anthropology, California State University, Sacramento.

Eshleman, J. A., R. S. Malhi, and D. G. Smith

2003 Mitochondrial DNA Studies of Native Americans: Conceptions and Misconceptions of the Population Prehistory of the Americas. *Evolutionary Anthropology* 12:7–18.

Eshleman, J. A., R. S. Malhi, J. R. Johnson, F. A. Kaestle, J. Lorenz, and D. G. Smith

2004 Mitochondrial DNA and Prehistoric Settlements: Native Migrations on the Western Edge of North America. *Human Biology* 76:55–75.

Esper, J., E. R. Cook, and F. H. Schweingruber

2002 Low Frequency Signals in Long Tree-Ring Chronologies for Reconstructing Past Temperature Variability. *Science* 295:2250–2253.

Estes, A., K. Brown, E. Strother, L. Valkenier, J. Allen, N. Summerlin, K. Popetz, M. Wells, and W. Self

2002 *Report on the Catellus Hercules Project Data Recovery, Burial Removal, and Construction Monitoring at Site CA-CCO-474/H, Hercules, California.* Vol. 1, *Data Recovery and Analysis.* William Self Associates, Orinda, California. Submitted to Catellus Residential, Hercules, California. Copies available from Northwest Information Center, Department of Anthropology, Sonoma State University, Rohnert Park, California.

Eugster, S. E.

1990 Freshwater Mussel Utilization at a Late Prehistoric Period Archaeological Site (CA-BUT-12) in the Northern Sacramento Valley, California. Master's thesis, Department of Anthropology, California State University, Chico.

Ezzo, J. A.

1994 *On the Trail to Avikwaame: Results of a Noncollection Class II Cultural Resources Survey of Quien Sabe/Big Maria Terrace, Riverside County, California.* Prepared by Statistical Research, Inc. for USDI Bureau of Reclamation, Lower Colorado Regional Office, Boulder City, Nevada.

Ezzo, J. A., and J. H. Altschul

1993 An Archaeological Survey of Pilot Knob, Imperial County, California: A Class III Cultural Resources Survey and Evaluation. In *Glyphs and Quarries of the Lower Colorado River Valley: The Results of Five Cultural Resources Surveys,* compiled by J. Ezzo and J. H. Altschul, Part 3 pp.1–162. Prepared by Statistical Research, for USDI Bureau of Reclamation, Lower Colorado Regional Office, Boulder City, Nevada.

Faegri, K., J. Iversen, P. E. Kaland, and K. Krzywinski

1989 *Textbook of Pollen Analysis.* Wiley, Chichester.

Fagan, B. M.

1987 *The Great Journey: The Peopling of Ancient America.* Thames & Hudson, New York.

1999 *Floods, Famines, and Emperors: El Niño and the Fate of Civilizations.* Basic Books, New York.

2000 *The Little Ice Age: How Climate Made History, 1300–1850.* Basic Books, New York.

2003 *Before California.* AltaMira Press, New York.

2004 The House of the Sea: An Essay on the Antiquity of Plank Canoes in Southern California. *American Antiquity* 69:7–16.

Fagan, J. L.

1988 Clovis and Western Pluvial Lakes Tradition Lithic Technologies at the Dietz Site in South-Central Oregon, In *Early Human Occupation in Far Western North America: The Clovis-Archaic Interface,* edited by J. A. Willig, C. M. Aikens, and J. L. Fagan, pp. 389–416. Nevada State Museum Anthropological Papers no. 21.

Fages, P.

1911 [1770] *Expedition to San Francisco Bay in 1770: Diary of Pedro Fages.* Publications of the Academy of Pacific Coast History 2:141–159.

1937 [1775] *A Historical, Political, and Natural Description of California (November 20, 1775).* Translated by H. E. Priestly. University of California Press, Berkeley.

Fairbanks, R. G.

1989 A 17,000-Year Glacio-Eustatic Sea Level Record: Influence of Glacial Melting Rates on the Younger Dryas Event and Deep-Ocean Circulation. *Nature* 342:637–642.

Farquhar, J. M.

2003 Organization of Flaked Stone Technology and Settlement Mobility on the South Central Coast of California: A Perspective from Diablo Canyon and Point Sal. Master's thesis, Department of Anthropology, California State University, Sacramento.

Farrell, N., T. Hannahs, and N. Stevens
2004 *Archaeological Investigations at CA-SLO-1914/H, Cayucos, San Luis Obispo County, California.* Cultural Resource Management Services, 829 Paso Robles Street, Paso Robles. Report on file, South Central Archaeological Information Center, Department of Anthropology, University of California, Santa Barbara.

Farris, G., K. E. Davis, and J. McAleer
1988 *The John Marsh House Archaeological Project.* Cultural Resources Support Unit, RPD. California State Parks, Sacramento.

Fedje, D. W., Q. Mackie, E. J. Dixon, and T. H. Heaton
2004 Late Wisconsin Environments and Archaeological Visibility on the Northern Northwest Coast. In *Entering America*, edited by D. B. Madsen, pp. 97–138. University of Utah Press, Salt Lake City.

Fenenga, F.
1973 Salvage Archaeology at CA-SJO-17 on Mormon Slough, Near Stockton, California. California State College, Long Beach. Submitted to the National Park Service, Washington, D.C.

Fenenga, G. L.
1992 Regional Variability in the Early Prehistory of the American Far West. Ph.D. dissertation, Department of Anthropology, University of California, Berkeley. University Microfilms, Ann Arbor.

Fentress, J.B.
1992 Prehistoric Rock Art of Alameda and Contra Costa Counties, California. Master's thesis, Department of Anthropology, California State University, Hayward.

Ferneau, J. A.
1998 Late Holocene Shellfish Exploitation on the Northern San Luis Obispo Coast, California. Master's thesis, Department of Anthropology, Sonoma State University.

Fiedel, S. J.
1999 Older Than We Thought: Implications for Corrected Dates for Paleoindians. *American Antiquity* 64:95–115.

Figgins, J. D.
1927 The Antiquity of Mankind in America. *Natural History* 27:229–239.

Fiore, C.M.
1998 These Old Houses: Aboriginal Domestic Structures at Eel Point, San Clemente Island. Master's thesis, Department of Anthropology, California State University, Northridge.

Fisher, L. E.
2002 Mobility, Search Modes, and Food-Getting Technology: from Magdalenian to Early Mesolithic in the Upper Danube Basin. In *Beyond Foraging and Collecting: Evolutionary Change in Hunter-Gatherer Settlement Systems*, edited by B. Fitzhugh and J. Habu, pp. 157–180. Kluwer Academic/Plenum, New York.

Fitzgerald, R. T.
1993 *Archaic Milling Cultures of the Southern San Francisco Bay Region.* Archives of California Prehistory 35. Coyote Press, Salinas.
1997 *Archaeological Data Recovery at the Salinas River Crossing Site, CA-SLO-1756, San Luis Obispo County, California.* Garcia and Associates, San Anselmo. Copies available from South Central Information Center, Department of Anthropology, University of California, Santa Barbara.
2000 *Cross Creek: An Early Holocene/Millingstone Site.* California State Water Project, San Luis Obispo County Archaeological Society Coastal Branch Series Paper no. 12.
2004 9000 Years of Prehistory and Beyond: A Survey of the Early Holocene Sites of the Central Coast of California Discovered Since Diablo Canyon. In *Emerging from the Ice Age Early Holocene Occupations on the California Central Coast, A Compilation in Honor of Roberta S. Greenwood*, edited by E. Bertrando and V. A. Levulett, pp. 5–16. San Luis Obispo County Archaeological Society, Occasional Papers no. 17.

Fitzgerald, R. T., and W. R. Hildebrandt
2002 Early Holocene Adaptations of the North Coast Ranges: New Perspectives on Old Ideas. *Proceedings of the Society for California Archaeology* 15:1–7.

Fitzgerald, R. T., and T. L. Jones
1999 The Milling Stone Horizon Revisited: New Perspectives from Northern and Central California. *Journal of California and Great Basin Anthropology* 21:65–93.
2003 On the Weight of the Evidence from Cross Creek: A Reply to Turner. *American Antiquity* 68:396–399.

Fitzgerald, R. T., and J. Porcasi
2003 The Metcalf Site (CA-SCL-178) and Its Place in Early Holocene California Prehistory. *Society for California Archaeology Newsletter* 37(4):27–31.

Fitzgerald, R. T., and A. Ruby
1997 *Archaeological Test Excavations at CA-SCR-117, the Davenport Landing Site.* Garcia and Associates, San Anselmo. Copies available from Northwest Archaeological Information Center, Department of Anthropology, Sonoma State University, Rohnert Park, California.

Fitzgerald, R. T., J. Farquhar, and N. Farrell
2000 *Archaeological Data Recovery at CA-SLO-809, Nipomo, San Luis Obispo, California.* Albion Environmental, Santa Cruz. Copies available from South Central Archaeological Information Center, Department of Anthropology, University of California, Santa Barbara.

Fitzgerald, R. T., T. L. Jones, and A. Schroth
2005 Ancient Long Distance Trade in Western North America: New AMS Radiocarbon Dates from Southern California. *Journal of Archaeological Science* 32:423–434.

Fitzgerald, R. T., J. L. Edwards, J. M. Farqhuar, and K. Loefller
1995 *Archaeological Test Excavation at CA-MNT-1765, for the Moro Cojo Standard Subdivision Project (SH 93001), Monterey County, California.* Report on file Northwest Archaeological Information Center, Department of Anthropology, Sonoma State University, Rohnert Park, California.

Fitzwater, R. J.
1962 Final Report on Two Seasons Excavations at El Portal Mariposa County, California. *University of California, Los Angeles Archaeological Survey Annual Report* 1961–1962:234–285.

Fladmark, K.
1979 Routes: Alternate Migration Corridors for Early Man in North America. *American Antiquity* 44:55–69.

Flenniken, J. Jeffrey, and Philip J. Wilke
1989 Typology, Technology, and Chronology of Great Basin Dart Points. *American Anthropologist* 9:149–158.

Fleschman, G. L.
1975 *Pit-and-Groove Rocks and Cupules in San Luis Obispo County. Papers on the Chumash.* San Luis Obispo County Archaeological Society Occasional Papers 9:89–115.

Forbes, J. D.
1963 Indian Horticulture West and Northwest of the Colorado River. *Journal of the West* 11:1–14.
1965 *Warriors of the Colorado: The Yumas of the Quechan Nation and Their Neighbors.* University of Oklahoma Press, Norman.

Forster, P., R. Harding, A. Torroni, and H. J. Bandelt
1996 Origin and Evolution of Native American mDNA Variation: A Reappraisal. *American Journal of Human Genetics* 59:935–945.

Fortescue, M.
1998 *Language Relations Across Bering Strait.* Cassell, London.

Foster, D., and J. Betts
1995 A Fluted Point from Sierra Valley. *Tularg Report* 8(9):304.

Foster, M. K.

1996 Language and the Culture History of North America. In *Languages,* edited by I. Goddard, pp. 64–110. Handbook of Native American Indians. Vol. 17. W. C. Sturtevant, general editor. Smithsonian Institution, Washington, D.C.

Fowler, C. S.

1972 Some Ecological Clues to Proto-Numic Homelands. In *Great Basin Cultural Ecology: A Symposium,* edited by D. D. Fowler, pp. 105–122. Desert Research Institute Publications in the Social Sciences no. 8.

1983 Lexical Clues to Uto-Aztecan Prehistory. *International Journal of American Linguistics* 49:224–257.

Fowler, C. S., and L. E. Dawson

1986 Prehistoric Basketry. In *Great Basin,* edited by W. d'Azevedo, pp. 705–737. Handbook of North American Indians. Vol. 11. W. G. Sturtevant, general editor. Smithsonian Institution, Washington, D.C.

Fowler, C. S., and S. Liljeblad

1986 Northern Paiute. In *Great Basin,* edited by W. L. d'Azevedo, pp. 435–465. Handbook of North American Indians. Vol. 11. W. C. Sturtevant, general editor. Smithsonian Institution, Washington, D.C.

Fredrickson, D. A.

1966 CCo-308: The Archaeology of a Middle Horizon Site in the Interior Contra Costa County, California. Master's thesis, Department of Anthropology, University of California, Davis.

1968 *Archaeological Investigations at CCo-30 near Alamo, Contra Costa County, California.* Center for Archaeological Research at Davis Publication no. 1. University of California, Davis.

1969 Technological Change, Population Movement, Environmental Adaptation, and the Emergence of Trade: Inferences on Culture Change Suggested by Midden Analysis. *University of California at Los Angeles Archaeological Survey Annual Reports* 11:101–125.

1973 Early Cultures of the North Coast of the North Coast Ranges, California. Ph.D. dissertation, Department of Anthropology, University of California, Davis.

1974a Cultural Diversity in Early Central California: A View from the North Coast Ranges. *Journal of California Anthropology* 1:41–54.

1974b Social Change in Prehistory: A Central California Example. In *'Antap: California Indian Political and Economic Organization,* edited by L. J. Bean and T. F. King, pp. 57–73. Ballena Press Anthropological Papers no. 2. Ballena Press, Menlo Park, California.

1984 The North Coastal Region. In *California Archaeology,* edited by M. J. Moratto, pp. 471–527. Academic Press, New York.

1989a *Prehistory of the Laguna: An Overview.* Submitted to David W. Smith Consulting, Oakland. Copies available from Northwest Information Center, Department of Anthropology, Sonoma State University, Rohnert Park, California.

1989b Spatial and Temporal Patterning of Obsidian Materials in the Geysers Region. In *Current Directions in California Obsidian Studies,* edited by R. E. Hughes, pp. 95–109. Contributions of the University of California Archaeological Research Facility no. 48.

1994a Spatial and Cultural Units in Central California Archaeology. In *Toward a New Taxonomic Framework for Central California Archaeology: Essays by James A. Bennyhoff and David A. Fredrickson,* edited by R. E. Hughes, pp. 25–48. Contributions of the University of California Archaeological Research Facility no. 52.

1994b Changes in Prehistoric Exchange Systems in the Alamo Locality, Contra Costa County, California. In *Toward a New Taxonomic Framework for Central California Archaeology: Essays by James A. Bennyhoff and David A. Fredrickson,* edited by R. E. Hughes, pp. 57–64. Contributions of the University of California Archaeological Research Facility no. 52.

1994c Central California Archaeology: The Concepts of Pattern and Aspect. In *Toward a New Taxonomic Framework for Central California Archaeology: Essays by James A. Bennyhoff and David A. Fredrickson,* edited by R. E. Hughes, pp. 75–79. Contributions to the University of California Archaeological Research Facility no. 52.

1994d Archaeological Taxonomy in Central California Reconsidered. In *Toward a New Taxonomic Framework for Central California Archaeology: Essays by James A. Bennyhoff and David A. Fredrickson,* edited by R. E. Hughes, pp. 91–103. Contributions of the University of California Archaeological Research Facility no. 52.

1996 Obsidian Studies, Social Boundaries, Theoretical Models, and the Development of Tribelet Structure in Central California. *Proceedings of the Society for California Archaeology* 9:25–29.

Fredrickson, D. A., and J. W. Grossman

1977 A San Dieguito Component at Buena Vista Lake, California. *Journal of California Anthropology* 4:173–190.

Fredrickson, D. A., and T. M. Origer

2002 Obsidian Hydration in the Borax Lake Basin, Lake County, California. In *Essays in California Archaeology: A Memorial to Franklin Fenenga,* edited by W. J. Wallace, and F. A. Riddell, pp. 148–165. Contributions to the University of California Archaeological Research Facility 60, Berkeley.

Fredrickson, D. A., and G. G. White

1988 The Clear Lake Basin and Early Complexes in California's North Coast Ranges. In *Early Human Occupation in Far Western North America: The Clovis-Archaic Interface,* edited by J. A. Willig, C. M. Aikens, and J. L. Fagan, pp. 75–86. Nevada State Museum Anthropological Papers no. 21.

Fredrickson, V. M.

1968 *Tice Valley: 500 Years of Human History [CA-Cco-309].* Privately published, Walnut Creek, California. Copies available from Northwest Information Center, Department of Anthropology, Sonoma State University, Rohnert Park, California.

1977 Painted Pebbles from a Shellmound on Brooks Island, Contra Costa County, California. *Journal of California Anthropology* 4:113–115.

Friddell, J. E., R. C. Thunell, T. P. Guilderson, and M. Kashgarian

2003 Increased Northeast Pacific Climatic Variability During the Warm Middle Holocene. *Geophysical Research Letters* 30:141–144.

Furlong, D. M.

2004 Spatial and Temporal Patterns of Artiodactyl Abundances During the Holocene in North Central California. Master's thesis, Department of Anthropology, California State University, Chico.

Gallegos, D. R.

1985 Batiquitos, Lagoon Revisited. *Coastal Papers* 2(1): Cultural Resource Management Center, Department of Anthropology, San Diego State University, San Diego.

1986 *Patayan II and Patayan III Occupation of IMP-4434 and IMP-5167, East Mesa, Imperial County, California.* WESTEC Services. Prepared for Ryerson Concrete Company.

1987 A Review and Synthesis of Environmental and Cultural Material for the Batiquitos Lagoon Region. In *San Dieguito-La Jolla: Chronology and Controversy,* edited by D. Gallegos, pp. 23–34. San Diego County Archaeological Society Research Paper no. 1.

1991 Antiquity and Adaptation at Agua Hedionda, Carlsbad, California. In *Hunter-Gatherers of Early Holocene Coastal California,* edited by J. M. Erlandson and R. H. Colten, pp. 19–41. Cotsen Institute of Archaeology, University of California, Los Angeles.

1992 Patterns and Implications of Coastal Settlement in San Diego County: 9000 to 1300 Years Ago. In *Essays on the Prehistory of Maritime California*, edited by T. Jones, pp. 205–216. Center for Archaeological Research at Davis no. 10. University of California, Davis.

2002 Southern California in Transition: Late Holocene Occupation of Southern San Diego County. In *Catalysts to Complexity: Late Holocene Societies of the California Coast,* edited by J. M. Erlandson and T. L. Jones, pp. 27–40. Cotsen Institute of Archaeology, University of California, Los Angeles.

Gallegos, D. R. (editor)

1980 *Class II Cultural Resource Inventory of the East Mesa and West Mesa Regions, Imperial Valley, California.* Prepared by WESTEC Services for the USDI, Bureau of Land Management, Riverside, California. Report on file, South Coast Information Center, San Diego State University.

Gallegos, D., and C. Kyle

1998 *Five Thousand Years of Maritime Subsistence at CA-SDI-48, on Ballast Point, San Diego County, California.* Archives of California Prehistory no. 40. Coyote Press, Salinas.

Gallucci, K. L.

2001 From the Desert to the Mountains: Salton Brownware Pottery in the Mountains of San Diego. Master's thesis, Department of Anthropology, San Diego State University.

Gamble, L. H.

1983 The Organization of Artifacts, Features, and Activities at Pitas Point: A Coastal Chumash Village. *Journal of California and Great Basin Anthropology* 5:103–129.

1991 Organization of Activities at the Historic Settlement of Helo': A Chumash Political, Economic, and Religious Center. Ph.D. dissertation, Department of Anthropology, University of California, Santa Barbara.

1995 Chumash Architecture: Sweatlodges and Houses. *Journal of California and Great Basin Anthropology* 17:54–92.

2002a Fact or Forgery: Dilemmas in Museum Collections. *Museum Anthropology* 25(2):3–20.

2002b Archaeological Evidence for the Origin of the Plank Canoe in North America. *American Antiquity* 67:301–315.

2004 New Perspectives on the Cuyamaca Complex: Archaeological Investigations at Camp Hual-Cu-Cuish, CA-SDI-945. *Proceedings of the Society for California Archaeology* 14:93–106.

2005 Culture and Climate: Reconsidering the Effect of Palaeoclimatic Variability Among Southern California Hunter-Gatherer Societies. *World Archaeology* 37:92–108.

Gamble, L. H., and C. King

1997 Middle Holocene Adaptations in the Santa Monica Mountains. In *Archaeology of the California Coast During the Middle Holocene*, edited by J. M. Erlandson and M. A. Glassow, pp. 61–72. Cotsen Institute of Archaeology, University of California, Los Angeles.

Gamble, L. H., and G. S. Russell

2002 A View from the Mainland: Late Holocene Cultural Developments Among the Ventureno Chumash and the Tongva. In *Catalysts to Complexity: Late Holocene Societies of the California Coast*, edited by J. M. Erlandson and T. L. Jones, pp. 101–126. Cotsen Institute of Archaeology, University of California, Los Angeles.

Gamble, L. H., P. L. Walker, and G. S. Russell

2001 An Integrative Approach to Mortuary Analysis: Social and Symbolic Dimensions of Chumash Burial Practices. *American Antiquity* 66:185–212.

2002 Further Considerations on the Emergence of Chumash Chiefdoms. *American Antiquity* 67:772–777.

Gardner, J. K.

2002 *Testing a Regional Model of Changing Settlement and Subsistence Patterns in the Western Mojave Desert: Results from the Coffee Break Site.* Coyote Press Archives of Great Basin Prehistory no. 6. Salinas, California.

2006 The Potential Impact of the Medieval Climatic Anomaly on Human Populations in the Western Mojave Desert. Ph.D. dissertation, Department of Anthropology, University of Nevada, Las Vegas.

Gardner, J. K., S. F. McGill, and M. Q. Sutton

2002 Buried Hearth Features Along the Garlock Fault. *Pacific Coast Archaeological Society Quarterly* 38(4).

Garfinkel, A. P.

2003 Dating "Classic" Coso Style Sheep Petroglyphs in the Coso Range and El Paso Mountains: Implications for Regional Prehistory. *Society for California Archaeology Newsletter* 37(4):34–37.

Garlinghouse, T. S.

2000 Human Responses to Insularity: The Intensification of a Marine Oriented Economy on San Clemente Island, California. Ph.D. dissertation, Department of Anthropology, University of California, Davis.

Gates, G. R.

1983 *Cultural Resource Overview, Modoc National Forest.* U.S. Forest Service, Pacific Northwest Region. Report on file, North Central Information Center, California State University, Sacramento.

Generaux, S., T. M. Niemi, and R. Burns

2003 Evidence for the Pleistocene-Holocene Transition from a 20.8 m Core Obtained from Vedanta Marsh, Olema, California (Abstract). North-Central Section Meeting of the Geological Society of America, Kansas City, MO. GSA Abstract with Program 35:53.

Gerow, B. A.

1954 The Problem of Culture Sequence in Central California Archaeology. Paper presented at the Annual Meeting of the American Association for the Advancement of Science, Berkeley.

1968 *An Analysis of the University Village Complex with a Reappraisal of Central California Archaeology.* Stanford University Press, Stanford. with R. Force.

1993 Implications of Physical Anthropology for Californian Prehistory. In *There Grows a Green Tree: Papers in Honor of David A. Fredrickson*, edited by G. White, P. Mikkelsen, W. R. Hildebrandt, and M. E. Basgall, pp. 397–410. Center for Archaeological Research at Davis no. 11. University of California, Davis.

Giambastiani, M. A.

2004 Prehistoric Obsidian Use on the Volcanic Tableland and Its Implications for Settlement Patterns and Technological Change in the Western Great Basin. Ph.D. dissertation, Department of Anthropology, University of California, Davis.

Giambastiani, M. A., and M. E. Basgall

2000 *Phase II Cultural Resource Evaluation for Sites CA-KER-4773/H and CA-KER-2016 in the Bissell Basin, Edwards Air Force Base, California.* Report submitted to the Department of the Army, Corps of Engineers, Sacramento.

Gibson, R. O.

1979a *Preliminary Inventory and Assessment of Indian Cultural Resources at Lodge Hill, Cambria, San Luis Obispo County, California.* Gibson's Archaeological Consulting, Paso Robles. Copies available from South Central Coast Information Center, Department of Anthropology, University of California, Santa Barbara.

1979b *Archaeological Investigations at SLO-187B: A Mitigation Project for the Cambria Water Transmission Facilities at San Simeon Creek/Van Gordon Road.* Gibson's Archaeological Consulting, Paso Robles. Copies available from South Central Coast Information Center, Department of Anthropology, University of California, Santa Barbara.

1981a *Cultural Resources Test Program at SLO-978, Morro Bay Sand Spit, San Luis Obispo County, California.* Gibson's Archaeological Consulting. Prepared for Department of Army Corps of Engineers, Los Angeles. Copies available from South Central Coast Archaeological Information Center, Department of Anthropology, University of California.

1981b Results of Archaeological Surface Survey and Subsurface Testing on the Sunset Palisades Project, Units Two Through Five, Tract 660 Pismo Beach, California. Prepared for Stanley Bell, 1036 Vista Collado, San Luis Obispo, California.

1983 Ethnography of the Salinan People: A Systems Approach. Master's thesis, Department of Anthropology, California State University, Hayward.

1991 *The Chumash.* Chelsea House, New York.

1996 *Results of Archaeological Monitoring for Unocal Soil Testing Program Along Pipelines Near Santa Margarita, San Luis Obispo County, California.* Gibson's Archaeological Consulting, Paso Robles. Report submitted to UNOCAL CERT, San Luis Obispo.

Gibson, R. O., and H. C. Koerper

2000 AMS Radiocarbon Dating of Shell Beads and Ornaments from CA-ORA-378. *Journal of California and Great Basin Anthropology* 20:342–352.

Gifford, E. W.

1916 Composition of California Shellmounds. *University of California Publications in American Archaeology and Ethnology* 12:1–29.

1931 The Kamia of Imperial Valley. *Smithsonian Institution Bureau of American Ethnology Bulletin 97.* United State Government Printing Office, Washington, D.C.

1936 California Balanophagy. In *Essays Presented to A. L. Kroeber*, edited by R. Lowie, pp. 87–98. University of California Press, Berkeley.

1940 Californian Bone Artifacts. *University of California Anthropological Records* 3:153–237.

1947 Californian Shell Artifacts. *University of California Anthropological Records* 9:1–132.

Gifford, D. P., and F. Marshall

1984 *Analysis of the Archaeological Assemblage from CA-SCR-35, Santa Cruz County, California.* Archives of California Prehistory 2. Coyote Press, Salinas.

Gillette, D. L., and T. M. Saltzman

2003 What's a PCN? *American Indian Rock Art* 29:105–110.

Gilreath, A. J.

1999a The Archaeology and Petroglyphs of the Coso Rock Art Landmark. *American Indian Rock Art* 25:33–44.

1999b *Chronological Assessment of the Coso Rock Art Landmark: An Obsidian Hydration Analysis.* Report submitted to Environmental Project Office, Naval Air Weapons Station, China Lake, California.

2003 Age and Function of Rock Art. In *Archaeological Testing of Fourteen Prehistoric Sites Within the Coso Target Range at Naval Air Weapons Station, North Range, China Lake, Inyo County, California,* by W. R. Hildebrandt and A. Ruby, pp. 209–214. Report submitted to Environmental Project Office, Naval Air Weapons Station, China Lake, California.

Gilreath, A. J., and W. R. Hildebrandt

1997 *Prehistoric Use of the Coso Volcanic Field.* Contributions of the University of California Archaeological Research Facility no. 56.

Gilreath, A. J., and E. Wohlgemuth

2004 *Investigations at the Lemmon's Quarry, CA-NAP-117/118.* Far Western Anthropological Research Group, Davis, California. Submitted to California Department of Forestry and Fire Protection. Copies available from Northwest Information Center, Department of Anthropology, Sonoma State University, Rohnert Park, California.

Glassow, M. A.

1979 An Evaluation of Models of Inezeño Chumash Subsistence and Economics. *Journal of California and Great Basin Anthropology* 1:155–161.

1980 Recent Developments in the Archaeology of the Channel Islands. In *The California Islands, Proceedings of a Multidisciplinary Symposium*, edited by D. M. Power, pp. 79–99. Santa Barbara Museum of Natural History, Santa Barbara.

1991 Early Holocene Adaptations on Vandenberg Air Force Base, Santa Barbara County. In *Hunter-Gatherers of Early Holocene Coastal California,* edited by J. M. Erlandson and R. H. Colten, pp. 113–124. Institute of Archaeology, University of California, Los Angeles.

1992 Changes in Prehistoric Subsistence, Settlement, and Technology at SBA-84 and SBA-117, El Capitan State Beach, California. In *Archaeological Investigations of Some Significant Sites on the Central Coast of California*, edited by H. Dallas and G. S. Breschini, pp. 109–132. Archives of California Prehistory 37. Coyote Press, Salinas.

1993a Changes in Subsistence on Marine Resources Through 7,000 Years of Prehistory on Santa Cruz Island. In *Archaeology on the Northern Channel Islands of California*, edited by M. A. Glassow, pp. 75–90. Archives of California Prehistory 34. Coyote Press, Salinas.

1993b The Occurrence of Red Abalone Shells in Northern Channel Island Archaeological Middens. In *Third California Island Symposium, Recent Advances in Research on the California Islands*, edited by F. G. Hochberg, pp. 567–576. Santa Barbara Museum of Natural History, Santa Barbara.

1996a *Purisimeno Chumash Prehistory Maritime Adaptations Along the Southern California Coast.* Harcourt Brace College Publishers, Fort Worth.

1996b The Significance to California Prehistory of the Earliest Mortars and Pestles. *Pacific Coast Archaeological Society* 32(4):14–26.

1997 Middle Holocene Cultural Development in the Central Santa Barbara Channel Region. In *The Archaeology of the California Coast During the Middle Holocene*, edited by J. M. Erlandson and M. A. Glassow, pp. 73–90. Cotsen Institute of Archaeology, University of California, Los Angeles.

1999 Measurement of Population Growth and Decline During California Prehistory. *Journal of California and Great Basin Anthropology* 21:45–66.

2002a Late Holocene Prehistory of the Vandenberg Region. In *Catalysts to Complexity: Late Holocene Societies of the California Coast*, edited by J. M. Erlandson and T. L. Jones, pp. 183–204. Cotsen Institute of Archaeology, University of California, Los Angeles.

2002b Prehistoric Chronology and Environmental Change at the Punta Arena Site, Santa Cruz Island, California. In *Proceedings of the Fifth California Islands Symposium*, edited by D. R. Browne, K. L. Mitchell, and H. W. Chaney, pp. 555–562. Santa Barbara Museum of Natural History, Santa Barbara.

2004a Applying the Method of Multiple Working Hypotheses to the Archaeology of Early Sites Along the Central Coast. In *Emerging from the Ice Age: Early Holocene Occupations on the California Central Coast*, edited by E. Betrando and V. A. Levulett, pp. 17–26. San Luis Obispo County Archaeological Society Occasional Papers no. 17.

2004b Identifying Complexity During the Early Prehistory of Santa Cruz Island, California. In *Foundations of Chumash Complexity*, edited by J. E. Arnold, pp. 17–24. Cotsen Institute of Archaeology, University of California, Los Angeles.

2005 Prehistoric Dolphin Hunting on Santa Cruz Island, California. In *The Exploitation and Cultural Importance of Sea Mammals*, edited by G. Monks, pp. 107–120. Oxbow Books, Oxford.

Glassow, M. A., J. R. Johnson, and J. M. Erlandson
1986 Mescalitan Island Archaeology and the Cañalino Period of Santa Barbara Prehistory. In *A New Look at Some Old Sites*, edited by G. S. Breschini and T. Haversat, pp. 9–20. Archives of California Prehistory. Coyote Press, Salinas.

Glassow, M. A., L. R. Wilcoxon, and J. M. Erlandson
1988 Cultural and Environmental Change During the Early Period of Santa Barbara Channel Prehistory. In *The Archaeology of Prehistoric Coastlines*, edited by G. Bailey and J. Parkington, pp. 64–77. Cambridge University Press, Cambridge.

Glassow, M. A., D. J. Kennett, J. P. Kennett, and L. R. Wilcoxon
1994 Confirmation of Middle Holocene Ocean Cooling Inferred from Stable Isotopic Analysis of Prehistoric Shells from Santa Cruz Island, California. In *The Fourth California Islands Symposium: Update on the Status of Resources*, edited by W. L. Halvorson and G. J. Maender, pp. 223–232. Santa Barbara Museum of Natural History, Santa Barbara.

Glassow, M. A., J. E. Arnold, G. A. Batchelder, D. T. Fitzgerald, B. Glenn, D. A. Guthrie, D. L. Johnson, and P. L. Walker
1991 *Archaeological Investigations on Vandenberg Air Force Base in Connection with the Development of Space Transportation Facilities*. 2 vols. Coyote Press, Salinas.

Glenn, B.
1991 Typological Analysis of Projectile Points Recovered from Excavations on Vandenberg Air Force Base, Santa Barbara County, California. Master's thesis, Archaeology Program, University of California, Los Angeles.

Glennan, W. S.
1971 Concave-base Lanceolate Fluted Points from California. *Masterkey* 45:27–32.
1987a Evidence for Paleoeastern Culture Type in the Southwestern Great Basin. In *Prehistory of the Antelope Valley, California: An Overview*, edited by R. W. Robinson, pp. 11–20. Antelope Valley Archaeological Society, Lancaster, California.
1987b Concave-based Lanceolate Fluted Projectile Points from California. In *Prehistory of the Antelope Valley, California: An Overview*, edited by R. W. Robinson, pp. 11–20. Antelope Valley Archaeological Society, Lancaster, California.

Gobalet, K. W., and T. L. Jones
1995 Prehistoric Native American Fisheries of the Central California Coast. *Transactions of the American Fisheries Society* 124:813–823.

Gobalet, K. W., P. D. Schulz, T. A. Wake, and N. Siefkin
2004 Archaeological Perspectives on Native Amercan Fisheries of California, with Emphasis on Steelhead and Salmon. *Transactions of the American Fisheries Society* 133:801–833.

Goddard, I.
1975 Algonquian, Wiyot, and Yurok: Proving a Distant Genetic Relationship. In *Linguistics and Anthropology: In Honor of C. F. Voegelin*, edited by M. D. Kinkade, K. L. Hale, and O. Werner, pp. 249–262. Peter de Ridder Press, Lisse, Holland.

Goddard, P. E.
1903 Life and Culture of the Hupa. *University of California Publications in American Archaeology and Ethnology* 1:1–88.

Goebel, T.
2002 The "Microblade Adaptation" and Recolonization of Siberia During the Late Upper Pleistocene. In *Thinking Small: Global Perspectives on Microlithization*, edited by R. G. Elston and S. L. Kuhn, pp. 117–132. Archaeological Papers of the American Anthropological Association no. 12.

Goebel, T., R. Powers, and N. Bigelow
1991 The Nenana Complex of Alaska and Clovis Origins. In *Clovis Origins and Adaptations*, edited by R. Bonnichsen and K. Turnmire, pp. 49–79. Center for the Study of the First Americans, Oregon State University, Corvallis.

Goebel, T., M. R. Waters, and M. Dikova
2003 The Archaeology of Ushki Lake, Kamchatka, and the Pleistocene Peopling of the Americas. *Science* 301:501–505.

Goerke, B., and R. Cowan
1983 The Pacheco Site (Marin-152) and the Middle Horizon in Central California. *Journal of New World Archaeology* 6:1–98.

Goldberg, S. K., and M. J. Moratto
1984 *Archaeological Investigations at Balsam Meadow, Fresno County, California: Data Recovery from Sites 04-Fre-811, 04-Fre-812, and 04-Fre-818*. INFOTEC Development, Sonora, California. Submitted to Southern California Edison Company, Rosemead. Report on file, Southern San Joaquin Valley Information Center, California State University, Bakersfield.

Goldberg, S. K., and E. J. Skinner
1990 *Cultural Resources of the Crane Valley Hydroelectric Project Area, Madera County, California*. Vol. 4, *Bass Lake Erosion Control Project, Limited Archaeological Site Data Recovery at CA-MAD-223, -244, and -392*. INFOTEC Research, Fresno, California. Submitted to Pacific Gas and Electric Company, San Francisco. Report on file, Southern San Joaquin Valley Information Center, California State University, Bakersfield.

Goldberg, S. K., S. S. Salzman, E. J. Skinner, J. Burton, M. E. Scully, J. J. Hobson, and M. J. Moratto
1986 *Cultural Resources of the Crane Valley Hydroelectric Project Area, Madera County, California*. Vol. 3, *Archaeological Testing, Resource, Evaluation, Impact Assessment, and Management Planning*. INFOTEC Research, Sonora, California. Submitted to Pacific Gas and Electric Company, San Francisco. Report on file, Southern San Joaquin Valley Information Center, California State University, Bakersfield.

Goldschmidt, W. R.
1951a Ethics and the Structure of Society: An Ethnological Contribution to the Sociology of Knowledge. *American Anthropologist* 53:506–524.
1951b Nomlaki Ethnography. *University of California Publications in American Archaeology and Ethnology* 42:303–443.

Golla, V.
1997 The Alsea-Wintu Connection. *International Journal of American Linguistics* 63:157–170.
2000a Language Families of North America. In *American Past, America Present: Genes and Languages in the Americas and Beyond*, edited by C. Renfrew, pp. 59–72. McDonald Institute for Archaeological Research, Cambridge.
2000b Language History and Communication Strategies in Aboriginal California and Oregon. In *Languages of the North Pacific Rim*. Vol. 5. Edited by O. Miyaoka, pp. 43–64. Faculty of Informatics, Osaka Gakuin University, Suita, Japan.

Goman, M., and L. Wells
2000 Trends in River Flow Affecting the Northeastern Reach of the San Francisco Bay Estuary over the Past 7000 Years. *Quaternary Research* 54:206–217.

Gorden, M.
1990 Cupule Petroglyphs in Tulare County, California. *American Indian Rock Art* 16:227–235.

Gordon, B. L.
1979 *Monterey Bay Area: Natural History, and Cultural Imprints*. Boxwood Press, Pacific Grove.

Gorsline, D. S., and L. S.-Y. Teng
1989 The California Continental Borderland. In *The Eastern Pacific Ocean and Hawaii (The Geology of North America, N.)*, edited by E. L. Winterer, D. M. Hussong, and R. W. Decker, pp. 471–487. Geological Society of America, Boulder.

Gould, R. A.
1964 Exploitative Economics and Culture Change in Central California. *University of California Archaeological Survey Reports* no. 62.

1966 *Archaeology of the Point St. George Site and Tolowa Prehistory.* University of California Publications in Anthropology 4.
1975 Ecology and Adaptive Response Among the Tolowa Indians of Northwest California. *Journal of California Anthropology* 2:148–170.

Grady, D. L., K. A. Latham, and V. A. Andrushko
1999 *Archaeological Investigations at CA-SCL-674, the Rubino Site, City of San Jose, Santa Clara County, California.* Vol. 2, *Human Skeletal Biology.* Archives of California Prehistory 50. Coyote Press, Salinas.

Graesch, A. P.
2004 Specialized Bead Making Among Island Chumash Households: Community Labor Organization During the Historic Period. In *Foundations of Chumash Complexity,* edited by J. E. Arnold, pp. 133–171. Perspectives in California Archaeology 7. Cotsen Institute of Archaeology, University of California, Los Angeles.

Graham, G. M.
1951 Ancient Man in Hidden Valley, California. *Masterkey* 25:79–82.

Graham, M. H., P. K. Dayton, and J. M. Erlandson
2003 Ice Ages and Ecological Transitions on Temperate Coasts. *Trends in Ecology and Evolution* 18:33–40.

Graham, N. E., and H. F. Diaz
2001 Evidence for Intensification of North Pacific Winter Cyclones Since 1948. *Bulletin of the American Meteorological Society* 82:1869–1893.

Grant, C.
1965 *The Rock Paintings of the Chumash.* University of California Press, Berkeley.

Grant, C., J. W. Baird, and J. K. Pringle
1968 *Rock Drawings of the Coso Range, Inyo County, California.* Maturango Museum Publication no. 4. Banning, California.

Graumlich, L. J.
1993 A 1000-year Record of Temperature and Precipitation in the Sierra Nevada. *Quaternary Research* 39:249–255.

Grayson, D. K., and D. J. Meltzer
2002 Clovis Hunting and Large Mammal Extinction: A Critical Review of the Evidence. *Journal of World Prehistory* 16:313–359.
2003 Requiem for North American Overkill. *Journal of Archaeological Science* 30:585–593.

Greene, H. G.
1977 Geology of the Monterey Bay Region. *United States Geological Survey Open File Reports* 77:1–718.

Greenwood, R. S.
1972 9000 Years of Prehistory at Diablo Canyon, San Luis Obispo County, California. San Luis Obispo County Archaeological Society Occasional Papers no. 7.
1978 Obispeño and Purisimeño Chumash. In *California,* edited by R. F. Heizer, pp. 520–523. Handbook of California Indians. Vol. 8. W. C. Sturtevant, general editor. Smithsonian Institution, Washington, D.C.
1979 Early Dwellers in Topanga Canyon. *Archaeology* 12:271–277.

Grenda, D. R.
1997 *Continuity and Change: 8,500 Years of Lacustrine Adaptation on the Shores of Lake Elsinore. Archaeological Investigations at a Stratified Site in Southern California.* Statistical Research, Inc. Technical Series 59. Tucson, Arizona.

Grenda, D. R., and J. A. Altschul
2002a A Moveable Feast: Isolation and Mobility Among Southern California Hunter-Gatherers. In *Islanders and Mainlanders: Prehistoric Context for the Southern California Bight,* edited by J. H. Altschul and D. R. Grenda, pp. 113–146. SRI Press, Tucson.
2002b Complex Cultures, Complex Arguments: Sociopolitical Organization in the Bight. In *Islanders and Mainlanders, Prehistoric Context for the Southern California Bight,* edited by J. H. Altschul and D. R. Grenda, pp. 147–178. SRI Press, Tucson.

Grenda, D. R., C. J. Doolittle, and J. H. Altschul
1998 *House Pits and Middens: A Methodological Study of Site Structure and Formation Processes at CA-ORA-116, Newport Bay, Orange County, California: An Innovative Study of Site Structure at an Intermediate Period Coastal Shell Midden Site in Southern California.* Statistical Research, Inc. Technical Series 69. Tucson, Arizona.

Grenda, D. R., J. A. Homburg, and J. H. Altschul (editors)
1994 *The Centinela Site (CA-LAN-60): Data Recovery at a Middle Period, Creek-Edge Site in the Ballona Wetlands, Los Angeles County, California.* Statistical Research, Inc. Technical Series 45. Tucson, Arizona.

Griset, S.
1996 Southern California Brown Ware. Ph.D. dissertation, Department of Anthropology, University of California, Davis.

Gross, G. T., and M. Sampson
1990 Archaeological Studies of Late Prehistoric Sites in the Cuyamaca Mountains, San Diego County, California. *Proceedings of the Society for California Archaeology* 3:135–148.

Grove, J. M.
1988 *The Little Ice Age.* Methuen, London.

Groza, R. G.
2002 An AMS Chronology for Central California *Olivella* Shell Beads. Master's thesis, Department of Anthropology, California State University, San Francisco.

Gruhn, R.
1994 The Pacific Coast Route of Initial Entry: An Overview. In *Method and Theory for Investigating the Peopling of the Americas,* edited by R. Bonnichsen and D. G. Steele, pp. 249–256. Center for the Study of the First Americans, Oregon State University, Corvallis.

Gruver, D.
2004 Results from the Excavation of a Rock Enclosure West of the Salton Sea. In *The Human Journey and Ancient Life in California's Deserts: Proceedings from the 2001 Millennium Conference,* edited by M. W. Allen and J. Reed, pp. 161–166. Maturango Museum Publication no. 15. Ridgecrest, California.

Guidon, N., and G. Delibrias
1986 Carbon-14 Dates Point to Man in the Americas 32,000 Years Ago. *Nature* 321:769–771.

Guilderson, T. P., P. J. Reimer, and T. A. Brown
2005 The Boon and Bane of Radiocarbon Dating. *Science* 307:362–364.

Gunnerson, J. H.
1962 Plateau Shoshonean Prehistory: A Suggested Reconstruction. *American Antiquity* 28:41–45.

Gursky, K.-H.
1966 On the Historical Position of Waikuri. *International Journal of American Linguistics* 32:41–45.

Hale, K., and D. Harris
1979 Historical Linguistics and Archeology. In *Southwest,* edited by A. Ortiz, 170–177. Handbook of North American Indians. Vol. 8. W. C. Sturtevant, general editor. Smithsonian Institution, Washington, D.C.

Hale, M. J.
2001 Technological Organization of the Millingstone Patterns in Southern California. Master's thesis, California State University, Sacramento.

Halford, F. K.
2001 New Evidence for Early Holocene Acquisition and Production of Bodie Hills Obsidian. *Society for California Archaeology Newsletter* 35(1):32–37.

Hall, J. T., R. Jurmain, and J. S. Nelson
1988 Preliminary Description of the Cemetery Complex at CA-ALA-343. *Proceedings of the Society for California Archaeology* 1:321–333.

Hall, M. C.
1983 Late Holocene Hunter-Gatherers and Volcanism in the Long Valley-Mono Basin Region: Prehistoric Culture Change in the Eastern Sierra Nevada. Ph.D. dissertation, Department of Anthropology, University of California, Riverside.
1993 *Archaeology of Seven Prehistoric Sites in Tiefort Basin, Fort Irwin, San Bernardino County, California.* Report submitted to the Department of the Army, Corps of Engineers, Los Angeles.

Hall, M. C., and M. E. Basgall
1994 Lessons to Learn from Newberry/Gypsum Period Archaeology of the Mojave Desert. In *Kelso Conference Papers 1987–1992: A Collection of Papers and Abstracts from the First Five Kelso Conferences on the Prehistory of the Mojave Desert,* edited by G. D. Everson and J. S. Schneider, pp. 82–94. California State University, Bakersfield, Museum of Anthropology Occasional Papers in Anthropology no. 4.

Hall, M. C., and R. J. Jackson
1984 Obsidian Hydration Rates in California. In *Current Directions in California Obsidian Studies,* edited by R. E. Hughes, pp. 31–58. Contributions of the University of California Archaeological Research Facility no. 48.

Hamilton, J. A.
1994 *Archaeological Survey of the Smith Ranch, Mendocino County, California.* Report on file Northwest Information Center, Department of Anthropology, Sonoma State University, Rohnert Park.

Hamusek-McGann, B.
1995 The Tuscan Obsidian Source of Northern California: Archaeological Implications and Geochemical Variability. *Proceedings of the Society for California Archaeology* 8:13–32.

Hamusek-McGann, B., E. Ritter, and J. Burcell
1998 Living on the Edge: Archaeological Signatures of the Eastern Shasta Valley Foothills, Siskiyou County, California. *Proceedings of the Society for California Archaeology* 11:102–111.

Haney, J. W., T. L. Jones, and J. Farquhar
2002 *Archaeological Evaluation of CA-MNT-879, Fort Hunter-Liggett, Monterey County, California.* Albion Environmental, Santa Cruz. Copies available from the Northwest Information Center, Department of Anthropology, Sonoma State University, Rohnert Park.

Hansen, H. P.
1942 A Pollen Study of Peat Profiles from Lower Klamath Lake of Oregon and California. In *Archaeological Researches in the Northern Great Basin,* edited by L. S. Cressman, pp. 103–114. Carnegie Institution of Washington Publication no. 538.

Harner, M. J.
1953 Gravel Pictographs of the Lower Colorado River Region. *University of California Archaeological Survey Reports* 20:1–29.

Harrington, J. P.
1928 Exploration of the Burton Mound at Santa Barbara, California. *Bureau of American Ethnology Annual Reports* 44:23–168. Smithsonian Institution, Washington, D.C.
1942 Culture Element Distributions: 19, Central California Coast. *University of California Anthropological Records* 7:1–146.

Harrington, M. R.
1938 Folsom Man in California. *Masterkey* 12:133–137.
1948 *An Ancient Site at Borax Lake, California.* Southwest Museum Papers no. 16.
1957 *Pinto Site at Little Lake.* Southwest Museum Papers no. 17.

Harrison, W. M., and E. S. Harrison
1966 An Archaeological Sequence for the Hunting People of Santa Barbara, California. In *UCLA Archaeological Survey Annual Report* 8, pp. 1–89. Department of Anthropology, University of California, Los Angeles.

Hartzell, L. L.
1991 Archaeological Evidence for Stages of Manufacture of *Olivella* Shell Beads in California. *Journal of California and Great Basin Anthropology* 13:29–39.
1992 Hunter-Gatherer Adaptive Strategies and Lacustrine Environments in the Buena Vista Lake Basin, Kern County, California. Ph.D. dissertation, University of California, Davis.

Hattori, E. M.
1982 *The Archaeology of Falcon Hill, Winnemucca Lake, Washoe County, Nevada.* Nevada State Museum Anthropological Papers no. 18.

Haury, E. W.
1950 *The Stratigraphy and Archaeology of Ventana Cave.* University of Arizona Press, Tucson.

Haury, E. W., E. B. Sayles, and W. W. Wasley
1959 The Lehner Mammoth Site, Southeastern Arizona. *American Antiquity* 25:2–30.

Hauswirth, W. W., C. D. Dickel, D. J. Rowold, and M. A. Hauswirth
1994 Inter- and Intrapopulation Studies of Ancient Humans. *Experientia (Basel)* 50:585–591.

Hayes, M. G., and D. H. O'Rourke
2001 Genetic Signatures of Migrations and Population Replacements During Human Colonization of the North American Arctic. *American Journal of Human Genetics* 69(4 Supplement):179.

Haynes, C. V., Jr.
1964 Fluted Projectile Points: Their Age and Dispersion. *Science* 145:1408–1413.
1991 Geoarchaeological and Paleohydrological Evidence for a Clovis-Age Drought in North America and Its Bearing on Extinction. *Quaternary Research* 35:438–450.
1993 Clovis-Folsom Geochronology and Climate Change. In *from Kostenki to Clovis, Upper Paleolithic–Paleo-Indian Adaptations,* edited by O. Soffer and N. D. Parslov, pp. 219–236.

Heaton, T. H., and F. Grady
1993 Fossil Grizzly Bears (*Ursus arctos*) from Prince of Wales Island, Alaska Offer New Insights into Animal Dispersal, Interspecific Competition, and Age of Deglaciation. *Current Research in the Pleistocene* 10:98–100.

Hedges, K.
1973 Rock Art in Southern California. *Pacific Coast Archaeological Society Quarterly* 8(4):1–28.
1981 Painted Pebbles from Lake Cahuilla, Imperial County, California. *American Indian Rock Art* 6:103–106.
1983 A Re-examination of Pomo Baby Rocks. *American Indian Rock Art* 9:10–21.
2001 Traversing the Great Gray Middle Ground: An Examination of Shamanistic Interpretation of Rock Art. *American Indian Rock Art* 27:123–136.
2002 Rock Art Styles in Southern California. *American Indian Rock Art* 28:25–40.
2005 Rock Art Sites at Palo Verde Point. *Proceedings of the Society for California Archaeology* 18:94–104.

Heizer, R. F.
1938 A Folsom-Type Point from the Sacramento Valley. *Masterkey* 12:180–182.
1941a Aboriginal Trade Between the Southwest and California. *Masterkey* 15:185–188.
1941b The Direct-Historical Approach in California Archaeology. *American Antiquity* 11:187–193.
1942a Massacre Lake Cave, Tule Lake Cave and Shore Sites. *Carnegie Institution of Washington Publicatinos* 538:121–134.
1942b Walla-Walla Indian Expeditions to the Sacramento Valley, 1844–1847. *California Historical Society Quarterly* 21(1):1–7.
1949 The Archaeology of Central California I: The Early Horizon. *University of California Anthropological Records* 12:1–84.
1953a The Archaeology of the Napa Region. *University of California Anthropological Records* 12:225–358.

1953b Sacred Rain-Rocks of Northern California. *University of California Archaeological Survey Reports* 2:33–38.
1958 Radiocarbon Dates from California of Archaeological Interest. *University of California Archaeological Survey Reports* 44:1–16.
1964 Archaeology of HUM-67, the Gunter Island Site in Humboldt Bay, California. *University of California Archaeological Survey Reports* 62:1–122.
1978 Introduction. In *California*, edited by R. F. Heizer, pp. 1–5. Handbook of North American Indians. Vol. 8. W. C. Sturtevant, general editor. Smithsonian Institution, Washington, D.C.

Heizer, R. F. (editor)
1978 *California*. Handbook of North American Indians. Vol. 8. W. C. Sturtevant, general editor. Smithsonian Institution, Washington, D.C.

Heizer, R. F., and M. A. Baumhoff
1962 *Prehistoric Rock Art of Nevada and Eastern California*. University of California Press, Berkeley.

Heizer, R. F., and C. W. Clewlow Jr.
1973 *Prehistoric Rock Art of California*. 2 vols. Ballena Press, Ramona, California.

Heizer, R. F., and A. B. Elsasser
1953 Some Archaeological Sites and Cultures of the Central Sierra Nevada. *University of California Archaeological Survey Reports* no. 21.
1980 *The Natural World of the California Indians*. University of California Press, Berkeley.

Heizer, R. F., and F. Fenenga
1939 Archaeological Horizons in Central California. *American Anthropologist* 41:378–399.

Heizer, Robert F., and M. A. Whipple (editors)
1951 *The California Indians: A Source Book*. University of California Press, Berkeley.

Helley, E. J., K. R. Lajoie, W. E. Spangle, and M. L. Blair
1979 Flatland Deposits of the San Francisco Bay Region, California: Their Geology and Engineering Properties, and Their Import. *United States Geological Survey Professional Paper* 943.

Helvenston, P. A., and P. G. Bahn
2005 *Waking the Trance Fixed*. Wasteland Press, Louisville, Kentucky.

Hendy, I., J. Kennett, E. B. Roark, and B. L. Ingram
2002 Apparent Synchroneity of Submillennial Scale Climatic Events Between Greenland and Santa Barbara Basin, California from 30–10 ka. *Quaternary Science Reviews* 21:1167–1184.

Hester, J. J.
1972 *Blackwater Locality No. 1: A Stratified Early Man Site in Eastern New Mexico*. Publication of the Fort Burgwin Research Center no. 8. Fort Burgwin, Taos, New Mexico.

Hester, J. J., and J. Grady
1982 *Introduction to Archaeology*. Holt, Rinehart, & Winston, New York.

Heusser, L. E.
1978 Pollen in the Santa Barbara Basin, California: A 12,000 Year Record. *Geological Society of America Bulletin* 89:673–678.
1995 Pollen Stratigraphy and Palecologic Interpretation of the 160-K.Y., edited by J. P. Kennett, J. G. Balduaf, and M. Lyle. Records from Santa Barbara Basin, Hole 893A. *Proceedings of the Ocean Drilling Program, Scientific Results*, 146:265–277.
1998 Direct Correlation of Millennial-Scale Changes in Western North American Vegetation and Climate with Changes in the California Current System over the Past ~60 kyr. *Paleoceanography* 13:252–262.

Heusser, L. E., and J. A Barron
2002 Holocene Patterns of Climate Change in Coastal Northern California. In *Proceedings of the 18th Annual Pacific Climate Workshop*, edited by G. J. West and L. D. Buffaloe, p. 157. Technical Report 69 of the Interagency Ecological Program for the San Francisco Estuary. California Department of Water Resources.

Heusser, L. E., and F. Sirocko
1997 Millennial Pulsing of Environmental Change in Southern California from the Past 24 k.y.: A Record of Indo-Pacific Enso events? *Geology* 25:243–246.

Hickman, J. C. (editor)
1993 *The Jepson Manual: Higher Plants of California*. University of California Press, Berkeley.

Hicks, B. A., M. E. Morgenstein, and S. Hamilton
2006 *Archeological Test and Data Recovery Excavations of Seven Sites in East Yosemite Valley, Yosemite National Park*. USDI National Park Service, Yosemite Research Center Publications in Anthropology 30.

Hildebrand, J. G.
2003 Ceramics Excavated from the Lower Colorado River Region by the North Baja Pipeline Project. In *A View Across the Cultural Landscape of the Lower Colorado Desert: Cultural Resource Investigations for the North Baja Pipeline Project*, edited by J. H. Cleland and R. M. Apple, pp. 245–259. Prepared by EDAW, for Tetra Tech FW, and North Baja Pipeline LLC.

Hildebrand, J. G., T. Gross, J. Schaefer, and H. Neff
2002 Patayan Ceramic Variability: Using Trace Elements and Petrographic Analysis to Study Brown and Buff Wares in Southern California. In *Ceramic Production and Circulation in the Greater Southwest: Source Determination by INNA and Complementary Mineralogical Investigations*, edited by D. M. Glowacki and H. Neff, pp. 121–139. Cotsen Institute of Archaeology, University of California, Los Angeles.

Hildebrandt, W. R.
1983 *Final Report, Archaeological Research of the Southern Santa Clara Valley Project: Based on a Data Recovery Program from Sites CA-SCL-54, CA-SCL-163, CA-SCL-178, CA-SCL-237 and CA-SCL-241 Located in the Route 101 Corridor, Santa Clara County, California*. Report on file, California Department of Transportation, Oakland.
1984 Late Period Hunting Adaptations on the North Coast of California. *Journal of California and Great Basin Anthropology* 6:189–206.
1997a The Relative Importance of Lacustrine and Estuarine Resources to Prehistoric Hunter-Gatherer Populations: A View from Southern Santa Clara Valley, California. *Journal of California and Great Basin Anthropology* 19:197–225.
1997b Late Holocene Use of Wetland Habitats in Central California: A Reply to Jones. *Journal of California and Great Basin Anthropology* 19:288–293.
2004 *Xonxon'ata, in the Tall Oaks: Archaeology and Ethnohistory of a Chumash Village in the Santa Ynez Valley*. Contributions in Anthropology 2. Santa Barbara Museum of Natural History, Santa Barbara.

Hildebrandt, W. R., and K. L. Carpenter
2006 California Animals. In *Environment, Origins, and Populations*, edited by B. Smith, pp. 284–291. Handbook of North American Indians. Vol. 3. W. C. Sturtevant, general editor. Smithsonian Institution, Washington, D.C.

Hildebrandt, W. R., and J. F. Hayes
1993 Settlement Pattern Change in the Mountains of Northwest California: A View from Pilot Ridge. In *There Grows a Green Tree: Papers in Honor of David A. Fredrickson*, edited by G. White, P. Mikkelsen, W. R. Hildebrandt, and M. E. Basgall, pp. 107–120. Center for Archaeological Research at Davis Publication no. 11. University of California, Davis.

Hildebrandt, W. R., and D. A. Jones
1998 *Archaeological Investigations at CA-MNT-1892: A Late Period Occupation Site at the Mouth of Limekiln Creek, Monterey*

County, California. Far Western Anthropological Research Group. Copies available from Northwest Archaeological Information Center, Department of Anthropology, Sonoma State University, Rohnert Park, California.

Hildebrandt, W. R., and T. L. Jones

1992 Evolution of Marine Mammal Hunting: A View from the California and Oregon Coasts. *Journal of Anthropological Archaeology* 11:360–401.

2002 Depletion of Prehistoric Pinniped Populations Along the California and Oregon Coasts: Were Humans the Cause? In *Wilderness and Political Ecology: Aboriginal Influences and the Original State of Nature,* edited by Charles E. Kay and Randy T. Simmons, pp. 72–110. University of Utah Press, Salt Lake City.

Hildebrandt, W. R., and J. H. King

2000 Projectile Point Variability Along the Northern California–Great Basin Interface: Results from the Tuscarora-Alturas Projects. In *Archaeological Investigations Along the California–Great Basin Interface: The Alturas Transmission Line Project,* edited by K. R. McGuire, pp. 221–252. Translated by Sierra Pacific Power Company. Far Western Anthropological Research Group, Davis, California.

2002 Projectile Point Variability Along the Northern California–Great Basin Interface: Results from the Tuscarora-Alturas Projects. In *Boundary Lands: Archaeological Investigations Along the California–Great Basin Interface,* edited by K. R. McGuire, pp. 5–28. Nevada State Museum Anthropological Papers no. 24, E. M. Hattori, general editor. Nevada Department of Cultural Affairs, Division of Museums and History, Carson City, Nevada.

Hildebrandt, W. R., and V. A. Levulett

1997 Middle Holocene Adaptations on the Northern California Coast: Terrestrial Resource Productivity and Its Influence on the Use of Marine Foods. In *Archaeology of the California Coast During the Middle Holocene,* edited by J. M. Erlandson and M. A. Glassow, pp. 143–150. Cotsen Institute of Archaeology, University of California, Los Angeles.

2002 Late Holocene Emergence of Advanced Maritime Cultures in Northwest California. In *The Archaeology of the California Coast During the Late Holocene,* edited by J. Erlandson and T. L. Jones, pp. 303–319. Cotsen Institute of Archaeology, University of California, Los Angeles.

Hildebrandt, W. R., and K. R. McGuire

2002 The Ascendance of Hunting During the California Middle Archaic: An Evolutionary Perspective. *American Antiquity* 67:231–256.

Hildebrandt, W. R., and P. J. Mikkelsen

1993 *Archaeological Test Excavations of Fourteen Sites Along Highway 101 and 152, Santa Clara and San Benito Counties, California.* Vol. 1, *Prehistory.* Far Western Anthropological Research Group, Davis. Copies available from California Department of Transportation, Sacramento.

1995 Projectile Point Typology. In *Archaeological Investigations PGT-PG&E Pipeline Expansion Project Idaho, Washington, Oregon, and California.* Vol. 5. Edited by R. U. Bryson, C. E. Skinner, and R. M. Pettigrew, pp. 1-1–1-40. Report submitted to Pacific Gas Transmission Company, Portland.

Hildebrant, W. R., K. Bethard, and D. Boe

1995 Archaeological Investigations at CA-SCL-714/H. *Archives of California Prehistory* 4:79–136. Coyote Press, Salinas.

Hildebrandt, W. R., M. J. Darcangelo, and T. Vaughn

2005 Extended Phase 1/Phase 2 Excavations and Determination of Eligibility on CA-SHA-571/H for the Sacramento River Bridge Replacement Project on Airport Road (Bridge #06C-0008), Near Anderson, Shasta County, California. Far Western Anthropological Research Group, Davis. Submitted to Shasta County Public Works, Redding. Copies available from Northeast Information Center, Department of Anthropology, California State University, Chico.

Hildebrandt, W. R., D. A. Jones, and K. Carpenter

2002 *Draft Report Prehistoric Coastal Occupations at Arroyo de los Chinos.* Far Western Anthropological Research Group, Davis, California. Prepared for California Department of Transportation, 50 Higuera Street, San Luis Obispo. Copies available from Far Western Anthropological Research Group.

Hildebrandt, W. R., J. Bizjak, R. Fitzgerald, R. Gillett, J. Hall, P. Hartsell, M. Hylkema, E. Kaufmann, L. Knott, J. Lopez, M. Maverick, S. Menkhus, B. Merrill, J. Nelson, J. O'Neil, and G. Wilson

1984 Prehistoric Hunting Patterns in Central California. *Papers on California Prehistory no. 1,* edited by G. Breschini and T. Haversat, pp. 43–67. Archives of California Prehistory 3. Coyote Press, Salinas.

Hill, J. H.

2001 Proto-Uto-Aztecan: A Community of Cultivators in Central Mexico? *American Anthropologist* 103:913–934.

2002 Proto-Uto-Aztecan Cultivation and Northern Devolution. In *Examining the Farming/Language Dispersal Hypothesis,* edited by P. Bellwood and C. Renfrew, pp. 331–340. McDonald Institute for Archaeological Research, Cambridge.

Hines, P.

1986 *The Prehistory of San Simeon Creek: 5800 B.P. to Missionization.* California Department of Parks and Recreation. Copies available from California Department of Parks and Recreation, Sacramento.

2004 The Results of an Archeological Survey Along the Southwestern Shores of Lake Cahuilla. In *The Human Journey and Ancient Life in California's Deserts: Proceedings from the 2001 Millennium Conference,* edited by M. W. Allen and J. Reed, pp. 153–160. Maturango Museum Publication no. 15. Ridgecrest, California.

Hinton, L.

1991 Takic and Yuman: A Study in Phonological Convergence. *International Journal of American Linguistics* 57:133–157.

Hitchcock, C. S., and E. J. Helley

2003 *Characterization of Subsurface Sediments, Southern San Francisco Bay Area.* National Earthquake Hazards Reduction Program, United States Geological Survey Award no. 99-HQ-GR-0097:1–30.

Hoffecker, J. F., W. R. Powers, and F. E. Goebel

1993 The Colonization of Beringia and the Peopling of the New World. *Science* 259:46–53.

Hofman, J. L., D. S. Amick, and R. O. Rose

1990 Shifting Sands: A Folsom-Midland Assemblage from a Campsite in Western Texas. *Plains Anthropologist* 35:221–253.

Holanda, K. L.

2000 Reversing the Trend: Late Holocene Subsistence Change in Northeastern California. In *Archaeological Investigations Along the California–Great Basin Interface: The Alturas Transmission Line Project,* edited by K. R. McGuire, pp. 282–295. Prepared for the Sierra Pacific Power Company. Report on file, Northeast Information Center of the California Historical Resources Information System, California State University, Chico.

Hollimon, S. E.

1990 Division of Labor and Gender Roles in Santa Barbara Channel Area Prehistory. Ph.D. dissertation, Department of Anthropology, University of California, Santa Barbara.

1995 Human Osteology. In *Final Report on the Archaeological Analysis of CA-SAC-43, Cultural Resources Mitigation for the Sacramento Urban Area Levee Reconstruction Project, Sacramento County, California,* edited by P. D. Bouey, pp. 301–339. Far Western Anthropological Research Group, Davis.

2004 The Role of Ritual Specialization in the Evolution of Prehistoric Chumash Complexity. In *Foundations of Chumash*

Complexity, edited by J. E. Arnold, pp. 53–64. Cotsen Institute of Archaeology, University of California, Los Angeles, California.

Holson, J., R. Gargett, S. Anton, L. Hager, R. Milliken, T. L. Jackson, J. A. Bennyhoff, S. Goddard, R. Orlins, E. Alexander, K. Gobalet, D. D. Simons, E. Skinner, and P. Ainsworth

2000 *Data Recovery Excavations for the Wildcat and San Pablo Creeks Flood Control and Water Resource Project at CA-CCO-269, -270, -600, and -601, Contra Costa County, California.* Pacific Legacy, Albany, and California Archaeological Consultants, Oakland. Submitted to the U.S. Army Corps of Engineers, Sacramento District. Copies available from Northwest Information Center, Department of Anthropology, Sonoma State University, Rohnert Park, California.

Hoover, R. L., and W. B. Sawyer

1977 *Los Osos Junior High School Site 4-SLO-214.* San Luis Obispo County Archaeological Society Occasional Papers no. 11.

Horai, S., R. Kondo, Y. Nakagawa-Hattori, S. Hayashi, S. Sonoda and K. Tajima

1993 Peopling of the Americas Founded by Four Major Lineages of Mitochondrial DNA. *Molecular Biology and Evolution* 10:23–47.

Hornbeck, D.

1983 *California Patterns: A Geographical and Historical Atlas.* Mayfield Publishing Company, California.

Horne, S. P.

1981 The Inland Chumash: Ethnography, Ethnohistory, and Archaeology. Ph.D. dissertation, Department of Anthropology, University of California Santa Barbara.

Houghton, J. G.

1969 *Characteristics of Rainfall in the Great Basin.* Desert Research Institute, Reno.

Howard, W. J., and L. M. Raab.

1993 *Olivella* Grooved Rectangle Beads as Evidence of a Mid-Holocene Southern Channel Islands Interaction Sphere. *Pacific Coast Archaeological Society Quarterly* 29(3):1–11.

Howe, C. B.

1968 *Ancient Tribes of Klamath Country.* Binfords and Mort, Portland, Oregon.

Hubbell, S. P.

2001 *The Unified Neutral Theory of Biodiversity and Biogeography.* Princeton University Press.

Hubbs, C. L., G. S. Bien, and H. E. Suess

1962 La Jolla Natural Radiocarbon Dates II. *Radiocarbon* 4:204–238.

Huberland, A. B.

1989 Etsel Ridge Archaeological Project: A Multi-Site Approach to Prehistoric Adaptation in the Middle Eel Uplands. *Proceedings of the Society for California Archaeology* 2:19–34.

Huckell, B. B., and C. V. Haynes, Jr.

2003 The Ventana Complex: New Dates and New Ideas on Its Place in Early Holocene Western Prehistory. *American Antiquity* 68:353–371.

Hudson, D. T.

1969 The Archaeological Investigations During 1935 and 1937 at ORA-237, ORA-238, and ORA-239, Santiago Canyon, Orange County, California. *Pacific Coast Archaeological Society Quarterly* 5(1).

1971 Proto-Gabrielino Patterns of Territorial Organizations in South Coastal California. *Pacific Coast Archaeological Society Quarterly* 7(2):49–76.

1981 To Sea or Not to Sea: Further Notes on the "Oceangoing" Dugouts of North Coastal California. *Journal of California and Great Basin Anthropology* 3:269–282.

Hudson, D. T., and T. C. Blackburn

1979 *The Material Culture of the Chumash Interaction Sphere.* Vol. 1, *Food Procurement and Transportation.* Ballena Press and the Santa Barbara Museum of Natural History, Los Altos.

1983 *The Material Culture of the Chumash Interaction Sphere.* Vol. 2, *Food Preparation and Shelter.* Ballena Press, Palo Alto, California.

1985 *The Material Culture of the Chumash Interaction Sphere.* Vol. 3, *Clothing, Ornamentation, and Grooming.* Ballena Press, Palo Alto, California.

1986 *The Material Culture of the Chumash Interaction Sphere.* Vol. 4, *Ceremonial Paraphernalia, Games, and Amusements.* Ballena Press, Palo Alto, California.

1987 *The Material Culture of the Chumash Interaction Sphere.* Vol. 5, *Manufacturing Processes, Metrology, and Trade.* Ballena Press, Palo Alto, California.

Hudson, D. T., and K. Conti

1981 The "Aquatic Motif" in Chumash Rock Art. *Journal of California and Great Basin Anthropology* 3:224–231.

1984 *The Rock Art of Indian Creek: Ritual Sanctuary of the Gifted Chumash. Papers on Chumash Rock Art.* San Luis Obispo County Archaeological Society, Occasional Papers 12:49–90.

Hudson, D. T., and G. Lee

1984 Function and Symbolism in Chumash Rock Art. *Journal of New World Archaeology* 6:26–47.

Hudson, D. T., and E. Underhay

1978 *Crystals in the Sky: An Intellectual Odyssey Involving Chumash Astronomy, Cosmology and Rock Art.* Ballena Press/Santa Barbara Museum of Natural History Cooperative Publication.

Hudson, T., J. Timbrook, and M. Rempe

1978 *Tomol: Chumash Watercraft as Described in the Ethnographic Notes of John P. Harrington.* Ballena Press Anthropological Papers no. 9. Ballena Press, Socorro, New Mexico.

Hughes, M. K., and P. M. Brown

1992 Drought Frequency in Central California Since 101 B.C. Recorded in Giant Sequoia Tree Rings. *Climate Dynamics* 6:161–167.

Hughes, M. K., and L. J. Graumlich

1996 Climatic Variations and Forcing Mechanisms of the Last 2000 Years. *Multi-Millenial Dendroclimatic Studies from the Western United States* 141:109–124. NATO ASI Series.

Hughes, M. K., P. M. Kelly, J. R. Pilcher, and V. C. LaMarche, Jr.

1982 *Climate from Tree Rings.* Cambridge University Press, Cambridge.

Hughes, R. E.

1977 *The Archaeology of the Burrell Site (CA-MOD-293), a Lowland Occupation Site in the Goose Lake Basin, Northeast California.* Report for the National Endowment for the Humanities.

1978 Aspects of Prehistoric Wiyot Exchange and Social Ranking. *Journal of California Anthropology* 5:53–66.

1982 Age and Exploitation of Obsidian from the Medicine Lake Highland, California. *Journal of Archaeological Science* 9:173–185.

1984 Obsidian Sourcing Studies in the Great Basin: Problems and Prospects. In *Obsidian Studies in the Great Basin*, edited by R. E. Hughes, pp. 1–19. Contributions of the University of California Archaeological Research Facility no. 45.

1985 Obsidian Sources. In *Nightfire Island: Late Holocene Lakemarsh Adaptation on the Western Edge of the Great Basin*, edited by C. G. Sampson, pp. 245–267. University of Oregon Anthropological Papers 33, Eugene.

1986a *Diachronic Variability in Obsidian Procurement Patterns in Northeastern California and Southcentral Oregon.* University of California Publications in Anthropology 17. University of California Press, Berkeley.

1986b Trace Element Composition of Obsidian Butte, Imperial County, California. *Bulletin of the Southern California Academy of Sciences* 85:35–45.

1988 The Coso Volcanic Field Reexamined: Implications for Obsidian Sourcing and Hydration Dating Research. *Geoarchaeology* 3:253–265.

1989 A New Look at Mono Basin Obsidians. In *Current Directions in California Obsidian Studies*, edited by R. E. Hughes, pp. 1–12. Contributions of the University of California Archaeological Research Facility 48.

1990 The Gold Hill Site: Evidence for a Prehistoric Socioceremonial System in Southwestern Oregon. In *Living with the Land: The Indians of Southwest Oregon*, edited by N. Hannon and R. K. Olmo, pp. 48–55. Southern Oregon Historical Society, Medford.

1992a California Archaeology and Linguistic Prehistory. *Journal of Anthropological Research* 48:317–338.

1992b Northern California Obsidian Studies: Some Thoughts and Observations on the First Two Decades. *Proceedings of the Society for California Archaeology* 5:113–122.

1994a Mosaic Patterning in Prehistoric California–Great Basin Exchange. In *Prehistoric Exchange Systems in North America*, edited by T. G. Baugh and J. E. Ericson, pp. 363–383. Plenum Press, New York.

1994b Intrasource Chemical Variability of Artefact-Quality Obsidians from the Casa Diablo Area, California. *Journal of Archaeological Science* 21:263–271.

1994c Editor's Introduction. In *Toward a New Taxonomic Framework for Central California Archaeology: Essays by James A. Bennyhoff and David A. Fredrickson*, edited by R. E. Hughes, pp. 1–3. Contributions of the University of California Archaeological Research Facility no. 52.

1998 On Reliability, Validity, and Scale in Obsidian Sourcing Research. In *Unit Issues in Archaeology: Measuring Time, Space, and Material*, edited by A. F. Ramenofsky and A. Steffen, pp. 103–114. University of Utah Press, Salt Lake City.

Hughes, R. E. (editor)

1994 *Toward a New Taxonomic Framework for Central California Archaeology: Essays by James A. Bennyhoff and David A. Fredrickson*. Contributions of the University of California Archaeological Research Facility 52.

Hughes, R. E., and J. A. Bennyhoff

1986 Early Trade. In *Great Basin*, edited by W. L. d'Azevedo, pp. 238–255. Handbook of North American Indians. Vol. 11. Smithsonian Institution, Washington, D.C.

Hughes, R. E., and R. L. Bettinger

1984 Obsidian and Prehistoric Sociocultural Systems in California. In *Exploring the Limits: Frontiers and Boundaries in Prehistory*, edited by S. P. DeAtley and F. J. Findlow, pp. 153–172. British Archaeological Reports International Series 223.

Hughes, R. E., and R. L. Smith

1993 Archaeology, Geology and Geochemistry in Obsidian Provenance Studies. In *Effects of Scale on Archaeological and Geoscientific Perspectives*, edited by J. K. Stein and A. R. Linse, pp. 79–91. Geological Society of America Special Paper 283.

Hughes, R. E., and D. L. True

1985 Perspectives on the Distribution of Obsidians in San Diego County, California. *North American Archaeologist* 6:325–339.

Hull, K. L.

2001 Reasserting the Utility of Obsidian Hydration Dating: A Temperature-Dependent Empirical Approach to Practical Temporal Resolution with Archaeological Obsidians. *Journal of Archaeological Science* 28:1025–1040.

2002 Culture Contact in Context: A Multiscalar View of Catastrophic Depopulation and Culture Change in Yosemite Valley, California. Ph.D. dissertation, Department of Anthropology, University of California, Berkeley.

2005 Process, Perception, and Practice: Time Perspectivism in Yosemite Native Demography. *Journal of Anthropological Archaeology* 24: 354–377.

Hull, K. L., C. K. Roper, and M. J. Moratto

1999 Prehistoric Economic Systems. In *Archeological Synthesis and Research Design, Yosemite National Park, California*, edited by K. L. Hull and M. J. Moratto, pp. 205–258. USDI National Park Service Yosemite Research Center Publications in Anthropology 21.

Hull, K. L., R. W. Bevill, W. G. Spaulding, and M. R. Hale

1995 *Archeological Site Subsurface Survey, Test Excavations, and Data Recovery Excavation for the Tuolumne Sewer Replacement Project in Tuolumne Meadows, Yosemite National Park, California.* USDI National Park Service, Yosemite Research Center Publications in Anthropology 16.

Hull, K. L., and M. J. Moratto, with contributions by H. McCarthy, C. K. Roper, W. G. Spaulding, M. R. Hale, and E. Nilsson

1999 *Archeological Synthesis and Research Design, Yosemite National Park, California.* USDI National Park Service Yosemite Research Center Publications in Anthropology 21.

Humphreys, K. H.

1994 Description and Analysis of the Glen Aulin and Pate Valley Obsidian Biface Caches. Master's thesis, Department of Anthropology, California State University, Sacramento.

Hunt, C. B.

1960 *Death Valley: Geology, Ecology, Archaeology*. University of California Press, Berkeley.

Hurd, G. S., G. E. Miller, and H. C. Koerper

1990 An Application of Neutron Activation Analysis to the Study of Prehistoric Californian Ceramics. In *Hunter-Gatherer Pottery from the Far West*, edited by J. M. Mack, pp. 201–220. Nevada State Museum Anthropological Papers no. 23.

Hutchins, J., and D. D. Simons

2000 Obsidian Studies in the Truckee Meadows. *Journal of California and Great Basin Anthropology* 22:151–163.

Huyer, A.

1983 Coastal Upwelling in the California Current System. *Progess in Oceanography* 12:259–284.

Hyder, W. D.

1989 *Rock Art and Archaeology in Santa Barbara County, California.* San Luis Obispo County Archaeological Society, Occasional Papers no. 13.

Hyder, W. D., and G. Lee

2003 Chapter 2: Research Background. In *Overview of Rock Art for California State Parks*. Report on file, California Department of Parks and Recreation, Sacramento.

Hyder, W. D., and M. Oliver

1986 Style and Chronology in Chumash Rock Art. *American Indian Rock Art* 10:86–101.

Hylkema, M. G.

1991 Prehistoric Native American Adaptations Along the Central California Coast of San Mateo and Santa Cruz Counties. Master's thesis, Department of Anthropology, San Jose State University.

1993 Some Perspectives on Upland Settlement Patterns of the Central Diablo Range of California. *Proceedings of the Society for California Archaeology* 6:99–119.

1995 *Archaeological Investigation at Mission Santa Clara (CA-SCL-30) for the Re-alignment of Route 82.* Report on file, California Department of Transportation, District 4, Oakland.

1998 *Seal Cove Prehistory: Archaeological Excavations at CA-SMA-134, Fitzgerald Marine Preserve, San Mateo County Park, California.* Copies available from Northwest Information Center, Department of Anthropology, Sonoma State University, Rohnert Park, California.

2002 Tidal Marsh, Oak Woodlands, and Cultural Florescence in the Southern San Francisco Bay Region. In *Catalysts to Complexity: Late Holocene Societies of the California Coast*, edited by J. M. Erlandson and T. L. Jones, pp. 233–262. Cotsen Institute of Archaeology, University of California, Los Angeles.

Hylkema, M. G. (editor)

2006 *Santa Clara Valley Prehistory: Archaeological Investigations at CA-SCL-690, the Tamien Station Site, San Jose, California.* Center for Archaeological Research at Davis Publication no. 15.

Imamura, K.
1996 *Prehistoric Japan: New Perspectives on Insular East Asia.* University of Hawaii Press, Honolulu.

Imbrie, J., and J. Z. Imbrie
1980 Modeling the Climate Response to Orbital Variations. *Science* 207:943–953.

Imbrie, J., E. A. Boyle, S. C. Clemens, A. Duffy, W. R. Howard, G. Kukla, J. Kutzbach, D. G. Martinson, A. McIntyre, A. C. Mix, B. Molfino, J. J. Morley, L. C. Peterson, N. G. Pisias, W. L. Prell, M. E. Raymo, N. J. Shackleton, and J. R. Toggwieler
1992 On the Structure and Origin of Major Glaciation Cycles: Linear Responses to Milankovitch Forcing. *Paleoceanography* 7:701–738.

Ingram, B. L.
1998 Differences in Radiocarbon Age Between Shell and Charcoal from a Holocene Shellmound in Northern California. *Quaternary Research* 49:102–110.

Ingram, B. L., and J. R. Southon
1996 Reservoir Ages in Pacific Coast Estuarine Waters. *Radiocarbon* 38:573–582.

Inman, D. L.
1983 Application of Coastal Dynamics to the Reconstruction of Paleocoastlines in the Vicinity of La Jolla, California. In *Quaternary Coastlines and Marine Archaeology*, edited by P. M. Masters and N. C. Flemming, pp. 1–49. Academic Press, London.

Inman, D. L., and R. Dolan
1989 The Outer Banks of North Carolina: Budget of Sediment and Inlet Dynamics Along a Migrating Barrier System. *Journal of Coastal Research* 5:193–237.

Inman, D. L., and J. D. Frautschy
1965 Littoral Processes and the Development of Shorelines. *Coastal Engineering, Santa Barbara Specialty Conference*, edited by T. Saville, pp. 511–536. American Society of Civil Engineers, New York.

Inman, D. L., and S. A. Jenkins
1997 Changing Wave Climate and Littoral Drift Along the California Coast. In *California and The World Ocean '97*, edited by O. T. Magoon, pp. 538–549. American Society of Civil Engineers, Reston, Virginia.
1999 Climate Change and the Episodicity of Sediment Flux of Small California Rivers. *Journal of Geology* 107:251–270.
2005 Climate Patterns in the Coastal Zone. In *Encyclopedia of Coastal Science*, edited by M. Schwartz, pp. 301–305. Kluwer Academic Publishers, Dordrecht, Netherlands.

Inman, D. L., and C. E. Nordstrom
1971 On the Tectonic and Morphologic Classification of Coasts. *Journal of Geology* 79:1–21.

Inman, D. L., P. M. Masters, and S. A. Jenkins
2005 Facing the Coastal Challenge: Modeling Coastal Erosion in Southern California. *California and the World Ocean '02*, edited by O. T. Magoon et al., pp. 38–52. American Society of Civil Engineers, Reston, Virginia.

Intermountain Research, Inc.
1995 *An Archaeological Treatment Plan for the Mount Rose Land Exchange.* Intermountain Research, Silver City, Nevada. Submitted to Humboldt and Toiyabe National Forests on behalf of the American Land Conservancy, San Francisco. Copies available from Humboldt-Toiyabe National Forest, Sparks, Nevada.

Ivanhoe, F.
1995 Secular Decline in Cranioskeletal Size over Two Millennia of Interior Central California Prehistory: Relation to Calcium Deficit in the Reconstructed Diet and Demographic Stress. *International Journal of Osteoarchaeology* 5:213–253.

Jack, R. N.
1976 Prehistoric Obsidian in California I: Geochemical Aspects. In *Advances in Obsidian Glass Studies: Archaeological and Geochemical Perspectives*, edited by R. E. Taylor, pp. 183–215. Noyes Press, Park Ridge, New Jersey.

Jackson, R. J., and H. S. Ballard
1999 *Once upon a Micron: A Story of Archaeological Site CA-ELD-145 Near Camino, El Dorado County, California.* Pacific Legacy, Cameron Park, California. Submitted to California Department of Transportation, District 3, Marysville.

Jackson, R. J., T. Jackson, C. Miksicek, K. Roper, and D. Simons
1994 *Framework for Archaeological Research and Management, National Forests of the North Central Sierra Nevada: Unit III, Special Studies and Research Data.* Vol. C, *Projectile Point Compendium.* Prepared by BioSystems Analysis, Sacramento. Submitted to USDA Forest Service, Eldorado National Forest, Placerville. Report on file, North Central Information Center, California State University, Sacramento.

Jackson, T. L.
1974 The Economics of Obsidian in Central California Prehistory: Applications of X-ray Fluorescence Spectrography in Archaeology. Master's thesis, Department of Anthropology, San Francisco State University, San Francisco.
1984 A Reassessment of Obsidian Production Analyses for the Bodie Hills and Casa Diablo Quarry Areas. In *Obsidian Studies in the Great Basin*, edited by Richard E. Hughes, pp. 117–134. Contributions of the University of California Archaeological Research Facility 45.
1986 Late Prehistoric Obsidian Exchange in Central California. Ph.D. dissertation, Department of Anthropology, Stanford University.
1988 Amending Models of Trans-Sierran Obsidian Tool Production and Exchange. *Journal of California and Great Basin Anthropology* 10:62–72.
1989a Late Prehistoric Obsidian Production and Exchange in the North Coast Ranges, California. In *Current Directions in California Obsidian Studies*, edited by R. E. Hughes, pp. 79–94. Contributions of the University of California Archaeological Research Facility no. 48.
1989b Reconstructing Migration in California Prehistory. *American Indian Quarterly* 13:359–368.
1991 Pounding Acorn: Women's Production as Social and Economic Focus. In *Engendering Archaeology: Women and Prehistory*, edited by J. M. Gero and M. W. Conkey, pp. 301–325. Basil Blackwell, Oxford.

Jackson, T. L., and S. A. Dietz
1984 *Archaeological Data Recovery Excavations at CA-FRE-798 and CA-FRE-805, Siphon Substation 33kV Distribution Line and Balsam Meadow Hydroelectric Project.* Archaeological Consulting and Research Services, Santa Cruz, California. Submitted to Southern California Edison, Rosemead.

Jackson, T. L., and J. E. Ericson
1994 Prehistoric Exchange Systems in California. In *Prehistoric Exchange Systems in North America*, edited by T. G. Baugh and J. E. Ericson, pp. 385–415. Plenum Press, New York.

Jackson, T. L., and C. Morgan
1999 *Archaeological Data Recovery Program Rush Meadow Archaeological District, Ansel Adams Wilderness, Inyo National Forest, California.* Pacific Legacy, Santa Cruz, California. Submitted to Southern California Edison Company, Rosemead, California.

Jackson, T. L., L. A. Shapiro, and J. H. King
1998 *Prehistoric Archaeological Resources Inventory and Evaluation at Naval Petroleum Reserve no. 1 (Elk Hills), Kern County, California.* Pacific Legacy, Aptos. Report on file, Southern San Joaquin Valley Information Center, California State University, Bakersfield.

Jacobs, R. A.
1975 *Syntactic Change: A Cupan (Uto-Aztecan) Case Study.* University of California Publications in Linguistics 79.

Jacobsen, W. H.

1986 Washoe Language. In *Great Basin*, edited by W. L. d'Azevedo, pp. 107–112. Handbook of North American Indians. Vol. 11. W. C. Sturtevant, general editor. Smithsonian Institution, Washington, D.C.

Jaffke, T. D.

1997 A Spatial and Temporal Analysis of Morphological Variation Among Gunther Barbed Projectile Points of the Central North Coastal Ranges, Mendocino County, California. Master's thesis, Department of Anthropology, Sonoma State University, Rohnert Park.

Jelinek, A. J.

1992 Perspectives from the Old World on the Habitation of the New. *American Antiquity* 57:345–347.

Jenkins, D. L.

1985 *Rogers Ridge (4-SBr-5250): A Fossil Spring Site of the Lake Mohave and Pinto Periods–Phase 2 Test Excavations and Site Evaluation.* Report on file, National Park Service, San Francisco.

1986 *Flood, Sweat, and Spears in the Valley of Death: Site Survey and Evolution in Tiefort Basin, Fort Irwin, San Bernardino County, California.* Limited edition technical report on file, National Park Service Interagency Archaeological Services, San Francisco, California.

1987 Dating the Pinto Occupation at Rogers Ridge: A Fossil Spring Site in the Mojave Desert, California. *Journal of California and Great Basin Anthropology* 9:214–231.

Jenkins, D. L., and J. M. Erlandson

1996 *Olivella* Grooved Rectangle Beads from a Middle Holocene Site in the Fort Rock Valley, Northern Great Basin. *Journal of California and Great Basin Anthropology* 18:296–302.

Jenkins, D. L., L. Largaespada, T. D. Largaespada, and M. A. McDonald

2004 Early and Middle Holocene Ornament Exchange Systems in the Fort Rock Basin of Oregon. In *Early and Middle Holocene Archaeology of the Northern Great Basin,* edited by D. L. Jenkins, T. J. Connolly, and C. M. Aikens, pp. 251–269. University of Oregon Anthropological Papers no. 62.

Jenkins, R. C.

1992 *Preliminary Report on the Archaeology of the Corral Site, CA-FRE-1346, Fresno County, California.* Copies available from California Department of Forestry and Fire Protection, Archaeology Office, Sacramento.

2001 The Archaeology of the Corral Site, CA-FRE-1346, Fresno County, California. In *Investigations of the Coalinga Archaeological Research Group 1988 to 1994*, edited by J. Betts and D. G. Foster. CDF Archaeological Reports no. 29.

2005 A Fluted Point from Siskiyou County, California. In *Archaeology Without Limits: Papers in Honor of Clement W. Meighan*, edited by B. D. Dillon and M. A. Boxt, pp. 61–68. Labyrinthos, Lancaster.

Jennings, S. A., and D. L. Elliot-Fisk

1993 Packrat Midden Evidence of Late Quaternary Vegetation Change in the White Mountains, California-Nevada. *Quaternary Research* 39:214–221.

Jensen, P. M., and A. Farber

1982 *Archaeological Data Recovery Program at CA-SIS-342 on 02-SIS-97 P.M. 41.5 to 42.3.* Department of Transportation, Redding, California. Report submitted to California Department of Transportation, Sacramento.

Jewell, D.

1987 *Indians of the Feather River: Tales and Legends of Concow Maidu of California.* Ballena Press, Menlo Park, California.

Jobson, R. W., and W. R. Hildebrandt

1980 The Distribution of Oceangoing Canoes on the North Coast of California. *Journal of California and Great Basin Anthropology* 2:165–175.

Joël, J.

1964 Classification of the Yuman Languages. In *Studies in Californian Linguistics*, edited by W. Bright, pp. 99–105. University of California Publications in Linguistics 34.

Johns, T., and M. Duquette

1991 Traditional Detoxification of Acorn Bread with Clay. *Ecology of Food and Nutrition* 25:221–228.

Johnson, B.

1985 *Earth Figures of the Lower Colorado and Gila River Deserts: A Functional Analysis.* Arizona Archaeological Society Publication 20. Phoenix.

2003 Geoglyphs Associated with the *Xam Kwatan* Trail in the Palo Verde Point Area, South of Blythe, California. In *A View Across the Cultural Landscape of the Lower Colorado Desert: Cultural Resource Investigations for the North Baja Pipeline Project*, edited by J. H. Cleland and R. M. Apple. Prepared for Tetra Tech FW, Santa Ana, California and North Baja Pipeline LLC, Portland Oregon. EDAW San Diego.

Johnson, D. L.

1989 Subsurface Stone Lines, Stone Zones, Artifact-Manuport Layers, and Biomantles Produced by Bioturbation via Pocket Gophers (*Thomomys bottae*). *American Antiquity* 54:370–389.

Johnson, J. J.

1967 *The Archaeology of the Camanche Reservoir Locality, California.* Sacramento Anthropological Society Paper no. 6.

1990 Cosumnes Brownware: A Pottery Type Centered on the Lower Cosumnes and Adjacent Sacramento Rivers in Central California. In *Hunter-Gatherer Pottery from the Far West*, edited by J. M. Mack, pp. 145–158. Nevada State Museum Anthropological Papers no. 23.

Johnson, J. J. (editor)

1976 Archaeological Investigations at the Blodgett Site (CA-SAC-267), Sloughhouse Locality, California. Archaeological Study Center, California State University, Sacramento and the Department of Anthropology at the University of California, Davis. Submitted to National Park Service, Western Region. Copies available from the North Central Information Center, Department of Anthropology, California State University, Sacramento.

Johnson, J. J., and S. B. Dondero

1990 *Excavations at Archaeological Site CA-TEH-10, Cemetery 1: Black Butte Lake, Glenn and Tehama Counties, California.* The Hornet Foundation, California State University, Sacramento. Submitted to U.S. Army Corps of Engineers, Sacramento. Copies available from the North Central Information Center, Department of Anthropology, California State University, Sacramento.

Johnson, J. J., and D. J. Theodoratus

1984 *Cottonwood Creek Project, Shasta and Tehama Counties, California: Dutch Gulch Lake Intensive Cultural Resource Survey.* Foundation of California State University, Sacramento and Theodoratus Cultural Research, Fair Oaks. Submitted to U.S. Army Corps of Engineers, Sacramento. On file, Northeast Information Center, California State University, Chico.

Johnson, J. J., D. J. Theodoratus, C. M. Blount, and S. B. Dondero

1984 *Black Butte Lake Intensive Cultural Resource Survey.* Prepared for the U.S. Army Corps of Engineers, Sacramento District. Report on file, Northeast Information Center of the California Historical Resources Information System, California State University, Chico.

Johnson, J. R.

1982 An Ethnohistoric Study of the Island Chumash. Master's thesis, Department of Anthropology, University of California, Santa Barbara.

1988 Chumash Social Organization: An Ethnohistoric Perspective. Ph.D. dissertation, University of California, Santa Barbara.

2000 Social Responses to Climate Change Among the Chumash Indians of South-Central California. In *The Way the Wind Blows: Climate, History, and Human Action*, edited by R. J. McIntosh, J. A. Tainter, and S. K. McIntosh, pp. 301–327. Columbia University Press, New York.

Johnson, J. R., and D. Crawford

1999 Contributions to Luiseno Ethnohistory Based on Mission Register Research. *Pacific Coast Archaeological Society Quarterly* 35(3):79–102.

Johnson, J. R., and J. G. Lorenz

2006 Genetics, Linguistics, and Prehistoric Migrations: An Analysis of California Indian Mitochondrial DNA Lineages. *Journal of California and Great Basin Anthropology* 26:33–64.

Johnson, J. R., T. W. Stafford, Jr., H. O. Ajie, and D. P. Morris

2002 Arlington Springs Revisited. In *Proceedings of the Fifth California Islands Symposium*, 2 vols., edited by D. R. Browne, K. L. Mitchell, and H. W. Chaney, pp. 541–545. Santa Barbara Museum of Natural History, Santa Barbara.

Johnson, K. L.

1980 Rainbow Point Revisited: Archaeological Investigations at Bucks Lake, Plumas County, California. Report on file, Northeast Information Center of the California Historical Resources Information System, California State University, Chico.

Johnston, S. E., and B. Price

2002 A Clovis Point from the Sierra National Forest. *Society for California Archaeology Newsletter* 36(1):15–16.

Jones, D. A.

1992 The Forager-Collector Model and Monterey Bay Prehistory. In *Essays on the Prehistory of Maritime California*, edited by T. L. Jones, pp. 105–113. Center for Archaeological Research at Davis no. 10. University of California, Davis.

Jones, D. A., and M. Darcangelo

2004 *Archaeological Survey Report for the South Halcyon Road Climbing Lane Project, Nipomo Mesa, San Luis Obispo County, California*. Far Western Anthropological Research Group, Davis. Copies available from South Central Information Center, Department of Anthropology, University of California, Santa Barbara.

Jones, D. A., and W. R. Hildebrandt

1990 *Archaeological Excavation at Sand Hill Bluff: Portions of Prehistoric Site CA-SCR-7, Santa Cruz County, California*. Far Western Anthropological Research Group, Davis. Copies available from Northwest Information Center, Department of Anthropology, Sonoma State University, Rohnert Park, California.

Jones, D. A., P. A. Mikkelsen, and W. R. Hildebrandt

2004 Prehistoric Occupations on Ancient Halcyon Bay/Estuary: Excavation Results from CA-SLO-832, and 1420. In *Emerging from the Ice Age: Early Holocene Occupations on the California Central Coast*, edited by Ethan Betrando and Valerie A. Levulett, pp. 71–80. San Luis Obispo County Archaeological Society Occasional Papers no. 17.

Jones, D. A., D. C. Young, and W. R. Hildebrandt

2001 *Phase II Archaeological Test Excavations at CA-SLO-832 and CA-SLO-1420, for the James Way/Price Street Road Improvement Project, San Luis Obispo County, California*. Far Western Anthropological Research Group, Davis, California.

2002 *Prehistoric Occupations on Ancient Halcyon Bay/Estuary: Excavations at Sites CA-SLO-832 and -1420, Pismo Beach, California*. San Luis Obispo Country Archaeological Society Occasional Papers no. 15.

Jones, G. T., and C. Beck

1990 An Obsidian Hydration Chronology of Late Pleistocene/Early Holocene Surface Assemblages from Butte Valley, Nevada. *Journal of California and Great Basin Anthropology* 12:84–100.

1992 Chronological Resolution in Distributional Archaeology. In *Space, Time, and Archaeological Landscapes*, edited by J. Rossignol and L. Wandsnider, pp. 167–192. Plenum Press, New York.

Jones, G. T., C. Beck, E. E. Jones, and R. E. Hughes

2003 Lithic Source Use and Paleoarchaic Foraging Territories in the Great Basin. *American Antiquity* 68:5–38.

Jones, T. L.

1991 Marine-Resource Value and the Priority of Coastal Settlement: A California Perspective. *American Antiquity* 56:419–443.

1992 Settlement Trends Along the California Coast. In *Essays on the Prehistory of Maritime California*, edited by T. L. Jones, pp. 1–37. Center for Archaeological Research at Davis Publication no. 10. University of California, Davis.

1993 Big Sur: A Keystone in Central California Culture History. *Pacific Coast Archaeological Society Quarterly* 29(1):1–78.

1995 Transitions in Prehistoric Diet, Mobility, Exchange, and Social Organization Along California's Big Sur Coast. Ph.D. dissertation, Department of Anthropology, University of California, Davis.

1996 Mortars, Pestles, and Division of Labor in Prehistoric California: A View from Big Sur. *American Antiquity*, 6:243–264.

1997 Lakes and Estuaries Reconsidered: A Comment on Lacustrine Intensification in the Southern Santa Clara Valley, California. *Journal of California and Great Basin Anthropology* 19:281–288.

2000 *Archaeological Evaluation of CA-MNT-237 and CA-MNT-519, Fort Hunter Liggett, Monterey County, California*. Albion Environmental, Santa Cruz. Copies available from Northwest Information Center, Department of Anthropology, Sonoma State University, Rohnert Park, California.

2002 Archaeology and Prehistoric Human Use. In *Changes in a California Estuary: A Profile of Elkhorn Slough*, edited by J. Caffrey, M. Brown, W. B. Tyler, and M. Silberstein, pp. 55–91. Elkhorn Slough Foundation, Moss Landing, California.

2003 Prehistoric Human Ecology of the Big Sur Coast, California. *Contributions of the University of California Archaeological Research Facility* no. 61.

Jones, T. L., and J. A. Ferneau

2002a *Prehistory at San Simeon Reef: Archaeological Data Recovery at CA-SLO-179 and -267, San Luis Obispo County, California*. San Luis Obispo County Archaeological Society Occasional Papers no. 16.

2002b De-intensification Along the Central Coast. In *Catalysts to Complexity: Late Holocene Societies of the California Coast*, edited by J. M. Erlandson and T. L. Jones, pp. 204–231. Cotsen Institute of Archaeology, University of California, Los Angeles.

Jones, T. L., and J. W. Haney

1997 *Archaeological Evaluation of CA-MNT-521, Fort Hunter Liggett, Monterey County, California*. Garcia and Associates, San Anselmo, California. Copies available from Northwest Information Center, Department of Anthropology, Sonoma State University, Rohnert Park, California.

2005 *Archaeological Evaluation of CA-MNT-910, -1748/H, 1919, and -2182, Fort Hunter Liggett Military Installation, Monterey County, California*. California Polytechnic State University, San Luis Obispo. Copies available from Northwest Information Center, Department of Anthropology, Sonoma State University, Rohnert Park, California.

Jones, T. L., and J. Hayes

1989 *Archaeological Data Recovery at CA-SON-120, Sonoma County, California*. Environmental Research Branch, California Department of Transportation, Oakland.

1993 Problems and Prospects in Sonoma County Archaeology. In *There Grows a Green Tree: Papers in Honor of David A. Fred-*

rickson, edited by G. White, P. Mikkelsen, W. R. Hildebrandt, and M. E. Basgall, pp. 197–216. Center for Archaeological Research at Davis Publication no. 11. University of California, Davis.

Jones, T. L., and W. R. Hildebrandt
1995 Reasserting a Prehistoric Tragedy of the Commons: Reply to Lyman. *Journal of Anthropological Archaeology* 14:78–98.

Jones, T. L., and M. G. Hylkema
1988 Two Proposed Projectile Point Types for the Monterey Bay Area: The Año Nuevo Long-Stemmed and Rossi Square-Stemmed. *Journal of California and Great Basin Anthropology* 10:163–186.

Jones, T. L., and D. A. Jones
1992 Elkhorn Slough Revisited: Reassessing the Chronology of CA-MNT-229. *Journal of California and Great Basin Anthropology* 10:163–186.

Jones, T. L., and D. J. Kennett
1999 Late Holocene Climate Change and Cultural Ecology of the Central California Coast. *Quaternary Research* 51:74–82.

Jones, T. L., and K. A. Klar
2005 Diffusionism Reconsidered: Linguistic and Archaeological Evidence for Prehistoric Polynesian Contact with Southern California. *American Antiquity* 70:457–484.

Jones, T. L., and J. R. Richman
1995 On Mussels: *Mytilus californianus* as a Prehistoric Resource. *North American Archaeologist* 16:33–58.

Jones, T. L., and G. Waugh
1995 *Central California Coastal Prehistory: A View from Little Pico Creek.* Cotsen Institute of Archaeology, University of California, Los Angeles.
1997 Climatic Consequences of Population Pragmatism? A Middle Holocene Prehistory of the Central California Coast. In *Archaeology of the California Coast During the Middle Holocene*, edited by J. M. Erlandson and M. A. Glassow, pp. 111–128. Cotsen Institute of Archaeology, University of California, Los Angeles.

Jones, T. L., W. R. Hildebrandt, D. J. Kennett, and J. F. Porcasi
2002 Prehistoric Marine Mammal Overkill in the Northeastern Pacific: A Review of New Evidence. *Journal of California and Great Basin Anthropology* 24:69–80.

Jones, T. L., J. F. Porcasi, K. W. Gobalet, and L. T. Laurie
2004 CA-SLO-215, A Late Milling Stone Site at Morro Bay, San Luis Obispo County, California. In *Out of the Ice Age: Papers in Honor of Roberta Greenwood*, edited by E. Bertrando and V. Levulett, pp. 57–70. San Luis Obispo County Archaeological Society Occasional Papers no. 17.

Jones, T. L., B. Rivers, A. M. Maliarik, T. L. Joslin, and D. Alger
2000 An Addendum to Harrington's Northern Salinan Place Names. *Journal of California and Great Basin Anthropology* 22:3–11.

Jones, T. L., T. M. Van Bueren, S. Grantham, J. Huddleston, and T. Fung
1996 *Archaeological Test Excavations for the Castroville Bypass Project, Monterey County, California.* Office of Cultural Studies, California Department of Transportation. Copies available from Northwest Information Center, Department of Anthropology, Sonoma State University, Rohnert Park, California.

Jones, T. L., S. Anderson, M. Brown, A. Garsia, K. Hildebrand, and A. York
1989 *Surface Archaeology at Landels-Hill Big Creek Reserve and the Gamboa Point Properties.* University of California Santa Cruz Environmental Field Program Publications 18.

Jones, T. L., K. Davis, G. Farris, T. Fung, S. Grantham, and B. Rivers
1994 *Toward a Prehistory of Morro Bay: Phase II Archaeological Investigations for the Highway 41 Widening Project, Caltrans Environmental Division.* San Luis Obispo. Report on file with Caltrans, Environmental Division.

Jones, T. L., R. T. Fitzgerald, D. J. Kennett, C. H. Miksicek, J. L. Fagan, J. Sharp, and J. M. Erlandson
2002 The Cross Creek Site (CA-SLO-1797) and Its Implications for New World Colonization. *American Antiquity* 67:213–230.

Jones, T. L., G. M. Brown, L. M. Raab, J. L. McVickar, W. G. Spaulding, D. J. Kennett, A. York, and P. L. Walker
1999 Environmental Imperatives Reconsidered: Demographic Crises in Western North America During the Medieval Climatic Anomaly. *Current Anthropology* 40:137–170.
2004 Environmental Imperatives Reconsidered: Demographic Crises in Western North America During the Medieval Climatic Anomaly. In *Prehistoric California: Archaeology and the Myth of Paradise*, edited by L. M. Raab and T. L. Jones, pp. 12–32. University of Utah Press, Salt Lake City.

Joslin, T. L.
2006 Late Prehistoric Coastal Adaptations Along the San Simeon Reef, San Luis Obispo County, California. Master's thesis, Department of Anthropology, University of California, Santa Barbara.

Jurmain, R.
1983 *The Skeletal Biology of CA-ALA-342.* Coyote Press, Salinas.
1990 Paleoepidemiology of a Central California Prehistoric Population from CA-ALA-329: Dental Disease. *American Journal of Physical Anthropology* 83:83–94.
1993 Paleodemography and Paleopathology. In *The Archaeology of the Guadalupe Corridor*, edited by R. Cartier, J. Bass, and S. Ortman, pp. 79–88. Santa Clara County Archaeological Society, Santa Clara, California, and Archaeological Resource Management, San Jose, California.
2001 Paleoepidemiolgical Patterns of Trauma in a Prehistoric Population from Central California. *American Journal of Physical Anthropology* 115:13–23.

Justice, N. D.
2002 *Stone Age Spear and Arrow Points of California and the Great Basin.* Indiana University Press, Bloomington.

Kaestle, F. A.
1998 Molecular Evidence for Prehistoric Native American Population Movement: The Numic Expansion. Ph.D. dissertation, Department of Anthropology, University of California, Davis.

Kaestle, F. A., and D. G. Smith
2001 Ancient Mitochondrial DNA Evidence for Prehistoric Population Movement: The Numic Expansion. *American Journal of Physical Anthropology* 115:1–12.

Kahrl, W. L. (editor)
1979 *The California Water Atlas.* Prepared by the Governor's Office of Planning and Research in cooperation with the California Department of Water Resources. Sacramento.

Kaufman, T.
1988 A Research Program for Reconstructing Proto-Hokan: First Gropings. In *Papers from the 1988 Hokan-Penutian Languages Workshop*, edited by S. DeLancey, pp. 50–168. Department of Linguistics, University of Oregon, Eugene.

Keefer, D. K., M. E. Moseley, and S. D. deFrance
2003 A 38,000-Year Record of Floods and Debris Flows in the Ilo Region of Southern Peru and Its Relation to El Niño Events and Great Earthquakes. *Palaeogeography, Palaeoclimatology, Palaeoecology* 194:41–77.

Keefer, D. K., S. D. deFrance, M. E. Moseley, J. B. Richardson III, D. R. Saterlee, and A. Day-Lewis
1998 Early Maritime Economy and El Niño Events at Quebrada Tacahuay, Peru. *Science* 281:1833–1835.

Keller, E. A., and L. D. Gurrola
2000 Earthquake Hazard of the Santa Barbara Fold Belt, California. Final Report, U.S. Geological Survey, National Earthquake Hazards Reduction Program.

Kelly, R. L.
1995 *The Foraging Spectrum: Diversity in Hunter-Gatherer Lifeways.* Smithsonian Institution Press, Washington, D.C.
Kelman, L. M., and Z. Kelman
1999 The Use of Ancient DNA in Paleontological Studies. *Journal of Vertebrate Paleontology* 19:8–20.
Kemp, B. M., J. A. Eshleman, and R. S. Malhi
2005 *Report on the Extraction of DNA from the LAN 949 Burial #4 Tooth.* Trace Genetics, Richmond.
Kennedy, M. A.
2005 An Investigation of Hunter-Gatherer Shellfish Foraging Practices: Archaeological and Geochemical Evidence from Bodega Bay, California. Ph.D. dissertation, Department of Anthropology, University of California, Davis.
Kennedy, M. A., A. D. Russell, and T. Guilderson
2005 A Radiocarbon Chronology of Hunter-Gatherer Occupation from Bodega Bay, California, U.S.A. *Radiocarbon* 47:1–29.
Kennett, D. J.
1998 Behavioral Ecology and the Evolution of Hunter-Gatherer Societies on the Northern Channel Islands. Ph.D. dissertation, Department of Anthropology, University of California, Santa Barbara.
2005 *The Island Chumash; Behavioral Ecology of a Maritime Society.* University of California Press, Berkeley.
Kennett, D. J., and C. A. Conlee
2002 Emergence of Late Holocene Sociopolitical Complexity on Santa Rosa and San Miguel Islands. In *Catalysts to Complexity: Late Holocene Societies of the California Coast*, edited by J. M. Erlandson and T. L. Jones, pp. 147–165. Cotsen Institute of Archaeology, University of California, Los Angeles.
Kennett, D. J., and J. P. Kennett
2000 Competitive and Cooperative Responses to Climate Instability in Coastal Southern California. *American Antiquity* 65:379–395.
Kennett, D. J., B. L. Ingram, J. M. Erlandson, and P. Walker
1997 Evidence for Temporal Fluctuations in Marine Radiocarbon Reservoir Ages in the Santa Barbara Channel, Southern California. *Journal of Archaeological Science* 28:941–950.
Kennett, J. P., and B. L. Ingram
1995 A 20,000-Year Record of Ocean Circulation and Climate Change from the Santa Barbara Basin. *Nature* 377:510–514.
Kerr, S. L.
2004 The People of the Southern Channel Islands: A Bioarchaeological Study of Adaptation and Population Change in Southern California. Ph.D. dissertation, Department of Anthropology, University of California, Santa Barbara.
Kerr, S. L., and G. M. Hawley
2002 Population Replacement on the Southern Channel Islands: New Evidence from San Nicolas Island. In *Proceedings of the Fifth California Islands Symposium*, edited by D. Browne, K. Mitchell, and H. Chaney, pp. 546–554. Santa Barbara Museum of Natural History.
Keswick, J. A.
1990 Archaeological Investigations of CA-SON-159, Southern Sonoma County, California. Master's thesis, Department of Anthropology, Sonoma State University, Rohnert Park, California.
Keter, T. S.
1995 *Environmental History and Cultural Ecology of the North Fork of the Eel River Basin, California.* Heritage Resource Program, Report on file, Pacific Southwest Region, Six Rivers National Forest, Eureka, California.
Kielusiak, C. Mary
1982 Variability and Distribution of Baked Clay Artifacts from the Lower Sacramento-Northern San Joaquin Valleys of California. Master's thesis, Department of Anthropology, California State University, Sacramento.
King, C. D.
1967 The Sweetwater Mesa Site (LAn-267) and Its Place in Southern California Prehistory. In *UCLA Archaeological Survey Annual Report* 9:25–76. Department of Anthropology, University of California, Los Angeles.
1974a Calendaruc Ethnohistory. In *An Assessment of the Lower Pajaro River Basin, California*, edited by R. Edwards and M. Farley. Report on file, Northwest Information Center, Department of Anthropology, Sonoma State University, Rohnert Park, California.
1974b The Explanation of Differences and Similarities Among Beads Used in Prehistoric and Early Historic California. In *Antap: California Indian Political and Economic Organization*, edited by L. J. Bean and T. F. King, pp. 75–92. Ballena Press Anthropological Papers no. 2. Ballena Press, Menlo Park, California
1976 Chumash Intervillage Economic Exchange. In *Native Californians: A Theoretical Retrospective*, edited by L. J. Bean and T. C. Blackburn, pp. 289–318. Ballena Press, Ramona.
1978 Protohistoric and Historic Archaeology. In *California*, edited by R. F. Heizer, pp. 58–68. Handbook of North American Indians. Vol. 8. W. C. Sturtevant, general editor. Smithsonian Institution, Washington, D.C.
1982 The Evolution of Chumash Society: A Comparative Study of Artifacts Used in Social System Maintenance in the Santa Barbara Channel Region Before A.D. 1804. Ph.D. dissertation, Department of Anthropology, University of California, Davis.
1984 Appendix 1, Ethnohistoric Background. In *Archaeological Investigations of the San Antonio Terrace, Vandenberg Air Force Base, California, in Connection with MX Facilities Construction*, edited by Chambers Consultants and Planners. Report on file at South Central Information Center, Department of Anthropology, University of California, Santa Barbara.
1990 *Evolution of Chumash Society: A Comparative Study of Artifacts Used for Social System Maintenance in the Santa Barbara Channel Region Before A.D. 1804.* Garland Publishing, New York.
1994 Central Ohlone Ethnohistory. In *The Ohlone Past and Present: Native Americans of the San Francisco Bay region*, edited by L. J. Bean, pp. 203–228. Ballena Press Anthropological Papers 42. Menlo Park, California.
1995 Beads and Ornaments from Excavations at Tahquitz Canyon (CA-RIV-45). In *Archaeological, Ethnographic, and Ethnohistoric Investigations at Tahquits Canyon, Palm Springs, California*, edited by L. J. Bean, J. Schaefer, and S. B. Vane, pp. X111-1–X-111-77. Limited distribution technical report prepared by Cultural Systems Research for Riverside County Flood Control and Water Conservation District, Riverside, California.
2000 *Native American Indian Cultural Sites in the Santa Monica Mountains.* Report prepared for the Santa Monica Mountains and Seashore Foundation, in possession of Topanga Anthropological Consultants, Topanga, California.
2004 *Beads from Rancho Cuyamaca State Park, San Diego County, California.* Letter Report prepared for San Diego State University by Chester King, Topanga Anthropological Consultants, January 29, 2004. Copy in possession of Randall Milliken.
King, C. D., T. Blackburn, and E. Chandonet
1968 The Archaeological Investigation of Three Sites on the Century Ranch, Western Los Angeles County, California. In *UCLA Archaeological Survey Annual Report* 10:12–161. Department of Anthropology, University of California, Los Angeles.
King, J.
2004 Re-Examining Coso Obsidian Hydration Rates. *Proceedings of the Society for California Archaeology* 14:135–142.

King, L. B.
1982 Medea Creek Cemetery: Late Inland Chumash Patterns of Social Organization, Exchange, and Warfare. Ph.D. dissertation, Department of Anthropology, University of California, Los Angeles.

King, T. F.
1970 *The Dead at Tiburon: Mortuary Customs and Social Organization on Northern San Francisco Bay*. Northwestern California Archaeological Society Occasional Papers no. 2.
1974a *Manos on the Mountain: Borax Lake Pattern High Altitude Settlement and Subsistence in the North Coast Ranges of California*. Report on file, Northwest Information Center of the California Historical Resources Inventory System, Sonoma State University, Rohnert Park, California.
1974b The Evolution of Status Ascription Around San Francisco Bay. In *Antap: California Indian Political and Economic Organization*, edited by L. J. Bean and T. F. King, pp. 35–54. Ballena Press Anthropological Papers no. 2. Ballena Press, Menlo Park, California.
1978 Don't That Beat the Band? Nonegalitarian Political Organization in Prehistoric Central California. In *Social Archeology: Beyond Subsistence and Dating*, edited by C. Redman et al., pp. 225–248. Academic Press, New York.
1998 *Cultural Resource Laws and Practice: An Introductory Guide*. Altamira Press, California.

King, T. F., and P. P. Hickman
1973 *The Southern Santa Clara Valley: A General Plan for Archaeology*. Treganza Anthropology Museum, San Francisco State University.

King, T. F., and W. F. Upson
1970 Protohistory on Limantour Sandspit: Archaeological Investigations at 4-Mrn-216 and 4-Mrn-298. In *Contributions to the Archaeology of Point Reyes National Seashore: A Compendium in Honor of Adan E. Treganza*, edited by R. E. Schenk, pp. 115–194. Treganza Museum Papers no. 6. San Francisco State University, San Francisco.

Kinkade, M. D., W. W. Elmendorf, B. Rigsby, and H. Aoki
1998 Languages. In *Plateau*, edited by D. E. Walker, pp. 49–72. Handbook of North American Indians. Vol. 12. W. C. Sturtevant, general editor. Smithsonian Institution, Washington, D.C.

Kirch, P. V.
2000 *On the Road of the Winds*. University of California Press, Berkeley.

Klar, K. A.
1980 Northern Chumash Numerals. In *American Indian and Indoeuropean Studies: Papers in Honor of Madison S. Beeler*, edited by K. A. Klar, M. Langdon, and S. Silver, pp. 113–119. The Hague, Mouton.
1992 *John P. Harrington's Phonetic Representations of Obispeño Chumash Palatal Consonants*. Southern Illinois University Occasional Papers in Linguistics 17:17–19.
2002 The Island Chumash Language: Implications for Interdisciplinary Work. In Proceedings of the Fifth California Islands Symposium, edited by D. R. Brown, K. C. Mitchell, and H. C. Chaney, pp. 654–658. Santa Barbara Museum of Natural History, Santa Barbara.

Klar, K. A., and T. L. Jones
2005 Linguistic Evidence for a Prehistoric Polynesia-Southern California Contact Event. *Anthropological Linguistics* 47:369–400.

Klimek, S.
1935 Culture Element Distributions, I: The Structure of California Indian Culture. *University of California Publications in American Archaeology and Ethnography* 37:1–70.

Klug, L. P., and V. S. Popper
1995 Macrobotanical Analysis of Samples from SDI-1074, SDI-4411, and SDI-13,325. In *Archaeological Testing Along San Mateo and San Onofre Creeks, Northwestern Camp Pendleton, San Diego County, California*, edited by B. F. Byrd, D. Pallette, and C. Serr, pp. 147–163. Report on file, South Coastal Information Center, San Diego State University.

Klug, L. P., and H. C. Koerper
1991 The Bioenvironment: Vegetation. In *Newport Coast Archaeological Project: Project Background and Research Design*, by R. D. Mason, pp. 44–75. Report on file, South Central Coastal Information Center, California State University, Fullerton.

Kniffen, F. B.
1928 *Achomawi Geography*. University of California Publications in American Archaeology and Ethnology no. 23. University of California Press, Berkeley.

Knott, J. R., and D. S. Eley
2006 Timing and Control of Early to Middle Holocene Coastal Dune and Estuarine Deposition Relative to Climate and Sea Level, Santa Maria Valley, California, U.S.A. *Physical Geography* 27:127–213.

Knudsen, K. L., J. M. Sowers, R. C. Witter, C. M. Wentworth, and E. J. Helley
2000 *Description of Mapping of Quaternary Deposits and Liquefaction Susceptibility, Nine-County San Francisco Bay Region, California*. U.S. Geological Survey Open-File Report 00-444.

Koch, P. L., and A. D. Barnosky
2006 Late Quaternary Extinctions: State of the Debate. *Annual Review of Ecology, Evolution, and Systematics* 37. In press.

Koehler, P. A., and R. S. Anderson
1994a Full-Glacial Shoreline Vegetation During the Maximum Highstand at Owens Lake, California. *Great Basin Naturalist* 54:142–149.
1994b The Paleoecology and Stratigraphy of Nichols Meadow, Sierra Nevada National Forest, California, U.S.A. *Palaeogeography, Palaeoclimatology, Palaeoecology* 112:1–17.
1995 Thirty Thousand Years of Vegetation Changes in the Alabama Hills, Owens Valley, California. *Quaternary Research* 43:238–248.

Koehler, P. A., R. S. Anderson, and W. G. Spaulding
2005 Development of Vegetation in the Central Mojave Desert of California During the Late Quaternary. *Palaeogeography, Palaeoclimatolog, Palaeoecology* 215:297–311.

Koerper, H. C.
1981 Prehistoric Subsistence and Settlement in the Newport Bay Area and Environs, Orange County, California. Ph.D. dissertation, Department of Anthropology, University of California, Riverside.

Koerper, H. C., and K. Hedges
1996 Patayan Anthropomorphic Figurines from an Orange County Site. *Journal of California and Great Basin Anthropology* 18:204–220.

Koerper, H. C., P. E. Langenwalter II, and A. Schroth
1991 Early Holocene Adaptations and the Transition Phase Problem: Evidence from the Allan O. Kelly Site, Agua Hedionda Lagoon. In *Hunter-Gatherers of Early Holocene Coastal California*, edited by J. M. Erlandson and R. H. Colten, pp. 43–62. Cotsen Institute of Archaeology, University of California, Los Angeles.

Koerper, H. C., R. D. Mason, and M. L. Petersen
2002 Complexity, Demography, and Change in Late Holocene Orange County. In *Catalysts to Complexity: Late Holocene of the California Coast*, edited by J. Erlandson and T. L. Jones, pp. 63–81. Cotsen Institute of Archaeology, University of California, Los Angeles.

Koerper, H. C., J. E. Ericson, C. E. Drover, and P. E. Langenwalter II
1986 Obsidian Exchange in Prehistoric Orange County. *Pacific Coast Archaeological Society Quarterly* 22(1):33–69.

Koerper, H. C., A. B. Schroth, R. D. Mason, and M. L. Peterson
1996 Arrow Projectile Point Types as Temporal Types: Evidence from Orange County, California. *Journal of California and Great Basin Anthropology* 18:258–283.
Koltermann, C. E., and S. M. Gorelick
1992 Paleoclimatic Signature in Terrestrial Flood Deposits. *Science* 256:1775–1782.
Koutavas, A., J. Lynch-Stieglitz, T. M. Marchitto Jr., and J. P. Sachs
2002 El Niño-Like Pattern in Ice Age Tropical Pacific Sea Surface Temperature. *Science* 297:226–230.
Kowta, M.
1969 *The Sayles Complex, A Late Milling Stone Assemblage from Cajon Pass and the Ecological Implications of Its Scraper Planes.* University of California Publications in Anthropology 6. University of California Press, Berkeley.
1988 *The Archaeology and Prehistory of Plumas and Butte Counties, California: An Introduction and Interpretive Model.* Report on file, North Central Information Center, Department of Anthropology, California State University, Sacramento.
Krantz, G.
1977 *The Peopling of Western North America.* Society for California Archaeology Occasional Papers in Method and Theory in California Archaeology 1:1–64.
Krauss, M. E., and V. Golla
1981 Northern Athapaskan Languages. In *Subarctic*, edited by J. Helm, pp. 67–85. Handbook of North American Indians. Vol. 6. W. C. Sturtevant, general editor. Smithsonian Institution, Washington, D.C.
Krieger, A. D.
1964 Early Man in the New World. In *Prehistoric Man in the New World*, edited by Jesse D. Jennings and Edward Norbeck, pp. 23–81. University of Chicago Press, Chicago.
Kroeber, A. L.
1907 Shoshonean Dialects of California. *University of California Publications in American Archaeology and Ethnology* 4:65–165.
1909 The Archaeology of California. In *Anthropological Essays Presented to Frederic Ward Putnam in Honor of his Seventieth Birthday, April 16, 1909, by His Friends and Associates*, pp. 1–42. Stechart, New York.
1915 Serian, Tequistlatecan, and Hokan. *University of California Publications in American Archaeology and Ethnology* 11:279–290.
1922 *Elements of Culture in Native California.* University of California Publications in American Archaeology and Ethnology 13(8).
1925 *Handbook of the Indians of California.* Smithsonian Institution, Bureau of American Ethnology Bulletin 78. Reprint (1976); Dover Publications, New York.
1929 *The Valley Nisenan.* University of California Publications in American Archaeology and Ethnology 24:253–90.
1931 *The Seri.* Southwest Museum Paper 6.
1932 *The Patwin and Their Neighbors.* University of California Publications in American Archaeology and Ethnology 29:254–423.
1934 *Yurok and Neighboring Kin Term Systems.* University of California Publications in American Archaeology and Ethnology 35:15–22.
1935 Preface. In *Culture Element Distributions, I: The Structure of California Indian Culture*, edited by S. Klimek, pp. 1–11. University of California Publications in American Archaeology and Ethnology 37.
1936 *Culture Element Distributions, III: Area and Climax.* University of California Publications in American Archaeology and Ethnology 37(3).
1939 *Cultural and Natural Areas of Native North America.* University of California Publications in American Archaeology and Ethnology 38:1–240.
1955 Nature of the Land-Holding Group. *Ethnohistory* 2:303–314.
1962 The Nature of Land-Holding Groups in Aboriginal California. In *Aboriginal California: Three Studies in Culture History*, pp. 81–120. Archaeological Research Facility, University of California, Berkeley.
Kuchler, A. W.
1977 Map of the Natural Vegetation of California. In *Terrestrial Vegetation of California*, edited by M. G. Barbour and J. Major. Wiley, New York.
Kudras, H. R., H. Erlenkeuser, R. Vollbrecht, and W. Weiss
1991 Global Nature of the Younger-Dryas Cooling Event Inferred from Oxygen Isotope Data from Sulu Sea Cores. *Nature* 349:406–409.
Kuehn, D. D.
2002 *Late Quaternary Stratigraphy and Geoarchaeology at Emerson Lake, MCAGCC, San Bernardino County, California: A View from the Southern Margin.* Report submitted to the Marine Corps Air Ground Combat Center, Twentynine Palms.
Kuhn, S. L.
2004 Upper Paleolithic Raw Material Economies at Ucagizli Cave, Turkey. *Journal of Anthropological Archaeology* 23:431–448.
Kutzbach, J. E., and P. J. Guetter
1986 The Influence of Changing Orbital Parameters and Surface Boundary Conditions on Climate Simulations for the Past 18,000 years. *Journal of Atmospheric Sciences* 43:1726–1759.
Kyle, C. E., A. Schroth, and D. R. Gallegos
1990 *Early Period Occupation at the Kuebler Ranch Site SDI-8654, Otay Mesa, San Diego County, California.* Gallegos & Associates, Carlsbad. Report on file, South Coast Information Center, California State University, San Diego.
1998 *Remington Hills, Archaeological Data Recovery Program for Prehistoric Site CA-SDI-11079, Otay Mesa, San Diego, California, DEP no. 93-0140.* Gallegos & Associates, Carlsbad. Copies available from Gallegos and Associates.
LaJeunesse, R. M., and J. M. Pryor
1996 *Skyrocket Appendices.* Report on file, Department of Anthropology, California State University, Fresno.
LaJeunesse, R. M., J. M. Pryor, and B. Wickstrom
1996 *The 1993 and 1994 California State University, Fresno Archaeological Field Class Investigations at CA-FRE-2364, CA-FRE-2365, and CA-FRE-2366, Fresno County, California.* Report on file, Southern San Joaquin Valley Archaeological Information Center, California State University, Bakersfield.
Lajoie, K. R.
1986 Coastal Tectonics. In *Active Tectonics*, pp. 95–124. National Academy Press, Geophysics Study Committee, Geophysics Research Forum, Commission on Physical Sciences, Mathematics, and Resources, National Research Council, Washington, D.C.
Lalueza-Fox, C., A. Perez-Perez, E. Prats, L. Cornudella, and D. Turbon
1997 Lack of Founding Amerindian Mitochondrial DNA Lineages in Extinct Aborigines from Tierra del Fuego-Patagonia. *Human Molecular Genetics* 6:41–46.
LaMarche, V. C., Jr.
1973 Holocene Climatic Variations Inferred from Treeline Fluctuations in the White Mountains, California. *Quaternary Research* 3:632–660.
Lamb, H. H.
1965 The Early Medieval Warm Epoch and Its Sequel. *Palaeogeography, Palaeoclimatology, Palaeoecology* 1:13–37.
Lamb, S. M.
1958 Linguistic Prehistory in the Great Basin. *International Journal of American Linguistics* 24:95–100.
Lambeck, K., T. M. Esat, and E.-K. Potter
2002 Links Between Climate and Sea Levels for the Past Three Million Years. *Nature* 419:199–206.

Lambert, P. M.
1994 War and Peace on the Western Front: A Study of Violent Conflict and Its Correlates in Prehistoric Hunter-Gatherer Societies of Coastal Southern California. Ph.D. dissertation, Department of Anthropology, University of California, Santa Barbara.
2002 The Archaeology of War: A North American Perspective. *Journal of Archaeological Research* 10:207–41.

Lambert, P. M., and P. L. Walker
1991 Physical Anthropological Evidence for the Evolution of Social Complexity in Coastal Southern California. *Antiquity* 65:963–973.

Lanning, E. P.
1963 Archaeology of the Rose Spring Site, INY-372. *University of California Publications in American Archaeology and Ethnology* 49:237–336.

Larson, D. O., and J. C. Michaelson
1989 *Climatic Variability: A Compounding Factor Causing Culture Change Among Prehistoric Costal Populations.* Report on file, Department of Anthropology, California State University, Long Beach.

Larson, D. O., J. R. Johnson, and J. C. Michaelsen
1994 Missionization Among the Coastal Chumash of Central California: A Study of Risk Minimization Strategies. *American Anthropologist* 96:263–299.

Latham, T. S., P. A. Sutton, and K. L. Verosub
1992 Non-Destructive XRF Characterization of Basalt Artifacts from Truckee, California. *Geoarchaeology* 7:81–101.

Lathrap, D. W., and R. L. Hoover
1975 *Excavations at Shilimaqshtush: SBA-205.* San Luis Obispo County Archaeological Society Occasional Papers no. 10.

Lathrap, D. W., and R. T. Troike
1984 California Historical Linguistics and Archaeology. *Journal of the Steward Anthropological Society* 15:99–157.

Laughlin, W. S., and J. S. Aigner
1966 Preliminary Analysis of the Anangula Unifacial Core and Blade Industry. *Arctic Anthropology* 3:41–56.

Lawson, A. C.
1894 The Geomorphogeny of the Coast of Northern California. *University of California Publications in Geology* 1:241–271.

Lawton, H. W., and L. J. Bean
1968 A Preliminary Reconstruction of Aboriginal Agricultural Technology Among the Cahuilla. *Indian Historian* 1:18–24, 29.

Laylander, D.
1994 *Phase III Data Recovery at the Elmore Site (CA-IMP-6427) Imperial County, California.* Report prepared by California Department of Transportation, District 11. Report on file, Southeast Information Center, Imperial Valley College Desert Museum, Ocotillo, California.
1995 The Question of Prehistoric Agriculture Among the Western Yumans. *Estudios Fronterizos* 35–36:187–203.
1997 The Last Days of Lake Cahuilla: The Elmore Site. *Pacific Coast Archaeological Society Quarterly* 33(1–2):1–138.
2002 Assessing the Magnitude of Hydration Chronology Error for Coso Obsidian in Western Inyo County. *Proceedings of the Society for California Archaeology* 15:61–65.

Laylander, D., and L. E. Christenson
1988 Corral Canyon and Late Prehistoric Exchange in Inland San Diego County, California. *Proceedings of the Society for California Archaeology* 1:135–157.

Laylander, D., and K. Victorino
2001 *Archaeological Evaluation of the Garlic Spring Sites (CA-SBR-8983, CA-SBR-8984, and CA-SBR-10, 310) Fort Irwin, San Bernardino County, California.* Report prepared for U.S. Army Corps of Engineers, Los Angeles District, by ASM Affiliates, San Bernardino Archeological Information Center, San Bernardino County Museum, Redlands, California.

Layton, T. N.
1985 Invaders from the South? Archaeological Discontinuities in the Northwestern Great Basin. *Journal of California and Great Basin Archaeology* 7:183–201.
1990 *Western Pomo Prehistory: Excavations at Albion Head, Nightbird's Retreat, and Three Chop Village, Mendocino County, California.* Cotsen Institute of Archaeology, Monograph 32. University of California, Los Angeles.

Leach, M.
1988 Subsistence Intensification and Settlement Change Among Prehistoric Hunters and Gatherers of the Northwestern Great Basin. Ph. D dissertation, Department of Anthropology, University of California, Los Angeles.

Leakey, L. S. B., R. D. Simpson, T. Clements, R. Berger, and J. Withoff
1972 *Pleistocene Man at Calico.* San Bernadino County Museum Association, Bloomington, California.

LeBlanc, S. A.
1999 *Prehistoric Warfare in the American Southwest.* University of Utah Press, Salt Lake City, Utah.

Lebow, C., M. C. Baloian, D. R. Harro, R. L. McKim, C. Denardo, J. Onken, E. Romanski, and B. A. Price
2001 *Final Report of Archaeological Investigations for Reaches 5B and 6 Coastal Branch Aqueduct, Phase II.* Applied Earthworks Fresno, California. Submitted to Central Coast Water Authority, Buellton, California. Copies available from California Department of Water Resources, Sacramento.

Lebow, C. G., and J. Onken
1997 *Preliminary Archaeological Testing at Swordfish Cave (CA-SBA-503).* Report on file, South Central Information Center, Department of Anthropology, University of California, Santa Barbara.

Lee, G.
1977 Chumash Myth in Paint and Stone. *Pacific Coast Archaeological Society Quarterly* 13(3):1–14.
1981a The Rock Art of *Soxtonocmu*, an Inland Chumash Village. *Journal of California and Great Basin Anthropology* 3:116–126.
1981b *The Portable Cosmos: Effigies, Ornaments, and Incised Stone from the Chumash Area.* Ballena Press Anthropological Papers no. 21.
1984 *Rock Art of the Sierra Madre Ridge. Papers on Chumash Rock Art.* San Luis Obispo County Archaeological Society Occasional Papers 12:13–48.

Lee, G., W. Hyder, and A. Benson
1988 *The Rock Art of Petroglyph Point and Fern Cave, Lava Beds National Monument.* Prepared for Lava Beds National Monument, Tulelake, California.

Legare, J.
1998 Results of Archaeobotanical Pilot Study. In *Archaeological Investigations at CA-MRN-254, The Dominican College Site, San Rafael, Marin County, California,* edited by D. G. Bieling, Appendix I. Holman and Associates, San Francisco. Submitted to Dominican College, San Rafael, California. Copies available from Northwest Information Center, Department of Anthropology, Sonoma State University, Rohnert Park, California.

Legg, M. R.
1991 Developments in Understanding the Tectonic Evolution of the California Continental Borderland. In *Shoreline to Abyss: Contributions in Marine Geology in Honor of Francis Parker Shepard*, edited by Robert H. Osborne, pp. 291–312. Society for Sedimentary Geology, Tulsa, Oklahoma.

Leonard, N. N., III
1968 Salvage Investigations at the Pico Creek Site: 4-SLO-179. *Robert E. Schenk Archives of California Archaeology* 4:1–40.

Leonard, N. N., III, and C. Drover
1980 Prehistoric Turquoise Mining in the Halloran Springs District, San Bernardino County, California. *Journal of California and Great Basin Anthropology* 2:245–256.

Leonhardy, F. C., and D. G. Rice
1970 A Proposed Culture Typology for the Lower Snake River Region, Southeastern Washington. *Northwest Anthropological Research Notes* 4(1):1–29.

Lerch, M. K.
1985 *The Desert Mojave: A Review of Ethnohistoric Data and Archaeological Implications.* Report on file, Department of Anthropology, University of California, Riverside.

Leventhal, A. M.
1993 A Reinterpretation of Some Bay Area Shell Mounds: A View from the Mortuary Complex, ALA-329. Master's thesis, Department of Social Sciences, San Jose State University, San Jose, California.

Leventhal, A. M., and G. Seitz
1989 Experimental Archaeology Mortar Replication Study: Description and Analysis. Appendix A, pp. 141–150. In *Results of the General Development Plan Archaeological Test Excavation conducted at CA-MNT-185/H, Garrapata State Park, Big Sur District, Central Coast Region*, by L. Motz, E. Abbink, P. Hines, M. G. Hylkema, E. Kimbo, A. M. Leventhal, R. Schwaderer, G. Seitz, and C. Swiden. Report on file, California Department of Parks and Recreation, Sacramento.

Levulett, V. A.
1985 The Prehistory of Southwestern Humboldt County: A Study of Coastal Archaeological Sites in the King Range National Conservation Area. Ph.D. dissertation, Department of Anthropology, University of California, Davis.

Levy, R. S.
1978a Costanoan. In *California*, edited by R. F. Heizer, pp. 485–495. Handbook of North American Indians. Vol. 8. W. C. Sturtevant, general editor. Smithsonian Institution, Washington, D.C.
1978b Eastern Miwok. In *California*, edited by Robert F. Heizer, pp. 398–413. Handbook of North American Indians. Vol. 8. W. C. Sturtevant, general editor. Smithsonian Institution, Washington, D.C.

Lewis, H. T.
1973 *Patterns of Indian Burning in California: Ecology and Ethnohistory.* Ballena Press, Ramona, California.

Lewis-Williams, J. D.
1986 Cognitive and Optical Illusions in San Rock Art Research. *Current Anthropology* 27:171–178.

Lewis-Williams, J. D., and T. A. Dowson
1988 The Signs of All Times: Entoptic Phenomena in Upper Paleolithic Art. *Current Anthropology* 29:201–245.

Lightfoot, K. G.
1997 Cultural Construction of Coastal Landscapes: A Middle Holocene Perspective from San Francisco Bay. In *Archaeology of the California Coast During the Middle Holocene*, edited by J. M. Erlandson and M. Glassow, pp. 129–141. Cotsen Institute of Archaeology, University of California, Los Angeles.

Lightfoot, K. G., and E. M. Luby
2002 Late Holocene in the San Francisco Bay Area: Temporal Trends in the Use and Abandonment of Shell Mounds in the East Bay. In *Catalysts to Complexity: Late Holocene Societies of the California Coast*, edited by J. M. Erlandson and T. L. Jones, pp. 263–281. Cotsen Institute of Archaeology, University of California, Los Angeles.

Lightfoot, K. G., T. A. Wake, and A. M. Schiff
1991 *The Archaeology and Ethnohistory of Fort Ross, California.* Contributions of the University of California Archaeological Research Facility 49. University of California Press, Berkeley.

Liljeblad, S., and C. S. Fowler
1986 Owens Valley Paiute. In *Great Basin*, edited by W. L. d'Azevedo, pp. 412–434. Handbook of North American Indians. Vol. 11. W. C. Sturtevant, general editor. Smithsonian Institution, Washington, D.C.

Lilllard, J. B., and W. K. Purves
1936 *The Archaeology of the Deer Creek-Cosumnes Area, Sacramento County, California.* Sacramento Junior College Department of Anthropology Bulletin 1.

Lillard, J. B., R. F. Heizer, and F. Fenenga
1939 *An Introduction to the Archeology of Central California.* Department of Anthropology Bulletin 2. Sacramento Junior College, Sacramento.

Lindström, S.
1982 *Archaeological Test Excavations at Oiyier Springs and Pi Pi Valley.* Prepared in cooperation with Far Western Anthropological Research Group. Submitted to Eldorado National Forest, Placerville. Copies available from Eldorado National Forest, Placerville.
1990 Submerged Tree Stumps as Indicators of Mid-Holocene Aridity in the Lake Tahoe Basin. *Journal of California and Great Basin Anthropology* 12:146–157.
1992 Great Basin Fisherfolk: Optimal Diet Breadth Modeling the Truckee River Aboriginal Subsistence Fishery. Ph.D. dissertation, Department of Anthropology, University of California, Davis.
2000 A Contextual Overview of Human Land Use and Environmental Conditions. In *Lake Tahoe Watershed Assessment*, vol. 1, edited by D. D. Murphy and C. M. Knopp, pp. 23–130. USDA Forest Service, Pacific Southwest Research Station General Technical Report PSW-GTR-175.

Lindström, S., and W. W. Bloomer
1994 *Evaluation of Site Data Potential for 26WA5322 (TY3437/05-19-280), Tahoe Meadows Prehistoric Site Complex, Segment 17 of the Tahoe Rim Trail Near Mt. Rose, Lake Tahoe, Nevada, Washoe County.* Submitted to USDA Forest Service, Toiyabe National Forest, Sparks, Nevada.

Livingston, S. D.
1986 Archaeology of the Humboldt Lakebed Site. *Journal of California and Great Basin Anthropology* 8:99–115.

Lloyd, A. H., and L. J. Graumlich
1997 Holcene Dynamics of Treeline Forests in the Sierra Nevada. *Ecology* 78:1199–1210.

Loechl, S. K., T. Britt, W. Meyer, R. R. Sands, A. Smith, J. L. Webster, and L. L. Whalley
2004 *Integrated Cultural Resources Management Plan for Edwards Air Force Base, California.* Edwards AFB Plan 32-7065. Report on file, Edwards Air Force Base.

Lorenz, J. G., and D. G. Smith
1994 Distribution of the 9-bp Mitochondrial DNA Region V Deletion Among North American Indians. *Human Biology* 66:777–788.
1996 Distribution of Four Founding mtDNA Haplogroups Among Native North Americans. *American Journal of Physical Anthropology* 101:307–323.
1997 Distribution of Sequence Variation in the mtDNA Control Region of Native North Americans. *Human Biology* 69:749–776.

Loubser, J., and D. S. Whitley
1999 *Recording Eight Places with Rock Imagery, Lava Beds National Monument, Northern California.* 2 vols. Report submitted to National Park Service, Arcata, California.

Loud, L. L.
1918 Ethnogeography and Archaeology of the Wiyot territory. *University of California Publications in American Archaeology and Ethnography* 14:221–436.

Love, B. (editor)
1996 *Archaeology on the North Shoreline of Ancient Lake Cahuilla.* Prepared by CRM TECH, Riverside, California, for U.S. Home Corporation, Tempe, Arizona.

Love, B., and M. Dahdul
2002 Desert Chronologies and the Archaic Period in the Coachella

Valley. *Pacific Coast Archaeology Society Quarterly* 38(2–3):65–86.

Luby, E. M.

1992 Social Organization and Symbolism at the Patterson Mound, Ala-328, Alameda County, California. *California Anthropologist* 18:45–52.

2004 Shell Mounds and Mortuary Behavior in the San Francisco Bay Area. *North American Archaeologist* 25:1–33.

Luby, E. M., and M. F. Gruber

1999 The Dead Must Be Fed: Symbolic Meanings of the Shellmounds of the San Francisco Bay Area. *Cambridge Archaeological Journal* 9:95–108.

Ludwig, B.

2005 The North Baja Pipeline Project: Lithic Artifact Studies. *Proceedings of the Society for California Archaeology* 18:119–129.

Luomala, K.

1978 Tipai and Ipai. In *California*, edited by Robert F. Heizer, pp. 592–609. Handbook of North American Indians. Vol. 8. W. C. Sturtevant, general editor. Smithsonian Institution, Washington, D.C.

Lyle, M., A. A. Mix, A. C. Ravelo, D. Andreasen, L. Heusser, and A. Olivarez

2000 Millennial-scale CaCO3 and C org Events Along the Northern and Central California Margins: Stratigraphy and Origins. In *Proceedings of the Ocean Drilling Program, Scientific Results* 167, edited by M. Lyle, I. Koizumi, C. Richter, and T. C. Moore Jr., pp. 163–182. Ocean Drilling Program, College Station, Texas.

Lyman, R. L.

1995 On the Evolution of Marine Mammal Hunting on the West Coast of North America. *Journal of Anthropological Archaeology* 14:45–77.

2003 Pinniped Behavior, Foraging Theory, and the Depression of a Local Population on the Southern Northwest Coast of North America. *Journal of Anthropological Archaeology* 22:376–388.

Lyneis, M. M.

1995 The Virgin Anasazi: Far Western Puebloans. *Journal of World Prehistory* 9:199–241.

Macgowan, K.

1950 *Early Man in the New World.* Macmillan, New York.

Mack, J. M.

1991 Upper Klamath River Canyon Prehistory. In *Klamath River Canyon Prehistory and Ethnology.* Cultural Resource Series no. 8. Report on file, U.S. Department of the Interior, Bureau of Land Management, Oregon State Office, Portland.

Mackey, E. M., and D. G. Sullivan

1991 Revised Final Report, Results of Palynological Investigations at Gabbott Meadow Lake, Alpine County, California. In *Cultural Resource Studies, North Fork Stanislaus River Hydroelectric Development Project,* edited by A. S. Peak and N. J. Neuenschwander, pp. 473–499. Peak and Associates, Sacramento. Copies available from Peak and Associates.

Macko, M. E.

1983 Beads, Bones, Baptisms, and Sweatlodges: Analysis of Collections from "Elijman" (CA-SBa-485), a Late Period Ynezeno Chumash Village in the Central Santa Ynez Valley, California. Master's thesis, Department of Anthropology, University of California, Santa Barbara.

1998 *Neolithic Newport: Executive Summary, Results of Implementing Mitigation Measures Specified in the Operation Plan and Research Design for the Proposed Newporter North Residential Development at ORA-64,* Macko, Huntington Beach. Copies available from Macko, Inc.

Macko, M. E., J. S. Couch, and H. R. Koerper

2005 Implications of Ritual Biface Caches from the Irvine Site. *Journal of California and Great Basin Anthropology* 25:93–108.

MacMahon, J., and F. Wagner

1985 The Mojave, Sonoran, and Chihuahuan Deserts of North America. In *Hot Deserts and Arid Shrublands,* edited by M. Evenari, I. Noy-Meir, and D. Goddall, pp. 105–202. Ecosystems of the World. Vol. 12A. Elsevier, Amsterdam.

MacNeish, R. S.

1971 Early Man in the Andes. *Scientific American* 224:74–85.

Madsen, D. B.

1999 Environmental Change During the Pleistocene-Holocene Transition and Its Possible Impact on Human Populations. In *Models for the Millennium: Great Basin Anthropology Today,* edited by C. Beck, pp. 75–82. University of Utah Press, Salt Lake City.

Madsen, D. B. (editor)

2004 *Entering America: Northeast Asia and Beringia Before the Last Glacial Maximum.* University of Utah Press, Salt Lake City.

Madsen, D. B., and D. Rhode (editors)

1994 *Across the West: Human Population Movement and the Expansion of the Numa.* University of Utah Press, Salt Lake City.

Magnuson, J. J.

1990 Long-term Ecological Research and the Invisible Present. *Bioscience* 40:495–501.

Malhi, R. S.

2001 Investigating Prehistoric Population Movements in North America with Ancient and Modern mtDNA. Ph.D. dissertation, Department of Anthropology, University of California, Davis.

Malhi, R. S., B. A. Schultz, and D. G. Smith

2001 Distribution of Mitochondrial DNA Lineages Among Native American Tribes of Northeastern North America. *Human Biology* 73:17–55.

Malhi, R. S., K. E. Breece, B. A. S. Shook, F. A. Kaestle, J. C. Chatters, S. Hackenberger, and D. G. Smith

2004 Patterns of mtDNA Diversity in Northwestern North America. *Human Biology* 76:33–54.

Malhi, R. S., H. M. Mortensen, J. A. Eshleman, B. M. Kemp, J. G. Lorenz, F. A. Kaestle, J. R. Johnson, C. Gorodezky, and D. G. Smith

2003 Native American mtDNA Prehistory in the American Southwest. *American Journal of Physical Anthropology* 120:108–124.

Malhi, R. S., J. A. Eshleman, J. A. Greenberg, D. A. Weiss, B. A. Shultz Shook, F. A. Kaestle, J. G. Lorenz, B. M. Kemp, J. R. Johnson, and D. G. Smith

2002 The Structure of Diversity Within New World Mitochondrial DNA Haplogroups: Implications for the Prehistory of North America. *American Journal of Human Genetics* 70:905–919.

Manaster Ramer, A.

1992 Tubatulabal "Man" and the Subclassification of Uto-Aztecan. *California Linguistic Notes* 23:30–31.

Maniery, M. L., and J. L. Brown

1994 *National Register Evaluation of CA-SAC-344/H: A Multicomponent Site Near Folsom, Sacramento County, California.* PAR Environmental Services. Submitted to Elliott Homes, Folsom, California. Copies available from the North Central Archaeological Information Center, Department of Anthropology, California State University, Sacramento.

Mann, D. H., and T. D. Hamilton

1995 Late Pleistocene and Holocene Paleoenviroments of the North Pacific Coast. *Quaternary Science Reviews* 14:449–471.

Mantua, N. J., and S. R. Hare

2002 The Pacific Decadal Oscillation. *Journal of Oceanography* 58:35–44.

Manual, D.

1989 *Exacavation and Analysis of CA-LAS-973: A Small Winter Village Site on the Modoc Plateau of Northeastern California.* Bureau of Land Management, Susanville District, Susanville, California.

Martin, P. S.
1967 Prehistoric Overkill. In *Pleistocene Extinctions: The Search for a Cause*, edited by P. S. Martin and H. E. Wright Jr., pp. 75–120. Yale University Press, New Haven.

Martin, S., and V. Popper
1998 Paleobotanical Analysis. In *3,000 years of Prehistory at the Red Beach Site, CA-SDI-811, Marine Corps Base, Camp Pendleton, California*, edited by K. Rasmussen and C. Woodman, pp. 203–209. Report on file, South Coast Information Center, San Diego State University.
1999 Macrobotanical Analysis. In *Archaeological Investigations Along the Lower Santa Margarita River, Marine Corps Base Camp Pendelton, California*, edited by A. York, C. Dolan, J. Underwood, and T. Wahoff. Report on file, South Coast Information Center, San Diego State University.

Martin, T. P.
1998 Archaeological Test Excavations at the Visitor Center Site, an Early Holocene Site in Lake Tahoe, California. Master's thesis, Department of Anthropology, Sonoma State University.

Martz, P.
1984 Social Dimensions of Chumash Mortuary Populations in the Santa Monica Mountains Region. Ph.D. dissertation, Department of Anthropology, University of California, Riverside.
1992 Status Distinctions Reflected in Chumash Mortuary Populations in the Santa Monica Mountains Region. In *Essays on the Prehistory of Maritime California*, edited by T. L. Jones, pp. 145–156. Center for Archaeological Research Publication 10. University of California, Davis.

Martz, P., and E. J. Rosenthal
2001 The Maritime Hunter-gatherers of San Nicolas Island, California: An Analogy to Rapa Nui? In *Pacific 2000: Proceedings of the Fifth International Conference on Easter Island and the Pacific*, edited by C. M. Stevenson, G. Lee, and F. J. Morin, pp. 59–70. Bearsville Press, Los Osos, California.

Mason, J. A.
1912 The Ethnology of the Salinan Indians. *University of California Publications in American Archaeology and Ethnology* 10:97–240.
1918 *The Language of Salinan Indians.* University of California Publications in Archaeology and Ethnology 14.

Mason, R. D., H. C. Koerper, and P. E. Langenwalter II
1997 Middle Holocene Adaptations on the Newport Coast of Orange County. In *Archaeology of the California Coast During the Middle Holocene,* edited by J. M. Erlandson and M. A. Glassow, pp. 35–60. Cotsen Institute of Archaeology, University of California, Los Angeles.

Masters, P. M.
1998 Paleo-Environmental Reconstruction of San Diego Bay, 10,000 B.P. to Present. In *Five Thousand Years of Maritime Subsistence at CA-SDI-48, on Ballast Point, San Diego County, California*, edited by D. Gallegos and C. Kyle, pp. 16–30. Archives of California Prehistory 40, Coyote Press, Salinas.
2006 Holocene Sand Beaches of Southern California: ENSO Forcing and Coastal Processes on Millennial Scales. *Palaeogeography, Palaeoclimatology, Palaeoecology* 232:73–95.

Masters, P. M., and D. Gallegos
1997 Environmental Change and Coastal Adaptations in San Diego County During the Middle Holocene. In *Archaeology of the California Coast During the Middle Holocene*, edited by J. M. Erlandson and M. A. Glassow, pp. 11–21. Cotsen Institute of Archaeology, University of California, Los Angeles.

Maxwell, D.
2003 Vertebrate Faunal Remains. In *At the Base of the Bluff, Archaeological Inventory and Evaluation Along Lower Centinela Creek, Marina del Rey, California.* Playa Vista Monograph Series Test Excavation Report 4, edited by J. H. Altschul, A. Q. Stoll, D. R. Grenda, and R. Ciolek-Torello, pp. 145–177. Statistical Research, Tucson, Arizona.

May, R. V.
1978 A Southern California Indigenous Ceramic Typology: A Contribution to Malcolm J. Rogers Research. *Journal of the Archaeological Survey Association of Southern California* 2(2).
2001 Ceramic Rims from the Rim of Lake Cahuilla. *San Bernardino County Museum Association Quarterly* 48(3):45–72.

MCAGCC
2002 *Integrated Cultural Resources Management Plan for the Marine Corps Air Ground Combat Center, Twentynine Palms, California*. Report prepared by NREA staff, Marine Corps Air Ground Combat Center, Twentynine Palms.

McCarten, N., and T. R. Van Devender
1988 Late Wisconsin Vegetation of Robber's Roost in the Western Mojave Desert, California. *Madrono* 35:226–237.

McCarthy, D. F.
1993 Prehistoric Land-Use at McCoy Spring: An Arid-Land Oasis in Eastern Riverside County, California. Master's thesis, Department of Anthropology, University of California, Riverside.

McCarthy, H.
1985 Linguistics and Its Implications for California Ethnography and Culture History. In *Ethnography and Prehistory of the North Coast Range, California*, edited by H. McCarthy, W. R. Hildebrandt, and L. K. Swenson, pp. 20–34. Center for Archaeological Research at Davis Publication no. 8. University of California, Davis.

McCarthy, H., and H. Scotten
2004 Ethnographic Context. In *Class I Cultural Resources Overview and Research Design for the Alturas, Eagle Lake, and Surprise Resource Areas*, edited by J. King, K. McGuire, K. Carpenter, M. L. Maniery, C. Baker, H. McCarthy, and H. Scotten, pp. 36–53. Bureau of Land Management, Surprise, Eagle Lake, and Alturas Field Offices, California.

McCarthy, H. C., C. M. Blount, and R. A. Hicks
1985 Appendix F: A Functional Analysis of Bedrock Mortars: Western Mono Food Processing in the Southern Sierra Nevada. In *Cultural Resources of the Crane Valley Hydroelectric Project Area, Madera County, California.* Vol. 1, *Ethnographic, Historic, and Archaeological Overviews and Archaeological Survey*, edited by S. K. Goldberg, pp. 189–214. INFOTEC Research, Sonora, California. Submitted to Pacific Gas and Electric Company, San Francisco.

McCarthy, H., W. R. Hildebrandt, and L. K. Swenson (editors)
1985 *Ethnography and Prehistory of the North Coast Range, California.* Center for Archaeological Research at Davis Publication no. 8. University of California, Davis.

McCawley, W.
1996 *The First Angelinos: The Gabrielino Indians of Los Angeles.* Malki Museum Press, Banning, and Ballena Press, Novato.

McClure, S. B.
2004 Small Mammal Procurement in Coastal Contexts: A California Perspective. *Journal of California and Great Basin Anthropology* 24:207–232.

McCulloch, D. S., and H. G. Greene
1989 Geologic Map of the Central California Continental Margin. In *California Continental Margin Geologic Map Series*, Central California Continental Margin, Map 5A (Geology), edited by H. G. Greene and M. P. Kennedy. California Division of Mines and Geology, San Francisco.

McDonald, A. M.
1992 Indian Hill Rockshelter and Aboriginal Cultural Adaptation in Anza-Borrego Desert State Park, Southeastern California. Ph.D. dissertation, Department of Anthropology, University of California, Riverside.

McDonald, A. M., and J. Eighmey
1998 Late Period Prehistory. In *Prehistoric and Historic Archaeology of Metropolitan San Diego: A Historic Properties Background Study.* Prepared for Metropolitan Wastewater District. Report on file, South Coast Information Center, San Diego State University.
McFarland, S. L.
2000 Changes in Obsidian Exchange in Southern California. Master's thesis, Department of Anthropology, San Diego State University.
McGonagle, R. L.
1966 The Cook Site: A Middle Horizon Site in Central California. Master's thesis, Department of Anthropology, University of California, Davis.
McGowan, C.
1982 *Ceremonial Fertility Sites in Southern California.* San Diego Museum of Man Papers no. 14.
McGuire, K. R.
1989 Incised Stones. Appendix D in *Prehistory of the Sacramento River Canyon, Shasta County, California,* edited by M. E. Basgall and W. R. Hildebrandt, pp. D.1–D.44. Center for Archaeological Research at Davis no. 9. University of California, Davis.
1995 *Test Excavations at CA-FRE-61, Fresno County, California.* Occasional Papers in Anthropology no. 5. Museum of Anthropology, California State University, Bakersfield.
1997a *Secret Valley.* Culture Change Along the Eastern Sierra Nevada/Cascade Front. Vol. 4. Far Western Anthropological Research Group, Davis, California. Report prepared for Tuscarora Gas Transmission Company. Reno, Nevada.
1997b *Fort Sage Uplands and Spanish Springs Valley.* Culture Change Along the Eastern Sierra Nevada/Cascade Front. Vol. 6. Far Western Anthropological Research Group, Davis, California. Report prepared for Tuscarora Gas Transmission Company, Reno.
2000 Prehistoric Archaeological Studies: The Pit River Uplands, Madeline Plains, Honey Lake and Secret Valley, and Sierran Front Project Segments. In *Archaeological Investigations Along the California–Great Basin Interface: The Alturas Transmission Line Project,* edited by K. R. McGuire. Vol. 1. Far Western Anthropological Research Group, Davis, California. Report prepared for Sierra Pacific Power Company, Reno.
McGuire, K. R. (editor)
2002 *Boundary Lands: Archaeological Investigations Along the California–Great Basin Interface.* Nevada State Museum Anthropological Papers no. 24.
McGuire, K. R., and W. Bloomer
1997 Middle Period Land-Use Patterns and Toolstone Preferences: A Model for the Martis Complex and Other North-central Sierran and Eastern Front Assemblages. In *Culture Change Along the Eastern Sierra/Cascade Front,* edited by K. McGuire, pp. 115–122. Far Western Anthropological Research Group, Davis, California. Report prepared for Tuscarora Gas Transmission Company.
McGuire, K. R., and M. C. Hall
1988 *The Archaeology of Tiefort Basin, Fort Irwin, San Bernardino, California.* Report on file, San Bernardino County Archaeological Information Center, San Bernardino County Museum, Redlands.
McGuire, K. R., and W. R. Hildebrandt
1994 The Possibilities of Women and Men: Gender and the California Millingstone Horizon. *Journal of California and Great Basin Anthropology* 16:41–59.
2005 Re-Thinking Great Basin Foragers: Prestige Hunting and Costly Signaling During the Middle Archaic Period. *American Antiquity* 70:695–712.
McGuire, K. R., A. P. Garfinkle, and M. E. Basgall
1982 *Archaeological Investigations in the El Paso Mountains of the Western Mojave Desert: The Bickel and Last Chance Sites (CA-Ker-250 and -261).* Far Western Anthropological Research Group, Davis, California. Report on file, Southern San Joaquin Valley Archaeological Information Center, California State University, Bakersfield.
McGuire, R. H., and M. B. Schiffer
1982 *Hohokam and Patayan, Prehistory of Southwestern Arizona.* Academic Press, New York.
McLendon, S., and J. R. Johnson
1999 *Cultural Affiliation and Lineal Descent of Chumash Peoples in the Channel Islands and Santa Monica Mountains.* 2 vols. Prepared for the Archaeology and Ethnography Program, National Park Service, Washington, D.C. Santa Barbara Museum of Natural History, Santa Barbara.
McRae, K. S.
1999 Soxtonokmu' (CA-SBA-167): An Analysis of Artifacts and Economic Patterns from a Late Period Chumash Village in the Santa Ynez Valley. Master's thesis, Department of Anthropology, University of Texas, San Antonio.
Meacham, C. M.
1979 *Halotis* Ornaments of the Windmiller Culture. Coyote Press, Salinas, California.
1984 A Great Basin Pecked Style Petroglyph in the North Coast Ranges. *Journal of California and Great Basin Anthropology* 6:260–265.
Meese, D. A., A. J. Gow, P. Grootes, P. A. Mayewski, M. Ram, M. Stuiver, K. C. Taylor, E. D. Waddington, and F. A. Zielinski
1994 The Accumulation Record from the GISP2 Core as an Indicator of Climate Change Throughout the Holocene. *Science* 266:1680–1682.
Mehringer, P. J., Jr., and P. E. Wigand
1987 Western Juniper in the Holocene. *Proceedings of the Pinyon-Juniper Conference, January 13–16, 1986, Reno, Nevada,* compiled by R. L. Everett, pp. 109–119. U.S. Forest Service, Intermountain Research Station, General Technical Report INT-215, Ogden, Utah.
Meighan, C. W.
1954 A Late Complex in Southern California Prehistory. *Southwestern Journal of Anthropology* 10:215–227.
1955 Archaeology of the North Coast Ranges, California. *University of California Archaeological Survey Reports* 30:1–39.
1959 The Little Harbor Site, Catalina Island: An Example of Ecological Interpretation in Archaeology. *American Antiquity* 24:383–405.
1969 A Ritual Cave in Topanga. *Masterkey* 43:112–117.
Meighan, C., and C. V. Haynes
1970 The Borax Lake Site Revisited. *Science* 167:1213–1221.
Meighan, C., D. A. Fredrickson, and A. Mohr
1953 Ground Stone. In *Archaeology of the Napa Region,* edited by R. F. Heizer, pp. 257–261. University of California Anthropological Records 12(6).
Meko, D. M.
2001 *Reconstructed Sacramento River System Runoff from Tree Rings.* Report prepared for the California Department of Water Resources. Laboratory of Tree-Ring Research, University of Arizona, Tucson. Copies available from Department of Water Resources, Sacramento.
Meko, D. M., M. D. Therrell, C. H. Paisan, and M. K. Hughes
2001 Sacramento River Flow Reconstructed to A.D. 869 from Tree Rings. *Journal of American Water Resources Association* 37:1029–1039.
Meltzer, D. J.
1988 Late Pleistocene Human Adaptations in Eastern North America. *Journal of World Prehistory* 2:1–52.

1993a *Search for the First Americans.* Smithsonian Institution, Washington, D.C.
1993b Is There a Clovis Adaptation? In *From Kostenki to Clovis, Upper Paleolithic–Paleo-Indian Adaptations*, edited by O. Soffer and N. D. Parslov, pp. 293–310. Plenum Press, New York.

Meltzer, D. J., D. K. Grayson, G. Ardila, A. W. Varker, D. F. Dincauze, V. Haynes, F. Mena, L. Nunez, and D. J. Stanford
1997 On the Pleistocene Antiquity of Monte Verde. *American Antiquity* 62:659–663.

Mensing, S.
2001 Late Glacial and Early Holocene Vegetation and Climate Change Near Owens Lake, Eastern California. *Quaternary Research* 55:57–67.

Menzies, A.
1924 [1792] Menzies' California Journal. *Quarterly of the California Historical Society* 2:265–340.

Merriam, C. H., and Z. Talbot
1974 *Boundary Descriptions of California Indian Stocks and Tribes.* Miscellaneous Publications of the University of California Archaeological Research Facility, Department of Anthropology, UC Berkeley.

Mester, A. M., and C. McEwan (editors)
1988 Archaeology and Linguistics. *Journal of the Steward Anthropological Society* 15:1–2.

Meyer, J.
1996 Geoarchaeological Implications of Holocene Landscape Evolution in the Los Vaqueros Area of Eastern Contra Costa County, California. Master's thesis, Department of Anthropology, Sonoma State University, Rohnert Park.
2005 *Geoarchaeological Study of the Marsh Creek Site (CA-CCO-18 and CA-CCO-548) Eastern Contra Costa County, California.* Anthropological Studies Center, Sonoma State University, Rohnert Park. Copies available from the Northwest Information Center, Sonoma State University, Rohnert Park.

Meyer, J., and J. S. Rosenthal
1997 *Archaeological and Goearchaeological Investigations at Eight Prehistoric Sites in the Los Vaqueros Reservoir Area, Contra Costa County, California.* Anthropological Studies Center, Sonoma State University Academic Foundation, Rohnert Park, California. Submitted to the Contra Costa Water District, Concord, California. Copies available from the Northwest Information Center, Sonoma State University, Rohnert Park.
1998 *An Archaeological Investigation of Artifacts and Human Remains from CA-CCO-637, Los Vaqueros Project Area, Contra Costa County, California.* Anthropological Studies Center, Sonoma State University Academic Foundation, Rohnert Park, California. Submitted to the Contra Costa Water District, Concord, California. Copies available from Northwest Information Center, Department of Anthropology, Sonoma State University, Rohnert Park, California.

Mikkelsen, P., and W. R. Hildebrandt
1990 *Archaeological Inventory and Evaluation for the Proposed Los Banos Grandes Reservoir, Merced County, California.* Report submitted to U.S. Bureau of Reclamation. Sacramento, California. Far Western Anthropological Research Group, Davis. Report on file, Central California Information Center, Department of Anthropology, California State University, Stanislaus, Turlock.

Mikkelsen, P., W. R. Hildebrandt, and D. A. Jones
2000 *Prehistoric Adaptations on the Shores of Morro Bay Estuary: Excavations at Site CA-SLO-165, Morro Bay, California.* San Luis Obispo County Archaeological Society Occasional Papers no. 14.

Mikkelsen, P., W. R. Hildebrandt, D. A. Jones, J. Rosenthal, and R. Gibson
2004 *Thirty Years After: 1974 Excavations at Kirk Creek, CA-MNT-238, on the Big Sur Coast.* Far Western Anthropological Research Group, Davis. Submitted to California Department of Transportation, District 5, San Luis Obispo. Report on file, Northwest Information Center, Department of Anthropology, Sonoma State University, Rohnert Park, California.

Miksicek, C. H.
1999 On the Cusp of History: Archaeobotanical Remains from CA-SOL-397. Appendix K in *Archaeological Investigations at SOL-397, Located on the University of California, Davis Campus, Yolo County, California,* edited by L. Shapiro and K. J. Tremaine, Pacific Legacy. Submitted to the University of California, Davis. Report on file, Northwest Information Center, Department of Anthropology, Sonoma State University, Rohnert Park, California.

Milburn, J. W., D. A. Fredrickson, M. Dreiss, L. Michael, and W. Van Dusen
1979 *A Preliminary Report on the Archaeology of CA-HUM-129.* Report on file, California Department of Parks and Recreation, Sacramento.

Miles, S. R., and C. B. Goudey
2005 *Ecological Subregions of California.* USDA Forest Service. www.fs.fed.us/r5/projects/ecoregions.

Millar, C. I., and W. B. Woolfenden
1999 Sierra Nevada Forests: Where Did They Come From? Where Are They Going? What Does It Mean? In *Transactions of the 64th North American Wildlife and Resources Conference,* edited by by R. E. McCabe and S. E. Loos, pp. 206–236. Wildlife Management Institute, Washington, D.C.

Millar, C. I., R. D. Westfall, D. L. Delany, J. C. King, and L. J. Groumlich
2004 Response of Subalpine Conifers in the Sierra Nevada, California, U.S.A., to 20th Century Warming and Decadal Climatic Variability. *Arctic, Antarctic, and Alpine Research* 36:181–200.

Miller, J. N.
1966 The Present and Past Molluscan Faunas and Environments of Four Southern California Coastal Lagoons. Master's thesis, Scripps Institution of Oceanography, University of California, San Diego.

Miller, W. R.
1983 Uto-Aztecan Languages. In *Southwest,* edited by A. Ortiz, 113–124. Handbook of North American Indians. Vol. 10. W. C. Sturtevant, general editor. Smithsonian Institution, Washington, D.C.
1984 The Classification of the Uto-Aztecan Languages Based on Lexical Evidence. *International Journal of American Linguistics* 50:1–24.

Milliken, R. T.
1981 Ethnohistory of the Rumsen: The Mission Period. In *Report of Archaeological Excavations at Nineteen Archaeological Sites for the Stage 1 Pacific Grove–Monterey Consolidation Project of the Regional Sewerage System,* edited by S. A. Dietz and T. L. Jackson, pp. 10–102. Archaeological Consulting and Research Services, Santa Cruz. Copies available from Northwest Information Center, Department of Anthropology, Sonoma State University, Rohnert Park, California.
1988 Ethnographic Context. In *Archaeological Investigations at Elkhorn Slough: CA-MNT-229, a Middle Period Site on the Central California Coast,* edited by S. A. Dietz, W. Hildebrandt, and T. L. Jones, pp. 57–94. Papers in Northern California Anthropology 3. Anthropological Research Group, Berkeley.
1995a *A Time of Little Choice: The Disintegration of Tribal Culture in the San Francisco Bay Area, 1769–1810.* Ballena Press, Menlo Park, California.
1995b *Report on the 1994 Archaeological Excavation on the Skirt of the Souza Mound, SAC-42, Sacramento County, California.* Far Western Anthropological Research Group. Submitted to the City of Sacramento. Copies available from North Central In-

formation Center, Department of Anthropology, California State University, Sacramento.

1999 Shell, Stone, and Bone Beads in the Owens Valley. In *The Changing Role of Riverine Environments in the Prehistory of the Central-Western Great Basin: Data Recovery Excavations at Six Prehistoric Sites in Owens Valley, California*, edited by M. G. Delacorte, pp. 65–108. Limited distribution technical report submitted to California Department of Transportation, District 9, by Far Western Anthropological Research Group, Davis, California.

Milliken, R. T., and J. A. Bennyhoff

1993 Temporal Changes in Beads as Prehistoric California Grave Goods. In *There Grows a Green Tree: Papers in Honor of David A. Fredrickson*, edited by G. White, P. Mikkelsen, W. R. Hildebrandt, and M. E. Basgall, pp. 381–395. Center for Archeological Research at Davis no. 11. University of California, Davis.

Milliken, R. T., and W. R. Hildebrandt

1997 *Culture Change Along the Eastern Sierra Nevada/Cascade Front.* Vol. 5, *Honey Lake Basin.* Report prepared for Tuscarora Gas Transmission Company. Reno.

Milliken, R. T., and J. R. Johnson

2005 *An Ethnogeography of Salinan and Northern Chumash–1769 to 1810.* Report prepared for Caltrans District 5. Far Western Anthropological Research Group, Davis. Copies available from California Department of Transportation, San Luis Obispo.

Milliken, R. T., and J. Meyer

1997 *Fire Damage Archaeological Mitigation at CA-FRE-2365 on Panoche Creek, Western Fresno County.* Report submitted to USDI Bureau of Land Management, Hollister, California.

Milliken, R. T., J. Nelson, W. R. Hildebrandt, and P. Mikkelsen

1999 *The Moss Landing Hill Site: A Technical Report on Archaeological Studies at CA-MNT-234.* Far Western Anthropological Research Group, Davis. Copies available from Northwest Information Center, Department of Anthropology, Sonoma State University, Rohnert Park, California.

Milliken, R. T., W. Bloomer, S. Stratton, J. Nelson, D. Furlong, D. C. Young, E. Wohlgemuth, J. Costello, P. Mikkelsen, T. Carpenter, and D. Jones

1997 *The Taylors Bar Site (CA-CAL-1180/H): Archaeological and Ethnohistoric Investigations in Calaveras County, California.* Far Western Anthropological Research Group, Davis. Report submitted to Calaveras County Water District, San Andreas.

Milliman, J. D., and K. O. Emery

1968 Sea Levels During the Past 35,000 years. *Science* 162:1121–1123.

Mills, W., M. Rondeau, and T. L. Jones

2005 A Fluted Projectile Point from Nipomo, San Luis Obispo County, California. *Journal of California and Great Basin Anthropology* 25:68–74.

Mitchell, V. L.

1976 The Regionalization of Climate in the Western United States. *Journal of Applied Meteorology* 15:920–927.

Mithun, M.

1999 *The Languages of Native North America.* Cambridge Language Surveys. Cambridge University Press, Cambridge.

Moberg, A., D. M. Sonechkin, K. Holmgren, N. M. Datsenko, and W. Karlén

2005 Highly Variable Northern Hemisphere Temperatures Reconstructed from Low- and High-Resolution Proxy Data. *Nature* 433:613–617.

Mohr, J. A., C. Whitlock, and C. Skinner

2000 Postglacial Vegetation and Fire History, Eastern Klamath Mountains, California, U.S.A. *Holocene* 10:587–601.

Moore, E.

1982 Continuity and Change in Central California Prehistory: The Material Record. Master's thesis, Department of Anthropology, California State University, Hayward.

Moratto, M. J.

1972 A Study of Prehistory in the Southern Sierra Nevada Foothills, California. Ph.D. dissertation, Department of Anthropology, University of Oregon, Eugene.

1973 Archaeology in the Far West. In *Archaeology in the 70's: Mitigating the Impact*, edited by C. H. Chapman. pp. 19–32. *Missouri Archaeologist* 35.

1981 *An Archeological Research Design for Yosemite National Park, California.* USDI National Park Service, Western Archeological and Conservation Center Publications in Anthropology 19.

1984 *California Archaeology.* Academic Press, New York.

1992 CRM in California: Retrospect on 25 Years of Progress. *Proceedings of the Society for California Archaeology* 5:39–57.

1999 Cultural Chronology 2: The Yosemite Data. In *Archeological Synthesis and Research Design, Yosemite National Park, California*, edited by K. L. Hull and M. J. Moratto, pp. 121–204. USDI National Park Service Yosemite Research Center Publications in Anthropology 21.

2002 Culture History of the New Melones Reservoir Area, Calaveras and Tuolumne Counties, California. In *Essays in California Archaeology: A Memorial to Franklin Fenenga*, edited by W. J. Wallace and F. A. Riddell, pp. 25–54. Contributions of the University of California Archaeological Research Facility no. 60.

2004 *California Archaeology.* New introduction. Coyote Press, Salinas, California.

Moratto, M. J., and M. R. Arguelles

1984 The Texas Charley Gulch Site, 04-CAL-S-286. In *Final Report of the New Melones Archaeological Project.* Vol. 4. Edited by Michael J. Moratto, Macus Arguelles, Susan Goldberg, Steven O'Brien, Lynn Riley, and William T. Singleton. Infotech Development. Submitted to the National Park Service, Washington, D.C.

Moratto, M. J., T. F. King, and W. B. Woolfenden

1978 Archaeology and California's Climate. *Journal of California Anthropology* 5:147–161.

Moratto, M. J., J. D. Tordoff, and L. H. Shoup

1988 *Culture Change in the Central Sierra Nevada, 8000 B.C.-A.D. 1950.* Final Report of the New Melones Archaeological Project 9, pp. 1–626. INFOTEC Research Sonora, California. Submitted to the USDI National Park Service, Washington, D.C.

Moriarty, J. R., III

1967 Transitional Pre-Desert Phase in San Diego County, California. *Science* 155:553–556.

Moriarity, J. R., III, and R. P. Burns

1962 *A Preliminary Reconnaissance of a Pre-Ceramic Site at Avila Beach, San Luis Obispo County, California.* San Diego Science Foundation Occasional Papers no. 3.

Moriarty, J. R., III, G. Shumway, and C. N. Warren

1959 Scripps Estates Site I (SDI-525): A Preliminary Report on an Early Site on the San Diego Coast. *University of California Archaeological Survey Annual Report 1958–1959*, pp. 185–216.

Motz, L., E. Abbink, P. Hines, M. Hylkema, E. Kimbro, A. Leventhal, P. D. Shulz, R. Schwaderer, G. Seitz, and C. Swidden

1989 *Results of the General Development Plan Archaeological Test Excavation Conducted at CA-MNT-185/H, Garrapata State Park, Big Sur District, Central Coast Region.* Copies available from California Department of Parks and Recreation, Sacramento.

Moy, C. M., G. O. Seltzer, D. T. Rodbell, and D. M. Anderson

2002 Variability of El Niño/Southern Oscillation Activity at Millennial Timescales During the Holocene Epoch. *Nature* 420:162–165.

Muir, J.

1894 *The Mountains of California.* Reprinted by Ten Speed Press, Berkeley, 1977.

1916 *The Mountains of California.* Houghton Mifflin, Boston.

Mullins, H. T., D. K. Nagel, and L. L. Dominguez
1985 Tectonic and Eustatic Controls of Late Quaternary Shelf Sedimentation Along the Central California (Santa Cruz) Continental Margin: High Resolution Seismic Stratigraphic Evidence. *Sedimentological Geolology* 45:327–347.

Munns, A. M., and J. E. Arnold
2002 Late Holocene Santa Cruz Island: Patterns of Continuity and Change. In *Catalysts to Complexity: Late Holocene Societies of the California Coast*, edited by J. M. Erlandson and T. L. Jones, pp. 127–146. Cotsen Institute of Archaeology, University of California, Los Angeles.

Munro, P.
1994 Gulf and Yuki-Gulf. *Anthropological Linguistics* 36:125–222.

Munz, P. A., and D. D. Keck
1959 *A California Flora*. University of California Press, Berkeley.

National Research Council
1999 *Improving American River Flood Frequency Analysis*. National Academy Press, Washington, D.C.

Nelson, D. E., R. E. Moreland, J. S. Vogel, J. R. Southon, and C. R. Harington
1986 New Radiocarbon Dates on Artifacts from the NorthernYukon Territory: Holocene Not Upper Pleistocene in Age. *Science* 232:749–751.

Nelson, J. S.
1991 Interpersonal Violence in Prehistoric Northern California: A Bioarchaeological Approach. Master's thesis, Department of Anthropology, California State University, Chico.

Nelson, N. C.
1910 The Ellis Landing Shellmound. *University of California Publications in American Archaeology and Ethnology* 7(5).

Nettle, D.
1998 Explaining Global Patterns of Language Diversity. *Journal of Anthropological Archaeology* 17:354–374.

Newsome, S., D. L. Phillips, B. J. Culleton, T. P. Guilderson, and P. L. Koch
2004 Dietary Reconstruction of an Early to Middle Holocene Human Population from the Central California Coast: Insights from Advanced Stable Isotope Mixing Models. *Journal of Archaeological Science* 31:1101–1115.

Nichols, J.
1990 Linguistic Diversity and the First Settlement of the New World. *Language* 66:475–521.
1992 *Linguistic Diversity in Space and Time*. University of Chicago Press, Chicago.
1997 Modeling Ancient Population Structures and Movement in Linguistics. *Annual Review of Anthropology* 26:359–384.
2000 Estimating Dates of Early American Colonization Events. In *Time Depth in Historical Linguistics*, edited by C. Renfrew, A. McMahon, and L. Trask, pp. 643–663. McDonald Institute for Archaeological Research, Cambridge.
2002 The First American Languages. In *The First Americans: The Pleistocene Colonization of the New World*, edited by N. G. Jablonski, pp. 273–293. Memoirs of the California Academy of Sciences 27.

Nichols, M. J. P.
1988 Old California Uto-Aztecan. *Journal of the Steward Anthropological Society* 15:22–46.

Nilsson, E. R., R. Bevill, and M. S. Kelly
2000 *Archaeological Investigations Along the California–Great Basin Interface: The Alturas Transmission Line Project*. Vol. 3, *Prehistoric Archaeological Studies: Alturas Segment*. Report prepared for Sierra Pacific Power Company, Reno, Nevada.

Nissen, K. M., and E. W. Ritter
1986 Cupped Rock Art in North Central California: Hypothesis Regarding Age and Social/Ecological Context. *American Indian Rock Art* 11:59–76.

Northrup, J. J., K. C. Long, J. Nadolski, and K. Ataman
1999 Toolstone Sources and Exchange Patterns. In *Post-modern Martis: New Archaeological Investigations in Martis Valley*, edited by Kathryn Ataman, pp. 8-1–8-18. Summit Envirosolutions, Reno, Nevada, and Pacific Legacy, Cameron Park, California. Submitted to U.S. Army Corps of Engineers, Sacramento, California, and California Department of Transportation, Marysville, California.

Noss, R. F. (editor)
2000 *The Redwood Forest*. Island Press, Washington, D.C.

O'Brien, S.
1984 The Redbud Site, 04-CAL-S-347. In *Final Report of the New Melones Archaeological Project*, edited by Michael J. Moratto, Macus Arguelles, Susan Goldberg, Steven O'Brien, Lynn Riley, and William T. Singleton. Vol. 4. Infotech Development Incorportaed. Submitted to the National Park Service, Washington, D.C.

O'Connell, J. F.
1971 The Archaeology and Cultural Ecology of Surprise Valley, Northeast California. Ph.D. dissertation, University of California, Berkeley.
1975 *The Prehistory of Surprise Valley*, edited by L. J. Bean. Anthropological Papers 4. Ballena Press, Romona, California.

O'Connell, J. F., and C. M. Inoway
1994 Surprise Valley Projectile Points and Their Chronological Implications. *Journal of California and Great Basin Anthropology* 16:162–198.

Odion, D., D. M. Storms, and F. Davis
1998 Appendix MP, The Modoc Plateau Region. In *California Gap Analysis: A Geographic Analysis of Biodiversity, Final Report*, edited by F. M. Davis, D. M. Storms, A. D. Hollander, K. A. Thomas, P. A. Stine, D. Odion, M. J. Borchert, J. H. Thorne, M. V. Gray, R. E. Walker, K. Warner, and J. Grace, pp. 1–9. University of California Santa Barbara Biogeography Laboratory. Submitted to the U.S. Geological Survey, Biological Resources Division, Menlo Park.

Olmsted, D. L.
1966 *Achumawi Dictionary*. University of California Publications in Linguistics 45.
1985 Linguistic Evidence Concerning Pomo Migrations. In *Ethnography and Prehistory of the North Coast Range, California*, edited by H. McCarthy, W. R. Hildebrandt, and L. K. Swenson, pp. 216–221. Center for Archaeological Research at Davis Publication no. 8. University of California, Davis.

Olmsted, D. L., and O. C. Stewart
1978 Achumawi. In *California*, edited by R. F. Heizer, pp. 225–235. Handbook of North American Indians. Vol. 8. W. C. Sturtevant, general editor. Smithsonian Institution, Washington, D.C.

Olsen, W. H.
1963 The Comparative Analysis of the King Brown Site (4-SAC-29). Master's thesis, Department of Anthropology, California State University, Sacramento.

Olsen, W. H., and L. A. Payen
1968 *Archeology of the Little Panoche Reservoir, Fresno County, California*. California Department of Parks and Recreation Archeological Report no. 11.
1969 *Archaeology of the Grayson Site*. California Department of Parks and Recreation Archaeological Report no. 12. Department of Parks and Recreation.
1983 Excavations at CA-MER-130: A Late Prehistoric Site in Pacheco Pass. In *Papers in Merced County Prehistory*, pp. 1–85. *University of California Archaeological Survey Reports* no. 21.

Olsen, W. H., and N. L. Wilson
1964 *The Salvage Archeology of the Bear Creek Site (SJO-112), a Terminal Central California Early Horizon Site*. Sacramento Anthropological Society Papers 1.

Olson, R. L.
1930 Chumash Prehistory. *University of California Publications in American Archaeology and Ethnology* 28:1–21.

Oppenheimer, S.
2003 *Out of Eden: The Peopling of the World.* Robinson, London.

Origer, T. M.
1982 Temporal Control in the Southern North Coast Ranges of California: The Application of Obsidian Hydration Analysis. Master's thesis, Department of Anthropology, San Francisco State University, San Francisco.
1989 Hydration Analysis of Obsidian Flakes Produced by Ishi During the Historic Period. In *Current Directions in California Obsidian Studies,* edited by R. E. Hughes, pp. 69–77. Contributions of the University of California Archaeological Research Facility 48.

Origer, T. M., and D. A. Fredrickson
1980 *The Laguna Archaeological Research Project, Sonoma County, California.* Cultural Resources Facility, Anthropological Studies Center, Sonoma State University, Rohnert Park, California. Submitted to Public Works Department, City of Santa Rosa.

Origer, T. M., and B. P. Wickstrom
1982 The Use of Hydration Measurements to Date Obsidian Materials from Sonoma County, California. *Journal of California and Great Basin Anthropology* 4:123–131.

Orme, A. R.
1990 The Instability of Holocene Coastal Dunes: The Case of the Morro Dunes, California. In *Coastal Dunes: Form and Process,* edited by K. F. Nordstrom, N. P. Psuty, and R. W. G. Carter, pp. 315–336. Wiley, New York.
2004 *Lake Thompson, Mojave Desert, California: A Desiccating Late Quaternary Lake System.* Monograph TR-03, U.S. Army Corps of Engineers, Engineering Research and Development Center and Cold Regions Research and Engineering Laboratory.

O'Rourke, D. H., M. G. Hayes, and S. W. Carlyle
2000 Spatial and Temporal Stability of mtDNA Haplogroup Frequencies in Native North America. *Human Biology* 72:15–34.

Orr, P. C.
1943 *Archaeology of Mescalitan Island and Customs of the Canalino.* Occasional Papers no. 5. Santa Barbara Museum of Natural History, Santa Barbara.
1962 The Arlington Springs Site, Santa Rosa Island, California. *American Antiquity* 27:417–419.
1968 *Prehistory of Santa Rosa Island.* Santa Barbara Museum of Natural History, Santa Barbara.

Orr, P. C., and R. Berger
1966 The Fire Areas on Santa Rosa Island, California. *Proceedings of the National Academy of Sciences* 56:1409–1416.

Ortiz, A. (editor)
1979 *Southwest.* Handbook of North American Indians. Vol. 9. W. C. Sturtevant, general editor. Smithsonian Institution, Washington, D.C.
1983 *Southwest.* Handbook of North American Indians. Vol. 10. W. C. Sturtevant, general editor. Smithsonian Institution, Washington, D.C.

Ostenaa, D. A., D. R. Levish, and D. R. H. O'Connell
1996 *Paleoflood Study for Bradbury Dam, Cachuma Project, California.* Seismotectonic Report 96-6. Technical Services Center, Bureau of Reclamation, Denver.

Oswalt, R. L.
1964 The Internal Relationships of the Pomo Family of Languages. *Actas y Memorias* 2: 413–427. 35th Congreso Internacional de Americanistas, Mexico.

Otte, J. R., Jr.
2001 Mobility and Technology in the Santa Ynez Valley, Santa Barbara, California: An Example from CA-SBA-485. Senior honors thesis, Department of Anthropology, University of California, Santa Barbara.

Owen, R. C., F. Curtis, and D. S. Miller
1964 The Glen Annie Canyon Site, SBa-142: An Early Horizon Coastal Site of Santa Barbara County. In *UCLA Archaeological Survey Annual Report* 6:431–520. Department of Anthropology, University of California, Los Angeles.

Oxendine, J.
2000 *Integrated Cultural Resources Management Plan for U.S. Army Yuma Proving Ground, Yuma, Arizona 1999–2003.* Prepared by the U.S. Army Engineer District, Fort Worth, Texas, and Earthtech, Colton, California.
2002 *The Archaeology of Barrel Springs.* Edited by Joan S. Schneider. California Department of Parks and Recreation, Sacramento, California.

Pahl, G. (editor)
2003 *The Archaeology of De Silva Island: CA-MRN-17.* Treganza Museum Publication no. 17. Tiburon Archaeological Research Group, San Francisco State University, San Francisco.

Parker, J.
1993 Ethnographic and Prehistoric Settlement Systems in the Clear Lake Basin. In *There Grows a Green Tree: Papers in Honor of David A. Fredrickson,* edited by G. White, P. Mikkelsen, W. R. Hildebrandt, and M. E. Basgall, pp. 303–322. Center for Archaeological Research at Davis Publication no. 11. University of California, Davis.
1996 *Cultural Resource Investigation of the Proposed Expansion of the Morro Shores Mobile Home Park Ramona Ave., Los Osos.* Prepared by Parker and Associates, P.O. Box 462, Cayucos, California. Copies available from Parker and Associates.
2000 *Archaeological Mitigation Report for the Elfin Forest Board Walk Project Covering Prehistoric Site CA-SLO-1122/1395.* Prepared for San Luis Obispo County Department of General Services. Copies available from Parker and Associates.
2002 *A 9,000 Year Old House Floor at CA-SLO-369: Archaeological Mitigation and Monitoring Report for APN 023-023012, 611 Warren Road, Cambria.* Parker and Associates, P.O. Box 462, Cayucos, California. Prepared for O'Sullivan Construction, 2471 Banbury Road, Cambria. Copies available from Parker and Associates.
2004 9,000 Years of Prehistory in Cambria: Cultural Ecology at CA-SLO-369. In *Emerging from the Ice Age: Early Holocene Occupations on California's Central Coast,* edited by E. Bertrando and V. A. Levulett, pp. 27–44. San Luis Obispo County Archaeological Society Occasional Papers no. 17.

Parkman, E. B.
1981 An Incised Tablet from Northern California. *Journal of California and Great Basin Anthropology* 3:286–289.
1983 Soapstone for the Cosmos: Archaeological Discoveries in the Cuyamaca Mountains. *Journal of California and Great Basin Anthropology* 5:140–155.
1994 Bedrock Milling Stations. In *The Ohlone Past and Present: Native Americans of the San Francisco Bay Region,* edited by L. J. Bean, pp. 43–63. Ballena Press, Menlo Park, California.

Parr, R. L., S. W. Carlyle, and D. H. O'Rourke
1996 Ancient DNA Analysis of Fremont Amerindians of the Great Salt Lake Wetlands. *American Journal of Physical Anthropology* 99:507–518.

Pastron, A. G.
1973 Aboriginal Warfare in Northern California. *Masterkey* 47:136–172.

Pastron, A. G. (editor)
1999 *Archaeological Investigations at CA-SCL-674, the Rubino Site, City of San Jose, Santa Clara County, California.* Vol. 2. Archeo-Tec, Oakland. Submitted to Kaufman & Broad-South Bay, Fremont. Copies available from Northwest Information Center, Sonoma State University, Rohnert Park.

Pastron, A. G., and M. R. Walsh
1988a *Archaeological Excavations at CA-SFR-112, the Stevenson Street Shellmound, San Francisco, California.* Archives of California Prehistory 21. Coyote Press, Salinas.
1988b *Archaeological Excavations at CA-SFR-113, the Market Street Shell Midden, San Francisco, California.* Archives of California Prehistory 25. Coyote Press, Salinas.
1989 Two Biface Clusters and Their Relation to Mortuary Practices in the San Francisco Bay Area. *Journal for California and Great Basin Anthropology* 11:74–88.

Pastron, A. G., A. Gottsfield, and A. Vanderslice
2004 *Final Archeological Report for the Jessie Square Garage Project, San Francisco, California.* Archeo-Tec, Oakland. Submitted to Jessie Square Garage Partners, San Francisco. Copies available from Northwest Information Center, Sonoma State University, Rohnert Park.

Payen, L.
1966 Prehistoric Rock Art in the Northern Sierra Nevada, California. Master's thesis, Department of Anthropology, California State University, Sacramento.

Peak and Associates
1984 Report on the Salvage of CA-SAC-42, Pocket Road Area of Sacramento City, California. Peak and Associates, Sacramento. Copies available from Peak and Associates.

Peak, A. S., and H. L. Crew
1990 Parts I and II: An Archaeological Data Recovery Project at CA-CAL-S342, Clarks Flat, Calaveras County, California. In *Cultural Resource Studies, North Fork Stanislaus River, Hydroelectric Development Project.* Vol. 2. Peak and Associates, Sacramento. Report prepared for Northern California Power Agency, Roseville.

Peak, A. S., and N. J. Neuenschwander
1991 *Archeological Data Recovery of CA-Alp-109, CA-Alp-149, CA-Alp-152, CA-Alp-192, CA-Alp-252, CA-Tuo-675, CA-Tuo-1289, CA-Tuo-1607, Upper Mountain Locale, Alpine and Tuolumne Counties, California.* Cultural Resource Studies, North Fork Stanislaus River Hydroelectric Development Project. Vol. 5. Peak and Associates, Sacramento. Submitted to Northern California Power Agency, Roseville.

Peak, A. S., and T. F. Weber
1978 *Archaeological Investigations at the Wolfsen Mound, CA-MER-215, Merced County, California.* Ann S. Peak and Associates, Consulting Archeology. Submitted to the City of Newman, Stanislaus County.

Peak, A. S., H. L. Crew, and R. A. Gerry
1984 *The 1971 Archaeological Salvage of the Bennett Mound, CA-SAC-16, Sacramento County, California.* Peak and Associates, Sacramento. Copies available from Peak and Associates.

Pendleton, L. S., and D. H. Thomas
1983 The Fort Sage Drift Fence, Washoe County, Nevada. *Anthropological Papers of the American Museum of Natural History* 58(2). American Museum of Natural History, New York.

Pendleton, L. S., L. Capper, J. Clevenger, T. Cooley, D. Kupel, J. Schaefer, R. Thompson, J. Townsend, and M. R. Waters.
1986 *Archaeological Investigations in the Picacho Basin.* Report prepared by Wirth Environmental Services for San Diego Gas and Electric. Report on file, Southeast Information Center Imperial Valley College Desert Museum, Ocotillo, California.

Perry, J. E.
2003 Changes in Prehistoric Land and Resource Use Among Complex Hunter-Gatherer-Fishers on Eastern Santa Cruz Island, California. Ph.D. dissertation, Department of Anthropology, University of California, Santa Barbara.
2004 Quarries and Microblades: Trends in Prehistoric Land and Resource Use on Eastern Santa Cruz Island. In *Foundations of Chumash Complexity*, edited by J. E. Arnold, pp. 113–132. Cotsen Institute of Archaeology, University of California, Los Angeles.

Pesnichak, L. M., and S. R. Evans
2005 *Results of Archaeological Monitoring and Burial Recovery: Avignon Housing Development (CA-SCl-478), San Jose, Santa Clara County, California.* Archaeological Resource Service, Petaluma. Submitted to Bayrock Residential, LLC. Copies available from Northwest Archaeological Information Center, Department of Anthropology, Sonoma State University, Rohnert Park, California.

Peterson, R. R.
1994 Archaeological Settlement Dynamics on the South Side of Santa Cruz Island. In *The California Islands: Proceedings of a Multidisciplinary Symposium: Update on the Status of Resources*, edited by W. L. Halvorson and G. J. Maender, pp. 215–222. Santa Barbara Museum of Natural History, Santa Barbara, California.

Pierce, A. M.
1979 Archaeological Investigations at SLO-177 and Vicinity, Cambria California. Master's thesis, Department of Anthropology, Stanford University.

Pigniolo, A.
1994 The Distribution of Piedra de Lumbre "Chert" in the Archaeological Record of Southern California. *Proceedings of the Society for California Archaeology* 7:191–198.
1995 The Rainbow Rock Wonderstone Source and Its Place in Regional Material Distribution Studies. *Proceedings of the Society for California Archaeology* 8:123–131.
2005 A Different Context: San Dieguito in the Mountains of Southern California. *Proceedings of the Society for California Archaeology* 18:247–254.

Pigniolo, A. R., J. Underwood, and J. H. Cleland
1997 *Where Trails Cross: Cultural Resources Inventory and Evaluation for the Imperial Project, Imperial County, California.* Prepared by KEA Environmental, San Diego, for the USDI Bureau of Land Management, El Centro, California.

Pigniolo, A. R., J. Dietler, I. C. Zepeda, and S. Murray
2001 *A Look at Silver Strand Prehistory: Cultural Resources Testing and Evaluation Report for the Coronado Undergrounding Project, City of Coronado, California.* Tierra Environmental Services, San Diego. Report on file, South Coast Information Center, San Diego State University.

Pilling, A. R.
1950 The Archaeological Implications of an Annual Coastal Visit for Certain Yokuts Groups. *American Anthropologist* 52:438–440.
1952 The British Museum Collection from Near Avila, California. *American Antiquity* 1:169–172.
1957 An Incised Pebble from Lassen County, California. *University of California Archaeological Survey Reports* 38(6).

Pilloud, M.
2005 The Medieval Climatic Anomaly and Its Impact on Health in the Pacific Rim: A Case Study from Canyon Oaks, California. Master's thesis, Department of Anthropology, Ohio State University.

Pippin, L. C., J. O. Davis, E. Budy, and R. G. Elston
1979 *Archaeological Investigations at the Pike's Point Site (4-LAS-537) Eagle Lake, Lassen County, California.* Social Sciences Center, Desert Research Institute, University of Nevada. Submitted to the U.S. Department of Agriculture, Forest Service, Lassen National Forest, Susanville, California.

Pisias, N. G.
1978 Paleoceanography of the Santa Barbara Basin During the Last 8000 Years. *Quaternary Research* 10:366–384.

Pisias, N. G., A. C. Mix, and L. Heusser
2001 Millennial Scale Climate Variability of the Northeast Pacific Ocean and of the Northwest North America based on Radiolaria and Pollen. *Quaternary Science Review* 20:1561–1576.

Pletka, S.
2001 The Economics of Island Chumash Fishing Practices. In *The Origins of a Pacific Coast Chiefdom: The Chumash of the Channel Islands*, edited by J. E. Arnold, pp. 221–244. University of Utah Press, Salt Lake City.

Pohorecky, Z. S.
1976 *Archaeology of the South Coast Ranges of California*. Contributions of the University of California Archaeological Research Facility no. 34. University of California, Berkeley.

Polanich, J.
2005 Textiles and Cordage. In *Final Report: Archaeological Evaluation and Mitigative Data Recovery at CA-YOL-69, Madison Aggregate Plant, Yolo County, California*, edited by R. S. Wiberg, pp. 12–22. Holman and Associates Archaeological Consultants, San Francisco. Submitted to Solano Concrete Company, Fairfield. Copies available from Northwest Information Center, Department of Anthropology, Sonoma State University, Rohnert Park, California.

Polansky, B.
1998 A Prehistoric Archaeological Settlement Pattern Model for the Point Reyes Peninsula. Master's thesis, Department of Anthropology, Sonoma State University, Rohnert Park, California.

Polk, M. R.
1972 Manufacture and Uses of Steatite Objects by the Diegueno. *Pacific Coast Archaeological Society Quarterly* 8(30):1–26.

Pope, K. O.
1997 Prehistoric Depostional Environment: Geology and Stratigraphy. In *Reconstructing 2000 Years of Environmental and Cultural Change on the CSULB Campus: Contributions from Midden Trace D, the Parking Structure Site,* edited by M. A. Boxt, pp. 88–116. Submitted to California State University Long Beach, Department of Physical Planning and Facilities Management.

Pope, K. O., O. K. Davis, M. R. Palacios-Fest, B. F. Byrd, and M. Trout
2004 Paleoenvironmental History of the Northern San Diego County Coast. In *Results of NSF-Funded Archaeological and Paleoenvironmental Investiagations at San Elijo Lagoon, San Diego County, California,* edited by B. F. Byrd, K. O. Pope, and S. N. Reddy, pp. 15–71. ASM Affiliates, Carlsbad, California. Report prepared for National Science Foundation Archaeology Program Grant BCS-00043902.

Porcasi, J. F.
2007 Subsistence Patterns of Prehistoric Coastal California: Investigating Variations of Early Maritime Adaptation. Ph.D. dissertation, School of Archaeology and Ancient History, Leicester University, Leicester.

Porcasi, J. F., and H. Fujita
2000 The Dolphin Hunters: A Specialized Prehistoric Maritime Adaptation in the Southern California Channel Islands and Baja California. *American Antiquity* 65:543–566.

Porcasi, J. F., T. L. Jones, and L. M. Raab
2000 Trans-Holocene Marine Mammal Exploitation on San Clemente Island: A Tragedy of the Commons Revisited. *Journal of Anthropological Archaeology* 19:200–220.

Potter, A.
2004 The Genetic Affinities of the Prehistoric People of San Clemente Island, California: An Analysis of Ancient DNA. Ph.D. dissertation, Department of Anthropology, University of Oregon.

Powell, J. W.
1891 Indian Linguistic Families of America North of Mexico. *Bureau of American Ethnology Annual Reports* 7:7–142.

Power, M. J.
1998 Paleoclimatic Interpretation of an Alpine Lake in South Central Sierra Nevada, California: Multiple Proxy Evidence. Master's thesis, Quaternary Studies Program, Northern Arizona University.

Powers, W. R., and J. Hoffecker
1989 Late Pleistocene Settlement in the Nenana Valley, Central Alaska. *American Antiquity* 54:263–287.

Preston, W.
1996 Serpent in Eden: Dispersal of Foreign Diseases into Pre-Mission California. *Journal of California and Great Basin Anthropology* 18:3–37.

Preziosi, A. M.
2001 Standardization and Specialization: The Island Chumash Microdrill Industry. In *The Origins of a Pacific Coast Chiefdom: The Chumash of the Channel Islands*, edited by J. E. Arnold, pp. 151–164. University of Utah Press, Salt Lake City.

Price, H., A. Arrigoni, J. Price, E. Strother, and J. Allan
2006 *Archaeological Investigations at CA-CCO-309, Rossmoor Basin, Contra Costa County, California*. Prepared for County of Contra Costa Department of Public Works, Martinez, California, by William Self Associates, Orinda, California.

Prior, C., D. W. Gray, and J. Sanders
1999 *Radiocarbon Analysis of the Upwelling Effect on Marine Shell from San Nicolas Island, Ventura County, California.* Statistical Research Technical Report 97–20. Redlands, California.

Pritchard, W. E.
1968 *Preliminary Archaeological Investigations at El Castillo, Presidio of Monterey, Monterey, California*. National Park Service, San Francisco. Copies available from Coyote Press, Salinas.
1970 *Archaeology of the Mejoulet Site, Merced County, California.* Archaeological Resources Section Report 13. California Department of Parks and Recreation, Sacramento.
1983 Archaeological Testing of Three Kahwatchwah Yokuts Dwelling Structures at the San Luis Forebay Site (CA-MER-119), Merced County, California. In *Papers in Merced County Prehistory*, pp. 86–103. *University of California Archaeological Survey Reports* no. 21.

Proulx, P.
1981 The Linguistic Evidence on Algonquian Prehistory. *Anthropological Linguistics* 22:1–21.
1994 Proto-Algic V: Doublets and Their Implications. *Kansas Working Papers in Linguistics* 19:115–182.

Quinlan, A. R.
2000a The Ventriloquist's Dummy: A Critical Review of Shamanism and Rock Art in Far Western North America. *Journal of California and Great Basin Anthropology* 22:92–108.
2000b Reply to Whitley. *Journal of California and Great Basin Anthropology* 22:129–132.

Quinn, W. H.
1999 Climate Variation in Southern California over the Past 2,000 Years based on the El Niño/Southern Oscillation. In *Trends and Extremes of the Past 2000 Years*, edited by M. R. Rose and P. E. Wigand, pp. 213–238. Proceedings of the Southern California Climate Symposium, October 25, 1991, Natural History Museum of Los Angeles County, Technical Report no. 11.

Quintero, L.
1987 Room and Board at Deer Springs: Faunal Analysis as an Aid to Settlement Studies. Master's thesis, Department of Anthropology, San Diego State University.

Raab, L. M.
1992 An Optimal Foraging Analysis of Prehistoric Shellfish Collecting on San Clemente Island, California. *Journal of Ethnobiology* 12:63–80.
1994 *The Dead at Calleguas Creek: A Study of Punctuated Cultural Evolution During the Middle-Late Period Transition in Southern California.* Center for Public Archaeology, California State University, Northridge. Copies available from South Central Coastal Information Center, Department of Anthropology, California State University, Fullerton.
1997 The Southern Channel Islands During the Middle Holocene: Trends in Maritime Cultural Evolution. In *Archaeology of*

California Coast During the Middle Holocene, edited by J. M. Erlandson and M. A. Glassow, pp. 23–34. Cotsen Institute of Archaeology, University of California, Los Angeles.

Raab, L. M., and W. J. Howard
2002 Modeling Cultural Connections Between the Southern Channel Islands and Western United States: The Middle Holocene Distribution of *Olivella* Grooved Rectangle Beads. In *Proceedings of the Fifth California Islands Symposium*, edited by D. R. Browne, K. L. Mitchell, and H. W. Chaney, pp. 590–597. Santa Barbara Museum of Natural History, Santa Barbara.

Raab, L. M., and T. L. Jones
2004 The Future of California Prehistory. In *Prehistoric California: Archaeology and the Myth of Paradise*, edited by L. M. Raab and T. L. Jones, pp. 204–211. University of Utah Press, Salt Lake City.

Raab, L. M., and D. O. Larson
1997 Medieval Climatic Anomaly and Punctuated Cultural Evolution in Coastal Southern California. *American Antiquity* 62:319–336.

Raab, L. M., and A. Yatsko
1992 Ancient Maritime Adaptations of the California Bight: A Perspective from San Clemente Island. In *Essays on the Maritime Prehistory of California*, edited by T. L. Jones, pp. 173–194. University of California, Davis, Publication 10. Center for Archaeological Research, Davis.

Raab, L. M., K. Bradford, and A. Yatsko
1994 Advances in Southern Channel Islands Archaeology: 1983–1993. *Journal of California and Great Basin Anthropology* 16:243–270.

Raab, L. M., K. Bradford, J. F. Porcasi, and J. Howard
1995 Return to Little Harbor, Santa Catalina Island, California: A Critique of the Marine Paleotemperature Model. *American Antiquity* 60:287–308.

Raab, L. M., A. Yatsko, T. S. Garlinghouse, J. F. Porcasi, and K. Bradford
2002 Late Holocene San Clemente Island: Notes on Comparative Social Complexity in Coastal Southern California. In *Catalysts to Complexity: Late Holocene of the California Coast*, edited by J. Erlandson and T. L. Jones, pp. 13–26. Cotsen Institute of Archaeology, University of California, Los Angeles.

Raab, L. M., and T. L. Jones (editors)
2004 *Prehistoric California: Archaeology and the Myth of Paradise.* University of Utah Press, Salt Lake City.

Rafferty, K.
1994 Archaeological Research in the Clark Mountains, San Bernardino County, California. In *Kelso Conference Papers 1987–1992, A Collection of Papers and Abstracts from the First Five Kelso Conferences on the Prehistory of the Mojave Desert*, edited by G. D. Everson and J. S. Schneider, pp. 1–14. California State University, Bakersfield, Museum of Anthropology Occasional Papers in Anthropology no. 4.

Ragir, S.
1972 The Early Horizon in Central California Prehistory. *Contributions of the University of California Archaeological Research Facility* 15.

Ramos, B. A.
2000 Prehistoric Obsidian Quarry Use and Technological Change in the Western Great Basin: Examining Lithic Procurement at the Truman/Queen Obsidian Source, California and Nevada. Ph.D. dissertation, Department of Anthropology, University of California, Davis.

Raven, C.
1984 Northeastern California. In *California Archaeology*, edited by M. J. Moratto, pp. 431–470. Academic Press, New York.
1986 *Rock Art North of Bishop.* Great Basin Foundation Occasional Papers no. 1.

Raven, P. H.
1988 The California Flora. In *Terrestrial Vegetation of California*, edited by M. G. Barbour and J. Major. Wiley, New York.

Ray, V. F.
1963 *Primitive Pragmatists: The Modoc Indians of Northern California.* University of Washington Press, Seattle.

Reddy, S. N.
1996a Experimental Ethnoarchaeological Study of *Donax gouldii* Exploitation. In *Coastal Archaeology of Las Flores Creek and Horno Canyon, Camp Pendleton, California*, edited by B. F. Byrd, pp. 231–240. ASM Affiliates, Carlsbad, California. Report on file, South Coast Information Center, San Diego State University.
1996b Paleoethnobotanical Investigations. In *Coastal Archaeology of Las Flores Creek and Horno Canyon, Camp Pendleton, California*, edited by B. F. Byrd, pp. 275–304. ASM Affiliates, Carlsbad, California. Prepared for U.S. Army Corps of Engineers, Los Angeles District, California. Report on file, South Coast Information Center, San Diego State University.
1997a Macrobotanical Remains and Shellmidden Paleoethnobotany. In *Coastal Archaeology at CA-SDI-10,728, Las Flores Creek, Camp Pendleton, California*, edited by B. F. Byrd, pp. 117–136. ASM Affiliates, Carlsbad, California. Report on file, South Coast Information Center, San Diego State University.
1997b Macrobotanical Remains and Paleoeconomy at Case Spring. In *Camping and Milling in the Highlands: Archaeological Investigation of Case Spring and Firebreak Sites on Camp Pendleton, San Diego County, California*, edited by S. N. Reddy. ASM Affiliates, Carlsbad, California. Report on file, South Coast Information Center, San Diego State University.
1999a *Shellfish on the Menu: Archaeology of Dinner Camps and Limited Activity Sparse Shell Scatters Along Coastal Camp Pendleton, San Diego County, California.* ASM Affiliates, Carlsbad, California. Report on file, South Coast Information Center, San Diego State University.
1999b Plant Usage and Prehistoric Diet: Paleoethnobotanical Investigations on Camp Pendleton, Southern California. *Pacific Coast Archaeological Society Quarterly* 35(4):25–44.
2001 Reconstructing Plant Usage at SDI-12,572. In *Evaluation of a Repeatedly Occupied Site (SDI-12,572) Along Santa Margarita River, Camp Pendleton, California*, edited by Seetha N. Reddy and Collin O'Neill. ASM Affiliates, Carlsbad, California. Report on file, South Coast Information Center, San Diego State University.
2003 Plants, Shell Middens, and Paleoethnobotany: A Study of Macrobotanical Remains from SDI-10,726 and SDI-15,254. In *Coastal Views of Prehistoric Middens: Archaeological Investigations and Paleoecological Reconstructions Along Las Flores Creek, Camp Pendleton, California*, edited by B. F. Byrd, pp. 171–192. ASM Affiliates, Carlsbad, California. Report on file, South Coast Information Center.
2004 *Opportunistic Gathering to Logistically Planned: Changes in Prehistoric Plant Use in Prehistoric California; Results of NSF-Funded Archaeological and Paleoenvironmental Investigation at San Elijo Lagoon, San Diego County, California*, edited by B. F. Byrd, K. O. Pope, and S. N. Reddy, pp. 228–262. Report on file, South Coastal Information Center, San Diego State University.

Reddy, S. N., and S. Berryman (editors)
1999a Cultural Dimensions of Time: New Perspectives on the Archaeology of Camp Pendleton, Southern California. *Pacific Coast Archaeological Society Quarterly* 35:1.
1999b Cultural Dimensions of Time: New Perspectives on the Archaeology of Camp Pendleton, Southern California, Part II. *Pacific Coast Archaeological Society Quarterly* 35:4.

Reitz, E. J., and E. S. Wing
1999 *Zooarchaeology*. Cambridge University Press, New York.
Reynolds, L. A.
1996 In the Dwelling Place of the Great Spirit: The Prehistory of the Pinyon-Juniper Woodland of the Inyo-White Mountain Range, Eastern California. Ph.D. dissertation, Department of Anthropology, University of Nevada, Reno.
Reynolds, R. D.
1959 Effect of Natural Fires and Aboriginal Burning upon the Forests of the Central Sierra Nevada. Master's thesis, Department of Geography, University of California, Berkeley.
Rhode, D.
2001 *Woodrat Midden Evidence of Holocene Paleoenvironment Change at Marine Corps Air Ground Combat Center, Twentynine Palms, California.* Report submitted to the Marine Corps Air Ground Combat Center, Twentynine Palms.
Ribeiro-Dos-Santos, A. K. C., S. E. B. Santos, A. L. Machado, V. Guapindaia, and M. A. Zago
1996 Heterogeneity of Mitochondrial DNA Haplotypes in Pre-Columbian Natives of the Amazon Region. *American Journal of Physical Anthropology* 101:29–37.
Richards, G. D.
1988 Human Osteological Remains from CA-SCl-294, a Late Period and Protohistoric Site, San Jose, California. In *Human Skeletal Biology: Contributions to the Understanding of California's Prehistoric Populations,* edited by G. D. Richards, pp. 97–178. Archives of California Prehistory 24. Coyote Press, Salinas.
Richardson, J. B., III
1998 Looking in the Right Places: Pre-5000 B.P. Maritime Adaptations in Peru and the Changing Environment. *Revista de Arquelogia Americana* 15:33–56.
Richardson, P. J., R. Boyd, and R. L. Bettinger
2001 Was Agriculture Impossible During the Pleistocene but Mandatory During the Holocene? A Climate Change Hypothesis. *American Antiquity* 66:387–411.
Rick, J. W., and T. L. Jackson
1992 A Funny Thing Happened on the Way from the Quarry . . . Analysis of the Great Blades Cache of Northern California. In *Stone Tool Procurement, Production, and Distribution in California Prehistory*, edited by J. E. Arnold, pp. 5–65. Cotsen Institute of Archaeology, University of California, Los Angeles.
Rick, T. C.
2004a Social and Economic Dynamics on Late Holocene San Miguel Island, California. In *Foundations of Chumash Complexity*, edited by J. E. Arnold, pp. 97–112. Cotsen Institute of Archaeology, University of California, Los Angeles.
2004b Daily Activities, Community Dynamics, and Historical Ecology on California's Northern Channel Islands. Ph.D. dissertation, Department of Anthropology, University of Oregon, Eugene.
2004c Red Abalone Bead Production and Exchange on California's Northern Channel Islands. *North American Archaeologist* 25:215–237.
Rick, T. C., and Jon M. Erlandson
2000 Early Holocene Fishing Strategies on the California Coast: Evidence from CA-SBA-2057. *Journal of Archaeological Science* 27:621–633.
Rick, T. C., J. M. Erlandson, and R. L. Vellanoweth
2001 Paleocoastal Fishing Along the Pacific Coast of the Americas: Evidence from Daisy Cave, San Miguel Island, California. *American Antiquity* 66:595–614.
2003 Early Cave Occupations of San Miguel Island, California. *Current Research in the Pleistocene* 20:70–72.
Rick, T. C., D. J. Kennett, and J. M. Erlandson
2005a Preliminary Report on the Archaeology and Paleoecology of the Abalone Rocks Estuary, Santa Rosa Island, California. *Proceedings of the Sixth California Islands Symposium,* edited by D. Garcelon and C. Schwemm. Santa Barbara Museum of Natural History. In press.
2005b Early Holocene Land Use and Subsistence on Eastern Santa Rosa Island, California. *Current Research in the Pleistocene.* In press.
Rickards, O., C. Martínez-Labarga, J. K. Lum, G. F. De Stefano, and R. L. Cann
1999 MtDNA History of the Cayapa Amerinds of Ecuador: Detection of Additional Founding Lineages for the Native American Populations. *American Journal of Human Genetics* 65:519–530.
Riddell, F. A.
1950 *An Archaeological Survey in Lassen County, California.* Report on file, North Central Information Center, California State University, Sacramento.
1951 The Archaeology of Site KER-74. *University of California Archeological Survey Reports* 10:1–28.
1956 Archaeological Research in Lassen County, California. *University of California Archaeological Survey Reports* 33:44–49.
1960a *Honey Lake Paiute Ethnography.* Nevada State Museum Anthropological Papers no. 4. Nevada State Museum, Carson City, Nevada.
1960b The Archaeology of the Karlo Site (LAS-7), California. *University of California Archaeological Survey Reports* 53.
1968 *The Archaeology of 4-MER-14 at San Luis Dam, Western Merced County, California.* Report on file, California Department of Parks and Recreation, Sacramento.
1978 Maidu and Konkow. In *Handbook of North American Indians.* Vol. 8. Edited by R. F. Heizer, pp. 370–386. W. C. Sturtevant, general editor. Smithsonian Institution, Washington, D.C.
Riddell, F. A., and W. H. Olsen
1969 An Early Site in the San Joaquin Valley, California. *American Antiquity* 34:121–130.
Rigby, J.
1985 A *Preliminary Report on the Excavations at the Nursery Site (4-SCLI-1215).* Report on file, Natural Resources Office, Naval Air Station North Island, San Diego.
Ritter, E. W.
1980 A Historic Aboriginal Structure and Its Associations, Panamint Mountains, California. *Journal of California and Great Basin Anthropology* 2:97–113.
Ritter, E. W., and E. B. Parkman
1992 Rock Art of the Foothills of the Northern Sierra Nevada–Southern Cascade Range Interface. *American Indian Rock Art* 18:81–104.
Ritter, E. W., B. W. Hatoff, and L. A. Payen
1976 Chronology of the Farmington Complex. *American Antiquity* 41:334–341.
Robbins-Wade, M.
1992 Prehistoric Settlement Pattern of Otay Mesa, San Diego County, California. *Proceedings of the Society for California Archaeology* 5:229–246.
Rodeffer, M. J., and J. R. Galm (editors)
1985 A Cultural Resources Survey and Site Testing of the Bonneville Power Administration's Malin-Warner 230kv Transmission Line, Klamath County, Oregon, and Modoc County, California. *Eastern Washington University Reports in Archaeology and History* 100–136.
Rogers, D. B.
1929 *Prehistoric Man of the Santa Barbara Coast.* Museum of Natural History, Santa Barbara.
Rogers, M. J.
1929 The Stone Art of the San Dieguito Plateau. *American Anthropologist* 31:454–467.
1945 An Outline of Yuman Prehistory. *Southwestern Journal of Anthropology* 1(2):167–198.

1966 *Ancient Hunters of the Far West.* Union-Tribune Publishing, San Diego.

Rogers, R. A.
1985 Wisconsin Glaciation and the Dispersal of Native Ethnic Groups in North America. In *Woman, Poet, Scientist: Essays in New World Anthropology Honoring Dr. Emma Lou Davis,* pp. 105–113. Ballena Press, Los Altos.

Romani, J., G. Romani, and D. Larson
1985 Archaeoastronomical Investigations at Burro Flats: Aspects of Ceremonialism at a Chumash Rock Art and Habitation Site. In *Earth and Sky: Papers from the Northridge Conference on Archaeoastronomy,* edited by A. Benson and T. Hoskinson, pp. 93–108. Slo'w Press, Thousand Oaks, California.

Rondeau, M. F.
1985 Lithic Techniques of the Tulare Lake Locality, California. *Current Research in the Pleistocene* 2:55–56.

Roop, W.
1976 Adaptation on Ben Lomond Mountain: Excavation at CA-SCR-20. Master's thesis, Department of Anthropology, San Francisco State University.

Roop, W., C. Gerike, and M. Duddy
1982 *Prehistoric Archaeological Survey Report.* Guadalupe Transportation Corridor, Santa Clara County, California. Archaeological Resource Service. Submitted to Santa Clara County Transportation Authority. Copies available from Northwest Information Center, Department of Anthropology, Sonoma State University, Rohnert Park, California.

Roosevelt, A. C., J. Douglas, and L. Brown
2002 The Migrations and Adaptations of the First Americans: Clovis and Pre-Clovis Viewed from South America, In *The First Americans: The Pleistocene Colonization of the New World,* edited by N. G. Jablonski, pp. 159–235. Memoirs of the California Academy of Sciences no. 27.

Roosevelt, A. C., M. Lima Da Costa, C. Lopes Machado, M. Michab, N. Mercier, H. Vallada, J. Feathers, W. Barnet, M. Imazio da Silveira, A. Henderson, J. Sliva, B. Chernoff, D. S. Reese, J. A. Holman, N. Toth, and K. Schick
1996 Paleoindian Cave Dwellers in the Amazon: The Peopling of the Americas. *Science* 272:373–384.

Roper-Wickstrom, C. K.
1992 A Study of High Altitude Obsidian Distribution in the Southern Sierra Nevada California. Master's thesis, Department of Anthropology, Sonoma State University.
1993 Spatial and Temporal Characteristics of High Altitude Site Patterning in the Southern Sierra Nevada. In *There Grows a Green Tree: Papers in Honor of David A. Fredrickson,* edited by G. White, P. Mikkelsen, W. R. Hildebrandt, and M. E. Basgall, pp. 285–301. Center for Archaeological Research at Davis no. 11. University of California, Davis.

Rosen, M. D.
1995 IMP-6427, A Lake Cahuilla Shell Bead Manufacturing Site. *Proceedings of the Society for California Archaeology* 8:87–104.

Rosenthal, J. S.
1996 A Cultural Chronology for Solano County, California. Master's thesis, Department of Anthropology, California State University, Sonoma, Rohnert Park.
2000 Madeline Plains. In *Archaeological Investigations Along the California–Great Basin Interface: The Alturas Transmission Line Project.* Vol. 1, *Prehistoric Archaeological Studies: The Pit River Uplands, Madeline Plains, Honey Lake and Secret Valley, and Sierran Front Project Segments,* edited by K. R. McGuire. Report submitted to Sierra Pacific Power Company, Reno, Nevada.
2001 *Archaeological Survey and Extended Phase I/Phase II Excavations at CA-ALA-485 and -486 in the Baumberg Ecological Mitigation Tract, Alameda County, California.* Far Western Anthropological Research Group, Davis. Copies available from Northwest Archaeological Information Center, Department of Anthropology, Sonoma State University, Rohnert Park, California.
2002 Projectile Point Typology and Chronology in the North Central Sierra Nevada. *North American Archaeologist* 23:157–183.

Rosenthal, J. S., and K. R. McGuire
2004 *Middle Holocene Adaptations in the Central Sierra Foothills: Data Recovery Excavations at the Black Creek Site, CA-CAL-789.* Far Western Anthropological Research Group, Davis. Copies available from Central California Information Center, Department of Anthropology, California State University, Stanislaus, Turlock.

Rosenthal, J. S., and J. Meyer
2000 A Middle Holocene *Olivella* Wall-Bead Assemblage from Central California. *Society for California Archaeology Newsletter* 34(4):27–28.
2004a *Landscape Evolution and the Archaeological Record: A Geoarchaeological Study of the Southern Santa Clara Valley and Surrounding Region.* Center for Archaeological Research at Davis Publication no.14. University of California, Davis.
2004b Cultural Resources Inventory of Caltrans District 10, Rural Conventional Highways. In *Geoarchaeological Study.* Vol. 3, *Landscape Evolution and the Archaeological Record of Central California.* Far Western Anthropological Research Group, Davis, California.

Rosenthal, J. S., and S. A. Waechter
2002 *Results of Phase-II Test Excavations at CA-ELD-616/H Near Cool, Western El Dorado County.* Far Western Anthropological Research Group, Submitted to California Department of Transportation, District 3, Marysville.

Rosenthal, J. S., and G. White
1994 *Archaeological Investigations at the Pheasant Run Site, CA-SOL-363.* Anthropological Studies Center, Sonoma State University, Rohnert Park. Submitted to Kaufman and Broad of Northern California, Roseville. Copies available from Northwest Information Center, Department of Anthropology, Sonoma State University, Rohnert Park, California.

Rosenthal, J. S., K. L. Carpenter, and D. C. Young
2001 *Archaeological Survey of Target Area Buffer Zones in the Airport Lake, Baker and George Ranges, Naval Air Weapons Station, China Lake, Inyo and Kern Counties, California.* Report submitted to the Southwest Division, Naval Facilities Engineering Command, San Diego.

Rosenthal, J. S., W. R. Hildebrandt, and J. H. King
2001 *Donax* Don't Tell: Reassessing Late Holocene Land Use in Northern San Diego County. *Journal of California and Great Basin Anthropology* 23:179–214.

Rosenthal, J. S., J. Meyer, and G. White
1995 *Archaeological Investigations at the Crazy Creek Site, CA-LAK-1682, and CA-LAK-1683, Lake County, California.* Report on file, Northwest Information Center, Sonoma State University, Rohnert Park, California.

Rosenthal, Y., and A. J. Broccoli
2004 In Search of Paleo-ENSO. *Science* 304:219–221.

Ross, B. E.
1977 The Pleistocene History of the San Francisco Bay Along the Southern Crossing. Master's thesis, Department of Geology, San Jose State University, San Jose, California.

Rowlands, P., H. Johnson, E. Ritter, and A. Endo
1982 The Mojave Desert. In *Reference Handbook on the Deserts of North America,* edited by G. L. Bender, pp. 103–162. Greenwood Press, Westport, Connecticut.

Rubicz, R., T. G. Schurr, P. L. Babb, and M. H. Crawford
2003 Mitochondrial DNA Variation and the Origins of the Aleuts. *Human Biology* 75:809–835.

Rucks, M. M.
1995 The Social Context and Cultural Meaning of Ground Stone Milling Among Washoe Women. Master's thesis, Department of Anthropology, University of Nevada, Reno.

Rudolph, J.
1985 Changing Shellfish Exploitation in San Luis Obispo County. *Journal of California and Great Basin Anthropology* 7:126–132.

Rypins, S., S. L. Reneau, R. Byrne, and D. Montgomery
1989 Palynological and Geomorphic Evidence for Environmental Change During the Pleistocene-Holocene Transition at Point Reyes Peninsula, Central Coastal California. *Quaternary Research* 32:72–87.

Sabin, A. L., and N. G. Pisias
1996 Sea Surface Temperature Changes in the Northeastern Pacific Ocean During the Past 20,000 Years and Their Relationship to Climate in Northwestern North America. *Quaternary Research* 46:48–61.

Salls, R. A.
1985a Fish Remains from the Marymount Site (LAn-61). In *The Loyola-Marymount Archaeological Project: Salvage Excavations at LAn-61A-C*, edited by D. Van Horn. Report on file, South Central Coastal Information Center, Department of Anthropology, California State University, Fullerton.
1985b The Scraper Plane: A Functional Interpretation. *Journal of Field Archaeology* 12:99–106.
1987 The Fish Fauna from the Del Rey Site, Appendix C. In *Excavations at the Del Rey Site (LAn-63) and the Bluff Site (LAn-64) in the City of Los Angeles*, edited by D. M. Van Horn, Archaeological Associates, Sun City.
1988 Prehistoric Fisheries of the California Bight. Ph.D. dissertation, Archaeology Program, University of California, Los Angeles.
1992 Prehistoric Subsistence Change on California's Channel Islands: Environmental or Cultural. In *Essays on the Prehistory of Maritime California*, edited by T. L. Jones, pp. 157–172. Center for Archaeological Research at Davis Publication no. 10. University of California, Davis.

Salls, R. A., and K. M. Cairns
1994 Piscine Faunal Remains. In *The Centinela Site (CA-LAN-60): Data Recovery at a Middle Period, Creek-Edge Site in the Ballona Wetlands, Los Angeles County, California*, edited by D. R. Grenda, J. A. Homburg, and J. H. Altschul, pp. 111–131. Statistical Research Technical Series no. 45.

Salls, R. A., L. M. Raab, and K. Bradford
1993 A San Clemente Island Perspective on Coastal Residential Structures and the Emergence of Sedentism. *Journal of California and Great Basin Anthropology* 15:176–194.

Sampson, C. G.
1985 *Nightfire Island: Later Holocene Lakemarsh Adaptation on the Western Edge of the Great Basin*. University of Oregon Anthropological Papers 33. Department of Anthropology, University of Oregon, Eugene.

Sampson, M.
1991 A Distinctive Flaked-Stone Tool Type from Tulare Lake Basin. In *Contributions to Tulare Lake Archaeology I: Background to a Study of Tulare Lake's Archaeological Past*, edited by W. J. Wallace and F. A. Riddell, pp. 53–60. Tulare Lake Archaeological Research Group, Redondo Beach.

Sandweiss, D. H.
2003 Terminal Pleistocene Through Mid-Holocene Archaeological Sites as Paleoclimatic Archives for the Peruvian Coast. *Palaeogeography, Palaeoclimatology, Palaeoecology* 194:23–40.

Sandweiss, D. H., K. A. Maasch, R. L. Burger, J. B. Richardson III, H. B. Rollins, and A. Clement
2001 Variation in Holocene El Niño Frequencies, Climate Records, and Cultural Consequences in Ancient Peru. *Geology* 29:603–606.

Sandweiss, D. H., H. McInnis, R. L. Burger, A. Cano, B. Ojeda, R. Paredes, M. D. C. Sandweiss, and M. Glascock
1998 Quebrada Jaguay: Early South American Maritime Adaptation. *Science* 281:1830–1833.

Sapir, E.
1913 Wiyot and Yurok: Algonkin Languages of California. *American Anthropologist* 15:617–646.
1925 The Hokan Affinity of Subtiaba in Nicaragua. *American Anthropologist* 27:402–435, 491–527.
1929 Central and North American Indian Languages. In *Encyclopedia Britannica*, 14th ed., 5:138–141.

Sawyer, J. O., and T. Keeler-Wolf
1995 *A Manual of California Vegetation*. California Native Plant Society, Sacramento.

Sawyer, J. O., and D. A. Thornburgh
1970 Extension of the Range of *Abies lasiocarpa* into California. *Madroño* 20:413–415.

Schaefer, J.
1986 *Late Prehistoric Adaptations During the Final Recessions of Lake Cahuilla: Fish Camps and Quarries on West Mesa, Imperial County, California*. Prepared by Mooney-Levine and Associates, San Diego, for the USDI Bureau of Land Management, El Centro, California.
1988 *Lowland Patayan Adaptations to Ephemeral Alkali Pans at Supersitition Mountain, West Mesa, Imperial County, California*. Prepared by Brian F. Mooney Associates for the Bureau of Land Management, El Centro Resource Area.
1992 *Hunter-Gatherer Settlement, Subsistence, and Symbolism at White Tanks, Yuma Proving Ground, Arizona*. Prepared by Brian F. Mooney Associates for U.S. Army Corps of Engineers, Los Angeles District.
1994a The Colorado Desert. In *Research Design for the Lower Colorado Region*, compiled by J. H. Altschul, pp. 21–38. Statistical Research Technical Report no. 93–19. Prepared for the U.S. Bureau of Reclamation, Lower Colorado Regional Office, Boulder City, Nevada.
1994b The Challenge of Archaeological Research in the Colorado Desert: Recent Approaches and Discoveries. *Journal of California and Great Basin Anthropology* 16:60–80.
1994c The Stuff of Creation: Recent Approaches to Ceramic Analysis in the Colorado Desert. In *Recent Research Along the Colorado River*, edited by J. A. Ezzo, pp. 81–100. Statistical Research Technical Series no. 51.
1995 Ceramics. In *Archaeological, Ethnographic, and Ethnohistoric Investigations at Tahquitz Canyon, Palm Springs, California*, by L. J. Bean, J. Schaefer, and S. B. Vane, pp IX.1–IX.73. Prepared by Cultural Systems Research, Menlo Park, California, for Riverside County Flood Control and Water Conservation District, Riverside, California.
2000a "Now Dead I Begin to Sing": A Protohistoric Clothes-burning Ceremonial Feature in the Colorado Desert. *Journal of California and Great Basin Anthropology* 22:186–211.
2000b *Archaeological Investigations at a Protohistoric Fish Camp on the Receding Shoreline of Ancient Lake Cahuilla, Imperial County, California*. Prepared for Imperial Irrigation District, Imperial, California.
2002 A Supplemental Bibliography for the Western Colorado Desert. In *The Archaeology of Barrel Springs*, by J. Oxendine, pp. C1–10. California Department of Parks and Recreation, Sacramento.

Schaefer, J., and G. Huckleberry
1995 Evidence of Agriculture and Irrigation at Tahquitz Canyon. In *Archaeological, Ethnographic, and Ethnohistoric Investigations at Tahquitz Canyon, Palm Springs, California*, by L. J. Bean, J. Schaefer, and S. B. Vane, pp. XX.1–53. Prepared by Cultural Systems Research, Menlo Park, California, for Riverside County Flood Control and Water Conservation District.

Schaefer, J., and K. Moslak
2001 *Archaeological Survey Report of Sections 31 and 33 at San Sebastian Marsh, Imperial County, California.* Prepared by ASM Affiliates for Caltrans, District 11, San Diego, California.

Schaefer, J. D., and D. Pallette
2003 *Results and Recommendations of a Class III Cultural Resource Inventory of the Proposed Mesquite Regional Landfill Project Area, Imperial County, California.* Prepared by Brian F. Mooney Associated for Environmental Solutions, Irvine, California.

Schaefer, J., S. N. Ghabhláin, and M. Becker
2003 *A Class III Cultural Resource Inventory and Evaluation for the Coachella Canal Lining Project: Prehistoric and Historic Sites Along the Northeastern Shore of Ancient Lake Cahuilla, Imperial and Riverside Counties, California.* Prepared by ASM Affiliates for Coachella Valley Water Authority, Coachella, California, and USDI, Bureau of Land Management, Boulder City, Nevada.

Schaefer, J., D. Huntley, and D. Pallette
2002 *Archaeological Investigations at the Cahuilla Village of Rincon, Agua Caliente Indian Reservation, Palm Springs, California.* Prepared by ASM Affiliates for the Agua Caliente Band of Cahuilla Indians, Palm Springs.

Schenck, W. E., and E. J. Dawson
1929 Archaeology of the Northern San Joaquin Valley. *University of California Publications in Archaeology and Ethnology* 25:289–413. University of California Press, Berkeley.

Schimmelmann, A., C. B. Lange, and B. J. Meggers
2003 Palaeoclimatic and Archaeological Evidence for a ~200-Yr Recurrence of Floods and Droughts Linking California, Mesoamerica, and South America over the Past 2000 Years. *Holocene* 13:763–778.

Schneider, J. S.
1989 The Archaeology of the Afton Canyon Site. *San Bernardino County Museum Association Quarterly* 36(1).
1993 Aboriginal Milling-Implement Quarries in Eastern California and Western Arizona: A Behavioral Perspective. Ph.D. dissertation, Department of Anthropology, University of California, Riverside.
1994 Milling-Implement Quarrying and Production Bordering the Lower Colorado and Lower Gila Rivers: Archaeological, Ethnographic, and Historical Evidence for an Aboriginal Industry. In *Recent Research Along the Lower Colorado River*, edited by J. A. Ezzo, pp. 101–117. Statistical Research Technical Series no. 51.

Schneider, J. S., H. C. L. Brewer, and M. C. Hall
2000 *Research, Inventory, and Management Strategies for At-Risk and Other Prehistoric Cultural Resources, Death Valley National Park, California: Program Design Report.* Report on file, Eastern Information Center, University of California, Riverside.

Schoenherr, A. A.
1992 *A Natural History of California.* University of California Press, Berkeley.

Scholes, R. J.
1990 Change in Nature and the Nature of Change: Interaction Between Terrestrial Ecosystems and the Atmosphere. *South African Journal of Science* 86:350–354.

Schroeder, A. H.
1958 Lower Colorado River Buffware. In *Pottery Types of the Southwest*, edited by H. S. Colton. Museum of Northern Arizona, Ceramic Series 3D.
1979 Prehistory: Hakataya. In *Southwest*, edited by A. Ortiz, pp. 100–107. Handbook of North American Indians. Vol. 9. W. C. Sturtevant, general editor. Smithsonian Institution, Washington, D.C.

Schroth, A. B.
1994 The Pinto Point Controversy in the Western United States. Ph.D dissertation, Department of Anthropology, University of California, Riverside.
1996 An Ethnographic Review of Grinding, Pounding, Pulverizing, and Smoothing with Stones. *Pacific Coast Archaeological Society Quarterly* 32(4):55–75.

Schulz, H.
1994 *Archaeology of the Miller Mound (CA-COL-1): A River Pa'twin Village.* Report on file, Department of Anthropology, University of California, Davis.

Schulz, P. D.
1970 *Solar Burial Orientation and Paleodemography in Central California Windmiller Tradition.* In Papers on California and Great Basin Prehistory, edited by E. W. Ritter, P. D. Schulz, and R. Kautz, pp. 185–198. Center for Archaeological Research at Davis Publication no. 2.
1981 Osteoarchaeology and Subsistence Change in Prehistoric Central California. Ph.D. dissertation, Department of Anthropology, University of California, Davis.

Schulz, P. D., H. M. Wagner, and D. P. Domning
1976 Vertebrate Fauna of Site CA-SAC-329, Sacramento County, California. Appendix I in *Archaeological Excavations at SAC-329 Near Walnut Grove, Sacramento County, California*, by William E. Soule. Archaeological Study Center of California State University, Sacramento. Submitted to the Army Corps of Engineers, Sacramento. Copies available from the North Central Information Center, Department of Anthropology, California State University, Sacramento.

Schurr, T. G.
2004a Molecular Genetic Diversity in Siberians and Native Americans Suggests an Early Colonization of the New World. In *Entering America*, edited by D. B. Madsen, pp. 187–238. University of Utah Press, Salt Lake City.
2004b An Anthropological Genetic View of the Peopling of the New World. In *The Settlement of the American Continents: A Multidisciplinary Approach to Human Biogeography*, edited by C. M. Barton, G. A. Clark, D. R. Yesner, and G. A. Pearson, pp. 11–27. University of Arizona Press, Tucson.

Schurr, T. G., S. W. Ballinger, Y. Y. Gan, J. A. Hodge, D. A. Merriwether, D. N. Lawrence, W. C. Knowler, K. M. Weiss, and D. C. Wallace
1990 Amerindian Mitochondrial DNAs Have Rare Asian Mutations at High Frequencies, Suggesting They Derived from Four Primary Maternal Lineages. *American Journal of Human Genetics* 46:613–623.

Schwaderer, R.
1992 Archaeological Test Excavation at the Duncans Point Cave, CA-SON-348/H. In *Essays on the Prehistory of Maritime California*, edited by T. L. Jones, pp. 55–71. Center for Archaeological Research at Davis no. 10. University of California, Davis.

Schwartz, D. L., H. T. Mullins, and D. F. Belknap
1986 Holocene Geologic History of a Transform Margin Estuary: Elkhorn Slough, Central California. *Estuarine, Coastal, and Shelf Science* 22:285–302.

Scuderi, L. A.
1993 A 2000-Year Tree Ring Record of Annual Temperatures in the Sierra Nevada Mountains. *Science* 259:1433–1436.

Seals, K.
1993 Charmstones and Charmstone Caches of the Tulare Lake Region. In *Contributions to Tulare Lake Archaeology II, Finding the Evidence: The Quest for Tulare Lake's Archaeological Past*, edited by W. J. Wallace and F. A. Riddell, pp. 65–72. Tulare Lake Archaeological Research Group, Redondo Beach.

Seck, S. M.
1980 The Archaeology of Trego Hot Springs: 26Pe118. Master's thesis, Department of Anthropology, University of Nevada, Reno.

Sehgal, L.
2003 CA-SBA-550 and Its Significance to Chumash Cosmology: A New Interpretation. *Rock Art Papers* 16:71–82. San Diego Museum Papers 41.

Sernander, R.
1910 Discussion. *International Geolological Congress 11 Compte Rendu* 1:404–409.

Setzler, F. M., and G. C. Marshall
1952 Seeking the Secret of the Giants. *National Geographic*, September, pp. 389–404.

Seymour, G. R.
1997 A Reevalution of Lower Colorado Buff Ware Ceramics: Redefining the Patayan in Southern Nevada. Master's thesis, Department of Anthropology, University of Nevada, Las Vegas.

Shackley, M. S.
1988 *Prehistoric Lithic Technology and Production in the Southern Chocolate Mountains: Data Recovery and Analysis at Mesquite Mine, Imperial County, California*. On file, Southeast Information Center, El Centro, California.
1994 Intersource and Intrasource Geochemical Variability in Two Newly Discovered Archaeological Obsidian Sources in the Southern Great Basin. *Journal of California and Great Basin Anthropology* 16:118–129.

Shalom, D.
2005 Climate Change and Cultural Response: A Study of Fish Remains from Pitas Point (CA-VEN-27). Master's thesis, Department of Anthropology, San Diego State University, San Diego.

Shapiro, W., and K. J. Tremaine
1995 *Final Report for the Archaeological Investigation of the Wiegand Property, Dixon, California*. Submitted to Lewis Homes of California, Sacramento. Biosystems Analysis, Sacramento. Copies available from the North Central Information Center, Department of Anthropology, California State University, Sacramento.

Shaul, D. L., and J. M. Andresen
1989 A Case for Yuman Participation in the Hohokam Regional System. *Kiva* 54:105–126.

Shaul, D. L., and J. H. Hill
1998 Tepimans, Yumans, and Other Hohokam. *American Antiquity* 63:375–396.

Sheeders, D. J.
1982 An Archaeological Analysis of the Whaley Site, CA-SAC-265. Master's thesis, Department of Anthropology, California State University, Sacramento.

Shelley, S. D., and J. H. Altschul
1989 *Paleoenvironments and Archaeology of the Trigo Mountains: Data Recovery in the Hart Mine and Cibola Quarry Areas, Yuma County, Arizona*. Statistical Research Technical Series no. 15. Tucson, Arizona.

Shelley, S. D., J. A. Homburg, A. R. Orme, and E. C. Brevik
2003 Environment, Soils, and Stratigraphy. In *At the Base of the Bluff, Archaeological Inventory and Evaluation Along Lower Centinela Creek, Marina del Rey, California*, edited by J. H. Altschul, A. Q. Stoll, D. R. Grenda, and R. Ciolek-Torrello, pp. 77–97. Statistical Research, Playa Vista Monograph Series, Test Excavation Report 4.

Shepard, F. P., and D. L. Inman
1950 Nearshore Water Circulation Related to Bottom Topography and Wave Refraction. *Transactions of the American Geophysical Union* 31:196–212.

Shields, G. F., A. M. Schmeichen, B. L. Frazier, A. Redd, M. I. Voevoda, J. K. Reed, and R. H. Ward
1993 MtDNA Sequences Suggest a Recent Evolutionary Divergence for Beringian and Northern North American Populations. *American Journal of Human Genetics* 53(3):549–562.

Shipek, F. C.
1989 An Example of Intensive Plant Husbandry: The Kumeyaay of Southern California. In *Foraging and Farming: The Evolution of Plant Exploitation*, edited by David R. Harris and Gordon C. Hillman, pp. 99–110. Unwin Hyman, London.

Shipley, W. F.
1978 Native Languages of California. In *California*, edited by R. F. Heizer, pp. 80–90. Handbook of North American Indians. Vol. 8. W. G. Sturtevant, general editor. Smithsonian Institution, Washington, D.C.

Shlemon, R. J., and E. L. Begg
1975 Late Quaternary Evolution of the Sacramento-San Joaquin Delta, California. In *Quaternary Studies*, edited by R. P. Suggate and M. M. Cresswell, pp. 259–265. The Royal Society of New Zealand Bulletin 13.

Shumway, G., C. L. Hubbs, and J. R. Moriarty
1961 Scripps Estates Site, San Diego, California: A La Jolla Site Dated 5460 to 7370 Years Before the Present. *Annals of the New York Academy of Sciences* 93:37–132.

Sickler-Hylkema, L.
2005 A Geo-Spatial Study of Prehistoric Land Use in California's Diablo Mountain Range. Master's thesis, Department of Anthropology, California State University, Hayward.

Siefkin, N.
1999 Archaeology of the Redtfeldt Mound (CA-KIN-66), Tulare Basin, California. Master's thesis, Department of Sociology and Anthropology, California State University, Bakersfield.

Sierra Nevada Ecosystem Project
1996 *Sierra Nevada Ecosystem Project: Final Report to Congress*. Vols. 1–3. University of California, Center for Water and Wildland Resources, Davis.

Silliman, S.
2000 Obsidian Studies in the Archaeology of 19th-Century California. *Society for California Archaeology Newsletter* 34(1):1, 26–29.

Simms, S.
1985 Acquisition Costs and Nutritional Data on Great Basin Resources. *Journal of California and Great Basin Anthropology* 7:117–125.

Simons, D. D.
1978 Terrestrial Vertebrates from the Wolfsen Mound (Mer-215), Merced County. In *Archaeological Investigations at the Wolfsen Mound, CA-MER-215, Merced County, California*, by Ann S. Peak and Tony F. Weber. Ann S. Peak and Associates Consulting Archeology. Submitted to the City of Newman, Stanislaus County. Copies available from the North Central Information Center, Department of Anthropology, California State University, Sacramento.
1992 Prehistoric Mammal Exploitation in the San Francisco Bay Area. In *Essays on the Prehistory of Maritime California*, edited by T. L. Jones, pp. 73–103. Center for Archaeological Research at Davis Publication no. 10. University of California, Davis.
2007 Vertebrate Faunal Remains. In *Santa Clara Valley Prehistory: Archaeological Investigations at CA-SCL-690, the Tamien Station Site, San Jose, California*, edited by M. Hylkema, pp. 353–386. Center for Archaeological Research at Davis no. 15. University of California, Davis.

Simons, D. D., T. N. Layton, and R. Knudson
1985 A Fluted Point from the Mendocino County Coast, California. *Journal of California and Great Basin Anthropology* 7:260–269.

Simpson, R. D.
1947 A Classic Folsom from Lake Mohave. *Southwest Museum Masterkey* 21(1):24–25.

Sims, J. D., M. J. Rymer, and J. A. Perkins
1988 Late Quaternary Deposits Beneath Clear Lake, California; Physical Stratigraphy, Age, and Paleogeographic Implica-

tions. In *Late Quaternary Climate, Tectonism, and Sedimentation in Clear Lake, Northern California Coast Ranges*, edited by J. D. Sims, pp. 21–44. Geological Society of America Special Paper no. 214. Boulder, Colorado.

Singer, C. A., and J. E. Ericson
1977 Quarry Analysis at Bodie Hills, Mono County, California. In *Exchange Systems in Prehistory*, edited by T. K. Earle and J. E. Ericson, pp. 171–190. Academic Press, New York.

Skowronek, R. K., R. L. Bishop, M. J. Blackman, S. Ginn, and M. G. Heras
2003 Chemical Characterization of Earthenware on the Alta California Frontier. *Proceedings of the Society for California Archaeology* 16:209–219.

Slater, R. A., D. S. Gorsline, R. L. Kolpack, and G. I. Shiller
2002 Post-Glacial Sediments of the Californian Shelf from Cape San Martin to the U.S.-Mexico Border. *Quaternary International* 92:45–61.

Smith, B.
1998 *The Emergence of Agriculture.* Scientific American Library, New York.
2001 Low-level Food Production. *Journal of Archaeological Research* 9:1–43.

Smith, C. R.
1978 Tubatulabal. In *California*, edited by R. F. Heizer, pp. 437–445. Handbook of North American Indians. Vol. 8. W. C. Sturtevant, general editor. Smithsonian Institution, Washington, D.C.

Smith, D. G., R. S. Malhi, J. Eshleman, J. G. Lorenz, and F. A. Kaestle
1995 Distribution of mtDNA Haplogroup X Among Native North Americans. *American Journal of Physical Anthropology* 110:271–284.

Smith, G. A., and S. M. Freers
1994 *Fading Images: Indian Pictographs of Western Riverside County.* Riverside Museum Press, Riverside, California.

Smith, G. A., and M. K. Lerch
1984 Cupule Petroglyphs in Southern California. *Quarterly San Bernardino County Museum Association* 32(1–2):1–17.

Smith, G. A., and M. Mosely
1962 Archaeological Investigations of the Mojave River Drainage, Part 1. *Quarterly of the San Bernardino County Museum Association* 9(3).

Smith, G. I., and F. A. Street-Perrott
1983 Pluvial Lakes of the Western United States. In *Late Quaternary Environments of the United States.* Vol. 1. Edited by H. E. Wright Jr., pp. 190–212. University of Minnesota Press, Minneapolis.

Smith, S. A., and R. S. Anderson
1992 Late Wisconsin Paleoecological Record from Swamp Lake, Yosemite National Park, California. *Quaternary Research* 38:91–102.

Soule, W. E.
1976 *Archaeological Excavations at SAC-329 Near Walnut Grove, Sacramento County, California.* Archaeological Study Center of California State University, Sacramento. Submitted to the Army Corps of Engineers, Sacramento. Copies available from the North Central Information Center, Department of Anthropology, California State University, Sacramento.

Spanne, L. W.
1975 Seasonal Variability in the Population of Barbareño Chumash Villages: An Exploratory Model. In *Papers on the Chumash*, pp. 25–63. San Luis Obispo County Archaeological Society Occasional Papers no. 9.

Spaulding, W. G.
1990 Vegetational and Climatic Development of the Mojave Desert: The Last Glacial Maximum to the Present. In *Packrat Middens: The Last 40,000 Years of Biotic Change*, edited by J. L. Betancourt, T. R. Van Devender, and P. S. Martin, pp. 166–199. University of Arizona Press, Tucson.
1995a Environmental Change, Ecosystem Responses, and the Late Quaternary Development of the Mojave Desert. In *Late Quaternary Environments and Deep History: A Tribute to Paul Martin*, edited by D. W. Steadman and J. I. Mead, pp. 139–164. Scientific Papers. Vol. 3, The Mammoth Site of Hot Springs, Hot Springs, South Dakota.
1995b The Environmental Setting. In *Prehistory of the Middle Pit River, Northeastern California: Archaeological Investigations at Lake Britton, Pit 3, 4 & 5 Project*, edited by J. H. Cleland. Vol. 1. Report submitted to Pacific Gas and Electric Company, San Francisco.
1999 Paleoenvironmental Studies. In *Archeological Synthesis and Research Design, Yosemite National Park, California*, by K. L. Hull and M. J. Moratto, pp. 29–64. USDI National Park Service Yosemite Research Center Publications in Anthropology 21.

Spier, R. F. G.
1978a Foothill Yokuts. In *California*, edited by R. F. Heizer, pp. 471–484. Handbook of North American Indians. Vol. 8. W. C. Sturtevant, general editor. Smithsonian Institution, Washington, D.C.
1978b Monache. In *California*, edited by R. F. Heizer, pp. 426–436. Handbook of North American Indians. Vol. 8. W. C. Sturtevant, general editor. Smithsonian Institution, Washington, D.C.

Sprague, J., and G. Grasse
2001 Lizard Cave: A Possible Solar Marker at CA-KER-5525. *American Indian Rock Art* 27:227–234.

Squier, R. J., and G. L. Grosscup
1952 *An Archaeological Survey of Lava Beds National Monument, California.* Report on file, Lava Beds National Monument, Tule Lake, California.
1954 *Preliminary Report of Archaeological Excavations in Lower Klamath Basin, California.* University of California Archaeological Survey Manuscript 183.

Stafford, T.W., Jr., A. J. T. Jull, K. Brendel, R. Duhamel, and D. Donahue
1987 Study of Bone Radiocarbon Dating Accuracy at the University of Arizona Accelerator Facility for Radioisotope Analysis. *Radiocarbon* 29:24–44.

Stahle, D. W., M. D. Therrell, M. K. Cleaveland, D. R. Cayan, M. D. Dettinger, and N. Knowles
2001 Ancient Blue Oaks Reveal Human Impact on San Francisco Bay Salinity. *Eos* 82:141, 144–145.

Stanford, D., and B. Bradley
2002 Ocean Trails and Prairie Paths? Thoughts About Clovis Origins. In *The First Americans: The Pleistocene Colonization of the New World*, edited by N. G. Jablonski, pp. 255–271. Memoirs of the California Academy of Sciences 27.

Starratt, S.
2002 Diatoms as Indicators of Freshwater Flow Variation in Central California. In *Proceedings of the 18th Annual Pacific Climate Workshop, March 18–21, 2001*, edited by G. J. West and L. D. Buffaloe, pp. 129–144. Technical Report 69 of the Interagency Ecological Program for the San Francisco Estuary. State of California Department of Water Resources.

Starratt, S. W., J. A. Barron, T. Kneeshaw, R. Larry Phillips, J. Brischoff, J. B. Lowernstern, and J. A. Wanket
2003 A Holocene Record from Medicine Lake, Siskiyou County, California: Preliminary Diatom, Pollen, Geochemical, and Sedimentological Data. In *Proceedings of the 19th Annual Pacific Climate Workshop, March 3–6, 2002, Asilomar*, edited by G. J. West and N. L. Blomquist. Technical Report 71 of the Interagency Ecological Program for the San Francisco Estuary.

Steffen, A., E. J. Skinner, and P. Ainsworth
1999 A View to the Core: Technological Units and Debitage Analysis. In *Unit Issues in Archaeology*, edited by A. F. Ramenofsky

and A. Steffen, pp. 131–146. University of Utah Press, Salt Lake City.

Stern, T.
1998 Klamath and Modoc. In *Plateau,* edited by D. E. Walker, pp. 446–466. Handbook of North American Indians. Vol 12. W. C. Sturtevant, general editor. Smithsonian Institution, Washington, D.C.

Stevens, N.
2002 Spatial and Temporal Patterning of Bedrock Mortar Sites in the Sierra Nevada: A Regional Exploration. *Proceedings of the Society for California Archaeology* 16:175–184.
2005 Changes in Prehistoric Land Use in the Alpine Sierra Nevada: A Regional Exploration Using Temperature-Adjusted Obsidian Hydration Rates. *Journal of California and Great Basin Anthropology* 25:187–205.

Stevens, N. E., R. T. Fitzgerald, N. Farrell, M. A. Giambastiani, J. M. Farquhar, and D. Tinsley
2004 *Archaeological Test Excavations at Santa Ysabel Ranch, Paso Robles, San Luis Obispo County, California.* Report submitted to Weyrich Development Company, LLC. Cultural Resource Management Services, Paso Robles.

Stevenson, C. M., M. Gottesman, and M. Macko
2000 Redefining the Working Assumptions of Obsidian Hydration Dating. *Journal of California and Great Basin Anthropology* 22:223–236.

Steward, J. H.
1929 Petroglyphs of California and Adjoining States. *University of California Publications in American Archaeology and Ethnology* 24(2).
1933 Ethnography of the Owens Valley Paiute. *University of California Publications in American Archaeology and Ethnology* 33(3).
1938 *Basin-Plateau Aboriginal Sociopolitical Groups.* Bureau of American Ethnology Bulletin 120, Smithsonian Institution, Washington, D.C.

Stewart, O.
2002 *Forgotten Fires: Native Americans and the Transient Wilderness.* University of Oklahoma Press, Norman.

Stewart, O. C.
1939 The Northern Paiute Bands. *University of California Anthropological Records* 2:127–149.

Stewart, S.
1993 Upper Archaic Diversity in the Warm Springs Locality, Sonoma County, California. Master's thesis, Department of Anthropology, Sonoma State University, Rohnert Park, California.
2003 *Archaeological Research Issues for the Point Reyes National Seashore–Golden Gate National Recreation Area, Part II: An Overview of Research Issues for Indigenous Archaeology for the PRNS-GGNRA.* Anthropological Studies Center, Sonoma State University, Rohnert Park, California. Submitted to the National Park Service Golden Gate National Recreation Area, San Francisco. Copies available from Northwest Information Center, Department of Anthropology, Sonoma State University, Rohnert Park, California.

Stewart, S., and C. Gerike
1994 *Test Excavations at CA-CAL-114/H, Mark Twain St. Joseph's Hospital, San Andreas, Calaveras County, California.* Submitted to Mark Twain St. Joseph's Hospital, San Andreas. Copies available from Central California Information Center, Department of Anthropology, California State University, Stanislaus, Turlock, California.

Stine, S.
1990 Late Holocene Fluctuations of Mono Lake, Eastern California. *Palaeogeography, Palaeoclimatology, Palaeoecology* 78:333–381.
1994 Extreme and Persistent Drought in California and Patagonia During Mediaeval Time. *Nature* 369:546–549.
2001 *The Great Droughts of Y1K.* Sierra Nature Notes 1. Yosemite Association, El Portal, California.

Stone, A. C., and M. Stoneking
1998 MtDNA Analysis of a Prehistoric Oneota Population: Implications for the Peopling of the New World. *American Journal of Human Genetics* 62:1153–1170.

Storer, T. I., and R. L. Usinger
1963 *Sierra Nevada Natural History.* University of California Press, Berkeley.

Storer, T. I., R. L. Usinger, and D. Lukas
2004 *Sierra Nevada Natural History.* Rev. ed. University of California Press, Berkeley.

Storlazzi, C. D., and G. B. Griggs
2000 Influence of El Niño–Southern Oscillation (ENSO) Events on the Evolution of Central California's Shoreline. *Geological Society of America Bulletin* 112:236–249.

Story, J. A., V. E. Wessels, and J. A. Wolfe
1966 Radiocarbon Dating of Recent Sediments in San Francisco Bay. *Mineral Information Service* 19:47–50.

Straus, L. G.
2000 Solutrean Settlement of North America? A Review of Reality. *American Antiquity* 65:219–226.

Strock, P. L.
1991 Imperialists Without a State: The Cultural Dynamics of Early Paleoindian Colonization As Seen from the Great Lakes Region. In *Clovis Origins and Adaptations*, edited by R. Bonnichsen and Karen L. Turnmire, pp. 153–162. Center for the Study of the First Americans, Corvallis.

Stromberg, G.
1992 *Shell Beads at the Patwin Site of Tebti.* Report on file, Department of Anthropology Museum, University of California, Davis.

Strong, W. D.
1929 Aboriginal Society in Southern California. *University of California Publications in American Archaeology and Ethnology* 26:1–358.

Strother, E.
2003 Songs of Insult: Study of Perimortem Cutmarks on Human Bone at CA-CCO-474/H. Master's thesis, Department of Anthropology, California State University, Hayward.

Strother, E., J. Price, A. Arrigoni, H. Price, T. Young, and K. Kearney
2005 *Data Recovery, Burial Removal and Construction Monitoring at the Canyon Oaks Site, CA-ALA-613/H Pleasanton, Alameda County, California.* Vol. 2, *Osteological Investigations.* William Self Associates, Orinda. Submitted to KB Home South Bay, Pleasanton. Copies available from Northwest Information Center, Sonoma State University, Rohnert Park.

Strub, P. T., J. S. Allen, A. Huyer, R. L. Smith, and R. C. Beardsley
1987 Seasonal Cycles of Currents, Temperatures, Winds, and Sea Level over the Northeast Pacific Continental Shelf: 35°N to 48°N. *Journal of Geophyical Research* 92:1507–1526.

Strudwick, I. H.
2005 The Use of Fired Clay Daub from CA-ORA-269 in the Identification of Prehistoric Dwelling Construction Methods, San Joaquin Hills, Orange County, California. *Proceedings of the Society for California Archaeology* 18:219–237.

Stuiver, M., and P. J. Reimer
1993 Extended ^{14}C Data Base and Revised CALIB 3.0 ^{14}C Age Calibration Program. *Radiocarbon* 35:215–230.
2000 Calib 4.3 Radiocarbon Calibration Program 2000. Quaternary Isotope Laboratory, University of Washington.

Stuiver, M., G. W. Pearson, and T. Braziunas
1986 Radiocarbon Age Calibrations of Marine Samples Back to 9000 CAL YR BP. *Radiocarbon* 28:980–1021.

Suchey, J. A.
1975 Biological Distance of Prehistoric Central California Populations Derived from Non-metric Traits of the Cranium.

Ph.D. dissertation, Department of Anthropology, University of California, Riverside.

Sundahl, E. M.
1982 The Shasta Complex in the Redding Area, California. Master's thesis, Department of Anthropology, California State University, Chico.
1984 Two Painted Stone Artifacts from Shasta County, California. *Journal of California and Great Basin Anthropology* 6:252–256.
1992 Cultural Patterns and Chronology in the Northern Sacramento River Drainage. In *Proceedings of the Society for California Archaeology 5*, edited by M. D. Rosen, L. E. Christenson, and D. Laylander, pp. 89–112. Society for California Archaeology, San Diego.

Sundahl, E. M., and W. Henn
1993 Borax Lake Pattern Assemblages on the Shasta-Trinity National Forests, North-Central California. *Journal of California and Great Basin Anthropology* 15:73–89.

Susia, M.
1962 The Soule Park Site (Ven-61). In *UCLA Archaeological Survey Annual Report 1961–1962*, pp. 157–234. Department of Anthropology, University of California, Los Angeles.

Sutton, M. Q.
1982 Kawaiisu Mythology and Rock Art: One Example. *Journal of California and Great Basin Anthropology* 4:148–154.
1986 Warfare and Expansion: An Ethnohistoric Perspective on the Numic Spread. *Journal of California and Great Basin Anthropology* 8:65–82.
1988 *An Introduction to the Archaeology of the Western Mojave Desert, California*. Archives of California Prehistory 14. Coyote Press, Salinas.
1989 Late Prehistoric Interaction Spheres in the Mojave Desert, California. *North American Archaeologist* 10:95–121.
1993 Midden and Coprolite Derived Subsistence Evidence: An Analysis of Data from the La Quinta Site, Salton Basin, California. *Journal of Ethnobiology* 13:1–15.
1994 The Numic Expansion as Seen from the Mojave Desert. In *Across the West: Human Population Movement and the Expansion of the Numa*, edited by D. B. Madsen and D. Rhode, pp. 133–140. University of Utah Press, Salt Lake City.
1996a The Current Status of Archaeological Research in the Mojave Desert. *Journal of California and Great Basin Anthropology* 18:221–257.
1996b A Charmstone Cache from the Southern San Joaquin Valley. *Pacific Coast Archaeological Society Quarterly* 32(4):41–54.
1998 Cluster Analysis of Paleofecal Data Sets: A Test of Late Prehistoric Settlement and Subsistence Patterns in the Northern Coachella Valley, California. *American Antiquity* 63:86–107.
2000 Prehistoric Movements of Northern Uto-Aztecan Peoples Along the Northwestern Edge of the Southwest: Impact on Southwestern Populations. In *The Archaeology of Regional Interaction: Religion, Warfare, and Exchange Across the American Southwest and Beyond*, edited by M. Hegmon, pp. 295–315. University Press of Colorado, Boulder.
2005 *The 1992 Excavations at Rustler Rockshelter, Eastern Mojave Desert, California*. California State University Bakersfield, Museum of Anthropology Occasional Papers no. 7.

Sutton, M. Q., and S. R. Jackson
1993 Archaeological Investigations CA-KER-2450, Rosamond, Kern County, California. In *Archaeological Studies in Rosamond, Western Mojave Desert, California*, edited by M. Q. Sutton, pp. 10–25. Museum of Anthropology Occasional Papers no. 3. California State University, Bakersfield.

Sutton, M. Q., and D. Rhode
1994 A History of the Numic Problem. In *Across the West: Human Population Movement and the Expansion of the Numa*, edited by D. B. Madsen and D. Rhode, pp. 6–15. University of Utah Press, Salt Lake City.

Sutton, M. Q., and P. Wilke
1984 New Observations on a Clovis Point from the Central Mojave Desert, California. *Journal of California and Great Basin Anthropology* 6:113–115.

Sutton, M. Q., J. S. Schneider, and R. M. Yohe II
1993 The Siphon Site (CA-SBR-6580): A Millingstone Horizon Site in Summit Valley, California. *San Bernardino County Museum Association Quarterly* 40(3).

Swadesh, M.
1954 Perspectives and Problems of Amerindian Comparative Linguistics. *Word* 10:306–332.
1959 Linguistics as an Instrument of Prehistory. *Southwestern Journal of Anthropology* 15:20–35.

Swartz, B. K., Jr.
1964 Archaeological Investigations at Lava Beds National Monument. Ph.D. dissertation, Department of Anthropology, University of Arizona, Tucson.

Swernoff, M.
1982 *Cultural Resources Survey, Upper Stony Creek, El Piojo, and San Antonio River Valleys, Fort Hunter Liggett, Monterey County, California*. Copies available from Northwest Information Center, Department of Anthropology, Sonoma State University, Rohnert Park, California.

Swetnam, T. W.
1993 Fire History and Climate Change in Giant Sequoia Groves. *Science* 262:885–889.

Swetnam, T. W., and J. L. Betancourt
1998 Mesoscale Disturbance and Ecological Response to Decadal Climatic Variability in the American Southwest. *Journal of Climate* 11:3128–3147.

Tainter, J. A.
1971a Climatic Fluctuations and Resource Procurement in the Santa Ynez Valley. *Pacific Coast Archaeological Society Quarterly* 11:27–40.
1971b *Salvage Excavations at the Fowler Site: Some Aspects of Social Organization of the Northern Chumash*. San Luis Obispo County Archaeological Society Occasional Papers no. 3.
1972 *Simulation Modeling of Inland Chumash Interaction*. University of California Archaeological Survey Report 14:79–106. Department of Anthropology, University of California, Los Angeles.
1975 Hunter-Gatherer Territorial Organization in the Santa Ynez Valley. *Pacific Coast Archaeological Society Quarterly* 11:27–40.

Taite, K. K.
1999 Resource Intensification and the Los Vaqueros Archaeofauna: A Test of the Distant Patch Hypothesis. Master's thesis, Department of Anthropology, California State University, Chico.

Tamez, S.
1978 A Preliminary Report on the Analysis of Three *Olivella* Bead Manufacturing Sites in Sonoma County. In *Archaeological Investigations at CA-Son-455, Sonoma County, California: A Compilation of Student Papers*, edited by D. A. Fredrickson. Department of Anthropology, Sonoma State University. Copies available from Northwest Information Center, Department of Anthropology, Sonoma State University, Rohnert Park, California.

Tankersly, K.
2002 *In Search of Ice Age Americans*. Gibbs Smith, Salt Lake City.

Taylor, R. E.
1983 Non-concordance of Radiocarbon and Amino Acid Racemization Age Estimates on Human Bone: Implications for the Dating of the Earliest *Homo sapiens* in the New World. *Radiocarbon* 25:647–654.

1991 Frameworks for Dating the Late Pleistocene Peopling of the Americas. In *The First Americans: Search and Research*, edited by T. D. Dillehay and D. J. Meltzer, pp. 77–111. CRC Press, Boca Raton, Florida.

Taylor, R. E., C. Vance Haynes Jr., and M. Stuiver
1996 Clovis and Folsom Age Estimates: Stratigraphic Context and Radiocarbon Calibration. *Antiquity* 70:515–525.

Taylor, R. E., L. A. Payen, C. A. Prior, P. J. Slota Jr., R. Gillespie, J. A. J. Gowlett, R. E. M. Hedges, A. J. T. Jull, T. H. Zabel, D. J. Donahue, and R. Berger
1985 Major Revisions in the Pleistocene Age Assignments for North American Human Skeletons by C-14 Accelerator Mass Spectrometry: None Older Than 11,000 C-14 Years. *American Antiquity* 50:136–140.

Taylor, T. T., D. L. Taylor, D. Alcorn, E. B. Weil, and M. Tambunga
1987 Investigations Regarding Aboriginal Stone Mound Features in the Mojave Desert: Excavations at CA-SBR-221 and CA-SBR-3186, San Bernardino County, California. In *Papers on the Archaeology of the Mojave Desert*, edited by M. Q. Sutton, pp. 79–114. Archives of California Prehistory 10, Coyote Press. Salinas.

Tenney, J. A.
1986 Trauma Among Early California Populations. *American Journal of Physical Anthropology* 69:271.

Theodoratus Cultural Research and Archaeological Consulting and Research Services
1984 *Cultural Resources Overview of the Southern Sierra Nevada: An Ethnographic, Linguistic, Archaeological, and Historical Study of the Sierra National Forest, Sequoia National Forest, and Bakersfield District of the Bureau of Land Management.* Submitted to the USDA Forest Service, Southern Central Contracting Office, Bishop, California.

Theodoratus, D. J., F. A. Riddell, C. M. Blount, D. A. Bell, and M. E. Peters
1979 *Anthropological Overview of a Portion of Lassen and Modoc Counties.* Vol. 1. Theodoratus Cultural Research, Fair Oaks, California. Submitted to the U.S. Department of the Interior Bureau of Land Management, Susanville, California.

Thomas, D. H.
1983 The Archaeology of Monitor Valley: 1, Epistemology. *Anthropological Papers of the American Museum of Natural History* 58(1).

Thomas, D. H., L. S. A. Pendleton, and S. C. Cappannari
1986 Western Shoshone. In *Great Basin*, edited by Warren L. d'Azevedo, pp. 262–283. Handbook of North American Indians. Vol. 11. William C. Sturtevant, general editor. Smithsonian Institution, Washington, D.C.

Thomas, T.
1983a Material Culture of Gatecliff Shelter: Incised Stones. In *The Archaeology of Monitor Valley 2: Gatecliff Shelter*, edited by D. H. Thomas, pp. 246–278. Anthropological Papers of the American Museum of Natural History 59, pt. 1.
1983b Rock Art of Gatecliff Shelter. In *The Archaeology of Monitor Valley 2: Gatecliff Shelter*, edited by D. H. Thomas, pp. 310–319. Anthropological Papers of the American Museum of Natural History 59, pt. 1.
1983c The Visual Symbolism of Gatecliff Shelter. In *The Archaeology of Monitor Valley 2: Gatecliff Shelter*, edited by D. H. Thomas, pp. 332–352. Anthropological Papers of the American Museum of Natural History 59, pt. 1.

Tiley, S.
2001 *Phase II Excavation of Prehistoric Site CA-SLO-1355, on the SLO/KER-46 Four-Lane Project, San Luis Obispo County, California.* Prepared for California Department of Transportation, Fresno. Copies available from Archaeological Research Center, Department of Anthropology, California State University, Sacramento.

Timbrook, J.
1993 Island Chumash Ethnobotany. In *Archaeology on the Northern Channel Islands of California, Studies of Subsistence, Economics, and Social Organization*, edited by M. A. Glassow. Archives of California Prehistory 34. Coyote Press, Salinas.

Titus, M. D.
1987 Evidence for Prehistoric Occupation of Sites on San Clemente Island by Hokan and Uto-Aztecan Indians. Master's thesis, Department of Anthropology, University of California, Los Angeles.

Torroni, A.
2000 Mitochondrial DNA and the Origin of Native Americans. In *American Past, American Present: Genes and Languages in the Americas and Beyond*, edited by C. Renfrew, pp. 77–87. McDonald Institute for Archaeological Research, Cambridge.

Torroni, A., T. G. Schurr, M. F. Cabell, M. D. Brown, J. V. Neel, M. Larsen, D. G. Smith, C. M. Vullo, and D. C. Wallace
1993 Asian Affinities and Continental Radiation of the Four Founding Native American mtDNAs. *American Journal of Human Genetics* 53:563–590.

Treganza, A. E.
1946 Possibilities of an Aboriginal Practice of Marginal Agriculture Among the Southern Diegueño. *American Antiquity* 12:169–173.
1947 *An Interesting Cache of Domesticated Seeds from Southern California.* Robert E. Schenk Memorial Archives of California Archaeology Paper no. 21. California State University, San Francisco.
1952 Archaeological Investigations in the Farmington Reservoir Area, Stanislaus County, California. *University of California Archaeological Survey Reports* 14:1–37.
1958 Topanga Culture, Final Report on Excavations, 1948. *Anthropological Records* 20(2). University of California Press, Berkeley.
1964 An Ethno-archaeological Examination of Samwell Cave. *Cave Studies* 12:1–29.

Treganza, A. E., and A. Bierman
1958 *The Topanga Culture, Final Report on Excavations, 1948.* Anthropological Records 20:2. University of California, Berkeley.

Treganza, A. E., and R. F. Heizer
1953 Additional Data on the Farmington Complex, a Stone Implement Assemblage of Probable Early Postglacial Date from Central California. *University of California Archaeological Survey Reports* 22:28–41.

Treganza, A. E., and C. G. Malamud
1950 The Topanga Culture, First Season's Excavation of the Tank Site, 1947. *Anthropological Records* 12(4). University of California, Berkeley.

Tremaine, K. J.
1993 Temporal Ordering of Artifact Obsidian: Relative Dating Enhanced Through the Use of Accelerated Hydration Experiments. In *There Grows a Green Tree: Paper in Honor of David A. Fredrickson*, edited by G. White, P. Mikkelsen, W. R. Hildebrandt, and M. E. Basgall, pp. 265–275. Center for Archaeological Research at Davis Publication no. 11. University of California, Davis.

Trigger, B.
1989 *A History of Archaeological Thought.* Cambridge University Press, New York.

True, D. L.
1966 Archaeological Differentiation of Shoshonean and Yuman Speaking Groups in Southern California. Ph.D. dissertation, Department of Anthropology, University of California, Los Angeles.
1993 Bedrock Milling Elements as Indicators of Subsistence and Settlement Patterns in Northern San Diego County, California. *Pacific Coast Archaeological Society Quarterly* 29(2):1–26.

True, D. L., and M. A. Baumhoff
1981 Pitted Rock Petroglyphs in Southern California. *Journal of California and Great Basin Anthropology* 3:257–268.
1985 Archaeological Investigations at Lake Berryessa, California: Berryessa II. *Journal of California and Great Basin Anthropology* 7:21–45.
True, D. L., and G. Waugh
1986 To-Vah: A Luiseno Power Cave. *Journal of California and Great Basin Anthropology* 8:269–273.
Turner, K.
1987 Aspects of Salinan Grammar. Ph.D. dissertation, Department of Linguistics, University of California, Berkeley.
Turner, T. H.
1993 *The Archaeology of Five Sites in the Northwest Truckee Meadows.* State of Nevada, Department of Transportation, Environmental Services Division, Cultural Resources Section. Nevada Department of Transportation Archaeological Technical Report Series no. 7.
Tushingham, S.
2005 An Ancient Campground: Archaeology on the Smith River. *Redwood Currents* 21:12–15.
Ugan, A.
2005 Does Size Matter? Body Size, Mass Collecting, and Their Implications for Understanding Prehistoric Foraging Behavior. *American Antiquity* 70:75–89.
Underwood, J.
2004 A Posited Patayan Travel Route Between Pilot Knob and Buttercup Pass. In *The Human Journey and Ancient Life in California's Deserts: Proceedings from the 2001 Millennium Conference*, edited by M. W. Allen and J. Reed, pp. 239–243. Maturango Museum Publication no. 15. Ridgecrest, California.
Valente, N.
1998a Resource Intensification and Foraging Efficiency at the Patrick Site (CA-BUT-1). Master's thesis, Department of Anthropology, California State University, Chico.
1998b Reptile, Bird, and Mammal Remains. In *Archaeological Investigations at CA-MRN-254, the Dominican College Site, San Rafael, Marin County, California.* Holman and Associates, San Francisco. Submitted to Dominican College, San Rafael, California. Submitted to Davidon Homes, Walnut Creek, California. Copies available from Northwest Archaeological Information Center, Sonoma State University, Rohnert Park.
Van Bueren, T. M.
1983 Archaeological Perspectives on Central Miwok Cultural Change During the Historic Period. Master's thesis, Department of Anthropology, San Francisco State University.
Van Devender, T. R.
1990 Late Quaternary Vegetation and Climate of the Sonoran Desert, United States and Mexico. In *Packrat Middens: The Last 40,000 Years of Biotic Change*, edited by J. L. Betancourt, T. R. Van Devender, and P. S. Martin, pp. 134–165. University of Arizona Press, Tucson.
Van Geen, A., S. N. Luoma, C. C. Fuller, R. Anima, H. E. Clifton, and S. Trumbore
1992 Evidence from Cd/Ca ratios in Foraminifera for Greater Upwelling off California 4,000 Years Ago. *Nature* 358:54–56.
Van Horn, D. M.
1987 Trade and Subsistence in Humaliwu: A Focused Review of Two Decades of Archaeology in the Conejo Corridor. *Pacific Coast Archaeological Quarterly* 23(1):59–77.
Vayda, A.
1967 Pomo Trade Feasts. In *Tribal and Peasant Economies,* edited by G. Dalton, pp. 494–500. Natural History Press, Garden City, New York.
Vellanoweth, R. L.
1995 New Evidence from San Nicholas Island on the Distribution of *Olivella* Grooved Rectangle Beads. *Pacific Coast Archaeological Society Quarterly* 31(4):13–22.
2001 AMS Radiocarbon Dating and Shell Bead Chronologies: Middle Holocene Trade and Interaction in Western North America. *Journal of Archaeological Science* 28:941–950.
Vellanoweth, R. L., and J. M. Erlandson
2000 Notes on a "Pleistocene" Millingstone Site at Tecolote Canyon, Santa Barbara, California. *Current Research in the Pleistocene* 17:85–87.
Vellanoweth, R., L. P. Martz, and S. .J. Schwartz
2002 Complexity and the Late Holocene Archaeology of San Nicolas Island. In *Catalysts to Complexity: Late Holocene Societies of the California Coast,* edited by J. Erlandson and T. L. Jones, pp. 82–100. Cotsen Institute of Archaeology, University of California, Los Angeles.
Vellanoweth, R. L., T. C. Rick, and J. M. Erlandson
2000 Middle and Late Holocene Maritime Adaptations on Northeastern San Miguel Island, California. In *Proceedings of the Fifth California Islands Symposium*, edited by D. Browne, K. Mitchell, and H. Chaney, pp. 607–614. Santa Barbara Museum of Natural History, Santa Barbara.
Voegelin, E. W.
1942 Cultural Element Distributions: XX, Northeast California. *University of California Anthropological Records* 7:47–252.
Von Post, L.
1916 Forest Tree Pollen in Southern Swedish Peat Bog Deposits. *Pollen et Spores* 9:378–401. Translated by M. B. Davis and K. Faegri.
Von Werlhof, J.
1987 *Spirits of the Earth: A Study of Earthen Art in the Northern American Deserts.* Vol. 1, *The North Desert.* Imperial Valley College Museum Society, El Centro, California.
2004a *Spirits of the Earth: That They May Know and Remember.* Vol. 2. Imperial Valley College Museum Society, Ocotillo, California.
2004b Native Exploitation Strategies for the West and East Mesa Shorelines of Lake Cahuilla, Imperial County. In *The Human Journey and Ancient Life in California's Deserts: Proceedings from the 2001 Millennium Conference*, edited by M. W. Allen and J. Reed, pp. 149–152. Maturango Museum Publication no. 15. Ridgecrest, California.
Waechter, S. A.
2002a *Report on Phase-II Test Excavations at CA-PLU-131 and CA-PLU-421 in Mohawk Valley, Southern Plumas County.* Prepared for the California Department of Transportation Whitehawk Realignment Project. Report on file, Northeast Information Center, California State University, Chico, California.
2002b *Report on Phase II Test Excavations at CA-PLU-1541/H and CA-PLU-130 Near Clio, Southern Plumas County.* Prepared for the California Department of Transporation Whitehawk Realignment Project. Report on file, Northeast Information Center, California State University, Chico, California.
2002c On the Cutting Edge: Basalt Toolstone Sourcing and Distribution in Northeastern California and Northwestern Nevada. In *Boundary Lands: Archaeological Investigations Along the California–Great Basin Interface,* edited by K. R. McGuire. Nevada State Museum Anthropological Papers no. 24.
2002d A Record of Cultural Upheaval: The Late-Period Residential Pattern in Crooks Canyon. In *Boundary Lands: Archaeological Investigations Along the California–Great Basin Interface,* edited by K. R. McGuire. Nevada State Museum Anthropological Papers no. 24.
2005 Late-Period Resource Intensification in Sierra Valley, Eastern Plumas County: A Response to the Medieval Climatic

Anomaly. *Proceedings of the Society for California Archaeology* 18:45–52.

Waechter, S. A., and D. Andolina

2005 *Ecology and Prehistory in Sierra Valley, California: Excavations at CA-PLU-1485.* Far Western Anthropological Research Group, Davis, California. Submitted to California Department of Transportation, Sacramento.

Waechter, S. A., and S. Mikesell

2002 *Phase-II Report for Excavations at Sites CA-PLU-1487/H (Plumas National Forest #05-11-51-825), CA-PLU-1486 (PNF #05-11-51-825), CA-PLU-1484/H, and CA-PLU-1485, Plumas County, California.* Far Western Anthropological Research Group, Davis, California. Prepared for the California Department of Transportation, District 2, Redding.

Wagner, H. R.

1929 *Spanish Voyages to the Northwest Coast of North America in the Sixteenth Century.* California Historical Society Special Publications 4.

Wahoff, T. L.

1999 Flaked Lithic Tools from Recent Investigations on the Salton Sea Test Base. *Proceedings of the Society for California Archaeology* 12:20–27.

Wake, T. A.

1999 Temporal Variation in Vertebrate Archaeofaunas from Camp Pendleton Marine Corps Base, San Diego County, California. *Pacific Coast Archaeological Society Quarterly* 35(4):45–64.

2001 Bone Tool Technology on Santa Cruz Island and Implications for Exchange. In *The Origins of a Pacific Coast Chiefdom: The Chumash of the Channel Islands*, edited by J. E. Arnold, pp. 183–198. University of Utah Press, Salt Lake City.

Wake, T. A., and D. D. Simons

2000 Trans-Holocene Subsistence Strategies and Topographic Change on the Northern California Coast: The Fauna from Duncans Point Cave. *Journal of California and Great Basin Archaeology* 22:295–320.

Walker, E. F.

1951 *Five Prehistoric Archaeological Sites in Los Angeles County, California.* Southwest Museum, F. W. Hodge Anniversary Publication Fund VI.

Walker, P. L.

1989 Cranial Injuries as Evidence of Violence in Prehistoric Southern California. *American Journal of Physical Anthropology* 80:313–323.

Walker, P. L., and P. Lambert

1989 Skeletal Evidence for Stress During a Period of Cultural Change in Prehistoric California. In *Advances in Paleopathology*, edited by L. Capasso, pp. 207–212. Journal of Paleopathology Monographic Publication 1. Marino Solfanelli, Chieti, Italy.

Walker, P. L., D. J. Kennett, T. L. Jones, and R. DeLong

2002 Archaeological Investigations at the Point Bennett Pinniped Rookery on San Miguel Island, California. In *Proceedings of the Fifth California Islands Symposium*, edited by D. Browne, K. Mitchell, and H. Chaney, pp. 628–632. Santa Barbara Museum of Natural History.

Wallace, D. C., M. D. Brown, and M. T. Lott

1999 Mitochondrial DNA Variation in Human Evolution and Disease. *Gene* [Amsterdam] 238:211–230.

Wallace, W. J.

1954 The Little Sycamore Site and the Early Milling Stone Cultures of Southern California. *American Antiquity* 20:112–123.

1955 A Suggested Chronology for Southern California Coastal Archaeology. *Southwestern Journal of Anthropology* 11:214–230.

1977 *Death Valley National Monument's Prehistoric Past: An Archaeological Overview.* Report on file, National Park Service Western Service Center, Tucson.

1978 Post-Pleistocene Archaeology, 9000 to 2000 B.C. In *California*, edited by R. F. Heizer, pp. 25–36. Handbook of North American Indians. Vol. 8. W. C. Sturtevant, general editor. Smithsonian Institution, Washington, D.C.

1986 Archaeological Research at Malaga Cove. In *Symposium: A New Look at Some Old Sites*, edited by G. S. Breschini and T. Haversat. Coyote Press Archives of California Archaeology 6:21–27. Coyote Press, Salinas.

1988 *Old Crump Flat and Ubehebe Craters: Two Rockshelters in Death Valley National Monument.* Monographs in California and Great Basin Anthropology no. 2.

1990 Another Look at Yokuts Pottery Making. In *Hunter-Gatherer Pottery from the Far West*, edited by J. M. Mack, pp. 171–178. Nevada State Museum Anthropological Papers no. 23.

1991 Tulare Lake's Archaeological Past. In *Background to a Study of Tulare Lake's Archaeological Past*, pp. 23–33. Contributions to Tulare Lake Archaeology 1.

Wallace, W. J., and D. W. Lathrop

1975 *West Berkeley (CA-ALA-307): A Culturally Stratified Shellmound on the East Shore of San Francisco Bay.* Contributions of the University of California Archaeological Research Facility no. 29.

Wallace, W. J., and F. A. Riddell

1988 Prehistoric Background of Tulare Lake California. In *Early Human Occupation in the Far Western North America: The Clovis-Archaic Interface*, edited by J. A. Willig, C. M. Aikens, and J. L. Fagan, pp. 87–101. Nevada State Museum Anthropological Papers no. 21.

Wallace, W., and F. A. Riddell (editors)

1991 *Contribution to Tulare Lake Archaeology I, Background to a Study of Tulare Lake's Archaeological Past.* Tulare Lake Archaeological Research Group, Redondo Beach.

Walsh, M. R.

2000 Beyond the Digging Stick: Women and Flaked Stone Tools in the Desert West. In *Archaeological Passages: A Volume in Honor of Claude Nelson Warren*, edited by J. S. Schneider, R. M. Yohe II, and J. K. Gardner, pp. 198–212. Publications in Archaeology no. 1. Western Center for Archaeology and Paleontology.

Wanket, J.

2002 Late Quaternary Vegetation and Climate of the Klamath Mountains. Ph.D. dissertation, Department of Geography, University of California, Berkeley.

Wanket, J., and H. Bills

2005 Preliminary Analysis of Holocene Changes in Mixed Evergreen Forest Composition from Frog Pond, Siskiyou County. California Geographic Society Annual Meeting Abstracts.

Warren, C. N.

1964 Cultural Change and Continuity on the San Diego Coast. Ph.D. dissertation, Department of Anthropology, University of California, Los Angeles.

1966 The San Dieguito Type Site: M.J. Rogers' 1938 Excavation on the San Dieguito River, San Diego. *San Diego Museum Papers* 5:1–39.

1967 The San Dieguito Complex: A Review and Hypothesis. *American Antiquity* 32:168–185.

1968 Cultural Tradition and Ecological Adaptation on the Southern California Coast. In *Archaic Prehistory in the Western United States*, edited by C. Irwin-Williams, pp. 1–14. Contributions in Anthropology 1(3). Eastern New Mexico University Paleo-Indian Institute, Portales.

1984 The Desert Region. In *California Archaeology*, edited by M. J. Moratto, pp. 339–430, Academic Press, Orlando.

1991 *Archaeological Investigations at Nelson Wash, Fort Irwin California.* Report submitted to the Interagency Archaeological Services, National Park Services, Western Region, San Francisco, California.

2000 The Age of Clovis Points at China Lake. Paper presented at the Great Basin Anthropological Conference, Ogden, Utah.

2002 Time, Form, and Variability: Lake Mojave and Pinto Periods in Mojave Desert Prehistory. In *Essays in California Archaeology: A Memorial to Franklin Fenenga*, edited by W. J. Wallace and F. A. Riddell, pp. 129–141. Contributions of the University of California Archaeological Research Facility 60, Berkeley.

2004 Data Recovery at Pleistocene Lake Mojave: Sites CA-SBR-140, CA-SBR-6566, CA-SBR-264. In *Kern River 2003 Expansion Project, California.* Vol. 2, *Cultural Resource Data Recovery Report*, pp. 39–78. Report on file with the Harry Reid Center for Environmental Studies, Las Vegas.

Warren, C. N., and R. H. Crabtree

1986 Prehistory of the Southwestern Area. In *Great Basin*, edited by W. L. d'Azevedo, pp. 183–193. Handbook of North American Indians. Vol. 11. W. C. Sturtevant, general editor. Smithsonian Institution, Washington, D.C.

Warren, C. N., and M. B. McKusick

1959 A Burial Complex from the San Joaquin Valley. *University of California Archaeological Survey Reports* 1958–1959:15–24.

Warren, C. N., and M. G. Pavesic

1963 Shell Midden Analysis of Site SDI-603 and Ecological Implications for Cultural Development of Batiquitos Lagoon, San Diego County. *University of California Archaeological Survey Reports* 5:411–438.

Warren, C. N., and C. Phagan

1988 Fluted Points in the Mojave Desert: Their Technology and Cultural Context. In *Early Human Occupation in the Far Western North America: The Clovis-Archaic Interface*, edited by J. A. Willig, C. M. Aikens, and J. L. Fagan, pp. 121–130. Nevada State Museum Anthropological Papers no. 21.

Warren, C. N., and A. J. Ranere

1968 Outside Danger Cave: A View of Early Man in the Great Basin. *Eastern New Mexico University Contributions in Anthropology* 1:6–18.

Warren, C. N., and J. S. Schneider

2000 *Phase II: An Archaeological Inventory of Joshua Tree National Park, Description and Analysis of Results of a Stratified Random Sample Inventory Conducted 1991–1992.* Report on file, Archaeological Information Center, San Bernardino County Museum, Redlands.

Warren, C. N., G. Siegler, and F. Dittner

1998 Paleoindian and Early Archaic Periods. In *Prehistoric and Historic Archaeology of Metropolitan San Diego: A Historic Properties Background Study.* Report on file, Metropolitan Wastewater Department, San Diego.

Warren, C. N., D. L. True, and A. A. Eudey

1961 Early Gathering Complexes of Western San Diego County: Results and Interpretations of an Archaeological Survey. *University of California, Los Angeles, Archaeological Survey Annual Report* 1960–1961:1–106.

Warter, J. K.

1976 Late Pleistocene Plant Communities: Evidence from the Rancho La Brea Tar Pits. In *Symposium Proceedings Plant Communities of Southern California*, edited by J. Latting, pp. 32–39. Special Publication no. 2. California Native Plant Society.

Watchman, A.

1992 Potential Methods for Dating Rock Paintings. *American Indian Rock Art* 18:43–52.

Waterman, T. T.

1910 The Religious Practices of the Diegueño Indians. *University of California Publications in American Archaeology and Ethnology* 8:271–358.

1920 Yurok Geography. *University of California Publications in American Archaeology and Ethnology* 16:177–314.

Waters, M. R.

1981 Holocene Lacustrine Chronology and Archaeology of Ancient Lake Cahuilla, California. Ph.D. dissertation, Department of Geosciences, University of Arizona.

1982a The Lowland Patayan Ceramic Tradition. In *Hohokam and Patayan: Prehistory of Southwestern Arizona*, edited by R. H. McGuire and M. B. Schiffer, pp. 275–297. Academic Press, New York.

1982b The Lowland Patayan Ceramic Typology. In *Hohokam and Patayan: Prehistory of Southwestern Arizona*, edited by R. H. McGuire and M. B. Schiffer, pp. 537–570. Academic Press, New York.

1982c Ceramic Data from Lowland Patayan Sites. In *Hohokam and Patayan: Prehistory of Southwestern Arizona*, edited by R. H. McGuire and M. B. Schiffer, pp. 571–580. Academic Press, New York.

1983 Late Holocene Lacustrine Chronology and Archaeology of Ancient Lake Cahuilla, California. *Quaternary Research* 19:373–387.

2002 Geological Investigation of the Anderson Flat Area. In *Culture History and Culture Change in Prehistoric Clear Lake Basin: Final Report of the Anderson Flat Project*, by G. White, D. A. Fredrickson, L. Hager, J. Meyer, J. Rosenthal, M. Waters, J. West, and E. Wohlgemuth, pp. 115–127. Center for Archaeological Research at Davis no. 13. University of California, Davis.

Waters, M. R., B. F. Byrd, and S. N. Reddy

1999 Geoarchaeological Investigations of San Mateo and Las Flores Creeks, California: Implications for Coastal Settlement Models. *Geoarchaeology* 14:289–306.

Watts, D.

1984 Bones Along the Bayshore: A Study of Mammalian Exploitation and Cultural Taphonomy of Faunal Assemblages from Two Bayshore Shellmounds, ALA-328 and ALA-329. Master's thesis, Department of Anthropology, California State University, Hayward.

Waugh, G.

1986 Intensification and Land-use: Archaeological Indication of Transition and Transformation in a Late Prehistoric Complex in Southern California. Ph.D. dissertation, Department of Anthropology, University of California, Davis.

1992 *Further Investigations at Pico Creek, CA-SLO-179, Phase II Archaeological Test for the Proposed Bridge Replacement at Pico Creek, State Route 1, San Luis Obispo County.* Office of Cultural Studies, California Department of Transportation, Sacramento.

Webb, M. C.

1974 Exchange Networks: Prehistory. *Annual Review of Anthropology* 3:357–383.

Wedel, W. R.

1941 *Archaeological Investigations at Buena Vista Lake, Kern County, California.* Bureau of American Ethnology Bulletin 130, Washington, D.C.

Weide, D. L.

1976 Regional Environmental History of the Yuha Desert. In *Background to Prehistory of the Yuha Desert Region*, edited by P. J. Wilke, pp. 9–20. Ballena Press Anthropological Papers no. 5. Ramona, California.

Weide, M. L.

1976 A Cultural Sequence for the Yuha Desert. In *Background to Prehistory of the Yuha Desert Region*, edited by P. J. Wilke, pp. 81–94. Ballena Press Anthropological Papers no. 5. Ramona, California.

Weigel, L. E.

1993 Prehistoric Burning in Northwestern California. In *There Grows a Green Tree: Papers in Honor of David A. Fredrickson*, edited by Gregory G. White, Patricia Mikkelsen, William

R. Hildebrandt, and Mark E. Basgall, 237–242. Center for Archaeological Research at Davis no. 11. University of California, Davis.

Weiss, E.

2002 Drought-Related Changes in Two Hunter-Gatherer California Populations. *Quaternary Research* 58:393–396.

Welden, B.

1990 The Physical Being and Lifeways of the Indians of the Llano Seco Site, CA-BUT-233, Butte County, California. Master's thesis, Department of Anthropology, California State University, Chico.

Wells, S. G., and D. Woodcock

1985 Full-Glacial Vegetation of Death Valley, California: Juniper Woodland Opening to *Yucca* Semidesert. *Madroño* 32:11–23.

Wells, S. G., W. G. Brown, Y. Enzel, R. Y. Anderson, and L. D. McFadden

2003 Late Quaternary Geology and Paleohydrology of Pluvial Lake Mojave, Southern California. In *Paleoenvironments and Paleohydrology of the Mojave and Southern Great Basin Deserts,* edited by Y. Enzel, S. G. Wells, and N. Lancaster, pp. 79–114. Special Paper 368. Geological Society of America, Boulder.

West, F. H.

1996 *American Beginnings: The Prehistory and Palaeoecology of Beringa.* University of Chicago Press, Chicago.

West, G. J.

1977 *Late Holocene Vegetation History of the Sacramento-San Joaquin Delta, California.* Report prepared by California Department of Parks and Recreation for the Department of Water Resources, Interagency Agreement B-50173.

1988 *Exploratory Pollen Analysis of Sediments from Elkhorn Slough.* In *Archaeological Investigations at Elkhorn Slough: CA-MNT-229, a Middle Period Site on the Central California Coast,* edited by S. A. Dietz, W. Hildebrandt, and T. L. Jones, pp. 25–56. Papers in Northern California Anthropology 3. Northern California Anthropological Research Group, Berkeley.

1989 Late Pleistocene/Holocene Vegetation and Climate. In *Prehistory of the Sacramento River Canyon, Shasta County, California,* edited by M. E. Basgall and W. R. Hildebrandt, pp. 36–50. Center for Archaeological Research at Davis Publication no. 9. University of California, Davis.

1990 Holocene Fossil Pollen Records of Douglas Fir in Northwestern California: Reconstruction of Past Climate. In *Proceedings of the Sixth Annual Pacific Climate (PACLIM) Workshop,* edited by J. L. Betancourt and A. M. MacKay, pp. 119–122. California Department of Water Resources Technical Report 23. Interagency Ecological Studies Program for the Sacramento-San Joaquin Estuary, Sacramento.

1993 The Late Pleistocene-Holocene Pollen Record and Prehistory of California's North Coast Ranges. In *There Grows a Green Tree: Papers in Honor of David A. Fredrickson,* pp. 219–236. Center for Archaeological Research at Davis Publication no. 11. University of California, Davis.

1997 A Late Glacial Age Pollen Biozone for Central California. In *Proceedings of the 14th Annual Pacific Climate Workshop,* edited by R. C. Wilson and V. L. Sharp, pp. 23–35. California Department of Water Resources Technical Report 57.

2001 Pollen Analysis of Late Pleistocene-Holocene Sediments from Core CL-73-5, Clear Lake, Lake County, California: A Terrestrial Record of California's Cismontane Vegetation and Climate Change Inclusive of the Younger Dryas Event. In *Proceedings of the 17th Annual Pacific Climate Workshop, Santa Catalina Island, May 22-25, 2000,* edited by G. J. West and L. D. Buffaloe, pp. 91–106. Technical Report 67, Interagency Ecological Program for the San Francisco Estuary, Sacramento.

2004 A Pollen Record of Late Pleistocene-Holocene Vegetation and Climate History, Lassen Volcanic National Park, California. In *Proceedings of the 20th Annual Pacific Climate Workshop. April 6–9, 2003,* edited by S. W. Starratt and N. L. Blomquist, pp. 65–80. Technical Report 72 of the Interagency Ecological Program for the San Francisco Estuary, Sacramento.

West, G. J., and K. R. McGuire

2004 9,500 Years of Burning Is Recorded in a High Desert Marsh. *Proceedings of the Spring-fed Wetlands: Important Scientific and Cultural Resources of the Intermountain Region, 2000.* www.wetlands.dri.edu.

West, G. J., and C. Slaymaker

1987 *An Archaeological Survey of the Proposed Enlarged Cachuma Reservoir, Santa Barbara County, California.* Report on file, South Central Information Center, Department of Anthropology, University of California, Santa Barbara.

West, G. J., and P. Welch

2001 *Descriptive Archaeology of CA-MOD-2640: A Stemmed Projectile Point Site at Clear Lake Reservoir, Modoc County, California.* Draft report. U.S. Bureau of Reclamation, Mid-Pacific Region, Sacramento, California.

West, G. J., O. K. Davis, and W. J. Wallace

1991 Fluted Points at Tulare Lake, California: Environmental Background. In *Background to a Study of Tulare Lake's Archaeological Past,* pp. 1–10. Contributions to Tulare Lake Archaeology 1. Tulane Lake Archaeological Research Group, Redondo Beach.

West, G. J., D. Hansen, and P. Welch

2001 A Geographic Information System Based Analysis of the Distribution of Prehistoric Archeological Sites in the Sacramento-San Joaquin Delta, California: A CALFED Planning Study. In *Along the Shores of Time, Proceedings from an International and Interdisciplinary Conference,* edited by R. E. Kelly and G. Franklin. March 31–April 3, 1999. National Park Service, Sausalito.

Whistler, K. W.

1977 Wintun Prehistory: An Interpretation Based on Linguistic Reconstruction of Plant and Animal Nomenclature. *Proceedings of the Annual Meeting of the Berkeley Linguistics Society* 3:157–174.

1979 Linguistic Prehistory in the Northwest California Culture Area. In *A Study of Cultural Resources in Redwood National Park,* edited by P. M. Bickel, pp. 11–26. Report to the National Park Service, Denver.

1984 Mystery Words in Northern Yokuts. Paper presented at the Annual Meeting of the American Anthropological Association, Denver, Colorado, November 15, 1984.

1988 Pomo Prehistory: A Case for Archaeological Linguistics. *Journal of the Steward Anthropological Society* 15 (1983–1984):64–98.

Whistler, K., and V. Golla

1986 Proto-Yokuts Reconsidered. *International Journal of American Linguistics* 52:317–358.

White, G. G.

1988 *Archaeological Investigations at Fort Mountain Rockshelter (CA-CAL-991), A Late Prehistoric Rockshelter Habitation Site in Central Calaveras County, California.* Submitted to the USDI Bureau of Land Management, Sacramento.

1989 *A Report of Archaeological Investigations at Eleven Native American Coastal Sites, MacKerricher State Park, Mendocino County, California.* Report prepared for the California Department of Parks and Recreation, Sacramento. Copies available from Northwest Information Center, Sonoma State University, Rohnert Park.

1991 New Finds on the Mendocino County Coast. *Society for California Archaeology Newsletter* 25(1):1–16.

2002 Social Complexity and Resource Abundance in Early Clear Lake Basin. In *Cultural Diversity and Culture Change in Prehistoric Clear Lake Basin: Final Report of the Anderson*

Flat Project, edited by G. White, pp. 523–537. Center for Archaeological Research at Davis Publication no. 13. University of California, Davis.
2003a Population Ecology of the Prehistoric Colusa Reach. Ph.D. dissertation, Department of Anthropology, University of California, Davis.
2003b *Testing and Mitigation at Four Sites on Level (3) Long Haul Fiber Optic Alignment, Colusa County, California.* Archaeological Research Program, California State University, Chico. Report prepared for Kiewit Pacific, Concord.
2005 Environment or Organization? California's Upper Archaic Artiodactyl Spike. *Newsletter of the Society for California Archaeology* 39(2):26–30.

White, G. G., and R. King
1993 Rethinking the Mostin Site. In *There Grows a Green Tree: Essays in Honor of David A. Fredrickson*, edited by G. G. White, P. Mikkelsen, W. R. Hildebrandt, and M. E. Basgall, pp. 121–140. Center for Archaeological Research at Davis Publication no. 11. University of California, Davis.

White, G. G., and L. Weigel
2006 *Final Report of Investigations CA-GLE-217, an Archaic Millingstone Site in Western Glenn County, California.* Archaeological Research Program, California State University, Chico. Report prepared for California Department of Transportation, Sacramento.

White, G. G., G. J. West, and J. Meyer
2005 *Archaeological Overview and Assessment and Archaeological Research Design, Lassen Volcanic National Park.* Archaeological Research Program, California State University, Chico. Submitted to Lassen Volcanic National Park, Mineral, California.

White, G. G., D. A. Fredrickson, L. D. Hager, J. Meyer, J. S. Rosenthal, M. R. Waters, G. J. West, and E. Wohlgemuth
2002 *Cultural Diversity and Culture Change in Prehistoric Clear Lake Basin: Final Report of the Anderson Flat Project.* Center for Archaeological Research at Davis Publication no. 13. University of California, Davis.

Whitley, D. S.
1987 Socioreligious Context and Rock Art in East-central California. *Journal of Anthropological Archaeology* 6:159–188.
1992 Shamanism and Rock Art in Far Western North America. *Cambridge Archaeological Journal* 2:89–113.
1994a Ethnography and Rock Art in the Far West: Some Archaeological Implications. In *New Light on Old Art: Recent Advances in Hunter-Gatherer Rock Art Research*, edited by David S. Whitley and L. L. Loendorf, pp. 13–36. Institute of Archaeology, University of California, Los Angeles.
1994b By the Hunter, for the Gatherer: Art, Social Relations, and Subsistence Change in the Prehistoric Great Basin. *World Archaeology* 25:356–373.
1994c Shamanism, Natural Modeling, and the Rock Art of Far Western North American Hunter-Gatherers. In *Shamanism and Rock Art in North America*, edited by Solveig A. Turpin, pp. 1–43. Special Publication 1, Rock Art Foundation, San Antonio, Texas.
1996 *A Guide to Rock Art Sites: Southern California and Southern Nevada.* Mountain Press Publishing Company. Missoula, Montana.
1997 Reading the Minds of Rock Artists. *American Archaeology* 1:19–23.
1998 Meaning and Metaphor in the Coso Petroglyphs: Understanding Great Basin Rock Art. In *Coso Rock Art: A New Perspective*, edited by Elva Younkin, pp. 109–174. Maturango Museum Publication no. 12.
2000a *The Art of the Shaman: Rock Art of California.* University of Utah Press, Salt Lake City.
2000b Response to Quinlan. *Journal of California and Great Basin Anthropology* 22:108–129.

Whitley, D. S., and R. I. Dorn
1987 Rock Art Chronology in Eastern California. *World Archaeology* 19:150–164.
1988 Cation-ratio Dating of Petroglyphs Using PIXE. *Nuclear Instruments and Methods in Physics Research* 35:410–414.

Whitley, D. S., J. M. Simon, and J. H. N. Loubser
2004 *Class II Inventory of the Carrizo Plain National Monument, San Luis Obispo County, California.* Prepared for Bureau of Land Management, Bakersfield, California. Contract no. BAP030092. Copies available from Bureau of Land Management, 3801 Pegasus Drive, Bakersfield.

Whitley, D. S., G. Gumerman IV, J. M. Simon, and E. H. Rose
1988 The Late Prehistoric Period in the Coso Range and Environs. *Pacific Coast Archaeological Society Quarterly* 24(1):2–10.

Whittaker, R. H.
1961 Vegetation History of the Pacific Coast States and the "Central" Significance of the Klamath Region. *Madroño* 16:5–19.

Wiberg, R. S.
1988 *The Santa Rita Village Mortuary Complex (CA-ALA-413): Evidence and Implications of a Meganos Intrusion.* Archives of California Prehistory 18. Coyote Press, Salinas.
1992 *Archaeological Data Recovery at Sites CA-SOL-69 and CA-SOL-315, Green Valley, Solano County, California.* Holman and Associates, San Francisco. Submitted to Duffel Financial and Construction Company, Concord. Copies available from Northwest Information Center, Sonoma State University, Rohnert Park.
1993 *Final Report: Archaeological Data Recovery at Prehistoric Site CA-SOL-355/H, Green Valley, Solano County, California.* Holman and Associates Archaeological Consultants, San Francisco. Submitted to Citation Northern Incorporated, Martinez. Copies available from Northwest Information Center, Sonoma State University, Rohnert Park.
1996a *Archaeological Excavations and Burial Removal at Sites CA-ALA-483, CA-ALA-483 Extension, and CA-ALA-555, Pleasanton, Alameda County, California.* Holman and Associates, San Francisco. Submitted to Davidon Homes, Walnut Creek. Copies available from Northwest Information Center, Sonoma State University, Rohnert Park.
1996b *Archaeological Excavations at Site CA-SOL-356, Fairfield, Solano County, California: Final Report.* Holman and Associates, San Francisco. Submitted to Citation Northern Incorporated, Martinez, California. Copies available from Northwest Information Center, Sonoma State University, Rohnert Park.
1997 *Archaeological Investigations at Site CA-ALA-42 Alameda County, California: Final Report.* Holman and Associates, San Francisco. Submitted to Standard Pacific of Northern California, Pleasanton. Copies available from Northwest Information Center, Sonoma State University, Rohnert Park.
2002 *Archaeological Investigations: Skyport Plaza Phase 1 (CA-SCL-478), San Jose, Santa Clara County, California.* Holman and Associates, San Francisco. Submitted to Spieker Properties, San Jose. Copies available from Northwest Information Center, Sonoma State University, Rohnert Park.
2005 *Final Report: Evaluation and Mitigative Data Recovery at CA-YOL-69, Madison Aggregate Plant, Yolo County, California.* Holman and Associates, San Francisco. Submitted to Solano Concrete Company, Fairfield. Report on file. Northwest Information Center, Sonoma State University, Rohnert Park.

Wiberg, R. S., and M. R. Clark.
2004 *Report of Phase II Section 106 Evaluative Test Excavations at CA-CCO-548, Vineyards at Marsh Creek Project Area, Brentwood, Contra Costa County, California.* Holman and Associates Archaeological Consultants, San Francisco. Report on file. Northwest Information Center, Sonoma State University, Rohnert Park.

Wickstrom, B. P.
1986 An Archaeological Investigation of Prehistoric Sites CA-SON-1250 and CA-SON-1251, Southern Sonoma County, California. Master's thesis, Department of Anthropology, Sonoma State University, Rohnert Park, California.

Wigand, P. E., and D. Rhode
2002 Great Basin Vegetation History and Aquatic Systems: The Last 150,000 Years. *Smithsonian Contributions to the Earth Sciences* 33:309–367.

Wilcoxon, L. R.
1993 Subsistence and Site Structure: An Approach for Deriving Cultural Information from Coastal Shell Middens. In *Archaeology on the Northern Channel Islands of California*, edited by M. A. Glassow, pp. 137–167. Archives of California Prehistory 34. Coyote Press, Salinas.

Wilde, J. D.
1985 Prehistoric Settlements in the Great Basin: Excavations and Collections Analysis in the Steens Mountain Area, Southeastern Oregon. Ph.D. dissertation, Department of Anthropology, University of Oregon, Eugene.

Wilke, P. J.
1978 *Late Prehistoric Human Ecology at Lake Cahuilla, Coachella Valley, California*. Contributions of the University of California Archaeological Research Facility no. 38.
1991 Lanceolate Projectile Points from Tulare Lake, California. In *Contributions to Tulare Lake Archaeology I: Background to A Study of Tulare Lake's Archaeological Past*, edited by W. J. Wallace and F. A. Riddell, pp. 41–52. Tulare Lake Archaeological Research Group, Redondo Beach.

Wilke, P. J., and H. Lawton
1975 Early Observations on the Cultural Geography of Coachella Valley, California. In *The Cahuilla Indians of the Colorado Desert: Ethnohistory and Prehistory*, pp. 9–44. Ballena Press, Ramona, California.

Wilke, P. J., and M. McDonald
1986 Flaked Stone Artifacts. In *Excavations at Indian Hill Rockshelter, Anza-Borrego Desert State Park, California, 1984–1985*, edited by P. J. Wilke, M. McDonald, and L. A. Payen, pp. 46–71. Archaeological Research Unit, University of California, Riverside.

Wilke, P. J., M. McDonald, and L. A. Payen
1986 *Excavations at Indian Hill Rockshelter, Anza-Borrego Desert State Park, California, 1984–1985*. Archaeological Research Unit, University of California, Riverside.

Wilke, P. J., T. W. Whitaker, and E. Hattori
1977 Prehistoric Squash (*Cucurbita pepo L.*) from the Salton Basin. *Journal of California Anthropology* 4:55–59.

Willey, G., and P. Phillips
1958 *Method and Theory in American Archaeology*. University of Chicago Press, Chicago.

Willig, J. A.
1988 Paleo-Archaic Adaptations and Lakeside Settlement Patterns in the Northern Alkali Basin. In *Early Human Occupation in Far Western North America: The Clovis-Archaic Interface*, edited by J. A. Willig, C. M. Aikens, and J. L. Fagan, pp. 417–482. Nevada State Museum Anthropological Papers no. 21.
1991 Clovis Technology and Adaptation in Far Western North America: Regional Pattern and Environmental Context. In *Clovis Origins and Adaptions*, edited by R. Bonnichsen and K. Turnmire, pp. 91–118. Center for the Study of the First Americans, Oregon State University, Corvalis.

Willig, J. A., and C. M. Aikens
1988 The Clovis-Archaic Interface in Far Western North America. In *Early Human Occupation in Far Western North America: The Clovis-Archaic Interface*, edited by J. A. Willig, C. M. Aikens, and J. L. Fagan, pp. 1–40. Nevada State Museum Anthropological Papers no. 21.

Wilson, G. B.
1993 *The Archaeological Collection from CA-ALA-329, the Ryan Mound, Alameda County, California*. Coyote Press, Salinas.
1999 *The Coyote Hills Area, Alameda County, California: A Settlement Pattern and Artifact Distribution Study*. Archives of California Prehistory 46. Coyote Press, Salinas.

Wilson, N. L.
1963 The Archaeology of the Loyalton Rock Shelter, Sierra County, California. Master's thesis, Department of Anthropology, Sacramento State College, California.

Wilson, N. L., and A. H. Towne
1978 Nisenan. In *California*, edited by R. F. Heizer, pp. 387–397. Handbook of North American Indians. Vol. 8. W. C. Sturtevant, general editor. Smithsonian Institution, Washington, D.C.

Winterbourne, J. W.
1967 Report of the Goff's Island Site Excavation, May 1, 1939 to January 22, 1940 (WPA). *Pacific Coast Archaeological Society Quarterly* 3(1):1–156.

Wirth Environmental Services
1985 *Mokelumne River Project Cultural Resources Evaluation Program*. WIRTH Environmental Services, San Diego. Submitted to Pacific Gas and Electric Company, San Francisco.

Wohlgemuth, E.
1978 *Preliminary Investigation and Evaluation of CA-LAS-345, Eagle Lake, Lassen County, California*. Report prepared for Lassen County Department of Public Works, Susanville, California.
1996 Resource Intensification in Prehistoric Central California: Evidence from Archaeobotanical Data. *Journal of California and Great Basin Anthropology* 18:81–103.
1997 Appendix H: Plant Remains. In *Archaeological and Goearchaeological Investigations at Eight Prehistoric Sites in the Los Vaqueros Reservoir Area, Contra Costa County, California*, edited by J. Meyer and J. S. Rosenthal, pp. H.1–H.36. Anthropological Studies Center, Sonoma State University Academic Foundation, Rohnert Park, California. Submitted to the Contra Costa Water District, Concord, California. Copies available from Northwest Information Center, Department of Anthropology, Sonoma State University, Rohnert Park, California.
2004 The Course of Plant Food Intensification in Native Central California. Ph.D. dissertation, Department of Anthropology, University of California, Davis.
2005 The Medieval Climatic Anomaly in Central Sierran Foothill Prehistory. *Proceedings of the Society for California Archaeology* 18:307–311.

Wohlgemuth, E., W. R. Hildebrandt, and K. Ballantyne
2002 *Data Recovery Excavations for Unanticipated Discovery at CA-MNT-1942, Big Creek Bridge (BR. NO. 44-56), Monterey County, California Highway 1, P.M. 28.1*. Far Western Anthropological Research Group, Davis. Copies available from the Northwest Information Center, Sonoma State University, Rohnert Park.

Wood, S. H.
1975 *Holocene Stratigraphy and Chronology of Mountain Meadows, Sierra Nevada, California*. Earth Resources Monograph 4. U.S. Forest Service, San Francisco.

Woodcock, D.
1986 The Late Pleistocene of Death Valley: A Climatic Reconstruction Based on Macrofossil Data. *Palaeogeography, Palaeoclimatology, Palaeoecology* 57:273–283.

Woodman, C. F., C. Cagle, P. de Barros, and T. P. Rudolph
1995 *Final Report: Archaeological Survey and Evaluation of the Honda Beach Site, SBA-530*. Science Applications International Corporation and Chambers Group, Santa Barbara. Submitted to USDI National Park Service, Western Region

Interagency Archaeological Services Branch, San Francisco, Contract no. 1443 CX 8000-92-010.

Woods, C. M., S. Raven, and C. Raven

1986 *The Archaeology of Creation: Native American Ethnology and the Cultural Resources at Pilot Knob.* On file, USDI, Bureau of Land Management, El Centro, California.

Woodward, A.

1932 Gigantic Intaglio Pictographs in the Californian Desert. *Illustrated London News*, September 10.

Woolfenden, W. B.

1996 Quaternary Vegetation History. In *Sierra Nevada Ecosystem Project: Final Report to Congress.* Vol. 2, *Assessments and Scientific Basis for Management Options,* pp. 47–70. Centers for Water and Wildland Resources, University of California, Davis.

2003 A 180,000-Year Pollen Record from Owens Lake, California: Terrestrial Vegetation Change on Orbital Scales. *Quaternary Research* 59:430–444.

Workman, J.

2003 The Unique Wave-Shaped Cupule Boulders of Western Riverside County. *Rock Art Papers* 16:87–99.

Wormington, H. M.

1965 [1957]*Ancient Man in North America.* 5th ed. Popular Series 4. Denver Museum of Natural History.

Wulf, E. L.

1997 An Analysis of Bone and Antler Artifacts from the Augustine Site (CA-SAC-127). Master's thesis, Department of Anthropology, California State University, Sacramento.

Yatsko, A.

2000 Late Holocene Paleoclimatic Stress and Prehistoric Human Occupation on San Clemente Island. Ph.D. dissertation, Department of Anthropology, University of California, Los Angeles.

Yesner, D. R.

1987 Life in the "Garden of Eden": Causes and Consequences of the Adoption of Marine Diets by Human Societies. In *Food and Evolution*, edited by M. Harris and E. B. Ross, pp. 285–310. Temple University Press, Philadelphia.

1996 Human Adaptations at the Pleistocene-Holocene Boundary (circa 13,000 to 8,000 BP) in Eastern Beringia. In *Humans at the End of the Ice Age*, edited by L. G. Strauss, B. V. Eriksen, J. M. Erlandson, and D. R. Yesner, pp. 255–276. Plenum Press, New York.

Yesner, D. R., and G. Pearson

2002 Microblades and Migrations: Ethnic and Economic Models in the Peopling of the Americas. In *Thinking Small: Global Perspectives on Microlithization*, edited by R. G. Elston and S. L. Kuhn, pp. 133–162. Archaeological Papers of the American Anthropological Association no. 12.

Yohe, R. M., II

1992a A Clovis-Like Point from the Rose Spring Site *(CA-INY-372). Journal of California and Great Basin Anthropology* 14:234–237.

1992b A Reevaluation of Western Great Basin Cultural Chronology and Evidence for the Timing of the Introduction of the Bow and Arrow to Eastern California Based on New Excavations at the Rose Spring Site (CA-INY-372). Ph.D. dissertation, Department of Anthropology, University of California, Riverside.

2000 "Rosegate" Revisited: Rose Spring Point Temporal Range in the Southwestern Great Basin. In *Archaeological Passages: A Volume in Honor of Claude Nelson Warren*, edited by J. S. Schneider, R. M. Yohe II, and J. K. Gardner, pp. 213–224. Publications in Archaeology no. 1. Western Center for Archaeology and Paleontology.

Yohe, R. M. II, and M. Q. Sutton

1998 Settlement, Subsistence, Environmental Change, and the Rose Spring Period in the Western Mojave Desert. Report on file, Department of Sociology and Anthropology, California State University, Bakersfield.

1999 Implications of Technological and Environmental Change in the Rose Spring Period in the Western Mojave Desert. Report on file, Department of Sociology and Anthropology, California State University, Bakersfield.

Yoklavich, M. M., G. M. Cailliet, J. P. Barry, D. A. Ambrose, and B. S. Antrim

1991 Temporal and Spatial Patterns in Abundance and Diversity of Fish Assemblages in Elkhorn Slough, California. *Estuaries* 14:465–480.

Young, D. C.

2002 Secondary Obsidian Sources of the Madeline Plains: Paleolandscapes and Archaeological Implications. In *Boundary Lands: Archaeological Investigations Along the California–Great Basin Interface,* edited by K. R. McGuire, pp. 75–83. Nevada State Museum Anthropological Papers no. 24.

Younkin, E. (editor)

1998 *Coso Rock Art: A New Perspective.* Maturango Museum Publication no. 12. Ridgecrest, California.

Zancanella, J. K.

1987 A Study of Projectile Points from the East Central Sacramento Valley, California. Master's thesis, Department of Anthropology, California State University, Chico.

Zeanah, D. W., and A. T. Leigh

2003 *Results of Phase II Investigations at 25 Archaeological Sites for the Aberdeen-Blackrock Four-Lane Project on Highway 395, Inyo County, California.* Pacific Legacy and Archaeological Research Center, California State University. Submitted to California Department of Transportation, Fresno.

Zepeda, C. I.

2004 Exchange Networks and Beads Among the Historic Kumeyaay. *Proceedings of the Society for California Archaeology* 14:125–132.

Zepeda-Herman, C., and J. Underwood

2005 *Draft Integrated Cultural Resources Management Plan for the Naval Air Facility, El Centro.* RECON. Prepared for Naval Facilities Engineering Command, Southwest, San Diego.

Zimmerman, K. L., C. L. Pruett, and M. Q. Sutton

1989 A Clovis-like Point from the Southern Sierra Nevada, California. *Journal of California and Great Basin Anthropology* 11:89–90.

Index of Sites

Note: Page numbers in *italics* refer to illustrations.

Index

Note: Page numbers in *italics* refer to illustrations. For cross references to site designations, please refer to the Index of Sites.

About the Editors and Contributors

ABOUT THE EDITORS

Terry L. Jones is associate professor of anthropology at California Polytechnic State University–San Luis Obispo, where he has taught since 1998. He holds an M.A. in cultural resources management from Sonoma State University (1982) and an M.A. (1989) and Ph.D. (1995) in anthropology from the University of California–Davis. He has conducted research along the central and southern coasts of California for the past twenty-five years.

Kathryn A. Klar is a lecturer in Celtic studies at the University of California–Berkeley, where she has taught since 1980. She holds an A.B. (1971), M.A. (1973), and Ph.D. (1977) in linguistics from the University of California–Berkeley and is a research associate at the Santa Barbara Museum of Natural History. She has done research in both Native California languages and Celtic studies for over thirty years.

ABOUT THE CONTRIBUTORS

Ivano W. Aiello is an assistant professor in geological oceanography at the Moss Landing Marine Laboratories. He received his Ph.D. from the University of Bologna (Italy) in 1997. His fields of expertise include marine geology, sedimentology and paleomagnetism of marine sediments, cyclostratigraphy, and paleoceanography.

Mark W. Allen was awarded a Ph.D. in anthropology from UCLA in 1994. He is currently an associate professor of anthropology at California State Polytechnic University, Pomona.

R. Scott Anderson received his Ph.D. in geosciences from the University of Arizona in 1987. He has been faculty member and administrator at Northern Arizona University since 1987, and he is presently a professor of environmental and quaternary sciences.

Mark E. Basgall obtained his Ph.D. in anthropology from the University of California–Davis in 1993. He is currently a professor in the Department of Anthropology, California State University–Sacramento, where he also serves as director of the Archaeological Research Center.

Viviana Bellifemine is a consulting archaeologist currently employed by Archeo-Tec in Oakland. She received her M.A. in archaeology from San Jose State University in 1997.

David G. Bieling works as an independent consulting archaeologist for projects in northern California. He received his M.A. in cultural resources management from Sonoma State University in 1992.

Brian F. Byrd received his Ph.D. from the University of Arizona in 1987. He is currently a principal investigator for Far Western Anthropological Research Group and is affiliated as a research associate with the Department of Anthropology, University of California–Davis.

Robert Cartier received his Ph.D. from Rice University in 1975. For the past thirty years he has focused on the prehistoric and historic resources of central California, particularly the Santa Clara Valley and the Monterey Bay region.

Jim Cassidy received his Ph.D. from the University of California–Santa Barbara in 2004, and is currently employed as an archaeologist for the Marine Corps Air Ground Combat Center in Twentynine Palms. He specializes in the study of California and maritime cultures of the north Pacific Rim.

Joseph L. Chartkoff is a professor of anthropology at Michigan State University, where he has served on the faculty since 1971. He received his Ph.D. from UCLA in 1974, and has been practicing professional archaeology in California since 1965.

Jon M. Erlandson earned his Ph.D. from the University of California–Santa Barbara in 1988. He has taught at the University of Oregon since 1990, where he is a professor of anthropology. He also serves as director of the University of Oregon Museum of Natural and Cultural History, and coeditor of the *Journal of Island and Coastal Archaeology.*

Jason A. Eshleman received his doctorate in biological anthropology from the University of California–Davis in 2002. He is a senior research scientist and cofounder of Trace Genetics as well as a research associate with the Department of Anthropology at the University of California–Davis.

Richard T. Fitzgerald received his M.A. in archaeology from San Jose State University in 1991. With twenty-five years of professional experience, he is currently employed as a state archaeologist for the California Department of Parks and Recreation in Sacramento.

David A. Fredrickson is both professor emeritus of anthropology and director emeritus of the Anthropological Studies Center at Sonoma State University, where he worked from 1967 to 1991. He received his M.A. in 1967 and his Ph.D. in 1973, both in anthropology from the University of California–Davis.

Lynn H. Gamble is associate professor and director of the Collections Management Program in the Department of Anthropology at San Diego State University. She received her Ph.D. in anthropology from the University of California–Santa Barbara in 1991.

Jill K. Gardner received her Ph.D. in 2006 from the University of Nevada–Las Vegas, and has been a professional archaeologist since 1994. She has served as the associate director of the Center for Archaeological Research at California State University–Bakersfield and as an adjunct professor in the Department of Anthropology.

Donna Gillette is an archaeologist and rock art specialist. She received her M.A. in anthropology from California State University–Hayward in 1998, and is currently a Ph.D. candidate at the University of California–Berkeley.

Amy J. Gilreath received an M.A. from Washington State University in 1983 and joined Far Western Anthropological Research Group in Davis in 1984, where she has served as a principal investigator since 1992.

Michael A. Glassow received his Ph.D. in 1972 from UCLA. He has been teaching at the University of California–Santa Barbara since 1969, where he is currently professor of anthropology.

Victor Golla is professor of anthropology at Humboldt State University and research associate in anthropology at the University of California–Davis. He holds a Ph.D. in linguistics from the University of California–Berkeley (1970).

Andrew Gottsfield is a project director for Archeo-Tec, a San Francisco Bay Area cultural resources management firm. He received his B.A. in anthropology from Northern Arizona University in 1996, and is currently pursuing graduate studies at the University of Kansas.

Randy Groza is a central California cultural resource manager/archaeologist. She received her M.A. in anthropology from San Francisco State University in 2002 and is currently working in Hawaii.

William R. Hildebrandt is president of Far Western Anthropological Research Group and an adjunct professor of anthropology at the University of California–Santa Cruz. He received a Ph.D. in anthropology from the University of California–Davis in 1981, and served as director of archaeology at San Jose State University until 1985. He joined Far Western in 1986.

Richard E. Hughes is director of Geochemical Research Laboratory in Portola Valley, California. He received a Ph.D. in anthropology from the University of California–Davis in 1983 and subsequently held faculty positions at the University of California–Davis, Sonoma State University, and California State University–Sacramento.

Kathleen L. Hull is currently assistant professor of anthropology at the University of California–Merced. She received her Ph.D. from the University of California–Berkeley in 2002, and has worked as a professional archaeologist for twenty-five years.

Mark G. Hylkema has over twenty-five years of experience in California archaeology with an emphasis on the prehistory and ethnography of the San Francisco Bay Area. He received his M.A. in anthropology from San Jose State University in 1991, and is currently employed as the Santa Cruz district archaeologist for California State Parks.

Deborah A. Jones is a senior staff archaeologist for Far Western Anthropological Research Group, where she serves as director of their Central Coast office. She received her M.A. in anthropology from the University of California–Davis in 1988. She has worked as a professional archaeologist for twenty-five years.

Don Laylander is a senior archaeologist with ASM Affiliates in Carlsbad. He earned an M.A. in anthropology from San Diego State University in 1987 and has worked as a professional archaeologist for twenty-eight years in governmental and private consulting positions.

Alan Leventhal (M.A.) is an archaeologist who has conducted fieldwork in the Great Basin and California. He has worked at San Jose State University as a staff member and lecturer for the past twenty-seven years with the departments of Anthropology, Urban and Regional Planning, and Office of the Dean, College of Social Sciences.

Patricia M. Masters holds an M.A. in anthropology and a Ph.D. in biology. She has published papers in biogeochemistry and reconstruction of coastal paleoenvironments. She is senior editor of the book *Quaternary Coastlines and Marine Archaeology,* and provided the content for the website http://coastalchange.ucsd.edu, part of a coastal modeling project at Scripps Institution of Oceanography in La Jolla, California.

Kelly R. McGuire received his M.A. in anthropology from the University of California–Davis in 1977. He is one of the founding partners of Far Western Anthropological Research Group in Davis, where he has worked for the past twenty-eight years.

Randall Milliken is an independent consultant in ethnohistory and prehistoric artifact seriation. He has worked in both fields since 1978, and received his M.A. in cultural resources management from Sonoma State University in 1983, and his Ph.D. in anthropology from the University of California–Berkeley in 1991.

Michael J. Moratto (Ph.D., University of Oregon, 1972) retired in 2005 from a teaching career that began in 1969 with the California State University system. He now works full-time as a senior archaeologist/environmental scientist for Applied EarthWorks.

Tom Origer began his career as an avocationalist in the late 1960s. His formal training began at Santa Rosa Junior College and led to an M.A. in anthropology from San Francisco State University in 1982. He now is the senior partner in a CRM firm, Origer and Associates.

Jennifer E. Perry is an assistant professor of anthropology at Pomona College. She has been involved with archaeology in southern California since 1992, and received her Ph.D. from the University of California–Santa Barbara in 2003.

Judith F. Porcasi has been a zooarchaeologist at the UCLA Cotsen Institute of Archaeology for fifteen years and is also an independent archaeofaunal consultant. She received an M.A. in anthropology from California State University–Northridge in 1995, and is currently a Ph.D. candidate in archaeology at Leicester University, United Kingdom.

L. Mark Raab is professor emeritus of anthropology at California State University–Northridge, where he taught for twenty-two years. He is currently an adjunct professor in the Departments of History and Geosciences at the University of Missouri–Kansas City.

Torben C. Rick received his Ph.D. in anthropology from the University of Oregon in 2004. He is currently assistant professor of anthropology at Southern Methodist University in Dallas, Texas. His major research interest is in the archaeology and historical ecology of the North American Pacific coast.

Michael F. Rondeau currently conducts research through Rondeau Archeological. He specializes in technological, use wear, and related forms of lithic analysis. He holds an M.A. in anthropology from California State University–Sacramento and has thirty years of professional experience in archaeology.

Jeffrey S. Rosenthal received an M.A. in cultural resources management from Sonoma State University in 1996. He has worked as a professional archaeologist for eighteen years, and is currently a principal investigator for Far Western Anthropological Research Group in Davis.

Glenn S. Russell received his M.A. in archaeology and Ph.D. in anthropology from UCLA. He currently serves as the chief of planning and land use for the County of San Diego.

Jerry Schaefer is a principal and senior archaeologist at ASM Affiliates in Encinitas, California. He has worked throughout California and the Southwest over the past twenty-five years since receiving his Ph.D. in anthropology from the University of Arizona in 1979.

David Glenn Smith received his M.A. and Ph.D. from the University of Colorado, Boulder. He is currently a professor of anthropology at the University of California–Davis.

Nathan E. Stevens received his M.A. in anthropology from California State University–Sacramento in 2002 and has ten years of professional experience in California and Great Basin archaeology. He is currently staff archaeologist for Applied Earthworks in Lompoc, California.

Eric Strother received his M.A. in anthropology from California State University–Hayward in 2004. He is currently a senior archaeologist at William Self and Associates in Orinda, California.

Mark Q. Sutton holds a Ph.D. (1987) in anthropology from the University of California–Riverside. He has been at California State University–Bakersfield since 1987, where he is now a professor of anthropology.

James A. Wanket is currently assistant professor of geography at Sacramento State University, where he codirects the Quaternary Paleoecology Laboratory. He received his Ph.D. in geography in 2002 from the University of California–Berkeley.

G. James West retired after twenty-five years as regional archaeologist for the U.S. Bureau of Reclamation, Sacramento, in 2004. He is currently a research associate in the Department of Anthropology, University of California–Davis. He received his Ph.D. in anthropology from the University of California–Davis in 1978.

Gregory G. White received his Ph.D. in anthropology from the University of California–Davis in 2003. He is currently director of the Archaeological Research Program at California State University–Chico, and has worked as a professional archaeologist for thirty-two years.

Randy S. Wiberg is a senior associate with Holman and Associates with over twenty-five years of experience in California archaeology. He received his M.A. in anthropology from San Francisco State University in 1984.

Wallace Woolfenden holds a Ph.D. in geosciences and anthropology from the University of Arizona (1996). He retired from the USDA Forest Service after thirty years in heritage resource and ecosystem management, and is a co-owner of Mountain Heritage Associates (MHA).